TO THE STUDENT: Three helpful supplemental study aids for this textbook are available:

- *Student Guide* by Dudley W. Curry and John K. Harris contains, for each chapter in this textbook, a detailed review of key ideas plus practice test questions and problems with solutions (ISBN 0-13-179540-6)

- *Review Manual for Classroom Exams: CPA and CMA Questions with Explanatory Answers* by John K. Harris contains efficient chapter-by-chapter review for classroom exams by means of CPA and CMA Questions (most of which are multiple choice), all with explanatory answers. (ISBN 0-13-179573-2)

- *Applications in Cost Accounting with the TWIN™/Lotus®1-2-3®* by David M. Buehlmann and Dennis P. Curtin is a book/disk package that provides a series of case problems—all drawn from various real-life industries—that relies heavily on managerial accounting concepts. The templates on the disk run with either the TWIN or Lotus 1-2-3 and are designed to help students solve the problems. (ISBN 0-13-179557-0)

If these supplements are not in your college bookstore, ask the manager to order them for you.

6TH EDITION

COST

ACCOUNTING
A Managerial Emphasis

Charles T. Horngren
Stanford University

George Foster
Stanford University

PRENTICE-HALL, INC., Englewood Cliffs, NJ 07632

Library of Congress Cataloging-in-Publication Data
HORNGREN, CHARLES T.
  Cost accounting.
  Bibliography: p.
  Includes index.
  1. Cost accounting. 2. Costs, Industrial.
I. Foster, George.   II. Title.
HF5686.C8H59 1987   658.1'511   86-21274
ISBN 0-13-179508-2

Editorial/production supervision: Esther S. Koehn
Interior design and cover design: Maureen Eide
Cover Photograph: © Chicago, Illinois, by Frank Cezus
Manufacturing buyer: Ray Keating

COST ACCOUNTING: A Managerial Emphasis, 6th Edition
Charles T. Horngren/George Foster

Printed in the United States of America

10 9 8 7 6 5 4 3 2

ISBN 0-13-179508-2 01

Prentice-Hall International (UK) Limited, *London*
Prentice-Hall of Australia Pty. Limited, *Sydney*
Prentice-Hall Canada Inc., *Toronto*
Prentice-Hall Hispanoamericana, S.A., *Mexico*
Prentice-Hall of India Private Limited, *New Delhi*
Prentice-Hall of Japan, Inc., *Tokyo*
Prentice-Hall of Southeast Asia Pte. Ltd., *Singapore*
Editora Prentice-Hall do Brasil, Ltda., *Rio de Janeiro*

To Professor William J. Vatter

ABOUT THE AUTHORS

Charles T. Horngren is the Edmund W. Littlefield Professor of Accounting at Stanford University. A graduate of Marquette University, he received his MBA from Harvard University and his Ph.D. from the University of Chicago. He has also received honorary doctorates from Marquette University and De Paul University.

A Certified Public Accountant, Horngren served on the Accounting Principles Board for six years, the Financial Accounting Standards Board Advisory Council for five years, and the Council of the American Institute of Certified Public Accountants for three years. He is currently serving as a trustee of the Financial Accounting Foundation.

A member of the American Accounting Association, Horngren has been its President and its Director of Research. He received the Outstanding Accounting Educator Award in 1973 when the association initiated this annual award.

The California Certified Public Accountants Foundation gave Horngren its Faculty Excellence Award in 1975 and its Distinguished Professor Award in 1983. He is the first person to have received both awards.

In 1985 the American Institute of Certified Public Accountants presented its first Outstanding Educator Award to Horngren.

Professor Horngren is also a member of the National Association of Accountants, where he was on its research planning committee for three years. He was a member of the Board of Regents, Institute of Certified Management Accountants, which administers the Certified Management Accountant examinations.

Horngren is co-author (with Gary L. Sundem) of two other books published by Prentice-Hall: *Introduction to Financial Accounting, Third Edition*, 1987, and *Introduction to Management Accounting, Seventh Edition*, 1987.

Charles T. Horngren is the Consulting Editor for the Prentice-Hall Series in Accounting.

George Foster is Professor of Accounting at Stanford University. He has a B.Ec. and M.Ec. from The University of Sydney and a Ph.D. from Stanford University. He has previously taught at The University of Sydney, The University of Chicago, and The University of New South Wales.

A member of the American Accounting Association, Foster has been awarded the association's Competitive Manuscript Award in 1975 and 1976. He chaired the Competitive Manuscript Award committee in 1986 and has made presentations at several of the Doctoral Consortiums of the AAA.

Active in the accounting research community, Professor Foster has been an Associate Editor of *The Accounting Review* and has served on the editorial boards of *The Australian Journal of Management, Journal of Accounting and Economics*, and *Journal of Accounting Research*.

Professor Foster is the author of *Financial Statement Analysis, Second Edition* (Prentice-Hall, 1986) and the co-author of *Security Analyst Multi-Year Earnings Forecasts and the Capital Market* (American Accounting Association, 1985). His articles have appeared in many journals including *Abacus, The Accounting Review, Journal of Accounting and Economics, Journal of Accounting Research*, and *Journal of Finance*. In 1981 and 1983 the American Institute of Certified Public Accountants presented its Notable Contributions to the Accounting Literature Award to Foster.

Contents

6 Flexible Budgets and Standards: Part I   179

7 Flexible Budgets and Standards: Part II   218

PART FIVE   DECISION MODELS AND COST INFORMATION

xiii

PART SEVEN COST ACCOUNTING, SYSTEMS CHOICE, AND MANAGEMENT CONTROL

Preface

Cost accounting provides data for three major purposes (1) planning and controlling routine operations; (2) nonroutine decisions, policy making, and long-range planning; and (3) inventory valuation and income determination. This book gives abundant consideration to all three of these, but emphasis is placed on the first two. Our major theme of "different costs for different purposes" is continually stressed throughout the book.

The topics emphasized from the outset are those that challenge students and spur their curiosity. Because the emphasis is on costs for planning and control, the following topics of prime managerial significance are introduced early: the role of the accountant in the organization; cost-volume-profit relationships; responsibility accounting; standard costs; flexible budgets; relevant costs for nonroutine decisions; determining how costs behave; and cost analysis for control and motivation. The favorable reaction to the format of previous editions is evidence that cost accounting courses can be enriched, relieved of drudgery, and broadened from coverage of procedures alone to a full-fledged treatment of concepts, analyses, and procedures that pays more than lip-service to accounting as a managerial tool.

STRENGTHS OF FIFTH EDITION RETAINED AND ENHANCED

Reviewers of the fifth edition cited the following strengths: clarity and understandability of the text; the inclusion of important topics; the numerous approaches used to enhance student learning; good quantity, quality, and range of assignment material; helpful Problems for Self-Study included at the end of each chapter; and a flexible organization via a modular approach. These features have been retained and enhanced.

The first eleven chapters can provide the essence of a one-term (quarter or semester) course. There is ample text and assignment materials in the book's twenty-eight chapters for a two-term course.

Comments on organization

The organizational structure of a textbook is a challenge. After sifting through countless course outlines and reviews of the fifth and earlier editions of this book we have reached the following conclusions:

1. Instructors disagree more markedly about the sequence of chapters in cost/management accounting textbooks than about any other aspect. A tightly integrated sequence may please a segment of instructors, but it narrows a teacher's options. Consequently, we have refrained from *maximizing the satisfaction* of a relatively small fraction of the teacher population; instead, we have tried to *minimize the dissatisfaction* of the teacher population as a whole.

2. If it is impossible to please all of the potential users all of the time, a logical attack is to present a modular, flexible approach that permits jumping around with minimal inconvenience. We have taken great pains to facilitate such hopping and skipping. *In a nutshell, our rationale is to provide a loosely constrained sequence to facilitate diverse approaches to teaching.*

3. As long as departing from a given structure causes no serious inconvenience, the organization of a text is not a central issue. The content and clarity of the chapters, and the quality of the assignment material, are far more important than organization. Teaching is highly personal and heavily influenced by the backgrounds and interests of assorted students and faculty in various settings. To satisfy this audience, a book must be a pliable tool, not a straitjacket. As one reviewer stated, "I have never understood the sequencing of chapters in the book, but it has never limited my usage of the book."

CHANGES IN CONTENT AND PEDAGOGY OF SIXTH EDITION

Many changes have been made in the sixth edition. Most chapters have been completely rewritten. The authors spent much time interacting with the business community to determine new uses of cost accounting data, and to gain insight into how changes in technology are affecting the role of cost accounting information.

Changes in content

Major changes to the content of the sixth edition are:

1. New text and problems on automation and robotics and their implications for cost accounting; Chapters 4, 13, and 20.

2. New text and problems on computer-based planning and control approaches; Chapters 19, 20, and 21.

3. New text and problems on just-in-time purchasing and just-in-time production; Chapters 17 and 21.

4. Increased emphasis on measuring the quality of products or services and of the diverse cost items associated with quality control programs; Chapters 16, 17, 21, and 26.

5. Increased recognition of the importance of nonfinancial measures of performance; Chapters 11, 17, 21, and 26.

6. Increased discussion of executive compensation and incentive schemes; Chapter 26.

7. New analysis of cost functions, such as the incremental unit time learning curve model, and more discussion of the use of nonlabor hour (cost) based independent variables when estimating cost functions in automated plants; Chapters 10, 13, and 23.

8. Added text and problems on how changing price and price level information can be incorporated into standard setting, cost estimation, capital budgeting, and performance evaluation; Chapters 6, 10, 20, and 26.

9. Added text and problems on government regulations, such as the Accelerated Cost Recovery System (ACRS), and the Financial Managers' Financial Integrity Act; Chapters 20 and 27.

Preface

XX

One indication of the new material added is that over 70% of all citations in the sixth edition are to articles or other books appearing subsequent to the publication of the fifth edition.

Added realism   Several approaches have been used to deepen student appreciation of actual company practice:

1. Greatly increased discussion of surveys of company practice; data from twenty recent surveys of company practice have been included in the sixth edition.
2. Increased use of examples from individual company management accounting systems; e.g., Celanese Corp (Chapter 21), Hewlett-Packard (Chapters 17 and 21), Holiday Inn (Chapter 26), and McCormick & Co. (Chapter 27).
3. Many new problems added to the sixth edition are based on actual organization situations or actual legal cases involving the use of accounting data.

In class-testing the sixth edition, students cited realism of the text and problem material as a major reason for their high level of interest in cost accounting.

Improvements in pedagogy and presentation   Several improvements have been made to increase student learning:

1. Additional use of step-by-step expositions of individual topics; overhead application (Chapter 4), cost estimation (Chapter 10), and capital budgeting (Chapter 19).
2. Additional use of numerical examples to unify the text of individual chapters, heighten student interest, and provide a more explicit link to the numerical assignment material; cost estimation (Chapters 10 and 23), transfer pricing (Chapter 25), and performance evaluation (Chapter 26).
3. Additional use of summary exhibits to highlight text material and provide more guidance in solving assignment material; Exhibit 4-10 (overhead cost disposition), Exhibit 11-3 (discretionary cost centers), Exhibit 12-2, (cost allocation), Exhibit 15-1 (job-order and process costing), Exhibit 17-3 (operation costing), Exhibit 17-5 (just-in-time costing), and Exhibit 23-6 (regression analysis).
4. The front page of each chapter now includes a summary of topics to be covered to provide students with a road map.
5. Terms defined in the Terms to Learn section and in the Glossary are cross-referenced to the exact text page in which the term is first defined. This eases the reader's task of checking the meaning of terms included in the book.

Additions to problem material   This edition continues the widely applauded tight linkage between text and problem material found in previous editions. The problem material aims to reinforce the text using as diverse a set of contexts as possible. The Solutions Manual provides an index of problems in the following categories to facilitate use of their increased diversity:

- Service sector
- Nonprofit sector
- International sector
- High technology/computer sector

Two areas that attract high student interest were targeted as important when developing new problem material. These areas are:

- Evolving changes in manufacturing and distribution technology
- Executive compensation/incentive

The Solutions Manual also presents an index of problems in each of these two areas.

Changes in sequencing of topics

The sequence of topics in Chapters 1 through 8 is unchanged from the fifth edition. Significant modifications in the sequence of chapters beyond Chapter 8 are:

- Old Chapter 11 (Relevance) is now Chapter 9.
- Old Chapters 12 and 13 (Capital Budgeting) are now Chapters 19 and 20. They are clustered with other chapters on decision models in a new section titled, "Decision Models and Cost Information" (Chapters 18 through 22).
- Old Chapters 19 (Transfer Pricing) and 20 (Division Performance Measurement) are now Chapters 25 and 26 in a new section titled "Cost Accounting, Systems Choice, and Management Control" (Chapters 25 through 27).

Chapter 17 is brand new. It extends job and process systems, covers nonmanufacturing settings, operation costing, project costing, and the implications for cost accounting of changes in underlying production systems.

SUPPLEMENTS TO THE SIXTH EDITION

A complete package of supplements is available to assist students and instructors in their use of this book. Supplements available to students are:

- *Student Guide* by Dudley W. Curry and John K. Harris. This is a chapter-by-chapter learning aid for students.
- *Review Manual for Classroom Exams: CPA and CMA Questions with Explanatory Answers* by John K. Harris. Actual professional examination material is aligned with the individual chapters of the textbook.
- *Applications in Cost Accounting with the TWIN™/Lotus® 1-2-3®* by David M. Buehlmann and Dennis P. Curtin. Personal computer applications are keyed to selected chapters of the textbook.

Supplements available to instructors are:

- *Solutions Manual* by Charles T. Horngren and George Foster. Includes comments on alternative teaching approaches as well as solutions to every assignment problem.
- *Test Bank* by Dudley W. Curry and John K. Harris. Includes quiz and examination material and is available in both hard copy and diskette form.
- *Instructor's Resource Outlines* by Jonathan Schiff. A guide for instructors that outlines day-to-day schedules and lectures.

We are grateful to the authors of all the above supplements.

ACKNOWLEDGMENTS

We are indebted to many for their ideas and assistance. The acknowledgments in the five previous editions contain a long list of our creditors. Our primary obligation is to Professor William J. Vatter to whom this book is dedicated. For those who know him, no words are necessary; for those who do not know him, no words will suffice.

Professors D. Curry and J. Harris aided us immensely at all stages in the development and production of this book, including a critique of the fifth edition, detailed review of the manuscript of this edition, and the essential task of proofing.

The following professors influenced this edition by their preparation of reviews of the preceding edition: A. Atkinson, L. Bamber, R. Barden, K. Chen, J. Collins, M. Duffy, D. Kleespie, and W. Stephens.

Many comments on chapters in draft form were provided by A. Atkinson, G. Clinch, E. Hubbard, and D. Then. Their care and attention to detail are greatly appreciated.

Incisive comments were received from C. Bailey, L. Bamber, S. Barty, N. Boyle, P. Brown, C. Canellos, J. Chen, B. Committe, M. Duffy, S. Finkler, M. Harrison, J. Horrigan, L. Jacobsen, D. Knutson, M. Lieberman, R. Manes, K. McGahran, C. Merz, D. Monson, M. Oliverio, R. Owens, R. Peterson, W. Pollard, V. Raval, E. Schwarz, J. Sheppard, G. Staubus, and J. Weiler. In addition, we have received helpful suggestions by mail from many users, unfortunately too numerous to mention here. The sixth edition was much improved by this feedback from users.

Many students have read the manuscript and worked the new problems to insure that they are as error free as possible. They have also contributed ideas and material for revising chapters and preparing new problems. Particular thanks go to T. Bryson, A. Dravid and J. Ring.

Our Stanford colleagues have continually stimulated our thinking on many topics in this book.

A special note of gratitude is extended to T. Bush, J. Ochoa, E. Young, and L. Yujuico for their skillful typing of much material in syllabus form.

We thank the people at Prentice-Hall: L. Drazien, E. Koehn, M. Lines, N. McDermott, and J. Warner.

Appreciation also goes to the American Institute of Certified Public Accountants, The National Association of Accountants, The Institute of Certified Management Accountants, the Society of Management Accountants of Canada, the Certified General Accountant's Association of Canada, the Financial Executives Institute of America, and to many other publishers and companies for their generous permission to quote from their publications. Problems from the Uniform CPA Examinations are designated (CPA); problems from the Certificate in Management Accounting examinations are designated (CMA); problems from the Canadian examinations administered by the Society of Management Accountants are designated (SMA); problems from the Certified General Accountants Association are designated (CGAA). Many of these problems are adapted to highlight particular points.

We are grateful to the professors who contributed assignment material for this edition. Their names are indicated in parentheses at the start of their specific problems.

Comments from users are welcome.

CHARLES T. HORNGREN AND GEORGE FOSTER

The Accountant's Role in the Organization

Purposes of management accounting and financial accounting • Elements of management control • Cost-benefit approach • The pervading duties of the management accountant

As this chapter is being written, former accountants are the top executives in many large companies, including General Motors and PepsiCo. Accounting duties played a key part in their rise to the management summit. Accounting cuts across all facets of the organization; the management accountant's duties are intertwined with executive planning and control.

The study of modern cost accounting yields insight and breadth regarding both the accountant's role and the manager's role in an organization. How are these two roles related? Where may they overlap? How can accounting help managers? This book tries to answer these questions. In this chapter we will try to get some perspective on where the accountant should fit in the organization. Then we will have a framework for studying the rest of the chapters.

PURPOSES OF MANAGEMENT ACCOUNTING AND FINANCIAL ACCOUNTING

Basic distinctions

Modern cost accounting is often called *management accounting*. Why? Because cost accountants look at their organizations through managers' eyes. Because managers want to know how accountants measure performance. Because managers often depend upon accounting data for guiding their decisions. By definition, decision making is the purposeful choosing from among a set of alternative courses of action in light of some objectives.

The accounting system is the major quantitative information system in almost every organization. It should provide information for three broad purposes:

1. Internal reporting to managers, for use in planning and controlling routine operations
2. Internal reporting to managers, for use in making nonroutine decisions and in formulating major plans and policies
3. External reporting to stockholders, government, and other outside parties, for use in investor decisions, income tax collections, and a variety of other applications

Both management and external parties share an interest in all three important purposes, but the emphasis differs. External reporting, the third purpose, emphasizes the historical, custodial, and stewardship aspects of accounting. This area is usually called **financial accounting,** which is heavily constrained by generally accepted accounting principles. On the other hand, internal reporting, the first two purposes, focuses on management planning and control. This area is usually called *management accounting,* which has looser constraints than financial accounting.

The distinction between financial accounting and management accounting became institutionalized in the United States in 1972 when the **National Association of Accountants (NAA),** the largest association of internal accountants in the United States, established a program leading to the Certificate in Management Accounting (CMA).[1] The **Certified Management Accountant (CMA)** is the internal accountant's counterpart of the CPA (Certified Public Accountant). Just like certified public accountants, management accountants are expected to adhere to a code of ethics.

Boundaries of cost accounting

Where does cost accounting fit within the above framework? Cost accounting is generally indistinguishable from management accounting because it serves the multiple purposes of internal reporting as described above. **Management accounting** is the identification, measurement, accumulation, analysis, preparation, interpretation, and communication of information that assists executives in fulfilling organizational objectives. A synonym is **internal accounting.**

A major purpose of cost accounting systems is to accumulate the costs of an organization's products and services. This **product-costing** purpose helps managers. For example, managers can use product costs to guide the setting of selling prices. In addition, these product costs are used for inventory valuation and income determination. Such information is reported to both internal and external parties. When viewed in this way, **cost accounting** *is* management accounting, plus a small part of financial accounting—to the extent that its product-costing function satisfies the requisites of external reporting.

We need not be greatly concerned with the boundaries of cost accounting. The major point is that the focus of a modern cost accounting system is on helping managers deal with both the immediate and the distant future. Its concern with the past is justified only insofar as it helps prediction and satisfies external reporting requirements.

---

[1]A key objective of this program is to establish management accounting as a recognized profession. For more information about the CMA program and other programs, see Chapter 28.

Is Shell's management control system better than Exxon's? Unilever's better than Nestlé's? A major purpose of this book is to develop a method for answering such questions. This section provides an overview of the nature of control systems.

Planning and control

Consider the following diagram:

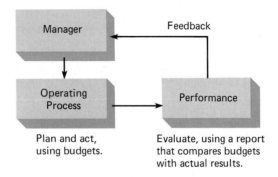

The diagram implies a rhythmic sequence that is sometimes called the management cycle of planning and control. There are countless definitions of planning and control. Here we define **planning** as a delineation of goals, predictions of potential results under various ways of achieving goals, and a decision of how to attain the desired results. *Control* is usually distinguished from planning. **Control** is (a) action that implements the planning decision and (b) performance evaluation that provides feedback of the results. This feedback concerns both the activities of the operating process (as a process) and the manager (as a professional manager).

The Operating Process box in the diagram includes planning plus the action phase of control as just defined. The Performance box and Feedback loops represent the remainder of this definition of control.

Two major accounting tools for helping managers are budgets and performance reports. A **budget** is a quantitative expression of a plan of action and an aid to coordination and implementation. **Performance reports** are measurements of activities. These reports often consist of comparisons of budgets with actual results. The deviations of actual results from budget are called **variances.** The latter help **management by exception,** which is the practice of concentrating on areas that deserve attention and ignoring areas that are presumed as running smoothly.

Planning and control are so strongly interlocked that it seems artificial to draw rigid distinctions between them. Managers certainly do not spend time drawing such rigid distinctions. In this book the narrow idea of control will not be used. Unless otherwise stated, control will be employed in its broadest sense to denote the entire management process of *both* planning and control. For example, instead of referring to a *management planning and control system,* we will refer to a *control system.* Similarly, we will refer to the *control purpose* of accounting instead of the more awkward *planning and control purpose* of accounting.

Well-conceived plans include enough flexibility or discretion so that the manager may feel free to seize any unforeseen opportunities. That is, in no case should control mean that managers cling to a preexisting plan when unfolding events indicate the desirability of actions that were not encompassed in the original plan.

Exhibit 1-1 demonstrates the basic elements of a **management control system.** The latter is a means of gathering data to aid and coordinate the process of making decisions throughout the organization. Note how our initial diagram is nested within a broader network:

1. A commonly used example of a planning and control cycle is the familiar room thermostat: Set temperature goal, measure existing temperature, compare with goal, activate the operating process, produce feedback, and if required, take corrective action. However, the automatic control of a room-heating or -cooling process is an example of *engineering control,* not management control. Exhibit 1-1 shows that there are generally at least two persons in a management control system. The major role of the superior is to oversee the work of subordinates. The control of *human* activity is what ordinarily distinguishes *management control* from *engineering control.* Visualize hundreds or thousands of Exhibits 1-1, all interrelated at both an instant of time and through time. Then you can appreciate the enormity of the problem of management control, which often entails vast numbers of humans making countless decisions in a world of uncertainty.

2. The subordinate, such as a sales manager, a train conductor, or a school principal, supervises an operating process or processes. A **process** is a collection of decisions or activities that should be aimed at some ends. For example, there are processes of selling, transporting, and teaching.

3. The **environment** is the set of uncontrollable factors that affect the success of a process. It is a level of uncertainty or risk as to whether predicted results or outputs will be achieved. Environmental (uncontrollable) variables might include absenteeism, condition of railroad tracks, weather, and competitor reactions. The role of the environ-

EXHIBIT 1-1
Basic Elements of Management Control System

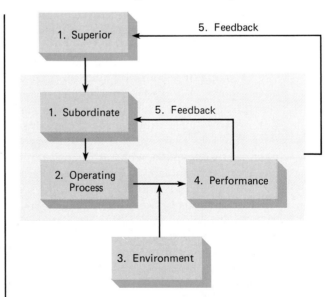

Source: *Adapted from H. Itami,* Adaptive Behavior: Management Control and Information Analysis *(Sarasota, Fla.: American Accounting Association), p. 9.*

ment (uncertainty or risk) is explored later, particularly in Chapter 18, which may be studied now if desired.

4. The Performance box highlights the regular evaluation of the results of the operating process and its managers. Executives are frequently helped here by various accounting reports regarding inputs or outputs or both.

5. The Feedback loops indicate how managers learn to improve the unending sequence of predictions and decisions that are embedded in the operating process.

In control systems, **feedback** often consists of a comparison of the budget with actual results. Feedback may be used for a variety of purposes, including the following:

CHANGING GOALS For example, based on an evaluation of past results, a hospital may decide not to offer open-heart surgery services.

SEARCHING FOR ALTERNATIVE MEANS For example, a state government may consider alternative ways of issuing drivers' licenses.

CHANGING METHODS FOR MAKING DECISIONS For example, a university may have traditionally based its maintenance decisions on how to minimize repair costs for the current year. Feedback may indicate that such a decision method is undoubtedly more expensive over the long run. The university may then base its decisions on a comparison of expected repair costs over a five-year period rather than a one-year period.

MAKING PREDICTIONS For example, a government contractor may use some new ways to predict materials and labor costs if its feedback indicates that a poor prediction record adversely affected its success in winning contracts. **In particular, note that feedback consists of historical information.** In addition, other information, such as trends in prices of materials, is also used in formulating predictions.

CHANGING THE OPERATING PROCESS For example, alter a management style by using more oral and less written communication.

CHANGING THE MEASURING AND REWARDING OF PERFORMANCE Rewards such as promotions and bonuses are often affected by performance reports. For example, individuals may act differently if their performance is measured by total sales rather than by total profits.

Feedback is obviously important. Yet many control systems are weak, not because the feedback is weak, but because of the managers themselves. *Managers are part of the system.* The feedback is usually available at low cost, but it is often ignored by managers. On the other hand, many successful managers actively support their control system by using feedback in a highly visible way. Both accountants and managers should periodically remind themselves that management control systems are not confined exclusively to technical matters such as data processing. **Management control is primarily a human activity that should focus on how to help other humans in their work.**

5

Focus on operating decisions

This textbook has a general approach to accounting that will be referred to as a **cost-benefit approach.** That is, the primary criterion for choosing among alternative accounting systems or methods is how well they help achieve management goals in relation to their costs.

Accounting systems are economic goods. They cost money, just like beer and milk. The old adage says that if you build a better mousetrap, people will beat a path to your door. But many sellers of mousetraps will testify that when the buyers get to the door, they say, "What is the price?" Thus, if the price is too high, buyers may be unwilling to pay, and the maker of better mousetraps may face financial ruin.

The costs of buying a new accounting system include the usual clerical and data-processing activities plus educational activities. **The costs of educating users of the system is frequently substantial, particularly when much management time is required and when the users have been reasonably satisfied with existing systems.**

Managers buy a more elaborate management accounting system when its perceived expected benefits exceed its perceived expected costs. **Although the benefits may take many forms, they can be summarized as collective sets of operating decisions that will better attain top-management desires.**

To illustrate this cost-benefit approach, consider the familiar story of the installation of a company's first budgeting system. Chances are high that the company had been using some historical recordkeeping and little formal planning. A major benefit from purchasing a budgeting system is to compel managers to plan and thus make a *different*, more profitable set of decisions than would have been generated by using only a historical system.

Admittedly, the measurement of these costs and benefits is seldom easy. Therefore you may want to call this approach an abstract theory rather than a practical guide. Nevertheless, the cost-benefit approach provides a starting point for analyzing virtually all accounting issues. Moreover, it is directly linked to a vast theoretical structure of information economics (the application of the microeconomic theory of uncertainty to questions of buying information).[2] Furthermore, managers and practicing accountants find its central ideas appealing, probably because they have been using such a "practical" notion for years. After all, a favorite justification for the status quo is that the new system is too costly in light of expected benefits.

The cost-benefit way of thinking is widely applicable even if the cost and benefits defy precise measurement. As stated by a motto in the System Analysis Office of the Department of Defense, "It is better to be roughly right than precisely wrong." For example, if two methods of accomplishing the same disease cure are available, the less costly is preferable. Similarly, if two proposals have equal costs, the proposal that is perceived to yield more benefits is preferable. This judgment can be achieved without a numerical measurement of the levels of benefits.[3]

---

[2]J. Demski, *Information Analysis*, 2nd ed. (Reading, Mass.: Addison-Wesley, 1980); and R. Magee, *Advanced Managerial Accounting* (New York: Harper & Row, 1986).

[3]See R. Anthony and D. Young, *Management Control in Nonprofit Organizations*, 3rd ed. (Homewood, Ill.: Richard D. Irwin, 1984), pp. 316–21.

Dependence on circumstances	A key question asked by the cost-benefit approach is, **How much would we be willing to pay for one system versus another?** For example, the same concert ticket at a given price may be a "good buy" for one person but a "bad buy" for another person when their circumstances are different. Similarly, a particular cost accounting system or method may be a good buy for General Motors but a bad buy for Ford. Thus the cost-benefit approach takes a skeptical view of such sweeping generalizations as "This budgeting technique is a vast improvement over other techniques. It is badly needed."

The choice of a technique or system inherently depends on specific circumstances. Therefore this book will concentrate on describing alternative techniques and systems and on how to go about making the choices between them. It will not present one cost accounting technique as being innately superior to another. Again, the human element is significant. The same system may work well in one organization and not in another. Why? Because the collective personalities and traditions differ between the two. Systems do not exist in a vacuum. Managers and accountants are integral parts of management control systems. Costs and benefits cannot be evaluated apart from the managers and accountants who will use and prepare systems and reports.

THE PERVADING DUTIES OF THE MANAGEMENT ACCOUNTANT

Overview of an organization	Exhibit 1-2 illustrates the general organizational relationships in a manufacturing company. The chief financial officer, who often has the title of financial vice-president or vice-president—finance, is an integral part of top management.[4] Two key accounting executives, the treasurer and the controller, usually report to the financial vice-president.

Note the distinction between production departments and service departments. The primary purpose of a factory is to produce goods. Therefore the production-line departments are usually termed *production* or *operating departments*. To facilitate production, most plants also have *service departments,* which exist to facilitate the tasks of the production departments.

Line and staff relationships	Most entities have the production and sale of goods or services as their basic objectives. Line managers are directly responsible for attaining these objectives as efficiently as possible. Staff activities of organizations exist because the scope of the line managers' responsibility and duties expands, so that they need specialized help to operate effectively. When a department's primary task is that of advice and service to other departments, it is a staff department.

Except for exerting line authority over their own departments, the chief financial officers generally fill a staff role in their companies, as contrasted with the line roles of sales and production executives. This staff role includes advice and help in the areas of budgeting, controlling, pricing, and special decisions. The accounting officers do not exercise direct authority over line departments.

Management literature is hazy on these distinctions, and we will not belabor them here. For example, some writers distinguish among three types of authority:

---

[4]"Heady Days for the Numbers Guys," *Fortune*, January 23, 1985, says: "The title of chief financial officer no longer evokes images of gray men in green eyeshades lurking among dusty ledgers far from the blood and guts of business."

EXHIBIT 1-2
Partial Organization Chart of Manufacturing Company

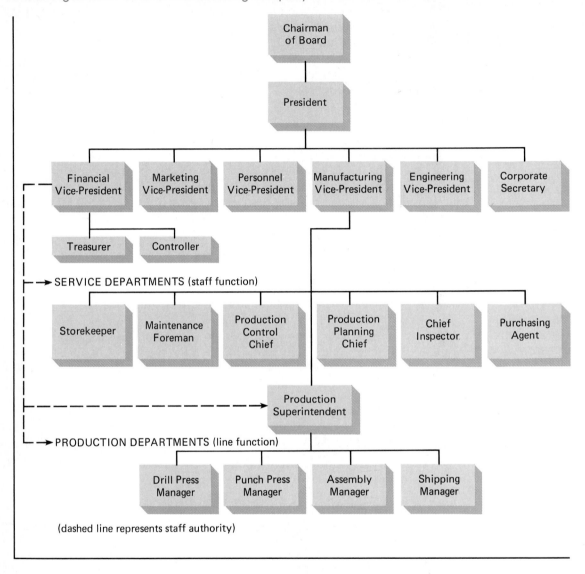

(dashed line represents staff authority)

line, staff, and functional. **Line authority** is exerted downward over subordinates. **Staff authority** is the authority to *advise* but not command others; it may be exercised laterally or upward. **Functional authority** is the right to *command* action laterally and downward with regard to a specific function or specialty.

Uniformity of accounting and reporting is often acquired through the delegation of authority regarding accounting procedures to the chief management accountant, the controller, by the top line management. Note carefully that when the controller prescribes the line department's role in supplying accounting information, he or she is speaking for top line management—not as the controller, a staff person. The uniform accounting procedure is authorized by the president and is installed by the controller.

Theoretically, the controller's decisions regarding the best accounting procedures to be followed by line people are transmitted to the president. In turn, the president communicates these procedures through a manual of instructions that comes down through the line chain of command to all people affected by the procedures.

Practically, the daily work of the controller is such that face-to-face relationships with the production superintendent or shipping manager may call for directing how production records should be kept or how time records should be completed.[5] The controller usually holds delegated authority from top line management over such matters.

Distinctions between controller and treasurer

Many people confuse the offices of controller and treasurer. The chief financial officer, vice-president—finance, typically oversees both the controllership and treasurership functions. The Financial Executives Institute, an association of corporate treasurers and controllers, distinguishes their functions as follows:

CONTROLLERSHIP	TREASURERSHIP
1. Planning and control	1. Provision of capital
2. Reporting and interpreting	2. Investor relations
3. Evaluating and consulting	3. Short-term financing
4. Tax administration	4. Banking and custody
5. Government reporting	5. Credits and collections
6. Protection of assets	6. Investments
7. Economic appraisal	7. Insurance

Note how managerial cost accounting is the controller's primary *means* of implementing the first three functions of controllership.

The **treasurer** is the financial executive who is primarily responsible for obtaining investment capital and managing cash. We will not dwell at length on the treasurer's functions. As the seven points indicate, treasurers are concerned mainly with financial, as distinguished from operating, problems. The exact division of various accounting and financial duties obviously varies from company to company.

The **controller** is the financial executive who is primarily responsible for both management accounting and financial accounting. The controller has been compared to the ship's navigator. The navigator, with the help of specialized training, assists the captain. Without the navigator, the ship may founder on reefs or miss its destination entirely, but the captain exerts the right to command. The navigator guides and informs the captain as to how well the ship is being steered. This navigator role is especially evident in points 1 through 3 of the controller's functions.

The controller: the chief management accountant

The word *controller* is applied to various accounting positions. The stature and duties of the controller vary from company to company. In some firms the controller is little more than a glorified bookkeeper who compiles data primarily for conventional balance sheets and income statements. In other firms—for example, General Electric—controllers are key executives who aid management planning and control in about two hundred subdivisions. In most firms the controller's status

---

[5]According to some writers, this would be exercising the *functional authority* described above.

is somewhere between these two extremes. For example, controllers' opinions on the tax implications of certain managerial decisions may be carefully weighed, yet their opinions on the other aspects of these decisions may not be sought.

Whatever the title, the controller is viewed in this book as the chief management accounting executive. The point of terminology here is that the modern controller does not do any controlling in terms of line authority except over his or her own department. Yet the modern concept of controllership maintains that the controller does control in a special sense. That is, by reporting and interpreting relevant data, the controller exerts a force or influence that impels management toward logical decisions consistent with objectives.

In sum, the modern controller plays a "two-count" role in organizations. The first count is responsibility to top management for the integrity (reliability) of the financial reports of the subunits. The second count is responsibility for helping the subunit managers in planning and controlling operations. Therefore controllers must balance their independence and objectivity against their necessary involvement in assisting line managers.

Division of duties **Accountants often face a dilemma because they are supposed to fulfill two conflicting roles simultaneously. First, they are seen as watchdogs for top managers. Second, they are seen as helpers for all managers. The "watchdog" role is usually performed via the "scorekeeping" task of accumulating and reporting to all levels of management. The "helper" role is usually performed via the tasks of directing managers' attention to problems and of assisting managers in solving problems.**[6]

The sheer volume of the scorekeeping task is often overwhelming; the day-to-day routines and endless deadlines shunt the helper role into the background and often into oblivion. To prevent the helper role from falling by the wayside, many organizations deliberately split the accountants' duties in ways similar to those in Exhibit 1-3.

The attention-directing and problem-solving tasks improve mutual understanding if a member of the controller's staff personally explains and interprets reports as they are presented to line managers. This attention-directing role (for example, explaining the differences between budgeted and actual performance) is often performed by experienced accountants who, at least to some degree, can talk the line manager's language. Indeed, the interpreters are the individuals who will establish the status of the controller's department in the company. Close, direct contacts between accountants and operating managers usually instill confidence in the reliability of the financial reports, which are the measuring devices of performance.

Many companies deliberately rotate their young accountants through scorekeeping, attention-directing, and problem-solving posts. In this way, accountants are more likely to appreciate the decision maker's viewpoint and are thus prone to keep the accounting system tuned to the users.

Two surveys of the 1980s have demonstrated that internal accountants have become increasingly involved in the ongoing management of the organization. For example, one survey report states: "Management accountants feel that they are

---

[6]H. A. Simon, H. Guetzkow, G. Kozmetsky, and G. Tyndall, *Centralization vs. Decentralization in Organizing the Controller's Department* (New York: Controllership Foundation, Inc.). This perceptive study is much broader than its title implies.

EXHIBIT 1-3
Organization Chart of a Controller's Department

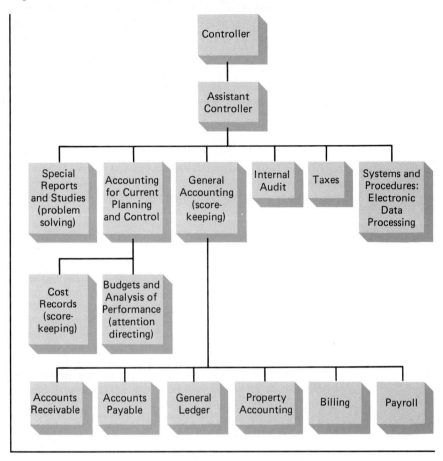

more active in decision making and have assumed more decision-making responsibility today than in the past."[7]

SUMMARY

In its fullest sense, management accounting is well named. It ties management with accounting. To maximize their value, accountants must focus on the operating managers' concerns and attitudes as much as on the technical aspects of accounting measurement.

[7]C. Lander, J. Holmes, M. Tipgos, and M. Wallace, *Profile of the Management Accountant* (Montvale, N.J.: National Association of Accountants, 1983), p. 8. Also see V. Sathe, *Controller Involvement in Management* (Englewood Cliffs, N.J.: Prentice-Hall, 1982). An additional illustration of involvement was described in "How Bob Pritzker Runs a $3 Billion Empire," *Business Week,* March 7, 1983, p. 65: "Indeed, every time Pritzker makes a visit to a unit, he spends time alone not only with its general manager but also with the controller. In addition, each controller reports directly to Chicago corporate headquarters, as well as to his or her own general manager." The best-known holding of the Pritzker family is the Hyatt Hotel chain. For additional discussion of controller involvement, see Chapter 27 of this book.

This chapter stressed the interrelationship of accounting information and management decisions. The first major part of this chapter provided a conceptual overview of this interrelationship. The second major part described how accountants fit into typical organizational settings.

Accounting information is an important input to many decision makers. In turn, the accountant frequently must choose what and how much information to provide. The choices among accounting techniques and systems are aimed at helping the collective operating decisions desired by top management.

The cost-benefit approach is a major theme of this book. In a most fundamental sense, the question of what accounting data, report, or system to buy must focus on how decisions (and resulting benefits) are going to be affected. The method of analysis is to ask what collective decisions throughout the organization will be affected by one costly accounting system or method versus another.

PROBLEMS FOR SELF-STUDY

(Try to solve these problems before examining the solutions that follow.)

problem 1   Reexamine the basic elements of a management control system in Exhibit 1-1. Describe how the ideas of planning and controlling and how the major accounting tools mesh with the system.

solution 1   Planning is most obviously linked with the operating process. Planning entails delineation of goals, predictions of potential results, and a decision of how to attain goals. The budget is the principal accounting tool that helps managers plan.
　　　　Controlling entails action, which is part of the Operating Process box in Exhibit 1-1. It also includes performance evaluation, often using a report that compares budgets with actual results. **This report provides major feedback, which is the essence of control.**

problem 2   Using the organization charts in this chapter (Exhibits 1-2 and 1-3), answer the following questions:
　　a. Do the following have line or staff authority over the assembly manager: maintenance foreman, manufacturing vice-president, production superintendent, purchasing agent, storekeeper, personnel vice-president, president, chief budgetary accountant, chief internal auditor?
　　b. What is the general role of service departments in an organization? How are they distinguished from operating or production departments?
　　c. Does the controller have line or staff authority over the cost accountants? The accounts-receivable clerks?
　　d. What is probably the *major duty* (scorekeeping, attention directing, or problem solving) of the following?

1. Payroll clerk	7. Budgetary accountant
2. Accounts-receivable clerk	8. Cost analyst
3. Cost-record clerk	9. Head of special reports and studies
4. Head of general accounting	10. Head of accounting for planning
5. Head of taxes	and control
6. Head of internal auditing	11. Controller

solution 2   a. The only executives having line authority over the assembly manager are the president, the manufacturing vice-president, and the production superintendent.
　　b. A typical company's major purpose is to produce and sell goods or services. Unless a department is directly concerned with producing or selling, it is called a service or staff department. Service departments exist only to help the production and sales departments with their major tasks: the efficient production and sale of goods or services.

c. The controller has line authority over all members of his or her own department, all of those shown in the controller's organization chart (Exhibit 1-3).

d. The major duty of the first five is typically scorekeeping. Attention directing is probably the major duty of 6, 7, and 8. Problem solving is probably the primary duty of the head of special reports and studies. **The head of accounting for planning and control and the controller should be concerned with all three duties: scorekeeping, attention directing, and problem solving. However, there is a perpetual danger that day-to-day pressures will emphasize scorekeeping. Therefore accountants and managers should constantly see that attention directing and problem solving are also stressed. Otherwise the major management benefits of an accounting system may be lost.**

Terms to Learn

Each chapter will include this section. Like all technical subjects, accounting contains many terms with precise meanings. To learn cost accounting with relative ease, pin down the definitions of new terms when you initially encounter them.

Before proceeding to the assignment material or to the next chapter, be sure you understand the following words or terms. Their meaning is explained in the chapter and also in the Glossary at the end of this book.

budgets (p. 3)   Certified Management Accountant (2)   CMA (2)
control (3)   controller (9)   cost accounting (2)
cost-benefit approach (6)   environment (4)   feedback (5)
financial accounting (2)   functional authority (8)   internal accounting (2)
line authority (8)   management accounting (2)   management by exception (3)
management control system (4)   NAA (2)
National Association of Accountants (2)   performance reports (3)
planning (3)   process (4)   product costing (2)
staff authority (8)   treasurer (9)   variances (3)

Special Points and Pitfalls

Many readers tend to skim the first chapter. After all, it contains neither financial statements nor discussions of various cost terms. Nevertheless, the chapter sets an important tone:

1. **Cost accounting is vital to management control, which entails human control of other humans.** Therefore cost accounting is far more than merely a technical subject. It often has an enormous impact on human behavior.

2. Cost accounting systems come in various shapes and sizes. **Managers buy one system or another, depending on perceptions of relative costs and benefits.**

3. Cost accounting systems are usually the responsibility of the controller, a staff officer. The controller must worry about the system's human aspects and its technical aspects.

Special note about the assignment material No attempt has been made to distinguish among questions, problems, and cases because distinctions among them are so often artificial. Many problems are based on actual business situations. To aid selection, most problems have individual short titles that describe their subject matter.

1-1 The accounting system should provide information for three broad purposes. Describe the three purposes.

1-2 Explain the meaning of the letters *NAA* and *CMA* as used in accounting.

1-3 "A major purpose of cost accounting systems is to accumulate the costs of an organization's products and services. This is the product-costing purpose." Identify two uses of product costs.

1-4 "Cost accounting *is* management accounting, plus a small part of financial accounting." Explain.

1-5 Identify the basic elements of a management control system.

1-6 Give at least three examples of the environment when it is regarded as a basic element of management control.

1-7 Feedback may be used for a variety of purposes. Identify at least five.

1-8 Management control has been compared to a room thermostat. What is the major distinction between them?

1-9 As a new controller, reply to this comment by a factory superintendent: "As I see it, our accountants may be needed to keep records for stockholders and Uncle Sam—but I don't want them sticking their noses in my day-to-day operations. I do the best I know how; no pencil-pusher knows enough about my responsibilities to be of any use to me."

1-10 In your own words, briefly describe the meaning of decision making.

1-11 Define *planning*. Distinguish it from *control*.

1-12 "Planning is really much more vital than control." Do you agree? Why?

1-13 "We need to record replacement costs because they are more accurate approximations of economic reality." How would an advocate of cost-benefit analysis react to this statement?

1-14 Which two major executives usually report to the vice-president—finance?

1-15 "The controller is both a line and a staff executive." Do you agree? Why?

1-16 "The modern concept of controllership maintains that the controller *does* control in a special sense." Explain.

1-17 What are some common causes of friction between line and staff executives?

1-18 How is cost accounting related to the concept of controllership?

1-19 Distinguish among line, staff, and functional authorities.

1-20 "The modern controller plays a two-count role in organizations." Explain.

1-21 Elements of control system. Examine Exhibit 1-1. Consider the operations of a manufacturing department. The department manager is the superior and the supervisor is the subordinate. Give at least one example of each of the other elements in the exhibit: operating process, environment, performance, and feedback.

1-22 Uses of feedback. A separate section in the chapter, page 5, identified six uses of feedback and provided an example of each:
  1. Changing goals
  2. Searching for alternative means
  3. Changing methods for making decisions
  4. Making predictions
  5. Changing the operating process
  6. Changing the measuring and rewarding of performance

Match the numbers with the appropriate following capital letters:
  A. The hiring of new sales personnel will include an additional step: an interview and evaluation by the company psychiatrist.
  B. Quality inspectors at General Motors are now being used in the middle of the process in addition to the end of the process.
  C. Procter & Gamble introduces a new soap.
  D. The California State University system adopts a WATS (Wide Area Telephone Service) method for making long-distance telephone calls.
  E. Sales commissions are to be based on gross profit instead of total revenue.
  F. The Ford Motor Company adjusts its elaborate way of forecasting demand for its cars by including the effects of expected changes in the price of crude oil.

1-23 Role of the accountant in the organization: line and staff functions.
  1. Of the following, who has line authority over a cost-record clerk: budgetary accountant; head of accounting for current planning and control; head of general accounting; controller; storekeeper; production superintendent; manufacturing vice-president; president; production-control chief?
  2. Of the following, who has line authority over an assembler: stamping manager; assembly manager; production superintendent; production-control chief; storekeeper; manufacturing vice-president; engineering vice-president; president; controller; budgetary accountant; cost-record clerk?

1-24 Draw an organization chart. Draw an organization chart for a company that has the following positions:

Vice-president, controller and treasurer	Foundry superintendent
Chief designer	Head of job evaluation
Receiving and stores superintendent	Vice-president, personnel
Branch A sales manager	Head of general accounting
Production superintendent	Budget director
Chief of finished stockroom	Tool-room superintendent
Shipping-room head	Chief purchasing agent
Chief of cost accumulation	Head of cost analysis
Maintenance superintendent	Inspection superintendent
Employment manager	Stamping superintendent
Welding and assembly superintendent	Head of research
Machining superintendent	President
Vice-president, manufacturing	Head of production control
Finishing-department superintendent	Vice-president, sales
Vice-president, chief engineer	

1-25 Scorekeeping, attention directing, and problem solving.   (Alternate is 1-26.) For each of the activities listed below, identify the *major function* (scorekeeping, attention directing, or problem solving). Also state whether the departments mentioned are production or service departments.

1. Analyzing, for a General Motors production superintendent, the impact on costs of some new drill presses.

2. Preparing a monthly statement of Australian sales for the IBM marketing vice-president.

3. Interpreting variances on the Stanford University purchasing department's performance report.

4. Preparing a schedule of depreciation for forklift trucks in the receiving department of a Hewlett-Packard factory in Scotland.

5. Analyzing, for a Mitsubishi international manufacturing manager, the desirability of having some auto parts made in Korea.

6. Interpreting why a Birmingham foundry did not adhere to its production schedule.

7. Explaining the stamping department's performance report.

8. Preparing, for the manager of production control of a U.S. Steel plant, a cost comparison of two computerized manufacturing control systems.

9. Preparing a scrap report for the finishing department of a Toyota part factory.

10. Preparing the budget for the maintenance department of Mount Sinai Hospital.

1-26 Scorekeeping, attention direction, and problem solving.   (Alternate is 1-25.) For each of the following, identify the major function the accountant is performing—i.e., scorekeeping, attention directing, or problem solving. *Also* state whether the departments mentioned are service departments.

1. Interpreting why a branch did not meet its IBM sales quota.

2. Interpreting variances on a machining manager's performance report at a Nissan plant.

3. Preparing the budget for research and development at a Du Pont division.

4. Preparing adjusting journal entries for depreciation on the personnel manager's office equipment at Citibank.

5. Preparing a customer's monthly statement for a Sears store.

6. Processing the weekly payroll for the Harvard University maintenance department.

7. Explaining the welding manager's performance report at a Chrysler factory.

8. Analyzing the costs of several different ways to blend raw materials in the foundry of a General Electric factory.

9. Tallying sales, by branches, for the sales vice-president of Unilever.

10. Analyzing, for the General Motors president, the impact of a contemplated new product on net income.

1-27 Financial and management accounting.   David Colhane, an able electrical engineer, was informed that he was going to be promoted to assistant factory manager. David was elated but uneasy. In particular, his knowledge of accounting was sparse. He had taken one course in "financial" accounting but had not been exposed to the "management" accounting that his superiors found helpful.

Colhane planned to enroll in a management accounting course as soon as possible. Meanwhile he asked Susan Hansley, an assistant controller, to state three or four of the principal distinctions between financial and management accounting, including some concrete examples.

As the assistant controller, prepare a written response to Colhane.

1-28 Effectiveness of controller.   A research team undertook the task of appraising the relative effectiveness of the controller's department in various organizations. Based on the general descriptions in the chapter, how would you proceed to accomplish this task?

1-29 Cost accounting in nonprofit institutions.   The bulk of the revenues of U.S. hospitals do not come directly from patients. Instead the revenues come through third parties such as insurance companies and governmental agencies. Until the early 1980s these payments were based on the hospital's costs of serving patients. However, such payments are now based on a flat fee for specified services. For example, the hospital might receive $4,000 for an appendectomy or $19,000 for heart surgery—no more, no less.

Required | Would the change in the method of payment change the cost accounting practices of hospitals? Explain.

1-30 Responsibility for analysis of performance. John Phillipson is the new controller of a multinational company that has just overhauled its organization structure. The company is now decentralized. Each division is under an operating vice-president who, within wide limits, has responsibilities and authority to run his division like a separate company.

Phillipson has a number of bright staff members, one of whom, Bob Garrett, is in charge of a newly created performance-analysis staff. Garrett and his fellow staff members prepare monthly divisional performance reports for the company president. These reports are divisional income statements, showing budgeted performance and actual performance, and are accompanied by detailed written explanations and appraisals of variances. Each of Garrett's staff members had a major responsibility for analyzing one division; each consulted with divisional line and staff executives and became generally acquainted with the division's operations.

After a few months, Bill Whisler, vice-president in charge of Division C, has stormed into the controller's office. The gist of his complaint follows:

"Your staff is trying to take over part of my responsibilities. They come in, snoop around, ask hundreds of questions, and take up plenty of our time. It's up to me, not you and your detectives, to analyze and explain my division's performance to central headquarters. If you don't stop trying to grab my responsibilities, I'll raise the whole issue with the president."

Required | 1. What events or relationships may have led to Whisler's outburst?
2. As Phillipson, how would you answer Whisler's contentions?
3. What alternative actions can Phillipson take to improve future relationships?

1-31 Accountant's role in planning and control. Dick Victor has been president of Sampson Company, a multinational textile company, for ten months. The company has an industry reputation as being conservative and having average profitability. Previously, Victor was associated with a very successful company that had a heavily formalized accounting system, with elaborate budgets and effective uses of performance reports.

Victor is contemplating the installation of a formal budgetary program. To signify its importance, he wants to hire a new vice-president for planning and control. This person would report directly to Victor and would have complete responsibility for implementing a system for budgeting and reporting performance.

Required | If you were the controller of Sampson Company, how would you react to Victor's proposed move? What alternatives are available to Victor for installing his budgetary program? In general, should all figure specialists report to one master figure expert, who in turn is responsible to the president?

1-32 Organization of accounting department: centralization or decentralization.[8] The following quotation is from an address made by an officer of the Ford Motor Company:

We can all, I think, take pride in the way cost accounting has kept pace with industrial development in this country. Tremendous strides have been made during the last quarter of a century, and I'm sure that much more progress will be made in the future. In fact, progress will *have* to be made if we are to keep the science of cost accounting abreast of the times. The whole of industry is now operating on a different level than we have known before—a higher plateau, on which cost accounting appears in a new light, becomes more and more significant as a factor in business management.

---

[8]From the *N.A.C.A. Bulletin*, Vol. 29, No. 7, Sec. II. This problem is a bit more challenging than the others in this group.

It is my experience that the function of cost determination is basic to every other function of a modern business. Cost factors thread their way through every phase of a business and to a large extent influence the makeup of the entire enterprise—its products, its markets, and its methods of operation.

We must, of necessity, have rather complex and extensive costing organizations, but the principle according to which they work is the same—finding out what each of the operations costs before it is too late to avoid doing the wrong thing.

I am sure you would be interested in knowing that the accounting office at Ford was formerly almost completely centralized and that we have begun to install a decentralized system. . . .

It is planned that after the decentralized and the local organizations are prepared to assume the responsibilities involved, these accounting offices will be placed under the direct jurisdiction of the managers of the operations which they serve. . . .

Under the decentralized system, each division has its own complete accounting service. . . . Each separate activity, such as each assembly plant, has been provided with an accounting office to compile its own internal operating reports for its own use, and to forward the financial statements required by the central office.

Required

1. *Decentralization* is frequently defined as the extension of decision-making power to the lowest possible levels of an organization. What accounting functions are the most likely candidates for centralization? For decentralization?
2. Draw three boxes on an organization chart, one each for the corporate controller, the plant controller, and the plant manager. Draw appropriate lines between the boxes that would accord with the system described in the quotation. Use a dashed line to denote "functional" authority and a solid line to denote "line" authority. Describe some major advantages and complications of the new organization arrangements.
3. Assume that accounting's service to management is maximized if it is decentralized as much as feasible, consistent with reasonable costs. Suppose you were to conduct research about the extent of decentralized accounting in a particular organization. What types of evidence would you examine?
4. As a college graduate newly hired by the plant controller's department, would you prefer that the plant controller have line responsibility to the corporate controller or to the plant manager? Explain.
5. "The controller must frequently fulfill two roles simultaneously, as a helper and as a spy." How can accountants' duties be organized to cope with these conflicting roles?

1-33 Professional ethics, quality control. (CMA) FulRange Inc. produces complex printed circuits for stereo amplifiers. The circuits are sold primarily to major component manufacturers, and any production overruns are sold to small manufacturers at a substantial discount. The small manufacturer market segment appears very profitable.

A common product defect that occurs in production is a "drift" that is caused by failure to maintain precise heat levels during the production process. Rejects from the 100% testing program can be reworked to acceptable levels if the defect is drift. However, in a recent analysis of customer complaints, George Wilson, the cost accountant, and the quality control engineer have ascertained that normal rework does not bring the circuits up to standard. Sampling shows that about one-half of the reworked circuits will fail after extended, high-volume amplifier operation. The incidence of failure in the reworked circuits is projected to be about 10% over one to five years' operation.

Unfortunately, there is no way to determine which reworked circuits will fail because testing will not detect this problem. The rework process could be changed to correct the problem, but the cost-benefit analysis for the suggested change in the rework process indicates that it is not feasible. FulRange's marketing analyst has indicated that this problem will have a significant impact on the company's reputation and customer satisfaction if the problem is not corrected. Consequently, the board of directors would interpret this problem as having serious negative implications on the company's profitability.

Wilson has included the circuit failure and rework problem in his report that has been prepared for the upcoming quarterly meeting of the board of directors. Due to the potential adverse economic impact, Wilson has followed a longstanding practice of highlighting this information.

After reviewing the reports to be presented, the plant manager and his staff were upset and indicated to the controller that he should control his people better. "We can't upset the board with this kind of material. Tell Wilson to tone that down. Maybe we can get it by this meeting and have some time to work on it. People that buy those cheap systems and play them that loud shouldn't expect them to last forever."

The controller called Wilson into his office and said, "George, you'll have to bury this one. The probable failure of reworks can be referred to briefly in the oral presentation, but it should not be mentioned or highlighted in the advance material mailed to the board."

Wilson feels strongly that the board will be misinformed on a potentially serious loss of income if he follows the controller's orders. Wilson discussed the problem with the quality control engineer, who simply remarked, "That's your problem, George."

Required

1. Discuss the ethical considerations that George Wilson should recognize in deciding how to proceed in this matter.
2. Explain what ethical responsibilities should be accepted in this situation by the (a) controller, (b) quality control engineer, and (c) plant manager and staff.
3. What should George Wilson do in this situation? Explain your answer.

An Introduction to Cost Terms and Purposes

2

Costs in general • Variable costs and fixed costs • Average costs and total costs •
Product costs and period costs • Some cost accounting language • Classifications of costs

Now we turn to the language—what cost means. We usually do not decide to buy a commodity without some idea of its makeup or characteristics. Similarly, if we acquire knowledge of the composition of cost data and systems, we will be in a better position to decide what types to "buy" in what situations. In this chapter we will learn some basic terminology, the jargon that every technical subject seems to possess. More important, we will quickly see that there are different costs for different purposes. When economically feasible, cost accounting systems are usually designed to serve multiple purposes.

This chapter contains several widely recognized cost concepts and terms. They are sufficient to demonstrate the multiple purposes that we will stress throughout the book. There are many other types of costs, but you will not be swamped by them in this chapter. For clarity, we ease into the subject matter of cost accounting; therefore we will postpone our discussion of many costs. For example, we explore the ideas of controllable and uncontrollable costs in Chapter 5 and opportunity cost in Chapter 9.

COSTS IN GENERAL

Cost objectives

Accountants usually define **costs** as resources sacrificed or forgone to achieve a specific objective. For now, consider costs as being measured in the conventional accounting way, as monetary units (for example, dollars) that must be paid for goods and services.

To guide decisions, managers want data pertaining to a variety of purposes. They want the cost *of something.* This something may be a product, a group of products, a service rendered to a hospital patient or a bank customer, a machine-hour, a social-welfare project, a mile of highway, or any conceivable activity. We call this something a **cost objective** and define it as any activity for which a separate measurement of costs is desired.[1] A synonym is **cost object.**

Cost systems

Cost accumulation is the collection of cost data in an organized way via an accounting system. The word *system* implies regularity—for example, the routine compilation of historical data in an orderly fashion. Other cost data may be gathered on occasion as desired (for example, replacement costs of certain equipment). Of course, continuous compilation is more expensive than occasional compilation; the relative elaborateness of systems is fundamentally a cost-benefit decision as to what data to "buy" on a regular basis.

Cost objectives are chosen not for their own sake but to help decision making. The most economically feasible approach to the design of a cost system is typically to assume some common classes of decisions (for example, inventory control and labor control) and to choose cost objectives (for example, products and departments) that relate to those decisions. Nearly all systems at least accumulate **actual costs,** which are amounts determined on the basis of costs incurred (historical costs), as distinguished from predicted or forecasted costs. The relationships are exemplified as in the accompanying chart.

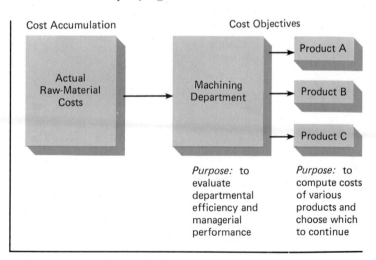

Years ago many cost accounting systems emphasized one purpose—product costing for inventory valuation and income determination—as if it were an end in itself. Consequently, many systems failed to collect the data in a form suitable for

[1]G. Staubus, *Activity Costing and Input-Output Accounting* (Homewood, Ill.: Richard D. Irwin, 1971), p. 1, stresses that in essence we are determining the cost of an activity or action:
"Costing is the process of determining the cost of doing something, e.g., the cost of manufacturing an article, rendering a service, or performing a function. . . . We may, however, find ourselves speaking of the cost of a product as an abbreviation for the cost of acquiring or manufacturing that product. . . ."

other purposes, such as judging departmental efficiency. Modern systems, however, have a more-balanced approach; obtaining the inventory cost of finished product units is regarded as only one purpose. Other purposes may be characterized as planning and control. They include getting a reliable basis for predicting the economic consequences of such decisions as the following:

1. Which products should we continue to make? Discontinue?
2. Should we manufacture a product component or should we acquire it outside?
3. What prices should we charge?
4. Should we buy the proposed equipment?
5. Should we change our manufacturing methods?
6. Should we promote this manager?
7. Should we expand this department?

VARIABLE COSTS AND FIXED COSTS

Costs and changes in activity

Variable and *fixed* costs are two basic types of cost. Each is defined in terms of how its *total* cost changes in response to fluctuations in the activity (often called *volume*) of a chosen cost objective. The activity or volume of the cost objective can be measured in units of product manufactured or sold, hours worked, miles driven, gallons consumed, patients seen, payroll checks processed, lines typed, sales dollars, or any other index of volume.

A **variable cost** is a cost that changes in total in direct proportion to changes in the related total activity or volume. A **fixed cost** is a cost that remains unchanged in total for a given time period despite wide changes in the related total activity or volume. Consider two examples:

1. If General Motors Company buys one type of special clamp at $1 for each of its M-1 model cars, then the total cost of clamps should be $1 times the number of cars produced. This is an example of a variable cost, a cost that is unchanged per unit of volume but changes *in total* in direct proportion to changes in activity (volume). Examples include most materials and parts, many types of assembly labor, sales commissions, and some factory supplies.

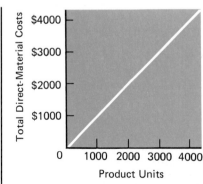

EXHIBIT 2-1
Direct Material Costs—
$1.00 Per Unit

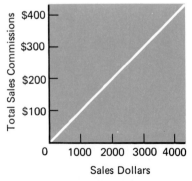

EXHIBIT 2-2
Sales Commissions—
10% of Sales

Variable-cost behavior can be plotted graphically. Exhibit 2-1 shows the relationship between direct-material costs and units produced; Exhibit 2-2 shows the relationship between sales commissions and dollar sales.

2. General Motors may incur $100 million in a given year for a factory's property taxes, executive salaries, rent, and insurance. These are examples of fixed costs, costs that are unchanged *in total* over a wide range of volume during a given time span but become progressively smaller on a per unit basis as production increases.

Relevant range

A **relevant range** is the band of activity (volume) in which a specific form of budgeted sales and cost (expense) relationships will be valid. A fixed cost is fixed only in relation to a given relevant range (usually large) and a given time (usually a particular budget period). For example, as Exhibit 2-3 shows, a fixed-cost level of $100,000 may apply to a relevant range of, say, 30,000 to 95,000 labor-hours per year. However, fixed costs may differ from one year to the next wholly because of changes in such items as rent terms, salary levels, and property tax rates.

Exhibit 2-3 also shows that operations on either side of the relevant range would result in major salary adjustments or the hiring or laying off of supervisory personnel. For instance, fixed costs may be reduced drastically if activity levels plummet. In some cases, an entire factory may be shut down, virtually eliminating the need for service and executive personnel.

Exhibit 2-4 illustrates how fixed costs are usually graphed in practice. The likelihood of volume being outside the relevant range is usually slight, so $100,000 becomes the fixed-cost level. That is, the three-level refinement in Exhibit 2-3 is not usually graphed. Instead the $100,000 total is extended back to the zero-volume axis. Such plotting causes no particular harm as long as operating decisions are limited to the relevant range.

Nonlinearity and volume measures

Nearly all organizations have some costs that can be classified as either variable or fixed. This book will explain why accountants and managers find this distinction

EXHIBIT 2-3
Total Annual Fixed Costs—Conceptual Analysis

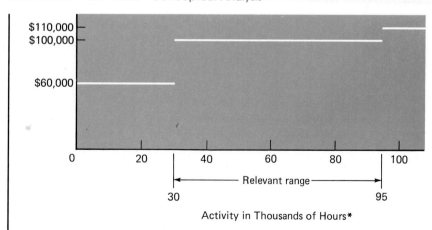

*$100,000 level between 30,000 and 95,000 hours.
$110,000 level in excess of 95,000 hours: hiring of additional supervision.
$60,000 level from shutdown (zero hours) to 30,000 hours: laying off of supervision.

EXHIBIT 2-4
Total Annual Fixed Costs as Plotted in Practice

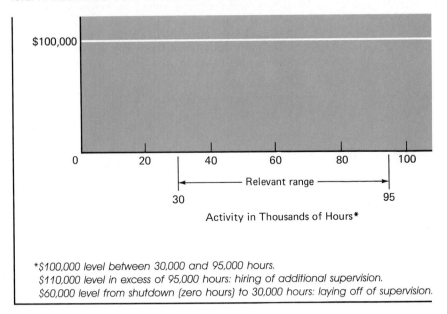

*$100,000 level between 30,000 and 95,000 hours.
$110,000 level in excess of 95,000 hours: hiring of additional supervision.
$60,000 level from shutdown (zero hours) to 30,000 hours: laying off of supervision.

helpful. However, variable and fixed costs are just two of an assortment of useful cost behavior patterns. For the time being, we will assume that all costs fall into either variable or fixed categories. In practice, of course, classification is difficult and nearly always necessitates some simplifying assumptions.

Linearity is a widespread assumption. That is, when plotted on simple graph paper, a total cost in relation to total volume will appear as an unbroken straight line. For instance, the unbroken line for fixed costs in Exhibit 2-4 demonstrates the assumption of linearity, whereas the broken line in Exhibit 2-3 demonstrates non-linearity.

The basic assumption of a relevant range also applies to variable costs. That is, outside the relevant range, some variable costs, such as raw materials used, fuel consumed, or labor used, may behave differently per unit of activity volume. For example, more raw materials and labor-hours may be wasted when learning occurs at low volumes or when crowding or fatigue occurs at high volumes. Exhibit 2-5 shows how variable costs may be affected outside the relevant range. The top graph shows how an economist would graph the likely behavior of total variable costs, whereas the bottom graph shows how the same costs are graphed in practice. Again, as in the case of fixed costs, such plotting does no harm as long as decisions are confined to the relevant range.

Another major simplifying assumption in practice is that the volume of activity is unidimensional; for example, solely units of product, solely labor hours, solely machine hours, solely sales dollars, or solely tons transported. Actually, however, total costs are affected by more than one factor. For example, the cost of fuel is affected by the weight of the vehicle, the weight of the load, and the distance traveled. These complications are explored in Chapters 10 and 23.

EXHIBIT 2-5
Total Variable Costs and the Relevant Range

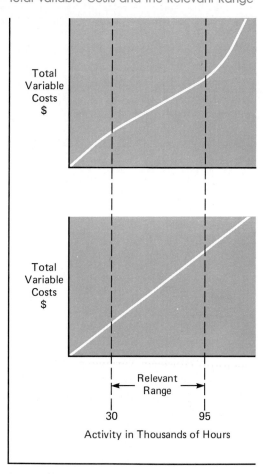

AVERAGE COSTS AND TOTAL COSTS

Helping
understanding

The preceding section concentrated on the behavior patterns of total costs in relation to chosen activity levels of the cost objective. Generally, the decision maker
should take a straightforward analytical approach by thinking in terms of total costs
rather than average costs. As we will see momentarily, average costs must be interpreted cautiously. Nevertheless, their use is essential in many decision contexts. For
example, the chairman of the social committee of a fraternity may be trying to
decide whether to hire a musical group for a forthcoming party. The total fee may
be predicted with certainty at $1,000. This knowledge is helpful for the decision,
but it may not be enough.

Before a decision can be reached, the decision maker must predict both the
total cost and the probable number of persons who will attend. Without knowledge
of both, he cannot decide intelligently on a possible admission price or even on
whether to have a party at all. So he computes an average cost by dividing the total

cost by the expected number of persons who will attend. If 1,000 people attend, the average cost is $1; if 100 attend, the average cost soars to $10 per person.

Unless the total cost is averaged (that is, "unitized"), the $1,000 cost is difficult to interpret; so the average cost (or unit cost) combines the total cost and the number of persons in a handy communicative way.

Meaning of average costs

An **average cost** is computed by dividing some total cost (the numerator) by some denominator. Often the denominator is a measure of activity that is most closely related to the total cost incurred. Examples of denominators include units of product, hours of service, student credit hours, pounds handled in a shipping department, and number of invoices processed or lines billed in a billing department. Generally, average costs are expressed in terms most informative to the people who are responsible for incurring the costs.

The average cost of making a finished good is frequently computed by accumulating manufacturing costs and then dividing the total by the number of units produced. For example:

Total costs of manufacturing 1,000 units (numerator)	$3,800
Divided by the number of units produced (denominator) ÷	1,000
Equals a unit cost (average cost) =	$3.80

Suppose that 800 units are sold and 200 units remain in ending inventory. The average-cost idea helps the assignment of a total cost to various accounts:

Cost of goods sold, 800 units × $3.80 =	$3,040
Ending inventory of finished goods, 200 units × $3.80 =	760

Unit costs are averages, and they must be interpreted with caution. For example, what does it mean to say that the unit cost for the musicians is $1 if 1,000 persons attend? In this case of fixed costs, the *total* cost of $1,000 is unaffected by the activity level, the size of the denominator. But the *unit* cost is strictly a function of the size of the denominator; it would be $1,000 per unit if one person attended, $1.00 per unit if 1,000 persons attended, and $.10 per unit if 10,000 persons attended.

In contrast, assume that the musicians agreed to perform for $1.00 per person. Then we would have a variable-cost situation. If one person attended, the *total* cost would be $1.00; if 1,000 attended, $1,000; if 10,000 attended, $10,000.

Note that for decision purposes the fixed cost per unit must be distinguished from the variable cost per unit. A common mistake is to regard all average costs indiscriminately—as if all costs were variable costs. **Changes in activity will affect *total* variable costs but not *total* fixed costs.** In our fraternity example, the committee chairman could use the $1.00 unit variable cost to predict the total costs. But using a $1.00 unit fixed cost to predict the total costs would be perilous. His prediction would be correct if, and only if, 1,000 persons attended—total fixed costs would be $1,000 regardless of the number attending. The moral is: **Average costs are often useful, but they should be interpreted with extreme caution, especially if they are in the form of fixed costs per unit.** These relationships are summarized below:

Chapter 2
26

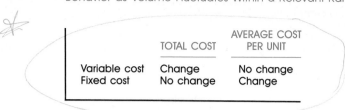

	TOTAL COST	AVERAGE COST PER UNIT
Variable cost	Change	No change
Fixed cost	No change	Change

PRODUCT COSTS AND PERIOD COSTS

Manufacturing and nonmanufacturing activities

Some form of cost accounting is applicable to any entity that has a goal, including manufacturing companies, railroads, retail stores, insurance companies, advertising agencies, government units, hospitals, and nearly all other organizations, whether or not they are operated for a profit goal. We will consider both manufacturing and nonmanufacturing companies throughout this book, but we will begin with the manufacturing company. Why? Because it provides the most general case— embracing production, marketing, and general administration functions. This approach develops a completely general framework of cost accounting for ready application to any organization.

Historically, accounting techniques for planning and control arose in conjunction with manufacturing rather than nonmanufacturing. Why? Because the measurement problems were less imposing and environmental factors such as economic conditions, customer reactions, and competitor activity were generally less influential. However, the basic concepts of planning and control are equally applicable to both manufacturing and nonmanufacturing activities. At the moment, we will examine manufacturing and nonmanufacturing from the viewpoint of inventory costing and income determination—the product-costing purpose when the cost objective is the unit of product.

Manufacturing is the transformation of materials into other goods through the use of labor and factory facilities. **Merchandising** is the selling of goods without changing their basic form. For example, assume that Jane Nentlaw wants to make shampoo and sell it directly to retailers. She may buy certain oils and fancy containers, purchase a factory and equipment, hire some workers, and manufacture thousands of units of finished product. This is her manufacturing function. But to persuade retailers to buy her shampoo, Nentlaw will have to convince the ultimate consumer that this product is desirable. This means advertising, including the development of a sales appeal, the selection of a brand name, the choice of media, and so forth. To maximize her success, Nentlaw must effectively manage both manufacturing and merchandising functions.

Three manufacturing-cost elements

Note the basic difference between the conventional income statements of Nentlaw's business and Crump's Department Store in Exhibit 2-6. In the cost-of-goods-sold section, the Nentlaw statement has a "cost of goods manufactured" line instead of the "purchases" line found in the Crump statement. The details of the cost of goods manufactured appear in the separate supporting schedule.

27

EXHIBIT 2-6 *(Place a clip on this page for easy reference.)*
Comparison of Income Statements ($000 omitted)

NENTLAW (A MANUFACTURER)			CRUMP'S (A RETAILER)		
Income Statement for the Year Ended December 31, 19_2			Income Statement for the Year Ended December 31, 19_2		
Sales		$210,000	Sales		$1,500,000
Less cost of goods sold:			Less cost of goods sold:		
Finished goods, December 31, 19_1	$ 22,000		Merchandise inventory, December 31, 19_1	$ 95,000	
Cost of goods manufactured (see schedule)	104,000		Purchases	1,100,000	
Cost of goods available for sale	$126,000		Cost of goods available for sale	$1,195,000	
Finished goods, December 31, 19_2	18,000		Merchandise inventory, December 31, 19_2	130,000	
Cost of goods sold		108,000	Cost of goods sold		1,065,000
Gross margin (or gross profit)		$102,000	Gross margin (or gross profit)		$ 435,000
Less selling and administrative expenses		80,000	Less selling and administrative expenses		315,000
Operating income*		$ 22,000	Operating income		$ 120,000

NENTLAW

Schedule of Cost of Goods Manufactured†

Direct materials		
Inventory, December 31, 19_1	$11,000	
Purchases of direct materials	73,000	
Cost of direct materials available for use	$84,000	
Inventory, December 31, 19_2	8,000	
Direct materials used		$ 76,000
Direct labor		18,000
Factory overhead (indirect manufacturing costs):		
Indirect labor	$ 4,000	
Supplies	1,000	
Heat, light, and power	1,500	
Depreciation—plant building	1,500	
Depreciation—equipment	2,500	
Miscellaneous	500	11,000
Manufacturing costs incurred during 19_2		$105,000
Add work-in-process inventory, December 31, 19_1		6,000
Manufacturing costs to account for		$111,000
Less work-in-process inventory, December 31, 19_2		7,000
Cost of goods manufactured† (to Income Statement)		$104,000

*Note that operating income is determined before the deduction of income taxes. Net income is operating income plus other income and minus other expenses and income taxes.

†Note that the term cost of goods manufactured refers to the cost of goods brought to completion (finished) during the year, whether they were started before or during the current year. Some of the manufacturing costs incurred are held back as costs of the ending work in process; similarly, the costs of the beginning work in process become a part of the cost of goods manufactured for 19_2.

Note too that this schedule can become a Schedule of Cost of Goods Manufactured and Sold simply by including the opening and closing finished-goods inventory figures in the supporting schedule rather than directly in the body of the income statement.

There are three major elements in the cost of a manufactured product:

1. **Direct materials costs**. The acquisition costs of all materials that are identified as a part of the finished goods and may be traced to the finished goods in an economically feasible manner. Examples are sheet steel and subassemblies for an automobile company. Direct materials often do *not* include minor items such as glue or tacks. Why? Because the costs of tracing insignificant items do not seem worth the possible benefits of having more accurate product costs. Such items are called *supplies* or *indirect materials* and are classified as a part of the indirect manufacturing costs described below.

2. **Direct labor costs.** The wages of all labor that can be identified in an economically feasible manner with the production of finished goods. Examples are the labor of machine operators and assemblers. **Indirect labor** is all factory labor wages other than for direct labor. These are labor costs that are impossible or impractical to trace to specific products. Examples are wages of janitors and plant guards.

3. **Indirect manufacturing costs.** All costs other than direct materials and direct labor that are associated with the manufacturing process. Other terms describing this category include **factory overhead, factory burden, manufacturing overhead,** and **manufacturing expenses.** The term *indirect manufacturing costs* is a clearer descriptor than *factory overhead*,[2] but the latter will be used throughout this book because it is briefer. Two subclassifications of factory overhead are

    a. *Variable factory overhead*. Examples are power, supplies, and most indirect labor. Whether the cost of a specific subcategory of indirect labor is variable or fixed depends on its behavior pattern in a given company. In this book, unless we specify otherwise, indirect labor will be considered a variable rather than a fixed cost.

    b. *Fixed factory overhead*. Examples are rent, insurance, property taxes, depreciation, and supervisory salaries.

Two of the three major elements are sometimes combined in cost terminology as follows: **Prime costs** consist of (1) + (2), direct materials plus direct labor. **Conversion costs** consist of (2) + (3), direct labor plus factory overhead. In sum, these new terms relate as follows:

Prime costs { 1. Direct materials
2. Direct labor
3. Factory overhead
   a. Variable factory overhead } Conversion costs
   b. Fixed factory overhead

How detailed is the tracking of costs? Managers judge whether the informational benefits exceed the expense of gathering specific costs. Where the costs of any one element become relatively insignificant, separate tracking of such costs may no longer be cost effective. For example, in highly automated factories direct labor is often less than 5% of total manufacturing costs. Many of these factories no longer track direct-labor costs separately. Consider Hewlett-Packard. Several of its plants collect direct labor and factory overhead in a single category termed *conversion costs*.[3]

---

[2]The term *overhead* is peculiar; its origins are unclear. Some accountants have wondered why such costs are not called "underfoot" rather than "overhead" costs. The answer probably lies in the organization chart. Lower departments ultimately bear all costs, including those coming from over their heads.

[3]R. Hunt, L. Garrett, and C. Merz, "Direct Labor Cost Not Always Relevant at H-P," *Management Accounting*, February 1985, pp. 58–62. For additional coverage, see Chapter 17.

Manufacturing companies also incur selling and administrative costs. These costs are accumulated by departments such as public relations, advertising, and legal. As the next section explains, these costs do not become a part of the inventory cost of the manufactured products.

Inventoriable costs

Accountants often distinguish between product costs and period costs. Equivalents for these product costs are merchandise purchases for a merchandising company and manufacturing costs for a manufacturing company. That is, **product costs** are those allocated to inventory when incurred. In turn, these inventoriable costs become expenses (as *cost of goods sold*) only when the units in inventory are sold, and this may occur in some period following their manufacture. A synonym for product costs is **inventoriable costs. Period costs** are always expensed in the same period in which they are incurred; they do not go through an inventory stage. Thus period costs can also be called noninventoriable costs; for example, selling and administrative expenses.

Exhibit 2-7 should help clarify the differences between product (inventoriable) and period (noninventoriable) costs. Study the top of the exhibit. A retailer or wholesaler buys goods for resale without changing their basic form. The *only* inventoriable cost is the cost of merchandise. Unsold goods are held as merchandise inventory whose cost is shown as an asset on the balance sheet. As the goods are sold, their costs become expenses in the form of "cost of goods sold."

A retailer or wholesaler also has a variety of selling and administrative expenses, which are the main examples of period costs (noninventoriable costs). These are called period costs because in the income statement they are deducted from revenue as expenses without ever having been regarded as a part of inventory.

A manufacturer, as the bottom half of Exhibit 2-7 shows, transforms direct materials into salable form with the help of direct labor and factory overhead. All these costs are product costs because they are allocated to inventory until the goods are sold. As in accounting for retailers and wholesalers, the manufacturer's selling and administrative expenses are regarded as period costs.

Effect on the balance sheet

As Exhibit 2-7 shows, balance sheets of manufacturers and merchandisers differ with respect to inventories. The merchandise inventory account is supplanted in a manufacturing company by three inventory classes, each depicting a stage in the production process:

1. **Direct-materials inventory.** Materials on hand and awaiting use in the production process.
2. **Work-in-process inventory.** Also sometimes called **work in progress** or **goods in process.** Goods undergoing the production process but not yet fully completed. Costs include the three major manufacturing costs (direct materials, direct labor, and factory overhead).
3. **Finished-goods inventory.** Goods fully completed but not yet sold.

The only essential difference between the structure of the balance sheet of a manufacturer and that of the balance sheet of a retailer or wholesaler would appear in

EXHIBIT 2-7
Relationships of Product Costs and Period Costs

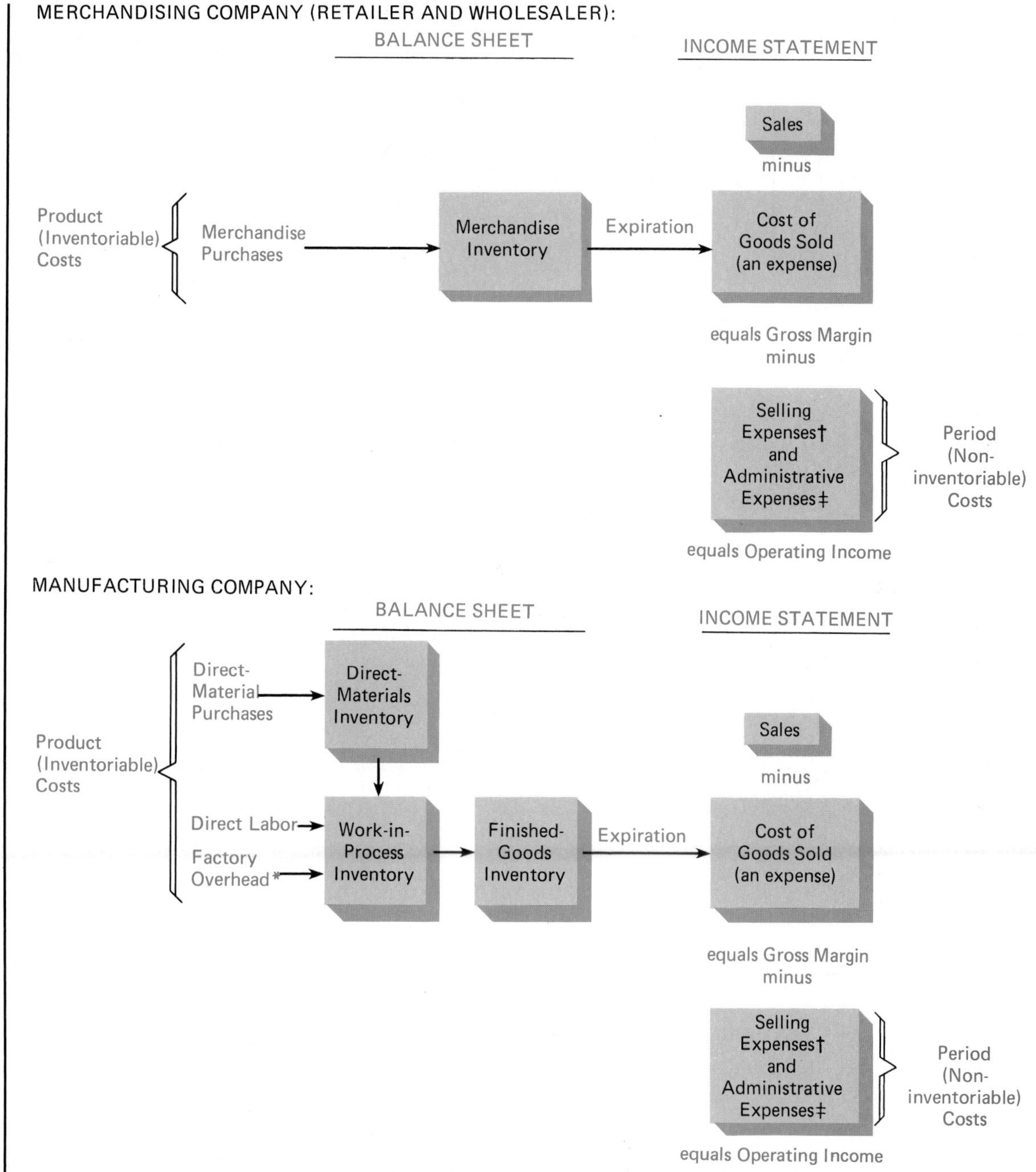

MERCHANDISING COMPANY (RETAILER AND WHOLESALER):

BALANCE SHEET | INCOME STATEMENT

Product (Inventoriable) Costs → Merchandise Purchases → Merchandise Inventory → Expiration → Cost of Goods Sold (an expense)

Sales
minus

equals Gross Margin
minus

Selling Expenses† and Administrative Expenses‡ } Period (Non-inventoriable) Costs

equals Operating Income

MANUFACTURING COMPANY:

BALANCE SHEET | INCOME STATEMENT

Product (Inventoriable) Costs:
- Direct-Material Purchases → Direct-Materials Inventory
- Direct Labor → Work-in-Process Inventory
- Factory Overhead* → Work-in-Process Inventory

Direct-Materials Inventory → Work-in-Process Inventory → Finished-Goods Inventory → Expiration → Cost of Goods Sold (an expense)

Sales
minus

equals Gross Margin
minus

Selling Expenses† and Administrative Expenses‡ } Period (Non-inventoriable) Costs

equals Operating Income

*Examples: indirect labor, factory supplies, insurance and depreciation on plant. (Note particularly that where insurance and depreciation relate to the manufacturing function, they are inventoriable; but where they relate to selling and administration, they are not inventoriable.)

†Examples: insurance on salesperson's cars, depreciation on salesperson's cars, salesperson's salaries.

‡Examples: insurance on corporate headquarters building, depreciation on office equipment, clerical salaries.

their respective current asset sections (numbers are assumed):

Current Asset Sections of Balance Sheets

MANUFACTURER			RETAILER OR WHOLESALER	
Cash		$ 4,000	Cash	$ 30,000
Receivables		5,000	Receivables	70,000
Finished goods	$12,000			
Work in process	2,000			
Materials	3,000			
Total inventories		17,000	Merchandise inventories	100,000
Prepaid expenses		1,000	Prepaid expenses	3,000
Total current assets		$27,000	Total current assets	$203,000

Perpetual and periodic inventories

There are two fundamental ways of accounting for inventories: perpetual and periodic. The **perpetual inventory method** requires a continuous record of additions to and reductions in materials, work in process, and finished goods, thus measuring on a day-to-day basis not only these three inventories but also the cumulative cost of goods sold. Indeed, computerized systems update these records instantly as inventories change. Such a record helps managerial control and preparation of interim financial statements. Physical inventory counts are usually taken at least once a year in order to check on the validity of the clerical records.

The **periodic inventory method** does not require a day-to-day record of inventory changes. Costs of materials used or costs of goods sold cannot be computed accurately until ending inventories, determined by physical count, are subtracted from the sum of the beginning inventory, purchases, and other purchasing costs. Costs are recorded by natural classifications, such as Material Purchases, Freight In, and Purchase Discounts. See Exhibit 2-8 for a comparison of perpetual and periodic inventory methods.

EXHIBIT 2-8
Summary Comparison of Periodic and Perpetual Inventory Methods
(Figures from Exhibit 2-6)

PERIODIC METHOD		PERPETUAL METHOD	
Beginning inventories (by physical count)	$ 22,000	Cost of goods sold (kept on a day-to-day basis rather than being determined periodically)*	$108,000
Add: Manufacturing costs (direct materials used, direct labor, factory overhead)	104,000		
Cost of goods available for sale	126,000		
Less ending inventories (by physical count)	18,000		
Cost of goods sold	$108,000		

*Such a condensed figure does not preclude the presentation of a supplementary schedule showing details of production costs similar to that in Exhibit 2-6.

Troublesome terms

There are many terms that have very special meanings in accounting. The meanings often differ from company to company; each organization seems to develop its own distinctive and extensive accounting language. This is why you will save much confusion and wasted time if you always find out the exact meaning of any strange jargon that you encounter.

Before proceeding, reflect on some commonly misunderstood terms that are displayed in Exhibits 2-6 and 2-7. Consider the misnomer *manufacturing expenses*, which is often used to describe the factory overhead shown in Exhibit 2-6. **Factory overhead is not an expense. It is part of product cost and will funnel into the expense stream only when the product costs are released as cost of goods sold.**

Also, *cost of goods sold* is a widely used term that is somewhat misleading when you try to pin down the meaning of *cost*. Cost of goods sold is every bit as much an *expense* as salespersons' commissions. Cost of goods sold is also often called *cost of sales*.

Distinguish clearly between the merchandising accounting and the manufacturing accounting for such costs as wages, depreciation, and insurance. As Exhibit 2-7 demonstrates, in merchandising accounting all such items are period costs (expenses of the current period). **In manufacturing accounting, many of such items are related to production activities and thus, as factory overhead, are inventoriable costs (and become expenses only as the inventory is sold).**

Both merchandising accounting and manufacturing accounting regard selling and general administrative costs as period costs. Therefore the inventory cost of a manufactured product excludes sales salaries, sales commissions, advertising, legal, public relations, and the president's salary. **Manufacturing overhead is traditionally regarded as a part of the cost of finished-goods inventory, whereas selling expenses and general administrative expenses are not.** The underlying idea is that the finished-goods inventory should *include* all costs of manufacturing functions necessary to get the product to a completed state but should *exclude* all non-manufacturing costs.

Pause and ponder Exhibit 2-6, page 28, in its entirety. The following T-accounts for a manufacturing inventory system may help clarify some key terms (in thousands):

Work-in-Process Inventory				Finished-Goods Inventory			Cost of Goods Sold
Bal. Dec. 31, 19_1	6	Cost of goods		Bal. Dec. 31, 19_1	22	Cost of goods	
Direct materials used	76	manufactured 104 ---------------------→104				sold 108 --- →108	
Direct labor	18			Available for sale	126		
Factory overhead	11						
To account for	111			Bal. Dec. 31, 19_2	18		
Bal. Dec. 31, 19_2	7						

In particular, the cost of goods manufactured is the cost of all goods completed during the reporting period. Such goods are usually transferred to finished-goods inventory. They become cost of goods sold either quickly or slowly, depending on the nature of the product, types of customers, and business conditions.

Labor-cost classifications vary among companies, but the following distinctions are generally found:

Direct labor (previously defined)
Factory overhead (examples of labor costs found as a subpart of factory overhead follow):
  Factory managers' salaries
  Indirect labor (wages):
    Janitors
    Plant guards
    Forklift truck operators (internal handling of materials)
    Rework time (time spent by direct laborers redoing defective work)
    Overtime premium (described below)
    Idle time (described below)
    Fringe benefits (described below)

All factory-labor wages other than for direct labor are usually classified as *indirect labor.* As the above list indicates, the term has many subclassifications to ease analysis of these costs.

Costs are classified in a detailed fashion primarily to associate a specific cost with its specific cause or reason for incurrence. Two classes of indirect labor need special mention. **Overtime premium** consists of the wages paid to all factory workers (for both direct labor and indirect labor) in *excess* of their straight-time wage rates. Overtime premium is usually considered a part of overhead. If a lathe operator, George Flexner, gets $12 per hour for regular time, and time and one-half for overtime, his *premium* would be $6 per overtime hour. If he works forty-four hours, including four overtime hours, in one week, his gross earnings would be classified as follows:

Direct labor:	44 hours × $12.	$528
Overtime premium (factory overhead):		
	4 hours × $6	24
Total earnings		$552

Why is overtime premium of direct labor usually considered an indirect rather than a direct cost? After all, it can usually be traced to specific batches of work. It is usually not considered a direct charge because the scheduling of production jobs is generally *random*. For example, assume that Jobs 1 through 5 are scheduled for a specific workday of ten hours, including two overtime hours. Each job requires two hours. Should the job scheduled during hours 9 and 10 be assigned the overtime premium? Or should the premium be prorated over all the jobs? The latter approach does not penalize a particular batch of work solely because it happened to be worked on during the overtime hours. **Instead the overtime premium is considered to be attributable to the heavy overall volume of work, and its cost is thus regarded as part of factory overhead, which is borne by all units produced.**

Sometimes overtime premium is not random. For example, a special or rush job may clearly be the sole source of the overtime. In such instances, the premium is regarded as a direct cost of the products made for that job.

Another subsidiary classification of indirect labor is the **idle time** of both direct and indirect factory labor. This typically represents wages paid for unproductive time caused by machine breakdowns, material shortages, sloppy production scheduling, and the like. For example, if the lathe operator's machine broke down for three hours, his earnings would be classified as follows:

Direct labor:	41 hours × $12	$492
Overtime premium (factory overhead):		
	4 hours × $6	24
Idle time (factory overhead):		
	3 hours × $12	36
Total earnings for 44 hours		$552

Payroll fringe costs

The classification of factory-payroll fringe costs, such as employer contributions to life insurance, health, pension, and miscellaneous other employee benefits, differs from company to company. In most companies these are classified as factory overhead. For instance, a direct laborer such as a drill press operator, whose gross paycheck is computed on the basis of a $12 regular-time hourly rate, may enjoy payroll fringe benefits totaling, say, $2 per hour. Most companies tend to classify the $12 as direct labor and the $2 as factory overhead. In some companies, however, the fringe benefits related to direct labor are charged as an additional direct-labor cost; these companies would classify the entire $14 as direct labor. The latter approach is conceptually preferable because these costs are also a fundamental part of acquiring labor services.

Chapters 4, 12, and 13 explain how the cost accounting system allocates factory overhead to products. An averaging technique ensures that all products bear their share of overhead, including the components just described.

Definitions and direct labor

We cannot overemphasize the importance of obtaining a solid understanding (the sooner, the better) of the cost accounting terms introduced in this chapter and later in this book. The terms may have various shades of meaning in various organizations. In the real world, therefore, key personnel should be sure that they share the same meaning of a technical term.

Our warning here has many practical payoffs—fewer misunderstandings among managers within an organization and fewer disputes with suppliers, customers, and income tax authorities.

Consider an illustration. The term *direct labor* is often used in cost accounting systems. A general definition was given earlier, but its meaning and measurement differ from organization to organization. Moreover, legal disputes frequently arise regarding the definition and quantification of direct labor costs.

The watchwords are to pin down, clearly and exhaustively, what direct labor means when cost reimbursement contracts or tax incentive laws are written. As an example of the latter, some countries offer zero or very low income tax rates to companies that locate factories there. To qualify, these companies must spend at least a specified percentage of the total manufacturing costs of their products on "direct labor" in that country. How should "total manufacturing costs" be defined? Where does "manufacturing" start? Stop? Disputes have arisen regarding how to compute the direct-labor percentage for qualifying for relief from ordinary income tax rates. Among the debated items are compensation for training time, idle time, vacations, sick leave, and extra compensation for overtime. Moreover, in addition to wages earned, should related fringe benefits such as employers' contributions to

35

pension, health, and life insurance be included? To prevent these disputes, contracts and laws should be as specific as feasible regarding definitions and measurements.[4]

CLASSIFICATIONS OF COSTS

This chapter has merely hinted at the vast number of classifications of costs that have proven useful for various purposes. Classifications can be made by

1. Time when computed
   a. Historical costs
   b. Budgeted or predetermined costs (via cost "prediction")
2. Behavior in relation to fluctuations in activity
   a. Variable costs
   b. Fixed costs
   c. Other costs
3. Degree of averaging
   a. Total costs
   b. Average unit costs (e.g., per student, per hour, per pound)
4. Management function
   a. Manufacturing costs
   b. Selling costs
   c. Administrative costs
5. Ease of traceability to cost objective
   a. Direct costs
   b. Indirect costs
6. Timing of charges against revenue
   a. Product costs
   b. Period costs

SUMMARY

Accounting systems should serve multiple decision purposes, and there are different measures of cost for different purposes. A frequent distinction that is made concerning cost accounting systems is between the purposes of providing costs for inventory valuation and providing costs for planning and control.

The most economically feasible approach to designing a management accounting system is to assume some common wants for a variety of decisions and choose cost objectives for routine data accumulation in light of these wants.

This chapter has concentrated on definitions and explanations of many widely used cost accounting terms and how they relate to income statements and balance sheets.

---

[4]The National Association of Accountants (NAA) has issued a series of *Statements on Management Accounting* that discuss objectives, ethics, terminology, and definitions. They are available from the NAA, Montvale, N.J. 07645–0433. For example, Statement 4C is "Definition and Measurement of Direct Labor Cost." This statement favors including as many related fringe benefits as feasible as a part of direct-labor costs.

(Try to solve this problem before examining the solution that follows.)

problem Consider the following data of the Laimon Company for the year 19_1:

Sandpaper	$ 2,000	Depreciation—equipment	$ 40,000
Material handling	40,000	Factory rent	50,000
Lubricants and coolants	5,000	Property taxes on equipment	4,000
Overtime premium	20,000	Fire insurance on equipment	3,000
Idle time	10,000	Direct materials purchased	460,000
Miscellaneous indirect labor	40,000	Direct materials, 12/31/_1	50,000
Direct labor	300,000	Sales	1,260,000
Direct materials, 12/31/_0	40,000	Sales commissions	60,000
Finished goods, 12/31/_1	150,000	Sales salaries	100,000
Finished goods, 12/31/_0	100,000	Shipping expenses	70,000
Work in process, 12/31/_0	10,000	Administrative expenses	100,000
Work in process, 12/31/_1	14,000		

Required

1. Prepare an income statement with a separate supporting schedule of cost of goods manufactured. For all items except sales, purchases of direct materials, and inventories, indicate by "V" or "F" whether each is basically a variable or a fixed cost. If in doubt, decide on the basis of whether the total cost will fluctuate substantially over a wide range of volume.
2. Suppose that both the direct-material and rent costs were related to the manufacturing of the equivalent of 900,000 units. What is the average unit cost for the direct materials assigned to those units? What is the average unit cost of the factory rent? Assume that the rent is a fixed cost.
3. Repeat the computation in requirement 2 for direct materials and factory rent, assuming that the costs are being predicted for the manufacturing of the equivalent of 1,000,000 units next year. Assume that the implied cost behavior patterns persist.
4. As a management consultant, explain concisely to the president why the unit costs for direct materials and rent differed in requirements 2 and 3.

solution

1. LAIMON COMPANY

Income Statement
for the Year Ended December 31, 19_1

Sales		$1,260,000
Less cost of goods sold:		
Finished goods, December 31, 19_0	$ 100,000	
Cost of goods manufactured (see schedule below)	960,000	
Cost of goods available for sale	$1,060,000	
Finished goods, December 31, 19_1	150,000	
Cost of goods sold		910,000
Gross margin		$ 350,000
Less selling and administrative expenses:		
Sales commissions	$ 60,000 (V)	
Sales salaries	100,000 (F)	
Shipping expenses	70,000 (V)	
Administrative expenses	100,000*	330,000
Operating income		$ 20,000

Probably a mixture of fixed and variable items.

LAIMON COMPANY

Schedule of Cost of Goods Manufactured
For the Year Ended December 31, 19_1

Direct materials:		
Inventory, December 31, 19_0		$ 40,000
Purchases of direct materials		460,000
Cost of direct materials available for use		$500,000
Inventory, December 31, 19_1		50,000
Direct materials used		$450,000 (V)
Direct labor		300,000 (V)
Indirect manufacturing costs:		
Sandpaper	$ 2,000 (V)	
Lubricants and coolants	5,000 (V)	
Material handling	40,000 (V)	
Overtime premium	20,000 (V)	
Idle time	10,000 (V)	
Miscellaneous indirect labor	40,000 (V)	
Factory rent	50,000 (F)	
Depreciation—equipment	40,000 (F)	
Property taxes on equipment	4,000 (F)	
Fire insurance on equipment	3,000 (F)	214,000
Manufacturing costs incurred during 19_1		$964,000
Add work in process, December 31, 19_0		10,000
Manufacturing costs to account for		$974,000
Less work in process, December 31, 19_1		14,000
Cost of goods manufactured (to Income Statement)		$960,000

2. Direct-material unit cost = Direct materials used ÷ Units produced
   = $450,000 ÷ 900,000 = $.50

   Factory-rent unit cost = Factory rent ÷ Units produced
   = $50,000 ÷ 900,000 = $.0556

3. The material costs are variable, so they would increase in total from $450,000 to 1,000,000 × $.50 = $500,000. However, their unit costs would be unaffected:

   Direct materials used = $500,000 ÷ 1,000,000 units = $.50

   In contrast, the factory rent is fixed, so it would not increase in total. However, if the rent is assigned to units produced, the unit costs would decline from $.0556 to $.05:

   Factory-rent unit cost = $50,000 ÷ 1,000,000 = $.05

4. The explanation would begin with the answer to requirement 3. The accountant should stress that the averaging (unitization) of costs having different behavior patterns can be misleading. A common error is to assume that a total unit cost, which is often a sum of some variable unit costs and some fixed unit costs, is an indicator that *total* costs change in a wholly variable way as activity fluctuates. The next chapter demonstrates the necessity for distinguishing between cost behavior patterns. Above all, the user must be wary about unit fixed costs. Too often, unit fixed costs are erroneously regarded as being indistinguishable from variable costs.

Special Points and Pitfalls

At this point your biggest task is to learn the meaning of the flock of new terms introduced in this chapter. In particular, see the "Troublesome Terms" section in this chapter.

Be sure you understand Exhibit 2-6, including the footnotes and the new terms. Newcomers to cost accounting are used to assuming that such costs as power, telephone, and depreciation are expenses unconnected with inventories. However, if these costs are related to manufacturing, they are factory overhead costs that most cost accounting systems regard as inventoriable.

QUESTIONS, PROBLEMS, AND CASES

2-1 What two major purposes of cost accounting were stressed in this chapter?

2-2 Distinguish between *manufacturing* and *merchandising*.

2-3 What are the three major elements in the cost of a manufactured product?

2-4 Define the following: *direct materials, direct labor, indirect materials, indirect labor, factory overhead, prime cost, conversion cost.*

2-5 Give at least four terms that may be substituted for the term *factory overhead.*

2-6 Distinguish among *direct labor, indirect labor, overtime premium,* and *idle time.*

2-7 What is the major difference between the balance sheets of manufacturers and merchandisers?

2-8 "Fixed costs decline as production increases." Do you agree? Explain.

2-9 "For purposes of income determination, insurance, depreciation, and wages should always be treated alike." Do you agree? Explain.

2-10 Why is the term *manufacturing expenses* a misnomer?

2-11 "Cost of goods sold is an expense." Do you agree? Explain.

2-12 Why is the unit-cost concept helpful in accounting?

2-13 Define *variable cost, fixed cost, relevant range.*

2-14 Give three examples of variable factory overhead.

2-15 Distinguish between *costing for inventory valuation* and costing for other purposes.

2-16 Give three examples of fixed factory overhead.

2-17 "Fixed costs are really variable. The more you produce, the less they become." Do you agree? Explain.

2-18 Why is overtime premium usually considered an indirect cost rather than direct?

2-19 Periodic or perpetual inventory methods. (SMA) The terms *periodic* and *perpetual inventories* are referred to frequently in presenting the accounting procedures that are followed by businesses in recording their business transactions in any given period of their operations. Discuss the difference between periodic and perpetual inventory procedures and indicate the advantages and disadvantages of each method.

2-20 Average costs and total costs. A fraternity hired a musical group for a party. The cost was to be a fixed sum of $1,000.

Required
1. Suppose 500 persons attend the party. What will be the total cost of the musical group? The cost per person?
2. Suppose 2,000 persons attend. What will be the total cost of the musical group? The cost per person?
3. For prediction of total costs, should the manager of the party use the unit costs in requirement 1? In requirement 2? What is the major lesson of this problem?

2-21 Straightforward manufacturing statement. Suppose XY Company supplies Ford Motor Company with auto parts. Use the accompanying data to answer the following questions on XY (in millions).

	INVENTORIES	
	12/31/_3	12/31/_4
Direct materials	$ 7	$ 5
Work in process	4	3
Finished goods	10	13

Manufacturing Costs Incurred During 19_4

Direct materials used		$30
Direct labor		13
Indirect manufacturing costs:		
Indirect labor	$ 5	
Utilities	2	
Depreciation—plant and equipment	3	
Other	6	16
Other		$59

1. Prepare a statement of cost of goods manufactured and sold.
2. Compare your statement with those in Exhibit 2-6, page 28. How does your statement differ from the Schedule of Cost of Goods Manufactured in Exhibit 2-6?
3. Compute the prime costs incurred during 19_4. Compute the conversion costs incurred during 19_4.
4. What is the difference in meaning between the terms "total manufacturing costs incurred in 19_4" and "cost of goods manufactured in 19_4"?
5. Draw a T-account for Work in Process. Enter the amounts shown on your financial statement into the T-account as you think they might logically affect Work in Process, assuming that the account was kept on a perpetual inventory basis. Use a single summary number of $16 million for entering any effects of the indirect manufacturing costs rather than entering the four individual amounts.

2-22 Statement of cost of goods manufactured. (Alternate is 2-24.)   The Mondavi Corporation has the following accounts (in millions of dollars):

Selling and administrative expenses	$100
Work in process, December 31, 19_1	10
Factory supplies used	10
Direct materials, December 31, 19_2	20
Factory utilities	30
Finished goods, December 31, 19_2	55
Indirect labor	60
Work in process, December 31, 19_2	5
Purchases of direct materials	125
Direct labor	200
Depreciation—factory building and equipment	80
Factory supervisory salaries	5
Miscellaneous factory overhead	35
Sales	700
Finished goods, December 31, 19_1	70
Direct materials, December 31, 19_1	45

Income statement and a schedule of cost of goods manufactured for the year ended December 31, 19_2. (For additional questions regarding these facts, see the next problem.)

2-23 Interpretation of statements.   Refer to the preceding problem.

1. How would the answer to the preceding problem be modified if you were asked for a schedule of cost of goods manufactured and sold instead of a schedule of cost of goods manufactured? Be specific.
2. Examine Exhibit 2-7. Would the sales manager's salary be accounted for any differently if the Mondavi Corporation were a merchandising company instead of a manufacturing company? Using the boxes in the exhibit, describe how an assembler's wages would be accounted for in this manufacturing company.
3. Factory supervisory salaries are usually regarded as indirect manufacturing costs. When might some of these costs be regarded as direct costs? Give an example.
4. Suppose that both the direct materials and the depreciation were related to the manufacture of the equivalent of one million units of product. What is the unit cost for the direct materials assigned to those units? For depreciation? Assume that yearly depreciation is computed on a straight-line basis.
5. Assume that the implied cost behavior patterns in requirement 4 persist. That is, direct material costs behave as a variable cost and depreciation behaves as a fixed cost. Repeat the computations in requirement 4, assuming that the costs are being predicted for the manufacture of the equivalent of 1.2 million units of product. How would the total costs be affected?
6. As a management accountant, explain concisely to the president why the unit costs differed in requirements 4 and 5.

2-24 Statement of cost of goods manufactured. (Alternate is 2-22.)   The following items pertain to Galvez Corporation (in dollars):

		FOR YEAR 19_2	
Work in process, Dec. 31, 19_2	2,000	Selling and administrative	
Finished goods, Dec. 31, 19_1	40,000	expenses (total)	70,000
Accounts receivable,		Direct materials purchased	80,000
Dec. 31, 19_2	30,000	Direct labor	70,000
Accounts payable, Dec. 31, 19_1	40,000	Factory supplies	6,000
Direct materials, Dec. 31, 19_1	30,000	Property taxes on factory	1,000
Work in process, Dec. 31, 19_1	10,000	Factory utilities	5,000
Direct materials, Dec. 31, 19_2	5,000	Indirect labor	20,000
Finished goods, Dec. 31, 19_2	12,000	Depreciation—plant	
Accounts payable, Dec. 31, 19_2	20,000	and equipment	9,000
Accounts receivable,		Sales	350,000
Dec. 31, 19_1	50,000	Miscellaneous factory overhead	10,000

Required   Prepare an income statement and a supporting schedule of cost of goods manufactured. (For additional questions regarding these facts, see the next problem.)

2-25 Interpretation of statements.   Refer to the preceding problem.

Required   1. How would the answer to the preceding problem be modified if you were asked for a schedule of cost of goods manufactured and sold instead of a schedule of cost of goods manufactured? Be specific.

2. Examine Exhibit 2-7. Would the sales manager's salary be accounted for any differently if the Galvez Corporation were a merchandising company instead of a manufacturing company? Using the boxes in the exhibit, describe how an assembler's wages would be accounted for in this manufacturing company.

3. Factory supervisory salaries are usually regarded as indirect manufacturing costs. When might some of these costs be regarded as direct costs? Give an example.

4. Suppose that both the direct materials and the depreciation were related to the manufacture of the equivalent of 1,000 units of product. What is the unit cost for the direct materials assigned to those units? For depreciation? Assume that yearly depreciation is computed on a straight-line basis.

5. Assume that the implied cost behavior patterns in requirement 4 persist. That is, direct material costs behave as a variable cost and depreciation behaves as a fixed cost. Repeat the computations in requirement 4, assuming that the costs are being predicted for the manufacture of the equivalent of 1,500 units of product. How would the total costs be affected?

6. As a management accountant, explain concisely to the president why the unit costs differed in requirements 4 and 5.

2-26 Compute cost of goods sold.   (SMA) A manufacturing company had inventories at the beginning and end of its most recent fiscal period as follows:

	BEGINNING	END
Raw materials	$22,000	$30,000
Work in process	40,000	48,000
Finished goods	25,000	18,000

During this period, the following costs and expenses were incurred:

Raw materials purchased	$300,000
Direct-labor cost	120,000
Indirect-labor cost (factory)	60,000
Taxes, utilities, and depreciation on factory building	50,000
Sales and office salaries	64,000

Cost of goods sold during the period was (choose one): (1) $514,000, (2) $521,000, (3) $522,000, (4) $539,000.

2-27 Finding unknown balances. An auditor for the Internal Revenue Service is trying to reconstruct some partially destroyed records of two taxpayers. For each of the cases in the accompanying list, find the unknowns designated by capital letters.

	CASE 1	CASE 2
Finished-goods inventory, 1/1	$ 5,000	$ 4,000
Direct material used	8,000	6,000
Direct labor	13,000	11,000
Factory overhead	7,000	D
Purchases of direct material	9,000	7,000
Sales	42,000	31,800
Accounts receivable, 1/1	2,000	1,400
Accounts receivable, 12/31	6,000	2,100
Cost of goods sold	A	22,000
Accounts payable, 1/1	3,000	1,700
Accounts payable, 12/31	1,800	1,500
Finished-goods inventory, 12/31	B	5,300
Gross profit	11,300	C
Work in process, 1/1	–0–	800
Work in process, 12/31	–0–	3,000

2-28 Finding unknown balances. An insurance investigator in Manchester, England, is reconstructing records of the Malkind Company. Some data were destroyed in a fire. Given the following for the fiscal year (in thousands of British pounds): cost of goods sold, 33,000; purchases of direct materials, 8,000; factory overhead, 13,000; sales commissions, 2,000; direct labor, 8,000; direct materials used, 3,600; finished-goods inventory, beginning, 7,800; gross profit, 12,000; accounts payable, beginning, 1,700 and end, 1,500; work in process, beginning, 1,300 and end, 300.

Required | In conjunction with evaluating a claim for a fire loss, compute the sales and the ending inventory of finished goods.

2-29 Fire loss, computing inventory costs. A distraught employee, Fang W. Arson, put a torch to a factory on a blustery February 26. The resulting blaze completely destroyed the plant and its contents. Fortunately, certain accounting records were kept in another building. They revealed the following for the period December 31, 19_1–February 26, 19_2:

Sales, $500,000
Direct labor, $180,000
Prime costs, $294,000
Gross profit percentage based on net sales, 20%
Cost of goods available for sale, $450,000
Direct materials purchased, $160,000
Work in process, 12/31/_1, $34,000
Direct materials, 12/31/_1, $16,000
Finished goods, 12/31/_1, $30,000
Factory overhead, 40% of conversion costs

The loss was fully covered by insurance. The insurance company wants to know the approximate cost of the inventories as a basis for negotiating a settlement, which is really to be based on replacement cost, not historical cost.

Required Calculate the cost of

1. Finished-goods inventory, 2/26/_2
2. Work-in-process inventory, 2/26/_2
3. Direct-materials inventory, 2/26/_2

2-30 Classification of costs. Classify each of the following as direct or indirect (D or I) with respect to product, and as variable or fixed (V or F) with respect to whether the cost changes in total as activity or volume changes. If in doubt, select on the basis of whether the item will vary over a wide range of activity. You will have two answers, D or I and V or F, for *each* of the ten items:

1. Food for a factory cafeteria
2. Factory rent
3. Salary of a factory storeroom clerk
4. Manager training program
5. Abrasives (sandpaper, etc.)
6. Cutting bits in a machinery department
7. Workmen's compensation insurance in a factory
8. Cement for a roadbuilder
9. Steel scrap for a blast furnace
10. Paper towels for a factory washroom

2-31 Classification of costs. (Alternate to 2-30.) Classify each of the following as direct or indirect (D or I) with respect to a specific product or service, and as variable or fixed (V or F) with respect to whether the cost changes in total as activity or volume changes. If in doubt, select on the basis of whether the item will vary over a wide range of actvitity. You will have two answers, D or I and V or F, for *each* of the ten items:

1. Sheet steel for General Electric's manufacture of refrigerators
2. Idle time, assembly department
3. Property taxes
4. Coolant for operating machines
5. Supervisory salaries, assembly department
6. Fuel pumps purchased by Ford assembly plant
7. Straight-line depreciation on machinery
8. Factory picnic
9. Fuel for forklift trucks
10. Welding supplies

2-32 Overtime and fringe costs. A city planning department had a flurry of work during a particular week. The printers' labor contract provided for payment to workers at a rate of 150% of the regular hourly wage rate for all hours worked in excess of 8 per day. Anthony Bardo worked 8 hours on Monday through Wednesday, 10 hours on Thursday, and 9 hours on Friday. His regular pay rate is $12 per hour.

Required

1. Suppose that the printing department works on various jobs. All costs of the jobs are eventually allocated to the users, whether the consumers be the property-tax department, the city hospital, the city schools, or individual citizens who purchase some publications processed by the department. Compute Bardo's wages for the week. How much, if any, of Bardo's wages should be classified as direct costs of particular printing jobs? Why?
2. The city pension plan provides for the city to contribute to an employee pension fund for all employees at a rate of 20% of gross wages (not considering pension benefits). How much, if any, of Bardo's retirement benefits should be classified as direct costs of particular printing jobs? Why?

2-33 Unknowns, T-accounts, schedules. (CPA, adapted) Mat Company's cost of goods sold for the month ended March 31, 19_4, was $345,000. Ending work-in-process inventory was 90% of beginning work-in-process inventory. Factory overhead was 50% of direct-labor cost. Other information pertaining to Mat Company's inventories and production for the month of March is as follows:

Beginning inventories—March 1	
Direct materials	$ 20,000
Work in process	40,000
Finished goods	102,000
Purchases of direct materials during March	110,000
Ending inventories—March 31	
Direct materials	26,000
Work in process	?
Finished goods	105,000

Required

(Hint: Use T-accounts.)

1. Prepare a schedule of cost of goods manufactured for the month of March.
2. Compute the prime costs incurred during March.
3. Compute the conversion costs charged to work in process during March.

2-34 Comprehensive problem on unit costs, product costs, variable and fixed costs, and budgeted income statement. The Donavan Company makes a single product. Costs are as follows (V stands for variable; F, for fixed):

Production in units	100,000
Costs incurred:	
Direct material used	$100,000 V
Direct labor	70,000 V
Power	5,000 V
Indirect labor	10,000 V
Indirect labor	20,000 F
Other factory overhead	8,000 V
Other factory overhead	20,000 F
Selling expenses	30,000 V
Selling expenses	20,000 F
Administrative expenses	50,000 F
Work-in-process inventory, December 31, 19_1	—
Direct-material inventory, December 31, 19_1	2,000 lbs.
Finished-goods inventory, December 31, 19_1	$ 20,970

Dollar sales were $318,500 in 19_1. There were no beginning inventories in 19_1. The company's ending inventory of finished goods was carried at the average unit cost of production for 19_1. Direct material prices have been stable throughout the year. Two pounds of direct material are used to make a unit of finished product.

Required

1. Direct-material inventory, total cost, December 31, 19_1.
2. Finished-goods inventory, total units, December 31, 19_1.
3. Unit sales price, 19_1.
4. Operating income, 19_1. Show computations.

For an additional question regarding these facts, see the next problem.

2-35 Budgeted income statement. This problem is more difficult than previous ones. Refer to the preceding problem. Management has asked that you prepare a budgeted income statement for 19_2, assuming that all unit prices for sales and variable costs will not change. Assume that sales will be 102,000 units and that ending inventory of finished goods, December 31, 19_2, will be 12,000 units. Assume also that fixed costs will remain the same. Show supporting computations, and include a schedule of cost of goods manufactured. The ending inventory of finished goods is to be carried at the average unit cost of production for 19_2.

Cost-Volume-Profit Relationships

3

The breakeven point • Cost-volume-profit assumptions • Interrelationships of cost, volume, and profits • Introduction to variable costing • The P/V chart • Effects of sales mix • Role of income taxes • Measuring volume • All data in dollars • Nonprofit institutions and cost-volume-revenue analysis • CVP models, personal computers, decision situations

The preceding chapter distinguished sharply between two major purposes of cost accounting systems: (a) decision making for planning and control and (b) product costing for inventory valuation and income determination. This chapter and the next will examine these two purposes in more depth. Cost-volume-profit analysis is a subject inherently appealing to most students of management. It gives a sweeping overview of the planning process. It provides a concrete example of the importance of understanding cost behavior—the response of costs to a variety of influences. That is why we consider this subject now, even though it could just as easily be studied later.

Managers are constantly faced with decisions about selling prices, variable costs, and fixed costs. Basically, managers must decide how to acquire and utilize economic resources in light of some organization goal. Unless they can make reasonably accurate predictions about cost and revenue levels, their decisions may yield undesirable or even disastrous results. These decisions are usually short run: How many units should we manufacture? How many nurses should we hire? Should we change our price? How many airplane tickets should we sell at a discount? Should we spend more on advertising? However, long-run decisions such as the purchase of plant and equipment also hinge on predictions of the resulting cost-volume-profit relationships.

At the outset, remember that we will be considering simplified versions of the real world. Are these simplifications justifiable? The answer depends on the facts in a particular organization. The manager has a method for deciding among courses of action, often called a *decision model*. Models of cost-volume-profit relationships are examples of decision models. The simpler model is always preferable provided that the management decisions will be unaffected by the buying of a more complicated model. That is, a more complicated model is attractive only when the resulting decisions will be improved in a net benefit sense.

THE BREAKEVEN POINT

We obtain an overview of decision models by examining the interrelationships of changes in costs, volume, and profits—sometimes too narrowly described as breakeven analysis. The breakeven point is often only incidental in these studies. Instead the focus is on the impact upon net income of various decisions that affect sales and costs. The **breakeven point** is that point of activity (sales volume) where total revenues and total expenses are equal; that is, there is neither profit nor loss. The terms *net income* and *net profit* are used interchangeably in this book.

This section shows three methods for calculating the breakeven point: the equation method, the contribution-margin method, and the graphic method. Consider the following example.

EXAMPLE

Elsie plans to sell colorful souvenir badges at the state fair. She can purchase these badges at 50¢ each with the privilege of returning all unsold badges. The booth rental is $200, payable in advance. The badges will be sold at 90¢ each. How many badges must be sold to break even? (Ignore income taxes, which we consider later in the chapter.)

Equation method

The first solution method for computing the breakeven point is the *equation method*. Every income statement can be expressed in equation form as follows:

$$\text{Sales} - \text{Variable expenses} - \text{Fixed expenses} = \text{Net income}$$

Or (Unit sales price × Units) − (Unit variable expense × Units)
$$- \text{ Fixed expenses} = \text{Net income}$$

This equation provides the most general and easy-to-remember approach to any breakeven or profit-estimate situation. For the example above:

Let X = Number of units to be sold to break even, where the breakeven point is defined as zero net income

$$\$.90X - \$.50X - \$200 = 0$$

$$\$.40X = \$200$$

$$X = \frac{\$200}{\$.40}$$

$$X = 500 \text{ units (or } \$450 \text{ total sales at } 90¢ \text{ per unit)}$$

Contribution-margin method

A second solution method emphasizes a formula. It is the *contribution-margin* or *marginal-income* method. **Contribution margin** is equal to sales minus *all variable* expenses. Sales and expenses are analyzed as follows:

1. *Unit contribution margin* to cover fixed expenses and target net income

$$= \text{Unit sales price} - \text{Unit variable expense} = \$.90 - \$.50 = \$.40$$

2. *Breakeven point* in terms of units sold

$$= \frac{\text{Fixed expenses}}{\text{Unit contribution margin}} = \frac{\$200}{\$.40} = 500 \text{ units}$$

Stop a moment and relate the contribution-margin method to the equation method. The key calculation was dividing $200 by $.40. Look at the third line in the equation solution. It reads:

$$X = \frac{\$200}{\$.40}$$

giving us a general formula:

$$\text{Breakeven point in units} = \frac{\text{Fixed expenses}}{\text{Unit contribution margin}}$$

The *contribution-margin* method is merely a restatement of the *equation* method in different form. Use either technique; the choice is a matter of personal preference.

A condensed income statement at the breakeven point could be presented as follows:

	TOTAL	PER UNIT
Sales, 500 units × $.90	$450	$.90
Variable expenses, 500 units × $.50	250	.50
Contribution margin	$200	$.40
Fixed expenses	200	
Net income	$ 0	

Graphic approach

The relationships in this example can be graphed by using three building blocks:

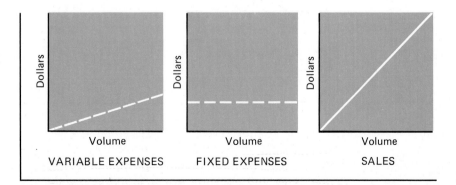

49

These three lines for our badge example are plotted as follows on the complete cost-volume-profit (CVP) chart in Exhibit 3-1:

1. To plot variable expenses, select a convenient sales volume, say 1,000 units. Plot the total variable expenses for that volume: 1,000 × $.50 = $500 (Point A). Draw the variable-expenses line from Point A to the origin Point O.
2. To plot fixed expenses, measure $200 on the vertical axis (Point B). Also add $200 to the $500 plot (Point A) at the 1,000 unit-volume level to get Point C, $700. Using those two points, draw the fixed-expenses line parallel to the variable-expenses line. The sum of the variable expenses plus the fixed expenses is the total expenses or total costs "function," that is, line BC.
3. To plot sales, select a convenient sales volume, say 1,000 units. Plot Point D for total sales dollars at that volume: 1,000 × $.90 = $900. Draw the total-sales line from Point D to the origin Point O.

The *breakeven point* is where the total-sales line and total-expenses line intersect. But note further that this graph shows the profit or loss outlook for a wide range of volume. The confidence we place in any particular cost-volume-profit chart is naturally a consequence of the relative accuracy of the cost-volume-profit relationships depicted.

Note that total sales and total variable expenses fluctuate in direct proportion to changes in physical volume, whereas fixed expenses are the same in total over the entire volume range.

Now combine the fixed and variable expenses in a single graph:

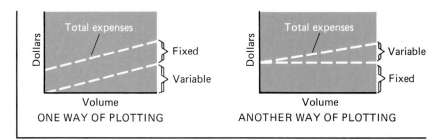

Note that the "total expenses" line is the same under either method. Now introduce the sales line:

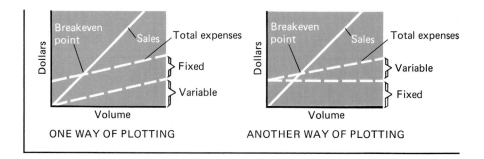

The graph that plots fixed expenses above the variable expenses is preferred by many accountants because it emphasizes the contribution-margin notion. On this graph, note that both the sales and variable expenses lines start at the origin; the vertical distance between them is the contribution margin. Whether operations are

EXHIBIT 3-1
Cost-Volume-Profit Chart

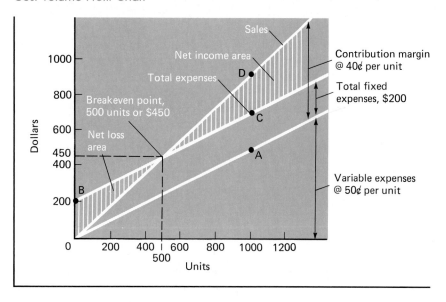

above or below the breakeven point, the vertical distance between the sales line and the variable expenses line always measures the total amount of the "contribution" that sales volume is making toward coverage of the fixed expenses.

The use of the chart in Exhibit 3-1 can also be depicted as follows:

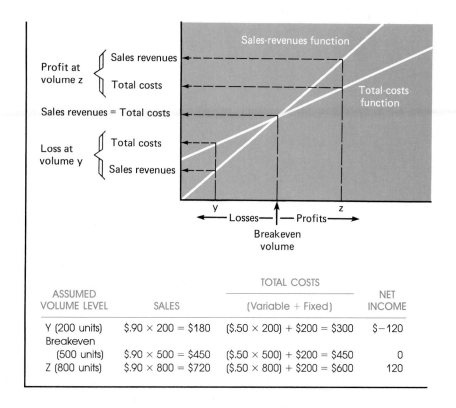

ASSUMED VOLUME LEVEL	SALES	TOTAL COSTS (Variable + Fixed)	NET INCOME
Y (200 units)	$.90 × 200 = $180	($.50 × 200) + $200 = $300	$−120
Breakeven (500 units)	$.90 × 500 = $450	($.50 × 500) + $200 = $450	0
Z (800 units)	$.90 × 800 = $720	($.50 × 800) + $200 = $600	120

Just as net income and net profit are synonyms, so are *costs* and *expenses* as used in CVP analysis. That is, costs refer to the costs expiring and thus becoming expenses during the period in question.

Target net income Let us introduce a profit element by asking, *How many badges must be sold to yield a net income of 20% of sales?* The same basic approach can be used. The equation method follows:

Let X = Number of units to be sold to yield target net income

Sales − Variable expenses − Fixed expenses = Target net income

$$\$.90X - \$.50X - \$200 = .20(\$.90X)$$

$$\$.90X - \$.50X - \$200 = \$.18X$$

$$\$.22X = \$200$$

$$X = 909 \text{ units}$$

Proof:		
	Sales, 909 × $.90	$818.10
	Variable expenses, 909 × $.50	454.50
	Contribution margin	$363.60
	Fixed expenses	200.00
	Net income	$163.60

The graph in Exhibit 3-1 indicates a net income at the 909-unit volume. The difference between sales and total expenses is the $163.60 net income.

Alternatively, the contribution-margin method could be used. The numerator now consists of fixed expenses plus the target net income;

$$X = \frac{\text{Fixed expenses} + \text{Target net income}}{\text{Unit contribution margin}}$$

$$X = \frac{\$200 + .20(\$.90X)}{\$.40}$$

$$\$.40X = \$200 + \$.18X$$

$$\$.22X = \$200$$

$$X = 909 \text{ units}$$

COST-VOLUME-PROFIT ASSUMPTIONS

Relevant range In a real-world situation, the cost-volume-profit chart can be drawn as shown in Exhibit 3-1. However, the many assumptions that underlie the chart are subject to change if actual volume falls outside the relevant range that was the basis for drawing the chart. It would be more realistic if the lines on these charts were not extended back to the origin, as shown on page 53.

The modified chart highlights the fact that tenuous, static assumptions underlie a graph of cost-volume-profit relationships. The sales and expense relationships are valid only within a band of activity called the *relevant range*.

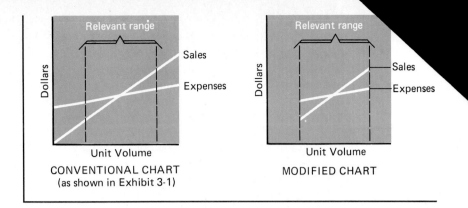

CONVENTIONAL CHART
(as shown in Exhibit 3-1)

MODIFIED CHART

Limitations of assumptions

Cost behavior is affected by the interplay of a number of factors. Physical volume is only one of these factors; others include unit prices of inputs, efficiency, changes in production technology, wars, strikes, legislation, and so forth. Any CVP analysis is based on assumptions about the behavior of revenue, costs, and volume. A change in expected behavior will alter the breakeven point; in other words, profits are affected by changes in other factors *besides volume*. A CVP chart must be interpreted in the light of the limitations imposed by its underlying assumptions. The real benefit of preparing CVP charts is in the enrichment of understanding of the interrelationships of all factors affecting profits, especially cost behavior patterns over ranges of volume.

The following underlying assumptions will limit the precision and reliability of a given cost-volume-profit analysis:

1. The behavior of total costs and total revenues has been reliably determined and is linear over the relevant range.[1]
2. All costs can be divided into fixed and variable elements.
3. Total fixed costs remain constant over the relevant volume range of the CVP analysis.
4. Total variable costs are directly proportional to volume over the relevant range.
5. Selling prices are to be unchanged.
6. Prices of the factors of production are to be unchanged (for example, material prices, wage rates).
7. Efficiency and productivity are to be unchanged.
8. The analysis either covers a single product or assumes that a given sales mix will be maintained as total volume changes. (This assumption will be discussed later in this chapter.)
9. Revenue and costs are being compared on a single activity base (for example, units produced and sold or sales value of production).
10. Perhaps the most basic assumption of all is that volume is the only relevant factor affecting cost. Of course, other factors also affect costs and sales. Ordinary cost-volume-profit analysis is a crude oversimplification when these factors are unjustifiably ignored.
11. The volume of production equals the volume of sales, or changes in beginning and ending inventory levels are insignificant in amount. (The impact of inventory changes on cost-volume-profit analysis depends on what inventory valuation method is used. This complexity is discussed in Chapter 8.)

---

[1]Economists do not assume linearity in CVP analysis. For example, they assume that sales price reductions may be needed to spur sales volume. Managers and accountants take comfort in knowing that most decisions are made within the relevant range of volume, where the linearity assumptions regarding sales and costs are likely to be good enough.

Business is dynamic, not static. The user of cost-volume-profit analysis must constantly challenge and reexamine assumptions in light of changes in business conditions, such as prices, factors of production, sales mixes, and factor mixes. Moreover, cost-volume-profit analysis need not adhere rigidly to the traditional assumptions of linearity and unchanging prices.

PS OF COST, VOLUME, AND PROFITS

Uncertainty and sensitivity analysis

Throughout much of this book we work with single-number "best estimates" in order to emphasize and simplify various important points. For example, our cost-volume-profit models, budget models, and capital-investment models make strong assumptions regarding the levels of variable costs, fixed costs, volume attainable, and so on. For purposes of introducing and using many decision models, we often conveniently assume a world of certainty.

Obviously, our estimates and predictions are subject to varying degrees of **uncertainty,** which is defined here as the possibility that an actual amount will deviate from an expected amount. How do we cope with uncertainty? There are many complex models available that formally analyze expected values in conjunction with probability distributions, as described in Chapter 18. But the application of *sensitivity analysis* to the certainty model is the most widely used approach.

Sensitivity analysis is a "what-if" technique that essentially asks how a result will be changed if the original predicted data are not achieved or if an underlying assumption changes. In the context of cost-volume-profit analysis, sensitivity analysis answers such questions as "What will net income be if volume changes from that originally predicted?" and "What will net income be if variable costs per unit increase by 10%?"

A tool of sensitivity analysis is the **margin of safety,** which is the excess of budgeted sales over the breakeven sales volume. It measures the amount that sales may fall below the budget level before net losses occur.

Changes in variable costs

Consider an example of sensitivity analysis. Both the unit contribution margin and the breakeven point are altered by changes in unit variable costs. Thus, in the badge example, if the cost of a badge increases from 50¢ to 70¢ and the sales price is unchanged at 90¢, the unit contribution decreases from 40¢ to 20¢, and the breakeven point increases from 500 to 1,000 units ($200 fixed expenses divided by $.20). A decrease in badge cost from 50¢ to 30¢ would change the unit contribution from 40¢ to 60¢. The new breakeven point would be 333 units ($200 fixed expenses divided by $.60).

Variable costs are subject to various degrees of control at different volumes because of psychological as well as other factors. When business is booming, management tends to be preoccupied with the generation of volume "at all costs." When business is slack, management tends to scrutinize costs. Decreases in volume are often accompanied by increases in selling expenses and lower selling prices; at the same time labor turnover falls, labor productivity increases and raw-material prices decrease. This is another illustration of the limitations of a CVP chart; conventional CVP charts assume directly proportional fluctuations of variable costs with volume. This assumption implies adequate and uniform control over costs, whereas in practice such control is often erratic.

Fixed costs are not static year after year. They may be deliberately increased to obtain more profitable combinations of production and distribution; these changes affect revenue, variable costs, and fixed costs. For example, a sales force may be established to reach markets directly instead of through wholesalers, thereby obtaining increased unit sales prices. More-complicated machinery may be bought to reduce unit variable costs. Increases in labor rates are likely to make it desirable for a firm to invest in labor-saving equipment. In some cases, on the other hand, it may be wise to reduce fixed costs to obtain a more favorable combination. Thus direct selling may be supplanted by the use of wholesalers. A company producing stoves may find it desirable to dispose of its foundry if the resulting reduction in fixed costs would more than counterbalance increases in the variable costs of purchased castings over the expected volume range.

When a major change in fixed costs is proposed, management uses forecasts of the effect on the targeted net income and the unit contribution margin as a guide toward a wise decision. The management accountant makes continuing analyses of cost behavior and redetermines breakeven points periodically. He or she keeps management informed of the cumulative effect of major and minor changes in the company's cost and revenue patterns.

Fixed costs are constant only over a contemplated range of activity for a given time period. The volume range rarely extends from shutdown levels to 100% capacity. Thus when a radical reduction in volume is foreseen, many fixed costs are "jarred loose" by managerial action. The slashing of fixed costs lowers the breakeven point and enables the firm to endure a greater decrease in volume before losses appear. The 1980s saw drastic reductions of fixed costs by automobile manufacturers such as General Motors, Ford, Chrysler, and Volkswagen. These cuts resulted in much lower breakeven points.

Managers are also more reluctant to add fixed costs. For example, the president of Emery Air Freight commented:

> We would prefer to keep out of the airline business and buy space from the existing airlines because that's a variable cost. If we don't have the need for capacity, we don't buy it, but if we have to own or charter airplanes, the costs become fixed and we're stuck with excess capacity sometimes.

INTRODUCTION TO VARIABLE COSTING

Two major methods of product costing will be emphasized in this book: absorption costing and variable costing. These methods differ in only one conceptual respect: whether fixed manufacturing overhead is an inventoriable cost. **Absorption costing** is a method of product costing where fixed manufacturing overhead is *included* in the inventoriable costs. **Variable costing** is a method of product costing where fixed manufacturing overhead is *excluded* from the inventoriable costs.

Exhibit 3-2 compares the flow of costs under absorption costing and variable costing. The top part of the exhibit should be familiar because it is the same approach to inventory valuation that was discussed in Chapter 2; nevertheless, the term *absorption costing* has not been used until now. Both absorption costing and variable costing apply variable manufacturing costs to products. However, as the bottom half of Exhibit 3-2 indicates, variable costing regards fixed manufacturing overhead as a period cost to be immediately charged against sales rather than as

EXHIBIT 3-2
Comparison of Flow of Costs

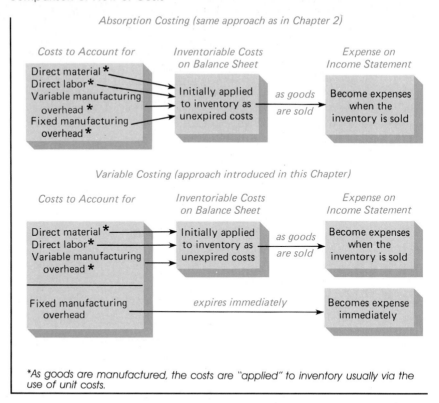

*As goods are manufactured, the costs are "applied" to inventory usually via the use of unit costs.

a product cost to be held back as inventory and charged against sales later as a part of cost of goods sold.

The term *variable costing* is an accurate description, but **direct costing** is also widely used to signify the exclusion of fixed factory overhead from inventories. *Direct costing* is an unfortunate choice of terms; after all, the approach includes in inventory not only direct material and direct labor but also *variable indirect* manufacturing costs. Indeed the term *variable costing* could be improved if it were called *variable manufacturing costing*. Why? Because the distinction centers on how to account for manufacturing costs. Variable selling and administrative costs are written off as period costs under both variable costing and absorption costing.

Variable costing has been a controversial subject among accountants. Why? Not so much because there is disagreement about the need for delineating between variable- and fixed-cost behavior patterns for management planning and control, but because there is a question about its theoretical propriety for *external* reporting. Proponents of variable costing maintain that the fixed part of factory overhead is more closely related to the *capacity* to produce than to the production of specific units. Opponents of variable costing maintain that inventories should carry a fixed-cost component because both variable and fixed manufacturing costs are necessary to produce goods; both of these costs should be inventoriable, regardless of their differences in behavior patterns. Neither the public accounting profession nor the Internal Revenue Service has approved of variable costing as a generally acceptable method of inventory valuation.

The traditional income statement uses absorption costing and classifies expenses primarily by *management function,* such as manufacturing, selling, and administrative expenses (numbers assumed in thousands):

Sales	$1,000
Less manufacturing cost of goods sold (including fixed manufacturing overhead)	600
Gross profit or gross margin	400
Less selling and administrative expenses	300
Net income	$ 100

In contrast, the variable costing income statement features *cost behavior* as the primary classification scheme. Indeed, the income statement is often called a *contribution* income statement instead of a *variable costing* income statement:

Sales		$1,000
Less variable expenses:		
Manufacturing	$360	
Selling	100	
Administrative	20	
Total variable expenses		480
Contribution margin		520
Less fixed expenses:		
Manufacturing	$240	
Selling	120	
Administrative	60	
Total fixed expenses		420
Net income		$ 100

These two income statements represent differing basic approaches to presenting the results of operations. However, there are hybrid approaches too. For example, some companies use absorption costing but include a few distinctions between variable and fixed costs. That is, these income statements retain the primary classifications by management function, but manufacturing overhead, selling, and administrative expenses are subclassified into variable and fixed categories.

The typical discussions of cost-volume-profit analysis assume that the units produced are equal to the units sold. That is, as assumed in this chapter, there are no changes in inventory levels. The implications of inventory changes regarding absorption costing and variable costing are explored more fully in Chapter 8, but for our immediate purposes they are unimportant.

Note that the absorption costing statement does not show any contribution margin. This raises analytical difficulties in the computation of the impact on net income of changes in sales. Fixed manufacturing overhead, under absorption costing procedures, is averaged (unitized) and assigned to products. Hence, as we will often see in later chapters, unit costs and gross-profit figures include fixed overhead that must be removed for a short-run cost-volume-profit analysis.

The contribution approach stresses the lump-sum amount of fixed costs to be recouped before net income emerges. This highlighting of total fixed costs helps to attract management attention to fixed-cost behavior and control when both short-run and long-run plans are being made. Keep in mind that advocates of this contribution approach do not maintain that fixed costs are unimportant or irrelevant, but they do stress that the distinctions between behaviors of variable and fixed costs are crucial for many decisions.

Avoid confusing the terms *contribution margin* and *gross margin* (which is often also called gross profit). As the preceding financial statements show, *contribution margin* is the excess of sales over *all* variable expenses, including variable manufacturing, selling, and administrative categories. In contrast, **gross margin** or **gross profit** is the excess of sales over the inventory cost of the goods sold. Therefore, in a manufacturing company, the manufacturing cost of goods sold (including *fixed* indirect manufacturing costs) is deducted from sales to obtain the gross margin.

In a manufacturing company, gross margin and contribution margin would almost always be different amounts. Such amounts would be equal only by an unlikely coincidence, whereby the fixed *manufacturing* costs included in cost of goods sold happened to equal variable *nonmanufacturing* costs. Even in retailing, where cost of goods sold consists entirely of variable costs, gross margin is not necessarily equal to the contribution margin. For example, suppose retail salespersons earn a 10% commission on sales (numbers assumed in thousands):

Sales	$100	Sales		$100
Cost of goods sold	55	Cost of goods sold	$55	
Gross margin	$ 45	Sales commissions	10	
		Total variable costs		65
		Contribution margin		$ 35

Both the contribution margin and the gross margin can be expressed as *totals,* as amounts *per unit,* or as *percentages of sales* in the form of ratios. For example, a **contribution-margin ratio** is the total contribution margin divided by the total sales. Similarly, the **variable-cost ratio** is the total variable costs divided by the total sales.

The advantages of knowing the contribution margins and ratios of corporate divisions and product lines include the following:

1.   Contribution-margin ratios often help management decide on which products to push and which to de-emphasize or to tolerate only because of the sales benefits that relate to other products.

2.   Contribution margins are essential for helping management decide whether a product line should be dropped. In the short run, if a product recovers more than its variable costs, it is making a contribution to overall profits. This information is provided promptly by the contribution approach. Under the traditional approach, the relevant information not only is difficult to gather but there is a danger that management may be misled by reliance on unit costs that contain an element of fixed cost.

3.   Contribution margins can be used to appraise alternatives that arise with respect to price reductions, special discounts, special advertising campaigns, and the use of premiums to spur sales volume. Decisions such as these are really determined by a comparison of the added costs with the prospective additions in sales revenue. Ordinarily, the higher the contribution-margin ratio, the better the po-

tential net benefit from sales promotion; the lower the ratio, the greater the increase in volume that is necessary to recover additional sales-promotion costs.

4.   When target profits are agreed upon, their attainability may be quickly appraised by computing the number of units that must be sold to secure them. The computation is easily made by dividing the fixed costs plus target profits by the unit contribution margin.

5.   Decisions must often be made on how to use a given set of resources (for example, machines or materials) most profitably. The contribution approach furnishes the data for a proper decision by determining the product that makes the largest total contribution to profits. (However, the solution to the problem of calculating the maximum contribution is not always intuitively obvious. This point is amplified in Chapters 9 and 22.)

6.   The contribution approach is helpful where selling prices are firmly established in the industry, because the principal problem for the individual company is how much variable cost is allowable (a matter most heavily affected in many companies by efficiency and design of products) and how much volume can be obtained.

7.   Advocates of the contribution approach maintain that the compilation of unit costs for products on a contribution basis helps managers understand the relationships among costs, volume, prices, and profits and hence leads to wiser pricing decisions. Ultimately, maximum prices are set by customer demand. Minimum short-run prices are sometimes determined by the variable costs of producing and selling a product. Pricing is discussed at greater length in Chapter 9.

THE P/V CHART

Exhibit 3-1 can be recast in simpler form as a so-called **P/V chart.** This is a profit-volume graph showing the impact of changes in volume on net income. This form is preferred by many managers who are interested mainly in the impact of such changes. The first graph in Exhibit 3-3 illustrates the chart, using the data in our example. The chart is constructed as follows:

1. The vertical axis is net income in dollars. The horizontal axis is volume, which can be expressed in units or in sales dollars.
2. At zero volume, the net loss would be the total fixed costs: $200 in this example.
3. A net-income line will slope upward from the −$200 intercept at the rate of the unit contribution margin of 40¢. The line will intersect the volume axis at the breakeven point of 500 units. Each unit sold beyond the breakeven point will add 40¢ to net income.

The P/V chart provides a quick condensed comparison of how alternatives on pricing, variable costs, or fixed costs may affect net income as volume changes. For example, the second graph in Exhibit 3-3 shows how net income and the breakeven point would be affected by a decrease in unit cost from 50¢ to 30¢ and an increase

EXHIBIT 3-3
P/V Chart

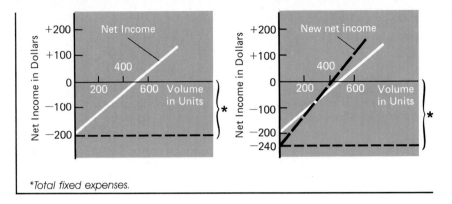

*Total fixed expenses.

in rent from $200 to $240. Unit contribution margin would become 60¢, and the breakeven point would fall from 500 units to 400 units:

$$\text{New breakeven point} = \$240 \div \$.60$$
$$= 400 \text{ units}$$

Note also the steeper slope of the new net-income line, which means that the net income will increase at a faster rate as volume increases.

EFFECTS OF SALES MIX

Sales mix is the relative combination of quantities of products that comprise total sales. If the mix changes, overall sales targets may still be achieved. However, the effects on profits depend on how the original proportions of low-margin or high-margin products have shifted.

For example, suppose that a two-product company had the following budget:

	A	B	TOTAL
Sales in units	120,000	40,000	160,000
Sales @ $5 and $10	$600,000	$400,000	$1,000,000
Variable expenses @ $4 and $3	480,000	120,000	600,000
Contribution margins @ $1 and $7	$120,000	$280,000	$ 400,000
Fixed expenses			300,000
Net income			$ 100,000

What would be the breakeven point? The usual answer assumes that the budgeted sales mix will not change. That is, three units of Product A will be sold for each unit of Product B:

$$\text{Let } B = \text{Number of units of Product B to break even}$$
$$3B = \text{Number of units of Product A to break even}$$
$$\text{Sales} - \text{Variable expenses} - \text{Fixed expenses} = \text{Zero net income}$$
$$\$5(3B) + \$10(B) - \$4(3B) - \$3(B) - \$300{,}000 = 0$$
$$\$25B - \$15B - \$300{,}000 = 0$$
$$\$10B = \$300{,}000$$
$$B = 30{,}000$$
$$3B = 90{,}000 = A$$

The breakeven point is 120,000 units, consisting of 90,000 units of A and 30,000 units of B. This is the only breakeven point for a sales mix of three units of A and one unit of B.

But the breakeven point is not a unique number. It obviously depends on the sales mix. For example, suppose only A were sold (its unit contribution margin is $1):

$$\$300{,}000 \div \$1.00 = 300{,}000 \text{ units (consisting exclusively of A)}$$

Similarly, if only B were sold (its contribution margin is $7):

$$\$300{,}000 \div \$7.00 = 42{,}857 \text{ units (consisting exclusively of B)}$$

Obviously, for any given sales volume, the higher the proportion of units having relatively high unit contribution margins, the higher the net income. To illustrate, suppose in this example that the actual results were sales of 160,000 units—exactly equal to the budget target for total sales volume in units. But sales of A were 100,000 units and B were 60,000 units. Net income would be $220,000, which is a hefty $120,000 higher than the $100,000 budgeted net income:

	A	B	TOTAL
Sales in units	100,000	60,000	160,000
Sales @ $5 and $10	$500,000	$600,000	$1,100,000
Variable expenses @ $4 and $3	400,000	180,000	580,000
Contribution margins @ $1 and $7	$100,000	$420,000	$ 520,000
Fixed expenses			300,000
Net income			$ 220,000

Managers naturally want to maximize the sales of all their products. Then why worry about the sales mix? The analysis of a change in mix often clarifies why actual and budgeted sales and profits differ. Coleco Industries provides a notorious example. In 1983 Coleco was budgeting enormous sales and profits from its Adam personal computer. At the same time, Coleco was expecting more modest sales from another major product, the Cabbage Patch doll. The Adam flopped, but the doll soared. This change in sales mix was the principal explanation for how actual profits differed from budgeted profits.

Despite their desire to maximize the sales of all products, managers must frequently cope with limited resources. For instance, additional production capacity may be unavailable. What products should be produced? As Chapters 9 and 22 explain in more detail, the decision is not necessarily to make the product having the highest percentage of unit contribution margin. After all, suppose a company can make ten units of Product A for each hour of capacity instead of one unit of Product B. Then Product A can generate a contribution margin of $10 \times \$1 = \$10$ per hour, whereas B can generate only $1 \times \$7 = \$7$ per hour.

In sum, cost-volume-profit analysis must be done carefully because so many initial assumptions may not hold. When the assumed conditions change, the break-even point and the expected net incomes at various volume levels also change. Of course, the breakeven points are frequently incidental data. Instead the focus is on the effects on net income under various production and sales strategies. Chapter 24 explores the subject of sales mix in more detail.

ROLE OF INCOME TAXES

When we introduced a profit element in our earlier souvenir badge example, the following income statement was shown (rounded to the nearest dollar):

Sales, 909 units × $.90	$818
Variable expenses, 909 × $.50	454
Contribution margin	$364
Fixed expenses	200
Net income	$164

Suppose we now want to compute the number of badges to be sold to earn net income of $164 *after* deducting income taxes at a rate of 30%. The only change in the general equation approach is to modify the target net income to allow for the impact of income taxes. Our previous equation approach was

$$\text{Sales} - \text{Variable expenses} - \text{Fixed expenses} = \text{Target income before taxes}$$

We now have to introduce income tax effects:

$$\text{Let } y = \text{Target income before taxes}$$

$$t = \text{Income tax rate (assumed .30)}$$

$$z = \text{Target after-tax net income}$$

Then   Target after-tax net income = Target income before taxes
$$-.30 \text{ (Target income before taxes)}$$

$$z = y - ty$$

$$z = y(1 - t)$$

$$y = \frac{\text{Target after-tax net income}}{1 - \text{Tax rate}} = \frac{z}{1 - .30}$$

The equation would now be

$$\$.90X - \$.50X - \$200 = \frac{\text{Target after-tax net income}}{1 - \text{Tax rate}}$$

$$\$.90X - \$.50X - \$200 = \frac{\$164}{1 - .30}$$

$$\$.90X - \$.50X - \$200 = \$234$$

$$\$.40X = \$434$$

$$X = 1{,}085 \text{ units}$$

Proof:		
	Sales, 1,085 × $.90	$976.50
	Variable expenses, 1,085 × $.50	542.50
	Contribution margin	$434.00
	Fixed expenses	200.00
	Income before income taxes	$234.00
	Income taxes, 30% of $234	70.20
	Net income	$163.80, or $164

Note that

$$\text{Target income before taxes} = \frac{\text{Target after-tax net income}}{1 - \text{Tax rate}}$$

$$\$234 = \frac{\$164}{1 - .30}$$

Suppose the target after-tax net income were set at $234, not $164. The needed volume would rise from 1,085 to 1,335 units:

$$\$.90X - \$.50X - \$200 = \frac{\$234}{1 - .30}$$

$$\$.40X - \$200 = \$334$$

$$\$.40X = \$534$$

$$X = 1{,}335 \text{ units}$$

A shortcut computation of the effects of volume on after-tax net income can use the formula:

$$\text{Change in after-tax net income} = \left(\begin{array}{c}\text{Change} \\ \text{in units}\end{array}\right) \times \left(\begin{array}{c}\text{Unit} \\ \text{contribution} \\ \text{margin}\end{array}\right) \times \left(1 - \text{Tax rate}\right)$$

63

In our example:

$$\text{Change in after-tax net income} = (1{,}335 - 1{,}085) \times \$.40 \times .70$$
$$= 250 \times \$.40 \times .70$$
$$= \$70, \text{ which would be the increase in target}$$

after-tax net income from $164 to $234

In short, each unit beyond the breakeven point adds to after-tax net income at the unit contribution margin multiplied by $(1 - \text{income tax rate})$.

Throughout our illustration, the breakeven point itself is unchanged. Why? Because there is no income tax at a level of zero income.

MEASURING VOLUME

In our examples so far, we have used units of product as a measure of volume. But "volume" is a general term for activity levels that can be measured in several ways. For example, the volume of hospital activity is often expressed in patient-days (number of patients multiplied by the average number of days each patient remained in the hospital). As another example, the volume of the teaching activity of a university is often expressed in terms of total student credit hours taken, not number of students enrolled.

Moreover, the breakeven point is frequently expressed in different forms in different industries. For example, a letter to the shareholders of Ozark Air Lines stated that personnel reductions and improved scheduling had lowered the company's "breakeven load factor from 52 percent to 50 percent." The latter is the percentage of seats occupied. Essentially, Ozark had improved its breakeven point by lowering fixed costs via personnel reductions and by running the airplanes more intensively.

ALL DATA IN DOLLARS

The most widely encountered aggregate measure of the volume of activity is sales dollars, a monetary rather than a physical calibration of activity. Few companies sell only one product. Apples and oranges can be added together in physical units, but such a sum is harder to interpret than their sales values in *dollars*. Similarly, the chief executive of a retailing chain such as Sears or Woolworth would get little help from knowing the total units sold of its thousands of products.

Cost-volume-profit analysis is basically the same whether it is anchored to units or to dollars.

Suppose the Ramirez Company has the following income statement:

Sales	$120,000	100%
Variable expenses	48,000	40%
Contribution margin	$ 72,000	60%
Fixed expenses	60,000	
Net income	$ 12,000	

The relationships in dollars may be expressed:

$$\text{Contribution margin ratio or percentage} = \frac{\text{Contribution margin}}{\text{Sales}} = 60\%$$

$$\text{Variable cost ratio or percentage} = \frac{\text{Variable expenses}}{\text{Sales}} = 40\%$$

Using the variable-cost ratio, the breakeven point could be calculated as follows:

Let X = Total sales dollars to break even

$$X - (\text{Variable cost ratio})X - \text{Fixed costs} = \text{Net income}$$

$$X - .40X - \$60,000 = 0$$

$$X - .40X = \$60,000$$

$$.60X = \$60,000$$

$$X = \frac{\$60,000}{.60} = \$100,000$$

Or using the contribution-margin ratio in a formula:

$$\text{Breakeven point} = \frac{\text{Fixed expenses}}{\text{Contribution-margin ratio}}$$

$$X = \frac{\$60,000}{.60} = \$100,000$$

Suppose we want to know the dollar sales needed to earn a net income before taxes of 20% of sales. The equation approach would be:

Let X = Sales in dollars

$$\text{Sales} - \text{Variable expenses} - \text{Fixed expenses} = \text{Target net income}$$

$$X - .40X - \$60,000 = .20X$$

$$.60X - \$60,000 = .20X$$

$$.40X = \$60,000$$

$$X = \$150,000$$

The equation approach just shown could also be recast in a formula that is frequently cited:

$$\text{Sales in dollars} = \frac{\text{Fixed expenses} + \text{Target net income}}{\text{Contribution-margin ratio}}$$

$$X = \frac{\$60,000 + .20X}{.60}$$

$$.60X = \$60,000 + .20X$$

$$.40X = \$60,000$$

$$X = \$150,000$$

Cost-volume analysis is not confined to profit-seeking institutions. For example, many private colleges in the United States are facing severe financial difficulties. Cost-volume-revenue analysis helps trustees and administrators to understand the potential economic consequences of their decisions.

Some institutions use cost-volume-revenue models for budget planning. Exhibit 3-4 displays the current budget of a college's costs and revenues. Most of the costs are fixed in the short run; for example, faculty and staff costs. Revenue is of two kinds, variable and fixed. For example, tuition and fees are variable in relation to the number of students, whereas gifts, grants, and contracts have no relationship to enrollment. Using assumed figures, Exhibit 3-4 indicates that the college will break even at a level of 2,300 students.

Exhibit 3-5 shows the effect of a decision to raise maintenance costs by $200,000. The breakeven point would increase to 2,350 students.

EXHIBIT 3-4
College Costs and Revenues

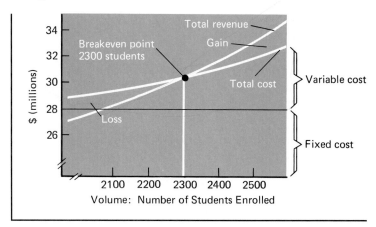

EXHIBIT 3-5
Effect of Increase in Maintenance Costs

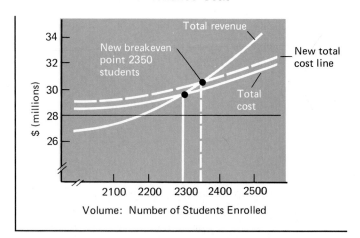

EXHIBIT 3-6
Effect of Increase in Tuition Costs

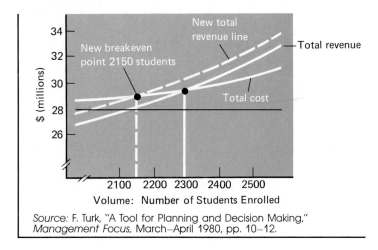

Source: F. Turk, "A Tool for Planning and Decision Making," *Management Focus*, March–April 1980, pp. 10–12.

Similarly, suppose the tuition per student were increased. If all other costs and revenues were unchanged, Exhibit 3-6 shows that the breakeven point would decrease to 2,150 students.

The cost-volume-revenue model can be used for many potential decisions, such as solicitations of annual gifts or increases in student aid. If several possible interactive changes should be analyzed simultaneously, a computerized planning model will undoubtedly be useful. Such models are based on assumptions regarding how various revenues and costs behave in relation to changes in the volume of students or programs.

Consider another example. Suppose a social welfare agency has a government budget appropriation for 19_1 of $900,000. The agency's major purpose is to help handicapped persons who are unable to hold jobs. On the average, the agency supplements each person's other income by $5,000 annually. The agency's fixed costs are $270,000. There are no other costs. The agency manager wants to know how many persons could be served in 19_1:

Let X = Number of persons

Revenue − Variable expenses − Fixed expenses = 0

$900,000 − \$5,000X − \$270,000 = 0$

$\$5,000X = \$900,000 − \$270,000$

$X = \$630,000 ÷ \$5,000$

$X = 126$

Suppose the manager is concerned that the total budget for 19_1 will be reduced by 15% to a new amount of .85($900,000) = $765,000. The manager wants to know how many handicapped persons will be helped. Assume the same amount of monetary support per person:

$$\$765,000 - \$5,000X - \$270,000 = 0$$

$$\$5,000X = \$765,000 - \$270,000$$

$$X = \$495,000 \div \$5,000$$

$$X = 99$$

Notice the two characteristics of the cost-volume-revenue relationships in this situation:

1. The percentage drop in service is $(126 - 99) \div 126$, or 21.4%, which is more than the 15% reduction in the budget.
2. If the relationships were graphed, the revenue amount would be a straight horizontal line of $765,000. The manager could adjust operations in one or more of three major ways: (a) cut the volume level, as calculated above; (b) alter the variable cost, the supplement per person; and (c) alter the total fixed costs.

CVP MODELS, PERSONAL COMPUTERS, DECISION SITUATIONS

The CVP model is widely used as a planning model. Moreover, the expanding use of personal computers has led to CVP applications in various organizations and situations. Managers test their plans on the computers, which quickly show changes both numerically and graphically. Managers study assorted combinations of changes in selling prices, unit variable costs, fixed costs, and target net incomes.

As the previous section demonstrates, computerized CVP planning models are used in nonprofit organizations. For instance, hospitals use the models to predict the financial effects of various patient mixes, nursing and other staff requirements, and patient volume.

Our illustrations in this chapter have concentrated on the sales of products and have assumed that variable and fixed costs can be clearly identified. In the real world, of course, which costs are variable and which are fixed depends heavily on the pertinent time span and the specific decision situation. To illustrate, the additional cost of driving a car five miles to a store is relatively small. In this instance, the car owner would regard nearly all costs of car ownership as fixed. On the other hand, as time lengthens and as volume of miles driven increases, more and more costs, such as tires, that are regarded as fixed in the very short run become variable in the longer run.

Lord Keynes once said that in the long run we are all dead. Similarly, many managers believe that in the long run all costs are variable. However, in many short-run situations managers believe their costs are all fixed. Of course, managers and accountants must cope with some short-run decisions and some long-run decisions. Accordingly, distinctions between variable costs and fixed costs have proven useful.

SUMMARY

Properly used, cost-volume-profit analysis offers essential aid for management decisions such as distribution channels, outside contracting, sales-promotion expenditures, and pricing strategies. It offers an overall view of costs and sales in relation to profit planning, and it provides clues to possible changes in management strategy. It is also the springboard for a different type of income statement, which emphasizes cost behavior patterns. This is often called the "contribution" income statement or the "variable costing" income statement. Such a statement differs from the traditional "absorption costing" statement because it excludes fixed factory overhead from inventories and it includes a contribution margin. Solution 3 in the "Problems for Self-Study" displays these latter distinctions.

Whenever the underlying assumptions of cost-volume-profit analysis do not correspond to a given situation, the limitations of the analysis must be clearly recognized. A single CVP graph is static because it is a picture of relationships that prevail under only one set of assumptions. If conditions change, a different set of cost-volume-profit relationships is likely to appear. The fluid nature of these relationships must be kept uppermost in the minds of executives and accountants.

_____PROBLEMS FOR SELF-STUDY_____

problem 1   A person wants to sell souvenir badges at a state fair. Booth rental is $200. The unit selling price is $.90, and the unit variable cost is $.50. How many badges must be sold to attain a target pretax net income of $300?

solution 1   The equation method follows:

$$\text{Let } X = \text{Number of units to be sold to earn target net income}$$

$$\$.90X - \$.50X - \$200 = \$300$$

$$\$.40X = \$500$$

$$X = 1{,}250 \text{ units}$$

problem 2   Here is the income statement of a British consulting firm (in British pounds, £):

Revenue		£500,000
Less expenses:		
Variable	£350,000	
Fixed	250,000	600,000
Net loss		£(100,000)

Assume that variable expenses will remain the same percentage of revenue:
  a. If fixed expenses are increased by £100,000, what amount of revenue will cause the firm to break even?
  b. With the proposed increase in fixed expenses, what amount of revenue will yield a pretax net income of £50,000?

solution 2   a. Let S = Breakeven revenue in British pounds
  S − Variable expenses − Fixed expenses = Target net income
  $$S - \frac{£350{,}000}{£500{,}000}S - (£250{,}000 + £100{,}000) = 0$$
  $$S - .70S - £350{,}000 = 0$$
  $$.30S = £350{,}000$$
  $$S = £1{,}166{,}667$$
  b. Let S = Revenue needed to earn £50,000
  $$S - .70S - £350{,}000 = £50{,}000$$
  $$.30S = £400{,}000$$
  $$S = £1{,}333{,}333$$

69   For additional explanation, see the "All Data in Dollars" section, page 64.

problem 3   Using the following data (in millions) for 19_3 for the Sprouse Company, prepare a variable-costing income statement and an absorption-costing income statement. Assume that there are no beginning or ending inventories. (The problem of changes in inventory levels and how they affect these statements is discussed in Chapter 8.)

Sales	$150	Variable factory overhead	$ 5
Variable selling expenses*	15	Direct labor	20
Variable administrative expenses	12	Direct materials used	50
Fixed selling expenses	20	Fixed administrative expenses	5
Fixed factory overhead	10		

*These and other expenses would be detailed.

solution 3

SPROUSE CO.

Variable-Costing Income Statement*
For the Year Ended Dec. 31, 19_3
(in millions of dollars)

Sales		$150
Less variable expenses:		
Direct materials used	$50	
Direct labor	20	
Variable factory overhead	5	
Total variable manufacturing costs	$75	
Variable selling expenses	15	
Variable administrative expenses	12	
Total variable expenses		102
Contribution margin		$ 48
Less fixed expenses:		
Fixed factory overhead	$10	
Fixed selling expenses	20	
Fixed administrative expenses	5	
Total fixed expenses		35
Net income		$ 13

SPROUSE CO.

Absorption-Costing Income Statement†
For the Year Ended Dec. 31, 19_3
(in millions of dollars)

Sales			$150
Less manufacturing cost of goods sold:			
Direct materials used		$50	
Direct labor		20	
Variable factory overhead		5	
Fixed factory overhead		10	85
Gross profit or gross margin			$ 65
Selling expenses:			
Variable	$15		
Fixed	20	$35	
Administrative expenses:			
Variable	$12		
Fixed	5	17	
Total selling and administrative expenses			52
Net income			$ 13

*Often called a "contribution" income statement.
†Often called a "traditional" or "functional" income statement. This type is described more fully in the preceding chapter.

Terms to Learn

This chapter and the Glossary contain definitions of the following important terms:

absorption costing (p. 55)   **breakeven point (48)**   **contribution margin (48)**
contribution-margin ratio (58)   **direct costing (56)**   **gross margin (58)**
gross profit (58)   **margin of safety (54)**   **P/V chart (59)**   **sales mix (60)**
sensitivity analysis (54)   **uncertainty (54)**   **variable costing (55)**
variable-cost ratio (58)

Clearly distinguish between *absorption costing*, which was introduced in Chapter 2, and *variable costing*, which was introduced in this chapter. As Exhibit 3-2 shows:

	INVENTORIABLE COST?	
	Absorption Costing	Variable Costing
Direct materials	yes	yes
Direct labor	yes	yes
Variable factory overhead	yes	yes
Fixed factory overhead	yes	no

Also see Solution 3 of the "Problems for Self-Study." Note especially that the contribution margin is the difference between sales and *all variable* expenses, including *variable* selling and *variable* administrative expenses. In contrast, gross profit or gross margin is the difference between sales and *the cost of manufacturing goods sold,* including the *fixed* factory overhead.

QUESTIONS, PROBLEMS, AND CASES

Special note: *To underscore the basic cost-volume-profit relationships, unless otherwise stated, this assignment material ignores income taxes.*

3-1 Identify three major methods of cost-volume-profit analysis.

3-2 Why is it often more desirable to plot fixed costs above the variable costs on a breakeven chart?

3-3 Why is it more accurate to describe the subject matter of this chapter as *cost-volume-profit relationships* rather than as *breakeven analysis?*

3-4 How is the margin of safety related to sensitivity analysis?

3-5 The term *variable costing* could be improved if it were called *variable manufacturing costing*. Explain.

3-6 "Advocates of the contribution approach maintain that fixed costs are unimportant." Do you agree? Explain.

3-7 "Gross margin is contribution margin minus fixed factory overhead." True or false? Explain.

3-8 "Even in retailing, where cost of goods sold consists entirely of variable costs, gross margin is not necessarily equal to the contribution margin." True or false? Explain.

3-9 "The variable cost ratio plus the contribution margin ratio will always equal 1.00." True or False? Explain.

3-10 "The heart of the difference between variable costing and absorption costing is fixed factory overhead." Do you agree? Explain.

3-11 What are the principal differences between the accountant's and the economist's breakeven charts?

3-12 Define *contribution margin, variable-cost ratio, contribution-margin ratio.*

3-13 "This breakeven approach is great stuff. All you need to do is worry about variable costs. The fixed costs will take care of themselves." Discuss.

3-14 A lithographic company follows a policy of high pricing each month until it reaches its monthly break-even point. After this point is reached, the company tends to quote low prices on jobs for the rest of the month. What is your opinion of this policy? As a regular customer, and suspecting this policy, what would you do?

3-15 Fill in blanks. In the data presented below, fill in the information that belongs in the blank spaces for each of the four unrelated cases.

	SALES	VARIABLE EXPENSES	FIXED EXPENSES	TOTAL COSTS	NET INCOME	CONTRIBUTION-MARGIN RATIO
a.	$1,500	$___	$300	$___	$___	.30
b.	___	500	___	800	1,200	___
c.	2,000	___	300	___	200	___
d.	1,000	700	___	1,000	___	___

3-16 Fill in blanks. Fill in the blanks for each of the following independent cases.

	(A) SELLING PRICE PER UNIT	(B) VARIABLE COST PER UNIT	(C) TOTAL UNITS SOLD	(D) TOTAL CONTRIBUTION MARGIN	(E) TOTAL FIXED COSTS	(F) NET INCOME
1.	$20	$14	—	$120,000	—	$10,000
2.	30	20	70,000	—	—	15,000
3.	25	—	180,000	900,000	800,000	—
4.	—	10	150,000	300,000	220,000	—

3-17 Changing the relationships. Reconsider the souvenir badge illustration in the chapter. Recall that the unit selling price was $.90 and the unit variable cost was $.50. Fixed expenses were $200.

Required

    1. Suppose the unit purchase cost of badges rises from 50¢ to 60¢, but the sales price is unchanged. What is the new breakeven point in units?

    2. Suppose the unit purchase cost of badges declines from 50¢ to 40¢, but the sales price is unchanged. What is the new breakeven point in units?

3-18 Exercises in cost-volume-profit relationships. The Best Buy Grocers Corporation owns and operates six supermarkets in and around Boston. You are given the following corporate budget data for next year.

Sales	$10,000,000
Fixed expenses	1,700,000
Variable expenses	8,200,000

Required

Compute expected income for each of the following deviations from budgeted data. (Consider each case independently.)

    a. 10% increase in total contribution margin, holding sales constant

    b. 10% decrease in total contribution margin, holding sales constant

    c. 5% increase in fixed costs

    d. 5% decrease in fixed costs

    e. 8% increase in sales volume

f. 8% decrease in sales volume

g. 10% increase in fixed costs and 10% increase in sales volume

h. 5% increase in fixed costs and 5% decrease in variable costs

3-19 Cost-volume-profit and shoe stores.   The Walk Rite Shoe Company operates a chain of rented shoe stores. The stores sell ten different styles of relatively inexpensive men's shoes with identical purchase costs and selling prices. Walk Rite is trying to determine the desirability of opening another store, which would have the following expense and revenue relationships:

	PER PAIR
Variable data:	
Selling price	$ 30.00
Cost of shoes	$ 19.50
Sales commissions	1.50
Total variable expenses	$ 21.00
Annual fixed expenses:	
Rent	$ 60,000
Salaries	200,000
Advertising	80,000
Other fixed expenses	20,000
	$360,000

Required

(Consider each question independently.)

1. What is the annual breakeven point in dollar sales and in unit sales?
2. If 35,000 pairs of shoes are sold, what would be the store's net income (loss)?
3. If the store manager were paid 30¢ per pair as commission, what would be the annual breakeven point in dollar sales and in unit sales?
4. Refer to the original data. If sales commissions were discontinued in favor of an $81,000 increase in fixed salaries, what would be the annual breakeven point in dollars and in unit sales?
5. Refer to the original data. If the store manager were paid 30¢ per pair as commission on each pair sold in excess of the breakeven point, what would be the store's net income if 50,000 pairs were sold?

3-20 Extension of preceding problem.   Refer to requirement 4 of the preceding problem.

1. Compute the point of indifference between a fixed salary plan and a commission plan. That is, calculate the volume level in units where the profit under each plan would be equal. Above that volume level, one plan would be more profitable than the other; below that level, the reverse would occur.
2. Compute the net income or loss under each plan at volume levels of 50,000 units and 60,000 units.
3. Suppose the target net income is $168,000. How many units must be sold to reach the target under (a) the commission plan and (b) the salary plan?

3-21 Sensitivity and inflation.   Refer to Problem 3-19. As president of Walk Rite, you are concerned that inflation may squeeze your profits. Specifically, you feel committed to the thirty-dollar selling price and fear that diluting the quality of the shoes in the face of rising costs would be an unwise marketing move. You expect cost prices of the shoes to rise by 10% during the forthcoming year. Therefore you are tempted to avoid the price rise by placing a noncancelable order with a large supplier that would provide 50,000 pairs of a specified quality for each store at $19.50 per pair. (To simplify this analysis, assume that all stores will face identical demands.)

These shoes could be acquired and paid for as delivered throughout the year. However, all shoes must be delivered to the stores by the end of the year.

As a shrewd merchandiser, you can foresee some risks in the sense that you deal exclusively in high-fashion goods that are subject to rapid obsolescence. If sales were less than 50,000 pairs, you feel that markdowns of the unsold merchandise would be necessary to move the goods. You predict that the average selling price of the leftover pairs would be $18.00 each. The regular sales commission of 5% of sales would be paid.

Required

1. Suppose that the actual demand for the year is 48,000 pairs and that you contracted for 50,000 pairs. What is the net profit for the store?
2. If you had had perfect knowledge, you would have contracted for 48,000 rather than 50,000 pairs. What would the net profit have been if you had ordered 48,000 pairs?
3. Given an actual volume of 48,000 pairs, by how much would the average purchase cost of a pair have had to rise before you would have been indifferent between having the contract for 50,000 pairs and not having the contract?

3-22 Miscellaneous relationships, margin of safety. Suppose the breakeven point is revenue of $100,000. Fixed costs are $40,000.

1. Compute the contribution margin ratio.
2. Compute the sales price per unit if variable costs are $12 per unit.
3. Suppose 8,000 units are sold. Compute the margin of safety.

3-23 Target prices and profits. (SMA) The Martell Company has recently established operations in a very competitive market. Management has been very aggressive in its attempt to establish a market share.

The price of its product was set at $5 per unit, well below the major competition's selling price. Variable costs were $4.50 per unit, and total fixed costs were $600,000 during the first year.

Required

1. Assume that the firm was able to sell 1,000,000 units in the first year. What was the profit (loss) for the year?
2. Assume that variable costs per unit and total fixed costs do not increase in the second year. Management has been successful in establishing its position in the market. What price must be set to achieve a profit of $25,000? Assume that output cannot be increased over the first-year level.

3-24 Target net incomes and contribution margins. The Blair Company has a maximum capacity of 200,000 units per year. Variable manufacturing costs are $12 per unit. Fixed factory overhead is $600,000 per year. Variable selling and administrative costs are $5 per unit, whereas fixed selling and administrative costs are $300,000 per year. Current sales price is $23 per unit.

Required

(Consider each situation independently.)

1. What is the breakeven point in (a) units? (b) dollar sales?
2. How many *units* must be sold to earn a target net income of $240,000 per year?
3. Assume that the company's sales for the year just ended totaled 185,000 units. A strike at a major supplier has caused a materials shortage, so that the current year's sales will reach only 160,000 units. Top management is planning to slash fixed costs so that the total for the current year will be $59,000 less than last year. Management is also thinking of either increasing the selling price or reducing variable costs, or both, in order to earn a target net income that will be the same dollar amount as last year's. The company has already sold 30,000 units this year at a sales price of $23 per unit with variable costs per unit unchanged. What contribution margin per unit is needed on the remaining 130,000 units in order to reach the target net income?

3-25 Channels of distribution. Chavez Co., a manufacturer of stationery supplies, has always sold its products through wholesalers. Last year its sales were $2 million and its net profit was $180,000.

As a result of the increase in stationery sales in department stores and discount houses, Chavez is considering eliminating its wholesalers and selling directly to retailers. It is estimated that this would result in a 40% drop in sales, but net profit would be $160,000 as a result of elimination of the wholesaler. Fixed expenses would increase from the present figure of $220,000 to $320,000, owing to the additional warehouses and distribution facilities required.

Required
1. Would the proposed change raise or lower the breakeven point in dollars? By how much?
2. What dollar sales volume must Chavez attain under the proposed plan to make as much profit as it made last year?

3-26 Effects of size of machines. Chan Pastries, Inc., is planning to manufacture doughnuts for its chain of pastry shops throughout Hong Kong. Two alternatives have been proposed for the production of the doughnuts—use of a semiautomatic machine or a fully automatic machine.

The shops now purchase their doughnuts from an outside supplier at a cost of 10¢ per doughnut.

	SEMIAUTOMATIC	AUTOMATIC
Annual fixed cost	$7,000	$13,000
Variable cost per doughnut	$ .05	$ .035

Required
The president has asked for the following information:

1. For each machine, the minimum annual number of doughnuts that must be sold in order to have the total annual costs equal to outside purchase costs
2. The most profitable alternative for 250,000 doughnuts annually
3. The most profitable alternative for 500,000 doughnuts annually
4. The volume level that would produce the same net income regardless of the type of machine owned

3-27 Choice of production method. (CMA, adapted) Candice Company has decided to introduce a new product. The new product can be manufactured by either a capital intensive method or labor intensive method. The manufacturing method will not affect the quality of the product. The estimated manufacturing costs by the two methods are as follows.

	CAPITAL INTENSIVE		LABOR INTENSIVE	
Raw materials per unit		$5.00		$5.60
Direct labor per unit	.5DLH @ $12	6.00	.8DLH @ $9	7.20
Variable overhead per unit	.5DLH @ $6	3.00	.8DLH @ $6	4.80
Directly traceable additional annual fixed manufacturing costs		$2,440,000		$1,320,000

Candice's market research department has recommended an introductory unit sales price of $30. The additional annual selling expenses are estimated to be $500,000 plus $2 for each unit sold regardless of manufacturing method.

Required
1. Calculate the estimated breakeven point in annual unit sales of the new product if Candice Company uses the (a) capital intensive manufacturing method, (b) labor intensive manufacturing method.
2. Determine the annual unit sales volume at which Candice Company would be indifferent between the two manufacturing methods. Explain the circumstances under which Candice should employ each of the two manufacturing methods.
3. Identify the business factors that Candice must consider before selecting the capital intensive or labor intensive manufacturing method.

3-28 Influence of relevant range on cost behavior. The Charne Company's cost behavior is as follows:

PRODUCTION RANGE IN UNITS	FIXED COSTS
0– 20,000	$160,000
20,001– 65,000	190,000
65,001– 90,000	210,000
90,001–100,000	250,000

At an activity of 70,000 units per year, variable costs total $280,000. Full capacity is 100,000 units per year.

Required

(Each case given below is independent of any other and should be considered individually.)

1. Production is now set at 50,000 units per year with a sales price of $7.50 per unit. What is the minimum number of additional units needed to be sold in an unrelated market at $5.50 per unit to show a total net profit of $3,000 per year?
2. Production is now set at 60,000 units per year. By how much may sales-promotion costs be increased to bring production up to 80,000 units and still earn a net profit of 5% of total sales if the selling price is held at $7.50?
3. If net profit is currently $10,000, with fixed costs at $160,000, and a 2% increase in price will leave units sold unchanged but increase profits by $5,000, what is the present volume in units?

3-29 Nonprofit institution. A city has a $100,000 lump-sum budget appropriation for a government agency to conduct a counseling program for drug addicts. All of the appropriation is spent. The variable costs for drug prescriptions average $400 per patient per year. Fixed costs are $60,000.

Required

1. Compute the number of patients that could be served in a year.
2. Suppose the total budget for the following year is reduced by 10%. Fixed costs are to be unchanged. The same level of service to each patient will be maintained. Compute the number of patients that could be served in a year.
3. As in requirement 2, assume a budget reduction of 10%. The drug counselor has discretion as to how much in drug prescriptions to give to each patient. She does not want to reduce the number of patients served. On the average, what is the cost of drugs that can be given to each patient? Compute the percentage decline in the annual average cost of drugs per patient.

3-30 Sales mix, two products. Goldman Company has two products, a standard (M) and a deluxe (N) version of a luggage carrier. The income budget follows.

	M	N	TOTAL
Sales in units	150,000	50,000	200,000
Sales @ $20 and $30	$3,000,000	$1,500,000	$4,500,000
Variable expenses @ $14 and $18	2,100,000	900,000	3,000,000
Contribution margins @ $6 and $12	$ 900,000	$ 600,000	$1,500,000
Fixed expenses			1,200,000
Net income			$ 300,000

Required

1. Compute the breakeven point in units, assuming that the planned sales mix is maintained.
2. Compute the breakeven point in units if (a) only M were sold and (b) if only N were sold.

3. Suppose 200,000 units were sold, but only 20,000 were N. Compute the net income. Compute the breakeven point if these relationships persisted in the next period. Compare your answers with the original plans and the answer in requirement 1. That is, what is the major lesson of this problem?

3-31 Sales mix, three products. The Bannister Company has three product lines of belts—A, B, and C—having contribution margins of $3, $2, and $1, respectively. The president is planning to sell 200,000 units in the forthcoming period, consisting of 20,000 A, 100,000 B, and 80,000 C. The company's fixed costs for the period are $255,000.

Required

1. What is the company breakeven point in units, assuming that the given sales mix is maintained?
2. If the mix is maintained, what is the total contribution margin at a volume of 200,000 units? Net income?
3. What would net income become if 20,000 units of A, 80,000 units of B, and 100,000 units of C were sold? What is the new breakeven point if these relationships persist in the next period?

3-32 Sales mix, three products. Esposito Company has three products, tote bags H, J, and K. The president plans to sell 200,000 units during the next period, consisting of 80,000 H, 100,000 J, and 20,000 K. The products have unit contribution margins of $2, $3, and $6, respectively. The company's fixed costs for the period are $406,000.

Required

1. Compute the planned net income. Compute the breakeven point in units, assuming that the given sales mix is maintained.
2. Suppose 80,000 units of H, 80,000 units of J, and 40,000 units of K were sold. Compute the net income. Compute the new breakeven point if these relationships persisted next period.

3-33 Breakeven analysis and the product-mix assumption. Suppose that the Blanton Company has the following budget data for 19_1:

	PRODUCT		
	X	Y	TOTAL
Selling price	$3	$6	
Variable expenses	1	2	
Contribution margin	$2	$4	
Total fixed expenses	$100,000	$120,000	
Number of units to be sold to break even	?	?	?
Number of units expected to be sold	30,000	50,000	80,000

Required

1. Compute the breakeven point for each product.
2. Suppose that Products X and Y were made in the same plant. Assume that a prolonged strike at the factory of the sole supplier of raw materials prevented the production of X for all of 19_1. Assume also that the Blanton fixed costs were unaffected.
   a. What is the breakeven point for the company as a whole, assuming that no X is produced?
   b. Suppose instead that the shortage applied so that only X and no Y could be produced. Then what is the breakeven point for the company as a whole?
3. Draw a breakeven chart for the company as a whole, using an average selling price and an average variable expense per unit. What is the breakeven point under this aggregate approach? What is the breakeven point if you add together the individual breakeven points that you computed in requirement 1? Why is the aggregate breakeven point different from the sum of the individual breakeven points?

3-34 Multiple choice, income taxes. (CMA) The statement of income for Davann Co. presented below represents the operating results for the fiscal year just ended. Davann had sales of 1,800 tons of product during the current year. The manufacturing capacity of Davann's facilities is 3,000 tons of product.

DAVANN CO.

Statement of Income
for the Year Ended December 31, 19_0

Sales	$900,000
Variable costs:	
Manufacturing	$315,000
Selling costs	180,000
Total variable costs	$495,000
Contribution margin	$405,000
Fixed costs:	
Manufacturing	$ 90,000
Selling	112,500
Administration	45,000
Total fixed costs	$247,500
Income before income taxes	$157,500
Income taxes (40%)	63,000
Net income after income taxes	$ 94,500

Required

(Choose the best answer. Each item is independent of every other item.)

1. The breakeven volume in tons of product for 19_0 is (a) 420 tons, (b) 1,100 tons, (c) 495 tons, (d) 550 tons, (e) some other amount.
2. If the sales volume is estimated to be 2,100 tons in the next year, and if the prices and costs stay at the same levels and amounts next year, the after-tax net income that Davann can expect for 19_1 is (a) $135,000, (b) $110,250, (c) $283,500, (d) $184,500, (e) some other amount.
3. Davann plans to market its product in a new territory. Davann estimates that an advertising and promotion program costing $61,500 annually would need to be undertaken for the next two or three years. In addition, a $25 per ton sales commission over and above the current commission to the sales force in the new territory would be required. How many tons would have to be sold in the new territory to maintain Davann's current after-tax income of $94,500? (a) 307.5 tons, (b) 1,095.0 tons, (c) 273.333 tons, (d) 1,545.0 tons, (e) some other amount.
4. Davann is considering replacing a highly labor intensive process with an automatic machine. This would result in an increase of $58,500 annually in manufacturing fixed costs. The variable manufacturing costs would decrease $25 per ton. The new breakeven volume in tons would be (a) 990 tons, (b) 1,224 tons, (c) 1,854 tons, (d) 612 tons, (e) some other amount.
5. Ignore the facts presented in requirement 4 and now assume that Davann estimates that the per ton selling price would decline 10% next year. Variable costs would increase $40 per ton and the fixed costs would not change. What sales volume in dollars would be required to earn an after-tax net income of $94,500 next year? (a) $1,140,000, (b) $825,000, (c) $1,500,000, (d) $1,350,000, (e) some other amount.

3-35 Role of income taxes. A person wants to sell souvenir badges at a state fair. The unit selling price is $.90, and the unit variable cost is $.50. Fixed expenses for the rental of a booth are $200. Assume an income tax rate of 40%. How many badges must be sold to reach the target after-tax net income of $300?

3-36 Role of income taxes. Here is the income statement of the Wilton Company, a British consulting firm (in British pounds, £):

	Revenue		£500,000
	Less expenses		
	Variable	£350,000	
	Fixed	350,000	700,000
	Net loss		£(200,000)

Assume that variable expenses will remain the same percentage of revenue. If fixed expenses are increased by £100,000, what amount of revenue will produce a target after-tax net income of £60,000? The income tax rate is 40%.

3-37 Role of income taxes. (D. Kleespie) The Bocka Company earned an after-tax net income of $8,000 in 19_1. The company had fixed costs of $80,000, and its variable cost ratio was 75%. The income tax rate in 19_1 was 60%.

Required

1. Determine the operating income before taxes in 19_1.
2. What was the amount of contribution margin in 19_1?
3. Determine the total sales volume in dollars for 19_1.
4. Determine the breakeven point in dollar sales.

3-38 Role of income taxes. (D. Kleespie) The Rory Corporation had a contribution margin of $200,000 in 19_1, and its after-tax income amounted to $8,000. The income tax rate in 19_1 was 60%, and the contribution margin ratio was 50%.

Required

1. What was the income before taxes in 19_1?
2. What were the total fixed expenses for 19_1?
3. Determine the total sales volume in dollars for 19_1.
4. Determine the breakeven point in dollar sales.

3-39 Restaurant income taxes. The Rapid Meal has two restaurants. Fixed costs for the two together total $490,000 per year. The average sales check for each customer is $4.00. The average cost of food and other variable costs for each customer is $1.60. The income tax rate is 30%. The desired net income after taxes is $245,000.

Required

1. Compute the total revenue needed to obtain the desired net income.
2. How many sales checks are needed to earn an after-tax income of $245,000? To break even?
3. Compute the net income if the number of sales checks were 400,000.

3-40 Cost-volume relationships, income taxes. (CMA) R. A. Ro and Company, maker of quality handmade pipes, has experienced a steady growth in sales for the past five years. However, increased competition has led Mr. Ro, the president, to believe that an aggressive advertising campaign will be necessary next year to maintain the company's present growth.

To prepare for next year's advertising campaign, the company's accountant has prepared and presented Mr. Ro with the following data for the current year, 19_2:

Variable costs (per pipe):	
Direct labor	$ 8.00
Direct materials	3.25
Variable overhead	2.50
Total variable costs	$13.75
Fixed costs:	
Manufacturing	$ 25,000
Selling	40,000
Administrative	70,000
Total fixed costs	$135,000
Selling price, per pipe	$25.00
Expected sales, 19_2 (20,000 units)	$500,000
Tax Rate: 40%	

1. What is the projected after-tax net income for 19_2?
2. What is the breakeven point in units for 19_2?
3. Mr. Ro has set the sales target for 19_3 at a level of $550,000 (or 22,000 pipes). He believes an additional selling expense of $11,250 for advertising in 19_3, with all other costs remaining constant, will be necessary to attain the sales target. What will be the after-tax net income for 19_3 if the additional $11,250 is spent?
4. What will be the breakeven point in dollar sales for 19_3 if the additional $11,250 is spent for advertising?
5. If the additional $11,250 is spent for advertising in 19_3, what is the required sales level in dollar sales to equal 19_2's after-tax net income?
6. At a sales level of 22,000 units, what maximum amount can be spent on advertising if an after-tax net income of $60,000 is desired?

3-41 Change in sales mix; income taxes. (CMA, adapted) Hewtex Electronics manufactures two products—tape recorders and electronic calculators—and sells them nationally to wholesalers and retailers. The Hewtex management is very pleased with the company's performance for the current fiscal year. Projected sales through December 31, 19_7, indicate that 70,000 tape recorders and 140,000 electronic calculators will be sold this year. The projected earnings statement, which appears below, shows that Hewtex will exceed its earnings goal of 9% on sales after taxes.

HEWTEX ELECTRONICS

Projected Earnings Statement for the Year Ended December 31, 19_7

| | TAPE RECORDERS | | ELECTRONIC CALCULATORS | | |
	Total Amount (000 omitted)	Per Unit	Total Amount (000 omitted)	Per Unit	Total (000 omitted)
Sales	$1,050	$15.00	$3,150	$22.50	$4,200.0
Production costs:					
Materials	$ 280	$ 4.00	$ 630	$ 4.50	$ 910.0
Direct labor	140	2.00	420	3.00	560.0
Variable overhead	140	2.00	280	2.00	420.0
Fixed overhead	70	1.00	210	1.50	280.0
Total production costs	$ 630	$ 9.00	$1,540	$11.00	$2,170.0
Gross margin	$ 420	$ 6.00	$1,610	$11.50	$2,030.0
Fixed selling and administrative					1,040.0
Net income before income taxes					$ 990.0
Income taxes (55%)					544.5
Net income					$ 445.5

The tape recorder business has been fairly stable the last few years, and the company does not intend to change the tape recorder price. However, the competition among manufacturers of electronic calculators has been increasing. Hewtex's calculators have been very popular with consumers. In order to sustain this interest in its calculators and to meet the price reductions expected from competitors, management has decided to reduce the wholesale price of its calculator from $22.50 to $20.00 per unit effective January 1, 19_8. At the same time the company plans to spend an additional $57,000 on advertising during fiscal year 19_8. As a consequence of these actions, management estimates that 80% of its total revenue will be derived from calculator sales as compared with 75% in 19_7. As in prior years, the sales mix is assumed the same at all volume levels. (That is, the sales mix in units for 19_8 will not necessarily be the same as in 19_7; however, the sales mix in 19_8 will be constant no matter what volume levels occur).

The total fixed overhead costs will not change in 19_8, nor will the variable overhead cost rates (applied on a direct-labor-hour base). However, the cost of materials and direct labor is expected to change. The cost of solid state electronic components will be cheaper in 19_8. Hewtex estimates that material costs will drop 10% for the tape recorders and 20% for the calculators in 19_8. However, direct-labor costs for both products will increase 10% in the coming year. Variable overhead rates will be unchanged at $2.00 per unit.

Required

1. How many tape recorder and electronic calculator units did Hewtex Electronics have to sell in 19_7 to break even?
2. How many tape recorder and electronic calculator units will Hewtex have to sell in 19_8 to break even?
3. How much total sales revenue is required if Hewtex Electronics is to earn a profit in 19_8 equal to 9% on sales after taxes?

3-42 Review of Chapters 2 and 3. For each of the following independent cases, find the unknowns designated by letters.

	CASE 1	CASE 2
Sales	$100,000	$ M
Direct materials used	29,000	55,000
Direct labor	10,000	25,000
Variable selling and administrative expenses	16,000	70,000
Fixed manufacturing overhead	30,000	Q
Fixed selling and administrative expenses	9,000	R
Gross profit	A	P
Finished-goods inventory, 1/1	0	0
Finished-goods inventory, 12/31	0	0
Contribution margin (dollars)	E	40,000
Direct-material inventory, 1/1	3,000	N
Direct-material inventory, 12/31	10,000	20,000
Variable manufacturing overhead	C	10,000
Work in process, 1/1	0	0
Work in process, 12/31	0	0
Purchases of direct materials	D	60,000
Breakeven point (in dollars)	F	S
Cost of goods manufactured	B	110,000
Net income	1,000	5,000

3-43 Review of Chapters 2 and 3. The Reader Co. makes deluxe bookcases to special order. The controller has given you, his newly hired assistant, the task of constructing a so-called contribution income statement for the year ended December 31, 19_5. You are troubled because all the data produced by the routine accounting system do not distinguish between variable and fixed costs.

After laboring with statistical regressions, you have identified various cost behavior patterns to your satisfaction. You have determined a breakeven point of $360,000; your computations were relatively easy because Reader's policy is not to carry any inventories. Instead the company finishes pending orders sometime in December and gives all employees vacations that end in early January.

The traditional income statement included a gross profit of $130,000, sales of $600,000, direct labor of $170,000, and direct materials used of $220,000.

The contribution margin was $150,000, and the variable manufacturing overhead was $20,000.

Required

You need not work these in sequence:

1. Fixed manufacturing overhead
2. Variable selling and administrative expenses
3. Fixed selling and administrative expenses

3-44 Contribution and absorption income statements. (Review of Chapters 2 and 3.) The Del Prado Company had the following data for the year 19_1. Assume that inventories are unchanged and that they can therefore be ignored.

Shipping expenses	$ 70,000	Fire insurance on	
Factory rent	50,000	equipment	$ 3,000
Sales	1,400,000	Material-handling labor	40,000
Administrative expenses (fixed)	100,000	Lubricants and coolants	3,000
Property taxes on		Idle time	10,000
equipment	4,000	Miscellaneous indirect	
Sales commissions	60,000	labor, variable	40,000
Depreciation—equipment	40,000	Overtime premium	20,000
Sandpaper used	1,000	Direct material used	380,000
Direct labor	300,000	Sales salaries	200,000

Required

1. Prepare a contribution income statement and an absorption income statement. Prepare a separate supporting schedule of indirect manufacturing costs subdivided between variable and fixed costs. If you are in doubt about any cost behavior pattern, decide on the basis of whether the individual cost in question will fluctuate substantially over a wide range of volume.
2. Suppose that total variable costs fluctuate directly in proportion to sales. Also suppose that total fixed costs are unaffected over a wide range of sales. What would operating income have been if sales had amounted to (a) $1,300,000 instead of $1,400,000? (b) $1,500,000 instead of $1,400,000? Which income statement did you use to arrive at your answer? Why?

3-45 Hospital cost-volume relationships. (CPA) Melford Hospital operates a general hospital but rents space and beds to separately owned entities rendering specialized services such as pediatrics and psychiatric. Melford charges each separate entity for common services such as patients' meals and laundry and for administrative services such as billings and collections. Space and bed rentals are fixed charges for the year, based on bed capacity rented to each entity. Melford charged the following costs to pediatrics for the year ended June 30, 19_2:

	PATIENT DAYS (Variable)	BED CAPACITY (Fixed)
Dietary	$ 600,000	—
Janitorial	—	$ 70,000
Laundry	300,000	—
Laboratory	450,000	—
Pharmacy	350,000	—
Repairs and maintenance	—	30,000
General and administrative	—	1,300,000
Rent	—	1,500,000
Billings and collections	300,000	—
Total	$2,000,000	$2,900,000

During the year ended June 30, 19_2, pediatrics charged each patient an average of $300 per day, had a capacity of 60 beds, and had revenue of $6 million for 365 days. In addition, pediatrics directly employed the following personnel:

	ANNUAL SALARIES
Supervising nurses	$25,000
Nurses	20,000
Aides	9,000

Melford has the following minimum departmental personnel requirements based on total annual patient days:

ANNUAL PATIENT DAYS	AIDES	NURSES	SUPERVISING NURSES
Up to 21,900	20	10	4
21,901 to 26,000	26	13	4
26,001 to 29,200	30	15	4

These staffing levels represent full-time equivalents. Pediatrics always employs only the minimum number of required full-time equivalent personnel. Salaries of supervising nurses, nurses, and aides are therefore fixed within ranges of annual patient days.

Pediatrics operated at 100% capacity on 90 days during the year ended June 30, 19_2. It is estimated that during these 90 days the demand exceeded 20 patients more than capacity. Melford has an additional 20 beds available for rent for the year ended June 30, 19_3. Such additional rental would increase pediatrics' fixed charges based on bed capacity.

Required

1. Calculate the minimum number of patient days required for pediatrics to break even for the year ended June 30, 19_3, if the additional 20 beds are not rented. Patient demand is unknown, but assume that revenue per patient day, cost per patient day, cost per bed, and salary rates will remain the same as for the year ended June 30, 19_2.
2. Assume that patient demand, revenue per patient day, cost per patient day, cost per bed, and salary rates for the year ended June 30, 19_3, remain the same as for the year ended June 30, 19_2. Prepare a schedule of increase in revenue and increase in costs for the year ended June 30, 19_3, in order to determine the net increase or decrease in earnings from the additional 20 beds if pediatrics rents this extra capacity from Melford.

3-46 Miscellaneous alternatives; contribution income statement. Study the income statement of the Hall Company. Commissions are based on sales dollars; all other variable expenses vary in terms of units sold.

The factory has a capacity of 150,000 units per year. The results for 19_1 have been disappointing. Top management is sifting a number of possible ways to make operations profitable in 19_2.

HALL COMPANY

Income Statement for the Year Ended December 31, 19_1

Sales (90,000 units @ $4.00)			$360,000
Cost of goods sold:			
Direct materials		$90,000	
Direct labor		90,000	
Factory overhead:			
Variable	$18,000		
Fixed	80,000	98,000	278,000
Gross margin			$ 82,000
Selling expenses:			
Variable:			
Sales commissions*	$18,000		
Shipping	3,600	$21,600	
Fixed:			
Advertising, salaries, etc.		40,000	$61,600
Administrative expenses:			
Variable		$ 4,500	
Fixed		20,400	24,900	86,500
Net loss			$ (4,500)

*Based on sales dollars, not physical units.

(Consider each situation independently.)

1. Recast the income statement into a contribution format. There will be three major sections: sales, variable expenses, and fixed expenses. Show costs per unit in an adjacent column. Allow adjacent space for entering your answers to requirement 2.
2. The sales manager is torn between two courses of action:
   a. He has studied the market potential and believes that a 15% slash in price would fill the plant to capacity.
   b. He wants to increase prices by 25%, to increase advertising by $150,000, and to boost commissions to 10% of sales. Under these circumstances, he thinks that unit volume will increase by 50%.

   Prepare the budgeted income statements, using a contribution margin format and two columns. What would be the new net income or loss under each alternative? Assume that there are no changes in fixed costs other than advertising.
3. The president does not want to tinker with the price. How much may advertising be increased to bring production and sales up to 130,000 units and still earn a target profit of 5% of sales?
4. A mail-order firm is willing to buy 60,000 units of product "if the price is right." Assume that the present market of 90,000 units at $4 each will not be disturbed. Hall Company will not pay any sales commission on these 60,000 units. The mail-order firm will pick up the units directly at the Hall factory. However, Hall must refund $24,000 of the total sales price as a promotional and advertising allowance for the mail-order firm. In addition, special packaging will increase manufacturing costs on these 60,000 units by 10¢ per unit. At what unit price must the mail-order chain business be quoted for Hall to break even on total operations in 19_2?
5. The president suspects that a fancy new package will aid consumer sales and ultimately Hall's sales. Present packaging costs per unit are all variable and consist of 5¢ direct materials and 4¢ direct labor; new packaging costs will be 30¢ and 13¢, respectively. Assuming no other changes in cost behavior, how many units must be sold to earn a net profit of $20,000?

3-47. Movie showings. Theater owners have to make competitive bids for the right to show a movie. They must send the film distributor a proposal with

1. The length of run they will provide.
2. The percentage of box office revenues that the theater will pay the distributor per week. This is usually on a sliding scale. The distributor may get up to 90% for the first week, 70% for the second, and so forth down to a minimum of 35%. Thus the longer the movie plays, the smaller the percentage the theater owner pays.

In addition, the theater owner must guarantee a minimum total payment to the film distributor, even if box office revenues are disastrously weak. For some "blockbuster" movies, the guarantee may exceed $100,000. This guarantee is a fixed cost as long as the accumulated sliding scale payments are less than the guarantee. Moreover, the sliding scale payments become variable costs only to the extent that they exceed the guarantee.

A theater owner, Myra Ripkin, is trying to decide how much to guarantee the distributor for a three-week run of *Rocky IX*. She has already decided to offer a 90%, 70%, and 50% sliding scale over the three-week period. The weekly fixed "house expenses" for rent, climate control, personnel, advertising, and other items are $5,000. The "house expenses" are fixed for the *entire* three-week run of the movie. Allowing for lower prices for children, senior citizens, and matinees, the average price per ticket is $6.

Ripkin expects to sell 8,000 tickets during the first week, 6,000 during the second, and 4,000 during the third. Her target operating income is $8,000 for the three-week run.

(For purposes of this problem, ignore concession operations, which ordinarily add significantly to a theater's profits.)

1. Using Ripkin's predictions of ticket sales, compute the maximum guarantee that she should bid.
2. Suppose Ripkin bids a guarantee of only $60,000. Compute the operating income for the three-week period if (a) her original target weekly revenues are attained, (b) 65%

of her original target weekly revenues are attained, and (c) 120% of her original target weekly revenues are attained.

3. Assume that Ripkin bids a $60,000 guarantee and attains her original target weekly revenues. Compute (a) the total number of tickets sold where her total costs are no longer affected by the guarantee, and (b) her breakeven point in terms of tickets sold. Hint: Compute (a) before (b). A graph could help.

Note: *See Chapter 18 for a discussion of cost-volume-profit analysis under uncertainty. Also see problems 18–15 and 18–17.*

4

Job, Process, and Operation Systems

Product-costing and control purposes • Job-order costing • Illustration of job-order accounting •
Control purpose in manufacturing and service industries • Responsibility center reporting •
Factory overhead application • Process and operation costing •
Appendix: Supplementary description of ledger relationships

This chapter examines a general approach to accounting for costs in a multiple-purpose accounting system. Two major cost objectives are discussed: responsibility centers and units of product. The former illustrates the control purpose of the system; the latter illustrates the product-costing purpose.

Here we must dwell heavily on techniques because they are an essential part of the accounting function. Equally important, we become familiar with many terms and fundamental ledger relationships that will aid understanding of the key subjects covered in Chapters 5 through 11.

If you have never worked in a factory, please study this chapter and its Appendix with care. The chapter was written for the reader with little business background. If you have had some business experience, the Appendix to this chapter will be familiar. If you want a more complete coverage of the bookkeeping aspects of cost accounting, see Chapters 15 and 17. The section on overhead accounting deserves special study.

PRODUCT-COSTING AND CONTROL PURPOSES

Ultimately, all costs are accumulated to help someone's decisions. But all these decisions cannot be foreseen, so systems are designed to fulfill general purposes that are commonplace among managers. **We will frequently distinguish between the *product-costing* purpose of a system and all other purposes. For convenience, we will sometimes refer to all other purposes as *planning and control purposes*, *budgetary-control purposes*, or, for brevity, as the *control purpose*.**

Aside from meeting the obvious external reporting demands for inventory valuation and income determination, managers want product costs for guiding their decisions regarding pricing and product strategies. In addition, managers want departmental costs (or costs of other parts of the organization) for judging the performance of their subordinates and the parts of the organization as economic investments.

Management accounting systems fulfill these general planning and control purposes by choosing parts of the organization as cost objectives. That is, top managers divide the work of the organization among **responsibility centers.** The latter are subunits of an organization whose managers are accountable for specified sets of activities. For example, costs are often routinely traced to a **cost center,** the smallest segment of activity or area of responsibility for which costs are accumulated. Typically, cost centers are departments, but in some instances a department may contain several cost centers. For example, although a machining department may be under one supervisor, it may contain various groups of machines, such as lathes, punch presses, and milling machines. Each group of machines is sometimes regarded as a separate cost center with its own assistant supervisor.

In sum, the system must trace costs to these two major cost objectives: departments and products. This tracing is frequently accomplished in two steps: (1) *accumulation* of costs by responsibility centers and (2) *application* of those costs to the physical units (or other measures of output) that pass through the departments. This second step is sometimes called cost *absorption* rather than cost *application*.

The following tabulation summarizes the main ideas of this chapter:

Control Purpose	Product-costing Purpose
1. Accumulate costs by:	2. Apply costs by:
Responsibility center	Job-order costing
Responsibility center	Process costing
Responsibility center	Operation costing

Note especially that no matter what label is used to describe how costs are applied for product costing, **first the costs are always accumulated by responsibility center for control purposes.** The three major ways of achieving product costing will be described in sequence.

JOB-ORDER COSTING

Job-order (or *job-cost* or *production-order* or *job*) **costing** systems are used by organizations whose products or services are readily identified by individual units or batches, each of which receives varying inputs of direct materials, direct labor, and factory overhead. Industries that commonly use job-order methods include construction, printing, aircraft, furniture, and machinery.

Although a manufacturing situation is illustrated in this chapter, the job-costing approach is used in nonmanufacturing organizations too. Examples include auto repair, auditing and consulting engagements, hospital cases, social-welfare cases, and research projects.[1]

Source documents

The basic document used by job-order costing to apply *product costs* is called the **job-order** or **job-cost record** or **job-cost sheet.** The file of job-cost records for the uncompleted jobs makes up the subsidiary ledger for Work-in-Process Control, the major product-costing account. Exhibit 4-1 illustrates a job-cost record.

Job-order manufacturers usually have several jobs passing through the plant simultaneously. Each job typically requires different kinds of materials and department effort. Thus jobs may have different routings, different operations, and different times required for completion. **Stores requisitions** (Exhibit 4-2) are forms used to charge job-cost records for direct materials used. **Work tickets** (Exhibit 4-3) are forms used to charge jobs for direct labor used. This work ticket (sometimes called *time ticket* or *time card*) indicates the time spent on a specific job. An employee

EXHIBIT 4-1
Job-Cost Record

			SAMPLE COMPANY	Job No. _____			
For stock_____Customer_____							
Product_____ Date started_____ Date completed _____							

Department A							
Direct Material			Direct Labor			Overhead	
Date	Reference (stores requisition number)	Amount	Date	Reference (work ticket number)	Amount	Date (based on budgeted overhead rate)	Amount

Department B							
Direct Material			Direct Labor			Overhead	
Date	Reference	Amount	Date	Reference	Amount	Date	Amount

Summary of Costs			
	Dept. A	Dept. B	Total
Direct material	xx	xx	xxx
Direct labor	xx	xx	xxx
Factory overhead applied	xx	xx	xxx
Total	xxx	xxx	xxx

[1]See "Job-Order Costing: Viewing the Patient as a Job," *Hospital Cost Accounting Advisor*, 1, No. 5 (October 1985), 1–5. Also see R. N. Anthony and D. W. Young, *Management Control in Nonprofit Organizations*, 3rd ed. (Homewood, Ill.: Richard D. Irwin, 1984). In nonprofit organizations the "job order" or class of services is often called a *program,* an identifiable segment of activities that often results in output in the form of services rather than goods. Examples are a drug-addict rehabilitation program and a safety program.

Chapter 4
88

EXHIBIT 4-2
Stores Requisition

Job No. _____ 41 _____			
Department _____ B _____		Date _____ 2/22 _____	
Debit Account _WORK IN PROCESS_			
Authorized by _____ GL _____			

Description	Quantity	Unit Cost	Amount
AT 462 BRACKETS	80	$2.50	$200.00

who is paid an hourly wage and who operates a lathe will have one **clock card** (Exhibit 4-4), which is a document used as a basis for determining individual earnings; but the worker will also fill out or punch several *work tickets* each day as he or she starts and stops work on particular jobs or operations. Many auto mechanics must account for their time in a similar way.

Of course, all the illustrated source documents may exist only in the form of computer records. As manufacturing and service industries become more automated, the time and materials used on jobs are recorded routinely without human intervention. For example, a stores requisition of direct material may be entered via a computer terminal, the materials may be picked from shelves and delivered directly to the factory floor by a robot or a conveyor, and the direct-labor time may be recorded by computer as each machine operation starts and stops.

Responsibility and control

The department responsibility for usage of direct materials and direct labor should be clearly drawn. Copies of direct-material requisitions and direct-labor work tickets are used for two purposes. One copy is used to post to job-cost records; another copy is used for fixing responsibility by departments. The department heads are usually kept informed of their direct-material and direct-labor performance by daily or weekly classified summaries of requisitions and work tickets charged to their departments.

The job-cost records also serve a control function. Comparisons are often made between predictions of job costs and the costs finally applied to the job. Deviations are investigated so that their underlying causes can be discovered.

EXHIBIT 4-3
Work Ticket

Employee No. _741_	Date _2/22_	Job No. _41_
Operation _drill_	Account _Work in Process_	Dept. _A_
Stop _4:45 P.M._	Rate _$12.00_	Pieces: Worked _15_
Start _4:00 P.M._	Amount _$9.00_	Rejected — Completed _15_

EXHIBIT 4-4
Clock Card

Date	AM		PM		Excess Hours		Total Hours
	In	Out	In	Out	In	Out	
2/22	7:58	12:01	1:00	5:01			8
2/23	7:55	12:00	1:00	5:02			8
2/24	8:00	12:02	12:58	5:00	6:00	9:00	11
2/25	7:58	12:02	12:59	5:03			8
2/26	7:56	12:01	12:59	5:01			8

Name __FRANK YOUNG__   Employee Number __741__

Department __A__   Week ending __2/26__

Regular Time ___43___ hrs. @ __$12.00__   __$516.00__

Overtime Premium __3__ hrs. @ __$6.00__   __$18.00__

Gross Earnings   __$534.00__

ILLUSTRATION OF JOB-ORDER ACCOUNTING

Because each job order often contains different materials and gets a different routing through departments, the time, costs, and attention devoted by departments to any given job may vary considerably. It is desirable, therefore, to keep a separate account for inventory purposes and another account, or other accounts, for department responsibility purposes. In practice, a Work-in-Process Control account, supported by a subsidiary ledger of individual job orders, is widely used for product-costing purposes. However, practice differs greatly as to the general-ledger accumulation of costs for department responsibility purposes.

Consider a specific example. Assume that a factory has two departments and uses the job-cost system. Department A is the machining department; Department B is the assembly department. Exhibit 4-5 (on pages 92–93) shows T-account relationships and relationships between the general and subsidiary ledgers.

The general-ledger section of Exhibit 4-5 gives a bird's-eye view of an entire cost accounting system. The subsidiary ledgers and the basic source documents, the section on the facing page of Exhibit 4-5, contain the underlying details—the worm's-eye view. The bulk of the clerical and computer time is spent on these source documents and the subsidiary ledger accounts; these are the everyday tools for systematically recording operating activities. However, the corresponding general-ledger entries are usually made monthly; they are summaries of the financial effects of hundreds or thousands of transactions recorded on the subsidiary ledgers and source documents.

Eight of the principal general-ledger entries for a typical job-cost system are given in journal form and explained here and on the pages following Exhibit 4-5. **Please be sure to trace each journal entry, step by step, to the accounts in both sections of Exhibit 4-5.**

1. To record purchases of direct and indirect materials:

Stores control*	60,000	
Accounts (or vouchers) payable		60,000

*The word "control," as used in journal entries and general-ledger accounts, has a narrow bookkeeping meaning. As contrasted with "control" in the management sense, "control" here means that the control account in question is supported by an underlying subsidiary ledger. To illustrate: In financial accounting, Accounts Receivable Control is supported by a subsidiary customers' ledger, with one account for each customer. The same meaning applies to the "Stores" account here; the stores subsidiary ledger consists of individual accounts for the various materials in inventory.

A summary of purchases of direct and indirect materials is charged to Stores Control because the storekeeper is accountable for them. The subsidiary records for Stores Control would be perpetual-inventory records called *stores records*. As a minimum, these records would contain quantity columns for receipts, issues, and balance. Exhibit 4-6 on page 94 is an illustration of a stores record.

2. To record issues of direct and indirect materials:

Work-in-process control	48,000	
Factory department overhead control (indirect materials)	4,000	
Stores control		52,000

Responsibility is fixed by using *stores requisitions* (sometimes called **material requisitions**) as a basis for charging departments. A stores requisition was shown in Exhibit 4-2. Requisitions are accumulated and journalized monthly.

Direct materials are charged to jobs; indirect materials (supplies) are charged to individual department-overhead cost records, which form a subsidiary ledger for Factory Department Overhead Control. In job-cost accounting, a single Factory Department Overhead Control account may be kept in the general ledger. The detail of factory overhead is charged to departments and recorded in subsidiary department-overhead ledgers (department-overhead cost records). (See Exhibit 4-7 on page 94.) In turn, the overhead is applied to jobs, as will be described later in this illustration.

3. To record incurrence of factory payroll costs:

Work-in-process control (direct labor)	39,000	
Factory department overhead control (indirect labor)	5,000	
Accrued payroll		44,000

EXHIBIT 4-5 *(Place a clip on this page for easy reference.)*
Job-Cost System, Diagram of Ledger Relationships

(Circled numbers refer to journal entries described more thoroughly in text.)

① Purchases, $60,000

② Usage of direct materials ($48,000) and indirect materials ($4,000)

③ Incurrence of direct labor ($39,000) and indirect labor ($5,000)

④ Payment of payroll liability, $44,000

⑤ Incurrence of other factory overhead, $18,000

⑥ Application of factory overhead, $26,460

⑦ Completion of goods $108,800

⑧ Cost of goods sold, $102,000

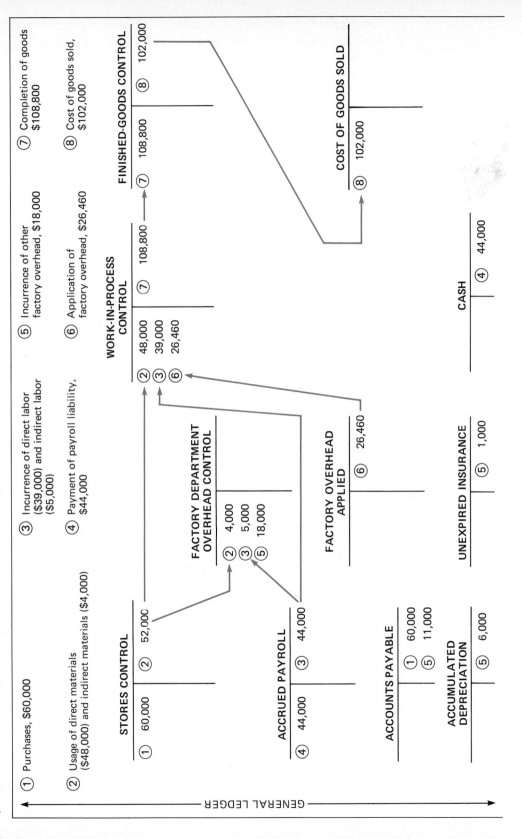

STORES CONTROL

① 60,000 | ② 52,000

FACTORY DEPARTMENT OVERHEAD CONTROL

② 4,000
③ 5,000
⑤ 18,000

ACCRUED PAYROLL

④ 44,000 | ③ 44,000

ACCOUNTS PAYABLE

| ① 60,000
| ⑤ 11,000

ACCUMULATED DEPRECIATION

| ⑤ 6,000

FACTORY OVERHEAD APPLIED

| ⑥ 26,460

UNEXPIRED INSURANCE

⑤ 1,000

WORK-IN-PROCESS CONTROL

② 48,000 | ⑦ 108,800
③ 39,000
⑥ 26,460

FINISHED-GOODS CONTROL

⑦ 108,800 | ⑧ 102,000

COST OF GOODS SOLD

⑧ 102,000

CASH

| ④ 44,000

— GENERAL LEDGER —

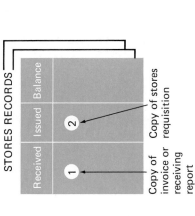
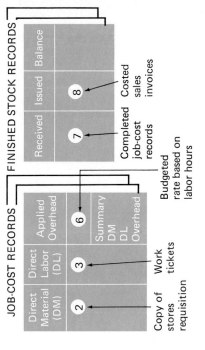
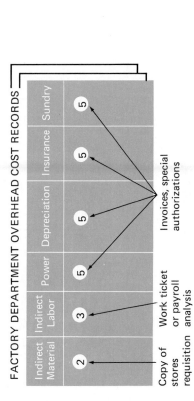

SUBSIDIARY LEDGER

STORES RECORDS

Received	Issued	Balance
1	2	

- Copy of invoice or receiving report → 1
- Copy of stores requisition → 2

JOB-COST RECORDS

Direct Material (DM)	Direct Labor (DL)	Applied Overhead
2	3	6
		Summary DM DL Overhead

- Copy of stores requisition → 2
- Work tickets → 3
- Budgeted rate based on labor hours → 6

FINISHED STOCK RECORDS

Received	Issued	Balance
7	8	

- Completed job-cost records → 7
- Costed sales invoices → 8

FACTORY DEPARTMENT OVERHEAD COST RECORDS

Indirect Material	Indirect Labor	Power	Depreciation	Insurance	Sundry
2	3	5	5	5	5

- Copy of stores requisition → 2
- Work ticket or payroll analysis → 3
- Invoices, special authorizations → 5

NOTE: Type of source document used is designated at the tail of the arrow. These entries would be shown in much more detail in the subsidiary ledger than in the general ledger.

EXHIBIT 4-6
Stores Record

		Received			Issued			Balance		
Date	Reference	Quantity	Unit Cost	Total Cost	Quantity	Unit Cost	Total Cost	Quantity	Unit Cost	Total Cost
2/10	V 1014	300	2.50	750				300	2.50	750
2/22	R41				80	2.50	200	220	2.50	550

Item _____ AF 462 Brackets _____

EXHIBIT 4-7
Factory Department Overhead Cost Record

Date	Source Document	Lubricants	Indirect Materials	Material Handling	Idle Time	Overtime Premium	Other Labor	Utilities	Insurance	Depr.
	Requisitions	xx	xx							
	Labor recap.			xx	xx	xx	xx			
	Invoices							xx		
	Special memos from chief accountant on accruals, pre-payments, etc.							xx	xx	xx

Payroll withholdings from employees are ignored in this example. Responsibility is fixed by using work tickets (Exhibit 4-3) or individual time summaries as a basis for tracing direct labor to jobs and direct and indirect labor to departments. Clock cards (Exhibit 4-4) are widely used as attendance records and as the basis for computation of payroll.

4. To record payment of payroll for the month:

Accrued payroll	44,000	
Cash		44,000

Actual payments and entries may be made weekly, even though payroll costs incurred (entry 3) are recorded monthly. The reason for this procedure is that paydays seldom coincide with the conventional accounting period (the month) for which costs are accumulated in the general ledger.[2] Thus the Accrued Payroll account typically appears as follows:

Accrued Payroll			
Payments	x	Gross Earnings:	x
	x		
	x		
	x		
		Balance represents wages earned but unpaid	x

5. To record incurrence of other factory-overhead costs:

Factory department overhead control*	18,000	
Accounts payable		11,000
Unexpired insurance		1,000
Accumulated depreciation—equipment		6,000

*Utilities, repairs, etc.	$11,000
Insurance	1,000
Depreciation	6,000
	$18,000

The detail of these costs is distributed to the appropriate columns of the individual department-overhead cost records that make up the subsidiary ledger for Factory Department Overhead Control. The basic documents for these distributions may be vouchers, invoices, or special memos from the responsible accounting officer.

6. To record application of factory overhead to job records:

Work-in-process control	26,460	
Factory overhead applied*		26,460

*Absorption costing is used here. As was explained in the preceding chapter, absorption costing is the common practice of applying both variable and fixed manufacturing overhead to products.

Applied overhead is factory overhead allocated to products (or services), usually by means of some budgeted (predetermined) rate. The budgeted overhead rate used here is $2.70 per direct-labor hour. The total amount of overhead ap-

---

[2]For a detailed treatment of the mechanics of payroll accounting, see Appendix 17, which may be studied now if desired without losing continuity.

plied to a particular job is dependent on the amount of actual direct-labor hours used on that job. It is assumed that 9,800 direct-labor hours were used for all jobs, resulting in a total overhead application of 9,800 × $2.70 = $26,460. This entry is explained further in a subsequent section of this chapter.

7. To record completion of Job Nos. 101–108:

Finished-goods control	108,800	
Work-in-process control		108,800

As job orders are completed, the job-cost records are totaled. Note especially that the totals consist of *actual* direct material, *actual* direct labor, and *applied* factory overhead. Some companies use the completed job-cost records as their subsidiary ledger for finished goods. Other companies use separate finished-stock cards or similar records to form a subsidiary ledger.

8. To record cost of goods sold:

Cost of goods sold (sometimes called cost of sales)	102,000	
Finished-goods control		102,000

The eight summary entries are usually made monthly. As already emphasized, the biggest share of data accumulated is devoted to compiling the day-to-day details that are recorded in subsidiary ledgers. There is a mass of daily detail that finds its way to subsidiary ledgers, in contrast to the summaries of the detail that are posted monthly to the general ledger. These "ledgers" are increasingly being stored on a computer rather than on loose-leaf pages.

At this point please pause and reexamine the entire eight entries in the illustration, step by step.

CONTROL PURPOSE IN MANUFACTURING AND SERVICE INDUSTRIES

The general-ledger illustration of prime costs—direct material and direct labor—has highlighted the product-costing purpose. Prime costs are applied to products as material and labor are identified with particular jobs. However, the job-cost record is used for more than just accumulating costs for inventory purposes. Planning and control purposes are also important. For example, the comparisons of budgeted and actual product costs may influence managers regarding future pricing and the relative emphasis given to various products or services.

The planning and controlling of job costs are similar in manufacturing, construction, and service industries. As each job is planned, the expected quantities of direct materials and the number of direct-labor hours are predicted. The appropriate prices and wage rates are multiplied by the related physical amounts. Overhead is also included, usually based on direct-labor hours or direct-labor dollars. The result is the total budgeted cost of the job.

To illustrate, consider a service such as an audit by a certified public accounting firm. A partner would plan the job, use the plans to quote a fee to the client, and monitor progress by comparing the hours logged to date against the original budget and the estimated hours remaining on the job. For more on this topic, see Chapter 17.

RESPONSIBILITY CENTER REPORTING

As mentioned early in this chapter, accountants accumulate costs by responsibility centers as well as by jobs. Why? To serve the planning and control purpose of cost accounting. Managers control by personally observing activities plus examining accounting reports.

Consider direct materials and direct labor, which are charged directly to jobs for product-costing purposes. The same stores requisitions and work tickets trace departmental responsibility for material and labor usage. These records are used for measuring departmental performance monthly. For example, a computer can easily obtain a sum of stores requisitions and work tickets coded by department for any given month. A departmental performance report can then be prepared that compares budgeted and actual costs for direct materials, direct labor, and factory overhead. Furthermore, direct-material usage might be reported hourly, whereas direct-labor usage might be reported daily, often in physical amounts only.

The scope of management accounting extends far beyond and far deeper than general and subsidiary ledger bookkeeping. Managers may want quick feedback on important costs like direct material or direct labor—too quick to await reports based on ledger balances. In such cases, there is little need for keeping a subsidiary multicolumn department-cost record for direct-material, direct-labor, and overhead items. **Instead the department overhead cost record is usually kept separately, whereas direct-material-usage and direct-labor-usage reports are automatically produced in summaries of requisitions and work tickets. Thus the source documents for direct materials and direct labor are used directly as a basis for control without necessarily having them formally summarized by department in either the subsidiary ledgers or the general ledger.**

FACTORY OVERHEAD APPLICATION

Assigning overhead to product

Entry 6 (see page 95) in our master illustration used a budgeted overhead rate to apply factory overhead to product. Direct materials and direct labor may be traced directly to physical units worked on through requisitions and work tickets. But, by its very nature, factory overhead cannot be traced directly to physical units. Yet the making of goods would be impossible without the incurrence of overhead costs such as depreciation, material moving, janitorial services, repairs, property taxes, heat, and light.

Overhead is *applied to* (*absorbed by*) products because of management's desire for a close approximation of costs of different products. If such product costs are to help management for product pricing, income determination, and inventory valuation, they must be timely as well as accurate. If the purpose were to apply all actual overhead to actual production for the year, the most accurate application of overhead could be made only at the end of the year, after actual results were determined. However, this timing would be too late. Managers want product-cost information throughout the year. Therefore overhead application *rates* are usually budgeted, that is, computed in advance of production.

Accountants have chosen an annual averaging process for applying factory overhead to products. The usual steps are

1. Select a rate base (a cost application base) that serves as a common denominator for all products. Examples include direct-labor hours, direct-labor costs, and machine-hours. The application base should be the best available measure of the cause and effect relationships between overhead costs and production volume.
2. Prepare a factory-overhead budget for the planning period, ordinarily a year. The two key items are (a) budgeted total overhead and (b) budgeted total volume of the rate base.
3. Compute the **budgeted factory overhead rate** by dividing the budgeted total overhead by the budgeted rate base.
4. Obtain the actual base data (such as direct-labor hours) as the year unfolds.
5. Apply the budgeted overhead to the jobs by multiplying the budgeted rate times the actual base data.
6. At the end of the year, account for any differences between the amount of overhead actually incurred and overhead applied to products.

To illustrate, a company may budget its factory overhead for the forthcoming year as shown in Exhibit 4-8. Assume that the forecast is based on a volume of activity expressed in direct-labor hours. Then, if detailed forecasts result in a prediction of total overhead of $324,000 for the next year at an anticipated 120,000-direct-labor-hour level of activity, the budgeted overhead rate would be

$$\frac{\text{Total budgeted overhead}}{\text{Total budgeted volume}} = \frac{\$324,000}{120,000} = \$2.70 \text{ per hour}$$

(This example assumes that a single plantwide overhead rate is appropriate. This calculation is an oversimplification. There are usually different budgeted overhead rates for different departments. These are illustrated and explained in Chapter 13, which can be studied now if desired.)

The $2.70 rate would be used for costing job orders. For example, suppose a job-cost record for Job 323 included the following information:

Actual direct-material cost	$100
Actual direct-labor cost	$280
Actual direct-labor hours	40

The overhead to be applied to Job 323 would be: 40 actual hours times the budgeted rate of $2.70, or $108. The total cost of Job 323 would be: $100 plus $280 plus $108, or $488.

EXHIBIT 4-8
Budget of Factory Overhead
for the Year Ended 19_1

Overhead predicted:	
Variable items:	
Lubricants	$ 8,000
Other supplies	40,000
Material moving*	21,000
Idle time†	4,000
Overtime premium	8,000
Other labor	65,000
Utilities and other variable overhead	58,000
Total variable overhead	$204,000
Fixed items:	
Insurance	$ 5,000
Depreciation	65,000
Supervision	31,000
Other fixed overhead	19,000
Total fixed overhead	$120,000
Total budgeted overhead	$324,000
Divided by:	
Budgeted direct-labor hours	120,000
Budgeted overhead rate per hour	$ 2.70

*Labor costs of moving direct and indirect materials.
†Labor costs incurred for employee time not devoted
to production. Causes include equipment failure, poor
scheduling, material shortages, and the like.

If actual results for the year conform to the prediction of the $324,000 over-head cost and the 120,000-direct-labor-hour level of volume, total overhead costs will have been exactly applied to products worked on during the year. **The basic idea of this approach is to use an annual average overhead cost per hour without changing this rate in costing jobs from day to day and from month to month.**

Annualized rate

Should overhead rates be set on the basis of weekly, or monthly, or yearly activity? Two major conditions have prompted the use of an annualized basis for a budgeted rate:

1. To overcome volatility in computed unit costs that would result because of fluctuations in the *level of volume* (the denominator reason) from month to month. This is the dominant reason.
2. To overcome the volatility in computed unit costs that would result because of seasonal, calendar, and other peculiar variations in the *level of total overhead costs* (the numerator reason) incurred each month.

THE DENOMINATOR REASON: FLUCTUATIONS IN MONTHLY ACTIVITY Some over-head costs are variable (for example, supplies and indirect labor), whereas others are fixed (for example, property taxes, rent, and depreciation). If production fluctuates from month to month, total variable overhead cost incurrence should change in close proportion to variations in production, whereas total fixed overhead will remain unchanged. These relationships mean that overhead rates based on monthly volume may differ greatly from month to month solely because of fluctuations in the volume over which fixed overhead is spread.

Exhibit 4-9 gives an example of a company that gears production of its single product to a highly seasonal sales pattern. Few people support the contention that an identical product should be inventoried with an $11.00 or $51.00 overhead rate at the end of July or August and only a $2.25 or $2.00 overhead rate at the end of March or April. These different overhead rates are not representative of typical, normal production conditions. Management has committed itself to a specific level of fixed costs in light of foreseeable needs far beyond a mere thirty days. Thus, where production fluctuates, monthly overhead rates may be volatile. An average, annualized rate based on the relationship of total annual overhead to total annual volume is more representative of typical relationships between total costs and volume than a monthly rate.

THE NUMERATOR REASON: PECULIARITIES OF SPECIFIC OVERHEAD ITEMS   Fluctuation in monthly volume rather than fluctuation in monthly costs incurred is the dominant reason for using an annualized overhead rate. Still, certain costs are

EXHIBIT 4-9
Monthly Versus Annual Overhead Rates

MONTH	TOTAL FACTORY OVERHEAD BUDGETED ($50,000 per month plus $1 per hour)	DIRECT-LABOR HOURS	MONTHLY RATE PER HOUR*	ANNUAL RATE PER HOUR†
January	$ 70,000	20,000	$ 3.50	$3.715
February	80,000	30,000	2.67	3.715
March	90,000	40,000	2.25	3.715
April	100,000	50,000	2.00	3.715
May	65,000	15,000	4.33	3.715
June	60,000	10,000	6.00	3.715
July	55,000	5,000	11.00	3.715
August	51,000	1,000	51.00	3.715
September	55,000	5,000	11.00	3.715
October	60,000	10,000	6.00	3.715
November	65,000	15,000	4.33	3.715
December	70,000	20,000	3.50	3.715
	$821,000	221,000	–	3.715

*Note that the fluctuation here is based solely on the presence of fixed overhead. By definition, variable overhead rates would be $1.00 regardless of whether monthly or annual rates were used.

†Can be subdivided as follows:

$$\text{Variable-overhead rate} = \frac{\$821,000 - (\$50,000 \times 12)}{221,000} = \$1.000$$

$$\text{Fixed-overhead rate} = \frac{\$600,000}{221,000} = 2.715$$

$$\text{Combined-overhead rate} = \$3.715$$

incurred in different amounts at various times of the year. If a month's costs alone were considered, the heating cost, for example, would be charged only to winter production and the air-conditioning cost only to summer production.

Typical examples of erratic behavior include repairs, maintenance, and certain indirect materials requisitioned in one month that will be consumed over two or more months. These items may be charged to a department on the basis of monthly repair orders or requisitions. Yet the benefits of such charges may easily extend over a number of months of production. The concepts of accrual accounting maintain that it would be illogical to load any single month with costs caused by several months of operations.

The calendar itself has an unbusinesslike design; some months have twenty workdays, while others have twenty-two or more. Is it sensible to say that a product made in February should bear a greater share of overhead like depreciation and property taxes than if made in March?

Other erratic items that distort monthly overhead rates are vacation and holiday pay, professional fees, subscriptions that may fall due in one month, extra costs of learning, and idle time related to the installation of a new machine or product line.

All the costs and peculiarities mentioned above are collected in the annual-overhead pool along with the kinds of overhead that do have uniform behavior patterns (for example, many indirect materials and indirect labor). In other words, accountants throw up their hands and say, "We have to start somewhere, so let's pool the year's overhead and develop an annual overhead rate regardless of month-to-month peculiarities of specific overhead costs." **Such an approach provides a *normal* product cost that is based on an annual average instead of a so-called actual product cost that is affected by month-to-month fluctuations in production volume and by erratic or seasonal behavior of many overhead costs.** Such a normal cost is often used as a point of departure for setting and appraising the selling prices of products.

Ledger procedure for overhead

Let us see how the notions above affect general and subsidiary ledger procedure. Some students have trouble in understanding this phase of product costing. **Special study of this section is warranted.**

As overhead costs are incurred by departments from month to month, these "actual" costs are charged in detail to department-overhead cost records (the subsidiary ledger) and in summary to Factory Department Overhead Control. These costs are accumulated weekly or monthly without regard to how factory overhead is applied to specific jobs. This ledger procedure serves the purpose of managerial control of overhead. These actual costs are compared with budgeted amounts in departmental performance reports.

Because a budgeted overhead rate (such as $3.715 per direct-labor hour) is an average used to apply costs to products, the daily, weekly, or monthly costing of *inventory* is independent of the actual incurrence of overhead costs by *departments*. For this reason, at any given time during the year, the balance in Factory Department Overhead Control is unlikely to coincide with the amount applied to product. Thus managerial control can be exercised by comparing, say, the actual cost of lubricants used with the budget for lubricants. The actual lubricants used are accumulated on the department-overhead cost record. For product costing, all overhead items are pooled together, a budgeted annual average overhead rate is computed, and this average rate is used on jobs for costing Work in Process. The use of an annual average results in inventories bearing a normalized share of factory overhead.

Most accountants stress this peculiarity of overhead accounting by confining Factory Department Overhead Control to the accumulation of "actual" overhead charges incurred. Accountants set up a separate account called *Factory Overhead Applied* (sometimes called Factory Overhead *Absorbed*), much as Accumulated Depreciation-Machinery is a separate account from Machinery. To illustrate:

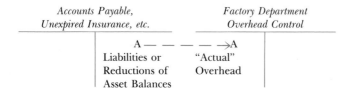

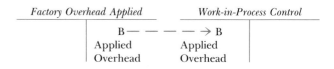

Underapplied or overapplied overhead

The workings of the ledger accounts for overhead may be more clearly understood if we pursue our master illustration (as shown in Exhibit 4-5, p. 92). Assume that the month's entries are for January, the first month of the company's year. Postings would appear as follows:

Factory Department Overhead Control			Factory Overhead Applied		
Jan. 31(2)	4,000			Jan. 31(6)	26,460
Jan. 31(3)	5,000				
Jan. 31(5)	18,000				
Jan. 31 Balance	27,000				

The monthly debits to Factory Department Overhead will seldom equal the monthly credits to Factory Overhead Applied. In January, for example, there is a $540 difference between the two balances. This $540 amount is commonly referred to as *underapplied* (or *underabsorbed*) *overhead*. **Overhead is underapplied when the applied balance is less than the incurred (actual) balance; it is overapplied when the applied balance exceeds the incurred balance.**

Although the month-end balances rarely coincide, the final year-end balances are ordinarily not too far apart. Consider the following cases for the year 19_2 (in thousands):

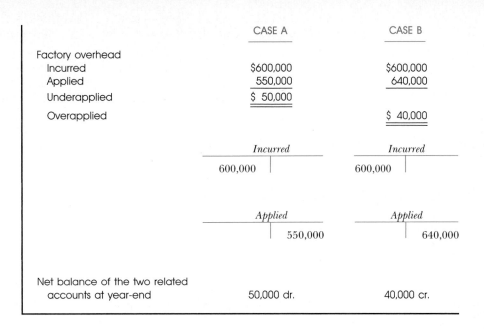

	CASE A	CASE B
Factory overhead		
Incurred	$600,000	$600,000
Applied	550,000	640,000
Underapplied	$ 50,000	
Overapplied		$ 40,000

Incurred		Incurred	
600,000		600,000	

Applied		Applied	
	550,000		640,000

	CASE A	CASE B
Net balance of the two related accounts at year-end	50,000 dr.	40,000 cr.

Accounting at end of year

What happens to the underapplied (or overapplied) overhead at the end of the year? Suppose the amount is small, say, less than 10% of the total amount incurred. Then most accountants favor closing the incurred and applied accounts out against one another; the net difference between the balances of the two related accounts is generally regarded as an adjustment of Cost of Goods Sold. In our example, the $50,000 underapplication would be accounted for as follows:

Cost of goods sold	50,000	
Factory overhead applied	550,000	
Factory department overhead control		600,000

To close the overhead accounts and to charge underapplied overhead to Cost of Goods Sold. (If overhead is overapplied, the overapplication would be credited to Cost of Goods Sold.)

Suppose the $50,000 underapplied overhead is judged as relatively large, either in relation to the total amount incurred, the total cost of goods sold, the total operating income, or some other test of materiality. Then accountants favor **proration,** the spreading of underapplied or overapplied overhead among various inventories and cost of goods sold. In this example, the $50,000 would be spread among three relevant accounts. Assume that the ending balances before proration are as shown in column (a) below. In column (b), the $50,000 is spread over the three pertinent accounts in proportion to their ending balances before proration, resulting in the adjusted balances in column (c):

103

	(a) UNADJUSTED BALANCE, END OF 19_1	(b) PRORATION OF UNDERAPPLIED OVERHEAD	(c) ADJUSTED BALANCE, END OF 19_1
Work in process	$ 125,000	125/1,250 × 50,000 = $ 5,000	$ 130,000
Finished goods	500,000	500/1,250 × 50,000 = 20,000	520,000
Cost of goods sold	625,000	625/1,250 × 50,000 = 25,000	650,000
	$1,250,000	$50,000	$1,300,000

The journal entry for this proration follows:

Work-in-process control	5,000	
Finished-goods control	20,000	
Cost of goods sold	25,000	
Factory overhead applied	550,000	
Factory department overhead control		600,000
To close the overhead accounts and to prorate		
underapplied overhead among the three		
relevant accounts.		

In practical situations, prorating is done only when inventory valuations would be significantly (materially) affected.

Exhibit 4-10 is a schematic comparison of the two methods of disposition of underapplied overhead at year-end. No matter which of the two methods is used, the underapplied overhead is not carried in the overhead accounts beyond the end of the year. That is, the ending balances in Factory Department Overhead Control and Factory Overhead Applied are closed and consequently become zero at the end of each year. (A section in Chapter 8 describes the accounting for underapplied and overapplied overhead on interim financial statements.)

Assumptions in practice

The proration method could be refined even further. Theoretically, the proration should be in proportion to the unadjusted *applied overhead* component in the three accounts described, not their unadjusted *ending balances*. The latter method is defective because it fails to recognize that the *proportions* of direct-material, direct-labor, and overhead costs are rarely constant among all jobs represented in the three accounts. For example, some furniture jobs may contain high proportions of valuable wood, whereas other jobs may contain inexpensive wood or plastic; yet the direct labor on each job may be approximately the same. After all, the fundamental objective of proration is to obtain a closer approximation of the "actual" costs of Work in Process, Finished Goods, and Cost of Goods Sold. Inasmuch as the *overhead* was applied using a *budgeted* rate, ideally all such overhead should be subject to adjustment to "actual" in whatever accounts the applied overhead now rests.

Modern companies are becoming increasingly conscious of inventory control,

EXHIBIT 4-10

Year-end Disposition of Underapplied Factory Overhead

(COGS = Cost of Goods Sold)

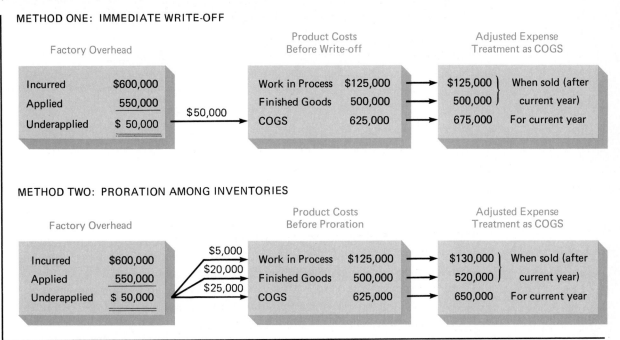

METHOD ONE: IMMEDIATE WRITE-OFF

Factory Overhead		Product Costs Before Write-off		Adjusted Expense Treatment as COGS	
Incurred	$600,000	Work in Process	$125,000	$125,000	When sold (after
Applied	550,000	Finished Goods	500,000	500,000	current year)
Underapplied	$ 50,000 → $50,000 →	COGS	625,000	675,000	For current year

METHOD TWO: PRORATION AMONG INVENTORIES

Factory Overhead		Product Costs Before Proration		Adjusted Expense Treatment as COGS	
Incurred	$600,000	$5,000 → Work in Process	$125,000	$130,000	When sold (after
Applied	550,000	$20,000 → Finished Goods	500,000	520,000	current year)
Underapplied	$ 50,000	$25,000 → COGS	625,000	650,000	For current year

which tends to increase the proportion of Cost of Goods Sold in relation to Work in Process and Finished Goods. Furthermore, the inventory balances of job-costing companies are usually relatively low because goods are made in response to specific sales orders. Consequently, the failure to prorate underapplied or overapplied overhead is unlikely to cause significant errors.

If you ponder the practical accounting for overhead, you can easily see the cost-benefit theme at work. Averages are used to obtain budgeted rates. In turn, these budgeted rates are used to measure the inventories and cost of goods sold, and direct write-offs of underapplied or overapplied overhead are used at year-end. Of course, proration of underapplied or overapplied overhead to inventories would give more accurate approximations of actual costs. However, most managers and accountants believe that such additional, often costly, attempts at accuracy would seldom provide additional useful information. **Thus, adjusting Cost of Goods Sold for all the underapplied or overapplied overhead is the most widely practiced treatment.**

Actual and normal absorption costing

The most difficult aspects of these early chapters are probably the flock of new terms and the accounting for overhead. This chapter illustrates *normal absorption costing*, which can be distinguished from *actual absorption costing*:

	Chapter 2 Approach, Called Actual Absorption Costing: Work-in-Process Inventory	Chapter 4 Approach, Called Normal Absorption Costing: Work-in-Process Inventory
Direct materials	actual costs	actual costs
Direct labor	actual costs	actual costs
Variable factory overhead	actual costs	actual inputs of the application base × budgeted overhead rates
Fixed factory overhead	actual costs	

The job-order system described in this chapter should be called a **normal costing** system, not an *actual* costing system, because the overhead is applied to products on an average or "normalized" basis to get representative inventory valuations. Hence the *normal cost* (perhaps more accurately called *normalized cost*) of the manufactured products is composed of *actual* direct material, *actual* direct labor, and applied overhead (using budgeted overhead rates times actual inputs).

The Chapter 2 approach would not apply overhead to the products until the end of a fiscal period. Then the actual overhead would be used for computing the costs of the products worked on. Reconsider the factory overhead cost in Exhibit 4-5 (page 92). Under actual costing, the Factory Overhead Applied would be $27,000 instead of the $26,460 used under normal costing. All costs actually incurred would be precisely offset by costs applied to Work in Process.

Normal costing has replaced actual costing in many companies because the latter fails to provide costs of products when they are manufactured. Of course, it is possible to use a normal costing system plus year-end adjustments to obtain final results that closely approximate the results under actual costing, as shown earlier in the proration of underapplied overhead. Thus, if managers desire yearly "actual" costing results, year-end prorations of underapplied or overapplied overhead may be used in conjunction with the normal costing that exists throughout the year.

Application bases: past and future

Most manufacturers use broad averages for applying overhead to products. For example, suppose a company has two departments, machining and assembly. Despite some basic differences in their departmental operations, many such companies have used a single plantwide overhead application rate. Moreover, surveys have consistently shown that a vast majority of manufacturers (in many surveys over 90%) use direct-labor hours or direct-labor dollars as their application base.

Why use different overhead rates for each department? Because it permits a more accurate linking of the actual resources used as a product moves through various departments. Consider automation, which has led to overhead becoming a much larger proportion of total manufacturing costs and direct labor a smaller proportion. Some companies have seen their factory overhead rates as a percentage of direct-labor cost soar from 20% in the 1940s to 1,500% and higher in the 1980s. Therefore many companies have developed many more departmental overhead bases *and* more overhead application rates within each department. As computers help reduce the costs of gathering more-detailed data, there will be several overhead rates within each department. Some departments will have an overhead rate related to the weight or cost of the direct materials used, a separate rate related to direct labor used, and a separate rate related to machine-hours used.[3]

PROCESS AND OPERATION COSTING

The two polar extremes of product costing are *job-order costing* and **process costing.** The latter is a system for applying costs to like products that are mass produced in continuous fashion through a series of production steps called *processes.* Process costing is most often found in such industries as chemicals, petroleum, textiles, paints, flour, canneries, rubber, steel, glass, food processing, mining, and cement.

The process-costing system is used in nonmanufacturing too. Examples include check clearing in banks, mail sorting in post offices, food preparation in fast-food outlets, and premium handling in insurance companies. In practice, there are often no clear lines between job-order and process costing. Instead many hybrid systems are found.

Product costing is averaging

The master illustration in this chapter has featured job-order costing. Whether a process-cost or a job-cost system is used, costs are accumulated for *control* in a similar way. However, the application of costs for *product costing* is typically much easier under process costing because individual jobs do not exist. The most important point is that product costing under both cost systems is an *averaging* process. The unit cost used for inventory purposes is the result of taking some accumulated cost and dividing it by some measure of production. The basic distinction between job-order costing and process costing is the size of the denominator: In job-order costing, it is small (for example, one painting, one hundred advertising circulars, or one special packaging machine); but in process costing, it is large (for example, thousands of pounds, gallons, or board feet).

Equivalent units

Assume that our sample company produced hand-held calculators in large quantities. Suppose it completed 10,000 units during January. Then the unit cost of goods completed would simply be $108,800 (from the Work-in-Process account in Exhibit 4-5, page 92) ÷ 10,000 = $10.88.

The major difficulty in process costing is in applying costs to uncompleted products, goods still in process at the end of the accounting period. For instance, suppose 1,000 calculators were in process at the end of the month; therefore 10,000 units were started, but only 9,000 were fully completed during January. All the parts had been made or requisitioned, but only half of the labor had been completed for each of the 1,000 calculators. What was the output for January?

An obvious answer would be 9,000 completed units plus 1,000 half-completed units. But we should hesitate to express the sum of the output as 10,000 units. Why? Because each of the partially completed units is not a perfect substitute for a completed unit. Therefore we express output not as *physical* units, but as *equivalent* units.

---

[3]Chapters 12 and 13 consider these issues in more detail. Also see H. R. Schwarzbach, "The Impact of Automation on Accounting for Indirect Costs," *Management Accounting,* December 1985, pp. 45–50, which reports on the practices of 112 manufacturing firms.

Equivalent units are measures of the output in terms of the quantities of each of the factors of production applied thereto. That is, an equivalent unit is a collection of inputs (work applications) necessary to produce one complete physical unit of output. In other words, an equivalent unit is a measure of the factors of production—direct materials, direct labor, and factory overhead.

Recall that direct labor plus factory overhead is called conversion costs. In terms of equivalent units of conversion costs, the ending work in process of 1,000 units half completed is equivalent to 500 units of work accomplished. In a like manner, an ending work in process of 750 units two-thirds completed is equivalent to 500 units of work accomplished.

The concept of equivalent units is not restricted to the task of applying costs to products. More fundamentally, it is a means of measuring activities or workload in terms of a common denominator. Equivalent units are all around us in all types of organizations, although perhaps not in the usual form portrayed by cost accounting texts. Examples are "full time equivalents" for measuring faculty positions and student enrollments. Breweries express their production in equivalent barrels even though most of their actual products may come in small cans and bottles.

Illustration of process costing

To illustrate basic process costing, for simplicity assume that all the costs in work in process in Exhibit 4-5 pertain to a one-department company:

		EQUIVALENT UNITS	
FLOW OF PRODUCTION	PHYSICAL UNITS	Direct Materials	Conversion Costs
Started and completed	9,000	9,000	9,000
Work in process, ending inventory:	1,000		
Direct materials added: 1,000 × 1		1,000	
Conversion costs added: 1,000 × ½			500
Total accounted for	10,000		
Total work done		10,000	9,500
Total costs to account for:	$113,460		
Direct materials added		$48,000	
Conversion costs added ($39,000 labor + $26,460 applied overhead)			$65,460
Divide by equivalent units of work done		10,000	9,500
Unit costs		$4.80	$6.89053

Costs are transferred from Work in Process to Finished Goods on the basis of costs per equivalent unit. Likewise, the balance of the ending Work in Process is based on costs per equivalent unit:

Total costs applied:		
To units completed and transferred to		
Finished Goods, 9,000 × ($4.80 + $6.89053) =		$105,215
To units still in Work in Process:		
Materials, 1,000 equivalent units × $4.80 =	$4,800	
Conversion costs, 500 equivalent units × $6.89053 =	3,445	
Ending work-in-process inventory		8,245
Total costs accounted for		$113,460

Using these data, the earlier journal entry (Number 7, page 96) would be revised because the cost of goods transferred would no longer be $108,800, as shown in Exhibit 4-5. The pertinent T-accounts would show:

Work-in-Process Control				Finished-Goods Control	
(2)	48,000	(7)	105,215 — — →(7)	105,215	
(3)	39,000				
(6)	26,460				
	113,460				
Bal.	8,245				

As you might expect, each manufacturing company develops its own hybrid accounting system to suit its own desires. For example, many companies employ a so-called **operation costing** system, which is used in the manufacture of goods that have some common characteristics plus some individual characteristics. In these systems, distinctions are made between batches of product, such as Model A calculators and Model B calculators. Materials are specifically allocated to the batches in the same way as a job-order costing system. Conversion costs are computed for each operation in the same way as a process-costing system. The final costs of Model A and Model B depend on their particular material components plus what operations were conducted in their manufacture. An operation is defined as a standardized production step, method, or technique that is repetitively performed. Obviously, the more materials and the more operations undergone, the more costs are applied to the specific product.

CHAPTERS 15 TO 17 DESCRIBE PROCESS COSTING, JOB COSTING, AND OPERATION COSTING IN MORE DETAIL. THEY CAN BE STUDIED NOW, IF DESIRED, WITHOUT BREAKING CONTINUITY. Chapter 17 also describes just-in-time costing, which is a hybrid of operation costing and process costing.

SUMMARY

The job-cost system described in this chapter illustrates how historical costs are compiled for evaluation of performance and for facilitating predictions of how various departments and managers will perform in forthcoming periods and of how various future jobs should be priced. Job-order costing is an expensive accounting system because of the detail underlying the recordkeeping required for each job. The number of departments and the number of overhead application rates used in this system depend on the perceived improvements in decisions in relation to the extra costs of more elaborate recordkeeping.

Scorekeeping for the purpose of planning and control consists largely of *accumulating* costs by departments; for the product-costing purpose, it consists largely of *applying* costs to products to obtain a representative indication of the relative costs of resources devoted to various physical units of product.

The two extremes of product costing are job-order costing and process costing. Many companies use some sort of hybrid, notably operation costing. Job-order costing was discussed at length in this chapter.

Many companies apply overhead at budgeted rates. The resultant product cost consists of "actual" direct materials, "actual" direct labor, and overhead applied using budgeted rates. Thus this total product cost should be called a *normal* cost rather than an *actual* cost. Therefore a given product-costing system can properly be called an *actual-cost* system or a *normal-cost* system (where budgeted rates are used to apply overhead). Within a given company, either a job-order-costing approach or a process-costing approach or some hybrid approach, such as *operation costing*, is tailored to needs.

Some thoughtful solving of homework at this stage will strengthen your understanding of basic relationships and terminology.

PROBLEMS FOR SELF-STUDY

Restudy the illustration of job-order accounting in this chapter. Then try to solve one or two straightforward job-order problems such as Problems 4-16 and 4-20. Then try to solve the following problem, which requires consideration of most of this chapter's important points.

problem 1 You are asked to bring the following incomplete accounts of a plant in a foreign country up to date through January 31, 19_2. Also consider the data that appear after the T-accounts.

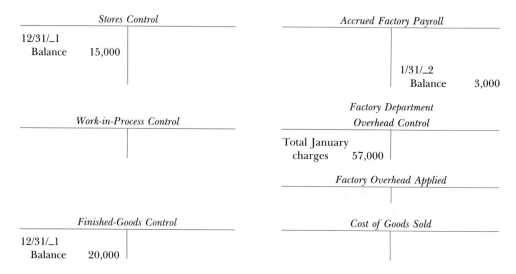

Stores Control			Accrued Factory Payroll	
12/31/_1 Balance	15,000		1/31/_2 Balance	3,000

Work-in-Process Control			Factory Department Overhead Control	
			Total January charges 57,000	

| | | | Factory Overhead Applied | |

Finished-Goods Control			Cost of Goods Sold	
12/31/_1 Balance	20,000			

ADDITIONAL INFORMATION

1. The overhead is applied using a budgeted rate that is set every December by forecasting the following year's overhead and relating it to forecast direct-labor costs. The budget for 19_2 called for $400,000 of direct labor and $600,000 of factory overhead.
2. The only job unfinished on January 31, 19_2, was No. 419, on which total labor charges were $2,000 (125 direct-labor hours) and total direct-material charges were $8,000.
3. Total materials placed into production during January were $90,000.
4. Cost of goods completed during January was $180,000.
5. January 31 balances on stores records totaled $20,000.
6. Finished-goods inventory as of January 31 was $15,000.
7. All factory workers earn the same rate of pay. Direct-labor hours for January totaled 2,500. Indirect labor and supervision totaled $10,000.
8. The gross factory payroll paid on January paydays totaled $52,000. Ignore withholdings.
9. All "actual" factory overhead incurred during January has already been posted.

Required

a. Materials purchased during January
b. Cost of goods sold during January
c. Direct-labor costs incurred during January
d. Overhead applied during January

e. Balance, Accrued Factory Payroll, December 31, 19_1

f. Balance, Work in Process, December 31, 19_1

g. Balance, Work in Process, January 31, 19_2

h. Overapplied or underapplied overhead for January

solution 1

a. Materials purchased: $90,000 + $20,000 − $15,000 = $95,000.

b. Cost of goods sold: $20,000 + $180,000 − $15,000 = $185,000.

c. Direct-labor rate: $2,000 ÷ 125 hours = $16 per hour (see 2). Direct-labor cost: 2,500 hours × $16 = $40,000 (see 7).

d. Overhead rate: $600,000 ÷ $400,000 = 150%. Overhead applied: 150% × $40,000 = $60,000.

e. Accrued factory payroll, Dec. 31: $52,000 + $3,000 − $40,000 − $10,000 = $5,000.

f. Work in process, Dec. 31: $180,000 + $13,000 − $90,000 − $40,000 − $60,000 = $3,000.

g. Work in process, Jan. 31: $8,000 + $2,000 + 150% of $2,000 = $13,000.

h. Overapplied overhead: $60,000 − $57,000 = $3,000.

Entries in T-accounts are numbered in accordance with the "additional information" in the problem and are lettered in accordance with the amounts required to be determined.

Stores Control

12/31/_1 Bal. (given)			15,000			
	(a)		95,000*	(3)		90,000
1/31/_2 Bal.	(5)		20,000			

Work-in-Process Control

12/31/_1 Bal.	(f)			3,000*	(4)	180,000
Direct materials	(3)			90,000		
Direct labor	(2)	(7)	(c)	40,000		
Overhead	(7)	(1)	(d)	60,000		
1/31/_2 Bal.	(2)	(g)		13,000		

Finished-Goods Control

12/31/_1 Bal. (given)			20,000			
	(4)		180,000	(6)	(b)	185,000
1/31/_2 Bal.	(6)		15,000			

Accrued Factory Payroll

(8)		52,000	12/31/_1 (e)	5,000*
			(7)	{40,000
				10,000
			1/31/_2 Bal. (given)	3,000

Factory Department Overhead Control

January charges (given)	57,000	

Factory Overhead Applied

		(7) (1) (d)		60,000

Cost of Goods Sold

(6) (b)		185,000	

111 *Can be computed only after all other postings in the account have been found, so (g) must be computed before (f).

A letter to the shareholders of Marantz, Inc., described many competitive troubles, including the following: "The reduced level of orders . . . resulted in increased unabsorbed costs . . . which further adversely affected the Company's overall competitive position."

| Using the terms introduced in this book, prepare a precise explanation of the quotation.

"Increased unabsorbed costs" means that the *applied* or *absorbed* factory overhead was less than the *actual* factory overhead. In other words, the underapplied or underabsorbed overhead becomes greater and greater if the company falls shorter and shorter of the volume level originally budgeted.

Marantz was confronted with a common difficulty. If sales drop precipitously, production must be cut back. At the same time, the fixed costs of factory facilities, such as rent, depreciation, and property taxes, are not easily reduced. These costs tend to be the bulk of the unabsorbed costs referred to in the quotation.

Terms to Learn

This chapter and the Glossary at the end of the book contain definitions of the following important terms:

applied overhead (p. 95) *budgeted factory overhead rate (98)*
clock card (89) *cost center (87)* *equivalent units (108)*
job-cost record (88) *job-cost sheet (88)* *job order (88)*
job-order costing (87) *material requisition (91)* *normal costing (106)*
operation costing (109) *overapplied overhead (102)* *process costing (107)*
proration (103) *responsibility center (87)* *stores requisition (88)*
underapplied overhead (102) *work ticket (88)*

Special Points and Pitfalls

This chapter focused on product costing, as distinguished from control. It introduced normal costing, which means that overhead is applied to product by multiplying a budgeted overhead rate by the *actual* amount of the application base. For example, a budgeted overhead rate would be multiplied by the actual number of direct-labor hours of input on a job.

In normal costing, throughout the fiscal year, Work in Process, Finished Goods, and Cost of Goods Sold are carried at actual direct materials, actual direct labor, and applied factory overhead. Underapplied or overapplied overhead usually accumulates in the accounts from month to month; its final amount is typically added to or subtracted from the Cost of Goods Sold at the end of the year. However, if the amount of underapplied or overapplied overhead is significant, it is prorated over Work in Process, Finished Goods, and Cost of Goods Sold.

APPENDIX: SUPPLEMENTARY DESCRIPTION OF LEDGER RELATIONSHIPS

This Appendix explains some of the work that underlies the general-ledger relationships described in this chapter. A factory setting is used to illustrate some of the basic manufacturing transactions and to show how source documents and auxiliary records can be used to facilitate the accumulation of data. Also included is an exhibit that summarizes sample accounting entries for job costing.

The general ledger is a summary device. Postings are made to it from totals and subtotals of underlying transactions. For example, the balance of the Stores Control may be supported by a voluminous file of stores records. Postings to the debit side of the Stores Control may be made from the Stores column in a special journal, such as a purchases journal or a voucher register. But the specific stores record in the subsidiary ledger is posted from a copy of a voucher or an invoice.

Source documents, such as voucher copies, stores requisitions, work tickets, clock cards, and other memoranda, are the primary means of recording business events. They are vital because all subsequent accounting classifications and reports are dependent on source documents. These documents are increasingly being kept on a computerized basis.

Direct-material-usage reports

A multicopy stores requisition may be made out by a supervisor. For example, separate copies may serve as follows:

Copy 1—Kept by storekeeper
Copy 2—Used by clerk or computer to post to job-cost record
Copy 3—Used by accounting department as a basis for a summary of requisitions

This summary is the support for the general-ledger entry:

Work-in-process control	xx	
Stores control		xx

This entry is usually made monthly, although it can be made more frequently if desired.

Copy 4—Used as a basis for departmental material-usage reports. If these reports are to prove useful for control, they must typically be prepared more often than once a month. Stale, month-old reports concerning major costs are not helpful. Daily or weekly reports are common. This is another reason why the general ledger is oriented toward product costing rather than toward costing for control. The reports for control are needed before formal postings can be made.
Copy 5—Retained by supervisor. Used as a cross-check against the usage reports sent by the accounting department.

The accounting department ordinarily uses requisitions that become part of a data base for computers. These may be sorted in many ways. For example:

Direct-Material Requisition Summary

REQUISITION NUMBER	JOB ORDER	DEPARTMENT	AMOUNT	JOB-COST SUBTOTALS	DEPARTMENT SUBTOTALS
501	1415	26	$ 32.00		
502	1415	27	51.00	$83.00	
503	1408	26	204.00		
504	1414	26	19.00		$255.00
505	1409	28	101.00		

Computers accumulate and tabulate data so that they can be classified, reclassified, summarized, and resummarized to provide the specific information needed by management. Thus a material-usage report can be submitted to the supervisor of Department 26 on a daily, weekly, or monthly basis:

Department 26
Direct-Material Usage
For the week ended _____

REQUISITION NUMBER	JOB ORDER	AMOUNT
501	1415	$ 32.00
503	1408	204.00
504	1414	19.00
510	1408	55.00
511	1412	122.00

Direct-labor-cost recapitulation

Similar analysis can be applied to the sorting of direct-labor costs, using the work ticket as the source document. Producing departments may have their labor classified by operations as well as by jobs. For example, the machining department may perform one or more of the following operations: milling, cleaning, grinding, and facing. Thus work tickets may be recapitulated as shown below.

This labor recapitulation can be used as a basis for the general-ledger entry that charges direct labor to product:

> Work in process   xx
>   Accrued payroll   xx
> This entry is usually made monthly, although it can
> be made more frequently if desired.

Direct-Labor-Cost Recapitulation

WORK TICKET NUMBER	EMPLOYEE ID NUMBER	JOB NUMBER	DEPT. NUMBER	OPERATION NUMBER	AMOUNT	JOB SUB-TOTALS	OPERATION SUBTOTALS	DEPT. SUB-TOTALS
P14	49	1410	26	6500	$20.00		$20.00	
15	49	1410	26	6501	6.00		6.00	$26.00
16	52	1410	27	7520	19.00		19.00	
17	53	1410	27	7522	16.00	$61.00		
18	30	1411	25	5298	30.00	30.00	30.00	30.00
19	61	1409	28	8414	24.60		24.60	24.60
20	52	1409	27	7522	9.75	34.35	25.75	44.75

The recapitulation also supplies the information for daily, weekly, or monthly usage reports to the department supervisor. These reports may be broken down by jobs or operations to suit the supervisor.

Work tickets may also be used for idle time (for example, caused by machine breakdowns or shortages of material), overtime premium, material moving, and so forth. A computer or timekeeper may prepare a daily reconciliation of employee clock cards with individual work tickets to see that all clock-card time is accounted for as direct labor, idle time, overtime premium, and so forth.

Sample entries

Exhibit 4-11 on pages 116–17 summarizes the accounting entries for job costing.

4-1 What are the two major cost objectives of a cost accounting system?

4-2 Give at least one synonym for the control purpose of a cost accounting system.

4-3 Give two examples of responsibility centers.

4-4 Give two uses of product costs.

4-5 Distinguish between cost accumulation and cost application.

4-6 "Job costing is confined to manufacturing." True or false. Explain.

4-7 Explain the role of a rate base in factory-overhead accounting.

4-8 Why is direct labor likely to become a lower proportion of total manufacturing costs?

4-9 Distinguish between a *clock card* and a *work ticket*.

4-10 What are the limitations of the general ledger as a cost accounting device?

4-11 What is a *normal product cost?*

4-12 Give two definitions of *control* as the word may be used by an accountant.

4-13 What is the purpose of a *department cost sheet?*

4-14 What is the principal difference between *job-cost* and *process-cost* accounting systems?

4-15 Journal entries. The Wisnenski Company uses a job-order cost system. The following relate to the month of March:
1. Direct materials issued to production, $96,000.
2. Direct-labor analysis, $78,000.
3. Manufacturing overhead is applied to production on the basis of $4 per direct-labor hour. There were 13,000 direct-labor hours incurred.
4. Total manufacturing overhead for the month was $54,000.
5. Job orders that cost $200,000 were completed during the month.
6. Job orders that cost $190,000 were shipped and invoiced to customers during the month at a profit of 20% based on cost.

Required | The beginning inventory of work in process was $30,000. Prepare the general-journal entries required to record this information. What is the ending balance of work in process?

4-16 Basic entries. (Alternate is 4-18.) The University of Chicago Press is wholly owned by the university. A job-order system is used for printing. The bulk of the work is done for other university departments, which pay as though the Press were an outside business enterprise. The Press also publishes and maintains a stock of books for general sale.

EXHIBIT 4-11

Job-Order-System Sample Entries

TRANSACTION	GENERAL-LEDGER EFFECTS	SUBSIDIARY LEDGERS	SOURCE DOCUMENTS	EXPLANATORY COMMENTS
1. Purchases of materials or supplies	Stores control Accounts payable	Dr. Stores records, "Received" column	Approved invoice	
2. Issuance of direct materials	Work-in-process control Stores control	Dr. Job cost records Cr. Stores records, "Issued" column	Stores requisition	Requisitions are summarized and classified by department for hourly, daily, weekly, or monthly, direct-material-usage reports
3. Issuance of indirect materials	Factory department overhead control Stores control	Dr. Department overhead cost records, appropriate columns Cr. Stores records, "Issued" column	Stores requisition	
4. Distribution of labor costs	Work-in-process control Factory department overhead control Accrued payroll	Dr. Job cost records Dr. Department overhead cost records, appropriate columns for various classes of indirect labor	Summary of work tickets or daily time analyses. This summary is sometimes called a labor cost distribution summary or a payroll recapitulation	
5. Payment of payroll (for a complete description see the appendix to Chapter 17	Accrued payroll Withholdings payable Cash		Summary of clock cards and individual withholdings as shown on payroll sheets	This entry is usually made weekly, while the cost distribution (the prior entry) is not necessarily made at the same time
6. Payment of withholdings	Withholdings payable Cash			Withholdings are usually broken down by type rather than lumped in one account
7. Employer payroll taxes	Factory department overhead control Employer payroll taxes payable	Dr. Department overhead costs records, appropriate columns	Accrual memoranda from accounting officer	

TRANSACTION	GENERAL-LEDGER EFFECTS	SUBSIDIARY LEDGERS	SOURCE DOCUMENTS	EXPLANATORY COMMENTS
8. Utilities	Factory department overhead control Accounts payable or Accrued utilities	Dr. Department overhead cost records, appropriate columns	Approved invoices or accrual memoranda	
9. Depreciation on factory equipment	Factory department overhead control Accumulated depreciation—equipment	Dr. Department overhead cost records, appropriate columns	Depreciation schedule	
10. Factory insurance write-off	Factory department overhead control Unexpired insurance	Dr. Department overhead cost records, appropriate columns	Insurance register or memoranda from accounting officer	
11. Application of overhead to product	Work-in-process control Factory overhead applied	Dr. Job-cost records	Budgeted overhead rate computed by using overhead budget	
12. Transfer completed goods to finished stock	Finished-goods control Work-in-process control	Dr. Finished stock records, "Received" column Cr. Job-cost records	Production report	Sometimes the completed job order serves as a finished stock record
13. Sales	Accounts-receivable control Sales	Dr. Customers' accounts	Copy of sales invoice	
14. Cost of goods sold	Cost of goods sold Finished-goods control	Dr. Cost of goods sold record (optional) Cr. Finished stock records	Copy of sales invoice plus costs as shown on finished stock records	
15. Yearly closing of overhead accounts	Factory overhead applied Factory department overhead control Cost of goods sold (cr. if overhead is overapplied; dr. if overhead is under-applied)		General ledger balances	

Dr. = debit; Cr. = credit

The following data pertain to 19_2 (in thousands):

Direct materials and supplies purchased on account	$ 800
Direct materials issued to the producing departments for production	710
Supplies issued to various producing departments	100
Labor used directly on production	2,600
Indirect labor incurred by various departments	900
Depreciation, buildings and equipment	400
Miscellaneous factory overhead* incurred by various departments (ordinarily would be detailed as repairs, photocopying, utilities, etc.)	550
Factory overhead applied at 80% of direct-labor cost	?
Cost of goods manufactured and transferred to finished goods	5,420
Sales	8,000
Cost of goods sold	5,320
Inventories, December 31, 19_1 (not 19_2):	
Stores control	100
Work-in-process control	60
Finished-goods control	500

*The term factory overhead is not used uniformly. Other terms that are often encountered in printing companies include job overhead and shop overhead.

Required

1. Prepare general journal entries to summarize 19_2 transactions. As your final entry, dispose of the year-end overapplied or underapplied factory overhead as a direct adjustment to Cost of Goods Sold. Number your entries. Explanations for each entry may be omitted.
2. Show posted T-accounts for all inventories, Cost of Goods Sold, Factory Department Overhead Control, and Factory Overhead Applied.
3. Sketch how the subsidiary ledger would appear for Factory Department Overhead Control. Assume that there are three departments: art, photo, and printing. You need not show any numbers.

4-17 Journal entries and source documents. Refer to Problem 4-16. For each journal entry, (a) indicate the most likely name of the source documents that would authorize the entry, and (b) give a description of the entry into the subsidiary ledgers affected, if any.

4-18 T-accounts. (Alternate is 4-16.) The following data relate to operations of the Donnell Printing Company for the year 19_5 (in millions):

Stores control, December 31, 19_4	$ 12
Work-in-process control, December 31, 19_4	3
Finished-goods control, December 31, 19_4	6
Materials and supplies purchased on account	150
Direct materials issued to the producing departments for production	145
Indirect materials (supplies) issued to various producing departments	10
Labor used directly on production	90
Indirect labor incurred by various departments	30
Depreciation—plant and equipment	19
Miscellaneous factory overhead incurred by various departments (ordinarily would be detailed as repairs, utilities, etc.)	9
Factory overhead applied at 70% of direct-labor cost	?
Cost of goods manufactured and transferred to finished stock	294
Sales	400
Cost of goods sold	292

1. Use T-accounts to record all transactions. Number your entries. What is the ending balance of Work-in-Process Control?
2. Sketch how the subsidiary ledger would appear for Factory Department Overhead Control, assuming that there are four departments. You need not show any numbers.
3. Show the journal entry for disposing of overapplied or underapplied overhead directly as a year-end adjustment to Cost of Goods Sold. Post the entry to T-accounts.

For more details concerning these data, see Problem 4-19.

4-19 Journal entries and source documents. Refer to Problem 4-18. Prepare journal entries. For each entry, (a) indicate the most likely name of the source documents that would authorize the entry, and (b) give a description of the entry into the subsidiary ledgers affected, if any.

4-20 Accounting for overhead; budgeted rates. (Alternate is 4-21.) The Aaron Company uses a budgeted overhead rate in applying overhead to production orders on a *labor-cost* basis for Department A and on a *machine-hour* basis for Department B. At the beginning of 19_1, the company made the following predictions:

	DEPT. A	DEPT. B
Direct-labor cost	$128,000	$ 35,000
Factory overhead	144,000	150,000
Direct-labor hours	16,000	5,000
Machine-hours	1,000	20,000

1. What is the budgeted overhead *rate* that should be used in Department A? In Department B?
2. During the month of January, the cost record for job order No. 200 shows the following:

	DEPT. A	DEPT. B
Materials requisitioned	$20	$40
Direct-labor cost	$32	$21
Direct-labor hours	5	3
Machine-hours	1	13

What is the *total overhead* cost of job order No. 200?
3. Assuming that Job No. 200 consisted of 20 units of product, what is the *unit cost* of Job No. 200?
4. At the *end* of 19_1, it was found that *actual* factory-overhead costs amounted to $160,000 in Department A and $138,000 in Department B. Suppose the actual direct-labor cost was $148,000 in Department A and the actual machine-hours were 18,000 in Department B. Compute the overapplied or underapplied overhead amount for each department and for the factory as a whole.

4-21 Accounting for overhead. (Alternate is 4-20.) The Lynn Company has made the following predictions for 19_4:

	MACHINING	ASSEMBLY
Factory overhead	$ 600,000	$ 800,000
Direct-labor cost	1,000,000	1,600,000
Direct-labor hours	100,000	200,000
Machine-hours	50,000	200,000

The company uses a budgeted overhead rate for applying overhead to production orders on a machine-hour basis in Machining and on a direct-labor-cost basis in Assembly.

1. Compute the budgeted overhead rate for each department.
2. During February the cost record for job #494 contained the following:

	MACHINING	ASSEMBLY
Direct materials requisitioned	$ 5,000	$15,000
Direct-labor cost	10,000	12,000
Direct-labor hours	1,000	1,500
Machine-hours	2,000	1,000

Compute the total overhead cost of job #494.
3. At the end of 19_4, the actual factory overhead costs were $680,000 in Machining and $725,000 in Assembly. Assume that 55,000 actual machine-hours were incurred in Machining and actual direct-labor cost in Assembly was $1,800,000. Compute the overapplied or underapplied overhead for each department.

4-22 Subsidiary and general ledgers, journal entries. The Knowles Custom Furniture Co. worked on only three jobs during September and October. The job-cost records are summarized as follows:

	410		411		412
	September	October	September	October	October
Direct materials	$19,000	$ —	$12,000	$8,000	$14,000
Direct labor	4,000	2,000	6,000	4,000	1,000
Factory overhead applied	12,000	?	18,000	?	?

Factory overhead is applied as a percentage of direct-labor costs. The balances in selected accounts on September 30 were: direct-materials inventory, $31,000; and finished-goods inventory, $42,000.

Other balances in selected accounts on September 30 were: cost of goods sold, $900,000; accrued payroll, $1,000; and factory overhead applied, $250,000.

Job 410 was completed, transferred to finished goods, and sold along with other finished goods by October 31, the end of the fiscal year. The total cost of goods sold during October was $75,000.

Job 411 was still in process at the end of October. Job 412 was also in process. It had begun on October 23.

1. Taken together, the job-cost records are the subsidiary ledger supporting the general-ledger balance of work in process. Prepare a schedule showing the balance of the work-in-process inventory, September 30.
2. Compute the overhead application rate.
3. Prepare summary general journal entries for all costs added to Work in Process during October. Also prepare an entry for all costs transferred from Work in Process to Finished Goods.
4. Post the journal entries to the appropriate T-accounts.
5. Prepare a schedule showing the balance of the work-in-process inventory, October 31.

4-23 Overhead balances. (SMA) Budgeted overhead, based on a budgeted volume of 100,000 direct-labor hours, was $255,000. Actual overhead costs amounted to $270,000, and actual direct-labor hours were 105,000. Overhead overapplied (underapplied) amounted to (choose one): (1) $2,250 overapplied, (2) ($2,250) underapplied, (3) $15,000 overapplied, or (4) ($15,000) underapplied.

4-24 Manufacturing statement. (CPA) The Helper Corporation manufactures one product and accounts for costs by a job-order cost system. You have obtained the following information for the year ended December 31, 19_3, from the corporation's books and records:

Total manufacturing cost added during 19_3 (sometimes called cost to manufacture) was $1,000,000 based on actual direct material, actual direct labor, and applied factory overhead on actual direct-labor dollars.

Cost of goods manufactured was $970,000 also based on actual direct material, actual direct labor, and applied factory overhead.

Factory overhead was applied to work in process at 75% of direct-labor dollars. Applied factory overhead for the year was 27% of the total manufacturing cost.

Beginning work-in-process inventory, January 1, was 80% of ending work-in-process inventory, December 31.

Required

Prepare a formal statement of cost of goods manufactured for the year ended December 31, 19_3, for Helper Corporation. Use actual direct material used, actual direct labor, and applied factory overhead. Show supporting computations in good form.

4-25 Applying overhead, job costing. (CMA, adapted) Baehr Company is a manufacturing company with a fiscal year that runs from July 1 to June 30. The company uses a job-order accounting system for its production costs.

A budgeted overhead rate based on direct-labor hours is used to apply overhead to individual jobs. A budget of overhead costs was prepared for the 19_7–_8 fiscal year as follows:

Direct-labor hours	120,000
Variable overhead costs	$390,000
Fixed overhead costs	216,000
Total overhead	$606,000

Company officials have determined 120,000 direct-labor hours as the expected volume for the year. The following information is for November, 19_7. Jobs 77-50 and 77-51 were completed during November.

Inventories, November 1, 19_7:	
Direct materials and supplies	$ 10,500
Work-in-process (Job 77-50)	54,000
Finished goods	112,500
Purchases of raw materials and supplies:	
Direct materials	$135,000
Supplies	15,000
Materials and supplies requisitioned for production:	
Job 77-50	$ 45,000
Job 77-51	37,500
Job 77-52	25,500
Supplies	12,000
	$120,000
Factory direct-labor hours:	
Job 77-50	3,500 DLH
Job 77-51	3,000 DLH
Job 77-52	2,000 DLH
Labor costs:	
Direct-labor wages	$ 51,000
Indirect-labor wages (4,000 hours)	15,000
Supervisory salaries	6,000
Building occupancy costs (heat, light, depreciation, etc.):	
Factory facilities	$ 6,500
Sales offices	1,500
Administrative offices	1,000
	$ 9,000

Factory equipment costs:	
Power	$ 4,000
Repairs and maintenance	1,500
Depreciation	1,500
Other	1,000
	$ 8,000

Answer the following multiple-choice questions.

1. The budgeted overhead rate to be used to apply overhead to individual jobs during the 19_7–_8 fiscal year is
(a) $3.25 per DLH   (b) $4.69 per DLH   (c) $5.05 per DLH
(d) $5.41 per DLH   (e) None of these.
Note: Without prejudice to your answer to Item 1, assume that the budgeted overhead rate is $4.50 per direct-labor hour. Use this amount in answering items 3 through 6.
2. At the end of the last fiscal year (June 30, 19_7), Baehr Company had the following account balances:

Cost of goods sold	$980,000
Work-in-process inventory	38,000
Finished-goods inventory	82,000

The most common treatment of the overapplied overhead of $1,000 would be to
(a) Prorate it between work-in-process inventory and finished-goods inventory
(b) Prorate it between work-in-process inventory, finished-goods inventory and cost of goods sold   (c) Carry it as a deferred credit on the balance sheet   (d) Carry it as miscellaneous operating revenue on the income statement or   (e) Credit it to cost of goods sold.
3. The total cost of job 77-50 is
(a) $81,750   (b) $135,750   (c) $142,750   (d) $146,750   (e) None of these.
4. The factory-overhead costs applied to job 77-52 during November were
(a) $9,000   (b) $47,500   (c) $46,500   (d) $8,000   (e) None of these.
5. The total amount of overhead applied to jobs during November was
(a) $29,250   (b) $38,250   (c) $47,250   (d) $56,250   (e) None of these.
6. Actual factory overhead incurred during November 19_7 was
(a) $38,000   (b) $41,500   (c) $47,500   (d) $50,500   (e) None of these.

4-26 Journal entries, year-end disposition of overhead.   Tuttle Company uses a job-order cost system. Factory overhead is applied at a rate of $2.50 per direct-labor hour. Both beginning and closing balances in work in process and finished goods are zero. You are given the following data for 19_4, and the fact that all goods manufactured are sold.

Direct-labor hours used	50,000
Direct materials used	$ 50,000
Direct labor used	100,000
Indirect labor used	25,000
Indirect supplies used	10,000
Rent—plant and equipment	50,000
Miscellaneous overhead	50,000
Cost of goods sold	275,000

All underapplied or overapplied overhead is allocated wholly to cost of goods sold at the end of the year.

1. Factory overhead applied.
2. Factory overhead incurred.
3. Prepare journal entries to record all the facts above, including all necessary entries to adjust for overapplied or underapplied overhead.

4-27 Accounting for overhead. On December 30, 19_2, the Mitchell Company has completed all jobs in process except for Job # 447; the job-cost sheet through that date showed direct materials of $40,000 and direct labor of $30,000. Total factory overhead incurred through December 30 was $900,000. The labor-cost recapitulation for the December 31 working day was: direct labor, $8,000; indirect labor, $2,000. In addition, miscellaneous factory overhead incurred on December 31 was $3,000. Direct materials of $2,000 were added to Job # 447.

The company's charges to Work in Process during 19_2 included direct labor for 19_2 of $720,000, excluding the December 31 working day described above. The factory overhead is applied to jobs at 120% of direct labor.

The balance in Finished-Goods Inventory, December 31, 19_2, was $112,000 and in Cost of Goods Sold was $2,000,000.

Required

1. Compute the *normal cost* of ending inventory, Work in Process, December 31, 19_2.
2. What is the underapplied or overapplied factory overhead for 19_2?

4-28 Application and proration of overhead. (SMA, heavily adapted) Nicole Limited is a company that produces machinery to customer orders, using a job-order cost system. Manufacturing overhead is applied to production using a budgeted rate. This overhead rate is set at the beginning of each fiscal year by forecasting the following year's overhead and relating it to direct-labor dollars. The budget for the company's last fiscal year was:

Direct labor	$280,000
Manufacturing overhead	$168,000

As of the end of the year, two jobs were incomplete. These were No. 1768B—total direct-labor charges were $11,000; and No. 1819C—total direct-labor charges were $39,000. On these jobs, machine-hours were 287 for No. 1768B, and 647 for No. 1819C. Direct materials issued to No. 1768B amounted to $22,000, and $42,000 to No. 1819C.

Total charges to the manufacturing-overhead control account for the year were $186,840; while direct-labor charges made to all jobs were $400,000, representing 20,000 direct-labor hours.

There were no beginning inventories. In addition to the ending work in process described above, the ending finished goods showed a balance of $72,000.

Sales for the year totaled $2,700,680; cost of goods sold totaled $648,000; and selling, general, and administrative expenses were $1,857,870.

The amounts for inventories and cost of goods sold were not adjusted for any overapplication or underapplication of manufacturing overhead to production. It is the company's practice to prorate any overapplied or underapplied overhead to inventories and cost of goods sold.

Required

1. Prepare a detailed schedule showing the ending balances in the inventories and cost of goods sold (before considering any underapplied or overapplied manufacturing overhead).
2. Assume that underapplied or overapplied manufacturing overhead is prorated in proportion to the ending balances (before the proration) in Work in Progress, Finished Goods, and Cost of Goods Sold. Prepare a detailed schedule showing the proration and the final balances after proration.
3. Assume that all the underapplied or overapplied manufacturing overhead was added to or subtracted from Cost of Goods Sold. Would operating income be higher or lower than the operating income that would result from the prorations in requirement 2 above? By what amount?

4-29 Proration of overhead. The Invincible Company has commercial and defense contracting business. A contracting officer for the United States Air Force has insisted that underapplied overhead should no longer be written off directly as an adjustment of Cost of Defense Goods Sold for a given year. His insistence was prompted by the fact that $40 million of underapplied overhead was added to the $400 million of unadjusted Cost of Goods Sold in 19_4. There were no beginning inventories.

123

Overhead is applied as a percentage of direct-labor dollars as contracts are produced. The air force had a large cost-plus-fixed-fee contract representing $300 million of the $400 million of defense production started and sold during 19_4; it had no other contracts pending with Invincible. An analysis of costs showed (in millions):

| | DEFENSE BUSINESS | | |
	Contracts in Progress	Finished-Goods Inventory	Cost of Goods Sold
Direct material used	$380	$20	$200
Direct-labor cost	90	10	100
Factory overhead applied	90	10	100
Total before adjustment	560	40	400*
Add: Underapplied overhead	—	—	40
Total after adjustment	$560	$40	$440

*Includes $300 million attributable to air force contract.

Required

1. What overhead rate based on direct-labor dollars would have resulted in factory overhead applied equaling factory overhead incurred?
2. As a judge trying to settle a dispute on the disposition of the overhead, what position would you favor? Why? Show computations and, assuming your answer would be formally recorded in the books of account, show a journal entry for the proration.
3. As the contracting officer, what proration of the underapplied overhead would you favor? Why? Show computations.

4-30 Incomplete data. The Fullerton Company uses perpetual inventories and a normal cost system. Balances from selected accounts were:

	BALANCES DECEMBER 31, 19_1	BALANCES DECEMBER 31, 19_2
Factory department overhead control		$ 56,000
Finished goods	$50,000	40,000
Cost of goods sold		180,000
Direct-materials stores	?	20,000
Factory overhead applied at 60% of direct-labor cost		72,000
Work in process	?	130,000

The cost of direct materials requisitioned for production during 19_2 was $100,000. The cost of direct materials purchased during 19_2 was $90,000.

Required

Before considering any year-end adjustments for overapplied or underapplied overhead, compute:

1. Direct-materials stores, December 31, 19_1
2. Work in process, December 31, 19_1

4-31 Overview of general-ledger relationships. The Blakely Company uses a job-order cost system. The total debits and credits in certain accounts at year-end are:

	Total Debits	Total Credits
Direct-material control	$100,000	$ 70,000
Work-in-process control	320,000	305,000
Factory department overhead control	85,000	—
Finished-goods control	325,000	300,000
Cost of goods sold	300,000	—
Factory department overhead applied	—	90,000

Note that "total debits" in the inventory accounts would include beginning inventory balances, if any.

The above accounts *do not* include the following:

a. The labor-cost recapitulation for the December 31 working day: direct labor, $5,000; and indirect labor, $1,000

b. Miscellaneous factory overhead incurred on December 30 and December 31: $1,000

ADDITIONAL INFORMATION

Factory overhead has been applied as a percentage of direct labor through December 30.

Direct-material purchases during 19_6 were $90,000.

There were no returns to suppliers.

Direct-labor costs during 19_6 totaled $150,000, not including the December 31 working day described above.

Required

1. Beginning inventories of direct material, work in process, and finished goods. Show T-accounts.
2. Prepare all adjusting and closing journal entries for the above accounts. Assume that all underapplied or overapplied overhead is closed directly to Cost of Goods Sold.
3. Ending inventories, after adjustments and closing, of direct material, work in process, and finished goods.

4-32 Overview of general-ledger relationships. Frantic Publishing Company has its own printing facilities. Frantic uses a job-order accounting system and normal costing. Its president has interviewed you recently. As a graduate of a correspondence school in accountancy, he has a longstanding suspicion of accounting courses as being too general. He commented, "Most students learn high-blown theory, but when they are confronted by a few basic facts produced by an accounting system, they can't piece them together. If they don't understand such fundamental relationships, they can't possibly use the data intelligently."

Because of his suspicions he has prepared an entrance examination for all prospective employees who seek a Frantic management position. He provides them with the following data for the year 19_2 (in thousands of dollars):

Accounts receivable, 1/1/19_2	65	Plant depreciation cost	130
Accounts receivable, 12/31/19_2	100	Direct labor	420
Accounts payable, 1/1/19_2	35	Factory heat and light cost	40
Accounts payable, 12/31/19_2	40	Gross profit*	350
Stores inventory, 1/1/19_2	70	Indirect labor	100
Stores inventory, 12/31/19_2	60	Purchases of direct materials and supplies	400
Finished goods, 1/1/19_2	50	Sales	1,230
Finished goods, 12/31/19_2	250	Supplies used	30
Accrued payroll, 1/1/19_2	20	Work-in-process inventory, 12/31/19_2	110
Accrued payroll, 12/31/19_2	70		

*This is after a separate correction (after cost of goods sold) has been made for overapplied factory overhead of 20.

The president asks you to compute the following. He says, "Use any technique you wish, but leave an audit trail so I can follow your work." You may use T-accounts if you wish.

1. Direct-material usage
2. Cost of goods sold (at normal cost)
3. Cost of goods completed and transferred to finished goods (at normal cost)
4. Factory overhead applied
5. Work in process, January 1, 19_2

4-33 Multiple choice; incomplete data. Some of the general-ledger accounts of the Sharman Manufacturing Company appear as follows on January 31, 19_1.

The accounts are incomplete because the accountant had an emergency operation for ulcers after he ate lunch in the company cafeteria on January 31. The treasurer, an old friend of yours, supplied you with the following incomplete accounts and three bits of additional information.

Direct-Material Stores Control			
Bal. Jan. 1	15,000		
	35,000		

Work-in-Process Control			
Bal. Jan. 1	1,000		40,000
Direct materials requisitioned	20,000		

Finished-Goods Control		
Bal. Jan. 1	10,000	20,000

Cost of Goods Sold	

Accrued Factory Payroll		
	Bal. Jan. 1	1,000
	Gross earnings of all factory workers	40,000

ADDITIONAL INFORMATION

a. Factory Overhead Applied is credited for all indirect costs that are applied to production orders.
b. Work tickets for the month totaled 5,500 direct-labor hours. All factory workers received $6 per hour.
c. Indirect costs are applied at a rate of $4 per direct-labor hour.

After giving you a few minutes to look over the data given, your old friend asks you the following (place all answers on an answer sheet; indicate your answer by letter):

1. The January 31 balance of Direct-Material Stores Control should be
   (a) $50,000 (b) $25,000 (c) $30,000 (d) $20,000 (e) $35,000 (f) None of these.
2. The amount of total direct-labor cost that should have been charged to all the individual production orders worked on during January should be
   (a) $40,000 (b) $41,000 (c) $55,000 (d) $30,000 (e) $33,000 (f) None of these.
3. The total *indirect* cost that should have been applied to production is
   (a) $17,000 (b) $75,000 (c) $40,000 (d) $33,000 (e) $24,000 (f) None of these.
4. The *total* factory-labor cost for the month of January is
   (a) $41,000 (b) $40,000 (c) $55,000 (d) $33,000 (e) $56,000 (f) None of these.
5. The January 31 balance of Work-in-Process Control should be
   (a) $75,000 (b) $77,000 (c) $76,000 (d) $36,000 (e) $35,000 (f) None of these.

6. The January 31 balance of Finished-Goods Control should be
(a) $5,000 (b) $10,000 (c) $20,000 (d) $25,000 (e) $30,000 (f) None of these.

7. The Cost of Goods Sold during January was
(a) $40,000 (b) $10,000 (c) $20,000 (d) $30,000 (e) $50,000 (f) None of these.

8. *Total* indirect costs actually incurred during the month amount to $24,000. The balance in Factory-Overhead Control at the end of January should be
(a) $24,000 (b) $17,000 (c) $26,000 (d) $41,000 (e) $22,000 (f) $2,000
(g) None of these.

9. The January 31 balance of Factory Overhead Applied should be
(a) $33,000 (b) $40,000 (c) $24,000 (d) $22,000 (e) $26,000 (f) $30,000
(g) None of these.

10. The amount of underapplied (or overapplied) costs for January is
(a) Underapplied by $1,000 (b) Underapplied by $2,000
(c) Overapplied by $1,000 (d) Overapplied by $2,000 (e) Overapplied by $3,000
(f) Neither overapplied nor underapplied (g) None of these.

4-34 General-ledger relationships; incomplete data. You are asked to bring the following incomplete Mexico Co. accounts up to date through May 19_1. Also consider the additional information (in dollars) that follows the T-accounts.

Stores Control			Accounts Payable	
5/31/_1				4/30/_1
Balance	18,000			Balance 10,000

Work-in-Process Control			Department Factory Overhead Control	
4/30/_1			Total	
Balance	2,000		charges	
			for May	15,000

| | | | Factory Overhead Applied | |

Finished-Goods Control			Cost of Goods Sold	
4/30/_1				
Balance	25,000			

ADDITIONAL INFORMATION

a. The overhead is applied by using a budgeted rate that is set at the beginning of each year by forecasting the year's overhead and relating it to forecasted direct-labor hours. The budget for 19_1 called for a total of 150,000 hours of direct labor and $225,000 of factory overhead.

b. The accounts payable are for direct materials only. The balance on May 31 was $5,000. Payments of $35,000 were made during May.

c. The finished-goods inventory as of May 31 was $22,000.

d. The cost of goods sold during the month was $65,000.

e. On May 31 there was only one unfinished job in the factory. Cost records show that $1,000 (400 hours) of direct labor and $2,000 of direct material had been charged to the job.

f. A total of 9,400 direct-labor hours were worked during the month of May. All factory workers earn the same rate of pay.

g. All "actual" factory overhead incurred during May has already been posted.

Required
1. Materials purchased during May
2. Cost of goods completed during May
3. Overhead applied during May

4. Balance, Work in Process, May 31, 19_1
5. Direct materials used during May
6. Balance, Stores Control, April 30, 19_1
7. Overapplied or underapplied overhead for May

4-35 Process costing: material introduced at start of process. A certain process incurred $37,600 of production costs during a month. Materials costing $22,000 were introduced at the start of processing, while conversion costs of $15,600 were incurred at a uniform rate throughout the production cycle. Of the 40,000 units of product started, 38,000 were completed; 2,000 were still in process at the end of the month, averaging one-half complete.

Required | In step-by-step fashion, prepare a production-cost report showing cost of goods completed and cost of ending work in process.

4-36 Process costs; single department. The following data pertain to the mixing department for July:

Units:	
Work in process, July 1	0
Units started	50,000
Completed and transferred to finishing department	35,000
Costs:	
Material P	$250,000
Material Q	$ 70,000
Direct labor and overhead	$135,000

Material P is introduced at the start of the process, while Material Q is added when the product reaches a three-fourths stage of completion. Conversion costs are incurred uniformly throughout the process.

Required | Cost of goods transferred during July. Cost of work in process as of July 31. Assume that ending work in process is two-thirds completed.

4-37 Process-operation cost accumulation. The Malaysia Co. produces a mechanical device called Rambo as its single product. The company maintains an "operation-process-cost" accounting system.

The process starts with Material A, a metal that is stamped and assembled with a purchased Part B. The resulting unit is enameled in the final operation.

Time and motion studies indicate that, of the total time needed to manufacture a complete unit, the first operation requires 40% of the labor cost; the assembly, 50%; and the enameling, 10 percent. Factory overhead is considered to follow the same pattern by operations as does labor.

The following data are presented to you as of March 31, the end of the first month of operation:

Material A purchased	$76,000
Part B purchased, 24,000 units	$24,000
Enamel used	$ 1,200
Direct labor and factory overhead	$60,000
Material A ending inventory	$ 4,600
Part B ending inventory	$10,000

	UNIT QUANTITY
Units of Rambo completed and sent to finished-goods warehouse	12,000
Inventories of Rambo in process at end of month:	
Units stamped but not assembled	3,000
Units assembled but not enameled	2,000
Total units in process	5,000

There was no spoilage or shrinkage.

1. Equivalent units of work performed for (a) Material A; (b) Part B; (c) enamel; (d) conversion costs
2. Cost of goods completed and transferred, divided into the four components: Material A, Part B, enamel costs, and conversion costs
3. Cost of goods stamped but not assembled
4. Cost of goods assembled but not enameled

4-38 Details of job costing. (CMA) Targon Inc. manufactures lawn equipment. A job-order system is used because the products are manufactured on a batch rather than a continuous basis. The balances in selected general-ledger accounts for the eleven-month period ended August 31, 19_2, are presented below.

Stores inventory	$ 32,000
Work-in-process inventory	1,200,000
Finished-goods inventory	2,785,000
Factory overhead control	2,260,000
Cost of goods sold	14,200,000

The work-in-process inventory consists of two jobs:

JOB NO.	UNITS	ITEMS	ACCUMULATED COST
3005-5	50,000	Estate sprinklers	$ 700,000
3006-4	40,000	Economy sprinklers	500,000
			$1,200,000

The finished-goods inventory consists of five items:

ITEMS	QUANTITY AND UNIT COST	ACCUMULATED COST
Estate sprinklers	5,000 units @ $22 each	$ 110,000
Deluxe sprinklers	115,000 units @ $17 each	1,955,000
Brass nozzles	10,000 gross @ $14 per gross	140,000
Rainmaker nozzles	5,000 gross @ $16 per gross	80,000
Connectors	100,000 gross @ $5 per gross	500,000
		$2,785,000

The factory cost budget prepared for the 19_1–_2 fiscal year is presented below. The company applies factory overhead on the basis of direct-labor hours.

The activities during the first eleven months of the year were quite close to the budget. A total of 367,000 direct-labor hours have been worked through August 31, 19_2.

FACTORY COST ANNUAL BUDGET
For the Year Ended
September 30, 19_2

Direct materials		$ 3,800,000
Purchased parts		6,000,000
Direct labor (400,000 hours)		4,000,000
Overhead		
Supplies	$190,000	
Indirect labor	700,000	
Supervision	250,000	
Depreciation	950,000	
Utilities	200,000	
Insurance	10,000	
Property taxes	40,000	
Miscellaneous	60,000	2,400,000
Total factory costs		$16,200,000

The September 19_2 transactions are summarized below.

1. All direct materials, purchased parts, and supplies are charged to stores inventory. The September purchases were as follows:

Materials	$410,000
Purchased parts	285,000
Supplies	13,000

2. The direct materials, purchased parts, and supplies were requisitioned from stores inventory as shown in the table below.

	PURCHASED PARTS	MATERIALS	SUPPLIES	TOTAL REQUISITIONS
3005-5	$110,000	$100,000	$ —	$210,000
3006-4	—	6,000	—	6,000
4001-3 (30,000 gross rainmaker nozzles)	—	181,000	—	181,000
4002-1 (10,000 deluxe sprinklers)	—	92,000	—	92,000
4003-5 (50,000 ring sprinklers)	163,000	—	—	163,000
Supplies	—	—	20,000	20,000
	$273,000	$379,000	$20,000	$672,000

3. The payroll summary for September is as follows:

	HOURS	COST
3005-5	6,000	$ 62,000
3006-4	2,500	26,000
4001-3	18,000	182,000
4002-1	500	5,000
4003-5	5,000	52,000
Indirect	8,000	60,000
Supervision	—	24,000
Sales and administration	—	120,000
		$531,000

4. Other factory costs incurred during September were:

Depreciation	$62,500
Utilities	15,000
Insurance	1,000
Property taxes	3,500
Miscellaneous	5,000
	$87,000

5. Jobs completed during September and the actual output were:

JOB NO.	QUANTITY	ITEMS
3005-5	48,000 units	Estate sprinklers
3006-4	39,000 units	Economy sprinklers
4001-3	29,500 gross	Rainmaker nozzles
4003-5	49,000 units	Ring sprinklers

6. The following finished products were shipped to customers during September:

ITEMS	QUANTITY
Estate sprinklers	16,000 units
Deluxe sprinklers	32,000 units
Economy sprinklers	20,000 units
Ring sprinklers	22,000 units
Brass nozzles	5,000 gross
Rainmaker nozzles	10,000 gross
Connectors	26,000 gross

Required

1. a. Calculate the overapplied or underapplied overhead for the year ended September 30, 19_2. Be sure to indicate whether the overhead is overapplied or underapplied.
   b. What is the appropriate accounting treatment for this overapplied or underapplied overhead balance? Explain your answer.
2. Calculate the dollar balance in the work-in-process inventory account as of September 30, 19_2.
3. Calculate the dollar balance in the finished-goods inventory as of September 30, 19_2, for the estate sprinklers using a FIFO basis.

4-39 Comprehensive review problem—job-order costs. This problem is intended to provide a summary of general-ledger and subsidiary-ledger relationships for factory costs under a job-order cost system. The facts are simplified because, in order to save student time, the tremendous detail and number of accounts in a real situation are not reproduced here. However, the solving of this problem should provide the student with a comprehensive view of the basic ledger framework.

The Garcia Company is a small manufacturer of metal products in Los Angeles. The company rents its factory building. It uses a job-order cost system because it has a wide variety of products that receive varying attention and effort in the two factory departments, Machining and Assembly.

Garcia has the following trial balance as of December 31, 19_0:

Cash	$ 15,000	
Accounts receivable	40,000	
Stores control	29,600	
Work-in-process control	4,000	
Finished-goods control	20,000	
Unexpired insurance	12,000	
Office equipment	20,000	
Accumulated depreciation—office equipment		$ 5,000
Factory equipment	950,000	
Accumulated depreciation—factory equipment		220,000
Accounts payable		23,000
Accrued payroll		1,000
Accrued utilities		2,000
Accrued property taxes		3,000
Capital stock		100,000
Retained earnings		736,600
	$1,090,600	$1,090,600

Detail on Subsidiary Records
as of December 31, 19_0

STORES:

CODE	QUANTITY	UNIT COST	AMOUNT
A	5,000	$2.00	$10,000
B	10,000	1.50	15,000
C	400	8.00	3,200
Supplies	Various	—	1,400
			$29,600

WORK IN PROCESS:

JOB-ORDER NUMBER	DEPARTMENT	DIRECT MATERIALS	DIRECT LABOR	FACTORY OVERHEAD	TOTAL
100	Machining	$1,800	$800	$900	$3,500
	Assembly	200	200	100	500
					$4,000

FINISHED GOODS:

STOCK NO.	REFERENCE	QUANTITY	UNIT COST	AMOUNT
X-1	Job 97	100	$80	$ 8,000
X-2	Job 99	1,000	12	12,000
				$20,000

The accompanying factory-overhead budget has been prepared for the coming year, 19_1. This budget has been prepared after careful consideration of the sales outlook for the coming year. The production schedules are geared to the forecast sales pattern.

FACTORY OVERHEAD BUDGET
For Year Ended
December 31, 19_1

	MACHINING	ASSEMBLY	TOTAL
FACTORY OVERHEAD:			
Variable:			
Supplies	$ 14,400	$ 5,400	$ 19,800
Indirect labor	22,800	16,800	39,600
Utilities	30,000	9,000	39,000
Repairs	24,000	6,000	30,000
Miscellaneous	22,800	12,000	34,800
	$114,000	$ 49,200	$163,200
Fixed:			
Insurance	$ 7,200	$ 2,400	$ 9,600
Depreciation	114,000	14,400	128,400
Rent	24,000	16,800	40,800
Property taxes	4,200	1,200	5,400
Supervision	14,400	19,200	33,600
	$163,800	$ 54,000	$217,800
Total factory overhead	$277,800	$103,200	$381,000

To cost jobs as they are worked on, a budgeted overhead rate is computed as follows:

	YEAR 19_1	
	Machining	Assembly
Factory overhead	$277,800	$103,200
Machine-hours	69,450	
Direct-labor cost		$206,400
Rate per machine-hour	$ 4.00	
Rate per direct-labor dollar		50%

These overhead rates will be used throughout the year by each department. All overhead will be applied to all jobs worked on during the year in proportion to the machine-hour or direct-labor cost factor devoted to each job. If management predictions are accurate, total overhead applied to the year's jobs through the use of budgeted rates should equal the total overhead costs actually incurred.

January data:

1. Purchases for stores (credit Accounts Payable):

	QUANTITY	UNIT COST	JANUARY
A	7,500	$2.00	$15,000
B	14,000	1.50	21,000
C	2,125	8.00	17,000
Supplies			3,000
			$56,000

2. Returns (debit Accounts Payable): 50 units of Material B.
3. The direct-material requisitions were summarized, and the following data were shown on a material-usage report. These reports were submitted weekly to department foremen, although monthly data are shown here.

Machining Department
Direct-Material Usage
For the Month Ended January 31, 19_1

REQUISITION	TYPE	JOB ORDER	QUANTITY	UNIT COST	AMOUNT
M89	B	101	1,500	$1.50	$ 2,250
M90	A	102	3,000	2.00	6,000
M91	A	103	1,000	2.00	2,000
M92	B	103	1,000	1.50	1,500
M93	B	102	3,000	1.50	4,500
M94	B	101	200	1.50	300
M95	A	104	2,000	2.00	4,000
					$20,550

Assembly Department
Direct-Material Usage
For the Month Ended January 31, 19_1

REQUISITION	TYPE	JOB ORDER	QUANTITY	UNIT COST	AMOUNT
A301	C	100	5	$8.00	$ 40
A302	C	103	200	8.00	1,600
A303	C	101	800	8.00	6,400
A304	C	102	1,500	8.00	12,000
A305	C	103	20	8.00	160
					$20,200

4. A summary of payroll costs incurred follows. Compare with item 7 below. Payments (settlements) are independent of recognition of cost incurrence. In other words, costs may be summarized monthly while settlements are made weekly.

Work Ticket*	Job Order	LABOR HOURS Machining	LABOR HOURS Assembly	COST Machining	COST Assembly	Total
ML480	101	4		$ 50	$	$ 50
ML481	101	300		3,750		3,750
ML482	103	200		2,500		2,500
ML483	102	240		3,000		3,000
ML484	104	100		1,250		1,250
ML485	103	20		250		250
AL60	100		4		40	40
AL61	102		1,400		14,000	14,000
AL62	101		100		1,000	1,000
AL63	103		200		2,000	2,000
AL64	102		40		400	400
Total direct labor		864	1,744	$10,800	$17,440	$28,240
Indirect labor				2,000	1,500	3,500
Supervision†				1,200	1,600	2,800
Total factory labor				$14,000	$20,540	$34,540
Selling and administrative wages						6,000
Total payroll costs						$40,540

*In practice, there would be many more of these. Often they are recapitulated daily and posted to each job in groups rather than as individual tickets.
†One supervisor oversees both departments; the costs have been split between the two departments based on the average time spent in each.

5. Apply overhead to jobs. Rates as calculated when overhead budget was prepared: Machining, $4.00 per machine-hour; Assembly, 50% of direct-labor cost. See data for item 6 to obtain machine-hours worked. A direct laborer operates more than one machine simultaneously.

6. Production and sales data:

JOB	UNITS COMPLETED	FINISHED	FINISHED STOCK NO.	UNITS SOLD	SOLD FOR	JANUARY MACHINE-HOURS WORKED IN MACHINING DEPT.
97	100	19_0	X-1	100	$ 9,300	
98	—	—	—	—	—	
99	1,000	19_0	X-2	1,000	16,000	
100	50	Jan. 5, 19_1	X-1	20	1,800	
101	1,750	Jan. 12, 19_1	X-2	900	14,400	3,000
102	1,000	Jan. 19, 19_1	X-3	950	55,000	2,000
103	100	Jan. 30, 19_1	X-4	50	6,500	150
104	Unfinished					800
					$103,000	5,950

7. Gross payroll paid in cash during month, $39,000.

8. The following additional overhead costs were incurred during January:

ITEM	TOTAL	DEPARTMENT Machining	Assembly	SELLING AND ADMINISTRATIVE	GENERAL-LEDGER ACCOUNT TO BE CREDITED
Supplies requisitioned	$ 2,000	$ 1,500	$ 400	$ 100	?
Utilities*	4,000	2,700	800	500	Accrued Utilities
Repairs by outsiders (parts and labor)	3,000	2,350	600	50	Accounts Payable
Miscellaneous	3,000	2,000	900	100	Accounts Payable
Insurance	1,000	600	200	200	?
Depreciation on equipment	11,000	9,500	1,200	300	?
Rent	4,000	2,000	1,400	600	Accounts Payable
Property taxes	500	350	100	50	Accrued Property Taxes
	$28,500	$21,000	$5,600	$1,900	

*Cost recognized on basis of usage estimates for month rather than on basis of invoices, which may cover other dates than a current calendar month.

9. Utility bills received, $2,900 (dr. Accrued Utilities and cr. Accounts Payable).
10. Utility bills paid, $2,525 (dr. Accounts Payable).
11. Other selling and administrative expenses, $15,000 (cr. Accounts Payable).
12. Payments on accounts payable, other than the $2,525 in (10), $65,300.
13. Collections on accounts receivable, $99,000.

Required

1. Enter beginning balances in general-ledger T-accounts.
2. Draw up stores records, job-cost records, and finished-goods stock records. Be sure to put in "reference" columns so that appropriate requisitions and work tickets, as well as dollar amounts, may be entered in the subsidiary ledger. See the accompanying sample stores record and job-cost record.

Finished-stock records would be similar in design to stores records.

The factory-overhead cost records have columns for date, reference, supplies, indirect labor, utilities, repairs, miscellaneous, insurance, depreciation on equipment, rent, property taxes, and supervision.

Post beginning balances to subsidiary records.

3. Journalize and post entries for January.
4. Prepare a trial balance as of January 31, 19_1. Also prepare schedules of subsidiary-ledger balances.
5. Prepare an income statement for January and a balance sheet as of January 31, 19_1. Underapplied overhead is treated as an addition to cost of goods sold on interim financial statements.
6. Prepare factory-overhead performance reports for January, one for Machining and one for Assembly. Show actual overhead, budgeted overhead, and variances. Assume arbitrarily that budget figures for January are one-twelfth of those shown in the annual overhead budget.

Stores Record

material A

	RECEIVED			ISSUED			BALANCE			
REFERENCE	quantity	unit cost	amount	quantity	unit cost	amount	date	quantity	unit cost	amount
(vouchers, invoices, or requisitions)							12/31/-0	5,000	$2.00	$10,000

job order no. 100

Machining Department

DIRECT MATERIAL				DIRECT LABOR				OVERHEAD	
reference	quantity	unit cost	amount	reference	quantity	unit cost	amount	machine-hours worked	amount
Req. #A88	900	$2.00	$1800	work tickets	64 hrs	$12.50	$800	225	$900

Assembly Department

DIRECT MATERIAL				DIRECT LABOR				OVERHEAD	
reference	quantity	unit cost	amount	reference	quantity	unit cost	amount	reference	amount
Req. #A300	25	$8.00	$200	work tickets	20 hrs	$10.00	$200	50% of direct labor	$100

Summary

	Machining	Assembly	Total
Direct material	$_____	$_____	$_____
Direct labor	_____	_____	_____
Factory overhead applied	_____	_____	_____
Total cost	$_____	$_____	$_____

7. Assume that operations continue for the remainder of 19_1. Certain balances at December 31, 19_1 follow:

Stores	$ 30,000	
Work in process	10,000	
Finished goods	30,000	
Cost of goods sold	960,000	
Factory-overhead control	400,000	
Factory overhead applied		$385,000

Prepare journal entries to close the factory-overhead accounts, assuming that
a. Underapplied overhead is treated as a direct adjustment of Cost of Goods Sold.
b. Underapplied overhead is spread over appropriate accounts in proportion to their unadjusted ending balances

Master Budget and Responsibility Accounting

5

Evolution of systems • Major features of budgets • Advantages of budgets • Types of budgets • Illustration of master budget • Sales forecasting—a difficult task • Financial planning models • Responsibility accounting • Responsibility and controllability • Human aspects of budgeting • Appendix 5A: The cash budget • Appendix 5B: Administering the budget

What is the most widely used type of accounting system among well-managed organizations today? Is it a historical cost system? No, although it is often referred to as such. Instead it is better described as a budgeting system, a system that includes *both* expected results and historical or actual results.

Budgeting has come of age. It is becoming increasingly important, and it is all around us. For some reason, however, accountants and managers seem reluctant to give it the respect it deserves. Still, there has been a steady increase in the prominence of budgeting in both nonprofit and profit-seeking organizations.

This chapter examines the master, or comprehensive, budget as a planning and coordinating device. The succeeding chapters, especially Chapters 6, 7, and 8, examine various aspects of budgeting decisions and their implementation.

EVOLUTION OF SYSTEMS

Ponder the evolution of control systems. As small organizations begin, there is usually a dominant means of control—personal observation. A manager sees, touches, and hears the relationships between inputs and outputs; he or she oversees the behavior of various personnel.

The next step is historical records. No fancy cost-benefit analysis is necessary to justify keeping some historical records for internal purposes. These records help answer essential operating questions, such as what are the amounts of sales, purchases, cash, inventories, receivables, and payables. Historical records also help answer other questions; for example, how a department performed in 19_3 versus 19_2. Analyses of past performance may help improve future performance. Managers must deal with a series of periods, not just one.

The next step is budgets. A manager would find it more helpful to compare *performance* in 19_3 with *plans* for 19_3. Budgeting systems evidently meet the cost-benefit test. Typically, they are purchased voluntarily rather than as a result of outside forces. Why? Because budgeting systems are looked at as good investments. They change human behavior (and decisions) in the ways sought by top management. For example, budgeting may prompt managers to extend their planning horizons much further. Therefore many prospective difficulties are foreseen and avoided. Without a budgeting system, many managers may veer from one crisis to another.

Do budgeting systems meet the cost-benefit test? Suppose we took a poll of one thousand executives, asking them to rank their favorite operating activities (e.g., talking with customers, designing a product, bargaining with suppliers, training subordinates, planning a new production system). The chances are good that budgeting would rank low on the managers' lists. Nevertheless, the poll would also probably show that few managers would be willing to discard their budgeting systems. Improve them? Yes. Abolish them? No.

In sum, managers plan and control with the help of

1. Personal observation (the basic means)
     plus
2. Historical records ⎤
     plus   ⎬ (the accounting system means)
3. Budgets   ⎦

MAJOR FEATURES OF BUDGETS

Definition and role of budgets

A **budget** is a quantitative expression of a plan of action and an aid to coordination and implementation. Budgets may be formulated for the organization as a whole or for any subunit. The **master budget** summarizes the objectives of all subunits of an organization—sales, production, distribution, and finance. It quantifies the expectations regarding future income, cash flows, financial position, and supporting plans. These are the culmination of a series of decisions resulting from a careful look at the organization's future.

The diagram at the top of page 140 shows how budgets and performance reports help managers.

Note how budgets can play a key role in the entire work of the manager. Our focus in this chapter will be on the planning function. However, budgets serve a variety of additional functions: evaluating performance, coordinating activities, implementing plans, and communicating, motivating, and authorizing actions. The last-named function seems to predominate in government budgeting and non-profit budgeting, where budget appropriations serve as authorizations and ceilings for management actions.

139

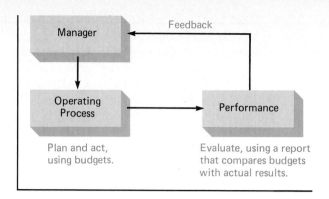

Well-managed organizations usually have the following budgetary cycle:

1. Planning the performance of the organization as a whole as well as its parts. The entire management team agrees as to what is expected.
2. Providing a frame of reference, a set of specific expectations against which actual results can be compared.
3. Investigating variances from plans. Corrective action follows investigation.
4. Planning again, considering feedback and changed conditions.

The master budget embraces the impact of both *operating decisions* (those concerning the acquisition and utilization of scarce resources) and *financing decisions* (those concerning the obtaining of funds for acquisition of resources). This book concentrates on how accounting helps the manager make operating decisions; the emphasis in this chapter is on operating budgets. Financing decisions and the role of cash budgets are covered in many finance texts. Appendix 5A provides a review of cash budgets. Incidentally, the leading corporations usually excel in both operating management and financial management. Business failures often arise because of weaknesses in one or the other of these responsibilities.

Wide use of budgets

Budgeting systems are more common in larger companies, where formalized techniques often serve management. Still, small concerns also use budgets. Small companies have a relatively high failure rate. More extensive use of budgets by such concerns would force entrepreneurs to quantify their dreams and directly face the uncertainties of their ventures.[1] For example, a small business with lofty hopes moved into a lush market for school equipment. However, failure to quantify the long collection periods, to forecast a maximum sales potential, and to control costs from the outset resulted in disaster within a year. As one commentator said: "Few businesses plan to fail, but many of those that flopped failed to plan."

Managers must grapple with uncertainty, either with a budget or without one. The advocates of budgeting maintain that the benefits from budgeting nearly always exceed the costs. Some budget program, at least, will be helpful in almost every organization.

---

[1]Dun & Bradstreet, *Business Failure Record* (1985), reports that the major cause of business failure is the inability to avoid conditions that result in inadequate sales or heavy operating expenses.

Budgets are a major feature of most control systems. When administered intelligently, budgets (a) compel planning, (b) provide performance criteria, and (c) promote communication and coordination.

Compelled short-term and long-term planning

"Planning ahead" is a redundant watchword for business managers and for every individual as well. Too often, executives practice "management by crisis." Everyday problems interfere with planning; operations drift along until the passage of time catches the firms or individuals in undesirable situations that should have been anticipated and avoided. Budgets compel managers to look ahead and be ready for changing conditions. **This forced planning is by far the greatest contribution of budgeting to management.**

Strategy, plans, and budgets

Budgeting is an integral part of both short-run (typically one year or less) planning and long-run planning. Both of these forms of planning may incorporate what some people glamorously call strategic aspects.[2] These aspects include the resources of the organization, the behavior of competitors, and especially the current and projected demands of the marketplace. A consultant commented that consideration of such aspects "is a blend of creativity, analysis, and operating knowledge." The resulting quantitative expression of plans, determined after consideration of such strategic aspects, would be called a budget.[3]

A diagram of our perspective follows:

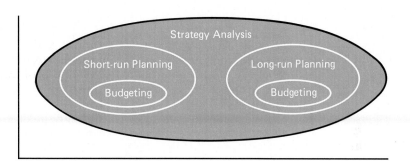

In sum, (a) strategic aspects should be analyzed for both the short run and the long run, (b) plans should be developed, and (c) budgets should then be formulated. Strategy, plans, and budgets are interrelated. Changes in thinking may occur as a result of any of these interacting steps. For example, Boise Cascade Corporation, a large forest products company, uses key budgets and elaborate revenue and expense projections as the starting points for discussing strategies.

---

[2]The term *strategic planning* is often regarded as a short description of overall long-run planning. Not all organizations undertake strategic analysis before or during the development of a budget. For example, some budgets in the nonprofit sector are merely based on last year's expenditures and then adjusted for an inflation factor.

[3]See A. Ishikawa, *Strategic Budgeting: A Comparison between U.S. and Japanese Companies* (New York: Praeger, 1985), for case studies on linkages between strategic analysis and budgeting.

Framework for judging performance	Employees do not like to fumble along not really knowing what their superiors anticipate or to see such expectations vary with, for example, the condition of the superior's sinus trouble. The budget helps meet this difficulty by letting employees know what is expected of them.

As a basis for judging actual results, budgeted performance is generally viewed as being a better criterion than past performance. The fact that sales are better than last year's, or that direct-labor costs are lower than last year's, may be encouraging—but it is by no means conclusive as a measure of success. For example, the news that a company sold 100,000 units this year as compared with 90,000 units in the previous year may not necessarily be greeted with joy. To keep pace with market growth, perhaps sales should have been 112,000 units this year. A major weakness of using historical data for judging performance is that inefficiencies may be buried in the past performance. Furthermore, the usefulness of comparisons with the past may be hampered by intervening changes in technology, personnel, products, competition, and general economic conditions.

Communication and coordination	*Coordination* is the meshing and balancing of all factors of production and of all the departments and functions so that organizational objectives can be attained.

The concept of coordination implies, for example, that purchasing officers integrate their plans with production requirements, and that production officers use the sales budget as a basis for planning personnel needs and utilization of machinery. Top managers want systems designed so that the self-interests of all managers do not conflict with the interests of the organization.

Budgets help management to coordinate in several ways:

1. The existence of a well-laid plan is the major step toward achieving coordination. Executives are forced to think of the relationships among individual operations and the company as a whole.
2. Budgets help to restrain the empire-building efforts of executives. Budgets broaden individual thinking by helping to remove unconscious biases on the part of engineers, sales managers, and production officers.
3. Budgets help to search out weaknesses in the organizational structure. The formulation and administration of budgets identify problems of communication, of fixing responsibility, and of working relationships.

The idea that budgets improve coordination and communication may look promising on paper, but it takes plenty of intelligent administration to achieve in practice. For instance, the use of budgets to judge performance may cause managers to wear blinders and concentrate more than ever on their individual departments. We will examine this problem in more detail later in the chapter.

Management support and administration	Budgets help managers, but budgets need help. **That is, top management must understand and enthusiastically support the budget and all aspects of the control system.** Consider a memo from the chief executive officer of the Bank of America: "Operating plans are contracts, and I want them met. If your revenue is off, you should cut your expenses accordingly." Referring to the chief executive officer of Wells Fargo Bank, a news story said: "Expense control is a state of mind around here. Carl is an absolute bear when it comes to meeting budgets."

Despite the quoted words, administration of budgets should not be rigid. Changed conditions call for changes in plans. The budget must receive respect, but it does not have to be so revered that it prevents a manager from taking prudent action. A department head may commit to the budget. But matters might develop so that some special repairs or a special advertising outlay would best serve the interests of the firm. Then the manager should feel free to request permission for such outlays, or the budget itself should provide enough flexibility to permit reasonable discretion in deciding how best to get the job done.

TYPES OF BUDGETS

Time coverage

Budgets may span a period of one year or less—or, in cases of plant and product changes, up to ten or more years. More and more companies use budgets as essential tools for long-range planning. The usual planning-and-control budget period is one year. The annual budget is often broken down by months for the first quarter and by quarters for the remainder of the year. The budgeted data for a year are frequently revised as the year unfolds. For example, at the end of the first quarter, the budget for the next three quarters is changed in light of new information. *Continuous budgets* are increasingly used, whereby a twelve-month forecast is always available by adding a month or quarter in the future as the month or quarter just ended is dropped. Continuous budgets are desirable because they constantly force management to think concretely about the forthcoming twelve months, irrespective of whether the month at hand is May or October. Arizona Public Service Co. has a budget that looks ahead two years but is updated every month. The choice of budget periods largely flows from the objectives, uses, and dependability of the budget data.

Classification of budgets

Various descriptive terms for budgets have arisen. Terminology varies among organizations. For example, budgeted financial statements are sometimes called **pro forma statements.** Some organizations, such as Hewlett-Packard, refer to *targeting* rather than budgeting. Indeed, to give a more positive thrust to the entire area, many organizations do not use the term *budget* at all. Instead, they use the term *profit planning.*

There are countless forms of budgets. Many special budgets and related reports are prepared, including:

- Comparisons of budgets with actual performance (performance reports)
- Reports for specific managerial needs—for example, cost-volume-profit projections
- Long-term budgets, often called "capital" or "facilities" or "project" budgets (see Chapter 19)
- Flexible budgets (see Chapter 6)

Exhibit 5-1 shows a simplified diagram of the various parts of the *master budget,* the comprehensive plan, a coordinated set of detailed financial statements and schedules for short periods, usually a year. As the diagram indicates, many supporting budget schedules are necessary in actual practice. The bulk of the diagram presents various elements that together are often called the **operating budget.**

143

EXHIBIT 5-1
Master Budget

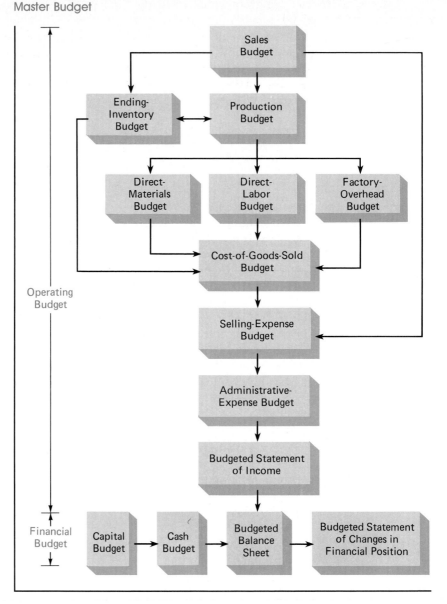

They focus on the income statement and its supporting schedules. In contrast, the **financial budget** is that part of the master budget that comprises the capital budget, cash budget, budgeted balance sheet, and budgeted statement of changes in financial position. It focuses on the impact on cash of operations and other factors, such as planned capital outlays for equipment.

For simplicity, Exhibit 5-1 does not show all the interrelationships among the various budgets. For instance, the amount of interest expense on the income statement is affected by the cash budget.

This illustration is largely mechanical, but remember that the master-budget process generates key top-management decisions regarding pricing, product lines, production scheduling, capital expenditures, research and development, management assignments, and so on. For instance, the first draft of the budget almost always leads to decisions that prompt further drafts before a final budget is chosen.

Basic data and requirements

The M Company in Hong Kong uses specified metal alloys for manufacturing aircraft replacement parts. The company has an absorption-costing system. Managers are ready to prepare a master budget for the year 19_2. Having carefully examined all relevant factors, the executives expect the following, expressed in U.S. dollars:

DIRECT MATERIALS:
Material 111	$1.20 per kilogram
Material 112	$2.60 per kilogram
Direct labor	$2.05 per hour

Factory overhead is applied on the basis of direct-labor hours

	PRODUCT F REGULAR AIRCRAFT PARTS	PRODUCT G HEAVY-DUTY AIRCRAFT PARTS
FINISHED GOODS: (content of each unit)		
Direct material 111	12 kilograms	12 kilograms
Direct material 112	6 kilograms	8 kilograms
Direct labor	14 hours	20 hours

Additional information regarding the year 19_2:

	FINISHED GOODS		
	F	G	TOTAL
Expected sales in units	5,000	1,000	
Selling price per unit	$ 105.40	$ 164.00	
Desired ending inventory in units	1,100	50	
Beginning inventory in units	100	50	
Beginning inventory in dollars	$8,670	$5,810	$14,480

	DIRECT MATERIALS	
	111	112
Beginning inventory in kilograms	5,000	5,000
Desired ending inventory in kilograms	6,000	1,000

For simplicity, work in process is negligible and is ignored.

At anticipated volume levels, the following costs will be incurred:

FACTORY OVERHEAD:	
Supplies	$ 30,000
Indirect labor	70,000
Payroll fringe costs	25,000
Power—variable portion	8,000
Maintenance—variable portion	20,000
Depreciation	25,000
Property taxes	4,000
Property insurance	500
Supervision	20,000
Power—fixed portion	1,000
Maintenance—fixed portion	4,500
	$208,000
SELLING AND ADMINISTRATIVE EXPENSES:	
Sales commissions	$ 20,000
Advertising	3,000
Sales salaries	10,000
Travel	5,000
Clerical wages	10,000
Supplies	1,000
Executive salaries	21,000
Miscellaneous	5,000
	$ 75,000

Required

Prepare an operating budget (budgeted income statement through operating income) for the year 19_2. Include the following detailed schedules:

1. Sales budget
2. Production budget, in units
3. Direct-material-purchases budget
4. Direct-labor budget
5. Factory-overhead budget
6. Ending-inventory budget
7. Cost-of-goods-sold budget
8. Selling and administrative-expense budget

Formulating the master budget

The master budget is fundamentally nothing more than the preparation of familiar financial statements. The major difference is in dealing with expected future data rather than with historical data. Therefore this illustration provides a review of the technical material covered in the previous chapters and culminates with a major part of the master budget, the income statement. **Thus we concentrate on the operating budget.** The financial budget, notably the ending balance sheet and the cash budget, is discussed in Appendix 5A.

Most organizations have a budget manual, which contains instructions and related information. For elaboration, see Appendix 5B. Although the details differ among organizations, the manual has the following nine basic steps for a manufacturing company. Try to prepare your own budget schedules, step by step, before looking at the solution after each step. In many cases, computer software is available to speed the computations associated with the preparation of budgets.

Step 1: *Revenue or sales budget.* **The sales forecast is the usual starting point for budgeting.** Why? Because production (and hence costs) and inventory levels are generally geared to the rate of sales activity.

The sales budget is:

Sales Budget
For the Year Ended December 31, 19_2

SCHEDULE 1	UNITS	SELLING PRICE	TOTAL SALES
Product F	5,000	$105.40	$527,000
Product G	1,000	164.00	164,000
Total			$691,000

The $691,000 is used as budgeted sales in the income statement. The sales budget is often the result of elaborate information gathering. A later section in this chapter (p. 151) discusses this activity.

In nonprofit organizations, forecasts of revenue or some target level of service are also the cornerstone of the master budget. Examples are hospital patient revenues and city police protection.

Occasionally, sales are limited by available production capacity. For example, there may be unusually heavy market demands, shortages of personnel or materials, and strikes. In such cases, the production capacity is the starting point for budgeting.

Step 2: *Production budget.* After sales are budgeted, the production budget (Schedule 2) can be prepared. The total units to be produced depend on planned sales and also expected changes in inventory levels, as shown in Schedule 2:

Production Budget * In Units
For the Year Ended December 31, 19_2

SCHEDULE 2	PRODUCTS	
	F	G
Budgeted sales (Schedule 1)	5,000	1,000
Target ending finished-goods inventory	1,100	50
Total needs	6,100	1,050
Less beginning finished-goods inventory	100	50
Units to be produced	6,000	1,000

*For simplicity, work in process is assumed negligible and is ignored.

Note that the production budget is stated in finished physical units. Frequently, production is stabilized throughout the year despite seasonal fluctuations in sales. Therefore inventory serves as a coordinating link between production and sales by providing a cushion that satisfies not only the marketing need for goods when demand is unusually heavy but also a manufacturing aim of stable utilization of personnel and facilities.

Step 3: *Direct-materials budget.* The units to be produced (Schedule 2) are the keys to computing the usage of direct materials in units and in dollars:

Budgeted Usage of Direct Materials in Kilograms and Dollars
For the Year Ended December 31, 19_2

SCHEDULE 3A	MATERIAL 111	MATERIAL 112	TOTAL
Product F (6,000 units × 12 and 6 kilograms)	72,000	36,000	
Product G (1,000 units × 12 and 8 kilograms)	12,000	8,000	
Total direct-material usage	84,000	44,000	
Multiply by price per kilogram	$1.20	$2.60	
Total cost of direct materials used	$100,800	$114,400	$215,200

Just like planning the production of finished units, the purchases of direct materials depend on both budgeted usage and inventory levels:

$$\text{Purchases in units} = \text{Usage} + \text{Target ending inventories} - \text{Beginning inventories}$$

The computations of direct-material purchases are in Schedule 3B.

Direct-Material-Purchases Budget
For the Year Ended December 31, 19_2

SCHEDULE 3B	MATERIAL 111	MATERIAL 112	TOTAL
Kilograms used in production (Schedule 3A)	84,000	44,000	
Target ending direct-material inventory in kilograms	6,000	1,000	
Total needs	90,000	45,000	
Less beginning direct-material inventory in kilograms	5,000	5,000	
Kilograms to be purchased	85,000	40,000	
Price per kilogram	$ 1.20	$ 2.60	
Purchase cost	$102,000	$104,000	$206,000

Step 4: *Direct-labor budget.* These costs depend on the types of products, labor rates, and methods:

Direct-Labor Budget
For the Year Ended December 31, 19_2

SCHEDULE 4	UNITS PRODUCED	DIRECT-LABOR HOURS PER UNIT	TOTAL HOURS	TOTAL BUDGET @ $2.05 PER HOUR
Product F	6,000	14	84,000	$172,200
Product G	1,000	20	20,000	41,000
Total			104,000	$213,200

Step 5: *Factory-overhead budget.* The total of these costs depends on how individual overhead costs behave as production fluctuates:

Factory-Overhead Budget*
For the Year Ended December 31, 19_2

SCHEDULE 5		AT ANTICIPATED ACTIVITY OF 104,000 DIRECT-LABOR HOURS:
Supplies	$30,000	
Indirect labor	70,000	
Payroll fringe costs	25,000	
Power—variable portion	8,000	
Maintenance—variable portion	20,000	
Total variable overhead		$153,000
Depreciation	$25,000	
Property taxes	4,000	
Property insurance	500	
Supervision	20,000	
Power—fixed portion	1,000	
Maintenance—fixed portion	4,500	
Total fixed overhead		55,000
Total factory overhead: ($208,000 ÷ 104,000 is $2.00 per direct-labor hour)		$208,000

*Data are from page 146.

Step 6. *Ending-inventory budget.* Schedule 6 shows the calculations of the desired ending inventories. This information is required not only for the production budget and the direct-material-purchases budget but also for detail on an income statement and a balance sheet.

Ending-Inventory Budget
December 31, 19_2

SCHEDULE 6	KILOGRAMS	PRICE PER KILOGRAM	TOTAL AMOUNT	
Direct materials:				
111	6,000*	$ 1.20	$ 7,200	
112	1,000*	2.60	2,600	$ 9,800

	UNITS	COST PER UNIT		
Finished goods:				
F	1,100†	$ 86.70‡	$95,370	
G	50†	116.20‡	5,810	101,180
Total				$110,980

*From Schedule 3B, second line.
†From Schedule 2, second line.
‡Computation of unit costs:

		PRODUCT F		PRODUCT G	
	COST PER KILOGRAM OR HOUR OF INPUT	Inputs	Amount	Inputs	Amount
Material 111	$1.20	12	$14.40	12	$ 14.40
Material 112	2.60	6	15.60	8	20.80
Direct labor	2.05	14	28.70	20	41.00
Factory overhead	2.00	14	28.00	20	40.00
Total			$86.70		$116.20

Step 7. *Cost-of-goods-sold budget.* The information gathered in Schedules 3 through 6 leads to Schedule 7:

Cost-of-goods-sold Budget
For the Year Ended December 31, 19_2

SCHEDULE 7	FROM SCHEDULE		
Finished-goods inventory, December 31, 19_1	Given*		$ 14,480
Direct materials used	3	$215,200	
Direct labor	4	213,200	
Factory overhead	5	208,000	
Cost of goods manufactured			636,400
Cost of goods available for sale			$650,880
Finished-goods inventory, December 31, 19_2			101,180
Cost of goods sold			$549,700

*Given in description of basic data and requirements.

Step 8. *Selling-and-administrative-expense budget.* Some of these expenses, such as sales commissions, may be directly affected by sales. Other expenses may be lump-sum appropriations, such as advertising, as determined by top management's discretion regarding the "correct" amount to spend:

Selling-and-Administrative-Expense Budget*
For the Year Ended December 31, 19_2

SCHEDULE 8		
Sales commissions	$20,000	
Advertising	3,000	
Sales salaries	10,000	
Travel	5,000	
Total selling expenses		$38,000
Clerical wages	$10,000	
Supplies	1,000	
Executive salaries	21,000	
Miscellaneous	5,000	
Total administrative expenses		37,000
Total selling and administrative expenses		$75,000

*Data are from page 146.

Step 9. *Budgeted income statement.* Schedules 1, 7, and 8 provide enough information for the income statement, identified here as Exhibit I. Of course, more details could be included in the income statement, and then fewer supporting schedules would be prepared:

M Company
Budgeted Income Statement
For the Year Ended December 31, 19_2

EXHIBIT I	FROM SCHEDULE	
Sales	1	$691,000
Cost of goods sold	7	549,700
Gross margin		$141,300
Selling and administrative expenses	8	75,000
Operating income		$ 66,300

SALES FORECASTING—A DIFFICULT TASK

Factors in sales forecasting

The term *sales forecast* is sometimes distinguished from *sales budget* as follows: The forecast is the estimate—the prediction—that may or may not become the sales budget. Indeed, companies often take up to four months to complete the forecasting process; sales forecasts are revised on an average of five times.[4] The forecast becomes the budget only if management accepts it as an objective. The forecast often leads to adjustments of managerial plans, so that the final sales budget differs from the original sales forecast.

The marketing vice-president usually has direct responsibility for the preparation of the sales budget, the foundation for the quantification of the entire business plan.

A sales forecast is made after consideration of many factors, including the following:

1. Past sales volume
2. General economic and industry conditions
3. Relationship of sales to economic indicators such as gross national product, personal income, employment, prices, and industrial production
4. Relative product profitability
5. Market research studies
6. Pricing policies
7. Advertising and other promotion
8. Quality of sales force
9. Competition
10. Seasonal variations
11. Production capacity
12. Long-term sales trends for various products

Forecasting procedures

An effective aid to accurate forecasting is to approach the task by several methods; each forecast acts as a check on the others. The three methods described below are usually combined in some fashion that is suitable for a specific company.

SALES STAFF PROCEDURES   As is the case for all budgets, those responsible should have an active role in sales-budget formulation. If possible, the budget data should

---

[4]E. A. Imhoff, Jr., *Sales Forecasting Systems* (Montvale, N.J.: National Association of Accountants, 1986). Surveys of company practices are often published in the *Journal of Forecasting*. Examples include J. R. Sparkes and A. K. McHugh, "Awareness and Use of Forecasting Techniques in British Industry," January–March 1984, pp. 37–42; and G. Assmus, "New Product Forecasting," April–June 1984, pp. 121–38.

flow from individual sales personnel or district sales managers upward to the marketing vice-president. A valuable benefit from the budgeting process is the holding of discussions, which generally result in adjustments and which tend to broaden participants' thinking.

STATISTICAL APPROACHES Trend, cycle projection, and correlation analysis are useful supplementary techniques. Correlations between sales and economic indicators help make sales forecasts more reliable, especially if fluctuations in certain economic indicators precede fluctuations in company sales. However, no firm should rely entirely on this approach. Too much reliance on statistical evidence is dangerous because chance variations in statistical data may completely upset a prediction. As always, statistical analysis can provide help but not outright answers.

GROUP EXECUTIVE JUDGMENT All top officers, including production, purchasing, finance, and administrative officers, may use their experience and knowledge to project sales on the basis of group opinion. This quick method dispenses with intricate statistical accumulations; however, it muddles responsibility for sales predictions and ignores the need for a tough-minded approach to this important task.

It is beyond the scope of this book to give a detailed description of all phases of sales-budget preparation, but its key importance should be kept in mind.

FINANCIAL PLANNING MODELS

A master budget can be regarded as a comprehensive planning model for the organization. As the budget is formulated, it is frequently altered via a step-by-step process as executives exchange views on miscellaneous aspects of expected activities and ask "what-if" questions. Such alterations are cumbersome by hand, but they are facilitated by the computer.

Computer-based **financial planning models** often use the master budget as their structural base. They are mathematical statements of the relationships among all operating and financial activities, as well as other major internal and external factors that may affect decisions. The models are used for budgeting, for revising budgets with little incremental effort, for conducting "what-if?" analysis, and for comparing a variety of decision alternatives as they affect the entire organization. Examples include Ralston Purina Co., where a 1% change in the price of a prime commodity causes a change in the company's cost models and a possible change in the whole corporate plan. At Dow Chemical Co., 140 separate cost inputs, constantly revised, are fed into its model. Such factors as major raw-material costs and prices by country and region are monitored weekly. Multiple contingency plans, rather than a single master plan, are used widely.

Computer models have various degrees of sophistication and usefulness, depending on how much an organization is willing to pay.[5] Rudimentary general-purpose models can be rented from consultants or software firms. These usually entail gathering specific firm data as input; the output consists of the conventional financial statements and supporting schedules. Personal computer users can purchase inexpensive budgeting software programs. At the other extreme, manage-

[5]See D. Sherwood, *Financial Modelling* (United Kingdom: Gee & Co., 1984); and J. W. Bryant, ed., *Financial Modelling in Corporate Management* (United Kingdom: John Wiley, 1982).

ment can have a special-purpose model designed that includes interactive capabilities, integrates detailed activities of all subunits of an organization, encompasses internal and external data, and permits probabilistic analyses.

As in all aspects of systems design, managers pursue cost-benefit approaches to using computer-based models. Some benefits were enumerated above, and the costs of using general-purpose models continue to decline. For example, some credit departments of banks now find it worthwhile to use a general-purpose model to monitor the progress of their borrowers. The borrowers' data are the input, which is updated periodically. The prospects of more widespread use of simple general-purpose models are excellent, but the costs of complex models are still too imposing to warrant predictions of their rapid adoption. Most corporations concentrate their attention on the eight to twelve variables most crucial to their industry—rate of inflation, consumer spending on nondurables, interest rates, and so on.

Other than sheer development costs, at least two factors prevent the widespread use of complex models:

1. The high rate of structural change in companies. For example, by the time the model is built, divisions are divested or new products are added.
2. Unimpressive performance in forecasting.

RESPONSIBILITY ACCOUNTING

This section emphasizes that management is essentially a human activity and that budgets exist, not for their own sake, but to help managers.

Managers supervise subordinates. To improve performance, top managers subdivide operating processes. Top managers also design an *organization structure*, which can be defined as an arrangement of lines of responsibility within an entity. For example, a company, such as Shell, may be organized primarily by business functions; exploration, refining, and marketing. Another company, such as General Foods, may be organized by product lines. If so, the managers of the individual coffee and cereal divisions would each have decision-making authority concerning both the manufacturing and the marketing functions of their divisions.

Definition of responsibility accounting

The organization structure is typically a pyramid where the lower levels of managers, in turn, report upward to layers of superiors. Each manager is placed in charge of a **responsibility center.** The latter is a part, or segment or subunit, of an organization whose manager is accountable for a specified set of activities. **Responsibility accounting** is a system that measures the plans and actions of each responsibility center. Four major types of responsibility centers have the following labels:

1. **Cost center**—accountable for costs only
2. **Revenue center**—accountable for revenues only
3. **Profit center**—accountable for costs and revenues
4. **Investment center**—accountable for costs, revenues, and investments

The following incident describes the dramatic impact on a manager's behavior of a responsibility accounting approach:

The sales department requests a rush production. The plant scheduler argues that it will disrupt his production and cost a substantial though not clearly determined amount of money. The answer coming from sales is: "Do you want to take the responsibility of losing the X Company as a customer?" Of course the production scheduler does not want to take such a responsibility, and he gives up, but not before a heavy exchange of arguments and the accumulation of a substantial backlog of ill feeling. Analysis of the payroll in the assembly department, determining the costs involved in getting out rush orders, eliminated the cause for argument. Henceforth, any rush order was accepted with a smile by the production scheduler, who made sure that the extra cost would be duly recorded and charged to the sales department—"no questions asked."

As a result, the tension created by rush orders disappeared completely; and, somehow, the number of rush orders requested by the sales department was progressively reduced to an insignificant level.[6]

Ideally, revenues and costs are recorded and automatically traced to the individual at the lowest level of the organization who shoulders primary day-to-day decision responsibility for the items. He or she is in the best position to make decisions, to implement decisions, to influence actions, and to gather and provide information.

Note the philosophy implied in the above incident. Top management has delegated the freedom to make decisions to a lower level. Instead of having to check with somebody before accepting a rush order, the manager of production scheduling has full discretion. Thus the manager is not subject to day-to-day monitoring of behavior (decisions). However, the manager is accountable for the results via responsibility accounting. So responsibility accounting is a mechanism that supplies the desired balance to the greater freedom of action that individual executives are given.

Illustration of responsibility accounting

The simplified organization chart in Exhibit 5-2 will be the basis for our illustration. We will concentrate on the manufacturing phase of the business. The lines of responsibility are easily seen in Exhibit 5-3, which is an overall view of responsibility reporting. Starting with the supervisor of the machining department, George Phelan, and working toward the top, we will see how these reports can be integrated through three levels of responsibility.

Note that each of three responsibility reports furnishes the department heads with figures on only those items subject to their control. Items not subject to his control are removed from these performance reports; they should not receive data that may clutter and confuse their decision making. For example, a fixed cost such as depreciation on the factory building is excluded.

Trace the $72,000 total from the machining department report in Exhibit 5-3 to the production vice-president's report. The vice-president's report merely summarizes the reports of the three individuals under her jurisdiction. She may also want copies of the detailed statements of each supervisor responsible to her.

Also trace the $116,000 total from the production vice-president's report to the report of Dudley Curry, the president. Curry's summary report includes data for his own office plus a summarization of the entire company's monthly cost-control performance.

---

[6]R. Villers, "Control and Freedom in a Decentralized Company," *Harvard Business Review*, XXXII, No. 2, 95. Another example is Citibank's responsibility accounting system for a check-processing department. On any given day, for every $1 million that is not delivered to the Federal Reserve Bank on time, the department is "fined" for the amount the parent company loses in potential interest.

EXHIBIT 5-2
Curry Co.: Simplified Organization Chart

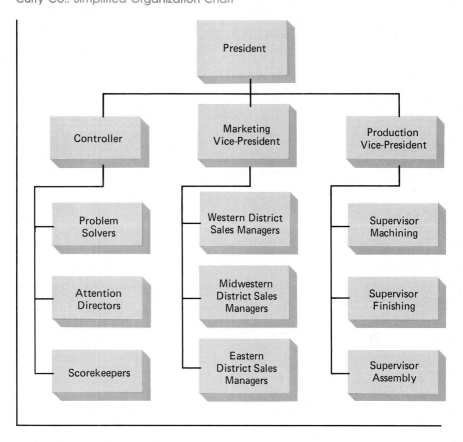

Format of feedback reports

This set of illustrative reports shows only the budgeted amount and the *variance*, which is defined as the difference between the budgeted and the actual amounts. This format focuses on the variances and illustrates *management by exception*, whereby the executive's attention is concentrated on the important deviations from budgeted items. In this way, managers do not waste time on those parts of the reports that indicate smoothly running phases of operations.

Exhibit 5-3 is only one way to present a report of performance. Another common reporting method shows three sets of dollar figures instead of two sets. The third set usually compares actual results for the current year with actual results of the previous year. Moreover, the variances could also be expressed in terms of percentages of budgeted amounts. For example, direct labor in the machining department could appear as follows:

	BUDGET		ACTUAL RESULTS		VARIANCE: FAVORABLE (UNFAVORABLE)		VARIANCE: PERCENT OF BUDGETED AMOUNT	
	This Month	Year to Date	This Month	Year to Date	This Month	Year to Date	This Month	Year to Date
Direct labor	$25,000	$75,000	$27,000	$82,000	$(2,000)	$(7,000)	(8.0%)	(9.4%)

The full performance report would contain a similar line-by-line analysis of all items. The exact format adopted in a particular organization depends heavily on user preferences.

EXHIBIT 5-3
Curry Co.

President's Monthly Responsibility Performance Report	BUDGET		VARIANCE: FAVORABLE, (UNFAVORABLE)	
	this month	year to date	this month	year to date
President's office	$ 6,000	$ 20,000	$ 100	$ 400
Controller	4,000	13,000	(200)	(1,000)
Production vice-president	116,000	377,000	(8,950)	(20,600)
Sales vice-president	40,000	130,000	(1,000)	(4,000)
Total controllable costs	$166,000	$540,000	$(10,050)	$(25,200)

Production Vice-President's Monthly Responsibility Performance Report	BUDGET		VARIANCE: FAVORABLE, (UNFAVORABLE)	
	this month	year to date	this month	year to date
Vice-president's office	$ 9,000	$ 29,000	$ (1,000)	$ (1,000)
Machining department	72,000	236,000	(2,950)	(11,600)
Finishing department	15,000	50,000	(2,000)	(3,000)
Assembly department	20,000	62,000	(3,000)	(5,000)
Total controllable costs	$116,000	$377,000	$ (8,950)	$(20,600)

Machining Department Supervisor's Monthly Responsibility Performance Report*	BUDGET		VARIANCE: FAVORABLE, (UNFAVORABLE)	
	this month	year to date	this month	year to date
Direct materials	$ 40,000	$140,000	$ (1,000)	$ (4,000)
Direct labor	25,000	75,000	(2,000)	(7,000)
Setup	4,000	12,000	400	100
Utilities	2,000	6,000	(200)	(100)
Supplies	200	600	(40)	(100)
Small tools	300	900	(50)	(100)
Other	500	1,500	(60)	(200)
Total controllable costs	$ 72,000	$236,000	$ (2,950)	$(11,600)

*Receives an itemized report of performance. Totals are carried to the report of immediate superior, whose results are, in turn, reported upward.

Feedback and fixing blame	Budgets coupled with responsibility accounting provide systematic help for managers, particularly if the feedback is interpreted carefully. **Discussions among managers, accountants, and students have repeatedly disclosed a tendency to "fix the blame"—as if the variance arising from a responsibility accounting system should pinpoint misbehavior and provide answers.** However, no accounting system or variances can provide answers by themselves alone. But variances can suggest questions or can direct attention to persons who should be asked to explain the variances. **In associating costs or variances with individuals, we should inquire** *who should be asked* in a specific situation—*not who should be blamed.*

RESPONSIBILITY AND CONTROLLABILITY

Definition of controllability	**Controllability** is the degree of influence that a specific manager has over the costs or revenues or other items in question. For instance, a **controllable cost** is any cost that is primarily subject to the influence of a given *manager* of a given *responsibility center* for a given *time span*. Ideally, responsibility accounting systems either will exclude all uncontrollable costs from a manager's performance report or will segregate such costs from the controllable costs. For example, a machining supervisor's performance report might be confined to usage of direct materials, direct labor, power, and supplies. In practice, controllability is difficult to pinpoint: 1. Few costs are clearly under the sole influence of one manager. For example, *prices* of direct materials may be influenced by a purchasing manager, whereas *quantities* used may be influenced by a production manager. Moreover, managers and others often work in groups or teams. 2. With enough time, virtually all costs will be controllable by somebody in the organization. But performance reports focus on periods of a year or less. Thus current managers may have to contend with inefficiencies in using direct materials and direct labor. Why? Because predecessors made undesirable contracts with suppliers or labor unions.
Emphasize information and behavior	Beware of overemphasis on controllability. For example, a time-honored theme of management is that responsibility should not be given without the accompanying authority. Such a guide is a useful first step, but responsibility accounting is more far-reaching. The basic focus should be *information* or *knowledge,* not control. The key question is, Who is the best informed? Put another way, Who is the person who can tell us the most about the specific item, regardless of ability to exert personal control? For instance, purchasing managers may be held accountable for the total purchase costs, not because of ability to affect prices but because of ability to predict uncontrollable prices and explain uncontrollable price changes. Performance reports for responsibility centers may also include uncontrollable items because such inclusion could **change behavior in the directions sought by top management.** For example, some companies have changed the accountability

of a cost center to a profit center. Why? Because the manager of, say, a factory behaves differently at the margin. In a cost center, the manager may emphasize efficiency and de-emphasize the pleas of sales personnel for faster service and rush orders. In a profit center, the manager is responsible for both costs *and* revenues. Thus even though control over sales personnel may be unchanged, the manager is more likely to weigh the impact of decisions on *profits* rather than solely on *costs*.

Importance of budget and MBO

The message given to managers is frequently *not* to *maximize* a single measure such as operating income. Instead the message is to *attain* a *budgeted* operating income of, say, $1 million, subject to simultaneously achieving additional goals such as a target share of a market. Budgets can be enormously helpful, versatile tools.

Intelligent budgeting can overcome many of the problems of human behavior that are inherent in commonly used performance measures such as income or return on investment. For example, many organizations have successfully used some form of **management by objectives (MBO).** Under this procedure, a subordinate and his or her superior jointly formulate the subordinate's set of goals and plans for attaining those goals for a subsequent period. For our purposes, *goals* and *objectives* are synonymous.

The plans are frequently crystallized in a responsibility accounting budget. In addition, various subgoals may be measured, such as levels of product innovation, quality, share of the market, and management training. The subordinate's performance is then evaluated in relation to these agreed-upon budgeted goals.

MBO is also used by nonprofit organizations. For example, in 1986 the Episcopal Diocese of Newark, New Jersey, started paying priests according to their performance. Under the merit-pay plan, priests can qualify for salary increases based on such goals as parish growth, education, and quality of sermons.

Responsibility and uncertainty

Managers live in an uncertain world. Actions and events outside and inside the organization affect the measures of managers' performance. An MBO approach can help overcome the problems and complaints regarding responsibility, uncertainties or risks, and lack of control. The focus is on *budgeted results,* given the degree of uncertainties, interdependencies, and limitations of accounting measurements.

The intelligent use of budgets gives desirable incentives to managers. For example, executives may be more willing to undertake risks. Thus a manager may more readily accept an assignment to a less-successful responsibility center. For example, the budgeted loss for a troubled division may be $50 million. Unless focus is on currently attainable results, able executives are less likely to accept responsibility for weak subunits.

In sum, distinctions between controllable and uncontrollable items should be made whenever feasible. However, financial responsibility may be assigned to managers even though controllability may be minimal. The final test is what information and what behavior will be generated by the measurement system. Put another way:

1. What do you want responsibility center managers to worry about? (they can't pay attention to costs that are not assigned) and

2. How much do you want them to worry? (the method of cost assignment may give them more or less direct control over the amount of costs charged to them).[7]

HUMAN ASPECTS OF BUDGETING

Why did we cover the two major topics, master budgets and responsibility accounting, in a single chapter? Primarily to emphasize that human factors are crucial parts of budgeting. Too often, students study budgeting as though it were a mechanical tool.

The budgeting techniques themselves are free of emotion; however, their administration requires education, persuasion, and intelligent interpretation. Many managers regard budgets negatively.[8] The word *budget* is about as popular as, say, *strike* or *layoff*. So top managers must convince their subordinates that the budget is a positive device designed to help managers choose and reach goals. But budgets are not cure-alls. They are not remedies for weak managerial talent, faulty organization, or a poor accounting system.

SUMMARY

Comprehensive budgeting is the expression of management's master operating and financing plan—the formalized outlining of company objectives and their means of attainment. When administered wisely, budgets (a) compel management planning, (b) provide definite expectations that are the best framework for judging subsequent performance, and (c) promote communication and coordination among the various segments of the business.

The foundation for budgeting is the sales forecast. Inventory, production, and cost incurrence are generally geared to the rate of sales activity.

Responsibility accounting systems identify various decision centers and trace financial data to the individual managers who are primarily responsible for the data in question.

---

[7]R. Vancil, *Decentralization: Managerial Ambiguity by Design* (New York: Financial Executives Research Foundation, 1979), p. 21. Also see R. Magee, *Advanced Managerial Accounting* (New York: Harper & Row, 1986), Chaps. 12 and 13; and S. Baiman, "Agency Research in Managerial Accounting: A Survey," *Journal of Accounting Literature*, 1 (Spring 1982), 154–213. An example of invoking shared responsibility was contained in an annual meeting address by the chairman of Carling O'Keefe Brewing: "It was just one year ago that I suggested that it was not I who should be congratulated for our record earnings, but rather the senior management of the Corporation who were responsible for the various segments of the business. This year, our earnings are at the other end of the spectrum, and I suggest a similar form of shared responsibility might be in order!"

[8]Surveys of practices in budgeting include W. P. Cress and J. B. Pettijohn, "A Survey of Budget-Related Planning and Control Policies and Procedures," *Journal of Accounting Education* 3, No. 2 (Fall 1985), 61–78. This large survey concluded that respondents heavily used recommended budgeting techniques. Nevertheless, wide participation of managers in the budgeting process was infrequent and statistical techniques were rarely used.

L. Daley, J. Jiambalvo, G. Sundem, and Y. Kondo, "Attitudes toward Financial Control Systems in the United States and Japan," *Journal of International Business Studies* (Fall 1985), surveyed controllers and line managers in Japan and the United States. The major findings suggest that the Japanese controllers and managers (a) prefer less participation, (b) have a more long-term planning horizon, (c) view budgets as more of a communication device, and (d) prefer more budget "padding" than their U.S. counterparts.

A budgeting system includes performance evaluation, which usually compares the planned data with the actual results. More will be said about budgeting systems in succeeding chapters.

PROBLEM FOR SELF-STUDY

Before trying to solve the homework problems, review the illustrations in this chapter.

Terms to Learn

The chapter, chapter Appendix, and Glossary contain definitions of the following important terms:

budget (p. 139)   cash budget (162)   cash cycle (164)   controllability (157) controllable cost (157)   cost center (153)   financial budget (144) financial planning model (152)   investment center (153)   master budget (139) management by objectives (158)   MBO (158)   operating budget (143) operating cycle (164)   profit center (153)   pro forma statements (143) responsibility accounting (153)   responsibility center (153) revenue center (153)   self-liquidating cycle (164)   working capital cycle (164)

Special Points and Pitfalls

This chapter began with a section on the evolution of control systems. Ponder the steps:

1. Personal observation
   +
2. Historical records
   +
3. Budgets

Budgeting systems are costly. They are bought because managers believe that the systems will help subordinates make better collective operating decisions.

Students are frequently overwhelmed by the variety of data required for preparing a master budget. The prediction of sales is almost always the best place to begin.

Because budgeting is loaded with technical trappings, accountants often forget the human aspects. The budget is usually a major tool for judging actual performance. Hence it often has an enormous influence on managers' behavior.

Some organizations mistakenly tend to use budgets and performance reports to pinpoint blame. The important question is who should be asked, *not* who should be blamed.

APPENDIX 5A: THE CASH BUDGET

The major illustration in the chapter featured the operating budget. The other major part of the master budget is the financial budget, which includes the capital budget, cash budget, budgeted balance sheet, and budgeted statement of changes in financial position. This Appendix focuses on the cash budget and the budgeted balance sheet. Capital budgeting is covered in Chapters 19 and 20; coverage of the statement of changes in financial position is beyond the scope of this book.

The balance sheet for the year just ended is as follows:

M Company
Balance Sheet
December 31, 19_1

ASSETS

Current assets:		
Cash	$ 10,000	
Accounts receivable	25,000	
Direct materials	19,000	
Finished goods	14,480	$ 68,480
Fixed assets:		
Land	$ 50,000	
Building and equipment	380,000	
Accumulated depreciation	(75,000)	355,000
Total assets		$423,480

EQUITIES

Current liabilities:		
Accounts payable	$ 8,200	
Income taxes payable	5,000	$ 13,200
Stockholders' equity:		
Common stock, no-par—25,000 shares outstanding	$350,000	
Retained income	60,280	410,280
Total equities		$423,480

Budgeted cash flows are:

	QUARTERS			
	1	2	3	4
Collections from customers	$125,000	$150,000	$160,000	$221,000
Disbursements:				
For direct materials	20,000	35,000	35,000	54,200
For other costs and expenses	25,000	20,000	20,000	17,000
For payroll	90,000	95,000	95,000	109,200
For income taxes	5,000	—	—	—
For machinery purchase	—	—	—	20,000

(The quarterly data are given for convenience. The figures are based on the cash effects of the operations formulated in Schedules 1 through 8 in the chapter).

The company desires to maintain a $15,000 minimum cash balance at the end of each quarter. Money can be borrowed or repaid in multiples of $500 at an interest rate of 10% per annum. Management does not want to borrow any more cash than is necessary and wants to repay as promptly as possible. In any event, loans may not extend beyond four quarters. Interest is computed and paid when the principal is repaid. Assume that borrowings take place at the beginning and repayments at the end of the quarters in question. Compute interest to the nearest dollar.

Use the above data and the other data contained in the solution in the chapter (pages 147–51). Try to solve this problem on your own. As you proceed, you may wish to check your work, step by step, against the solution that follows.

1. Prepare a cash budget. That is, prepare a statement of cash receipts and disbursements by quarters, including details of borrowings, repayments, and interest.
2. Prepare a budgeted balance sheet.
3. Prepare a budgeted income statement, including the effects of interest expense and assumed income taxes for 19_2 of $20,000.

solution

1. The **cash budget** (Exhibit II) is a schedule of expected cash receipts and disbursements. It predicts the effects on cash position of the levels of operation above. The illustrative cash budget is presented by quarters to show the impact of cash-flow timing on bank loan schedules. In practice, monthly—and sometimes weekly—cash budgets are very helpful for cash planning and control. Cash budgets aid in avoiding unnecessary idle cash and unnecessary cash deficiencies. The astute mapping of a financing program keeps cash balances in reasonable relation to needs. Ordinarily, the cash budget has the following main sections:

   a. The beginning cash balance plus cash receipts yields the total cash available for needs, before financing. Cash receipts depend on collections of accounts receivable, cash sales, and miscellaneous recurring sources such as rental or royalty receipts.

M Company
Budgeted Statement of Cash Receipts and Disbursements
For the Year Ending December 31, 19_2

EXHIBIT II

		QUARTERS				FOR THE YEAR AS A WHOLE
		1	2	3	4	
	Cash balance, beginning	$ 10,000	$ 15,000	$ 15,000	$ 15,325	$ 10,000
	Add receipts:					
	Collections from customers	125,000	150,000	160,000	221,000	656,000
(a)	Total available before current financing	$135,000	$165,000	$175,000	$236,325	$666,000
	Less disbursements:					
	For direct materials	$ 20,000	$ 35,000	$ 35,000	$ 54,200	$144,200
	For other costs and expenses	25,000	20,000	20,000	17,000	82,000
	For payroll	90,000	95,000	95,000	109,200	389,200
	For income taxes	5,000	—	—	—	5,000
	For machinery purchase	—	—	—	20,000	20,000
(b)	Total disbursements	$140,000	$150,000	$150,000	$200,400	$640,400
	Minimum cash balance desired	15,000	15,000	15,000	15,000	15,000
	Total cash needed	$155,000	$165,000	$165,000	$215,400	$655,400
	Excess of total cash available over total cash needed before current financing (deficiency)	$(20,000)	$ —	$ 10,000	$ 20,925	$ 10,600
	Financing:					
	Borrowings (at beginning)	$ 20,000	$ —	$ —	$ —	$ 20,000
	Repayments (at end)	—	—	(9,000)	(11,000)	(20,000)
	*Interest (at 10% per annum)	—	—	(675)	(1,100)	(1,775)
(c)	Total effects of financing	$ 20,000	$ —	$ (9,675)	$(12,100)	$ (1,775)
(d)	Cash balance, end (a + c − b)	$ 15,000	$ 15,000	$ 15,325	$ 23,825	$ 23,825

*The interest payments pertain only to the amount of principal being repaid at the end of a given quarter. Note that the remainder of the $20,000 loan must be repaid by the end of the fourth quarter. Also note that depreciation does not necessitate a cash outlay. The specific computations regarding interest are: $9,000 × .10 × 3/4 = $675 and $11,000 × .10 = $1,100.

M Company
Budgeted Balance Sheet
December 31, 19_2

EXHIBIT III

ASSETS

Current assets:

Cash (from Exhibit II)		$ 23,825	
Accounts receivable (1)		60,000	
Direct materials (2)		9,800	
Finished goods (2)		101,180	$194,805

Fixed assets:

Land (3)		$ 50,000	
Building and equipment (4)	$400,000		
Accumulated depreciation (5)	100,000	300,000	350,000
Total assets			$544,805

EQUITIES

Current liabilities:

Accounts payable (6)		$ 70,000	
Income taxes payable (7)		20,000	90,000

Stockholders' equity:

Common stock, no-par, 25,000 shares outstanding (8)		$350,000	
Retained income (9)		104,805	454,805
Total equities			$544,805

Notes:
Beginning balances are used as a start for most of the following computations:
(1) $25,000 + $691,000 sales − $656,000 receipts = $60,000.
(2) *From Schedule 6, page 149.*
(3) *From beginning balance sheet, page 161.*
(4) $380,000 + $20,000 purchases.
(5) $75,000 + $25,000 depreciation.
(6) $8,200 + ($206,000 direct-materials purchases, $213,200 direct labor, $183,000 factory overhead,* $75,000 selling and administrative expenses) − ($144,200 direct materials, $82,000 other costs and expenses, and $389,200 payroll) = $70,000.
(7) $5,000 + $20,000 current year − $5,000 payment.
(8) *From beginning balance sheet.*
(9) $60,280 + $44,525 net income.
*$208,000 from Schedule 5 minus depreciation of $25,000.

Studies of the prospective collectibility of accounts receivable are needed for accurate predictions. Key factors include bad-debt experience and average time lag between sales and collections.

b. Cash disbursements:

(1) Direct-material purchases—depends on credit terms extended by suppliers and bill-paying habits of the buyer.

(2) Direct labor and other wage outlays—depends on payroll dates.

(3) Other costs and expenses—depends on timing and credit terms. **Note that depreciation does not entail a cash outlay.**

(4) Other disbursements—outlays for fixed assets, long-term investments.

c. Financing requirements depend on how the total cash available for needs, keyed as (a) in Exhibit II, compares with the total cash needed. Needs include disbursements, keyed as (b), plus the ending cash balance desired, keyed as (d). The financing plans will depend on the relationship of cash available to cash required. If there is an excess, loans may be repaid or temporary investments made. The pertinent outlays for interest expenses are usually shown in this section of the cash budget.

d. The ending cash balance. The effect of the financing decisions on the cash budget, keyed as (c) in Exhibit II, may be positive (borrowing) or negative (repayment), and the ending cash balance, (d), equals (a) + (c) − (b).

The cash budget in Exhibit II shows the pattern of short-term "self-liquidating cash loans." Seasonal peaks of production or sales often result in heavy cash disbursements for purchases, payroll, and other operating outlays as the products are produced and sold. Cash receipts from customers typically lag behind sales. The loan is *self-liquidating* in the sense that the borrowed money is used to acquire resources that are combined for sale, and the proceeds from the sale are used to repay the loan. This cycle (sometimes called the **self-liquidating cycle, working-capital, cash,** or **operating cycle**) is the movement from cash to inventories to receivables and back to cash.

Cash budgets help managers avoid having unnecessary idle cash, on the one hand, and unnecessary nerve-racking cash deficiencies on the other.

2. Budgeted balance sheet (Exhibit III). Each item is projected in light of the details of the business plan as expressed in the previous schedules. For example, the ending balance of Accounts Receivable would be computed by adding the budgeted sales (from Schedule 1) to the beginning balance (given) and subtracting cash receipts (given and in Exhibit II).

3. The budgeted income statement is in Exhibit IV. It is merely the income statement in Exhibit I, page 151, but now includes interest and income taxes.

M Company
Budgeted Income Statement
For the Year Ending December 31, 19_2

EXHIBIT IV	SOURCE	
Sales	Schedule 1	$691,000
Cost of goods sold	Schedule 7	549,700
Gross margin		$141,300
Selling and administrative expenses	Schedule 8	75,000
Operating income		$ 66,300
Interest expense	Exhibit II	1,775
Income before income taxes		$ 64,525
Income taxes	Assumed	20,000
Net income		$ 44,525

For simplicity, the cash receipts and disbursements were given explicitly in this illustration. Frequently, there are lags between the items reported on an accrual basis in an income statement and their related cash receipts and disbursements. For example, sales may consist of 90% credit and 10% cash sales. In turn, half the total credit sales may be collected in each of the two months subsequent to the sale. Using assumed figures, supporting schedules would be constructed as follows:

	MAY	JUNE	JULY	AUGUST
SCHEDULE A: SALES BUDGET				
Credit sales, 90%	$81,000	$72,000	$63,000	
Cash sales, 10%	9,000	8,000	7,000	
Total sales, 100%	$90,000	$80,000	$70,000	
SCHEDULE B: CASH COLLECTIONS				
Cash sales this month	$ 9,000	$ 8,000	$ 7,000	
Credit sales last month		40,500*	36,000†	$31,500
Credit sales two months ago			40,500*	36,000†
Total collections	$_____	(affected by three months of sales‡)		

*.50 × $81,000 = $40,500.
†.50 × 72,000 = $36,000.
‡The data here provide a total for July of $83,500; not enough data are here for obtaining totals for the other months.

Of course, such schedules of cash collections depend on credit terms, collection histories, and expected uncollectible accounts. Similar schedules can be prepared for operating expenses and their related cash disbursement.

APPENDIX 5B: ADMINISTERING THE BUDGET

Budget director

Although line management has the ultimate responsibility for the preparation of individual budgets, there is also an evident need for technical, unbiased help and overall responsibility for the budget program. This need is usually satisfied by assigning responsibility to a budget director for establishing preparatory procedures, designing forms, *effective educating and selling,* collecting and coordinating data, verifying information, and reporting performance. The budget director is usually the controller or somebody who is responsible to the controller. The budget director serves as the staff expert, the person upon whom line management depends for technical guidance. He or she may also be a valuable communications official between line and staff departments.

The able budget director typically has warm rapport with line management. He or she particularly avoids grabbing line authority—an easy trap to fall into when a person has the position of company expert on budgetary matters.

Budget committee

A budget committee usually serves as a consulting body to the budget officer. Members generally include the budget director and the top-level line executives. However, very large businesses often exclude line executives other than the president from their budget committees; membership is confined to the budget director, the treasurer, the economist, and the president. Special budget committees are formed also—for example, a sales-budget committee and a production-budget committee.

The budget committee is concerned with developing and scrutinizing long-term operating and financial plans, offering advice, reconciling divergent views, and coordinating budgetary activities. The committee's very existence lends an aura of formality and prestige to the budget program.

The budget committee generally has an advisory role only; yet its advice is usually very influential. Initially, the committee usually assembles, reviews, and transmits underlying economic conditions and assumptions in relation to the ensuing budget period. It reviews departmental budgets and makes recommendations. It scrutinizes periodic reports comparing actual performance with the budget. As a result, it submits a variety of recommendations for top-management decision making.

Budget manual

It is usually desirable to have policies, organizational structure, and designations of responsibility and authority expressed in writing. The budget manual is a written set of instructions and pertinent information that serves as a rule book and a reference for the implementation of a budget program. It tells what to do, how to do it, when to do it, and which form to do it on. The effort and time needed for the manual's preparation are justified by its long-run usefulness, its tendency to crystallize all aspects of a budget program, and its documentation of procedures that otherwise are carried around in the heads of individuals who will not have the same job forever.

Follow-up is important

The investigation of budget deviations is the line manager's responsibility. The controller may assist to a very great extent, but the actual preparation of individual department budgets and decisions on deviations should be the responsibility of line management.

Ineffective budgetary systems are marked by failure to develop and use budgets to their fullest potential. That is, budgets are often used as tools for *planning* only. Great benefits from budgeting lie in the quick investigation of deviations and in the subsequent corrective action. Budgets should not be prepared in the first place if they are ignored, buried in files, or improperly interpreted. Again this points up the dire need for the education of company personnel.

QUESTIONS, PROBLEMS, AND CASES

5-1 Identify three major steps in the evolution of management control systems.

5-2 "*Strategic planning* and *long-term planning* are synonyms." Do you agree? Explain.

5-3 "Operating plans are contracts, and I want them met. If your revenue is off, you should cut your expenses accordingly." Do you agree? Explain.

5-4 Distinguish between *sales forecast* and *sales budget*.

5-5 "A common reporting method shows three sets of dollar figures instead of two sets." Identify the likely three sets.

5-6 What are the two major features of a budgetary program? Which feature is more important? Why?

5-7 What are the elements of the budgetary cycle?

5-8 Define *continuous budget, pro forma statements*.

5-9 "The sales forecast is the cornerstone for budgeting." Why?

5-10 Enumerate four common duties of a budget director.

5-11 What is the function of a *budget committee*? A *budget manual*?

5-12 "Budgets are half-used if they serve only as a planning device." Explain.

5-13 Define *responsibility accounting*.

5-14 Define *controllable cost*. What two major factors help an evaluation of whether a given cost is controllable?

5-15 "An action once taken cannot be changed by subsequent events." What implications does this have for the cost accountant?

5-16 "Budgets are wonderful vehicles for communication." Comment.

5-17 "Budgets meet the cost-benefit test. They force managers to act differently." Do you agree? Explain.

5-18 "Budgeted performance is a better criterion than past performance for judging managers." Do you agree? Explain.

5-19 "The major purpose of responsibility accounting is to fix blame." True or false? Explain.

5-20 Distinguish between *responsibility center, responsibility accounting, cost center, revenue center, profit center,* and *investment center.*

5-21 "The basic focus of responsibility accounting should be on information or knowledge, not control." Do you agree? Explain.

5-22 "Performance reports by responsibility centers may also include uncontrollable items." Do you agree? Explain.

5-23 "Management by objectives (MBO) prevents the overemphasis on a single goal." Do you agree? Explain.

5-24 Responsibility of purchasing agent. (R. Villers, adapted) Richards is the purchasing agent for the Hart Manufacturing Company. Sampson is head of the production planning and control department. Every six months, Sampson gives Richards a general purchasing program. Richards gets specifications from the engineering department. He then selects suppliers and negotiates prices.

When he took this job, Richards was informed very clearly that he bore responsibility for meeting the general purchasing program once he accepted it from Sampson.

During Week No. 24, Richards was advised that Part No. 1234—a critical part—would be needed for assembly on Tuesday morning, Week No. 32. He found that the regular supplier could not deliver. He called everywhere, finally found a supplier in the Middle West, and accepted the commitment.

He followed up by mail. Yes, the supplier assured him, the part would be ready. The matter was so important that on Thursday of Week No. 31, Richards checked by phone. Yes, the shipment had left in time. Richards was reassured and did not check further. But on Tuesday of Week No. 32, the part was not in the warehouse. Inquiry revealed that the shipment had been misdirected by the railroad company and was still in Chicago.

Required | What department should bear the costs of time lost in the plant? Why? As purchasing agent, do you think it fair that such costs be charged to your department?

5-25 Responsibility for downtime. Two of several departments at A. O. Smith Co. performed successive operations in the manufacture of automobile frames. The frames were transported from department to department via an overhead conveyor system that was paced in accordance with budgeted time allowances. Each department manager had responsibility for the budgeted costs and budgeted output of his department.

On Tuesday morning Department D had some equipment failure that caused the manager to ask the manager of Department C to stop the conveyor system. The Department C manager refused, so workers in Department D had to remove the frames, stack them, and return the frames to the conveyor later when production resumed.

The manager of Department D was bitter about the incident and insisted that the manager of Department C should bear the related labor and overhead costs of $11,345. In contrast, the manager of Department C said, "I was just doing my job as specified in the budget."

167

Required | As the controller, how would you account for the $11,345? Why?

5-26 Fixing responsibility. (Adapted from a description by Harold Bierman, Jr.) The city of Mountainvale had hired its first city manager four years ago. She favored a "management by objectives" philosophy and accordingly had set up many profit responsibility centers, including a sanitation department, a city utility, and a repair shop.

For many months, the sanitation manager had been complaining to the utility manager about wires being too low at one point in the road. There was barely clearance for large trucks. The sanitation manager asked the repair shop to make changes in the clearance. The repair shop manager asked, "Whom should I charge for the $2,000 cost of making the adjustment, the sanitation or the utility department?" Both departments refused to accept the charge, so the repair department refused to do the work.

Late one day the top of a truck caught the wires and ripped them down. The repair department made an emergency repair at a cost of $2,600. Moreover, the city lost $1,000 of utility revenue (less variable costs) because of the disruption of service.

Investigation disclosed that the truck had failed to clamp down its top properly. The extra two inches of height caused the catching of the wire.

Both the sanitation and utility managers argued strenuously about whether they should bear the $2,600 cost. Moreover, the utility manager demanded reimbursement from the sanitation department of the $1,000 of lost contribution.

Required | As the city controller in charge of the responsibility accounting system, how would you favor accounting for these costs? Specifically, what would you do next? What is the proper role of responsibility accounting in determining the blame for this situation?

5-27 A study in responsibility accounting. The David Machine Tool Company is in the doldrums. Production volume has fallen to a ten-year low. The company has a nucleus of skilled tool-and-die workers who could find employment elsewhere if they were laid off. Three of these workers have been transferred temporarily to the building and grounds department, where they have been doing menial tasks such as washing walls and sweeping for the past month. They have earned their regular rate of $13 per hour. Their wages have been charged to the building and grounds department. The supervisor of building and grounds has just confronted the controller as follows: "Look at the cockeyed performance report you pencil pushers have given me." The helpers' line reads:

	BUDGET	ACTUAL	DEVIATION	
Wages of helpers	$4,704	$7,644	$2,940	Unfavorable

"This is just another example of how unrealistic you bookkeepers are! Those tool-and-die people are loafing on the job because they know we won't lay them off. The regular hourly rate for my three helpers is $8. Now that my regular helpers are laid off, my work is piling up, so that when they return they'll either have to put in overtime or I'll have to get part-time help to catch up with things. Instead of charging me at $13 per hour, you should charge about $6—that's all those tool-and-die slobs are worth at their best."

Required | As the controller, what would you do *now*? Would you handle the accounting for these wages any differently?

5-28 Responsibility accounting and costs of quality. A St. Regis Co. factory makes grocery bags. A suburban Los Angeles plant produces 8 million to 9 million bags daily, supplying supermarket chains in eleven western states. Machines, which are 25-feet long, turn out bags in batches of 25 or 50. Machine operators inspect their own production by riffling each batch through their hands.

The company has been concerned that as much as 6% of production has been bad, resulting in an intolerable level of sales returns. An employee has suggested signature bags. A plate would be engraved with each employee's signature on it. Workers would slip their nameplate into the bag machines. Each bag would bear the inscription "personally inspected by . . ."

Required | Evaluate the suggestion. Is this an example of responsibility accounting? Explain.

5-29 Sales and production budget. The Ramos Company expects 19_2 sales of 100,000 units of serving trays. Ramos's beginning inventory for 19_2 is 8,000 trays; target ending inventory, 11,000 trays. Compute the number of trays budgeted for production.

5-30 Sales and production budget. The Gallo Company had a December 31, 19_2, target inventory of 80,000 four-liter bottles of burgundy wine. Gallo's beginning inventory was 60,000 bottles, and its budgeted production was 900,000 bottles. Compute the budgeted sales in number of bottles.

5-31 Direct-materials budget. Inglenook Co. produces wine. The company expects to produce 1,500,000 two-liter bottles of chablis in 19_3. Inglenook purchases empty glass bottles from an outside vendor. Its target ending inventory of such bottles is 50,000; its beginning inventory is 30,000. For simplicity, ignore breakage. Compute the number of bottles to be purchased in 19_3.

5-32 Direct-materials budget. Angeli Co. produces frozen pizzas. The company expects to purchase 910,000 cartons in 19_2. Beginning inventory is 35,000 cartons; target ending inventory, 46,000. For simplicity, ignore damaged cartons. Compute the number of cartons to be used in production in 19_2.

5-33 Budgeted manufacturing costs. The Bridget Company has budgeted sales for 100,000 units of its product for 19_1. Expected unit costs, based on past experience, should be $60 for direct materials, $40 for direct labor, and $30 for manufacturing overhead. Assume no beginning or ending inventory in process. Bridget begins the year with 40,000 finished units on hand but budgets the ending finished-goods inventory at only 10,000 units. Compute the budgeted costs of production for 19_1.

5-34 Budgeting material purchases. The X Company has prepared a sales budget of 42,000 finished units for a three-month period. The company has an inventory of 22,000 units of finished goods on hand at December 31 and has a target finished-goods inventory of 24,000 units at the end of the succeeding quarter.

It takes three gallons of direct materials to make one unit of finished product. The company has an inventory of 100,000 gallons of raw material at December 31 and has a target ending inventory of 110,000 gallons. How many gallons of direct materials should be purchased during the three months ending March 31?

5-35 Budgeting material quantities. (SMA) A sales budget for the first five months of 19_3 is given for a particular product line manufactured by Arthur Guthrie Co. Ltd.

	SALES BUDGET IN UNITS
January	10,800
February	15,600
March	12,200
April	10,400
May	9,800

The inventory of finished products at the end of each month is to be equal to 25% of the sales estimate for the next month. On January 1, there were 2,700 units of product on hand. No work is in process at the end of any month.

Each unit of product requires two types of materials in the following quantities:

Material A: 4 units
Material B: 5 units

Materials equal to one-half of the next month's requirements are to be on hand at the end of each month. This requirement was met on January 1, 19_3.

Prepare a budget showing the quantities of each type of material to be purchased each month for the first quarter of 19_3.

5-36 Sales, production, and purchases budget. The Suzuki Co. in Japan has a division that manufactures two-wheel motorcycles. Its budgeted sales for Model G in 19_3 is 800,000 units. Suzuki's target ending inventory is 100,000 units, and its beginning inventory is 120,000 units. The company's budgeted unit selling price to its distributors and dealers is 400,000 yen.

Suzuki buys all its wheels from an outside supplier. No defective wheels are accepted. (Suzuki's needs for extra wheels for replacement parts are ordered by a separate division of the company.) The company's target ending inventory is 30,000 wheels, and its beginning inventory is 24,000 wheels. The budgeted purchase price is 16,000 yen per wheel.

Required

1. Compute the budgeted sales in yen. (For your general information, during the 1980s the exchange rate fluctuated between 170 and 280 yen per U.S. dollar. This rate is not necessary to solve this problem.)
2. Compute the number of motorcycles to be produced.
3. Compute the budgeted purchases of wheels in units and in yen.

5-37 Budgeting conversion costs and cost of goods manufactured. Jose Co. is preparing a budget for 19_4 conversion costs regarding Product LMG, a part used heavily by computer manufacturers. The historical record for 19_3 indicates that an average of 5 painstaking direct-labor hours was necessary for each finished unit. The direct-labor rate was $20 per hour. The applied factory overhead rate was 200% of direct-labor cost.

Plans for 19_4 called for more automation, which would reduce direct-labor time per unit by 20%. However, increases in repairs, utilities, depreciation, and other factory over-head costs will increase the applied factory overhead rate to 500% of direct-labor cost. More-over, wage increases will increase the direct-labor rate per hour by 5%.

The company plans to produce 20,000 units of LMG in 19_4. Direct materials will cost $700 per unit.

Required

Prepare a budget of cost of goods manufactured. Show supporting computations. For simplicity, assume that there are no work-in-process inventories.

5-38 Sales and production budgets. (CPA) The Scarborough Corporation in Singapore manufactures and sells two products, Thingone and Thingtwo. In July 19_7, Scarborough's budget depart-ment gathered the following data in order to project sales and budget requirements for 19_8:

19_8 PROJECTED SALES:

PRODUCT	UNITS	PRICE
Thingone	60,000	$ 70
Thingtwo	40,000	$100

19_8 INVENTORIES—IN UNITS:

PRODUCT	EXPECTED JANUARY 1, 19_8	DESIRED DECEMBER 31, 19_8
Thingone	20,000	25,000
Thingtwo	8,000	9,000

To produce one unit of Thingone and Thingtwo, the following raw materials are used:

RAW MATERIAL	UNIT	AMOUNT USED PER UNIT	
		Thingone	Thingtwo
A	lbs.	4	5
B	lbs.	2	3
C	each		1

Projected data for 19_8 with respect to raw materials are as follows:

RAW MATERIAL	ANTICIPATED PURCHASE PRICE	EXPECTED INVENTORIES JANUARY 1, 19_8	DESIRED INVENTORIES DECEMBER 31, 19_8
A	$8	32,000 lbs.	36,000 lbs.
B	$5	29,000 lbs.	32,000 lbs.
C	$3	6,000 each	7,000 each

Projected direct-labor requirements for 19_8 and rates are as follows:

PRODUCT	HOURS PER UNIT	RATE PER HOUR
Thingone	2	$3
Thingtwo	3	$4

Overhead is applied at the rate of $2 per direct-labor hour.

Required Based on the above projections and budget requirements for 19_8 for Thingone and Thingtwo, prepare the following budgets for 19_8:

1. Sales budget (in dollars)
2. Production budget (in units)
3. Raw-materials purchase budget (in quantities)
4. Raw-materials purchase budget (in dollars)
5. Direct-labor budget (in dollars)
6. Budgeted finished-goods inventory at December 31, 19_8 (in dollars)

5-39 Budget for production and direct labor. (CMA, adapted) Roletter Company makes and sells artistic frames for pictures of weddings, graduations, christenings, and other special events. Bob Anderson, controller, is responsible for preparing Roletter's master budget and has accumulated the information below for 19_5.

	19_5				
	January	February	March	April	May
Estimated unit sales	10,000	12,000	8,000	9,000	9,000
Sales price per unit	$50.00	$47.50	$47.50	$47.50	$47.50
Direct-labor hours per unit	2.0	2.0	1.5	1.5	1.5
Wage per direct-labor hour	$8.00	$8.00	$8.00	$9.00	$9.00

Labor-related costs include pension contributions of $.25 per hour, workers' compensation insurance of $.10 per hour, employee medical insurance of $.40 per hour, and social security taxes. Assume that as of January 1, 19_5, the social security tax rates are 7% for employers and 6.7% for employees. The cost of employee benefits paid by Roletter on its employees is treated as a direct-labor cost.

Roletter has a labor contract that calls for a wage increase to $9.00 per hour on April 1, 19_5. New labor-saving machinery has been installed and will be fully operational by March 1, 19_5.

Roletter expects to have 16,000 frames on hand at December 31, 19_4, and has a policy of carrying an end-of-month inventory of 100% of the following month's sales plus 50% of the second following month's sales.

Required

Prepare a production budget and a direct-labor budget for Roletter Company by month and for the first quarter of 19_5. Both budgets may be combined in one schedule. The direct-labor budget should include direct-labor hours and show the detail for each direct-labor-cost category.

5-40 Comprehensive review of income budget schedules, incorporating budget revisions.   (CMA, adapted) Molid Company was founded by Mark Dalid three years ago. The company produces a modulation-demodulation unit (modem) for use with minicomputers and microcomputers. Business has expanded rapidly since the company's inception.

Bob Wells, the company's general accountant, prepared a budget for the fiscal year ending August 31, 19_4. The budget was based on the prior year's sales and production activity because Dalid believed that the sales growth experienced during the prior year would not continue at the same pace. The pro forma (that is, budgeted) statements of income and cost of goods sold that were prepared as part of the budget process are presented below.

Molid Company
Pro Forma Statement of Income
For the year Ended August 31, 19_4

Net sales		$31,248,000
Cost of goods sold		20,765,000
Gross profit		$10,483,000
Operating expenses:		
Marketing	$ 3,200,000	
General and administrative	2,200,000	5,400,000
Income from operations before income taxes		$ 5,083,000

Molid Company
Pro Forma Statement of Cost of Goods Sold
For the Year Ended August 31, 19_4

Direct materials:		
Materials inventory, 9/1/19_3	$ 1,360,000	
Materials purchased	14,476,000	
Materials available for use	15,836,000	
Materials inventory, 8/31/19_4	1,628,000	
Direct materials consumed		$14,208,000
Direct labor		1,134,000
Factory overhead:		
Indirect materials	$ 1,421,000	
General factory overhead	3,240,000	4,661,000
Cost of goods manufactured		$20,003,000
Finished goods inventory, 9/1/19_3		1,169,000
Cost of goods available for sale		$21,172,000
Finished goods inventory, 8/31/19_4		407,000
Cost of goods sold		$20,765,000

On December 10, 19_3, Dalid and Wells met to discuss the first-quarter operating results (i.e., results for the period September 1–November 30, 19_3). Wells believed that several changes should be made to the original budget assumptions that had been used to prepare the pro forma statements. Wells prepared the following notes that summarized the changes that did not become known until the first-quarter results had been compiled. The following data were submitted to Dalid.

a. The estimated production in units for the fiscal year should be revised upward from 162,000 units to 170,000 units, with the balance of production being scheduled in equal segments over the last nine months of the fiscal year. Actual first-quarter production was 35,000 units.

b. The planned ending inventory for finished goods of 3,300 units at August 31, 19_4, remains unchanged. The finished-goods inventory of 9,300 units as of September 1, 19_3, had dropped to 9,000 units by November 30, 19_3.

c. Direct materials sufficient to produce 16,000 units were on hand at the beginning of the fiscal year. The plans for direct-materials inventory to have the equivalent of 18,500 units of production at the end of each of the remaining quarters and of the fiscal year-end remain unchanged. Direct-materials inventory is valued on a first-in, first-out basis. Direct materials equivalent to 37,500 units of output were purchased for $3,300,000 during the first quarter of the fiscal year. Molid's suppliers have informed the company that direct-material prices will increase 5% on March 1, 19_4. Direct materials needed for the rest of the fiscal year will be purchased evenly throughout the last nine months.

d. The direct-labor rate will increase 8% as of June 1, 19_4, as a consequence of a new labor agreement that was signed during the first quarter. When the original pro forma statements were prepared, the expected effective date for this new labor agreement had been September 1, 19_4.

e. On the basis of historical data, indirect-material cost is projected at 10% of the cost of direct materials consumed.

f. One-half of general factory overhead and all of marketing and general and administrative expenses are considered fixed. The variable component of general factory overhead varies as a function of units produced; it is projected on the basis of expected unit production.

g. The finished-goods inventory at the end of the fiscal year will be valued at the average manufacturing cost for the year.

Required

1. Based on the revised data presented by Bob Wells, calculate the following for the year ended August 31, 19_4:
   a. Sales budget in dollars
   b. Production budget in units (also report production for each quarter of the fiscal year)
   c. Direct-materials purchases budget
   d. Direct-labor budget
   e. Factory-overhead budget
   f. Ending-inventory budget
   g. Cost-of-goods-sold budget
   h. Marketing-general-administrative-expense budget
   i. Budgeted income statement

2. The finished-goods inventory in the budget is valued at the average manufacturing cost during the year. How might further refinements be made in calculating the cost of finished-goods inventory?

5-41 Cash receipts and payments, multiple choice. (CMA) Read Appendix 5A. Information pertaining to Noskey Corporation's sales revenue is presented in the following table.

	NOVEMBER 19_5 (ACTUAL)	DECEMBER 19_5 (BUDGET)	JANUARY 19_6 (BUDGET)
Cash sales	$ 80,000	$100,000	$ 60,000
Credit sales	240,000	360,000	180,000
Total sales	$320,000	$460,000	$240,000

Management estimates that 5% of credit sales are uncollectible. Of the credit sales that are collectible, 60% are collected in the month of sale and the remainder in the month following the sale. Purchases of inventory each month are 70% of the next month's projected total sales. All purchases of inventory are on account; 25% are paid in the month of purchase, and the remainder are paid in the month following the purchase.

Required

1. Noskey's budgeted cash collections in December 19_5 from November 19_5 credit sales are (a) $144,000, (b) $136,800, (c) $96,000, (d) $91,200, (e) none of these.
2. Noskey's budgeted total cash receipts in January 19_6 are (a) $240,000, (b) $294,000, (c) $299,400, (d) $239,400, (e) none of these.
3. Noskey's budgeted total cash payments in December 19_5 for inventory purchases are (a) $405,000, (b) $283,500, (c) $240,000, (d) $168,000, (e) none of these.

5-42 Collections and disbursements. (CPA) Read Appendix 5A. The following information was available from Montero Corporation's books:

19_2	PURCHASES	SALES
Jan.	$42,000	$72,000
Feb.	48,000	66,000
Mar.	36,000	60,000
Apr.	54,000	78,000

Collections from customers are normally 70% in the month of sale, 20% in the month following the sale, and 9% in the second month following the sale. The balance is expected to be uncollectible. Montero takes full advantage of the 2% discount allowed on purchases paid for by the tenth of the following month. Purchases for May are budgeted at $60,000, while sales for May are forecasted at $66,000. Cash disbursements for expenses are expected to be $14,400 for the month of May. Montero's cash balance at May 1 was $22,000.

Required

Prepare the following schedules:

1. Expected cash collections during May
2. Expected cash disbursements during May
3. Expected cash balance at May 31

5-43 Comprehensive budget; fill in schedules. Read Appendix 5A. Ignore income taxes. Following is certain information relative to the position and business of the Newport Stores Company.

Current assets as of Sept. 30:	
Cash on deposit	$ 12,000
Inventory	63,600
Accounts receivable	10,000
Fixed assets—net	100,000
Current liabilities as of Sept. 30	None
Recent and anticipated sales:	
September	$ 40,000
October	48,000
November	60,000
December	80,000
January	36,000

Credit sales: Sales are 75% for cash, and 25% on credit. Assume that credit accounts are all collected within 30 days from sale. The accounts receivable on September 30 are the result of the credit sales for September (25% of $40,000).

Gross profit averages 30% of sales. Purchase discounts are treated on the income statement as "other income" by this company.

Expenses: Salaries and wages average 15% of monthly sales; rent, 5%; all other expenses, excluding depreciation, 4%. Assume that these expenses are disbursed each month. Depreciation is $1,000 per month.

Purchases: There is a basic inventory of $30,000. The policy is to purchase each month additional inventory in the amount necessary to provide for the following month's sales. Terms on purchases are 2/10, n/30. Assume that payments are made in the month of purchase, and that all discounts are taken.

Fixtures: In October, $600 is spent for fixtures, and in November, $400 is to be expended for this purpose.

Assume that a minimum cash balance of $8,000 is to be maintained. Assume also that all borrowings are effective at the beginning of the month and all repayments are made at the end of the month of repayment. Loans are repaid when sufficient cash is available. Interest is paid only at the time of repaying principal. Interest rate is 18% per annum. Management does not want to borrow any more cash than is necessary and wants to repay as soon as possible when cash is available.

Required | On the basis of the facts as given above:

1. Complete Schedule A.

Schedule A
Budgeted Monthly Dollar Receipts

ITEM	SEPTEMBER	OCTOBER	NOVEMBER	DECEMBER
Total sales	$40,000	$48,000	$60,000	$80,000
Credit sales	10,000	12,000		
Cash sales				
Receipts:				
Cash sales		$36,000		
Collections on accounts receivable		10,000		
Total		$46,000		

2. Complete Schedule B. Note that purchases are 70% of next month's sales.

Schedule B
Budgeted Monthly Cash Disbursements for Purchases

ITEM	OCTOBER	NOVEMBER	DECEMBER	TOTAL
Purchases	$42,000			
Less 2% cash discount	840			
Disbursements	$41,160			

3. Complete Schedule C.

Schedule C
Budgeted Monthly Cash Disbursements for Operating Expenses

ITEM	OCTOBER	NOVEMBER	DECEMBER	TOTAL
Salaries and wages	$ 7,200			
Rent	2,400			
Other expenses	1,920			
Total	$11,520			

4. Complete Schedule D.

Schedule D
Budgeted Total Monthly Disbursements

ITEM	OCTOBER	NOVEMBER	DECEMBER	TOTAL
Purchases	$41,160			
Operating expenses	11,520			
Fixtures	600			
Total	$53,280			

5. Complete Schedule E.

Schedule E
Budgeted Cash Receipts and Disbursements

ITEM	OCTOBER	NOVEMBER	DECEMBER	TOTAL
Receipts	$46,000			
Disbursements	53,280			
Net cash increase				
Net cash decrease	$ 7,280			

6. Complete Schedule F (assume that borrowings must be made in multiples of $1,000).

Schedule F
Financing Required by Newport Stores Company

ITEM	OCTOBER	NOVEMBER	DECEMBER	TOTAL
Opening cash	$12,000	$ 8,720		
Net cash increase				
Net cash decrease	7,280			
Cash position before financing	4,720			
Financing required	4,000			
Interest payments				
Financing retired				
Closing balance	$ 8,720			

7. What do you think is the most logical means of arranging the financing needed by Newport Stores Company?

8. Prepare a budgeted (pro forma) income statement for the fourth quarter and a balance sheet as of December 31. Ignore income taxes.

9. Certain simplifications have been introduced in this problem. What complicating factors would be met in a typical business situation?

5-44 Cash budget. bankruptcy setting. (CPA) Read Appendix 5A. Mayne Manufacturing Co. has incurred substantial losses for several years, and has become insolvent. On March 31, 19_5, Mayne petitioned the court for protection from creditors and submitted the following statement of financial position.

Mayne Manufacturing Co.
Statement of Financial Position
March 31, 19_5

	BOOK VALUE	LIQUIDATION VALUE
ASSETS:		
Accounts receivable	$100,000	$ 50,000
Inventories	90,000	40,000
Plant and equipment	150,000	160,000
Total	$340,000	$250,000
LIABILITIES AND STOCKHOLDERS' EQUITY:		
Accounts payable—general creditors	$600,000	
Common stock outstanding	60,000	
Deficit	(320,000)	
Total	$340,000	

Mayne's management informed the court that the company has developed a new product, and that a prospective customer is willing to sign a contract for the purchase of 10,000 units of this product during the year ended March 31, 19_6, 12,000 units of this product during the year ended March 31, 19_7, and 15,000 units of this product during the year ended March 31, 19_8, at a price of $90 per unit. This product can be manufactured using Mayne's present facilities. Monthly production with immediate delivery is expected to be uniform within each year. Receivables are expected to be collected during the calendar month following sales.

Unit production costs of the new product are expected to be as follows:

Direct materials	$20
Direct labor	30
Variable overhead	10

Fixed costs (excluding depreciation) will amount to $130,000 per year.

Purchases of direct materials will be paid during the calendar month following purchase. Fixed costs, direct labor, and variable overhead will be paid as incurred. Inventory of direct materials will be equal to 60 days' usage. After the first month of operations, 30 days' usage of direct materials will be ordered each month.

The general creditors have agreed to reduce their total claims to 60% of their March 31, 19_5 balances, under the following conditions:

Existing accounts receivable and inventories are to be liquidated immediately, with the proceeds turned over to the general creditors.

The balance of reduced accounts payable is to be paid as cash is generated from future operations, but in no event later than March 31, 19_7. No interest will be paid on these obligations.

Under this proposed plan, the general creditors would receive $110,000 more than the current liquidation value of Mayne's assets. The court has engaged you to determine the feasibility of this plan.

Required

Ignoring any need to borrow and repay short-term funds for working capital purposes, prepare a cash budget for the years ended March 31, 19_6 and 19_7, showing the cash expected to be available to pay the claims of the general creditors, payments to general creditors, and the cash remaining after payment of claims.

5-45 Cash budgeting. Read Appendix 5A. On December 1, 19_1, the XYZ Wholesale Co. is attempting to project cash receipts and disbursements through January 31, 19_2. On this latter date, a note will be payable in the amount of $10,000. This amount was borrowed in September to carry the company through the seasonal peak in November and December.

The trial balance on December 1 shows in part:

Cash	$ 1,000	
Accounts receivable	28,000	
Allowance for bad debts		$1,580
Inventory	8,750	
Accounts payable		9,200

Sales terms call for a 2% discount if paid within the first ten days of the month after purchase, with the balance due by the end of the month after purchase. Experience has shown that 70% of the billings will be collected within the discount period, 20% by the end of the month after purchase, and 8% in the following month, and that 2% will be uncollectible. There are no sales for cash.

The unit sales price of the company's one product is $10. Actual and projected sales are:

October actual	$ 18,000
November actual	25,000
December estimated	30,000
January estimated	15,000
February estimated	12,000
Total estimated for year ended June 30	150,000

All purchases are payable within fifteen days. Thus approximately 50% of the purchases in a month are due and payable in the next month. The unit purchase cost is $7. Target ending inventories are 500 units plus 25% of the next month's unit sales.

Total budgeted selling and administrative expenses for the year are $40,000. Of this amount, $15,000 is considered fixed (includes depreciation of $3,000). The remainder varies with sales. Both fixed and variable selling and administrative expenses are paid as incurred.

Required | Prepare a columnar statement of budgeted cash receipts and disbursements for December and January.

Flexible Budgets and Standards: Part I

Analysis levels 0 and 1: static budget • Analysis level 2: flexible budget •
Analysis level 3: detailed variances • Standards for materials and labor • Impact of inventories •
General-ledger entries • Standards for control • Controllability and variances •
When to investigate variances • Appendix: Inflation and price variances

The preceding chapter focused on the general ideas of budgeting and the use of responsibility accounting to help plan performance. A key element of the control system is feedback—the comparison of actual performance with planned performance. Now we focus on how managers use flexible budgets and standard costs as aids for planning and controlling.

The bulk of the chapter deals with standard costs, which are predetermined measures of what costs should be under specified conditions. The analysis of the variances of actual costs from standard costs can assist managers in judging and improving performance. The basic analysis is illustrated for the price and efficiency variances of direct-material costs and direct-labor costs.

To stress some fundamental ideas, we assume throughout this chapter (unless otherwise stated) no beginning or ending inventories of work in process or finished goods. Chapter 8 explores the implications of inventories for the measurement of performance.

ANALYSIS LEVELS 0 AND 1: STATIC BUDGET

When managers evaluate performance, they seek various levels of detail. For example, consider the Webb Company. Suppose for simplicity that the company manufactures a single product, a finely crafted, heavy ashtray made of a special alloy having a unique color and luster. Webb has a budgeting system, basing its budget on last year's performance, general economic conditions, and its expected share of predicted industry sales.

Exhibit 6-1 begins the variance analysis that will be covered throughout this and the next chapter. The exhibit presents two successive depths of detail of variance analysis. *Level 0* has the least depth, and *Level 1* has more depth.[1]

The top of Exhibit 6-1 presents a *Level 0* analysis of variances. Most observers, unless they are totally passive, would not be satisfied with such a skimpy report. Merely knowing that a relatively huge unfavorable variance exists ($110,600, or 98.7% of budgeted operating income) is not enough. Instead, as a minimum, managers would seek the *Level 1* analysis shown in Exhibit 6-1. That is, actual results are compared with the original budget, line by line, for at least the total revenue, variable costs, contribution margin, fixed costs, and operating income. If desired, a detailed analysis could be conducted for subclassifications of variable and fixed costs.

EXHIBIT 6-1
Webb Company
Overview of Variance Analysis
For the Month Ended April 30, 19_1

ANALYSIS LEVEL 0

		%
Actual operating income	$ 1,400	1.3
Budgeted operating income	112,000	100.0
Static-budget variance	$110,600 U	98.7

ANALYSIS LEVEL 1	(1) ACTUAL RESULTS	%	(2) STATIC (MASTER) BUDGET	%	(3) (1)–(2) VARIANCE
Units	10,000	—	12,000	—	2,000 U
Revenue (sales)	$720,000	100.00	$840,000	100.0	$120,000 U
Variable costs	546,600	75.9	552,000	65.7	5,400 F
Contribution margin	173,400	24.1	288,000	34.3	114,600 U
Fixed costs	172,000	23.9	176,000	21.0	4,000 F
Operating income	$ 1,400	0.2	$112,000	13.3	$110,600 U

↑ Static-budget variance* ↑
$110,600 U

F = Favorable; U = Unfavorable effect on operating income
*The static budget variance shown here is the variance in operating income.

---

[1] J. Shank and N. Churchill, "Variance Analysis: A Management-oriented Approach," *Accounting Review*, October 1977, pp. 950–57. In practice, there are wide varieties of cost systems and variance analyses. In any event, standard cost systems for manufacturing are used widely. For example, a survey of 112 manufacturing firms indicated that 85% used standard costs. See H. Schwarzbach, "The Impact of Automation on Accounting for Indirect Costs," *Management Accounting*, December 1985.

The *Level 1* analysis indicates that the *Level 0* analysis stops too soon. A total unfavorable variance of $110,600 in operating income may be the result of many factors that are frequently offsetting. Percentages are often used to highlight relationships, as is illustrated by both the *Level 0* and the *Level 1* analysis. In this instance, only 10,000 units were sold instead of the original target of 12,000. But the shortfall in sales was not accompanied by a corresponding fall in variable costs, which decreased by only $5,400 and amounted to 75.9% of sales instead of the 65.7% that was budgeted.[2] Thus the contribution-margin percentage was only 24.1% instead of the budgeted 34.3%.

The *Level 1* analysis assumes that the budgeted amounts were those originally formulated in the master budget for April. That is, the master budget is *static* because it has a single planned volume level. By definition, a **static budget** is not adjusted or altered, regardless of changes in volume or other conditions during the budget period. For example, the *Level 1* comparison aligns the originally budgeted sales volume of 12,000 units against the 10,000 units actually sold.

The *Level 1* combination of percentage analyses and absolute dollar amounts of variances tells the manager much more about underlying performance than the *Level 0* analysis. But most managers would consider *Level 1* as not being sufficiently informative.

ANALYSIS LEVEL 2: FLEXIBLE BUDGET

Adjusting for changes in volume

The chief executive of the Webb Company would probably want a flexible budget to help provide an explanatory trail between the static budget and the actual results. A **flexible budget** (also called a **variable budget**) is a budget that is adjusted for changes in volume. The flexible budget is based on a knowledge of how revenue and costs should behave over a range of activity.

Exhibit 6-2 shows how the flexible-budget data might appear for the Webb Company for a relevant range of 9,000 to 13,000 units. The costs in Exhibit 6-2 can be graphed as in Exhibit 6-3. These exhibits are based on a study of cost behavior patterns that lead to a mathematical function or formula: $176,000 fixed cost per month plus $46 variable cost per unit of product. Note especially that the graph in Exhibit 6-3 can be transformed to become the familiar cost-volume-profit graph by merely drawing the sales line, which is not shown there. Thus, in its fullest form, the flexible budget is an expression of the cost-volume-profit relationships already described in Chapter 3.

Flexible budgets can be useful either before or after a specific period in question. They can be helpful when managers are trying to choose a level of volume for planning purposes. They can also be helpful at the end of the period when managers are trying to analyze actual results.

To recapitulate, the flexible budget prepared at the end of the period is the budget that *would have been* formulated if all the managers were perfect forecasters of the activity volume; there would never be any difference between the budgeted volume and the actual volume achieved. In our example, if the managers could

---

[2]Managers and others tend to watch these percentages regularly. Comparisons are made from period to period and from company to company. For example, consider the U.S. airline industry. In 1986, the labor cost per available seat mile was 3.44 cents for Delta and 0.68 cents for People Express.

EXHIBIT 6-2
Webb Company
Flexible-Budget Data
Relevant Range of Activity (Volume)
For the Month Ended April 30, 19_1

	BUDGETED AMOUNT PER UNIT	VARIOUS LEVELS OF VOLUME		
Units		9,000	11,000	13,000
Revenue (sales)	$70	$630,000	$770,000	$910,000
Variable costs:				
Direct material	20	180,000	220,000	260,000
Direct labor	16	144,000	176,000	208,000
Variable factory overhead	3	27,000	33,000	39,000
Variable manufacturing costs	39	351,000	429,000	507,000
Variable selling and administrative costs*	7	63,000	77,000	91,000
Total variable costs	46	414,000	506,000	598,000
Contribution margin	$24	216,000	264,000	312,000
Fixed costs:				
Manufacturing†		96,000	96,000	96,000
Selling and administrative‡		80,000	80,000	80,000
Total fixed costs		176,000	176,000	176,000
Total costs		590,000	682,000	774,000
Operating income		$ 40,000	$ 88,000	$136,000

*Examples: Sales commissions, shipping, photocopying.
†Examples: Supervision, depreciation, property taxes.
‡Examples: Advertising, supervision, accounting.

EXHIBIT 6-3
Webb Company
Graph of Flexible Budget of Costs

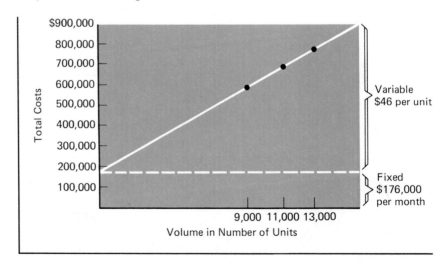

EXHIBIT 6-4   *(Place a clip on this page for easy reference.)*

Webb Company
Summary of Performance
For the Month Ended April 30, 19_1

ANALYSIS LEVEL 2	(1) ACTUAL RESULTS	(2) (1)–(3) FLEXIBLE- BUDGET VARIANCES	(3) FLEXIBLE BUDGET*	(4) (3)–(5) SALES VOLUME VARIANCES	(5) STATIC (MASTER) BUDGET
Physical units of output	10,000	—	10,000	2,000 U	12,000
Revenue (sales)	$720,000	$20,000 F	$700,000	$140,000 U	$840,000
Variable costs	546,600	86,600 U	460,000	92,000 F	552,000
Contribution margin	173,400	66,600 U	240,000	48,000 U	288,000
Fixed costs	172,000	4,000 F	176,000	—	176,000
Operating income	$ 1,400	$62,600 U	$ 64,000	$ 48,000 U	$112,000

Flexible-budget variances,   Sales volume variances,
$62,600 U $48,000 U

Static-budget variances, $110,600 U

*Amounts are computed using the formula for the flexible budget: 10,000 × $70, $46, and
$24, respectively. Fixed costs are budgeted at $176,000 per month.

have foreseen that actual volume would be 10,000 units, a master budget would have been geared to that level.

The flexible budget is the path to the more-penetrating *Level 2* variance analysis in Exhibit 6-4. The $110,600 static budget variance is split into two major categories: (a) sales volume variances and (b) flexible-budget variances. Brief definitions follow:

Sales volume variance—the difference between the flexible-budget amounts and the static (master) budget amounts. Held constant are selling prices and unit variable costs.
Flexible-budget variance—the difference between actual amounts and the flexible-budget amounts for the actual output achieved.

Sales volume variances

Exhibit 6-4 clearly shows how the variances due to the level of *sales volume* ($48,000 U) are unaffected by any changes in unit prices. Why? Because both the flexible budget and the static budget are constructed using budgeted prices. Thus the final three columns in Exhibit 6-4 focus on effects of sales volume changes while holding unit prices constant.

The total of the sales volume variances in *Level 2* tells the manager that operating income would be $48,000 lower than originally budgeted ($64,000 instead of $112,000). The tabulation in Exhibit 6-4, column 4, shows that the underachievement of sales by 2,000 units and $140,000 would decrease contribution margin by $48,000 and hence decrease operating income by $48,000.

In summary, the following explanation is offered by *Level 2* analysis. The budgeted unit contribution margin as indicated in Exhibit 6-2 is $70 − $46 = $24:

$$\text{Sales volume variance of operating income} = \begin{pmatrix} \text{Flexible-budget units} \\ -\text{Static-budget units} \end{pmatrix} \times \begin{pmatrix} \text{Budgeted unit} \\ \text{contribution margin} \end{pmatrix}$$

$$= (10,000 - 12,000) \times \$24$$

$$= \$48,000 \text{ U}$$

For now, we stop at *Level 2* for the sales volume variances. Such variances can be analyzed in much more detail. For example, Chapter 24 explores how variances can be compiled for intervening changes in sales mix, market size, and market share.

Who has responsibility for the sales volume variance? Fluctuations in sales are attributable to many factors, but the executive in charge of marketing is usually in the best position to explain why the volume achieved differs from the volume in the static budget.

Effectiveness and efficiency

When evaluating performance, some managers like to distinguish between effectiveness and efficiency:

Effectiveness—the degree to which a predetermined objective or target is met
Efficiency—the degree to which inputs are used in relation to a given level of outputs

Performance may be both efficient and effective, but either condition can occur without the other. For example, Webb Company set a static-budget goal of producing and selling 12,000 units. Subsequently, only 10,000 units were produced and sold. Performance would be judged ineffective. Whether performance was efficient is a separate question. The degree of efficiency is measured by comparing actual outputs achieved (10,000 units) with actual inputs (such as quantities of direct material and direct labor). In Webb's case, as we will see later, performance was also inefficient.

How do these ideas of effectiveness and efficiency relate to variances? The sales volume variance is a measure of effectiveness. The flexible-budget variance is often a measure of efficiency; however, it is also affected by changes in unit prices (such as an unforeseen change in selling prices or wage rates). Of course, all variances are affected by the care used in formulating the budgeted or standard amounts.

Flexible-budget variances

The first three columns of Exhibit 6-4 compare the actual results (that is, actual total revenue and actual total costs) with the flexible-budget amounts. The flexible-budget variances are the differences between columns 1 and 3. The following summary explanation is offered by *Level 2* analysis:

$$\text{Flexible-budget variance of operating income} = \begin{pmatrix} \text{Actual operating} \\ \text{income} \end{pmatrix} - \begin{pmatrix} \text{Flexible-budget} \\ \text{operating income} \end{pmatrix}$$

$$= \$1,400 - \$64,000$$

$$= \$62,600 \text{ U}$$

Most managers are not satisfied with such a sparse summary. They want at least a line-by-line listing of revenues, costs, and their flexible-budget variances. The static-budget variance in revenue for a single-product firm is attributable

EXHIBIT 6-5 *(Place a clip on this page for easy reference.)*

Webb Company
Cost Control Performance Report
For the Month Ended April 30, 19_1

	ACTUAL RESULTS	FLEXIBLE BUDGET*	FLEXIBLE-BUDGET VARIANCES†	EXPLANATORY COMMENTS
Units	10,000	10,000	—	
Variable costs:				
Direct material	$270,000	$200,000	$ 70,000 U	Excess price and usage‡
Direct labor	171,600	160,000	11,600 U	Lower price but excess usage‡
Variable factory overhead	32,000	30,000	2,000 U	Miscellaneous reasons
Total variable manufacturing costs	473,600	390,000	83,600 U	
Variable selling and administrative costs	73,000	70,000	3,000 U	Use of air freight
Total variable costs	546,600	460,000	86,600 U	
Fixed costs:				
Fixed manufacturing costs	92,000	96,000	4,000 F	Fewer pay raises
Fixed selling and administrative costs	80,000	80,000	—	
Total fixed costs	172,000	176,000	4,000 F	
Total variable and fixed costs	$718,600	$636,000	$ 82,600 U	

F = Favorable; U = Unfavorable
*Variable costs are 10,000 × $20, $16, $3, and $7, respectively, as shown in Exhibit 6-2.
†This represents a line-by-line breakdown of the variances in column 2 of Exhibit 6-4.
‡This type of analysis is described later in this chapter.

to two causes, volume and price. The sales volume variance has already been discussed. A **price variance** is defined as the difference between actual unit prices and budgeted unit prices multiplied by the actual quantity of goods or services in question (for example, purchased or used.) The flexible-budget revenue variance is wholly explained by changes in unit sales prices. To illustrate, the *Level 2* analysis indicates that sales prices were raised by an average $2 per unit (from $70 to $72 that is, $720,000 ÷ 10,000 units = $72) after the original budget was formulated:

Price variance = (Difference in price) × (Actual quantity of units)

= (Actual price − Budgeted price) × (Actual quantity of units)

= ($72 − $70) × 10,000 units

= $20,000 F, where F means a favorable effect on operating income

A *Level 2* analysis of costs can be conducted for variable and fixed costs on a line-by-line basis, as shown in Exhibit 6-5. If desired, even more details could be gathered. For example, the actual costs and the flexible budgeted amounts of subclassifications of direct material and direct labor might be routinely reported.

Compare the *Level 1* analysis on page 180 with the *Level 2* analysis on page 185. Note how the variable costs had favorable variances when a static budget was used as a basis for comparison. Exhibit 6-1, *Level 1*, shows a favorable variance of $5,400. But the flexible budget provides a more revealing picture. Exhibits 6-4 and 6-5 pinpoint unfavorable variable-cost variances of $86,600, which were partially offset by favorable fixed-cost variances of $4,000.

ANALYSIS LEVEL 3: DETAILED VARIANCES

In most organizations, top management tends to be satisfied with a *Level 2* depth of variance analysis. Subordinate managers, however, tend to seek more detail. For example, marketing managers may want to know sales price variances by sales territory. In our Webb Company illustration, a *Level 3* analysis might indicate that half the sales price variances were attributable to each of two territories. However, the price might also have been raised in one territory and not in the other. For example, suppose half the unit sales were in each territory. A price of $74 in Territory A and $70 in Territory B would produce an average price of $72 and thus the same total sales variance of $20,000 F. The *Level 2* sales price variance would be unchanged, but the *Level 3* sales price variances would change:

	DETAILED SALES PRICE VARIANCES	
ANALYSIS LEVEL 3	If Uniform Price Changes	If Price Change in Territory A Only
Territory A	$10,000 F	$20,000 F
Territory B	10,000 F	—
Total sales price variances	$20,000 F	$20,000 F

For perspective, you may wish to refer to Exhibit 6-6 occasionally. It provides an overall road map of where we have been and where we are going. *Level 0* and *Level 1* are reproductions of Exhibit 6-1. *Level 2* is a reproduction of Exhibit 6-4. *Level 3* was just discussed regarding revenues.

Please do not attach too much importance to the labels *Level 0, Level 1*, and so forth. By themselves such labels have no universal meaning in the field of cost accounting. They merely represent increasingly detailed analysis. We will not probe beyond *Level 3* in this chapter; however, many more levels of detail could be specified. For example, sales price variances might be subdivided within territories by customer, by sales personnel, by product color, by week, and by season of the year. Chapter 24 illustrates how analysis beyond *Level 3* can be informative in various sales and production settings.

The flexible-budget variances for costs are also candidates for further analysis. The remainder of this chapter will show how a *Level 3* analysis uses standards to subdivide these variances into price and efficiency components. Two major catego-

EXHIBIT 6-6 *(Place a clip on this page for easy reference.)*
Webb Company
Overview of Variance Analysis
For the Month Ended April 30, 19_1

ANALYSIS LEVEL 0

		%
Actual operating income	$ 1,400	1.3
Budgeted operating income	112,000	100.0
Static-budget variance	$110,600 U	98.7

ANALYSIS LEVEL 1

	(1) ACTUAL RESULTS	%	(2) STATIC (MASTER) BUDGET	%	(3) (1)–(2) VARIANCE
Units	10,000	—	12,000	—	2,000 U
Revenue (sales)	$720,000	100.0	$840,000	100.0	$120,000 U
Variable costs	546,600	75.9	552,000	65.7	5,400 F
Contribution margin	173,400	24.1	288,000	34.3	114,600 U
Fixed costs	172,000	23.9	176,000	21.0	4,000 F
Operating income	$ 1,400	0.2	$112,000	13.3	$110,600 U

↑ Static budget variance ↑
$110,600 U

ANALYSIS LEVEL 2

	(1) ACTUAL RESULTS	(2) (1) – (3) FLEXIBLE-BUDGET VARIANCES	(3) FLEXIBLE BUDGET	(4) (3) – (5) SALES VOLUME VARIANCES	(5) STATIC (MASTER) BUDGET
Physical units of output	10,000	—	10,000	2,000 U	12,000
Revenues (sales)	$720,000	$20,000 F*	$700,000	$140,000 U‡	$840,000
Variable costs	546,600	86,600 U†	460,000	92,000 F	552,000
Contribution margin	173,400	66,600 U	240,000	48,000 U	288,000
Fixed costs	172,000	4,000 F†	176,000	—	176,000
Operating income	$ 1,400	$62,600 U	$ 64,000	$ 48,000 U	$112,000

Flexible-budget variances, $62,600 U ↑   Sales volume variances, $48,000 U ↑

↑ Static-budget variance, $110,600 U ↑

ANALYSIS LEVEL 3

*DETAILED SALES PRICE VARIANCES		†DETAILED COST VARIANCES	‡DETAILED SALES VOLUME VARIANCES
Territory A	$ 10,000 F	Price and efficiency	Sales quantity variances
Territory B	10,000 F	variances for materials,	Sales mix variances
Sales price variances	$ 20,000 F	labor, and other costs	(These aspects are
		(Covered in this chapter.)	covered in Chapter 24.)

F = Favorable, U = Unfavorable effect on operating income.

187

ries of costs will be explored, direct materials and direct labor. The next chapter explains variance analysis for factory overhead.

STANDARDS FOR MATERIALS AND LABOR

Distinction between budgets and standards

Many organizations have budgeting systems that are confined to a static budget. That is, a master budget is prepared and performance is not evaluated beyond the *Level 1* analysis in Exhibit 6-6. However, when an organization invests in a flexible budgeting system, it typically develops standards for major costs such as direct material and direct labor.

Standard costs are carefully predetermined costs that are usually expressed on a per-unit basis; they are target costs, costs that should be attained. Standard costs help to build budgets, gauge performance, obtain product costs, and save bookkeeping costs. Standard costs are the building blocks of a flexible budgeting and feedback system.

A set of standards outlines how a task should be accomplished and how much it should cost. As work is being done, actual costs incurred are compared with standard costs to reveal variances. This feedback helps discover better ways of adhering to standards, of altering standards, and of accomplishing objectives.

What is the difference between a standard amount and a budgeted amount? If standards are currently attainable, as they are assumed to be in this book, there is no conceptual difference. The term *standard cost* usually refers to a *single* finished unit of output. In contrast, *budgeted cost* usually refers to a *total* amount. For example, suppose the Webb Company's standard for direct materials is four pounds of input allowed at $5 per pound, or 4 × $5 = $20 per unit of output. The standard cost in Exhibit 6-2 shows:

	BUDGET FORMULA PER UNIT	VARIOUS LEVELS OF VOLUME		
		9,000	11,000	13,000
Units	1	9,000	11,000	13,000
Direct material	$20	$180,000	$220,000	$260,000

The standard cost is $20 per finished unit. The budgeted cost is $180,000 if 9,000 units are to be produced. Think of a standard as a budget for a single unit. In many companies, the terms *budgeted performance* and *standard performance* are used loosely and often interchangeably.

Cost-benefit approach to variances

Exhibits 6-5 and 6-6 underscore the cost-benefit approach to management accounting systems. Some costs may receive heavy analysis; others, almost no analysis. For example, the direct-material and direct-labor variances in Exhibit 6-5 can be subdivided into price and efficiency variances, as will be shown; direct-material costs constitute 37.6% ($270,000/$718,600) of the total actual costs and direct labor 23.9% ($171,600/$718,600) of total actual costs in Exhibit 6-5. Webb Company managers may decide not to have subdivisions of the other costs, such as fixed manufacturing costs, beyond the flexible-budget variances in Exhibit 6-5; fixed manufacturing costs constitute only 12.8% ($92,000/$718,600) of total actual costs.

In addition, they may decide to analyze materials on a daily basis, labor on a weekly basis, and overhead on a monthly basis.[3]

Standard costs allowed

Consider the following standards for the manufacture of the Webb Company's units:

Direct materials	Four pounds of input allowed @ $5 = $20 per unit of output
Direct labor	Two hours of input allowed @ $8 = $16 per unit of output

In addition to the preceding data, the following data were compiled regarding *actual* performance:

Good units produced	10,000	Direct-labor costs	$171,600
Direct-material costs	$270,000	Hours of input	22,000
Pounds of input purchased and used	50,000	Labor price per hour	$7.80
Price per pound	$5.40		

These additional data permit the subdivision of the flexible-budget variances in Exhibit 6-5 into separate price and efficiency variances:

	ACTUAL COSTS INCURRED	FLEXIBLE BUDGET	FLEXIBLE BUDGET VARIANCE	PRICE VARIANCE*	EFFICIENCY VARIANCE*
Direct material	$270,000	$200,000	$70,000 U	$20,000 U	$50,000 U
Direct labor	171,600	160,000	11,600 U	$ 4,400 F	$16,000 U
*Computations to be explained shortly.					

The flexible-budget totals for variable costs such as direct materials and direct labor are also sometimes expressed as *total standard costs allowed*. They are computed as follows:

$$\text{Units of good output} \times \text{Input allowed per unit of output} \times \text{Standard unit price of input} = \text{Total standard cost allowed}$$

Direct materials: 10,000 units of good output × 4 pounds × $5 per pound = $200,000

Direct labor: 10,000 units of good output × 2 hours × $8 per hour = $160,000

---

[3]In other organizations, the cost-benefit approach can imply that a detailed variance analysis be made of direct materials and fixed manufacturing costs, but not of labor costs. For example, some organizations with highly automated production operations do not even record labor costs as an identifiable cost category due to their being such a small component of total costs; labor costs are combined with other indirect manufacturing costs into a single "conversion cost" category. See A. Seed, "Cost Accounting in the Age of Robotics," *Management Accounting*, October 1984, pp. 39–43. Further discussion of this area is in Chapters 12, 13, and 17.

Before proceeding, note especially that the flexible-budget amounts (that is, the total standard costs allowed) are keyed to an initial question: What was the *output* achieved? No isolation of efficiency variances in a standard-cost system can occur without the measurement of *outputs* as well as *inputs*.

Definitions of price and efficiency variances

Price variance was defined and discussed earlier in conjunction with revenue. Its definition also holds with respect to costs. The other component of the flexible-budget variance is the efficiency variance. Definitions follow:

Price variance—the difference between actual unit prices and budgeted unit prices multiplied by the actual quantity of goods or services in question (for example, purchased or used)

Efficiency variance—the difference between the quantity of actual inputs used (such as pounds of materials) and the quantity of inputs that *should have been used* (the flexible budget for any quantity of *units of good output achieved*), multiplied by the budgeted price

Generally, these variances separate the factors subject to the manager's direct influence from those that are not. Therefore price factors are distinguished from efficiency factors. Why? Because price factors are usually less subject to quick control, mainly because of external events such as general economic conditions and unpredictable price fluctuations. Although price factors are frequently regarded as uncontrollable, separating them excludes their often confusing effect on other variances.

Price variances are computed not only for their own sake but to obtain a sharper focus on efficiency. In this way, efficiency can be measured by holding unit prices constant. Thus managers' judgments about efficiency are unaffected by price changes. Efficiency variances have an important underlying assumption: All unit prices are standard prices that are sometimes called *budgeted, estimated,* or *predetermined prices.*

Price and efficiency variance computations

When calculating the price variance, hold inputs constant at the actual inputs purchased. When calculating efficiency variances, hold price constant at the standard unit price of inputs.

Consider the price variance:

$$\text{Price Variance} = \left(\begin{array}{c} \text{Difference in unit} \\ \text{price of inputs} \end{array} \right) \times \begin{array}{c} \text{Actual inputs} \\ \text{purchased} \end{array}$$

For direct materials:

$$= (\$5.40 - \$5.00) \times 50,000 \text{ pounds}$$

$$= \$20,000 \text{ Unfavorable (U)}$$

For direct labor:

$$= (\$7.80 - \$8.00) \times 22,000 \text{ hours}$$

$$= \$4,400 \text{ Favorable (F)}$$

Consider the efficiency variance: For any given level of output (that is, actual units produced), the efficiency variance is the difference between the inputs that should have been used and the inputs that were actually used—holding unit input prices constant at the standard unit price:[4]

$$\begin{array}{l} \dfrac{\text{Efficiency}}{\text{variance}} = \left(\dfrac{\text{Inputs}}{\text{actually used}} - \dfrac{\text{Inputs that should}}{\text{have been used}} \right) \times \dfrac{\text{Standard unit}}{\text{price of inputs}} \\[2em] \dfrac{\text{Efficiency}}{\text{variance}} = \left(\dfrac{\text{Actual pounds}}{\text{or hours used}} - \dfrac{\text{Standard pounds or hours}}{\text{allowed for good output}} \right) \times \dfrac{\text{Standard unit}}{\text{price of inputs}} \end{array}$$

Direct materials:

$$= [50{,}000 - (10{,}000 \text{ units} \times 4 \text{ pounds})] \times \$5.00$$

$$= (50{,}000 - 40{,}000) \times \$5.00$$

$$= \$50{,}000 \text{ U}$$

Direct labor:

$$= [22{,}000 - (10{,}000 \text{ units} \times 2 \text{ hours})] \times \$8.00$$

$$= (22{,}000 - 20{,}000) \times \$8.00$$

$$= \$16{,}000 \text{ U}$$

Measuring and expressing output

Exhibit 6-7 is a graphical representation of the analysis of direct labor. The cost function is linear, sloping upward at a standard price of $8.00 per hour. We can read the total standard costs that would be allowed for any given quantity of output. Note that quantity is expressed in hours rather than in physical units of product. *This is commonly done because most departments have an assortment of products; hours become a useful common denominator for measuring the total level of all production.*

Standard-cost systems frequently do not express output as, say, 10,000 ash-trays. Instead output is expressed as 20,000 **standard hours allowed** (also called **standard hours earned, standard hours worked,** or, most accurately, **standard hours of input allowed for good output produced**). This is another key concept in standard costing, so be sure to grasp it before reading on.

Standard hours allowed are the number of standard hours that should have been used to obtain any given quantity of output (that is, actual goods produced or actual outputs achieved).

---

[4]Algebraically, these variances are

$$V_p = (AP - SP) \times AQ$$

and

$$V_e = (AQ - SQ) \times SP$$

V_p = price variance, V_e = efficiency variance, AP = actual unit price of inputs, SP = standard unit price of inputs, AQ = actual quantity of inputs, SQ = standard quantity of inputs allowed for good output.

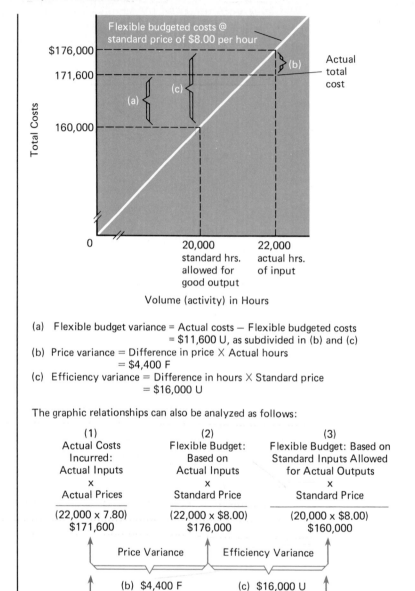

(a) Flexible budget variance = Actual costs − Flexible budgeted costs
        = $11,600 U, as subdivided in (b) and (c)
(b) Price variance = Difference in price × Actual hours
        = $4,400 F
(c) Efficiency variance = Difference in hours × Standard price
        = $16,000 U

The graphic relationships can also be analyzed as follows:

(1) Actual Costs Incurred: Actual Inputs × Actual Prices	(2) Flexible Budget: Based on Actual Inputs × Standard Price	(3) Flexible Budget: Based on Standard Inputs Allowed for Actual Outputs × Standard Price
(22,000 x 7.80) $171,600	(22,000 x $8.00) $176,000	(20,000 x $8.00) $160,000

Price Variance   Efficiency Variance

(b) $4,400 F   (c) $16,000 U
Flexible Budget Variance

(a) $11,600 U

U = Unfavorable; F = Favorable

Substitute terminology

To underscore their basic similarity, the two primary variances for both direct material and direct labor are designated here as price and efficiency variances. In practice, however, be alert for a variety of terms that are sometimes used to designate these variances. Substitute terminology includes:

For price variance: **Rate variance** (popular term with respect to direct labor)
For efficiency variance: **Quantity variance** or **usage variance** (popular term with respect to direct material)

In standard-cost systems, the concept of flexible budget, in contrast to static budget, is a key to the analysis of variances. **For brevity, the term *budget variance* will frequently be used henceforth instead of *flexible-budget variance*. For example, Exhibit 6-7 might have used *budget variance* instead of *flexible-budget variance*.**

IMPACT OF INVENTORIES

To concentrate on fundamentals, our Webb Company illustration assumed:

1. There were no finished-goods inventories at the beginning or end of the accounting period. All units were produced and sold in the same accounting period.
2. There were no direct-materials inventories. All direct materials were purchased and used in the same accounting period.

Suppose production and sales are unequal. Then the sales volume variance is the difference between the master budget and the flexible budget for *the number of units sold*. Chapter 8 provides details about the effects of inventories on a standard cost system.

Suppose the quantity of direct materials purchased and the quantity used are unequal. Generally, managers desire rapid feedback for control. They want to pinpoint variances as early as practical. In the case of material prices, that control point is when materials are purchased rather than when they are used. **Consequently, direct-material price variances are usually based on the quantities purchased, and direct-material efficiency variances are always based on the quantities used.**

Reconsider our illustration by assuming that 55,000 pounds were acquired by the purchasing department during the month, although only 50,000 pounds were used by the production department. The price variance would be 55,000 pounds $\times$ ($5.40 − $5.00) = $22,000, unfavorable.

GENERAL-LEDGER ENTRIES

Illustrative entries

General-ledger accounting for direct material and direct labor has been straightforward until this chapter. Two major inventory accounts have included:

Stores		*Work-in-Process*	
Actual costs of direct material purchased		Actual costs of direct material and direct labor used	

The general-ledger procedures in standard-cost systems introduce some separate accounts for variances.

General-ledger entries for standard-cost systems are usually *monthly* summaries of detailed variance analyses that were computed from day to day.

Using the data in our earlier illustration, but assuming the 55,000-pound purchases just described, the actual quantities of direct materials purchased are charged to Stores at standard prices. As Entry 1a shows, this approach isolates (that is, separately identifies) price variances for direct materials as early as feasible:

1a. Stores (55,000 lbs. × $5.00)	275,000	
Direct-material price variance (55,000 lbs. × $.40)	22,000	
Accounts payable (55,000 lbs. × $5.40)		297,000
To record direct materials purchased.		

The direct-materials efficiency variance is isolated when standard quantities allowed times standard unit prices are debited to Work in Process:

1b. Work in process (40,000 lbs. × $5.00)	200,000	
Direct-material efficiency variance (10,000 lbs. × $5.00)	50,000	
Stores (50,000 lbs. × $5.00)		250,000
To record direct materials used.		

Note that unfavorable variances are always debits and favorable variances are always credits.

Accrued Payroll is accounted for at *actual* wage rates. Work in Process is charged at standard quantities allowed times *standard rates*, and the direct-labor variances are recognized:

2. Work in process	160,000	
Direct-labor efficiency variance	16,000	
Direct-labor price variance		4,400
Accrued payroll		171,600
To record liability for direct-labor costs.		

T-accounts would appear as follows:

Stores		Direct-Material Price Variance	
1a. Actual quantity purchased × standard unit price, 275,000	1b. Actual quantity used × standard unit price, 250,000	1a. Actual quantity purchased × difference in unit price, 22,000	

194

Work-in-Process		Direct-Material Efficiency Variance	
Standard quantity used × standard unit price; 1b. 200,000 2. 160,000		1b. Difference in quantity used × standard unit price, 50,000	

Direct-Labor Price Variance		Direct-Labor Efficiency Variance	
	2. Actual quantity purchased × difference in unit price, 4,400	2. Difference in quantity used × standard unit price, 16,000	

The major advantage of this system is its stress on the control feature of standard costs, whereby all variances are isolated as early as feasible.

Disposition of variances

Like the disposition of underapplied or overapplied overhead discussed in Chapter 4, price and efficiency variances are either written off immediately to cost of goods sold or prorated among the inventories and cost of goods sold. A full discussion is found in Chapter 8, pages 268–73.

Costs of data gathering

At first glance, it might appear that standard-cost systems would always be more costly to operate than other systems. Obviously, a startup investment must be made to develop the standards; but the ongoing costs can be even less than so-called actual-cost systems. For example, it is more economical to simply carry all inventories at standard unit prices. Thus this system avoids the difficulty and extra data collection costs and confusion of making cost-flow assumptions such as first-in, first-out, or last-in, first-out.

Of course, standard-cost systems will be more costly if they are run in complete parallel with an actual-cost system (see Chapter 2) or normal-cost system (see Chapter 4). For instance, if actual direct-material costs and actual direct-labor costs continue to be traced to individual products even though a standard-cost system is in use, the costs of recordkeeping will increase.

On the other hand, many standard-cost systems have been adopted for the *major* purpose of saving recordkeeping costs. A standard-cost system can be designed so that

1. No "actual" costs of stores, work in process, and finished goods are traced to batches of product on a day-to-day basis. Only records of physical counts are kept.
2. Actual consumption of direct material and direct labor can be totaled by operation or department for, say, a month without tracing such consumption to jobs. Feedback on performance can be based on these actual totals of input compared with the total standard allowed inputs for the output during the month. However, the major advantage of this procedure is the simplicity of data collection.

Current attainability

How demanding should standards be? Should they express perfection, or should they allow for the various factors that prevent perfect performance?

Perfection, ideal, maximum efficiency, or *theoretical standards* reflect industrial engineers' dreams of a "factory heaven." Perfection standard costs are the absolute minimum costs that are possible under the best conceivable operating conditions, using existing specifications and equipment. Perfection standards, like other standards, are used where the management feels that they provide psychologically productive goals.

Currently attainable standards are standards that should be reached under very efficient operating conditions. They are difficult but possible to achieve. Attainable standards are looser than perfection standards because of allowance for normal spoilage, ordinary machine breakdowns, and lost time. However, attainable standards are usually set tight enough so that the operating people will consider the achievement of standard performance to be a satisfying accomplishment. In other words, variances are more likely to be slightly unfavorable than favorable—but favorable variances may be attained by a little better than expected efficiency.

Currently attainable standards are the most widely used because the resulting standard costs can serve many purposes simultaneously and because they have the most appealing motivational impact on employees.[5]

Expected variances

Currently attainable standards may be used simultaneously for product costing, master budgets, and motivation. Throughout the illustrations and problems in this book, unless otherwise stated, currently attainable standards are assumed to be in use.

If standards are not currently attainable because they are perfection standards, the amount budgeted for financial (cash) planning purposes should differ from the standard. Otherwise projected income and cash disbursements will be forecast incorrectly. In such cases, perfection standards may be used for compiling performance reports, but **expected variances** are stipulated in the budget for cash planning. For example, if unusually strict labor standards are used, the standard cost per finished unit may be $16 even though top management anticipates an unfavorable efficiency variance of, say, $1.60 per unit. In the master budget the total labor costs allowed would be $17.60 per unit: $16.00 plus an expected variance of $1.60. In our example, a master budget could conceivably include the following item:

Direct labor:	
Budget allowance shown on departmental performance report	$160,000
Expected variance that will appear in cash budget	16,000
Total budget allowance for cash planning	$176,000

[5]W. Cress and J. Pettijohn, in "A Survey of Budget-related Planning and Control Policies and Procedures," *Journal of Accounting Education,* 3, No. 2 (Fall 1985), 74, report that 50% of the companies surveyed use expected actual (but difficult to attain) standards; 42%, standards based on average past performance; and 8%, maximum efficiency (theoretical or perfection) standards. The same issue contains articles by J. Hughes on variance analyses for local governments and J. Lere on alternative standard-cost entries.

Developing the standards	The standard-setting and budget-setting process in an organization often is primarily the responsibility of the line personnel directly involved. The relative tightness of the budget is the result of face-to-face discussion and bargaining between the manager and his or her immediate superior. The budgetary accountants, the industrial engineers, and the market researchers should extend all desired technical assistance and advice, but the final decisions ordinarily should not be theirs. The line manager is the person who is supposed to accept and live with the budget or standard.

The job of the accounting department is (a) to price the physical standards—that is, to express the physical standards in the form of dollars and cents; and (b) to report operating performance in comparison with standards.

Textbooks generally give the impression that standard costs are always based on technical engineering studies and rigorous specifications. Accurate measurement is indeed the foundation for control. However, although a rigorous approach is desirable, it should be remembered that less-scientific standards may still provide a useful way of presenting information to stimulate corrective action.

Trade-offs among variances	Managers sometimes make bargain purchases or combine available resources to save overall costs. For example, a quantity of raw material having a few inferior characteristics (perhaps a lower grade of lumber) might be consciously acquired at an unusually low price. This material might lead to unusually heavy spoilage or excessive labor times in order to produce a finished product that will meet the standard quality specifications. Nevertheless, the manager may have enough discretion to proceed. The aim would be to reduce the *total* costs of manufacturing by obtaining favorable material price variances at the cost of a smaller amount of expected unfavorable material and labor efficiency variances.

A standard-cost system should not be a straitjacket that prevents the manager from looking at the overall company objectives. Too often, each unfavorable variance is regarded as obviously bad; and each favorable variance is regarded as obviously good. If the manager guesses wrong, and the unfavorable material and labor efficiency variances exceed the favorable material price variance, the outcome of the bargain purchase was unfavorable despite the favorable label pinned on the price variance. Similarly, if the manager guesses correctly, so that the favorable price variance exceeds the unfavorable efficiency variances, the outcome was favorable despite the unfavorable label pinned on the efficiency variances. There are many interdependencies among activities; a particular "unfavorable" or a "favorable" label should not lead the manager to jump to conclusions about what happened. By themselves, such labels are attention directors, not answer givers.

CONTROLLABILITY AND VARIANCES

Responsibility for material variances	In most companies, the *acquisition* of materials or merchandise entails different control decisions than their *use*. Thus the responsibility for explaining price variances usually rests with the purchasing officer, and the responsibility for explaining efficiency variances usually rests with the production manager or sales manager.

Price variances are often regarded as measures of forecasting ability rather than of failure to buy at specified prices. Some control over the price variance is obtainable by getting many quotations, buying in economical lot sizes, taking advantage of cash discounts, and selecting the most economical means of delivery. Price variances may lead to improvements in methods of forecasting and decisions to change suppliers or freight carriers. (The chapter Appendix explores inflation and price variances.)

However, failure to meet price standards may result from a sudden rush of sales orders or from unanticipated changes in production schedules, which in turn may require the purchasing officer to buy at uneconomical prices or to request delivery by air freight. In such cases, the responsibility for explaining the price variance may rest with the sales manager or the head of production scheduling, rather than with the purchasing officer.

When competition intensifies or financial crises loom, managers often search for improvements in their control systems. For example, consider the purchasing function. A few companies accept prices as market-driven and essentially uncontrollable. However, most companies believe that skillful managers can obtain goods and services at favorable prices and also obtain other key results. Examples of the latter are meeting schedules, meeting quality requirements, forecasting prices accurately, guiding make-or-buy decisions, and obtaining appropriate packaging, modes and costs of delivery, and extended payment terms.

Consider another example, General Motors (GM). In negotiations with key suppliers, GM requests justification via a "piece-parts explosion," which consists of dividing the part into its individual components. When a supplier seeks an increase in price, GM expects the supplier to provide evidence regarding which components of the part are increasing in cost.

Responsibility for labor variances

In most companies, because of union contracts or other predictable factors, labor prices can be foreseen with much greater accuracy than can prices of materials. Therefore labor price variances tend to be relatively insignificant.

Labor, unlike material and supplies, cannot be stored for later use. The purchase and use of labor occur simultaneously. For this reason, labor price variances are usually charged to the same manager who is responsible for labor usage.

Labor price variances may be traceable to faulty predictions of the labor rates. However, the more likely causes include (1) the use of a single average standard labor price for a given operation that is, in fact, performed by individuals earning different rates because of seniority; (2) the assignment of a worker earning, perhaps, $12 per hour to a given operation that should be assigned to a less-skilled worker earning, say, $10 per hour; and (3) the payment of hourly rates, instead of prescribed piece rates, because of low productivity.

Material efficiency

The physical "engineered" relationship of inputs to outputs is central to the development of standards for direct material, direct labor, or any other factor of production. Therefore daily and weekly reports to first-line supervisors are often expressed in physical terms only—gallons used, pounds consumed, hours of input, and so on. An efficiency variance may be expressed in dollars by multiplying the physical quantity variance by the standard unit price.

Exhibit 6-8 is a **standard bill of materials.** It specifies the physical quantities allowed for manufacturing a specified number of acceptable finished units. In many companies, when production of a product is about to begin, the standard bill becomes the stores requisition. The storeroom then issues the standard amount of materials allowed. As production occurs, any *additional* materials needed may be

EXHIBIT 6-8
Standard Bill of Materials

Assembly No. b		Description Tray Table
Part Number	Number Required	Description
A 1426	4 sq. ft.	Plastic sheet — Pearl grey
455	1/8 lb.	Adhesive
642	1	Table top
714	4	Steel legs
961	1	Nut and bolt kit

withdrawn from stores only by submitting an **excess materials requisition.** This is a form filled out by production employees to obtain any materials needed in excess of the standard amount allowed for the scheduled output. The supervisor must sign the requisition, so he or she is immediately informed of excess usage.

A periodic summary of excess materials requisitions provides the total unfavorable efficiency variance. If performance is better than standard, special returned-materials forms are used to calculate favorable efficiency variances. Possible reasons for efficiency variances include quality, workmanship, choice of materials, mix of materials, and faulty standards.

Mutual effects   Exhibit 6-9 shows how the $20,000 original price variance for materials could be subdivided:

1. Pure price variance = Difference in price × Standard quantity (instead of Actual quantity)
2. Combined price-efficiency variance = Difference in price × Difference in quantity

1. Pure price variance = $.40 × 40,000	=	$16,000 U
2. Combined variance = $.40 × 10,000	=	4,000 U
Price variance as originally calculated	=	$20,000 U

The importance of this refinement depends on the significance and usefulness of isolating the combined variance (also called a joint variance or a budget variance). Where executive bonuses depend on variances, this refinement may be necessary. For example, an unfavorable total-price variance, as ordinarily computed, could be partially attributable to inefficient usage. Thus a part of the price variance in our example would not have arisen if quantities used had not exceeded standard: (50,000 lbs. − 40,000 lbs.)($5.40 − $5.00) = $4,000. In this book, we will not refine our analysis this far; all of the $20,000 is called price variance. That is, we will consider the price variance to be the sum of the pure price variance and the combined price-efficiency variance. The philosophy of responsibility accounting supports this practice. Why? Because the responsibility of the purchasing manager

EXHIBIT 6-9
Graphic Analysis of Variances

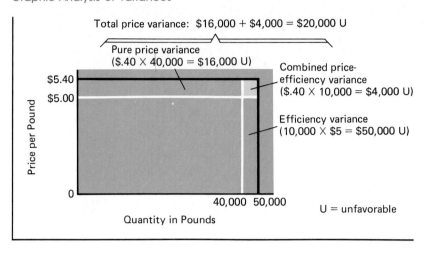

EXHIBIT 6-10
Operations Routing Sheet

MASTER OPERATIONS LIST

Part Name _____ Fuel pump body with bushings _____ Part Number _____ B-489 _____

Stock Specifications _____ Grey iron casting _____ Standard Quantity _____ 200 _____

Operation Number	Department Number	Standard Time Allowed in Minutes		Description of Operation
		Setup	Operation Per Unit	
20	27	90	10.2	Drill, bore, face, chamfer and ream
25	29	18	.7	Face and chamfer hub
30	29	12	1.5	Mill eng. fit pad
35	31	18	8.0	Drill and tap complete
40	29	12	1.5	Mill clearance
45	29	—	1.8	Clean and grind hose connection
50	29	12	2.3	Press in 2 bushings G-98 and face flange on mandrel
	13			Inspect
	21			To stockroom

is usually deemed to include buying for *all* needs regardless of whether the materials are used efficiently.

The human element makes the setting of labor efficiency standards (also called *time, usage, quantity,* or *performance* standards) a complicated task. As may be expected, disputes over proper standards are much more likely to arise over labor efficiency standards than over material efficiency standards.

Time standards are usually set for each operation. In turn, **master operations lists,** such as the Operations Routing Sheet in Exhibit 6-10, may be compiled for routing and scheduling a variety of products through a series of operations or processes.

The source documents for variance reports are usually some form of work ticket showing the actual time used. These work tickets are analyzed and variances are coded and classified. The classifications are almost always by responsibility (that is, by cost center), and often by operations, products, orders, and causes. Thus a work ticket may have a number designating departmental responsibility and another number designating the cause of the variance. Examples of causes include machinery breakdowns, rework, faulty material, use of nonpreferred equipment, and use of nonpreferred workers.

Absenteeism can dramatically affect efficiency. A General Motors executive has commented:

> When deer season opens, production drops from 70 to 35 cars per hour. Workers are shifted around to handle unfamiliar jobs. Quality declines. And the workers get paid overtime. . . . We have begun computerizing medical excuses signed by local doctors to determine if any definitive pattern exists among the chronic absentees.

Setup time is the time needed to prepare equipment and related resources for producing a specified number of finished units or operations. Machines and accessory equipment often must be adjusted and "made ready" before a particular operation or job can commence. This setup time is easily traceable to an operation or a job, yet its total cost is seldom affected by whether 100 pieces or 2,000 pieces are subsequently processed. The question then is whether setup costs should be treated as direct labor or as a part of factory overhead. No categorical answer can be given. It seems clear that if the length of production runs fluctuates wildly, setup costs should not ordinarily be regarded as direct labor, because the cost *per unit* of product would fluctuate solely because of the length of production run.

For analytical purposes and for cost-control follow-up, setup costs should not be commingled and averaged with the regular direct-labor costs even if it appears desirable to trace setup costs to specific jobs or operations. Most standard-cost systems have economic (standard) lot sizes for production runs. Often setup costs are allowed for in the standard direct-labor cost per unit by allocating the setup labor for each operation over the quantity in the economic lot. This practice may be suitable for product-costing purposes; but it has drawbacks for cost-control purposes, especially where economic lot sizes are seldom adhered to, because it mixes together two dissimilar elements that are subject to different control features. As a minimum, then, setup costs should always be coded so that they can be sharply distinguished from operating-labor costs. In this book, we will assume that setup costs are classified as a part of overhead (and ideally, separately identified).

When should variances be investigated? Frequently the answer is based on subjective judgments, or rules of thumb. **The most troublesome aspect of feedback is deciding when a variance (either favorable or unfavorable) is significant enough to warrant management's attention.** For some items, a small deviation may prompt follow-up. For other items, a minimum dollar amount or 5%, 10%, or 25% deviations from budget may be necessary before investigations commence. Of course, a 4% variance in a $1 million material cost may deserve more attention than a 20% variance in a $10,000 repair cost. Therefore rules such as "Investigate all variances exceeding $5,000, or 25% of standard cost, whichever is lower" are common.

Variance analysis is subject to the same cost-benefit test as other phases of a control system. The trouble with the foregoing rules of thumb is that they are too frequently based on subjective assessments, guesses, or hunches. The field of statistics offers tools that can help decisions regarding variance analysis. These tools help answer the cost-benefit question, and they help to separate variances caused by random events from variances that are controllable.

Accounting systems have traditionally implied that a standard is a single acceptable measure. Practically, accountants (and everybody else) realize that the standard is a *band* or *range* of possible acceptable outcomes. Consequently, accountants expect variances to fluctuate randomly within some normal limits.

By definition, a random variance per se is within this band or range. It calls for no corrective action to an existing process; random variances are attributable to chance rather than to management's implementation decisions. For a further discussion, see Chapter 24.

SUMMARY

Standard-cost systems aid management predictions and provide a framework for judging performance. Actual costs are compared with standard costs to obtain variances. Variances raise questions that lead to improvements in operations.

Currently attainable standards are the most widely used because they usually have the most desirable motivational impact and because they can be used for a variety of accounting purposes, including financial planning, as well as for monitoring departmental performance.

When standards are currently attainable, there is no real difference between standards and budgets. A standard is a *unit* concept, whereas a budget is a *total* concept. In a sense, the standard is the budget for one unit.

Material and labor variances are primarily divided into two categories: (a) price and (b) efficiency. Price variances are computed by multiplying differences in price by actual quantities purchased. Efficiency variances are computed by multiplying differences in quantities by standard prices.

General-ledger treatments for standard costs vary considerably. Variances should be isolated quickly for prompt management attention.

Variances should be assigned to the person primarily responsible. Otherwise the investigative follow-ups of reported variances—where the real payoff lies—will be fruitless.

problem 1 Consider some changed data in the Webb Company illustration in the chapter. All the necessary original and changed data follow:

Actual unit selling price for all units sold, $75	
Unit sales, 10,800	
Budgeted or standard amounts per unit:	
Selling price	$70
Direct material (4 pounds @ $5.00)	20
Direct labor (2 hours @ $8.00)	16
Variable factory overhead (2 hours @ $1.50)	3
Variable selling and administrative costs	7
Budgeted fixed factory overhead, $96,000	
Actual fixed factory overhead, $92,000	
Budget and actual fixed selling and administrative costs, $80,000	
Actual variable selling and administrative costs, $73,000	
Other actual data:	
Direct-material costs $270,000	
Direct-labor costs, $171,600	
Variable factory overhead, $32,000	

Required | Prepare an exhibit similar to Exhibit 6-4, page 183.

solution 1 The solution is in Exhibit 6-11. Note that the dramatic effect of the sales price increase is ($75 − $70) × 10,800 units = $54,000, favorable. Thus the expected operating income of $83,200 at the achieved volume level was exceeded despite the $49,800 of unfavorable variable-cost variances.

EXHIBIT 6-11
Summary of Performance
For the Month Ended April 30, 19_1

	(1) ACTUAL RESULTS	(2) (1)–(3) FLEXIBLE-BUDGET VARIANCES	(3) FLEXIBLE BUDGET	(4) (3)–(5) SALES VOLUME VARIANCES	(5) STATIC (MASTER) BUDGET
Physical units of output	10,800	—	10,800	1,200 U	12,000
Revenue (sales)	$810,000	$54,000 F	$756,000	$84,000 U	$840,000
Variable costs	546,600*	49,800 U	496,800‡	55,200 F	552,000
Contribution margin	263,400	4,200 F	259,200	28,800 U	288,000
Fixed costs	172,000†	4,000 F	176,000	—	176,000
Operating income	$ 91,400	$ 8,200 F	$ 83,200	$28,800 U	$112,000

Flexible-budget variances, $8,200 F ↑   Sales volume variances, $28,800 U ↑

↑ Static-budget variances, $20,600 U ↑

*Direct material	$270,000	†Fixed factory overhead	$ 92,000
Direct labor	171,600	Fixed selling and administrative costs	80,000
Variable factory overhead	32,000	Total fixed costs	$172,000
Selling and administrative costs	73,000		
Total variable costs	$546,600	‡10,800 × ($20 + $16 + $3 + $7) = $496,800	

Consider the following for the O'Shea Company for April, when 2,000 finished units were produced:

Direct materials used, 4,400 pounds. The standard allowance per finished unit is two pounds at $5 per pound. Six thousand pounds were purchased at $5.50 per pound, a total of $33,000.

Actual direct-labor hours were 6,500 at a total cost of $40,300. The standard labor cost per finished unit was $18. Standard labor time allowed is three hours per unit.

Required

1. Journal entries for a "normal"-cost system as described in Chapter 4. That is, "actual" amounts for direct materials and direct labor are charged to Work in Process.
2. Use the format shown at the bottom of Exhibit 6-7, page 192, to calculate the direct-material price and efficiency variances and the direct-labor price and efficiency variances. The direct-material price variance will be based on a flexible budget for actual quantities purchased, but the efficiency variance will be based on a flexible budget for actual quantities used.
3. Journal entries for a "standard"-cost system that isolates variances as early as feasible.

solution 2 1.

	NORMAL-COST SYSTEM	
Stores or direct-material inventory	33,000	
Accounts payable		33,000
Work in process (4,400 × $5.50)	24,200	
Stores		24,200
Work in process (6,500 × $6.20)	40,300	
Accrued payroll		40,300

2. Exhibit 6-12 presents a general framework for analyzing variances. It may seem awkward at first, but upon review you will discover that it provides perspective and insight.

EXHIBIT 6-12
Framework for Analysis of Variances

	(1) ACTUAL COSTS INCURRED: ACTUAL INPUTS × ACTUAL PRICE	(2) FLEXIBLE BUDGET: BASED ON ACTUAL INPUTS × STANDARD PRICE		(3) FLEXIBLE BUDGET: BASED ON STANDARD INPUTS ALLOWED FOR ACTUAL OUTPUTS × STANDARD PRICE
DIRECT MATERIALS	(6,000 × $5.50) $33,000	(6,000 × $5.00) $30,000	(4,400 × $5.00) $22,000	(4,000 × $5.00) $20,000
	(6,000 × $.50) Price Variance, $3,000 U		(400 × $5.00) Efficiency Variance, 2,000 U	
DIRECT LABOR	(6,500 × $6.20) $40,300	(6,500 × $6.00) $39,000		(2,000 × $18.00) or (6,000 × $6.00) $36,000
	(6,500 × $.20) Price Variance, $1,300 U		(500 × $6.00) Efficiency Variance, $3,000 U	

Stores or direct-material inventory (6,000 × $5.00)	30,000	
Direct-material price variance	3,000	
Accounts payable		33,000
Work in process (4,000 × $5.00)	20,000	
Direct-material efficiency variance	2,000	
Stores (4,400 × $5.00)		22,000
Work in process (2,000 × $18.00)	36,000	
Direct-labor price variance	1,300	
Direct-labor efficiency variance	3,000	
Accrued payroll		40,300

Terms to Learn

This chapter and the Glossary at the end of the book contain definitions of the following important terms:

> *currently attainable standards (p. 196)*   *effectiveness (184)*   *efficiency (184)*
> *efficiency variance (190)*   *excess materials requisition (199)*
> *expected variance (196)*   *flexible budget (181)*   *flexible-budget variance (183)*
> *master operations lists (201)*   *price variance (190)*   *quantity variance (193)*
> *rate variance (193)*   *sales volume variance (183)*   *setup time (201)*
> *standard bill of materials (198)*   *standard costs (188)*
> *standard hours allowed (191)*   *standard hours earned (191)*
> *standard hours of input allowed for good output produced (191)*
> *standard hours worked (191)*   *static budget (181)*   *usage variance (193)*
> *variable budget (181)*

Special Points and Pitfalls

The flexible-budget variance enables the manager to separate the effects of sales volume from other explanations of why the original (static) budget was not achieved.

In turn, the flexible-budget variance is often subdivided into its price and efficiency components. Efficiency is measured by comparing inputs with outputs. Therefore a common measure of inputs and outputs is necessary to obtain an efficiency variance.

Price variances enhance understanding of the influence of prices on actual results. In addition, price variances permit the exclusion of price effects from *other* variances. The definitions of efficiency *and* sales volume variances have a noteworthy common assumption: All unit prices are *standard* or *budgeted* prices.

As a minimum, be sure to solve the problems for self-study before proceeding to the next chapter. Inevitably, the first question to ask in solving standard-cost problems is, What was the good output achieved? The second question is, What were the standard direct-labor hours allowed for the good output achieved? Because more than one product is frequently produced, output is usually expressed in terms of standard hours allowed, which is also called standard hours earned.

Accounting for price changes (regardless of whether they are called price fluctuations, inflation, deflation, escalation, or by some other name) can be encompassed within a flexible-budget and standard-cost system. The challenge is to develop credible standards that provide useful information for planning and for judging performance.

Even when general inflation eases, prices of many materials fluctuate wildly from month to month and year to year. Examples are petroleum, many metals, lumber, and computer chips.

Materials and services acquired from outsiders are often a large percentage of a company's total manufacturing costs. Skillful management of the purchasing function can save costs, enhance quality, and smooth operations throughout a company. Significant price changes in materials and parts are among the major problems that periodically plague top management. The traditional explanations for unfavorable price variances include general inflation or uncontrollable price boosts by suppliers. But such answers are unsatisfying. Some companies have invested in control systems that try to get more thorough control over price variances. The phrase "whip inflation now" (WIN) vividly expresses the combat-zone mentality that some organizations attempt to develop in their purchasing offices with respect to proposed increases in raw materials prices by suppliers.

Consider an illustration based on an actual company's experience.[6] First, representatives of top management negotiate with the purchasing manager regarding their "price offset" or "inflation offset" target for the budget year. The offset is the target for beating the inflation rate, where the word "inflation" is used to describe an objective measurement, such as the average change in an index number supplied for a particular commodity by the U.S. Bureau of Labor Statistics (BLS). For example, suppose an offset percentage is negotiated as 4%, and the forecasted (anticipated) average inflation rate is 15%, then the purchasing manager would have a target price increase of 15% − 4% = 11%.

But what if the actual inflation rate differs from the forecasted rate? Forecasts may be used for planning purposes, but actual price changes should be used for judging performance after the fact. Exhibit 6-13 demonstrates the thinking behind this approach. Consider the steps shown in the exhibit:

1. At the end of 19_1, a commodity had a unit price of $1.00. Purchases of one thousand units are planned for 19_2. Step 1 shows a standard at 19_1 prices of 1,000 × $1.00 = $1,000.

2. The forecasted 19_2 inflation rate (the term used by this company to describe the BLS rate for this commodity) was 15%. Step 2 shows the standard cost as adjusted for anticipated inflation: $1,000 + .15($1,000) = $1,150.

3. The 19_2 standard price that would be used by the accounting system is based on a price increase of 15% − 4% or 11%, or $1.00 + $.11 = $1.11 per unit. The purchasing manager would plan to cope with the problem accordingly. That is, the manager has committed to a currently attainable standard ($1.11) that incorporates a 4% offset.

[6]For a thorough exploration of these issues, see International Harvester 9-181-090 (Boston: Mass.: Harvard Business School Case Services).

EXHIBIT 6-13
Standards or Budgets Under Inflation

1. Original standard based on 19_1 price, 1,000 units × $1.00 = $1,000
2. Adjust for anticipated average 19_2 inflation, 1,000 × [$1.00 + .15 ($1.00)], or 1,000 × $1.15 = $1,150
3. Adjust for amount of offset, 1,000 × [$1.15 − .04 ($1.00)], or a 19_2 standard cost for purchases: 1,000 × $1.11 = $1,110
4. Computation of price variance:

ACTUAL COSTS INCURRED: ACTUAL INPUTS PURCHASED × ACTUAL PRICE	FLEXIBLE BUDGET: BASED ON ACTUAL INPUTS PURCHASED × STANDARD PRICE
(1,000 × $1.16) $1,160	(1,000 × $1.11) $1,110

↑ (1,000 × $.05) ↑
Material price variance, $50 U

5. Detailed analysis of the $50 unfavorable material price variance:

Standard costs of purchases		$1,110
Variance attributable to unanticipated inflation:		
Anticipated average inflation rate	15%	
Actual average inflation rate	13	
Variance in inflation rate	2%	
Total amount 1,000 × $.02		20 F
Standard costs adjusted for unanticipated inflation		$1,090
Actual costs		1,160
"Controllable" price variance		$ 70 U

4.   Assume that actual prices were $1.16, leading to an unfavorable price variance of 1,000 × ($1.16 − $1.11), or $50.

5.   A more-detailed analysis of the $50 unfavorable variance should focus on the effects of unanticipated inflation on performance. Suppose there is a 13% actual inflation rate instead of the 15% anticipated rate. Thus there was an unanticipated inflation effect of 2%. Indeed, the appropriate standard for judging performance should really be 13% minus a 4% offset, or 9%. Stated differently, with perfect foresight the 19_2 standard costs would have been 1,000 × $1.09 = $1,090 rather than 1,000 × $1.11, or $1,110. Therefore the "controllable" price variance should be $70, unfavorable.

Critics of the latter approach have suggested that a predetermined offset rate of 4% is too rigid for judging subsequent performance. Instead the rate should be flexible. In this case, the 4% offset rate was supposed to offset a 15% anticipated rate, or 4% ÷ 15% = 26.67% of the inflation rate. Accordingly, if the actual rate is 13%, the offset rate should be 26.67% of 13%, or 3.47% (instead of 4%).

The final message here is that some managers may want detailed analysis beyond the calculation of the usual price and efficiency variances. Our illustration has shown special techniques for planning and evaluating performance. The latter focused on updating or restating the standard price so that uncontrollable and controllable factors could be identified.

6-1 "The idea of comparing performance at one activity level with a plan that was developed at some other activity level must be pertinent in judging the effectiveness of planning and control." Comment.

6-2 What are standard costs? Why is their use superior to comparisons of actual data with past data?

6-3 List and briefly describe two different types of standards.

6-4 What are the key questions in deciding how variances should be collected and analyzed?

6-5 Why do techniques for overhead control differ from techniques for control of direct materials and direct labor?

6-6 When can't the terms *budgeted performance* and *standard performance* be used interchangeably?

6-7 List the major factors that affect control procedures for material quantities.

6-8 Define *standard bill of materials, excess materials requisition, operations list.*

6-9 "Cost control means cost reduction." Do you agree? Why?

6-10 List four common causes of material-price variances.

6-11 "Setup costs are easily traceable to specific jobs. Therefore they should be classified as direct-labor costs." Do you agree? Why?

6-12 "Standard costing is OK for big companies that can afford such an elaborate system. But our company relies on an 'actual' system because it saves clerical costs." Comment.

6-13 List five purposes of standard costs.

6-14 Who is responsible for developing standards?

6-15 Why do budgeted variances arise?

6-16 When will budgets differ from standards? When will they be the same?

6-17 How does management decide when a variance is large enough to warrant investigation?

6-18 Flexible budget. Fontana Company made 200,000 units of product in a given year. The total manufacturing costs of $400,000 included $180,000 of fixed costs. Assume that no price changes will occur in the following year and that no changes in production methods are applicable. Compute the total budgeted cost for producing 220,000 units in the following year.

6-19 Flexible budget. The head of an army motor pool is trying to estimate the costs of operating a fleet of twenty trucks. Two major concerns are fuel, 18¢ per mile, and depreciation per truck per year, $8,000. Prepare the flexible-budget amounts for fuel and depreciation for twenty trucks at a level of 10,000, 20,000, and 30,000 miles per truck.

6-20 Flexible budget. The following data are for April:

	BUDGETED AMOUNT PER UNIT	VARIOUS LEVELS OF VOLUME		
Units		18,000	20,000	22,000
Sales	$30	$?	$?	$?
Variable costs:				
Direct material	?	360,000	?	?
Fuel	2	?	?	?
Fixed costs:				
Executive salaries		?	?	40,000
Depreciation		?	60,000	?

Required

1. Fill in the unknowns.
2. Draw a freehand graph of the flexible budget for the items shown here.

6-21 Basic flexible budget. The budgeted prices for direct materials and direct labor per unit of finished product are $10 and $4, respectively. The production manager is pleased with the following data:

	ACTUAL COSTS	STATIC (MASTER) BUDGET	VARIANCE
Direct materials	$91,000	$100,000	$9,000 F
Direct labor	39,000	40,000	1,000 F

Required

Is the manager's pleasure justified? Good output was 8,800 units. Prepare a performance report that uses a flexible budget and a static budget.

6-22 Price and sales volume variances (CMA) JK Enterprises sold 550,000 units during the first quarter ended March 31, 19_1. These sales represented a 10% increase over the number of units budgeted for the quarter. In spite of the sales increase, profits were below budget, as shown in the condensed income statement presented below.

JK Enterprises
Income Statement
For the First Quarter Ended March 31, 19_1
($000 omitted)

	BUDGET	ACTUAL
Sales	$2,500	$2,530
Variable costs:		
Cost of goods sold	$1,475	$1,540
Selling	400	440
Total variable costs	$1,875	$1,980
Contribution margin	$ 625	$ 550
Fixed costs:		
Selling	$ 125	$ 150
Administration	275	300
Total fixed costs	$ 400	$ 450
Income before taxes	$ 225	$ 100
Income taxes (40%)	90	40
Net income	$ 135	$ 60

The accounting department always prepares a brief analysis that explains the difference between budgeted net income and actual net income. This analysis, which has not yet been completed for the first quarter, is submitted to top management with the income statement.

Required | Prepare an explanation of the $125,000 unfavorable variance between the first quarter budgeted and actual before-tax income for JK Enterprises by calculating a single total amount for each of the following:

1. Sales price variance
2. Variable unit cost price variance
3. Sales volume variance for the contribution margin
4. Fixed cost variance

6-23 Material variances. Assume that a table manufacturer uses plastic tops. Plastic is purchased in large sizes, cut down as needed, and then glued to the tables. A given-sized table will require a specified amount of plastic. If the amount of plastic needed per Type-F TV table is 4 square feet and the cost per square foot is 65¢, then the standard cost of plastic for a single TV table would be $2.60. But a certain production run of 1,000 tables results in purchases and usage of 4,300 square feet at 70¢ per square foot, a total cost of $3,010.

Required | Compute the price variance and the efficiency variance.

6-24 Efficiency variances. Assume that 10,000 units of a particular item were produced. Suppose the standard direct-material allowance is two pounds per unit, at a cost per pound of $3. Actually, 21,000 pounds of materials (input) were used to produce the 10,000 units (output).

Similarly, assume that it is supposed to take four direct-labor hours to produce one unit, and that the standard hourly labor cost is $3. But 42,000 hours (input) were used to produce the 10,000 units in this Hong Kong factory.

Required | Compute the efficiency variances for direct material and direct labor.

6-25 Material and labor variances. Consider the following data:

	DIRECT MATERIAL	DIRECT LABOR
Actual price per unit of input (pounds and hours)	$15	$ 9
Standard price per unit of input	$12	$10
Standard inputs allowed per unit of output	5	2
Actual units of input	48,000	22,000
Actual units of output (product)	10,000	10,000

Required | 1. Compute the price, efficiency, and flexible-budget variances for direct material and direct labor. Use *U* or *F* to indicate whether the variances are unfavorable or favorable.
2. Prepare a plausible explanation for the performance.

6-26 Material and labor variances. Consider some changed data in the Webb Company illustration in the chapter. All the necessary original and changed data follow:

Units produced, 10,800
Budgeted or standard amounts per unit:
   Direct material (4 pounds @ $5.00) $20
   Direct labor (2 hours @ $8.00)   16

Actual data:

Direct-material costs	$270,000	Direct-labor costs	$171,600
Pounds of input purchased and used	50,000	Hours of input	22,000
Price per pound	$ 5.40	Labor price per hour	$ 7.80

1. Compute (a) price and efficiency variances for direct material and (b) price and efficiency variances for direct labor. Present your answer in a format similar to the analysis that appears in Exhibit 6-12, page 204.

2. Suppose that the Webb Company control system were designed to isolate material price variances upon purchase rather than upon usage of the materials. Suppose further that 60,000 pounds of material were purchased during April, but only 50,000 pounds were issued to production. Compute the purchase-price variance that would be reported by the control system.

6-27 Material and labor variances. (SMA, adapted) The Carberg Co. manufactures and sells a single product for $20. The company uses a standard-cost system, isolating all variances as soon as possible. The standards for one finished unit include:

Direct materials (1 kg. at $2)	$2.00
Direct labor (.6 hr. at $10)	6.00

Actual results for November were:

Units produced	5,100
Direct materials purchased at $2.10 per kg.	5,200 kg.
Direct materials used in production	5,300 kg.
Direct labor at $10.20 per hr.	3,200 hrs.

Required | Compute the price and efficiency variances for direct material and direct labor.

6-28 General journal entries for materials. Consider the following data compiled by the manufacturer of 1,000 television tables:

Actual quantity purchased	6,000 square feet
Standard quantity allowed	4,000 square feet
Actual quantity used	4,300 square feet
Standard price per square foot	$.65
Actual price per square foot	$.62

Required

1. The manager of purchasing wants early monitoring of price variances, and the manager of production wants early detection of efficiency variances. Prepare journal entries that would most closely reflect the timing of the isolation of each variance. Price variances are isolated upon purchase of direct materials, and efficiency variances upon the use of excess-materials requisitions.

2. Another company has the same process, but its managers are less concerned about early isolation of variances. Instead price variances are isolated upon issuance of direct material to the producing departments. In this way, the production department's efficiency can still be measured because price volatility will not affect the efficiency variance. This company does not isolate efficiency variances until after production is completed. Prepare journal entries that would most closely reflect the timing of the isolation of each variance. Show T-accounts.

6-29 Journal entries for direct labor. The Grafton Company had a standard rate (price) of $16.00 per direct-labor hour. Actual hours in July were 10,300 at an actual price of $15.80 per hour. The standard direct-labor hours allowed for the output achieved were 10,000.

Required | Prepare general-journal entries that isolate price and efficiency variances. Prepare one entry whereby Work in Process is carried at standard hours allowed times standard prices. Then prepare a second set of entries whereby (a) price variances are isolated as labor costs are originally journalized, and (b) efficiency variances are isolated as units are transferred from Work in Process to Finished Goods.

6-30 Analysis of variances. Chemical, Inc., has set up the following standards for materials and direct labor:

	PER FINISHED BATCH
Materials: 10 lbs. @ $3.00	$30.00
Direct labor: .5 hours @ $20.00	10.00

The number of finished units budgeted for the period was 10,000; 9,810 units were actually produced.
Actual results were:

Materials: 98,073 lbs. used	
Direct labor: 4,900 hrs.	$102,900

Required

During the month, purchases amounted to 100,000 lbs. at a total cost of $310,000. Price variances are isolated upon purchase.

1. Give journal entries to record the data above.
2. Show computations of all material and labor variances.
3. Comment on each of the variances.

6-31 Comparison of general-ledger entries for direct materials and direct labor. The Lee Co. in Korea has the following data for the month of March, when 1,100 finished units were produced:

Direct materials used, 3,600 pounds. The standard allowance per finished unit is 3 pounds at $3.00 per pound. Five thousand pounds were purchased at $3.25 per pound, a total of $16,250.

Direct labor, actual hours, was 2,450 hours at a total cost of $9,800. The standard labor cost per finished unit was $7.60. Standard time allowed is 2 hours per unit.

Required

1. Prepare journal entries for a "normal"-cost system.
2. Prepare journal entries for a "standard"-cost system. Support your entries with a detailed variance analysis, using the columnar analytical format illustrated in the chapter.
3. Show an alternative approach, including journal entries, to the way you quantified the material price variance in requirement 2. Which way is better, and why?

6-32 Flexible-budget preparation. The managing partner of Hess Music Box Fabricators has become aware of the disadvantages of static budgets and has asked you to prepare a flexible budget for October for its main style of music box. The following partial data are available for the actual operations in a recent typical month:

Boxes produced and sold	4,500
Direct-material costs	$45,000
Direct-labor costs	$67,500
Depreciation and other fixed manufacturing costs	$50,700
Average selling price per box	$ 50
Fixed selling and administrative expenses	$31,350

A 10% increase in the selling price is expected. The only variable selling expense is a 10% commission paid to the manufacturer's representatives, who bear all their own expenses of traveling, entertaining customers, and so on. The only variable overhead is a patent royalty of $2 per box manufactured. Salary increases that will become effective in October are $12,000 per year for the production superintendent and $15,000 per year for the sales manager. A 10% increase in direct-material prices is expected to become effective in October. No changes are expected in direct-labor wage rates or in the productivity of the direct-labor personnel.

1. Prepare a flexible budget for October, showing expected results at each of three levels of volume: 4,000 units, 5,000 units, 6,000 units.
2. Draw a freehand sketch of a graph for your flexible-budget costs. *Hint:* See Exhibits 6-2 and 6-3, page 182.

6-33 Basic variance analysis. Cash Management Printers, Inc., produces luxury checkbooks with three checks and stubs on each page. Each checkbook is designed for an individual customer and is ordered through the customer's bank. The company's operating budget for September included these data:

Number of checkbooks	15,000
Selling price, each	$ 20
Variable costs per book	$ 8
Total fixed costs for the month	$145,000

The actual results for September were:

Number of checkbooks produced and sold	12,000
Average selling price, each	$ 21
Variable costs per book	$ 7
Total fixed costs for the month	$150,000

The executive vice-president of the company observed that the operating income for September was much less than anticipated, despite a higher-than-budgeted selling price and a lower-than-budgeted variable cost per unit. You have been asked to provide explanations for the disappointing results in September.

Required

1. Prepare analyses of September performance. Prepare a *Level 1* and a *Level 2* analysis.
2. Comment briefly on your findings.

6-34 Overview of variance analysis. You have been hired as a consultant by Mary Flanagan, the president of a small manufacturing company that makes automobile parts. Flanagan is an excellent engineer, but she has been frustrated by not having adequate cost data.

You helped install flexible budgeting and standard costs. Flanagan has asked you to consider the following May data and recommend how variances might be computed and presented in performance reports:

Budgeted selling price per unit	$ 40
Budgeted variable costs per unit	$ 25
Budgeted total fixed costs per month	$200,000
Static budget in units	20,000
Actual units produced and sold	23,000
Actual revenue	$874,000
Actual variable costs	$630,000
Favorable variance in fixed costs	$ 3,000

Flanagan was disappointed: Although volume exceeded expectations, operating income had not.

Assume that there were no beginning or ending inventories.

Required

1. You decide to present Flanagan with alternative ways to analyze variances so that she can decide what level of detail she prefers. The reporting system can then be designed accordingly. Prepare an analysis similar to Levels 0, 1, and 2 in Exhibit 6-6, page 187.
2. What are some likely causes for the variances?

6-35 Cost control performance. You have just received a long-distance telephone call from a client in Bombay who is in a near panic concerning the operating costs of his company for the month just ended. He insists that a cost control performance report be sent immediately by special air courier. Because of a poor telephone connection, the data he provided you are incomplete, but you must nevertheless prepare the report now without being able to obtain any additional information.

Here are the notes you made during the telephone conversation:

a. Product units actually produced and sold last month   6,000

b. Actual total costs:

Direct materials	$150,000
Fixed selling and administrative costs	23,600
Variable and fixed costs (total)	645,300

c. Flexible-budget total costs:

Direct labor	$249,000
Fixed manufacturing costs	110,800
Total fixed costs	135,200
Total variable costs	474,400

d. Costs per product unit:

Direct materials, budgeted	$	23
Variable factory overhead, budgeted		7
Direct labor, actual		42

e. The only difference between actual and budgeted fixed manufacturing costs was an extra termination payment of $14,300 made to a supervisor during the month.

f. The only difference between actual and budgeted fixed selling and administrative costs was the replacement of two clerks at a total decrease in compensation of $800 for the month.

g. Higher electricity rates caused variable overhead costs to go over the budget by 15%.

h. The change in variable selling and administrative costs was caused by changes in sales commission rates. (The direction and amount of these is not known because of garbled communication.)

i. The increased speed of better-trained direct-labor workers did not justify their higher wage rates.

Required | Prepare the cost control performance report as completely as you can, showing all supporting computations clearly. *Hint:* See Exhibit 6-5, page 185.

6-36 Elementary variance analysis and graph.   Consider the following data regarding the manufacture of units (pairs) of boots:

	STANDARDS
Direct materials	Two pounds of input at $4 per pound, or $8 per unit of output
Direct labor	One-half hour of input at $10 per hour, or $5 per unit of output

The following data were compiled regarding actual performance: good units produced, 20,000; pounds of input acquired and used, 37,000; price per pound, $4.10; direct-labor costs, $88,200; actual hours of input, 9,000; labor rate per hour, $9.80.

Required | **1.** Show computations of price and efficiency variances for direct materials and for direct labor. Prepare a plausible explanation of why the variances arose.

2. Sketch a graphical analysis of the direct-labor variance, using the vertical axis for total costs and the horizontal axis for volume or activity in hours. Indicate what vertical distances represent the flexible-budget variance, price variance, and efficiency variance.

3. Suppose 60,000 pounds of materials were purchased even though only 37,000 pounds were used. Suppose further that variances are identified with their most likely control point; accordingly, direct-material purchase-price variances are isolated and traced to the purchasing department rather than to the production department. Compute the price and efficiency variances under this approach.

6-37 Flexibility in budgets. Refer to Problem 6-36. Suppose the original budget was for 24,000 units of output. The general manager is gleeful about the following report:

	ACTUAL COSTS	ORIGINAL BUDGET	VARIANCE
Direct materials	$151,700	$192,000	$40,300 F
Direct labor	$ 88,200	$120,000	$31,800 F

Required

Is the manager's glee warranted? Prepare a report that might provide a more-detailed explanation of why the original budget was not achieved. Good output was 20,000 units.

6-38 Journal entries and T-accounts. Prepare journal entries and T-accounts for all transactions in Problem 6-36, including requirement 3. Summarize how these journal entries differ from the normal costing entries as described in Chapter 4.

6-39 Material and labor variances. (CPA, adapted) Vogue Fashions, Inc., manufactures ladies' blouses of one quality, produced in lots to fill each special order from its customers, composed of department stores located in various cities. Vogue sews the particular stores' labels on the blouses. The standard prime costs for a dozen blouses are:

Direct materials	24 yards @ $1.10	$26.40
Direct labor	3 hours @ $4.90	14.70

During June, Vogue worked on three orders, for which the month's job-cost records disclose the following:

	LOT NO.		
	22	23	24
Units in lot (dozens)	1,000	1,700	1,200
Materials used (yards)	24,100	40,440	28,825
Actual hours worked	2,980	5,130	2,890

The following information is also available:

1. Vogue purchased 95,000 yards of material during June at a cost of $106,400. The materials price variance is recorded when goods are purchased. All inventories are carried at standard cost.

2. Direct labor during June amounted to $55,000. According to payroll records, production employees were paid $5.00 per hour.

3. There was no work in process at June 1. During June, lots 22 and 23 were completed. All material was issued for lot 24, which was 80% completed as to direct labor.

1. Prepare a schedule showing the computation of the materials price variance for June. Indicate whether the variance is favorable or unfavorable.
2. Prepare a schedule showing, for each lot produced during June, computations of the
   a. Materials efficiency variance in yards
   b. Labor efficiency variance in hours
   c. Labor price variance in dollars

Indicate whether each variance is favorable or unfavorable.

6-40 Developing standard costs per unit (CMA, adapted) Ogwood Company is a small manufacturer of wooden household items. Al Rivkin, corporate controller, plans to implement a standard-cost system for Ogwood. Rivkin has information from several co-workers that will assist him in developing standards for Ogwood's products.

One of Ogwood's products is a wooden cutting board. Each cutting board requires 1.25 board feet of lumber and 12 minutes of direct-labor time to prepare and cut the lumber. The cutting boards are inspected after they are cut. Because the cutting boards are made of a natural material that has imperfections, one board is normally rejected for each five that are accepted. Four rubber foot pads are attached to each good cutting board. A total of fifteen minutes of direct-labor time is required to attach all four foot pads and finish each cutting board. The lumber for the cutting boards costs $3.00 per board foot, and each foot pad costs $.05. Direct labor is paid at the rate of $8.00 per hour.

Develop the standard cost for the direct cost components of the cutting board. The standard cost should identify the

1. Standard quantity
2. Standard rate, and
3. Standard cost per unit

for each direct cost component of the cutting board.

6-41 Solving for unknowns. The city of Chicago has a maintenance shop where all kinds of truck repairs are performed. Through the years, various labor standards have been developed to judge performance. However, during a March strike, some labor records vanished. The actual hours of input were 1,000. The direct-labor flexible-budget variance was $1,700, favorable. The standard labor price was $14.00 per hour; however, a recent labor shortage had necessitated using higher-paid workers for some jobs and had produced a labor-price variance for March of $400, unfavorable.

1. Actual labor price per hour
2. Standard hours allowed for output achieved

6-42 Solving for unknowns. (SMA, adapted) King Corporation manufactures a special type of metal alloy. Budgeted sales for 19_8 were 10,000 kilos at $50 per kilo. Standard variable production and selling costs were $30 per kilo. Fixed costs were budgeted at $50,000 for 19_8.

Actual fixed costs in 19_8 were $50,000, but the market price realized was $55 per kilo due to an international shortage. Operating income was below the static-budget figure amount by $50,000. The sales-volume variance for revenue for 19_8 was $100,000, unfavorable. Contribution-margin price variance was $20,000, unfavorable.

Determine the following:

1. Revenue price variance
2. Variable-cost price variance
3. Variable-cost efficiency variance
4. Contribution-margin efficiency variance
5. Variable-cost sales-volume variance
6. Contribution-margin sales-volume variance
7. Operating income sales-volume variance

6-43 Responsibility for purchase-price variances. The Chester Company uses standard costs. The purchasing manager, Amy Strotz, is responsible for material-price variances, and the production manager, Juan Morales, is responsible for material-efficiency variances and direct-labor price and efficiency variances.

The standard price for metal used as a principal raw material was $2 per pound. The standard allowance was six pounds per finished unit of product.

The standard rate for direct labor was $14 per hour. The standard allowance was one-half hour per finished unit of product.

During the past week, 10,000 good finished units were produced. However, labor trouble caused the production manager to use much nonpreferred personnel. Actual labor costs were $78,000 for 6,500 actual hours; 80,000 pounds of metal were acquired for $1.80 per pound; and 71,000 pounds of metal were consumed during production.

Required

1. Compute the material purchase-price variance, material-efficiency variance, direct-labor price variance, and direct-labor efficiency variance.
2. As a supervisor of both the purchasing manager and the production manager, how would you interpret the feedback provided by the computed variances?
3. What are the budget allowances for the production manager for direct materials and direct labor? Would they be different if production were 7,000 good finished units?
4. Prepare a condensed responsibility performance report for the production manager for the 10,000 units produced. Show three columns: charges to department, budget, and variance.

6-44 Combined or joint price-efficiency variances and incentives. The MTT Company had a long history of using bonuses that were specifically tied to performance. Minimal inventories of any kind were kept. The purchasing manager was given a bonus of 5% of the favorable purchase-price variance for the year. The production manager was given a bonus of 5% of the favorable direct-material efficiency variance for the year plus additional bonuses regarding labor and overhead variances.

In 19_4, the performance regarding Material A, an important chemical ingredient, was:

lbs = 1 unit

> Standard pounds allowed @ $1.00, one per finished unit
> Actual pounds consumed, 500,000
> Actual production, 520,000 finished units
> Actual unit purchase price, $.90

Required

1. Compute the material price and efficiency variances.
2. Split the price variance into a "pure" price variance and a combined price-efficiency variance. As the purchasing manager, would you be pleased by the favorable efficiency variance? Why? Would your attitude change if the actual unit price were $1.10?
3. As the production manager, what would be your attitude toward the bonus system?
4. Given that top management is committed to a bonus system based on variances, what modifications in the bonus system would you favor? Why?

6-45 Inflation and price variances. Study Appendix 6. The Frenesi Co. buys and cuts plastic sheets for covering table tops in the course of furniture manufacturing. The company's original standard was based on its 19_1 price, which was $10 per sheet. The economist for the furniture trade association has published a predicted 14% price increase for these plastic sheets during 19_2.

The Frenesi manufacturing vice-president and the head of purchasing have agreed that Frenesi should be able to attain a 2% "offset" against the predicted 14% anticipated price increase.

During 19_2, Frenesi acquired 90,000 sheets at an average price of $11.50 per sheet.

Required

Compute the total price variance for 19_2. Analyze the variance, distinguishing between the amount attributable to the variance in the inflation rate and the amount attributable to "controllable" factors.

7

Flexible Budgets and Standards: Part II

Variable factory overhead: control and product costing •
Fixed factory overhead: control and product costing • Journal entries for overhead •
Standard, normal, and actual costing • Analysis of fixed-factory-overhead variances •
Combined-overhead rate and two-way and three-way analysis • Overhead variances in the ledger

This chapter continues the *Level 3* analysis of manufacturing costs introduced in the preceding chapter. We analyze variable and fixed factory overhead. We also compare the effects of the *budgetary control* purpose and the *product-costing* purpose of accounting for overhead.

In addition, this chapter covers some widely used methods of budgeting overhead, applying overhead, and analyzing overhead variances. Practices vary, depending on the preferences of the individual managers concerned.

Please proceed slowly as you study this chapter. Pause frequently. Trace the data to the graphs in a systematic manner. In particular, ponder how fixed factory overhead is accounted for in one way for budgetary control purposes and in a different way for product-costing purposes. The accounting for fixed factory overhead is usually the most puzzling aspect of the study of flexible budgets and standards.

This chapter concentrates on production, not selling. So we focus on units produced, not units sold. Thus we do not contend with the sales volume variance that was examined in the preceding chapter. (For more on the sales volume variance, see Chapter 24.)

Direct material and direct labor have traditionally received more thorough analyses than factory overhead. Examples are price and efficiency variances. Most companies have not monitored individual overhead items to the same extent. Why? Because it is too expensive, that is, it does not pass the cost-benefit test. Consequently, many companies compute budget variances for overhead but do not divide such variances into subvariances.

As automation increases, corresponding overhead items (such as costs of energy, supplies, and repairs) have become a higher fraction of total manufacturing costs.[1] Hence, companies are giving more attention to the analysis and control of overhead today than in past decades. For example, managers now get insights by subdividing the flexible-budget variance for variable overhead.

Standards and flexible budgets

Consider a continuation of the Webb Company illustration of the preceding chapter. Standard costing for variable overhead entails the following:

1. Choose the volume base that is most highly correlated with variable-factory-overhead costs, direct-labor hours in this case.
2. Estimate the inputs that should be used to produce one unit of good output, which is two hours in the Webb case.
3. Develop a budgeted variable-overhead rate per direct-labor hour, which is $1.50 in the Webb case: $36,000 ÷ (12,000 units × 2 hours) = $1.50.
4. Apply the variable overhead to work in process, using the budgeted rate multiplied by the standard hours allowed for the good output. For one unit of output, the standard cost is $1.50 × 2 hours, or $3.00. For 10,000 Webb units, the flexible budget would be $1.50 × (10,000 × 2 hours), or $30,000.

A summary of the Webb data follows:

Budgeted variable overhead rate per direct-labor hour	$1.50
Standard direct-labor hours allowed per unit of finished product	2
Budgeted variable overhead rate per unit of finished product, $1.50 × 2 hours	$3.00
Flexible budget for 20,000 standard hours allowed, or 10,000 units	$30,000

The control purpose

Variable factory overhead typically consists of many items, including energy costs, repairs, indirect labor, idle time, and fringe benefits such as employer payroll taxes. The most convincing way to discover why overhead performance did not agree with a budget is to investigate possible causes, line item by line item.

The price-efficiency distinction provides a starting point for analysis. However, the two tidy categories of "price" and "efficiency" are a crude split for variable factory overhead. Keep their limitations in mind. In practice, a fragile assumption frequently underlies the efficiency variance computation for variable overhead items: Variable overhead fluctuates in direct proportion to some measure of pro-

---

[1]See J. G. Miller and T. E. Vollmann, "The Hidden Factory," *Harvard Business Review*, September–October 1985, pp. 142–51. See Chapter 13 for further discussion.

duction volume, such as direct-labor hours or direct-labor costs. Webb Company uses direct-labor hours.

Recall that in April the company had good output achieved of 10,000 finished units of product. Standard direct-labor hours allowed were 10,000 × 2 = 20,000. However, actual direct-labor hours of input were 22,000. Using a format similar to that at the bottom of Exhibit 6-7 (page 192):

(1)	(2)	(3)
		FLEXIBLE BUDGET: BASED ON
ACTUAL COSTS INCURRED	FLEXIBLE BUDGET: BASED ON ACTUAL INPUTS	STANDARD INPUTS ALLOWED FOR ACTUAL OUTPUTS
Given $32,000	22,000 × $1.50 = $33,000	20,000 × $1.50 = $30,000
↑ Price variance, $1,000 F ↑	Efficiency variance, $3,000 U	↑
↑	Flexible budget variance, $2,000 U	↑

The efficiency variance for variable overhead is a measure of the extra overhead (or savings) incurred *solely* because the *actual direct-labor hours* of input differed from the *standard hours allowed*:

$$\text{Variable-overhead efficiency variance} = \left(\begin{array}{c} \text{Actual} \\ \text{direct-labor} \\ \text{hours used} \end{array} - \begin{array}{c} \text{Standard} \\ \text{hours} \\ \text{allowed} \end{array} \right) \times \begin{array}{c} \text{Budgeted} \\ \text{rate per} \\ \text{hour} \end{array}$$

$$= (22,000 - 20,000) \times \$1.50$$

$$= \$3,000 \text{ U}$$

To be more specific, suppose the variable overhead consisted wholly of supplies such as polishing cloths. The above analysis shows that, because direct labor was inefficiently used, the related usage of supplies would be expected to be proportionately excessive. Whether in fact this clear-cut relationship exists depends on particular circumstances.

The $1,000 "price" variance labeled in the analytical format shown above is usually called a variable-overhead **spending variance.** It is defined as the actual amount of overhead incurred minus the expected amount based on the flexible budget for actual inputs.

The "price" variance is really a glob. It is the remaining part of the flexible-budget variance that is unexplained by the efficiency variance. For this reason, most practitioners call this type of overhead variance a spending variance rather than merely a price variance:

$$\text{Variable overhead spending variance} = \text{Flexible-budget variance} - \text{Efficiency variance}$$

$$\$1,000 \text{ F} = \$2,000 \text{ U} - \$3,000 \text{ U}$$

Note that the spending variance in this case could result exclusively from favorable unit price changes for polishing cloths. But it could also arise exclusively from careful use of these supplies. Thus this "price variance" could be partially or completely traceable to the efficient use of supplies, even though it is labeled as a spending variance. In particular, variable-overhead costs may be affected by specific control of the items themselves, as distinguished from specific control of related direct labor.

The product-costing purpose

Consider some graphical displays of how variable factory overhead relates to (1) responsibility budgeting for planning and control purposes and (2) product-costing purposes. The graphs for variable factory overhead are:

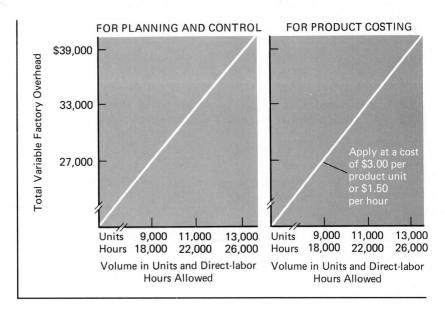

The lines on the two graphs are identical. Either graph can be used as a basis for predicting how total costs will behave. Variable factory overhead will increase at a rate of:

$$\$27,000 \div 9,000 = \$3.00 \text{ per unit}$$

$$\$33,000 \div 11,000 = \$3.00 \text{ per unit}$$

$$\$39,000 \div 13,000 = \$3.00 \text{ per unit}$$

Thinking in terms of *total costs* is the most popular way to exert budgetary control over operations at various levels of volume. In contrast, thinking in terms of *unit costs* is the most popular way to apply costs for product-costing purposes. For example, managers tend to say that their budget for 10,000 units is $30,000, and their cost per unit is $3.00.

FIXED FACTORY OVERHEAD: CONTROL AND PRODUCT COSTING

The control purpose

The Webb Company illustration indicates that budgeted fixed factory overhead was $96,000. By definition, this is a lump sum that is not expected to vary as volume fluctuates within the relevant range. Fixed costs are frequently a component of a flexible budget, as shown in Exhibit 6-2 (page 182). However, the "flex" in the flexible budget is attributable to the variable costs, not the fixed costs. Indeed, the flexible-budget formula for Webb Company factory is:

$$\text{Flexible budget for factory overhead} = \text{Budgeted fixed factory overhead} + \text{Budgeted variable factory overhead}$$

	= $96,000 per month	+ $1.50 per direct-labor hour or $3.00 per unit of output
For 9,000 units	= $96,000	+ $3.00 (9,000) = $123,000
For 13,000 units	= $96,000	+ $3.00 (13,000) = $135,000

Budgetary control of fixed factory overhead concentrates on line-by-line plans for such typical items as supervision, depreciation, insurance, property taxes, and rentals. Chapter 11 discusses these aspects in more detail. Fixed factory overhead is generally not subject to as much day-to-day (or month-to-month) influence as variable overhead. The variances of actual costs from fixed-overhead budgets tend to be relatively small.

The product-costing purpose

Until this point, our description of standard-cost systems pertains equally to all product costing, regardless of whether absorption costing or variable costing is used.[2] However, the remainder of this chapter pertains only to absorption costing. Why? Because fixed factory overhead is applied to products under absorption costing but not under variable costing. The basic procedure for applying overhead is the same as that introduced in Chapter 4. The budgeting and computation of the overhead rate are usually done annually. The budgeted rate for applying fixed factory overhead is computed as follows:

Budgeted fixed-factory-overhead rate for applying costs to product

$$= \frac{\text{Budgeted total fixed factory overhead}}{\text{Some preselected production volume level for the budget period}}$$

$$= \frac{\$96,000 \times 12 \text{ months}}{12,000 \text{ units} \times 12 \text{ months}}$$

$$= \frac{\$1,152,000}{144,000 \text{ units}} = \$8 \text{ per unit}$$

$$\text{or} = \frac{\$1,152,000}{144,000 \text{ units} \times 2 \text{ hours}} = \frac{\$1,152,000}{288,000 \text{ hours}} = \$4 \text{ per hour}$$

---

[2]About 65% of the American companies that use standard-costing systems use absorption costing. The other 35% use variable costing, which is discussed in the next chapter. See J. S. Chiu and Y. Lee, "A Survey of Current Practice in Overhead Accounting and Analysis," *Proceedings of the 1980 Western Regional Meeting of the American Accounting Association* (O. R. Whittington, San Diego State University, School of Accounting, 1980). The survey received usable responses from 327 of the *Fortune 500* American industrial firms. Of these, 75% either did not use standard costs or did not have factory operations. Of the companies that use standard costs, 70% maintained accounts that separated factory overhead into variable and fixed elements. An extensive survey by W. Cress and J. Pettijohn, "A Survey of Budget-related Planning and Control Procedures," *Journal of Accounting Education*, Vol. 3, No. 2 (Fall 1985), showed similar results. For example, 82% of the respondents identify the fixed and variable components of manufacturing overhead.

The preselected volume level in this case is based on the originally expected production volume for the year. It can be expressed as either 144,000 units or 288,000 hours per year, or 12,000 units or 24,000 hours per month.

Denominator volume is defined as the preselected production volume level used to set a budgeted fixed-factory-overhead rate for applying costs to product. Synonyms are **denominator activity** and **denominator level.**

For inventory purposes, as each unit is produced, an $8 fixed-factory-overhead cost will be applied thereto. Thus the first 5,000 units would bear a total *product cost* for fixed factory overhead of $40,000. The next 5,000 units would bear an additional $40,000, as the next graphs demonstrate:

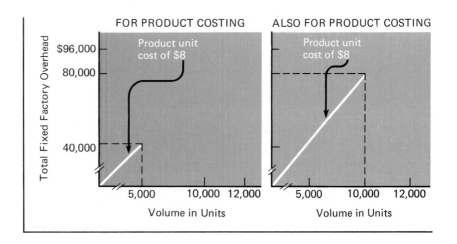

To recapitulate, the first of the following graphs shows that the focus for budgetary *control* is on the $96,000 lump-sum total of fixed factory overhead. However, the second graph shows how, for *product-costing* purposes, the total costs in the first graph are typically "unitized" by using some denominator volume:

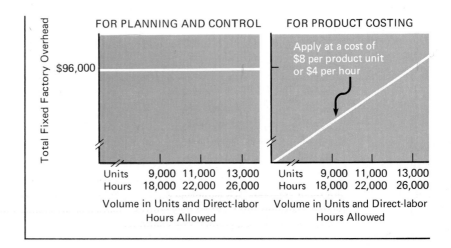

The *total* fixed factory overhead for budgetary control is unaffected by the specific preselected production volume used as a denominator. However, if fixed factory overhead is sizable, the choice of a denominator level can have a significant effect on *unit* product costs:

(1) TOTAL ANNUAL COSTS	(2) TOTAL VOLUME LEVEL FOR YEAR	(1) ÷ (2) BUDGETED FIXED-OVERHEAD RATE FOR PRODUCT COSTING
$1,152,000	9,000 × 12 = 108,000	$10.67
1,152,000	11,000 × 12 = 132,000	8.73
1,152,000	13,000 × 12 = 156,000	7.38

A graphical depiction of these data on a monthly basis follows:

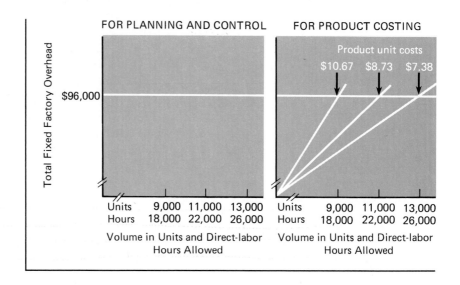

The right-hand graph clearly demonstrates that the unit cost depends on the production volume level chosen as the denominator in the computation; the higher the denominator volume, the lower the product cost per unit. The costing difficulty is troublesome because managers usually want a single representative unit fixed cost despite month-to-month fluctuations in production volume.

The two graphs underscore how the two purposes differ. The planning and control purpose regards fixed costs in accordance with their actual cost behavior pattern, costs that arise in chunks rather than in finely granulated portions. In contrast, absorption product costing views these *fixed* costs *as though* they had a *variable* cost behavior pattern. Therefore absorption costing seemingly transforms a fixed cost into a variable cost, and for product-costing purposes, *all manufacturing costs* are routinely regarded as variable.

The choice of an appropriate denominator level for the budgeting of fixed-overhead rates is a matter of judgment rather than science. The most widely used

Choosing the denominator level

EXHIBIT 7-1
Comparison of Approaches to Absorption Costing

COST CATEGORY	CHAPTER 2 APPROACH, CALLED ACTUAL ABSORPTION COSTING: WORK-IN-PROCESS INVENTORY	CHAPTER 4 APPROACH, CALLED NORMAL ABSORPTION COSTING: WORK-IN-PROCESS INVENTORY	CHAPTER 7 APPROACH, CALLED STANDARD ABSORPTION COSTING: WORK-IN-PROCESS INVENTORY
Direct materials	Actual inputs × Actual prices	Actual inputs × Actual prices	Standard inputs allowed for actual output × Standard prices
Direct labor	Actual inputs × Actual prices	Actual inputs × Actual prices	Standard inputs allowed for actual output × Standard prices
Variable factory overhead	Actual inputs × Actual overhead rates	Actual inputs × Budgeted overhead rates	Standard inputs allowed for actual output × Budgeted overhead rates
Fixed factory overhead	Actual inputs × Actual overhead rates	Actual inputs × Budgeted overhead rates	Standard inputs allowed for actual output × Budgeted overhead rates

The framework that was used at the beginning of this chapter to analyze variable overhead is arranged in Exhibit 7-2 so that it may easily be compared with the framework for fixed overhead.

Ponder the differences. For all variable costs, the *flexible-budget* allowance will *always* equal the amount *applied* to products. Thus the amount of the flexible-budget variance for variable overhead will always be identical to underapplied (or overapplied) variable overhead, $2,000 U in this example. In contrast, except when actual output achieved equals the denominator level, the *flexible budget* for fixed factory overhead will *never* equal the amount of fixed overhead *applied* to products. Thus the amount of the flexible-budget variance for fixed overhead will rarely be identical to underapplied (or overapplied) fixed overhead, $4,000 F versus $12,000 U in this example.

Finally, note that an efficiency variance is computed for variable but not fixed overhead. Why? Because efficiency variances are measures to help the short-run control of performance. Efficient use of direct materials, direct labor, and variable factory overhead can affect actual costs, but short-run fixed overhead is unaffected by efficiency.

Production volume variance

In an absorption-costing system, the first step in analyzing fixed overhead is to calculate the underapplied or overapplied amounts:

Actual of $92,000 − Applied of $80,000 = Underapplied fixed overhead of $12,000 U

This $12,000 can be subdivided into two variances, the flexible-budget variance of $4,000 F, plus a *production volume variance* of $16,000 U. A **production volume variance** arises only in an absorption-costing system. It is a measure of the cost of departing from the denominator level of volume that was used to set the fixed-overhead rate.

EXHIBIT 7-2
Framework for Analyzing Variable- and Fixed-Factory-Overhead Variances

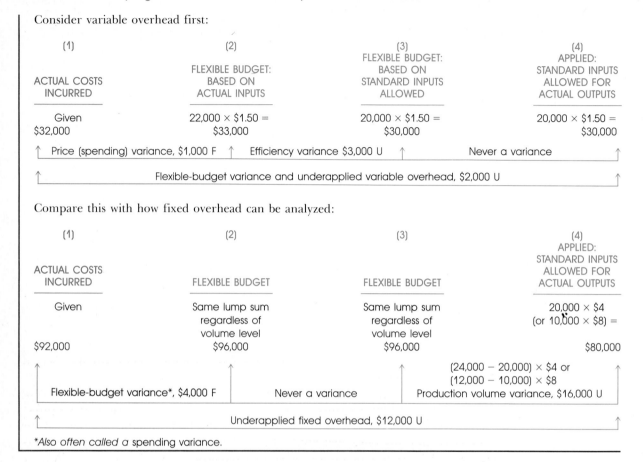

Consider variable overhead first:

(1) ACTUAL COSTS INCURRED	(2) FLEXIBLE BUDGET: BASED ON ACTUAL INPUTS	(3) FLEXIBLE BUDGET: BASED ON STANDARD INPUTS ALLOWED	(4) APPLIED: STANDARD INPUTS ALLOWED FOR ACTUAL OUTPUTS
Given $32,000	22,000 × $1.50 = $33,000	20,000 × $1.50 = $30,000	20,000 × $1.50 = $30,000

↑ Price (spending) variance, $1,000 F ↑ Efficiency variance $3,000 U ↑   Never a variance   ↑

↑   Flexible-budget variance and underapplied variable overhead, $2,000 U   ↑

Compare this with how fixed overhead can be analyzed:

(1) ACTUAL COSTS INCURRED	(2) FLEXIBLE BUDGET	(3) FLEXIBLE BUDGET	(4) APPLIED: STANDARD INPUTS ALLOWED FOR ACTUAL OUTPUTS
Given	Same lump sum regardless of volume level	Same lump sum regardless of volume level	20,000 × $4 (or 10,000 × $8) =
$92,000	$96,000	$96,000	$80,000

↑	↑	↑	(24,000 − 20,000) × $4 or (12,000 − 10,000) × $8 ↑
Flexible-budget variance*, $4,000 F		Never a variance	Production volume variance, $16,000 U

↑   Underapplied fixed overhead, $12,000 U   ↑

*Also often called a spending variance.

Exhibit 7-3 is a graph showing the $16,000 production volume variance. **When actual volume achieved is less than the denominator volume, the production volume variance is unfavorable.** It is viewed as a cost of idle capacity and is measured in Exhibit 7-3. Computations can be expressed in product units or in hours. Using hours:

$$\text{Production volume variance} = \left(\text{Denominator volume} - \text{Actual volume of output achieved}\right) \times \left(\text{Budgeted fixed-overhead rate}\right)$$

$$= (24,000 - 20,000) \times \$4$$

$$= \$16,000 \text{ U}$$

or

$$\text{Production volume variance} = \text{Budget} - \text{Applied}$$

$$= \$96,000 - (20,000 \times \$4)$$

$$= \$96,000 - \$80,000$$

$$= \$16,000 \text{ U}$$

EXHIBIT 7-3
Production Volume Variance

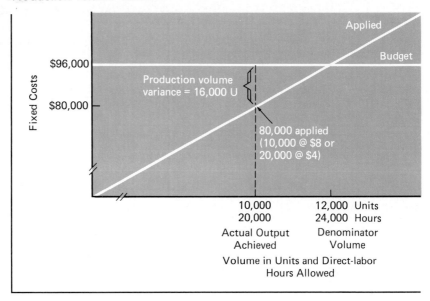

When actual production volume exceeds denominator volume, the production volume variance is favorable. It is viewed as a benefit of better-than-expected utilization of facilities.

There is no production volume variance for variable overhead. The concept of production volume variance arises for fixed overhead because of the conflict between accounting for planning and control (by budgets) and accounting for product costing (by budgeted application rates). Note again that the fixed-overhead budget serves the planning and control purpose, whereas the development of a product-costing rate results in the treatment of fixed overhead as if it were a variable cost. In other words, the applied line in Exhibit 7-3 is artificial in the sense that, for product-costing purposes, it seemingly transforms a fixed cost into a variable cost. This bit of magic forcefully illustrates the distinction between accounting for planning and control and accounting for product costing.

To summarize, the production volume variance arises because the actual production volume level achieved usually does not coincide with the volume level used as a denominator for selecting a budgeted product-costing rate for fixed factory overhead.

No efficiency variance for fixed overhead

The position in this chapter has been to distinguish between fixed and variable overhead as separate management problems. This distinction contrasts with the tendency among many accountants to analyze variable costs and fixed costs in a parallel manner. For instance, an efficiency variance for fixed overhead is often computed, just as it is for the other variable manufacturing costs:

$$\text{Efficiency variance} = \left(\begin{array}{c}\text{Actual hours} - \\ \text{Standard hours allowed}\end{array}\right) \times \begin{array}{c}\text{Hourly fixed-} \\ \text{overhead rate}\end{array}$$

However, the resulting variance is very different from the efficiency variances for direct materials, direct labor, and variable overhead. Efficient usage of these three factors can affect actual cost, but short-run fixed-overhead cost is not affected by efficiency. Furthermore, the managers responsible for inefficiency will be aware of its existence through reports on variable-cost control, so there is little to gain from expressing ineffective utilization of facilities in historical dollar terms.[3]

Economic meaning of unfavorable production volume variance

The economic meaning of the flexible-budget variance for fixed factory overhead is relatively straightforward. The amounts actually incurred are compared with the lump-sum amounts budgeted.

In contrast, the economic meaning of the production volume variance is less clear. The Webb Company variance in April is $(12,000 - 10,000) \times \$8 = \$16,000$, unfavorable. Remember that the variance is a creature of the "unitizing" of fixed costs. Does the production volume variance measure the economic cost to Webb Company of producing and selling 10,000 rather than 12,000 units in April? The presence of idle facilities has no bearing on the amount of fixed costs currently incurred.

How should the costs of idle capacity be measured? The economic impacts of the inability to reach a target denominator volume are often directly measured by lost contribution margin, even if it must be approximated. In the Webb Company example, Exhibit 6-4 (page 183) revealed that the lost contribution margin was 2,000 units $\times$ \$24 = \$48,000. Managers tend to understand the meaning of the latter, but they find the production volume variance less informative.[4]

The use of unit historical fixed-overhead costs might be justified in an economic sense on the following grounds: "We cannot regularly maintain measurements of lost contribution margin per unit. Therefore, as a practical but crude substitute, we use unit historical fixed-overhead costs instead."

Impact of choice of denominator volume

The economic meaning of the production volume variance is also clouded because its amount is affected by the choice of the denominator volume. For example, consider Webb's April operations:

---

[3]Some accountants favor computing production volume variance on the basis of the difference between the fixed-overhead budget (\$96,000) and (actual hours worked $\times$ fixed-overhead rate). In this example, the production volume variance would then become $\$96,000 - (22,000 \times \$4)$, or \$8,000 unfavorable instead of \$16,000 unfavorable. The remaining variance of \$8,000 unfavorable [(*actual* hours − standard hours) $\times$ \$4 overhead rate] is sometimes called the fixed-overhead *efficiency* or *effectiveness* variance—the measure of the ineffective use or waste of facilities because of off-standard labor performance. This breakdown of the production volume variance really attempts to separate the cost of *misused* facilities from the cost of *unused* facilities.

The authors think this refinement is unnecessary in most cases because (a) in the short run, total fixed costs incurred are *not* changed by efficiency changes, and (b) if the budget uses standard hours as a base, the production volume variance is more logically calculated by comparing standard hours achieved with the denominator volume that was used as a basis for setting the budgeted overhead rate.

The Chiu and Lee survey, *op. cit.*, indicated that 23% of their relevant respondents calculate an efficiency variance for fixed factory overhead.

[4]For an elaboration of these ideas, see C. Horngren, "A Contribution Margin Approach to the Analysis of Capacity Utilization," *Accounting Review*, XLII, No. 2, pp. 254–64.

(1) Budgeted fixed factory overhead	$96,000	$96,000	$96,000
(2) Denominator volume	10,000	11,000	12,000
(3) Budgeted fixed-overhead rate per unit of product	$ 9.60	$ 8.73	$ 8.00
(4) Applied fixed overhead (10,000 units of output × $9.60, $8.73, $8.00)	$96,000	$87,300	$80,000
(5) Production volume variance (1) − (4)	0	$ 8,700 U	$16,000 U

The table illustrates three of many possible denominator volumes. The choice of a denominator volume might reasonably fall anywhere within the relevant range of, say, 9,000 to 13,000 units per month. Thus the choice of denominator level results in different amounts of applied fixed overhead. Therefore it can affect inventory valuations and, if inventory levels change, operating income—even if all other facts and conditions are the same.

Different terminology

Production volume variances have a number of widely used synonyms: **capacity variance, idle capacity variance, activity variance, denominator variance,** and just plain **volume variance.** The last term is particularly popular, but we use *production volume variance* here. Why? To distinguish the *production* volume variance, which is unique to absorption costing, from *sales* volume variances. The latter were explained in the preceding chapter. Sales volume variances are encountered in *all* accounting systems and in *all* types of organizations, including service industries and nonprofit entities.

_____PROBLEM FOR SELF-STUDY_____

problem 1

Exhibit 7-4 shows a flexible budget for variable and fixed factory overhead for a machining department. Note how the "flex" in the flexible budget is confined to variable costs. The flexible budget for fixed costs is the same regardless of the volume level.

EXHIBIT 7-4
M Company
Machining Department
Simplified Flexible Factory-Overhead Budget for Anticipated Monthly Activity Range

Standard direct-labor hours allowed	8,000	9,000	10,000	11,000
Variable factory overhead:				
Material handling	$ 8,000	$ 9,000	$10,000	$11,000
Idle time	800	900	1,000	1,100
Rework	800	900	1,000	1,100
Overtime premium	400	450	500	550
Supplies	3,600	4,050	4,500	4,950
Total	$13,600	$15,300	$17,000	$18,700
Variable-overhead rate, $1.70 per DLH				
Fixed factory overhead:				
Supervision	$ 2,700	$ 2,700	$ 2,700	$ 2,700
Depreciation—plant	1,000	1,000	1,000	1,000
Depreciation—equipment	5,000	5,000	5,000	5,000
Property taxes	1,000	1,000	1,000	1,000
Insurance—factory	300	300	300	300
Total	$10,000	$10,000	$10,000	$10,000

The variable-overhead rate is $1.70 per standard direct-labor hour. The denominator volume used to set the fixed-overhead rate for product costing is 10,000 hours.

The actual hours of input were 7,900. Four standard hours are allowed per unit of product. There were 2,000 units of product produced, which are often expressed as 8,000 standard hours allowed or standard hours earned. Exhibit 7-5 lists the actual costs incurred.

EXHIBIT 7-5

M Company
Machining Department
Actual Factory Overhead Costs For the Month Ended March 31, 19_1

Variable overhead:		Fixed overhead:	
Material handling	$ 8,200	Supervision	$ 2,700
Idle time	600	Depreciation—plant	1,000
Rework	850	Depreciation—equipment	5,000
Overtime premium	600	Property taxes	1,150
Supplies	4,000	Insurance—factory	350
Total	$14,250	Total	$10,200

Required

1. Compute in summary form the variable-factory-overhead spending variance and efficiency variance. "Summary form" means to analyze all the variable overhead as a single-line item. For example, the actual variable costs incurred are $14,250.
2. Compute in summary form the fixed-factory-overhead spending budget variance (also called flexible-budget variance) and the production volume variance.

solution 1 See Exhibit 7-6 for the answers to both requirements. This analysis uses the analytical framework introduced earlier in this chapter (p. 228).

Some additional aspects of this problem are explored in subsequent sections.

EXHIBIT 7-6
Framework for Analysis of Factory-Overhead Variances

	(1) ACTUAL COSTS INCURRED	(2) FLEXIBLE BUDGET: BASED ON ACTUAL INPUTS	(3) FLEXIBLE BUDGET: BASED ON STANDARD INPUTS ALLOWED	(4) APPLIED: STANDARD INPUTS ALLOWED FOR ACTUAL OUTPUTS
Variable Overhead	Given $14,250	(7,900 × $1.70) $13,430	(8,000 × $1.70) $13,600	(8,000 × $1.70) $13,600
	↑ Spending variance, $820 U ↑	Efficiency variance, $170 F* ↑	Never a variance	↑
	↑	Underapplied variable overhead, $650 U		↑
Fixed Overhead	$10,200	$10,000	$10,000	(8,000 × $1.00†) $8,000
	↑ Spending variance, $200 U ↑	Never a variance	↑	Production volume variance, $2,000 U‡ ↑
	↑	Underapplied fixed overhead, $2,200 U		↑

*Or (8,000 − 7,900) × $1.70 = 170 F.

†Budgeted fixed-overhead rate = $\dfrac{\$10,000}{10,000 \text{ hours}}$ = $1.

‡*Alternative explanation: Multiply the difference between denominator volume and actual volume of output achieved times the product-costing rate*, (10,000 − 8,000) × $1 = $2,000 U.

Combined rate Many companies, while separating variable overhead and fixed overhead for planning and control purposes, combine them for product-costing purposes and use a single budgeted overhead rate. In the preceding example, such a rate would be $2.70, which is the variable-overhead rate of $1.70 plus the fixed-overhead rate of $1.00. In such cases, the overhead-variance analysis would merely show less detail than computed earlier. Do not attempt to study this section until you are thoroughly familiar with the earlier material in this chapter.

Two-way and three-way analysis Exhibit 7-7 provides a comprehensive analysis of all relationships among the combined-overhead analysis and its variable and fixed parts. Study it slowly, step by step. Begin at the bottom with the one-way analysis. Then move up.

EXHIBIT 7-7
Overhead Variance Analysis: Three Ways

	ACTUAL COSTS INCURRED	FLEXIBLE BUDGET: BASED ON ACTUAL INPUTS	FLEXIBLE BUDGET: BASED ON STANDARD INPUTS ALLOWED	APPLIED: STANDARD INPUTS ALLOWED FOR ACTUAL OUTPUTS
Total Overhead	($14,250 + $10,200) $24,450	($13,430 + $10,000) $23,430	($13,600 + $10,000) $23,600	($13,600 + $8,000) $21,600
3-way analysis	↑ Spending variance, $1,020 U*	↑Efficiency variance, $170 F↑	Production volume variance, $2,000 U	↑
2-way analysis	↑	Flexible-budget variance, $850 U	↑ Production volume variance, $2,000 U	↑
1-way analysis	↑	Total variance, $2,850 U (i.e., underapplied overhead of $2,850)		↑

*Note that this is the total of the variable-overhead spending variance and the fixed-overhead spending variance from Exhibit 7-6.

Even when the actual overhead costs cannot be separated into variable and fixed components, it is still possible to generate almost all of the flexible-budget analysis illustrated in the chapter. The only variances that could not be derived are the separate variable-overhead spending variance and the separate fixed-overhead spending variance (flexible-budget variance).

Note the distinction between the so-called two-way and three-way overhead analysis. The three-way analysis is the method that was used earlier in the chapter, where three different variances were computed: spending, efficiency, and production volume variances. The two-way analysis computes only two: flexible-budget (sometimes called the *controllable variance*) and production volume variances. The budget variance, as is clear in Exhibit 7-7, is simply the difference between actual costs and the budget allowance based on standard hours allowed. The two-way analysis stops there; it does not subdivide the budget variance into spending and efficiency variances.[5]

Exhibit 7-7 also illustrates how the flexible budget for the combined factory overhead is based on a formula with fixed and variable components: $10,000 +

---

[5]The respondents to the Chiu and Lee survey, *op. cit.*, indicated that 40% used the two-way analysis; 37%, the three-way; and 23%, some other way.

$1.70 per direct-labor hour. Such a formula can be developed by analyzing the budgeted behavior of costs as they change between two levels of volume. For example, in Exhibit 7-6:

$$\text{Variable overhead rate} = \frac{\text{Change in total combined overhead}}{\text{Change in production volume}}$$

$$= \frac{\$23,600 - \$23,430}{8,000 - 7,900} = \frac{\$170}{100} = \$1.70$$

Choose either level of volume to compute the fixed-overhead component:

$$\text{Fixed-overhead component} = \$23,600 - 8,000\ (\$1.70) = \$10,000$$

or

$$\text{Fixed-overhead component} = \$23,430 - 7,900\ (\$1.70) = \$10,000$$

OVERHEAD VARIANCES IN THE LEDGER

There are several ways of accounting for overhead variances. The easiest way is probably to allow the department-overhead control accounts and applied accounts to cumulate month-to-month postings until the end of the year. Monthly variances would not be isolated formally in the accounts, although monthly variance reports would be prepared. Assume that the data in Exhibit 7-6 are for the *year* rather than for the *month*. At the year-end, isolating (that is, separately identifying) and closing entries could be made as follows:

1. Variable factory overhead applied	13,600	
Variable-overhead spending variance	820	
Variable-overhead efficiency variance		170
Variable factory-overhead control		14,250
To isolate variances for the year.		
2. Fixed factory overhead applied	8,000	
Fixed-overhead spending (flexible budget) variance	200	
Fixed-overhead production volume variance	2,000	
Fixed factory-overhead control		10,200
To isolate variances for the year.		
3. Income summary (or Cost of goods sold)	650	
Variable-overhead efficiency variance	170	
Variable-overhead spending variance		820
To close.		
4. Income summary (or Cost of goods sold)	2,200	
Fixed-overhead spending (flexible budget) variance		200
Fixed-overhead production volume variance		2,000
To close.		

If desired, the isolation entries for the variances could be made monthly, although the closing entries are usually confined to the year-end.

Of course, rather than being closed directly to the Income Summary or Cost of Goods Sold, in certain cases the overhead variances may be prorated at the year-end, as shown in the next chapter.

The general ledger is designed mainly to serve purposes of product costing. Yet management's major purpose, that of planning and control, is aided by using flexible-budget figures, which are not highlighted in general-ledger balances. As is often the case, conventional general-ledger bookkeeping for overhead often provides only minimal information for control.

SUMMARY

This chapter has highlighted and contrasted two major purposes that must be served in accounting for overhead—planning and control via the use of flexible budgets and product costing via the use of budgeted overhead rates.

When analyzing overhead variances, managers regard the budget variance as controllable, at least to some degree. Managers generally regard production volume variance as less subject to control.

The general-ledger entries in this chapter sharply distinguish between fixed and variable overhead. This treatment is more effective for management than combining the two because it emphasizes the basic differences in cost behavior of these two kinds of overhead. Such basic differences are often important in influencing managerial decisions. The final section demonstrates that these distinctions can be maintained even if a combined overhead rate is used for product costing.

The worksheet analysis illustrated in Exhibits 7-6 and 7-7 provides a useful approach to the analysis of overhead variances. The first step is to obtain the underapplied or overapplied overhead, the total overhead variance. Then any further variance breakdowns can be added algebraically and checked against the total variance.

PROBLEMS FOR SELF-STUDY

The first problem for self-study appears earlier in this chapter. The following problem reviews both this and the preceding chapter. The numbers have deliberately been kept small to simplify the computations.

problem 2 The McDermott Furniture Company has established standard costs for the cabinet department, in which one size of a single four-drawer style of dresser is produced. The standard costs are used in evaluating actual performance. The standard costs of producing one of these dressers are shown below:

Standard-Cost Record
Dresser, Style AAA

Direct materials: Lumber—50 board feet @ $.20	$10.00
Direct labor: 3 hours @ $6.00	18.00
Factory overhead:	
Variable costs—3 hours @ $1.00	3.00
Fixed costs—3 hours @ $.50	1.50
Total per dresser	$32.50

The costs of operations to produce 400 of these dressers during January are stated below (there were no initial inventories):

Direct materials purchased:	25,000 board feet @ $.21	$5,250.00
Direct materials used:	19,000 board feet	
Direct labor:	1,100 hours at $5.90	6,490.00
Factory overhead:		
Variable costs		1,300.00
Fixed costs		710.00

The flexible budget for this department at the monthly volume level used to set the fixed-overhead rate called for 1,400 direct-labor hours of operation. At this level, the variable overhead was budgeted at $1,400, and the fixed overhead at $700.

Required

All journal entries for January. Compute the following variances from standard cost. Label your answers as *favorable* (F) or *unfavorable* (U).

1. Material price, isolated at time of purchase
2. Material efficiency
3. (a) Direct-labor price
   (b) Direct-labor efficiency
4. (a) Variable-overhead flexible-budget variance
   (b) Fixed-overhead spending (flexible budget) variance
   (c) Fixed-overhead production volume variance
5. (a) Variable-overhead spending variance
   (b) Variable-overhead efficiency variance

solution 2 Journal entries are supported by pertinent variance analysis.

1. Stores control (25,000 @ $.20)	5,000	
Material price variance (25,000 @ $.01)	250	
Accounts payable (25,000 @ $.21)		5,250
2. Work-in-process control (400 units × 50 board		
feet × $.20)	4,000	
Material-efficiency variance (1,000 × $.20)		200
Stores control (19,000 × $.20)		3,800
3. Work-in-process control (400 units × $18.00)	7,200	
Direct-labor price variance (1,100 hrs. × $.10)		110
Direct-labor efficiency variance (100 hrs. × $6.00)		600
Accrued payroll (1,100 hrs. × $5.90)		6,490
For analysis of variances, see Exhibit 7-8.		
4. Variable-overhead control	1,300	
Accounts payable and other accounts		1,300
Work-in-process control	1,200	
Variable overhead applied (400 × 3 × $1.00)		1,200
5. Fixed-overhead control	710	
Accounts payable and other accounts		710
Work-in-process control	600	
Fixed overhead applied (400 × 3 × $.50)		600

EXHIBIT 7-8 *(Place a clip on this page for easy reference.)*
McDermott Furniture Company
Analysis of Manufacturing Costs

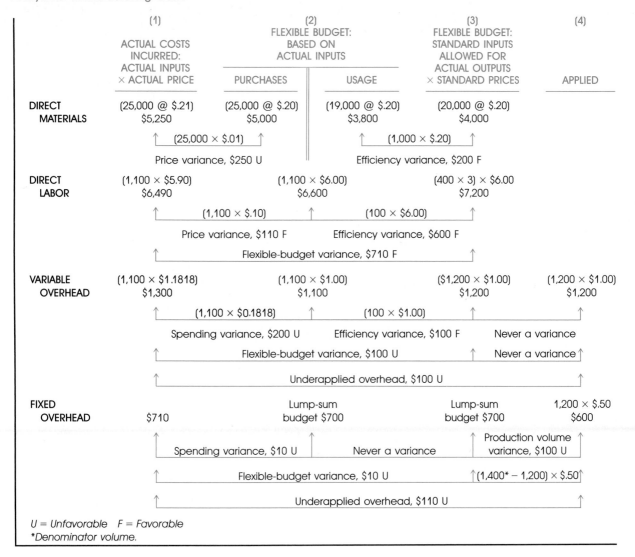

	(1) ACTUAL COSTS INCURRED: ACTUAL INPUTS × ACTUAL PRICE	(2) FLEXIBLE BUDGET: BASED ON ACTUAL INPUTS		(3) FLEXIBLE BUDGET: STANDARD INPUTS ALLOWED FOR ACTUAL OUTPUTS × STANDARD PRICES	(4) APPLIED
		PURCHASES	USAGE		
DIRECT MATERIALS	(25,000 @ $.21) $5,250	(25,000 @ $.20) $5,000	(19,000 @ $.20) $3,800	(20,000 @ $.20) $4,000	
		↑ (25,000 × $.01) ↑ Price variance, $250 U		↑ (1,000 × $.20) ↑ Efficiency variance, $200 F	
DIRECT LABOR	(1,100 × $5.90) $6,490		(1,100 × $6.00) $6,600	(400 × 3) × $6.00 $7,200	
		↑ (1,100 × $.10) ↑ Price variance, $110 F	↑ (100 × $6.00) ↑ Efficiency variance, $600 F		
		↑ Flexible-budget variance, $710 F ↑			
VARIABLE OVERHEAD	(1,100 × $1.1818) $1,300		(1,100 × $1.00) $1,100	($1,200 × $1.00) $1,200	(1,200 × $1.00) $1,200
		↑ (1,100 × $0.1818) ↑ Spending variance, $200 U	↑ (100 × $1.00) ↑ Efficiency variance, $100 F	↑ Never a variance	↑
		↑ Flexible-budget variance, $100 U ↑		↑ Never a variance ↑	
		↑ Underapplied overhead, $100 U			↑
FIXED OVERHEAD	$710	Lump-sum budget $700		Lump-sum budget $700	1,200 × $.50 $600
		↑ Spending variance, $10 U ↑	Never a variance	↑ Production volume variance, $100 U ↑	
		↑ Flexible-budget variance, $10 U ↑		↑(1,400* − 1,200) × $.50↑	
		↑ Underapplied overhead, $110 U ↑			

U = Unfavorable   F = Favorable
*Denominator volume.

     The analysis of variances in Exhibit 7-8 summarizes the characteristics of different cost behavior patterns. The approaches to direct labor and variable overhead are basically the same. Furthermore, there is no fundamental conflict between the planning and control and product-costing purposes; that is, the applied amounts in column (4) also equal the flexible-budget allowances. In contrast, the behavior patterns and control features of fixed overhead require a different analytical approach. The budget is a lump sum. There is no efficiency variance for fixed factory overhead because short-run performance cannot ordinarily affect incurrence of fixed factory overhead. Finally, there will nearly always be a conflict between the planning-and-control and product-costing purposes because the applied amount in column (4) for fixed overhead will differ from the lump-sum budget allowance. The latter conflict is highlighted by the production volume variance, which measures the effect of working at other than the denominator volume used to set the product-costing rate.

Terms to Learn

This chapter and the Glossary at the end of the book contain definitions of the following important terms:

activity variance (p. 231)   capacity variance (231)
denominator activity (223)   denominator level (223)
denominator variance (231)   denominator volume (223)
idle capacity variance (231)   production volume variance (227)
spending variance (220)   volume variance (231)

Special Points and Pitfalls

This chapter is probably the most technically demanding so far. The solving of a few homework problems is necessary for understanding. Before beginning any assigned problems, review the graphs, the Problems for Self-Study, and Exhibits 7-6 and 7-7 showing the worksheet summary. Students tend to become especially confused if they fail to:

1. Compute the actual output achieved and the standard hours allowed for that output before proceeding with any other part of their solution. The Applied column in the analytical framework is based on actual outputs or standard inputs allowed.
2. Clearly distinguish between variable factory overhead, which has an efficiency variance but no production volume variance, and fixed factory overhead, which has a production volume variance but no efficiency variance.
3. Remember that a production volume variance can be computed in either of two main ways: (a) Budget − Applied or (b) Fixed-overhead rate × (Denominator volume − Actual volume achieved).
4. Remember that the flexible budget for fixed factory overhead is a lump sum that is unaffected by either actual hours of input or standard hours of input allowed for actual output achieved.

The following tabulation is a capsule review of the key variances presented in this and the preceding chapter.

	DIRECT MATERIALS	DIRECT LABOR	VARIABLE FACTORY OVERHEAD	FIXED FACTORY OVERHEAD
Price variance?	Yes	Yes	No	No
Spending variance?	No	No	Yes	Yes*
Efficiency variance?	Yes	Yes	Yes	No
Flexible-budget variance?	Yes	Yes	Yes	Yes
Denominator volume concept?	No	No	No	Yes
Production volume variance?	No	No	No	Yes

*The flexible-budget variance and the spending variance for fixed overhead are always equal.

QUESTIONS, PROBLEMS, AND CASES

7-1 "The two tidy categories of price and efficiency are a crude split for analyzing variable-factory-overhead variances," Explain.

7-2 "A favorable variable-factory-overhead efficiency variance would be better described as a favorable variable-overhead labor efficiency variance." Do you agree? Explain.

7-3 "The price variance for variable factory overhead is really a glob." Explain.

7-4 Give two synonyms for *denominator volume*.

7-5 Explain how the accounting for fixed factory overhead in absorption cost systems differs between the planning and control purpose and the product-costing purpose.

7-6 Give three synonyms for *production volume variance*.

7-7 Why is it better to use the term *production volume variance* instead of *volume variance?*

7-8 "The spending variance and the flexible-budget variance for fixed factory overhead will always be identical amounts." Explain.

7-9 What is the essential difficulty in applying fixed overhead to product?

7-10 "There should be an efficiency variance for fixed overhead. A foreman can inefficiently use his fixed resources." Comment.

7-11 Why is the title "flexible budget" a misnomer?

7-12 What two basic questions should be asked in approaching the control of overhead?

7-13 Fill in the blanks. Use the given factory overhead data to fill in the blanks:

	VARIABLE	FIXED
Actual costs incurred	$11,800	$5,900
Applied to product	9,000	4,500
Flexible budget: Standard hours allowed for actual output achieved	9,000	5,000
Flexible budget: Based on actual hours of input	10,000	5,000

Use *F* for favorable and *U* for unfavorable:

	VARIABLE	FIXED
1. Spending variance	$ _____	$ _____
2. Efficiency variance	_____	_____
3. Production volume variance	_____	_____
4. Flexible-budget variance	_____	_____

7-14 Fill in the blanks. Using the given factory overhead data and *F* for favorable and *U* for unfavorable, fill in the blanks:

239

	FIXED	VARIABLE
Budget for actual hours of input	$60,000	$40,000
Applied	55,000	36,000
Budget for standard hours allowed for actual output achieved	?	?
Actual costs incurred	59,200	43,000
1. Spending variance	$_____	$_____
2. Efficiency variance	_____	_____
3. Production volume variance	_____	_____
4. Underapplied overhead	_____	_____
5. Flexible-budget variance	_____	_____

7-15 Flexible-budget, spending, and efficiency variances. John Eastman, the manager of a medical testing laboratory, has been under pressure from the director of a large clinic, Dr. Elvira Coleman, to get more productivity from his employees.

Eastman had been provided with some industry standards for various tests and had compiled a budgeted cost behavior pattern for direct labor and indirect costs. Some selected variable-cost items for a recent four-week period were:

	BUDGETED COST BEHAVIOR PATTERN PER DIRECT-LABOR HOUR	BUDGET BASED ON 4,000 ACTUAL LABOR HOURS	ACTUAL COSTS INCURRED	VARIANCE Amount	VARIANCE Percentage of Budget
Direct labor	$8.00	$32,000	$32,000	—	—
Supplies	2.00	8,000	6,400	1,600	20%
Indirect labor	1.00	4,000	3,000	1,000	25
Miscellaneous	2.00	8,000	6,000	2,000	25

Eastman was pleased with his budgetary performance, but Coleman was not happy. She asked you to reconstruct the performance report, saying, "This report seems incomplete. I want a better pinpointing of the degree of basic efficiency in that department."

Your investigation of the industry literature and your discussion with a management consultant in health care revealed that standard times have been developed for these clinical procedures. Although the standard times were open to criticism if examined on an hour-by-hour or day-by-day basis, in the aggregate over a week they provided a fairly reliable benchmark for measuring outputs against inputs. Your study of the output showed that about 2,600 standard direct-labor hours should have been allowed for the output actually achieved by the laboratory.

Required | Prepare a performance report based on the flexible budget for standard hours allowed for the output achieved. For each line item, show two final columns, one for spending variance and one for efficiency variance. Is this report better than the performance report shown above? Explain.

7-16 Price and spending variances. The Angelo Company used a flexible budget and standard costs. In March, the company produced 7,000 units of its finished product. Assume that 15,000 actual hours were used at an actual hourly rate of $8.20. Two direct-labor hours is the standard allowance for producing one unit. The standard-labor rate is $8 per hour. The flexible budget for miscellaneous supplies is based on a formula of $1.20 per unit, which can also be expressed as 60¢ per direct-labor hour. The actual cost of supplies was $9,400.

Required | 1. Compute the "price" and "efficiency" variances for direct labor and for supplies.
2. The "price" variance for supplies is rarely labeled as such. Instead it is often called a spending variance. The plant manager has made the following comments: "I have

been troubled by the waste of supplies for months. I know that the prices are exactly equal to the budgeted prices for every supply item, because a two-year stock of supplies was bought a year ago in anticipation of prolonged inflation. Consequently, we used known prices for preparing our budgets. Given these facts, please explain how a price or spending variance can arise for miscellaneous supplies. Why doesn't all waste appear as an efficiency variance?" Respond to the manager's comments. Be clear and specific; the manager is impatient with muddled explanations, and your next pay raise will be affected by her appraisal of your explanation.

7-17 Detailed analysis of variable overhead. A department is scheduled to produce 10,000 units of product in 5,000 standard direct-labor hours. However, it has taken 6,000 actual direct-labor hours to produce the 10,000 units. The variable-factory-overhead items are as follows:

	BUDGET FORMULA PER STANDARD DIRECT-LABOR HOUR ALLOWED	ACTUAL COSTS INCURRED
Indirect labor	$2.00	$11,700
Maintenance	.20	1,150
Lubricants	.10	600
Cutting tools	.16	1,500
	$2.46	$14,950

The actual direct-labor rate is $16.20 per hour; the standard rate is $16.00.

Required

1. Prepare a performance report with separate lines for direct labor, indirect labor, maintenance, lubricants, and cutting tools. Show three columns: actual costs incurred, flexible budget, and flexible-budget variance.
2. Prepare a more detailed version of your answer to requirement 2, showing six columns: actual costs incurred, actual quantities × standard prices, flexible budget, flexible-budget variance, price or spending variance, and efficiency variance.
3. Explain the similarities and differences between the direct-labor and the variable-overhead variances.

7-18 Variable overhead related to labor dollars. The following items are the variable factory overhead for October for the O'Leary Company:

ACTUAL COSTS		BUDGET RATE PER DIRECT LABOR DOLLAR
$ 66,000	Material handling (indirect) labor	10%
268,100	Employer payroll taxes, pensions, etc.	35
117,000	Power	15
40,000	Overtime premium	5
93,000	Factory supplies	15
$584,100	Total	80%

Actual direct-labor hours of input were 60,000. The standard direct-labor rate is $12. The use of less-experienced workers resulted in an actual direct-labor rate of $11. The standard direct-labor allowance was 4 hours per unit produced. The total units produced in October were 13,500.

Required

1. Prepare a detailed line-by-line performance report for direct labor and the *individual* variable factory overhead costs. Use three columns: actual costs, flexible budget, and flexible-budget variances.

241

2. Prepare a summary analysis of direct labor and the *total* variable-factory-overhead costs, using the framework of Exhibit 7-8, page 237.
3. What insights can you draw from your answers in requirements 1 and 2?

7-19 Comprehensive, straightforward problem on a standard-cost system. The Singapore division of a Canadian company uses a standard-cost system. The month's data regarding its lone product follow:

Fixed-overhead costs incurred, $6,150
Variable overhead applied at $.90 per hour
Standard direct-labor cost, $4.00 per hour
Standard material cost, $1.00 per pound
Standard pounds of material in a finished unit, 3
Denominator volume per month, 2,500 units
Standard direct-labor hours per finished unit, 5
Materials purchased, 10,000 lbs., $9,500
Materials used, 6,700 lbs.
Direct-labor costs incurred, 11,000 hours, $41,800
Variable-overhead costs incurred, $9,500
Fixed-overhead budget variance, $100, favorable
Finished units produced, 2,000

Required | Prepare journal entries. Prepare schedules of all variances, using the analytical framework illustrated in Exhibit 7-8, page 237. Material price variances are isolated as materials are purchased.

7-20 Graphs and overhead variances. The Carvelli Company is a manufacturer of footwear. The company uses a standard absorption-costing system. The budget for 19_2 included:

Variable factory overhead	$9 per direct-labor hour
Fixed factory overhead	$12,000,000
Denominator volume based on expected direct-labor hours allowed for budgeted output	4,000,000 hours

Required |
1. Prepare four freehand graphs, two for variable overhead and two for fixed overhead. Each pair should display how total costs will fluctuate for (a) planning and control purposes and (b) product-costing purposes.
2. Suppose 3,500,000 standard direct-labor hours were allowed for the production actually achieved in 19_2. However, 3,800,000 actual hours of input were used. Actual factory overhead was: variable, $36,100,000; fixed, $12,200,000. Compute (a) variable-overhead spending and efficiency variances and (b) fixed-overhead flexible-budget variance and production volume variance. Use the analytical framework illustrated in Exhibit 7-8, page 237.
3. Prepare a graph for fixed factory overhead that shows a budget line and an applied line. Indicate the production volume variance on the graph.
4. What is the amount of the underapplied variable overhead? Fixed overhead? Why are the flexible-budget variance and the underapplied overhead always the same amount for variable factory overhead but rarely the same amount for fixed factory overhead?
5. Suppose the denominator volume level was 3,000,000 rather than 4,000,000 hours. What variances in requirement 2 would be affected? What would be their new amounts?

7-21 Journal entries. Refer to the preceding problem, requirement 2. Consider variable factory overhead and then fixed factory overhead. Prepare the journal entries for (a) the incurrence of overhead, (b) the application of overhead, and (c) the isolation and closing of overhead variances for the year.

7-22 Straightforward overhead analysis. The Lopez Company uses a standard-cost system. Its standard cost of Product Y, based on a denominator activity of 40,000 units per year, included six hours of variable overhead at $.80 per hour and six hours of fixed overhead at $1.50 per hour. Actual output achieved was 44,000 units. Actual variable factory overhead was $245,000. Actual hours of input were 284,000. Actual fixed overhead was $373,000.

Prepare journal entries. Prepare an analysis of all variable-overhead and fixed-overhead variances, using the approach illustrated in Exhibit 7-6, page 232.

7-23 Characteristics of fixed-overhead variances. Fox Company executives have studied their operations carefully and have been using a standard-cost system for years. They are now formulating standards for 19_1. They agree that the standards for direct materials will amount to $10 per finished unit produced and that the standards for direct labor and variable overhead are to be $9 and $1 per direct-labor hour, respectively. Total fixed overhead is expected to be $600,000. Two hours of direct labor is the standard time for finishing one unit of finished product.

Required

1. Graph the budgeted fixed overhead for 400,000 to 800,000 standard allowed direct-labor hours of activity, assuming that the total budget will not change over that activity level. What would be the appropriate product-costing rate per standard direct-labor hour for fixed overhead if denominator activity is 500,000 hours? Graph the applied fixed-overhead line.
2. Assume that 250,000 units of product were produced. How much fixed overhead would be applied to product? Would there be a production volume variance? Why? Assume that 200,000 units were produced. Would there be a production volume variance? Why? Show the latter volume variance on a graph. In your own words, define *production volume variance*. Why does it arise? Can a volume variance exist for variable overhead? Why?
3. Assume that 220,000 units are produced. Fixed-overhead costs incurred were $617,000. What is the total fixed-overhead variance? Flexible-budget variance? Volume variance? Use the analytical technique illustrated in the chapter.
4. In requirement 1 (ignoring requirements 2 and 3), what would be the appropriate product-costing rate per standard direct-labor hour for fixed overhead if denominator volume is estimated at 400,000 hours? At 600,000 hours? At 800,000 hours? Draw a graph showing budgeted fixed overhead and three "applied" lines, using the three rates just calculated. If 200,000 units are produced, and the denominator volume is 600,000 standard direct-labor hours, what is the volume variance? Now compare this with the volume variance in your answer to requirement 2; explain the difference.
5. Specifically, what are the implications in requirements 1 and 4 regarding (a) the setting of product-costing rates for fixed overhead, (b) the meaning of budget and volume variances, and (c) the major differences in planning and control techniques for variable and fixed costs?

7-24 Flexible budget, overhead variances. (CMA, adapted) Nolton Products developed its overhead application rate from the current annual budget. The budget is based on an expected actual output of 720,000 units requiring 3,600,000 direct-labor hours (DLH). The company is able to schedule production uniformly throughout the year.

A total of 66,000 units requiring 315,000 DLH was produced during May. Actual overhead costs for May amounted to $375,000. The actual cost as compared with the annual budget and one-twelfth of the annual budget are shown below.

Nolton uses a standard absorption-costing system and applies factory overhead on the basis of DLH.

Schedule for Problem 7-24

	ANNUAL BUDGET				ACTUAL
	Total Amount	Per Unit	Per DLH	MONTHLY BUDGET	COSTS FOR MAY 19_3
VARIABLE					
Indirect labor	$ 900,000	$1.25	$ .25	$ 75,000	$ 75,000
Supplies	1,224,000	1.70	.34	102,000	111,000
FIXED					
Supervision	648,000	.90	.18	54,000	51,000
Utilities	540,000	.75	.15	45,000	54,000
Depreciation	1,008,000	1.40	.28	84,000	84,000
Total	$4,320,000	$6.00	$1.20	$360,000	$375,000

Required

Calculate the following amounts for Nolton Products for May 19_3:

1. Absorbed overhead costs
2. Variable overhead spending variance
3. Fixed overhead spending variance
4. Variable overhead efficiency variance
5. Production volume variance

Be sure to identify each variance as favorable (F) or unfavorable (U).

7-25 Find the unknowns. Consider each of the following situations independently. Data refer to operations for a week in April. For each situation assume a standard product-cost system. Also assume the use of a flexible budget for control of variable and fixed overhead based on standard direct-labor hours.

	CASES		
	A	B	C
(1) Actual fixed overhead	$10,600	—	$12,000
(2) Actual variable overhead	7,000	—	—
(3) Denominator volume in hours	5,000	—	11,000
(4) Standard hours allowed for good output	—	6,500	—
Flexible-budget data:			
(5) Fixed factory overhead	—	—	—
(6) Variable factory overhead (per standard hour)	—	85¢	50¢
(7) Budgeted fixed factory overhead	10,000	—	11,000
(8) Budgeted variable factory overhead*	—	—	—
(9) Total budgeted factory overhead*	—	12,525	—
(10) Standard variable overhead applied	7,500	—	—
(11) Standard fixed overhead applied	10,000	—	—
(12) Production volume variance	—	500 U	500 F
(13) Variable-overhead spending variance	950 F	-0-	350 U
(14) Variable-overhead efficiency variance	—	-0-	100 U
(15) Fixed-overhead budget variance	—	300 F	—
(16) Actual hours of input	—	—	—

*For standard hours allowed for output achieved.

Required

Fill in the blanks under each case. Prepare your answer by (a) listing the numbers that are blank for each case and (b) putting the final answers next to the numbers. Prepare supporting computations on a separate sheet. For example, your answer to Case A would contain a vertical listing of the numbers 4, 5, 6, 8, 9, 12, 14, 15, and 16, with answers next to the appropriate numbers. *Hint:* Prepare a worksheet similar to that in Exhibit 7-6, page 232. Fill in the knowns and then solve for the unknowns.

7-26 Two-way and three-way analysis. The Wilson Company has a standard absorption-costing system. A single hourly rate is used to apply factory overhead to product. However, a flexible-budget formula is used for budgetary-control purposes: $8,000,000 per year plus $7 per direct-labor hour.

For 19_1, the denominator volume for developing a product-costing rate was the expected volume of 1,600,000 direct-labor hours. The actual factory overhead was $18,000,000. Direct-labor hours were: standard allowed for actual output achieved, 1,300,000; actual hours of input, 1,500,000.

Required | Prepare an analysis of all overhead variances. Use the format of Exhibit 7-7 to display a two-way analysis and a three-way analysis. See page 233.

7-27 Combined overhead rate, three variances. (SMA, adapted) The Ballentine Company produces a single product, an intricate disposable medical sensor.
Monthly flexible-budget data follow:

Volume in units of product	15,000	25,000
Direct material costs	$ 30,000	$ 50,000
Direct labor	180,000	300,000
Factory overhead:		
✓ Indirect material	15,000	25,000
✓ Indirect labor	30,000	50,000
✓ Supervision	26,250	33,750
✓ Heat, light, and power	15,250	22,750
✓ Depreciation	63,000	63,000
✓ Insurance and taxes	8,000	8,000
Total overhead	157,500	202,500
Total manufacturing costs	$367,500	$552,500

OTHER INFORMATION

The standard time for one unit of product is 1.5 direct-labor hours. The denominator activity is 30,000 direct-labor hours. Actual data during June 19_1:

Units produced	22,000
Actual direct-labor hours of input	32,000
Overhead incurred	$191,000

Standard factory-overhead rates are based on direct-labor hours.

Required | 1. Prepare a summary factory-overhead variance analysis (using three variances) for June 19_1. Show all computations.
2. What possible courses of action are open to management to investigate the variances?

7-28 Hospital overhead variances. The Sharon Hospital, a large metropolitan health-care complex, has had much trouble in controlling its accounts receivable. Bills for patients, for various government agencies, and for private insurance companies have frequently been inaccurate and late. This has led to intolerable levels of bad debts and investments in receivables.

You were employed by the hospital as a consultant on this matter. After conducting a careful study of the billing operation, you developed some currently attainable standards that were implemented in conjunction with a flexible budget four weeks ago. You had divided costs into fixed and variable categories. You regarded the bill as the product, the unit of output.

You have reasonable confidence that the underlying source documents for compiling the results have been accurately tallied. However, the bookkeeper has had some trouble summarizing the data and has provided the following:

Variable costs, including all billing operators, whose compensation is regarded as variable, allowance per standard hour	$ 10
Fixed-overhead budget variance, favorable	200
Combined budgeted costs for the bills produced	22,500
Production volume variance, favorable	900
Variable-cost "spending" variance, unfavorable	2,000
Variable-cost efficiency variance, favorable	2,000
Standard hours allowed for the bills produced, 1,800	

Required

1. Actual hours of input
2. Fixed-overhead budget
3. Standard fixed overhead applied
4. Denominator volume in hours

7-29 Combined overhead rate. The Wright-Patterson Air Force Base contained an extensive repair facility for jet engines. It had developed standard costing amd flexible budgets for this activity. Budgeted *variable* overhead at a 16,000 standard monthly direct-labor-hour level was $64,000; budgeted *total* overhead at a 20,000 standard direct-labor-hour level was $197,600. The standard cost applied to repair output included a combined overhead rate of 120% of standard direct-labor cost.

Total actual overhead for October was $250,000. Direct-labor costs actually incurred were $202,440. The direct-labor price variance was $9,640, unfavorable. The direct-labor budget variance was $14,440, unfavorable. The standard labor price was $8.00 per hour. The denominator variance was $14,000, favorable.

Required

Direct-labor efficiency variance. Combined overhead spending, efficiency, and denominator variances. Also compute the denominator volume. (*Hint:* See Exhibit 7-7.)

7-30 Combined overhead variances. (SMA, adapted) The Weser Company uses a predetermined total overhead rate of $4 per unit based on a denominator volume of 600,000 units a year, or 50,000 units a month.

During October, the company produced 52,000 units and experienced the following combined overhead variances:

Overhead flexible-budget variance	$2,500 unfavorable
Overhead production volume variance	$5,000 favorable

During November, unit production was 49,000 units and the actual overhead cost incurred was $2,000 less than October's overhead.

Determine the overhead budget variance and production volume variance for the month of November.

7-31 Normal costing and overhead analysis. The Blaney Company had *budgeted* the following performance for 19_4:

Units	10,000
Sales	$120,000
Total variable production costs, including variable factory overhead of $5,000	60,000
Total fixed production costs	25,000
Gross margin	35,000
Beginning inventories	None

It is now December 31, 19_4. The factory-overhead rate that was used throughout the year was $3 per unit. Total factory overhead incurred was $30,000. Underapplied factory overhead was $900. There is no work in process.

Required

1. How many units were produced during 19_4?
2. Nine thousand units were sold at regular prices during 19_4. Assuming that the predicted cost behavior patterns implicit in the budget above have conformed to the plan (except for variable factory overhead), and that underapplied factory overhead is written off directly as an adjustment of cost of goods sold, what is the gross margin for 19_4? How much factory overhead should be assigned to the ending inventory if it is to be carried at "normal" cost?
3. Explain *why* overhead was underapplied by $900. In other words, analyze the variable- and fixed-overhead variances as far as the data permit.

Special review material for chapters 6 and 7

7-32 Fundamental variance analysis. (CPA, adapted) The Beal Company uses a standard-costing system. At the beginning of 19_6, Beal adopted the following standards:

	INPUT	TOTAL
Direct materials	3 lbs. @ $2.50 per lb.	$ 7.50
Direct labor	5 hrs. @ $7.50 per hr.	37.50
Factory overhead:		
Variable	$3.00 per direct-labor hour	15.00
Fixed	$4.00 per direct-labor hour	20.00
Standard cost per unit		$80.00

Normal volume per month is 40,000 standard direct-labor hours. Beal's January 19_6 flexible budget, set up on January 1, was based on normal volume. Beal's actual January production was 7,800 units. The records for January indicated the following:

Direct materials purchased	25,000 lbs. @ $2.60
Direct materials used	23,100 lbs.
Direct labor	40,100 hrs. @ $7.30
Total actual factory overhead (variable and fixed)	$300,000

Required

1. Prepare a schedule of total standard production costs for the production of 7,800 units in January.
2. For the month of January 19_6, compute the following variances, indicating whether each is favorable (F) or unfavorable (U):
   a. Direct-materials price variance, based on purchases
   b. Direct-materials efficiency (usage) variance
   c. Direct-labor price (rate) variance
   d. Direct-labor efficiency variance
   e. Total-factory-overhead spending variance
   f. Variable-factory-overhead efficiency variance
   g. Total-factory-overhead production volume variance

7-33 Miscellaneous aspects of standard costing. (D. Kleespie) The J/M Company manufactures a single product in a single department and utilizes a standard-cost system. Standard costs per unit of finished product include a total direct-materials cost of $20, which consists of 4 pounds of direct material at $5 per pound. Two hours of direct labor are required per unit of finished product. The standard direct-labor-hour rate is $5 per hour. The following represents a condensed monthly flexible factory-overhead budget for the firm:

247

STANDARD DIRECT-LABOR HOURS ALLOWED	30,000 HRS.	40,000 HRS.	50,000 HRS.
Variable manufacturing overhead:			
Supplies	$ 9,000	$ 12,000	$ 15,000
Indirect labor	22,000	33,000	44,000
Other variable overhead	17,000	19,000	21,000
	$ 48,000	$ 64,000	$ 80,000
Fixed manufacturing overhead:			
Supervision	$ 48,000	$ 48,000	$ 48,000
Depreciation	40,000	40,000	40,000
Other fixed overhead	17,000	17,000	17,000
	$105,000	$105,000	$105,000
Total budgeted manufacturing overhead	$153,000	$169,000	$185,000

The company uses a combined manufacturing-overhead rate (fixed and variable) of $8.20 per finished unit for product-costing purposes. Data for a certain month's production follow:

20,000 units produced (there were no units in process at either the beginning or the end of the month)

Direct labor, 41,000 actual direct-labor hours at $5.50 per hour

Direct material purchased, 96,000 pounds at $5.20 per pound

Direct material used in production, 90,000 pounds

Total actual manufacturing-overhead costs incurred, $176,000, of which $104,000 were fixed-overhead costs

Required

(Show supporting computations for your answers.)
For items 1 through 3 you are to determine the total dollar amounts of the indicated variances. Use *F* or *U* to designate favorable or unfavorable.

1. Labor efficiency variance.
2. Variable-overhead spending variance.
3. Fixed-overhead production volume variance.
4. Amount that should be debited to Work in Process for *total* factory overhead applied for this month.
5. Total amount that should be debited to Work in Process for direct labor used during this month.
6. Monthly denominator activity expressed in standard direct-labor hours.
7. Total amount of manufacturing overhead that would be *budgeted* for a month in which 22,000 *units of product* were expected to be produced.
8. Total dollar amount debited to the finished-goods inventory for the units produced this month. (Assume that all variances are closed directly to cost of goods sold, i.e., reported on the monthly income statement.)

7-34 Normal costing. Refer to the preceding problem.
What is the total dollar amount debited to the finished-goods inventory for the units produced this month if a "normal"-costing system had been used instead of the standard cost system described in requirement 8 above? (You may assume that any overhead that was overapplied or underapplied would be closed to cost of goods sold.)

7-35 Working backward from given variances. The Mancuso Company uses a flexible budget and standard costs to aid planning and control. At a 60,000-direct-labor-hour level, budgeted variable overhead is $30,000 and budgeted direct labor is $480,000.
The following are some results for August:

Variable-overhead budget variance	$ 10,500 U
Variable-overhead efficiency variance	9,500 U
Actual direct-labor costs incurred	574,000
Material purchase-price variance (based on goods purchased)	16,000 F
Material-efficiency variance	9,000 U
Fixed-overhead incurred	50,000
Fixed-overhead budget variance	2,000 U

The standard cost per pound of direct materials is $1.50. The standard allowance is one pound of direct materials for each unit of finished product. Ninety thousand units of product were made during August. There was no beginning or ending work in process. In July, the material-efficiency variance was $1,000, favorable, and the purchase-price variance was $.20 per pound, unfavorable. In August, the purchase-price variance was $.10 per pound.

In July, labor troubles caused an immense slowdown in the pace of production. There had been an unfavorable direct-labor efficiency variance of $60,000; there was no labor-price variance. These troubles had persisted in August. Some workers quit. Their replacements had to be hired at higher rates, which had to be extended to all workers. The actual average wage rate in August exceeded the standard average wage rate by $.20 per hour.

Required

For August:

1. Total pounds of direct materials purchased during August
2. Total number of pounds of excess material usage
3. Variable-overhead spending variance
4. Total number of actual hours of input
5. Total number of standard hours allowed for the finished units produced

7-36 Variance analysis from fragmentary evidence. Being a bright young person, you have just landed a wonderful job as assistant controller of Gyp-Clip, a new and promising Singapore division of Croding Metals Corporation. The Gyp-Clip Division has been formed to produce a single product, a new-model paper clip. Croding Laboratories has developed an extremely springy and lightweight new alloy, Clypton, which is expected to revolutionize the paper-clip industry.

Gyp-Clip has been in business one month; it is your first day on the job. The controller takes you on a tour of the plant and explains the operation in detail: Clypton wire is received on two-mile spools from the Croding mill at a fixed price of $40 a spool, which is not subject to change. Clips are bent, cut, and shipped in bulk to the Croding packaging plant. Factory rent, depreciation, and all other items of fixed factory overhead are handled by the home office at a set rate of $100,000 per month. Ten thousand tons of paper clips have been produced, but this is only 75% of denominator volume since demand for the product must be built up.

The controller has just figured out the month's variances; she is looking for a method of presenting them in clear, logical form to top management at the home office. You say that you know of just the method, and promise to have the analysis ready the next morning.

Filled with zeal and enthusiasm, feeling that your future as a rising star in this growing company is secure, you decide to take your spouse out to dinner to celebrate the trust and confidence that your superior has placed in you.

Upon returning home, with the flush of four martinis still upon you, you are horrified to discover your dog happily devouring the controller's figure sheet. You manage to salvage only the fragments shown on the next page.

You remember that the $35,000 variance did not represent the grand total of all variances. You also recall that variance analysis was easier to tackle by expressing items in terms of inputs (such as hours) rather than outputs.

Required

Don't let the controller think you're a knucklehead; go ahead and make up your analysis of all variances.

7-37 Variance analysis. (J. Patell) During 19_6, the T–M Division of Acro-Cel Tool and Machine had specialized in the production of a single heavy-duty motorcycle component. Original engineering estimates and the use of Acro-Cel's *Total Overhead* Flexible Budget had yielded the following standard cost per unit:

	STANDARD COST		FLEXIBLE BUDGET—TOTAL OVERHEAD	
			Labor Hours	Expected Cost
Materials	10 lbs. @ 1.50 per lb.	= $15.00	16,000	$ 96,000
Labor	2 hours @ $6.00 per hr. =	12.00	18,000	$ 98,000
Variable overhead	2 hours @ $1.00 per hr. =	2.00	20,000	$100,000
Fixed overhead	2 hours @ $4.00 per hr. =	8.00	22,000	$102,000
Total standard cost		$37.00		

Tom, the T–M Division shop foreman, tends to communicate in brief, blunt reports. His analysis of 19_6 is reproduced below:

> As usual, the yo-yos in Purchasing and Personnel goofed and are trying to pass the buck to us. Your hotshot planners predicted an average wage rate of $6.00, and then your bleeding heart labor negotiators conceded to $6.60 an hour, for a 10% overrun. On top of that, Purchasing paid $1.80 per pound for materials they should have gotten for $1.50, or a whopping 20% overexpenditure. Given that kind of incompetence, I feel the T–M production line deserves a big thank-you for holding actual total costs per unit down to $41.58, which works out to 12.4% over standard.

Actual expenditures:

Materials	$226,800	Total cost	$498,920
Labor	166,320	Actual output	12,000 units
Variable overhead	24,800	Actual cost per unit	$41.58
Fixed overhead	81,000		
Total costs	$498,920		

Required

For ease of computation, assume that both the beginning and ending material inventory balances were zero. Indeed, Acro-Cel uses a just-in-time inventory system, which means that no materials inventories are carried by Acro-Cel. Instead materials are delivered to the factory one to two hours before use.

1. Rework Tom's report into a complete variance analysis. Compute and *label* price, spending, and efficiency variances for direct material, direct labor, and variable overhead, as well as budget and production volume variances for fixed overhead.

2. Tom's report is also difficult to reconcile with a complaint from the controller's office that the T–M Division's cash expenditures were almost 35% higher than originally budgeted and had placed a severe strain on Acro-Cel's relationships with the bank. What was the original (static) budget figure for the T–M Division's total costs?

7-38 Interpretation of variances. Refer to the preceding problem. Analyze the quotation therein. Is Tom correct? Be specific, supplying as many numbers as possible. *Hint:* Remember the display in Exhibit 6-4, page 183.

8

Income Effects of Alternative Product-Costing Methods

Variable and absorption costing • Comparison of standard variable and standard absorption costing • Breakeven points and absorption costing • The central issue: a question of timing • Role of various denominator levels in absorption costing • Standard-cost variances and the income statement • Adjusting inventories for external reporting • Variances and interim reporting • Appendix 8A: Standard-cost variances: a more accurate approach to proration • Appendix 8B: Comparison of variance prorations, normal and standard costing

When an accounting system is designed, managers and accountants must choose an inventory-costing method. This decision is vital for many reasons, including its effects on reported income in any given fiscal period, on the evaluation of managers' performance, and on pricing decisions.

The major purposes of this chapter are to **examine and compare the effects of some costing alternatives on the measurements of product costs and income.** Other decision implications of these alternatives are also mentioned, but they are discussed more fully in subsequent chapters.

We consider three major topics: (a) variable and absorption costing, (b) the role of various denominator levels in absorption costing, and (c) standard-cost variances and the income statement. Chapter Appendixes cover additional discussions of prorations of variances. These topics are related sufficiently to warrant their being considered in a single chapter. *However, they may be studied independently.* Consequently, each of the Problems for Self-Study in this chapter is placed at the end of the appropriate major section. Pause at the end of each section and solve the pertinent Problem for Self-Study.

VARIABLE AND ABSORPTION COSTING

Impact of fixed factory overhead

The rudiments of *variable costing* (also called *direct costing*) and *absorption costing* were compared in Chapter 3, pages 55–58 and 70. You may wish to refresh your memory by rereading that discussion.

The basic impact of variable and absorption costing on income is deceptively simple. Differences arise because fixed factory overhead is not inventoried under variable costing and is inventoried under absorption costing. Using simple numbers, suppose that fixed factory overhead incurred was $2,200 for the year 19_1. Also suppose that 1,100 units were produced, but only 1,000 units were sold. Assuming the denominator volume for absorption costing was 1,100 units, the fixed overhead rate would be $2,200 ÷ 1,100 = $2.00 per unit. The following chart summarizes the differences in accounting:

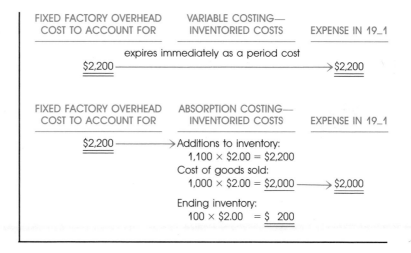

FIXED FACTORY OVERHEAD COST TO ACCOUNT FOR	VARIABLE COSTING— INVENTORIED COSTS	EXPENSE IN 19_1
	expires immediately as a period cost	
$2,200	————————————————————→	$2,200

FIXED FACTORY OVERHEAD COST TO ACCOUNT FOR	ABSORPTION COSTING— INVENTORIED COSTS	EXPENSE IN 19_1
$2,200 ————→	Additions to inventory: 1,100 × $2.00 = $2,200	
	Cost of goods sold: 1,000 × $2.00 = $2,000 ————→	$2,000
	Ending inventory: 100 × $2.00 = $ 200	

The chart contains only one item, fixed factory overhead, because *all* other manufacturing costs are accounted for exactly alike under both variable and absorption costing. That is, direct materials, direct labor, and variable factory overhead are always inventoriable.

Trace the $2,200 to Exhibit 8-1 where additional information is presented. The variable-costing statement deducts the lump sum as an expense in 19_1. In contrast, the absorption-costing statement regards each finished unit as bearing $2 of fixed factory overhead. The variable manufacturing costs are accounted for the same in either statement.

The general format of these income statements should be familiar. The new feature is explained in the second footnote in Exhibit 8-1. If inventory levels change, income will differ because of the different accounting for fixed factory overhead.

Never overlook the heart of the matter. The differences between variable costing and absorption costing center on how to account for fixed factory over-

EXHIBIT 8-1

Comparison of Variable and Absorption Costing
B Company
Income Statements for the Year Ended Dec. 31, 19_1

(Data assumed; there is no beginning inventory; the unit *variable* manufacturing cost is $6.00.)

VARIABLE (DIRECT) COSTING

Sales: 1,000 units @ $10.00		$10,000
Variable manufacturing cost of goods		
available for sale: 1,100 units @ $6.00	$6,600*	
Less ending inventory: 100 units @ $6.00	600†	
Variable manufacturing cost of goods sold	$6,000	
Add variable selling and administrative		
expenses	400	
Total variable costs charged against sales		6,400
Contribution margin‡		$ 3,600
Less fixed costs:		
Fixed manufacturing costs	$2,200	
Fixed selling and administrative expenses	500	2,700
Operating income		$ 900†

*Composed of

	UNIT COST	TOTAL
Direct materials	$3.00	$3,300
Direct labor	2.00	2,200
Variable overhead	1.00	1,100
Variable manufacturing costs	$6.00	$6,600

ABSORPTION COSTING

	UNIT COST	TOTAL	
Sales			$10,000
Cost of goods sold:			
Variable manufacturing costs:			
1,100 units	$6.00	$6,600*	
Fixed manufacturing costs	2.00	2,200	
Cost of goods available			
for sale	$8.00	$8,800	
Less ending inventory:			
100 units	8.00	800†	
Gross margin‡			$ 8,000
Less total selling and			
administrative expenses,			
including $400 of			
variable expenses			$ 2,000
			900
Operating income			$ 1,100†

†The $200 difference in operating income is caused by the $200 ($800 − $600) difference in ending inventories. Under absorption costing, $200 of the $2,200 fixed manufacturing costs is held back in inventory, whereas under variable costing the $200 is released immediately as a charge against sales.
‡The contribution margin and the gross margin are two important intermediate amounts that highlight the conflict of the underlying concepts of variable costing and absorption costing.

head. Instead of sales of 1,000 units, suppose sales were 900, 1,000, and 1,100 units, respectively. Fixed factory overhead would be included in expense as follows:

	EXPENSE IN 19_1
Variable costing, whether sales are 900, 1,000, or 1,100 units	$2,200
Absorption costing, where sales are:	
900 units, $400 held back in inventory	$1,800
1,000 units, $200 held back in inventory	$2,000
1,100 units, all $2,200 of 19_1 fixed overhead	$2,200

Versatility of variable costing

Exhibit 8-1 presents the general features of variable and absorption costing. Using a Work-in-Process account, a capsule comparison of six alternative product-costing systems is presented in Exhibit 8-2.

The boxes represent the debits to Work in Process (that is, the amounts applied to product) under alternative cost systems. The major systems in use are the standard-costing systems, which were introduced in the preceding two chapters, and the normal-costing systems, which were introduced in Chapter 4. As the boxes indicate, variable costing or absorption costing may be combined with actual, normal, or standard costing. **Variable costing signifies that fixed factory overhead is *not* inventoried.**

Variable (direct) costing has been a controversial subject among accountants—not so much because there is disagreement about the need for delineating between variable- and fixed-cost behavior patterns for management planning and control, but because there is a question about its theoretical propriety for *external* reporting. Proponents of variable costing maintain that the fixed portion of factory overhead is more closely related to the *capacity* to produce than to the production of specific

EXHIBIT 8-2
Capsule Comparison of Six Alternative Product-Costing Systems

		WORK-IN-PROCESS INVENTORY		
		ACTUAL COSTING	NORMAL COSTING	STANDARD COSTING
(1) { (2) {	DIRECT MATERIALS AND DIRECT LABOR	Actual inputs × Actual prices	Actual inputs × Actual prices	Standard inputs allowed for actual output achieved × Standard prices
	VARIABLE FACTORY OVERHEAD	Actual inputs × Actual overhead rates	Actual inputs × Budgeted overhead rates	Standard inputs allowed for actual output achieved × Budgeted overhead rates
	FIXED FACTORY OVERHEAD	Actual inputs × Actual overhead rates	Actual inputs × Budgeted overhead rates	Standard inputs allowed for actual output achieved × Budgeted overhead rates

(1) Absorption Costing—Includes All Boxes
(2) Variable (Direct) Costing—Excludes Bottom Boxes Representing Fixed Factory Overhead

units. Opponents of variable costing maintain that inventories should carry a fixed-cost component, because both variable and fixed manufacturing costs are necessary to produce goods; both of these costs should be inventoriable, regardless of their differences in behavior patterns. Neither the public accounting profession nor the Internal Revenue Service has approved of variable costing as a generally acceptable method of inventory valuation. However, variable costing is not prohibited for such purposes in Canada.

Absorption costing is much more widely used than variable costing, although the growing use of the contribution approach in performance measurement and cost analysis has led to increasing use of variable costing for *internal* purposes. A survey of *Fortune 500* industrial corporations indicated that 35% of the companies that use standard costing have adopted standard variable costing.[1]

COMPARISON OF STANDARD VARIABLE AND STANDARD ABSORPTION COSTING

The following problem illustrates the implications of accounting for fixed factory overhead in more depth.

problem   Stassen Company began business on January 1, 19_1. It is now the end of 19_2. The company uses standard absorption costing. The president is trying to decide whether to adopt standard variable costing for measuring management performance. She has asked you to prepare comparative income statements for 19_1 and 19_2 under absorption and variable costing.

The following simplified data are available:

	19_1	19_2
Beginning inventory	—	4,000
Production	6,000	900
Sales	2,000	3,000
Ending inventory	4,000	1,900

OTHER DATA:

Variable manufacturing costs per unit	$ 2
Fixed manufacturing costs	$10,000
Denominator volume in units	10,000
Fixed manufacturing costs per unit	$ 1
Fixed selling and administrative costs	$ 1,400
Variable selling and administrative costs per unit sold	$ .50
Selling price per unit	$ 8.50

[1]J. S. Chiu and Y. Lee, "A Survey of Current Practice in Overhead Accounting and Analysis," *Proceedings of the 1980 Western Regional Meeting of the American Accounting Association* (O. R. Whittington, San Diego State University, School of Accounting, 1980), p. 239. Also see E. A. Imhoff, "Management Accounting Techniques: A Survey," *Management Accounting*, LX, No. 5, which summarizes 53 responses from a survey of 105 publicly traded companies.

There were no inventories of work in process or raw materials. There were absolutely no standard cost variances in any variable costs. Production was far below expected volume in 19_2 because of persistent shortages of raw materials.

Required

1. Prepare the requested comparative income statements.
2. Explain the difference in operating income between absorption costing and variable costing in each of the two years.
3. Sales rose in 19_2. Did operating income rise? Explain.

Comparative income statements

Exhibit 8-3 contains the comparative income statements, as requested by requirement 1. The format shown is commonly encountered. The statement begins with all items valued at standard. All variances are grouped and shown as adjustments to

EXHIBIT 8-3 *(Place a clip on this page for easy reference.)*
Stassen Company
Comparative Income Statements
For the Years 19_1 and 19_2

	19_1	19_2
VARIABLE COSTING		
Sales 2,000 units and 3,000 units at $8.50	$17,000	$25,500
Beginning inventory at $2	—	$ 8,000
Add variable cost of goods manufactured at $2	12,000	1,800
Available for sale	12,000	9,800
Deduct ending inventory	8,000	3,800
Variable manufacturing cost of goods sold	4,000	6,000
Variable selling costs at $.50 per unit sold	1,000	1,500
Total variable costs	5,000	7,500
Contribution margin	12,000	18,000
Fixed factory overhead	10,000	10,000
Fixed selling and administrative costs	1,400	1,400
Total fixed costs	11,400	11,400
Operating income	$ 600	$ 6,600
ABSORPTION COSTING		
Sales	$17,000	$25,500
Beginning inventory at $3	—	12,000
Add absorption cost of goods manufactured	18,000	2,700
Available for sale	18,000	14,700
Deduct ending inventory	12,000	5,700
Cost of goods sold—at standard	6,000	9,000
Production volume variance*	4,000 U	9,100 U
Adjusted cost of goods sold	10,000	18,100
Gross margin or gross profit—at "actual"	7,000	7,400
Selling and administrative costs†	2,400	2,900
Operating income	$ 4,600	$ 4,500

*Computation of production volume variance based on denominator volume of 10,000 units:

19_1	$ 4,000 underapplied (10,000 − 6,000) × $1
19_2	9,100 underapplied (10,000 − 900) × $1
Two years together	$13,100 underapplied (20,000 − 6,900) × $1
†19_1	$ 1,400 fixed + 2,000 units × $.50 = $2,400
19_2	$ 1,400 fixed + 3,000 units × $.50 = $2,900

EXHIBIT 8-4
Stassen Company
Analysis of Fixed Factory Overhead in 19_2

	INVENTORY		EXPENSE
VARIABLE COSTING			
No fixed factory overhead carried over from 19_1			
Fixed factory overhead incurred in 19_2	$10,000 ─────────────────────→		$10,000

ABSORPTION COSTING		UNITS	DOLLARS	
Fixed factory overhead in beginning inventory	$ 4,000	4,000	$4,000	
Fixed factory overhead incurred in 19_2	10,000			
To account for:	$14,000			
Applied to product, 900 × $1 =		900	900	
Available for sale		4,900	$4,900	
Contained in standard cost of goods sold	$ 3,000	3,000	3,000 ──→	$ 3,000
In ending inventory	1,900	1,900	$1,900	
Not applied, so becomes production volume variance		9,100 ─────────────────→		9,100
Fixed factory overhead charged against 19_2 operations				$12,100
Fixed factory overhead accounted for in 19_2	$14,000			
Difference in 19_2 factory overhead charged to expense, $12,100 − $10,000				$ 2,100
This is the same as the difference in 19_2 operating income, $6,600 − $4,500				$ 2,100

standard cost of goods sold (as the production volume variance is shown here). Alternatively, such variances may be shown as adjustments to "operating income before variances" or "gross margin" or some other intermediate item on an income statement.

Trace the facts from the problem to Exhibit 8-3, step by step. In particular, consider the effects of absorption costing on income:

1. The unit product cost is $3, not $2, because variable manufacturing costs ($2) plus fixed factory overhead ($1) are applied to product.
2. The $1 application rate was based on a denominator volume of 10,000 units. Whenever *production* (not sales) deviates from the denominator volume, a production volume variance arises. The measure of the variance is $1 multiplied by the difference between the actual volume of production and the denominator volume.
3. All variances, including the production volume variances, are usually accounted for as deductions from (or additions to) operating income of the current fiscal period. Exhibit 8-4 gives a detailed analysis of the effects of fixed factory overhead in 19_2.
4. The absorption-costing statement in Exhibit 8-3 does not differentiate between the variable and fixed costs. Costs are often not classified as fixed or variable in absorption-costing statements, although such a classification is possible. Managers who are accustomed to looking at operations from a breakeven-analysis and flexible-budget viewpoint find that the absorption income statement fails to dovetail with cost-volume-profit relationships. They are then forced to take time trying to reconcile and interpret two or more sets of figures that portray a single operating situation. Variable-costing proponents say that it is more efficient to present important cost-volume-profit relationships as integral parts of the major financial statements.

The answer to requirement 2 is numbered below as point (5) because it is an addition to points (1) through (4) of the preceding section:

5. If inventories increase during a period, the variable-costing method will generally report less operating income than absorption costing; when inventories decrease, variable costing will report more operating income than absorption costing. These differences in operating income are due *solely* to the moving of fixed factory overhead in and out of inventories as they increase and decrease, respectively.[2]

To illustrate this important point, assume that all variances are written off completely as period costs, no change occurs in work-in-process inventory, and no change occurs in the budgeted overhead rate (budgeted fixed overhead divided by the units of denominator volume). Then the difference between the operating incomes under absorption and variable costing may be shown by formulas:

Formula (1)

$$\begin{pmatrix} \text{Absorption-} \\ \text{costing} \\ \text{operating} \\ \text{income} \end{pmatrix} - \begin{pmatrix} \text{Variable-} \\ \text{costing} \\ \text{operating} \\ \text{income} \end{pmatrix} = \begin{pmatrix} \text{Units} \\ \text{produced} \\ \text{minus} \\ \text{units} \\ \text{sold} \end{pmatrix} \times \begin{pmatrix} \text{Budgeted} \\ \text{fixed} \\ \text{overhead} \\ \text{rate} \end{pmatrix}$$

or

Formula (2)

$$\begin{pmatrix} \text{Difference in} \\ \text{operating income} \end{pmatrix} = \begin{pmatrix} \text{Increase or} \\ \text{decrease in} \\ \text{inventory units} \end{pmatrix} \times \begin{pmatrix} \text{Budgeted} \\ \text{fixed overhead} \\ \text{rate} \end{pmatrix}$$

The use of these formulas is illustrated by the data from Exhibit 8-3:

USING FORMULA (1)

19_1	$4,600 − $600	= (6,000 − 2,000 units) × $1
	$4,000	= $4,000
19_2	$4,500 − $6,600	= (900 − 3,000 units) × $1
	$−2,100	= $−2,100

USING FORMULA (2)

19_1	$ 4,000	= (Increase in inventory of 4,000 units) × $1
19_2	$−2,100	= (Decrease in inventory of 2,100 units) × $1

The answer to Requirement 3 is numbered below as point 6 because it is an addition to the previous five points:

6. Under variable costing, operating income is tied directly to fluctuations in sales. Operating income should rise as sales rise, and vice versa, at the rate of the contribution margin per unit:

$$\begin{pmatrix} \text{Increase in operating} \\ \text{income from 19\_1 to 19\_2} \end{pmatrix} = \begin{pmatrix} \text{Contribution margin} \\ \text{of \$8.50 − \$2.50} \end{pmatrix} \times \begin{pmatrix} 3{,}000 \text{ units} \\ \text{sold in 19\_2} \end{pmatrix} - \begin{pmatrix} 2{,}000 \text{ units} \\ \text{sold in 19\_1} \end{pmatrix}$$

$$= \$6.00 \times 1{,}000 = \$6{,}000$$

---

[2]The illustrations assume that the fixed-overhead rate per unit is unchanged from fiscal period to fiscal period. If the rate changes significantly, these generalizations may not hold.

Under absorption costing, operating income is tied to both sales *and* production. For example, in 19_1 income is higher than under variable costing because production exceeded sales. The opposite effect occurred in 19_2. Moreover, in 19_2 sales rose over the 19_1 level. Nevertheless, under absorption costing, operating income fell from $4,600 to $4,500. Why? Because 19_2 had to bear some of the fixed overhead carried over in inventory from 19_1. In addition, 19_2 bore the effects of production being below denominator volume. Thus, *production* schedules affect operating income under absorption costing but not under variable costing. The detailed effects of fixed factory overhead on 19_2 operations are shown in Exhibit 8-4.

For absorption costing we have seen that, under some circumstances, operating income could fall even though sales rise. **Heavy reductions of beginning inventory levels might combine with low production and a large production volume variance. This could result in unusually large amounts of fixed overhead being charged to a single period. Thus, under absorption costing, an increase in sales could be accompanied by a lower reported income, which could result in a confusing and misleading portrayal of operating results.**

Exhibit 8-5 is a concise presentation of the preceding six points regarding variable and absorption costing.

EXHIBIT 8-5
Comparative Income Effects

	VARIABLE COSTING	ABSORPTION COSTING	COMMENTS
1. Fixed factory overhead inventoried?	No	Yes	Basic theoretical question of when this cost should become an expense
2. Production volume variance?	No	Yes	Choice of denominator volume affects measurement of operating income under absorption costing.
3. Treatment of other variances?	Same	Same	Underscores the fact that the basic difference is the accounting for fixed factory overhead, not the accounting for any variable manufacturing costs.
4. Classifications between variable and fixed costs are routinely made?	Yes	No	However, absorption cost can be modified to obtain subclassifications of variable and fixed costs, if desired.
5. Usual effects of changes in inventory levels on operating income:			Differences are attributable to timing of the transformation of fixed factory overhead into expense.
Production = sales	Equal	Equal	
Production > sales	Lower*	Higher†	
Production < sales	Higher	Lower	
6. Cost-volume-profit relationships	Tied to sales	Tied to production *and* sales	Management control benefit: Effects of changes in volume on operating income are easier to understand under variable costing.

*That is, lower than absorption costing.
†That is, higher than variable costing.

Cost-volume-profit analysis was introduced in Chapter 3. The typical discussion assumes (a) the use of variable costing or (b) the use of absorption costing with no changes in beginning or ending inventory levels.

If variable costing is used, the breakeven point is computed in the usual manner. It is unique; there is only one breakeven point. Moreover, income is a function of sales. As sales rise, income rises, and vice versa. In our Stassen illustration for 19_2:

$$\text{Breakeven sales in units} = \frac{\text{Total fixed costs incurred during period}}{\text{Unit contribution margin}}$$

Let Q_s = Breakeven sales in units

$$Q_s = \frac{\$10,000 + \$1,400}{\$8.50 - (\$2.00 + \$.50)} = \frac{\$11,400}{\$6} = 1,900$$

In contrast, if absorption costing is used, income is a function of *both* sales and production. Therefore changes in inventory levels can dramatically affect income, as demonstrated by our illustration. The breakeven point is not unique. There may be several combinations of sales and production that produce an income of zero.[3]

---

[3] A formula for computing the breakeven point under absorption costing is similar to that under variable costing. However, the numerator must include the fixed-factory-overhead rate multiplied by the difference between the number of units sold and units produced. In our Stassen Company illustration for 19_2:

$$\text{Breakeven sales in units} = \frac{\text{Total fixed costs incurred during period} + \text{Fixed overhead rate}\left(\text{Breakeven sales in units} - \text{Units produced}\right)}{\text{Unit contribution margin}}$$

Let Q_s = Breakeven sales in units

$$Q_s = \frac{(\$10,000 + \$1,400) + \$1.00(Q_s - 900)}{\$8.50 - (\$2.00 + \$.50)}$$

$$\$6.00\, Q_s = \$11,400 + \$1.00 Q_s - \$900$$

$$\$5.00\, Q_s = \$10,500$$

$$Q_s = 2,100$$

Proof of 19_2 breakeven point:

Gross margin:		
(Sales price − unit cost of goods sold) × units sold,		
($8.50 − $3.00) × 2,100 =		$11,550
Production volume variance, as before	$9,100	
Selling and administrative costs:		
Variable, $.50 × 2,100	1,050	
Fixed	1,400	11,550
Operating income		$ 0

You can readily see that the breakeven point depends on the units sold, the units produced, and the denominator volume chosen to set the fixed overhead rate. In this case, the numbers were 2,100 sold, 900 produced, and 10,000 denominator volume.

Thus variable costing dovetails precisely with cost-volume-profit analysis. The user of variable costing can easily compute the breakeven point or any effects that changes in sales volume may have on income. In contrast, the user of absorption costing must consider both sales volume and production volume before making such computations.

Consider an additional example. Suppose in our illustration that actual production in 19_2 were equal to denominator volume, 10,000 units. Also suppose that there were no sales and no selling and administrative costs. All the production would be placed in inventory. Then all the fixed factory overhead would be lodged in inventory. There would be no production volume variance. Thus the company could break even if it sold nothing at all.[4] In contrast, under variable costing the operating loss would be equal to the fixed costs.

Absorption costing enables a manager to affect reported income for a given fiscal period by (a) choosing a production schedule and (b) choosing a denominator level of volume. Given such opportunities, a few managers may manipulate income. Such temptations are not available under variable costing.

THE CENTRAL ISSUE: A QUESTION OF TIMING

Nearly all accountants agree that distinctions between variable and fixed costs are helpful for a wide variety of managerial decisions. Absorption costing recognizes this possibility but takes the position that such information may be supplied without changing the conventional methods of income determination. Adherents of variable costing maintain that the importance of variable- and fixed-cost behavior should be spotlighted not only by changing the format of the financial statement but also by changing the basic principles or concepts, whereby fixed factory overhead would be written off in the period incurred rather than funneled into inventory as an integral part of inventory costs. Thus the central question becomes, What is the proper *timing* for expensing of fixed factory overhead as expense: at the time of incurrence, or at the time that the finished units to which the fixed overhead relates are sold? **The issue thus narrows to the propriety of excluding fixed factory overhead from inventory.** The focus must be on relating fixed overhead to the definition of an asset.[5]

_____PROBLEM FOR SELF-STUDY_____

problem   Reconsider the facts in Exhibit 8-3, page 257.

Required   1. Suppose there were a total of $1,000 unfavorable price, spending, and efficiency variances for variable costs in 19_2. These variances are regarded as adjustments to cost of goods sold. Compute the operating income under variable costing and absorption costing.
2. Ignore requirement 1. Suppose production in 19_2 were 5,900 instead of 900 units, but sales were unchanged. Compute the operating income under variable costing and absorption costing.

_____
[4]For an expanded discussion, see D. Solomons, "Breakeven Analysis under Absorption Costing," *Accounting Review*, XLIII, No. 3, pp. 447–52.

[5]See G. Sorter and C. Horngren, "Asset Recognition and Economic Attributes—The Relevant Costing Approach," *Accounting Review*, Vol. XXXVII, No. 3, pp. 391–99, for a discussion of the role of fixed overhead in the valuation of inventory.

1. Variable costing and absorption costing do not differ regarding price, spending, and efficiency variances. Therefore the operating income under each method would be lowered by $1,000:

	VARIABLE COSTING	ABSORPTION COSTING
Operating income per Exhibit 8-3	$6,600	$4,500
Price, spending, and efficiency variances for variable costs	1,000 U	1,000 U
Operating income	$5,600	$3,500

The $1,000 variances would appear as a line item in the income statement, ordinarily as an addition to the standard cost of goods sold.

2. The operating income under variable costing would be unaffected by the units produced, so it would be $6,600, as before. Why? Because operating income under variable costing is a function of units sold.

The operating income under absorption costing would be affected. The production volume variance would be $4,100 unfavorable instead of $9,100 unfavorable. Therefore operating income would be higher by $5,000:

Sales, as before	$25,500
Beginning inventory, as before	12,000
Add absorption cost of goods manufactured, $2,700 before, now 5,900 × $3, or	17,700
Available for sale	29,700
Deduct ending inventory, $5,700 before, now 6,900 × $3, or	20,700
Cost of goods sold—at standard	9,000
Production volume variance (10,000 − 5,900) × $1	4,100 U
Adjusted cost of goods sold	13,100
Gross margin, at "actual"	12,400
Selling and administrative costs	2,900
Operating income	$ 9,500

ROLE OF VARIOUS DENOMINATOR LEVELS IN ABSORPTION COSTING

Chapter 7 pointed out that product costs and income can be significantly affected by the choice of a particular volume level (also called *activity* level) as a denominator in the computation of fixed-overhead rates. We now study how various alternative levels of activity can affect operating income under absorption costing. As fixed manufacturing costs become a more prominent part of an organization's total costs, the importance of this choice becomes greater.

Characteristics of capacity

The choice of a capacity size is usually the result of capital-budgeting decisions, which are reached after studying the expected impact of these capital outlays on operations over a number of years. The choice may be influenced by a combination of two major factors, each involving trade-off decisions and each heavily depending on long-range forecasts of demand, material costs, and labor costs:

1. Provision for *seasonal* and *cyclical fluctuations* in demand. The trade-off is between (a) additional costs of physical capacity and (b) the costs of inventory stockouts and/or the carrying costs of inventory safety stocks of such magnitude to compensate for seasonal and cyclical variations, the costs of overtime premium, subcontracting, and so on.
2. Provision for upward *trends* in demand. The trade-off is between (a) the costs of constructing too much capacity for initial needs and (b) the later extra costs of satisfying demand by alternative means. For example, should a factory designed to make computer components have an area of 100,000, 150,000, or 200,000 square feet?

Although it can be defined and measured in a particular situation, capacity is an illusive concept. To most people, the term *capacity* implies a constraint, an upper limit. We sometimes hear, "I'm working at capacity now. I simply can't do more." This same notion of capacity as a constraint is commonly held in industry.

Although the term *capacity* is usually applied to plant and equipment, it is equally applicable to other resources, such as people and materials. A shortage of direct labor, executive time, or materials may be critical in limiting company production or sales.

The upper limit of capacity is seldom absolutely rigid, at least from an engineering viewpoint. That is, ways—such as overtime, subcontracting, or paying premium prices for additional materials—can usually be found to expand production. But these ways may be totally unattractive from an economic viewpoint. **Hence the upper limit of capacity is *specified* by management for current planning and control purposes after considering engineering *and* economic factors.** In this way, the upper limit is usually imposed by management, not by external forces.

Measurement of capacity

Measurement of capacity usually begins with **theoretical capacity** (also called *maximum* or *ideal* capacity) that assumes the production of output 100% of the time. Then deductions are made for Sundays, holidays, downtime, changeover time, and similar items to attain a measure of **practical capacity.** The latter is defined as the maximum level at which the plant or department can operate efficiently. Practical capacity often allows for unavoidable operating interruptions such as repair time or waiting time (downtime).

Two other commonly used levels of capacity utilization are

1. **Normal volume,** the level of capacity utilization (which is less than 100% of practical capacity) that will satisfy average consumer demand over a span of time (often five years) that includes seasonal, cyclical, and trend factors
2. **Master-budget volume,** the anticipated level of capacity utilization for the coming year

A survey of *Fortune 500* companies disclosed that the denominator volume bases shown at the top of the next page were used among 247 respondents[6]:

---

[6]Chiu and Lee, *op. cit.* Percentages are from their Table 3, p. 242. The sketch was added here. Also see various publications of the Cost Accounting Standards Board (Washington, D.C.) for descriptions of overhead practices.

	PERCENTAGE USED
THEORETICAL CAPACITY	1.6%
PRACTICAL CAPACITY	21.1
NORMAL VOLUME	18.2
MASTER-BUDGET VOLUME (varies from year to year)	57.5
NO RESPONSE	1.6
	100.0%

There are apt to be differences in terms used between companies, so be sure to obtain their exact meaning in a given situation. For example, *master-budget volume* is often called **budgeted volume** or **expected annual volume** or **expected annual capacity** or **expected annual activity** or **master-budget activity.**

Inventory and income effects

Consider the data below for comparing the choices of a denominator volume:

	DENOMINATOR BASED ON		
	Master-Budget Volume	Normal Volume*	Practical Capacity
Budgeted fixed factory overhead for 19_1	$450,000	$450,000	$450,000
Volume in standard direct labor hours	75,000	90,000	100,000
Budgeted fixed-factory-overhead rate per hour	$6.00	$5.00	$4.50
*Expected average volume per year for the next five years.			

We will deal with fixed factory overhead only. Why? Because variable overhead fluctuates with changes in activity but fixed overhead does not. The entire problem of choosing among practical capacity, normal volume, or master-budget volume is raised by the presence of fixed overhead. Recall that the production volume variance in Chapter 7 was confined to fixed overhead.

In 19_1, 70,000 units were produced (in 70,000 actual and standard hours allowed) and 60,000 units were sold. There was no beginning inventory. Exhibit 8-6 compares the effects of choosing different denominators for setting the budgeted fixed-factory-overhead rate. There are different inventory valuations, different operating incomes. Further, the measure of utilization of facilities, the production volume variance, will differ markedly. In Exhibit 8-6, income is lowest where practical capacity is the denominator volume and highest when master-budget volume is the denominator volume, because a smaller portion of overhead is held back as an asset in inventory when a lower overhead rate is used.

265

EXHIBIT 8-6

Income-Statement Effects of Using Various Volume Bases as Denominators for Overhead Application

	MASTER-BUDGET VOLUME (75,000 HOURS) Using a $6.00 Fixed Overhead Rate		NORMAL VOLUME (90,000 HOURS) Using a $5.00 Fixed Overhead Rate		PRACTICAL CAPACITY (100,000 HOURS) Using a $4.50 Fixed Overhead Rate	
Sales		$ xxx		$ xxx		$ xxx
Production costs:						
Direct materials, direct labor, variable overhead	$ xxx		$ xxx		$ xxx	
Fixed overhead applied to product*	420,000		350,000		315,000	
Total production costs, 70,000 units	$ xxx		$ xxx		$ xxx	
Ending inventory, fixed-overhead component, 10,000 units†	60,000		50,000		45,000	
Total fixed-overhead component of cost of goods sold		360,000		300,000		270,000
Production volume variance, unfavorable‡		30,000		100,000		135,000
Total fixed overhead charged to the period's sales		$390,000		$400,000		$405,000
Operating income		Highest		Middle		Lowest
Recapitulation:						
Total fixed overhead to account for§		$450,000		$450,000		$450,000
Accounted for as follows:						
Charged to cost of goods sold (expense)		$360,000		$300,000		$270,000
Charged to production volume variance		30,000		100,000		135,000
Charged to ending inventory (asset)		60,000		50,000		45,000
Overhead accounted for		$450,000		$450,000		$450,000

*70,000 × $6.00 and 70,000 × $5.00 and 70,000 × $4.50, respectively.
†10,000 × $6.00 and 10,000 × $5.00 and 10,000 × $4.50, respectively.
‡(75,000 − 70,000) × $6.00 and (90,000 − 70,000) × $5.00 and (100,000 − 70,000) × $4.50, respectively. This amount is sometimes called "loss from idle capacity."
§Assumed here that actual and budgeted fixed overhead were $450,000.

The exhibit also indicates that the accounting effects of using practical capacity are lower unit costs for inventory purposes and the steady appearance of an unfavorable production volume variance or "Loss from idle capacity" on the income statement.

The journal entry at the end of 19_1 would be:

	DENOMINATOR BASED ON		
	MASTER-BUDGET VOLUME	NORMAL VOLUME	PRACTICAL CAPACITY
Fixed factory overhead applied	420,000	350,000	315,000
Production volume variance (to be closed to Income Summary)	30,000	100,000	135,000
Fixed factory overhead control	450,000	450,000	450,000

Practical capacity Management often wants to keep running at full capacity, which really means practical capacity. "Normal volume" for applying fixed costs becomes "practical capacity"; anything less reduces profits and is undesirable. Where product costs are used as guides for pricing, some managers say that this policy results in more competitive pricing, which maximizes both volume and profits in good times and bad. Of course, profits also depend on factors other than physical volume—for example, the elasticity of demand. The accounting effects of using practical capacity are lower unit costs for inventory purposes and the almost perpetual appearance of an unfavorable production volume variance, sometimes described on the income statements as loss from idle capacity.

Using practical capacity as a denominator volume has become increasingly popular with American businesses. As indicated earlier, over 21% of the surveyed companies use practical capacity. A major reason is probably the position of the Internal Revenue Service, which forbids variable costing but permits the use of practical capacity as a denominator volume in conjunction with absorption costing. As compared with normal volume or master-budget volume, the practical-capacity denominator volume results in the faster write-offs of fixed factory overhead as a tax deduction.

There is no requirement that American companies use the same denominator volumes for internal management purposes and for income tax purposes. Nevertheless, the economies of recordkeeping often lead to the same denominator choice for management and tax purposes.

Normal volume versus master-budget volume

Master-budget volume is the denominator for applying all fixed overhead to products on a year-to-year basis, while the denominator based on *normal* volume attempts to apply fixed overhead by using a *longer-run* average expected activity. Conceptually, the *normal rate* results in overapplications in above-average-volume years that are offset by under-applications in below-average-volume years.

A major reason for choosing master-budget volume over normal volume as a denominator is the overwhelming forecasting problem that accompanies the determination of normal volume. Sales not only fluctuate cyclically but have trends over the long run. In effect, the use of normal volume implies an unusual talent for accurate long-run forecasting. Many accountants and executives who reject the normal volume as a denominator claim that the nature of their company's business precludes sufficiently accurate forecasts beyond one year.

Where companies use normal volume, the objective is to choose a period long enough to average out sizable fluctuations in volume and to allow for trends in sales. The uniform rate for applying fixed overhead supposedly provides for "recovery" of fixed costs over the long run. Companies expect that overapplications in above-average volume years will be offset by underapplications in below-average-volume years.

Conceptually, when normal volume is the denominator, the yearly overapplied or underapplied overhead should be carried forward on the balance sheet. Practically, however, year-end balances are closed directly to Income Summary, because the accounting profession (and the Internal Revenue Service) generally views the year as being the terminal time span for allocation of underapplied or overapplied overhead.

Significance of denominator volume for product costing and control

Obviously the choice of a denominator volume for product costing is a matter of judgment. The selection of a denominator probably becomes crucial where product costs heavily influence managerial decisions. For example, in a cyclical industry, the use of master-budgeted rather than normal volume as a denominator would tend to cause a company to quote low prices in boom years and high prices in recession years—in obvious conflict with good business judgment. That is why normal volume may make more sense as a denominator when there are wide swings in business volume through the years, even though the yearly overapplied and underapplied overhead is not carried forward in the balance sheet.

In the realm of planning and control for the current year, however, normal volume is an empty concept. Normal volume is used as a basis for long-range plans. It depends on the time span selected, the forecasts made for each year, and the weighting of these forecasts. In Exhibit 8-6, a comparison of the 70,000-hour master-budget volume with the 90,000-hour normal volume might be suggested as the best basis for auditing long-range planning. **However, normal volume is an average that has no particular significance with respect to a follow-up for a particular year.** The pertinent comparison is a particular year's actual volume with the volume level originally predicted in the authorization for the acquisition of facilities. This comparison may be done project by project. It need not be integrated in the accounting system on a routine basis. Furthermore, attempting to use normal volume as a reference point for judging current performance is an example of misusing a long-range measure for a short-range purpose.

The master-budget volume, rather than normal volume or practical capacity, is more germane to the evaluation of current results. The master budget is the principal short-run planning and control tool. Managers feel much more obligated to reach the levels stipulated in the master budget, which should have been carefully set in relation to the maximum opportunities for sales in the current year. In contrast, normal volume and practical capacity are not so pertinent to current operating problems, because they are not usually incorporated into the comprehensive or master budget—the focus of attention.

STANDARD-COST VARIANCES AND THE INCOME STATEMENT

Proration to achieve actual costs

Managers and accountants tend to think of "actual" costs as somehow representing absolute truths. Therefore they believe that "normal" or "standard costs" provide valuations that are somehow untrue unless month-end or year-end variances are prorated among the affected accounts to get corrected valuations that better approximate "actual" costs.[7] Of course, in all cases immaterial variances (however defined) can be written off immediately as adjustments to cost of goods sold.

How do companies dispose of their variances at year-end? A survey of 247 large companies regarding overhead variances showed:[8]

Closed to cost of goods sold	53.1%
Closed to income account	10.5
Subtotal affecting current income	63.6
Prorated (apportioned) among	
Work in Process, Finished Goods, and Cost of Goods Sold	33.6
Carried forward to next year	1.2
No response	1.6
Total	100.0%

[7]For example, see Standard #407, "Use of Standard Costs for Direct Material and Direct Labor," of the Cost Accounting Standards Board, Washington, D.C.

[8]Chiu and Lee, *op. cit.*, Table 4, p. 242. Similar results are reported in F. Rayburn and A. Stewart, "An Analysis of Standard Costs in Practice," *Cost and Management*, January–February 1981, pp. 30–32.

The disposition of *overhead* variances at year-end was initially described in Chapter 4, page 103. The same concepts and procedures apply to *all* variances. First, decide whether *proration* should occur. This decision usually depends on judgments about whether the variances are significant. Second, if proration is desired, find out where the related "standard" costs are now lodged. Use the sum of these standard costs as bases for apportioning the variances. For example, suppose that all variances are unfavorable and total $120,000 at year-end. The proration would be in proportion to the balances (assumed) in the accounts where the related standard costs now exist:

	WORK IN PROCESS	FINISHED GOODS	COST OF GOODS SOLD
Unadjusted balances (before proration), $1,000,000	$100,000	$300,000	$600,000
All variances, $120,000 unfavorable	12,000*	36,000*	72,000*
Adjusted balances (after proration), $1,120,000	$112,000	$336,000	$672,000

*$120,000 ÷ $1,000,000 = 12%; 12% × $100,000 = $12,000; or $100,000 ÷ $1,000,000 = 10%; 10% × $120,000 = $12,000; etc.

The journal entry would be:

Work in process	12,000	
Finished goods	36,000	
Cost of goods sold	72,000	
Cost variance accounts (would be detailed)		120,000
To prorate variances.		

The case against proration

Some accountants, industrial engineers, and managers reject the idea that actual costs represent absolute truth. Instead they claim that currently attainable standard costs are the "true costs" in the sense that such costs are the only costs that may be carried forward as assets or unexpired costs. They contend that variances are measures of inefficiency or abnormal efficiency. Therefore variances are not inventoriable and should be completely charged or credited against sales of the period instead of being prorated among inventories and cost of goods sold. In this way, inventory valuations will be more representative of desirable and attainable costs. **In particular, there is no justification for carrying costs of inefficiency as assets, which is what proration accomplishes.**

Varieties of proration

Variations of proration methods may be desirable under some conditions. For instance, efficiency variances may be viewed as being currently avoidable and therefore nonproratable. Similarly, price variances may be viewed as being unavoidable and therefore proratable. Conceptually, this is superior to the other methods because the costs of avoidable inefficiency are written off, whereas unavoidable costs are not. This treatment is correct because the costs of avoidable inefficiency do not qualify as assets under any economic test.

    The authors believe that unfavorable variances do not have to be inventoried as long as standards are currently attainable. However, if standards are not up to date, or if they reflect perfection (ideal) performance rather than expected performance under reasonably efficient conditions, then conceptually the variances should be split between the portion that reflects departures from currently attainable standards and the portion that does not. The former should be written off as period charges; the latter should be prorated to inventories and cost of goods sold. For example, assume that an operation has a perfection standard time allowed of 50 minutes, which is reflected in a formal standard-cost system. The currently attainable standard is 60 minutes. Now if it takes, say, 75 actual minutes to perform the operation, the conceptual adjustment would call for writing off the cost of 15 minutes of the 25-minute variance as a period cost and for treating the cost of the remaining 10-minute variance as a product cost.

The prorations of variances can have significant effects on the measurement of operating income, particularly where inventories have increased or decreased substantially and where the variances are relatively large. The Problem for Self-Study (p. 272) demonstrates these effects. Also see Appendixes 8A and 8B for additional discussions of prorations.

ADJUSTING INVENTORIES FOR EXTERNAL REPORTING

To satisfy external reporting requirements, companies often make adjustments to inventory accounts. Examples include (a) converting a variable-costing inventory valuation to absorption costing and (b) prorating variances. Typically, these companies do *not* alter their ongoing inventory records. Instead, for external reporting they create a separate but related "inventory adjustment" valuation account that bears a host of labels, some short, some long.

To illustrate the use of such an account, assume that a company adjusts its Finished-Goods Inventory of $700,000 upward by $100,000. The adjustment may be (a) to convert the inventory from variable costing to absorption costing or (b) to restate the inventory because of a proration of unfavorable variances. The journal entry would be:

a. Finished-goods inventory adjustment account   100,000
      Fixed factory overhead   100,000

or

b. Finished-goods inventory adjustment account   100,000
      Cost variance accounts (detailed)   100,000

Under first-in, first-out assumptions, the adjustment account would disappear in the subsequent period when the related inventories are sold. For example:

Cost of goods sold (from inventory adjustment account)   100,000
      Finished-goods inventory adjustment account   100,000

Effects of objectives

Interim reporting is far from uniform. Some companies write off all variances monthly or quarterly as additions to or subtractions from Cost of Goods Sold. Others prorate the variances among inventories and Cost of Goods Sold. For example, consider the practices of 247 companies in a survey concerning interim accounting for overhead variances (underapplied or overapplied overhead):[9]

Closed to cost of goods sold	60.3%
Closed to income account	11.3
Subtotal affecting current income	71.6%
Prorated (apportioned) among Work in Process, Finished Goods, and Cost of Goods Sold	23.1
Carried forward to next period	4.1
No response	1.2
Total	100.0%

Most companies follow the same practices for both interim and annual financial statements. They apparently favor the first of two major conflicting objectives of interim reporting.

> *Objective 1:* The results for each interim period should be computed in the same way as if the interim period were an annual accounting period. For example, the interim underapplied overhead would be written off or prorated just like the annual underapplied overhead.
>
> *Objective 2:* Each interim period is an integral part of the annual period. For example, a February repair cost may be regarded as benefiting the entire year's operations. Suppose the repair is the major cause of the underapplied overhead. Then the underapplied overhead should be deferred and spread over the entire fiscal year.

Supporters of the second objective argue that the central idea of overhead application is the use of a budgeted annual rate. There are bound to be random month-to-month underapplications or overapplications that may come near to offsetting one another by the end of the year. The most frequent causes of these month-to-month deviations are (a) operations at different levels of volume; and (b) the presence of seasonal costs, such as heating, that are averaged in with other overhead items in setting an annual overhead rate.

If underapplied manufacturing overhead is carried forward during the year, it would appear on an interim balance sheet as a current asset, a "prepaid expense." Similarly, overapplied overhead would be a current liability, a "deferred credit."

External reporting

The rules for external reporting distinguish among the types of standard-cost variances. In general, the same reporting procedures should be used for interim and annual statements. However, Accounting Principles Board Opinion No. 28 pinpoints direct-material price variances and factory-overhead production volume

---

[9]Chiu and Lee, *op. cit.*, p. 242.

variances for special treatment. If these interim variances are expected to be offset by the end of the annual period, they should "ordinarily be deferred at interim reporting dates."

The latter overhead variances are often called *planned variances*. They are especially common in seasonal businesses. Deferral is favored because such amounts are expected to disappear by the end of the year via the use of averaging as costs are applied to the product. However, "unplanned" or unanticipated under-applied or overapplied overhead should be reported "at the end of an interim period following the same procedures used at the end of a fiscal year."[10]

This approach of Opinion 28 represents a compromise between Objectives 1 and 2 above. Why? Because "unplanned" and "planned" overhead variances are accounted for differently.

_____PROBLEM FOR SELF-STUDY_____

problem   The final illustration in this chapter presented these unadjusted balances of standard costs at year-end (before proration):

Work in process	$ 100,000
Finished goods	300,000
Cost of goods sold	600,000
	$1,000,000

Assume now that variances were:

Production Volume Variance	Other Variances
30,000	150,000

Management has decided that the $30,000 production volume variance (loss from idle capacity) should be written off as an adjustment to current cost of goods sold. However, the other variances should be prorated in proportion to the unadjusted balances in work in process, finished goods, and cost of goods sold.

Required   **1.** Prepare a schedule that prorates the "other" variances.
         2. Prepare a journal entry that closes all variance accounts.
         3. What is the justification for writing off some variances but prorating others?

solution   1.

	WORK IN PROCESS	FINISHED GOODS	COST OF GOODS SOLD
Unadjusted balances (before proration), $1,000,000	$100,000	$300,000	$600,000
"Other" variances, $150,000	15,000*	45,000*	90,000*
Adjusted balances (after proration), $850,000	$ 85,000	$255,000	$510,000†

*$150,000 ÷ $1,000,000 = 15%; 15% × $100,000, $300,000, and $600,000, respectively.
†The $30,000 production volume variance will be added to this balance.

[10]Accounting Principles Board Opinion No. 28, *Interim Financial Reporting*, Paragraph 14(d). Also see the latest pronoucements of the Financial Accounting Standards Board.

2. Other variances   150,000

Work in process	15,000
Finished goods	45,000
Cost of goods sold ($90,000 − $30,000)	60,000
Production volume variance	30,000

3. The major justification for writing off the production volume variance (the cost of idle capacity) is that it does not fit the definition of an asset. That is, it is a "lost cost," not a future benefit. In contrast, the other variances may be dominated by price changes or efficiency factors that should have been embedded in the standard costs when they were set at the beginning of the year. Therefore these variances may indeed fit the definition of an asset. That is, the variances are costs that benefit future operations.

SUMMARY

Absorption costing and variable costing have different effects on income when inventory levels fluctuate. Differences occur because fixed factory overhead is inventoried only under absorption costing. Operating income is influenced by sales under variable costing, but by sales *and* production under absorption costing.

Three commonly used denominator volumes for developing product-costing fixed-overhead rates are (a) master-budget volume for the year, (b) normal volume over three to five years, and (c) practical capacity. The selection is essentially a matter of judgment. The choice will influence inventory valuations and resultant timing of income recognition.

If they are significant, standard-cost variances are usually prorated among various inventory accounts and cost of goods sold. In this way, better approximations of "actual" costs are achieved.

The advocates of currently attainable standard costs for product costing maintain that the results are conceptually superior to the results under "actual" or "normal" product-costing systems. They contend that the costs of inefficiency are not inventoriable.

Terms to Learn

This chapter and the Glossary at the end of the book contain definitions of the following important terms:

budgeted volume (p. 265)   *expected annual activity (265)*
expected annual capacity (265)   *expected annual volume (265)*
master-budget activity (265)   *master-budget volume (264)*
normal volume (264)   *practical capacity (264)*   *theoretical capacity (264)*

Special Points and Pitfalls

Variable costing and absorption costing are completely general in the sense that there may be:

actual variable costing	actual absorption costing
normal variable costing	normal absorption costing
standard variable costing	standard absorption costing

Standard-costing systems have the same cost variances regardless of whether variable costing or absorption costing is used, with one exception: Production volume variances are not present when variable costing is used because all fixed factory overhead is regarded as a period cost rather than an inventoriable cost.

Master-budget volume is the most popular denominator volume, followed by practical capacity and normal volume, respectively.

APPENDIX 8A: STANDARD-COST VARIANCES: A MORE ACCURATE APPROACH TO PRORATION

The approach to proration as described in the body of the chapter is relatively simple. More accurate approaches are explored in this Appendix, not for accuracy's sake alone, but also to review a standard-costing system in its entirety.

Illustration of proration

The following facts are the basis for an extended discussion of the general approach to proration. To keep the calculations manageable, the numbers are deliberately small.

problem Morales Company uses absorption costing. It has the following results for the year:

Purchases of direct materials (charged to Stores at standard prices), 200,000 lbs. @ $.50	$100,000
Direct-material price variance, 200,000 lbs. @ $.05	10,000
Direct materials—applied at standard prices, 160,000 lbs. @ $.50	80,000
Direct-material efficiency variance, 8,000 lbs. @ $.50	4,000
Direct labor incurred	45,000
Direct labor—applied at standard rate, 2,000 hrs. @ $20	40,000
Direct-labor price variance, 2,200 hrs @ $.4545	1,000
Direct-labor efficiency variance, 200 hrs. @ $20	4,000
Manufacturing overhead applied—at standard rate per labor hour	40,000
Manufacturing overhead incurred	45,000
Underapplied manufacturing overhead	5,000
Sales	135,000
Selling and administrative expenses	20,000

Assume that there is no ending work in process. Assume also that one uniform product is made, that 40% of the production is in the ending inventory of finished goods, and that 60% of the production has been sold. All variances are unfavorable.

There were no beginning inventories. The unadjusted balances (before proration) at the end of the year are based on the data given above:

		PERCENT
Work in process	$ 0	0%
Finished goods, 40% of the total standard costs applied for material, labor, and overhead ($80,000 + $40,000 + $40,000): 40% of $160,000	64,000	40
Cost of goods sold, 60% of $160,000	96,000	60
Total	$160,000	100%

An analysis of the data regarding direct materials follows:

	POUNDS	TOTAL COSTS AT $.50 STANDARD PRICE PER POUND	PERCENTAGE
To account for	200,000	$100,000	100%
Now present in:			
Direct-material efficiency variance	8,000	$ 4,000	4%
Finished goods	64,000	32,000	32
Cost of goods sold	96,000	48,000	48
Remainder, in stores	32,000	16,000	16
Accounted for	200,000	$100,000	100%

Required A comparative analysis of the effects on operating income (1) without proration of any variances and (2) with proration of all variances.

solution The solution is in Exhibit 8-8, which appears on page 279.

General guidelines for proration

The following general guidelines are illustrated:

1. The assumption is often made that standard costs are present in uniform proportions in Work in Process, Finished Goods, and Cost of Goods Sold. If the assumption is invalid and significant, then the direct materials, direct labor, and factory-overhead components should be *separately* identified; the related variances should then be prorated in proportion thereto.

First, confine our analysis to direct labor and factory overhead. These elements (only) are presented in T-accounts. The following entries are numbered in accordance with the logical flows of the amounts through the accounts:

Work in Process			
1. Direct labor 40,000		2. Transferred*	80,000
1. Overhead applied 40,000			

Finished Goods			
2.	80,000	3. Sold,* 60% of 80,000 or	48,000

Cost of Goods Sold	
3. 48,000	

Factory Overhead Control	
4. Incurred 45,000	

Factory Overhead Applied		
	1.	40,000

Direct-labor Price Variance	
1. 1,000	

Cash, Current Liabilities, etc.		
	1. Direct labor	45,000
	4. Overhead	45,000

Direct-labor Efficiency Variance	
1. 4,000	

*Transferred as a part of the total standard costs transferred

In our example, there is no ending work in process. Finished goods represents 40% of total manufacturing costs; costs of goods sold, 60%. Therefore all direct-labor and factory-overhead variances may be prorated accordingly. See the final three prorations in Exhibit 8-7 on page 278.

	TOTAL VARIANCE	FINISHED GOODS 40%	COST OF GOODS SOLD 60%
Direct-labor price variance	$1,000	$ 400	$ 600
Direct-labor efficiency variance	4,000	1,600	2,400
Factory-overhead variance	5,000	2,000	3,000

For simplicity, the factory-overhead variance of $5,000 has not been subdivided into components such as spending, efficiency, or production volume variances.

Based on the proration of these variances, a journal entry would be made:

Finished goods	4,000	
Cost of goods sold	6,000	
Factory overhead applied	40,000	
Direct-labor price variance		1,000
Direct-labor efficiency variance		4,000
Factory overhead control		45,000
To prorate variances and to close overhead accounts.		

2. The direct-material variances should be prorated slightly differently than direct labor and factory overhead. Why? Because direct material is inventoried before use, whereas the other elements of production cannot be inventoried before use.

Some key T-accounts follow regarding the movement of the direct-material cost (only) through the accounts:

Stores				Work in Process		
1. Purchased	100,000	2. Issued	84,000	2.	80,000	3. Transferred* 80,000

Finished Goods				Cost of Goods Sold	
3.	80,000	4. Sold*	48,000	4.	48,000
Bal. material cost only	32,000				

	Direct-Material Price Variance	
1.	10,000	

Accounts Payable			Direct-Material Efficiency Variance	
1.	110,000	2.	4,000	

*Transferred as a part of the total standard costs transferred.

The most critical proration is the material price variance. To be most accurate, its proration in our illustration should be traced at 5 cents per pound to wherever the 200,000 pounds have been charged at standard prices. As the analysis in the body of the problem indicates, the pounds are not only in Finished Goods and Cost of Goods Sold. **They are also in Stores and in the Direct-Material Efficiency Variance account.** Hence we begin with a proration of the material price variance to four accounts, using the percentages shown for direct materials in the problem data on page 275:

Direct-material price variance		$10,000
Allocated to:		
Direct-material efficiency variance, 4%	$ 400	
Finished-goods inventory, 32%	3,200	
Cost of goods sold, 48%	4,800	
Stores, 16%	1,600	
Total allocated		$10,000

The following journal entry prorates the price variance:

Direct-material efficiency variance	400	
Finished goods	3,200	
Cost of goods sold	4,800	
Stores	1,600	
Direct-material price variance		10,000

After posting the proration of the direct-material price variance, the direct-material efficiency variance account would be:

Direct-Material Efficiency Variance

Unadjusted balance	4,000	
Proration of direct-material price variance	400	
Adjusted balance	4,400	

In turn, the adjusted material efficiency variance is allocated to:

Finished goods inventory, 40%	$1,760
Cost of goods sold, 60%	2,640
Total allocated	$4,400

The following journal entry prorates the efficiency variance:

Finished goods	1,760	
Cost of goods sold	2,640	
Direct-material efficiency variance		4,400
To prorate the efficiency variance.		

EXHIBIT 8-7
EXHIBIT 8-7
Morales Company
Comprehensive Schedule of Prorations of Variances
(All Variances Are Unfavorable)

TYPE OF VARIANCE	(1) TOTAL VARIANCE	(2) TO STORES	(3) TO DIRECT MATERIAL EFFICIENCY VARIANCE	(4) TO FINISHED GOODS	(5) TO COST OF GOODS SOLD
Direct-material price	$10,000*	$1,600	$ 400	$3,200	$ 4,800
Direct-material efficiency					
Unadjusted balance	4,000		4,000		
Adjusted balance			$4,400†	1,760	2,640
Direct-labor price	1,000†			400	600
Direct-labor efficiency	4,000†			1,600	2,400
Factory overhead	5,000†			2,000	3,000
Total variances prorated	$24,000	$1,600		$8,960	$13,440
*Percentages used for proration	100%	16%	4%	32%	48%
†Percentages used for proration	100%			40%	60%

Exhibit 8-7 is a comprehensive schedule of all the variance prorations explained here. The T-accounts for inventories and cost of goods sold after proration are:

Stores			
Purchased	100,000	Issued	84,000
Proration of direct-material price variance	1,600		
Adjusted balance	17,600		

Work in Process			
Direct materials	80,000	Transferred	160,000
Direct labor	40,000		
Overhead applied	40,000		

Finished Goods			
Transferred	160,000	Sold	96,000
Proration of direct-labor and overhead variances	4,000		
Proration of direct-material price variance	3,200		
Proration of direct-material efficiency variance	1,760		
Adjusted balance	72,960		

Cost of Goods Sold			
Sold	96,000		
Proration of direct-labor and overhead variance	6,000		
Proration of direct-material price variance	4,800		
Proration of direct-material efficiency variance	2,640		
Adjusted balance	109,440		

EXHIBIT 8-8
Morales Company
Effects of Prorations of Variances on Operating Income

	STANDARD ABSORPTION COSTING	
	Without Proration	With Proration
Sales	$135,000	$135,000
Cost of goods sold—at standard	96,000	96,000
Total variances (from column 1, Exhibit 8-7)	24,000	
Prorated variances (from column 5, Exhibit 8-7)		13,440
Cost of goods sold—adjusted for variances	120,000	109,440
Selling and administrative expenses	20,000	20,000
Total charges against revenue	140,000	129,440
Operating income (loss)	$ (5,000)	$ 5,560

Exhibit 8-8 shows how proration affects operating income. Because all the variances are unfavorable, no proration reduces operating income by $24,000 instead of $13,440, a difference of $10,560. Hence operating income without proration is a negative $5,000; with proration, a positive $5,560, a relatively significant difference indeed.

APPENDIX 8B: COMPARISON OF VARIANCE PRORATIONS, NORMAL AND STANDARD COSTING

The main goal of this Appendix is to provide a comparative review of standard, normal, and actual cost systems. The principal vehicle for this review is the Morales Company illustration of how variances are prorated (Appendix 8A).

Exhibit 8-8 shows the effects of standard absorption costing on operating income, without and with variance prorations. We now compare these effects with those that would result using normal costing and actual costing.

Exhibit 8-9 on page 280 compares the entries that would be made to Work in Process under standard costing, normal costing, and actual costing. Exhibit 8-10 on page 281 assumes that the variances affect Finished Goods and Cost of Goods Sold in the same proportions under all alternative prorations.

Note that full prorations under standard costing and normal costing will yield accurate amounts of "actual" costs. Exhibit 8-10 also shows that proration, as compared with no proration, generates significant differences in inventories and cost of goods sold (and operating income). Of course, the size of the differences depends on the relative magnitude of the variances and the affected accounts. Compare the cost-of-goods-sold amounts (in dollars):

| | STANDARD COSTING | | NORMAL COSTING | | ACTUAL HISTORICAL COSTING |
	Without Proration	With Proration	Without Proration	With Proration	
Cost of goods sold	120,000	109,440	109,840	109,440	109,440

EXHIBIT 8-9
Comparative Work in Process Accounts, Absorption Costing

Work in Process (Standard Costing)

Direct materials, 160,000 lbs. @ $.50	80,000	Transferred	160,000
Direct labor, 2,000 hrs. @ $20	40,000		
Overhead applied, 2,000 hrs. @ $20	40,000		
	160,000		

Work in Process (Normal Costing)

Direct materials, 168,000 lbs. @ $.55	92,400*	Transferred	181,400
Direct labor, 2,200 hrs. @ $20.4545	45,000*		
Overhead applied, 2,200 hrs. @ $20	44,000†		
	181,400		

Work in Process (Actual Costing)

Direct materials	92,400*	Transferred	182,400
Direct labor	45,000*		
Overhead, actual	45,000‡		
	182,400		

*Actual quantities of material and labor at actual prices.
†Actual overhead rate base at budgeted application rate.
‡Actual overhead rate base at actual application rate.

EXHIBIT 8-10
Comparative Effects of Dispositions of Variances in Absorption Costing (in dollars)

	VARIANCES	DEBITS TO WORK IN PROCESS	ENDING BALANCES Finished Goods	ENDING BALANCES Cost of Goods Sold
Standard costing		160,000	64,000	96,000
Total variances not prorated*	24,000		—	24,000
Balances, end of year			64,000	120,000
Standard costing		160,000	64,000	96,000
Prorated variances ($24,000 − $1,600 to Stores)*	22,400		8,960	13,440
Balances, end of year			72,960	109,440
Normal costing		181,400	72,560	108,840
Underapplied overhead, not prorated, $45,000 actual − $44,000 applied	1,000		—	1,000
Balances, end of year			72,560	109,840
Normal costing		181,400	72,560	108,840
Prorated underapplied overhead	1,000		400	600
Balances, end of year			72,960	109,440
Actual historical costing		182,400	72,960	109,440

*Exhibits 8-7 and 8-8 (pp. 278–79) have more details. When variances are prorated, they are allocated 40% to Finished Goods and 60% to Cost of Goods Sold.

QUESTIONS, PROBLEMS, AND CASES

8-1 "Differences in operating income between variable costing and absorption costing are due solely to accounting for fixed costs." Do you agree? Explain.

8-2 Give an example of how, under absorption costing, operating income could fall even though sales rise.

8-3 List the three factors that affect the breakeven point under absorption costing.

8-4 "In the realm of planning and control for the current year, normal volume is an empty concept." Do you agree? Explain.

8-5 How do U.S. rules for external quarterly reporting distinguish among variances?

8-6 Why is *direct costing* a misnomer?

8-7 List three different types of denominator volumes.

8-8 "The central issue in variable costing is *timing*." Explain.

8-9 "The main trouble with variable costing is that it ignores the increasing importance of fixed costs in modern business." Do you agree? Why?

8-10 "The depreciation on the paper machine is every bit as much a part of the cost of the manufactured paper as the cost of the raw pulp." Do you agree? Why?

8-11 Straightforward variable costing income statement. Prepare a variable-costing income statement (through operating income) for Riordan Company. Use the following data: No beginning inventories of work in process or finished goods; no ending inventories of work in process. Production was 500,000 units, of which 400,000 were sold for $35 each. Unit direct-material cost was $6; unit direct-labor cost was $8; variable manufacturing cost was $1 per unit; fixed manufacturing cost was $2,000,000. Variable selling and administrative cost was $1 per unit sold; fixed selling and administrative cost was $2,500,000.

8-12 Absorption and variable costing. (CMA) Osawa Inc. planned and actually manufactured 200,000 units of its single product in 19_5, its first year of operations. Variable manufacturing costs were $30 per unit of product. Planned and actual fixed manufacturing costs were $600,000 and selling and administrative costs totaled $400,000 in 19_5. Osawa sold 120,000 units of product in 19_5 at a selling price of $40 per unit. Multiple choice:
1. Osawa's 19_5 operating income using absorption costing is (a) $200,000, (b) $440,000, (c) $600,000, (d) $840,000, (e) none of these.
2. Osawa's 19_5 operating income using variable (direct) costing is (a) $200,000, (b) $440,000, (c) $800,000, (d) $600,000, (e) none of these.

8-13 Comparison of actual costing methods. The AX Company sells its product at $2 per unit. The company uses a first-in, first-out, actual costing system. That is, a new fixed-factory-overhead application rate is computed each year by dividing the actual fixed factory overhead by the actual production. The following data relate to its first two years of operation:

	YEAR 1	YEAR 2
Sales	1,000 units	1,200 units
Production	1,400 units	1,000 units
Costs:		
Factory—variable	$700	$500
—fixed	700	700
Selling—variable	100	120
Administrative—fixed	400	400

Required
1. Income statements for each of the years based on absorption costing.
2. Income statements for each of the years based on direct or variable costing.
3. A reconciliation or explanation of the differences in the operating income for each year resulting from the use of the methods required above.

8-14 Income statements. (SMA) The Mass Company manufactures and sells a single product. The following data cover the two latest operating years:

	19_3	19_4
Selling price per unit	$ 40	$ 40
Sales in units	25,000	25,000
Opening inventory in units	1,000	1,000
Closing inventory in units	1,000	5,000
Fixed manufacturing costs	120,000	120,000
Fixed selling and administrative costs	90,000	90,000
Standard variable costs per unit:		

Materials	$10.50	Variable selling and
Direct labor	9.50	administrative	$1.20
Variable overhead	4.00	

The denominator activity is 30,000 units per year. Mass Company accounting records produce direct-costing information, and year-end adjustments are made to produce external reports showing absorption-costing data. Any variances are charged to cost of sales.

Required

1. Ignoring income taxes, prepare two income statements for 19_4, one under the direct-costing method and one under the absorption-costing method. Present your answer in good format.
2. Explain briefly why the net income figures computed in requirement 1 agree or do not agree.
3. Give two advantages and two disadvantages of using direct costing for internal reporting.

8-15 Variable versus absorption costing. The Mavis Company uses an absorption-costing system based on standard costs. Variable manufacturing costs, including material costs, were $3 per unit; the standard production rate was ten units per hour. Total budgeted and actual fixed factory overhead were $420,000. Fixed factory overhead was applied at $7 per hour ($420,000 ÷ 60,000 hours of denominator activity). Sales price is $5 per unit. Variable selling and administrative costs, which are related to units sold, were $1 per unit. Fixed selling and administrative costs were $120,000. Beginning inventory in 19_2 was 30,000 units; ending inventory was 40,000 units. Sales in 19_2 were 540,000 units. The same standard unit costs persisted throughout 19_1 and 19_2. For simplicity, assume that there were no price, spending, or efficiency variances.

Required

1. Prepare an income statement for 19_2 assuming that all underapplied or overapplied overhead is written off directly at year-end as an adjustment to Cost of Goods Sold.
2. The president has heard about variable (direct) costing. She asks you to recast the 19_2 statement as it should appear under variable costing.
3. Explain the difference in operating income as calculated in requirements 1 and 2.
4. Prepare a freehand graph of how *fixed factory* overhead was accounted for under absorption costing. That is, there will be two lines—one for the budgeted fixed overhead (which also happens to be the actual fixed factory overhead) and one for the product application rate. Show how the overapplied or underapplied overhead might be indicated on the graph.

8-16 Breakeven under absorption costing. Refer to the preceding problem.

Required

1. What is the breakeven point (in units) under variable costing? Explain.
2. What is the breakeven point (in units) under absorption costing? Explain.
3. Suppose production were exactly equal to the denominator activity, but no units were sold. Fixed factory costs are unaffected. However, assume that *all* selling and administrative costs were avoided. Compute operating income under (a) variable costing and (b) absorption costing. Explain the difference in your answers.

8-17 Absorption and variable costing. (CMA) BBG Corporation is a manufacturer of a synthetic element. Gary Voss, president of the company, has been eager to get the operating results for the just completed fiscal year. He was surprised when the income statement revealed that income before taxes has dropped to $885,000 from $900,000 even though sales volume had increased 100,000 kg. This drop in net income had occurred even though Voss had implemented the following changes during the past twelve months to improve the profitability of the company:

- In response to a 10% percent increase in production costs, the sales price of the company's product was increased by 12%. This action took place in December 1, 19_1.

- The managements of the selling and administrative departments were given strict instructions to spend no more in fiscal 19_2 than in fiscal 19_1.

BBG's accounting department prepared and distributed to top management the comparative income statements presented below. The accounting staff also prepared related financial information that is presented in the accompanying schedule to assist management in evaluating the company's performance. BBG uses the FIFO inventory method for finished goods.

BBG Corporation
Statements of Operating Income
For the years ended November 30, 19_1 and 19_2
($000 omitted)

	19_1	19_2
Sales revenue	$9,000	$11,200
Cost of goods sold	$7,200	$ 8,320
Manufacturing volume variance	(600)	495
Adjusted cost of goods sold	$6,600	$ 8,815
Gross margin	$2,400	$ 2,385
Selling and administrative expenses	1,500	1,500
Income before taxes	$ 900	$ 885

BBG Corporation
Selected Operating and Financial Data

	19_1	19_2
Sales price	$ 10/kg.	$11.20/kg.
Material cost	$1.50/kg.	$ 1.65/kg.
Direct-labor cost	$2.50/kg.	$ 2.75/kg.
Variable-overhead cost	$1.00/kg.	$ 1.10/kg.
Fixed-overhead cost	$3.00/kg.	$ 3.30/kg.
Total fixed-overhead costs	$3,000,000	$3,300,000
Selling and administrative (all fixed)	$1,500,000	$1,500,000
Sales volume	900,000 kg.	1,000,000 kg.
Beginning inventory	300,000 kg.	600,000 kg.

Required

1. Explain to Gary Voss why BBG Corporation's net income decreased in the current fiscal year despite the sales price and sales volume increases.
2. A member of BBG's accounting department has suggested that the company adopt variable (direct) costing for internal reporting purposes.
   a. Prepare an operating income statement through income before taxes for the year ended November 30, 19_2, for BBG Corporation using the variable (direct) costing method.
   b. Present a numerical reconciliation of the difference in income before taxes using the absorption-costing method as currently employed by BBG and the variable (direct) costing method as proposed.

8-18 The All-Fixed Company in 1996. (R. Marple, adapted) It is the end of 1996. The All-Fixed Company began operations in January 1995. The company is so named because it has no variable costs. All its costs are fixed; they do not vary with output.

The All-Fixed Company is located on the bank of a river and has its own hydroelectric plant to supply power, light, and heat. The company manufactures a synthetic fertilizer from air and river water and sells its product at a price that is not expected to change. It has a small staff of employees, all hired on an annual-salary basis. The output of the plant can be increased or decreased by adjusting a few dials on a control panel.

The following are data regarding the operations of the All-Fixed Company:

	1995	1996*
Sales	10,000 tons	10,000 tons
Production	20,000 tons	—
Selling price	$30 per ton	$30 per ton
Costs (all fixed):		
Production	$280,000	$280,000
General and administrative	$ 40,000	$ 40,000

*Management adopted the policy, effective January 1, 1996, of producing only as the product was needed to fill sales. During 1996, sales were the same as for 1995 and were filled entirely from inventory at the start of 1996.

Required

1. Prepare three-column income statements for 1995, 1996, and the two years together, using
   a. Variable (direct) costing
   b. Absorption costing
2. What is the breakeven point under (a) variable costing and (b) absorption costing?
3. What inventory costs would be carried on the balance sheets at December 31, 1995 and 1996, under each method?
4. Comment on the results in requirements 1 and 2. Which costing method appears more useful?

8-19 The Semi-Fixed Company in 1996. The Semi-Fixed Company began operations in 1995 and differs from the All-Fixed Company (described in Problem 8-18) in only one respect: It has both fixed and variable production costs. Its variable costs are $7 per ton and its fixed production costs $140,000 per year. Normal activity is 20,000 tons per year.

Required

1. Using the same data as in Problem 8-18 except for the change in production-cost behavior, prepare three-column income statements for 1995, 1996, and the two years together, under
   a. Variable costing
   b. Absorption costing
2. Why did the Semi-Fixed Company earn a profit for the two-year period while the All-Fixed Company in Problem 8-18 suffered a loss?
3. What inventory costs would be carried on the balance sheets at December 31, 1995 and 1996, under each method?
4. How may the variable-costing approach be reconciled with the definition of an asset as being "economic service potential"?

8-20 Comparison of variable costing and absorption costing. Consider the following data:

MELDER COMPANY
Income Statement for the Year Ended December 31, 19_4

	VARIABLE COSTING	ABSORPTION COSTING
Sales	$7,000,000	$7,000,000
Costs applied to goods sold (at standard)	$3,660,000	$4,575,000
Fixed manufacturing overhead	1,000,000	—
Manufacturing variances (all unfavorable):		
Direct material	50,000	50,000
Direct labor	60,000	60,000
Variable overhead	30,000	30,000
Fixed overhead:		
Spending or budget	100,000	100,000
Production volume	—	400,000
Total selling expenses	1,000,000	1,000,000
Total administrative expenses	500,000	500,000
Total expenses	$6,400,000	$6,715,000
Operating income	$ 600,000	$ 285,000

The inventories, carried at standard costs, were:

	VARIABLE COSTING	ABSORPTION COSTING
December 31, 19_3	$1,320,000	$1,650,000
December 31, 19_4	60,000	75,000

Required

1. Malcolm Melder, president of the Melder Company, has asked you to explain why the income for 19_4 is less than that for 19_3, despite the fact that sales have increased 40% over last year.
2. At what percentage of denominator volume was the factory working during 19_4?
3. Prepare a numerical reconciliation and explanation of the difference between the operating incomes under absorption costing and variable costing.

8-21 Inventory techniques and management planning. It is November 30, 19_4. Given the following for a company division's operations for January through November, 19_4:

Division H
Income Statement for Eleven Months Ended November 30, 19_4

	UNITS		DOLLARS
Sales @ $1,000	1,000		1,000,000
Less cost of goods sold:			
Beginning inventory, December 31, 19_3, @ $800	50	40,000	
Manufacturing costs @ $800, including $600 per unit for fixed overhead	1,100	880,000	
Total standard cost of goods available for sale	1,150	920,000	
Ending inventory, November 30, 19_4, @ $800	150	120,000	
Standard cost of goods sold*	1,000		800,000
Gross margin			200,000
Other expenses:			
Variable, 1,000 units @ $50		50,000	
Fixed, @ $10,000 monthly		110,000	160,000
Operating income			40,000

There are absolutely no variances for the eleven-month period considered as a whole.

Production in the past three months has been 100 units monthly. Practical capacity is 125 units monthly. To retain a stable nucleus of key employees, monthly production is never scheduled at less than 50 units.

Maximum available storage space for inventory is regarded as 195 units. The sales outlook for the next four months is 70 units monthly. Inventory is never to be less than 45 units.

The company uses a standard absorption-costing system. Denominator production volume is 1,200 units annually. All variances are disposed of at year-end as an adjustment to Standard Cost of Goods Sold.

Required

1. The division manager is given an annual bonus that is geared to operating income. Given the data above, assume that the manager wants to maximize the company's operating income for 19_4. How many units should the manager schedule for production in December? Note carefully that you do not have to (*nor should you*) compute the exact income for 19_4 in this or in subsequent parts of this question.
2. Assume that standard variable costing is in use rather than standard absorption costing. Would variable-costing operating income for 19_4 be higher, lower, or the same as

standard absorption-costing income, assuming that production for December is 80 units and sales are 70 units? Why?

3. If standard variable costing were used, what production schedule should the division manager set? Why?

4. Assume that the manager is interested in maximizing his performance over the long run, and that performance is being judged on an after-income-tax basis. Given the data in the beginning of the problem, assume that income tax rates will be halved in 19_5, and assume that the year-end write-offs of variances are acceptable for income tax purposes. Assume that standard absorption costing is used. How many units should be scheduled for production in December? Why?

8-22 Some additional requirements to problem 8-21; absorption costing and production volume variances.
Refer to Problem 8-21.

1. What operating income will be reported for 19_4 as a whole, assuming that the implied cost behavior patterns will continue in December as they did in January through November, and assuming—without regard to your answer to requirement 1 in Problem 8-21—that production for December is 80 units and sales are 70 units?

2. Assume the same conditions as in requirement 1 except that practical capacity was used in setting fixed-overhead rates for product costing throughout 19_4. What production volume variance would be reported for 19_4?

8-23 Executive incentives; relevant costing.   The data below pertain to the B. E. Company:

	YEAR 19_1
Selling price per unit	$ 2.00
Total fixed cost—production	$ 8,400,000.00
Total fixed costs—selling and administrative	$ 600,000.00
Variable cost per unit—selling and administrative	$ .50
Sales in units	17,000,000
Production in units	17,000,000
Normal activity in units (based on three-to five-year demand)	30,000,000
Operating loss	$ 500,000.00
No opening or closing inventories.	

The board of directors has approached a competent outside executive to take over the company. He is an optimistic soul and he agrees to become president at a token salary, but his contract provides for a year-end bonus amounting to 10% of operating profit (before considering the bonus or income taxes). The annual profit was to be certified by a public accounting firm.

The new president, filled with rosy expectations, promptly raised the advertising budget by $3,500,000, stepped up production to an annual rate of 30,000,000 units ("to fill the pipelines," the president said). As soon as all outlets had sufficient stock, the advertising campaign was launched, and sales for 19_2 increased—but only to a level of 25,000,000 units.

The certified income statement for 19_2 contained the following data:

Sales, 25,000,000 × $2		$50,000,000
Production costs:		
Variable, 30,000,000 × $1	$30,000,000	
Fixed	8,400,000	
Total	$38,400,000	
Inventory, 5,000,000 units (1/6)	6,400,000	
Cost of goods sold		32,000,000
Gross margin		$18,000,000
Selling and administrative expenses:		
Variable	$12,500,000	
Fixed	4,100,000	
		16,600,000
Operating profit		$ 1,400,000

The day after the statement was certified, the president resigned to take a job with another corporation having difficulties similar to those that B. E. Company had a year ago. The president remarked, "I enjoy challenges. Now that B. E. Company is in the black, I'd prefer tackling another knotty difficulty." His contract with his new employer is similar to the one he had with B. E. Company.

Required

1. As a member of the board, what comments would you make at the next meeting regarding the most recent income statement? Maximum production capacity is 40,000,000 units per year.
2. Would you change your remarks in requirement 1 if (consider each part independently):
   a. Sales outlook for the coming three years is 20,000,000 units per year?
   b. Sales outlook for the coming three years is 30,000,000 units per year?
   c. Sales outlook for the coming three years is 40,000,000 units per year?
   d. The company is to be liquidated immediately, so that the only sales in 19_3 will be the 5,000,000 units still in inventory?
   e. The sales outlook for 19_3 is 45,000,000 units?
3. Assuming that the $140,000 bonus is paid, would you favor a similar arrangement for the next president? If not, and you were outvoted, what changes in a bonus contract would you try to have adopted?

8-24 Overhead rates and cyclical business. It is a time of severe business depression throughout the capital-goods industries. A division manager for a large corporation in a heavy-machinery industry is confused and unhappy. The manager is distressed with the controller, whose cost department keeps feeding the manager costs that are of little use because they are higher than ever before. At the same time, the manager has to quote lower prices than before in order to get any business.

Required

1. What activity base is probably being used for application of overhead?
2. How might the overhead be applied in order to make the cost data more useful in making price quotations?
3. Would the product costs furnished by the cost department be satisfactory for the costing of the annual inventory?

8-25 Income taxes and practical capacity. In the United States there is nothing illegal or immoral about keeping multiple sets of accounting records, one to satisfy income tax reporting requirements, one to satisfy investor reporting requirements, one to satisfy manager decision requirements, and so on. Nevertheless, real or imagined costs versus benefits lead most companies to have one or, at most, two sets of records. Income tax regulations have heavy effects on accounting systems because records must be kept to satisfy tax laws.

For years the Internal Revenue Service was liberal regarding the tendency of companies to write off many indirect manufacturing costs, particularly depreciation on equipment, as charges against income immediately. However, in 1975 new income tax regulations (see the Regulations 1.471-11) forced industry to hold back more indirect costs as "inventoriable" costs. In short, the regulations came down hard against the variable- or direct-costing approach to inventory valuation and in favor of absorption costing.

The regulations insist that any significant underapplied or overapplied overhead be prorated among the appropriate inventory accounts and cost of goods sold. However, the regulations explicitly approve a "practical capacity concept." This permits the immediate write-off (rather than proration) of the production volume variance that results from using a fixed overhead rate based on a practical capacity denominator volume level.

Corporation X operates a stamping plant with a theoretical capacity of 60 units per hour. The plant is actually open 1,960 hours per year based on an 8-hour day, 5-day week and 15 shutdown days for vacations and holidays. A reasonable allowance for downtime (the time allowed for ordinary and necessary repairs and maintenance) is 5% of theoretical capacity. The latter is defined as the level of production that the manufacturer could reach if all machines and departments were operated continuously for the 1,960 hours at peak efficiency.

| Required | 1. Compute practical capacity in units per year. Assume no loss of production during starting up, closing down, or employee work breaks.
| | 2. Assume that 75,000 units are produced for the year and that budgeted and actual fixed indirect production costs totaled $14,523,600. Also assume that 7,500 units are on hand at the end of the taxable year and that there were no beginning inventories. Compute the amount of fixed indirect costs that would have been applied to production during the year. What amount will be allowed as a deduction in the computation of income taxes for the year? Label your computations.

8-26 Effects of denominator choice.

The Chang Company installed standard costs and a flexible budget on January 1, 19_3. The president had been pondering on how fixed manufacturing overhead should be applied to product. He decided to wait for the first month's results before making a final choice of what denominator volume should be used from that day forward.

In January, the company operated at an activity of 70,000 standard hours allowed for the good units actually produced. If the company had used practical capacity as a denominator volume, the budget variance would have been $10,000, unfavorable, and the production volume variance would have been $36,000, unfavorable. If the company had used "normal" activity as a denominator volume, the production volume variance would have been $20,000, favorable. Budgeted fixed overhead was $120,000 for the month.

| Required | 1. Denominator volume, assuming "normal" activity as the denominator.
| | 2. Denominator volume, assuming practical capacity as the denominator.

8-27 Proration of variances, multiple choice.

(CPA, adapted) Tolliver Manufacturing Company uses a standard-cost system in accounting for the cost of production of its only product, Product A. The standards for the production of one unit of Product A are as follows:

Direct materials: 10 feet of item 1 at $.75 per foot and 3 feet of item 2 at $1.00 per foot
Direct labor: 4 hours at $15.00 per hour
Manufacturing overhead: applied at 150% of standard direct-labor costs

There was no inventory on hand at July 1, 19_2. Following is a summary of costs and related data for the production of Product A during the year ended June 30, 19_3:

100,000 feet of item 1 were purchased at $.78 per foot
30,000 feet of item 2 were purchased at $.90 per foot
8,000 units of Product A were produced, which required 78,000 feet of item 1; 26,000 feet of item 2; and 31,000 hours of direct labor at $16.00 per hour
6,000 units of Product A were sold

At June 30, 19_3, there are 22,000 feet of item 1, 4,000 feet of item 2, and 2,000 completed units of Product A on hand. All purchases and transfers are "charged in" at standard.

| Required | Choose the best answers:

1. For the year ended June 30, 19_3, the total debits to the raw-materials account for the purchase of item 1 would be (a) $78,000, (b) $75,000, (c) $58,500, (d) $60,000.
2. For the year ended June 30, 19_3, the total debits to the work-in-process account for direct labor would be (a) $496,000, (b) $512,000, (c) $480,000, (d) $465,000.
3. Before allocation of standard variances, the balance in the material-efficiency-variance account for item 2 was (a) $2,000 debit, (b) $2,600 debit, (c) $600 debit, (d) $1,000 credit.
4. If all standard variances were prorated to inventories and cost of goods sold, the amount of material-efficiency variance for item 2 to be prorated to raw-materials inventory would be (a) $0, (b) $333 credit, (c) $333 debit, (d) $500 debit.
5. If all standard variances were prorated to inventories and cost of goods sold, the amount of material-price variance for item 1 to be prorated to raw-materials inventory would be (a) $0, (b) $647 debit, (c) $660 debit, (d) $600 debit.

289

8-28 Straightforward proration. Consider the following unadjusted balances of standard costs (before proration) at the end of the year: work in process, $200,000; finished goods, $800,000; cost of goods sold, $1,000,000. The production volume variance was $50,000, favorable. All other variances were $330,000, unfavorable. Management has decided to prorate all variances in proportion to the unadjusted balances in work in process, finished goods, and cost of goods sold.

Required

1. Prepare a schedule that prorates the variances.
2. Prepare a journal entry that closes all variance accounts.
3. The major justification for proration is the attempt to approximate the "actual" cost of the units produced. What is the most likely inaccuracy in the proration here? Explain.

8-29 Proration of variances and income effects of standard costs. The Moraine Company began business on January 1, 19_1. A standard absorption-costing system has been in use. Balances in certain accounts at December 31, 19_1, are as follows:

At standard unit prices:	
Stores	$ 20,000
Work in process	10,000
Finished goods	30,000
Cost of goods sold	60,000
Total	$120,000
Variances (unfavorable):	
Direct-material efficiency	$ 10,000
Direct-material purchase price	12,000
Direct-labor price	2,000
Direct-labor efficiency	10,000
Underapplied overhead	5,000
Total	$ 39,000
Sales	$150,000

The executives have asked you to compute the gross margin (after deductions for variances, if any), assuming first that no variances are prorated, and second that all variances are prorated.

Assume that all variances that are not prorated are considered direct adjustments of standard cost of goods sold. Assume that prorations are based on the ending balances of the applicable accounts affected, even though more-refined methods would be possible if additional data were available. There are not enough data about the direct-material components in the various accounts to warrant the proration of some of the direct-material purchase-price variance to the direct-material efficiency variance; therefore prorate the price variance directly to Stores, Work in Process, Finished Goods, and Cost of Goods sold.

Required

1. Prepare a comprehensive schedule of proration of all variances.
2. Prepare a compound journal entry for the proration.
3. Prepare comparative summary statements of gross margin under each of the two assumptions specified by the company's executives.

8-30 Proration of direct-materials variances. (D. Kleespie, adapted) Study Appendix 8A. The J/E Lahtinen Company manufactures a single product. The company prorates its direct-material price and efficiency variances to the appropriate accounts in proportion to the cost components in those accounts. The price variance is $2,800, unfavorable; efficiency variance, $1,200, unfavorable.

The company had no beginning materials inventory. Purchases were 14,000 pounds. The standard allowance is 2 pounds per finished unit. Units produced, 6,000. Units sold, 5,000. The standard unit price for the direct material is $4 per pound.

1. Compute the excess material used in pounds.
2. Compute the ending inventory, Stores, in pounds.
3. Compute the amounts of the price variance prorated to finished goods and to cost of goods sold.
4. Compute the amounts of the "adjusted" efficiency variance prorated to finished goods and to cost of goods sold.
5. Explain why the price variance is prorated before the efficiency variance is prorated.

8-31 Proration of variances and income effects of standard costs. Study Appendix 8A. The Pearson Company uses a standard absorption-costing system, which shows the following unadjusted account balances at December 31, 19_2:

Stores (direct materials only), ending inventory	$175,000
Work in process, ending inventory	100,000
Finished goods, ending inventory	300,000
Cost of goods sold	600,000
Direct-materials price variance	64,000
Direct-materials efficiency variance	25,000
Direct-labor price variance	5,000
Direct-labor efficiency variance	25,000
Factory overhead incurred	210,000
Factory overhead applied, at standard rate	170,000
Sales	900,000
Selling and administrative expenses	180,000

Materials price variances are measured when the material is purchased rather than when it is used. Assume that Work in Process, Finished Goods, and Cost of Goods Sold contain standard costs in uniform proportions of direct material, direct labor, and factory overhead. The direct-material component represented 60% of the ending balance in Work in Process, Finished Goods, and Cost of Goods Sold. All variances are unfavorable. There are no beginning inventories.

Required

1. Prepare a comprehensive schedule of proration of all variances.
2. Prepare a compound journal entry for the proration.
3. Prepare comparative summary income statements based on a standard absorption-costing system:
   a. Without proration of any variances
   b. With proration of all variances
4. Compute the amount of direct-labor cost included in the unadjusted balance of finished goods, ending inventory.

8-32 Comparative income effects of variance prorations. Study Appendix 8B. Refer to the data in the preceding problem for Pearson Company, which uses absorption costing. Overhead is applied as a percentage of direct-labor dollars.

The chief executive officer is curious regarding how ending balances of Work in Process, Finished Goods, and Cost of Goods Sold would be affected under each of the assumptions listed below:
   a. Standard costing without proration of any variances
   b. Standard costing with proration of all variances
   c. Normal costing without proration of underapplied overhead
   d. Normal costing with proration of underapplied overhead
   e. Actual historical costing—that is, no budgeted overhead rate used

Required

1. Summarize postings into Work in Process under standard costing, normal costing, and actual costing.
2. Prepare a comparison of the effects of the assumptions listed above. What would be the final balances in Work in Process, Finished Goods, and Cost of Goods Sold? *Hint:* See Exhibits 8-9 and 8-10, pp. 280–81.

3. Analyze the results in requirement 2. Which assumption writes costs off to expense most quickly? What other generalizations about the five assumptions can be made? Were Pearson's standards currently attainable? Explain.

4. What approach would you take if you had more data and wanted a more accurate proration of variances?

8-33 Multiple-choice interim reporting. (CPA) The following annual flexible budget has been prepared for use in making decisions relating to Product X.

	100,000 UNITS	150,000 UNITS	200,000 UNITS
Sales volume	$800,000	$1,200,000	$1,600,000
Manufacturing costs:			
Variable	$300,000	$ 450,000	$ 600,000
Fixed	200,000	200,000	200,000
	$500,000	$ 650,000	$ 800,000
Selling and other expenses:			
Variable	$200,000	$ 300,000	$ 400,000
Fixed	160,000	160,000	160,000
	$360,000	$ 460,000	$ 560,000
Income (or loss)	$ (60,000)	$ 90,000	$ 240,000

The 200,000-unit budget has been adopted and will be used for allocating fixed manufacturing costs to units of Product X; at the end of the first six months the following information is available:

	UNITS
Production completed	120,000
Sales	60,000

All fixed costs are budgeted and incurred uniformly throughout the year, and all costs incurred coincide with the budget.

Overapplied and underapplied fixed manufacturing costs are deferred until year-end. Annual sales have the following seasonal pattern:

	PORTION OF ANNUAL SALES
First quarter	10%
Second quarter	20
Third quarter	30
Fourth quarter	40
	100%

Required **1.** The amount of fixed factory costs applied to product during the first six months under absorption costing would be (a) equal to the fixed costs incurred, (b) overapplied by $20,000, (c) underapplied by $40,000, (d) underapplied by $80,000, (e) none of these.

2. Reported net income (or loss) for the first six months under absorption costing would be (a) $160,000, (b) $40,000, (c) $80,000, (d) ($40,000), (e) none of these.

3. Reported net income (or loss) for the first six months under direct costing would be (a) $144,000, (b) $72,000, (c) ($36,000), (d) $0, (e) none of these.

Chapter 8

292

4. Assuming that 90,000 units of Product X were sold during the first six months and that this is to be used as a basis, the revised budget estimate for the total number of units to be sold during this year would be (a) 360,000, (b) 240,000, (c) 200,000, (d) 120,000, (e) none of these.

8-34 Interim reporting. Alberti Company had the following data for the quarter ended March 31, 19_1:

	ACTUAL	FLEXIBLE BUDGET	FLEXIBLE-BUDGET VARIANCES
Variable factory overhead	$200,000	$178,000	$22,000 U
Fixed factory overhead:			
Applied		300,000	
Production volume variance		50,000	
Total	355,000	350,000	5,000 U
Total factory overhead	$555,000	$528,000	$27,000 U
Operating income	$110,000	$180,000	$70,000 U

For simplicity, assume that there are no beginning or ending inventories.

Required

1. Does the company use variable or absorption costing? Explain your answer.
2. Suppose the company had "planned" production volume variances. That is, volume fluctuated from month to month, but by the end of the year the total production volume variance was expected to be negligible. Under this approach, what "actual" operating income would be shown for the quarter? Explain your answer.
3. If variable costing is used, what "actual" operating income would be reported? Explain.

8-35 Prepare income statement on variable-costing basis. A fire partially destroyed the records of the McBee Manufacturing Company on December 31, 19_1. You have been asked to prepare a comparative statement of the original budgeted income statement for the year and the actual results. Even though the company has kept records on an absorption-costing basis, you have decided to prepare a statement on the variable-costing basis.

On an absorption-costing basis, the unfavorable production volume variance for fixed factory overhead was $13,650, and 52,000 units were produced and sold at an average selling price of $20 per unit. The standard contribution margin was $5 per unit. Budgeted and actual fixed costs were the same for both manufacturing ($122,850) and nonmanufacturing ($80,000). The total price, spending, and efficiency variances were $36,000, unfavorable. On an absorption-costing basis, fixed factory overhead had been applied on the basis of the expected volume level used in the master budget.

8-36 Difficult comparison of variable and absorption costing. Assume that operating income for 19_2 was $600,000 under variable costing and $800,000 under absorption costing. The end-of-year cost of the inventory under standard variable costing was $60,000. The beginning-of-year cost of the inventory under standard absorption costing was $25,000 higher than the cost of the beginning-of-year inventory under standard variable costing. Compute the end-of-year cost of inventory under standard absorption costing.

SPECIAL REVIEW MATERIAL FOR CHAPTERS 6 THROUGH 8

8-37 Comparison of actual costing, normal costing, and standard costing. The Vatner Company began business on January 1, 19_1. It manufactured a single product that was easy to standardize, so a standard-cost system was adopted. Price variances for raw material were isolated upon purchase, and Work in Process, Finished Goods, and Cost of Goods Sold were carried at standard cost. The standard cost per finished unit was based on one pound of raw material usage, ¼ hour of direct-labor time, and an overhead rate as related to labor time.

The standard price for raw material was $1 per pound; for direct labor, $16 per hour. The factory overhead budget for 19_1 was $200,000; 100,000 units were scheduled for production during 19_1. Any budgeted overhead rates were to be based on a denominator volume of 25,000 hours.

The following are the actual results for 19_1:

Sales	$1,000,000
Material purchases, 160,000 pounds @ $1.10	176,000
Material inputs, 110,000 pounds	
Direct-labor inputs, 30,000 hours	480,000
Factory overhead incurred	215,000
Nonmanufacturing expenses	300,000
Finished units produced, 100,000	
Finished units sold, 70,000	

Amy Vatner, the president, decided to use some form of absorption costing. She realized that because hers was a new company she had some latitude in deciding how to report the results of operations to investors and to the Internal Revenue Service. Moreover, she also realized that her choice would set a precedent regarding the method of reporting in subsequent years. Finally, she recognized that she could continue to use standard costing for internal reporting purposes without being obliged to use it for external purposes.

Required

(T-accounts may be helpful)

1. Vatner has asked you to prepare three comparative income statements in columnar form. The columns would be based on the following assumptions: (a) actual costing, (b) normal costing, and (c) standard costing. All variances are to be written off against revenue.
2. By how much do the net incomes in columns (b) and (c) differ from column (a)? Fully explain each difference.
3. Which of the three alternatives should Vatner choose for reporting to investors? For reporting to the Internal Revenue Service? Why?

8-38 Comparison of alternative income statements. Alternative income statements for the same company for a given year follow:

A   V

	A	B	C
Sales	$100,000	$100,000	$100,000
Cost of goods sold	40,000	30,000	42,000
	$ 60,000	$ 70,000	$ 58,000
Variances:			
Direct material	(1,500)	(1,500)	
Direct labor	(500)	(500)	
Factory overhead	(4,000)	—	(4,000)
	$ 54,000	$ 68,000	$ 54,000
Other operating expenses (all fixed)	40,000	54,000	40,000
Operating income	$ 14,000	$ 14,000	$ 14,000

Required

Write a brief explanation for each of your answers:

1. Which cost system: (1) actual cost, (2) standard absorption cost, (3) standard variable cost, or (4) historical cost with budgeted overhead rates was used for A? For B? For C?
2. Did the inventory: (1) increase, (2) decrease, (3) remain unchanged for A? For B? For C?

3. What was the selling and administrative expense for the year?
4. What would you expect the net operating income to be if sales volume increased 10% and selling prices remained the same? Assume that all variable costs will be at standard—in other words, no variances are to be budgeted for material, labor, or variable overhead for any production.
5. Was the production volume for the year higher than, lower than, or equal to the predetermined volume?
6. What was the fixed factory overhead for the year?
7. Was the variable factory overhead for the year more than, less than, or equal to the budget?

8-39 Comprehensive review of absorption costing and variable costing. A fire destroyed most of the assets and records of the Salinas Division of a large corporation on December 31, 19_2. The division manufactured a single product and used a standard-cost system together with a flexible budget. Salinas must try to reconstruct its records to help establish the amount of an insurance claim and its loss for income tax purposes. Unfortunately, the records are in chaos. Moreover, the division manager had been thinking of switching from an absorption (full) costing to variable (direct) costing. As an experiment, parallel records were being kept throughout 19_2 on both the absorption-costing and variable-costing basis.

You have been asked to collect the known data in one place. You have compiled the following:

(a) Direct-material purchases, at standard prices, $90,000.
(b) Actual and budgeted selling and administrative expenses (all fixed), $20,000; there are no variable selling and administrative costs.
(c) Notes receivable from Gilroy Division, $8,000.
(d) Sales, $300,000.
(e) Cash on hand, December 31, 19_2, $6,000.
(f) Standard variable manufacturing costs per unit, $2.00.
(g) Variances from standard of all variable manufacturing costs, $20,000, unfavorable.
(h) Total notes payable December 31, 19_2, $57,000.
(i) Unfavorable budget variance, fixed manufacturing costs, $3,000.
(j) Contribution margin, at standard (before deducting any variances), $120,000.
(k) Direct material used, at standard, $108,000.
(l) Actual fixed manufacturing costs, $73,000.
(m) Operating income, absorption-costing basis, $6,200.
(n) Accounts receivable December 31, 19_2, $47,000.
(o) Gross profit, absorption costing at standard (before deducting variances), $48,000.
(p) All standard *unit* costs have remained unchanged throughout 19_1 and 19_2. Variances are not prorated among inventories and cost of goods sold.

Required

Ignore income taxes. Solve for the following items. Various alternative approaches might be taken to obtain some of the items, so the items need not be solved in any particular order. Double-check your arithmetic. The avoidance of arithmetic errors is crucial and checks are available; therefore an arithmetic error here is a more serious transgression than in an ordinary case or problem. Your work will be used to help establish the amount of insurance claim and the amount of income taxes. Compute:

1. Operating income on a variable-costing (direct-costing) basis.
2. Variable manufacturing cost of goods sold, at standard prices.
3. Number of units sold.
4. Manufacturing cost of goods sold at standard prices, absorption costing.
5. Number of units produced.
6. Number of units used as the denominator to obtain fixed indirect manufacturing-cost application rate per unit on an absorption-costing basis.
7. Did inventory (in units) increase or decrease? Explain.
8. By how much in dollars did the inventory level change (a) under absorption costing; (b) under variable costing?

8-40 Comprehensive comparison of standard, normal, and actual costing. (W. Richards, Jr.) Milano Manufacturing, Inc., has just completed its second year of operations. It is a single-product firm and the standard-cost record applicable for both years is as follows:

Raw materials, 4 lbs. @ $.50/lb.	$2.00
Direct labor, ½ hr. @ $6.00/hr.	3.00
Manufacturing overhead, ½ hr. @ $14.00/hr.*	7.00

This is also the hourly rate used for normal absorption costing.

All variances (and/or overapplied or underapplied overhead) are charged directly to Cost of Goods Sold at the end of each year. The same denominator volume was used for each year. The first-in, first-out inventory method is appropriate where a cost flow assumption is necessary. There were no Raw-Material or Work-in-Process inventories for either year. Assorted data follow:

	FOR YEAR ENDED DECEMBER 31	
	19_4	19_5
Finished goods, beginning inventory	-0-	2,000 units
Production	10,000 units	14,000 units
Finished goods, ending inventory	2,000 units	4,000 units
Sales	$150,000	$240,000
Direct-labor price variance	1,000 F	-0-
Raw-materials price variance	-0-	-0-
Actual and budgeted fixed-selling and administrative expense	$ 5,000	$ 5,000
Actual and budgeted variable-selling and administrative expense	10% of sales	10% of sales
Production volume variance	$ 25,000 U	$ 5,000 U
Actual manufacturing costs:		
Raw materials	$ 21,000	$ 28,000
Direct labor	32,000	45,000
Variable manufacturing overhead	21,000	25,000
Fixed manufacturing overhead	70,000	84,000

Required | Determine operating income for each of the two years under each of the following assumptions.

OPERATING INCOME FOR:	VARIABLE COSTING	ABSORPTION COSTING
Standard costing, 19_4		
Standard costing, 19_5		
Normal costing, 19_4		
Normal costing, 19_5		
Actual costing, 19_4		
Actual costing, 19_5		

9

Relevance, Pricing, and the Decision Process

Information and the decision process • Meaning of relevance •
Illustration of relevance: choosing volume levels • Pricing decisions and cost data •
Effects of antitrust laws on pricing • Other illustrations of relevance and the contribution approach •
Opportunity costs, relevance, and accounting records • Irrelevance of past costs •
How managers behave • Appendix 9A: Cost of prediction error •
Appendix 9B: Cost terms used for different purposes

We have already seen how the contribution approach, with its emphasis on cost behavior patterns, helps cost analysis and the evaluation of performance. Our study has focused on two purposes:

1. Product costing
2. Costing for routine planning and control of operations

In this chapter we turn to a third purpose:

3. Costing for special nonroutine decisions

Examples of decisions related to this third purpose include the addition or deletion of a product line, the manufacture or purchase of component parts (make or buy), the acceptance or rejection of a special order, and the replacement of equipment. Executives commonly use teamwork in reaching these decisions, which are often fusions of the thinking of engineers, economists, production managers, sales managers, mathematicians, and accountants. Cost analysis is nearly always helpful, and therefore the cost accountant plays an important role in these special decisions.

Years ago the word *relevant* was not overused. Now it seems to be applied in every situation imaginable. Nevertheless, *relevant* is particularly apt for our purposes, so we will stress the word in this chapter. When is an item relevant to a particular management decision? When is it irrelevant? This distinction is crucial to the making of intelligent decisions. The contribution approach, combined with the ability to distinguish relevance from irrelevance, enables accountants and managers to reach correct conclusions in this challenging area. A commentator expressed the importance of relevance by saying: "If accounting had been a profession soon after Adam and Eve left the Garden of Eden, it could have placed relevance above all else and even might have gotten it included in the Ten Commandments."

INFORMATION AND THE DECISION PROCESS

The manager has a method for deciding among courses of action, often called a decision model. A **decision model** is a formal method for making a choice that often involves quantitative analysis. For now, let us focus on what accounting information can provide, given any form of decision model.

Predictions and models

Consider a decision whether to rearrange a production line in order to save operating labor costs. Assume that the only alternatives are "do not rearrange" or "rearrange." The rearrangement is predicted to cost $30,000. The predicted output of 200,000 units for the next year will be unaffected by the decision. Also unaffected by the decision is direct materials cost per unit, predicted to be $5 per unit, and the selling price of $10 per unit.

At this point, study Exhibit 9-1. Its analysis puts in perspective the role of accounting in predicting the labor-cost savings. The historical labor cost of $1.95 per unit of output is the starting point for *predicting* the labor costs per unit of output under both alternatives. The prediction under the "do not rearrange" alternative is $2.00, reflecting a recently negotiated increase in employee benefits. The prediction under the "rearrange" alternative is $1.80 per product unit because of expected reductions in labor usage.

The specific predictions are fed forward as inputs to a decision model, which might consist of a comparison of the total predicted labor savings against the required additional investment of $30,000.

Models and feedback

Assume that management chooses the "rearrange" alternative and this decision is implemented. The subsequent evaluation of actual performance provides feedback. In turn, the feedback might affect the future predictions, the prediction method itself, the decision model, or the implementation.

In our illustration, the actual results of the plant rearrangement may show that the new labor costs are $2.50 per product unit rather than the $1.80 originally predicted. This feedback may lead to better implementation (step 4 in Exhibit 9-1), such as a change in supervisory behavior, in employee training, or in personnel, so that the $1.80 target is achieved. On the other hand, the feedback may convince the decision maker that the prediction method, rather than the implementation, was faulty. Perhaps the prediction method for similar decisions in the future should be modified to allow for worker training or learning time.

Appendix 9A discusses three sources of prediction errors: faulty conceptual analysis, faulty data analysis, and uncertainty of the outcome. A three-step ap-

EXHIBIT 9-1
Accounting Information and the Decision Process

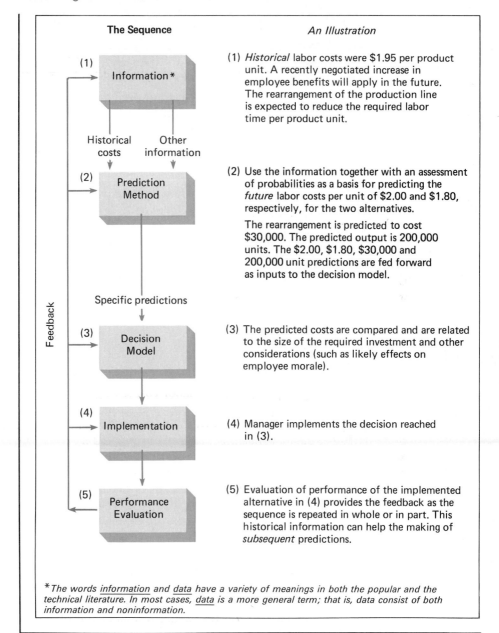

	The Sequence	An Illustration

(1) Information*

(1) *Historical* labor costs were $1.95 per product unit. A recently negotiated increase in employee benefits will apply in the future. The rearrangement of the production line is expected to reduce the required labor time per product unit.

Historical costs   Other information

(2) Prediction Method

(2) Use the information together with an assessment of probabilities as a basis for predicting the *future* labor costs per unit of $2.00 and $1.80, respectively, for the two alternatives.

The rearrangement is predicted to cost $30,000. The predicted output is 200,000 units. The $2.00, $1.80, $30,000 and 200,000 unit predictions are fed forward as inputs to the decision model.

Specific predictions

(3) Decision Model

(3) The predicted costs are compared and are related to the size of the required investment and other considerations (such as likely effects on employee morale).

(4) Implementation

(4) Manager implements the decision reached in (3).

(5) Performance Evaluation

(5) Evaluation of performance of the implemented alternative in (4) provides the feedback as the sequence is repeated in whole or in part. This historical information can help the making of *subsequent* predictions.

Feedback

*The words <u>information</u> and <u>data</u> have a variety of meanings in both the popular and the technical literature. In most cases, <u>data</u> is a more general term; that is, data consist of both information and noninformation.

proach to calculating the cost of a prediction error is outlined and illustrated using the Exhibit 9-1 example.

To highlight and simplify various points throughout this chapter, we assume that dollar amounts of future revenues and future costs are certain. In practice, the forecasting of these figures is generally the most difficult aspect of decision analysis. Chapter 18 discusses uncertainty and ways to incorporate it into decision making.

Historical data and predictions

Exhibit 9-1 shows that every decision deals with the future—whether it be ten seconds ahead (the decision to adjust a dial) or twenty years ahead (the decision to plant and harvest pine trees). **A decision always involves a prediction. Therefore the function of decision making is to select courses of action for the future. Nothing can be done to alter the past.**

Relevant costs (relevant revenues) are those *expected future costs (expected future revenues) that will differ* among alternatives. In Exhibit 9-1, the $2.00 and $1.80 expected future labor costs are relevant. The only role that the $1.95 past labor cost plays is in preparing the $2.00 and $1.80 forecasts. *Historical costs in themselves are irrelevant to the decision, although they may be the best available basis for predicting future costs.*

The data underlying the choice of the "do not rearrange" and the "rearrange" alternatives are presented in Exhibit 9-2.[1] We can safely ignore the revenues and the direct-materials cost because neither differs between the alternatives. Concentrating solely on relevant costs in this example may eliminate bothersome irrelevancies and may sharpen both the accountant's and the manager's thinking regarding costs for decision making. A key question in determining relevance is, What difference will it make? (Of course, irrelevant costs or irrelevant revenues may be included in comparisons for decisions, provided that they are included properly under both alternatives and do not mislead the decision maker.) The data

EXHIBIT 9-2
Determining Relevant Revenues and Relevant Costs

	ALL DATA		RELEVANT DATA	
	Alternative 1: Do Not Rearrange	Alternative 2: Rearrange	Alternative 1: Do Not Rearrange	Alternative 2: Rearrange
Revenues	$2,000,000*	$2,000,000*	$ —	$ —
Costs:				
Direct materials	1,000,000†	1,000,000†	—	—
Direct labor	400,000‡	360,000§	400,000‡	360,000§
Rearrangement of plant	—	30,000	—	30,000
Total costs	$1,400,000	$1,390,000	$400,000	$390,000
Operating income	$ 600,000	$ 610,000		

$10,000 Difference

$10,000 Difference

*200,000 × $10.
†200,000 × $ 5.
‡200,000 × $ 2.
§200,000 × $ 1.80.

[1]The time value of money is discussed in Chapters 19 and 20. When interest factors are introduced, expected future costs and future revenues with the same magnitude but different timing can be relevant.

in Exhibit 9-2 indicate that the alternative of rearranging the production line will increase operating income by $10,000.

In summary, **relevant costs** for decisions are expected future costs that will differ under alternatives; **relevant revenues** are expected future revenues that will differ under alternatives. Historical data, although helpful in predicting relevant costs or relevant revenues, are always irrelevant per se.

The definition of relevance is the major conceptual lesson in this chapter. This idea of relevance, coupled with the contribution approach, arms the manager and the accountant with a powerful weapon for making nonroutine decisions. The rest of this chapter will show how to apply these notions to some commonly encountered decisions. Note particularly that the analytical approach is consistent regardless of the particular decision encountered.

A commonly used term in decision making is **incremental cost**. An incremental cost is the difference in total cost between two alternatives. A synonym for incremental cost is **differential cost**. In Exhibit 9-2, the incremental cost between Alternative 1 and Alternative 2 is $10,000.

Qualitative and quantitative factors

The consequences of each alternative can be divided into two broad categories: *qualitative* and *quantitative*. Qualitative factors are those that are difficult to measure in numerical terms. A qualitative factor may easily be given more weight than the measurable cost savings. For example, a militant union that opposes the introduction of some labor-saving machinery may cause an executive to defer or to reject completely the contemplated installation of machinery. Another example is the chance to manufacture some product components at a cost below a particular supplier's quotations; it may be rejected because of a long-run dependency on that supplier for other important subassemblies.

Quantitative factors are those that can be expressed in numerical terms, such as projected alternative costs of direct materials, direct labor, and factory overhead. The accountant and statistician increasingly try to express as many decision factors as feasible in quantitative terms.

ILLUSTRATION OF RELEVANCE: CHOOSING VOLUME LEVELS

Decisions that affect volume levels are made under a given set of conditions, including existing plant capacity, equipment, and basic operating conditions. Such decisions are essentially short run in nature, but they have long-run overtones that should never be overlooked. At the outset, we stress the decision alternative that maximizes the chosen objective of an organization (typically long-run profitability in our illustrations).

Danger of full costs

The accounting system should produce information that leads managers toward correct decisions regarding either selection among courses of action or evaluation of performance. Intelligent analysis of costs often depends on explicit distinctions between cost behavior patterns, which are more likely to be made via the contribution approach than via absorption-costing methods. The general tendency toward indiscriminate full-cost allocations raises analytical dangers.

A bakery distributed its products through route sales representatives, each of whom loaded a truck with an assortment of products in the morning and spent the day calling on customers in an assigned territory. Believing that some items were more profitable than others, management asked for an analysis of product costs and sales. The accountants to whom the task was assigned allocated all manufacturing and marketing costs to products to obtain a net profit for each product. The resulting figures indicated that some of the products were being sold at a loss, and management discontinued these products. However, when this change was put into effect, the company's overall profit declined. It was thus seen that, by dropping some products, sales revenues had been reduced without commensurate reduction in costs because the joint manufacturing costs and route-sales costs had to be continued in order to make and sell the remaining products.[2]

The special order   Management sometimes faces the problem of price quotations on special orders when there is idle capacity.

EXAMPLE

X Company manufactures slippers. The current operating level, which is below full capacity of 110,000 pairs per year, is expected to show the results for the year as contained in Exhibit 9-3. (Note that these are predictions.)

A mail-order chain offers to buy 20,000 pairs at $7.50 per pair, for a total of $150,000. The buyer will pay for the shipping expenses. The acceptance of this special order will not affect regular sales. The president is reluctant to accept that order because the $7.50 price is below the $8.125 manufacturing unit cost. Should the offer be accepted?

Exhibit 9-3 has an absorption-costing format. In contrast, Exhibit 9-4 has a contribution approach that might be presented as a guide for decision making. The relevant costs are those that will be affected by taking the special order—the variable manufacturing costs. The fixed manufacturing costs and all selling expenses are irrelevant; they will not change in total if the order is accepted. Therefore the only relevant items here are sales and variable manufacturing costs.

EXHIBIT 9-3
Budgeted Income Statement for the Year:
Absorption Format

		PER UNIT‡
Sales—80,000 pairs @ $10.00	$800,000	$10.000
Manufacturing cost of goods sold*	650,000	8.125
Gross profit or gross margin	$150,000	$ 1.875
Selling expenses†	120,000	1.500
Operating income	$ 30,000	$ .375

*Includes fixed costs of $250,000. The remaining $400,000 is for variable costs of $5.00 per pair.
†Includes fixed costs of $80,000. The remaining $40,000 consists only of shipping expenses of $.50 per pair.
‡One pair equals one unit.

[2]W. McFarland, "The Field of Management Accounting," *NAA Bulletin,* XLV, No. 10, Sec. 3, p. 19.

Exhibit 9-4 also illustrates the frequent irrelevance of fixed costs in a decision of this kind. If the fixed costs of $330,000 remain the same under each alternative (acceptance or rejection), they are irrelevant. You can substitute $1 or $1,000,000 wherever the $330,000 fixed-cost amount is shown without changing the net difference in result.

Note also that the absorption unit cost at the 80,000-unit activity level is $8.125. If such a cost were used as a guide in deciding, a manager might unwisely reject the offer; after all, the $7.50 prospective selling price is well below the $8.125 unit cost. **In most cases (as demonstrated here), it is safer to compare total amounts of costs and revenues rather than unit amounts.** The spreading of the $250,000 fixed manufacturing cost over 100,000 units, instead of 80,000 units, will lower the average unit cost for all units produced. *But how fixed costs are allocated to units of product has no bearing on this decision, because the total fixed costs are unaffected by this decision.*

Frequently, the decision alternatives are compared, as in Exhibit 9-4, by preparing a separate income statement for each alternative, as well as by showing the differences. But shortcut reports may emphasize *differences* to spotlight only the relevant factors that influence the final results. A shortcut analysis would confine itself to the "difference" column in Exhibit 9-4.

Concentration on relevant items does not necessarily mean that the final reports submitted to the decision-making executives should contain only these *differential* items. The final reports should be tailored to managerial quirks and wants. There is no single "best" way to present reports. However, the contribution approach tends to help understanding.

EXHIBIT 9-4
Comparative Predicted Income Statements for the Year
Contribution Format, Two Decision Alternatives

	WITHOUT SPECIAL ORDER, 80,000 UNITS		WITH SPECIAL ORDER, 100,000 UNITS	
	Per Unit	Total	Total	DIFFERENCE
Sales	$10.000	$800,000	$950,000	$150,000*
Variable costs:				
Manufacturing	$ 5.000	$400,000	$500,000	$100,000†
Selling	.500	40,000	40,000	—
Total variable costs	$ 5.500	$440,000	$540,000	$100,000
Contribution margin	$ 4.500	$360,000	$410,000	$ 50,000
Fixed costs:				
Manufacturing	$ 3.125	$250,000	$250,000	—
Selling	1.000	80,000	80,000	—
Total fixed costs	$ 4.125	$330,000	$330,000	—
Operating income	$ .375	$ 30,000	$ 80,000	$ 50,000

*20,000 @ $7.50.
†20,000 @ $5.00.

Confusing terminology

Many different terms are used to describe the costs of specific products and services. For instance, the major distinction between variable costing and absorption costing was described in several earlier chapters (for example, see pages 55–56): Variable costing regards *fixed manufacturing* costs as expenses immediately when incurred, and not as costs of the product.

In a specific situation, be sure to get the exact meaning of the terms used. A particularly troublesome term is **full cost** or **fully distributed cost** or **fully allocated cost.** These terms are sometimes used as synonyms for *absorption cost*. In pricing situations, however, "full cost" per unit usually means absorption cost *plus* an allocation of selling and administrative cost. For example, using the amounts in column 1 of Exhibit 9-4, three different unit costs can be computed:

	COST PER UNIT		
Variable manufacturing cost	$5.000	$5.000	$5.000
Variable selling cost	.500		.500
Total variable costs	$5.500		
Fixed manufacturing cost		3.125	3.125
Absorption cost		$8.125*	
Fixed selling cost			1.000
Full cost (also called fully allocated or distributed cost)			$9.625

*This amount must be used by U.S. companies for inventory valuation in reports to shareholders and income tax authorities. (Selling costs are never inventoriable.)

Short run and long run

Avoid jumping to the conclusion that all variable costs are relevant and all fixed costs are irrelevant. This approach may be handy, but it is far from foolproof. For instance, in this special-order situation, although the selling costs are variable, they are irrelevant because the buyer will bear them. Moreover, fixed costs are often affected by a decision. For example, plans to buy a second car for family use should be most heavily influenced by the new set of fixed costs that would be incurred. Moreover, if the total family mileage were unaffected, the variable costs could conceivably be wholly irrelevant to the decision to buy a second car.

If the length of time under consideration is long enough, no type of cost is fixed. As a practical matter, management faces the task of making decisions when the length of time under consideration is short enough so that many conditions and costs are fixed. What role should fixed costs play in decision making? No categorical answer can be given to this question. About the most useful generalization is that fixed costs should be considered when they are expected to be altered, either immediately or in the future, by the decision at hand. If volume levels change so that additional supervision, plant, equipment, insurance, and property taxes are needed, these new fixed costs are relevant. For example, sales or production may expand to the point where a new delivery truck must be bought.

PRICING DECISIONS AND COST DATA

The special-order decision is merely one example of a pervasive difficulty that confronts managers: the pricing decision. This decision is the subject of an extensive literature in economics and marketing.[3] We will concentrate on only a few aspects here. Our major purpose is to put the role of costs in perspective with regard to the pricing decision.

Major influences on pricing

There are three major influences on pricing decisions: customers, competitors, and costs.

CUSTOMERS The manager must always examine pricing problems through the eyes of customers. A customer potentially may reject the company's product and choose one from a competitor. Alternatively, a customer may choose a substitute product that meets the desired quality specifications in a more cost-effective way; an example is the substitution of aluminum beer cans for steel beer cans. Some companies incorporate customer preferences into the development of products at all stages of the design and production process.[4]

COMPETITORS Rivals' reactions or lack of reactions will influence pricing decisions. In guessing a competitor's reactions, analysis of that competitor's costs can be very useful. Knowledge of the rival's technology, plant size, and operating policies can help sharpen estimates of such costs. Increasingly, competition should be viewed in an international context. Overcapacity of firms in some parts of the globe can lead to the adoption of aggressive pricing policies by those firms in their export markets.

COSTS The maximum price that may be charged is the one that does not drive the customer away. The minimum price is zero. Occasionally, companies will virtually give their products away in order to enter a market or to obtain a profitable long-run relationship with a customer. A more practical guide is gleaned from the study of cost-volume-profit relationships. In the short run, if the minimum price quoted exceeds the additional costs of accepting orders, short-run income will increase.

Surveys of practice report that companies weigh these three factors differently. Firms operating in highly competitive markets where products cannot be differentiated must accept the price as determined by market forces. For example, a company mining copper or gold has little ability to affect selling prices. Here cost data help decide the level and mix of output that can best attain the chosen objective (for example, to maximize long-run profitability of the company).

Where managers have some discretion in setting prices, numerous cost-based formulas are available for guiding the pricing decision. These include:

1. Variable production cost plus margin
2. Total variable cost plus margin
3. Total production cost plus margin
4. Total cost plus margin

The "margin" component of each of these pricing formulas could be a percentage of the associated cost figure or a fixed dollar amount. The next section illustrates

---

[3] An excellent starting point on this literature is D. Lund, K. Monroe, and P. Choudhury, *Pricing Policies and Strategies: An Annotated Bibliography* (Chicago: American Marketing Association, 1982).

[4] The importance of the customer is emphasized (and emphasized and emphasized . . .) in T. Peters and R. Waterman, *In Search of Excellence* (New York: Harper & Row, 1982); and in T. Peters and N. Austin, *Passion for Excellence* (New York: Random House, 1985).

305

how a contribution approach can be more informative for pricing decisions than an absorption-costing approach.

When used intelligently, the contribution approach generally offers more help than the absorption-costing approach for guiding a pricing decision.

First, the contribution approach provides more-detailed information than the absorption-costing approach. Why? Because variable- and fixed-cost behavior patterns are separately presented. The contribution approach measures cost-volume-profit relationships; therefore it eases the preparation of price schedules for different volume levels. Be aware that use of the target-pricing approach with absorption costing presumes a given volume level. When volume changes, the fixed cost allocated to each unit in an absorption-costing approach will also change.

Second, a "normal" or "target" pricing formula can be developed as easily under the contribution approach as under absorption costing for the "usual" or "nonincremental" situations. With a contribution approach, the percentage markup on cost would be based on variable costs. This percentage could, for instance, be a target ratio of operating profit to variable cost for the division as a whole. Suppose a division with three products had a ratio of division total operating profits to division total variable costs of 1.4 to 1 in the most recent year. Assume that the target next year is set at 1.5 to 1. This could be translated into the following target unit selling prices per product:

	PRODUCT A	PRODUCT B	PRODUCT C
Expected variable cost per unit	$ 8.00	$ 5.00	$ 9.00
Target overall markup (150%)	12.00	7.50	13.50
Target selling price per unit	$20.00	$12.50	$22.50

The target ratio of division total operating profits to division total variable costs can be set so that the total contribution margin both "recoups" the division fixed costs and makes a contribution to operating profits.

Third, as the example in Exhibits 9-3 and 9-4 shows, the contribution approach offers insight into short-run versus long-run effects of cutting prices on special orders. Generally, a manager can weigh such decisions by judging the expected long-run benefits of not cutting the price. Are the benefits worth a present "investment" equal to the immediate contribution to operating income ($50,000 in Exhibit 9-4 on p. 303) that would otherwise be sacrificed? Under absorption costing, the manager must conduct a detailed study to find the immediate effects of accepting a special order; under the contribution approach, the system will routinely provide such information.

Exhibit 9-5 shows an actual price-quote format used by the president and sales manager of a small job shop that bids on special machinery orders under highly competitive conditions. This approach is a tool for flexible pricing. Note that the *maximum* price is not a matter of cost at all; it is what you think you can get. The *minimum* price is set by the total variable costs. Note also in Exhibit 9-5 that the costs are classified and tailored especially for the pricing task. Pricing duties may be in the hands of a number of different executives. Often it is a joint effort on the part of the sales manager, production manager, and general manager (who has the final authority). The accountant's task is to present a format that not only is understand-

EXHIBIT 9-5
Quote Sheet
(Data Assumed)

Direct materials (materials only, at cost)	$ 75,000
Direct labor and variable overhead (3,000 direct-labor hrs. × $20) =	60,000
Commission (varies with job)	6,000
Total variable costs—minimum price	141,000
Add fixed costs applied (3,000 direct-labor hrs. × $15) =	45,000
Total costs (including share of fixed costs)	186,000
Add desired profit	27,000
Selling price (what you think you can get—maximum price)	$213,000

This quote sheet shows two prices, maximum and minimum. Any amount you can get above the minimum price is a contribution margin.

able but involves a minimum of computations. Under such a format, direct labor and variable overhead are often lumped together in one overall rate. All fixed costs, whether factory, engineering, selling, or administrative, are often lumped together for the same reason.

Surveys of practice

Surveys of executives report that both market data and cost data play important roles in many pricing decisions. For example, the following survey results from a questionnaire study were reported for 103 firms in the dry-cleaning and laundry industry:[5]

- 43% reported cost data as the primary source of information for pricing decisions; 83% of this group of respondents noted that market data play a secondary role.
- 39% reported market data as the primary source of information for pricing decisions; 75% of this group of respondents noted that cost data play a secondary role.
- 18% reported that both cost data and market data were primary sources of information for pricing decisions.

Internal sources of information on markets include reports from the company's sales staff, customer surveys, and explicit tracking of competition (e.g., comparison shopping). External sources of information on markets include market research studies, advisory agencies, and newspapers.

Executives most frequently report that the cost data used in their pricing decisions are absorption cost rather than variable cost or contribution margin data.[6] Why? Several reasons have been offered:

1. In the long run, all costs must be recovered to stay in business. Some managers believe that this is best achieved by having every product priced above its absorption or total unit cost.

---

[5] J. Goetz, "The Pricing Decision: A Service Industry's Experience," *Journal of Small Business Management,* April 1985, pp. 61–67.

[6] The results of a questionnaire study are reported in V. Govindarajan and R. Anthony, "How Firms Use Cost Data in Price Decisions," *Management Accounting,* July 1983, pp. 30–36. Thirty-three percent of the 501 respondents reported using a cost-plus approach based on "total unit production cost," while 41% reported using cost-plus based on "total unit cost." Total unit production cost includes fixed production overhead. Total unit cost also includes fixed selling, general, and administrative costs.

2. Because of its simplicity, absorption-cost or total-cost-formula pricing meets the cost-benefit test for some managers. It is costly to undertake individual cost-volume analysis for the many products (sometimes thousands) that a company offers. Some managers believe that the benefits from using these individual cost-volume studies do not exceed the costs of developing them. Unit data based on absorption costing are readily available in most accounting systems at minimal cost.

3. There is much uncertainty about the shape of the demand curves. Full-cost pricing copes with this uncertainty by not encouraging managers to take marginal business.

4. Absorption-cost or total-cost-formula pricing is believed to promote price stability. Managers prefer price stability because it makes planning more programmable.

A study of manufacturing executives in eleven companies reported use of both full-cost and variable-cost information in pricing decisions.[7] In-depth interviews with executives were conducted. Among the findings: "The full-vs.-variable-cost pricing controversy is not one of either black or white. The companies we surveyed used both approaches. . . . Some companies use full-cost pricing in some lines of business and variable costing in other lines of business (p. 59)." Areas where variable-cost information was used included:

1. Determining appropriate response to competition
2. Making product mix decisions
3. Setting the price on a new product
4. Accepting or rejecting a special order
5. Pricing bids in both sealed and open bid contexts
6. Setting the price of products sold under private label

The conclusion was that "the situations cited in modern management accounting texts" described many of the situations in which variable-cost data are actually used in pricing decisions.

EFFECTS OF ANTITRUST LAWS ON PRICING

To comply with American antitrust laws, such as the Sherman Act, the Clayton Act, and the Robinson-Patman Act, pricing must not be predatory. **Predatory pricing** involves temporary price cuts intended to eventually restrict supply and then to raise prices rather than to enlarge demand or meet competition.[8]

---

[7]T. Bruegelmann, G. Haessly, C. Wolfangel, and M. Schiff, "How Variable Costing Is Used in Pricing Decisions," *Management Accounting*, April 1985, pp. 58–61, 65. See also by the same authors, *The Use of Variable Costing in Pricing Decisions* (Montvale, N.J.: National Association of Accountants, 1986).

[8]See D. Greer, *Industrial Organization and Public Policy* (New York: Macmillan, 1984), pp. 316–17.

Recent court decisions have been influenced by a classic article by Areeda and Turner,[9] which argued that:

- A price at or above reasonably anticipated short-run marginal and average variable costs should be deemed nonpredatory.
- Unless at or above average cost, a price below reasonably anticipated (1) short-run marginal costs or (2) average variable costs should be deemed predatory.[10]

The case of *Adjustor's Replace-a-Car* v. *Agency Rent-a-Car* illustrates how the courts are willing to use variable cost information in decisions concerning predatory pricing.[11] *Agency Rent-a-Car* (the defendant) used selective price cuts to enter the Austin and San Antonio, Texas, car-rental market; cars were rented to customers for extended time periods. *Adjustor's* (the plaintiff) claimed that it was forced to depart from these markets because *Agency* had engaged in predatory pricing. A circuit court judge reaffirmed a lower court decision that *Agency* "did not predatorily price its service by underselling a competing service in light of the facts that its charges were above average variable cost and there were no significant entry barriers to the market." Evidence presented by *Adjustor's* included income statements of *Agency* showing that it had operated its outlets in Austin and San Antonio at a "net operating loss"; these statements included an allocated portion of the overhead cost of *Agency's* headquarters.

The circuit court judge ruled it was sufficient (in regard to cost justification) for *Agency* "to demonstrate that the price it charged for a rental car never dropped below its average variable cost." The judge noted:

> Agency's expert testified that Agency's average variable costs in San Antonio and Austin during the relevant time periods fluctuated between approximately $3.65 and approximately $5.00 (a day). Thus, Agency's price was always at least 40% greater than its average variable cost. The expert also testified that Agency's average variable costs in Austin were $5.23 when Agency went to a $9.00 price; the price was thus 72% above average variable cost. This testimony cut to the quick of plaintiff's predatory pricing claim.

The circuit court judge rejected Adjustor's claim that "a net loss from operations" on an income statement including an allocation of Agency's headquarters' overhead was "effectively an admission of predatory pricing."

The variable-cost guidelines proposed by Areeda and Turner, while having the support of several recent court decisions, are not explicitly incorporated into the statute law. Caution should always be used when generalizing from individual legal cases. Managers and cost accountants who are concerned with their conform-

---

[9]P. Areeda and D. Turner, "Predatory Pricing and Related Practices under Section 2 of the Sherman Act," *Harvard Law Review*, 88 (1975), 697–733. See also F. Scherer, "Predatory Pricing and the Sherman Act: A Comment," *Harvard Law Review*, 89 (1976), 869–903.

For an overview of case law, see *ABA Antitrust Section, Antitrust Law Developments* (2nd ed., 1984). See also the "Legal Developments" sections of the *Journal of Marketing* for summaries of court cases.

[10]Areeda and Turner, "Predatory Pricing," p. 733.

[11]Adjustor's Replace-a-Car, Inc. v. Agency Rent-a-Car, 735 F.2nd 884 (1984).

ance to antitrust laws would be prudent to have a system with the following characteristics:

1. Collect data in such a manner as to permit relatively easy compilation of variable costs.
2. Review all proposed prices below variable costs, in advance, with a presumption of claims of predatory intent.
3. Keep as detailed a set of records as feasible, not only of manufacturing costs but also of distribution costs such as advertising, warehousing, and transportation. In this way, a company will be prepared for inquiries by regulatory agencies.

OTHER ILLUSTRATIONS OF RELEVANCE AND THE CONTRIBUTION APPROACH

Contribution per unit of constraining factor

When a multiproduct plant is operated at capacity, decisions must often be made regarding which orders to accept. The contribution approach supplies the data for a proper decision because that decision is determined by the product that makes the largest *total* contribution to profits. This approach does not necessarily imply that the products to be pushed are those with the biggest contribution margin per unit of product or biggest contribution-margin ratios per sales dollar. **The objective is to maximize total profits, which depends on getting the highest contribution margin per unit of the constraining (that is, scarce, limiting, or critical) factor.** Consider an example. Suppose a company has two products:

	PRODUCT A	PRODUCT B
Selling price per unit	$10	$15
Variable expenses per unit	7	9
Contribution margin per unit	$ 3	$ 6
Contribution-margin ratio	30%	40%

At first glance, Product B looks more profitable than Product A. However, if you were the division manager, had 1,000 hours of production capacity available, and knew that you could turn out three units of A per hour and only one unit B per hour, your choice should be A because it contributes the most margin *per hour,* the constraining factor in this example:

	PRODUCT A	PRODUCT B
Units produced per hour	3	1
Contribution margin per unit	$ 3	$ 6
Contribution margin per hour	$ 9	$ 6
Total contribution for 1,000 hours	$9,000	$6,000

The constraining factor is the item that restricts or limits the production or sale of a given product. Thus *the criterion for maximum profits, for a given capacity, is the greatest possible contribution to profit per unit of the constraining factor.* The constraining factor in the example above may be machine-hours or direct-labor hours. In other decisions it may be cubic feet of display space.

EXHIBIT 9-6

	REGULAR DEPARTMENT STORE	DISCOUNT DEPARTMENT STORE
Retail price	$4.00	$3.50
Cost of merchandise	3.00	3.00
Contribution to profit per unit	$1.00(25%)	$ .50(14+%)
Units sold per year	20,000	44,000
Total contribution to profit	$20,000	$22,000

The success of the suburban discount department stores illustrates the concept of the contribution to profit per unit of constraining factor. These stores have been satisfied with subnormal markups because they have been able to increase turnover and thus increase the contribution to profit per unit of space. Exhibit 9-6 demonstrates this point and assumes that the same total selling space is used in each store.

As you can imagine, in most cases there will be many constraining factors that must be utilized by each of a variety of products. The problem of formulating the most profitable production schedules and the mixes of raw materials is essentially that of maximizing the contribution in the face of *many* constraints. These complications may be solved by linear-programming techniques, which are discussed in Chapter 22.

Make or buy, and idle facilities

Manufacturers often confront the question of whether to make or buy a product; that is, whether to manufacture their own parts and subassemblies or buy them from suppliers. Qualitative factors may be paramount in such decisions. Sometimes the manufacture of parts requires special know-how, unusually skilled labor, scarce materials, and the like. The desire to control the quality of parts often results in the decision to make them. In many instances, companies hesitate to destroy mutually advantageous long-run relationships by the erratic order giving that comes from making parts during slack times and buying them during prosperous times. Companies may have difficulty in obtaining any parts during boom times when there are shortages of materials and workers and no shortage of sales orders.

What are the quantitative factors relevant to the decision of whether to make or buy? The answer, again, depends on the context. A key factor is whether there are idle facilities. Many companies make parts only when their facilities cannot be used to better advantage.

Assume that the following costs are reported by El Cerrito Company:

	COST OF MAKING PART NO. 300	
	Total Costs for 10,000 Units	Costs per Unit
Direct materials	$ 10,000	$ 1
Direct labor	80,000	8
Variable overhead applied	40,000	4
Fixed overhead applied	50,000	5
Total costs	$180,000	$18

Another manufacturer offers to sell El Cerrito Company the same part for $16. Should El Cerrito Company make or buy the part?

The unit cost of $18 seemingly indicates that the company should buy. However, the answer is rarely obvious. The key question is the difference in relevant costs between the alternatives. Consider the fixed overhead. The total applied to the part is $50,000. Perhaps $30,000 of this fixed overhead represents those costs (for example, depreciation, property taxes, insurance, and allocated salaries of manufacturing personnel) that will continue at the same amount regardless of the decision. If so, the $30,000 is irrelevant, which amounts to $3 per unit for the 10,000-unit volume.

Again avoid saying categorically that only the variable costs are relevant. Perhaps, as we assume here, $20,000 of the fixed costs will be saved if the parts are bought instead of made. In other words, fixed costs that may be avoided in the future are relevant.

For the moment, suppose the capacity now used to make parts will become idle if the parts are purchased. The computations of relevant costs follow:

	TOTAL COSTS		PER-UNIT COSTS	
RELEVANT ITEMS	Make	Buy	Make	Buy
Outside purchase of parts		$160,000		$16
Direct materials	$ 10,000		$ 1	
Direct labor	80,000		8	
Variable overhead	40,000		4	
Fixed overhead that can be avoided by not making	20,000		2	
Total relevant costs	$150,000	$160,000	$15	$16
Difference in favor of making	$10,000		$1	

Essence of make or buy: utilization of facilities

The choice in our example is not really whether to make or buy; it is how best to utilize available facilities. Although the data above indicate that making the part is the better choice, the figures are not conclusive—primarily because we have no idea of what can be done with the manufacturing facilities if the component part is bought. Only if the released facilities are to remain idle are the above figures valid.

Perhaps the released facilities can be used advantageously in some other manufacturing activity or can be rented out. Then these alternatives must also be considered. Suppose the released facilities either can be used to manufacture other products with a contribution margin of $19,000 or can be rented out for $5,000. The original two courses of action have now become four (figures are in thousands):

	MAKE	BUY AND LEAVE FACILITIES IDLE	BUY AND USE FACILITIES FOR OTHER PRODUCTS	BUY AND RENT
Rent revenue	$ —	$ —	$ —	$ 5
Contribution margin from other products	—	—	19	—
Obtaining of parts	(150)	(160)	(160)	(160)
Net relevant costs	$(150)	$(160)	$(141)	$(155)

The analysis indicates that buying the parts and using the vacated facilities for the production of other products would yield the best results.

<table>
<tr><td>Beware of unit costs</td><td>

Unit costs should always be analyzed with care in decision making. Unit cost data can mislead in two major ways:

1. The inclusion of irrelevant costs. An example is the $3-per-unit allocation of fixed costs in the original make-or-buy comparison, which would result in a total unit cost of $18 instead of the relevant unit cost of $15.

2. Comparisons of unit costs not computed on the same volume. Generally, use total costs rather than unit costs. Then, if desired, the total can be unitized. Machinery sales personnel, for example, often brag about the low unit costs of using their new machines. Sometimes they neglect to say that the unit costs are based on outputs far in excess of the volume of their prospective customer. The unitization of fixed costs in this manner can be particularly misleading. The lesson here is to use total costs, not unit costs, in relevant cost analysis.

Recognition of how the use of otherwise idle resources can increase profitability occurred at a Chinese machine-repairing factory of the Beijing Engineering Machinery Company. The *China Daily* noted that workers are "busy producing electric plaster-spraying machines" even though the unit cost exceeded the selling price.

> According to the prevailing method of calculating its cost, each sprayer costs 1,230 yuan, but is sold for 985 yuan. After a five percent discount to pay taxes, the factory loses 294 yuan on each machine.

> Although the factory loses money on products, it continues to put them out to meet market demand. In addition, because workers and machines would otherwise be idle, the production of these sprayers, even at a loss, actually helps cut the factory deficit.

> Out of one sprayer's cost of 1,230 yuan, 759 yuan would have to be paid even if nothing had been produced. So because the factory did not have enough work to do, it would have lost even more money, leaving workers and equipment idle, than if it had not produced sprayers.

</td></tr>
</table>

OPPORTUNITY COSTS, RELEVANCE, AND ACCOUNTING RECORDS

Ideally, a decision maker should be able to make an exhaustive list of alternatives and then compute the expected results under each, giving full consideration to interdependent and long-run effects. Practically, the decision maker sifts among the possible alternatives, quickly discards many as being obviously unattractive, probably overlooks some attractive possibilities, and concentrates on a limited number. **The idea of an opportunity cost arises because some alternatives are excluded from formal consideration.**

<table>
<tr><td>Sale of inventory</td><td>

Suppose a company uses copper as an input for four products. At the beginning of the period, there are 1,000 units in copper inventory that were acquired for $110 per unit. Assume further that if the company decides not to use the 1,000 units on hand as inputs to various products, they can be sold to a salvage yard for $95 per unit. Another salvage yard has offered $90. There are many alternative end-

</td></tr>
</table>

product uses for the copper. Another alternative would be to throw the units in the city dump. A "total-alternatives" approach to the analysis follows (in thousands of dollars):

	CHOICES						
	Use Copper in Product				Salvage		Throw Away
	A	B	C	D	1	2	
Expected future revenues	$220	$204	$186	$170	$95	$90	—
Expected future costs:							
Labor and overhead	90	70	60	100	—	—	—
Excess of future revenues over future costs	$130	$134	$126	$ 70	$95	$90	

Use of the copper as an input to Product B is the preferred alternative.

Suppose, instead of the above analysis, the number of alternatives under formal consideration is limited to choices A through D above; the "salvage" and "throw away" alternatives are not to be analyzed in the same format. Then an opportunity-cost approach is desirable. **Opportunity cost** *is the maximum contribution that is forgone by using limited resources for a particular purpose.*

The use of opportunity cost is a practical means of reducing the number of alternatives under consideration; the solution reached is still the same as that given by a more complete "total-alternatives" approach. The decision maker says, "There are many alternatives that I want to reject without conducting a thorough analysis. Therefore I will take the *best* of these reject alternatives, compute its contribution (sell for salvage of $95 in this example), and use that as the cost of the scarce resource (copper in this example) when I explicitly analyze the remaining alternatives."

Under the opportunity-cost approach, the decision maker would organize the analysis of the remaining alternatives as follows (in thousands of dollars):

	CHOICES			
	Use Copper in Product			
	A	B	C	D
Expected future revenues	$220	$204	$186	$170
Expected future costs:				
Opportunity cost of salvaging copper	95	95	95	95
Outlay costs: Labor and overhead	90	70	60	100
Total future costs	185	165	155	195
Net advantage of future revenues over future costs	$ 35	$ 39	$ 31	$ (25)

Note that the *best* of the alternatives excluded from the previous analysis is included as an opportunity cost in the formal comparison. The other two (or more) excluded alternatives are not in this analysis. The possible uses of the copper in

Products A, C, and D also may become excluded alternatives eventually, but they should be excluded only after formal consideration in the decision model used.

An opportunity cost is not ordinarily incorporated into formal accounting reports to shareholders. Such costs represent contributions *forgone* by rejecting the best alternative; therefore opportunity costs do not entail cash receipts or disbursements. Accountants usually confine their systematic recording of costs to the outlay costs requiring exchanges of assets. **An outlay cost is a cost that requires a cash disbursement sooner or later.** Accountants confine their history to alternatives selected rather than those rejected, primarily because of the infeasibility of accumulating appropriate data on what might have been.

Holding costs of inventory

The opportunity cost notion can also be illustrated with a raw-material purchase order decision:

Estimated raw-material requirements for the year	120,000 units
Unit cost, orders below 120,000 units	$ 10.00
Unit cost, orders equal to or greater than 120,000 units; $10.00 minus 2% discount	$ 9.80
Alternatives under consideration:	
A: Buy 120,000 units at start of year	
B: Buy 10,000 units per month	
Average investment in inventory	
A: (120,000 units × $9.80) ÷ 2	$588,000
B: (10,000 units × $10.00) ÷ 2	$ 50,000

There is a substantial difference in the average investment in inventory under Alternatives A and B: $588,000 − $50,000 = $538,000. At a minimum, $538,000 could be invested in risk-free government bonds and return, say, .06 × $538,000 = $32,280 for the year.

This $32,280 is an opportunity forgone when Alternative A is chosen. This $32,280 is the opportunity cost of the 120,000-unit purchase order. Note that the $32,280, being a *forgone* cost rather than an outlay cost, would not ordinarily be recorded in the accounting system.

IRRELEVANCE OF PAST COSTS

As defined earlier, a *relevant cost* is (a) an expected future cost that (b) will differ among alternatives. The illustrations in this chapter have shown that expected future costs that will not differ among alternatives are irrelevant. Now we return to the idea that all past costs are irrelevant.

Book value of existing equipment

Consider an example of equipment replacement. The irrelevant cost illustrated here is the **book value** (original cost less any accumulated depreciation) of the existing equipment. Assume that the Toledo Company is considering replacement of an existing machine used for finishing products. Annual revenue of $100,000 will not change regardless of the decision. Summary data on the existing machine and the new machine are as follows:

EXISTING MACHINE

1. Initial cost of $120,000 (purchase made eight years ago)
2. Current book value of $40,000 ($120,000 minus accumulated depreciation of $80,000 using the straight-line method)
3. Current disposal value of $4,000
4. Estimated remaining useful life of four years with zero terminal disposal value
5. Variable operating costs per year of $80,000

NEW MACHINE

1. Current purchase price of $60,000
2. Estimated useful life of four years with zero terminal disposal value
3. Variable operating costs per year of $56,000

Exhibit 9-7 presents a cost comparison of the two machines. Some managers would not replace the old machine because it would entail recognizing a $36,000 "loss on disposal"; retention would allow spreading the $40,000 book value over the next four years in the form of "depreciation expense" (a more-appealing term than "loss on disposal").

EXHIBIT 9-7
Cost Comparison—Replacement of Machine,
Including Relevant and Irrelevant Items
(In Thousands of Dollars)

	FOUR YEARS TOGETHER		
	Keep	Replace	Difference
Sales	$400	$400	$ —
Expenses:			
Variable	320	224	96
Old machine (book value):			
Periodic write-off as depreciation	40	—	—
or			
Lump-sum write-off	—	40*	—
Disposal value	—	−4*	4
New machine, written off periodically as depreciation	—	60	−60
Total expenses	$360	$320	$ 40
Operating income	$ 40	$ 80	$ 40

The advantage of replacement is $40,000 for the four years together.

*In a formal income statement, these two items would be combined as "loss on disposal" of $36,000.

We can apply our definition of relevance to four commonly encountered items in equipment replacement decisions such as the one facing the Toledo Company:

1. *Book value of old equipment.* Irrelevant, because it is a past (historical) cost. All past costs are down the drain. Nothing can change what has already been spent or what has already happened.
2. *Disposal value of old equipment.* Relevant, because it is an expected future cash inflow that usually differs between alternatives.
3. *Gain or loss on disposal.* This is the algebraic difference between items 1 and 2. It is therefore a meaningless combination of book value, which is irrelevant, and disposal value, which is relevant. The combination form, *loss or gain on disposal,* blurs the distinction between the irrelevant book value and the relevant disposal value. Consequently, it is best to think of each separately.
4. *Cost of new equipment.* Relevant, because it is an expected future cash outflow that will differ between alternatives.

Exhibit 9-7 should clarify the above assertions. Book value of the old equipment is irrelevant regardless of the decision-making technique used. The Difference column in Exhibit 9-7 shows that book value of old equipment is not an element of difference between alternatives and could be completely ignored for decision-making purposes. *No matter what the timing of the charge against revenue, the amount charged is still $40,000 regardless of the available alternative.*

In either event, the undepreciated cost will be written off with the same ultimate effect on operating income. The $40,000 enters into the income statement either as a $40,000 offset against the $4,000 proceeds to obtain the $36,000 *loss on disposal* in the current year, or as $10,000 depreciation in each of the next four years. But how it appears is irrelevant to the replacement decision. *In contrast, the $60,000 cost of the new equipment is relevant because the total $60,000 may be avoided by not replacing.*

Exhibit 9-8 concentrates on relevant items only. Note that the same answer (the $40,000 net difference) will be produced even though the book value is com-

EXHIBIT 9-8
Cost Comparison—Replacement of Machine:
Relevant Items Only
(In Thousands of Dollars)

| | FOUR YEARS TOGETHER | | |
	Keep	Replace	Difference
Variable expenses	$320	$224	$ 96
Disposal value of old equipment	—	−4	4
Depreciation—new equipment	—	60	−60
Total relevant expenses	$320	$280	$ 40

pletely omitted from the calculations. The only relevant items are the variable operating costs, the disposal value of the old equipment, and the cost of the new equipment (represented as depreciation in Exhibit 9-8).

HOW MANAGERS BEHAVE

Consider our equipment replacement example in light of the sequence in Exhibit 9-1, page 299.

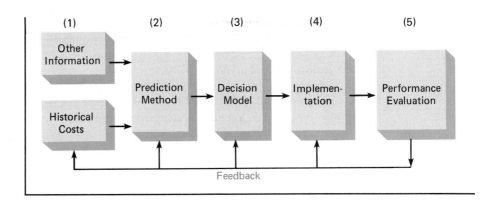

Impact of loss

Suppose the *decision model* (box 3) says to choose the alternative that will minimize total costs over the life span of the equipment. The analysis in Exhibit 9-7 favors replacing rather than keeping. In the "real world" would the manager replace? The answer often depends on the manager's perceptions of whether the decision model is consistent with the performance evaluation model (box 5).

Managers tend to favor the alternative that improves the measures used in the performance evaluation model. If there is an inconsistency between the decision model and the performance model, the latter often wins in terms of how managers behave. For example, top management may *say* it favors the decision model in Exhibit 9-7. But the subordinate manager may believe otherwise. That is, if the subordinate's promotion or bonus is perceived to hinge on short-run performance, the temptation not to replace will be overwhelming. Why? Because the ordinary accrual accounting model for measuring performance will show a first-year operating loss if the old machine is replaced:

	FIRST YEAR	
	Keep	Replace
Sales	$100	$100
Expenses:		
Variable	80	56
Depreciation	10	15
Loss on disposal	—	36
Total charges against sales	90	107
Operating income	$ 10	$ (7)

Faced with this performance evaluation model, what might go through the manager's mind?

Among the possibilities:

1. If I keep the equipment, my performance very likely will be in accord with my original predictions. I'll look much better in the first year by keeping the old machine than by replacing it and showing a loss.
2. Even if top management's goals try to pinpoint long-run considerations, I'll probably be transferred next year anyway. So my concern is naturally with the short run.

Synchronizing the models

The conflict between the decision models and performance evaluation models just described is frequently a baffling problem in practice. In theory, resolving the difficulty seems obvious: merely design consistent models. Consider our replacement example. Year-by-year income effects of replacement can be budgeted over the planning horizon of four years. The first year would be expected to be poor, the next three years much better.

The practical difficulty is basically that systems rarely track each decision in this fashion, one at a time. Performance evaluation focuses on responsibility centers for a specific period, not on projects or individual items of equipment for their entire useful lives. Therefore the impacts of many assorted decisions are combined in a single performance report. In such instances, the manager may predict the first-year effects and be less inclined to take the longer view that may be preferred by top management. Top management, through the reporting system, is rarely made aware of particular desirable alternatives *not* chosen by subordinates.

Chapters 25 and 26 further discuss problems of synchronizing decision models and performance evaluation models.

SUMMARY

The accountant's role in special decisions is basically that of a technical expert on cost analysis. The manager should be supplied with relevant data for guiding decisions. The ability to distinguish relevant from irrelevant items and the use of the contribution approach to cost analysis are twin foundations for tackling many decisions.

To be relevant to a particular decision, a cost must meet two criteria: (a) it must be an expected *future* cost; and (b) it must be an element of *difference* between alternatives. The key question is, What difference does it make? If the objective of the decision maker is to maximize long-run net income, all past (historical) costs are irrelevant to any decision about the future.

The role that past costs play in decision making is an auxiliary one. Past (irrelevant) costs are useful because they provide empirical evidence that often helps sharpen *predictions* of future relevant costs. But the expected future costs are the *only* cost ingredients in any decision model per se.

For a given set of facilities or resources, the key to maximizing operating income is to obtain the largest possible contribution per unit of the constraining factor.

Generally, in cost analysis, use total costs not unit costs; unitized fixed costs are often erroneously interpreted as if they behaved like unit variable costs. Incremental or differential costs are the differences in total costs under each alternative.

Cost reports for special decisions may concentrate on relevant items only (Exhibit 9-8), or they may encompass both relevant and irrelevant items (Exhibit 9-7). The best format depends on individual preferences. The shortcut approach concentrates only on the difference column because it summarizes the relevant items.

The problem of uncertainty, which is discussed in Chapter 18, complicates prediction and is easily the most formidable challenge in decision making.

_____PROBLEM FOR SELF-STUDY_____

problem The San Carlos Company is an electronics company having eight product lines. Income data for one of the products for the year just ended follow:

Sales—200,000 units @ average price of $100		$20,000,000
Variable costs:		
Direct materials @ $35	$7,000,000	
Direct labor @ $10	2,000,000	
Variable factory overhead @ $5	1,000,000	
Sales commissions @ 15% of selling price	3,000,000	
Other variable costs @ $5	1,000,000	
Total variable costs @ $70		14,000,000
Contribution margin		$ 6,000,000
Fixed costs:		
Discretionary (see Chapter 11) @ $15	$3,000,000	
Committed (see Chapter 11) @ $10	2,000,000	
Total fixed costs		5,000,000
Operating income		$ 1,000,000

Required

1. The electronics industry had severe price competition throughout the year. Near the end of the year, Abrams Co., which was experimenting with various components in its regular product line, offered $80 each for 3,000 units. The latter would have been in addition to the 200,000 units actually sold. The acceptance of this special order by San Carlos would not affect regular sales. The sales representative hoped that the order might provide entrance into a new application, so he told George Holtz, the product manager, that he would accept a flat commission of $6,000 if the order were accepted. If Holtz had accepted the offer, what would operating income have been?

2. Holtz pondered for a day, but he was afraid of the precedent that might be set by cutting the price. He said, "The price is below our full costs of $95 per unit. I think we should quote a full price, or Abrams Co. will expect favored treatment again and again if we continue to do business with them." Do you agree with Holtz? Explain.

3. The Gregorio Company had offered to supply San Carlos Company with a key part (M-I-A) for $20 each. One M-I-A is used in every finished unit. The San Carlos Company had made these parts for variable costs of $18 plus some additional fixed costs of $200,000 for supervision and other items. What would operating income have been if San Carlos purchased rather than made the parts? Assume that the discretionary costs for supervision and other items would have been avoided if the parts were purchased.

4. The company could have purchased the M-I-A parts for $20 each and used the vacated space for the manufacture of a different electronics component on a subcontracting basis for Hewlett-Packard, a much larger company. Assume that 40,000 special components could have been made for Hewlett-Packard (and sold in addition to the 200,000 regular units through regular channels) at a unit variable cost of $150, exclusive of parts. Part M-I-A would be needed for these components as well as the regular production. No sales commission would have to be paid. All the fixed costs pertaining to the M-I-A parts would have continued, including the supervisory costs, because they related mainly to the facilities used. What would operating income have been if San Carlos had made and sold the components to Hewlett-Packard for $170 per unit and bought the M-I-A parts?

1. Analysis of special order:

Additional sales of 3,000 units @ $80		$240,000
Direct materials—3,000 units @ $35	$105,000	
Direct labor—3,000 units @ $10	30,000	
Variable factory overhead—3,000 units @ $5	15,000	
Other variable costs—3,000 units @ $5	15,000	
Sales commission	6,000	
Total variable costs		171,000
Contribution margin		$ 69,000

Note that the variable costs, except for commissions, are affected by physical units of volume, not dollar revenue.

Operating income would have been $1,000,000 plus $69,000, or $1,069,000.

2. Whether Holtz is making a correct decision depends on many factors. He is incorrect if the capacity would otherwise be idle and if his objective is to increase operating income in the short run. If the offer is rejected, San Carlos is willing to invest $69,000 in immediate gains forgone (an opportunity cost) to preserve the long-run selling-price structure. Holtz is correct if he thinks future competition or future price concessions to customers will hurt San Carlos's operating income by more than $69,000.

3.

	MAKE	PURCHASE
Purchase cost @ $20		$4,000,000
Variable costs @ $18	$3,600,000	
Avoidable discretionary costs	200,000	
Total relevant costs	$3,800,000	$4,000,000

Operating income would have fallen by $200,000, or from $1,000,000 to $800,000, if San Carlos had purchased the parts.

4.

Sales would increase by 40,000 units @ $170			$6,800,000
Additional costs to the company as a whole:			
Variable costs exclusive of M-I-A parts would increase by 40,000 units @ $150		$6,000,000	
Effects on overall costs of M-I-A parts:			
Cost of 240,000 parts purchased @ $20	$4,800,000		
Less cost of making 200,000 parts @ $18 (only the variable costs are relevant because fixed costs continue)	3,600,000		
Additional cost of parts		1,200,000	7,200,000
Disadvantage of making components			$ (400,000)

Operating income would decline by $400,000, from $1,000,000 to $600,000.

Terms to Learn

This chapter and the Glossary contain definitions of the following important terms:

book value (p. 315) ***decision model (298)*** ***differential cost (301)*** ***full cost (304)*** ***fully allocated cost (304)*** ***fully distributed cost (304)*** ***incremental cost (301)*** ***opportunity cost (314)*** ***outlay cost (315)*** ***predatory pricing (308)*** ***relevant cost (301)*** ***relevant revenue (301)***

Special Points and Pitfalls

Exhibit 9-1, page 299, is important because it provides an overview of the role of accounting data in management decisions. The first step, the gathering of information, entails the examination of historical data, such as feedback in the form of performance reports. In addition, this step entails enough search to assure the manager that central problems and their probable alternative solutions are correctly identified. For example, if machinery seems obsolete because of the appearance of a superior machine, the manager should search sufficiently to be sure of what other machines or methods are available now or in the near future. Of course, search is costly, so managers tend to concentrate on obvious alternatives.

The gathering of information is succeeded by several additional steps. An example of a prediction method is the use of a learning curve (see Chapter 10) to forecast the cost of specified factory operations. An example of a decision model is the comparison of operating costs under each of two alternatives and the choice of the alternative having the lesser cost. An example of a performance evaluation model is a report that compares actual results with expected (budgeted) results. The latter model provides the feedback information that is a major basis for improving future predictions and decisions.

Top management faces a persistent challenge: making sure that the performance evaluation model is consistent with the decision model. A common inconsistency is (a) to tell subordinates to take a multiple-year view in making decisions, but (b) to judge performance based only on the first year.

APPENDIX 9A: COST OF PREDICTION ERROR

As Exhibit 9-1 on page 299 illustrates, all decisions involve predictions. Many of these predictions will, after the fact, turn out to be incorrect in the sense that the actual value differs from the predicted value. This Appendix discusses sources of prediction errors and then illustrates the use of a three-step procedure to calculate the cost of a prediction error.

Sources of prediction errors

One source of prediction error is *conceptual*—a failure to focus on relevant costs and relevant revenues. Chapter 9 illustrates how a preoccupation with unit costs and past costs or a failure to recognize opportunity costs can cloud the analysis when predicting the magnitude of relevant costs and relevant revenues.

A second source of prediction error occurs in *data analysis*. An example is the use of a technique for estimating cost behavior patterns that does not fully exploit all the information in the available data. Chapters 10 and 23 illustrate alternative approaches to examining the behavior of costs over time or across activity levels.

A third source of prediction error is *uncertainty of the outcome*. All decisions are made under uncertainty. No matter how good the conceptual or data analysis, events can arise outside the control of the decision maker that cause the actual value of a cost or revenue to differ from the predicted value. Chapter 18 elaborates on uncertainty and ways to incorporate it into decision making.

Calculating
the cost of a
prediction error

A three-step procedure can be used to calculate the cost of a prediction error:

Step One: Compute the monetary outcome from the best action that could have been taken, given knowledge of the actual value of the variable or item of uncertainty (cost, sales price, quantity sold, etc.).

Step Two: Compute the monetary outcome from the planned course of action when the decision is based on the predicted value of the variable. When calculating this monetary outcome, the actual value of the variable should be used. Why? Because this result is what will occur when the decision is implemented.

Step Three: Compute the difference between the monetary outcome from Step One and the monetary outcome from Step Two. Note that if the same action is taken in Step One and Step Two, there will be no difference in their monetary outcomes, and hence a zero cost of prediction error.

These three steps can be illustrated by the decision of whether to rearrange the production line (see Exhibits 9-1 and 9-2 pp. 299 and 300). Assume that unforeseen problems arise in moving items between stages of the new production line. The actual direct-labor cost is $1.90 per unit rather than the predicted $1.80 per unit. The cost of this prediction error of $.10 per unit is calculated as follows:

Step One: Monetary Outcome of Best Action, Given Actual Value of Predicted Variable. The "rearrange" alternative provides a reduction in direct-labor costs of $20,000 [200,000 units × ($2.00 less $1.90)] but costs $30,000 for the rearrangement. Thus, in this situation the "do not rearrange" alternative is the best action. The monetary outcome of "do not rearrange" is an operating income of $600,000 (see Exhibit 9-2).

Step Two: Monetary Outcome of Action Based on Incorrect Value of Predicted Variable. Using the incorrect $1.80 prediction, the "rearrange" alternative is chosen (see Exhibit 9-2). The monetary outcome from this action is:

Revenues		$2,000,000
Costs:		
Direct materials	$1,000,000	
Direct labor (200,000 × $1.90)	380,000	
Rearrangement cost	30,000	1,410,000
Operating income		$ 590,000

In particular, note that the actual labor cost per unit of $1.90 is used to compute the monetary outcome in Step Two.

Step Three: Difference between Monetary Outcomes of Step One and Step Two.

	MONETARY OUTCOME
Step one	$600,000
Step two	590,000
Difference	$ 10,000

This $10,000 cost of prediction error arises because the action chosen with the $1.90 actual value differs from the action chosen with the $1.80 predicted value.

APPENDIX 9B: COST TERMS USED FOR DIFFERENT PURPOSES

Because costs must be tailored to the decision at hand, many terms (too many!) have arisen to describe different types of cost. The authors believe that the variety of terms is more confusing than illuminating; yet the varying usage of such terms necessitates a familiarity with them. Whenever you are confronted by these terms in practice, you will save much confusion and wasted time if you find out their exact meaning in the given case. For that matter, this word of caution applies to all the accounting terms used from company to company. Individual companies frequently develop their own extensive and distinctive accounting language. This language is not readily understood by accountants outside the company. The following terms will be related to other terms used previously in this book.

An *imputed cost* is the result of a process that recognizes a cost as it pertains to a particular situation, although the cost may not be routinely recognized by ordinary accounting procedures. Imputed costs attempt to make accounting better dovetail with economic reality.

Imputed costs may be either opportunity costs or outlay costs. A common example of the opportunity cost is the inclusion among divisional or departmental expenses of "interest expense" on ownership equity. Some outlay costs are also imputed costs, but not all outlay costs are imputed costs. For example, if $3,000 is paid for labor, it is an outlay cost but not an imputed cost, because it would be routinely recognized by ordinary accounting processes. By itself, the $3,000 measures the economic impact of that particular event.

On the other hand, suppose $100,000 is loaned to a supplier at simple interest of 2% when loans of comparable risk in the free market are being made at 16%. Such a loan may be partial consideration under a purchase contract for supplier products at lower than the prevailing market prices. An accurate accounting would require recognizing that a part of the $100,000 loan is really an additional cost of the products purchased during the contract term. This would create an initial loan discount, which would be amortized as interest income over the life of the note. Thus this transaction illustrates the imputation of part of an outlay of $100,000 as a cost of product.

To illustrate, consider a one-year loan of $100,000 to a supplier. The note has a face amount of $100,000 with a stated interest rate of 2%. The note could be sold outright to a bank for $86,000 at the beginning of the year. These facts would require imputation and the following journal entries:

Note receivable	100,000	
Direct-materials inventory (stores)	14,000	
Discount on note receivable		14,000
Cash		100,000

To record the loan to a supplier of $100,000, bearing a nominal interest rate of 2%. The current value of the note is $86,000. Therefore the $14,000 difference has been imputed as an additional cost of materials acquired or to be acquired.

Discount on note receivable	14,000	
Cash	102,000	
Note receivable		100,000
Interest income		16,000

To record the collection of a note.

In sum, imputation applies to both outlay costs and opportunity costs. The aim is to get better recognition of the economic impact of a particular event or decision and not to take things at face value.

Out-of-pocket costs, a short-run concept, are those costs that entail current or near-future outlays for the decision at hand. For example, the acceptance of an order so that otherwise idle facilities may be used would entail a compilation of the out-of-pocket costs that could otherwise be avoided by not accepting the order; the depreciation on the machinery and equipment used for production would be irrelevant because it does not entail out-of-pocket outlays as a result of the decision.

Postponable costs are those that may be shifted to the future with little or no effect on the efficiency of current operations. The best example of these is maintenance and repairs. Railroads sometimes go on an economy binge and cut their sizable maintenance budgets. But it is really a matter of deferral and not avoidance. Eventually some overhauls must be made and tracks must be repaired.

Avoidable costs are those that may be saved by not adopting a given alternative. For example, by not adopting a new product line, additional direct-material, direct-labor, and overhead costs could be avoided. The criterion here is the question, Which costs can be saved by not adopting a given alternative?

Sunk cost is another term for a past cost that is unavoidable because it cannot be changed no matter what action is taken. We dislike this term because it often obscures the distinction between historical and future costs. However, *sunk cost* is discussed here because it is one of the most widely used terms in nonroutine-decision situations.

To illustrate, if old equipment has a book value of $600,000 and a scrap value of $70,000, what is the sunk cost? There are two ways of looking at the $600,000 book value of old equipment. We agree with a minority view maintaining that the entire $600,000 is sunk because it represents an outlay made in the past that cannot be changed: the $70,000 disposal value is a future factor, to be considered apart from the $600,000 sunk cost. The majority view maintains that $530,000 of the $600,000 is sunk, whereas $70,000 is not sunk because it is immediately recoverable through disposal: thus the sunk part of a historical cost is what is irrecoverable in a given situation. This majority view is that the two factors (book value and present disposal value) are complementary in replacement decisions; that is, book value minus disposal value equals sunk cost.

325

In our opinion, the term *sunk cost* should not be used at all. It muddles the task of collecting proper costs for decision making. Because all past costs are irrelevant, it is fruitless to introduce unnecessary terms to describe past costs. The issue of what part of past cost is sunk need not arise. The essence of the distinction between costs, past and future, irrelevant and relevant, was described earlier in this chapter. These distinctions are all that are needed for approaching special decisions. The term *sunk cost* is often more befuddling than enlightening. If it is going to be used, *sunk cost* should have the same meaning as *past cost*.

QUESTIONS, PROBLEMS, AND CASES

9-1 Distinguish briefly between *quantitative* and *qualitative* factors in decision making.

9-2 Define *relevant cost* as the term is used in this chapter. Why are historical costs irrelevant?

9-3 "All future costs are relevant." Do you agree? Why?

9-4 Define *opportunity cost*.

9-5 What are the three major influences on pricing decisions?

9-6 Suppose you are a senior manager with many years of experience. A new employee makes the following comment during a heated disagreement over the pricing of a new product: "No amount of rhetoric is going to change the fact that all your experience and knowledge is about the past and all your decisions are about the future." How would you respond?

9-7 What are three sources of prediction errors made by decision makers?

9-8 Questions on disposal of assets.
1. A company has an inventory of 1,000 assorted missile parts for a line of missiles that has been junked. The inventory cost $100,000. The parts can be either (a) remachined at total additional costs of $30,000 and then sold for a total of $35,000 or (b) scrapped for $2,000. What should be done?
2. A truck, costing $10,000 and uninsured, is wrecked the first day in use. It can be either (a) disposed of for $1,000 cash and replaced with a similar truck costing $10,200 or (b) rebuilt for $8,500 and be brand-new as far as operating characteristics and looks are concerned. What should be done?

9-9 The careening bookkeeping machine. (W. A. Paton)   A young lady in the accounting department of a certain business was moving a bookkeeping machine from one room to another. As she came alongside an open stairway, she carelessly slipped and let the machine get away from her. It went careening down the stairs with a great racket and wound up at the bottom in some thousands of pieces, completely wrecked. Hearing the crash, the office manager came rushing out and turned rather white when he saw what had happened. "Someone tell me quickly," he yelled, "if that is one of our fully amortized units." A check of the equipment cards showed that the smashed machine was, indeed, one of those that had been written off. "Thank God!" said the manager.

Required | Explain and comment on the point of Professor Paton's anecdote.

9-10 Inventory decision, opportunity cost.   A manufacturer of lawn mowers predicts that 240,000 spark plugs will have to be purchased during the next year. A supplier quotes a price of $8 per spark plug. The supplier also offers a special discount option: If all 240,000 spark plugs are purchased at the start of the year, a discount of 5% off the $8 price will be available. The manufacturer can invest its cash at 8% per year.

Required
1. What is the opportunity cost of purchasing all 240,000 units at the start of the year instead of in twelve monthly purchases of 20,000 per order?
2. Would this opportunity cost ordinarily be recorded in the accounting system? Why?

9-11 Multiple choice. (CPA) Choose the best answer:
1. Woody Company, which manufactures sneakers, has enough idle capacity available to accept a special order of 20,000 pairs of sneakers at $6.00 a pair. The normal selling price is $10.00 a pair. Variable manufacturing costs are $4.50 a pair, and fixed manufacturing costs are $1.50 a pair. Woody will not incur any selling expenses as a result of the special order. What would the effect on operating income be if the special order could be accepted without affecting normal sales? (a) $0, (b) $30,000 increase, (c) $90,000 increase, (d) $120,000 increase.
2. The Reno Company manufactures Part No. 498 for use in its production cycle. The cost per unit for 20,000 units of Part No. 498 is as follows:

Direct materials	$ 6
Direct labor	30
Variable overhead	12
Fixed overhead applied	16
	$64

The Tray Company has offered to sell 20,000 units of Part No. 498 to Reno for $60 per unit. Reno will make the decision to buy the part from Tray if there is a savings of $25,000 for Reno. If Reno accepts Tray's offer, $9 per unit of the fixed overhead applied would be totally eliminated. Furthermore, Reno has determined that the released facilities could be used to save relevant costs in the manufacture of Part No. 575. To have a savings of $25,000, the amount of relevant costs that would be saved by using the released facilities in the manufacture of Part No. 575 would have to be (a) $80,000, (b) $85,000, (c) $125,000, (d) $140,000.

9-12 Relevance of equipment costs. The Auto Wash Company has just installed a special machine for polishing cars at one of its several outlets. It is the first day of the company's fiscal year. The machine cost $20,000. Its annual operating costs total $15,000, exclusive of depreciation. The machine will have a four-year useful life and no residual value.

After the machine has been used one day, a machine salesperson offers a different machine that promises to do the same job at a yearly operating cost of $9,000, exclusive of depreciation. The new machine will cost $24,000 cash, installed. The "old" machine is unique and can be sold outright for only $10,000, less $2,000 removal cost. The new machine, like the old one, will have a four-year useful life and no residual value.

Sales, all in cash, will be $150,000 annually and other cash expenses will be $110,000 annually, regardless of this decision.

For simplicity, assume there is a world of no income taxes and no interest.

Required
1. Prepare a statement of cash receipts and disbursements for each of the four years under both alternatives. What is the cumulative difference in cash for the four years taken together?
2. Prepare statements of income for each of the four years under both alternatives. Assume straight-line depreciation. What is the cumulative difference in net income for the four years taken together?
3. What are the irrelevant items in each of your presentations in requirements 1 and 2? Why are they irrelevant?
4. Suppose the cost of the "old" machine was $1 million rather than $20,000. Nevertheless, the old machine can be sold outright for only $10,000, less $2,000 removal cost. Would the net differences in requirements 1 and 2 change? Explain.

5. "To avoid a loss, we should keep the old equipment." What is the role of book value in decisions about replacement of equipment?

6. You are the mayor of a small town. You purchased some new lawn-mowing equipment yesterday. Assume the same facts as in requirements 1 and 2; however, no operating revenues exist. Would any of your answers to requirements 1 through 5 change? How? Why?

9-13 An argument about pricing. A column in a newspaper contained the following:

> Dear Miss Lovelorn: My husband and I are in constant disagreement because he drives 10 miles to work every day and drives a mile in the opposite direction to pick up and deliver the man who rides with him. Therefore the total daily mileage is 24 for the round trip. For this service the man pays $6 every other week toward gas. Bus fare would cost $16 each week. I say this fellow should pay at least $8 each week, which would be one-half the cost for the week's gas. But my husband says he can't just ask him for the money, so he settles for this arrangement month after month. We have three children and are in debt for several thousand dollars, and even this $8 a week would really help, as we live on a very tight budget. Am I reasonable to think the gas expense should be split 50-50?

Required | As Miss Lovelorn, write a reply.

9-14 Contribution approach to pricing. The Dill Company had the following operating characteristics in 19_4:

Basic production data at standard cost:	
Direct materials	$1.30
Direct labor	1.50
Variable overhead	.20
Fixed overhead ($150,000 ÷ 150,000 units of denominator volume)	1.00
Total factory cost at standard	$4.00

Sales price, $5.00 per unit.
Selling and administrative expense is assumed for simplicity as being all fixed at $65,000 yearly, except for sales commissions at 5% of dollar sales.

In 19_4, a Dill Company salesperson had asked the president for permission to sell 1,000 units to a particular customer for $3.80 per unit. The president refused, stating that the price was below factory cost.

Required | Based solely on the information given, compute the effect of the president's decision on 19_4 net income. Specifically, what would be the reasoning of the contribution approach to such a decision?

9-15 Contribution approach to pricing. A company has a budget for 19_2; the absorption-costing approach follows (figures assumed):

Sales	$100,000	100%
Factory cost of goods sold, including $20,000 fixed costs	60,000	60
Gross profit	$ 40,000	40%
Operating expenses, including $20,000 fixed costs	30,000	30
Net income target	$ 10,000	10%

Normal or target markup percentage:
$40,000 ÷ $60,000 = 66.7% of absorption cost

1. Recast the income statement in a contribution format. Indicate the normal or target markup percentage based on total variable costs.
2. Assume the same cost behavior patterns as above. Assume further that a customer offers $540 for some units that have a factory cost of goods manufactured of $600 and total variable costs of $500. Should the offer be accepted? Explain.
3. Under what circumstances would you adopt a contribution approach to pricing as a part of your usual accounting system? That is, the system would routinely provide data using the contribution format.

9-16 Considering three alternatives. (CMA)   Auer Company had received an order for a piece of special machinery from Jay Company. Just as Auer Company completed the machine, Jay Company declared bankruptcy, defaulted on the order, and forfeited the 10% deposit paid on the selling price of $72,500.

Auer's manufacturing manager identified the costs already incurred in the production of the special machinery for Jay as follows:

Direct materials used		$16,600
Direct labor incurred		21,400
Overhead applied:		
Manufacturing		
Variable	$10,700	
Fixed	5,350	16,050
Fixed selling and administrative		5,405
Total cost		$59,455

Another company, Kaytell Corp., would be interested in buying the special machinery if it is reworked to Kaytell's specifications. Auer offered to sell the reworked special machinery to Kaytell as a special order for a net price of $68,400. Kaytell has agreed to pay the net price when it takes delivery in two months. The additional identifiable costs to rework the machinery to the specifications of Kaytell are as follows:

Direct materials	$ 6,200
Direct labor	4,200
	$10,400

A second alternative available to Auer is to convert the special machinery to the standard model. The standard model lists for $62,500. The additional identifiable costs to convert the special machinery to the standard model are:

Direct materials	$ 2,850
Direct labor	3,300
	$ 6,150

A third alternative for the Auer Company is to sell, as a special order, the machine as is (i.e., without modification) for a net price of $52,000. However, the potential buyer of the unmodified machine does not want it for 60 days. The buyer offers a $7,000 down payment with final payment upon delivery.

The following additional information is available regarding Auer's operations:

Sales commission rate on sales of standard models is 2% while the sales commission rate on special orders is 3%. All sales commissions are calculated on net sales price (i.e., list price less cash discount, if any).

Normal credit terms for sales of standard models are 2/10, n/30 (2/10 means a discount of 2% is given if payment is made within 10 days; n/30 means full amount is due within

30 days). Customers take the discounts except in rare instances. Credit terms for special orders are negotiated with the customer.

The application rates for manufacturing overhead and the fixed selling and administrative costs are as follows:

Manufacturing:	
Variable	50% of direct-labor cost
Fixed	25% of direct-labor cost
Selling and administrative:	
Fixed	10% of the total of direct-material, direct-labor, and manufacturing-overhead costs

Normal time required for rework is one month.

A surcharge of 5% of the sales price is placed on all customer requests for minor modifications of standard models.

Auer normally sells a sufficient number of standard models for the company to operate at a volume in excess of the breakeven point.

Auer does not consider the time value of money in analyses of special orders and projects whenever the time period is less than one year because the effect is not significant.

Required

1. Determine the dollar contribution that each of the three alternatives will add to the Auer Company's before-tax profits.
2. If Kaytell makes Auer a counteroffer, what is the lowest price Auer Co. should accept for the reworked machinery from Kaytell? Explain your answer.
3. Discuss the influence that fixed-factory-overhead cost should have on the sales prices quoted by Auer Company for special orders when (a) a firm is operating at or below the breakeven point; (b) a firm's special orders constitute efficient utilization of unused capacity above the breakeven volume.

9-17 Cost comparisons of airlines, unit costs vs. contribution approach. Charles Smith is chief operating officer for Oceanic United, an international airline operating two roundtrip flights between San Francisco and Nandi, Fiji, each week. Oceanic's capacity level is three roundtrip flights each week. The only other competitor on this 5,600-mile route is South Pacific Express; it operates three roundtrip flights between San Francisco and Nandi each week. Both Oceanic and South Pacific offer only one class of seats (tourist class) on their planes. Assume that no one-way tickets are sold.

Several months ago Smith hired a consulting firm to compare the costs of Oceanic United and South Pacific. The consultant's report includes the following summary cost comparison as its "punch line":

	OCEANIC UNITED	SOUTH PACIFIC EXPRESS
Total annual costs:		
Variable costs	$ 6,240,000	$17,160,000
Fixed costs	12,480,000	9,360,000
	$18,720,000	$26,520,000
Total passengers carried	20,800	34,320
Total unit cost per passenger	$ 900	$ 773

The data analysis underlying these numbers is:

	OCEANIC UNITED	SOUTH PACIFIC EXPRESS
Seating capacity per plane	360	310
Roundtrip flights per week	2	3
Roundtrip flights per year	104	156
Average passengers per roundtrip	200	220
Average price per roundtrip	$ 1,000	$ 950
Variable cost per roundtrip	$ 60,000	$ 110,000
Annual fixed costs	$12,480,000	$9,360,000

The variable costs associated with each passenger on a given flight are viewed as being "close to zero."

Smith is dismayed by the consultant's report but finds it less than informative. He is reminded of the comment that "a consultant is someone who will take your watch off your wrist and tell you what time it is."

Required
1. Would you choose an activity level measure different than the number of passengers? Why?
2. Critically evaluate the cost comparison analysis presented by the consultant.
3. Present a more informative financial comparison between Oceanic United and South Pacific Express based on your preferred activity measure. Include in your analysis: differences in the cost structures of the two airlines, activity levels at which total costs (for the two airlines) are equal, contribution margins, and implications of your analysis for pricing decisions.

9-18 Operating decisions for an airline, special order decision, and pricing decision. (Continuation of question 9-17)   Assume same facts as in question 9-17.

A. Oceanic United receives a proposal from a charter group wishing to sell package tours to Fiji. The proposal involves chartering a *plane* once every two weeks to make a roundtrip flight (i.e., a separate flight will be used by the charter group). The tours in Fiji last two weeks, so the tour group would be able to utilize the plane at both the San Francisco end and the Nandi end of each roundtrip flight. The charter group offers to pay Oceanic $700 per passenger, with a minimum guarantee of 120 passengers per roundtrip flight. Smith is reluctant to accept the proposal: *$700 is below the $900 unit total cost per passenger reported by the consultant.* In your answer to the following questions, assume that there will be no effect on current demand, and ignore the intermediate period of the first two weeks.

Required
1. How much will Oceanic United be better off from each roundtrip charter flight if only 120 passengers travel on a charter roundtrip?
2. What advice would you give Smith concerning the charter group proposal? Include in your answer comment(s) on Smith's concern that the "$700 price is below the $900 unit total cost per passenger reported by the consultant."

B. Smith hears that the Fijian government has recently negotiated landing rights in San Francisco for Air Fiji; only one roundtrip flight per week is permitted under the agreement negotiated by the Fijian government. Air Fiji is managed by Asian Airlines and has a very low cost structure. Smith estimates that its variable cost per roundtrip flight will be $50,000 and that its annual fixed-cost structure will be $3 million a year. Air Fiji plans to offer the one roundtrip flight a week between San Francisco and Nandi and has a seating capacity of 350 per plane. Smith anticipates a price-cutting war on this route and seeks your advice.

Required
1. How low can Oceanic price a roundtrip ticket and still break even, assuming that the demand it faces stays at its existing volume level of 104 roundtrip flights and an average of 200 passengers on each flight?

331

2. Assume that South Pacific Express does not start a price war. Would you advise Oceanic United to start one? Why?

9-19 Selection of most profitable product. The Reductio Co. produces two basic types of reducing equipment, G and H. Pertinent data follow:

	PER UNIT	
	G	H
Sales price	$100.00	$70.00
Expenses:		
Direct materials	$ 28.00	$13.00
Direct labor	15.00	25.00
Variable factory overhead*	25.00	12.50
Fixed factory overhead*	10.00	5.00
Selling expenses (all variable)	14.00	10.00
	$ 92.00	$65.50
Net margin	$ 8.00	$ 4.50

*Applied on the basis of machine-hours.

The reducing craze is such that enough of either G or H can be sold to keep the plant operating at full capacity. Both products are processed through the same production centers.

Required Which product should be produced? If more than one should be produced, indicate the proportions of each. Briefly explain your answer.

9-20 Opportunity cost. (H. Schaefer) Wolverine Corp. is working at full production capacity producing 10,000 units of a unique product, Rosebo. Standard costs per unit for Rosebo are:

Direct material	$ 2
Direct labor	3
Factory overhead	5
	$10

The unit overhead cost is based on a variable cost per unit of $2 and fixed costs of $30,000 (at full capacity of 10,000 units). The nonmanufacturing costs, all variable, are $4 per unit and the sales price is $20 per unit.

A customer, the Miami Co., has asked Wolverine to produce 2,000 units of a modification of Rosebo to be called Orangebo. Orangebo would require the same manufacturing processes as Rosebo, and the Miami Co. has offered to share equally the nonmanufacturing costs with Wolverine. It is expected that Orangebo will have a sales price of $15 per unit.

Required
1. What is the opportunity cost to Wolverine of producing the 2,000 units of Orangebo? (Assume no overtime is worked.)
2. The Buckeye Corp. has offered to produce 2,000 units of Rosebo for Wolverine so that Wolverine may accept the Orangebo offer. Buckeye would charge Wolverine $14 per unit for the Rosebo. Should Wolverine accept the Buckeye offer? (Support with specific analysis.)
3. Suppose Wolverine had been working at less than full capacity producing 8,000 units of Rosebo at the time the Orangebo offer was made. What is the *minimum* price Wolverine should accept for Orangebo under these conditions? (Ignore the $15 price above.)

9-21 Make or buy, unknown level of volume. (A. Atkinson)   Oxford Engineering manufactures small engines. The engines are sold to manufacturers who install them in products such as lawn mowers. The company currently manufactures all the parts used in these engines but is considering a proposal from an external supplier who wishes to supply the starter assembly used in these engines.

The starter assembly is currently manufactured in Division 3 of Oxford Engineering. The costs relating to Division 3 for the last twelve months were as follows:

Direct materials	$200,000
Direct labor	150,000
Overhead	400,000
Total	$750,000

Over the past twelve-month period, Division 3 manufactured 150,000 engines; the average cost for the starter assembly is computed as $5 ($750,000/150,000).

Further analysis of overhead revealed the following information. Of the total overhead reported, only 25% is considered variable. Of the fixed costs, $150,000 is an allocation of general factory overhead that would remain unchanged if production of the starter assembly is abandoned. A further $100,000 of the fixed overhead is avoidable if self-manufacture of the starter assembly is discontinued. The balance of the current fixed overhead, $50,000, is the division manager's salary. If self-manufacture of the starter assembly is discontinued, the manager of Division 3 will be transferred to Division 2 at the same salary. This will allow the company to save $40,000 that otherwise would be paid to attract an outsider to this position.

Required

1. Tidnish Electronics, a reliable supplier, has offered to supply starter assembly units at $4 per unit. Since this price is less than the current average cost of $5 per unit, the vice-president of manufacturing is eager to accept this offer. Should the outside offer be accepted?
2. How, if at all, would your response to requirement 1 change if the company could use the vacated factory space for storage and, in so doing, avoid $50,000 of outside storage charges currently incurred? Why is this information relevant or irrelevant?

9-22 Make or buy, relevant costs. (CMA)   GianAuto Corporation manufactures automobiles, vans, and trucks. Among the various GianAuto plants around the United States is the Denver Cover Plant. Coverings made primarily of vinyl and upholstery fabric are sewn at the Denver Cover Plant and are used to cover interior seating and other surfaces of GianAuto products.

Ted Vosilo is the plant manager for Denver Cover. The Denver Cover Plant was the first GianAuto plant in the region. As other area plants were opened, Vosilo, in recognition of his management ability, was given responsibility for managing them. Vosilo functions as a regional manager, although the budget for him and his staff is charged to the Denver Cover Plant.

Vosilo has just received a report indicating that GianAuto could purchase the entire annual output of Denver Cover from outside suppliers for $30 million. Vosilo was astonished at the low outside price because the budget for Denver Cover's operating costs for the coming year was set at $52 million. Vosilo believes that GianAuto will have to close down operations at Denver Cover in order to realize the $22 million in annual cost savings.

The budget for Denver Cover's operating costs for the coming year is presented below. Additional facts regarding the plant's operations are as follows:

- Due to Denver Cover's commitment to use high-quality fabrics in all its products, the purchasing department was instructed to place blanket purchase orders with major suppliers to ensure the receipt of sufficient materials for the coming year. If these orders are canceled as a consequence of the plant closing, termination charges would amount to 15% of the cost of direct materials.
- Approximately 700 plant employees will lose their jobs if the plant is closed. This includes all the direct laborers and supervisors as well as the plumbers, electricians, and other skilled workers classified as indirect plant workers. Some would be able to find new jobs while many others would have difficulty. All employees would have

333

difficulty matching Denver Cover's base pay of $9.40 per hour that is the highest in the area. A clause in Denver Cover's contract with the union may help some employees; the company must provide employment assistance to its former employees for twelve months after a plant closing. The estimated cost to administer this service would be $1 million for the year.

- Some employees would probably elect early retirement because GianAuto has an excellent pension plan. In fact, $3 million of the 19_6 pension expense would continue whether Denver Cover is open or not.
- Vosilo and his staff would not be affected by the closing of Denver Cover. They would still be responsible for administering three other area plants.
- Denver Cover considers equipment depreciation to be a variable cost and uses the units-of-production method to depreciate its equipment; Denver Cover is the only GianAuto plant to use this depreciation method. However, Denver Cover uses the customary straight-line method to depreciate its building.

Denver Cover Plant
Budget For Operating Costs
For the Year Ended December 31, 19_6
($000 omitted)

Materials		$12,000
Labor:		
Direct	$13,000	
Supervision	3,000	
Indirect plant	4,000	20,000
Overhead:		
Depreciation—equipment	$ 5,000	
Depreciation—building	3,000	
Pension expense	4,000	
Plant manager and staff	2,000	
Corporate allocation	6,000	20,000
Total budgeted costs		$52,000

Required

1. Without regard to costs, identify the advantages to GianAuto Corporation of continuing to obtain covers from its own Denver Cover Plant.
2. GianAuto Corporation plans to prepare a numerical analysis that will be used in deciding whether to close the Denver Cover Plant. Identify
   a. The recurring annual budgeted costs that can be avoided by closing the plant
   b. The recurring annual budgeted costs that are not relevant to the decision, and explain why they are not relevant
   c. Any nonrecurring costs that arise due to the closing of the plant, and explain how they affect the decision
   d. Any revenues or costs not specifically mentioned in the text that GianAuto should consider before making a decision

9-23 Which school(s) in a school district to close, relevant cost analysis, opportunity costs. Naomi Lance, the superintendent of the Palo Alto School District, faces a difficult decision. Declining student enrollment in the district appears to necessitate closing between one and three elementary or junior-high (middle) schools over the next four years. At present there are seven elementary schools (students of age 6–12 years), and three junior-high schools (students of age 13–14 years). Schools in one category can be converted to a school in the other category, although typically at a considerable one-time conversion cost. Eight of the ten schools are on land owned by the school district. Stanford elementary school and Leland middle school are on land leased from Stanford University. The school district pays Stanford University an annual $10,000 lease payment for Stanford elementary school and an annual $15,000 lease payment for Leland middle school.

Lance predicts that over the next four years demand for student places will decline from the current level of 5,000 (also the current capacity) to 4,100. Much of the decline in enrollment will first be reflected in the elementary schools. The following schools have been widely mentioned in the local press as likely to be closed by the school district:

1. *Addison* elementary school (200-student capacity). Located in the downtown shopping area, this is the smallest of the schools in the district. It was built at a cost of $1.2 million twenty years ago. A shopping mall developer has offered the school district $25 million for the property.

2. *Duveneck* elementary school (500-student capacity). The oldest of the schools in the district, it was built at a cost of $1 million thirty years ago. It is situated in an exclusive residential part of the district. A local developer has offered $8 million for the property. Two years ago the school district finished a $3 million renovation of Duveneck that made it a showpiece of all elementary schools in California.

3. *Stanford* elementary school (600-student capacity). This school, built at a cost of $5 million ten years ago, is on land leased from Stanford University. There are eighty-nine years remaining on the lease. The lease requires a $10,000 lease payment each year. The land will immediately revert to Stanford University if the school is closed before the lease term expires.

4. *Jane Lathrop* middle school (800-student capacity). This school, built at a cost of $7 million eight years ago, was formerly an elementary school. Last year it was converted to a junior high school at a cost of $1.5 million. A land developer has offered $9 million for the property. It is especially attractive to the developer due to its having large amounts of open space. It is the only school in the district with six playing fields for athletics.

OTHER INFORMATION

a. If Stanford elementary is not closed, it will require a $2 million capital investment this year to upgrade the classrooms, parking area, and playing fields.

b. If Jane Lathrop is closed, it will cost $1.8 million to convert an existing elementary school to a junior-high school. Three junior-high schools are necessary in the district.

c. Palo Alto School District has a central headquarters' administrative staff of twelve people. The superintendent is paid $50,000 a year (including benefits). The senior assistant is paid $35,000 a year. Each school has one assistant at the central administrative headquarters paid $20,000 a year.

Required

1. Lance believes that the following alternatives warrant further analysis:
   a. Close no schools
   b. Close Addison and Duveneck
   c. Close Addison and Stanford
   d. Close Jane Lathrop

   Prepare a quantitative comparison of these four alternatives. Present your analysis focusing on relevant costs and other relevant cash inflows and outflows. Distinguish between recurring items and one-time-only items.

2. Lance receives a letter from a concerned parent who lives close to Jane Lathrop. The letter presses strongly for closing both Addison and Stanford elementary. It argues that "Stanford is the only school in current need of additional capital investment" and notes that "the school district could avoid a $2 million outlay by immediately closing Stanford elementary school." The letter also points out that "the school district will have to pay Stanford University $890,000 over the next eighty-nine years if it keeps Stanford elementary; in contrast, no cash outflow arises if the school district retains Jane Lathrop." Do you agree with this parent's argument?

3. What cost figures mentioned in the question are irrelevant to the school-closing decision? Explain your reasoning.

4. Other than the costs outlined in requirement 1, what other factors would you recommend that Lance consider in her school-closing decision?

9-24 Continue operations versus subcontract, relevant cost analysis. (CMA) VAR Association is a professional educational organization with affiliates located throughout the United States. The organization publishes a monthly magazine, offers continuing education courses, and conducts research that is then published in report or monograph form. All of these operations are provided out of VAR's office in Los Angeles.

VAR has over 250 research reports and monographs in print. These are available to members and the general public at selling prices ranging from $2.50 to $35.00 each. Approximately 12–20 titles are released during each fiscal year. The printing of all publications takes place in the Los Angeles metropolitan area.

The association processes an average of 1,500 orders a month. The processing and filling of orders has become an increasingly burdensome task for the association staff. The association's publication director has suggested that VAR contract with an outside service to handle the inventorying, order processing, shipping, and billing for publication orders.

VAR has contacted ProEd Book Service to determine the kind of service it offers and the cost. ProEd is located in Cincinnati and inventories and distributes books and monographs for several other professional organizations. ProEd would be willing to inventory VAR's complete stock of research publications and process, ship, and bill all direct-mail orders. ProEd would charge VAR an inventory storage fee, processing and recordkeeping fees at the rate of $10 per hour, and for the cost of mailing supplies and shipping charges.

VAR's publication director asked a member of the association's staff to prepare an analysis to determine the feasibility of using ProEd Book Service. The preliminary cost analysis and narrative report are reproduced below:

Monthly Cost Savings Analysis
ProEd Book Service

RENTAL SAVINGS

1. Outside warehouse (4,000 square feet @ $8.40 per square foot ÷ 12)	$2,800	
2. Basement storeroom (900 square feet @ $12.00 per square foot ÷ 12)	900	
3. Stockroom (100 square feet @ $21.00 per square foot ÷ 12)	175	$3,875

LABOR SAVINGS

4. Order clerk (150 hours @ $8.50 per hour)	$1,275	
5. Shipping clerk (150 hours @ $7.00 per hour)	1,050	
6. Storeroom clerk (60 hours @ $7.50 per hour)	450	
7. Stockroom clerk		
a. Inventory function (16 hours @ $8.50 per hour)	136	
b. Replenishing stock room (30 hours @ $8.50 per hour)	255	
8. Mailroom supervisor (50 hours @ $10.00 per hour)	500	3,666
Total Savings		$7,541

COSTS

9. ProEd storage fees (4,000 square feet @ $4.20 per square foot ÷ 12)	$1,400	
10. Process/recordkeeping fees (456 hours @ $10.00 per hour)	4,560	
11. Additional supplies (1500 orders @ [$.50 − .40])	150	6,110
Net monthly savings		$1,431

RENTAL SAVINGS If the services of ProEd Book Service are used, the outside warehouse would no longer be required. Space in the basement storeroom and the upstairs stockroom now used for research publications would be used to provide additional space for storage of affiliate supplies and educational materials. Currently, these items are stored in space too crowded for easy access. The quantities of affiliate and educational supplies would not be increased, but the accessibility to materials would be improved. The cost used in the analysis is based on the current rental charge for the space.

LABOR SAVINGS The services of an order clerk and a shipping clerk would not be needed if ProEd's services are employed. The activities of the other three positions identified in the analysis cannot be combined. The stockroom clerk would still be required to take inventory of all materials and replenish stock when needed. A portion of the released time of the mailroom supervisor would be devoted to shipping new titles to ProEd. The remaining released time of these individuals would allow them to do their other regularly assigned duties on a more timely basis. The labor analysis is based on the hourly wage plus employee benefits of each individual and a normal work month of 150 hours.

STORAGE COSTS ProEd has indicated that the VAR inventory can be stored in 4,000 square feet in its warehouse. The annual charge for this space is $4.20 per square foot.

PROCESSING AND RECORDKEEPING COSTS Order processing and recordkeeping would be charged at the actual hours required. ProEd has not provided an estimate of the time required for these activities. Therefore the labor-hours saved by the VAR staff were used in the analysis.

SUPPLY COSTS VAR uses three different shipping packages depending on the size of the order—i.e., envelope (cost of $.10 each), corrugated mailing pouch (cost of $.30 each), or cardboard carton (cost of $.75 each). An average cost of $.40 per order was used in the analysis. The carton ProEd uses costs $.50 each.

OTHER INFORMATION Shipping costs to customers were not included in the analysis. These should be reduced because ProEd is more centrally located.

The startup cost related to the movement of the present inventory to ProEd's warehouse in Cincinnati would consist of costs related to loading, shipping, and unloading. Total cost should not exceed $3,500.

CONCLUSIONS Considering all costs, VAR should save over $17,000, exclusive of startup costs, during the course of a year by using ProEd. Due to ProEd's central location, shipping costs should be less. Thus these cost savings along with the freeing of storage space and personnel time for other purposes are excellent reasons for using the services of ProEd Book Service.

Required

Review the cost analysis and narrative report regarding the use of ProEd Book Service by VAR Association.

1. For each of the eleven items identified in the cost analysis, discuss whether the item and amount are appropriate or inappropriate for the analysis.
2. Identify and explain cost items, if any, that were omitted but should have been incorporated into the cost analysis and narrative report.
3. Identify and explain additional qualitative items, if any, that VAR Association should consider in its analysis.

9-25 Pricing of a textbook, relevant costs, timing differences. Julie Flair, a former sales representative, has been promoted to be Accounting Series editor of Gulf Publishing. Her first task concerns the pricing of the third edition of *Financial Statement Analysis* by Scott Leland, hereafter *FSA* (3E). A new edition of this book appears every four years. Summary data relating to the second edition are:

	YEAR 1	YEAR 2	YEAR 3	YEAR 4
Printed (units)	20,000	25,000	25,000	—
Sales (units)	16,000	18,000	16,000	10,000
Complimentaries distributed (units)	3,000	1,000	500	500
Wholesale price per copy	$16	$18	$18	$20

Summary data relating to production costs for the manuscript of the third edition are:

1.	Payment to Leland to cover development costs	$10,000
2.	In-house manuscript preparation costs at Gulf Publishing (production editor, proofing, etc.)	18,000
3.	Subcontracting for typesetting, page layouts, and color graphics	50,000
4.	Subcontracting of index preparation	2,000
		$80,000

These costs of $80,000 have already been incurred. The $10,000 payment to Leland was made two years ago. Assume that the $18,000, $50,000, and $2,000 payments were just made. It is now the start of year 1 of *FSA* (3E). The book will be printed next week and will be on the bookshelves two months later.

Printing costs will depend on the size of the print-run. The cost schedule from Adept Printing for the first printing of *FSA* (3E) is:

PRINT-RUN	TOTAL COST	
5,000	$ 50,000	
10,000	85,000	
15,000	115,000	
20,000	140,000	
25,000	160,000	
Above 25,000	160,000	plus $3 per copy above 25,000

Adept Printing requires payment of the printing charge at the start of the year in which the print-run is made.

Flair intends to spend $20,000 in year 1 for the marketing of *FSA* (3E); $10,000 will be spent each year in years 2, 3, and 4 of the third edition. These amounts are paid at the start of each year.

Flair's assistant has prepared the following schedule to support a year 1 wholesale price of $33 for *FSA* (3E).

Pricing Schedule for Year 1 of FSA (3E)	
Manuscript preparation cost	$ 80,000
Marketing cost	20,000
Printing cost (based on a print-run of 20,000 copies)	140,000
	$240,000
Estimated sales in year 1 (based on year 1 sales of 2E)	16,000
Cost per copy in year 1: $240,000 ÷ 16,000	$ 15
Markup (120% of cost, including a 10% royalty payment to the author of $3.30)	18
Wholesale price per copy in year 1	$ 33

Flair has a gut-feel that $33 per copy is way out of line. It is at least 50% above the year 4 wholesale price of the second edition. Using the widely followed university bookstore markup of 25% on wholesale price, the cost per copy to students would run at $41.25. No textbook in the financial statement analysis market has yet gone through the $40 barrier; Flair is most reluctant for Gulf Publishing to be the first. Sales payments from retailers are received by Gulf Publishing at the end of each year. Royalty payments are made to authors at the end of each year.

One of the sales representatives of Gulf Publishing confirms to Flair a widely circulating rumor that Homewood Press, a major competitor, is going to bring out the first edition of a *Financial Statement Analysis* text in three months' time. The author of the new Homewood Press competitor is the author of the current leading text in the Intermediate Accounting market. Homewood Press's highly successful strategy is to price textbooks at the low end of the spectrum and to aim for high sales volume.

Required

1. Criticize the Pricing Schedule for Year 1 of *FSA* (3E) prepared by Flair's assistant.
2. Prepare a Pricing Schedule(s) that you think will be most informative to Flair in her pricing decision for the third edition of *Financial Statement Analysis*.
3. What cost and other information would you recommend that Flair consider in her pricing decision?
4. Assume that Gulf orders a production run of 70,000 in year 1. What relevant cost(s) might arise from this decision that would not be recorded by the external financial reporting system? What are the pros and cons of making a print-run of 70,000 in year 1?

9-26 Multiple choice; comprehensive problem on relevant costs. The following are the Class Company's *unit* costs of making and selling a given item at a level of 20,000 units per month:

Manufacturing:	
Direct materials	$1.00
Direct labor	1.20
Variable indirect cost	.80
Fixed indirect cost	.50
Selling and other:	
Variable	1.50
Fixed	.90

The following situations refer only to the data given above—there is *no connection* between the situations. Unless stated otherwise, assume a regular selling price of $6 per unit.

Required

Choose the answer corresponding to the most nearly acceptable or correct answer in each of the eight items. Support each answer with summarized computations.

1. In presenting an inventory of 10,000 items on the balance sheet, the unit cost conventionally to be used is (a) $3.00, (b) $3.50, (c) $5.00, (d) $2.20, (e) $5.90.
2. The unit cost relevant to setting a *normal* price for this product, assuming that the implied level of operations is to be maintained, is (a) $5.00, (b) $4.50, (c) $3.50, (d) $5.90, (e) $3.00.
3. This product is usually sold at the rate of 240,000 units per year (an average of 20,000 per month). At a sales price of $6.00 per unit, this yields total sales of $1,440,000, total costs of $1,416,000, and a net margin of $24,000, or 10¢ per unit. It is estimated by market research that volume could be increased by 10% if prices were cut to $5.80. Assuming the implied cost behavior patterns to be correct, this action, if taken, would (a) decrease profits by a net of $7,200; (b) decrease profits by 20¢ per unit, $48,000, but increase profits by 10% of sales, $144,000; net, $96,000 increase; (c) decrease unit fixed costs by 10% or 14¢ per unit and thus decrease profits by 20¢ − 14¢, or 6¢ per unit; (d) increase sales volume to 264,000 units, which at the $5.80 price would give total sales of $1,531,200; costs of $5.90 per unit for 264,000 units would be $1,557,600, and a loss of $26,400 would result; (e) none of these.
4. A cost contract with the government (for 5,000 units of product) calls for the reimbursement of all costs of production plus a fixed fee of $1,000. This production is part of the regular 20,000 units of production per month. The delivery of these 5,000 units of product increases profits from what they would have been, were these units not sold, by (a) $1,000, (b) $2,500, (c) $3,500, (d) $300, (e) none of these.
5. Assume the same data as in 4 above except that the 5,000 units will displace 5,000 other units from production. The latter 5,000 units would have been sold through regular channels for $30,000 had they been made. The delivery to the government increases (or decreases) net profits from what they would have been, were the other

5,000 units sold by (a) $4,000 decrease, (b) $3,000 increase, (c) $6,500 decrease, (d) $500 increase, (e) none of these.

6. The company desires to enter a foreign market, in which price competition is keen. An order for 10,000 units of this product is being sought on a minimum unit-price basis. It is expected that shipping costs for this order will amount to only 75¢ per unit, but the fixed costs of obtaining the contract will be $4,000. Domestic business will be unaffected. The minimum basis for breakeven price is (a) $3.50, (b) $4.15, (c) $4.25, (d) $3.00, (e) $5.00.

7. The company has an inventory of 1,000 units of this item left over from last year's model. These must be sold through regular channels at reduced prices. The inventory will be valueless unless sold this way. The unit cost that is relevant for establishing the minimum selling price would be (a) $4.50, (b) $4.00, (c) $3.00, (d) $5.90, (e) $1.50.

8. A proposal is received from an outside supplier who will make and ship this item directly to the Class Company's customers as sales orders are forwarded from Class's sales staff. Class's fixed selling costs will be unaffected, but its variable selling costs will be slashed 20%. Class's plant will be idle, but its fixed factory overhead would continue at 50% of present levels. To compare with the quotation received from the supplier, the company should use a unit cost of (a) $4.75, (b) $3.95, (c) $2.95, (d) $5.35, (e) none of these.

9-27 **Make or buy.** (Continuation of 9-26)   Assume the same facts as in requirement 8 of Problem 9-26 except that if the supplier's offer is accepted, the present plant facilities will be used to make a product whose unit costs will be:

Variable manufacturing costs	$5.00
Fixed manufacturing costs	1.00
Variable selling costs	2.00
Fixed selling costs (new increment)	.50

Total fixed factory overhead will be unchanged, while fixed selling costs will increase as indicated. The new product will sell for $9. This minimum desired net profit on the two products taken together is $50,000 per year.

Required | What is the maximum purchase cost per unit that the Class Company should be willing to pay for subcontracting the old production? (There are no multiple-choice answers supplied.)

Determining How Costs Behave

General approach to estimating cost functions • Steps in estimating a cost function • Alternative estimation approaches • Data collection issues • Nonlinearity and cost functions • Learning curves and cost functions • Costs and benefits • Appendix: Inflation and cost estimation.

Know your costs. Throughout this book, again and again we see that knowledge of how costs behave can frequently mean the difference between wise and unwise decisions. Such information is important in planning and control decisions. For example, some firms attempt to position themselves as low-cost producers in their industry and compete on the basis of low price.[1] Knowledge of their own costs and of how they compare with their competitors is a key input for decisions in this area. Cost behavior information also plays a key role in other planning decisions, such as bidding for contracts. Decisions in the control area, such as the setting of standards and the interpretation of variances, also rely heavily on knowledge of cost behavior.

GENERAL APPROACH TO ESTIMATING COST FUNCTIONS

Basic terms and assumptions

Accountants and statisticians often distinguish between **cost estimation** and **cost prediction.** The former denotes the attempt to measure historical cost relationships; the latter deals with the forecasting or prediction of costs. This distinction is not

---

[1]The following statements are typical of those found in annual reports: "Our goal is to become a low-cost producer, focusing only on those products and market segments in which Scott has unique competitive advantages" (Scott Paper); and "[Dana is committed] to be number one in technology, quality, and low production costs (at 90% of our major world-wide competitors' costs) in our global markets" (Dana Corporation).

universal; many managers often use *estimated cost* and *cost estimation* to describe forecasts or predictions. Consequently, be sure of the meaning of *cost estimation* in a specific situation.

Two assumptions are frequently used in the estimation of cost behavior:

1. Cost behavior can adequately be approximated by a linear function.
2. Variations in the total cost level can be explained by variations in a single variable (such as direct-labor hours or machine-hours).

These assumptions are used throughout much of this chapter; the final sections give examples of nonlinear behavior. Chapter 23 discusses how variations in two or more variables (say, direct-labor hours, machine-hours, and units produced) can be used to explain variations in the total cost level. **The question of which set of assumptions adequately approximates the underlying relationship is one that can be answered only in actual situations, on a case-by-case basis.**

Given the assumptions of linearity and a single explanatory variable, each cost has some underlying cost behavior pattern, more technically described as a *cost function*. Its expected value, $E(y)$, has the form

$$E(y) = A + Bx$$

where A and B are the underlying (but unknown) parameters. (A **parameter** is a constant, such as A, or a coefficient, such as B, in a model or system of equations.)

Working with historical data, the cost analyst can develop a linear formula to estimate the underlying relationship:

$$y' = a + bx$$

where y' is the estimated value, as distinguished from the observed value y, and a (termed the *intercept* or *constant*) and b (termed the *slope coefficient*) are the estimates of the underlying A and B. **The intercept a is the estimated component of total costs that, in the relevant range, does not vary with the activity level of the explanatory variable. The slope coefficient b is the amount of change in y for each unit change in x. The *relevant range* is the span of activity or volume over which the cost function is expected to be valid.**

Examples of cost functions

Exhibit 10-1 on p. 343 illustrates variations of the basic formula, $y' = a + bx$.

Graph 1 in Exhibit 10-1 presents the familiar *variable cost,* which is often referred to as being *proportionately variable, strictly variable,* or *directly variable.* Its total fluctuates in direct proportion to changes in x within the relevant range because the intercept (a) is zero.

Graph 2 presents the familiar *fixed cost.* Its total does not fluctuate within the relevant range because b is zero.

Graph 3 presents a **mixed cost,** sometimes called a **semivariable cost.** As the name implies, a mixed cost has both fixed and variable elements. Its total fluctuates as x changes within the relevant range, but not in direct proportion to the changes.

Nature of mixed costs

The fixed element of a mixed cost represents the minimum cost of supplying a good or service (within the relevant range). The variable element is the portion of the mixed cost that is influenced by changes in activity. Examples of mixed costs are

EXHIBIT 10-1
Examples of Cost Functions

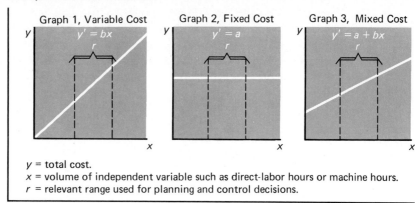

Graph 1, Variable Cost   Graph 2, Fixed Cost   Graph 3, Mixed Cost

$y' = bx$ $y' = a$ $y' = a + bx$

y = total cost.
x = volume of independent variable such as direct-labor hours or machine hours.
r = relevant range used for planning and control decisions.

the rentals of delivery trucks and photocopying machines for a fixed cost per month plus a variable cost based on the volume of usage.

Ideally, there should be no single ledger account for mixed costs. All such costs should be subdivided into two accounts, one for the variable portion and one for the fixed portion. In practice, however, these distinctions are rarely made in the recording process because of the difficulty of analyzing day-to-day cost data into variable and fixed portions. Costs such as power, indirect labor, repairs, maintenance, and clerical labor generally are accounted for in total in respective ledger accounts.

STEPS IN ESTIMATING A COST FUNCTION

There are six steps in estimating a cost function: (1) choose the estimation approach, (2) choose the dependent variable, (3) choose the independent variable(s), (4) collect data on the dependent and independent variables, (5) plot the data, and (6) evaluate the estimated cost function. **Frequently, the cost analyst will proceed through these six steps several times before concluding that an acceptable cost function has been identified.**

1. *Choose the Estimation Approach.* The approaches normally considered include:
   a. Industrial engineering
   b. Account analysis
   c. Visual fit
   d. Regression analysis
   e. Two-point (typically high-low)

These approaches are described in the next section. They differ in the cost of conducting the analysis, the assumptions they make, and the evidence they yield about the adequacy of the estimated cost function. These approaches are not mutually exclusive. In many organizations a combination of several may be used simultaneously.

343

2. *Choose the Dependent Variable.* Choice of the **dependent variable** (the cost to be predicted), usually called *y*, will be guided by the decision for which the cost information is to be used. For example, if the aim is to predict overhead costs on a production line, then all those costs that are classified as being overhead with respect to the production line should be incorporated into *y*. Ideally, all the individual items in the dependent variable will have a similar relationship with the independent variables. Where a single relationship does not exist, the possibility of estimating more than one cost function should be investigated.

3. *Choose the Independent Variable(s).* The **independent variable,** often denoted by *x*, is sometimes termed the **controllable** or **explanatory** variable. In cost accounting contexts, it is usually a measure of volume subject to the influence of a decision maker. The possibilities include:

Units of production	Units of sales
Direct-labor hours	Dollar sales volume
Direct-labor dollars	Weight of materials
Machine-hours	Miles driven

Ideally, the independent variable(s) chosen should have economic plausibility and should be accurately measurable. The range of the independent variable for which the relationship expressed by the cost function is valid is termed the *relevant range*.

4. *Collect Data on the Dependent and Independent Variables.* This is usually the most difficult step in cost analysis. The ideal data base would contain numerous observations for a firm whose operations have not been influenced by any economic or technological change. Moreover, the time period (e.g., daily, weekly, or monthly) used to measure both the dependent and independent variables would be identical. A subsequent section of this chapter gives examples of frequently encountered departures from this ideal data base.

5. *Plot the Data.* This step is critical in estimating cost relationships. **The expression "a picture is worth a thousand words" adequately conveys the benefits that come from plotting the data.** The general relationship between the independent variable and the dependent variable can readily be observed in a plot of the data. Moreover, extreme observations are highlighted. These extreme observations can then be checked to determine whether they arise from an error in recording the data, from an unusual event such as a strike, or from any other event that would prevent them from being representative of the normal relationship between the two variables. Plotting the data can also provide insight into the relevant range of the cost function.

6. *Evaluate the Estimated Cost Function.* In evaluating a cost function, the analyst should retain the following perspective:

1. *Economic Plausibility.* The relationship between the dependent and independent variables must be plausible. That is, they must be logical and appeal to common sense. When possible, physical observation, such as an engineering study, provides the best evidence of a valid relationship.

2. *Goodness of Fit.* The cost analyst tests past data to see which of the plausible cost functions best describes cost behavior patterns. Sometimes these tests employ measures such as the coefficient of determination (r^2) described in Chapter 23.

Economic plausibility and goodness of fit serve as checks on one another. For example, data may show that a clerical overhead cost is more closely related (correlated) to fluctuations in the price of electricity than to the number of documents processed. But there may be no logical cause-and-effect relationship that supports such closeness of fit. Therefore a manager, for example, should be reluctant to use a cost function based on electricity prices to predict how clerical overhead cost will behave. There is greater confidence in an observed statistical relationship persisting in subsequent periods if there is an economic plausibility to that relationship.

ALTERNATIVE ESTIMATION APPROACHES

Alternative estimation approaches will be illustrated with an example involving direct labor. Direct labor is often regarded as a classic example of a variable cost. However, many companies do not refine their direct-labor cost accounts for each job or batch of products to distinguish between the time for original setup, the time for intervening adjustment of machinery during a production run, and the time for actually producing the units of output.

Suppose a manufacturer, Southern Rugs, is troubled by apparent fluctuations in efficiency and wants to determine how direct-labor costs are related to volume (units produced). Southern Rugs produces large woven rugs. The workers set up their own jobs on complex machinery. The data in Exhibit 10-2 on p. 346 show the results for the twelve most recent weekly time periods. Note that the data are paired. For example, week 12 has 24 units produced (independent variable) with an *associated* direct-labor cost (dependent variable) of $275. We will use these data to illustrate alternative estimation approaches.

Industrial engineering approach

The **industrial engineering approach**, often called the *engineering* or *analytic* or *work measurement* approach, is used widely by companies having standard-cost systems.[2] The relationships between inputs and outputs are analyzed and quantified in physical terms—hours of direct labor, kilograms of material, gallons of fuel, number of records processed, and so forth. Time and motion studies may be employed, and the physical measures are then transformed into standard or budgeted costs. The engineering approach is costly, but its benefits are often dramatic. It is increasingly being used in nonmanufacturing as well as manufacturing activities.[3]

In our example, management could have industrial engineers study the direct labor and carefully specify the amounts of time for setup and for individual operations regarding various levels of output. But suppose management is unwilling to invest in the engineering approach. It may be deemed too costly to use for controlling the particular direct labor in question. Moreover, the engineering approach is seldom feasible for planning and controlling many types of overhead costs. Physical

---

[2]The industrial engineering approach is also used by companies bidding on government defense contracts. An excellent set of papers, including case studies of this and other cost-estimation approaches, can be found in G. McNichols, *Cost Analysis* (Arlington, Va.: Operations Research Society of America, 1984).

[3]For a more-detailed description of the industrial engineering approach, see "Cost Estimation: Engineering Methods," in R. Magee, *Advanced Managerial Accounting* (New York: Harper & Row, 1986), Chap. 5.

EXHIBIT 10-2
Explaining Direct-labor Cost Behavior at Southern Rugs

WEEK NUMBER	DIRECT-LABOR COSTS (y)	UNITS PRODUCED (x)
1	$340	34
2	346	44
3	287	31
4	262	36
5	220	30
6	416	49
7	337	39
8	180	21
9	376	41
10	295	47
11	215	34
12	275	24

relationships between inputs and outputs may be difficult or impossible to specify for a host of individual overhead items.

Account analysis approach

The *account analysis* or *account classification* approach entails proceeding through ledger accounts and classifying each account into one of three categories: variable, fixed, or mixed. Such classifications may be based on superficial feelings ("I just know how these costs behave!"), on inspection of cost behavior for at least a few past periods, or on intuition and past experience. In our illustration, many managers might automatically classify direct labor as variable without undertaking further analysis.

Visual fit approach

As noted in the previous section, plotting the data is an essential step. Exhibit 10-3 demonstrates this step in determining cost behavior in our example. Inspection of the scatter of points will indicate the degree of relationship (often called **correlation**) between cost and volume. The scatter diagram is a key to deciding whether the relationship can be estimated by a linear approximation. In this illustration, the answer is yes. A straight line could indeed be fitted through the points.

In some cases, the cost analyst will use the scatter diagram to identify the cost function. An advantage of visual fit is that all sample points are used in determining the cost function. This procedure may provide more accurate estimates than using a casual summary or only two observations. Nevertheless, a visual fit has no objective measure to ensure that the line (or curve, if nonlinear) is the most accurate representation of the underlying data. Furthermore, visual fit ignores information that may be valuable about the quality of the fit.

Regression analysis approach

Regression analysis uses a statistical model to measure the *average* amount of change in the dependent variable (direct-labor cost in our example) that is associated with a unit change in the amounts of one or more independent variables (units produced in our example). When specific assumptions hold, it provides reliable measures of probable error. The most widely used regression model is *ordinary least squares*. Regression is discussed at length in Chapter 23.

EXHIBIT 10-3
Visual Analysis via a Plot of the Data

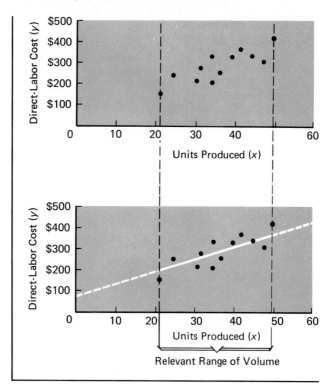

Using least-squares regression, the second graph in Exhibit 10-3 shows the line of best possible fit. Placing the amounts for a and b in the equation, we have

$$y' = \$77.08 + \$6.10x$$

where y' is the estimated direct-labor cost for any volume of output level (x). The constant or intercept term of the regression is $77.08 while the slope coefficient is $6.10.

This equation can be used for budgeting direct-labor costs. For instance, production of 40 units would be expected to have direct-labor costs on the average of $77.08 + $6.10(40) = $321 (rounded to the nearest dollar).

The line in the second graph in Exhibit 10-3 is deliberately extended to the left and right as a dashed line to emphasize the focus on the relevant range. The manager typically is interested in cost levels *within the relevant range*, not with the cost levels outside the relevant range. Therefore keep the $77.08 constant or intercept term in perspective. It is not a fixed cost per se. *Instead it is the constant component of the formula that provides the best available linear approximation of how a cost behaves within the relevant range.*

Two-point approach

Very simplified approaches are occasionally used in practice. An example is the **high-low approach**, which entails using only the highest and lowest values of the *independent variable* within the relevant range.[4] The line connecting these two points becomes the estimated cost function.

Using the Exhibit 10-2 data in our illustration:

	UNITS PRODUCED (X)	DIRECT-LABOR COST (Y)
High (H)	49	$416
Low (L)	21	180
Difference	28	$236

$$\text{Variable rate} = \frac{y_H - y_L}{x_H - x_L} = \frac{\$236}{28} = \$8.43 \text{ per unit}$$

If
$$y = a + bx$$

then
$$a = y - bx$$

Constant component = Total cost minus Variable component

At x_H: Constant component = \$416 − \$8.43(49) = \$3.00

At x_L: Constant component = \$180 − \$8.43(21) = \$3.00

Therefore the high-low estimate of the cost function is[5]:

$y = \$3.00$ constant component $+ \$8.43$ per unit variable component

Compare the high-low formula with the least-squares formula, which was $77.08 + $6.10 per units produced. At a 45-unit level of volume, cost predictions would be:

Least squares: $77.08 + $6.10(45) = $351.58

High-low: $ 3.00 + $8.43(45) = $382.35

In this illustration, the difference of $30.77 between these two approaches is 8.8% of the least-squares estimate. This difference may be significant to a decision.

There is an obvious danger of relying on only two points. They may not be

---

[4]In some cases, the highest (lowest) observation of the independent variable will not coincide with the highest (lowest) observation of the dependent variable. An example would be a company that is experiencing declining production that is more than offset by inflation in the cost inputs. Given that any causality runs from the independent variable to the dependent variable in a cost function, choosing the high-low observations of the *independent variable* is appropriate.

The high-low method sometimes is modified so that the two points chosen are a "representative high" and a "representative low." The motivation is to avoid the cost function's being affected by extreme observations that arise from abnormal events. Even with such a modification, this approach ignores information on all but two observations when estimating the cost function. Moreover, the approach does not provide any of the valuable diagnostic information provided by regression analysis (see Chapter 23).

[5]The constant or intercept component in the high-low method is sometimes called the fixed-cost component. As discussed in more detail in Chapter 23, the constant component should only be interpreted as the fixed-cost component if the relevant range incorporates a zero volume level.

EXHIBIT 10-4
Dangers of High-Low Method

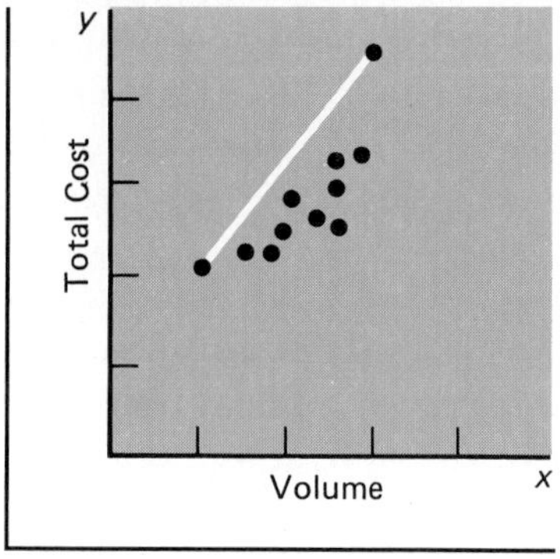

representative of all the points. Always plot all the data. The graph in Exhibit 10-4 illustrates the danger of mechanically applying the high-low method. It shows why simply picking the highest and lowest volume level can result in an estimated cost function that poorly describes the underlying cost relationship.

DATA COLLECTION ISSUES

Ideally, the cost analyst will obtain many observations of the dependent and independent variables, and there will be considerable fluctuations in the values of those variables.[6] When examining the behavior of costs over time, there are two approaches to obtaining a large number of observations:

1. Obtain observations from many very short time periods. For example, when examining costs over a twelve-month period, weekly costs will yield considerably more observations for analysis than will monthly costs.

   The time periods should be short enough to avoid the averaging of fluctuations in production within a period. Averages also tend to hide the true relationship between cost and output. For example, month-to-month comparisons may overlook some important changes in production *within* particular months.

   The time periods should be long enough to permit the recording procedures to link output with the cost incurred because of that output. For example, allowance should be made for lags in recording costs. The recording of production in one period, and related costs such as supplies or indirect labor in another, will obscure the true underlying relationship.

2. Obtain observations from many past time periods. For example, use of monthly observations over the past five years, rather than monthly observations

---

[6]For excellent discussions of data collection issues, see G. Benston, "Cost Measurement," in S. Davidson and R. Weil, *Handbook of Cost Accounting* (New York: McGraw-Hill, 1978), pp. 5.1–5.32); R. Kaplan, *Advanced Management Accounting* (Englewood Cliffs, N.J.: Prentice-Hall, 1982), Chaps. 2–4; C. Chow, "Regression Cost Analysis and the Collection and Use of Accounting Data," *Industrial Accountant,* October–December 1983; and R. Magee, *Advanced Managerial Accounting* (New York: Harper & Row, 1986), Chaps. 5–7.

over the past year, will result in a sizable increase in the data base. However, going back further in time runs the risk that technological change may have occurred. An example is the substitution of machinery for labor as a plant becomes more automated. Such a substitution can result in a different cost function being descriptive of the operations after the new machinery is installed.

Frequently
encountered data
problems

In most cases, a cost analyst will encounter one or more of the following problems:

1.   Costs are not properly matched with the independent variable. This problem often arises when accounting records are not kept on an accrual basis. For example, suppose factory supplies are purchased sporadically and stored in a manufacturing department for later use. If records are kept on a cash basis, it will appear that zero factory supplies are used in many months, whereas in the other months very sizable amounts of supplies are used. Accrual accounting typically will result in a better matching of costs with the independent variable.

2.   Fixed costs are allocated as if they were variable. For example, such costs as depreciation, insurance, or rent may be allocated on a per-unit-of-output basis. The danger is to regard these costs as variable rather than fixed. They may seem to be variable because of the allocation methods used.

3.   The same basic unit of time is not used for all the items included in the dependent and independent variables. For example, labor costs could be accumulated on a monthly basis, whereas volume could be accumulated on a weekly basis.

4.   Nonavailability of data. Missing observations frequently arise from a clerical failure to record a cost, or from the recording of a cost in a wrong classification. Misplaced files can also give rise to missing observations.

5.   Extreme values of observations occur. These extreme values can arise from errors in recording costs (for instance, a misplaced decimal point), from nonrepresentative time periods (for instance, from a period in which a major machine breakdown occurred), or from observations made outside the relevant range.

6.   Inflation has occurred in the dependent variable or in an independent variable. The Appendix to this chapter outlines two approaches that can be used to reduce problems arising from such inflation. A related problem arises when a variable is an aggregate of several individual cost items and these individual cost items are subject to differing inflation rates. For example, the cost-of-goods-sold figure for a brewing company is a composite of the costs of items such as labor, raw materials (malt, corn, barley, and hops), fuel, and depreciation. Over time, the individual inflation rates of these items have differed significantly.

NONLINEARITY AND COST FUNCTIONS

Limits of linearity

Almost without exception, accountants and managers use linear cost functions to approximate the relationships of total costs to a given range of inputs or outputs.

EXHIBIT 10-5
Cost Behavior, Nonlinear

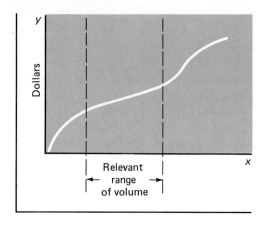

There are several assumptions that are sufficient conditions for linearity to exist when total costs are related to output:

1. The technological relationships between inputs and outputs must be linear; for example, each unit of finished product must contain the same amount of raw materials.
2. The inputs acquired must equal the inputs used; for example, each worker hired must be fully utilized.
3. The cost of acquiring each input must be a linear function of the quantity acquired; for example, the unit price of raw materials must be identical regardless of the amount purchased.

As Exhibit 10-5 shows, *the relevant range of output under consideration may permit a linearity assumption within specified limits of output.* Outside this range the cost of production may increase much faster or slower than the assumed linear rate.

Examples of nonlinearity

Nonlinear cost behavior can be caused by a variety of circumstances; for example, economies or diseconomies of scale. Even direct-material costs are not always linear variable costs. For example, consider the availability of quantity discounts, as in Exhibit 10-6; the cost per unit falls as the level of each price break is reached.

EXHIBIT 10-6
Effects of Quantity Discounts

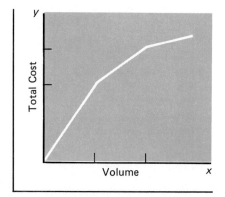

The graph in Exhibit 10-6 shows how *total* cost increases at a decreasing rate. A graph of the *unit* cost (not shown) would appear as a stair-step pattern with three steps going downward from left to right across the *x*-axis.

Few costs are variable in the strict sense of fluctuating in direct proportion to changes in volume. As already mentioned, many raw-material costs provide examples of this proportionately variable cost behavior, as shown in the left-hand side graph in Exhibit 10-7.

The right-hand side graph in Exhibit 10-7 exemplifies a **step-function cost,** whereby the cost of the input is constant over various small ranges of output, but the cost increases by discrete amounts (that is, in steps) as activity moves from one range to the next. This steplike behavior occurs when the input is acquired in discrete quantities but is used in fractional quantities. For example, labor costs of all sorts—direct or indirect, manufacturing or administrative—often represent step-variable costs. These costs increase or decrease abruptly at various intervals of activity because their acquisition comes in indivisible chunks. Labor services cannot be stored for future use; they are either utilized or lost as the workday ends. They cannot be turned on or off like a faucet.

A popular objective in the planning and control of step costs is usually to attain activity or utilization at the highest volume for any given step. This action will maximize returns for each dollar spent because the services involved will be fully utilized and their unit cost will be lowest. That is why a "linear approximation" of the step-variable cost behavior is often used for budgetary control purposes, as the second graph in Exhibit 10-7 shows.

The width and height of the steps may vary among the types of labor services. For instance, the number of hours worked by each direct laborer may be closely geared to production. The use of overtime, part-time help, or short workweeks may cause the direct-labor-cost steps to be narrow and small, so that they approximate a pure variable-cost behavior pattern. On the other hand, failures to use part-time help, to gear the workweek to current needs, and to use overtime tend to widen and heighten the labor-cost steps.

EXHIBIT 10-7
Variable Cost Behavior

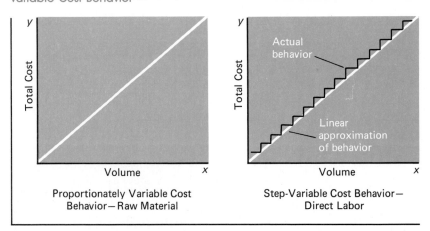

Proportionately Variable Cost Behavior—Raw Material

Step-Variable Cost Behavior— Direct Labor

EXHIBIT 10-8
Step-Fixed Cost Behavior: Supervision Costs

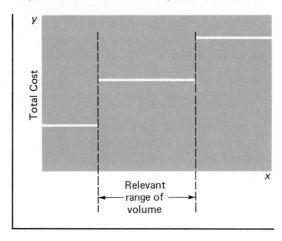

As the steps in a cost pattern widen, a so-called step-variable cost may become a "step-fixed" or even a "fixed" cost. Exhibit 10-7 shows how direct labor may be regarded as a variable cost because only a small error is caused by using a straight line instead of a step function. On the other hand, Exhibit 10-8 demonstrates how supervision costs may have wider steps, so that a fixed-cost approximation would be more accurate than a variable-cost approximation for the bulk of the relevant range under consideration.

LEARNING CURVES AND COST FUNCTIONS

This section continues the analysis of nonlinear cost functions via a discussion of learning curves.

Effects of learning on productivity

"Practice makes perfect" is a familiar saying, but it is rarely true. Perfection is seldom attainable. "Practice increases efficiency" is an unfamiliar saying, but it is frequently true. When new products or processes are begun, learning also begins. Efficiency gradually improves in a nonlinear manner. The sources of learning include increased dexterity by workers doing repetitive tasks, improvements in the scheduling of workers, and more efficient utilization of the operating facility.

The effect of learning on output per labor-hour is usually depicted by a learning curve, which helps managers to predict how labor-hours (or labor costs) will change as more units are produced. A **learning curve** is a function that shows how labor-hours per unit decline as units of output are increased.[7]

---

[7]The learning curve was originally observed with respect to labor-hours in assembly operations. More recently, the learning curve notion has been extended to include other areas of costs, such as marketing, distribution, and administration. The term **experience curve** is often used to describe this broader application of the learning curve notion. For an excellent introduction to the literature, see A. Belkaoui, *The Learning Curve: A Management Accounting Tool* (Westport, Conn.: Quorum Books, 1986).

One of two assumptions is usually made when incorporating learning into the estimation of cost functions:

1. Cumulative average time per unit is reduced by a constant percentage each time the cumulative quantity of units produced is doubled; this is termed the **cumulative average-time learning model.**
2. Incremental unit time (the time needed to produce the last unit) is reduced by a constant percentage each time the cumulative quantity of units produced is doubled; this is termed the **incremental unit-time learning model.**

Both assumptions will be illustrated in this section.[8] The improvements in efficiency that are portrayed by learning curve cost functions do not happen automatically. They require constant effort at all levels in the organization.

Cumulative average-time learning model

Exhibit 10-9 illustrates the cumulative average-time model with an 80% learning curve; the assumption is that when the quantity of units produced is doubled from X to $2X$, the cumulative average time per unit for the $2X$ units is 80% of the cumulative average time per unit for the X units. The graph on the left side plots the average time *per unit* as a function of units produced. The graph on the right side plots the *total* number of labor-hours as a function of units produced. The observations underlying Exhibit 10-9, and details of their calculation, are presented in Exhibit 10-10. The cumulative total time is obtained by multiplying the cumulative average time by the cumulative number of units produced.

Incremental unit-time learning model

Exhibit 10-11 on page 356 illustrates the incremental unit-time model with an 80% learning curve. The assumption is that when the quantity of units produced is doubled from X to $2X$, the time needed to produce the *last* unit at $2X$ production level is 80% of the time needed to produce the *last* unit at X production level. The graph on the left side plots the average time *per unit* as a function of units produced. The graph on the right side plots the *total* number of labor-hours as a function of units produced. The observations underlying Exhibit 10-11, and details of their calculation, are presented in Exhibit 10-12, also on page 356. The cumulative total time is obtained by summing the individual unit times.

The incremental unit-time model predicts a higher cumulative total time required to produce two or more units as compared with the predictions of the cumulative average-time model. Which of these two models is preferable? The one that more accurately approximates the behavior of labor-hour usage as volume levels increase. The choice can only be decided on a case-by-case approach. Plots of the data can provide useful information. Engineers, plant managers, and workers are good sources of information on the amount of learning actually occurring as output increases.

Setting budgets and standards

Predictions of costs should allow for the effects of learning. Consider the data on page 355 for the cumulative average-time model. Suppose the variable costs subject to learning effects consisted of direct labor and related overhead totaling $50 per direct-labor hour. Then the costs shown at the top of page 357 could be predicted.

---

[8]For further discussion, see J. Chen and R. Manes, "Distinguishing the Two Forms of the Constant Percentage Learning Curve Model," *Contemporary Accounting Research*, Spring 1985, pp. 242–52; and Belkaoui, *Learning Curve*, Chaps. 1 and 2.

EXHIBIT 10-9
Cumulative Average-time Learning Model

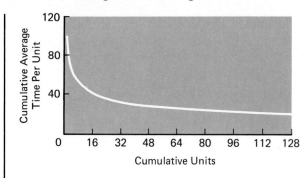

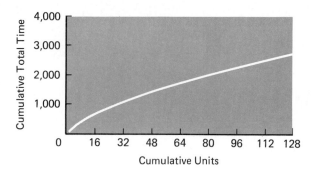

EXHIBIT 10-10
Cumulative Average-time Learning Model

(1) CUMULATIVE NUMBER OF UNITS	(2) CUMULATIVE AVERAGE TIME PER UNIT (y)	(3) = (1) × (2) CUMULATIVE TOTAL TIME	(4) INDIVIDUAL UNIT TIME FOR Xth UNIT
1	100.00	100.00	100.00
2	80.00 (100 × .8)	160.00	60.00
3	70.21	210.63	50.63
4	64.00 (80 × .8)	256.00	45.37
5	59.57	297.85	41.85
6	56.17	337.02	39.17
7	53.45	374.15	37.13
8	51.20 (64 × .8)	409.60	35.45
·	·	·	
16	40.96 (51.2 × .8)	655.36	28.06

NOTE: *The mathematical relationship underlying the cumulative average-time learning model is*

$$y = aX^b$$

where y = *cumulative average time per unit,*
X = *cumulative number of units produced,*
a = *time required to produce the first unit, and*
b = *the index of learning.*

The value of b is calculated as $b = \dfrac{\ln\ (\%\ learning)}{\ln\ 2}$

For an 80% learning index: $b = \dfrac{-.2231}{.6931} = -.3219$

As an illustration, when X = 3, a = 100, and b = −.3219:

$$y = 100 \times 3^{-.3219} = 70.21 \ hours.$$

The cumulative total time when X = 3 is 70.21 × 3 = 210.63 hours.

The individual unit times in column (4) are calculated using the data in column (3). For example, the individual unit time of 50.63 hours for the third unit is calculated as 210.63 minus 160.00.

EXHIBIT 10-11
Incremental Unit-time Learning Model

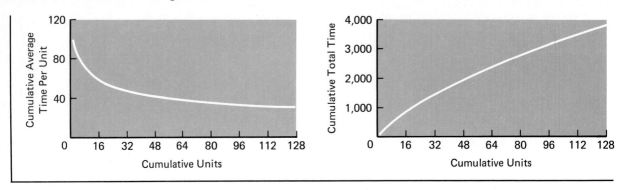

EXHIBIT 10-12
Incremental Unit-time Learning Model

(1) CUMULATIVE NUMBER OF UNITS	(2) INDIVIDUAL UNIT TIME FOR Xth UNIT (m)	(3) CUMULATIVE TOTAL TIME	(4) = (3) ÷ (1) CUMULATIVE AVERAGE TIME PER UNIT
1	100.00	100.00	100.00
2	80.00 (100 × .8)	180.00	90.00
3	70.21	250.21	83.40
4	64.00 (80 × .8)	314.21	78.55
5	59.57	373.78	74.76
6	56.17	429.95	71.66
7	53.45	483.40	69.06
8	51.20 (64 × .8)	534.60	66.82
.	.	.	.
.	.	.	.
16	40.96 (51.2 × .8)	892.00	55.75

NOTE: *The mathematical relationship underlying the incremental unit-time learning model is*

$$m = aX^b$$

where m = *time taken to produce the last single unit,*
X = *cumulative number of units produced,*
a = *time required to produce the first unit, and*
b = *the index of learning.*
For an 80% learning curve, b = −.3219 (see Exhibit 10-10).
As an illustration, when X = 3, a = 100, and b = −.3219:

$$m = 100 \times 3^{-.3219} = 70.21 \ hours$$

The cumulative total time when X = 3 is 100 + 80 + 70.21 = 250.21 hours.

These data on the effects of the learning curve could be used for many different purposes. The data can have a major influence on decisions. For example, a company might set a deliberately low price in order to generate sufficiently high demand to "ride the product down the learning curve" and establish a high share of the market. Moreover, subject to legal and other considerations, the company

CUMULATIVE NUMBER OF UNITS	CUMULATIVE TOTAL TIME	CUMULATIVE COSTS		ADDITIONS TO CUMULATIVE COSTS
1	100	$ 5,000	(100 × $50)	$ 5,000
2	160	8,000	(160 × $50)	3,000
4	256	12,800	(256 × $50)	4,800
8	409.60	20,480	(409.6 × $50)	7,680
16	655.36	32,768	(655.36 × $50)	12,288

might set a low price on the final eight units. After all, its labor and related cost per unit is predicted to be only $12,288 ÷ 8 units = $1,536, which is much lower than the $5,000 cost per unit of the first unit produced.

Uses and limitations

Assume that a firm predicts learning will occur over production of the first 10,000 units and then steady-state conditions (no learning) for labor time exist. Standards for labor during the learning period should not be based on steady-state conditions. Use of such a standard can lead to faulty cash planning and production scheduling because of failure to allow for the unusually high costs and time consumption of startups.

In addition, the inappropriate standards may have an unfavorable motivational impact. If the unfavorable discrepancy between the steady-state standard and actual performance is large and persistent, employees may reject the standards as being unattainable.

Of course, the opposite effect may also occur. That is, the learning curve might be ignored, resulting eventually in outdated standards that are not stringent enough.[9]

The learning curve concept has many ramifications for business strategies. For example, competitive bidding in defense contracting would be affected by the predicted learning effects. The expected volume could have a dramatic influence on the unit price. The cost per airplane is typically much less if five hundred are manufactured than if only fifty are manufactured.

COSTS AND BENEFITS

The subject of estimating cost functions should be viewed from the perspective of the sensitivity of the results to the decisions. Ideally, the decision maker wants to know the "real" or "exact" impact of a variety of actions and events on costs. In most instances, that impact cannot be known with certainty. Instead the statistician or accountant estimates some cost function that is a simplification of the underlying relationships. The discussion in cost accounting books is often couched in terms of obtaining more accuracy, as if more accuracy were always desirable. But obtaining more accuracy may be too expensive relative to the benefits.

The central question is whether the resulting approximation, which is nearly

---

[9]For an illustration of how learning curves can be incorporated into standard-cost variance analysis, see D. Harvey and S. Soliman, "Standard Cost Variance Analysis in a Learning Environment," *Accounting and Business Research*, Summer 1983, pp. 181–89.

always a linear function, is good enough for the purpose at hand. The answer to that question is often difficult to establish with much confidence. Nevertheless, it is a cost-benefit question that cannot be avoided. By the very act of using the cost function, the manager has made an information decision. He or she may have faced the decision squarely and explicitly by saying, "Yes, I can use this cost function for my prediction rather than a simpler or more complicated cost function." Or the manager may have reached the same conclusion implicitly by proceeding with the given function with no questions asked. For example, when a manager uses an overhead rate of $5 per direct-labor hour as a part of the accumulation of costs for a pricing decision—even though this manager knows that overhead is affected by labor-hours, machine-hours, weight of materials, and weather conditions—he or she made an information decision. The manager has decided that the simple $5 cost function is good enough for the specific pricing decision.

SUMMARY

Predictions of how costs will behave in response to various actions usually affect many decisions. Two assumptions are widely used in cost analysis. First, linear approximations to cost functions are "good enough" for most purposes. Second, cost behavior can be explained by a single independent variable. Where these assumptions are not descriptive of the underlying cost relationship, it may be cost effective to estimate a nonlinear cost function or to include more than one independent variable.

The most difficult task in cost analysis typically is collecting "high-quality" data on the dependent and independent variables. Problems associated with the recorded costs being mismatched with the chosen independent variable(s), inflation, missing data, and outlier data observations are frequently encountered.

Approaches available to estimate cost functions include industrial engineering, account analysis, visual fit, regression analysis, and high-low. Ideally, more than one of these approaches to cost estimation should be used so that each approach serves as a check on the other approaches. The chosen cost function should satisfy both economic plausibility criteria and goodness-of-fit criteria.

PROBLEMS FOR SELF-STUDY

problem 1   Suppose a linear approximation is used for flexible budgeting, as in the accompanying graph. The "true" cost function is the nonlinear function as shown:

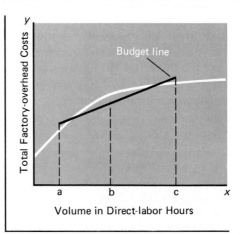

Will the flexible budget be higher or lower than what the budgeted "true" costs would be at *a*, *b*, and *c*? What are the decision implications of using the linear approximations at each point?

solution 1   Budgeted factory-overhead costs will be higher at *a* and *c*, and lower at *b*. The decision implications depend heavily on the particular situation and organization. The linear approximation may be good enough in the vast majority of cases in the sense that, for example, the more accurate approximation will not result in changing any decisions regarding pricing or choice of product lines. In terms of the credibility of budgets and their motivational effects, the use of linear approximations may influence the attitudes and beliefs of managers regarding this part of the accounting system or the system as a whole. In other words, a little inaccuracy, by itself, may be unimportant in one decision situation or with respect to one class of costs. But more accuracy may be preferable to less when the system as a whole is judged in relation to a host of decisions and attitudes that might be affected.

problem 2   Reg Gasnier is a cost analyst at Aero Construction Enterprises (ACE). The company is considering bidding on a contract for eight airplanes. A major area of uncertainty is the estimated total labor-hours to produce the eight airplanes. Gasnier observes that in the past a cumulative average-time learning model, with a 70% learning coefficient, has provided a good approximation of how labor-hours have behaved at ACE. It is estimated that the first airplane will take 50 hours of labor. How many hours of labor will it take to produce the eight airplanes?

solution 2   One approach is to use the table format illustrated on page 355 for the cumulative average-time learning model:

CUMULATIVE NUMBER OF UNITS	CUMULATIVE AVERAGE TIME PER UNIT	CUMULATIVE TOTAL TIME
1	50.00	50.00
2	35.00 (50.00 × .7)	70.00
4	24.50 (35.00 × .7)	98.00
8	17.15 (24.50 × .7)	137.20

This estimate of 137.20 hours for the eight airplanes is highly dependent on the applicability of the 70% cumulative average-time learning model to the construction of all eight airplanes.[10]

Terms to Learn

This chapter and the Glossary contain definitions of the following important terms:

controllable variable (p. 344)   *correlation (346)*   *cost estimation (341)*
cost prediction (341)   *cumulative average-time learning model (354)*
dependent variable (344)   *experience curve (353)*   *explanatory variable (344)*
high-low approach (347)   *incremental unit-time learning model (354)*
independent variable (344)   *industrial engineering approach (345)*
intercept (342)   *learning curve (353)*   *mixed cost (342)*   *parameter (342)*

---

[10]An alternative approach to estimating the cumulative average time per unit for 8 units is the formula in Exhibit 10-10. For a 70% learning curve, $b = -.5146$. Thus, with $a = 50$ and $X = 8$: $y = aX^b = 50 \times 8^{-.5146} = 17.15$, and the total time for 8 airplanes is $17.15 \times 8 = 137.20$ hours.

Special Points and Pitfalls

There are six steps in estimating a cost function: (1) choose the estimation approach, (2) choose the dependent variable, (3) choose the independent variable(s), (4) collect data on the dependent and independent variables, (5) plot the data, and (6) evaluate the estimated cost function. In most applications, the cost analyst will proceed through these steps several times before concluding that an acceptable cost function has been identified.

The major concern in the analysis of cost behavior should be how a cost fluctuates within the relevant range.

In contexts where learning is occurring, a nonlinear cost function may be appropriate. The cost analyst should (a) select a specific form of the learning curve model (cumulative average time vs. incremental unit time), and (b) estimate the learning coefficient (coefficients between 80% and 90% are often encountered).

APPENDIX: INFLATION AND COST ESTIMATION

Inflation can exist in either the dependent or independent variables in a cost function. The result is that there may not be a uniform relationship between the dependent and independent variables over time. Several approaches can be used, either individually or in combination, when inflation is encountered.

Approach 1

Deflate the variable(s) subject to inflation by an appropriate price index. Exhibit 10-13 illustrates this approach. The graph on the left side plots quarterly observations at Cybernetics Corporation of indirect manufacturing costs and machine-hours for the past nine quarters. These observations are reported in the second and third columns of Exhibit 10-14. Although a positive correlation of .75 exists between indirect manufacturing costs and machine-hours, there is considerable variation around the cost function estimated with a regression model: $y' = \$19.22 + (\$.56 \times \text{machine-hours})$.

EXHIBIT 10-13
Cost Functions and Inflation Adjustments

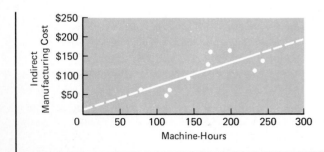
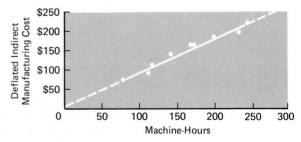

EXHIBIT 10-14
Cost Behavior at Cybernetics Corporation

QUARTER (1)	INDIRECT MANUFACTURING COSTS (2)	MACHINE HOURS (3)	INDEX OF INDUSTRY MACHINE AND MAINTENANCE COSTS (Quarter 9 = 1,000) (4)	DEFLATED INDIRECT MANUFACTURING COSTS (5) = (2) ÷ (4)
1	$ 52	110	.578	$ 90
2	113	231	.595	190
3	66	115	.601	110
4	139	242	.647	215
5	95	141	.694	137
6	130	168	.809	161
7	164	198	.913	180
8	67	76	.942	71
9	161	172	1.000	161

The fourth column of Exhibit 10-14 presents an index of industry machine construction and maintenance costs. Over these nine quarters, the index has increased 73%. The fifth column of Exhibit 10-14 presents the deflated indirect manufacturing cost series. It is calculated by dividing each indirect manufacturing cost observation in column (2) by the corresponding value of the index in column (4). Thus the deflated cost figure of $90 in quarter 1 is calculated as $52 ÷ .578 = $90. The graph on the right side of Exhibit 10-13 plots the deflated indirect manufacturing cost series against machine-hours; also presented is the cost function estimated with a regression model: $y' = \$10.64 + (\$.84 \times \text{machine-hours})$. The correlation between deflated indirect manufacturing costs and machine-hours is .98. The deflation approach has successfully controlled much of the variation around the fitted cost function that is observed when the (nominal) indirect manufacturing cost series is used.

One limitation of using the index approach in Exhibits 10-13 and 10-14 to control for inflation is that appropriate indexes may not be available for all the individual cost series used to estimate cost functions. Readily available indexes (such as the Consumer Price Index) may fail to capture adequately the price changes affecting items included in the costs of individual organizations.

Approach 2   Use observations drawn from a period with less variation in inflation. For example, instead of using the nine quarterly observations in Exhibit 10-14 (with a total inflation rate of 73%), an analyst could examine nine monthly observations covering quarters 7, 8, and 9. The total inflation rate in quarters 7, 8, and 9 is only 7%.

_____QUESTIONS, PROBLEMS, AND CASES_____

10-1 What factors must management consider in the year-to-year planning of fixed costs?

10-2 Give two examples of a mixed cost.

10-3 List six factors besides volume that can cause costs to vary.

10-4 Name three assumptions that are sufficient conditions for linearity.

10-5 List the six steps in estimating a cost function. Which step typically is the most difficult for a cost analyst?

10-6 Discuss three frequently encountered problems when collecting cost data on variables included in a cost function.

10-7 Define *learning curve*. Outline two models that can be used when incorporating learning into the estimation of cost functions.

10-8 Division of mixed costs into variable and fixed components. The controller of the Ijiri Co. wants you to approximate the fundamental variable- and fixed-cost behavior of an account called Maintenance from the following:

MONTHLY ACTIVITY IN MACHINE-HOURS	MONTHLY MAINTENANCE COSTS INCURRED
4,000	$3,000
7,000	3,900

10-9 Linear approximations. Suppose the following situation existed:

VOLUME LEVEL IN DIRECT-LABOR HOURS	TOTAL ACTUAL OVERHEAD COST BEHAVIOR
30,000	$340,000
40,000	400,000
50,000	435,000
60,000	477,000
70,000	529,000
80,000	587,000

Required

1. Compute the formula for the flexible-budget line, using only two "representative" volumes of 40,000 hours and 70,000 hours, respectively.
2. What would be the predicted cost for 50,000 labor-hours using the flexible budget developed in requirement 1? Using a nonlinear flexible budget equal to the "actual cost behavior" curve? For 80,000 hours? Plot the points and draw the flexible-budget line and the "actual cost behavior" curve.
3. The manager had a chance to accept a special order that would have boosted production from 40,000 to 50,000 hours of activity. Suppose the manager, guided by the linear flexible-budget formula, rejected a sales order that would have brought a total increase in contribution of $38,000 less the predicted increase in total overhead cost. What is the total contribution forgone?
4. If you were an operating manager responsible for budgetary control of overhead, would you regard the linear budget allowances at 50,000 hours and at 80,000 hours as too tight or too loose as compared with the nonlinear budget? Why?
5. Does the intercept of the flexible-budget line represent the fixed-overhead costs? Why?
6. In your own words, summarize the major lessons of this problem.

10-10 Various cost behavior patterns. (CPA, adapted)   Select the graph on p. 363 that matches the numbered factory-cost or expense data. You are to indicate by letter which of the graphs best fits each of the situations or items described.

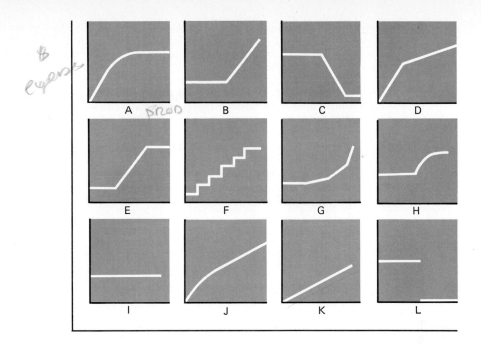

The vertical axes of the graphs represent *total* dollars of expense, and the horizontal axes represent production during a calendar year. In each case the zero point is at the intersection of the two axes. The graphs may be used more than once.

1. Depreciation of equipment, where the amount of depreciation charged is computed by the machine-hours method.
2. Electricity bill—a flat fixed charge, plus a variable cost after a certain number of kilowatt hours are used.
3. City water bill, which is computed as follows:

First 1,000,000 gallons or less	$1,000 flat fee
Next 10,000 gallons	.003 per gallon used
Next 10,000 gallons	.006 per gallon used
Next 10,000 gallons	.009 per gallon used
etc.	etc.

4. Cost of lubricant for machines, where cost per unit decreases with each pound of lubricant used (for example, if one pound is used, the cost is $10; if two pounds are used, the cost is $19.98; if three pounds are used, the cost is $29.94) with a minimum cost per pound of $9.25.
5. Depreciation of equipment, where the amount is computed by the straight-line method. When the depreciation rate was established, it was anticipated that the obsolescence factor would be greater than the wear-and-tear factor.
6. Rent on a factory building donated by the city, where the agreement calls for a fixed-fee payment unless 200,000 man-hours are worked, in which case no rent need be paid.
7. Salaries of repairpersons, where one person is needed for every 1,000 machine-hours or less (that is, 0 to 1,000 hours requires one person, 1,001 to 2,000 hours requires two people, and so forth).
8. Cost of raw materials used.
9. Rent on a factory building donated by county, where the agreement calls for rent of $100,000 less $1 for each direct-labor hour worked in excess of 200,000 hours, but minimum rental payment of $20,000 must be paid.

10-11 Matching graphs with descriptions of cost behavior. (D. Green)   Given below are a number of charts, each indicating some relationship between cost and another variable. No attempt has been made to draw these charts to any particular scale; the absolute numbers on each axis may be closely or widely spaced.

You are to indicate by number which of the charts best fits each of the situations or items described. Each situation or item is independent of all the others; all factors not stated are assumed to be irrelevant. Only one answer will be counted for any item. Some charts will be used more than once; some may not apply to any of the situations. Note that category 14, "No relationship," is not the same as 15, "Some other pattern."

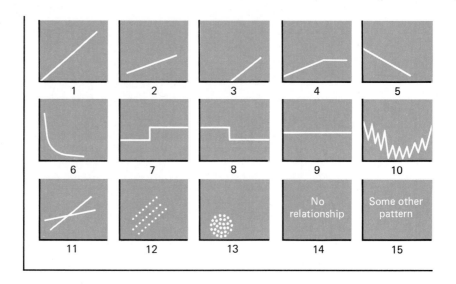

A. Taking the horizontal axis as representing the rate of activity over the year and the vertical axis as representing *total cost* or *revenue*, indicate the pattern or relationship for each of the following items:
1. Direct-material cost.
2. Federal Social Security tax, as legally assessed, per worker, with workers earning over $42,000 per year, which is the maximum subject to tax.
3. Supervisor's salaries.
4. A breakeven chart.
5. Total average unit cost.
6. Mixed costs—for example, electric power *demand charge* plus usage rate.
7. Average versus variable cost.
8. Depreciation of plant, computed on a straight-line, time basis.
9. Data supporting the use of a variable-cost rate, such as $2 per direct-labor hour.
10. Vacation pay accrued for all workers in a department or plant.
11. Data indicating that an indirect-cost rate based on the given activity measure is spurious.
12. Variable costs *per unit* of output.
13. Incentive bonus plan, operating only above some level of activity.
14. Interest charges on money borrowed to finance acquisition of plant, before any payments on principal.

B. Taking the horizontal axis as representing a *time series of weeks* during a year and the vertical axis as representing *total cost per week*, match the following items with the relationship shown by the charts:
15. Direct-labor cost under stable production.
16. Direct materials purchased in small quantities during a period of widely fluctuating prices (inventory held at zero).
17. Effect of declining production volume over the year.

18. Result of a shutdown because of vacations, a serious casualty, or complete failure of demand. The shutdown continues to the end of the year.
19. Underapplied or overapplied factory overhead, taken weekly over the year, when a volume varies widely and the cost rate is assumed to be correct.
20. Seasonal fluctuation in the use of fuel for heating the plant building over the year.

C. Taking the horizontal axis as representing a *time series of weeks or months* during a year, but the vertical axis as representing *unit-product cost* as determined by conventional methods, that is, by using indirect-cost rates, match the charts with each of the following items:

21. Upward revision during the year of the variable indirect-cost rate, because of changes in price, or other factors, expected to be permanent.
22. Indirect materials acquired for immediate use in small quantities at fluctuating prices.
23. Unusual repair charges caused by careless operation of the machinery.
24. A downward revision of the fixed indirect-cost rate because of greater volume than was anticipated; the higher volume is expected to continue over the rest of the year.

10-12 Data collection issues, use of high-low approach. Trevor Kennedy, the cost analyst at United Packaging's can manufacturing plant, is seeking to develop a cost function(s) that relates engineering support (E.S.) costs to machine-hours. These costs have two components: (1) labor (which is paid monthly) and (2) materials and parts (which are purchased from an outside vendor every three months). He collects the following monthly data from the accounting records kept at the factory:

	ENGINEERING SUPPORT: REPORTED COSTS			
MONTH	Labor	Materials and Parts	Total	MACHINE-HOURS
March	$347	$847	$1,194	30
April	521	0	521	63
May	398	0	398	49
June	355	961	1,316	38
July	473	0	473	57
August	617	0	617	73
September	245	821	1,066	19
October	487	0	487	53
November	431	0	431	42

Required

1. Present plots of the data for the following three cost functions:

Dependent Variable	Independent Variable
(i) E.S. labor costs	Machine-hours
(ii) E.S. materials and parts costs	Machine-hours
(iii) E.S. total costs	Machine-hours

Comment on the plots.

2. Compute estimates of each of the three cost functions in requirement 1 using the high-low approach.
3. Cite two factors that could explain the pattern of monthly E.S. costs for materials and parts. For each factor you cite, explain its implications for examining cost behavior patterns.

10-13 Cost behavior and budgets. (M. Strecker) The president of Shuz, Inc., summoned the vice-presidents in charge of sales and of production. Together they constructed two budgets—one optimistic, one pessimistic. These are shown in columns 1 and 2 below. The actual results are shown in column 3. The company's cost accountant was perplexed as to how to present an analysis. Consequently, he produced variances of actual against both the optimistic projection and the pessimistic projection, columns 4 and 5. Favorable variances are in parentheses.

	(1) OPTIMISTIC	(2) PESSIMISTIC	(3) ACTUAL	(4) OPTIMISTIC VARIANCE	(5) PESSIMISTIC VARIANCE
Units	200,000	75,000	135,000	65,000	(60,000)
Sales	$2,000,000	$750,000	$1,350,000	$650,000	$(600,000)
Direct material	$ 200,000	$ 75,000	$ 140,000	$ (60,000)	$ 65,000
Direct labor	400,000	150,000	285,000	(115,000)	135,000
Indirect labor	106,000	43,500	72,000	(34,000)	28,500
Maintenance	20,000	20,000	22,000	2,000	2,000
Supplies	28,000	15,500	21,000	(7,000)	5,500
Power	160,000	60,000	108,000	(52,000)	48,000
Heat	50,000	50,000	53,000	3,000	3,000
Light	7,000	4,500	5,900	(1,100)	1,400
Rent	80,000	80,000	80,000	-0-	-0-
Insurance	20,000	13,750	17,000	(3,000)	3,250

Required

The company president is baffled by the analysis. She has asked you for a more understandable performance report. In the columns below, in clear and orderly fashion, prepare a new report. Explain your work to the president. Show computations as needed.

BUDGET ITEM	BUDGET ITEM FORMULA	BUDGET REVISION	ACTUAL PERFORMANCE	VARIANCES
Units			135,000	
Sales			$1,350,000	
Direct materials			$ 140,000	
Direct labor			285,000	
(and so forth)			(and so forth)	

10-14 Planned variances, changes in labor mix. (CMA)   The Lenco Co. employs a standard-cost system as part of its cost-control program. The standard cost per unit is established at the beginning of each year. Standards are not revised during the year for any changes in material or labor inputs or in the manufacturing processes. Any revisions in standards are deferred until the beginning of the next fiscal year. However, in order to recognize such changes in the current year, the company includes planned variances in the monthly budgets prepared after such changes have been introduced.

The following labor standard was set for one of Lenco's products effective July 1, 19_1, the beginning of the fiscal year:

Class I labor	4 hrs.	@ $ 6.00	$24.00
Class II labor	3 hrs.	@ 7.50	22.50
Class V labor	1 hr.	@ 11.50	11.50
Standard labor cost per 100 units			$58.00

The standard was based on the quality of material that had been used in prior years and what was expected to be available for the 19_1–_2 fiscal year. The labor activity is performed by a team consisting of four persons with Class I skills, three persons with Class II skills, and one person with Class V skills. This is the most economical combination for the company's processing system.

The manufacturing operations occurred as expected during the first five months of the year. The standard costs contributed to effective cost control during this period. However, there were indications that changes in the operations would be required in the last half of the year. The company had received a significant increase in orders for delivery in the spring. There were an inadequate number of skilled workers available to meet the increased production. As a result, the production teams, beginning in January, would be made up of more Class I labor and less Class II labor than the standard required. The teams would consist of six Class I persons, two Class II persons, and one Class V person. This labor team would be less efficient than the normal team. The reorganized teams work more slowly, so that only 90 units are produced in the same time period that 100 units would normally be produced. No raw materials will be lost as a result of the change in the labor mix. Completed units have never been rejected in the final inspection process as a consequence of faulty work; this situation is expected to continue.

In addition, Lenco was notified by its material supplier that a lower-quality material would be supplied after January 1. One unit of raw material normally is required for each good unit produced. Lenco and its supplier estimated that 5% of the units manufactured would be rejected upon final inspection due to defective material. Normally, no units are lost due to defective material.

Required

1. How much of the lower-quality material must be entered into production in order to produce 42,750 units of good production in January with the new labor teams? Show your calculations.
2. How many hours of each class of labor will be needed to produce 42,750 good units from the material input? Show your calculations.
3. What amount should be included in the January budget for the planned labor variance due to the labor team and material changes? What amount of this planned labor variance can be associated with (1) the material change and (2) the team change? Show your calculations. *Hint:* Planned or budgeted variances are discussed on page 196.

10-15 Guaranteed minimum wages and cost behavior patterns. The Lavin Company had a contract with a labor union that guaranteed a minimum wage of $2,000 payable monthly to direct laborers with at least twelve years' service. One hundred workers currently qualified for such coverage. All direct-labor employees are paid $20 per hour.

The budget for 19_1 was based on the usage of 400,000 hours of direct labor, a total of $8,000,000. Of this amount, $2,400,000 (100 workers × $2,000 × 12 months) was regarded as fixed.

Data on performance for the first three months of 19_1 follow:

	JANUARY	FEBRUARY	MARCH
Direct-labor hours actually worked	22,000	32,000	42,000
Standard direct-labor hours allowed*	22,000	32,000	42,000
Direct-labor costs budgeted	$508,000	$648,000	$788,000
Direct-labor costs incurred	440,000	640,000	840,000
Variance (U = unfavorable; F = favorable)	68,000 F	8,000 F	52,000 U

*Note that perfect efficiency is being assumed.

The factory manager was perplexed by the results, which showed favorable variances when production was low and unfavorable variances when production was high. He felt that his control over labor costs was consistently good.

Required

1. Why did the variances arise? Use amounts and diagrams, as necessary, to explain.
2. Assume that only 5,000 standard and actual hours were utilized in a given month and that all of the most senior workers were used. Does this direct-labor budget provide a basis for evaluating direct-labor performance? What variances would arise under the approach used in requirement 1? What variances would arise under the approach you recommend?
3. Suppose 5,500 actual hours of input were used but only 5,000 standard hours were allowed for the work accomplished. What variances would arise under the approach used in requirement 1? Under the approach you recommend?

10-16 Operation costing and setup costs. Variances may be computed in various levels of detail. The following is an excerpt from a company's cost accounting manual:

Setup costs as an element of the standard product costs are to be separated from the other costs. Standard setup times are to be established for each part and a standard setup cost based on applicable cost rates for labor and overhead calculated.

Recognizing setup costs on a per-piece basis requires a standard lot size (the number of pieces that are expected to run through the machine before the setup is changed). The standard lot sizes are to be established by the production control department. The standard setup cost per piece will be calculated by dividing the standard lot size into the applicable standard setup costs.

Production runs varying from the standard lot size will create a lot size variance, as follows:

$$\text{Lot size variance} = \text{Standard setup cost} \times \left(\frac{\text{Actual run size} - \text{Standard lot size}}{\text{Standard lot size}} \right)$$

Lot size variance is to be calculated only in the primary cost centers. If an alternating routing is used, lot size variance will not be calculated but will create an alternate routing variance. The following example illustrates the lot size variance calculation.

Part number:	0109306	
Actual run size:	500 pieces	
Standard lot size:	1,000 pieces	

COST CENTER	OPERATION DESCRIPTION	STANDARD DIRECT-LABOR HOURS ALLOWED PER SETUP	STANDARD RATES PER SETUP HOUR			STANDARD OPERATION COST PER PIECE		
			Direct Labor	Factory Overhead	Total	Direct Labor	Factory Overhead	Total
411	MAM Lathe	24.00	$20.88	$19.12	$40.00	$.125	$.115	$.24

Required | Compute the lot size variance. Construct an appropriate journal entry that would identify the lot size variance. *Hint:* Setup costs are discussed on page 201.

10-17 Cost estimation, cumulative average-time learning curve. The Nautilus Company, which is under contract to the navy, assembles submarines. As part of its research program, it completes the assembly of the first of a new model (PT109) of submarines. The navy is impressed with the PT109. It requests that Nautilus submit a proposal on the cost of producing another seven PT109s.

The accounting department at Nautilus reports the following cost information for the first PT109 assembled by Nautilus:

Direct materials	$100,000
Direct labor (10,000 hours @ $30)	300,000
Tooling cost*	50,000
Variable overhead†	200,000
Other overhead‡	75,000
	$725,000

*Tooling can be reused, even though all of its cost was assigned to the first submarine.

†Variable-overhead incurrence is directly affected by direct-labor hours; a rate of $20 per hour is used for purposes of bidding on contracts.

‡Other overhead is assigned at a flat rate of 25% of direct-labor cost for purposes of bidding on contracts.

Nautilus uses an 85% cumulative average-time learning curve as a basis for forecasting direct-labor hours on its assembling operations. (An 85% learning curve implies $b = -.2345$.)

Required Prepare a prediction of the total expected costs for producing the seven PT109s for the navy. (Nautilus will keep the first submarine produced, costed at $725,000, as a demonstration model for other potential purchasers.)

10-18 Cost estimation, incremental unit-time learning curve. Assume the same information for the Nautilus Company as that in Problem 10-17 with one exception. This exception is that Nautilus uses an 85% incremental unit-time learning curve as a basis for forecasting direct-labor hours on its assembling operations.

Required Prepare a prediction of the total expected costs for producing the seven PT109s for the navy. If you solved Problem 10-17, compare your cost prediction there with the one you made here.

10-19 Make or buy, relevant costs, cumulative average-time learning curve. The Oceanic Exploration Company has, in the past, purchased oil rigs from McDermont Inc. The price has increased considerably in recent years and has reached $800,000 per rig for the coming year. Oceanic will require eight new oil rigs (one every six weeks) in the forthcoming year. The production manager at Oceanic proposes that the oil rigs be assembled internally. He notes that the space necessary for the assembling is readily available and would otherwise remain idle. The equipment necessary for the assembling is already available at Oceanic. The incremental depreciation on the plant and equipment (due to the extra wear and tear from producing the oil rigs) will be adequately covered by the variable-overhead rate of 250% of the combined assembly and supervisory labor cost.

One extra production manager would be required at a total annual compensation package of $60,000; this manager could supervise the assembly workers who are paid an hourly rate ($40 per hour including benefits). This production manager could supervise the assembling of up to twelve oil rigs each year; one rig could be assembled every four weeks. No change in general and administrative costs is anticipated. The fixed factory overhead represents a lease payment under a long-term lease agreement. The space leased will not be used elsewhere if the rigs are purchased from McDermont Inc.

The engineering and accounting departments of Oceanic estimate the total cost of assembling each oil rig internally to be $1,806,200. It was recommended that Oceanic continue purchasing the oil rigs from McDermont.

Cost Estimate For Each Oil Rig

Components (outside purchases)	$ 130,000
Assembly labor (7,500 hours at $40 per hour)	300,000
Supervisory labor	60,000
Factory overhead*	1,152,000
General and administrative overhead†	164,200
	$1,806,200

*Factory overhead is applied on the basis of "labor cost," defined as the combined assembly and supervisory labor cost:

Fixed factory overhead	70% of "labor cost"
Variable factory overhead	250% of "labor cost"
Factory overhead rate	320% of "labor cost"

†General and administrative overhead is applied at 10% of the total costs of production.

Required 1. Evaluate the cost analysis done by the engineering and accounting departments. Do you agree with their recommendation to continue using McDermont as the oil rig supplier?

2. Assume Oceanic could experience assembly labor-hour improvements on each oil rig consistent with an 80% cumulative average-time learning curve. Oceanic will require eight new oil rigs in the forthcoming year. Should Oceanic reconsider its decision to purchase oil rigs from its outside supplier, McDermont? Explain your answer.

10-20 Make or buy, incremental unit-time learning curve. Assume the same information for the Oceanic Exploration Company as that in Problem 10-19 with one exception. The exception is that Oceanic expects an 80% incremental unit-time learning curve to describe labor-hour improvements during the assembly of the eight new oil rigs in the forthcoming year.

Required | Should Oceanic assemble the rigs itself or purchase them from McDermont? Explain your answer.

10-21 Cost predictions, incremental unit-time learning curve, and pricing. Piper Corporation is an aircraft manufacturer. One of its specialties is the manufacture of small planes that have a low level of demand. Its Aerojoy division is currently developing a new type of aircraft for which the demand is predicted to range between 20 and 30 units. The actual demand will be determined by both the ultimate aircraft characteristics and, more importantly, the aircraft price.

Aerojoy has already spent $3 million on developing and testing the new technology that the aircraft will utilize. It is also constructing a new $2 million specialized production facility, which would become totally obsolete after production of the planes is completed. The engineering department has predicted that an additional $1 million will have to be spent on further development and testing before the aircraft is ready for production. Piper Corporation's accounting policy is to capitalize all development and equipment costs until production actually starts.

The division has made detailed predictions of the aircraft's production costs. These predictions have proven to be extremely accurate on previous projects of this type. All the aircraft parts requirements are subcontracted for fabrication. Aerojoy has already contracted for parts for twenty aircraft, which will cost $300,000 per aircraft. These contracts have a provision for parts for an additional ten aircraft, at a 10% decrease in cost per aircraft on these additional ten aircraft.

Direct labor is the most significant element of production costs. Labor costs are substantial in an absolute sense. A $40-per-hour rate (including benefits) is paid to workers. The direct-labor hours required to assemble the first plane are 20,000. An 80% incremental unit-time learning curve, found to be descriptive of labor-hours behavior on production runs for past projects, is believed to apply to the current project. The predicted labor-hours for each additional plane (m), and the cumulative total time for the manufacture of up to thirty planes, are (based on the formula $m = aX^b$, where $a = 20,000$ and $b = -.3219$):

PLANES MANUFACTURED	INDIVIDUAL LABOR-HOURS FOR XTH UNIT	CUMULATIVE TOTAL LABOR-HOURS	PLANES MANUFACTURED	INDIVIDUAL LABOR-HOURS FOR XTH UNIT	CUMULATIVE TOTAL LABOR-HOURS
1	20,000	20,000	16	8,192	178,410
2	16,000	36,000	17	8,034	186,444
3	14,043	50,043	18	7,888	194,332
4	12,800	62,843	19	7,752	202,084
5	11,913	74,756	20	7,625	209,709
6	11,234	85,990	21	7,506	217,215
7	10,690	96,680	22	7,394	224,609
8	10,240	106,920	23	7,289	231,898
9	9,860	116,780	24	7,190	239,088
10	9,531	126,311	25	7,096	246,184
11	9,243	135,554	26	7,007	253,191
12	8,988	144,542	27	6,923	260,114
13	8,759	153,301	28	6,842	266,956
14	8,552	161,853	29	6,765	273,721
15	8,365	170,218	30	6,692	280,413

The general manager and the controller of the Aerojoy division use these data as a basis for predicting costs and setting unit selling prices for the aircraft. They decide that the fixed costs applicable to the program that must be recovered include $6 million plus whatever incremental general and administrative costs are incurred. Their prediction of the latter is $750,000 if twenty planes are assembled and $900,000 if thirty planes are assembled.

Required

1. What price must be set to break even, assuming twenty planes are sold? Assuming thirty planes are sold?
2. Suppose Aerojoy sets a price of $1.2 million per plane. This price has produced orders for twenty planes. The marketing department now reports that a potential new customer will purchase ten planes, but only if the price is $1 million or less. This price reduction would have to be made retroactive and applied to all customers. Should Aerojoy accept the new order?

10-22 Cost predictions, cumulative average-time learning curve, and pricing. Assume the same information as that for the Aerojoy division of Piper Corporation in Problem 10-21, with one exception. The exception is that Aerojoy predicts that an 80% cumulative average-time learning curve will describe the behavior of labor-hours as production of the new aircraft is increased.

Required

What price must be set to break even, assuming twenty planes are sold? Assuming thirty planes are sold?

10-23 Standards in hospital. Some management consultants have developed standards for the clerical work force in a large local hospital. Some estimates of overhead behavior also were developed. The standard variable-overhead rate per billing in the billing department was $.12. Five bills per hour is regarded as standard productivity per billing clerk. The actual total overhead incurred was $97,000, of which $70,000 was fixed. There were no variances for fixed overhead. The variable-overhead spending variance was $3,000, favorable. The variable-overhead budget variance was $600, favorable.

Required

Compute (1) variable-overhead efficiency variance, (2) actual hours of input, and (3) standard hours allowed for output achieved.

10-24 Nonlinear costs. See the preceding problem. Suppose that cost studies had developed the following approximation for relating overhead to labor-hours (L):

$$\text{Total overhead} = \$68{,}000 + \$.40L + \$30\sqrt{L}$$

Required

If this cost function was used as a flexible-budget formula (instead of the linear budget used in the preceding problem), what would be the efficiency variance in this case? (Round your square root to the nearest hour.)

10-25 Inflation adjustments, use of high-low approach. (See Appendix 10) Paul Sellinger is examining cost behavior patterns at the Jos. Schlitz Brewing Company. He collects the following information covering the most recent ten-year period.

YEAR	REPORTED COST OF SALES (millions)	BARRELS SOLD (millions)	WHOLESALE PRICE INDEX OF BEER (Year 10 = 1.000)
1	$ 594	16.7	.611
2	686	18.9	.612
3	783	21.3	.623
4	922	22.7	.719
5	1,047	23.3	.759
6	1,102	24.2	.769
7	1,073	22.1	.794
8	1,047	19.6	.848
9	1,050	16.8	.933
10	998	15.0	1.000

The cost of sales is an aggregate of cost items such as labor, raw materials (malt, corn, barley, hops, etc.), and depreciation. The wholesale price index of beer is calculated at the brewing industry level and is based on the price at which wholesalers sell a barrel of beer to retail outlets.

1. Plot the relationship between reported cost of sales and barrels sold over this period. What patterns are apparent in the data?
2. Use the high-low approach to compute the cost function relating cost of sales to barrels sold. Comment on the representativeness of the two points used to estimate the cost function with the high-low approach.
3. Use the wholesale price index of beer to deflate reported cost of sales of Schlitz each year. Plot the relationship between deflated cost of sales and barrels sold over this period.
4. Use the high-low approach to compute the cost function relating deflated cost of sales to barrels sold. Compare the cost function with that calculated in requirement 2.
5. What alternatives to the use of the wholesale price index of beer might Sellinger consider to minimize any problems that inflation causes when estimating cost functions?

11

Systems Choice: Discretionary and Nonmanufacturing Costs

Criteria for Judging Systems • Engineered, Discretionary, and Committed Costs •
Control of Discretionary Costs • Promoting Efficiency and Effectiveness in a Discretionary-Cost Center •
Budgeting for Discretionary Costs • Nonmanufacturing Work Measurement •
Budgeting of Nonmanufacturing Costs •
Efficiency and Effectiveness Measures for a Personnel Department •
Appendix: More on Systems Choice and the Organization Behavior Literature

This chapter begins with an overview of how management control systems should be chosen. It then compares various budgetary techniques. Special focus is on discretionary and nonmanufacturing costs, particularly those costs that are significant in service industries and nonprofit organizations.

Behavioral issues are central to cost and management accounting. Managers and accountants do not choose a particular system in the abstract. Sooner or later, the question of how the collective set of decisions in an organization will be affected by the choice of a particular information system must be considered. Often there will not be a pat answer, or in some cases even a systematic method of studying the question.

When examining an organization, we choose the "rational approach" as our point of departure. A key assumption in this approach is that both individuals and organizations are goal-oriented in their behavior; decisions of individuals and organizations aim to maximize the attainment of these goals.

CRITERIA FOR JUDGING SYSTEMS

Executives and accountants often judge management control systems using technical considerations such as characteristics of data processing and vulnerability to fraud. However, a broader focus is preferable. **Systems exist primarily to improve** the collective decisions within an organization. Because decisions entail human behavior, our emphasis rightly belongs on human rather than technical considerations.

Cost, congruence, effort

What is a useful starting point for judging a control system? *Obtain a specification of top management's goals for the organization as a whole.* To keep our focus manageable, assume that organization goals either are given or can be determined. An observer may disagree with the goals specified by top management, but a control system should be judged in light of how well it helps achieve a given set of goals. For example, the main goal might be maximization of short-run income, a goal regarded as unworthy by many; nevertheless, if top management chooses such a goal, the system should be appraised in relation to it.

The primary criterion for judging System A versus System B is cost-benefit. Control systems are commodities. They benefit an organization by helping collective decision making. They cost money. The system with the largest favorable difference between benefits and costs should be chosen. Determining benefits and costs of individual systems can be an imposing task. Two secondary criteria useful in making the cost-benefit criterion more concrete are *goal congruence* and *effort.*

Goal congruence *exists when individuals and groups aim at the organization goals desired by top management.* Congruence is obtained when managers, working in their own perceived best interests, make decisions that further the overall goals of top management.[1]

Effort *is defined here as exertion toward a goal.* Effort is not confined to its common meaning of a worker producing at a faster rate; it embraces all conscientious actions (such as watching or waiting) that accompany the behavior of individuals. This effort can be guided toward the attainment of tangible goals such as dollars, cars, and clothing, or intangible items such as fun, self-esteem, and power.

Motivation

Considered together, goal congruence and effort are really subparts of *motivation:*

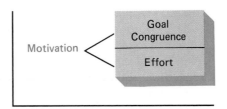

Motivation is the desire for a selected goal (the goal congruence aspect) together with the resulting drive or pursuit (the effort aspect) toward that goal.

Goal congruence and effort are often reinforcing aspects of motivation, but each can exist without the other. Thus a manager can share an organization goal of reaching a target sales level or a product quality level. But the manager may pursue such goals unenthusiastically. Similarly, a manager may pursue a personal

---

[1]The notion that individuals are guided by their own self-interest is viewed as objectionable by some. Terms such as *selfish* and *self-centered* are used to describe such behavior. It is not the job of the system designer to pass judgment on the motivations of individuals, but rather to predict how they will behave as changes are made in the management control system.

goal, such as playing golf instead of working, with great effort that is incongruent with organization goals.

In summary, the primary criterion is cost-benefit. To apply that criterion, the motivational effects of System A versus System B deserve center attention. Why? Because the measurement of benefits requires consideration of how individuals will be motivated by each system under evaluation. The task of the information system designer is more ill-structured, more complex, and more affected by human behavior than many people realize. *There is a strong link between the seemingly foreign ideas of motivation and the design of accounting systems, even though the relationship may initially appear farfetched.* (There is truth in the comment that "a successful controller earns a Ph.D. in psychology merely by engaging in the profession.")

<table>
<tr><td>

Formal and informal control systems

</td><td>

The formal control system of an organization includes those explicit rules, procedures, performance evaluation measures, and incentive systems that guide the behavior of its managers and employees. The management accounting system is one of several information systems that collectively constitute a formal control system. For example, other information systems pertain to employee relations, production quality, and compliance with environmental regulations.

The informal control system includes aspects not included in the formal control system. Examples are the shared values, loyalties, and mutual commitments among members of the organization (or subsets thereof), and the unwritten norms about acceptable behavior for promotion. Companies have developed slogans, readily understandable to individuals in diverse parts of the organization, to reinforce these values and loyalties; for example, "IBM means service" and "At Ford, Quality is Job 1."[2]

Most control systems will include both quantitative and qualitative components. The mix between the two components can vary considerably. Moreover, what appears, on the surface, as a heavily quantitative approach may actually operate differently in practice. Some multinational companies place such heavy emphasis on foreign subsidiaries meeting financial targets that the phrase "managing by the numbers" is used to describe their control systems. However, a closer examination may reveal a policy of frequent rotating of senior managers across different countries. In addition, there may be frequent visits by headquarters' management to the foreign affiliates. By this rotation and visiting process, and the use of meetings, top management may convey many of the qualitative aspects of the control system that (at first glance) appear to receive little emphasis.[3]

</td></tr>
<tr><td>

Importance of informal systems

</td><td>

Even if personal goals agree with organization goals, the formal management control system may be dominated by an informal system. Many executives, including top managers, rely on rules of thumb and accumulated experience rather than on the output of formal systems such as accounting reports. This method often proves satisfactory because the executives are evaluating the information wisely and are making decisions that keep their companies competitive.

As companies grow, however, managers become more dependent on formal

</td></tr>
</table>

---

[2]A sizable literature has explored the role of shared values and loyalties in much detail. See the studies in P. Frost, L. Moore, M. Louis, C. Lundberg, and J. Martin, *Organizational Culture* (Beverly Hills, Calif.: Sage Publications, 1985).

[3]Y. Doz and C. Prahalad, "Headquarters Influence and Strategic Control in MNCs," *Sloan Management Review,* Fall 1981, pp. 15–29.

rather than informal information systems. A formal system provides a crutch for the orderly succession of management. Large companies, with mobile executives who typically move frequently, must have such a system; after all, most managers do not have thirty years of experience as a basis for their decisions.

A prime challenge for systems designers is to discover whether some or all of the informal information system is leading to successful decisions. If so, the designer should attempt to formalize those parts of the informal system. For example, the formal system should aim at incorporating the key numbers or events that a manager may be monitoring informally. Consider pricing decisions. The data compiled by the formal system may be ignored when setting prices because the manager's experience and understanding of industry or economic data are the keys to decisions. The designer should then try to crystallize the manager's decision model explicitly so that the critical data may be supplied by the formal system. In this way, the formal system can become the key information system, can engender sincere top-management support, and can ease the tasks of management succession as promotions, transfers, and turnovers occur. Hence collective decisions are likely to be improved.

This book emphasizes one part of the formal control system, the cost and management accounting system, in much detail. However, the accounting system is only one of many sources of information for managers. The importance of cost accounting depends on many factors, including the stage of development of the system and of the organization, and on the managerial style of the key senior managers (see Chapter 25).

System goals, individual behavior, and risk sharing

Individuals behave in relation to their own personal goals, as well as in relation to the formal and informal control systems. Clearly, it is not enough for the control system simply to specify subgoals so that they harmonize with top-management goals. Ideally, management should also design the system to lead the individual managers toward *acceptance* of those subgoals as their own personal goals. For example, how important is attainment of a budget prediction? If managers view attainment as important (because they believe it says "I am competent"), and if accounting feedback is regarded as the most important source on whether attainment is achieved, the budget will be a crucial part of the control system.

What is the role of risk in the design of systems?[4] The potential of bearing risk changes behavior. For instance, if you suddenly realize that you have not paid your annual auto insurance premium, you will undoubtedly drive your car more cautiously. Indeed, you may decide not to drive the car at all until the premium is paid.

To further illustrate how different risk-sharing arrangements can change behavior, consider an accounting firm with offices in many different cities. Assume that the executive committee in New York has decided that the firm's best long-run interest calls for aggressively seeking banking industry clients. Suppose a Milwaukee bank seeks competitive bids for its audit. The Milwaukee managing partner of the accounting firm may agree with the firm's goal but may be unwilling to make a competitive bid for the audit. The internal cost to the Milwaukee office of preparing a bid is $20,000. The partner views the likelihood of winning the audit engagement to be no more than one in four, even if a billing rate 10% below its normal

---

[4]A very active line of research is examining this topic. See the studies discussed in M. Namazi, "Theoretical Developments of Principal-Agent Employment Contract in Accounting: The State of the Art," *Journal of Accounting Literature*, Spring 1985, pp. 113–63.

rate is bid. How can the executive committee encourage the Milwaukee office to take the one-in-four chance of winning the new audit client?

The executive committee in New York can take several steps to reduce the risks facing the Milwaukee office. For example, it could:

1. Fully reimburse the Milwaukee office for the $20,000 cost of preparing the bid, irrespective of whether it is awarded the audit engagement
2. Award the Milwaukee office its normal billing rate via a subsidy, even though the actual billing rate to the banking client is below normal

The effect of items 1 and 2 is to shift a major portion of the risks of bidding on the audit engagement from the Milwaukee office to the accounting firm as a whole. Ideally, the control system should encourage the local partner to accept or avoid the risks as desired by top management.

General guidelines

A favorite pastime of accountants, managers, and professors regarding management control systems is fault finding. But the heart of judging a system is not in assessing its degree of imperfection. The central question should be, *How can the existing system, with all its imperfections, be improved?* A system exists to help managers in their collective making of decisions in organizations. **Top managers should predict how System A will affect the collective actions of managers in comparison with System B. To make such predictions, managers must be conscious of the likely motivational effects (goal congruence and managerial effort) of systems.**

Many influential variables, such as organizational structure and management style, affect a system. Hence the most desirable system greatly depends on the specific organization. What is good for Organization A may be bad for Organization B. The influential variables are dynamic. Therefore many aspects of a system may be changed through time. What is good in the late 1980s may be bad in the early 1990s.

Chapters 25 and 26 contain additional discussion of how influential variables can affect the choice of management control systems.

ENGINEERED, DISCRETIONARY, AND COMMITTED COSTS

The general guidelines of cost-benefit and motivation can help management make intelligent choices among systems. We now explore some more concrete avenues for exercising control. Exhibit 11-1 presents three categories of costs that have

EXHIBIT 11-1
Types of Cost

TYPE OF COST	HORIZON FOR PLANNING AND FEEDBACK	MAJOR ACCOUNTING TECHNIQUES FOR CONTROL
1. Engineered	Short	Flexible budgets and standards
2. Discretionary	Longer	Negotiated static budgets
3. Committed	Longest	Capital expenditure budgets

377

differences in the time horizon for planning and feedback, as well as in the techniques used for their control.

Engineered costs

Engineered costs are costs that result specifically from a clearcut measured relationship between inputs and outputs. This relationship is usually personally observable and is established by work measurement. Examples are direct-material costs, energy costs, and many labor costs.

The major accounting techniques for controlling engineered costs are flexible budgets and standards. Chapters 5 through 8 provide a detailed discussion of these techniques. The feedback time is short. For example, direct-material waste may be monitored as each unit is produced.

Discretionary costs

Discretionary costs (sometimes called **managed costs** or **programmed costs**) are costs that (1) arise from periodic (usually yearly) appropriation decisions regarding the maximum amounts to be incurred and (2) have no well specified function relating inputs (as measured by the costs) and outputs (as measured by revenue or other objectives such as students' knowledge or patients' health). Examples include advertising, public relations, executive training, teaching, research, health care, and management consulting services.

The most noteworthy aspect of discretionary costs is that one is seldom confident that the "correct" amount is being spent. One is unsure of how much is enough. Subsequent sections of this chapter discuss techniques used to control discretionary costs.

Committed costs

Committed costs are costs that arise from having property, plant, equipment, and a functioning organization. The capital expenditure budget is the principal accounting technique for control. The planning horizon is long, as is the feedback time. Examples of such costs are depreciation, property taxes, insurance, and long-term lease rentals. There can often be a high level of uncertainty about the benefits or cash inflows associated with such long-term capital expenditure decisions.

Chapters 19 and 20 outline formal decision models (such as discounted cash flow) used to assist managers' choices. Committed costs are relatively difficult to influence by short-run actions. These costs are affected primarily by long-run sales forecasts that, in turn, indicate the long-run capacity targets. Hence careful long-range planning, rather than day-to-day monitoring, is the key to managing committed costs.

Once a building has been erected and equipment has been installed, little can be done in day-to-day operations to affect the *total level* of committed costs. From a control standpoint, the objective is usually to increase current utilization of facilities because this will ordinarily increase net income.

CONTROL OF DISCRETIONARY COSTS

Exhibit 11-2 compares engineered costs with discretionary costs. The exhibit focuses on the following characteristics:

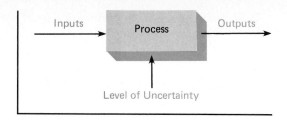

Inputs → Process → Outputs

↑ Level of Uncertainty

EXHIBIT 11-2
Comparison of Engineered and Discretionary Costs*

CHARACTERISTIC	ENGINEERED COST	DISCRETIONARY COST
1. Primary inputs	Physical and human resources	Human resources
2. Process	a. Detailed and physically observable	a. Black box (because knowledge of process is sketchy or unavailable)
	b. Repetitive	b. Often nonrepetitive or nonroutine
3. Primary outputs	a. Products or quantifiable services	a. Information
	b. Value easy to determine	b. Value difficult to determine
	c. Quality easy to ascertain	c. Quality difficult to ascertain
4. Level of uncertainty	Moderate or small (e.g., production setting)	Great (e.g., marketing, lawsuit, research settings)

*This exhibit is a modification of one suggested by H. Itami.

As Exhibit 11-2 indicates, the primary inputs that affect engineered costs are both physical and human resources. Examples are materials and labor. In contrast, the primary inputs that affect discretionary costs are human resources. Examples are salaries and fees paid for professional services rendered by people inside or outside the organization.

Exhibit 11-2 shows how processes that are detailed, repetitive, and personally observable are main candidates for using engineered-cost techniques. In contrast, discretionary costs are associated with processes that are sometimes labeled as *black boxes*. The latter can be defined as processes that are not easily understood. Knowledge of the precise process may be sketchy, unmeasurable, or unavailable. Examples include activities like executive education, public relations, and research and development.

The contrast between engineered and discretionary costs is also evident when outputs are considered. *In particular, Exhibit 11-2 points out that the outputs linked with many discretionary-cost centers are types of information.* Examples are oral or written reports or advice from various accounting, legal, marketing, personnel, and research staffs. Value and quality are much more difficult to ascertain for discretionary costs than for engineered costs.

The level of uncertainty also helps determine whether a cost may be engineered or discretionary. *Uncertainty* is defined here as the possibility that an actual amount will deviate from an expected amount. The degree of uncertainty may be small or large, depending on whether the relationship between inputs and outputs is highly predictable. The exploration budget of a natural resource company is a classic example of a discretionary cost. There is a high level of uncertainty about the relationship between the spending of $10 million on exploring for oil or natural gas in a high-risk frontier area and the discovery of a particular amount of crude oil or natural gas.[5]

Engineered costs are more likely to be found in manufacturing settings than in nonmanufacturing settings. It is much easier to specify that three kilograms of material will be necessary to produce a finished product than to specify that a twelve-hour training program in communications skills will be necessary to produce a supervisor who can communicate well.

PROMOTING EFFICIENCY AND EFFECTIVENESS IN A DISCRETIONARY-COST CENTER

Exhibit 11-3 outlines eight approaches that are used in varying combinations to promote the *efficiency* or *effectiveness* with which costs are managed in discretionary-cost centers.[6] Chapter 6 gave the following definitions of these two key concepts:

- *Efficiency*—the relationship between inputs used and outputs obtained. The fewer the inputs used to obtain a given output, the greater the efficiency.
- *Effectiveness*—the attainment of a predetermined goal.

This chapter examines the first two approaches in Exhibit 11-3. The use of budgets to promote efficiency and effectiveness is discussed in the next three sections of this chapter. The use of financial and nonfinancial measures to promote efficiency and effectiveness in a personnel department is discussed in the final section.

Subsequent chapters of this textbook cover topics related to several other approaches in Exhibit 11-3. Organization design and the competitive forces of the market are discussed in Chapter 25. Rewards for performance are covered in Chapter 26.

Several of the approaches in Exhibit 11-3—leadership, administrative approval mechanisms, and organization culture—typically use little accounting information. This in no way diminishes their importance. Indeed, leadership is likely to be the single most important approach of the eight listed in Exhibit 11-3. However, it is dangerous to rely on leadership alone. Leaders can resign and join a competitor, can be transferred within the organization, or can have a heart attack and be unable to work for an extended period of time.

---

[5]Diamond Shamrock made the following comment relating to a $194 million write-off for an exploration venture in which it was a copartner: "The past year we joined with some of the nation's leading oil companies in drilling an unusually promising high-stakes exploratory well off the North Slope of Alaska. . . . The Alaskan Exploratory Venture demonstrated the risk and the potential of frontier exploration: The well encountered a vast reservoir which once held possibly billions of barrels of oil. However, the reservoir lacked an essential geologic feature—a trapping mechanism to seal the oil in place—allowing the oil to leak out long ago. It was a dry hole."

[6]Exhibit 11-3 draws on research studies of many different types of discretionary-cost centers. Examples include N. Lothian, *How Companies Manage R & D* (London: Institute of Cost and Management Accountants, 1984); and K. Merchant, "Organizational Control and Discretionary Program Decision Making: A Field Study," *Accounting, Organizations and Society,* 10, No. 1 (1985), pp. 67–85.

EXHIBIT 11-3

Approaches to Promoting and Monitoring
The Efficiency or Effectiveness of Discretionary-Cost Centers

TYPE OF APPROACH	EXAMPLES
1. Detailed analysis when preparing financial budgets	• Government departments using zero-base budgeting
2. Monitoring financial and non-financial indicators of efficiency or effectiveness on an ongoing basis	• University departments monitoring input success indicators (e.g., the ratio of student acceptances to offers of admission made) or output success indicators (e.g., the starting salaries of graduates) • Supervisor in a warehouse using work-measurement standards, e.g., number of trucks loaded each day
3. Organization design	• Keeping corporate (headquarters) functions to a minimum by, for example, allowing each division to have its own computer service center that reports to the president of the division rather than to a vice-president of computer services at headquarters
4. Exposing discretionary-cost centers to competitive forces of the market place	• Prices charged to divisions for company-run executive development programs being limited by the prices charged by external programs • Divisions of a company being given the option to purchase computer services or legal services from outside firms
5. Rewards for performance	• "Fraction of the action" programs, e.g., (1) R & D staff having a percentage of the operating profits associated with the commercial development of their R & D activity, and (2) exploration geologists having a percentage of the revenues from the proved oil and gas reserves they discover
6. Leadership	• Head of a project team in an advertising agency being a charismatic and creative individual who promotes a high team spirit and a willingness in team members to work long productive hours
7. Administrative approval mechanisms	• Detailed approval procedures for the hiring of new personnel, upgrading of classifications, or working of overtime
8. Promotion of organization culture	• High-technology firms promoting shared norms of strong loyalty and a commitment to technological leadership • "New ideas" programs in which much publicity is given to individuals with innovative ideas

BUDGETING FOR DISCRETIONARY COSTS

The most common accounting technique for controlling discretionary costs is a **negotiated static budget**. This is a budget in which a fixed amount of costs is appropriated based on negotiations at the start of the budget period.

Negotiated static budgets can be classified as ordinary incremental, priority incremental, and zero-base. Each will be discussed in turn.

Ordinary incremental budgets consider the previous period's budget and actual results. The budget amount is then changed in accordance with experience during the previous period and expectations for the next period. This is the most popular type of negotiated static budget. For instance, a budget for a research department might be increased because of salary raises, the addition of personnel, and the introduction of a new project.

Priority incremental budgets are similar to incremental budgets, with the addition of a description of what incremental activities or changes would occur, first, if the budget were increased by, say, 10% and, second, if the budget were decreased by a similar percentage. In this way, superiors can better ensure goal congruence because they can check their own priorities against those of subordinates. Furthermore, the act of establishing some priorities forces the manager to think more carefully and concretely about operations. In a way, priority budgeting can be considered a simple and economical compromise between ordinary incremental budgeting and zero-base budgeting.

Zero-base budgeting (ZBB) is budgeting from the ground up as though the budget were being initiated for the first time. ZBB gets at bedrock questions by requiring managers to take and document the following major steps:

1. Determine objectives, operations, and costs of all activities under the manager's jurisdiction.
2. Explore alternative means of conducting each activity.
3. Evaluate alternative budget amounts for various levels of effort for each activity.
4. Establish measures of workload and performance.
5. Rank all activities in the order of their importance to the organization.

Many of the issues that arise in using ordinary incremental and priority incremental budgets were discussed in Chapter 5. We now discuss issues that arise in using ZBB.

Zero-base budgeting typically begins with the decision units that are at the lowest levels in an organization for which a budget is prepared. A set of *decision packages* is prepared for each unit. These packages describe various levels of service that may be rendered by the decision unit. The set must usually include a package of one level lower than the current level of operations. At Stanford University, the ZBB documentation includes the specification of the objectives, the description of the alternative means of accomplishing objectives, and the financial effects of four different levels of service (two of which must be below the current levels of services).[7]

ZBB has its boosters and its critics. The strengths that successful adopters of ZBB cite include many of the following:[8]

---

[7]See K. Bennett, L. Owen, and T. Warner, "Implementing Zero-Base Budgeting at Stanford University," *Business Officer*, May 1980, pp. 21–27.

[8]The early literature on ZBB invariably cited the same one or two "success stories" (especially Texas Instruments), but recently the number of reports on ZBB implementation and the resultant improvements and problems has been increasing. For representative reports, see P. Moore, "Zero-Base Budgeting in American Cities," *Public Administration Review*, May/June 1980, pp. 253–58; T. Lauth, "Performance Evaluation in the Georgia Budgetary Process," *Public Budgeting and Finance*, Spring 1985, pp. 67–82; and S. Reed, "The Impact of Budgetary Roles upon Perspectives," *Public Budgeting and Finance*, Spring 1985, pp. 83–96.

1. Goals have been more sharply established and alternative means have been explicitly considered.
2. Managers have become more heavily involved in a well-structured budget process that fosters communication and consensus.
3. Priorities among activities have been better pinpointed.
4. Knowledge and understanding of inputs and outputs have been enhanced. The budget process is generally more rational and less political than most.
5. Resources have been reallocated more efficiently and effectively.

There are many critics of ZBB. Common complaints include the following:

1. The time and cost of preparing the budget are much higher than in less-elaborate budgeting processes. Indeed, in some organizations the heavy paperwork involved in ZBB is referred to as "Zerox-Base Budgeting."
2. The determination of performance measures is difficult.
3. The specification of service levels, especially the minimum levels of service, is threatening to many managers.
4. Top managers fail to follow through and use the ZBB information. In short, they do not really support the process.

Most of these weaknesses or problems may result from a rigid application of ZBB without tailoring the technique to the peculiarities of a specific organization. Criticisms of all types of budgeting are often misdirected. They are aimed at a budget *technique* or *process* (such as ZBB), when instead they should be aimed at the *administration* of the technique.

Conclusions about ZBB

What major conclusions should we draw about ZBB in relation to other forms of budgeting? Consider the following:

1. The cost-benefit test will probably not be met if ZBB is conducted by all departments annually. However, ZBR (or zero-base "review" as distinguished from "budgeting") deserves serious consideration if it is conducted for all departments sequentially every five years or so. Meanwhile, incremental priority budgeting deserves annual use.
2. Unlike incremental budgeting, ZBB forces managers to consider alternative ways of accomplishing objectives systematically (e.g., to use inside or outside computer services). This is a desirable attribute of any budgeting system for discretionary costs.
3. Although ZBB might be applied to all kinds of costs, its major potential contribution is in the area of discretionary costs. ZBB has received the most attention from nonprofit organizations because they tend to have higher proportions of discretionary costs.
4. The biggest benefit of the notoriety of ZBB will probably be indirect. That is, if ZBB acquires a bad name and fades away, it will nevertheless have made one major contribution. Today, more than ever, there has been a decided increase in the prominence of budgeting in general. Inasmuch as intelligent budgeting is a help rather than a hindrance to management, almost any increase in attention to budgeting is a worthwhile contribution.

NONMANUFACTURING WORK MEASUREMENT

Work measurement is the careful analysis of a task, its size, the method used in its performance, and its efficiency. The objective of work measurement is to determine the workload in an operation and the number of workers needed to perform that work efficiently. The techniques used include time and motion study, observation of a random sample of the work (i.e., work sampling), and the estimation, by a work-measurement analyst and a line supervisor, of the amount of time required for the work (i.e., time analysis). The workload is expressed in *control-factor units,* which are used in formulating the budget. A **control-factor unit** is a measure of workload.

For example, the control-factor units in a payroll department might include operations performed on time records, on notices of change in labor rate, on notices of employee promotion, on new employment and termination reports, and on routine weekly and monthly reports. All of these operations would be measured. The estimated workload would then be used to determine the required labor force and budgetary allowance.

Other examples of control-factor units include the following:

OPERATION	CONTROL-FACTOR UNIT
Billing	Lines per hour
Warehouse labor	Pounds or cases handled per day
Packing	Pieces packed per hour
Posting accounts receivable	Postings per hour
Mailing	Pieces mailed per hour

Standards for certain order-filling activities, such as packing or driving a delivery truck, may necessarily be less refined than for such manufacturing activities as assembly work, but they still provide the best available formal tool for planning and control.[9]

Dayton-Hudson, a U.S. retailer, is an enthusiastic advocate of nonmanufacturing work-measurement techniques. The areas it measures on a per hour basis include cartons handled, invoices processed, and store items ticketed. The cost savings from productivity gains in these areas are substantial. For example, the Target chain division of Dayton-Hudson increased the number of accounts payable processed from 9.7 to 15.0 per hour over a five-year period. (The total number of accounts payable processed each year by the Target chain division exceeds 4 million.)

Return to Exhibit 11-2. A hallmark of the evolution of control is the attempt to apply engineered-cost techniques to costs that were formerly subjected to discretionary-cost techniques. The first candidates for this shift in application were manufacturing costs, largely because many manufacturing processes are observable and repetitive, the inputs and outputs are measurable, and the uncertainty of the relationship between inputs and outputs is relatively small. The next candidates have been those nonmanufacturing costs that are subject to credible measurements of the relationship between inputs and outputs. Examples are the loading of trucks and the transportation of mail.

There is nothing hallowed about the distinctions in Exhibit 11-2. Many costs are neither innately engineered nor discretionary. *Whether they become one type or the other often depends on management's policies of planning and control.* The history of cost accounting reveals a steady movement from the discretionary cate-

---

[9]Examples of research in this area include Ernst & Whinney, *Warehouse Accounting and Control Guidelines for Distribution and Financial Managers* (Oak Brook, Ill.: National Council of Physical Distribution Management, 1985); and J. Magee, W. Copacino, and D. Rosenfield, *Modern Logistics Management* (New York: John Wiley, 1985).

gory to the engineered category. Indeed, the management consulting arms of public accounting firms, and many industrial engineering firms, have flourished by replacing discretionary-cost systems with engineered-cost systems.

BUDGETING OF NONMANUFACTURING COSTS

There is much disagreement about how some nonmanufacturing costs should be controlled. Advocates of work measurement favor a more rigorous approach, which essentially regards these costs as engineered variable costs. In contrast, a discretionary-cost approach, which basically regards these costs as fixed, is more often found in practice.[10]

To illustrate these two approaches, assume that five clerks are employed by Construction Enterprises, Inc., and that each clerk's operating efficiency *should be* the processing of the pay records of 1,000 employees per month. In the month of June, 4,700 individual pay records were processed by these clerks. Each clerk earns $1,200 per month. The variances shown by the engineered-cost approach and the discretionary-cost approach are tabulated below and graphed in Exhibit 11-4.

The engineered variable-cost approach

The engineered approach to the control of payroll-clerk labor bases the budget formula on the unit cost of the individual pay record processed: $1,200 ÷ 1,000 records, or $1.20. Therefore the flexible-budget allowance for payroll-clerk labor would be $1.20 × 4,700, or $5,640. Assuming that the five employees worked throughout the month at $1,200 per month (giving an actual cost of $6,000), the following performance report would be prepared:

	ACTUAL COST	FLEXIBLE BUDGET: TOTAL STANDARD COST ALLOWED FOR GOOD UNITS PRODUCED	FLEXIBLE-BUDGET VARIANCE
Payroll-clerk labor	$6,000	$5,640	$360 U

A graphic representation of what has occurred (Exhibit 11-4) may yield insight. For simplicity, the flexible-budget variance is not divided into price and efficiency variances here.

Essentially, two decisions must be made in this operation. The *first* is a policy decision. How many clerks do we desire? How flexible should we be? How divisible is the task? Should we use part-time help? Should we hire and lay off as the volume of work fluctuates? The implications of these questions are that once the hiring decision has been made, the total costs incurred can easily be predicted: $6,000 in our example.

---

[10]One survey of controllers of U.S. manufacturing companies (with 223 responses) reported the following on the approach that "best describes your company's experience with setting standards for nonmanufacturing costs":
  a. Extensive use is made = 1.7%
  b. Moderate use is made = 16.2%
  c. Setting of standards tried, but found not to be of significant benefit = 3.9%
  d. Setting of standards not yet attempted = 78.2%
See W. Cress and J. Pettijohn, "A Survey of Budget-Related Planning and Control Policies and Procedures," *Journal of Accounting Education*, Fall 1985, pp. 61–78.

EXHIBIT 11-4

Engineered and Discretionary Costs

	Budget as an Engineered Cost (perfection)	Budget as a Discretionary Cost (currently attainable)
Actual cost incurred	$6,000	$6,000
Budget allowance	5,640*	6,000
Variance	360 U	0

*Rate = $6,000 ÷ 5,000 records or $1.20 per record;
Total = 4,700 records @ $1.20 = $5,640.

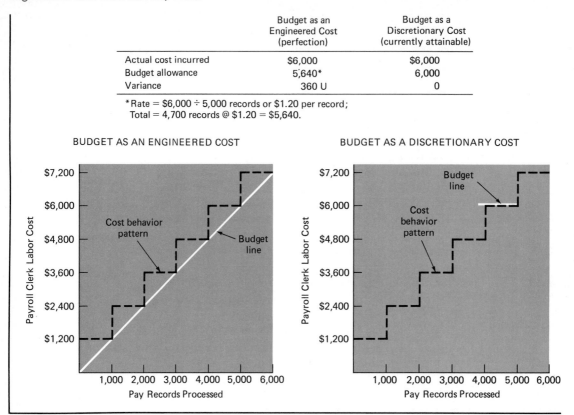

The *second decision* concentrates on day-to-day control, on how efficiently and effectively the given resources are being utilized. The work-measurement approach formally attempts to measure the utilization of resources by:

1. Assuming a proportionately variable-cost budget and the complete divisibility of the workload into small units. Note that the *budget line* on the engineered-cost graph in Exhibit 11-4 is variable, even though costs are actually incurred in steps.
2. Generating a flexible-budget variance that assumes a comparison of actual costs with a perfection standard—the cost that would be incurred if payroll-clerk labor could be hired on an hour-by-hour basis. In this case, the unfavorable variance of $360 informs management that there was overstaffing (that is, the step of the cost behavior pattern from $4,800 to $6,000 on the graph in Exhibit 11-4 was only partially utilized). The workload capability was 5,000 pay records, not the 4,700 actually processed. The extra cost of $360 resulted from operating in a way that did not attain the lowest possible cost. This result may not be from a conscious decision; it may merely be the effect of producing a volume in response to the actual total monthly demand. Advocates of work measurement maintain that such a variance shows where the managers should be alert for cost reduction opportunities because options may be available. Such an approach provides a measure ($360) of the amount that management is currently investing to provide stability in the work force.

The use of a tight budget based on perfection standards generates variances that upon investigation will reveal either or both of the following: (a) the cost of a management policy of deliberately retaining personnel to service long-run needs even though the volume of the current workload is insufficient (for instance, the maximum work available for payroll-clerk labor may be 4,700 individual payroll records and the individual work may have been performed with complete efficiency); or (b) the inefficient use or underutilization of available personnel (for instance, perhaps 5,000 individual payroll records had to be processed, and other clerks or supervisors had to pitch in to get all the work done).

The discretionary fixed-cost approach

Work-measurement techniques are not used in connection with discretionary fixed costs in the vast majority of organizations. Consequently, the tendency is to rely on personal observation as the primary means of control. That is, the experience of the department head is used to judge the size of the work force needed to carry out the department's functions. There is a genuine reluctance to overhire because there is a corresponding reluctance to discharge or lay off people when volume slackens. Consequently, occasional peak loads are often met by hiring temporary workers or by having the regular employees work overtime.

In most cases, the relevant range of volume during the budget period can be predicted with assurance, and the work force needed for the marketing and administrative functions can readily be determined. If management refuses, consciously or unconsciously, to control costs rigidly in accordance with short-run fluctuations in activity, these costs become fixed and unresponsive to short-run variations in volume.

Hence there is a conflict between common practice and the objective of work measurement, which is to treat most costs as engineered and subject them to short-range management control. *The moral is that management's attitudes and its planning and controlling decisions often determine whether a cost is fixed or variable. A change in policy can transform a fixed cost into a variable cost and vice versa.*

Moreover, management may regard a cost as a discretionary fixed cost for *cash-planning purposes* in the preparation of the master budget but may use the variable-cost approach for *control purposes* in the preparation of flexible budgets for performance evaluation. These two views may be reconciled within the same overall system. In our example, a master budget could conceivably include the following items:

Payroll-clerk labor:

Flexible-budget allowance for control	$5,640
Expected flexible-budget variance (due to conscious overstaffing)	360
Total budget allowance for cash planning	$6,000

Follow-up analysis under discretionary fixed costs

Control may be exercised (a) in the commonly accepted sense of the day-to-day follow-up that is associated with engineered costs, and (b) in the special sense of periodically evaluating an expenditure, relating it to the objectives sought, and carefully planning the total amount of the cost for the ensuing period. The latter approach does not mean that day-to-day follow-up is neglected; follow-up is necessary to see that the available resources are being used fully and efficiently. It does mean that perceptive planning is stressed and that daily control *via a formal work-*

387

measurement system is de-emphasized. Reliance is placed more on hiring capable people and less on frequent checking up on them.

The practical effects of the discretionary fixed-cost approach are that the budgeted cost and the actual cost tend to be the same amount, so that resulting budget variances are zero. Follow-ups to see that the available resources are being fully and efficiently utilized are regarded as the manager's responsibility. This duty can be achieved by face-to-face control and by nonfinancial records. For example, physical quantities (such as pounds handled per day in a warehouse or pieces mailed per hour in a mailing room) may be tallied but not formally integrated into the accounting records in dollar terms.

Difficulties in applying work measurement

The success of the work-measurement, engineered variable-cost approach to some nonmanufacturing costs is limited by the nature of the work being performed. Attempts have been made to measure the work of legal personnel and claims adjusters in insurance companies, of economists in a Federal Reserve Bank, and of stock clerks in retail stores. Such attempts have achieved only limited success because of (a) the inability to develop a satisfactory control-factor unit, (b) the diversity of tasks and objectives of such personnel, or (c) the difficulty of measuring the output of lawyers or economists.

For example, consider the attempt to measure the work of clerks and stock helpers in a food store. Their tasks are routine and repetitive, but they are often fragmented. Attempts at measuring employee work have shown volatile results. The trouble is that each employee usually performs a variety of tasks on a variety of items. The worker may unpack, price-mark, stock shelves, operate a cash register, bag groceries, cart groceries to automobiles, sweep floors, and watch for shoplifters.

Whether the engineered-cost approach is "better" than the discretionary-cost approach must be decided on a case-by-case basis, *using a cost-benefit approach that focuses on how much operating decisions will be improved.* Of course, the consultants who want to install work-measurement systems will typically try to demonstrate that their more costly formal systems will generate net benefits in the form of cost savings and better customer service.

EFFICIENCY AND EFFECTIVENESS MEASURES FOR A PERSONNEL DEPARTMENT

This section discusses the second approach in Exhibit 11-3 to promoting efficiency and effectiveness in a discretionary cost center, i.e., monitoring financial and nonfinancial indicators on an ongoing basis. A personnel department is used to illustrate this approach.

Personnel departments have responsibility for activities such as staffing, employee relations, compensation design, and employee training and development. Labor cost is typically the largest single item in the total costs of the personnel department budget. The benefits from a well-functioning personnel department appear as higher revenues or lower costs in *other* departments and divisions of the organization; these benefits arise from higher-quality and more strongly motivated employees being hired and retained by the organization.

What is the optimal amount of resources to spend on the personnel function in an organization? How can top management assess whether a personnel department is increasing the efficiency or effectiveness of its operation? Few organizations ask such questions, in part due to the difficulty of answering them. However, an emerging trend is the use of quantitative measures to monitor efficiency and, to a lesser degree, effectiveness.

Efficiency measures

Exhibit 11-5 illustrates three variables used to monitor the efficiency of the hiring function of a personnel department. Consider the cost-per-hire ratio. Total costs of hiring include:[11]

1. Cost of advertising vacant positions
2. Fees paid to third parties to locate potential job applicants
3. Cost of the time and resources (e.g., phone calls) of the personnel department in interviewing and processing applicants
4. Travel and related costs for staff and applicants
5. Relocation costs (if any) of hired employees
6. Cost of the time and resources used by nonpersonnel department individuals in interviewing job applicants

Two approaches are used to make inferences about the efficiency of hiring:

- Time-series approach: comparison of the values of the cost-per-hire ratio over time
- Cross-sectional approach: comparison of the cost-per-hire ratio of one organization with the values of the same ratio for comparable organizations at the same time

Exhibit 11-6 illustrates both approaches for the recruiting of graduating college students by Accounting Professionals Inc. (AP), a medium-sized public accounting firm. Also included in Exhibit 11-6 are summary data for a comparable set of accounting firms. Such data on comparables may be available from an industry trade association or from a commercial organization.[12]

EXHIBIT 11-5
Illustrative Variables Used to Monitor the Efficiency
of the Hiring Function of a Personnel Department

1. Cost per hire $= \dfrac{\text{Total hiring costs}}{\text{Total number of hirees}}$

2. Acceptance ratio $= \dfrac{\text{Number of job offers accepted}}{\text{Number of job offers extended}}$

3. Average time to fill each vacancy = Numbers of days, on average, between the day the approved vacant position requisition is received and the day the new hire starts work

Source: Saratoga Institute, Saratoga, Calif., 1986

---

[11]For further discussion of the costs of hiring, see J. Fitz-enz, *How to Measure Human Resources Management* (New York: McGraw-Hill, 1984). See also E. Flamholtz, *Human Resource Accounting*, 2nd ed. (San Francisco: Jossey-Bass, 1985), pp. 152–70.

[12]Data on comparables for the personnel function of firms for a broad cross-section of industries are in the "Human Resource Effectiveness Survey" of the Saratoga Institute Inc. of Saratoga, California.

EXHIBIT 11-6

Cost-per-Hire Data for Accounting Professionals Inc. and Comparable Firms

	COST PER HIRE				
	19_1	19_2	19_3	19_4	19_5
Accounting Professionals Inc.	$3,800	$3,500	$3,300	$3,200	$2,800
Comparable firms*					
.25 percentile	$1,800	$2,000	$2,100	$2,400	$2,900
.50 percentile	3,600	3,900	4,400	4,500	4,800
.75 percentile	6,400	6,500	6,900	7,300	8,000

*Data for comparable firms are collected by an industry association body. The .25 percentile (.50, .75) is that point on the cost-per-hire distribution at which 25% (50%, 75%) of all respondents fall below. For example, in 19_1, 75% of the firms spent more than $1,800 per hire.

Using the data in Exhibit 11-6, the personnel department of AP increased the efficiency of its hiring practices in the 19_1 to 19_5 period:

a. AP decreased its cost per hire from $3,800 in 19_1 to $2,800 in 19_5.
b. Comparable firms increased their cost per hire in the same period; for each of the .25, .50, and .75 percentiles in Exhibit 11-6, the cost per hire systematically increased over the 19_1 to 19_5 period.
c. In 19_1, the cost per hire for AP was above the .50 percentile of comparable firms. In 19_5, the cost per hire for AP was below the .25 percentile of comparable firms.

The cost-per-hire ratio and the other two measures in Exhibit 11-5 focus only on the cost and speed with which the personnel department operates its hiring function. None of these measures indicate the "quality" of the people hired.

Effectiveness measures

Did the increase in the efficiency of AP's hiring practices come at the expense of a decline in the effectiveness of its hiring practices? (Effectiveness means the hiring of "high-quality and strongly motivated" employees.) **In a discretionary-cost center such as personnel, short-run increases in efficiency indicators need not imply anything about effectiveness.** For example, the group of graduating students most likely to accept a job offer from AP are those who are actively seeking employment but have as yet had no alternative job offers. In the short run, AP could reduce many of the individual hiring cost items by interviewing only students with no other offers of employment. Such an approach would surely be counterproductive in terms of hiring quality employees. Yet, in the short run, it would probably decrease the cost-per-hire ratio.

Quantitative measures of effectiveness in discretionary-cost centers often have a long-term focus. There are two measures of interest to AP that can be computed only after a considerable lapse of time:

$$\text{Retention ratio} = \frac{\text{Employees hired as entry-level staff in year 19\_X and still with AP in year 19\_Y}}{\text{Total employees hired as entry-level staff in year 19\_X}}$$

$$\text{Promotion-to-manager ratio} = \frac{\text{Employees hired as entry-level staff in year 19\_X and subsequently promoted to manager in year 19\_Y}}{\text{Total employees hired as entry-level staff in year 19\_X}}$$

EXHIBIT 11-7
Measures of Effectiveness at Accounting Professionals Inc. and Comparable Firms

	19_6	19_7	19_8	19_9	19_0
A. RETENTION RATIO FOR 19_5 HIREES					
Accounting Professionals Inc.	.80	.65	.55	.50	.40
Comparable firms*					
.25 percentile	.70	.58	.47	.42	.35
.50 percentile	.78	.66	.58	.51	.49
.75 percentile	.88	.74	.67	.58	.55
B. PROMOTION-TO-MANAGER RATIO FOR 19_5 HIREES					
Accounting Professionals Inc.	.00	.02	.07	.10	.12
Comparable firms*					
.25 percentile	.00	.01	.02	.03	.08
.50 percentile	.00	.02	.06	.09	.11
.75 percentile	.02	.06	.10	.14	.17

Data for comparable firms are collected by an industry association body. The .25 percentile (.50, .75) is that point on the distribution at which 25% (50%, 75%) of all respondents fall below. For example, for every 10 hirees in 19_5, .80 × 10 = 8 were still with Accounting Professionals in 19_6. In contrast, 25% of comparable firms had retained .70 × 10 = 7 for the same time span.

Higher levels of effectiveness are associated with higher levels of the retention ratio, and higher levels of the promotion-to-manager ratio. (It is assumed that AP has some absolute standard for promotion to manager.)

Exhibit 11-7 illustrates these two ratios, and data for comparable firms, in the 19_6 to 19_0 period. Over this period, both AP's retention ratio and its promotion-to-manager ratio were very similar to the .50 percentile for comparable firms. There is no evidence of a decline in the effectiveness of its recruiting policy in 19_5, which was done at a decreased cost-per-hire ratio (see Exhibit 11-6). Note that the two effectiveness measures in Exhibit 11-7 reflect a combination of many factors. These include (1) the effectiveness of the hiring decision in 19_5, (2) the actions of the supervisors of each hiree in years subsequent to 19_5, (3) the in-house training and development program of AP, and (4) the competitiveness of the salaries paid by AP.

Interfirm comparisons

Interfirm comparisons, such as those in Exhibits 11-6 and 11-7, are one means of gaining insight about the relative efficiency or effectiveness of discretionary-cost centers. Such comparisons highlight whether a firm is an outlier, in terms of differing markedly from other firms in the comparison set, (without any prejudgment than it is inappropriate to be an outlier). Several factors limit their widespread use:

1. Nonavailability of data on comparables. In some cases, comparables may not exist. In other cases, comparables exist but the data are not made public, either individually or as part of a summary report.
2. Inconsistencies across firms in the way they collect and report data. For instance, public accounting firms may differ in how they record the cost of the time of non-personnel department individuals who interview potential employees.

Interfirm comparisons provide evidence only on *relative* efficiency or effectiveness. Be careful to consider the importance of any changes in the total set of comparables when making interfirm comparisons.

Return to Exhibit 11-5 on p. 389. This exhibit illustrates several points that apply generally to the problems of measuring performance:

1. Only a subset of the variables monitored will be financial. Moreover, for these variables the accounting system may not include the appropriate total costs. Consider the cost-per-hire ratio in Exhibit 11-5. Many accounting systems do not include the costs of the time and resources of non-personnel department individuals interviewing applicants. Failure to include them in the numerator of the cost-per-hire ratio can lead to sizable underestimation of the actual cost to hire each new employee.

2. In the long run, the nonfinancial measures (the other two variables in Exhibit 11-5) may be more important than the cost per hire. Nonfinancial measures are important aids in obtaining a more complete monitoring of performance.

SUMMARY

Management control systems exist primarily to improve the collective decisions within an organization. All systems are imperfect. The central question usually is, How can a system, with all its defects, be improved? Using a cost-benefit philosophy, top managers must be conscious of the motivational effects of a chosen system. That is, how does System A affect goal congruence and managerial effort in comparison with System B?

For budgetary-control purposes, costs are frequently divided into three categories: engineered, discretionary, and committed. Different mixes of management control techniques are used in each category. Discretionary costs are especially difficult to control because, by definition, well-specified relationships between inputs and outputs do not exist.

A diverse set of approaches is used to promote efficiency and effectiveness in discretionary-cost centers. These include the use of budgets, the monitoring of financial and nonfinancial indicators, organization design, competitive forces of the market, rewards for performance, leadership, administrative approval mechanisms, and the promotion of an organization culture. Accounting data play a key role in several of these approaches; these include the use of budgets and the monitoring of financial indicators of efficiency or effectiveness.

PROBLEM FOR SELF-STUDY

problem

The Bombay Co. has many small accounts receivable. Work measurement of billing labor has shown that a billing clerk can process 2,000 customers' accounts per month. The company employs 30 billing clerks at an annual salary of $9,600 each. The outlook for next year is for a decline in the number of customers, from 59,900 to 56,300 per month.

Required

1. Assume that management has decided to continue to employ the 30 clerks despite the expected drop in billings. Show two approaches, the engineered-cost approach and the discretionary fixed-cost approach, to the budgeting of billing labor. Show how the performance report for the year would appear under each approach.
2. Some managers favor using tight budgets as motivating devices for controlling operations. In these cases, the managers really expect an unfavorable variance and must allow, in cash planning, for such a variance so that adequate cash will be available as needed. What would be the budgeted variance, also sometimes called expected variance, in this instance?
3. Assume that the workers are reasonably efficient. (a) Interpret the budget variances under the engineered-cost approach and the discretionary fixed-cost approach. (b) What should management do to exert better control over clerical costs?

solution   **1.** Engineered-cost approach:

Standard unit rate = $\$9,600 \div 2,000 = \$4.80$ **per customer per year**
or $= \$.40$ **per customer per month**

	ACTUAL COST	FLEXIBLE BUDGET: TOTAL STANDARD COST ALLOWED FOR GOOD UNITS PRODUCED	FLEXIBLE-BUDGET VARIANCE
	$(30 \times \$9,600)$	$(56,300 \times \$.40 \times 12 \text{ months})$	
Billing-clerk labor	$288,000	$270,240	$17,760 U

Discretionary fixed-cost approach:

	ACTUAL COST	FLEXIBLE BUDGET: A LUMP SUM	FLEXIBLE-BUDGET VARIANCE
Billing-clerk labor	$288,000	$288,000	$0

2. The budgeted variance would be $17,760, unfavorable. The master budget for financial planning must provide for labor costs of $288,000; therefore, if the engineered-cost approach were being used for control, the master budget might specify:

Billing-clerk labor:	
Flexible-budget allowance	$270,240
Expected flexible-budget variance	17,760
Total budget allowance for cash planning	$288,000

3. As the chapter explains, management decisions and policies are often of critical importance in classifying a cost as either fixed or variable. If management refuses, as in this case, to control costs rigidly in accordance with short-run fluctuations in activity, these costs are discretionary. The $17,760 variance represents the price that management, consciously or unconsciously, is willing to pay currently in order to maintain a stable work force geared to management's ideas of "normal needs."

Management should be given an approximation of such an extra cost. There is no single "right way" to keep management informed on such matters. Two approaches were demonstrated in the previous parts of this problem. The important point is that clerical workloads and capability must be measured before effective control may be exerted. Such measures may be formal or informal. The latter is often achieved through a supervisor's regular observation of how efficiently work is being performed.

Terms to Learn

This chapter, chapter appendix, and the Glossary contain definitions of the following important terms:

authoritative budgeting (p. 394)   *committed costs (378)*
control-factor unit (384)   *discretionary costs (378)*   *effort (374)*

Special Points and Pitfalls

The task of the formal control system is to help attain goal congruence and managerial effort. Behavioral and organizational considerations deserve front and center attention.

Few firms currently invest many resources in the setting of standards for nonmanufacturing costs; most adopt a discretionary-cost approach rather than an engineered-cost approach. However, some firms are now spending more resources on their accounting systems in the nonmanufacturing cost area. By the use of work measurement and other standard-setting techniques, many control approaches used with engineered costs can be used in the nonmanufacturing area. No particular cost item should be viewed as inherently discretionary (or, indeed, engineered or committed).

This book stresses that accounting information is only one of many sources of information used in the planning and control of organizations. This observation is especially true in the discretionary-cost area.

APPENDIX: MORE ON SYSTEMS CHOICE AND THE ORGANIZATION BEHAVIOR LITERATURE

This appendix covers several topics that are related to organization behavior issues raised previously in the chapter.

Top-management support

Budgets and standards are major facets of a formal management control system. The motivational influence of a formal system varies from organization to organization and from individual manager to individual manager. For example, some professional personnel, such as research scientists, are often most affected by their personal or group goals. The scientist's feedback sources are more likely to be informal than formal. The opinions of colleagues and external critics may count heavily.

Personal goals, to the extent that acceptance of goals (such as budget goals) can be affected by formal systems within the organization, are likely to be heavily influenced by how higher executives support the system. *Without massive top-management backing, the goals specified by the system, which should aim at goal congruence, are less likely to gain acceptance as group goals or as personal goals.* Note too that acceptance is the key; acceptance may be best achieved in some cases by authoritative processes, and in other cases by participative processes.

Participative budgeting

Two polar types of management processes are *authoritative* and *participative*. In an **authoritative budgeting** approach, top management imposes the budget on all managers without consulting them. In a **participative budgeting** approach, the individuals influenced by the budget are fully involved in the setting of the budget. Research has sought to isolate factors that determine the likely adoption of authoritative or participative budgeting. Brownell outlines the following factors based on a survey of numerous individual studies:[13]

1. *Cultural variables* such as nationality, race, and religion. For example, because of cultural reasons, a participative approach rather than an authoritative approach is more likely to exist in the kibbutz organizations found in Israel.

2. *Organizational variables* such as environmental stability, location of critical information, and organization structure. For example, where information held by subunits of an organization is critical to budget allocations by top management, participative budgeting is used frequently.

3. *Interpersonal variables* such as group size. For example, an authoritative approach, rather than a participative approach, is used in large organizations, such as in the armed forces.

4. *Individual* level variables such as personality. For example, one study found that individuals who feel their destinies are under their control prefer high participation, while those placing faith in luck or chance prefer low participation.[14]

Emphasis on short run

The accounting system is dominant as a means for setting goals and influencing management behavior in most organizations. Goals outside the accounting system, even though meritorious, are regarded as supplementary unless top management follows through and acts as if they are actually as important as short-run financial performance.

EXAMPLE

The Soviet Union provides many cases where overstress on one or two aspects of the measurement system may lead to uneconomical behavior that focuses on a subgoal without considering overall organizational goals. To illustrate, taxi drivers were put on a bonus system based on mileage. Soon the Moscow suburbs were full of empty taxis barreling down the boulevards to fatten their bonuses. In response to bonuses based on tonnage norms, a Moscow chandelier factory produced heavier and heavier chandeliers until they started pulling ceilings down.

The most common instance of overemphasis is the short-run maximization of net income or sales that hurts long-run results. There are many questionable ways to improve short-run performance. One common method is stinting on repairs, quality control, advertising, research, or training; or a manager may successfully exert pressure on employees for more productivity for short spurts of time, which may have some unfavorable long-run overtones.

As we explore various facets of systems design and techniques, we see the importance of goal congruence in example after example. Top management must explicitly face the job of goal setting and coordination; it should not be a product of chance or a byproduct of the day-to-day extinguishing of business brush fires.

Accurate recordkeeping

Textbooks do not devote much space to the problems of obtaining accurate source documents. Yet this problem is easily one of the most pervasive, everlasting con-

---

[13]P. Brownell, "Participation in the Budgeting Process: When It Works and When It Doesn't," *Journal of Accounting Literature*, Spring 1982, pp. 124–53.

[14]P. Brownell, "Participation in Budgeting, Locus of Control and Organizational Effectiveness," *Accounting Review*, October 1981, pp. 844–60.

cerns in collecting information. An accounting system cannot help managers predict and make decisions if its recordkeeping is haphazard.

Pressures may spur managers to encourage their subordinates to record time erroneously or to tinker with scrap or usage reports.

EXAMPLE

The maintenance crews of one telephone company regularly performed recurring short-term maintenance and repair work on various projects. At other times, the same crews would be concerned with huge construction projects—installing or building plant and equipment. The company had weekly reports on performance of the regular maintenance work but had only loose control over the construction projects. An investigation disclosed that the supervisor was encouraging the workers to boost the time on the construction projects and to understate the time on the regular maintenance projects. Thus the supervisor's performance on the latter always looked good. The situation was corrected when the emphases on maintenance and on construction were balanced so that both were currently budgeted and controlled.

Accurate recordkeeping is essentially a problem of motivation. The accountant and manager should be more sensitive to possible errors, and more conscious of the natural tendency of individuals to report their activities so as to minimize their personal bother and maximize their own showing. Chapter 27, "Accounting Systems and Internal Control," describes several well-documented cases of management improving the accounting measures of their performance by so-called cooking the books techniques.

QUESTIONS, PROBLEMS, AND CASES

11-1 "Considered together, congruence and effort are really subparts of motivation." Do you agree? Explain.

11-2 "Clearly, the bearing of risk changes behavior." Give an example.

11-3 Give three examples of committed costs.

11-4 Give three examples of discretionary costs.

11-5 Give three examples of engineered costs.

11-6 What are two synonyms for *discretionary costs?*

11-7 What are the most common outputs linked with discretionary costs?

11-8 What are four approaches used to promote efficiency and effectiveness in a discretionary-cost center?

11-9 What are the most obvious candidates for work measurement?

11-10 "The central purpose of a management accounting system is to improve the collective decisions within an organization." Do you agree? Explain.

11-11 Give an example of how a control system can motivate a manager to behave against the best interests of the company as a whole.

11-12 "I'm majoring in accounting. This study of human relations is fruitless. You've got to be born with a flair for getting along with others. You can't learn it!" Do you agree? Why?

11-13 Budgets as motivators. "Budgets and responsibility accounting and other modern accounting techniques foster a policed, departmental orientation rather than a positive, overall organizational orientation." Do you agree? Explain.

11-14 Budgets as pressure devices. Sord and Welsch have stated: "It should be recognized that pressure on supervisors need not come from control techniques, assuming that standards of performance are not unfair or too high. Pressure on supervisors comes from the responsibilities inherent in the supervisor's job." Do you agree? Why?

11-15 Budgets as motivators. "To accept budgets as motivators is to imply that supervisors do not have adequate interest in their job. This is seen as an insult to a person's integrity, and the factory supervisors resent it strongly." Do you agree? Why?

11-16 Goals of public accounting firms. All personnel, including partners, of public accounting firms must usually turn in biweekly time reports, showing how many hours were devoted to their various duties. These firms have traditionally looked unfavorably on idle or unassigned staff time. They have looked favorably on heavy percentages of chargeable (billable) time because this maximizes revenue. What effect is such a policy likely to have on the behavior of the firm's personnel? Can you relate this practice to the problem of harmony of goals that was discussed in the chapter? How?

11-17 Performance evaluation. Consider the following excerpt from a company employee newsletter. It announces the creation of a Perpetual Trophy that will be awarded to the branch with the most outstanding performance during a fiscal year.

> The Trophy will be several feet high and will be designed to be moved from branch to branch each year. Additionally, a small replica of the trophy will be awarded to the manager of the winning branch.
>
> The Trophy will be awarded to the branch with the best combination of sales percentage increase and net operating percentage increase. The actual calculation will be to take the sales percentage increase, plus the net operating profit percentage increase, and divide those two numbers by two, giving equal weight to both sales and profit growth. Only independent branches achieving a minimum 15% sales increase will be eligible.

Required | What is your personal evaluation of the way outstanding performance is measured?

11-18 Governmental and business budgets. (CMA) The term *budget* and the concept of budgeting can have different connotations depending upon the use and situation. A fundamental difference between governmental and business budgets lies in the appropriation nature of the governmental budget. However, a business organization could choose to base its budgeting process on a basis similar to the governmental approach.

Required
1. Describe the characteristics that exist in the governmental sector that encourage or require the use of appropriation budgeting.
2. If a business were to adopt an appropriation basis for its budgeting process:
   a. Describe the probable effect on a manager's behavior, and
   b. Explain why a manager would behave in this manner.
3. Explain how governmental budgeting could be modified in order to be more effective for managerial control purposes.

397

11-19 Control of discretionary costs, work-measurement. The manager of a warehouse for a mail-order firm is concerned with the control of her fixed costs. She has recently applied work-measurement techniques and an engineered-cost approach to the staff of order clerks and is wondering if a similar technique could be applied to the workers who collect merchandise in the warehouse and bring it to the area where orders are assembled for shipment.

The warehouse foreman contends that this should not be done, because the present work force of twenty persons should be viewed as a fixed cost necessary to handle the usual volume of orders with a minimum of delay. These employees work a forty-hour week at $15 per hour.

Preliminary studies show that it takes an average of twelve minutes for a worker to locate an article and take it to the order-assembly area, and that the average order is for two different articles. At present the volume of orders to be processed is 1,800 per week.

Required

1. For the present volume of orders, develop a discretionary-cost and an engineered-cost approach for the weekly performance report.
2. Repeat requirement 1 for volume levels of 1,600 and 1,400 orders per week.
3. What other factors should be compared with the budget variances found in requirements 1 and 2 in order to make a decision on the size of the work force?

11-20 Work measurement. The Hayward Company has installed a work-measurement program for its billing operations. A standard billing cost of $2 per bill has been used, based on hourly labor rates of $16 and an average processing rate of 8 bills of 10 lines each per hour. Each clerk has a 7½-hour workday and a 5-day workweek.

The supervisor has received the following report of performance from his superior—the office manager, Ann Davis—for a recent 4-week period regarding his clerks:

	ACTUAL	BUDGET	VARIANCE Amount	VARIANCE Equivalent Persons
Billing labor (5 clerks)	$12,000	$7,400 (3,700 bills × $2.00)	$4,600 U	1.9

The supervisor knows that he must explain the unfavorable variance and offer suggestions regarding how to avoid such an unfavorable variance in the future. Because of a recession, the office manager is under severe pressure to cut staff. In fact, she had penciled a question on the report: "Looks as if we can get along with two less clerks?"

Anticipating the pressures, the supervisor had taken a random sample of 400 of the 3,700 bills that were prepared during the period under review. His count of the lines in the sample totaled 5,200.

Required

As the supervisor, prepare a one-page explanation of the $4,600 unfavorable variance, together with your remedial suggestions.

11-21 Work measurement. The administrator of the Singapore Hotel has established a budget for the laundry department. The department's equipment consists of a washer that can process 500 pounds an hour. For every 100 pounds of linen processed, soap costs of 15¢ and water costs of 5¢ are incurred. One man operates the laundry. He works eight hours daily, six days per week, at $2 per hour, a good wage in Singapore. There is no premium paid for overtime.

The depreciation on the machine is $1,950 per year. The budget drawn by the administrator calls for $100 of overhead to be charged to the laundry for every four-week period. When the budget was established, the administrator thought that the expenses for the normal volume of linen would be $802 for a four-week period, including fixed expenses.

During the last four weeks, the laundry processed 72,000 pounds of linen and incurred $814 in expenses, of which $145 was for soap and $35 was for water. The man in charge of the laundry says he is doing a good job, because the budget calls for expenses of $802, and he incurred only $814.

Required
1. What volume of laundry did the administrator use for his $802 budget for the four-week period?
2. Prepare a performance report that will give the administrator a method for evaluating the laundry.

11-22 Commission plan for new-car sales personnel. As an automobile dealer, you are faced with the problem of formulating a commission plan for new-car sales personnel. You have listed the following alternatives:
  a. Commissions based on a flat percentage of dollar sales.
  b. Commissions based on varying percentages of dollar sales. The higher the sales price of a deal, the higher the commission rate. Also, commissions will vary depending on the accessories sold.
  c. Commissions based on net profit after allocation of a fair share of all operating expenses.

Required
Evaluate these alternatives. Are there other methods that deserve consideration?

11-23 Budgets and motivation. You are working as a supervisor in a manufacturing department that has substantial amounts of personnel and equipment. You are paid a "base" salary that is actually low for this type of work. The firm has a very liberal bonus plan, which pays you another $1,000 each time you "make the budget" and 2% of the amount you are able to save. Your past experiences have been as follows:

MONTH	JAN.	FEB.	MAR.	APR.	MAY	JUNE
Budget	$40,000	$40,000	$39,000	$36,000	$36,000	$36,250
Actual	41,000	39,500	37,000	37,000	36,500	36,000
Variance	$ 1,000 U	$ 500 F	$ 2,000 F	$ 1,000 U	$ 500 U	$ 250 F

Required
1. What would you do as a "rational person" if you were starting the job all over again from period 1 with the above information?
2. What would you recommend, if anything, be done to the system if you are now promoted to a higher job in management and required to handle the "bonus system" in this department?

11-24 Budgets and motivation. Christine Everette operates a chain of health centers. One of the largest is in the heart of Chicago. Everette used the services of three managers, Dave, Nick, and Sid. Each had charge of a group of exercise and apparatus rooms similar in all regards. She offered three methods of weekly payment to the men:

Method X. A base rate of $6 per hour and 30% of all reductions in expenses below a "norm" of $600 per week

Method Y. A flat wage of $7 per hour

Method Z. No base rate, but a bonus of $300 for meeting the "norm," plus 10% of all reductions in expenses below the norm

The men chose their method of compensation before starting employment. Assume a 40-hour week. The record for the past six weeks for the three areas follows (all data are in dollars):

	WEEKS					
	1	2	3	4	5	6
Dave:						
Utilities	250	250	250	250	250	250
Supplies	180	20	20	260	100	20
Repairs & misc.	305	250	220	265	260	200
Total	735	520	490	775	610	470
Nick:						
Utilities	250	250	250	250	250	250
Supplies	100	100	100	100	100	100
Repairs & misc.	250	200	265	220	260	305
Total	600	550	615	570	610	655
Sid:						
Utilities	250	250	250	250	250	250
Supplies	100	100	100	100	100	100
Repairs & misc.	250	250	250	250	250	250
Total	600	600	600	600	600	600

Required

Which payment methods were most likely chosen by Dave, Nick, and Sid? Base your answer on an analysis of cost behavior patterns. Assume that each man picked a different plan. (Giving your final answer is not enough; briefly explain your choices.)

11-25 Risk sharing, motivation, new clients for advertising agency. The Media Impact Group (MIG) is the second largest advertising agency in Canada with offices in Vancouver, Calgary, Edmonton, Regina, Winnipeg, Toronto, Montreal, Quebec City, and Halifax. The head office is in Toronto. The partners of the firm have agreed to place high priority on developing a larger client base in the lodging industry.

Quality Inns is a major motel chain with over 100 motels across Canada. Its headquarters is in Vancouver. The managing director has called for bids for its advertising account. Quality Inns' current advertising has been described in advertising circles as "uninspiring, nonmemorable, and without focus."

Trent Natham, the partner in charge of MIG's Vancouver office, is unenthusiastic about devoting large amounts of the resources of the Vancouver office to bidding on the Quality Inns account. He views the minimum cost of preparing a credible bid to be $100,000. Moreover, Quality Inns has informed all potential bidders that it will not consider any bid with an average billing rate higher than $60 an hour. The Vancouver office of MIG currently averages $70 an hour on its billing rate to its clients. Moreover, Natham estimates that only 20% of the revenues of the Quality Inns account would be received by the Vancouver office. The Toronto and Montreal offices would jointly receive over 50% of the revenues of the Quality Inns account if MIG wins the bidding. Competition for the account will be intense with at least six other advertising agencies willing to prepare bids.

Each office of MIG is viewed by the head office as a profit center. Over 50% of Natham's annual bonus is based on profitability for that year at the Vancouver office. The current year has been a highly successful one for the Vancouver office; many partners have worked 60 hours each week for extended periods of time.

Required

1. Why might Natham be unenthusiastic about making a serious bid for the Quality Inns advertising account?
2. How might Natham be encouraged by the head office in Toronto to make a serious bid for the Quality Inns advertising account?

11-26 Participative budgetary process, government department. (CMA) Scott Weidner, the controller in the Division of Social Services for the state, recognizes the importance of the budgetary process for planning, control, and motivation purposes. He believes that a properly implemented participative budgeting process for planning purposes and a management by exception reporting procedure based on the participative budget will motivate his subordinates to improve productivity within their particular departments. Based on this philosophy, Weidner has implemented the following budget procedures:

- An appropriation target figure is given to each department manager. This amount is the maximum funding that each department can expect to receive in the next fiscal year.
- Department managers develop their individual budgets within the following spending constraints as directed by the controller's staff:
  1. Expenditure requests cannot exceed the appropriation target.
  2. All fixed expenditures should be included in the budget. Fixed expenditures would include such items as contracts and salaries at current levels.
  3. All government projects directed by higher authority should be included in the budget in their entirety.
- The controller's staff consolidates the departmental budget requests from the various departments into one budget that is to be submitted for the entire division.
- Upon final budget approval by the legislature, the controller's staff allocates the appropriation to the various departments on instructions from the division manager. However, a specified percentage of each department's appropriation is held back in anticipation of potential budget cuts and special funding needs. The amount and use of this contingency fund is left to the discretion of the division manager.
- Each department is allowed to adjust its budget when necessary to operate within the reduced appropriation level. However, as stated in the original directive, specific projects authorized by higher authority must remain intact.
- The final budget is used as the basis of control for a management by exception form of reporting. Excessive expenditures by account for each department are highlighted on a monthly basis. Department managers are expected to account for all expenditures over budget. Fiscal responsibility is an important factor in the overall performance evaluation of department managers.

Weidner believes his policy of allowing the department managers to participate in the budget process and then holding them accountable for their performance is essential, especially during these times of limited resources. He further believes the department managers will be motivated positively to increase the efficiency and effectiveness of their departments because they have provided input into the initial budgetary process and are required to justify any unfavorable performances.

Required
1. Explain the operational and behavioral benefits that generally are attributed to a participative budgeting process.
2. Identify deficiencies in Scott Weidner's participative budgetary policy for planning and performance evaluation purposes. For each deficiency identified, recommend how the deficiency can be corrected. Use the following format in preparing your response.

Deficiency   *Recommendation*
a.   a.
b.   b.
etc.

11-27 Practical work measurement. A team of job analysts has been studying a U.S. Air Force maintenance base in Ohio. The aim is to apply flexible budgeting to determine how many workers are required.

A repair parts stockroom has been under study. The stockroom has used a perpetual inventory system. The stockroom has a manager plus two clerks. A second clerk had been added in the middle of the preceding year at the manager's request.

During the month of March, a job analyst spent several days reviewing and timing the tasks of the stockroom personnel. She classified all workloads as either tasks that vary with the volume of activity or tasks that are necessary regardless of volume.

Variable operations in the stockroom depend on receipts and issuances of repair parts. The job analyst established the following five operations and time allowances. All time allowances have been adjusted for personal time and fatigue:

OPERATION NUMBER	DESCRIPTION	STANDARD TIME ALLOWANCE IN MINUTES
1	Issuing repair parts	15
2	Recording issues on stores ledger cards and pricing	9
3	Checking parts received and preparing receiving reports	5
4	Recording receipts on stores ledger cards	3
5	Placing parts in stock	10

The analyst also computed time allowances for "standby" activities, which were defined as those activities independent of fluctuations in volume. They were attributed solely to the manager for a four-week period:

	MINUTES
Testing, expediting, supervising	3,000
Inventory control problems	1,800
Physical counts and comparisons with records	900
Total	5,700

Each four-week period normally had 20 working days of 8 hours each. Therefore each worker would have $20 \times 8 \times 60 = 9,600$ minutes of available work time. Records of actual time spent performing stockroom operations during a recent four-week period showed:

EMPLOYEE	VARIABLE OPERATION NUMBER					OTHER	TOTAL
	1	2	3	4	5		
Manager	600		700			8,300	9,600
Clerk #1		3,800		1,000		4,800	9,600
Clerk #2	5,600		1,000		3,000		9,600
Total	6,200	3,800	1,700	1,000	3,000	13,100	28,800

The "other" time consisted of:

	MINUTES
Manager:	
Testing, expediting, and supervising	5,000
Inventory control problems	3,300
Clerk #1:	
Rearranging items in stock	3,800
Physical inventory counts	1,000

The volume of activity consisted of 350 requisitions filled and processed for parts issued. In addition, 250 receiving reports were prepared and recorded for parts received and placed in stock.

Required

1. Based on the level of activity during the period, prepare a performance report in minutes. For each operation, including standby operations, present the appropriate total standard time allowance, the actual time recorded, and the variance.

2. Fill in the question marks:

Total available work time	?
Deduct: total standby workload time allowance	?
Variable workload time available	?
Deduct: total variable workload time allowance	?
Excess time available	?

3. How many excess employees are working in the stockroom?

4. Suppose management decides to reduce the stockroom personnel to two persons, the manager plus one clerk. What activities offer the best opportunities for improving efficiency?

5. Assume that the manager earns a salary of $26,000 per year and each clerk is paid $10 per hour. Prepare a budget for the next operating year for compensation. Use (a) a discretionary-cost approach and (b) an engineered work-measurement approach. Show how you arrived at your numbers.

6. Describe at least two "useful generalizations" about work measurement that are illustrated by this situation.

11-28 Motivation and control of costs. The Sharp Company develops, manufactures, and markets several product lines of low-cost consumer goods. Top management of the company is attempting to evaluate the present method and a new method of charging the different production departments for the services they receive from one of the engineering departments, which is called Manufacturing Engineering Services (MES).

The function of MES, which consists of about thirty engineers and ten draftsmen, is to reduce the costs of producing the different products of the company by improving machine and manufacturing process design while maintaining the required level of quality. The MES manager reports to the engineering supervisor, who reports to the vice-president, manufacturing. The MES manager, George Amershi, may increase or decrease the number of engineers under him. He is evaluated on the basis of several variables, one of which is the annual incremental savings to the company brought about by his department in excess of the costs of operating his department. These costs consist of actual salaries, a share of corporate overhead, the cost of office supplies used by his department, and a cost of capital charge. An individual engineer is evaluated on the basis of the ratio of the annual savings he or she accomplishes in relation to the engineer's annual salary. The salary range of an engineer is defined by personnel classification; there are four classifications, and promotion from one classification to another depends on the approval of a panel that includes both production and engineering personnel.

Production department managers report to a production supervisor, who reports to the vice-president, manufacturing. The production department for each product line is treated as a profit center, and engineering services are provided at a cost, according to the following plan. When a production department manager and an engineer agree on a possible project to improve production efficiency, they sign a contract that specifies the scope of the project, the estimated savings to be realized, the probability of success, and the number of engineering hours of each personnel classification required. The charge to the particular production department is determined by the product of the number of hours required times the "classification rate" for each personnel classification. This rate depends on the average salary for the classification involved and a share of the engineering department's other costs. An engineer is expected to spend at least 85% of his time on specific, contracted projects; the remainder may be used for preliminary investigations of potential cost-saving projects or

403

self-improving study. A recent survey showed that production managers have a high degree of confidence in the MES engineers.

A new plan has been proposed to top management, in which no charge will be made to production departments for engineering services. In all other respects the new system will be identical to the present. Production managers will continue to request engineering services as under the present plan. Proponents of the new plan say that under it, production managers will take a greater advantage of existing engineering talent. Regardless of how engineering services are accounted for, the company is committed to the idea of production departments being profit centers.

Required Evaluate the strong and weak points of the present and proposed plans. Will the company tend to hire the optimal quantity of engineering talent? Will this engineering talent be used as effectively as possible?

11-29 Discretionary-cost center, university schools, efficiency and effectiveness measures. Judith Kennedy, the president of Western University, is preparing for her annual report to the board of trustees of the university. This report must include recommendations on the budget to be allocated in 19_5 to each of the nine schools at Western University (Business, Dentistry, Earth Sciences, Education, Engineering, Humanities and Sciences, Law, Medicine, and Nursing). The report must also include a detailed evaluation of the "health and resource requirements for the next three years" of three of the nine schools. This year Kennedy must report on the Business, Dentistry, and Engineering schools. Western University's goal is to be a center of education and research excellence.

At the time of writing the report, Kennedy only had data involving the 19_1 to 19_3 period for a broad set of variables covering the students and faculty at each school. Exhibit 11-8 presents a subset of these data for each school over this period. Dentistry was a big concern to Kennedy. At the end of 19_2, the leading dental researcher at Western resigned to accept an endowed chair at the nation's highest-ranked school of dentistry. The researcher noted that this school had a budget six times that of the School of Dentistry at Western University, but a faculty only three times as large, and a student body only twice as large.

Kennedy, prior to becoming president, had been a highly respected scholar on management control in nonprofit organizations. Her first major administrative appointment was dean of the Business School at Western University. During her tenure as dean she became an influential spokesperson on the financial aspects of the entire university. Terms such as discretionary-cost center, efficiency measure, and effectiveness measure had become part of the university jargon at many meetings.

Required
1. What are the characteristics of a discretionary-cost center? From Kennedy's perspective, would you view each of the nine individual schools as a discretionary-cost center?
2. Using the data in Exhibit 11-8, make a report on (a) the efficiency and (b) the effectiveness of each of the Business, Dentistry, and Engineering schools.
3. What are the strengths and weaknesses of the quantitative measures you use in requirement 2 to measure efficiency and effectiveness?
4. One option Kennedy plans to raise at the board of trustees' meeting is whether to discontinue the Dentistry school at Western. What information other than that in Exhibit 11-8 would you recommend that Kennedy present to the board of trustees when outlining this option?

11-30 Zero-base budgeting, business school of a university. For many years Western University has used an incremental approach to deciding the amounts budgeted for each of the nine schools (Business, Dentistry, Earth Sciences, Education, Engineering, Humanities and Sciences, Law, Medicine, and Nursing). The new president of Western University is a strong advocate of zero-base budgeting (ZBB). She decides that the School of Business will be used to illustrate implementation of ZBB. Exhibit 11-8 (from Problem 11-29) presents summary information pertaining to the School of Business.

EXHIBIT 11-8
Western University: Summary Data Over 19_1 to 19_3 Period

YEAR	SCHOOL OF BUSINESS			SCHOOL OF DENTISTRY			SCHOOL OF ENGINEERING		
	19_1	19_2	19_3	19_1	19_2	19_3	19_1	19_2	19_3
Total budget spent (millions)	$17.4	$18.7	$20.2	$10.6	$10.3	$9.1	$88.7	$92.6	$98.7
Number of academic faculty	62	63	66	28	26	25	183	187	192
Number of students	642	638	649	260	258	237	2010	2060	2035
Student Admissions Data:									
Applicants-per-slot ratio	10.5	12.3	14.7	6.2	6.5	6.6	4.2	3.9	3.6
Acceptances-to-offers-made ratio	.57	.58	.64	.26	.20	.18	.37	.38	.41
Mean percentile of admitted class on national test such as GMAT	98	97	98	83	81	77	89	91	93
Graduating Student Data:									
Mean starting annual salary	$38,000	$42,300	$45,200	$29,200	$31,300	$31,400	$27,300	$29,100	$31,600
Mean job offers per graduating student	5.4	4.7	6.4	2.6	2.5	2.2	1.8	1.8	1.7
Faculty Data:									
Mean teaching evaluation (How effective is this teacher? 1–7 scale)	5.80	5.93	5.87	5.38	5.43	5.47	4.95	5.15	5.10
Mean refereed publications per faculty	1.7	1.6	1.8	3.5	3.2	2.1	2.7	2.6	2.9
Average page length per published article	14.1	13.2	15.5	3.6	4.1	3.9	5.8	6.2	5.7
Mean number of citations per faculty in four leading academic journals	3.1	3.4	3.6	3.8	3.6	2.4	2.5	2.7	2.6
Total books published by faculty	8	7	8	2	2	1	4	7	6
National ranking of school by deans of comparable departments in other universities	2	1	1	11	12	15	8	8	6

1. How is ZBB different from the incremental approach to budgeting?
2. Describe how you would implement ZBB at the School of Business at Western University.
3. What are the likely advantages and disadvantages of using ZBB for the School of Business?

11-31 Discretionary-cost center, research and development function of a computer software company. Susan Teece, president of Software Advance Inc., has a set of problems many of her competitors would love to have. Teece has a large cash fund of $50 million that can potentially be allocated to research and development. Her twin problems are (a) how much of the $50 million to spend on R & D, and (b) how to ensure that the amount budgeted for R & D is efficiently and effectively spent.

The sales, operating income, and R & D expenditures of Software Advance over the last four years (19_1 to 19_4) are (in $ millions):

	19_1	19_2	19_3	19_4
Sales	2	12	47	86
R & D	0.5	2	8	15
Operating income	(1)	3	11	16

Software's success is based almost exclusively on Insight 1-2-3, a spreadsheet program for personal computers. The Insight program was developed by Jeff Moore, a major shareholder in Software Advance and head of its research and development department. Over 30% of the R & D budget in 19_3 and 19_4 was paid to independent contractors who operate out of their own homes or private offices. Despite $23 million being spent on R & D in 19_3 and 19_4, Software Advance has not been successful in developing a second generation of products to continue its recent high growth rate of sales.

The 19_3 and 19_4 R & D budgets were based on the 19_2 percentage of R & D to sales, the year in which the Insight 1-2-3 program was developed. Teece used this mechanical percentage-of-sales approach because it seemed a convenient way to reach a decision quickly. Moreover, the percentage approach allowed Teece to handle her many pressing marketing problems of 19_3 and 19_4.

The electronics industry trade association reports the following 19_4 summary data for 33 software development companies, classified by firm size:

	FIRM SIZE CATEGORY BY SALES ($ millions)			
	1–5	5–10	10–20	20–100
Number of firms	18	5	5	5
R & D as a percentage of sales	25.9%	18.4%	15.0%	7.4%

1. Why might the R & D department of Software Advance Inc. be viewed as a discretionary-cost center?
2. What limitations arise from use of the fixed percentage-of-sales approach to deciding the size of the annual R & D budget?
3. How might the industry trade association data be useful in the R & D decisions facing Teece?
4. How might Teece and Moore help ensure that the R & D budget of Software Advance is efficiently and effectively spent? Show evidence of using Exhibit 11-3 (p. 381) in your answer.

11-32 Discretionary cost center, personnel department of a public accounting firm, efficiency and effectiveness measures. KLM, a large and reputable public accounting firm, is in a period of transition. Rich Elliot, the new managing partner, was elected on the promise of increasing efficiency and effectiveness in all phases of the business. KLM's revenues are derived from three areas: auditing (70%), tax (20%), and consulting (10%). Like many similar firms, KLM

EXHIBIT 11-9
University Recruiting Data for KLM

	19_1	19_2	19_3	19_4	19_5	19_6
COST PER HIRE						
Graduate Accounting	$2,000	$1,600	$2,000	$2,100	$1,900	$1,800
Graduate Business	2,400	3,600	3,900	5,800	8,200	9,000
Undergraduate	1,100	1,200	1,400	1,700	1,800	1,850
RETENTION RATIO						
Graduate Accounting:19_1 Hirees	—	.75	.60	.50	.44	.40
Graduate Business :19_1 Hirees	—	.60	.40	.32	.26	.24
Undergraduate :19_1 Hirees	—	.85	.70	.62	.57	.50
Graduate Accounting:19_3 Hirees	—	—	—	.76	.63	.54
Graduate Business :19_3 Hirees	—	—	—	.50	.35	.26
Undergraduate :19_3 Hirees	—	—	—	.86	.69	.63
PROMOTION-TO-MANAGER RATIO						
Graduate Accounting:19_1 Hirees	—	.02	.08	.13	.17	.24
Graduate Business :19_1 Hirees	—	.04	.20	.22	.24	.22
Undergraduate :19_1 Hirees	—	.01	.02	.07	.11	.18
Graduate Accounting:19_3 Hirees	—	—	—	.02	.09	.15
Graduate Business :19_3 Hirees	—	—	—	.04	.21	.23
Undergraduate :19_3 Hirees	—	—	—	.01	.02	.08

is experiencing declining profit margins in its audit activities. The tax and consulting business areas are more profitable and have not experienced any erosion in profit margins in recent years.

Jody Mitchell, the newly appointed senior partner in charge of personnel at KLM, fully agrees with Elliot's efficiency and effectiveness philosophy. Mitchell gathers some data on recruiting over the last five years. She classifies the universities at which KLM recruits into three categories:

1. Graduate Accounting: candidates graduating with a master's degree in accounting
2. Graduate Business: candidates graduating with a master's degree in business
3. Undergraduate: candidates graduating with a bachelor's degree in an area such as accounting, business, or economics

Exhibit 11-9 presents information on the cost per hire, retention ratio, and promotion-to-manager ratio for these three recruiting categories over the 19_1 to 19_6 period. Mitchell wants to use more quantitative measures when deciding how to allocate the resources KLM spends on recruiting.

Required

1. Why might the personnel department of a public accounting firm be viewed as a discretionary-cost center?
2. What items would be included in KLM's costs of hiring university graduates?
3. What inferences would you make about the efficiency and effectiveness of KLM's recruiting in each area: (a) Graduate Accounting, (b) Graduate Business, and (c) Undergraduate?
4. What information, other than that in Exhibit 11-9, would you collect to evaluate the efficiency and effectiveness of KLM's recruiting?

11-33 Discretionary cost center, oil exploration division, efficiency and effectiveness measures. In 19_8 Wildcat Inc. and Energy Inc., two companies concentrating on high-risk oil exploration, merged to form a new company called Risky Business. Randy Savage, the president of Risky Business, was trying to choose between the two top candidates for the position of manager of exploration for the new company:

Scott Magee, oil exploration manager of Wildcat Inc.

Bob Ellis, oil exploration manager of Energy Inc.

Savage collected the information in Exhibit 11-10 that pertains to the 19_1 to 19_7 period.

Magee and Ellis were senior executives of their respective companies. They were both in their early forties and had been members of their respective boards of directors. Both Wildcat and Energy subcontracted the majority of their exploration to independent oil service companies that conducted activities such as sinking exploratory holes and seismic evaluation. Magee and Ellis were in daily communication with these oil service companies. Both Wildcat and Energy employed an independent oil production firm that extracts the discovered oil and sells it to third parties for a total fee to the exploration company of $3 per barrel produced.

Magee, in an interview with Savage, proudly noted that the annual net income of Wildcat Inc. had always been positive and that it had increased in five of the last six years. Magee derisively noted the loss years in 19_4 and 19_6 at Energy Inc. He stressed that he had always been able to stay within the annual cost budget that the board of directors of Wildcat set for the exploration division. His final observation was that in 19_7 Wildcat averaged $12.63 exploration cost for each barrel of oil discovered compared with an average of $18.42 exploration cost per barrel for Energy.

Ellis, in an interview with Savage, stressed that the exploration function of an oil company should not be evaluated on a year-by-year net income basis. There is a high level of uncertainty in finding oil reserves. A company that made two big finds in seven years might be highly successful, irrespective of the stability of its year-by-year net income. Ellis stressed that a benefit of the long-range focus he had implemented at Energy Inc. was a lower average cost to drill each exploratory wellhole. He noted that from 19_1 to 19_7, the total

EXHIBIT 11-10
Operating Data for Wildcat Inc. and Energy Inc.

WILDCAT INC.	19_1	19_2	19_3	19_4	19_5	19_6	19_7
Revenues ($000's)	10,000	8,400	11,500	13,500	11,440	13,600	13,500
Exploration costs ($000's)	2,600	1,300	1,900	3,100	2,000	4,700	4,800
Net income ($000's)	800	830	860	940	950	930	960
Barrels of oil sold (000's)	625	420	500	750	520	800	900
Average price per barrel sold	$16	$20	$23	$18	$22	$17	$15
Barrels of oil discovered (000's)	120	220	360	160	310	260	380
Wellholes drilled	8	3	5	9	5	12	14

ENERGY INC.	19_1	19_2	19_3	19_4	19_5	19_6	19_7
Revenues ($000's)	12,000	18,400	20,900	16,660	21,850	15,980	12,600
Exploration costs ($000's)	3,000	3,800	4,000	3,600	5,000	4,300	3,500
Net income ($000's)	900	1,900	3,300	(1,040)	3,350	(1,520)	900
Barrels of oil sold (000's)	800	920	950	980	950	940	900
Average price per barrel sold	$15	$20	$22	$17	$23	$17	$14
Barrels of oil discovered (000's)	1,375	620	1,320	340	450	1,700	190
Wellholes drilled	10	12	13	12	16	13	12

exploration cost per wellhole drilled averaged approximately $309,000 for Energy Inc. compared with $364,000 for Wildcat Inc.

1. Why might the exploration division of an oil company be regarded as a discretionary-cost center?
2. What are the limitations of using the current year's net income to evaluate the efficiency or effectiveness of the current year's exploration activity?
3. What conclusions about the exploration ability of Magee would you make from his ability to stay within the annual cost budget that the board of directors of Wildcat set for exploration?
4. Compute the following two measures of efficiency for Wildcat and Energy for each year from 19_1 to 19_7 and for the entire seven-year period:

$$\text{Cost per wellhole drilled} = \frac{\text{Total exploration cost per year}}{\text{Wellholes drilled in year}}$$

$$\text{Cost per barrel of oil discovered} = \frac{\text{Total exploration cost for year}}{\text{Barrels of oil discovered in year}}$$

What inferences can you draw from these two measures?

5. Compute the following measure of effectiveness for Wildcat and Energy for each year from 19_1 to 19_7:

$$\frac{\text{Gross margin}}{\text{per barrel}} = \left(\frac{\text{Selling price}}{\text{per barrel}}\right) - \left(\frac{\text{Exploration cost}}{\text{per barrel}}\right) - \left(\frac{\text{Production cost}}{\text{per barrel}}\right)$$

What inferences can you draw from this measure? (For simplicity use the selling price each company actually obtained in 19_X for oil discovered in 19_X.)

6. Would you choose Magee or Ellis as exploration manager of Risky Business? Explain your choice.

Cost Allocation: Part I

12

Terminology • Purposes of Cost Allocation • Criteria to Guide Cost Allocation Decisions • The General Process of Allocation • Allocating Costs from One Department to Another • Allocating Costs of Service Departments • Allocation of Common Costs •

Cost allocation is an inescapable problem in nearly every organization and in nearly every facet of accounting. How should the costs of fixed assets be allocated to months, years, departments, and products or services? Accounting for depreciation is essentially a problem of cost allocation. Or, how should the costs of shared services be allocated among departments? How should university costs be split among undergraduate programs, graduate programs, and research? How should the costs of expensive medical equipment, facilities, and staff be allocated in a hospital?

Inevitably, these are tough questions. The answers often are not clearly right or clearly wrong. Nevertheless, we will try to obtain some insight into the pervasive problem of cost allocation—at least to understand the dimensions of the problem, even if the answers seem elusive. The chances are considerable that you will be directly faced with this problem sometime during your career.

This chapter first examines the purposes served by cost allocation and the general process of cost allocation. It then focuses on the allocation of costs to departments. Chapter 13 discusses topics related to the allocation of indirect department costs to individual products, services, or projects (such as a government contract). There is much overlap in the material in Chapters 12 and 13. The reader should avoid any attempt to place the topics in these two chapters into separate isolated categories.[1]

TERMINOLOGY

The terms relating to cost allocation vary throughout the literature and among organizations. Be sure to get mutual agreement on definitions when you deal with allocation problems in practice. This book uses **cost allocation** in a general sense: the assignment and reassignment of a cost or group of costs to one or more cost objectives.[2] A cost objective is any activity for which a separate measurement of costs is desired. Allocation encompasses the assignment of both direct and indirect costs.

A cost item is a **direct cost** if it can be identified specifically with a single cost objective in an economically feasible manner. An example of direct-cost allocation is the allocation of direct materials to a department and then to the various jobs worked on within that department.

A cost item is an **indirect cost** if it cannot be identified specifically with a single cost objective in an economically feasible manner.[3] An example of indirect-cost allocation is the allocation of insurance costs to individual departments. Insurance premiums for firms typically are not quoted on an individual-department basis, let alone a single-item basis such as an individual finished product. Firms seek some reasonable basis, such as square footage of buildings covered by the insurance, when allocating the total insurance-premium cost to individual departments.

PURPOSES OF COST ALLOCATION

Exhibit 12-1 outlines and illustrates four purposes for allocating costs: economic decisions, motivation, income and asset measurement for external parties, and cost justification or reimbursement. Ideally, a single-cost allocation would satisfy all purposes simultaneously. An example would be the acquisition cost of a direct material such as an airplane engine by an airplane manufacturer; all four purposes would imply that this acquisition cost should be allocated to the cost of assembling the airplane. In contrast, the salary of a scientist in a central corporate research department of IBM may be allocated to satisfy purpose 1 (economic decisions), may

---

[1]For a superb overview of cost allocation issues, see A. Atkinson, *Intrafirm Cost and Resource Allocations: Theory and Practice* (Society of Management Accountants of Canada and Canadian Academic Accounting Association Research Monograph, 1987). This study includes a literature review, an analysis of questionnaire responses from 245 large Canadian firms, an analysis of responses from a more-detailed questionnaire returned by 15 firms, and six case studies based on plant visits to each firm.

[2]There are other terms that may be used with assorted shades of meaning: **cost reallocation**, **cost assignment** and **reassignment**, **cost apportionment** and **reapportionment**, **cost distribution** and **redistribution**, and **cost tracing** and **retracing**.

The terms *cost application* and *cost absorption* have a fairly uniform usage. They are confined to a *special type* of cost allocation, the final assignment of costs to *products,* as distinguished from departments, divisions, territories, or cost centers.

[3]The definitions of *direct cost* and *indirect cost* used in this chapter are similar to those in "Statement on Management Accounting No. 4B—Allocation of Service and Administrative Costs" by the Management Accounting Practices Committee of the National Association of Accountants in *Management Accounting,* September 1985.

EXHIBIT 12-1
Purposes of Cost Allocation

PURPOSE	ILLUSTRATIONS
1. Economic decisions for resources allocation	To decide how to allocate available capacity among products. To decide whether to add a new airline flight.
2. Motivation	To encourage or discourage use of services such as computers, accounting, market research, or legal. To decrease the rate of growth of corporate overhead expenditures.
3. Income and asset measurement for external parties	To cost products for stockholder and income tax reporting. Under generally accepted accounting principles, these costs include the allocation of indirect manufacturing costs to products.
4. Cost justification or reimbursement	To cost products or services as a basis for establishing a "fair" price. Used in defense contracting, health care, and public utility rate regulations to obtain cost reimbursements. To reimburse operating parties in joint-venture agreements.

or may not be allocated to satisfy purpose 2 (motivation), must not be allocated to inventory to satisfy purpose 3 (income and asset measurement for external parties), and, depending on the laws or regulations, may or may not be allocated to a government contract based on cost reimbursement to satisfy purpose 4 (cost justification). When all four purposes are unattainable simultaneously, the accountant and manager should initially tackle the problem by identifying the purpose that should dominate in the specific situation faced.

Executives frequently cite the economic decisions and motivation purposes as important reasons for allocating indirect costs. For example, one survey reported the following reasons:

1. To remind profit center managers that indirect costs exist and that profit center earnings must be adequate to cover some share of those costs.
2. To encourage use of central services that would otherwise be underutilized.
3. To stimulate profit center managers to put pressure on central managers to control service costs.[4]

A poll of Canadian executives on "the primary objective" of allocating indirect costs reported the following:[5]

PRIMARY OBJECTIVE	PERCENTAGE OF RESPONDENTS
1. Motivation	42%
2. Provide signals for resource allocation	32
3. Other	
Cost determination	19
Overhead recovery	5
Equity	2

[4] J. Fremgen and S. Liao, *The Allocation of Corporate Indirect Costs* (New York: National Association of Accountants, 1981).

[5] Atkinson, *Intra-firm Cost and Resource Allocations: Theory and Practice*, p. 9.

Consider the motivation purpose. Cost allocation typically will not be the only approach to controlling service costs or the reduction of indirect-cost items such as power and electricity. Other approaches include top-management edicts and the involvement of all affected managers in the budgeting process. *Organizations rarely ask which single approach to motivating managers is best. Rather, they view the challenge as designing a collective set of motivation mechanisms that reinforce each other.*

Cost allocations for motivation need not be "full" or "tidy" allocations in the sense that all the costs assigned to a chosen pool are 100% allocated to the cost objectives.[6] Indeed, partial allocation of some service department costs may encourage use of the central service but still remind divisional managers that costs are actually incurred.

Exhibit 12-1 demonstrates a major theme of this book: different costs for different purposes. Consider the *income and asset measurement for external parties* purpose. Under generally accepted accounting principles for financial reporting, indirect manufacturing costs, but *not* indirect selling costs, are allocated to products. Yet, indirect selling costs may be allocated to products in decisions relating to purpose 1 in Exhibit 12-1—e.g., pricing decisions and product promotion decisions.

Consider the *cost justification or reimbursement* purpose in Exhibit 12-1. Allocation of indirect costs to products (projects, services, etc.) increases profitability. Why? Because where contracts permit the recovery of indirect costs, managers would be negligent not to incorporate them into the computation of reimbursable cost.

CRITERIA TO GUIDE COST ALLOCATION DECISIONS

Exhibit 12-2 outlines and illustrates four criteria used to guide decisions relating to cost allocations. **The criterion chosen in a specific decision should be guided by the dominant purpose to be served by the cost allocation. This text emphasizes the superiority of the cause-and-effect criterion when the purpose of cost allocation is related to resource allocation decisions or motivation.**

The benefits-received and equity criteria are explicitly included in the regulations governing U.S. federal government procurement. The Federal Acquisition Regulation (FAR) includes the following definition of "allocability" (in FAR 31.201-4):

> A cost is allocable if it is assignable or chargeable to one or more cost objectives on the basis of relative benefits received or other equitable relationship. Subject to the foregoing, a cost is allocable to a Government contract if it—
>
> (a) Is incurred specifically for the contract;
>
> (b) Benefits both the contract and other work, and can be distributed to them in reasonable proportion to the benefits received; or
>
> (c) Is necessary to the overall operation of the business, although a direct relationship to any particular cost objective cannot be shown.[7]

---

[6]The phrase "tidy allocation" is taken from J. Demski, "Cost Allocation Games" in *Joint Cost Allocations*, ed. S. Moriarity (Norman: University of Oklahoma, 1981), pp. 142–73.

[7]See J. Bedingfield and L. Rosen, *Government Contract Accounting* (Washington, D.C.: Federal Publications Inc., 1985), p. 7.13.

EXHIBIT 12-2
Criteria to Guide Cost Allocation Decisions

1. *CAUSE AND EFFECT.* This criterion identifies the outputs of the cost pool (any grouping of individual costs) and allocates the costs in proportion to the services provided. This relationship is usually easy to establish for direct manufacturing costs such as material and labor. Specific causes and effects of factory overhead and nonmanufacturing costs often are difficult to pinpoint with assurance. As a practical matter, relationships are sought to relate the cost objective and the cost incurred. The preferable relationship or cost function is one that helps the prediction of changes in total costs.

2. *BENEFITS RECEIVED.* This criterion identifies the beneficiaries of the outputs of the cost pool and allocates the costs in proportion to the benefits received. An example is a corporatewide advertising program that promotes the general image of a corporation rather than any individual product. The costs of such programs may be allocated on the basis of division sales in the belief that divisions with higher sales levels are more likely to benefit than divisions with lower sales levels.

3. *FAIRNESS OR EQUITY.* This criterion is often cited in government contracting where cost allocations are the means for establishing a mutually satisfactory price. The allocation here is viewed as a "reasonable" or "fair" means of establishing a selling price in the minds of the contracting parties. For most allocation decisions, fairness is a lofty objective rather than an operational criterion.

4. *ABILITY TO BEAR.* This criterion advocates allocating costs in proportion to the cost objective's ability to bear. An example is the allocation of corporate executive salaries on the basis of divisional profitability; the presumption is that the more profitable divisions have a greater ability to absorb corporate headquarters' costs. Note the similarity of this criterion to the justifications given by legislators for progressive income tax rates.

An authoritative work on U.S. Government Contract Accounting includes the following comment on cost allocation criteria:

> Benefits received, when measurable and traceable, provide guidance for allocation. Benefits received should be interpreted as meaning the receiving of services or goods by the activity represented by the cost objectives to which the costs are being allocated. Where benefits are not reasonably traceable or measurable because of the nature of the cost or its remoteness from the cost objectives to which it is to be allocated, equity must supplant benefit.[8]

Further discussion of the contract reimbursement purpose of cost allocation is presented in Chapter 13 (pp. 455–57).

THE GENERAL PROCESS OF ALLOCATION

The three facets of cost allocation

There are essentially three facets of cost allocation:

1. Choosing the cost objective (the independent variable), which is essentially an *action*.[9] Examples are products, services, processes, contracts, departments, or divisions, all of which represent various actions.

---

[8]Ibid., p. 7.14.

[9]See Chapter 2 for an introductory coverage of cost objectives. Further discussion can be found in J. Demski and G. Feltham, *Cost Determination: A Conceptual Approach* (Ames: Iowa State University Press, 1976), especially Chaps. 5 and 6.

2. Choosing and accumulating (pooling) the *costs* (the dependent variable) that relate to the cost objective. Examples are the direct materials, direct labor, and overhead costs of making a product, as well as the nonmanufacturing selling and administration expenses. A **cost pool** is any grouping of individual costs.

3. Choosing a **cost allocation base,** which is a systematic means of relating a given cost or cost pool with a cost objective. For example, direct-labor hours or direct-machine hours are commonly used as allocation bases for applying indirect manufacturing costs (the cost pool) to products (the cost objective).

This chapter and the next will concentrate mainly on the question of how to allocate an **indirect cost pool,** which can be defined as any grouping of individual costs that cannot be identified directly with a single cost objective in an economically feasible manner. This chapter discusses the allocation of indirect costs to departments producing products or services. Chapter 13 discusses the allocation of indirect department costs to the individual products or services themselves.

Intermediate and final cost objectives

Sometimes cost objectives are divided into "intermediate" and "final" categories. For example, the final cost objective may be a job order. It is "final" in the sense that the accumulated costs are not allocated further except perhaps to the units of product within the job. That is, a job may cost $1,000 for 1,000 units; if 400 were sold and 600 were still held in inventory, then $600 of the $1,000 would be allocated to inventory.

The overhead allocated to that job order may follow a circuitous route involving many cost objectives. Consider the salary of the supervisor of a factory building maintenance department. That person's salary may be charged directly to the building maintenance department, which is only an intermediate cost objective as far as product costing is concerned. The salary usually becomes part of a larger grouping of overhead costs—often called an *overhead pool*—that are allocated to two or more subsequent cost objectives. Exhibit 12-3 illustrates these relationships.

Note that an individual cost usually qualifies initially as a *direct* cost to at least one cost objective because it can be identified specifically therewith. But the allocation process then proceeds so that costs lose their directness (individuality). They become part of indirect cost groups, so that subsequent allocations are made of *cost pools,* not *individual* costs. Thus the supervisor's salary is not allocated separately to other service and production departments. Instead, the aggregated building maintenance costs are allocated as a group or pool.

EXHIBIT 12-3
Intermediate and Final Cost Objectives

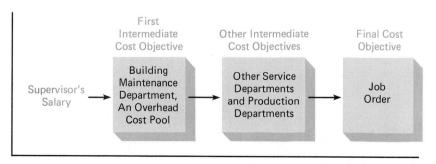

As an illustration of the diverse items that fall under the indirect-cost umbrella, consider Computer Horizons. Computer Horizons has two divisions:

- The Microcomputer Division, which manufactures three related products: (1) the Plum Computer (sold mostly to college students and for use in small offices and in homes); (2) the Portable Plum (smaller version of the Plum that can be carried in a briefcase), and (3) the Super Plum (has a larger memory and more capabilities than the Plum and is targeted at the business market).

- The Peripheral Equipment Division, which manufactures printers, plotters, and other items that can be used with the Plum line of microcomputers.

Exhibit 12-4 illustrates the kinds of indirect costs that typically are incurred at corporate and division levels. The Computer Horizons example will be used in several subsequent sections of Chapters 12 and 13.

Several of the departments in Exhibit 12-4 frequently are labeled as service

EXHIBIT 12-4
Examples of Indirect Costs (With Respect to Individual Products)
Typically Incurred at Corporate and Division Levels

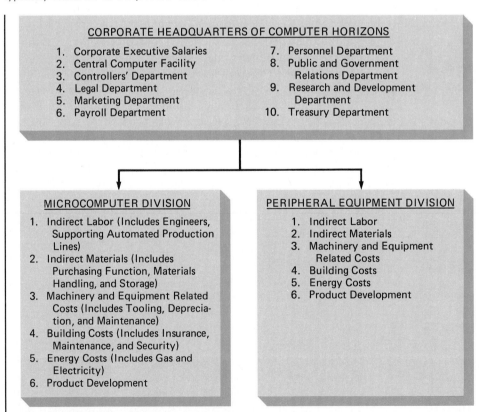

CORPORATE HEADQUARTERS OF COMPUTER HORIZONS

1. Corporate Executive Salaries
2. Central Computer Facility
3. Controllers' Department
4. Legal Department
5. Marketing Department
6. Payroll Department
7. Personnel Department
8. Public and Government Relations Department
9. Research and Development Department
10. Treasury Department

MICROCOMPUTER DIVISION

1. Indirect Labor (Includes Engineers, Supporting Automated Production Lines)
2. Indirect Materials (Includes Purchasing Function, Materials Handling, and Storage)
3. Machinery and Equipment Related Costs (Includes Tooling, Depreciation, and Maintenance)
4. Building Costs (Includes Insurance, Maintenance, and Security)
5. Energy Costs (Includes Gas and Electricity)
6. Product Development

PERIPHERAL EQUIPMENT DIVISION

1. Indirect Labor
2. Indirect Materials
3. Machinery and Equipment Related Costs
4. Building Costs
5. Energy Costs
6. Product Development

departments. Examples include the legal and personnel departments. Two criteria are most frequently used by organizations to "identify" a **service department**:

1. The main (and in some cases exclusive) rationale of the department is the provision of services to other departments in the organization.
2. There is a traceable cause-and-effect relationship between the costs of the service department and the services provided to other departments.

Service departments create special cost allocation problems when individual service departments provide reciprocal services to each other, as well as to producing departments. An example of reciprocal services in Computer Horizons would be the legal department providing services to the personnel department (e.g., advice on compliance with labor laws) and the personnel department providing services to the legal department (e.g., the hiring of lawyers and secretaries). Alternative methods of allocating service department costs are described in a subsequent section of this chapter. The Problem for Self-Study at the end of this chapter illustrates three methods of allocating the legal and personnel department costs of Computer Horizons to its two production divisions.

Be cautious here. First, organizations differ in the departments located at the corporate and division levels. Some departments located at corporate headquarters of Computer Horizons (e.g., research and development) are located at the division level in other organizations. Second, organizations differ in the meaning attached to the term *service department*. Always try to ascertain the precise meaning of this term when analyzing data including allocations of "service department" costs.

Examples of indirect cost allocation bases

Most companies allocate some indirect corporate costs or central-service costs to divisions (departments, profit centers, etc.). In one survey, 84% of the firms stated that they allocated at least part of their corporate indirect costs to their profit centers.[10]

Examples of cost allocation bases used for several of the corporate headquarters' cost pool categories in Exhibit 12-4 include the following:

COST POOL	ALLOCATION BASE
Corporate Executive Salaries	Sales
Legal Department	Estimated time or usage
Marketing Department	Sales
Payroll Department	Number of employees Payroll dollars
Personnel Department	Number of employees
Treasury Department (interest cost on debt)	Identifiable assets

Examples of cost allocation bases used for several of the division cost pool categories in Exhibit 12-4 include the following:

---

[10]Fremgen and Liao, *Allocation of Corporate Indirect Costs*, p. 33.

COST POOL	ALLOCATION BASE
Indirect Materials	Cost of direct materials
	Number of direct-material units
Machinery and Equipment Costs	Machine-hours
Building Costs (includes insurance, maintenance, and security)	Relative square footage
	Relative cubic footage
Energy Costs	Installed horsepower
	Relative square footage

The above allocation bases are illustrative only. The base preferred by an organization will depend on the purpose served by the cost allocation (see Exhibit 12-1) and the costs of implementing alternative allocation bases.

ALLOCATING COSTS FROM ONE DEPARTMENT TO ANOTHER

When allocating costs from one department to another, management must decide (a) whether to use a single-cost pool or multiple-cost pools (e.g., a fixed-cost pool and a variable-cost pool) for the costs of the department, (b) whether to use standard prices and standard quantities or actual prices and actual quantities when collecting the costs of the department, and (c) whether to use budgeted volume or actual volume as the allocation base for a given cost pool.

The purpose of the cost allocation should guide decisions related to items a, b, and c. This section illustrates how the following guidelines can help achieve the economic and motivation purposes where economically feasible:

1. Use multiple-cost pools, in which a distinction is made between fixed costs and variable costs.
2. Use standard prices and standard quantities allowed when collecting the department costs to be allocated.
3. Use budgeted volume as the allocation base for a given fixed-cost pool, and use actual volume as the allocation base for a given variable-cost pool.

These guidelines are presented as useful starting points. (We note in this section how recognition of the risks facing providers or users of services can complicate decisions on how to allocate costs.)

Single- vs. multiple-cost pools

One of two approaches is used by most organizations when allocating service department costs:

1. Collect costs for the department into a single-cost pool. This approach, termed the single-rate method, makes no distinction between fixed and variable costs.
2. Collect costs for the department into two or more cost pools. One cost pool could include the fixed costs; the second cost pool could include the variable costs of the department. Where two cost pools are used, this approach is termed the **dual-rate method.** Further refinement is possible by using more than one variable-cost pool, with different allocation bases used for each pool.

To illustrate these two methods, consider the Central Computer Facility Department of Computer Horizons (see Exhibit 12-4). For simplicity, assume that the only users of this facility are the Microcomputer Division and the Peripheral Equipment Division. The following data apply to the forthcoming budget year:

1. Fixed cost of operating the facility — $300,000
2. Total capacity available in hours — 2,000
3. Budgeted usage in hours:
   - Microcomputer Division — 800
   - Peripheral Equipment Division — 400
   - Total for both divisions — 1,200
4. Estimated variable standard cost per hour in the 1,000- to 1,500-hour relevant range — $200 per hour

Under the single-rate method, the costs of the Central Computer Facility would be allocated as follows:

$$\text{Total costs: } \$300,000 + (1,200 \times \$200) = \$540,000$$
$$\text{Budgeted usage} = 1,200 \text{ hours}$$
$$\text{Cost per hour: } \frac{\$540,000}{1,200} = \$450$$
$$\text{Microcomputer Division} = \$450 \text{ per hour}$$
$$\text{Peripheral Equipment Division} = \$450 \text{ per hour}$$

Use of the single-cost pool, when combined with the budgeted volume base, transforms what is a fixed cost to the Central Computer Facility (and to Computer Horizons) into a variable cost to users of that facility.

Under the dual-rate method, the costs of the Central Computer Facility would be allocated as follows (assuming fixed costs are allocated using budgeted volume and variable costs are allocated using actual volume):

Microcomputer Division

$$\text{Fixed-cost pool: } \left(\frac{800}{1,200} \times \$300,000 \right) = \$200,000$$
$$\text{Variable-cost pool} = \$200 \text{ per hour}$$

Peripheral Equipment Division

$$\text{Fixed-cost pool: } \left(\frac{400}{1,200} \times \$300,000 \right) = \$100,000$$
$$\text{Variable-cost pool} = \$200 \text{ per hour}$$

To illustrate these two methods, assume that the Microcomputer Division actually uses 900 hours and the Peripheral Equipment Division actually uses 300 hours. The costs allocated to these two departments would be as follows:

Single-Rate Method

$$\text{Microcomputer Division: } 900 \times \$450 = \$405,000$$
$$\text{Peripheral Equipment Division: } 300 \times \$450 = \$135,000$$

Dual-Rate Method

Microcomputer Division: $200,000 + (900 \times \$200) = \$380,000$

Peripheral Equipment Division: $100,000 + (300 \times \$200) = \$160,000$

The dual-rate method may provide better information for economic decisions. Suppose that in midyear an external vendor offers the Microcomputer Division comparable computer services at $300 per hour. The fixed costs are unavoidable and will remain the same. Since the single-rate method results in a charge of $450 per hour, the Microcomputer Division would prefer to use the external vendor. However, this is not in the best interests of the company. In contrast, the $200-per-hour variable rate by the dual-rate method correctly signals to the Microcomputer Division that Computer Horizons will save $100 per hour by using the internal computer facility. (Chapter 25 provides further discussion of the pricing of internally used goods and services.)

The benefit of using a single-cost pool is its low cost of implementation. It avoids the often expensive analysis necessary to classify the individual cost items of a department into fixed and variable categories. This benefit can appear very attractive to organizations that are reluctant to invest in fancier accounting systems unless the prospects of better operating decisions are obvious.

Standard vs. actual prices and quantities

Departmental costs can be allocated using standard prices and standard quantities allowed or actual prices and actual quantities. A major benefit of standard prices and standard quantities is that the user department knows the cost in advance. Users are then better equipped to decide about the amount of the service to request, and (if the option exists) whether to use the internal department source or an external vendor.

Standard prices and standard quantities also help motivate the manager of the service department to improve efficiency. The service department bears the risk of any unfavorable price or efficiency variances, not the user department.

Some organizations recognize that it may not always be best to impose *all* the risks of changes from standards completely on the service department (as when costs are allocated using standard quantities and standard prices) or completely on the user department (as when costs are allocated using actual quantities and actual prices). For example, both departments may agree to share the risk (via an explicit formula) of a large uncontrollable increase in the price of a material used by the service department.

Budgeted vs. actual volume allocation bases

There are motivational benefits from basing departmental fixed-cost allocations on budgeted volume rather than actual volume. To illustrate, consider the budget of $300,000 fixed costs at the Central Computer Facility of Computer Horizons. Assume that actual and budgeted fixed costs are equal. The effect of using the budgeted and actual usage figures to allocate the $300,000 can be illustrated for three different cases: that the actual usage of the Peripheral Equipment Division equals, exceeds, or is less than the budgeted usage. Assume the actual and budgeted usage of the Microcomputer Division are always equal. The allocation of the total fixed costs (TFC) of $300,000 to each department would be:

	ALLOCATION BASE	
CASE	Budgeted Volume	Actual Volume
1. Microcomputer uses 800 hours	$\$200,000\left(\dfrac{800}{1,200} \times \text{TFC}\right)$	$\$200,000\left(\dfrac{800}{1,200} \times \text{TFC}\right)$
Peripheral Equipment uses 400 hours	$\$100,000\left(\dfrac{400}{1,200} \times \text{TFC}\right)$	$\$100,000\left(\dfrac{400}{1,200} \times \text{TFC}\right)$
2. Microcomputer uses 800 hours	$\$200,000\left(\dfrac{800}{1,200} \times \text{TFC}\right)$	$\$160,000\left(\dfrac{800}{1,500} \times \text{TFC}\right)$
Peripheral Equipment uses 700 hours	$\$100,000\left(\dfrac{400}{1,200} \times \text{TFC}\right)$	$\$140,000\left(\dfrac{700}{1,500} \times \text{TFC}\right)$
3. Microcomputer uses 800 hours	$\$200,000\left(\dfrac{800}{1,200} \times \text{TFC}\right)$	$\$240,000\left(\dfrac{800}{1,000} \times \text{TFC}\right)$
Peripheral Equipment uses 200 hours	$\$100,000\left(\dfrac{400}{1,200} \times \text{TFC}\right)$	$\$60,000\left(\dfrac{200}{1,000} \times \text{TFC}\right)$

With actual usage as the allocation base in case 3, the Microcomputer Division will see its fixed-cost allocation increase by $40,000 relative to what it expected at the start of the year. Yet the actual usage by the Microcomputer Division is exactly the same as it budgeted. By allocating fixed costs on the basis of actual usage, fluctuations in usage in one department can affect the fixed costs allocated to other departments. When actual volume is the allocation base, user departments will not know their allocated costs until the end of the budget year.

When budgeted volume is the allocation base, user departments will know their allocated costs in advance. This information helps both short-run and long-run planning by user departments. The main justification given for the use of budgeted volume to allocate fixed costs is related to long-run planning. Firms make decisions on committed costs (such as the fixed costs of a service department) using a long-run planning horizon; the use of budgeted volume to allocate these fixed costs is consistent with this long-run horizon.

If fixed costs are allocated on the basis of long-run commitments or plans, some managers will be tempted to underestimate their planned usage. In this way, they will bear a lower fraction of the total costs. Top management can counteract these tendencies by systematically comparing actual usage with planned usage. In some organizations there may be clear-cut rewards in the form of salary increases and promotions for managers who are accurate forecasters. In addition, some cost allocation methods include penalties for underpredictions of budgeted usage; for instance, a higher variable rate may be charged after a department exceeds its budgeted usage.

A common allocation base is sales revenue. As with the above discussion for production or usage, budgeted sales typically are preferable to actual sales as an allocation base. This practice avoids the short-run costs of one department being affected by fluctuations in the actual sales of the other departments. The use of sales revenue as an allocation base is often justified on an ability-to-bear criterion; in many cases where it is used, it does not capture a cause-and-effect relationship.[11]

---

[11]Actual sales may be an appropriate allocation base where there is an identifiable cause-and-effect relationship between a cost item and actual sales. An example is sales commissions that are a predetermined percentage of actual sales.

Top managers may resort to seemingly arbitrary cost allocations, ranging from zero to a high price above full cost. Why? Because the allocation is used as a major means of getting subordinates to behave as desired by top managers. An example would be the charging of operating divisions for central costs such as basic research even though cause-and-effect justifications are weak. Some top managers will insist that such allocation practices get division managers to take a desired interest in, say, central research activities. Thus an "arbitrary" cost allocation scheme may be chosen because the formal accounting system provides the best way to get desired actions. This practice may be desirable to the extent that this objective is reached without causing confusion in cost analysis, and resentment about the methods of cost allocation.

Are there any service departments whose costs should not be allocated even though they are clearly needed by the other parts of the organization? Consider the internal-auditing department or the legal department as examples. Ordinarily, where the other department managers have no discretion over their consumption of such services, the argument in favor of allocation rests on the assumption that the costs should be allocated anyway, and that managers generally do not become too concerned about such allocation as long as all departments are subject to a uniform cost allocation procedure. The argument against the allocation of such costs rests on the assumption that no costs should be allocated unless the manager has some direct influence over their amount.

In some organizations, however, operating managers may have much leeway over their usage of such services. Charging for the internal auditing or legal services on the basis of the amount provided may discourage their use, even though such use may be desirable from the standpoint of the organization as a whole. In such instances, either no charge may be involved or a flat annual fee may be involved regardless of the quantity of services consumed. For instance, a large automobile-manufacturing company does not charge for internal auditing because it wants to encourage its managers to utilize such services.

As a general rule, the same objective will be attained by allocating a flat sum to the various departments regardless of actual use. It reminds the managers that the costs do exist. A possible advantage of this procedure is its retainer-fee effect; the payment of the retainer fee motivates the user to utilize the service. Of course, there is always the danger that a few managers may demand too much of what they would then regard as a "free" service. Then some priority system must be instituted, and a method of charging on the basis of services consumed may finally be adopted.

The morale effects of allocation procedures on employees of service departments, as well as on employees of production departments, should be considered. Service department managers report that if other departments are not charged for the services they provide, the service department staff can feel that it lacks the status of first-class citizenship and is not an integral part of the organization.

ALLOCATING COSTS OF SERVICE DEPARTMENTS

In many organizations, there are relationships not only between individual service departments but also between service departments and production departments. Assume, for example, that a company has four departments. The two service de-

EXHIBIT 12-5
Data for Service Department Cost Allocation Example

	SERVICE DEPARTMENTS		PRODUCTION DEPARTMENTS		TOTAL
	Factory Administration	Repair	Machining	Assembly	
Budgeted overhead costs before any interdepartment cost allocations	$600,000	$116,000	$400,000	$200,000	$1,316,000
Proportions of service furnished:					
By Factory Administration					
Budgeted labor-hours	—	16,000	24,000	40,000	80,000
Proportion	—	2/10	3/10	5/10	10/10
By Repair					
Budgeted repair-hours	2,000	—	16,000	2,000	20,000
Proportion	1/10	—	8/10	1/10	10/10

partments are factory administration and repair. The two production departments are machining and assembly. Overhead costs are accumulated by department responsibility for control purposes. For product-costing purposes, however, the service department costs must be allocated to production departments. The data for our example are in Exhibit 12-5.

Three service department allocation methods will be illustrated: *direct, step-down,* and *reciprocal.* These methods have the following four common phases:

1. Prepare budgets for each department.
2. Choose allocation bases.
3. Allocate (reallocate) service department costs.
4. Develop budgeted overhead application rates for the output of each production department.

To highlight concepts, the example in Exhibit 12-5 uses a single-cost pool to collect the costs of each department. (The ideal motivation for this assumption, given the prior discussion in this chapter, is that all the costs of both service departments are variable.) The Problem for Self-Study at the end of this chapter illustrates the use of multiple-cost pools when allocating service department costs.

Direct allocation method

The **direct allocation method** (often abbreviated as the **direct method**) is the most widely used method for allocation of service department costs. This method ignores any service rendered by one service department to another; it allocates each service department's total costs directly to the production departments. Exhibit 12-6 presents this method for the data in Exhibit 12-5. Note how this method ignores the service rendered by the factory administration department to the repair department, and also the service rendered by repair to factory administration. For example, the base used for allocation of factory administration is the budgeted total labor-hours worked in the production departments: 24,000 + 40,000 = 64,000 hours. This excludes the 16,000 hours of service provided to the repair department by factory administration. Similarly, the base used for allocation of

EXHIBIT 12-6
Direct Method of Allocating Service Department Costs

	SERVICE DEPARTMENTS		PRODUCTION DEPARTMENTS		TOTAL
	Factory Administration	Repair	Machining	Assembly	
Budgeted overhead costs before any interdepartment cost allocations	$600,000	$116,000	$400,000	$200,000	$1,316,000
Allocation of Factory Administration: (3/8, 5/8)*	(600,000)		225,000	375,000	
	$0				
Allocation of Repair: (8/9, 1/9)†		(116,000)	103,111	12,889	
		$0			
Total overhead of production departments			$728,111	$587,889	$1,316,000

*Base is (24,000 + 40,000), or 64,000 hours; 24,000/64,000 = 3/8; 40,000/64,000 = 5/8.
†Base is [16,000 + 2,000], or 18,000 hours; 16,000/18,000 = 8/9; 2,000/18,000 = 1/9.

repair costs is $16,000 + 2,000 = 18,000$ hours; this excludes the 2,000 hours of service rendered to factory administration by the repair department.

The benefit of the direct method is its simplicity. There is no need to predict the usage of service department resources by other service departments.

Step-down allocation method

Some companies use the **step-down allocation method** (sometimes called the **step** or **sequential** method), which allows for limited recognition of services rendered by service departments to other service departments.[12] This method is more complex than the direct method because a sequence of allocations must be chosen. The sequence often begins with the department that renders the highest percentage of its total services to other service departments. The sequence continues in step-by-step fashion and ends with the allocation of the costs of the service department that renders the lowest percentage of its total services to other service departments.[13]

Exhibit 12-7 illustrates use of the step-down method. Note that factory administration costs are allocated to the other service department as well as to the production departments. Note also that after the first department's costs are allocated, repair costs include a share of such costs: $120,000. The new total for repair, $236,000, is then allocated to *subsequent* departments only. The allocation base is

---

[12]The step-down method was approved for use by hospitals seeking reimbursement from health-care agencies in the United States. A change in the reimbursement approach (to a prospective payment system) has meant that the reimbursement motive for use of this method by hospitals no longer exists. See S. Finkler, "The Future of Product Costing and Cost Allocation," *Hospital Cost Accounting Advisor*, June 1985, p. 1.

[13]An alternative approach to selecting the sequence of allocations is to begin with the department that renders the highest dollar amount of services to other service departments. The sequence ends with the allocation of the costs of the department that renders the lowest dollar amount of services to other service departments.

EXHIBIT 12-7
Step-Down Method of Allocating Service Department Costs

	SERVICE DEPARTMENTS		PRODUCTION DEPARTMENTS		TOTAL
	Factory Administration	Repair	Machining	Assembly	
Budgeted overhead costs before any interdepartment cost allocations	$600,000	$116,000	$400,000	$200,000	$1,316,000
Allocation of Factory Administration: (2/10, 3/10, 5/10)*	(600,000) $0	120,000	180,000	300,000	
Allocation of Repair: (8/9, 1/9)†		(236,000) $0	209,778	26,222	
Total overhead of production departments			$789,778	$526,222	$1,316,000

*Base is (16,000 + 24,000 + 40,000), or 80,000 hours; 16,000/80,000 = 2/10; 24,000/80,000 = 3/10; 40,000/80,000 = 5/10.

†Base is (16,000 + 2,000), or 18,000 hours; 16,000/18,000 = 8/9; 2,000/18,000 = 1/9.

the total service units provided to the departments to which the cost will be allocated. Note that once a service department's costs have been allocated, no subsequent service department costs are reallocated or recirculated back to it.

Reciprocal allocation method

The **reciprocal method** allocates costs by explicitly including the mutual services rendered among all departments. The reciprocal method is also called the **cross-allocation** method, the **matrix method**, and the **double-distribution** method. The direct method and the step-down method theoretically are not accurate when service departments render services to one another reciprocally. For example, the factory administration department serves the employees of the repair department, while the factory administration department receives some services from the repair department.

Three stages are involved in implementing the reciprocal allocation method.

STAGE 1: Express service department costs and service department reciprocal relationships in linear equation form. Let F be the complete reciprocated costs of factory administration and R be the complete reciprocated costs of repair. Then the data in Exhibit 12-5 can be expressed as follows:

$$(1): F = \$600,000 + .1R$$

$$(2): R = \$116,000 + .2F$$

By **complete reciprocated cost** in equations (1) and (2) we mean the actual incurred cost of the department plus a part of the costs of the other service departments that provide services to it. This complete reciprocated cost figure is sometimes labeled the **"artificial" cost** of the service department.

425

STAGE 2: Solve the system of linear equations to obtain the complete reciprocated cost of each service department. Where there are a small number of service departments, the following substitution approach can be used:

Substituting equation (2) into equation (1):

$$F = \$600,000 + .1(\$116,000 + .2F)$$

$$F = \$600,000 + \$11,600 + .02F$$

$$.98F = \$611,600$$

$$F = \$624,082$$

Substituting into equation (2):

$$R = \$116,000 + .2(\$624,082) = \$240,816$$

Where there are a large number of departments with many reciprocal relationships, computer programs can be used to calculate the complete reciprocated cost of each service department.

STAGE 3: Allocate the complete reciprocated cost of each service department to all other departments (both service and production departments), using the computed usage proportions (based on total units of service provided to all departments). Consider the repair department, which has a complete reciprocated cost of $240,816. This complete reciprocated cost would be allocated as follows:

To Factory Administration ($\frac{1}{10}$) =	$ 24,082
Machining ($\frac{8}{10}$) =	192,652
Assembly ($\frac{1}{10}$) =	24,082
	$240,816

Exhibit 12-8 presents summary data pertaining to the reciprocal method.

One source of confusion to some managers with the reciprocal cost allocation method is why the complete reciprocated costs of the service departments ($624,082 and $240,816 in Exhibit 12-8) exceed their actual costs ($600,000 and $116,000). This phenomenon occurs because the allocations are simultaneous; the total costs allocated to the production department are still only $716,000.

Overview of methods

Assume that the total budgeted overhead of each production department in the example in Exhibits 12-5 to 12-8 is applied to individual products based on budgeted machine-hours for the machining department (40,000 hours) and budgeted direct-labor hours for the assembly department (30,000 hours). The budgeted overhead application rates associated with each service department allocation method are:

ALLOCATION METHOD	TOTAL BUDGETED OVERHEAD COSTS AFTER ALLOCATION OF ALL SERVICE DEPARTMENT COSTS		BUDGETED OVERHEAD RATE PER HOUR FOR PRODUCT-COSTING PURPOSES	
	Machining	Assembly	Machining (40,000 machine-hours)	Assembly (30,000 labor-hours)
Direct	$728,111	$587,889	$18.20	$19.60
Step-down	789,778	526,222	19.74	17.54
Reciprocal	779,877	536,123	19.50	17.87

Differences in product costs resulting from the use of different service department cost allocation methods may have infinitesimal decision consequences in some situations but may have substantial consequences in other situations. These could include decisions involving pricing, internal or external purchases of services, setting levels of output, or product choice. Also cost-reimbursement contracts such as those for defense industries, universities, and hospitals would obviously be affected.

The reciprocal method is theoretically the most defensible. The advantage of the direct and step-down methods is that they are relatively simple to compute and understand. However, with the ready availability of computer software to solve systems of linear equations, the extra costs of using the reciprocal method will in most cases be minimal. The more likely roadblocks to the reciprocal method being widely adopted are: (1) many managers find it difficult to understand, and (2) the numbers obtained by using the reciprocal method differ little in some cases from those obtained by using the direct or step-down methods.

EXHIBIT 12-8
Reciprocal Method of Allocating Service Department Costs

	SERVICE DEPARTMENTS		PRODUCTION DEPARTMENTS		TOTAL
	Factory Administration	Repair	Machining	Assembly	
Budgeted overhead costs before any interdepartment cost allocations	$600,000	$116,000	$400,000	$200,000	$1,316,000
Allocation of Factory Administration: (2/10, 3/10, 5/10)*	(624,082)	124,816	187,225	312,041	
Allocation of Repair: (1/10, 8/10, 1/10)†	24,082	(240,816)	192,652	24,082	
	$0	$0			
Total overhead of production departments			$779,877	$536,123	$1,316,000

*Base is (16,000 + 24,000 + 40,000), or 80,000 hours; 16,000/80,000 = 2/10; 24,000/80,000 = 3/10; 40,000/80,000 = 5/10.

†Base is (2,000 + 16,000 + 2,000), or 20,000 hours; 2,000/20,000 = 1/10; 16,000/20,000 = 8/10; 2,000/20,000 = 1/10.

427

A **common cost** is a cost of operating a facility that is shared by two or more users. For example, consider the fixed costs of the mailroom facility that is shared by the *Financial Accounting Standards Board* (FASB) and the *Governmental Accounting Standards Board* (GASB). The FASB was set up in 1972 to issue standards governing financial reporting by profit-seeking corporations. The GASB was set up in 1984 to issue standards governing financial reporting by public-sector organizations. Both organizations occupy the same building. A single mailroom facility serves both the FASB and the GASB. Variable costs of mailing are readily identifiable and kept in separate cost pools that are charged to the user. The fixed costs of the mailroom, however, cannot be identified with each individual user on the basis of a cause-and-effect relationship. How should these fixed costs be allocated between the two users?

Suppose that the fixed costs of the mailroom facility for the next year are budgeted at $500,000. If the GASB was not using the mailroom, the fixed operating costs would be $480,000. An outside vendor offers to provide mailroom services to the FASB for a fixed fee of $600,000 plus variable costs. The same vendor offers to provide mailroom services to the GASB for a fixed fee of $200,000 plus variable costs.

Two methods have been proposed for allocating common costs to individual users:

1. *Incremental Common Cost Allocation Method.* This method requires that one user be viewed as the primary party and the second user be viewed as the incremental party. The incremental party is allocated only that component of the common cost attributable to having both users as opposed to only the primary user. In the extreme, the incremental party may receive zero allocation of the common costs. For the mailroom example, the FASB would be allocated $480,000 and the GASB $20,000.

Under the incremental method, the user viewed as the primary party typically will receive the highest allocation of the common costs. Not surprisingly, most parties in common cost allocation disputes propose themselves as the incremental user.

Advocates of the incremental method often stress a motivation rationale. For example, incremental parties are often newly formed organizations, or new subparts of a corporate family (a new product line or a new sales territory). Their short-term survival may be promoted if they bear a relatively low allocation of common costs.

2. *Stand-Alone Common Cost Allocation Method.* This method allocates the common cost on the basis of each user's percentage of the total of the individual stand-alone costs. In the mailroom example, the total of the individual stand-alone costs is $800,000 ($600,000 for FASB and $200,000 for GASB). The common cost of the internally run mailroom facility is allocated thus:

$$\text{FASB: } \frac{\$600,000}{\$800,000} \times \$500,000 = \$375,000$$

$$\text{GASB: } \frac{\$200,000}{\$800,000} \times \$500,000 = \$125,000$$

Advocates of the stand-alone method often emphasize an equity or fairness rationale; they argue that fairness requires that each user pay a percentage of actual common costs based on its share of the total of the stand-alone costs.

Several of the allocation bases described previously in this chapter have also been used in allocating common costs. For instance, relative revenues are sometimes adopted as an allocation base; an ability-to-bear criterion is the most commonly given rationale for the relative revenues allocation base. Also, common fixed costs can be allocated based on the users' estimates of their long run service requirements.

SUMMARY

Costs are allocated for four major purposes: (1) economic decisions for resource allocation, (2) motivation, (3) income and asset measurement for external parties, and (4) cost justification or reimbursement. When allocation issues arise, a good basic question is, What is the dominant purpose of the cost allocation in this particular instance?

There are essentially three facets of cost allocation: (1) choosing the cost objective (some action or activity), (2) choosing how to accumulate or pool costs, and (3) choosing the allocation base that relates the two. These three choices should be made simultaneously because they are interdependent.

For purposes of guiding economic decisions and motivation, where feasible, variable costs should be allocated by using budgeted rates for the services *used*. Fixed costs should be allocated by using budgeted lump sums for providing a *basic capacity* to serve.

Three major methods are available to allocate service department costs to other departments: direct, step-down, and reciprocal. The last is the most defensible, but the direct and step-down methods are more widely used.

Chapter 13 continues the analysis of cost allocation topics. Two major points stressed in Chapter 13 have already been noted in this chapter's discussion of allocating costs of one department to another: (1) choices of how to allocate costs have an important impact on managers' behavior, and (2) cost allocations often substitute for market prices as a way of obtaining mutually satisfactory selling or contract prices.

PROBLEM FOR SELF-STUDY

problem   Computer Horizons budgets the following concerning the capacity of two service departments (legal and personnel) to service each other and the two producing divisions—the Microcomputer Division (MCD) and the Peripheral Equipment Division (PED):

	BUDGETED CAPACITY				
	Legal	Personnel	MCD	PED	Total
Legal—hours	—	250	1,500	750	2,500
—proportions	—	.10	.60	.30	1.00
Personnel—hours	2,500	—	22,500	25,000	50,000
—proportions	.05	—	.45	.50	1.00

Details on actual usage:

		ACTUAL USAGE			
	Legal	Personnel	MCD	PED	Total
Legal—hours	—	400	400	1,200	2,000
—proportions	—	.20	.20	.60	1.00
Personnel—hours	2,000	—	26,600	11,400	40,000
—proportions	.05	—	.665	.285	1.00

The actual costs were:

	FIXED	VARIABLE
Legal	$360,000	$200,000
Personnel	$475,000	$600,000

Fixed costs are allocated on the basis of budgeted capacity. Variable costs are allocated on the basis of actual usage.

Required What service department costs for legal and personnel will be allocated to MCD and PED using (a) the direct method, (b) the step-down method (allocating the legal department costs first), and (c) the reciprocal method?

solution Exhibit 12-9 presents the computations for allocating the fixed and variable service department costs. A summary of these costs follows.

		MICROCOMPUTER DIVISION (MCD)	PERIPHERAL EQUIPMENT DIVISION (PED)
A.	Direct Method		
	Fixed costs	$465,000	$370,000
	Variable costs	470,000	330,000
		$935,000	$700,000
B.	Step-Down Method		
	Fixed costs	$458,053	$376,947
	Variable costs	488,000	312,000
		$946,053	$688,947
C.	Reciprocal Method		
	Fixed costs	$462,513	$372,487
	Variable costs	476,364	323,636
		$938,877	$696,123

EXHIBIT 12-9
Dual-Rate Service Department Cost Allocation Methods

ALLOCATION METHOD	SERVICE DEPARTMENTS		PRODUCTION DEPARTMENTS	
	Legal	Personnel	MCD	PED
A. DIRECT METHOD				
Fixed Costs	$360,000	$475,000		
Legal (6/9, 3/9)	(360,000)		$240,000	$120,000
Personnel (225/475, 250/475)		(475,000)	225,000	250,000
			$465,000	$370,000
Variable Costs	$200,000	$600,000		
Legal (.25, .75)	(200,000)	—	$ 50,000	$150,000
Personnel (.7, .3)		(600,000)	420,000	180,000
			$470,000	$330,000
B. STEP-DOWN METHOD				
(Legal Department First)				
Fixed Costs	$360,000	$475,000		
Legal (.10, .60, .30)	(360,000)	36,000	$216,000	$108,000
Personnel (225/475, 250/475)		(511,000)	242,053	268,947
			$458,053	$376,947
Variable Costs	$200,000	$600,000		
Legal (.20, .20, .60)	(200,000)	40,000	$40,000	$120,000
Personnel (.7, .3)		(640,000)	448,000	192,000
			$488,000	$312,000
C. RECIPROCAL METHOD				
Fixed Costs	$360,000	$475,000		
Legal (.10, .60, .30)	(385,678)	38,568	$231,407	$115,703
Personnel (.05, .45, .50)	25,678	(513,568)	231,106	256,784
			$462,513	$372,487
Variable Costs	$200,000	$600,000		
Legal (.20, .20, .60)	(232,323)	46,465	$46,465	$139,393
Personnel (.05, .665, .285)	32,323	(646,465)	429,899	184,243
			$476,364	$323,636

The simultaneous equations for the reciprocal method are shown here.

FIXED COSTS

$$L = \$360,000 + .05 \, P$$

$$P = \$475,000 + .10 \, L$$

$$L = \$360,000 + .05(\$475,000 + .10L)$$

$$= \$385,678$$

$$P = \$475,000 + .10(\$385,678)$$

$$= \$513,568$$

VARIABLE COSTS

$$L = \$200,000 + .05\ P$$

$$P = \$600,000 + .20\ L$$

$$L = \$200,000 + .05(\$600,000 + .20L)$$

$$= \$232,323$$

$$P = \$600,000 + .20(\$232,323)$$

$$= \$646,465$$

Terms to Learn

This chapter and the Glossary at the end of the book contain definitions of the following important terms:

"artificial" cost (p. 425)   *common cost (428)*
complete reciprocated cost (425)   *cost allocation (411)*
cost allocation base (415)   *cost apportionment (411)*   *cost assignment (411)*
cost distribution (411)   *cost pool (415)*   *cost reallocation (411)*
cost reapportionment (411)   *cost reassignment (411)*
cost redistribution (411)   *cost retracing (411)*   *cost tracing (411)*
cross-allocation method (425)   *direct allocation method (423)*
direct cost (411)   *direct method (423)*
double-distribution allocation method (425)   *dual-rate method (418)*
indirect cost (411)   *indirect cost pool (415)*   *matrix-allocation method (425)*
reciprocal allocation method (425)   *sequential allocation method (424)*
service department (417)   *step allocation method (424)*
step-down allocation method (424)

Special Points and Pitfalls

Exhibit 12-1 (Purposes of Cost Allocation) is the most important exhibit in this chapter. The purpose of allocating a cost to a given cost objective should always guide choices relating to how cost pools are defined and what allocation bases are used.

The problem of cost allocation is closely tied to the issues discussed in Chapters 10 and 23, which concentrate on various patterns of cost behavior such as variable, fixed, and mixed. Managers should especially be on guard regarding cost allocations that make the fixed costs in one department appear to be a variable cost in other departments.

Disputes over cost allocation issues can be frustrating to all parties. There will often be no clearly right or clearly wrong solution. Where the purpose of the allocation is related to economic decisions or motivation, the cause-and-effect criterion is a useful guide in choosing an allocation method.

QUESTIONS, PROBLEMS, AND CASES

12-1 Distinguish between a direct cost and an indirect cost.

12-2 "Every indirect cost was at one stage a direct cost." Do you agree? Explain.

12-3 "A given cost allocation may be performed for one or more purposes." List at least three purposes.

12-4 Cite four criteria that may be used to guide cost allocation decisions.

12-5 "There are essentially three facets of cost allocation." What are they?

12-6 What is a cost pool? Give an example.

12-7 Give four examples of cost objectives.

12-8 What is the major reason for having a cost allocation base?

12-9 Why use a dual-rate cost allocation method when it is less costly to use a single-cost pool method?

12-10 "Service department costs shouldn't be allocated." Do you agree? Why?

12-11 What are the criteria for selecting among allocation bases for service department costs?

12-12 What is the theoretically most defensible method for allocating service department costs?

12-13 Allocation of travel costs. Joan Ernst, a graduating senior at a university near Denver, received an invitation to visit a prospective employer in Omaha. A few days later she received a similar invitation to visit North Platte, Nebraska. She decided to combine her visits, traveling from Denver to Omaha to North Platte to Denver.

Joan received job offers from both locations. Upon her return, she decided to accept the Omaha offer. She was puzzled about how to allocate her travel costs between the two prospective employers. She gathered the following data:

Roundtrip sedan service, dormitory to Denver airport	$ 26
Regular roundtrip fares from Denver to:	
Omaha	348
North Platte	294
Actual airfare paid	396

Required | How much should each employer pay for Joan Ernst's travel costs? Why? Explain. Show computations.

12-14 Allocation of advertising. (SMA) The H Company allocates national magazine advertising cost to sales territories on the basis of circulation, weighted by an index that measures relative buying power in the territories. Does this method give cost and profit figures appropriate for the following decisions? Indicate clearly why or why not.
   1. For deciding whether or not to close an unprofitable territory
   2. For deciding whether or not a territorial manager has obtained sufficient sales volume
   3. For determining how efficiently the territorial manager has operated his territory
   4. For determining whether or not advertising costs are being satisfactorily controlled

12-15 Alternative allocation methods. (W. Crum, adapted) Kona Company has a power plant designed and built to serve its three factories. Data for 19_1 follow:

	USAGE IN KILOWATT HOURS	
FACTORY NUMBER	Budget	Actual
1	100,000	80,000
2	60,000	120,000
3	40,000	40,000

Actual fixed costs of the power plant were $1 million in 19_1; actual variable costs, $2 million.

Required
1. Using a single-cost pool, compute the amount of power cost that would be allocated to Factory 2. Use two alternative allocation bases.
2. Using multiple-cost pools, compute the amount of power cost that would be allocated to Factory 2. Use two alternative allocation bases.

12-16 Alternative allocation methods. The power plant that services all factory departments has a budget for the forthcoming year. This budget has been expressed in the following terms, for a normal month:

| | KILOWATT HOURS | |
FACTORY DEPARTMENTS	Needed at Practical Capacity Production Volume*	Average Expected Monthly Usage
A	10,000	8,000
B	20,000	9,000
X	12,000	7,000
Y	8,000	6,000
Totals	50,000	30,000

*This was the most influential factor in planning the size of the power plant.

The expected monthly costs for operating the department during the budget year are $15,000: $6,000 variable and $9,000 fixed.

Required
1. Assume that a single-cost pool is used for the power plant costs. What dollar amounts will be allocated to each factory department? Use (a) practical capacity provided and (b) average expected monthly usage as the allocation base.
2. Assume a dual-rate method; separate cost pools for the variable and fixed costs are used. Variable costs are allocated on the basis of expected usage. Fixed costs are allocated on the basis of practical capacity provided. What dollar amounts will be allocated to each factory department? Why might you prefer the dual-rate method?

12-17 Allocation of service department costs. Atherton Machining Company has one service department (electric power) and two production departments in its factory. The flexible-budget formula for allocating the service department costs for the next fiscal year is $6,000 monthly plus $.40 per machine-hour in the production departments. Fixed costs are allocated on a lump-sum basis, 60% to Production Department 1 and 40% to Production Department 2. Variable costs are allocated at the budgeted unit rate of $.40 per machine-hour.

Required
1. Assume that the actual costs coincided exactly with the flexible-budgeted amount. Departments 1 and 2 each worked at 4,000-hour levels. Tabulate the allocations of all costs.
2. Assume the same facts as in requirement 1 except that the fixed costs were allocated on the basis of actual hours rather than capacity available. Tabulate the allocations of all costs. As the manager of Department 2, would you prefer the method in requirement 1 or in requirement 2? Why?
3. Suppose the service department had inefficiencies at an 8,000-hour level, incurring costs that exceeded budget by $800. How would this change your answers in requirements 1 and 2? Be specific.

12-18 Allocation of service department costs. For simplicity, suppose there is one service department (maintenance) plus two production departments. The flexible budget of the service department is $24,000 monthly plus $1 per machine-hour. Assume that the total service department capacity was originally acquired with the expected "long-run" usage of 75% by Department M and 25% by Department N.

Required

1. Indicate the dual rates for allocating the service department's costs to each production department.
2. Assume that actual costs coincided exactly with the flexible-budgeted amount. Departments M and N each worked at 8,000-hour levels. Tabulate the allocation of all costs.
3. Assume the same facts as in requirement 2 except that the fixed costs were allocated on the basis of actual hours worked by each department rather than on the basis of long-run usage. Tabulate the allocation of all costs. As the manager of Department N, would you prefer the method in requirement 2 or in requirement 3? Why?
4. Suppose the service department had inefficiencies at a 16,000-hour level, incurring costs that exceeded budget by $6,000. How would this change your answers in requirements 2 and 3? Be specific.

12-19 Approaches to allocation. A computer service department of a large university serves two major users, the School of Engineering and the School of Humanities and Sciences (H&S).

Required

1. When the computer equipment was initially installed, the procedure for cost allocation was straightforward. The actual monthly costs were compiled and were divided between the two schools on the basis of the time used by each. In October the costs were $100,000. H&S used 100 hours and Engineering used 100 hours. How much cost would be allocated to each school? Suppose costs were $110,000 because of various inefficiencies in the operation of the computer department. How much cost would be allocated? Does such allocation seem justified? If not, what improvement would you suggest?
2. Use the same approach as in requirement 1. The actual cost behavior pattern of the computer department was $80,000 per month plus $100 per hour used. In November, H&S used 50 hours and Engineering used 100 hours. How much cost would be allocated to each school? Use a single-rate method.
3. As the computer service department developed, the size and composition of the equipment was affected by a committee that included representatives of H&S and Engineering. They agreed that planning should be based on long-run average utilization of 180 hours monthly by H&S and 120 hours monthly by Engineering. In requirement 2, suppose fixed costs are allocated via a budgeted monthly lump sum based on long-run average utilization; variable costs are allocated via a budgeted standard unit rate of $100 per hour. How much cost would be allocated to each school? What are the advantages of this method over other methods?
4. What are the likely behavioral effects of lump-sum allocations of fixed costs? For example, if you were the representative of H&S on the facility planning committee, what would your biases be in predicting long-run usage? How would top management counteract the bias?

12-20 Using revenue as a basis for allocating costs. The Mideastern Transportation Company has had a longstanding policy of fully allocating all costs to its various divisions. Among the costs allocated were general and administrative costs in central headquarters, consisting of office salaries, executive salaries, travel expense, accounting costs, office supplies, donations, rents, depreciation, postage, and similar items.

All these costs were difficult to trace directly to the individual divisions benefited, so they were allocated on the basis of the total revenue of each of the divisions. The same basis was used for allocating general advertising and miscellaneous selling costs. For example, in 19_3 the following allocations were made:

| | DIVISIONS | | | |
	A	B	C	TOTAL
Revenue (in millions)	$50.0	$40.0	$10.0	$100.0
Costs allocated on the basis of revenue	6.0	4.8	1.2	12.0

In 19_4, Division A's revenue was expected to rise. But the division encountered severe competitive conditions; its revenue remained at $50 million. In contrast, Division C enjoyed explosive growth in traffic because of the completion of several huge factories in its area; its revenue rose to $30 million. Division B's revenue remained unchanged. Careful supervision kept the total costs allocated on the basis of revenue at $12 million.

Required

1. What costs will be allocated to each division in 19_4?
2. Using the results in requirement 1, comment on the limitations of using revenue as a basis for cost allocation.

12-21 Allocating costs of a central telephone reservation system. Helena Park, the chief operating officer of Happy Inns, faces a difficult problem. The manager of the most prestigious motel in the five-motel chain is upset about her proposed cost allocation scheme for the central telephone reservation system. Until one year ago, each motel handled its own reservations. Then Happy Inns leased a central telephone reservation system. The annual lease payment paid by Happy Inns is $84,000 per year. The variable costs of operating the system are paid by Happy Inns. During the first year of operations, Happy Inns allocated none of the $84,000 fixed cost and none of the $56,000 variable costs of operating the system. Summary data for the first year of operating the central reservation system are:

MOTEL	RESERVATIONS MADE VIA CENTRAL SYSTEM	TOTAL NUMBER OF ROOM NIGHTS AVAILABLE FOR RENTAL FOR YEAR	TOTAL NUMBER OF ROOM NIGHTS ACTUALLY RENTED DURING YEAR	AVERAGE RATE PER ROOM NIGHT	TOTAL ROOM REVENUES FOR YEAR
Vancouver	5,000 (12.5%)	28,000 (11.7%)	20,000 (10.8%)	$60	$ 1,200,000 (8.6%)
Halifax	4,000 (10.0)	31,000 (12.9)	25,000 (13.5)	76	1,900,000 (13.6)
Toronto	8,000 (20.0)	37,000 (15.4)	30,000 (16.2)	50	1,500,000 (10.7)
Jasper	3,000 (7.5)	32,000 (13.3)	30,000 (16.2)	100	3,000,000 (21.4)
Quebec City	20,000 (50.0)	112,000 (46.7)	80,000 (43.3)	80	6,400,000 (45.7)
	40,000	240,000	185,000		$14,000,000

The total number of rooms actually rented includes those made through the central reservation system, those made by direct dial to the individual motel, and those made by walk-in clientele. During the first year of operations, approximately 100,000 phone calls were made to the central reservation service.

Park decides to allocate the central telephone costs to each motel. She proposes that the fixed and variable costs be combined in a single pool and be allocated on the basis of actual total room revenues for the year.

Each Happy Inn manager receives a fixed salary plus a percentage of the net income of the individual motel.

Required

1. What costs would have been allocated to each motel under the relative percentage of actual total room revenues proposal of Park in the first year of operation of the central reservation system? Why might the manager of the Jasper Happy Inn oppose Park's proposal?
2. What limitations are associated with the proposed cost allocation method of Park in requirement 1?
3. Park considers alternative cost allocation systems. She decides to retain a single-cost pool, but to consider alternative allocation bases. What costs would have been allocated to each motel under each of the following bases: (a) reservations made via central system, (b) total number of room nights available for rental, and (c) total number of room nights actually rented during the year?

12-22 Allocation of central corporate costs to divisions. Dusty Rhodes, the corporate controller of Richfield Oil Company, is about to make a presentation to the senior corporate executives and the presidents of its four divisions. These divisions are:

1. **Oil & Gas Upstream**—the exploration, production, and transportation of oil and gas
2. **Oil & Gas Downstream**—the refining and marketing of oil and gas
3. **Chemical Products**
4. **Copper Mining**

Under the existing internal accounting system, costs incurred at central corporate headquarters are collected in a single pool and allocated to each division on the basis of the actual revenues of each division. The central corporate costs for the most recent year are (in millions of dollars):

Interest on debt	$2,000
Corporate salaries	100
Accounting and control	100
General marketing	100
Legal	100
Research and development	200
Public affairs	208
Personnel and payroll	192
	$3,000

Public affairs includes the public relations staff, the lobbyists, and the sizable donations Richfield makes to numerous charities and nonprofit institutions.

Summary data relating to the four divisions for the most recent year are (in millions of dollars):

	OIL & GAS UPSTREAM	OIL & GAS DOWNSTREAM	CHEMICAL PRODUCTS	COPPER MINING	TOTAL
Revenues	$7,000	$16,000	$4,000	$3,000	$30,000
Operating costs	3,000	15,000	3,800	3,200	25,000
Operating income	$4,000	$ 1,000	$ 200	$ (200)	$ 5,000
Identifiable assets	$14,000	$6,000	$3,000	$2,000	$25,000
Number of employees	9,000	12,000	6,000	3,000	30,000

The senior managers of each division share in a divisional income bonus pool. *Divisional income* is defined as operating income less allocated central corporate costs.

Rhodes is about to propose a change in the method used to allocate central corporate costs. He favors collecting these costs in four separate pools:

Cost Pool 1: Allocated using identifiable assets of division
Cost Item: Interest on debt

Cost Pool 2: Allocated using revenues of division
Cost Items: Corporate salaries, accounting and control, general marketing, legal, research and development

Cost Pool 3: Allocated using operating income (if positive) of division, with only divisions with positive operating income included in the allocation base
Cost Item: Public affairs

Cost Pool 4: Allocated using number of employees in division
Cost Item: Personnel and payroll

Required

1. What purposes might be served by the allocation of central corporate costs to each division at Richfield Oil?
2. Compute the divisional income of each of the four divisions when central corporate costs are allocated using revenues of each division.

3. Compute the divisional income of each of the four divisions when central corporate costs are allocated via the four cost pools.
4. What are the pros and cons of Rhodes's proposal relative to the existing single-cost pool method?

12-23 Division managers' reactions to the allocation of central corporate costs to divisions. (Continuation of Problem 12-22) Dusty Rhodes presents his proposal (outlined in Problem 12-22) for the use of four separate cost pools to allocate central corporate costs to the divisions. The comments of the presidents of each of the four divisions include the following:

(a) By the president of Oil & Gas Upstream Division: "The multiple pool method of Rhodes is absurd. We are the only division generating a substantial positive cash flow, and this is ignored in the proposed (and indeed the existing) system. We could pay off any debt very quickly if we were not a cash cow for the rest of the dog divisions in Richfield Oil."

(b) By the president of Oil & Gas Downstream Division: "Rhodes's proposal is the first sign that the money we spend in the accounting and control function at corporate headquarters is justified. The proposal is fair and equitable."

(c) By the president of Chemical Products Division: "I oppose any cost allocation scheme. Last year I was the only major player in the chemical industry to show a positive operating profit. We are operating at the bare bones level. Last year I saved $300,000 by making everyone travel economy class. This created a lot of dissatisfaction, but we finally managed to get it accepted. Then at the end of the year we get a charge of $400 million for corporate central costs. What's the point of our division economy drives when they get swamped by allocations of corporate largess?"

(d) By the president of Copper Mining Division: "I should probably get concerned, but frankly I view it all as bookkeeping entries. If we were in the black, certain aspects would really infuriate me. For instance, why should corporate research and development costs be allocated to the Copper Division? The only research corporate does for us is how to best prepare our division for divestiture."

Required | How should Rhodes respond to these comments?

12-24 Allocating costs of service departments; step-down and direct methods. The X Company has prepared departmental overhead budgets for normal activity levels before allocations, as follows:

Service departments:		
Building and grounds	$ 10,000	
Personnel	1,000	
General factory administration	26,090	
Cafeteria—operating loss	1,640	
Storeroom	2,670	
		41,400
Production departments:		
Machining	34,700	
Assembly	48,900	
		83,600
		$125,000

Management has decided that the most sensible product costs are achieved by using departmental overhead rates. These rates are developed after appropriate service department costs are allocated to production departments.

Bases for allocation are to be selected from the following:

DEPARTMENT	DIRECT-LABOR HOURS	NUMBER OF EMPLOYEES	SQUARE FEET OF FLOOR SPACE OCCUPIED	TOTAL LABOR-HOURS	NUMBER OF REQUISITIONS
Building & grounds	—	—	—	—	
Personnel*		—	2,000	—	
General factory administration		35	7,000	—	
Cafeteria—operating loss		10	4,000	1,000	
Storeroom		5	7,000	1,000	
Machining	5,000	50	30,000	8,000	2,000
Assembly	15,000	100	50,000	17,000	1,000
	20,000	200	100,000	27,000	3,000

*Basis used is number of employees.

Required

1. Using a worksheet, allocate service department costs by the step-down method. Develop overhead rates per direct-labor hour for machining and assembly. Allocate the service departments in the order given in this problem. Use the allocation base for each service department you think is most appropriate.
2. Same as in requirement 1, using the direct method.
3. Using the following information about two jobs, prepare two different total-overhead costs for each job, using rates developed in requirements 1 and 2 above.

	DIRECT-LABOR HOURS	
	Machining	Assembly
Job 88	18	2
Job 89	3	17

12-25 Service department cost allocations; single-department cost pools; direct, step-down, and reciprocal methods. The Manes Company has two products. Product 1 is manufactured entirely in Department X. Product 2 is manufactured entirely in Department Y. To produce these two products, the Manes Company has two service departments: A (a material-handling department) and B (a power-generating department).

An analysis of the work done by Departments A and B in a typical period follows:

	USER				TOTAL UNITS OF WORK
SOURCE	A	B	X	Y	DONE
Material handling (Dept. A)	0	20	50	30	100
Power (Dept. B)	50	0	10	40	100

Each work unit for Department A represents a direct-labor hour of material handling time. Each work unit for Department B represents a kilowatt-hour of power.

The costs of the service departments during this typical period are as follows:

	A	B
Variable labor and material costs	$ 7,000	$1,000
Supervision	1,000	1,000
Depreciation	2,000	2,000
	$10,000	$4,000
	+ Power costs	+ Material-handling costs

Supervisory costs represent salary costs. Depreciation in B represents the straight-line depreciation of power-generation equipment in its nineteenth year of an estimated twenty-five-year life; it is old but well-maintained equipment.

Required

1. What are the allocations of costs of Service Departments A and B to Production Departments X and Y using the direct method, two different sequences of the step-down method, and the reciprocal method of reallocation?
2. The power company has offered to supply all the power needed by the Manes Company and to provide all the services of the present power department. The cost of this will be $40 per kilowatt-hour of power. Should Manes accept?

12-26 Allocating costs of service departments; dual rates; direct, step-down, and reciprocal methods. Magnum T.A. Inc. specializes in the assembly and installation of high-quality security systems for the home and business segments of the market. The four departments at its highly automated state-of-the-art assembly plant are:

SERVICE DEPARTMENTS	ASSEMBLY DEPARTMENTS
Engineering Support	Home Security Systems
Information Systems Support	Business Security Systems

The *budgeted* level of service relationships at the start of the year was:

	ENGINEERING SUPPORT	INFORMATION SYSTEMS SUPPORT	HOME SECURITY SYSTEMS	BUSINESS SECURITY SYSTEMS
Engineering Support	—	.10	.40	.50
Information Systems Support	.20	—	.30	.50

The *actual* level of service relationships during the year was:

	ENGINEERING SUPPORT	INFORMATION SYSTEMS SUPPORT	HOME SECURITY SYSTEMS	BUSINESS SECURITY SYSTEMS
Engineering Support	—	.15	.30	.55
Information Systems Support	.25	—	.15	.60

Magnum collects fixed costs and variable costs of each department in separate cost pools. The actual costs in each pool for the year were:

	FIXED-COST POOL	VARIABLE-COST POOL
Engineering Support ($000's)	2,700	8,500
Information Systems Support ($000's)	8,000	3,750

Fixed costs are allocated on the basis of the budgeted level of service. Variable costs are allocated on the basis of the actual level of service.

The service department costs allocated to each assembly department are allocated to products on the basis of units assembled. The units assembled in each department during the year were:

Home Security Systems	7,950 units
Business Security Systems	3,750 units

1. Allocate the service department costs to the assembly departments using a dual-rate system and (a) the direct method, (b) the step-down method (allocate information systems support first), (c) the step-down method (allocate engineering support first), and (d) the reciprocal method. Present results in a format similar to Exhibit 12-9.
2. Compare the service department costs allocated to each home security systems unit assembled and each business security systems unit assembled under *a, b, c,* and *d* in requirement 1.
3. What factors might explain the very limited adoption of the reciprocal method by many organizations?

12-27 Cost justification for a contract; analysis of service department cost allocations. Solve problem 13-25, which could have been placed here.

12-28 Reciprocal cost allocations. (D. Green) The Prairie State Paper Company located a plant near one of its forests. At the time of construction, there were no utility companies equipped to provide this plant with water, power, or fuel. Therefore, included in the original facilities were (1) a water plant, which pumped water from a nearby lake and filtered it; (2) a coal-fired boiler room that produced steam, part of which was used for the manufacturing process and the balance for producing electricity; and (3) an electric plant.

An analysis of these activities has revealed that 60% of the water is used for the production of steam and 40% is used in manufacturing. Half of the steam produced is used for the production of electric power and half for manufacturing. Twenty percent of the electric power is used by the water plant and 80% goes to manufacturing.

For the year 19_9, the costs charged to these departments were:

	VARIABLE	FIXED	TOTAL
Water plant	$ 2,000	$ 8,000	$10,000
Steam room	18,000	12,000	30,000
Electric plant	6,000	9,000	15,000
			$55,000

1. How would you allocate these costs in an absorption product-cost determination situation? Use the reciprocal method.
2. A new power company has offered to sell electricity to Prairie State for two cents a kilowatt-hour. In 19_9, the electric plant generated 600,000 kilowatt-hours. The manager of the electric plant has advised that the offer be rejected, since (he says) "our variable costs were only one cent per kilowatt-hour in 19_9." Was this the right answer? Show computations.

12-29 Service department cost allocation and motivation. Solve Problem 11-28 (Sharp Company), which could have been placed here.

12-30 Allocation of computer costs. Salquist, Inc., is an international ethical pharmaceutical manufacturer that specializes in hormone research and the development and marketing of hormone-base products. The 22 different wholly owned subsidiaries and separate divisions that constitute the organization are highly decentralized, but they receive overall direction from a small corporate staff at parent-corporation headquarters in Palo Alto. The laboratories division, research division, and all corporate offices are located at the home-office site. Each of the divisional functional areas operates as a cost center. That is, labs accounting, labs production, labs sales, research accounting, and research operations are separate cost centers. Corporate purchasing, employee relations, office services, and computer (Electronic Data Processing: EDP) systems also function as individual cost centers, and they provide their services to Research, Labs, and the other divisions as necessary.

Until recently, no costs of the corporate service cost centers were allocated to the divisional cost centers; they were simply lumped together as central corporate overhead. Recently, however, it was decided to start charging the operating units (that is, the cost centers) for their EDP usage. Prior to this time, EDP services were simply requested as desired by the cost centers; priorities were determined by negotiations, with ultimate recourse to an EDP control committee (each cost center was represented); and all charges were absorbed as corporate overhead.

EDP systems contain both systems programming services and computer operations. In the current "charge-back" system, the EDP director prepares a budget at the start of each quarter based upon his estimates of user demand. Using full absorption costing, he then computes an hourly charge rate, which he promulgates to the user cost centers. The users prepare their budgets utilizing his charge rate and their estimates of the services they think they will be needing. When a user desires to undertake any specific project or use EDP services, he negotiates an agreement with EDP on the hours (thus cost) that he will be charged. The user is free to reject the EDP "bid" and obtain outside services if he does not feel the EDP job estimates are reasonable. Also, since many projects last a year or more but service agreements are arranged on a quarterly basis, the user can drop a project in midstream at the end of a quarter if his overall budget should become too tight. If the actual hours needed to complete a given job exceed those contracted for, the EDP center must absorb the extra cost as an unfavorable overhead variance.

The performance of all cost centers is evaluated on the basis of how closely their actual results match budget. Thus the EDP director must ensure not only that his actual expenditures coincide with those that were budgeted but that he is able to bill other centers for all his actual charges. He must be sure that he contracts for enough projects from the users to absorb his budget.

The shift to the charge-back method was imposed by the corporate financial vice-president for the "purpose of putting control and responsibility for expenditures where the benefits are received." The VP also felt the move was necessary to avoid a "mushrooming of the EDP group" and to make users more aware of the costs they were incurring. An additional factor mentioned was an almost irresistible tide of "allocationism" prevalent in local industry because of the overpowering influence of government contracting there. He does feel he will resist allocating the other services, however, with the possible exception of printing and reproduction, which has grown to be quite costly in the last few years. The major rationale for not allocating the other services is that they are all uniform, predictable functions, whereas the EDP services are more spasmodic and project-oriented.

The head of the EDP group is strongly opposed to the new system. He believes that there is "too much lip service paid to the specialized nature of computers" and that the new system is reducing the effectiveness of the EDP group to the corporation as a whole. He and several of the user-directors believe the shift was simply a political maneuver on the part of the VP to consolidate the EDP empire under the aegis of the corporate staff. The head of the EDP group believes a nonchargeable system administered by the EDP control committee would yield better results.

Required

1. What are the motivational and operational effects of this change on users, EDP group, and corporation?
2. Evaluate the impact of having coexistence of allocated and nonallocated services.
3. Evaluate the operation of this particular allocation system.

12-31 Common cost allocation, theater facility with multiple users. The Downtown Theater is owned by the city of Los Angeles. It has seating capacity of 2,500. The use of the theater is shared by two companies:

Civic Light Opera Company: Agreement with the city enables it to use the facilities on Friday, Saturday, and Sunday nights 50 weeks a year. It has used the Downtown Theater each year for the last ten years.

Experimental Drama Company: Agreement with the city enables it to use the facilities on Tuesday, Wednesday, and Thursday nights 50 weeks a year. This company was organized last year and has used the Downtown Theater for one year.

Data for the most recent year are:

	CIVIC LIGHT OPERA	EXPERIMENTAL DRAMA
Nights theater available	150	150
Nights theater used	120	80
Average attendance per night	2,000	500
Average price per ticket	$15	$10
Revenues	$3,600,000	$400,000
Cost identifiable with		
each company	$2,200,000	$250,000

The common costs of the Downtown Theater are the $200,000 annual fixed rent payment to the city and the annual fixed operating costs of $800,000.

If the Civic Light Opera Company was the only user of the theater, the fixed costs of the Downtown Theater are estimated to be $875,000 ($200,000 fixed rent payment + $675,000 fixed operating costs). Both companies can use the facilities of other theaters providing they sign a one-year lease contract. The Civic Light Opera Company could use the Santa Monica Theater at an annual rent payment of $900,000. The Experimental Drama Company could use the University of Southern California Theater facility for an annual rent payment of $300,000.

Required

1. How will the common cost of $1,000,000 for the Downtown Theater be allocated between the two companies using the following allocation bases: (a) relative capacity (nights theater available), (b) relative use (nights theater used), (c) relative revenues, and (d) relative identifiable costs? What criterion might be invoked to justify methods *a, b, c,* and *d* individually?
2. How will the common cost of $1,000,000 be allocated using (e) the incremental common cost allocation method (assuming Civic Light Opera is the primary user), and (f) the stand-alone common cost allocation method? What criterion might be invoked to justify methods *e* and *f* individually?
3. What is the operating income of each of the two companies under methods *a, b, c, d, e,* and *f,* respectively? *Operating income* is defined as revenues minus identifiable costs minus common cost allocations.
4. The mayor of Los Angeles proposes to use the incremental method as calculated in requirement 2. The manager of the Civic Light Opera Company comments that if the city wants to promote experimental drama, it should provide a direct subsidy to the Experimental Drama Company rather than use a cost allocation method that is unfair to the Civic Light Opera Company. How should the mayor respond to the manager of the Civic Light Opera Company?

Cost Allocation: Part II

Chapter 12 introduced four purposes of cost allocation and discussed the allocation of costs from corporate and other service departments to production departments. Chapter 13 continues our exploration of this topic. The focus is on the allocation of the indirect costs of production departments to individual products, services, or jobs (such as a government contract); these indirect costs can include the already allocated costs of corporate and other service departments. The final sections of Chapter 13 discuss the contribution approach to cost allocation and specific issues that arise in the cost justification or reimbursement purpose of cost allocation.

MAGNITUDE OF FACTORY-OVERHEAD COSTS

Two related trends in the cost structure of many manufacturing companies have been observed:[1]

1. Factory-overhead costs have been increasing as a percentage of total manufacturing costs.
2. Direct-labor costs have been decreasing as a percentage of total manufacturing costs.

---

[1]See J. Miller and T. Vollmann, "The Hidden Factory." *Harvard Business Review*, September–October 1985, pp. 142–50.

EXHIBIT 13-1

Relative Magnitude of Factory-Overhead Costs to Total Cost of Goods Sold for Nine Segments of the U.S. Electronics Industry

SEGMENT OF THE U.S. ELECTRONICS INDUSTRY (NUMBER OF FIRMS IN SURVEY)	COST CATEGORY AS A PERCENTAGE OF COST OF GOODS SOLD			COST OF GOODS SOLD AS A PERCENTAGE OF SALES
	Factory Overhead	Direct Materials	Direct Labor	
Semiconductor (33)	53.8%	25.3%	20.9%	55.1%
Active components (39)	34.0	44.1	21.9	64.7
Electronic Systems (138)	33.3	42.8	23.9	70.3
Instruments (97)	32.4	54.5	13.1	47.3
Production Equipment (37)	30.0	55.5	14.5	53.0
Passive Components (41)	29.8	48.6	21.6	61.9
Computer Peripheral (67)	27.5	62.3	10.2	62.4
Computers (41)	26.0	67.5	6.5	56.7
Software (34)	11.0	42.8	46.2	49.9

Source: 1985–86 Operating Ratios Survey (Palo Alto, Calif.: American Electronics Association, 1985).

Exhibit 13-1 illustrates the relative magnitude of factory-overhead costs in nine segments of the U.S. electronics industry. The range is from 53.8% of cost of goods sold for semiconductor manufacturers to 11.0% for software firms. For many segments of the electronics industry, and in many other areas of manufacturing, factory overhead is now a major cost category.[2] There is heightened interest both in how to control the magnitude of overhead costs and in how these costs are allocated to individual products or services.

Indirect costs of nonmanufacturing organizations also are of great interest to many parties. For example, the indirect costs charged by some U.S. universities for government-sponsored research projects exceed 60% of the direct costs.[3] Many individual researchers and government officials claim that such indirect-cost rates are excessive and serve to reduce the total amount of research activity undertaken by universities.

CHOOSING COST POOL CATEGORIES

Costs allocated to individual products or services are a function of:

1. The aggregate costs in each cost pool
2. The measure used as the allocation base for each cost pool

---

[2] One survey reports that for a sample of 112 manufacturing firms, the percentage of indirect manufacturing costs to total manufacturing costs ranged from a low of 2% to a high of 67%; the average was 29%. H. Schwarzbach, "The Impact of Automation on Accounting for Indirect Costs," *Management Accounting*, December 1985, pp. 45–50.

[3] A 60% indirect-cost charge means that if a research project has a direct-cost budget of $100,000, the researcher must apply for a grant of $160,000 ($60,000 of which goes to the university to cover its overhead costs associated with providing the research facilities).

This section discusses issues related to the choice of cost pools. Subsequent sections discuss the choice of allocation bases.

A cost pool is *homogeneous* if each activity whose costs are included therein has the same or a similar cause-and-effect relationship to a cost objective as the other activities whose costs are included in the cost pool. One consequence of using a **homogeneous cost pool** is that the costs allocated using that pool will be the same as those that would be made if costs were separately collected for each individual activity in the homogeneous pool. Cost allocation will best reflect cause-and-effect relationships if each cost pool is a homogeneous one.

Plantwide versus departmental cost pools

Most manufacturing plants produce more than one product. Different products may require different attention and effort, different material usages, and different production routings. Consider the Peripheral Equipment Division of the Computer Horizons example that was introduced in Chapter 12. This division has a single plant. The two main products manufactured are plotters and printers. Both products are routed through two departments: machining and finishing. The machining department is heavily mechanized with costly semiautomatic and automatic equipment. The finishing department contains a few simple tools and is dependent on skilled workers. Overhead costs are relatively large in machining and small in finishing. Assume the following production requirements:

	MACHINING	FINISHING
Plotter	1 direct-labor hour	10 direct-labor hours
Printer	9 direct-labor hours	2 direct-labor hours

Computer Horizons can use one of two approaches in collecting the machining and finishing department indirect costs when allocating them to individual products:

1. Use a single plantwide cost pool, in which the machining and finishing department indirect costs lose their individual identity.
2. Use separate cost pools for the machining department and the finishing department. (This approach was illustrated in Chapter 12, pages 418–20.)

Exhibit 13-2 illustrates the use of both plantwide and departmental cost pools; indirect costs of all cost pools in this illustration are allocated on the basis of direct-labor hours. The indirect costs allocated to each product are:

	PLANTWIDE COST POOL	DEPARTMENTAL COST POOLS
Plotter	$59.40 per unit	$18.00 per unit
Printer	$59.40 per unit	$91.60 per unit

The use of separate departmental cost pools can result in a more accurate linking of overhead with specific jobs when products do not receive uniform time in each production department. The machining and finishing departmental rates are $10.00 and $0.80 per direct-labor hour, respectively. Compare these with the $5.40

EXHIBIT 13-2
Plantwide Versus Departmental Cost Pools

	MACHINING DEPARTMENT	FINISHING DEPARTMENT	PLANTWIDE TOTAL
Budgeted indirect costs	$100,000	$ 8,000	$108,000
Budgeted direct-labor hours	10,000	10,000	20,000
Budgeted rate per DLH	$ 10.00	$ 0.80	$ 5.40
Indirect Costs Allocated to Each Plotter:			
Using plantwide cost pool: 11 DLH × $5.40			$59.40
Using department cost pools: $10.00 + $8.00			$18.00
(1 DLH of machining × $10.00 = $10.00)			
(10 DLH of finishing × $0.80 = $8.00)			
Indirect Costs Allocated to Each Printer:			
Using plantwide cost pool: 11 DLH × $5.40			$59.40
Using department cost pools: $90.00 + $1.60			$91.60
(9 DLH of machining × $10.00 = $90.00)			
(2 DLH of finishing × $0.80 = $1.60)			

plantwide rate. The latter may mislead managers. They would be inclined to misjudge relative product profitabilities.

In Exhibit 13-2, **departmental cost pools are preferable to the plantwide cost pool; they provide a more-refined picture of cost relationships for each product.** Note that in this example the same allocation base (direct-labor hours) is used for each department. Further refinement of the cost allocations may be desirable. For example, machine-hours might be used for allocating machining department indirect costs while direct-labor hours might be used for allocating the finishing department indirect costs.

Furthermore, two or more allocation bases might be desirable within each department. For instance, the finishing department may want to use direct materials as an allocation base for some overhead items and direct-labor hours for others.

COST POOL CATEGORIES AND TECHNOLOGICAL CHANGE

The trend in some industries is toward the use of highly capital intensive plants, and in some cases the extensive utilization of automated machinery. This trend has implications for the choice of cost pools. **Two changes in the traditional cost pool categories of direct materials, direct labor, and factory overhead are being experimented with: (a) adding a fourth cost pool category termed** *machining costs,* **and (b) combining two of the traditional cost pool categories (direct labor and overhead) into a single cost pool category (termed** *conversion costs*).

ADDITION OF A SEPARATE MACHINING COST POOL CATEGORY. Machining costs are a major cost item in some organizations. Variable machining costs include energy, lubricants, maintenance and repair, and the component of depreciation that is a function of machine use. Fixed components of machining costs include facilities rental (if not purchased), property tax, insurance, and the component of depreciation that is constant for the period irrespective of machine use. Fixed costs of machining will often be a large proportion of total machining costs. Unlike some components of direct labor, robots and automated machine tools cannot be laid off when business activity declines.

One company experimenting with the addition of a machining cost pool category keeps separate records for each of the key machines in its plant.[4] Such records can include precise details on machine-operating time (in minutes or even seconds), energy usage, and labor-hours of the machine operators associated with their use. Low-cost microprocessors, digital clocks, and counters make it economically feasible to maintain such records on an ongoing basis in some plants.

Obtaining precise estimates of equipment depreciation costs, a major component in a machining cost pool category, will often be a difficult and costly task. For example, refined estimates of useful life may require the employment of industrial engineers. A problem sometimes encountered is that the depreciation method used is based on taxation guidelines rather than on any reduction in the economic service potential of the machine.

The second Problem for Self-Study, at the end of this chapter, illustrates how a separate machine cost pool for robotic-related costs can be used when allocating materials-handling department costs to finished-goods units. This problem also illustrates how the use of robots can increase the information available about allocation bases that best captures cause-and-effect relationships.

COMBINING OF DIRECT-LABOR AND OVERHEAD COST POOL CATEGORIES INTO A SINGLE CONVERSION COST POOL CATEGORY. When labor costs constitute a minimal percentage of total manufacturing costs, it may no longer be economically feasible to collect them separately in an individual cost pool category. Chapter 2 cited the example of a Hewlett-Packard plant that eliminated the direct-labor cost pool category and now includes such costs in the manufacturing-overhead cost pool.[5] In a highly automated plant of Anchor Hocking, the labor costs of machine operators have been switched from being a separate cost pool to being part of the variable-overhead cost pool.[6]

This separate conversion cost pool can be defined at either the plant or the departmental level. Where departments differ sizably in the cost of purchasing or maintaining machines, the use of department conversion cost pools would yield more-refined applications of costs to individual products than would the use of a plant conversion cost pool.

CHOOSING COST ALLOCATION BASES

A cost allocation base is a systematic means of relating a given cost or cost pool to a cost objective. The choice of the allocation base should be guided by (a) the purpose to be served by the cost allocation, and (b) the necessary clerical costs and effort in allocation. To illustrate, suppose a manager wants to predict how total overhead costs fluctuate. The ideal allocation base would have a *cause-and-*

---

[4]H. Schwarzbach and R. Vangermeersh, "Why We Should Account for the 4th Cost of Manufacturing," *Management Accounting*, July 1983, pp. 24–28.

[5]R. Hunt, L. Garrett, and C. Merz, "Direct Labor Cost Not Always Relevant at H-P," *Management Accounting*, February 1985, pp. 58–62.

[6]G. Hakala, "Measuring Costs with Machine Hours," *Management Accounting*, October 1985, pp. 57–61.

effect relationship between changes in total costs and changes in the allocation base. Chapter 23 further explores some general approaches to choosing allocation bases (the independent variables) for aid in predicting how total costs (the dependent variable) will fluctuate. Plotting the relationship between alternative allocation bases and total costs can provide much insight.

Examples of factory-overhead allocation bases

Four factory-overhead cost allocation bases encountered in practice are:

1. **DIRECT-LABOR HOURS**   This is a commonly used basis for two reasons. First, indirect labor and supplies usage in many cases is closely related to the input of direct-labor hours. Second, information on the number of direct-labor hours associated with each product is readily available in many organizations. Time is traced to specific products by using work records for direct labor. Budgeted overhead rates are developed by dividing budgeted total overhead by budgeted total direct-labor hours.

2. **DIRECT-LABOR COST**   If labor rates are nearly uniform for every operation, the use of a labor-*dollar* base for overhead application would yield the same results as the use of direct-labor hours. Otherwise, in theory, direct-labor *hours* would be better (using a cause-and-effect criterion) in most instances, particularly where the senior and junior workers in an organization are equally efficient and therefore use the same amount of overhead services per hour. For example, a senior worker may earn $20 per hour while a junior worker may earn $14 per hour. If a 200-percent-of-direct-labor-cost rate is in effect, the applied overhead cost of a given job requiring one hour of direct labor would be $40 if the senior worker were used, and $28 if the junior worker were used. Standard or average labor rates generally prevent such strange results.

   Direct-labor *dollars* as an overhead base may be conceptually better than labor *hours* where many overhead items represent fringe labor costs, which are primarily tied to direct-labor *cost,* or where high-cost laborers make the greatest use of high-cost facilities and complex machinery.

3. **MACHINE-HOURS**   Where production is highly mechanized, depreciation, supplies usage, and indirect labor are frequently more closely related to machine utilization than to direct-labor usage. In theory, then, machine time may be the most accurate base for overhead application. In the past, machine-time statistics for each individual product have not always been collected on a systematic basis. However, the increasing use of computerized machine controls is substantially reducing the (marginal) costs of collecting this information. (More discussion of this base appears in the next section.)

4. **DIRECT-MATERIAL COST OR WEIGHT**   Use of these bases typically is restricted to allocating materials management costs such as purchasing, receiving, incoming inspection, inventory control, and material-handling costs.

   Surveys of practice consistently report widespread use of direct-labor hours or direct-labor dollars as the allocation base for factory-overhead costs. To illustrate, one survey of 112 manufacturing firms reported the following (some firms use more than one base, so the percentages exceed 100):[7]

ALLOCATION BASE	PERCENTAGE OF FIRMS USING BASE
Direct-labor dollars	58.0%
Direct-labor hours	35.7
Machine-hours	27.7
Direct-material cost	18.8
Weight	11.6

Exhibit 13-1 presented data on the magnitude of factory-overhead costs in nine segments of the U.S. electronics industry. Direct labor (either hours or dollars) is the most frequently used allocation base in many of these segments. The following summary data relate to several segments.

INDUSTRY SEGMENT	PERCENTAGE OF FIRMS USING DIRECT LABOR (HOURS OR DOLLARS) AS ALLOCATION BASE	AVERAGE FACTORY OVERHEAD AS A PERCENTAGE OF DIRECT-LABOR DOLLARS
Semiconductor	66.7%	405%
Electronic Systems	46.8	246
Instruments	62.8	337
Computer Peripheral	55.2	392
Computers	48.5	474

COST ALLOCATION BASES AND TECHNOLOGICAL CHANGE

Implementation of an automated or computer-assisted production line can dramatically affect cost relationships within a factory. Unless management changes the cost allocation system to recognize the new cost relationships, the resulting cost figures can be misleading. **Operating managers may quickly lose confidence in the internal accounting system if it produces numbers that they fervently believe fail to capture cost behavior patterns at the operating level.**

A useful distinction in highly capital intensive operations, when choosing an allocation base, is between labor-paced manufacturing environments and machine-paced manufacturing environments:[8]

Labor-Paced Manufacturing Environments: Worker dexterity and productivity determine the speed of production. Machines function as tools that aid production workers. Often the use of direct-labor hours or direct-labor costs as an allocation base can still capture cause-and-effect relationships in such environments. Allocation rates of

---

[7]Schwarzbach, "Impact of Automation on Accounting for Indirect Costs," p. 48. For additional evidence on the widespread use of direct-labor dollars or hours as an allocation base, see Chapter 8 ("Allocation Costs to Specific Objectives") of J. Bedingfield and L. Rosen, *Government Contract Accounting* (Washington, D.C.: Federal Publications Government Contract Text, 1985).

[8]A. Seed, "Cost Accounting in the Age of Robotics," *Management Accounting*, October 1984, pp. 39–43.

500% or more of direct-labor costs can be observed where the machines used to assist workers have very high acquisition and maintenance costs.

Machine-Paced Manufacturing Environments: Machines conduct most (or all) phases of production, such as shipment of materials to the production line, assembly and other activities on the production line, and shipment of finished goods to the delivery dock areas. Machine workers in such environments may tend more than one machine. Workers focus their activity on the minimization of machine problems rather than on the actual operation of the machines. Computer specialists and industrial engineers are the real "controllers" of the speed of production.

Firms in machine-paced environments are experimenting with one or more of the following allocation bases:

1. Machine-hours. One firm using this allocation base keeps detailed records on machine usage: distinctions are made between idle time, setup time, and operating time for each machine.[9]
2. Units of production. Where there is a single product or an appropriate physical measure to combine multiple products into a single-unit measure (such as a per-ton basis for paper mills), units of production can serve as an allocation base.
3. Standard direct conversion costs. This base can include direct labor, energy, operating supplies, and costs of operating machinery and equipment.
4. Total standard variable costs. This base includes standard variable conversion costs and standard variable material costs.

Consequences of inappropriate use of an allocation base

When a firm switches from a labor-paced to a machine-paced environment, direct-labor hours or direct-labor costs are unlikely to continue having a strong cause-and-effect relationship to the incurrence of factory overhead. Firms that continue to use direct-labor hours or dollars as an allocation base can expect to encounter:

1. Substantial increases in the budgeted overhead rate per direct-labor hour or per direct-labor dollar. A senior executive commented: "We've been brought up to manage in a world where burden rates (the ratios of overhead costs to direct-labor costs) are 100% to 200% or so. But now some of our plants are running with burden rates of over 1,000%. We don't even know what that means!"[10]
2. Substantial changes (variation) in month-to-month unit product costs for firms that allocate overhead on the basis of actual labor-hours rather than standard labor-hours. This variation will magnify when firms do not distinguish between operating labor-hours and labor-hours for machine maintenance and repair. Manufacturing managers may justifiably complain that computed unit product costs fail to measure the cost relationships that must be managed in the automated production setting.

Use of direct-labor hours as an allocation base in machine-paced manufacturing environments has reportedly prompted a variety of decisions that conflict with maximizing total company profits.[11] These include

1. Product managers' use of external vendors for parts that require a labor-intensive process when produced internally, even though it is more cost effective to produce the part internally. The high number of direct-labor hours will attract a high overhead charge even though the part does not actually use that much overhead.

---

[9]Hakala, "Measuring Costs with Machine Hours," pp. 57–61.

[10]Miller and Vollmann, "The Hidden Factory," p. 142.

[11]R. Kaplan, "Accounting Lag: The Obsolescence of Cost Accounting Systems," *California Management Review,* Winter 1986.

2. Excessive attention by product managers to controlling labor-hours relative to the attention paid to controlling the more costly categories of materials and machining. Managers can control the accounting numbers allocated by controlling direct-labor use. However, this does not control the actual incurrence of the larger materials and machining amounts.

3. Managers' attempts to classify manufacturing engineers as indirect labor rather than direct labor, resulting in part of their costs being allocated to other products.

Further discussion Chapter 17 (pp. 588–93) includes additional discussion of how changes in production technology can lead to changes in the accounting system that best passes the cost-benefit test.

THE CONTRIBUTION APPROACH TO COST ALLOCATION

In general, *contribution approach* means internal financial reporting and analysis that distinguishes between variable and fixed costs and includes the contribution margin described in Chapter 3. The contribution approach can be employed for nonroutine decisions and for performance evaluation.

The contribution approach to cost allocation, as shown in Exhibit 13-3, attempts to respond simultaneously to the purposes of economic decisions and motivation. Exhibit 13-3 is an important exhibit. It stresses cost behavior patterns in relation to individuals and segments of an organization. A **segment** is any line of activity or part of an organization for which separate determinations of costs or revenues or both are desired. A synonym for *segment* is **subunit.**

Failure to distinguish cost behavior patterns creates a big roadblock in cost analysis. Two different types of segments are illustrated in Exhibit 13-3: divisions and products. As you read across Exhibit 13-3, the focus becomes narrower; from the company as a whole, to Divisions A and B, and then to the products in Division B only.

Revenues, variable costs, and contribution margins The allocations of revenues and variable costs are usually straightforward. Each item is directly identifiable with a specific segment of activity. (We assume no intersegment sales in this section. Issues associated with the pricing of such sales are discussed in Chapter 25.) The contribution margin, item (1) in Exhibit 13-3, is particularly helpful for predicting the impact that short-run changes in volume have on income. Changes in income can quickly be calculated by multiplying the change in units by the unit contribution margin, or by multiplying the increment in dollar sales by the contribution-margin ratio. For example, the contribution-margin ratio of Product 1 is $120/$300 = 40%. The increase in pretax income resulting from a $20,000 increase in its sales volume can readily be computed as .40 × $20,000, or $8,000. This calculation assumes no changes in selling prices, operating efficiency, or fixed costs. Some portion of fixed costs may be avoidable or escapable in short-run decisions. (See pages 301–304 of Chapter 9.)

Contributions by managers and segments Items (2) and (3) in Exhibit 13-3 distinguish between the performance of the manager as a professional executive and the segment as a long-run economic investment, respectively.

Controllability is the degree of influence that a specific manager has over the costs or revenues in question. Distinctions between controllable and uncontrollable items are helpful when feasible. They aid motivation and the analysis of perform-

EXHIBIT 13-3

The Contribution Approach: Model Income Statement by Segments
(In Thousands of Dollars)

	COMPANY AS A WHOLE	COMPANY BREAK-DOWN INTO TWO DIVISIONS		POSSIBLE BREAKDOWN OF DIVISION B ONLY				
		Division A	Division B	Not Allocated	Product 1	Product 2	Product 3	Product 4
Net revenues	1,500	500	1,000		300	200	100	400
Variable manufacturing cost of goods sold	780	200	580		120	155	45	260
Manufacturing contribution margin	720	300	420		180	45	55	140
Variable selling and administrative costs	220	100	120		60	15	25	20
(1) Contribution margin	500	200	300		120	30	30	120
Fixed costs controllable by segment managers, (certain advertising, sales promotion, salespersons' salaries, engineering, research, management consulting, and supervision costs)	190	110	80	45*	10	6	4	15
(2) Contribution controllable by segment managers	310	90	220	(45)	110	24	26	105
Fixed costs controllable by others (such as depreciation, property taxes, insurance, and the division manager's salary)	70	20	50	20	3	15	4	8
(3) Contribution by segments	240	70	170	(65)	107	9	22	97
Unallocated costs (not clearly or practically allocable to any segment except by some questionable allocation base)	135							
(4) Income before income taxes	105							

*Only those costs clearly identifiable with a product line should be allocated.

ance. For example, unless discrimination is made between the manager and the responsibility center as an economic entity, the skillful executive will be reluctant to accept troublesome responsibilities. Sometimes it takes a miracle worker to get a limping segment up to a minimally acceptable level of operating income.

The controllable contribution, keyed as item (2) in Exhibit 13-3, should be interpreted in conjunction with the contribution margin. *Managers can often influence some fixed costs, particularly discretionary fixed costs.* (Examples of these costs are given in Exhibit 13-3.) The incurrence of discretionary costs may affect variable costs. For example, heavier outlays for maintenance, engineering, or management consulting may reduce repairs, increase machine speeds, or heighten labor productivity. Also, decisions on advertising, research, and sales-promotion budgets are necessarily related to expected impacts on sales volumes.

The distinction between controllable and uncontrollable costs must be drawn on a company-by-company basis. For example, management may prefer to deduct depreciation on some classes of plant and equipment when computing the controllable contribution, item (2). Getting agreement as to these classifications may be bothersome, but it is not a herculean task.

The income statement in Exhibit 13-3 has four numbered measures of performance, ranging from contribution margin to income before income taxes. There is nothing hallowed about these four illustrative measures; some organizations may want to use only two or three such measures. For instance, Reckett & Colman, a large British manufacturer and seller of housewares, has a classification of sales, contribution before marketing costs, marketing costs, contribution after marketing costs, fixed costs, and trading profit.

The distinction between item (2) and item (3) in Exhibit 13-3 is seldom found in practice. Why? Because it is difficult to draw fine distinctions in identifying which fixed costs are controlled by which managers. Nevertheless, distinctions between the performances of the manager and the segment are still accomplished via intelligent budgeting. For example, the manager's objective for the forthcoming year may be agreed upon: "I'll reduce this division's loss from $5 million to $3 million." If this objective is attained, the manager may subsequently be judged as successful. However, the division may continue to be regarded as a miserable investment.

Allocations to segments

There may be a limit to the allocation of a given cost in a given income statement. Although many discretionary costs can easily be traced to divisions, they may not all be directly traceable to products. Some advertising expenses for Division B may be common to all products. For example, Products 1, 2, and 3 may be consumer items that all benefit from the same advertisements, while Product 4 may be an item sold to manufacturers by a separate sales force with its own fixed selling costs.

Discretionary and committed costs may or may not be allocated, *depending on the segments in question. Discretionary costs* are costs arising from periodic or budget appropriation decisions that directly reflect top-management decisions. *Committed costs* are fixed costs that arise from having property, plant, equipment, and a basic organization.

Assume that a sales salary is easily identified with a particular territory. However, if more than one product is sold, the allocation of the salary among the products can be questionable. Consequently, there may be a limit to the allocation of a given cost in a given income statement. For instance, the divisions in Exhibit 13-3 could be territories. The sales salary just described could readily be allocated to Division A or B (a territory), but it could not be allocated convincingly among the products. *A given cost may be allocated with respect to one segment of the organization and unallocated with respect to another.*

Unallocated costs

Consider the next-to-last line in Exhibit 13-3. An unallocated cost is common to all the segments in question and is not clearly or practically assignable except on some questionable basis. Examples of unallocated costs include the salaries of the president and other top officers, basic research and development, and some central corporate costs like public relations or corporate-image advertising. Unless the general company costs are clearly traceable to segments, allocations are not made under the contribution approach. For example, income taxes typically are not allocated under the contribution approach because of the difficulty of tracing them to individual segments.

This refusal to allocate some costs is the most controversial aspect of the contribution approach income statement. Accountants and managers are accustomed to the whole being completely subdivided into parts that can be added up again to equal the whole. In *traditional* segment income statements, all costs are fully allocated, so that the segments show final net incomes that can be summed to equal the net income for the company as a whole.

Of course, if for some reason management prefers a whole-equals-the-sum-of-its-parts statement, the unallocated costs may be allocated so that the segments show income figures that will cross-add to equal the income for the company as a whole. **The important point is that the contribution approach distinguishes between various degrees of objectivity in cost allocations.** As you read downward and to the right in Exhibit 13-3, you become less and less confident about the cost allocations. A dozen independent accountants would most likely agree on how the variable costs should be allocated and would least likely agree on whether and how the unallocated costs should be accounted for.

COST JUSTIFICATION AND REIMBURSEMENT

Cost data are often used in the setting of contract prices. Examples include

1. A contract between the Department of Defense and a company assemblying fighter planes; the price paid is based on the contractor's cost plus a preset fixed fee.
2. A contract between two oil companies in a joint venture; the costs of operating a shared oil-refining facility are allocated between the companies on the basis of expected usage of the refinery.
3. A contract between an energy-consulting firm and a hospital; the consulting firm receives a fixed fee plus a share of the energy cost savings associated with implementing the consulting firm's recommendations.

To reduce the areas of dispute between parties to such contracts, the "rules of the game" should be explicit (preferably in written form) and well understood at the time the contract is signed. Such "rules of the game" include the definition of cost items allowed, the cost pools, and the permissible allocation base(s) for each cost pool.

Contracting with the U.S. government

The U.S. government reimburses most contractors in one of two ways:[12]

1. **Fixed-Price Contract.** The price to be received by the contractor is established at the outset. It is not subject to any adjustment due to the actual cost experience of the contractor.
2. **Cost-Reimbursement Contract.** The price to be received by the contractor is based on the actual costs incurred by the contractor. There are many variants of this contract—e.g., cost-plus-fixed-fee reimbursement and cost-plus-incentive-fee reimbursement.

The cost accounting rules to be followed in U.S. federal government procurement are governed by the Federal Acquisition Regulation (FAR), which became effective in 1984. The most-detailed cost accounting rules underlying this regula-

---

[12]Detailed works in this area include F. Alston, F. Johnson, M. Worthington, L. Goldsman, and F. DeVito, *Contracting with the Federal Government* (New York: John Wiley, 1984); and H. Wright and J. Bedingfield, *Government Contract Accounting*, 2nd ed. (Washington, D.C.: Federal Publications, 1985).

tion were issued by the **Cost Accounting Standards Board (CASB)**, which was created by Congress in 1970.

U.S. government agencies have considerable power to investigate the internal accounting records of contractors. In some cases, the agencies can subpoena even the internal audit reports of contractors. It is imperative that contractors maintain a high level of control over internal accounting policies. Firms operate in an environment in which politicians seek to publicize any appearance of "misbehavior" by government contractors. Firms found guilty of overcharging on government contracts have been fined and, in some cases, prohibited from bidding on subsequent government contracts for a designated period.

Cost accounting standards board

The CASB was established against a backdrop of systematic cost overruns by contractors on cost-reimbursement contracts, and allegations that contractors were overstating their costs.[13] The aim of the CASB was to "promulgate cost accounting standards designed to achieve *uniformity* and *consistency* in the cost accounting principles followed by defense contractors and subcontractors under federal contracts." In October 1980, after issuing twenty cost accounting standards, the CASB ceased operations. The immediate cause of its demise was a congressional refusal to appropriate $1.5 million dollars for the CASB's annual budget. The standards issued by the CASB continue to have the full force of law.

Exhibit 13-4 lists the titles of selected accounting standards issued by the CASB. Several of the CASB standards (e.g., 402) cover general issues relating to

EXHIBIT 13-4
CASB Standards & Interpretations

<table>
<tr><td colspan="2" align="center">COST ACCOUNTING
STANDARDS & INTERPRETATIONS</td></tr>
<tr><td>CAS 401</td><td>Consistency In Estimating, Accumulating & Reporting Costs*</td></tr>
<tr><td>CAS 402</td><td>Consistency In Allocating Costs Incurred For The Same Purpose*</td></tr>
<tr><td>CAS 403</td><td>Allocation Of Home Office Expenses To Segments*</td></tr>
<tr><td>CAS 404</td><td>Capitalization Of Tangible Assets</td></tr>
<tr><td>CAS 405</td><td>Accounting For Unallowable Costs</td></tr>
<tr><td>CAS 406</td><td>Cost Accounting Period</td></tr>
<tr><td>CAS 407</td><td>Use Of Standard Cost For Direct Material & Direct Labor</td></tr>
<tr><td>CAS 408</td><td>Accounting For Costs Of Compensated Personal Absence</td></tr>
<tr><td>CAS 409</td><td>Depreciation Of Tangible Capital Assets</td></tr>
<tr><td>CAS 410</td><td>Allocation Of Business Unit General & Administrative Expense To Final Cost Objectives</td></tr>
<tr><td>CAS 411</td><td>Accounting For Acquisition Costs Of Material</td></tr>
<tr><td>CAS 412</td><td>Composition & Measurement Of Pension Costs</td></tr>
<tr><td>CAS 413</td><td>Adjustment & Allocation Of Pension Cost</td></tr>
<tr><td>CAS 414</td><td>Cost Of Money As An Element Of The Cost Of Facilities Capital</td></tr>
<tr><td>CAS 415</td><td>Accounting For The Cost Of Deferred Compensation</td></tr>
<tr><td>CAS 416</td><td>Accounting For Insurance Costs</td></tr>
<tr><td>CAS 417</td><td>Cost Of Money As An Element Of The Cost Of Capital Assets Under Construction</td></tr>
<tr><td>CAS 418</td><td>Allocation Of Direct & Indirect Costs</td></tr>
<tr><td>CAS 420</td><td>Accounting For Independent Research & Development Costs And Bid & Proposal Costs</td></tr>
<tr><td colspan="2">*Indicates Standard for which an Interpretation was issued.</td></tr>
</table>

[13]For example, an examination of 2,271 Air Force contracts in 1967 and 1968 revealed that 66% required price adjustments, and 90% of those adjustments were upward shifts. See M. Trubnick, "Premature Death of an Agency: The Case of the CASB," *Mid-Atlantic Journal of Business,* Winter 1984/85, pp. 55–62.

EXHIBIT 13-5

Illustrative Allocation Bases Suggested by CASB
for Centralized Home-Office Service Functions

SERVICE RENDERED	COST-ALLOCATION BASES
1. Personnel administration	1. Number of personnel, labor-hours, payroll, number of hires
2. Data-processing services	2. Machine time, number of reports
3. Centralized purchasing and subcontracting	3. Number of purchase orders, value of purchases, number of items
4. Centralized warehousing	4. Square footage, value of material, volume
5. Company aircraft service	5. Actual or standard rate per hour, mile, passenger mile, or similar unit
6. Central telephone service	6. Usage costs, number of telephones

the definition of cost items and the prohibition of double-counting; double-counting occurs when a cost item is included both as a direct-cost item and as a part of overhead or an indirect-cost pool that is allocated to the contract using a budgeted rate. Other standards cover either the allocation of direct (e.g., 407) or indirect (e.g., 403) costs to government contracts.

Standard 403 ("Allocation of Home Office Expenses to Segments") illustrates the CASB approach to determining cost pools and the allocation bases for these pools:

> The allocation of centralized service functions shall be governed by a hierarchy of preferable allocation techniques which represent beneficial or causal relationships. The preferred representation of such relationships is a measure of the activity of the organization performing the function. Supporting functions are usually labor-oriented, machine-oriented, or space-oriented.

Exhibit 13-5 gives examples of the allocation bases presented in Standard 403 for individual home office expense cost pools.

Fairness for pricing

The entire field of negotiated government contracts is marked by the attempt to use *cost* allocations as a means for establishing a mutually satisfactory *price*. There is a subtle but important distinction here. A *cost* allocation may be difficult to defend on the basis of any cause-effect reasoning. However, an allocation may be a "reasonable" or "fair" *means of establishing a selling price* in the minds of the affected parties. Various costs become "allowable," whereas others are "unallowable." If cost allocations are to be used in lieu of market-based pricing, much argument and litigation are avoided when the allocation rules are made as explicit as is feasible in writing in advance.

COMPREHENSIVE ILLUSTRATION OF ALLOCATION

Exhibit 13-6 presents a comprehensive illustration of cost allocation that draws on the material in Chapters 12 and 13. There are three service departments and three production departments in Exhibit 13-6:

EXHIBIT 13-6

Sample Company

Factory-Overhead Budget: Step-Down Method of Allocation for Application to Product for the Year Ended December 31, 19_1 (Lines 1–17 are in thousands)

LINE	SERVICE DEPARTMENTS			PRODUCTION DEPARTMENTS			
	Repair and Maintenance	Building and Grounds	Factory Administration	Machining	Assembly	Finishing	Total
1. Indirect labor (direct to departments [payroll analysis or work tickets])	$ 400	$ 960	$2,200	$ 4,900	$1,000	$ 360	$ 9,820
2. Supplies (direct to departments [requisitions])	640	700	240	3,500	400	1,400	6,880
3. Power (meters or horsepower ratings)	130	1,600	25	1,800	200	500	4,255
4. Payroll taxes (department payrolls)	200	50	200	1,300	300	100	2,150
5. Overtime premium (department payrolls)	100	—	60	600	140	50	950
6. Rework (direct to responsible department)	—	—	—	300	150	40	490
7. Fuel	—	100	—	—	—	—	100
8. Total variable overhead	$1,470	$3,410	$2,725	$12,400	$2,190	$2,450	$24,645
9. Property taxes and insurance	140	770	760	600	100	100	2,470
10. Depreciation	150	700	300	2,300	400	300	4,150
11. Supervision and miscellaneous	700	220	4,015	1,800	1,010	550	8,295
12. Total department-overhead budgets before allocation of service department costs to production departments	$2,460	$5,100	$7,800	$17,100	$3,700	$3,400	$39,560
Allocation of service department costs (see Note A on p. 459):							
13. Repair and maintenance (maintenance service, current month)	$2,460	492	25	1,476	246	221	
14. Building and grounds (square footage occupied)		$5,592	559	3,355	1,119	559	
15. Factory administration (direct-labor hours)*			$8,384	6,708	838	838	
16. Total production-department overhead				$28,639	$5,903	$5,018	$39,560
17. Application bases— budgeted standard direct-labor hours				2,400	300	300	
18. Budgeted overhead rate per standard direct-labor hour allowed				$11.933	$19.677	$16.727	

*Other possible bases might be number of employees or total labor-hours, or total costs excluding factory administration, or any measure that best represents the activity being managed.

EXHIBIT 13-6 *Continued*

| LINE | SERVICE DEPARTMENTS | | | PRODUCTION DEPARTMENTS | | | |
	Repair and Maintenance	Building and Grounds	Factory Administration	Machining	Assembly	Finishing	Total
Note A: Allocation bases:							
19. Repair and maintenance, based on specific maintenance service	100%	20%	1%	60%	10%	9%	
20. Building and grounds, based on square footage in each department			100,000	600,000	200,000	100,000	1,000,000
21. Using rate method, $5,592,000 ÷ 1,000,000 sq. ft. = $5.592 per sq. ft. or							
			(5.592 × 100,000), (5.592 × 600,000), (5.592 × 200,000), (5.592 × 1,000,000)				
22. Percentages based on square footage		100%	10%	60%	20%	10%	
23. Factory administration, based on direct-labor hours			100%	80%	10%	10%	

SERVICE DEPARTMENTS	PRODUCTION DEPARTMENTS
Repair and maintenance	Machining
Building and grounds	Assembly
Factory administration	Finishing

The step-down method of service department cost allocation is used. Exhibit 13-6 comprises four steps:

1. Prepare departmental budgets. (Lines 1–12)
2. Choose allocation bases. (Lines 19–23)
3. Allocate (reallocate) service department costs to production departments, using the step-down method. (Lines 13–16)
4. Develop budgeted overhead application rates for the output of each production department. (Lines 17–18)

Lines 1–11 provide the details of the department-overhead budgets. The total overhead on line 12 is then allocated, using the step-down method. Repair and Maintenance Department costs are allocated first because they render more service to Building and Grounds than the latter renders to Repair and Maintenance.

Lines 20–22 of Exhibit 13-6 show two computation techniques for allocation. Building and Grounds is allocated on the basis of the departmental percentage of total square footage. An alternative method would be to develop a rate per square foot, as shown on line 21. Then the square footage in each department would be multiplied by the rate. The two calculations are logically identical, and they give the same results. Personal preference determines the arithmetical method used in a specific case.

Besides demonstrating how service department costs are allocated, Exhibit 13-6 also illustrates how budgeted overhead application rates for the production departments are developed. The bases used in this illustration are standard direct-labor hours allowed in each department. Note that overhead application rates for product costing are used only for production departments because products flow only through those departments.

459

Indirect manufacturing (factory overhead) costs are an increasing percentage of total manufacturing costs in many industries. Decisions about the number of cost pools and the base used to allocate each cost pool can greatly affect the unit-cost figures reported for each product.

Technological change, such as an increase in automation on a production line, has implications for the design of cost accounting systems. Accountants should examine whether changes in the existing cost pools or the allocation bases used are warranted. Some firms are experimenting with adding a separate cost pool for machining costs. Another area of experimentation is the combining of the traditionally separate direct-labor and factory-overhead cost pools into a single conversion cost pool. Increased use of automation is also leading firms to experiment more with allocation bases other than direct-labor hours or direct-labor costs; alternative allocation bases include machine-hours, standard direct conversion costs, and standard variable costs.

The contribution approach to the income statement and to the problems of cost allocation helps management to evaluate performance and make decisions. Allocations are made with thoughtful regard to the purpose of the information being compiled.

Cost data often aid the setting of contract prices. The legal agreement between the contracting parties should be explicit as to the allowable cost items, the cost pools to be used, and the allocation base for each cost pool.

PROBLEMS FOR SELF-STUDY

problem 1 Sierra Lumber is a large forest products company. At its Klamath Falls, Oregon, plant, Sierra produces the following three products, each in different departments: (1) lumber for building and housing construction, (2) wooden poles for electric utility companies, and (3) newsprint for newspaper companies.

Materials handling is performed by a fleet of operator-driven forklift trucks. These trucks transport logs from an on-site rail receiving yard to the production lines associated with each department. The finished product from each department is transported to rail trucks in the shipping yard.

There is a two-stage process for allocating costs of materials handling to each product:
a. Allocate total materials-handling costs to each department on the basis of tons of raw material transported from the receiving yard to the production line, *and* tons of finished product transported to the shipping yard from each department.
b. Allocate materials-handling costs of each department to products on the basis of tons of finished product transported from that department to the shipping yard.

The receiving yard and the shipping yard have a weighing station to record tons carried by each forklift driver. Partly finished wood products (mainly odd ends and chips) are also transported from the Lumber and Utility Poles departments to the Newsprint department, but a record of tons carried is not maintained.

For the most recent month, materials-handling costs were $2 million. Details of recorded tons carried by forklift drivers are:

DEPARTMENT	TONS OF RAW MATERIAL TRANSPORTED FROM RECEIVING YARD TO DEPARTMENT	TONS OF FINISHED PRODUCT TRANSPORTED FROM DEPARTMENT TO SHIPPING YARD
(1)	(2)	(3)
Lumber	40,000	25,000
Utility Poles	60,000	30,000
Newsprint	20,000	25,000

1. Compute the materials-handling cost allocated to each ton of finished product of each department.

2. What limitations might arise from how Sierra allocates materials-handling costs to each department?

solution 1   **1.** *A. Allocation of materials-handling costs to each department.*

DEPARTMENT	TONS OF RAW MATERIAL TRANSPORTED FROM RECEIVING YARD TO DEPARTMENT	TONS OF FINISHED PRODUCT TRANSPORTED FROM DEPARTMENT TO SHIPPING YARD	TOTAL RECORDED TONS TRANSPORTED	PERCENTAGE OF TOTAL RECORDED TONS TRANSPORTED	ALLOCATION OF THE $2 MILLION MATERIALS-HANDLING COSTS TO DEPARTMENTS
(1)	(2)	(3)	(4) = (2) + (3)	(5)	(6) = (5) × $2 mill.
Lumber	40,000	25,000	65,000	32.5%	$ 650,000
Utility Poles	60,000	30,000	90,000	45.0%	900,000
Newsprint	20,000	25,000	45,000	22.5%	450,000
					$2,000,000

B. Materials-handling cost of each department allocated to each ton of finished product

DEPARTMENT	MATERIALS-HANDLING COSTS ALLOCATED TO DEPARTMENT	TONS OF FINISHED PRODUCT TRANSPORTED	MATERIALS-HANDLING COST PER TON OF FINISHED PRODUCT
(1)	(2)	(3)	(4) = (2) ÷ (3)
Lumber	$650,000	25,000	$26
Utility Poles	900,000	30,000	30
Newsprint	450,000	25,000	18

2. Sierra's use of tons of raw materials and tons of finished goods as the allocation base assumes a high degree of homogeneity regarding usage of the materials-handling facilities—e.g., the same distance is traveled between the receiving yard and between each department in transporting the raw materials. The allocation base understates the usage of the materials-handling facility by the Newsprint department; no account is taken of materials shipped by forklift operators from the Lumber and Utility Poles departments to the Newsprint department.

problem 2   Suppose Sierra Lumber makes a major change in its materials-handling department. It switches to robotic forklifts. Machine operators in the plant control each robotic forklift. The main motivation for the change was to eliminate the high number of personal injuries occurring at the operator-driven forklift truck operations.

 The use of robots has several implications for cost accounting at the Klamath Falls plant. First, a high proportion of the materials-handling cost now consists of machine-related costs. Second, more-detailed information is available regarding differential usage of the materials-handling function by each department. Sierra decides to allocate materials-handling costs to each department using two separate cost pools:

1. Robotic related costs. Allocated to each department using hours of robot-operating time.

2. Other materials-handling costs. Allocated to each department using tons of raw materials, partly finished product, and finished goods transported by robots.

In the most recent month, robotic-related costs were $1.6 million and other materials-handling costs were $675,000. Operating data relating to the robots for this month are:

DEPARTMENT	HOURS OF ROBOT-OPERATING TIME ATTRIBUTABLE TO DEPARTMENT	TONS OF PRODUCT (RM, WIP, & FG) TRANSPORTED BY ROBOTS AND ATTRIBUTABLE TO DEPARTMENT	TONS OF FINISHED PRODUCT TRANSPORTED FROM DEPARTMENT TO SHIPPING YARD
(1)	(2)	(3)	(4)
Lumber	400	75,000	35,000
Utility Poles	250	100,000	35,000
Newsprint	350	50,000	30,000

Required | Compute the materials-handling costs allocated to each ton of finished product of each department.

solution 2 | *A. Allocation of materials-handling costs to each department*

DEPARTMENT	PERCENTAGE OF TOTAL ROBOT-OPERATING HOURS	ALLOCATION OF THE $1.6 MILLION ROBOTIC-RELATED COSTS	PERCENTAGE OF TOTAL TONS OF PRODUCT TRANSPORTED	ALLOCATION OF THE $675,000 OTHER MATERIALS-HANDLING COSTS	TOTAL COSTS ALLOCATED TO DEPARTMENT
(1)	(2)	(3) = (2) × $1.6 mm	(4)	(5) = (4) × $675,000	(6) = (3) + (5)
Lumber	40%	$ 640,000	33% (3/9)	$225,000	$ 865,000
Utility Poles	25%	400,000	45% (4/9)	300,000	700,000
Newsprint	35%	560,000	22% (2/9)	150,000	710,000
		$1,600,000		$675,000	$2,275,000

B. Allocation of department materials-handling costs to each ton of finished product

DEPARTMENT	MATERIALS-HANDLING COSTS ALLOCATED TO DEPARTMENT	TONS OF FINISHED PRODUCT	MATERIALS-HANDLING COST PER TON OF FINISHED PRODUCT
(1)	(2)	(3)	(4) = (2) ÷ (3)
Lumber	$865,000	35,000	$24.71
Utility Poles	700,000	35,000	20.00
Newsprint	710,000	30,000	23.67

Special Points and Pitfalls

The use of homogeneous cost pools helps cost allocations to capture cause-and-effect relationships. Department cost pools will typically be more homogeneous than plantwide cost pools.

When examining the implications of technological change for the design of cost accounting systems, be aware of inappropriate generalizations. In highly capital intensive plants, direct-labor hours may be an inappropriate allocation base in machine-paced manufacturing environments, but an appropriate allocation base in labor-paced manufacturing environments. It is inappropriate to generalize that direct-labor hours are an improper allocation base in all capital-intensive plants.

Cost allocations in cost-reimbursement contracts mainly serve as a means of establishing a mutually satisfactory price. In such contracts, both parties may agree to include individual cost items for which cause-and-effect relationships are not easily established.

Accountants and managers should understand the assumptions underlying the allocations of costs in their organizations. They will then be better able to judge the relevance of costs for particular classes of decisions. Skepticism is appropriate, especially when somebody adamantly maintains that "the cost of this product or service is exactly $48.57."

QUESTIONS, PROBLEMS, AND CASES

13-1 Why are departmental overhead rates generally preferable to plantwide rates?

13-2 How is homogeneity in cost allocation measured?

13-3 "To obtain higher homogeneity, have more rather than fewer cost pools." Do you agree? Why?

13-4 "The traditional three cost categories of direct materials, direct labor, and overhead are outdated. It's time all firms recognized that the machining cost component of overhead should be separately reported as a fourth cost category." Do you agree? Why?

13-5 What is the most frequently used cost allocation base?

13-6 "Manufacturing firms that are highly capital intensive should abandon the use of direct-labor cost as an allocation base." Do you agree? Why?

13-7 List at least three subtotals that might be highlighted in a contribution income statement by segments.

13-8 Name two ways that firms get reimbursed under government contracts.

13-9 Plant managers and accounting reports. Six months ago, a firm switched from a highly manual-driven to a highly machine-driven automated production line. One of its plant managers makes the following comment on the monthly accounting report on individual product costs: "Nobody at the plant level now understands the unit-cost figures. They are both too high and too volatile. We gave up trying to understand or use them months ago." What advice would you give the accountant?

13-10 Factory cost allocation, use of a separate machining cost pool category. Mahitsu Motors is a manufacturer of motorcycles. Production and cost data for 19_1 are:

	500 CC BRAND	1,000 CC BRAND
Units produced	10,000	20,000
Direct-labor hours per unit	2	4
Machine-hours per unit	8	8

A single-cost pool is used for factory overhead. For 19_1, factory overhead was $6,400,000. Mahitsu allocates factory-overhead costs on the basis of direct-labor hours per unit.
 Mahitsu's accountant proposes that two separate pools be used for overhead costs:

- Machining cost pool ($3,600,000 in 19_1)
- General factory cost pool ($2,800,000 in 19_1)

Machining costs are to be allocated using machine-hours per unit, while general factory costs are to be allocated using direct-labor hours per unit.

Required

1. Compute the overhead costs allocated per unit to each brand of motorcycle in 19_1 using the current single-cost pool approach of Mahitsu.
2. Compute the machining costs and general factory costs allocated per unit to each brand of motorcycle assuming the accountant's proposal for two separate cost pools is used in 19_1.
3. What benefits might arise from the accountant's proposal for separate pools for machining costs and general factory costs?

13-11 Factory cost allocation, use of a conversion cost pool category, automation. Medical Technology Products manufactures a wide range of medical instruments. Two testing instruments (101 and 201) are produced at its highly automated Quebec City plant. Data for December 19_1 are:

	INSTRUMENT 101	INSTRUMENT 201
Direct materials	$100,000	$300,000
Direct labor	$ 10,000	$ 20,000
Units produced	5,000	20,000
Actual direct-labor hours	500	1,000

Factory overhead is allocated to each instrument on the basis of actual direct-labor hours per unit for that month. Factory-overhead cost for December 19_1 is $270,000. The production line at the Quebec City plant is a machine-paced one. Direct labor is for workers minimizing machine problems rather than actually operating the machines. The machines in this plant are operated by computer specialists and industrial engineers.

Required

1. Compute the cost per unit in December 19_1 for Instrument 101 and Instrument 201 under the existing cost accounting system.
2. The accountant at Medical Technology proposes combining direct-labor costs and factory-overhead costs into a single conversion cost pool. Conversion costs would be allocated to each unit on the basis of direct-materials costs. Compute the cost per unit in December 19_1 for Instrument 101 and Instrument 201 under the accountant's proposal.
3. What are the benefits of combining direct-labor costs and factory-overhead costs into a single conversion cost pool?

13-12 Choice of cost pools and allocation bases. (CPA, adapted) You have been engaged to install a cost system for the Martin Company. Your investigation of the manufacturing operations of the business discloses these facts:

1. The company makes a line of lighting fixtures and lamps. The material cost of any particular item ranges from 15% to 60% of total factory cost, depending on the kind of metal and fabric used in making it.
2. The business is subject to wide cyclical fluctuations, for the sales volume follows new-housing construction.
3. About 60% of the manufacturing is normally done in the first quarter of the year.
4. For the whole plant, the wage rates range from $12.75 to $25.85 an hour. However, within each of the eight individual departments, the spread between the high and low wage rates is less than 5%.
5. Each of the products made use of all eight of the manufacturing departments but not proportionately.
6. Within the individual manufacturing departments, factory overhead ranges from 30% to 80% of conversion cost.

Required

Based on the information above, you are to prepare a statement or letter for the president of the company, explaining whether in its cost system Martin Company should use

a. A denominator volume tied to normal volume or master-budget volume (see Chapter 8)
b. A plantwide overhead rate or a departmental overhead rate
c. A method of factory-overhead application based on direct-labor hours, direct-labor cost, or prime cost.

Include the reasons supporting *each* of your three recommendations.

13-13 Comparison of departmental and plantwide overhead rates. (CGAA) The Sayther Company manufactured two products, A and B, during the first year of its operations. For purposes of product costing, an overhead rate of application of $1.70 per direct-labor hour was used, based on budgeted factory overhead of $340,000 and 200,000 budgeted direct-labor hours, as follows:

	BUDGETED OVERHEAD	BUDGETED HOURS
Department 1	$240,000	100,000
Department 2	100,000	100,000
Total	$340,000	200,000

The number of labor hours required to manufacture each of these products was:

	PRODUCT A	PRODUCT B
In Department 1	4	1
In Department 2	1	4
Total	5	5

At the end of the year, there was no work in process and there were 2,000 and 6,000 finished units, respectively, of Products A and B on hand. Assume that budgeted activity was attained.

Required

1. What was the effect on the company's income of using a plantwide overhead rate instead of departmental overhead rates?
2. Assume that material and labor costs per unit of Product A are $10 and that the selling price is established by adding 40% of absorption costs to cover profit and selling and administrative expenses. What difference in selling price would result from the use of departmental overhead rates?

3. Explain briefly but clearly why departmental overhead rates are generally preferable to plantwide rates.

13-14 Plantwide versus department cost pools. (CMA) MumsDay Corporation manufactures a complete line of fiberglass attaché cases and suitcases. MumsDay has three manufacturing departments—molding, component, and assembly—and two service departments—power and maintenance.

The sides of the cases are manufactured in the molding department. The frames, hinges, locks, etc., are manufactured in the component department. The cases are completed in the assembly department. Varying amounts of materials, time, and effort are required for each of the various cases. The power department and maintenance department provide services to the three manufacturing departments.

MumsDay has always used a plantwide overhead rate. Direct-labor hours are used to assign the overhead to its product. The predetermined rate is calculated by dividing the company's total estimated overhead by the total estimated direct-labor hours to be worked in the three manufacturing departments.

Whit Portlock, manager of Cost Accounting, has recommended that MumsDay use departmental overhead rates. The planned operating costs and expected levels of activity for the coming year have been developed by Portlock and are presented by department in the schedules (000 omitted) in the accompanying tables.

	MANUFACTURING DEPARTMENTS		
	Molding	Component	Assembly
Departmental activity measures:			
Direct-labor hours	500	2,000	1,500
Machine-hours	875	125	—
Departmental costs:			
Raw materials	$12,400	$30,000	$ 1,250
Direct labor	3,500	20,000	12,000
Variable overhead	3,500	10,000	16,500
Fixed overhead	17,500	6,200	6,100
Total departmental costs	$36,900	$66,200	$35,850
Use of service departments:			
Maintenance			
Estimated usage in labor-hours for coming year	90	25	10
Power (in kilowatt hours)			
Estimated usage for coming year	360	320	120
Maximum allotted capacity	500	350	150

	SERVICE DEPARTMENTS	
	Power	Maintenance
Departmental activity measures:		
Maximum capacity	1,000 KWH	Adjustable
Estimated usage in coming year	800 KWH	125 hours
Departmental costs:		
Materials and supplies	$ 5,000	$1,500
Variable labor	1,400	2,250
Fixed overhead	12,000	250
Total service department costs	$18,400	$4,000

1. Calculate the plantwide overhead rate for MumsDay Corporation for the coming year using the same method as used in the past.
2. Whit Portlock has been asked to develop departmental overhead rates for comparison with the plantwide rate. The following steps are to be followed in developing the departmental rates:
   a. The maintenance department costs should be allocated to the three manufacturing departments using the direct method.
   b. The power department costs should be allocated to the three manufacturing departments using the dual method, i.e., the fixed costs allocated according to long-term capacity and the variable costs according to planned usage.
   c. Calculate departmental overhead rates for the three manufacturing departments using a machine-hour base for the molding department and a direct-labor hour base for the component and assembly departments.
3. Should MumsDay Corporation use a plantwide rate or departmental rates to assign overhead to its products? Explain your answer.

13-15 Plantwide versus department cost pools; year-end disposition of underapplied or overapplied overhead. (D. Jacques Grinnell) A manufacturing company is divided into three producing departments, A, B, and C. All production is to customer's order. Budgeted manufacturing costs for 19_1 are as follows:

	DEPT. A	DEPT. B	DEPT. C	TOTAL
Direct material				$170,000
Direct labor	$40,000	$20,000	$60,000	120,000
Manufacturing overhead	10,000	40,000	30,000	80,000

The actual material and labor cost of producing a particular order (order #162) during 19_1 was as follows:

Direct material		$1,500
Direct labor:		
Dept. A	$200	
Dept. B	190	
Dept. C	240	630

Manufacturing overhead is applied to product on the basis of direct-labor cost. Overhead rates are predetermined at the beginning of the year using annual budget data.

1. Determine the total manufacturing cost associated with order #162 assuming that (a) a factorywide manufacturing overhead rate is used to apply cost to product, and (b) departmental rates are used to apply cost to product.
2. *Actual* manufacturing costs for 19_1 were as follows:

	DEPT. A	DEPT. B	DEPT. C	TOTAL
Direct material				$180,000
Direct labor	$44,000	$19,000	$72,000	135,000
Manufacturing overhead	12,000	36,000	39,000	87,000

Determine the underapplied or overapplied overhead for the year assuming
   a. The use of the factorywide overhead rate
   b. The use of the departmental overhead rates
3. Consider the information provided in requirement 2 above. Assume that the firm chose to use departmental rates to apply overhead to product. Also assume that at the beginning of 19_1 there were no work-in-process or finished-goods inventories. At the

end of 19_1 the work-in-process and finished-goods inventories were represented by the following balances:

Work in process	$19,500
Finished goods	60,500

The balances include actual direct-material costs, actual direct-labor costs, and applied overhead costs; that is, no year-end adjustments have been made for underapplied or overapplied overhead. Assuming the company desires to prorate underapplied or overapplied overhead between ending inventories and cost of goods sold in proportion to their unadjusted balances, compute the correct prorated amount to be assigned to cost of goods sold.

13-16 Allocation of robotic costs to products; alternative depreciation measures for a robotic cost pool. Consumer Electrics assembles three models of refrigerators (standard, deluxe, and supreme) at its Nashville plant. The plant has 20 robots on its assembly line. There are four factory cost pools: (1) direct materials, (2) direct labor, (3) robotics-related costs, and (4) general factory overhead.

The robotics cost pool for July totaled $900,000:

Depreciation	$380,000
Operating and maintenance	520,000
Total robotic costs	$900,000

Robotic costs are allocated to each refrigerator unit using the average actual robot-operating hours per unit for that model in the month times the average actual robotic cost per robot-operating hour in the month. Operating data for July are:

MODEL	TOTAL NUMBER OF ROBOT-OPERATING HOURS ATTRIBUTABLE TO REFRIGERATOR MODEL	TOTAL UNITS OF MODEL PRODUCED
Standard	10,000	5,000
Deluxe	12,000	4,000
Supreme	8,000	2,000

The 20 robots were purchased eighteen months ago for a total of $12 million. Under an income tax law designed to encourage investment, Consumer Electrics can claim 25% of cost as depreciation in year 1, 38% as depreciation in year 2, and 37% as depreciation in year 3. These tax-based depreciation rates are also used for internal reporting purposes and product cost accumulation at Consumer Electrics.

Required

1. Compute the total robotic cost allocated in July to each unit of (a) standard, (b) deluxe, and (c) supreme refrigerator.
2. An industrial engineer at the plant observes that the robots are superbly maintained. Consequently, the three-year useful life underestimates their economic life to Consumer Electrics. She suggests that the "true" depreciation expense is better measured using the straight-line method, a five-year estimate of useful life (from the initial purchase date), and total disposal value at the end of five years of $3 million for the 20 robots. Compute how this measure of depreciation would affect the robotic costs allocated in July to each unit of (a) standard, (b) deluxe, and (c) supreme refrigerator. (Assume the straight-line method had been used from the time the asset was first purchased.)
3. What are the pros and cons of relying on tax rules to measure the robotic depreciation cost that is allocated to an individual refrigerator unit?

13-17 Allocation of standard costs to products, automation. Photocopy Plus is a manufacturer and distributor of quality photocopying units. Consider its product line at the high-price range. It features color options and reduction/enlargement options. There are three brands in this line of products. The wholesale price of each brand and the units produced in the most recent month are:

BRAND NAME	WHOLESALE PRICE	UNITS PRODUCED (AUGUST)
Regal	$ 3,000	2,000
Royal	8,000	3,000
Monarch	30,000	5,000

These products are assembled at a highly automated plant in Biloxi, Mississippi.

For internal accounting purposes, Photocopy Plus uses a standard absorption-costing system. Costs at the Biloxi plant are collected into four pools:

A. *Direct-materials costs.* Standard costs are based on the standard materials used in assembling each photocopying unit times the standard price for that part.

B. *Direct-labor costs.* Standard costs are based on standard direct-labor hours for each unit (from an engineering study) times the standard rate of $20 per labor-hour.

C. *Machining costs.* Standards are based on standard direct machine-hours for each unit (from an engineering study) times the standard rate of $50 per machine-hour.

D. *General factory costs.* Standard rate is 80% of the total of the direct-materials costs, direct-labor costs, and machining costs.

Standard unit production costs are calculated as the sum of A, B, C, and D.

The following information underlies the standard unit production costs for each photocopying unit:

	REGAL	ROYAL	MONARCH
Direct materials	$800	$2,000	$4,000
Direct labor	5 hours	10 hours	30 hours
Machining	6 hours	20 hours	70 hours

Required

1. Compute the standard unit production costs for the Regal, Royal, and Monarch photocopying units.

2. What percentage of total standard production cost for August is each cost pool?

3. Wendy Reichter, the controller at the Biloxi plant, attends a conference on "Cost Accounting and the Automated Plant." A speaker at the conference proposes eliminating direct-labor costs as a separate cost pool and including all labor costs in indirect factory costs. What factors should Reichter consider in evaluating this proposal for the Biloxi plant?

13-18 Factory overhead rates, production scheduling. Steve Morris is the sales manager at Wood Restoration Inc. He was both furious and puzzled. Rod Reddy, the production manager, had just told him there would be a one-week delay on Job #78 for one of Morris's most-valued customers. Moreover, the quoted price seemed excessive. Although he believed the customer would finally approve the price quote for this job, Morris was fully expecting complaints about price gouging and a threat to resort to other contractors in the future.

What puzzled Morris most was that Wood Restoration had just installed a series of high-speed, state-of-the-art finishing machines that included microcomputer monitoring of all inputs and machine time. An investment of over $10 million had been made in the new machines. Faster turnaround to customers was one of the supposed benefits of the investment. Prior to the installation of the new machines, direct materials had averaged 25% of factory costs; direct labor, 40%; and factory overhead, 35%. It was predicted that with the new machines, direct materials would average 20% of factory costs; direct labor, 15%; and factory overhead, 65%. In light of these predicted changes, the overhead applied to each job had been increased from 100% of direct-labor cost to 400% of direct-labor cost, irrespective of which machine is used on the job.

Wood Restoration used a job-costing approach for quoting prices. The price quoted was calculated as the sum of A, B, C and D:

A. Estimated material cost
B. Estimated actual labor-hours × $20 per hour standard rate
C. Overhead charge: 400% of B
D. Markup: 20% of (A + B + C)

Morris made some informal inquiries via a friend who worked in the factory. The friend said that ten old machines had been retained during the switchover; they were still being run by Reddy at full capacity. The new machines were only being used 40% of the time. Morris's friend estimated the following for Job #78:

	USING OLD MACHINES	USING NEW MACHINES
Direct materials	$1,000	$800
Direct-labor time	40 hours	18 hours

Job #78 was scheduled by Reddy for the old machine in ten days' time; two jobs already scheduled would require the full capacity of the old machines for the next ten days. No jobs were currently scheduled for the new machines.

Required

1. What price did Reddy quote Morris for Job #78?
2. What price would have been quoted for Job #78 had the job been scheduled to be done on the new machines?
3. What problems might arise from Reddy's job-scheduling approach?
4. Why might Reddy favor using the old machines?

13-19 Contribution approach to cost allocation: income statement by segments. Stuart Philatelic Sales, Inc., is engaged in the business of selling postage stamps and supplies to collectors on a retail basis. Stuart also makes up packets of inexpensive stamps that it sells on a wholesale basis to stamp departments of various stores.

Stuart's retail division has two stores, A and B, each of which has a stamp department and an albums and supplies department. Stuart had total net sales in 19_4 of $960,000; cost of merchandise sold was $490,000; and variable operating expenses were $120,000. The company's nonvariable costs, which it fully allocated to its two divisions, were $105,000 of advertising expense and $120,000 of various committed costs. Stuart's joint discretionary and committed costs were $35,000.

The costs of merchandise sold and variable operating expenses allocated to the retail division were $190,000 and $50,000, respectively. Net sales of Retail were $390,000, two-thirds of which were Store A's net sales. Sixty percent of Retail's merchandise costs and 54% of its variable operating expenses were allocated to Store A. Advertising costs of $40,000 were allocated to Retail, which in turn allocated 45% directly to Store A and 5% to Store B; the rest of the $40,000 was unallocated. Of the $120,000 separable committed costs, 50% were allocated to Retail, which in turn allocated 50% of its committed costs to Store A, had $25,000 of unallocated costs, and allocated the rest to Store B.

OTHER INFORMATION

1. Allocations to Store B—stamp department:

Net sales	$100,000
Cost of merchandise sold	$ 58,000
Variable operating expenses	$ 17,000

Allocations to Store B—albums and supplies department:

Net sales	$ 30,000
Cost of merchandise sold	$ 18,000
Variable operating expenses	$ 6,000

2. One-half of Store B's allocated advertising expenses could not be further allocated either to the stamp department or to the albums and supplies department; the other half of B's allocated advertising expenses was equally divided between the two departments.

3. Sixty percent of Store B's committed costs were unallocated; three-fourths of the rest was allocated to the stamp department and one-fourth to the albums and supplies department.

Required

1. What was operating income before taxes for the company as a whole?
2. Determine the contribution margin, contribution controllable by division managers, and contribution by segments for each of the following
   a. Company as a whole
   b. Wholesale division
   c. Retail division
   d. Store A of the retail division
   e. Store B of the retail division
   f. Stamp department of Store B
   g. Albums and supplies department of Store B

13-20 Product-line and territorial income statements. The Delvin Company shows the following results for the year 19_1:

Sales	$1,000,000	100.0%
Manufacturing costs of goods sold	$ 675,000	67.5%
Selling and advertising*	220,000	22.0%
Administrative (all nonvariable)	35,000	3.5%
Total expenses	$ 930,000	93.0%
Income before income taxes	$ 70,000	7.0%

*All nonvariable except for $40,000 freight-out cost.

The sales manager has asked you to prepare statements that will help him assess the company efforts by product line and by territories. You have gathered the following information:

	PRODUCT			TERRITORY		
	A	B	C	north	central	eastern
Sales*	25%	40%	35%			
Product A				50%	20%	30%
Product B				15%	70%	15%
Product C				14/35	8/35	13/35
Variable manufacturing and packaging costs†	68%	55%	60%			
Nonvariable separable costs:						
Manufacturing	$15,000	$14,000	$21,000	(not allocated)		
Selling and advertising	40,000	18,000	42,000	$48,000	$32,000	$40,000
Freight out		(not allocated)		13,000	9,000	18,000

Note. All items not directly allocated were considered common costs.
*Percent of company sales.
†Percent of product sales.

Required

1. Prepare a product-line income statement, showing the results for the company as a whole in the first column and the results for the three products in adjoining columns. Show a contribution margin and a product margin, as well as net income.

2. Repeat requirement 1 on a territorial basis. Show a contribution margin and a territory margin.

3. Should salespeople's commissions be based on contribution margins, product margins, territorial margins, net income, or dollar sales? Explain.

13-21 Contribution approach to cost allocation. (CMA) Caprice Company manufactures and sells two products—a small portable office file cabinet that it has made for over fifteen years and a home/travel file introduced in 19_1. The files are made in Caprice's only manufacturing plant. Budgeted variable production costs per unit of product are as follows.

	OFFICE FILE	HOME/TRAVEL FILE
Sheet metal	$ 3.50	—
Plastic	—	$3.75
Direct labor (@ $8 per DLH)	4.00	2.00
Variable manufacturing overhead (@ $9 per DLH)	4.50	2.25
	$12.00	$8.00

Variable manufacturing overhead costs vary with direct-labor hours. The annual fixed manufacturing overhead costs are budgeted at $120,000. A total of 50% of these costs are directly traceable to the office file department, and 22% of the costs are traceable to the home/travel file department. The remaining 28% of the costs are not traceable to either department.

Caprice employs two full-time salespersons—Pam Price and Robert Flint. Each salesperson receives an annual salary of $14,000 plus a sales commission of 10% of his or her total gross sales. Travel and entertainment expense is budgeted at $22,000 annually for each salesperson. Price is expected to sell 60% of the budgeted unit sales for each file, and Flint the remaining 40%. Caprice's remaining selling and administrative expenses include fixed administrative costs of $80,000 that cannot be traced to either file plus the following traceable selling expenses.

	OFFICE FILE	HOME/TRAVEL FILE
Packaging expenses per unit	$ 2.00	$ 1.50
Promotion	$30,000	$40,000

Data regarding Caprice's budgeted and actual sales for the fiscal year ended May 31, 19_4, are presented in the following schedule. There were no changes in the beginning and ending balances of either finished-goods or work-in-process inventories.

	OFFICE FILE	HOME/TRAVEL FILE
Budgeted sales volume in units	15,000	15,000
Budgeted and actual unit sales price	$29.50	$19.50
Actual unit sales:		
Pam Price	10,000	9,500
Robert Flint	5,000	10,500
Total units	15,000	20,000

Data regarding Caprice's operating expenses for the year ended May 31, 19_4, follow:

• There were no increases or decreases in raw materials inventory for either sheet metal or plastic, and there were no usage variances. However, sheet metal prices were 6% above budget, and plastic prices were 4% below budget.

- The actual direct-labor hours worked and costs incurred were as follows:

	HOURS	AMOUNT
Office file	7,500	$ 57,000
Home/Travel file	6,000	45,600
	13,500	$102,600

- Fixed-manufacturing-overhead costs attributable to the office file department were $8,000 above the budget. All other fixed-manufacturing-overhead costs were incurred at the same amounts as budgeted, and all variable-manufacturing-overhead costs were incurred at the budgeted hourly rates.
- All selling and administrative expenses were incurred at budgeted rates or amounts except the following items.

Nontraceable administrative expenses		$ 34,000
Promotion:		
Office files	$32,000	
Home/Travel files	58,000	90,000
Travel and entertainment:		
Pam Price	$24,000	
Robert Flint	28,000	52,000
		$176,000

Required

1. Prepare a segmented income statement of Caprice Company's actual operations for the fiscal year ended May 31, 19_4. The report should be prepared in a contribution-margin format by product and should reflect total income (loss) for the company before income taxes.
2. Identify and discuss any additional analyses that could be made of the data presented that would be of value to Caprice Company.

13-22 Cost allocation and contribution margin.[14] In discussing the costs incident to various types of operations, the analogy was drawn of the restaurant that adds a rack of peanuts to the counter, intending to pick up a little additional profit in the usual course of business. This analogy was attacked as an oversimplification. However, the accuracy of the analogy is evident when one considers the actual problem faced by the Restaurateur (Joe) as revealed by his Accountant–Efficiency-Expert.

EFF EX: Joe, you said you put in these peanuts because some people ask for them, but do you realize what this rack of peanuts is *costing* you?

JOE: It ain't gonna cost. 'Sgonna be a profit. Sure, I hadda pay $25 for a fancy rack to hold bags, but the peanuts cost 6¢ a bag and I sell 'em for 10¢. Figger I sell 50 bags a week to start. It'll take 12½ weeks to cover the cost of the rack. After that I gotta clear profit of 4¢ a bag. The more I sell, the more I make.

EFF EX: That is an antiquated and completely unrealistic approach, Joe. Fortunately, modern accounting procedures permit a more accurate picture which reveals the complexities involved.

JOE: Huh?

EFF EX: To be precise, those peanuts must be integrated into your entire operation and be allocated their appropriate share of business overhead. They must share a proportionate part of your expenditure for rent, heat, light, equipment depreciation, decorating, salaries for your waitresses, cook . . .

JOE: The *cook*? What's he gotta do wit'a peanuts? He don' even know I got 'em!

[14]Originated by Rex H. Anderson. Versions of this situation have been printed many times.

EFF EX:	Look Joe, the cook is in the kitchen, the kitchen prepares the food, the food is what brings people in here, and the people ask to buy peanuts. That's why you must charge a portion of the cook's wages, as well as a part of your own salary to peanut sales. This sheet contains a carefully calculated cost analysis which indicates the peanut operation should pay exactly $1,278 per year toward these general overhead costs.
JOE:	The peanuts? $1,278 a year for overhead? The nuts?
EFF EX:	It's really a little more than that. You also spend money each week to have the windows washed, to have the place swept out in the mornings, keep soap in the washroom, and provide free cokes to the police. That raises the total to $1,313 per year.
JOE:	[Thoughtfully] But the peanut salesman said I'd make money . . . put 'em on the end of the counter, he said . . . and get 4¢ a bag profit . . .
EFF EX:	[With a sniff] He's not an accountant. Do you actually know what the portion of the counter occupied by the peanut rack is worth to you?
JOE:	Ain't worth nothing—no stool there . . . Just a dead spot at the end.
EFF EX:	The modern cost picture permits no dead spots. Your counter contains 60 square feet and your counter business grosses $15,000 a year. Consequently, the square foot of space occupied by the peanut rack is worth $250 per year. Since you have taken that area away from general counter use, you must charge the value of the space to the occupant.
JOE:	You mean I gotta add $250 a year more to the peanuts?
EFF EX:	Right. That raises their share of the general operating costs to a grand total of $1,563 per year. Now then, if you sell 50 bags of peanuts per week, these allocated costs will amount to 60¢ per bag.
JOE:	*What?*
EFF EX:	Obviously, to that must be added your purchase price of 6¢ per bag, which brings the total to 66¢. So you see by selling peanuts at 10¢ per bag, you are losing 56¢ on every sale.
JOE:	Somethin's crazy!
EFF EX:	Not at all! Here are the *figures.* They *prove* your peanuts operation cannot stand on its own feet.
JOE:	[Brightening] Suppose I sell *lotsa* peanuts . . . thousand bags a week 'stead of fifty.
EFF EX:	[Tolerantly] Joe, you don't understand the problem. If the volume of peanuts sales increases, our operating costs will go up . . . you'll have to handle more bags with more time, more depreciation, more everything. The basic principle of accounting is firm on that subject: "The Bigger the Operation, the More General Overhead Costs That Must Be Allocated." No, increasing the volume of sales won't help.
JOE:	Okay, you so smart, *you* tell *me* what I gotta do.
EFF EX:	[Condescendingly] Well . . . you could first reduce operating expenses.
JOE:	How?
EFF EX:	Move to a building with cheaper rent. Cut salaries. Wash the windows biweekly. Have the floor swept only on Thursday. Remove the soap from the washrooms. Decrease the square-foot value of your counter. For example, if you can cut your expenses 50 percent, that will reduce the amount allocated to peanuts from $1,563 to $781.50 per year, reducing the cost to 36¢ per bag.
JOE:	[Slowly] That's better?
EFF EX:	Much, much better. However, even then you would lose 26¢ per bag if you only charge 10¢. Therefore, you must also raise your selling price. If you want a net profit of 4¢ per bag you would have to charge 40¢.
JOE:	[Flabbergasted] You mean even after I cut operating costs 50 percent I still gotta charge 40¢ for a 10¢ bag of peanuts? Nobody's that nuts about nuts! Who'd buy 'em?
EFF EX:	That's a secondary consideration. The point is, at 40¢ you'd be selling at a price based upon a true and proper evaluation of your then reduced costs.
JOE:	[Eagerly] Look! I gotta better idea. Why don't I just throw the nuts out . . . put 'em in the ashcan?
EFF EX:	Can you afford it?

JOE:	Sure. All I got is about 50 bags of peanuts . . . cost about three bucks . . . so I lose $25 on the rack, but I'm outa this nutsy business and no more grief.
EFF EX:	[Shaking head] Joe it isn't that simple. You are *in* the peanut business! The minute you throw those peanuts out you are adding $1,563 of annual overhead to the rest of your operation. Joe . . . be realistic . . . *can you afford to do that?*
JOE:	[Completely crushed] It's unbelievable! Last week I was making money. Now I'm in trouble . . . just because I think peanuts on a counter is gonna bring me some extra profit . . . just because I believe 50 bags of peanuts a week is easy.
EFF EX:	[With raised eyebrow] That is the object of modern cost studies, Joe . . . to dispel those false illusions.

Required

1. Is Joe losing 56¢ on every sale of peanuts? Explain.
2. Do you agree that if the volume of peanut sales is increased, operating losses will increase? Explain.
3. Do you agree with the "Efficiency Expert" that, in order to make the peanut operation profitable, the operating costs in the restaurant should be decreased and the selling price of the peanuts should be increased? Give reasons.
4. Do you think that Joe can afford to get out of the peanut business? Give reasons.
5. Do you think that Joe should eliminate his peanut operations? Why or why not?

13-23 Overhead disputes. (Suggested by Howard Wright) The Azure Ship Company works on U.S. Navy vessels and commercial vessels. General yard overhead (for example, the cost of the purchasing department) is allocated to the jobs on the basis of direct-labor costs.

In 19_3 Azure's total $150 million of direct-labor cost consisted of $50 million navy and $100 million commercial. The general yard overhead was $30 million.

Navy auditors periodically examine the records of defense contractors. The auditors investigated a nuclear submarine contract, which was based on cost-plus-fixed-fee pricing. The auditors later claimed that the navy was entitled to a refund because of double-counting of overhead in 19_3.

The government contract included the following provision:

Par. 15-202. Direct Costs.

(a) A direct cost is any cost which can be identified specifically with a particular cost objective. Direct costs are not limited to items which are incorporated in the end product as material or labor. Costs identified specifically with the contract are direct costs of the contract and are to be charged directly thereto. Costs identified specifically with other work of the contractor are direct costs of that work and are not to be charged to the contract directly or indirectly. When items ordinarily chargeable as indirect costs are charged to the contract as direct costs, the cost of like items applicable to other work must be eliminated from indirect costs allocated to the contract.

A special expediting purchasing group, the SE group, had been formed to do work (in addition to that rendered by the central purchasing group) on obtaining materials for the nuclear submarine only. Their direct costs, $5 million, had been included as direct labor of the nuclear work. Accordingly, overhead was applied to the contracts in the usual manner. The SE costs of $5 million were not included in the yard overhead costs. The auditors claimed that no overhead should have been applied to these SE costs.

Required

1. Compute the amount of the refund that the navy would claim.
2. Suppose that later the navy also discovered that $4 million of general yard overhead was devoted exclusively to commercial engine-room purchasing activities. Compute the additional refund that the navy would probably claim. (*Note:* This $4 million was never classified as "direct labor." Furthermore, the navy would claim that it should be reclassified as a "direct cost" but not as "direct labor.")

13-24 Cost justification for a contract; dispute over direct-labor and direct-materials cost components.
P. C. Products specializes in the development of software for accounting applications. The company organizes its activities into four departments:

SERVICE DEPARTMENTS	MANUFACTURING DEPARTMENTS
Product Development	Inventory Accounting Software Manufacture
Computer Systems	Project-Costing Software Manufacture

P. C. Products is approached by Titan Software, a foreign retailer, which offers to buy 5,000 units of its recently developed Project-Costing Software II package. The contract calls for Titan Software to reimburse P. C. Products on a basis of unit product cost plus 20% profit margin. A clause in the contract permits Titan Software to investigate the accounting records of P. C. Products to verify the unit-cost calculations. Unit product costs are defined in the contract to include four components:

A. "Direct-materials cost as incurred"
B. "Direct-labor cost as incurred"
C. "Service Department costs attributable to the Project-Costing Software Manufacture Department"
D. "Project-Costing Department overhead rate, calculated as 400% of direct labor cost in B"

At the end of the period, P. C. Products submits the following bill to Titan Software:

Unit Product Cost Determination Based on
Total Production of 13,250 Units (Packages)

A. Total direct materials	$1,060,000
B. Total direct labor	397,500
C. Total service department costs attributable to Project-Costing Manufacture Department	2,694,393
D. Total overhead applied: 400% × 397,500	1,590,000
Total product cost	$5,741,893
Unit product cost: $5,741,893 ÷ 13,250	$ 433.35

Titan purchases 5,000 of the 13,250 units produced.

Titan Software sends Jessie Ventura to investigate the accounting records of P. C. Products. She reports that P. C. Products incorrectly classified $99,375 as a direct-labor cost that should have been classified as indirect labor. Indirect labor was to be reimbursed using the 400% of direct-labor cost rate included in the contract. P. C. Products recognizes that a misclassification has been made and offers to adjust the price to be charged to Titan Software accordingly.

Ventura also finds that the direct-materials cost includes $198,750 attributable to the purchase of a defective batch of iron-oxide material by P. C. Products. Ventura believes that this $198,750 should be excluded from the unit-cost determination for the contract. P. C. Products strongly disagrees and points out that the contract specifies inclusion of "direct-materials cost as incurred." Ventura admits her argument would not hold up to a legal challenge.

Required

1. What adjustment in the price should be made by P. C. Products for the misclassification of the labor-cost item?
2. If the $198,750 item was excluded as an allowable cost of the 5,000-unit contract, what further adjustment in the price would be made?
3. Ventura wonders what can be done in the future to prevent Titan Software's reimbursing P. C. Products for P. C.'s purchasing inefficiencies or materials usage inefficiencies. What advice would you give her?

13-25 Review of Chapters 12 and 13, cost justification for a contract, analysis of service department cost allocations. Jessie Ventura is investigating the costs charged by P. C. Products to Titan Software under a cost-plus reimbursement contract (see preceding problem). An allowable cost item in the contract is "Service department costs attributable to the Project-Costing Software Manufacture Department." P. C. Products organizes its activities into four departments:

SERVICE DEPARTMENTS	MANUFACTURING DEPARTMENTS
Product Development	Inventory Accounting Software Manufacture
Computer Systems	Project-Costing Software Manufacture

P. C. Products reports that the "total service department costs attributable (allocated) to the Project-Costing Software Manufacture Department" were $2,694,393.50:

Fixed costs of service departments allocated	$1,524,706.00
Variable costs of service departments allocated	1,169,687.50
	$2,694,393.50

Ventura discovers that P. C. Products allocates the fixed costs of service departments on the basis of budgeted usage; variable costs of service departments are allocated on the basis of actual usage.

The budgeted usage relationship between the four departments was:

	PRODUCT DEVELOPMENT	COMPUTER SYSTEMS	INVENTORY ACCOUNTING SOFTWARE	PROJECT-COSTING SOFTWARE
Product Development	—	20%	40%	40%
Computer Systems	15%	—	25%	60%

The actual usage relationships between the four departments was:

	PRODUCT DEVELOPMENT	COMPUTER SYSTEMS	INVENTORY ACCOUNTING SOFTWARE	PROJECT-COSTING SOFTWARE
Product Development	—	15%	45%	40%
Computer Systems	20%	—	30%	50%

The actual costs incurred at the two service departments were:

	FIXED COSTS	VARIABLE COSTS
Product Development	$ 600,000	$ 850,000
Computer Systems	1,700,000	1,200,000

Required

1. What method did P. C. Products use to allocate service department costs to the Project-Costing Software Manufacture Department? (*Hint:* It was not the reciprocal method.)
2. Ventura reads that the reciprocal method of cost allocation is "the most defensible theoretically." How would this method affect the costs allocated to the Project-Costing Software Manufacture Department?
3. Ventura views the contract clause that an allowable cost item is "service department costs attributable to the Project-Costing Software Manufacture Department" as being excessively vague. It provides P. C. Products the opportunity to manipulate the costs allocated to the Titan Software contract. What areas of vagueness may arise with this clause? How might each area of vagueness be reduced (and possibly be eliminated)?

Cost Allocation: Joint Products and Byproducts

Meaning of terms • Why allocate joint costs? • Methods of allocating joint costs • Irrelevance of joint costs in decision making • Accounting for byproducts •

Joint costs plague the accountant's work. This chapter examines methods for allocating joint costs to products and services. Many of the topics discussed in this chapter are related to issues already covered in Chapters 12 and 13. Before reading on, be sure you are comfortable with pages 411–13 on Terminology and Purposes of Cost Allocation.

MEANING OF TERMS

A **joint cost** is a cost of a single process that yields two or more products (or services) simultaneously. These products are classified individually into one of two categories: joint-product category or byproduct category.

Joint products are two or more products that (1) have relatively significant sales values and (2) are not separately identifiable as individual products until their split-off point. **Byproducts** are products that (1) have minor sales values as compared with the sales value of the major product(s) and (2) are not separately identifiable as individual products until their split-off point.

The **split-off point** is the juncture of production where the joint products and byproducts become individually identifiable. Any costs beyond this point are called **separable costs** because they are not part of the joint production process; they are identifiable with individual products.

478

Examples of single processes that simultaneously yield two or more separable products abound in many industries. For example:

INDUSTRY	SEPARABLE PRODUCTS AFTER SPLIT-OFF POINT
1. Agriculture Industries	
• Dairy	• Milk, cream, and butter
• Hogs	• Pork, hides, bones, and fat
2. Extractive Industries	
• Crude oil	• Naphtha, kerosene, jet fuel, and gasoline
• Copper ore	• Copper, silver, lead, and zinc
3. Chemical Industries	
• Base chemical	• Ethylene, propylene, and benzene
4. Semiconductor Industry	
• Fabrication of silicon wafers	• Memory chips of different quality as to the number of chips per module, speed, life expectancy, and temperature tolerance

In each example, no individual product can be produced without an accompanying appearance of the other products, although sometimes in variable proportions.[1] A meatpacking company cannot kill a pork chop; it has to slaughter a hog that supplies various cuts of dressed meat, hides, bones, and fat.

WHY ALLOCATE JOINT COSTS?

The reasons for allocating joint costs to individual products or services are similar to the reasons for cost allocation in general (see Exhibit 12-1 on page 412). They include:

1. Inventory valuation and cost-of-goods-sold computations for external financial reporting and for reporting to taxation authorities.
2. Inventory valuation and cost-of-goods-sold computations for internal financial reporting. One use of such reports is in computing executive compensation.
3. Cost reimbursement under contracts where only a portion of the jointly produced products or services is sold or delivered to a single customer.
4. Rate regulation where only a subset of the jointly produced products or services is subject to price regulation. For example, both crude oil and natural gas are jointly produced, but only natural gas is subject to price regulation in the United States.[2]

---

[1] For a case study, see W. Cats-Baril, J. Gatti, and D. Grinnell, "Joint Product Costing in the Semiconductor Industry," *Management Accounting*, February 1986, pp. 28–35.

[2] J. Crespi and J. Harris, "Joint Cost Allocation under the Natural Gas Act: An Historical Review," *Journal of Extractive Industries Accounting*, Summer 1983, pp. 133–42. This article provides a lucid case study of several methods of joint-cost allocation in the natural gas industry.

The allocation of joint product costs serves the four useful purposes described above. Nevertheless, managers and accountants should beware when using such allocations for economic decisions. A subsequent section illustrates how joint-cost allocations can provide misleading data in decisions about product mix and whether to sell at the split-off point, or process beyond the split-off point.

METHODS OF ALLOCATING JOINT COSTS

There are three basic approaches to valuing inventory (and computing cost of goods sold) in joint-cost situations:

1. Allocate cost using market selling-price data. Examples of this approach are the sales value at split-off method, the estimated net realizable value (NRV) method, and the constant gross-margin percentage NRV method.
2. Allocate cost using a physical measure.
3. Do not allocate cost; market selling-price data are used to guide inventory valuation.

In the simplest situation, the joint products are sold at the split-off point without further processing. We consider this case first. Then we consider situations involving further processing beyond the split-off point.[3]

EXAMPLE 1. Suppose a chemical company processes a single input up to the split-off point, at which stage two products (A and B) are obtained. The joint cost prior to the split-off point is $900. Both A and B are sold without undergoing any separate additional processing:

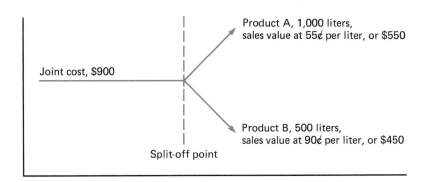

Assume that 40% of the output of Product A is unsold at the end of the month and 20% of the output of Product B is unsold at the end of the month. How should the accountant value Product A and Product B for inventory purposes? The $900

---

[3] There are many variations within the three basic approaches to joint-cost allocation. For example, see J. Hardy, B. Orton, and L. Pope, "The Sales to Production Ratio: A New Approach to Joint Cost Allocation," *Journal of Accountancy*, October 1981, pp. 105–10, and correspondence in the September 1982 issue.

cannot physically be identified or traced to either product. Why? Because the products themselves were not separated before the split-off point.

Example 1 will be used to illustrate the joint-cost allocation methods of sales value at split-off point and physical measure.

Sales value at split-off method

The **sales value at split-off method** allocates joint costs on the basis of the products' relative sales value at the split-off point. In Example 1, the sales value at split-off is $550 for Product A and $450 for Product B:

	PRODUCT A	PRODUCT B	TOTAL
1. Sales value at split-off (A, 1,000 × 55¢; B, 500 × 90¢)	$550	$450	$1,000
2. Weighting	$\dfrac{550}{1,000} = .55$	$\dfrac{450}{1,000} = .45$	
3. Joint costs allocated (A, .55 × $900; B, .45 × $900)	$495	$405	$900

Note that this method uses the sales value of the entire production including the unsold portion, not just the actual sales. Exhibit 14-1 presents the product-line income statement using this method of joint-cost allocation.

An advantage of the sales value at split-off point method is its simplicity. The allocation base (sales value) is expressed in terms of a common denominator (dollars) that is systematically recorded in the accounting system. Many managers cite a second advantage: the costs are allocated in proportion to a measure of the relative revenue-generating power identifiable with the individual products.

Physical measure method

The **physical measure method** allocates joint costs on the basis of their relative proportions at the split-off point, using a common physical measure such as weight or volume. In Example 1, the $900 cost produced 1,500 liters of the two

EXHIBIT 14-1
Product-Line Income Statement
Joint Costs Allocated Using Sales Value at Split-Off Method

	PRODUCT A	PRODUCT B	TOTAL
Sales (A, 600 × 55¢; B, 400 × 90¢)	$330	$360	$690
Joint costs:			
Production costs (A, .55 × $900; B, .45 × $900)	495	405	900
Less ending inventory (A, 40%; B, 20%)	198	81	279
Cost of goods sold	297	324	621
Gross margin	$ 33	$ 36	$ 69
Gross-margin percentage	10%	10%	10%

products on a physical quantity basis; therefore the costs are allocated as follows:

	PRODUCT A	PRODUCT B	TOTAL
1. Physical measure of production (liters)	1,000	500	1,500
2. Weighting	$\frac{1,000}{1,500} = .667$	$\frac{500}{1,500} = .333$	
3. Joint costs allocated (A, .667 × $900; B, .333 × $900)	$600	$300	$900

This method uses the same unit cost for each product: $900 ÷ 1,500 = 60¢ per liter. Thus the joint-cost allocations shown here could be computed alternatively as follows:

$$\text{Product A: } 1,000 \times 60¢ = \$600$$

$$\text{Product B: } \quad 500 \times 60¢ = \$300$$

Exhibit 14-2 presents the product-line income statement using this method of joint-cost allocation.

The physical weights used for allocating joint costs may have no relationship to the revenue-producing power of the individual products. Consider a mine that extracts ore jointly containing gold, silver, and lead. Use of a common physical measure (tons) would result in almost all the costs being allocated to the product that weighs the most but has the lowest revenue-producing power (lead). As a second example, if the joint cost of a hog were assigned to its various products on the basis of weight, center-cut pork chops would have the same cost per pound as pigs' feet, lard, bacon, ham, and so forth. Fabulous "profits" would be shown for some products, but "losses" would consistently be shown for others.

Use of the physical measure method requires a common denominator to allocate joint costs. Adjustment factors may be required to yield this common base. An example is where one joint product is a liquid while another is a solid. To illustrate, crude oil and natural gas typically are converted into equivalent units of energy (British thermal unit, or Btu's) when allocating the joint costs of producing oil and gas.

EXHIBIT 14-2
Product-Line Income Statement
Joint Costs Allocated Using Physical Measure Method

	PRODUCT A	PRODUCT B	TOTAL
Sales (A, 600 × 55¢; B, 400 × 90¢)	$330	$360	$690
Joint costs:			
Production costs (A, .667 × $900; B, .333 × $900)	600	300	900
Less ending inventory (A, 40%; B, 20%)	240	60	300
Cost of goods sold	360	240	600
Gross margin	$ (30)	$120	$ 90
Gross-margin percentage	(9.1%)	33.3%	13.0%

One rationale offered for the use of physical measures is that they avoid cost allocations being influenced by highly volatile market prices. Physical measures also are sometimes used in rate-regulation settings where the object is to set a fair selling price. Why? Because it is circular reasoning to use selling prices as a basis for determining a selling price.

EXAMPLE 2: Assume the same facts as in Example 1 except that both Product A and Product B can be further processed and sold in more-refined form. One thousand liters of Product A can be further processed to yield 1,000 liters of Super A at an incremental production and selling cost of $300; Super A sells for $1.80 per liter. Five hundred liters of Product B can be further processed to yield 500 liters of Super B at an incremental production and selling cost of $200; Super B sells for $1.40 per liter. These data are summarized in the following diagram:

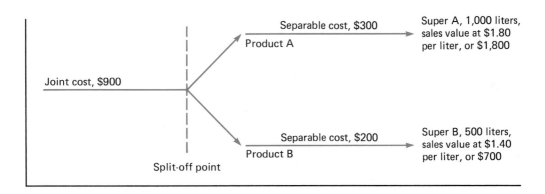

The company decides to further process Product A and Product B into Super A and Super B. Assume that 20% of the output of each of Super A and Super B is unsold at the end of the month.

Example 2 will be used to illustrate the estimated net realizable value method of joint-cost allocation, the constant gross-margin percentage NRV method, and the no-allocation of joint-cost alternative.

Estimated net realizable value method

The **estimated net realizable value method** allocates joint costs on the basis of their *relative estimated net realizable value* (predicted final sales value in the ordinary course of business less the predicted separable costs of production and selling). Joint costs would be allocated as follows:

	SUPER A	SUPER B	TOTAL
1. Expected sales value of production (Super A, 1,000 × $1.80; Super B, 500 × $1.40)	$1,800	$700	$2,500
2. Deduct expected separable costs to complete and sell	300	200	500
3. Estimated net realizable value at split-off point	$1,500	$500	$2,000
4. Weighting	$\frac{1,500}{2,000} = .75$	$\frac{500}{2,000} = .25$	
5. Joint cost allocated (Super A, .75 × $900; Super B, .25 × $900)	$ 675	$225	$ 900

483

EXHIBIT 14-3
Product-Line Income Statement
Joint Costs Allocated Using Estimated Net Realizable Value Method

	SUPER A	SUPER B	TOTAL
Sales (Super A, 800 × $1.80; Super B, 400 × $1.40)	$1,440	$560	$2,000
Cost of goods sold:			
Joint costs (Super A, .75 × $900; Super B, .25 × $900)	675	225	900
Separable costs to complete and sell	300	200	500
Cost of goods available for sale	975	425	1,400
Less ending inventory (Super A, 20%; Super B, 20%)	195	85	280
Cost of goods sold	780	340	1,120
Gross margin	$ 660	$220	$ 880
Gross-margin percentage	45.83%	39.29%	44%

Note the use of expected sales value of the total production of the period and *not* the actual sales of the period. Exhibit 14-3 presents the product-line income statement using the estimated net realizable value method. The gross-margin percentages are 45.83% for Super A and 39.29% for Super B.

The estimated net realizable value method presupposes the exact number of subsequent steps for which further processing is undertaken. In some plants, there may be numerous subsequent steps possible. Firms may make frequent changes in further processing to exploit fluctuations in the separable costs of each processing stage or in the selling prices of individual products. Under the estimated net realizable method, each such change would imply a change in the joint-cost allocation percentages.[4]

Constant gross-margin percentage NRV method

The **constant gross-margin percentage NRV method** allocates joint costs so that the overall gross-margin percentage is identical for each individual product. This method entails three steps:

Step 1: Computing the overall gross-margin percentage

Step 2: Using the overall gross margin percentage, deduct the gross margin from the sales values to obtain the total costs that each product should bear

Step 3: Deducting the separable costs from the total costs to obtain the joint-cost allocation

For the data in Example 2, the joint cost of $900 would be allocated as follows:

Step 1:

Total sales value: (1,000 × $1.80) + (500 × $1.40)	= $2,500
Deduct joint and separable costs: ($900 + $300 + $200)	= 1,400
Gross margin	$1,100
Gross-margin percentage ($1,100 ÷ $2,500)	44%

---

[4] The estimated net realizable value method is clear-cut where there is only one split-off point. However, where there are multiple split-off points, additional allocations may be required where processes subsequent to the initial split-off point remerge with each other to create a second joint-cost situation. See F. Lowenthal, "Multiple Splitoff Points" (Working Paper, California State University, Hayward, 1985).

Chapter 14

484

	SUPER A	SUPER B	TOTAL
Expected sales value of production (Super A, 1,000 × $1.80; Super B, 500 × $1.40)	$1,800	$700	$2,500
Step 2: Gross margin, using overall gross-margin percentage (44%)	792	308	1,100
Cost of goods sold	1,008	392	1,400
Step 3: Deduct separable costs to complete and sell	300	200	500
Joint costs allocated	$ 708	$192	$ 900

Exhibit 14-4 presents the product-line income statement for the constant gross-margin percentage NRV method. The gross-margin percentage for each product (44%) is equal by construction.

The tenuous assumption underlying the constant gross-margin percentage NRV method is that there is a uniform relationship between cost and sales value at the individual product level. Such a relationship is rarely observed in companies producing multiple products that do not involve joint costs.[5]

EXHIBIT 14-4
Product-Line Income Statement
*Joint Costs Allocated Using Constant
Gross-Margin Percentage NRV Method*

	SUPER A	SUPER B	TOTAL
Sales (Super A, 800 × $1.80; Super B, 400 × $1.40)	$1,440.0	$560.0	$2,000.0
Cost of goods sold:			
Joint costs (see above)	708.0	192.0	900
Separable costs to complete and sell	300.0	200.0	500
Cost of goods available for sale	1,008.0	392.0	1,400
Less ending inventory (Super A, 20%; Super B, 20%)	201.6	78.4	280
Cost of goods sold	806.4	313.6	1,120
Gross margin	$ 633.6	$246.4	$ 880
Gross-margin percentage	44%	44%	44%

No allocation of joint cost

The foregoing methods all allocate joint costs to individual products. The various schemes for joint-cost allocations are subject to valid criticisms. Therefore many companies refrain from the attempt entirely. Instead they carry all inventories at estimated net realizable value, which has the effect of recognizing profits as production is completed. Industries using variations of this method include meatpacking, canning and mining.

Exhibit 14-5 presents the income statement for this method for Example 2. The separable costs are allocated first to highlight the cause-and-effect relationship. Furthermore, the contribution line in Exhibit 14-5 reminds managers that

---

[5] The joint costs allocated to each individual product need not always be positive under the constant gross-margin percentage NRV method. Some products may receive negative allocations of joint costs to bring their gross-margin percentages up to the overall company average.

EXHIBIT 14-5
Income Statement for No Allocation of Joint Cost

	SUPER A	SUPER B	TOTAL
Produced and sold:			
(Super A, 800 × $1.80; Super B, 400 × $1.40)	$1,440	$560	$2,000
Produced but not sold:			
(Super A, 200 × $1.80; Super B, 100 × $1.40)	360	140	500
Total sales value of production	1,800	700	2,500
Separable costs to complete and sell	300	200	500
Contribution to joint costs and profits	$1,500	$500	$2,000
Joint costs			900
Gross margin			$1,100
Gross-margin percentage			44%

their product choices at and beyond split-off must focus on additional revenue in comparison with separable costs. Finally, the joint costs are not allocated to Super A and Super B as individual products.

Accountants ordinarily criticize carrying inventories at estimated net realizable values. Why? Because profit is recognized *before* sales are made. Partly in response to this criticism, some companies using this no-allocation approach carry their inventories at net realizable values less a normal profit margin.

Comparison of the methods

What method of allocating joint costs should be chosen? Each has weaknesses. Due to the joint nature of the costs, the cause-and-effect criterion is not helpful in making this choice. The authors advocate the use of sales value at split-off method, where such selling-price data are available, for the following reasons:

1. *No anticipation of subsequent management decisions.* The sales value at split-off point method does not presuppose the exact number of subsequent steps for which further processing is undertaken.

2. *Availability of an informative common denominator to compute the weighting factors.* The denominator of the sales value at split-off method (dollars) is an informative one. In contrast, the physical measure method may lack an informative common denominator for *all* the separable products.

3. *Simplicity.* The sales value at split-off point is a simple method. In contrast, the estimated net realizable value method can be very complex in operations with multiple products and multiple split-off points. The sales value at split-off point is unaffected by any change in the production process subsequent to the split-off point.

Where sales values at the split-off point are not available, a second-best method is sought. Individual industries differ in terms of the complexity of using the estimated net realizable value method and in the availability of an informative common physical measure. The same joint-cost allocation method is unlikely to pass the cost-benefit test in all industries. For example, a survey of the joint-cost allocation methods used by U.K. chemical and oil refining companies reported the following:[6]

[6] K. Slater and C. Wootton, *A Study of Joint and By-Product Costing in the U.K.* (London, U.K.: Institute of Cost and Management Accountants, 1984).

TYPE OF COMPANY	PREDOMINANT JOINT-COST ALLOCATION METHOD USED
• Petrochemicals	• Sales value at split-off method or estimated net realizable value method
• Coal processing	• Physical measure method
• Coal chemicals	• Physical measure method
• Oil refining	• No allocation of joint cost

The authors of the survey noted that "it was considered by the majority of oil refineries that the complex nature of the process involved, and the vast number of joint product outputs, made it impossible to establish any meaningful cost apportionment between products."[7]

IRRELEVANCE OF JOINT COSTS IN DECISION MAKING

No technique for allocating joint product costs should be used for judging the performance of product lines or for managerial decisions regarding whether a product should be sold at the split-off point or processed beyond split-off. When a product is an inherent result of a joint process, the decision to process further should not be influenced by either the size of the total joint costs or the portion of the joint costs allocated to particular products.

Sell or process further

The decision to incur additional costs beyond split-off is a matter of determining the incremental income attainable beyond the split-off point. Example 2 on page 483 implicitly assumed that it was profitable for both Product A and Product B to be separately processed into Super A and Super B. The computation underlying this decision can be illustrated by the following incremental analysis for Product A and Super A:

	ALTERNATIVE 1 (Sell Product A at Split-off)	ALTERNATIVE 2 (Further Process Product A into Super A)	DIFFERENCE
Sales	$550	$1,800	$1,250
Deduct separable costs	—	300	300
Contribution to income	$550	$1,500	$ 950

A similar computation shows that processing Product B into Super B yields incremental sales of $250 ($700 − $450) and incremental costs of $200. The amount of joint costs incurred up to split-off ($900), and how they are allocated, is irrelevant with respect to the decision to further process Product A or Product B. Why? Because the joint costs of $900 cannot be traced to separate products by definition.

Many manufacturing companies constantly face the decision of whether to further process a joint product. Meat products may be sold as cut or may be smoked, cured, frozen, canned, and so forth. Petroleum refiners are perpetually trying to adjust to the most profitable product mix. The refining process necessi-

[7] Ibid., p. 101.

tates separating all products from crude oil, even though only one or two may be desired. The refiner must decide what combination of processes to use to get the most profitable quantities of gasoline, lubricants, kerosene, naphtha, fuel oil, and the like. In addition, the manager may occasionally find it profitable to purchase distillates from some other refiner and process them further.

In serving management for these decisions, the accountant must concentrate on opportunity costs rather than on how historical joint costs are to be split among various products. The only relevant items are the incremental revenue as compared with incremental cost. In turn, these increments must be compared with the revenue forgone by rejecting other alternatives.

To illustrate the importance of the incremental cost viewpoint, consider another example.

EXAMPLE 3: A perfume company is jointly processing a chemical that yields 200 pints each of two salable products: Lotion X and Lotion Y. The sales values per pint at split-off are $1.60 for X and $0.80 for Y. The joint costs to the split-off point are $440. The manager now has the option of further processing 200 pints of Lotion Y to yield 200 pints of Lotion Z. The total additional costs of converting Lotion Y into Lotion Z would be $50, while the selling price per pint would be $1.20. The question is whether Y should be converted into Z. The following diagram summarizes these data:

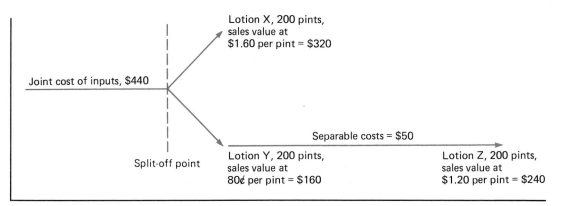

The correct approach to deciding whether to convert Lotion Y into Lotion Z is to compare the incremental revenue with the incremental costs:

Incremental revenue of Z, ($1.20 − $.80) × 200 pints	$80
Incremental costs of Z, further processing	50
Incremental income from converting Y into Z	$30

Another way of looking at the same problem is:

Lotion Z revenue, 200 pints × $1.20		$240
Costs:		
Further processing of Z	$ 50	
Opportunity cost, forgoing of Lotion Y sales (200 × $.80)	160	210
Difference in favor of further processing of Y into Z		$ 30

We can prove the validity of this approach:

Total Income Computations

| | ALTERNATIVE 1 | ALTERNATIVE 2 | |
	Sell Lotions X and Y	Sell Lotions X and Z	DIFFERENCE
Sales	($320 + $160) $480	($320 + $240) $560	$80
Total costs	440	($440 + $ 50) 490	50
Operating income	$ 40	$ 70	$30

> *In summary, it is profitable to extend processing or to incur additional distribution costs on a joint product as long as the incremental revenue exceeds incremental explicit costs and incremental implicit opportunity costs.*

Conventional methods of joint-cost allocation may serve to mislead managers relying on unit cost data to guide their sell-or-process-further decisions. For example, allocating via physical measures would split the $440 joint cost as follows:

PRODUCT	PINTS PRODUCED	WEIGHTING	JOINT COST	ALLOCATION
Lotion X	200	200/400 = .5	.5 × $440 =	$220
Lotion Y	200	200/400 = .5	.5 × $440 =	$220
	400			$440

The product-line income statement for the alternative of selling Lotion X and Lotion Z would *erroneously* imply that a loss was made on Lotion Z:

	LOTION X	LOTION Z
Sales	$320	$240
Costs		
Joint costs allocated	220	220
Separable costs	—	50
Total cost of goods sold	220	270
Gross margin	$100	$ (30)

Pricing decisions

Similarly, pricing decisions generally should not be influenced by allocations of joint costs.[8] The circular reasoning is particularly obvious under the estimated net realizable value method (prices used to set costs and costs then used to set prices). Nevertheless, regulated firms have been subjected to this reasoning as a justification for not permitting them to increase their prices. For example, many critics have claimed that shortages of natural gas in the United States have been caused by the approach that the Federal Power Commission (FPC) has taken to regulate natu-

---

[8] An exception would be a government contract for a joint product that lacks competitive markets. Negotiations for a mutually acceptable price may be based on the allocation of joint-product costs. In such instances, the cost allocation is a means of substituting for market prices.

ral gas prices. The FPC based prices on old competitive natural gas prices. Meanwhile, unregulated oil prices rose, resulting in lower proportions of joint costs being allocated to natural gas, thus restricting natural gas prices and providing less incentive for finding natural gas.

ACCOUNTING FOR BYPRODUCTS

The distinction between joint products, byproducts, and scrap is largely influenced by the relative sales values of the products in question. However, these distinctions are not firm; the variety of terminology and accounting practice is bewildering. For example, brass turnings may be called scrap in one company and valuable byproducts in another. Many sewage plants that formerly regarded their products as waste have developed the waste into joint-products stature as valuable fertilizer.

Byproducts are products of joint processes that have minor sales value compared with the sales value of the joint or main product(s). Examples are mill ends of cloth and carpets; cotton meal and cotton hulls in the processing of cottonseed oil; and tar and naphtha in gasoline production. The distinction between scrap and byproducts is often difficult to establish. A view that is sometimes helpful is that byproducts (a) have relatively more sales value than scrap and (b) are often subject to additional costs beyond the split-off point, whereas scrap is usually sold outright. The basic accounting for scrap and for byproducts is the same. *The estimated net realizable values of both are best treated as deductions from the cost of the main products.* The rest of this discussion is confined to accounting for byproducts.

Accounting methods for byproducts

The two basic methods of accounting for byproducts first recognize the byproduct in the general ledger at either (1) the time of sale or (2) the time of production. Exhibit 14-6 shows one version of each of the basic methods.

METHOD ONE   Net revenue from byproduct *sold* is gross revenue from byproduct sold less separable costs *incurred,* such as additional manufacturing and marketing costs. This net revenue is deducted from the cost of the main product(s) *sold.*

METHOD TWO   Estimated net realizable value of the byproduct *produced* is sales value of the byproduct produced less separable costs *applicable,* whether already incurred or to be incurred. This net realizable value is deducted from the cost of the main product(s) *produced.*[9]

Many variations and combinations of these two methods are used in practice. Exhibit 14-7 presents journal entries based on the data in Exhibit 14-6 to help clarify the distinctions between the two methods.

Essentially, Method One has practical appeal, but conceptually it fails to match the value of the byproduct with the cost of the products simultaneously

---

[9]One version of Method Two deducts the estimated net realizable value of the byproduct(s) from the total production cost (joint costs + separable costs). Another version of Method Two deducts the estimated net realizable value of the byproduct(s) from the joint costs before they are allocated to individual main products. Where there is only one main product, both versions yield the same result.

EXHIBIT 14-6
Two Accounting Methods for Byproducts

DATA FOR ILLUSTRATION

	MAIN PRODUCT		BYPRODUCT	
	19_1	19_2	19_1	19_2
Beginning inventory in units	0	1,000	0	300
Production in units	10,000	0	1,000	0
Sales in units	9,000	1,000	700	300
Ending inventory in units	1,000	0	300	0
Sales revenue @ $15.00 and @ $1.50	$135,000	$15,000	$ 1,050	$ 450
Separable disposal costs @ $.30	—	—	210	90
Net revenue from byproduct sold	—	—	840	360
Net realizable value of byproduct produced:				
1,000 units @ ($1.50 − $.30)	—	—	1,200	—

PARTIAL INCOME STATEMENTS (IN DOLLARS)

	METHOD (SEE TEXT FOR DESCRIPTION)			
	Method One		Method Two	
	19_1	19_2	19_1	19_2
Sales revenues from main product	$135,000	$15,000	$135,000	$15,000
Cost of main product sold:				
Beginning inventory of main product		$10,000		$ 9,880
Total production costs (assumed)	$100,000		$100,000	
Net realizable value of byproduct produced			1,200	
Net production costs	$100,000		$ 98,800	
Ending inventory of main product (10%)	10,000		9,880	
Cost of main product sold (gross)	$ 90,000	$10,000	$ 88,920	$ 9,880
Net revenue from sale of byproduct	840	360		
Cost of main product sold (net)	$ 89,160	$ 9,640	$ 88,920	$ 9,880
Gross margin	$ 45,840	$ 5,360	$ 46,080	$ 5,120
Gross margin for both years	$51,200		$51,200	

produced. Alternative approaches to reporting byproduct income (that is, byproduct revenue less separable costs incurred) under this method include the following:

a. Treat as an "other sales" item in the top section of the income statement, or

b. Treat as an "other income" item near the bottom of the income statement, or

c. Treat as a deduction from the cost of main products *sold*, which is illustrated in Exhibit 14-6 for Method One.

Method One (and variations thereof) is often justified on the grounds that byproducts are incidental and do not warrant costly accounting procedures. Unsold byproducts are inventoried at zero value, although procedures may be adopted for control of physical quantities.

Method Two tries to relate the estimated net realizable value of the byproducts *produced* to the cost of the main products *produced,* as is illustrated by Method Two in Exhibit 14-6. This method eliminates the effect of lag between production

EXHIBIT 14-7
Journal Entries for Byproducts

	19_1 Debit	19_1 Credit	19_2 Debit	19_2 Credit
METHOD ONE				
At time of production:				
No entry				
At time of sale:				
Separable disposal costs	210*		90§	
Cash		210		90
Cash	1,050†		450‖	
Revenue from sale of byproduct		1,050		450
Net revenue from sale of byproduct	($1,050 − $210 = $840)		($450 − $90 = $360)	
Note that the valuation (cost) of the byproduct inventory is always zero				
METHOD TWO				
At time of production:				
Byproduct inventory				
(1,000 × ($1.50 − $0.30))	1,200			
Work in process		1,200		
At time of sale:				
Separable disposal costs	210*		90§	
Cash		210		90
Cash	1,050†		450‖	
Revenue from sale of byproduct		1,050		450
Cost of byproduct sold	840‡		360#	
Byproduct inventory		840		360
Valuation (cost) of the ending byproduct inventory	($1,200 − $840 = $360)		($360 − $360 = 0)	
Note that no net revenue from the sale of byproduct is recognized; for example, net revenue in 19_1 = $1,050 − $210 − $840 = 0				

*700 × $0.30.   §300 × $0.30.
†700 × $1.50.   ‖300 × $1.50.
‡700 × $1.20.   #300 × $1.20.

and sales and directly matches the cost-reduction power of byproducts with the production costs of the main product. The byproduct inventory is carried at estimated net realizable value (plus separable manufacturing costs incurred, if any).[10]

[10] A variation of Method Two would use net realizable value *less normal profit margin* of byproducts produced (minus separable manufacturing costs incurred, if any). This version is more conservative because the byproducts would be valued lower than their estimated net realizable value. Thus the costs of main products would be higher, and a "normal profit" would be shown for the byproduct as it is sold. This version would shift income to a future period to the extent that the byproduct in question is not sold in the current period. This version has conceptual appeal, but it implies that the byproduct is important enough to warrant treatment as a separate product line. In short, the product is treated like a joint product instead of a byproduct.

Both methods in Exhibit 14-6 recognize that byproducts somehow reduce the costs of the main products. Method Two is more correct about the timing of such cost reductions. The two periods taken together show the same combined income for the two methods (there being no beginning inventories for the first period and no ending inventories for the second period). The variations in methods raise some provocative theoretical problems concerning the matching of revenues and expenses. But cost-benefit comparisons in choosing among the accounting alternatives usually lead to whatever alternative seems expedient. By definition, byproducts should have minor sales values, and thus their effect on income should be immaterial.

The illustration in Exhibit 14-6 assumes that the separable costs of the byproduct are confined to disposal costs (marketing costs). If any significant separable manufacturing costs were incurred, they would be deducted from the byproduct revenue under Method One. This treatment would be a violation of the matching principle if all the separable manufacturing costs incurred were applicable to the 1,000 units produced rather than to only the 700 units sold. Under Method Two, the separable manufacturing costs would be deducted in computing the estimated net realizable value of the byproduct produced.

Sometimes byproducts are used internally as fuel or even as a component of a new batch of raw materials for the main product. For example, steel companies will often remelt scrap and byproducts along with purchased scrap metal as a part of producing new steel ingots. In these cases, the byproducts are frequently accounted for at estimated net realizable values or replacement values; in turn, the cost of the main product is reduced by the same amount. For instance, scrap metal would be valued at replacement cost, and byproducts such as gas and tar derivatives would be valued at the cost of fuel oil that would otherwise be used to yield equivalent heat units.

SUMMARY

Joint costs permeate accounting. Viewed in their broadest sense, costs are joint with respect to time, facilities, products, and services. Accountants attempt to allocate joint costs among products having relatively important sales values. Where a product produced in a joint process is valueless (for example, waste), all costs are applied to the main product(s). Where a product produced in a joint process has minor value, it is often called a byproduct: Its estimated net realizable value or net revenue is frequently deducted from the cost of the main product.

The major purposes for allocating joint costs are inventory valuation and the determination of costs for contract reimbursement or rate regulation. Where external parties are involved, perceptions about the propriety of joint-cost allocations are quite naturally influenced by self-interest. For instance, taxpayers may favor one method, whereas income tax collectors may favor another method. Accounting methods available in joint-cost situations include sales value at split-off, estimated net realizable value, constant gross-margin percentage NRV, physical measure, and no-allocation.

Only opportunity costs, incremental costs, and incremental revenues are relevant to decisions on whether to incur additional separable costs beyond the split-off point. As long as the incremental revenue exceeds the incremental costs (including the opportunity costs), further processing will be warranted.

problem   The Alden Oil Company buys crude vegetable oil. The refining of this oil results in four products: A, B, and C, which are liquids, and D, which is a heavy grease. Joint costs in 19_9 total $97,600 ($27,600 for crude oil plus $70,000 conversion costs). The output and sales for the four products in 19_9 were as follows:

PRODUCT	OUTPUT	SALES	SEPARABLE PROCESSING COST
A	500,000 gal.	$115,000	$30,000
B	10,000 gal.	10,000	6,000
C	5,000 gal.	4,000	—
D	9,000 gal.	30,000	1,000

Required   **1.** Assume that the estimated net realizable value method of allocating joint costs is used. What is the gross margin for Products A, B, C, and D?
2. The company had been tempted to sell at split-off directly to other processors. If that alternative had been selected, sales per gallon would have been: A, 15¢; B, 50¢; C, 80¢; and D, $3. What would the gross margin have been for each product under this alternative? Assume that the sales value at split-off method of allocating joint costs is used.
3. The company expects to operate at the same level of production and sales in the forthcoming year. Could the company increase gross margin by altering its processing decisions? If so, what would be the expected overall gross margin? Which products should be further processed and which should be sold at split-off? Assume that all costs incurred after split-off are variable.

solution   **1.**

	(a) Sales Value	(b) Separable Costs	Estimated Net Realizable Value at Split-off	(c) Allocation of Joint Costs	(a) − (b) − (c) Gross Margin
A	$115,000	$30,000	$ 85,000	85/122 × $97,600 = $68,000	$17,000
B	10,000	6,000	4,000	4/122 × 97,600 = 3,200	800
C	4,000	—	4,000	4/122 × 97,600 = 3,200	800
D	30,000	1,000	29,000	29/122 × 97,600 = 23,200	5,800
	$159,000	$37,000	$122,000	$97,600	$24,400

2.

	(a) Sales Value at Split-off	(b) Allocation of Joint Costs	(a) − (b) Gross Margin
A	500,000($ .15) = $ 75,000	75/111 × $97,600 = $65,947	$ 9,053
B	10,000($ .50) = 5,000	5/111 × 97,600 = 4,396	604
C	5,000($ .80) = 4,000	4/111 × 97,600 = 3,517	483
D	9,000($3.00) = 27,000	27/111 × 97,600 = 23,740	3,260
	$111,000	$97,600	$13,400

3. Note that comparing 1 and 2 in the manner computed above is irrelevant. For example, Product C's gross margin above is $483 or $800, despite the fact that the same amount is sold at the same price in either case. The only proper way to compare is to use an incremental approach:

	SALES AFTER FURTHER PROCESSING	SALES AT SPLIT-OFF	INCREMENTAL SALES	SEPARABLE COSTS OF FURTHER PROCESSING	INCREMENTAL GROSS MARGIN (OR LOSS)
A	$115,000	$75,000	$40,000	$30,000	$10,000
B	10,000	5,000	5,000	6,000	(1,000)
D	30,000	27,000	3,000	1,000	2,000
Increase in gross margin from further processing					$11,000

Based on the given data, the company gross margin, before considering cost of capital for further processing, could be improved by $1,000 by selling Product B at the split-off point instead of processing it further. That is, B's current incremental loss of $1,000 would be avoided by selling B at the split-off point.

An alternative approach to illustrating the effect on the gross margin of the proposed (Alternative 1) and the existing (Alternative 2) product mix is:

	ALTERNATIVE 1		ALTERNATIVE 2	
	Sell B and C at Split-off Further Process A and D		Sell C at Split-off Further Process A, B, and D	
Sales	$115,000 + $5,000 + $4,000 + $30,000 = $154,000		$115,000 + $10,000 + $4,000 + $30,000 = $159,000	
Deduct total costs	$97,600 + $30,000 + $1,000 = $128,600		$97,600 + $30,000 + $6,000 + $1,000 = $134,600	
Gross margin	$ 25,400		$ 24,400	

Terms to Learn

This chapter and the Glossary contain definitions of the following important terms:

byproduct (p. 478)   constant gross-margin percentage NRV method (484)
estimated net realizable value method (483)   joint cost (478)
joint product (478)   physical measure method (481)
sales value at split-off method (481)   separable cost (478)
split-off point (478)

Special Points and Pitfalls

Joint-product costs provide a splendid illustration of why there is no "true" cost of a product that may be used for all purposes. A cost that is suitable for inventory valuation may be unsuitable for decisions of which products to manufacture and which processes to use.

The sales value at split-off method has several advantages—simplicity, a meaningful common denominator, and no anticipation of subsequent management decisions. The major obstacle to its widespread adoption is that selling prices for some products at the split-off point are not readily available.

Where joint-cost data are used in the setting of prices, such as in rate regulation, allocation methods that rely on current market selling-price data should not be used.

QUESTIONS, PROBLEMS, AND CASES

14-1 What is a joint cost?

14-2 What is the split-off point?

14-3 Give two examples of industries in which joint costs are found. For each example, what are the separable products at the split-off point?

14-4 Name four methods of allocating joint costs among main products.

14-5 Many oil refineries do not allocate joint costs among their products. What reasons could explain this choice?

14-6 Define *estimated net realizable value*.

14-7 Briefly describe the two basic methods of accounting for byproducts.

14-8 "The sales value at split-off method of joint-cost allocation is the best method for managerial decisions regarding whether a product should be sold or processed further." Do you agree? Why?

14-9 Difference between joint products and byproducts. (CPA)
1. Explain the basic difference between the method of accounting for joint products and that for byproducts.
2. State the conditions under which an item should be treated as a byproduct rather than as a joint product.

14-10 Estimated net realizable value method.   A company produces two joint products, A and B. The joint cost is $24,000. Added processing costs: A, $30,000; B, $7,500. A sells for $50 per unit; B sells for $25 per unit.

If the company produces 1,000 units of A and 500 units of B, what is the proper amount of joint cost that should be allocated to B, assuming that the estimated net realizable value method of allocation of joint costs is used?

14-11 Alternative joint-cost allocation methods, further process decision.   The Wood Spirits Company produces two products, turpentine and methanol (wood alcohol), by a joint process. Joint costs amount to $12,000 per batch of output. Each batch totals 10,000 gallons, being 25% methanol and 75% turpentine. Both products are processed further without gain or loss in volume. Added processing costs: methanol, 30¢ per gallon; turpentine, 20¢ per gallon. Methanol sells for $2.10 per gallon; turpentine sells for $1.40 per gallon.

Required
1. What joint costs per batch should be assigned to the turpentine and methanol, assuming that joint costs are assigned on a physical-volume basis?
2. If joint costs are to be assigned on an estimated net realizable value basis, what amounts of joint cost should be assigned to the turpentine and to the methanol?
3. Prepare product-line income statements per batch for requirements 1 and 2. Assume no beginning or ending inventory.

4. The company has discovered an additional process by which the methanol (wood alcohol) can be made consumable and into a pleasant-tasting alcoholic beverage. The new selling price would be $6 a gallon. Additional processing would increase separable costs 90¢ a gallon, and the company would have to pay taxes of 20% on the new selling price. Assuming no other changes in cost, what is the joint cost applicable to the wood alcohol (using the net realizable value method)? Should the company use the new process?

14-12 Alternative methods of joint-cost allocation, further process decision, chemicals. Inorganic Chemicals purchases salt and processes it into more-refined products such as caustic soda, chlorine, and PVC (poly vinyl chloride). In the most recent month (July), Inorganic purchased and processed salt with a purchase cost of $40,000. Conversion costs of $60,000 were incurred up to the split-off point, at which time two salable products were produced: caustic soda and chlorine. Chlorine can be further processed into PVC.

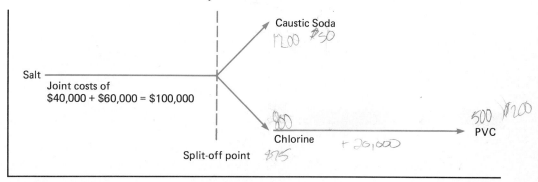

The July production and sales information is:

	PRODUCTION	SALES	SALES PRICE PER TON
Caustic soda	1,200 tons	1,200 tons	$ 50
Chlorine	800 tons		
PVC	500 tons	500 tons	$200

All the 800 tons of chlorine were further processed, at an incremental cost of $20,000, to yield 500 tons of PVC. There are no byproducts or scrap from this further processing of chlorine. There were no beginning or ending inventories of caustic soda, chlorine, or PVC in July.

There is an active market for chlorine. Inorganic Chemical could have sold all its July production of chlorine at $75 a ton.

Required

1. Calculate how the joint cost of $100,000 would be allocated between caustic soda and chlorine under each of the following methods: (a) sales value at split-off, (b) physical measure (tons), (c) estimated net realizable value, and (d) constant gross-margin percentage NRV method.

2. What is the gross-margin percentage of caustic soda and PVC under methods *a, b, c,* and *d,* respectively, in requirement 1?

3. Lifetime Swimming Pool Products offers to purchase the 800 tons of chlorine in August at $75 a ton. Assume that the production and sales relationships in July also hold in August. This sale of chlorine would mean that no PVC would be produced in August. What is the effect on August net income of accepting this offer?

14-13 Net realizable value cost allocation method, further process decision. (W. Crum) Tuscania Company crushes and refines mineral ore into three products in a joint-cost operation. Costs and production for 19_8 were as follows:

Department 1: Initial joint costs $420,000 producing 20,000 pounds of Alco, 60,000 pounds of Devo, 100,000 pounds of Holo

Department 2: Processes Alco further at a cost of $100,000

Department 3: Processes Devo further at a cost of $200,000

Results for 19_8:

Alco: 20,000 pounds completed; 19,000 pounds sold for $20 per pound; final inventory, 1,000 pounds

Devo: 60,000 pounds completed; 59,000 pounds sold for $6 per pound; final inventory, 1,000 pounds

Holo: 100,000 pounds completed; 99,000 pounds sold for $1 per pound; final inventory, 1,000 pounds; Holo required no further processing

Required

1. Use the estimated net realizable value method to allocate the joint costs of the three products.
2. Compute the total costs and unit costs of ending inventories.
3. Compute the individual gross-margin percentages of the three products.
4. Suppose Tuscania had an offer to sell all of its Devo product at the split-off before going through Department 3 for a price of $2 per pound, just as it comes off the line in Department 1, F.O.B. Tuscania plant. Would Tuscania have been better off by selling Devo that way last year rather than by processing it through Department 3 and selling it as it did? Show computations to support your answer. Disregard all other factors not mentioned in the problem.

14-14 Alternative methods of joint-cost allocation, ending inventories. The Darl Company operates a simple chemical process to reduce a single basic material into three separate items, here referred to as X, Y, and Z (all three end products being separated simultaneously at a single split-off point).

Products X and Y are ready for sale immediately upon split-off without further processing or any other additional cost. Product Z, however, is processed further before being sold. There is no available market price for Z at the split-off point.

The selling prices quoted below have not changed for three years, and no future changes are foreseen.

During 19_3, the selling prices of the items and the total number sold were as follows:

X—120 tons sold for $1,500 per ton

Y—340 tons sold for $1,000 per ton

Z—475 tons sold for $700 per ton

There were no beginning inventories of X, Y, or Z.

The total joint manufacturing costs for the year were $400,000. An additional $200,000 was spent in order to finish Product Z.

At the end of the year, the following inventories of completed units were on hand: X, 180 tons; Y, 60 tons; Z, 25 tons. There was no beginning or ending work in process.

Required

1. What will be the cost of inventories of X, Y, and Z for balance sheet purposes and the cost of goods sold for income statement purposes as of December 31, 19_3, using (a) estimated net realizable value joint-cost allocation method, and (b) constant gross-margin percentage NRV cost allocation method?
2. For *a* and *b* in requirement 1, compare the gross-margin percentages for X, Y, and Z.

14-15 Estimated net realizable value cost allocation method, further process decision. (CPA) The Mikumi Manufacturing Company produces three products by a joint production process. Raw material is put into production in Department A, and at the end of processing in this department three products appear. Product X is immediately sold at the split-off point, with no further processing. Products Y and Z require further processing before they are sold. Product Y is processed in Department B, and Product Z is processed in Department C. The Company uses the estimated net realizable value method of allocating joint production costs. Following is a summary of costs and other data for the year ended September 30, 19_2.

There were no inventories on hand at September 30, 19_1, and there was no raw material on hand at September 30, 19_2. All the units of product on hand at September 30, 19_2, were fully complete as to processing:

	PRODUCTS		
	X	Y	Z
Pounds sold	10,000	30,000	40,000
Pounds on hand at September 30, 19_2	20,000	-0-	20,000
Sales revenues	$15,000	$81,000	$141,750

	DEPARTMENTS		
	A	B	C
Raw-material cost	$56,000	-0-	-0-
Direct-labor cost	24,000	$40,450	$101,000
Manufacturing overhead	10,000	10,550	36,625

Required

1. Determine the following amounts for each product: (a) estimated net realizable value as used for allocating joint costs, (b) joint costs allocated, (c) cost of goods sold, and (d) finished-goods inventory costs, September 30, 19_2.
2. Assume that the entire output of Product X could be processed further at an additional cost of $2.00 per pound and then sold at a price of $4.30 per pound. What is the effect on operating income if all the Product X output for the year ended September 30, 19_2, had been processed further and sold, rather than all being sold at the split-off point?

14-16 Alternative methods of joint-cost allocation, product-mix decisions. The Sunshine Oil Company buys crude vegetable oil. The refining of this oil results in four products at the split-off point: A, B, C, and D. Product C is in fully processed form at this split-off point. Products A, B, and D can individually be further refined into Super A, Super B, and Super D. In the most recent month (December), the output at the split-off point was:

Product A	300,000 gallons
Product B	100,000 gallons
Product C	50,000 gallons
Product D	50,000 gallons

The joint cost of purchasing the crude vegetable oil and its processing was $100,000.

Sunshine had no beginning or ending inventories. Sales of Product C in December were $50,000. Total output of Products A, B, and D was further refined and then sold. Data relating to December are:

	SEPARABLE PROCESSING COST TO MAKE SUPER PRODUCTS	SALES REVENUES
Super A	$200,000	$300,000
Super B	80,000	100,000
Super D	90,000	120,000

Sunshine had the option of selling Products A, B, and D at the split-off point. This alternative would have yielded the following sales revenues for the December production:

Product A	$50,000
Product B	30,000
Product D	70,000

Required

1. What is the gross-margin percentage for each product sold in December, using the following methods for allocating the $100,000 joint cost: (a) sales value at split-off, (b) physical measure, and (c) estimated net realizable value.
2. Could Sunshine have increased its December net income by making different decisions about the further refining of Products A, B, or D? Show the effect on net income of any changes you recommend.

14-17 Joint and byproducts, estimated net realizable value method. (CPA)   The Harrison Corporation produces three products—Alpha, Beta, and Gamma. Alpha and Gamma are joint products while Beta is a byproduct of Alpha. No joint cost is to be allocated to the byproduct. The production processes for a given year are as follows:

A. In Department One, 110,000 pounds of raw material, Rho, are processed at a total cost of $120,000. After processing in Department One, 60% of the units are transferred to Department Two, and 40% of the units (now Gamma) are transferred to Department Three.

B. In Department Two, the material is further processed at a total additional cost of $38,000. Seventy percent of the units (now Alpha) are transferred to Department Four and 30% emerge as Beta, the byproduct, to be sold at $1.20 per pound. Selling expenses related to disposing of Beta are $8,100.

C. In Department Four, Alpha is processed at a total additional cost of $23,660. After this processing, Alpha is ready for sale at $5 per pound.

D. In Department Three, Gamma is processed at a total additional cost of $165,000. In this department, a normal loss of units of Gamma occurs which equals 10% of the good output of Gamma. The remaining good output of Gamma is then sold for $12 per pound.

Required

1. Prepare a schedule showing the allocation of the $120,000 joint cost between Alpha and Gamma using the estimated net realizable value method. The estimated net realizable value of Beta should be treated as an addition to the sales value of Alpha.
2. Independent of your answer to requirement 1, assume that $102,000 of total joint costs were appropriately allocated to Alpha. Assume also that there were 48,000 pounds of Alpha and 20,000 pounds of Beta available to sell. Prepare a statement of gross margin for Alpha using the following facts:
   a. During the year, sales of Alpha were 80% of the pounds available for sale. There was no beginning inventory.
   b. The net realizable value of Beta available for sale is to be deducted from the cost of producing Alpha. The ending inventory of Alpha is to be based on the net cost of production.
   c. All other cost, selling-price, and selling-expense data are those listed in A through D above.

14-18 Joint costs and byproducts. (W. Crum)   Caldwell Company processes an ore in Department 1, out of which come three products, L, W, and X. Product L is processed further through Department 2; Product W is sold without further processing. X is considered a byproduct and is processed further through Department 3. Costs in Department 1 are $800,000 in total; Department 2 costs are $100,000; Department 3 costs are $50,000. Processing 600,000 pounds in Department 1 results in 50,000 pounds of Product L being produced, with 300,000 pounds of Product W and 100,000 pounds of Product X.

Product L sells for $10 per pound; Product W sells for $2 per pound; Product X sells for $3 per pound. The company wants to make a profit margin of 10% on Product X and also allow 25% for selling and administrative expenses.

Required

1. Compute unit costs per pound for Products L, W, and X, treating X as a byproduct. Use the estimated net realizable value method for allocating joint costs. Deduct the estimated net realizable value of the byproduct from the joint cost of the two main products produced.
2. Compute unit costs per pound for Products L, W, and X, treating all three as joint products and allocating cost by the estimated net realizable value method.

14-19 Estimated net realizable value method, byproducts. (CMA, adapted)   Doe Corporation grows, processes, cans, and sells three main pineapple products—sliced pineapple, crushed pineapple, and pineapple juice. The outside skin is cut off in the cutting department and processed as animal feed. The skin is treated as a byproduct. Doe's production process is as follows:

Pineapples are initially processed in the cutting department. The pineapples are washed, and the outside skin is cut away. Then the pineapples are cored and trimmed for slicing. The three *main products* (sliced, crushed, juice) and the *byproduct* (animal feed) are recognizable after processing in the cutting department. Each product is then transferred to a separate department for final processing.

The trimmed pineapples are forwarded to the slicing department where the pineapples are sliced and canned. The juice generated during the slicing operation is packed in the cans with the slices.

The pieces of pineapple trimmed from the fruit are diced and canned in the crushing department. Again, the juice generated during this operation is packed in the can with the crushed pineapple.

The core and surplus pineapple generated from the cutting department are pulverized into a liquid in the juicing department. There is an evaporation loss equal to 8% of the weight of the good output produced in this department that occurs as the juice is being heated.

The outside skin, the byproduct, is chopped into animal feed in the feed department.

The Doe Corporation uses the estimated net realizable value method to assign costs of the joint process to its main products. The byproduct is inventoried at its market value. *Corporate policy is to subtract the estimated net realizable value of the byproduct produced from the joint costs to be allocated.*

A total of 270,000 pounds were entered into the cutting department during May. The schedule presented below shows the costs incurred in each department, the proportion by weight transferred to the four final processing departments, and the selling price of each end product.

DEPARTMENT	COSTS INCURRED	PROPORTION OF PRODUCT BY WEIGHT TRANSFERRED TO DEPARTMENTS	SELLING PRICE PER POUND OF FINAL PRODUCT
Cutting	$60,000	—	None
Slicing	4,700	35%	$.60
Crushing	10,580	28	.55
Juicing	3,250	27	.30
Animal feed	700	10	.10
Total	$79,230	100%	

Required

1. Calculate:
   a. The pounds of pineapple that result as departmental output for pineapple slices, crushed pineapple, pineapple juice, and animal feed.

b. The estimated net realizable value at the split-off point of the three main products.

c. The amount of the cost of the cutting department assigned to each of the three main products and to the byproduct in accordance with corporate policy.

d. The gross margins for each of the three main products.

2. Comment on the significance to managerial decisions of the gross-margin information by main product.

14-20 Byproducts, journal entries. (CPA) Lares Confectioners, Inc., makes a candy bar called Rey, which sells for $.50 per pound. The manufacturing process also yields a product known as Nagu. Without further processing, Nagu sells for $.10 per pound. With further processing, Nagu sells for $.30 per pound. During the month of April, total joint manufacturing costs up to the point of separation consisted of the following charges to work in process:

Direct materials	$150,000
Direct labor	120,000
Factory overhead	30,000

Production for the month aggregated 394,000 pounds of Rey and 30,000 pounds of Nagu. To complete Nagu during the month of April and obtain a selling price of $.30 per pound, further processing of Nagu during April would entail the following additional costs:

Direct materials	$2,000
Direct labor	1,500
Factory overhead	500

Required

Prepare the April journal entries for Nagu if Nagu is

1. Transferred as a byproduct at sales value to the warehouse without further processing, with a corresponding reduction of Rey's manufacturing costs.

2. Further processed as a byproduct and transferred to the warehouse at estimated net realizable value, with a corresponding reduction of Rey's manufacturing costs.

3. Further processed and transferred to finished goods, with joint costs being allocated between Rey and Nagu based on relative sales value at the split-off point.

14-21 Allocating joint costs, Christmas trees. S. Claus is a retired gentleman who has rented a lot in the center of a busy city for the month of December 19_0 at a cost of $5,000. On this lot he sells Christmas trees and wreaths. He buys his trees by the bundle for $20 each. A bundle is made up of two big trees (average height, seven feet), four regular-sized trees (average height, five feet), and broken branches. The shipper puts in the broken branches merely to make all the bundles of uniform size for shipping advantages. The amount of branches varies from bundle to bundle.

Mr. Claus gets $2 a foot for the trees. He takes home the broken branches. He and Mrs. Claus, Donner, Blitzen, and the rest sit around the fire in the evenings and make wreaths, which Mr. Claus sells for $8 each. Except for Christmas Eve, these evenings are a time when there is nothing else to do; therefore their labor is not a cost.

During the course of the season, Mr. Claus buys 1,000 bundles of trees and makes 2,000 wreaths. In addition to the broken branches, the wreaths contain pine cones (100 pounds, total cost $200), twine (4,000 yards @ 10¢ a yard), and miscellaneous items amounting to $400.

In 19_0 Claus sold 1,800 of the seven-foot trees, all the regular-sized ones, and half the wreaths (the local Boy Scouts were also selling wreaths). The department store next door says that it will buy the rest of the wreaths, if Claus will preserve them, for $3 each. The preservative spray costs $2,000 for enough to do the job.

Required

1. What unit cost should Claus assign to each of his items? Use the estimated net realizable value method of allocating joint costs.

2. What is the inventory cost on January 1, 19_1, if he doesn't sell to the department store?

3. Should he sell to the department store?

14-22 Sell or process further; allocation of fixed costs. The Space Parts Co. receives cold-worked steel in sheet form from a nearby steel mill. The company has a special patented machine that takes the sheet steel and produces three missile parts simultaneously. Part A is taken from the machine and further processed to make it available for sale at $3.50; the additional processing cost for part A is $495. Parts B and C are run through a vat containing a secret "dip" developed by one of the company engineers to make them heat-resistant. This dip costs 20¢ per cubic foot of product. Part B sells for $5 and part C for $8.25.

ADDITIONAL INFORMATION

Materials	$ 8,000
Direct labor	1,600
Maintenance and depreciation	1,200
	$10,800 cost of running special machine for month

Month's production and sales (which is the typical product mix):

Part A	600 units
Part B	800 units
Part C	1,000 units

Part B has a volume of .50 cu ft.
Part C has a volume of .75 cu ft.

The vat is being depreciated at the rate of $60 per month, requires two part-time persons for its operation at a total combined salary of $1,500 per month, and necessitates other operating expenses of $165 per month. All these costs are fixed.

Required

1. Joint costs assignable to each part for the month's operations. Use the estimated net realizable value method.

2. The company has a chance to sell part B undipped at split-off at $4.70 each on a long-run basis. Should the company adopt this alternative?

14-23 Analysis of joint-cost allocation data in decisions. (CMA, adapted) Talor Chemical Company is a highly diversified chemical-processing company. The company manufactures swimming pool chemicals, chemicals for metal-processing companies, specialized chemical compounds for other companies, and a full line of pesticides and insecticides.

Currently, the Noorwood plant is producing two derivatives, RNA-1 and RNA-2 from the chemical compound VDB developed by Talor's research labs. Each week, 1,200,000 pounds of VDB are processed at a cost of $246,000 into 800,000 pounds of RNA-1 and 400,000 pounds of RNA-2. The proportion of these two outputs is fixed and cannot be altered. RNA-1 has no market value until it is converted into a product with the trade name Fastkil. The cost to process RNA-1 into Fastkil is $240,000. Fastkil wholesales at $70 per 100 pounds.

RNA-2 is sold as is for $80 per hundred pounds. However, Talor has discovered that RNA-2 can be converted into two new products through further processing. The further processing would require the addition of 400,000 pounds of compound LST to the 400,000 pounds of RNA-2. The joint process would yield 400,000 pounds each of DMZ-3 and Pestrol—the two new products. The additional direct material and related processing costs of this joint process would be $120,000. DMZ-3 can be sold for $65 per 100 pounds. Pestrol can be sold for $50 per 100 pounds.

Talor management receives a consultant's report that recommends against processing the RNA-2 further. This report includes the following:

	ALTERNATIVE 1: SELL RNA-2	ALTERNATIVE 2: PROCESS RNA-2 INTO DMZ-3 AND PESTROL		
		DMZ-3	Pestrol	Total
Revenue	$320,000	$260,000	$200,000	$460,000
Allocated VDB costs*	$ 82,000	$ 61,500	$ 61,500	$123,000
Allocated costs of LST materials and further processing of RNA-2†	—	$ 60,000	$ 60,000	$120,000
Total costs	$ 82,000	$121,500	$121,500	$243,000
Weekly gross margin	$238,000	$138,500	$ 78,500	$217,000

*Allocated using the physical measure of pounds: 400,000 pounds for RNA-2; 400,000 pounds for DMZ-3; and 400,000 pounds for Pestrol.

†Allocated using the physical measure of pounds: 400,000 pounds for DMZ-3; and 400,000 pounds for Pestrol.

A new staff accountant reviewed the consultant's report. He criticized the method used to allocate joint cost and commented that "product costing of products such as these should be done on an estimated net realizable value basis, not a physical measure basis." He also questioned whether the chosen physical measure basis had been correctly used by the consultants.

Required

1. Discuss whether the use of the estimated net realizable value method of joint-cost allocation would provide data more relevant for the decision of whether to market DMZ-3 and Pestrol.
2. Critique the consultant's analysis and make any revisions that are necessary. Your critique and analysis should include discussion of (a) whether Talor Chemical Company received the correct recommendation, and (b) the gross savings (loss) per week of not processing RNA-2 further, if you disagree with the consultant's analysis.

14-24. Joint costs; change in product mix. The Laissez Faire Perfume Company processes a secret blend of flower petals into three products. The process works in such a way that the petals are broken down into a high-grade perfume, Charm, and a low-grade flower oil. The flower oil is then processed into a low-grade perfume, Wild Scent, and a cologne, Personally.

The company used 10,000 pounds of petals last month. The costs involved in reducing the petals into Charm and flower oil were:

Direct materials	$150,000
Direct labor	90,000
Indirect costs	60,000
	$300,000

The cost of producing Wild Scent and Personally from the flower oil were:

Direct materials	$15,000
Direct labor	35,000
Indirect costs	20,000
	$70,000

Total production for the month, with no ending work-in-process inventory, was:

Charm	10,000 ounces
Wild Scent	20,000 ounces
Personally	50,000 ounces

The sales price of Charm is $40 an ounce; of Wild Scent, $10 an ounce; and of Personally, $1 an ounce.

Additional costs, entirely separate for each product, of processing and selling are:

Charm	$ 20,000
Wild Scent	160,000
Personally	40,000
	$220,000

Required

1. Joint cost of Charm, Wild Scent, and Personally, using the estimated net realizable value method.
2. Product-line income statement, assuming no beginning or ending inventories.
3. The management, completely ignorant of cost accounting, is considering the possibility of increasing the quality of Wild Scent, at an increase in final processing cost of $2 per ounce. The selling price would increase to $12 per ounce. This decision would result in a different product mix of Wild Scent and Personally. Every 10,000 pounds of petals would then result in 10,000 ounces of Charm, 18,000 ounces of Wild Scent, and 60,000 ounces of Personally. The separable costs of Personally and Wild Scent are completely variable. All prices and costs not specifically mentioned will remain unchanged. Should this alternative be selected?

14-25 Alternative methods of joint-cost allocation, further process decision, memory chips. AMC is a semiconductor firm that specializes in the production of extended life memory chips. The first stage of the manufacturing operation is fabrication in which raw silicon wafers are first photolithographed and then baked at high temperatures. This process yields three individual products at a common split-off point. For each batch of 1,600 raw silicon wafers, these products are:

1. 300 high-density (HD) memory chips
2. 900 low-density (LD) memory chips
3. 400 defective memory chips

The density of a memory chip is based on the number of good memory bits on each chip, with HD chips having more memory bits per chip than LD chips. The 400 defective memory chips from each batch have zero salvage value. The joint cost of purchasing and processing the 1,600 raw silicon wafers to the split-off point is $5,000.

AMC has two options for each grade of good memory chip at the split-off point:

1. Sell immediately. HD chips have a sales price of $10 each. LD chips have a sales price of $5 each.
2. Process further into extended life memory chips. This processing step exposes the chips to extreme conditions (e.g., as to temperature), and those that survive are sold as extended life memory chips. Data pertaining to this further processing stage include
   a. Extended life high-density (EL–HD) chips: From a batch of 300 HD chips, the yield is 200 EL–HD chips. The 100 defective chips from this further processing step have zero salvage value. The separable cost to further process the 300 HD chips is $1,000. The sales price for each EL–HD chips is $30.
   b. Extended life low-density (EL–LD) chips: From a batch of 900 LD chips, the yield is 500 EL–LD chips. The 400 defective chips from this further processing step have zero salvage value. The separable cost to further process the 900 LD chips is $3,000. The sales price for each EL–LD chip is $18.

AMC has consistently followed the policy of further processing the entire output of both the HD and LD chips into their EL–HD and EL–LD forms.

1. State how the joint cost of $5,000 would be allocated between HD and LD chips under each of the following methods: (a) sales value at split-off, (b) physical measure (number of good chips at split-off point), (c) estimated net realizable value, and (d) constant gross-margin percentage NRV. Assume that AMC has no beginning or ending inventories.

2. What is the gross-margin percentage of EL–HD and EL–LD chips under methods a, b, c, and d, respectively, in requirement 1?

3. Peach Computer Systems offers to buy 900 LD memory chips from AMC at $5 a chip. What is the effect on operating income of accepting this offer as opposed to AMC's current policy of further processing the LD chips into the EL–LD form?

Process-Costing Systems 15

Nature of process costing • Five major steps • Weighted-average method • First-in, first-out method • Comparison of FIFO and weighted-average methods • Standard costs and process costs • Transfers in process costing • Additional aspects of process costing • Appendix 15A: Sample entries for process costing • Appendix 15B: Alternative format for process costing

Process-costing systems are used for inventory costing when there is continuous mass production of like units, in contrast to the production of tailor-made or unique goods produced under job-order systems. This chapter covers the major *product-costing* methods that may be used in process-cost systems. It will be concerned only incidentally with *planning* and *control* because the latter techniques are discussed in other chapters and are applicable to *all* product-costing systems regardless of whether process costing or job-order costing or some hybrid system is used.

A basic description of process costing, including the key concept of equivalent units, appears in Chapter 4 (pages 107–109). **Please review that material before proceeding.**

NATURE OF PROCESS COSTING

All product costing uses averaging to determine costs per unit of production. The average unit cost may be relatively narrow, as in the production of a particular printing order in job-order costing. In contrast, the average may be relatively broad, as in the production of beer in process costing. *Process costing* **is a system**

507

that applies costs to like products that are usually mass produced in continuous fashion through a series of production steps.

The principal difference between job costing and process costing arises from the type of products that are the cost objectives. Job-order costing is found in industries such as printing, construction, and furniture manufacturing, where each unit or batch (job) of product tends to be unique and easily identifiable. Process costing is found where there is mass production through a sequence of several processes, such as mixing and cooking. Examples include chemicals, flour, glass, and paint.

Exhibit 15-1 shows the major differences between job-order costing and proc-

EXHIBIT 15-1
Comparison of Job-order and Process Costing

JOB-ORDER COSTING: Examples include printing, construction, auditing, repairing, and jewelry

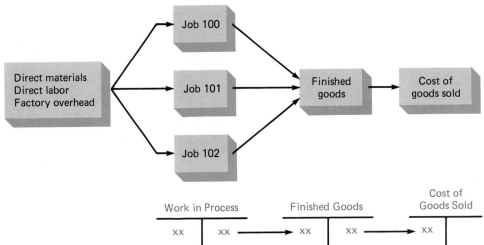

PROCESS COSTING: Examples include flour, glass, paint, paper, and silicon wafers

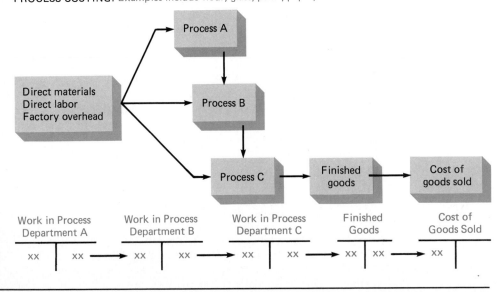

ess costing. Several work-in-process accounts are used in process costing. As goods move from process to process, their costs are transferred accordingly.

The process-costing approach is less concerned with distinguishing among individual units of product. Instead accumulated costs for a period, say a month, are divided by quantities produced during that period to get broad, average unit costs. Process costing may be adopted in nonmanufacturing activities as well as in manufacturing activities. Examples include dividing the costs of giving state automobile driver's license tests by the number of tests given and dividing the costs of an X-ray department by the number of X-rays processed.

Process-costing systems are usually simpler and less expensive than job-order costing. Individual jobs do not exist. There are no individual job cost records. The unit cost for inventory purposes is calculated by accumulating the costs of each processing department and dividing the total cost by an appropriate measure of output. For instance, the accumulated cost of a cooking department may be divided by the number of items processed.

The relationships of the inventory accounts are (amounts in millions):

Work in Process—Cooking		*Work in Process—Freezing*	
Direct materials 30	Transfer cost of goods completed to next department 55	Cost transferred in from Cooking 55 Additional costs 8 —— 63	Transfer cost of goods completed to finished goods 60
Direct labor 10			
Factory overhead 20 —— 60			
Ending inventory 5		Ending inventory 3	

The journal entries are similar to those for the job-order costing system. That is, direct materials, direct labor, and factory overhead are accounted for as before. However, now there is more than a single Work-in-Process account for all units being manufactured. There are two or more Work-in-Process accounts, one for each processing department. Journal entries are illustrated later in this chapter.

FIVE MAJOR STEPS

The easiest way to learn process cost accounting is by example. The data in Example 1 will be used. The weighted-average method will be illustrated first, followed by the first-in, first-out method.

EXAMPLE 1

A plastics company uses two processes, forming (in Department A) and finishing (in Department B), for making a high-volume children's toy. Direct material is introduced at the *beginning* of the process in Department A, and additional direct material is added at the *end* of the process in Department B. Conversion costs are applied evenly throughout both processes. As the process in Department A is completed, goods are immediately transferred to Department B; as goods are completed in Department B, they are transferred to Finished Goods.

Data for Department A for the month of March 19_1 are:

Work in process,		
Beginning inventory:		10,000 units
Direct materials	$4,000	
Conversion costs (40%)*	1,110	$5,110
Units completed and transferred out during March		48,000
Units started during March		40,000
Work in process, ending inventory		2,000(50%)*
Direct-material cost added during March		$22,000
Conversion costs added during March:		
Direct labor	$ 6,000	
Factory overhead applied	12,000	$18,000

*This means that each unit in process is regarded as being fractionally complete with respect to the conversion costs of the present department only, at the dates of the work-in-process inventories.

Required

Compute the cost of goods transferred out of Department A. Compute ending-inventory costs for goods remaining in the department. Use (a) weighted-average product costing and (b) first-in, first-out (FIFO) product costing. Show journal entries for the transfers to Department B.

Five major steps in accounting for process costs will be described:

Step 1: Summarize the flow of physical units
Step 2: Compute output in terms of equivalent units
Step 3: Summarize the total costs to account for, which are the total debits in Work in Process
Step 4: Compute unit costs
Step 5: Apply total costs to units completed and to units in ending work in process

Although shortcuts are sometimes taken, the methodical procession through each of the five steps minimizes errors. The first two steps concentrate on what is occurring in physical or engineering terms. The dollar impact of the production process is measured in the final three steps.

Step 1: summarize physical units

Step 1 traces the physical units of production. (Where did units come from? Where did they go?) In other words, (a) how many units are there to account for? and (b) how are they accounted for? Draw flow charts as a preliminary step, if necessary. Exhibit 15-2 shows these relationships, which may also be expressed as an equation:

Beginning inventories + Units started = Units transferred + Ending inventories

The total of the left side of the equation is shown as the units to account for: 10,000 + 40,000 = 50,000 in Exhibit 15-2. The total of the right side is shown as the units accounted for: 10,000 + 38,000 + 2,000 = 50,000 in Exhibit 15-2.

There are 10,000 physical units in process at the start of the period. In addition, 40,000 units were begun during the current period. Of the total of 10,000 + 40,000 = 50,000 units to account for, 2,000 units remained in process at the end of the period. Therefore 48,000 units were completed during the period, consisting

EXHIBIT 15-2
Step 1: Summarize Physical Units

Work in process, beginning inventory	10,000 (40%)*
Started during current period	40,000
To account for	50,000
Completed and transferred out during current period:†	
From beginning inventory	10,000
Started and completed currently	38,000
Work in process, ending inventory	2,000 (50%)*
Accounted for	50,000

*Degrees of completion, for conversion costs of this department only, at the dates of the work-in-process inventories.

†"Current period" is used as a general term. In this example, the current period is one month, March.

of the 10,000 units from the beginning work in process plus 38,000 units from the 40,000 units started.

All costs incurred are debited to a department account that simultaneously serves as an inventory account, Work in Process—Department A. As goods are completed and transferred, costs are shifted from one Work-in-Process account to the next, usually by monthly entries. For purposes of our example, this account will show units as well as dollars:

Work in Process—Department A

	PHYSICAL UNITS	DOLLARS		PHYSICAL UNITS	DOLLARS
Beginning inventory	10,000	?	Transferred out	48,000	?
Started	40,000	?	Ending inventory	2,000	?
To account for	50,000	?	Accounted for	50,000	?

WEIGHTED-AVERAGE METHOD

Step 1 is the same for each inventory method, but Steps 2 through 5 are affected by the choice of method. This section describes the weighted-average method.

Recall that **equivalent units** measure the output in terms of the quantities of each of the factors of production applied thereto. That is, an equivalent unit is a collection of inputs (work applications) necessary to produce one complete physical unit of product.

In process costing, costs are often divided into only two main classifications: direct materials and conversion costs. Direct labor is seldom a major part of total costs, so it is combined with factory-overhead costs (such as the costs of energy, repairs, and material handling) as a major classification called conversion costs.

Step 2: compute output in equivalent units

Express the physical units in terms of work done. Because direct materials and conversion costs are usually applied differently, the equivalent output is divided into direct-material and conversion-cost categories. For example, instead of thinking of output in terms of physical units, think of output in terms of direct-material doses of work and conversion-cost doses of work. **Disregard dollar amounts until equivalent units are computed.**

In Department A of this example, direct materials are introduced at the beginning of the process. Therefore both the physical units completed and the physical units in the ending work in process are "fully completed" in terms of equivalent units of work done regarding direct materials. Note especially that the direct-material component of work in process is fully completed as soon as work is started. Why? Because all doses of direct material are applied at the initial stage of the process. Specific computations follow:

	DIRECT MATERIALS
Completed and transferred out, 48,000 × 100%	48,000
Work in process, end, 2,000 × 100%	2,000
Total equivalent units of work done	50,000

Exhibit 15-3 is a sketch of the weighted-average approach to the computation of equivalent units. For conversion costs, the physical units completed and transferred out are fully completed. The physical units in ending work in process are 50% completed; therefore they will be weighted accordingly:

	CONVERSION COSTS
Completed and transferred out, 48,000 × 100%	48,000
Work in process, end, 2,000 × 50%	1,000
Total equivalent units of work done	49,000

Exhibit 15-4 combines Steps 1 and 2. It summarizes the computation of output in terms of equivalent units.

The weighted-average method focuses on the total work done to date regardless of whether that work was done before or during the current period. Conse-

EXHIBIT 15-3
Sketch of Underlying Computations of Equivalent Units
Weighted-average Computations

		Beginning Inventory 10,000	Started during Current Period 40,000		
Physical Units		Transferred Out 48,000		Ending Inventory 2,000	
Equivalent Units	Direct Materials*	48,000 × 100% = 48,000		2,000 × 100% = 2,000	Total 50,000
	Conversion Costs*	48,000 × 100% = 48,000		2,000 × 50% = 1,000	Total 49,000

*Expressed in terms of work done in current and previous periods (that is, work done to date.)

EXHIBIT 15-4

Department A
Computation of Output in Equivalent Units
For the Month Ended March 31, 19_1
Weighted-average Method

| | (STEP 1) | (STEP 2) EQUIVALENT UNITS | |
FLOW OF PRODUCTION	Physical Units	Direct Materials	Conversion Costs
Work in process, beginning	10,000(40%)*		
Started in March	40,000		
To account for	50,000		
Completed and transferred out during current period	48,000	48,000	48,000
Work in process, end:	2,000(50%)*		
Direct materials: 2,000 × 100%		2,000	
Conversion costs:			
2,000 × 50%			1,000
Accounted for	50,000		
Work done to date		50,000	49,000

*Degrees of completion for conversion costs of this department only, at the dates of the work-in-process inventories.

quently, the equivalent units include the work completed before March as well as the work done during March. Thus the stage of completion of the March beginning work in process is not used in this computation.

Step 3: summarize total costs to account for

Exhibit 15-5 summarizes the total costs to account for, that is, the total debits in Work in Process. The debits consist of the beginning balance, $5,110, plus the current costs, $40,000, added during March.

Step 4: compute unit costs

Exhibit 15-6 shows the computation of unit costs. The weighted-average method has been called a "roll-back" method because the averaging of costs includes the work done in the preceding period on the current period's beginning inventory of work in process. Thus the total costs and the equivalent units mingle the applicable work begun in the preceding period with the work started during the current period. Thus the total costs include the cost of the work in process at the beginning

EXHIBIT 15-5

Step 3: Summarize Total Costs to Account For
(The Total Debits in Work in Process)

Work in Process—Department A

	PHYSICAL UNITS	DOLLARS		PHYSICAL UNITS	DOLLARS
Beginning inventory	10,000	$ 5,110	Transferred out	48,000	?
Started:	40,000		Ending inventory	2,000	?
Direct materials		22,000	Accounted for	50,000	?
Conversion costs		18,000*			
To account for	50,000	$45,110			

*Direct labor + factory overhead applied: $6,000 + $12,000 = $18,000.

EXHIBIT 15-6
Step 4: Compute Unit Costs
Weighted-average Method

	TOTALS	DETAILS Direct Materials	DETAILS Conversion Costs	Equivalent Whole Unit
Work in process, beginning inventory	$ 5,110	$ 4,000	$ 1,110	
Current costs added	40,000	22,000	18,000	
Total costs to account for (Step 3)	$45,110	$26,000	$19,110	
Divide by equivalent units for work done to date (from Exhibit 15-4)		÷50,000	÷49,000	
Cost per equivalent unit		$.52	$.39	$.91

of the current period. Note that the equivalent units also include all work done to date, including the work done on beginning work in process before the current period.

Step 5: apply total costs

Exhibit 15-7 shows how the unit costs computed in Step 4 are the basis for applying total costs to units completed and in ending work in process. The 48,000 units completed and transferred out bear a unit cost of $.52 plus $.39 equals $.91. The 2,000 units in ending work in process bear 2,000 equivalent units of materials at $.52 and 1,000 equivalent units of conversion costs at $.39. Note how the total costs accounted for can be checked against one another in Steps 3 and 5. The $45,110 in Exhibit 15-5 agrees with the $45,110 in Exhibit 15-7.

A **production-cost report** is a report of the units manufactured during a specified period together with their related costs (Steps 3, 4, and 5). Such a report may be highly summarized or extensively detailed. Supporting schedules are often provided also. Exhibit 15-8 is a sample of a production-cost report for the weighted-average method.

EXHIBIT 15-7
Step 5: Apply Total Costs to Units Completed and in Ending Work in Process
Weighted-average Method

	TOTALS	DETAILS Direct Materials	DETAILS Conversion Costs
Units completed and transferred out (48,000)	$43,680	48,000($.91)	
Work in process, end (2,000)			
Direct materials	$ 1,040	2,000($.52)	
Conversion costs	390		1,000($.39)
Total cost of work in process	$ 1,430		
Total costs accounted for	$45,110		

EXHIBIT 15-8
Department A
Production-Cost Report
For the Month Ended March 31, 19_1
Weighted-average Method

		TOTALS	Direct Materials	Conversion Costs	Equivalent Whole Unit
			DETAILS		
	Work in process, beginning inventory	$ 5,110	$ 4,000	$ 1,110	
	Current costs added	40,000	22,000	18,000	
(STEP 3)	Total costs to account for	$45,110	$26,000	$19,110	
	Divide by equivalent units*		÷50,000	÷49,000	
(STEP 4)	Cost per equivalent unit		$ .52	$ .39	$ .91
(STEP 5)	Application of total costs: Total costs of work completed and in process:				
	Units completed and transferred out (48,000)	$43,680			48,000(.91)
	Work in process, ending inventory (2,000):				
	Direct materials	$ 1,040	2,000($.52)		
	Conversion costs	390		1,000($.39)	
	Total work in process	$ 1,430			
	Total costs accounted for	$45,110			

*For work done to date. For more details, see Exhibit 15-4.

Journal entries

Process-costing journal entries are basically like those for the job-order costing system. That is, direct materials, direct labor, and factory overhead are accounted for as before. The main difference is that there is more than one Work-in-Process account.

The data in our weighted-average illustration would be journalized as follows:

1. Work in process—Department A 22,000
   Direct materials (or Stores) 22,000
   To record requisitions of direct materials for March.

2. Work in process—Department A 6,000
   Accrued payroll 6,000
   To record direct labor for March.

3. Work in process—Department A 12,000
   Factory overhead applied 12,000
   To record application of factory overhead for March.

4. Work in process—Department B 43,680
   Work in process—Department A 43,680
   To record cost of goods completed and transferred from Department A to Department B.

EXHIBIT 15-9
Flow of Costs
Process-Costing System

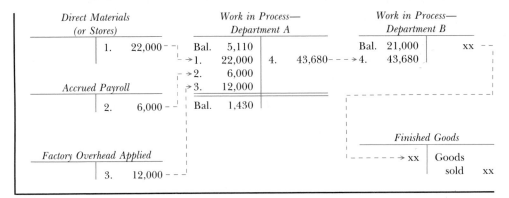

Exhibit 15-9 shows a general sketch of the flow of costs through the T-accounts. The key T-account, Work in Process—Department A, shows an ending balance of $1,430:

Work in Process—Department A					
	PHYSICAL UNITS	DOLLARS		PHYSICAL UNITS	DOLLARS
Beginning inventory	10,000	$ 5,110	Transferred out	48,000	$43,680
Started:	40,000		Ending inventory	2,000	1,430
Direct materials		22,000	Accounted for	50,000	$45,110
Conversion costs		18,000*			
To account for	50,000	$45,110			
Ending inventory	2,000	$ 1,430			

*Direct labor plus factory overhead applied: $6,000 + $12,000 = $18,000.

FIRST-IN, FIRST-OUT METHOD

Steps 1 and 2: physical units and equivalent units

The first-in, first-out (FIFO) method regards the beginning inventory as if it were a batch of goods separate and distinct from the goods started *and* completed by a process during the current period. Step 1, the analysis of physical units, is unaffected by this method. However, subsequent steps are affected.

Step 2, the computation of the output in terms of equivalent units, is the same as under the weighted-average method—except for a final computation. As Exhibit 15-10 shows, the work done to date is exactly the same as that computed in Exhibit 15-4. Under FIFO, however, a deduction must be made for the work done on the beginning inventory prior to the current period; *thus the equivalent units are confined to work done during the current period only.*

What work was done before March on the 10,000 units of the beginning work in process? All the direct materials and 40% of the conversion costs. Therefore Exhibit 15-10 deducts 10,000 equivalent units of direct materials and 4,000 equivalent units of conversion costs to compute the work done during March only.

EXHIBIT 15-10

Department A
Computation of Output in Equivalent Units
For the Month Ended March 31, 19_1
FIFO Method

	FLOW OF PRODUCTION	(STEP 1) Physical Units	(STEP 2) EQUIVALENT UNITS Direct Materials	Conversion Costs
Same as in Exhibit 15-4, p. 513	Work in process, beginning	10,000(40%)*		
	Started in March	40,000		
	To account for	50,000		
	Completed and transferred out during current period	48,000	48,000	48,000
	Work in process, end:	2,000(50%)*		
	Direct materials: 2,000 × 100%		2,000	
	Conversion costs: 2,000 × 50%			1,000
	Accounted for	50,000		
	Work done to date		50,000	49,000
	Less equivalent units for work done on beginning inventory in previous periods:			
	Direct materials: 10,000 × 100%		10,000	
	Conversion costs: 10,000 × 40%			4,000
	Remainder, work done during current period only		40,000	45,000

Degrees of completion for conversion costs of this department only, at the dates of the work-in-process inventories.

An alternative computation to that in Exhibit 15-10 produces the same answers:

FLOW OF PRODUCTION	PHYSICAL UNITS	DIRECT MATERIALS	CONVERSION COSTS
Completed and transferred out during current period:			
From beginning work in process	10,000	—	6,000*
Started and completed currently	38,000	38,000	38,000
Work in process, ending inventory	2,000	2,000	1,000†
Accounted for	50,000		
Work done in current period only		40,000	45,000

*10,000 × (100% − 40%) = 10,000 × 60% = 6,000.
†2,000 × 50% = 1,000.*

This approach and format is an acceptable substitution for the computations of equivalent units in Exhibit 15-10. Indeed, it often serves as a check or proof of the accuracy of the calculations in Exhibit 15-10. However, the rest of the chapter will follow the approach in Exhibit 15-10.

Exhibit 15-11 is the production-cost report for the FIFO method. It presents Steps 3, 4, and 5. Concentrate for now on Steps 3 and 4. The divisor for computing unit costs is confined to the work done during the current period. Therefore the current costs (only) are divided by the equivalent units for work done during the current period (only). Thus the $5,110 beginning inventory costs and the equivalent units of work done on the beginning inventory in the preceding period are excluded from the computation of unit costs.

The bottom half of Exhibit 15-11 shows how the unit costs computed in Step 4 are the basis for Step 5: applying costs to units completed and in ending work in process. The exhibit presents two ways to compute the costs of goods completed and transferred out. The first and quicker way is to calculate the $1,500 ending work in process and then simply deduct it from the $45,110 total costs to account for, obtaining the $43,610.

To check accuracy, a second way is used. The $2,400 cost of the work done on the beginning inventory during March is computed and added to the $5,110 beginning inventory balance. The $36,100 cost of the goods started and completed within March is then added to obtain the $43,610.

Finally, why does the $.9085 average unit cost of goods transferred out differ

EXHIBIT 15-11
DEPARTMENT A
Production-Cost Report
For the Month Ended March 31, 19_1
FIFO Method

			DETAILS	
	TOTALS	Direct Materials	Conversion Costs	Equivalent Whole Unit
Work in process, beginning inventory	$ 5,110	(costs of work done prior to current period)		
Current costs	40,000	$22,000	$18,000	
Total costs to account for (Step 3)	$45,110			
Divisor, equivalent units for work done during current period only (from Exhibit 15-10)		÷40,000	÷45,000	
Cost per equivalent unit (Step 4)		$.55	$.40	$.95
Application of total costs (Step 5): Work in process, March 31				
Direct materials	$ 1,100	2,000*($.55)		
Conversion costs	400		1,000*($.40)	
Total work in process (2,000 units)	$ 1,500			
Completed and transferred out (48,000 units), $45,110 − $1,500	43,610†			
Total costs accounted for	$45,110			

*Equivalent units of work done. See Exhibit 15-10.

†Check: Work in process, beginning inventory	$ 5,110
Additional costs to complete, beginning work in process, conversion costs of (100% − 40%) of 10,000 × $.40	2,400
Started and completed, 48,000 − 10,000 = 38,000; 38,000 × ($.55 + $.40), or 38,000 × $.95	36,100
Total cost transferred	$43,610
Average unit cost transferred, $43,610 ÷ 48,000 = $.9085	

from the $.95 unit cost of units started and completed during March? Department A uses FIFO to distinguish between monthly batches of production. Succeeding departments, however, such as Department B, "cost in" these goods at the *one* average unit cost ($.9085 in this illustration). If the latter averaging were not done, the attempt to trace costs on a strict FIFO basis throughout a series of processes would be too cumbersome for managers to find useful.

In summary, although the so-called FIFO method is sometimes used in process-costing situations, only rarely is an application of strict FIFO ever encountered. It should really be called a *modified* or *departmental* FIFO method. Why? Because, while FIFO is applied within a department to compile the cost of goods transferred *out*, the goods transferred *in* during a given period usually bear a single average unit cost as a matter of convenience.

COMPARISON OF FIFO AND WEIGHTED-AVERAGE METHODS

The key difference between FIFO and the weighted-average methods is how equivalent units are computed. Ponder the difference in Exhibit 15-10, page 517:

> Weighted-average—total work done to date (full weight given to all units completed and transferred out during current period *plus* partial weights for work done on ending work in process).
> FIFO—work done during current period only (same as weighted-average amount *minus* work done in previous period on beginning work in process).

In turn, differences in equivalent units generate differences in unit costs. Accordingly, there are differences in costs applied to goods completed and still in process. In our example:

	WEIGHTED AVERAGE*	FIFO†
Cost of goods transferred out	$43,680	$43,610
Ending work in process	1,430	1,500
Total costs accounted for	$45,110	$45,110

*From Exhibit 15-8, p. 515.
†From Exhibit 15-11.

In this example, the FIFO ending inventory is higher than the weighted-average ending inventory by only $70, or 4.9% ($70 ÷ $1,430 = 4.9%). The difference is attributable to variations in unit costs of direct materials and conversion costs in different months. The unit cost of the work done in March only was $.55 + $.40 = $.95, as shown in Exhibit 15-11. In contrast, Exhibit 15-8 shows the weighted-average unit cost of $.52 + $.39 = $.91. Therefore the FIFO method results in a larger work-in-process inventory, March 31, and a smaller March cost of goods transferred out.

The difference in unit costs from month to month is ordinarily even less significant than the small difference illustrated here. Fluctuations in unit costs are usually caused by volatile direct-materials prices, not conversion costs. The latter tend to be relatively stable.

519

In process-costing industries, the physical inventory levels of work in process tend not to change much from month to month. They also tend to be relatively small in relation to the total number of units completed and transferred. These conditions also help to explain why unit costs do not differ much between the FIFO and weighted-average methods.

The FIFO measurements of work done during the current period only are essential for judging current period performance, March in this illustration. A major advantage of FIFO is that the efficiency of performance in March can be judged independently from the performance in February. In brief, the "work done during the current period" is vital information for planning and control purposes as well as for FIFO inventory valuation purposes. Standard costing, which is described next in this chapter, uses "work done during the current period only" as a basis for comparing actual costs of the current period with budgeted or standard costs of the current period.

In sum, standard costing is by far the dominant process-costing method used in practice today. Weighted-average costing is a lagging second choice. FIFO is rarely encountered for *product costing*. However, FIFO computations of *equivalent units* are an essential ingredient for standard costing. That is the main justification for learning the FIFO method of process costing.

STANDARD COSTS AND PROCESS COSTS

This section assumes that you have already studied Chapters 6, 7, and 8. If you have not studied these chapters, proceed to the next major section, "Transfers in Process Costing," page 524.

Standards are useful

Previous chapters demonstrated that the use of standard costing is completely general; that is, it can be used in job-order situations or process-costing situations, and with absorption costing or variable costing. However, standard-cost procedures tend to be most effective when they are adapted to process costing. Mass, continuous, and repetitive production conditions lend themselves rather easily to setting appropriate physical standards. Price tags may then be applied to the physical standards to develop standard costs. Such standard costs would allow for normal shrinkage, waste, evaporation, or spoilage.

The intricacies and conflicts between weighted-average and FIFO costing methods are eliminated by using standard costs. Further, weighted-average and FIFO methods become very complicated when used in industries that produce a variety of products. Many observers have stressed that standard costing is especially useful where there are various combinations of materials, operations, and product sizes. For example, a steel-rolling mill uses various steel alloys and produces sheets of various sizes and of various finishes. The items of direct material are not numerous; neither are the operations performed. But used in various combinations, they yield too great a variety of products to justify the broad averaging procedure of historical process-cost accounting. Elsewhere, similar conditions are frequently found—as, for example, in plants manufacturing rubber goods, textiles, ceramics, paints, and packaged food products.

Standard costing is growing in importance in industries where process costing is used. Therefore, because of its conceptual and practical appeal, standard costing deserves our study. Because we have already seen how standard costing aids planning and control, we will concentrate on its product-costing aspects.

Computations under standard costing

The facts in Example 2 are basically the same as those for Department A in Example 1 except that standard costs have been developed for the process as follows:

EXAMPLE 2

	PER UNIT
Direct materials, introduced at start of process	$ .53
Conversion costs, incurred evenly throughout process	.37
Standard cost per unit	$ .90
Work in process, beginning, 10,000 units, 40% completed (materials, $5,300; conversion costs, $1,480)	$ 6,780
Units completed during March	48,000
Units started during March	40,000
Work in process, end	2,000, 50% completed

Required

1. Compute the standard cost of goods completed and of ending work-in-process inventory.
2. "Actual" direct-material costs added during the month were $22,000. Conversion costs were $18,000. Compute the total direct-material variance and total conversion-cost variance.

A standard-cost system greatly simplifies process-cost computations. There is a similarity between the FIFO and standard-cost methods in one important respect. Both use the "work done during current period only" in Exhibit 15-10, page 517, as the basis for computing equivalent units.

Steps 1 and 2 are the same for FIFO and standard costing. Exhibit 15-10 shows work done during the current period: direct materials, 40,000 equivalent units; and conversion costs, 45,000 equivalent units.

Steps 3, 4, and 5 are easier for standard costing than for the FIFO method. Why? Because the cost per equivalent unit does not have to be computed, as was done for the FIFO method. Instead the cost per equivalent unit is the standard cost. The latter is the key to computing the total costs to account for, the costs transferred out, and the ending work-in-process inventory. Exhibit 15-12 summarizes all these calculations. Exhibit 15-13 illustrates a production-cost report.

Accounting for variances

Standard-cost systems usually accumulate actual costs separately from the inventory accounts. The following is an example. The actual data are recorded in the first two entries, and the variances are recorded in the next two entries. Exhibit 15-14 shows how the costs flow through the accounts.

1. Department A cost control (at actual)	22,000	
Direct materials (or Stores)		22,000
To record requisitions of direct materials for March.		
2. Department A cost control (at actual)	18,000	
Accrued payroll, accounts payable, etc.		18,000
To record conversion costs for March.		

EXHIBIT 15-12
Standard Costs in Process Costing
For the Month Ended March 31, 19_1

Work in Process—Department A (at standard)

	PHYSICAL UNITS	DOLLARS		PHYSICAL UNITS	DOLLARS
Beginning inventory	10,000	$ 6,780*	Transferred out	48,000	$43,200‡
Started:	40,000		Ending inventory	2,000	1,430§
Direct materials		21,200†	Accounted for	50,000	$44,630
Conversion costs		16,650			
To account for	50,000	$44,630			
Ending inventory	2,000	$ 1,430			

*10,000 × $.53 = $5,300
40% of 10,000 × $.37 = 1,480
$6,780

†40,000 × $.53 = $21,200
45,000 × $.37 = $16,650
‡48,000 × ($.53 + $.37) = $43,200
§2,000 × $.53 = $1,060
50% of 2,000 × $.37 = 370
$1,430

3. Work in process—Department A (at standard)	21,200	
Direct-material variances	800	
Department A cost control		22,000
To record product costs and direct-material variances.		

4. Work in process—Department A (at standard)	16,650	
Conversion-cost variances	1,350	
Department A cost control		18,000
To record product costs and direct-material variances.		

5. Work in process—Department B	43,200	
Work in process—Department A		43,200
To record cost of goods completed and transferred at standard cost from Department A to Department B.		

Variances can be measured and analyzed in little or great depth in the same manner as that described in the earlier chapters on standard costs.

A standard-cost system not only eliminates the intricacies of weighted-average versus FIFO inventory methods but also erases the need for burdensome computations of costs per equivalent unit. The standard cost *is* the cost per equivalent unit. In addition, a standard-cost approach helps control operations.

Note how the equivalent units for the current period provide the key measures of the work accomplished during March. Again we see that the analysis of the

EXHIBIT 15-13
Department A
Production-Cost Report
For the Month Ended March 31, 19_1
Standard-Cost System

	TOTALS	DETAILS Direct Materials	DETAILS Conversion Costs
Standard cost per equivalent unit (given)		$.53	$.37
Work done in current period only (Exhibit 15-10, p. 517)		× 40,000	× 45,000
Current costs applied at standard prices	$37,850	$21,200	$16,650
Work in process, beginning inventory	6,780	$ 5,300	$ 1,480
Total costs to account for	$44,630		
Summary of costs:			
Units completed and transferred out 48,000 × ($.53 + $.37)	$43,200*		
Work in process, ending inventory (2,000):			
Direct materials	$ 1,060	2,000 × $.53	
Conversion costs (half-completed)	370		1,000 × $.37
Total work in process	$ 1,430		
Total costs accounted for	$44,630		
Summary of variances for current performance:			
Current output in equivalent units		40,000	45,000
Current output at standard costs applied		$21,200	$16,650
Actual costs		$22,000	$18,000
Total variance (which could be subdivided if more data were available)		$ 800 U	$ 1,350 U

Additional details could be provided.

Work in process, beginning inventory, which is transferred out first	$ 6,780	
Additional costs to complete: (100% − 40%) of 10,000 × $.37	2,220	
Cost of units started and completed this month: (48,000 − 10,000)($.53 + $.37)	34,200	
Total cost of goods completed and transferred out	$43,200	

523

EXHIBIT 15-14
Flow of Costs
Standard Process-Costing System

	Department A Cost Control				Work in Process— Department A				Work in Process— Department B
				Bal.	6,780				
1.	22,000	3.	22,000- - - →3.	21,200	5.	43,200 - - → 5.	43,200
2.	18,000	4.	18,000┐- - -↓→4.	16,650			
					44,630			
				Bal.	1,430			

Direct Materials (or Stores)				Direct-Material Variances
	1.	22,000	⌐→3.	800

Accrued Payroll Accounts Payable, etc.				Conversion- Cost Variances
	2.	18,000- - - →4.	1,350

physical units and equivalent units in Exhibit 15-10, page 517, is vital for evaluating current period performance. The equivalent units are used to value inventories and to measure variances.

TRANSFERS IN PROCESS COSTING

Many process-cost situations have two or more departments or processes in the production cycle. Ordinarily, as goods move from department to department, related costs are also transferred by monthly accounting entries. If standard costs are used, the accounting for such transfers is relatively simple. However, if FIFO or weighted-average is used, the accounting can become more complex.

To make the ideas concrete, we now extend Example 1 to encompass Department B.

EXAMPLE 1 EXTENDED TO ENCOMPASS DEPARTMENT B

A plastics company uses two processes, forming (in Department A) and finishing (in Department B), for making a high-volume children's toy. Direct material is introduced at the *beginning* of the process in Department A, and additional direct material is added at the *end* of the process in Department B. Conversion costs are applied evenly throughout both processes. As the process in Department A is completed, goods are immediately transferred to Department B; as goods are completed in Department B, they are transferred to Finished Goods.

Data for Department B for the month of March 19_1 are:

Work in process,		
Beginning inventory:		12,000 units
Transferred-in costs	$10,920	
Conversion costs (66⅔%)*	10,080	$21,000
Units completed during March		44,000
Units started during March		?
Work in process, ending inventory		16,000(37½%)*
Direct-material cost added during March		$13,200
Conversion costs added during March:		
Direct labor	$15,750	
Factory overhead applied	47,250	$63,000
Costs transferred in during March:		
Weighted-average method		$43,680
FIFO method		$43,610

*This means that each unit in process is regarded as being fractionally complete with respect to the conversion costs of the present department only, at the dates of the work-in-process inventories.

Required

Compute the cost of goods transferred out of Department B. Compute ending-inventory costs for goods remaining in the department. Use (a) weighted-average product costing and (b) first-in, first-out (FIFO) product costing. Show journal entries for the transfers to Finished Goods.

Transfers and weighted-average method

The five-step procedure described earlier still pertains when transfers into a department are accounted for. Exhibit 15-15 shows for Department B the initial two steps that analyze physical units and compute equivalent units. Note that direct-material costs have no degree of completion regarding the ending work in process. Why? Because in Department B direct materials are introduced at the *end* of the

EXHIBIT 15-15
Department B
Computations of Output in Equivalent Units
For the Month Ended March 31, 19_1
Weighted-average Method

	(STEP 1)	(STEP 2) EQUIVALENT UNITS		
FLOW OF PRODUCTION	PHYSICAL UNITS	Transferred-in Costs	Direct Materials	Conversion Costs
Work in process, February 28	12,000 (66⅔%)*			
Transferred in during March	48,000			
To account for	60,000			
Completed and transferred out during current period	44,000	44,000	44,000	44,000
Work in process, March 31	16,000 (37½%)*	16,000	—	6,000†
Units accounted for	60,000			
Work done to date		60,000	44,000	50,000

*Degrees of completion for conversion costs at the dates of inventories.
†16,000 × .375 = 6,000.

process. However, the equivalent units for transferred-in costs are, of course, fully completed because they are always introduced at the beginning of the process.

Transferred-in costs tend to give students much trouble, so special study is needed here. **Transferred-in costs** (or **previous department costs**) are costs incurred in a previous department that have been received by a subsequent department. They are similar but not identical to additional direct-material costs bought from an outside supplier and added in the subsequent department. Thus Department B's computations must provide for transferred-in costs, as well as for any new direct-material costs added in Department B, and for conversion costs added in Department B.

The essential difference between the weighted-average method as applied to Department A (Exhibit 15-4, page 513) and Department B is the accounting for transferred-in costs in B. In our example, Steps 1 and 2 are unchanged. Exhibit 15-16 displays the computations of output in equivalent units.

Exhibit 15-16 is a production-cost report. It shows Steps 3, 4, and 5. It presents the total costs to account for. Equivalent unit costs are computed and then applied to the units completed and in ending work in process.

Examine Exhibit 15-16 closely and note the following points: (1) The weighted-average method, unlike the FIFO method, necessitates the subdivision of the costs of beginning work in process into its components. (2) In this way, these components can be combined with the costs added currently to obtain a total

EXHIBIT 15-16

Department B
Production-Cost Report
For the Month Ended March 31, 19_1
Weighted-average Method

		TOTAL	Transferred-in Costs	Direct Materials	Conversion Costs
	Work in process, beginning inventory	$ 21,000	$10,920	$ —	$10,080
	Current costs	119,880	43,680	13,200	63,000
(Step 3)	Total costs to account for	$140,880	$54,600	$13,200	$73,080
	Divide by equivalent units for work done to date (from Step 2, Exhibit 15-15)		÷60,000	÷44,000	÷50,000
(Step 4)	Cost per equivalent unit	$2.6716	$.91	$.30	$1.4616
(Step 5)	Application of total costs: Units completed and transferred out (44,000)($2.6716)	$117,550			
	Work in process, ending inventory (16,000):				
	Transferred-in costs	$ 14,560	16,000($.91)		
	Direct materials	—		—	
	Conversion costs	8,770			6,000($1.4616)
	Total work in process	$ 23,330			
	Total costs accounted for	$140,880			

EXHIBIT 15-17

DEPARTMENT B
Summary of Costs Accounted For
For the Month Ended March 31, 19_1
Weighted-average Method

Work in Process—Department B					
	PHYSICAL UNITS	DOLLARS		PHYSICAL UNITS	DOLLARS
Beginning inventory	12,000	$ 21,000	Transferred out	44,000	$117,550
Transferred-in:	48,000		Ending inventory	16,000	23,330
Transferred-in costs		43,680	Accounted for	60,000	$140,880
Direct materials		13,200			
Conversion costs		63,000			
To account for	60,000	$140,880			
Ending inventory	16,000	$ 23,330			

amount for each cost element: transferred-in costs, direct materials, and conversion costs. (3) Thus the unit costs of each cost element will be weighted averages.

Note again that the total costs to account for are divided by the equivalent units for the "work done to date." For instance, the divisor for conversion costs is 50,000 units.

Exhibit 15-17 is a T-account portrayal of the total costs to account for (the total debits in work in process) and how they are accounted for.

Production-cost reports may also be presented in a briefer form than that shown in Exhibit 15-16. For example, the data in Exhibit 15-16 could be the supporting computations for a summary production-cost report. The latter would really be a formal presentation of the effects on the Work in Process—Department B account (see Exhibit 15-18).

The journal entry for the transfer out to finished-goods inventory would be:

Finished-goods inventory	117,550	
Work in process—Department B		117,550
To transfer units to finished goods.		

EXHIBIT 15-18

Department B
Summary Production-Cost Report
For the Month ended March 31, 19_1
Weighted-average Method

FLOW OF PRODUCTION	PHYSICAL UNITS	TOTAL COSTS
Work in process, beginning inventory	12,000	$ 21,000
Transferred in during March	48,000	119,880
To account for	60,000	$140,880
Completed and transferred out	44,000	$117,550
Work in process, ending inventory	16,000	23,330
Accounted for	60,000	$140,880

Sometimes a problem requires that the Work-in-Process account be split into Work in Process—Direct Materials, Work in Process—Direct Labor, and Work in Process—Factory Overhead. In these cases, the journal entries would contain this greater detail, even though the underlying reasoning and techniques would be unaffected.

Appendix 15A presents a complete set of sample entries for a process-costing system.

<table>
<tr><td>Transfers
and FIFO method</td><td>Exhibit 15-19 shows the initial two steps for the FIFO method. The method of computation of equivalent units is basically the same as for FIFO in Department A. However, transferred-in costs are a component that must now be considered.</td></tr>
</table>

Exhibit 15-20, the production-cost report, shows Steps 3, 4, and 5. Note again how the divisor equivalent units for FIFO differ from the divisor equivalent units for the weighted-average method. FIFO uses equivalent units for work done in the current period only.

Exhibit 15-21 summarizes the entries to Work in Process—Department B. As shown in Exhibit 15-20, the cost of goods transferred out would be $117,273, and the ending inventory would be $23,537.

Remember that in a series of interdepartmental transfers, each department is regarded as a distinct accounting entity. All transferred-in costs during a given

EXHIBIT 15-19
Finishing Department B
Computation of Output in Equivalent Units
For the Month Ended March 31, 19_1
FIFO Method

	FLOW OF PRODUCTION	(STEP 1) PHYSICAL UNITS	(STEP 2) EQUIVALENT UNITS Transferred-in Costs	Direct Materials	Conversion Costs
Same as in Exhibit 15-15, p. 525	Work in process, February 28	12,000 (66⅔%)*			
	Transferred in during March	48,000			
	To account for	60,000			
	Completed and transferred out during current period	44,000	44,000	44,000	44,000
	Work in process, March 31	16,000 (37½%)*	16,000	—	6,000†
	Units accounted for	60,000			
	Work done to date		60,000	44,000	50,000
	Less equivalent units for work done on beginning work in process prior to the current period		12,000‡	—	8,000§
	Work done during current period only		48,000	44,000	42,000

*Degrees of completion for conversion costs at the dates of inventories.
†16,000 × 37.5% = 6,000.
‡12,000 × 100% = 12,000.
§12,000 × 66⅔% = 8,000.

EXHIBIT 15-20
Department B
Production-Cost Report
For the Month Ended March 31, 19_1
FIFO Method

		TOTALS	Transferred-in Costs	Direct Materials	Conversion Costs
				DETAILS	
(Step 3)	Work in process, February 28	$ 21,000	(costs of work done prior to March)		
	Current costs added	119,810	$43,610	$13,200	$63,000
	Total costs to account for	$140,810			
(Step 4)	Divide by equivalent units		÷48,000	÷44,000	÷42,000
	Unit costs of work done during March only	$2.70845	$.90854*	$ .30	$ 1.50
(Step 5)	Application of total costs: Work in process, March 31				
	Transferred-in costs	$ 14,537	16,000($.90854)		
	Direct materials	—		—	
	Conversion costs	9,000			6,000†($1.50)
	Total work in process (16,000 units)	23,537			
	Completed and transferred out (44,000 units), $140,810 − $23,537	117,273‡			
	Total costs accounted for	$140,810			

*The unit costs are carried to several decimal places in these exhibits. Of course, they could be rounded with no harm done. However, small discrepancies in totals caused by rounding will occur.
†Equivalent units of work done. See Exhibit 15-19 for details.
‡Check:

Work in process, February 28	$ 21,000
Additional costs to complete;	
Direct materials, 12,000 × $.30 =	3,600
Conversion costs, 12,000 × .333 × $1.50 =	6,000
Started and completed 44,000 − 12,000 = 32,000; 32,000 × $2.70854 =	86,673
Total cost of goods completed and transferred	$117,273
Unit cost transferred, $117,273 ÷ 44,000 = $2.6653	

period are carried at one unit cost, regardless of whether weighted-average or FIFO methods were used by previous departments.

Common mistakes   Avoid some common pitfalls when accounting for transferred costs:

1. Remember to include transferred-in costs from previous departments in your calculations. Such costs should be treated as if they were another kind of direct-material cost added at the beginning of the process. In other words, when successive departments are involved, transferred goods from one department become all or a part of the direct materials of the next department, although they are called *transferred-in costs*, not direct materials.

2. In calculating costs to be transferred on a first-in, first-out basis, do not overlook the costs attached at the beginning of the period to goods that were in process but are now included in the goods transferred. For example, do not overlook the $21,000 in Exhibit 15-21.

3. Unit costs may fluctuate between periods. Therefore transferred goods may contain batches accumulated at different unit costs (see point 2). These goods, when trans-

EXHIBIT 15-21
Summary of Total Costs to Account For
(The Total Entries to Work in Process)
FIFO Method

Work in Process—Department B

	PHYSICAL UNITS	DOLLARS		PHYSICAL UNITS	DOLLARS
Beginning inventory	12,000	$ 21,000	Transferred out	44,000	$117,273
Transferred in:	48,000		Ending inventory	16,000	23,537
Transferred-in costs		43,610	Accounted for	60,000	$140,810
Direct materials		13,200			
Conversion costs		63,000			
To account for	60,000	$140,810			
Ending inventory	16,000	$ 23,537			

ferred to the next department, are typically valued by that next department at *one* average unit cost.

4. Units may be expressed in terms of kilograms in one department and liters in the next. Consider each department separately. Unit costs would be based on kilogram measures in the first department and liters in the second. As goods are received by the second department, they may be converted to the liter unit of measure.

ADDITIONAL ASPECTS OF PROCESS COSTING

Estimating degree of completion

This chapter's illustrations plus almost all process-cost problems blithely mention various degrees of completion for inventories in process. The accuracy of these estimates depends on the care and skill of the estimator and the nature of the process. Estimating the degree of completion is usually easier for direct materials than for conversion costs. The conversion sequence usually consists of a number of standard operations or a standard number of hours, days, weeks, or months for mixing, heating, cooling, aging, curing, and so forth. Thus the degree of completion for conversion costs depends on what proportion of the total effort needed to complete one unit or one batch has been devoted to units still in process. In industries where no exact estimate is possible, or, as in textiles, where vast quantities in process prohibit costly physical estimates, all work in process in every department is assumed to be ⅓ or ½ or ⅔ complete. In other cases, continuous processing entails little change of work-in-process levels from month to month. Consequently, in such cases, work in process is safely ignored and monthly production costs are assigned solely to goods completed.

This is another example of a cost-benefit approach, whereby a simplified system is used because management decisions will be unaffected by a more elaborate cost accounting system. Surveys of practice have shown that work-in-process inventories, as distinguished from completed goods, are typically ignored in process-costing systems.

Standard costing is used with process costing far more than either historical weighted-average or FIFO. The FIFO method is used the least. Process-costing problems appear on professional examinations with some regularity.[1]

[1]See the supplement to this textbook: John K. Harris. *Review Manual for Classroom Exams* (Englewood Cliffs, N.J.: Prentice-Hall, Inc., 1987).

Overhead and budgeted rates	Direct labor and factory overhead applied tend to be lumped together as conversion costs for process-costing purposes. In many process-cost industries, continuous, even production results in little fluctuation of total factory overhead from month to month. In such cases, there is no need to use budgeted overhead rates. Of course, where overhead costs and production vary from period to period, budgeted overhead rates are used in order to get representative unit costs.
Overhead and cost flow	In general, factory overhead is applied using budgeted rates in the same manner as was introduced in Chapter 4. The assumption that all conversion costs are incurred evenly in proportion to the degree of product completion is difficult to justify on theoretical grounds. For example, this implies that a wide variety of factory-overhead cost incurrence is directly related to direct-labor cost incurrence. Although such a direct cause-and-effect relationship may not exist, refinements of overhead application beyond this assumption are usually deemed too costly. When more precision is attempted, it is usually confined to developing a budgeted overhead rate to be loaded on direct-material cost to cover such indirect costs as purchasing, receiving, storing, issuing, and transferring materials. In such cases, one overhead rate would be applied along with direct-material costs while a separate overhead rate would be applied along with direct-labor costs.

SUMMARY

Process costing is used for inventory costing when there is continuous, mass production of like units. The key concept in process costing is that of equivalent units, the expression of output during a given period in terms of doses or amounts of work applied thereto.

Five basic steps may be used in solving process-cost problems. Process costing is complicated by varying amounts of cost factors, by the presence of beginning inventories, and by the presence of costs transferred in from prior departments.

Two widely advocated process-costing methods are known as *weighted-average* and *first-in, first-out*. However, standard costs are the most widely used; they are simpler and more useful than other techniques for both product-costing and control purposes.

PROBLEMS FOR SELF-STUDY

Review each example in this chapter and obtain the solutions on your own. Then check your work against the solutions, which appear in the various exhibits.

Terms to Learn

This chapter and the Glossary at the end of the book contain definitions of the following important terms:

equivalent units (p. 511)   **previous-department costs (526)**
production-cost report (514)   **transferred-in costs (526)**

In practice, standard costing is the most widely used method of process costing.

The five-step technique is not the only or the fastest way to solve process-cost problems. Nevertheless, it is logical and has built-in checks. By applying the five-step approach, you will develop confidence and comprehension. Armed with this approach, you should be able to handle any process-cost situation adequately. Shortcuts should be applied wherever feasible. But it is difficult to generalize on shortcut methods, because they differ depending upon the specific problem and the accountant's ability to use them.

APPENDIX 15A: SAMPLE ENTRIES FOR PROCESS COSTING

The appendix to Chapter 4 presented a set of entries for a job-order system. In parallel fashion, Exhibit 15-22 presents some typical process-costing transactions, general-ledger effects, subsidiary-ledger effects, and source documents. To demonstrate the variety of accounting practices that may be encountered, an *actual* rather than a *normal* cost system is illustrated. That is, all actual costs are charged to Work in Process as incurred; no budgeted overhead rates are used, as entry 5 indicates. The use of actual rather than normal overhead is more likely to be used by companies that have steady production levels from month to month.

Note also that all costs are charged to a department account that simultaneously serves as an inventory account, Work in Process—Department A. As goods are completed and transferred, costs are shifted from one department to the next, as entry 6 indicates.

APPENDIX 15B: ALTERNATIVE FORMAT FOR PROCESS COSTING

The chapter exhibits showed one of several possible formats for reports on process costing. Exhibit 15-23 presents an alternative format.[2] The substance of the exhibit does not differ from that of Exhibit 15-8, page 515. Steps 3, 4, and 5 are labeled so that the formats will be easier to compare.

Some accountants prefer the format of Exhibit 15-23 because it is somewhat more tightly knit than that of Exhibit 15-8. In particular, the cost of the goods completed is simply deducted from the total costs (the total debits to work in process) to obtain the cost of the ending work in process. Nevertheless, it is advisable to check the accuracy of these computations by the following proof:

Direct materials (2,000 × $.52)	$1,040
Conversion costs (2,000 × .5 × $.39)	390
Total	$1,430

---

[2]Various accountants favor different formats. For example, see S. H. Dinius, "A Matrix Solution to Process Cost Problems," *Proceedings of American Accounting Association Western Regional Meeting, 1983*, pp. 46–53.

EXHIBIT 15-22
Process Cost System—Sample Entries

TRANSACTION	GENERAL-LEDGER EFFECT*	SUBSIDIARY-LEDGERS EFFECT†	SOURCE DOCUMENTS
1. Purchases of direct materials and supplies	Stores control Accounts payable	Dr. Stores record, "Received" column	Approved invoice

2. Issuance of direct materials	Work-in-process control—
	  Department A
	  Stores control
		Dr. Department A cost record—appropriate columns
		  Cr. Stores record, "Issued" column
			Stores requisition

3. Payroll costs	Work-in-process control—
	  Department A
	  Accrued payroll
		Dr. Department A cost record—appropriate labor cost columns	Clock cards that are summarized and classified by natural classification (for example, supervision, inspection, mixers). This summary is sometimes called *payroll recapitulation, a labor distribution,* or a *payroll summary.*

4. Payroll payments	Accrued payroll Cash		Clock cards that are summarized on payroll sheets each pay period to compute individual payouts.

5. Other costs, such as utilities, insurance, and depreciation	Work-in-process control—
	  Department A
	  Accounts payable
	  Unexpired insurance
	  Allowance for depreciation—equipment
		Dr. Department A cost record—appropriate columns for utilities, insurance, and depreciation	Approved invoices, insurance registers, and depreciation schedules. Accruals, write-offs, and other charges may be authorized by a top accounting executive.

6. Transfer of completed goods to next department	Work-in-process control—
	  Department B
	  Work-in-process control—
	  Department A
		Dr. Department B cost record—
		"Costs Transferred-In" column
		  Cr. Department A cost record—"Costs Transferred-Out" column
			Production-cost report

7. Operating costs of Department B	Same types of entries as (2)–(5)		

8. Transfer of completed goods to finished stock	Finished goods
	  Work-in-process control—
	  Department B
		Dr. Finished stock record, "Received" column
		  Cr. Department B cost record—"Costs Transferred-Out" column
			Production-cost report

9. Sales	Accounts receivable
	  Sales
	Cost of sales
	  Finished goods
		Dr. Customers ledger
		  Cr. Sales ledgers (if any)
		Dr. Cost of sales ledger (if any)
		  Cr. Finished stock record, "Issued" column
			Sales invoices

*These entries are in summary form and are usually posted monthly.
†Subsidiary ledgers are not necessarily kept for every general-ledger account. Consequently, there are no entries in subsidiary ledgers for some transactions.

EXHIBIT 15-23
Department A
Application of Costs to Products: Weighted-Average Method
For the Month Ended March 31, 19_1

	(STEP 3)*			(STEP 4)	
	Work in Process, Beginning	Current Costs	Total Costs	Equivalent Units†	Average Unit Costs
Direct materials	$4,000	$22,000	$26,000	50,000	$.52
Conversion costs	1,110	18,000	19,110	49,000	.39
	$5,110	$40,000	$45,110		$.91

(Step 5)	Goods completed:		
	48,000 units × $.91		43,680
(Step 5)	Work in process, end, 2,000 units		$ 1,430

*See Exhibit 15-4 for Steps 1 and 2, p. 513.
†The divisor for computing unit costs depends on the inventory method. For the weighted-average method, this is the total work done to date as computed in Exhibit 15-4.

_____QUESTIONS, PROBLEMS, AND CASES_____

15-1   Name three industries that use process-costing systems.

15-2   Give three different examples of equivalent units that could be used in various organizations.

15-3   What feature of the first two steps of the five-step uniform technique distinguishes them from the final two steps?

15-4   "There is no need for using budgeted-overhead rates for product costing in process-cost industries." Do you agree? Why?

15-5   Why should the accountant distinguish between *transferred-in costs* and *new direct-material* costs for a particular department?

15-6   "Previous department costs are those incurred in the preceding fiscal period." Do you agree? Explain.

15-7   "Standard-cost procedures are particularly applicable to process-costing situations." Do you agree? Why?

15-8   What are some virtues of standard costs as used in process costing?

15-9 Weighted-average equivalent units.   Consider the following:

FLOW OF PRODUCTION	PHYSICAL UNITS
Work in process, beginning inventory	20,000*
Started in current period	70,000
To account for	90,000
Completed and transferred out	?
Work in process, ending inventory	5,000†
Accounted for	90,000

*Degree of completion: direct materials, 60%;
conversion costs, 30%.

†Degree of completion: direct materials, 80%;
conversion costs, 40%.

Required | Prepare a schedule of equivalent units for direct materials and conversion costs under the weighted-average method.

15-10 FIFO equivalent units. The Gagliano Company had computed a portion of the physical units for Department A, for the month of April, as follows:

Units completed:	
From work in process on April 1	10,000
From April production	30,000
	40,000

Direct materials are added at the beginning of the process. Units of work in process at April 30 were 8,000. The work in process at April 1 was 80% complete as to conversion costs, and the work in process at April 30 was 60% complete as to conversion costs. What are the equivalent units of production for the month of April using the FIFO method? Choose one of the following combinations:

		DIRECT MATERIALS	CONVERSION COSTS
	a.	38,000	38,000
	b.	48,000	44,800
	c.	48,000	48,000
	d.	38,000	36,800

15-11 Weighted-average and FIFO equivalent units. Consider the following data for May:

	PHYSICAL UNITS
Started in May	50,000
Completed in May	46,000
Ending inventory, work in process	12,000
Beginning inventory, work in process	8,000

The beginning inventory was 90% complete regarding direct materials and 40% complete regarding conversion costs. The ending inventory was 60% complete regarding direct materials and 20% complete regarding conversion costs.

Required | Prepare a single schedule of equivalent units for the work done to date (for the weighted-average method) and the work done during May only (for the FIFO method). See Exhibit 15-10, page 517.

15-12 Weighted-average and FIFO equivalent units. This problem is more difficult than 15-11. Consider these September data for physical units in Department C: beginning work in process, 15,000; transferred in from Department B during September, 9,000; ending work in process, 5,000. Direct materials are added at the 80% stage of completion of the process in Department C. Conversion costs are incurred evenly throughout the process. At the inventory dates, the beginning inventory was 60% completed as to conversion costs; the ending inventory was 20% completed. See Exhibit 15-19, page 528.

Required | Prepare a single schedule of equivalent units for the work done to date (for the weighted-average method) and the work done during September only (for the FIFO method). Include computations of equivalent units for transferred-in costs as well as for conversion costs and direct materials.

15-13 Weighted-average unit cost. (CPA) Barnett Company adds direct materials at the beginning of the process in Department M. Conversion costs were 75% complete as to the 8,000 units in work in process at May 1, 19_3, and 50% complete as to the 6,000 units in work in process at May 31. During May 12,000 units were completed and transferred to the next department. An analysis of the costs relating to work in process at May 1 and to production activity for May is as follows:

	COSTS	
	Direct Materials	Conversion
Work in process, 5/1	$ 9,600	$ 4,800
Costs added in May	15,600	14,400

Using the weighted-average method, the total cost per equivalent unit for May was (choose one): (a) $2.47, (b) $2.50, (c) $2.68, (d) $3.16.

15-14 Multiple choice, transfers in, weighted-average. (CPA) On April 1, 19_7, the Collins Company had 6,000 units of work in process in Department B, the second and last stage of their production cycle. The costs attached to these 6,000 units were $12,000 of costs transferred in from Department A, $2,500 of (direct) material costs added in Department B, and $2,000 of conversion costs added in Department B. Materials are added in the beginning of the process in Department B. Conversion was 50% complete on April 1, 19_7. During April, 14,000 units were transferred in from Department A at a cost of $27,000; and material costs of $3,500 and conversion costs of $3,000 were added in Department B. On April 30, 19_7, Department B had 5,000 units of work in process 60% complete as to conversion costs. The costs attached to these 5,000 units were $10,500 of costs transferred in from Department A, $1,800 of material costs added in Department B, and $800 of conversion costs added in Department B.

Required | Choose the best answer for each question:

1. Using the weighted-average method, what were the equivalent units for the month of April?

	TRANSFERRED IN FROM DEPARTMENT A	DIRECT MATERIALS	CONVERSION
a.	15,000	15,000	15,000
b.	19,000	19,000	20,000
c.	25,000	25,000	20,000
d.	20,000	20,000	18,000

2. Using the weighted-average method, what was the cost per equivalent unit for conversion costs? (a) $4,200 ÷ 15,000, (b) $5,800 ÷ 18,000, (c) $5,000 ÷ 18,000, (d) $5,800 ÷ 20,000.

15-15 Multiple choice, FIFO. (SMA) Choose the best answer for each of the following three multiple-choice questions. Show your supporting computations. The company uses FIFO.

1. With an opening inventory consisting of 1,000 units 80% complete as to direct materials and 30% complete as to conversion work; 11,000 units completed and transferred; no lost units; and a closing inventory of 900 units, 40% complete as to direct materials and 20% complete as to conversion; the total cost of the opening inventory before completion was $8,000; and current unit costs being $2 for direct materials and $8 for conversion; the total current direct materials costs amounted to (a) $21,800, (b) $21,120, (c) $22,200, (d) $22,720, (e) $23,400.

2. Total current conversion costs amounted to (a) $86,390, (b) $86,680, (c) $87,040, (d) $89,380, (e) $89,440.

3. Costs allocated to the goods transferred out amounted to (a) $6,000, (b) $14,000, (c) $110,000, (d) $114,000, (e) $120,000.

15-16 Weighted-average method. A toy manufacturer buys wood as its direct material for its forming department. The department processes one type of toy. The toys are transferred to the finishing department, where hand shaping and metal are added. Consider the following data:

Units:

Work in process, March 31, 3,000 units, 100% completed for direct materials but only 40% completed for conversion costs

Units started in April, 22,000

Units completed during April, 20,000

Work in process, April 30, 5,000 units, 100% completed for direct materials but only 25% completed for conversion costs

Costs:

Work in process, March 31:		
Direct materials	$7,500	
Conversion costs	2,125	$ 9,625
Direct materials added during April		70,000
Conversion costs added during April		42,500
Total costs to account for		$122,125

Required | Use the weighted-average method. Prepare a schedule of output in equivalent units. Prepare a production-cost report for the forming department for April. (For journal entries, see the next problem.)

15-17 Journal entries. Refer to the preceding problem. Prepare a set of summarized journal entries for all April transactions affecting Work in Process—Forming Department. Conversion costs consisted of $10,625 direct labor and $31,875 factory overhead applied. Set up a T-account, Work in Process—Forming, and post the entries therein.

15-18 FIFO computations. Repeat Problem 15-16, using FIFO and 4 decimal places for unit costs.

15-19 Transfers in, weighted-average. A toy manufacturer has two departments, forming and finishing. Consider the finishing department, which processes the formed toys through the addition of hand shaping and metal. Although various direct materials might be added at various stages of finishing, for simplicity here suppose all additional direct materials are added at the end of the process.

537 The following is a summary of the April operations in the finishing department:

Units:

Work in process, March 31, 5,000 units, 60% completed
for conversion costs
Units transferred in during April, 20,000
Units completed during April, 21,000
Work in process, April 30, 4,000 units, 30% completed
for conversion costs

Costs:

Work in process, March 31 (transferred-in costs, $17,750; conversion costs, $7,250)	$ 25,000
Transferred-in costs from forming department during April	104,000
Direct materials added during April	23,100
Conversion costs added during April	38,400
Total costs to account for	$190,500

Required

1. Use the weighted-average method. Prepare a schedule of output in equivalent units. Prepare a production-cost report for the finishing department for April.
2. Prepare journal entries for April transfers from the forming department to the finishing department and from the finishing department to finished goods.

15-20 FIFO costing. Refer to the preceding problem. Using FIFO costing, repeat the requirements.

15-21 Transferred-in costs, weighted-average and FIFO. Consider a finishing department that processes formed toys through the addition of hand shaping and metal. For simplicity, assume that all additional materials are added at the end of the process.
The April operations in the finishing department were:

Units:

Work in process, March 31, 5,000 units, 80% completed
for conversion costs
Units transferred in during April, 20,000
Units completed during April, 21,000
Work in process, April 30, 4,000 units, 40% completed
for conversion costs

Costs:

Work in process, March 31 ($29,000 transferred-in costs, $9,060 conversion costs)	$ 38,060
Transferred-in costs from forming department during April	96,000
Direct materials added during April	25,200
Conversion costs added during April	38,400
Total costs to account for	$197,660

Required

1. Compute the equivalent units for direct materials and conversion costs. Use (a) weighted-average method and (b) FIFO method.
2. Assume the weighted-average method is used for the finishing department. Prepare (a) a schedule of output in equivalent units and (b) a production-cost report. Headings for the exhibits may be omitted.
3. Assume the FIFO method is used for the finishing department. Compute the unit costs for applying April costs to products.

15-22 Comparing weighted-average and FIFO methods. (D. Kleespie) The Estevan Company manufactures "Smitties" and uses actual costs in a weighted-average process-cost accounting system. In Department 1 the direct materials are added at the beginning of processing, and conversion costs are considered to be added evenly throughout the processing. Consider the following information regarding the month of May:

	UNITS
Beginning inventory of work in process	
($620 conversion cost)	100 (60%)*
Completed and transferred out	3,000
Ending inventory of work in process	200 (50%)*
Equivalent unit cost for conversion cost, $10 per unit	

*Degree of completion of each unit

Direct-materials cost information has been omitted in order to simplify the problem.

Required

1. How many units were started in production in Department 1 during May?
2. How many equivalent units were used in determining the unit cost for conversion efforts?
3. What is the total dollar amount of the conversion-cost portion of the ending work-in-process inventory?
4. What is the total dollar amount of the conversion-cost portion being transferred out of Department 1?
5. What is the total amount of conversion cost charged to Department 1 during May?
6. Assume instead that the company had used the FIFO method. How many equivalent units would have been used to determine the unit cost for conversion efforts?
7. Assume as in requirement 6 that the company had used the FIFO method. What is the total amount of conversion cost charged to Department 1 during May?

15-23 Weighted-average method. (CPA) Lakeview Corporation is a manufacturer that uses the weighted-average process-cost method to account for costs of production. Lakeview manufactures a product that is produced in three separate departments: molding, assembling, and finishing. The following information was obtained for the assembling department for the month of June 19_0.

Work in process, June 1—2,000 units composed of the following:

	AMOUNT	DEGREE OF COMPLETION
Transferred in from the molding department	$32,000	100%
Costs added by the assembling department:		
Direct materials	$20,000	100%
Direct labor	7,200	60%
Factory overhead applied	5,500	50%
	32,700	
Work in process, June 1	$64,700	

The following activity occurred during the month of June:

10,000 units were transferred in from the molding department at a cost of $160,000. $150,000 of costs were added by the assembling department:

Direct materials	$ 96,000
Direct labor	36,000
Factory overhead applied	18,000
	$150,000

539   8,000 units were completed and transferred to the finishing department.

At June 30, 4,000 units were still in work in process. The degree of completion of work in process at June 30, was as follows:

Direct materials	90%
Direct labor	70%
Factory overhead applied	35%

Required

Prepare in good form a cost of production report for the assembling department for the month of June. Show supporting computations in good form. The report should include (a) equivalent units of production, (b) total manufacturing costs, (c) cost per equivalent unit, (d) dollar amount of ending work in process, (e) dollar amount of inventory cost transferred out.

15-24 Alternative format. (W. Crum) Study Appendix 15B. The Doral Company has the following data for the month of October:

	DEPARTMENT A	DEPARTMENT B
Beginning inventory in process:	2,000 units	2,000 units
Prior department cost*	0	$4,600
Direct materials added last month	$2,000 (100%)	$3,200 (80%)
Conversion costs added last month	$900 (60%)	$800 (40%)
Units put in process this month	30,000	29,000
Direct materials added this month	$30,968	$56,580
Conversion costs added this month	$41,800	$29,803
Units completed and transferred	29,000	30,000
Ending inventory in process:	3,000 units	1,000 units
Direct materials content	90%	50%
Conversion costs	50%	30%

*These are transferred-in costs.

Required

Using weighted-average costing, prepare a production-cost report for each department. Show the cost of goods completed and transferred and also show the cost of the ending work in process. Carry any decimals to 5 places.

15-25 FIFO costing. Refer to the preceding problem. Using FIFO costing, repeat the requirements.

15-26 Two departments; two months. (W. Vatter) One of the products of this company is manufactured by passing it through two processes. The (direct) materials are started into production at the beginning of Process 1 and are passed directly from Process 1 to Process 2 without inventory between the processes. Operating data for two months are as follows:

January

Process 1.   No initial work in process. During the month, 800 units were put into process and $8,000 was charged to this account for direct materials. Conversion costs incurred during the month were $2,800. Six hundred units were finished and transferred to Process 2. The work in process at January 31 was one-half finished.

Process 2.   No work in process on January 1. The work transferred from Process 1 was received and conversion costs of $2,000 were incurred to complete 300 units. At the end of the month, 300 units one-third finished remained in process.

February

Process 1.   Six hundred units of direct material were put into process at a total cost of $6,000. Conversion costs incurred were $2,550. At the end of the month, there were 300 units still in the process, two-thirds finished.

Process 2.   Conversion costs charged to this process for February were $2,640. On February 28, there were 300 units still in the process, two-thirds finished.

There is no spoilage in either of the processes; all units unfinished at the beginning of the month are completed within that month.

Required Prepare production-cost reports for each process for each month on a weighted-average basis.

15-27 FIFO costing. Refer to the preceding problem. Using FIFO costing, repeat the requirements.

15-28 Weighted-average process costing. The following information relates to one department operating under a process-cost system: Work in process, December 1, 19_1, 1,000 units, 40% complete, consisting of $8,703 of direct materials and $5,036 of conversion costs. Production completed for December, 8,200 units; work in process, December 31, 19_1, 800 units, 20% complete.

All direct materials are introduced at the start of the process, while conversion costs are incurred evenly throughout the process. Direct materials added during December were $72,000; conversion costs were $83,580.

Required Using weighted averages, show a schedule of equivalent units and a production-cost report. Also prepare a summary entry for the transfer of completed goods to finished stock. Carry decimals to 3 places.

15-29 FIFO costing. Refer to the preceding problem. Using FIFO costing, repeat the requirements.

15-30 Standard process costs. Refer to the preceding problem. Assume standard costs per finished unit as follows: direct materials, $8.50; conversion costs, $10.00.

1. Compute standard costs of goods transferred and still in process.
2. Give the total variances for current performance on direct materials and conversion costs.

15-31 Weighted-average process costing. (CPA) You are engaged in the audit of the December 31, 19_8, financial statements of Spirit Corporation, a manufacturer of a digital watch. You are attempting to verify the costing of the ending inventory of work in process and finished goods, which was recorded on Spirit's books as follows:

	UNITS	COST
Work in process (50% complete as to labor and overhead)	300,000	$ 660,960
Finished goods	200,000	$1,009,800

Materials are added to production at the beginning of the manufacturing process, and overhead is applied to each product at the rate of 60% of direct-labor costs. There was no finished-goods inventory on January 1, 19_8. A review of Spirit's inventory-cost records disclosed the following information:

	UNITS	COSTS Materials	Labor
Work in process, January 1, 19_8 (80% complete as to labor and overhead)	200,000	$ 200,000	$ 315,000
Units started in production	1,000,000		
Material costs, current period		$1,300,000	
Labor costs, current period			$1,995,000
Units completed	900,000		

Required 1. Prepare schedules as of December 31, 19_8, to compute the following:
a. Equivalent units of production using the weighted-average method
b. Unit costs of production of materials, labor, and overhead

c. Costing of the finished-goods inventory and work-in-process inventory

2. Prepare the necessary journal entry to correctly state the inventory of finished goods and work in process, assuming the books have not been closed. (Ignore income tax considerations.)

15-32 Basic standard costing. Grand Clock Company uses a standard-cost accounting system for manufacturing some of the parts used in making large clocks. Below is a summary of the June operations of the first process for one of these parts:

Beginning inventory of work in process	none
Units started in June	1,300
Ending inventory, 100% completed for direct materials, 70% completed for conversion costs	200
Standard unit costs:	
Direct materials	$ 6
Direct labor and factory overhead	$ 10
Total "actual" costs incurred during June:	
Direct materials	$ 8,050
Conversion costs	$12,960

Required

1. Compute the total standard cost of units transferred out in June and the total standard cost of the June 30 inventory of work in process.
2. Compute the total June variances for direct-materials cost and conversion cost.

15-33 Standard costing with beginning and ending work in process. The Victoria Corporation uses a standard-costing system for its manufacturing operations. Standard costs for the Cooking Process are $2 per unit for direct materials and $3 per unit for conversion costs. All direct materials are introduced at the beginning of the process, but conversion costs are incurred uniformly throughout the process. The operating summary for May included the following data for the Cooking Process:

> Work-in-process inventories:
>   May 1, 3,000 units, 60% completed
>   May 31, 5,000 units, 50% completed
> Units started in May, 20,000
> Units completed and transferred out of Cooking in May, 18,000
> Additional ("actual") costs incurred for Cooking during May:
>   Direct materials, $41,500
>   Conversion cost, $57,000

Required

1. Compute the total standard cost of units transferred out in May and the total standard cost of the May 31 inventory of work in process.
2. Compute the total May variances for direct-materials cost and conversion cost.

15-34 Weighted averages. The Dyer Processing Company had work in process at the beginning and end of 19_1 as follows:

	PERCENTAGE OF COMPLETION	
	Direct Materials	Conversion Costs
January 1, 19_1—3,000 units	40%	10%
December 31, 19_1—2,000 units	80%	40%

The company completed 40,000 units of finished goods during 19_1. Manufacturing costs incurred during 19_1 were: direct materials, $242,600; conversion costs, $445,200.

Inventory at January 1, 19_1, was carried at a cost of $10,600 (direct materials, $7,000; conversion costs, $3,600).

Assuming weighted average:

Required

1. Compute equivalent production for 19_1 for (a) direct materials and (b) conversion costs.
2. What is the proper cost of ending goods in process?

15-35 Standard process costs.   Refer to the preceding problem. If the standard cost for direct materials is $5 per finished unit and the standard cost for conversion costs is $10 per finished unit, what would be the total standard cost of work performed during 19_1?

Spoilage, Waste, Reworked Units, and Scrap

Terminology • Spoilage in general • Process costing and spoilage • Job costing and spoilage • Reworked units • Accounting for scrap • Comparison of accounting for spoilage, rework, and scrap • Some applications to standard costs • Appendix: A closer look at spoilage under process costing

Problems of spoilage, waste, reworked units, and scrap are widespread. This chapter describes a general approach to this entire area. Managerial cost accounting must distinguish between normal and abnormal spoilage, mainly for keeping management informed, but also for product costing.

In recent years, managers have paid more attention to the cost of spoilage, waste, and reworked units. Dramatic reductions in these costs have been reported as justifications for firms investing in techniques such as just-in-time (JIT) inventory systems, computer-integrated manufacturing (CIM), and materials resources planning (MRP). Accounting systems that record these costs in a timely and detailed way help management make more-informed decisions about investing in techniques such as JIT, CIM, and MRP. (See chapters 17 and 21 for more discussion about the techniques.)

TERMINOLOGY

The definitions and accounting in this area vary considerably from organization to organization. This chapter distinguishes between the various terms as follows:

Spoilage. Unacceptable units of production that are discarded and sold for disposal value. Spoilage may be partially completed or fully completed units. Net spoilage cost is the total of the costs applied to the point of rejection, and either plus disposal costs or less net disposal value.

Waste. Inputs that do not become part of the outputs. The most common example is material that is lost or evaporates or shrinks or is a residue with no economic value. Examples are gases, dust, and toxic residues. Sometimes waste disposal is costly; for instance, nuclear waste.

Reworked Units. Unacceptable units of production that are subsequently reworked and sold as acceptable finished goods. Such units may be sold through regular marketing channels or alternate channels, depending on the characteristics of the product and on the available alternatives.

Scrap. Inputs that do not become part of the outputs but have relatively minor economic values. Scrap may be either sold or reused. Examples are shavings and short lengths from woodworking operations and sprues, ingots, and flash from a casting operation in a foundry.

Some causes of spoilage, rework, waste, or scrap are largely beyond the control of management. An example is a mining company that processes batches of ore having a varying mix of valuable metals and waste products. Many other causes can be controlled by management; for example, consider production workers paying inadequate attention to quality, poorly maintained machines being used, and inadequate lighting.

SPOILAGE IN GENERAL

Management implications and factor combination

The problem of spoilage is important from many aspects, the most important being that of managerial planning and control.[1] Managers must first attempt to select the most economical production method or process. Then they must see that spoilage is controlled within chosen predetermined limits so that excessive spoilage does not occur.

Much experimentation has occurred to see whether the near elimination of spoilage is economically justified. After all, spoilage affects other costs, including material handling, storage, and costs of disruptions in production. The problem of spoilage is regarded as a subpart of a larger problem. For instance, a division of the IBM Corporation compiles an analysis of costs called the "costs of quality." Included in the latter are comparisons through time and between manufacturing techniques of the current costs of spoiled goods, waste, reworked units, scrap, material-handling costs, storage costs, and warranty costs. (See Chapter 21 for further discussion of accounting for the cost of quality.)

There is an unmistakable trend in manufacturing to increase quality. Why? Because managers have found that improved quality and intolerance for high spoilage have lowered overall costs and increased sales.[2] The procedures described in this chapter help identify the costs of spoilage as special management problems.

---

[1]The helpful suggestions of Samuel Laimon, University of Saskatchewan, are gratefully acknowledged.

[2]See L. McAulay, "Reporting Systems for Quality Cost Variance," *Management Accounting,* Great Britain, February 1985, p. 62.

That is, spoilage costs are not ignored or buried as an unidentified part of the costs of good product.

Normal spoilage

Working within the selected set of production conditions, management must establish the rate of spoilage that is to be regarded as *normal*. **Normal spoilage is what arises under efficient operating conditions; it is an inherent result of the particular process and is thus uncontrollable in the short run.** Costs of normal spoilage are typically viewed as a part of the costs of *good* production, because the attaining of good units necessitates the simultaneous appearance of spoiled units. In other words, normal spoilage is planned spoilage, in the sense that the choice of a given combination of factors of production entails a spoilage rate that management is willing to accept.

Abnormal spoilage

Abnormal spoilage is spoilage that is not expected to arise under efficient operating conditions; it is not an inherent part of the selected production process. Most of this spoilage is usually regarded as controllable, in the sense that the first-line supervisor can exert influence over inefficiency. Such causes as machinery breakdowns, accidents, and inferior materials are typically regarded as being subject to some manager's influence. Costs of abnormal spoilage are the costs of inferior products that should be written off directly as losses for the period in which detection occurs. For the most informative feedback, the Loss from Abnormal Spoilage account should appear on a detailed income statement as a separate line item and not be buried as an indistinguishable part of the cost of goods manufactured.

General accounting procedures for spoilage

Before discussing debits and credits for spoiled goods, let us try to relate spoiled goods to two major purposes of cost accounting: control and product costing. Accounting for control is primarily concerned with charging responsibility centers for costs *as incurred*. Product costing is concerned with *applying* to inventory or other appropriate accounts the costs *already incurred*. Where does costing for spoiled goods fit into this framework? First, it must be made clear that the costs of both normal and abnormal spoiled goods are, at least in concept, *product costs*. But abnormal spoilage is a cost of bad product. So it really is not regarded as an inventoriable cost. Instead, abnormal spoilage is written off as a loss immediately when it is detected:

	GOOD-PRODUCT COSTS—INVENTORIABLE	BAD-PRODUCT COSTS— CHARGED OFF AS A LOSS IMMEDIATELY
Cost of spoiled goods—normal	Yes	No
Cost of spoiled goods—abnormal	No	Yes

The existence of spoiled goods does not involve any additional cost beyond the amount already incurred before detection of spoilage.[3] Therefore, in account-

[3]Where spoilage is not detected until completion of goods, spoiled units require the same effort as good units. In other words, a laborer can be performing with equal efficiency on all goods and yet turn out some spoiled units because of inferior materials, worn cutting tools, and the like. So labor efficiency may be very satisfactory, but spoilage may nevertheless be a major problem. Thus a worker can efficiently turn out spoiled goods.

ing for spoiled goods, we are not dealing with new cost incurrence. Our objectives are

1. To accumulate data to spotlight the cost of spoilage so that management is made aware of its magnitude
2. To identify the *nature* of the spoilage and distinguish between costs of normal spoilage and abnormal spoilage

Depending on the product(s) or departments involved, there is a bewildering mass of treatments in practice, which vary from the inexcusable to the highly informative. This chapter cannot possibly cover all the theoretical and practical ramifications. It will try to contrast conceptual treatments with some methods used in practice.

A study of the entries in the conceptual treatment in Exhibit 16-1 will show that when a product is spoiled, some debit must be made to balance the necessary credit to Work in Process. Furthermore, some means must be found to charge normal spoilage to good inventory and abnormal spoilage to a loss account. The entries in the conceptual treatment use a Cost of Spoiled Goods account to high-

EXHIBIT 16-1
General Accounting for Spoilage

Assume: Units worked on		1,100	Assume a unit cost $10, not including any spoilage allowance. Total costs to account for are 1,100 × $10, or $11,000.
Good units completed	1,000		
Normal spoilage	30		
Abnormal spoilage	70	1,100	

CONCEPTUAL TREATMENT			PRACTICAL TREATMENT		
	Debit	Credit		Debit	Credit
1. Work in process	11,000		1. (Same.)		
Stores, accrued payroll, overhead applied		11,000			
1,100 units worked on.					
2. Cost of spoiled goods	1,000		2,3,4. Finished goods	10,300	
Work in process		1,000	Work in process		10,300
100 units spoiled.			1,000 good units		
3. Finished goods	10,000		completed @ $10		
Work in process		10,000	plus normal spoil-		
1,000 good units			age of 30 units		
completed.			@ $10. Total costs		
			of 1,000 good units		
4. Finished goods	300		is thus $10,300.		
Cost of spoiled goods		300			
Normal-spoilage					
allowance, 30 units.					
5. Loss from abnormal			5. Loss from abnormal		
spoilage	700		spoilage*	700	
Cost of spoiled goods		700	Work in process		700
Abnormal spoilage,			Abnormal spoilage,		
70 units.			70 units.		

*In practice, abnormal spoilage is often not isolated at all. Instead the $700 cost is erroneously lumped with the other costs to show a total cost of $11,000 and a unit cost of $11 for the 1,000 good units produced. However, the $700 abnormal spoilage should not be concealed as a part of the cost of the good product.

light the nature of the problem and to stress the notion that the costs applied to Work in Process are initially product costs that are then transferred either to Finished Goods or to a loss account. In practice, Cost of Spoiled Goods is not used, and the second set of entries in Exhibit 16-1 is more likely to be found. Notice that the two sets would produce the same account balances.

PROCESS COSTING AND SPOILAGE

Although this discussion of process costing will emphasize accounting for spoilage, the ideas here are equally applicable to waste (shrinkage, evaporation, or lost units). Again we must distinguish between control and product costing. For control, most companies use some version of estimated or standard costs that incorporates an allowance for normal spoilage, shrinkage, or waste into the estimate or standard. This section emphasizes product costing in so-called actual or normal process-costing systems.[4]

Count all spoilage

As a general rule, accumulate the costs of spoilage separately from other product costs. Then allocate normal spoilage costs to finished goods or work in process, depending on where in the production cycle the spoilage is assumed to take place. Spoilage is typically assumed to occur at the stage of completion where inspection takes place, because spoilage is not detected until this point. **Normal spoilage need not be allocated to units that have failed to reach this point in the production process, because the spoiled units are related solely to the units that have passed the inspection point.**

Many writers on process costing advocate ignoring the computation of equivalent units for spoilage, shrinkage, or waste. The reason cited in favor of this short-cut technique is that it automatically spreads normal-spoilage costs over good units through the use of higher equivalent unit costs. However, the results of this short-cut are not as accurate.

Consider the example of direct materials. Suppose $1,800 of direct materials are introduced at the start of a process. Production data are: 1,000 units started, 500 good units completed, 100 units spoiled (all normal spoilage), and 400 units in ending work in process. Spoilage is detected upon completion.

The direct-material unit costs would be computed and then applied, as shown on the top of the next page.

Ignoring the equivalent units for spoilage decreases equivalent units; hence a higher unit cost is computed. Therefore a $2.00 unit cost (instead of a $1.80 unit cost) is applied to work in process that has not reached the inspection point. Simultaneously, the direct-material costs applied to good units completed are too low ($1,000 instead of $1,080). Consequently, the 400 units in ending work in process contain costs of spoilage of $80 ($800 − $720) in this example that do not pertain to such units and that in fact belong with the good units completed. The 400 units in work in process undoubtedly include some units that will be detected as spoiled in a subsequent period. In effect, these units will bear two charges for spoilage. The ending work in process is being charged for spoilage in the current period, and it

[4]This section assumes that you have studied Chapter 15.

	ACCURATE METHOD: COUNT EQUIVALENT UNITS FOR SPOILAGE	INACCURATE METHOD: IGNORE EQUIVALENT UNITS FOR SPOILAGE
Costs to account for	$1,800	$1,800
Equivalent units	1,000	900
Costs per equivalent unit	$ 1.80	$ 2.00
Applied to:		
Good units completed, 500 × $1.80 =	$ 900	$1,000*
Add: Normal spoilage, 100 × $1.80 =	180	—
Costs transferred out	$1,080	$1,000
Work in process, ending, 400 × $1.80 =	720	800†
Costs accounted for	$1,800	$1,800

*500 × $2.00 = $1,000.
†400 × $2.00 = $800.

will be charged anew when inspection occurs as the units are completed. Such cost distortions would not occur under the accurate method: including spoiled units in computing equivalent units.

Base for computing normal spoilage

Normal spoilage should be computed from the good output, or from the *normal input*—not from the total input. Total input includes the abnormal as well as the normal spoilage and is therefore unacceptable as a basis for computing normal spoilage. For example, if the normal rate of spoilage of polio vaccine is sloppily stated as 5% of input, an input of 100,000 cubic centimeters would be expected to produce 5,000 cubic centimeters of spoilage. Now, if 85,500 cubic centimeters of good units are produced, normal spoilage is not 5,000 centimeters (5% of 100,000), because it should have taken only 90,000 cubic centimeters of input to get 85,500 cubic centimeters of good vaccine (85,500 ÷ 95% = 90,000). If normal spoilage is precisely expressed as 5% of normal input, the good output should be 95% of normal input. In this case, normal spoilage would be 4,500 cubic centimeters (5% of 90,000) and abnormal spoilage would be 10,000 cubic centimeters (100,000 minus 90,000). These relationships are summarized:

			RELATIONSHIPS	
Input	100,000 c.c.			
Output:				
Good units	85,500 c.c.		95%	
Normal spoilage	4,500 c.c.	90,000 c.c.*	5%	100%
Abnormal spoilage		10,000 c.c.		
		100,000 c.c.		

*Normal input.

Thus, in this case we should express the normal-spoilage rate more accurately either as 5% of *normal input* or as ⁵⁄₉₅ of good output.

Illustrative problem

EXAMPLE 1

One of a company's products is manufactured in the processing department. Direct materials for this product are put in at the beginning of the production cycle: conversion costs are incurred evenly over the cycle. Some units of this product are spoiled as a result of defects not ascertainable before inspection of finished units. Normally the spoiled units are 10% of the good output.

At January 1, the inventory of work in process of this product was $29,600, representing 2,000 pounds of direct material ($15,000) and conversion cost of $14,600 representing 80% completion. During January, 8,000 pounds of material ($61,000) were put into production. Direct labor of $40,200 was charged to the process. Factory overhead is assigned at the rate of 100% of direct-labor cost. Therefore the total conversion costs for January were $40,200 + $40,200 = $80,400. The inventory at January 31 consisted of 1,500 pounds, 66⅔% finished. Seventy-two hundred pounds of good product were transferred to finished goods after inspection.

Spoiled units were 2,000 + 8,000 − 1,500 − 7,200 = 1,300. Normal spoilage was 10% of the 7,200 good units completed, or 720. Thus abnormal spoilage was 1,300 − 720 = 580 units.

<table>
<tr><td>Required</td><td>Using weighted-average and then FIFO, show calculations of</td></tr>
</table>

1. Equivalent units of production for January
2. The dollar and unit amount of the abnormal spoilage during January
3. Total product costs transferred to finished-goods inventory
4. The cost of work-in-process inventory at January 31
5. Journal entries for transfers out of work-in-process inventory

Weighted-average and spoilage

The answers to requirements 1 through 4 under the weighted-average method are shown in Exhibit 16-2. The basic five-step procedure introduced in the preceding chapter needs only slight modification to handle spoilage. The following observations pertain to both the weighted-average and FIFO methods:

Step 1: Summarize physical units. Identify both normal and abnormal spoilage.

Step 2: Compute output in terms of equivalent units. Compute equivalent units for spoilage in the same way as for good units. Because inspection occurs upon completion in Example 1, the same amount of work was done on each spoiled unit and each completed good unit.

Step 3: Summarize total costs to account for. The details of this step do not differ from those in the preceding chapter.

Step 4: Compute unit costs. The details of this step do not differ from those in the preceding chapter. **However, the divisor includes the work applicable to the spoiled units.**

Step 5: Apply total costs to units completed and in process. This step now includes computation of the cost of spoiled goods in the same manner as the cost of good units.

As shown in Exhibit 16-2, the costs of abnormal spoilage are assigned to a loss account, 580 units × $17.60 = $10,208. The costs of normal spoilage, $12,672, are added to the costs of their related good units.[5]

An alternative way to think about spoilage would be in terms of the normal spoilage cost per good unit passing inspection: $17.60 ÷ 10 units = $1.76. In Ex-

---

[5]This illustration assumes inspection upon completion. In contrast, inspection may take place at some other stage—say, at the halfway point in the production cycle. In such a case, normal-spoilage costs would be added to completed goods and to the units in process that are more than half completed.

EXHIBIT 16-2

A Processing Department
Production-Cost Report
For the Month Ended January 31, 19_1
Weighted-Average Method

			(STEP 2) EQUIVALENT UNITS	
FLOW OF PRODUCTION	(STEP 1) PHYSICAL UNITS	Direct Materials	Conversion Costs	
Work in process, beginning inventory	2,000 (80%)*			
Started	8,000			
To account for	10,000			
Abnormal spoilage	580	580	580	
Normal spoilage	720	720	720	
Good units completed and transferred out	7,200	7,200	7,200	
Work in process, ending inventory	1,500 (66⅔%)*	1,500	1,000	
Accounted for	10,000			
Total work done to date		10,000	9,500	

				DETAILS	
COSTS	TOTALS	Direct Materials	Conversion Costs	Equivalent Whole Unit	
(Step 3) Work in process, beginning inventory	$ 29,600	$15,000	$14,600		
Current costs	141,400	61,000	80,400		
Total costs to account for	$171,000	$76,000	$95,000		
(Step 4) Divide by equivalent units		÷10,000	÷9,500		
Cost per equivalent unit		$ 7.60	$ 10.00	$17.60	
(Step 5) Apply total costs to units completed and in process:					
Abnormal spoilage (580)	$ 10,208			580($17.60)	
Units completed and transferred out (7,200):					
Costs before adding spoilage	$126,720			7,200($17.60)	
Normal spoilage	12,672			720($17.60)	
Total cost transferred out	$139,392				
Work in process, ending inventory (1,500):					
Direct materials	$ 11,400	1,500($7.60)			
Conversion costs	10,000		1,000($10.00)		
Total work in process	$ 21,400				
Total costs accounted for	$171,000				

*Degree of completion for conversion costs of this department at the dates of the work-in-process inventories. Note that direct-material costs are fully completed at each of these dates, because in this department materials are introduced at the beginning of the process.

hibit 16-2, the application of normal spoilage costs to the goods completed would be computed as 7,200 units × $1.76 = $12,672.

To provide an overall picture, Exhibit 16-2 shows the results of all five steps in a single exhibit. Obviously, Steps 1 and 2 could be presented in a separate exhibit, as was done in the preceding chapter.

Managers should try to have inspection as early in the production process as technically possible. This will reduce the direct materials and conversion costs applied to spoiled units. Thus, in the Exhibit 16-2 example, if inspection can occur when units are 80% complete as to conversion costs and 100% complete as to direct materials, the company can avoid incurring the final 20% of conversion costs on the spoiled units.

FIFO method and spoilage

As explained in Chapter 15, except for a final subtraction for the equivalent units of work done on the beginning work in process prior to the current period, Steps 1 and 2 are unaffected by using FIFO instead of the weighted-average method. Therefore equivalent units are computed as follows:

	DIRECT MATERIALS	CONVERSION COSTS
Total work done to date (from Exhibit 16-2)	10,000	9,500
Less equivalent units for work done on beginning inventory in previous period:		
Direct materials, 2,000 × 100%	2,000	
Conversion costs, 2,000 × 80%		1,600
Work done during current period only (Step 2)	8,000	7,900

Exhibit 16-3 is the production-cost report. As before, Step 3 computes the total costs to account for; Step 4, unit costs; and Step 5, the application of costs to units completed and in ending work in process.

Journal entries

A summary production-cost report is shown in Exhibit 16-4. It is confined to physical units and the total costs that flow through the Work in Process account. If managers prefer, the supporting computations could be embodied in a more elaborate production-cost report like Exhibit 16-2.

The information in Exhibit 16-4 supports the following journal entries (the answers to requirement 5 of the illustrative problem):

	WEIGHTED AVERAGE		FIFO	
	Debit	Credit	Debit	Credit
Finished goods	139,392		139,060	
Work in process—processing department		139,392		139,060
To transfer good units completed in January.				
Loss from abnormal spoilage	10,208		10,325	
Work in process—processing department		10,208		10,325
To recognize abnormal spoilage in January.				

EXHIBIT 16-3

A Processing Department
Production-Cost Report
For the Month Ended January 31, 19_1
First-in, First-Out Method

	TOTALS	DETAILS Direct Materials	DETAILS Conversion Costs	DETAILS Equivalent Whole Unit
(Step 3) Work in process, beginning inventory	$ 29,600	(costs incurred on work done in preceding period)		
Current costs	141,400	$61,000	$80,400	
Total costs to account for	$171,000			
(Step 4) Divide by equivalent units		÷8,000	÷7,900	
Cost per equivalent unit		$7.6250*	$10.1772*	$17.8022*
(Step 5) Apply total costs to units completed and in process:				
Work in process, end:				
Direct materials	$ 11,438	1,500 ($7.6250)		
Conversion costs	10,177		1,000 ($10.1772)	
Total work in process (1,500 units)	21,615			
Abnormal spoilage (580 units)	10,325			580 ($17.8022)
Completed and transferred (7,200 units):				
$171,000 − $21,615 − $10,325	139,060†‡			
Total costs accounted for	$171,000			

*Unit costs are carried out to several decimal places to prevent rounding errors later.
†The accuracy of computing the cost of goods completed and transferred can be proven as follows:

Work in process, beginning, which is transferred out first	$ 29,600
Additional cost to complete:	
Conversion costs: 2,000 × (1 − .80) × $10.1772	4,071
Cost of units started and completed this month	
(7,200 − 2,000) × $17.8022	92,571
Normal spoilage (720 × $17.8022)	12,818§
Total cost of goods completed and transferred out	$139,060

‡The average cost of these is $139,060 ÷ 7,200 units = $19.3139.
§For convenience we assume that all spoilage relates to units completed during this period.

Assumptions for allocating normal spoilage

Spoilage might actually *occur* at various points or stages of the production process, but spoilage is typically not *detected* until one or more specific points of inspection. The cost of spoiled units is assumed to be all cost incurred prior to inspection. The unit costs of abnormal and normal spoilage are the same when both are detected simultaneously. However, situations might arise where abnormal spoilage is detected at a different point than normal spoilage. In such cases, the unit cost of abnormal spoilage would differ from the unit cost of normal spoilage.

Various assumptions prevail regarding how to allocate the cost of normal spoilage between completed units and the ending inventory of work in process. A popular approach follows.

When normal spoilage is presumed to occur at a specific point in the production process, allocate its cost (e.g., a unit cost of $17.60 in Exhibit 16-2) over all units

553

EXHIBIT 16-4
A Processing Department
Summary Production-Cost Report
For the Month Ended January 31, 19_1

| | | TOTAL COSTS | |
FLOW OF PRODUCTION	PHYSICAL UNITS	Weighted-average Method	FIFO
Work in process, beginning inventory	2,000	$ 29,600	$ 29,600
Started	8,000	141,400	141,400
To account for	10,000	$171,000	$171,000
Good units completed and transferred out	7,200 ⎫		
Normal spoilage	720 ⎰	$139,392	$139,060
Abnormal spoilage	580	10,208	10,325
Work in process, ending inventory	1,500	21,400	21,615
Accounted for	10,000	$171,000	$171,000

that have passed this point. In our example, spoilage is presumed to occur upon completion, so no cost of normal spoilage is allocated to the ending work in process.

Whether the cost of normal spoilage is allocated to the units in ending work in process strictly depends on whether they have passed the point of inspection. For example, if the inspection point is presumed to be the halfway stage of conversion, work in process that is 70% completed would be allocated a full measure of normal-spoilage cost. But work in process that is 40% completed would not be allocated any normal-spoilage cost.

So the point of inspection is the key to the application of spoilage costs. Avoid the idea that normal spoilage costs attach solely to units transferred out. Thus, if units in ending work in process have passed inspection, they should have normal spoilage costs added to them.

The appendix to this chapter contains additional discussion concerning various assumptions about spoilage.

JOB COSTING AND SPOILAGE

Job-cost accounting for spoilage in practice varies considerably. Where spoiled goods have a disposal value, the net cost of spoilage is computed by deducting disposal value from the costs of the spoiled goods accumulated to the point of inspection.

Spoilage is often considered as a normal characteristic of a given production cycle. For example, machines might malfunction at random. Then the causes of spoilage would be attributable to work done on all jobs. Net spoilage cost is budgeted in practice as a part of factory overhead, so that the budgeted overhead rate includes a provision for normal-spoilage cost. Therefore normal-spoilage cost is spread, through overhead application, over all jobs rather than being loaded on particular jobs only.

To illustrate, assume that five pieces out of a lot of fifty were normally spoiled. Costs accumulated to the point of inspection were $100 per unit. Disposal value is estimated at \$30 per unit. As the normal spoilage is detected, the spoiled goods are inventoried, overhead control is debited for the net cost of spoilage, and work in process is credited for the costs applied to the goods up to the point of inspection:[6]

Stores control (spoiled goods at disposal value)	150	
Department factory-overhead control (normal spoilage)	350	
Work in process (particular job)		500

Items in parentheses indicate subsidiary postings.

Another method used, where management finds it helpful for control or for pricing, is to credit specific jobs with only the disposal value of normally spoiled units, thus forcing the remaining good units in the job to bear net normal-spoilage costs. Under this method, the budgeted overhead rate would *not* include a provision for normal-spoilage cost because the spoilage would be viewed as being directly attributable to the specifications of particular jobs instead of being attributable to general factory conditions or processes. The journal entry, with the same data as were just used, follows:

Stores control (spoiled goods at disposal value)	150	
Work in process (particular jobs)		150

REWORKED UNITS

Reworked units are unacceptable units of production that are subsequently reworked and sold as "firsts" or "seconds." Management needs effective control over such actions, because supervisors are tempted to rework rather than to junk unacceptable units. If control is not exercised, supervisors may rework many bad units instead of having them sold outright at a greater economic advantage. Rework should be undertaken only if incremental revenue is expected to exceed incremental costs.

Unless there are special reasons for charging rework to the jobs or batches that contained the bad units, the cost of the extra materials, labor, and so on, are in practice usually charged to factory overhead.[7] Thus, once again we see that rework is usually spread over all jobs or batches as a part of a budgeted overhead rate. Assume that the five spoiled pieces used in our prior illustration are reworked and sold as firsts through regular marketing channels. Entries follow:

---

[6]Conceptually, the prevailing treatment just described can be criticized primarily because *product costs* are being charged back to Department Factory-Overhead Control, which logically should accumulate only *costs incurred*, rather than both cost incurrence and product costs.

[7]The criticisms of the practical treatment for spoiled goods are also applicable to the treatment described here. The overhead-incurred and overhead-applied accounts may be padded for amounts that in themselves did not necessitate overhead incurrence.

Original cost accumulations:	Work-in-process control	500	
	Stores control		200
	Accrued payroll		200
	Factory overhead applied		100
Rework (figures assumed):	Departmental factory-overhead control (rework)	190	
	Stores control		40
	Accrued payroll		100
	Factory overhead applied		50
Transfer to finished stock:	Finished-goods control	500	
	Work-in-process control		500

ACCOUNTING FOR SCRAP

Scrap is input that does not become part of the output but has relatively minor economic value. There are two major aspects of accounting for scrap: control and product costing. Items like metal chips, filings, and wood shavings should be quantified by weighing, counting, or some other expedient means. Norms or standards should be determined because excessive scrap indicates inefficiency. *Scrap records* are prepared as source documents for periodic scrap reports that summarize the amount of scrap and compare it with budgeted norms or standards. Scrap should be returned to the storeroom to be held for sale or for reuse. Scrap should be accounted for in some manner, not only from the point of view of efficiency but because scrap is often a tempting source for theft or manipulation.

There are many methods of accounting for scrap. Typically, scrap is not assigned any cost; instead its sales value is regarded as an offset to factory overhead, as follows:

Scrap returned to storeroom:	No journal entry.		
	(Memo of quantity received is entered on the perpetual record.)		
Sale of scrap:	Cash or Accounts receivable	xx	
	Department factory-overhead control		xx
	Posting made to subsidiary record—"Sale of Scrap" column on departmental cost record.		

This method is both simple and accurate enough in theory to justify its wide use. A normal amount of scrap is an inevitable result of production operations. Basically, this method does not link scrap with any particular physical product; instead, because of practical difficulties, all products bear regular production costs without any particular credit for scrap sales except in an indirect manner. What really happens in such situations is that sales of scrap are considered when budgeted overhead rates are being set. Thus the budgeted overhead rate is lower than it would be if no credit for scrap sales were allowed in the overhead budget.

An alternative method in a job-cost situation would be to trace sales of scrap to the jobs that yielded the scrap. This method is used only when it is feasible and economically desirable. For example, there may be agreements between the company and particular customers that provide for charging specific, difficult jobs with all rework or spoilage costs and crediting such jobs with all scrap sales arising therefrom. Entries follow:

Scrap returned to storeroom: No journal entry.
                  (Memo of quantity received and related job is entered on the perpetual record.)

Sale of scrap:
          Cash or Accounts receivable   xx
               Work in process   xx
          Posting made to specific job order.

The illustrations above assume that no inventory value is assigned to scrap as it is returned to the storeroom. However, sometimes the value is significant and there is a noteworthy time lag between storing scrap and selling it. Then there is justification for inventorying scrap at some conservative estimate of net realizable value so that production costs and related scrap recovery may be recognized in the same period.

Some companies tend to delay sales of scrap until the price is most attractive. Volatile price fluctuations are typical for scrap metal. In these cases, if scrap inventory becomes significant, it should be inventoried at some "reasonable" value—a difficult task in the face of volatile market prices.

Scrap is sometimes reused as direct material rather than being sold as scrap. Then it should be debited to Stores as a class of direct material and carried at its net realizable value.[8]

COMPARISON OF ACCOUNTING FOR SPOILAGE, REWORK, AND SCRAP

The basic approach to the accounting for spoilage, rework, and scrap should distinguish among the normal amount that is common to all jobs, the normal amount that is attributable to specific jobs, and abnormal amounts. The following entries recapitulate the preceding examples. Note the parallel approach to the three categories:

---

[8]Kaplan observed that "it is customary to assign to scrap at least its raw-material value were it to be purchased or sold on the open market. Perhaps, however, the scrap value should be reduced by the increased materials handling and storage costs, plus the cost of disrupting the production schedule, when defective output is produced. This places more of a premium on eliminating defective items in the production process." R. Kaplan, "Measuring Manufacturing Performance: A New Challenge for Managerial Accounting Research," *Accounting Review,* October 1983, p. 701.

SPOILAGE COST (NET $350)

Normal (common to all jobs)	Stores	150	
	Departmental factory overhead control	350	
	Work in process		500
Normal (peculiar to specific jobs)	Stores	150	
	Work in process		150
Abnormal	Stores	150	
	Special loss account	350	
	Work in process		500

REWORK COST (ASSUMED AT $190)

Normal (common to all jobs)	Departmental factory overhead control	190	
	Stores		40
	Accrued payroll		100
	Factory overhead applied		50
Normal (peculiar to specific jobs)	Same as preceding entry except that the debit of $190 would be to Work in Process		
Abnormal	Same as preceding entry except that the debit of $190 would be to Special Loss account		

SCRAP VALUE RECOVERED ($100)

Normal (common to all jobs)	Stores or Cash or Accounts receivable	100	
	Departmental factory overhead control		100
Abnormal (peculiar to specific jobs)	Same as preceding entry except that the credit would be to Work in Process		

Although these journal entries have used job-order costing as an illustration, similar entries pertain to process costing. Of course, process costing, by definition, has no specific jobs for the identification of costs. Practices vary considerably from company to company.

SOME APPLICATIONS TO STANDARD COSTS

Waste

When standard-cost systems are used, allowance is made in the standard product costs for expected waste or scrap. Actual waste is usually computed by working back from product output. Waste in excess of standard is a direct-material efficiency (usage) variance. Unlike spoilage and scrap, waste can seldom be tagged and traced by physical identification.

Examples of waste that are not traced and specifically costed include paint or varnish adhering to the sides of its container, mill ends, shavings, and evaporation. Excess-material consumption is usually revealed through excess-material requisitions or through standard-yield percentages for such materials as lumber, chemicals, and ores. Thus, where 15,000 gallons of raw chemicals ordinarily produce 12,000 gallons of good finished product, the standard-yield percentage could be expressed as 80% of normal input. On the other hand, the waste percentage could be expressed as 20% of normal input or as 25% of good output.

Note that these percentages provide a physical standard that can be used without worrying about price changes. Furthermore, such a standard is easily understood and can readily be used as a timely index of efficiency—on an hourly or batch basis if desired.

Scrap

Material-efficiency standards usually include allowances for scrap. Although the allowance can be computed in various ways, standards are based on a careful study of the operation(s), not on historical data alone or on wild guesses. The standard cost of direct materials thus becomes (a) standard unit price times the standard input per finished unit, less (b) standard scrap price per unit times standard scrap weight loss per finished unit.

To illustrate, assume that a metal rod is fed into an automatic screw machine. About five inches (ten ounces) at one end of each 105-inch rod (210 ounces) are clutched by the chuck and cannot be used. This results in a "crop loss." It takes five ounces of metal to produce a finished unit that weighs four ounces. Thus each rod, after the crop loss of ten ounces, weighs 200 ounces and can produce $200 \div 5 = 40$ units. The standard starting lot size is 4,040 units, but the first 40 units are scrapped in setting up the run. Therefore the standard *finished* lot size is only 4,000 units, and the scrap piece loss is $40 \div 4,000 = 1\%$ of good output. Standard-cost computations follow:

	OUNCES	ASSUMED PRICE PER OUNCE	UNIT COST
Standard cost per unit:			
Finished piece	4.00		
Turnings	1.00		
Crop loss (10 oz. ÷ 40 units per rod)	0.25		
Subtotal, before scrap piece loss	5.25*		
Add 1% scrap piece loss	0.0525		
Total	5.3025	$.12	$.6363
Less credit for scrap (1.00 + 0.25 + 0.0525)	1.3025	.04	.0521
Standard cost per finished unit	4.00		$.5842

Or 210 ÷ 40 = 5.25 ounces, including turnings and crop loss.

Although standards for direct materials are built in this way for each operation, it is usually inexpedient to trace scrap to specific lots or operations. Reports are usually limited to monthly, or sometimes weekly, comparisons of standard costs of good units produced with the total "actual" charges to the department.

Spoilage

In practice, allowances for net spoilage cost and for rework are often incorporated into the flexible budget for overhead. Spoiled units are removed from Work in Process at standard costs and charged to Factory Overhead. Periodic comparisons of budget allowances with actual spoilage provide summary information for managerial control. If no spoilage is allowed, the budget provided may be zero. Rework is controlled in a similar manner. Day-to-day control is aided by spoilage tags prepared at the point of inspection. These tags, or a summary thereof, are promptly shown to the supervisor and other interested parties.

This procedure really spotlights spoilage and rework as special managerial problems, as opposed to, say, direct-material efficiency variances that are related to good units. For example, assume that the standard cost for a particular product is as follows:

Direct materials, 1 pound	$ 5.00
Direct labor, .1 hour	3.00
Factory overhead—variable	1.50
Factory overhead—fixed	1.50
Standard cost per unit	$11.00

Assume that no spoilage occurs, but that it takes 1,150 pounds of direct material to produce 1,000 good units:

Direct materials:		
Actual, 1,150 pounds @ $5.00		$5,750
Standard, 1,000 pounds @ $5.00		5,000
Efficiency variance		$ 750

Assume, instead, that 1,100 units were produced, but that 100 were spoiled because of careless machine operation. There would be two alternatives for analyzing such a variance. First consider the figures presented in the following table:

	COSTS INCURRED	STANDARD COSTS— GOOD OUTPUT	TOTAL VARIANCE
*Direct materials, 1,150 lbs.	$ 5,750	$ 5,000	$ 750 U
Direct labor, 110 hours	3,300	3,000	300 U
Factory overhead—variable	1,650	1,500	150 U
Factory overhead—fixed	1,650	1,500	150 U
	$12,350	$11,000	$1,350 U
*Standard materials allowed for good units		1,000 lbs.	
Standard materials allowed for spoiled units, which were spoiled by careless labor		100 lbs.	
Excess materials used in producing 1,100 units		50 lbs.	
Total		1,150 lbs.	

ANALYSIS ONE Analyze variances on the basis of good output only. This is the familiar way:

Direct-material efficiency variance	$5,750 − $5,000	$ 750
Direct-labor efficiency variance	$3,300 − $3,000	300
Variable-overhead total variance	$1,650 − $1,500	150
Fixed-overhead total variance	$1,650 − $1,500	150
Total variance explained		$1,350

ANALYSIS TWO Isolate a separate variance for spoilage, $1,100 (10% spoilage × $11,000), consisting of the four elements shown above. This approach would entail setting up a special Spoilage Variance account in the ledger. This account would represent the standard cost of spoiled work. Thus the other variance accounts would not reflect any spoilage effects:

	SPOILAGE VARIANCE	OTHER VARIANCES		TOTAL VARIANCE EXPLAINED
Direct materials	$ 500	Efficiency	$250 U	$ 750
Direct labor	300	—		300
Variable overhead	150	—		150
Fixed overhead	150	—		150
	$1,100		$250	$1,350

Recall that Chapter 6 provided an overview of variance analysis, pointing out that desired levels of detail may vary from organization to organization. Analysis One stops at one level, whereas Analysis Two pushes one step further. Consider the direct materials:

	ACTUAL COSTS INCURRED	ACTUAL INPUTS × STANDARD PRICES	STANDARD COSTS ALLOWED FOR GOOD AND SPOILED OUTPUT	STANDARD COSTS ALLOWED FOR GOOD OUTPUT
	1,150 lbs. × $5 $5,750	1,150 lbs. × $5 $5,750	1,100 lbs. × $5 $5,500	1,000 lbs. × $5 $5,000

ANALYSIS ONE ↑ Price variance, $0 ↑   Efficiency variance, $750 U   ↑
(150 lbs. × $5)

ANALYSIS TWO   Nonspoilage-related efficiency variance, $250 U ↑   Spoilage-related efficiency variance, $500 U ↑
↑ Price variance, $0 ↑   (50 lbs. × $5)   (100 lbs. × $5)

The key difference between the two analyses is centered on how output is measured. Analysis One measures output in terms of good units only. Analysis Two measures output in terms of good units and good units plus spoiled units. This permits the breakdown of the efficiency variance into a spoilage-related efficiency variance and another variance, here called a "nonspoilage-related efficiency" variance. The journal entry would be:

Work in process	5,000	
Direct-material spoilage-related efficiency variance		
(or Cost of spoiled goods)	500	
Direct-material nonspoilage-related efficiency variance	250	
Stores		5,750

To record material usage and isolate the cost of spoiled goods.

Nearly every manufacturing company has some problems of spoilage, waste, rework, or scrap as a consequence of management's choice of those factors of production that will render the most economic benefit. Hence some of these problems are a normal result of efficient production. Yet there is a need to distinguish between, for example, normal and abnormal spoilage. Standards or norms must be computed so that performance may be judged and costs properly accounted for. Normal spoilage, then, is spoilage that is unavoidable under a given set of efficient production conditions: abnormal spoilage is spoilage that is not expected to arise under efficient conditions. Laxity in setting currently attainable standards often results in too liberal allowances for normal spoilage.

Accounting for spoilage, rework, and the like, varies considerably. Practically, most of these net costs are allowed for in budgeted overhead rates; or, where standard costs are employed, scrap and normal spoilage allowances are often incorporated into the standard costs for direct materials, direct labor, and overhead.

Conceptually, some practical treatments are faulty because they muddle the distinction between product costs and costs for control by charging product costs back to Department Factory-Overhead Control.

PROBLEMS FOR SELF-STUDY

Review each example in this chapter and obtain the solutions on your own. Then check your work against the solutions, which appear in the text.

Terms to Learn

This chapter and the Glossary contain definitions of the following important terms:

abnormal spoilage (p. 546)   *normal spoilage (546)*   *reworked units (545)*
scrap (545)   *spoilage (544)*   *waste (545)*

Special Points and Pitfalls

When spoilage occurs, trace the units spoiled as well as the units finished and in process. Compute both normal and abnormal spoiled units separately. Build separate costs of spoiled units. Then add normal-spoilage cost to good units passing inspection; charge off abnormal-spoilage costs as a loss. Even if no abnormal spoilage exists, it is helpful to compute normal-spoilage costs separately. In this way, management will be constantly reminded of the normal-spoilage cost of a given process.

The allocation of the cost of normal spoilage usually depends on where spoilage is detected. If spoilage is detected at the final stage of completion, then no cost of normal spoilage is added to ending work in process. This assumption was used in the illustrations of the weighted-average and FIFO methods. In contrast, inspection may take place at some other stage—say, at the halfway point in the production cycle. In such a case, some normal-spoilage cost would also be added to the units in process that are more than half completed. This solution is illustrated in the chapter appendix.

This appendix extends the discussion in the body of this chapter regarding spoilage assumptions and computations.[9] Consider the following illustrative problem for a processing department for the month of January:

	PHYSICAL UNITS
Work in process, beginning inventory	11,000 (25%)*
Started	74,000
To account for	85,000
Completed during current period:	
From beginning inventory	11,000
Started and completed	50,000
Good units completed	61,000
Spoiled units	8,000
Work in process, ending inventory	16,000 (75%)*
Accounted for	85,000

*Degree of completion for conversion costs of this department at the dates of the work-in-process inventories. Direct materials are added at the start of production.

Inspection occurs when production is 50% completed. Normal spoilage is 10% of good units passing inspection.

The following cost data are available:

Beginning inventory:		
Direct materials	$220,000	
Conversion costs	40,000	$ 260,000
Current costs added:		
Direct materials		1,480,000
Conversion costs		1,115,000
Cost to account for		$2,855,000

Required

Prepare a detailed production-cost report. Use the weighted-average method. Distinguish between normal and abnormal spoilage.

When accuracy is desired, the calculation of the good units passing inspection during the current period is critical. The number of units inspected depends on the amount of conversion work done on them during the current period. Depending on their stage of completion, units in work in process may or may not have passed inspection in January. In this instance:

---

[9]Professors A. Atkinson and W. Stephens made helpful suggestions.

Work in process, beginning inventory	11,000
Started and completed	50,000
Work in process, ending inventory	16,000
Good units passing inspection during current period	77,000
Spoiled units	8,000
Normal spoilage, 10% of 77,000 units passing inspection	7,700
Abnormal spoilage	300

Exhibit 16-5 is the detailed production-cost report. Consider Steps 1 and 2 in Exhibit 16-5. The calculation of equivalent units of work done on the spoiled units depends on how much direct-material and conversion costs were incurred to get the units to the point of inspection. In the illustration, the spoiled units would have a full count of direct materials and a 50% count of conversion costs.

Steps 3 and 4 are similar to earlier illustrations of the weighted-average method. Note how an erroneous computation of equivalent units would affect all steps beyond Step 2. Why? Because the unit costs computed in Steps 3 and 4 would be inaccurate.

Step 5 is also similar to earlier illustrations. However, there is one important difference. Note how the ending work in process has passed the point of inspection. Therefore these units bear a normal-spoilage cost just like the units that have been completed and transferred.

Reconsider the facts in the illustration. Suppose inspection had occurred at the 100% or at the 10% conversion stage. How would the computations have been affected?

The number of abnormally spoiled units would change:

	INSPECTION AT STAGE OF COMPLETION	
	at 100%	at 10%
Work in process, beginning inventory	11,000	—
Started and completed	50,000	50,000
Work in process, ending inventory	—	16,000
Good units passing inspection during current period	61,000	66,000
Spoiled units	8,000	8,000
Normal spoilage, 10% of good units passing inspection	6,100	6,600
Abnormal spoilage	1,900	1,400

If abnormal spoilage increases, more of the total costs to account for would be written off currently as a loss.

Note the effect of the point of inspection on the ending work in process. Normal-spoilage costs would be applied thereto only if the ending units in process had passed inspection. In our illustration, the units are 75% completed. Therefore, if inspection occurs at the 100% stage, no normal spoilage costs would be added to the ending inventory. In contrast, if inspection occurs at the 10% stage, normal-spoilage costs would be added to the ending inventory.

EXHIBIT 16-5

B Company
Production-Cost Report
For the Month Ended January 31, 19_1
Weighted-Average Method

	FLOW OF PRODUCTION	(STEP 1) PHYSICAL UNITS	(STEP 2) EQUIVALENT UNITS Direct Materials	Conversion Costs
	Work in process, beginning inventory	11,000 (25%)*		
	Started	74,000		
	To account for	85,000		
	Abnormal spoilage	300	300	150
	Normal spoilage	7,700	7,700	3,850
	Good units completed and transferred out	61,000	61,000	61,000
	Work in process, ending inventory	16,000 (75%)*	16,000	12,000
	Accounted for	85,000		
	Total work done to date		85,000	77,000

	COSTS	TOTALS	DETAILS Direct Materials	Conversion Costs	Equivalent Whole Unit
	Work in process, beginning inventory	$ 260,000	$ 220,000	$ 40,000	
	Current costs	2,595,000	1,480,000	1,115,000	
(Step 3)	Total costs to account for	$2,855,000	$1,700,000	$1,155,000	
(Step 4)	Divide by equivalent units		÷85,000	÷77,000	
	Cost per equivalent unit		$ 20.00	$ 15.00	$35.00
(Step 5)	Apply total costs to units completed and in process				
	Abnormal spoilage (300)	$ 8,250	300($20)	150($15)	
	Units completed and transferred out (61,000):				
	Costs before adding spoilage	$2,135,000			61,000($35)
	Normal spoilage	167,750	6,100($20)	3,050($15)	
	Total cost transferred out	$2,302,750			
	Work in process, ending inventory (16,000):				
	Direct materials	$ 320,000	16,000($20)		
	Conversion costs	180,000		12,000($15)	
	Normal spoilage	44,000	1,600($20)	800($15)	
	Total work in process	$ 544,000			
	Total costs accounted for	$2,855,000			

*Degree of completion for conversion costs of this department at the dates of the work-in-process inventories. Note that direct-material costs are fully completed at each of these dates, because in this department materials are introduced at the beginning of the process.

An alternative approach to that displayed in Exhibit 16-5 is to conceive of a spoilage unit cost as applied to production at time of inspection. For example, in Exhibit 16-5, the cost of each spoiled unit would be $27.50 ($20 for direct materials + 50% of $15, or $7.50 for conversion costs). Then the normal-spoilage cost per good unit passing inspection would be $27.50 ÷ 10 units = $2.75 per unit. In Exhibit 16-5, the application of normal spoilage costs to the goods completed would be computed as 61,000 × $2.75 = $167,750; of work in process, 16,000 × $2.75 = $44,000.

_____QUESTIONS, PROBLEMS, AND CASES_____

16-1 "Spoilage costs are only one facet of the costs of quality control." Do you agree? Explain.

16-2 "Management has two major planning and control problems regarding spoilage." What are the two problems?

16-3 "Normal spoilage is planned spoilage." Discuss.

16-4 "Costs of abnormal spoilage are lost costs." Explain.

16-5 "In accounting for spoiled goods, we are dealing with cost application and allocation rather than cost incurrence." Explain.

16-6 "Total input includes the abnormal as well as the normal spoilage and is therefore irrational as a basis for computing normal spoilage." Do you agree? Why?

16-7 "The point of inspection is the key to the application of spoilage costs." Explain.

16-8 "The practical treatments of spoilage in job-order costing can be criticized on conceptual grounds." What is the major criticism?

16-9 Describe the general accounting for scrap where no inventory value is assigned to scrap.

16-10 How is scrap usually accounted for under standard costing?

16-11 Two ways of accounting for spoilage. (CPA)   In manufacturing activities, a portion of the units placed in process is sometimes spoiled and becomes practically worthless. Discuss two ways in which the cost of such spoiled units could be treated in the accounts, and describe the circumstances under which each method might be used.

16-12 Process costing, spoilage.   The following information is for a company that uses the weighted-average method of process costing. Fill in the twelve blank spaces (on lines marked A, B, C, D, E, F).

	DIRECT MATERIALS	CONVERSION COSTS
Units to be accounted for:		
Beginning inventory, 30% finished	1,000	
Input	10,000	
	11,000	
Units accounted for:		
Output	8,000	8,000
Spoilage, detected at end of process	1,000	1,000
Ending inventory, 60% completed	2,000	1,200
	11,000	10,200
Cost to be accounted for:		
Beginning inventory	$ 2,000	$ 900
Current input	20,000	29,700
	$22,000	$30,600

Cost allocation (to good and spoiled units):

Unit costs	$ _____	$ _____	A
Cost of spoiled units	$ _____	$ _____	B
Ending inventory	_____	_____	C
Output without spoilage included	_____	_____	D
Total cost	$22,000	$30,600	

Costs reallocated with the spoilage cost applied to the cost of good units:

	DIRECT MATERIALS	CONVERSION COSTS	
Ending inventory	$ _____	$ _____	E
Output	_____	_____	F
Total cost	$22,000	$30,600	

16-13 Allocating normal spoilage. The ABC Company operates under a process-cost system for one of its products. During the period in question for this product, 3,850 units were put into production. During the period, 3,000 finished units were completed and transferred out. Inspection of this product occurs at the halfway point in the process. Normally, spoilage amounts to 10% of the good units passed. The inspector informs you that the process did in fact function normally during this period. The production supervisor estimates that units still in process are on the average two-thirds complete. All, however, are at least one-half complete. Assume that there were no beginning inventories. Costs for the period were:

Direct materials	$38,500	—Applied at the beginning of the process
Conversion cost	35,080	—Applied evenly during the process
	$73,580	

Determine the cost of goods completed and the cost of the ending inventory of work in process.

16-14 Normal and abnormal spoilage. The Van Brocklin Company manufactures one style of long, tapered wax candle, which is used on festive occasions. Each candle requires a two-foot-long wick and one pound of a specially prepared wax. Wick and melted wax are placed in molds and allowed to harden for twenty-four hours. Upon removal from the molds, the candles are immediately dipped in a special coloring mixture that gives them a glossy lacquer finish. Dried candles are inspected, and all defective ones are pulled out. Because the coloring mixture penetrates into the wax itself, the defective candles cannot be salvaged for reuse. They are destroyed in an incinerator. Normal spoilage is regarded as 3% of the number of candles that pass inspection.

Cost and production statistics for a certain week were as follows:

Direct materials requisitioned (including wicks and wax)	$3,340.00
Direct labor and overhead costs (applied at a constant rate during the hardening process)	1,219.50
Total cost	$4,559.50

During the week, 7,800 candles were completed; 7,500 passed inspection, and the remainder were defective. At the end of the week, 550 candles were still in the molds; they were considered 60% complete. There was no beginning inventory. Show computations.

Required

1. Which of the following is the cost of the 7,500 candles that passed inspection? (a) $4,333.73, (b) $4,125.00, (c) $4,217.85, (d) $4,248.75, (e) $4,290.00.
2. Which of the following is the cost of the candles still in the molds at the end of the week? (a) $393.25, (b) $185.13, (c) $269.50, (d) $274.72, (e) $300.30.

16-15 Weighted average and spoilage. The Alston Company operates under a process-cost system. It has two departments, cleaning and milling. For both departments, conversion costs are applied in proportion to the stage of completion. But direct materials are added at the *beginning* of the process in the cleaning department, and additional direct materials are added at the *end* of the milling process. Following are the costs and unit production statistics for May. All unfinished work at the *end* of May is 25% completed. All beginning inventories (May 1) were 80% completed as of May 1. All completed work is transferred to the next department.

BEGINNING INVENTORIES	CLEANING	MILLING
Cleaning: $1,000 direct materials, $800 conv. costs	$1,800	
Milling: $6,450 previous dept. cost (transferred-in cost) and $2,450 conv. costs		$8,900
CURRENT COSTS		
Direct materials	$9,000	$ 640
Conversion costs	$8,000	$4,950
PHYSICAL UNITS		
Units in beginning inventory	1,000	3,000
Units started this month	9,000	7,400
Total units finished and transferred	7,400	6,000
Normal spoilage	500	400
Abnormal spoilage	500	0

ADDITIONAL FACTORS

1. Spoilage is assumed to occur at the *end* of *each* of the two processes when the units are inspected.

2. Assume that there is no waste, shrinkage, evaporation, or abnormal spoilage other than that indicated in the tabulation above.

3. Carry unit-cost calculations to three decimal places where necessary. Calculate final totals to the nearest dollar.

Required

Using the weighted-average method, show for *each* department:

1. Analysis of physical units and an analysis of equivalent units
2. Calculations of *unit* costs
3. *Detailed* presentation of the *total* costs assigned to goods transferred out and the total costs assigned to ending work in process

16-16 FIFO. Redo Problem 16-15, using FIFO.

16-17 FIFO process costing, normal and abnormal spoilage. (D. Kleespie)   The CeeKay Company uses actual costs in a FIFO process-cost accounting system. Materials are added at the beginning of processing in the mixing department; inspection takes place at the end of the process. Conversion costs are added evenly throughout the process. Operating data for August include:

	POUNDS
Beginning inventory of work in process, 30% complete as to conversion costs ($13,500 conversion cost)	500
Normal spoilage	60
Abnormal spoilage	40
Good units transferred out	2,000
Ending inventory of work in process, 60% complete as to conversion costs	600
Equivalent unit cost for conversion costs, $100 per pound	

Required

1. How many units were started in production in the mixing department during August?
2. How many equivalent units were used in determining the unit cost for conversion?
3. What is the total dollar amount of the conversion-cost portion of the ending work-in-process inventory?
4. What is the total dollar amount of the conversion-cost portion being transferred out of the mixing department?
5. What is the total amount of conversion cost charged to the mixing department this period?
6. Assume instead that the CeeKay Company had used the weighted-average method. How many divisor equivalent units would have been used to determine the average unit cost for conversion?
7. Assume as in requirement 6 that the CeeKay Company had used the weighted-average method. What is the total amount of conversion cost charged to the mixing department this period? Assume the weighted-average conversion cost per equivalent unit is $100.

16-18 Process costs; weighted-average; abnormal spoilage. (SMA)   The Quebec Manufacturing Company produces a single product. There are two producing departments, Departments 1 and 2, and the product passes through the plant in that order.

There were no work-in-process inventories at the beginning of the year.

In January, direct materials for 1,000 units were issued to production in Department 1 at a cost of $5,000. Direct-labor and factory-overhead costs for the month were $2,700. During the month, 800 units were completed and transferred to Department 2. The work-in-process inventory at the end of the month contained 200 units, complete in materials and one-half complete in labor and overhead.

Direct labor and factory overhead in Department 2 amounted to $6,250 in January. During the month, 500 units were completed and transferred to finished stock. At the end of the month, 200 units remained in process, one-quarter complete. Ordinarily, in Department

2, spoilage is recognized upon inspection at the end of the process, but in January there was an abnormal loss of 50 units when one-half complete. The effect of abnormal loss is not to be included in inventory.

Required Prepare a detailed production-cost report for the month of January. Use the weighted-average method.

16-19 Process costs; weighted-average; spoilage. (CMA) Ranka Company manufactures high-quality leather products. The company's profits have declined during the past nine months. Ranka has used unit-cost data that were developed eighteen months ago in planning and controlling its operations. In an attempt to isolate the causes of poor profit performance, management is investigating the manufacturing operations of each of its products.

One of Ranka's main products is fine leather belts. The belts are produced in a single, continuous process in the Bluett Plant. During the process leather strips are sewn, punched, and dyed. Buckles are attached by rivets when the belts are 70% complete as to direct labor and overhead (conversion costs). The belts then enter a final finishing stage to conclude the process. Labor and overhead are applied evenly during the process.

The leather belts are inspected twice during the process: (1) right before the buckles are attached (70% point in the process), and (2) at the conclusion of the finishing stage (100% point in the process). Ranka uses the weighted-average method to calculate its unit costs.

The leather belts produced at the Bluett Plant wholesale for $9.95 each. Management wants to compare the current manufacturing costs per unit with the prices that exist on the market for leather belts. Top management has asked the Bluett Plant to submit data on the cost of manufacturing the leather belts for the month of October. This cost data will be used to evaluate whether modifications in the production process should be initiated or whether an increase in the selling price of the belts is justified. The cost per equivalent unit which is being used for planning and controlling purposes is $5.35 per unit.

The work-in-process inventory consisted of 400 partially completed units on October 1. The belts were 25% complete as to conversion costs. The costs included in the inventory on October 1 were as follows:

Leather strips	$1,000
Conversion costs	300
	$1,300

During October 7,600 leather strips were placed in production. A total of 6,800 good leather belts were completed. A total of 300 belts were identified as spoiled at the two inspection points—100 at the first inspection point (before buckle is attached) and 200 at the final inspection point (after finishing). This quantity of spoiled belts was considered normal. In addition, 200 belts were removed from the production line when the process was 40% complete as to conversion costs because they had been damaged as a result of a malfunction during the sewing operation. This malfunction was considered an unusual occurrence, and consequently the spoilage was classified as abnormal. Spoiled units are not reprocessed and have zero salvage value. The work-in-process inventory on October 31 consisted of 700 belts which were 50% complete as to conversion costs.

The costs charged to production during October were as follows:

Leather strips	$20,600
Buckles	4,550
Conversion costs	20,700
	$45,850

Required 1. In order to provide cost data regarding the manufacture of leather belts in the Bluett Plant to the top management of Ranka Company, determine for the month of October (a) the equivalent units for each type of material and conversion costs; (b) the cost per equivalent unit for each type of material and conversion costs; (c) the assignment of

total production costs to the work-in-process inventory and to goods transferred out; (d) the average unit cost of the 6,800 good leather belts completed and transferred to finished goods.

2. If Ranka Company decided to repair (rework) the 300 belts that were considered normal spoilage, explain how the company would account for the rework costs.

16-20 Process costing, inspection at 70% stage. (CMA)   APCO Company manufactures various lines of bicycles. Because of the high volume of each type of product, the company employs a process-cost system using the weighted-average method to determine unit costs. Bicycle parts are manufactured in the molding department. The parts are consolidated into a single bike unit in the molding department and transferred to the assembly department where they are partially assembled. After assembly the bicycle is sent to the packing department.

Cost per unit data for the 20-inch dirt bike has been completed through the molding department. Annual cost and production figures for the assembly department are presented in the accompanying schedules.

Defective bicycles are identified at an inspection point when the assembly labor process is 70% complete; all assembly material has been added prior to this point of the process. The normal rejection percentage for defective bicycles is 5% of the bicycles reaching the inspection point. Any defective bicycles over and above the 5% quota are considered as abnormal. All defective bikes are removed from the production process and disposed of with zero net disposal value.

ASSEMBLY DEPARTMENT COST DATA

	TRANSFERRED IN FROM MOLDING DEPARTMENT	ASSEMBLY MATERIAL	ASSEMBLY CONVERSION COST	TOTAL COST OF DIRT BIKE THROUGH ASSEMBLY
Prior period costs	$ 82,200	$ 6,660	$ 11,930	$ 100,790
Current period costs	1,237,800	96,840	236,590	1,571,230
Total costs	$1,320,000	$103,500	$248,520	$1,672,020

ASSEMBLY DEPARTMENT PRODUCTION DATA

		PERCENT COMPLETE		
	BICYCLES	Transferred In	Assembly Material	Assembly Conversion
Beginning inventory	3,000	100	100	80
Transferred in from molding department during year	45,000	100	—	—
Transferred out to packing department during year	40,000	100	100	100
Ending inventory	4,000	100	50	20

Required

1. Compute the number of defective bikes that are considered to be
   a. A normal amount of defective bikes
   b. An abnormal amount of defective bikes
2. Compute the equivalent units of production for the year for
   a. Bicycles transferred in from the molding department
   b. Bicycles produced with regard to assembly material
   c. Bicycles produced with regard to assembly conversion
3. Compute the cost per equivalent unit for the fully assembled dirt bike.
4. Compute the amount of the total production cost of $1,672,020 that will be associated with the following items:
   a. Normal defective units
   b. Abnormal defective units
   c. Good units completed in the assembly department
   d. Ending work-in-process inventory in the assembly department

5. Describe how the applicable dollar amounts for the following items would be presented in the financial statements:
   a. Normal defective units
   b. Abnormal defective units
   c. Completed units transferred into the packing department
   d. Ending work-in-process inventory in the assembly department

16-21 Different ways of accounting for spoilage. (CPA) The D. Hayes Cramer Company manufactures Product C, whose cost per unit is $1 of (direct) materials, $2 of (direct) labor, and $3 of overhead costs. During the month of May, 1,000 units of Product C were spoiled. These units could be sold for 60¢ each.

The accountant said that the entry to be made for these 1,000 lost or spoiled units could be one of the following four:

ENTRY NO. 1

Spoiled goods	600	
Work in process—materials		100
Work in process—labor		200
Work in process—overhead		300

ENTRY NO. 2

Spoiled goods	600	
Manufacturing expenses	5,400	
Work in process—materials		1,000
Work in process—labor		2,000
Work in process—overhead		3,000

ENTRY NO. 3

Spoiled goods	600	
Loss on spoiled goods	5,400	
Work in process—materials		1,000
Work in process—labor		2,000
Work in process—overhead		3,000

ENTRY NO. 4

Spoiled goods	600	
Receivable	5,400	
Work in process—materials		1,000
Work in process—labor		2,000
Work in process—overhead		3,000

Required | Indicate the circumstance under which each of the four solutions above would be appropriate.

16-22 Job-cost spoilage and scrap. (F. Mayne) Santa Cruz Metal Fabricators, Inc., has a large job, No. 2734, which calls for producing various ore bins, chutes, and metal boxes for enlarging a copper concentrator. The following charges were made to the job in November 19_9:

Direct materials	$26,951
Direct labor	15,076
Factory overhead	7,538

The contract with the customer called for the price to be based on a cost-plus approach. The contract defined *cost* to include direct materials, direct labor, and overhead to be applied at 50% of labor. The contract also provided that the total costs of all work spoiled were to be removed from the billable cost of the job, and that the benefits from scrap sales were to reduce the billable cost of the job.

Required

1. In accordance with the stated terms of the contract, record the following two items in general journal form:
   a. A cutting error was made in production. The up-to-date job-cost record for the batch of work involved showed materials of $650, direct labor of $500, and applied overhead of $250. Since fairly large pieces of metal were recoverable, it was estimated that the salvage value was $600 and that the materials recovered would be used on other jobs. The spoiled work was sent to the warehouse.
   b. Small pieces of metal cuttings and scrap in November 19_9 amounted to $1,250, which was the price quoted by a scrap dealer. You may assume that there were no entries made with regard to the scrap until the price was quoted by the scrap dealer. The scrap dealer's offer was immediately accepted.
2. Consider the issue of normal versus abnormal spoilage that was discussed in the chapter. Suppose the contract described above had instead contained the clause "a normal spoilage allowance of 1% of the job cost will be included in the billable cost of the job."
   a. Is this clause really specific enough to define exactly how much spoilage is normal and how much is abnormal? *Hint:* Consider the inputs versus outputs distinction that was presented in the material on page 549.
   b. Repeat requirement 1a with this "normal spoilage of 1%" clause in mind. You should be able to provide two slightly different entries.

16-23 Spoilage and job costing. (L. Bamber) Bamber Kitchens produces a variety of items in accordance with special orders of hospitals, factories, and food manufacturers. The following $6 cost per case pertains to an order for 2,500 cases of chicken "à la king": direct materials, $3; direct labor, $2; and factory overhead applied, $1. The overhead rate includes a provision for normal spoilage.

Required

1. Assume that a laborer dropped and totally destroyed 200 cases. Prepare a journal entry to record this event. What is the unit cost of the remaining 2,300 cases?
2. Reconsider requirement 1. Suppose part of the 200 cases could be salvaged and sold to a nearby prison for $200 cash. How would your answers in requirement 1 change?
3. Refer to the original data. Tasters reject 200 of the 2,500 cases, and the 200 rejected cases are destroyed. Assume this rejection rate is considered normal. Prepare a journal entry to record this event, and calculate the unit cost if
   a. The rejection is attributable to exacting specifications of this particular job
   b. The rejection is characteristic of the production process and is not attributable to this specific job
4. Reconsider requirement 3. Suppose part of the 200 cases could be salvaged and sold to a nearby welfare agency for $400. How would your answers in requirement 3 change?
5. Refer to the original data. Tasters rejected 200 cases that had insufficient salt. The product can be placed in a vat, salt added, and reprocessed into jars. This operation will cost $200; it is considered a normal phenomenon because of the difficulty in seasoning processed chicken items. Prepare a journal entry to record this event. What is the average unit cost of all the cases?
6. How would your answer in requirement 5 change if the rejection was because of the exacting specifications of this particular job?
7. How would your answer in requirement 5 change if the rejection occurred because a worker simply forgot to add the salt?

16-24 Weighted-average, spoilage at 80% completion. (A. Atkinson) Ottawa Manufacturing produces a single product, X, in a two-stage manufacturing operation. The company uses a weighted-average process-costing system. During the month of June, the following data were recorded for Department 2:

Units of beginning inventory	10,000
% completion of opening units	25%
Cost of direct materials in beginning inventory	$ 0
Units started	70,000
Units completed	50,000
Units in ending inventory	20,000
% completion of ending units	95%
Spoiled units	10,000
Current direct-materials cost	$655,200
Current labor cost	$635,600
Current overhead cost	$616,000
Conversion costs in beginning inventory	$ 42,000
Cost of units, transferred in	$ 82,900
Cost of current units, transferred in	$647,500

Conversion costs are incurred evenly throughout the process. Direct-material costs are incurred when production is 90% complete. Inspection occurs when production is 80% complete. Normal spoilage is 10% of all good units that pass inspection.

Required | Prepare a production-cost report for the month of June. Show supporting computations.

16-25 Standard process costing and spoilage. Refer to the preceding problem. Suppose you are provided with the following standard per unit cost data for Department 2:

Direct materials (5 pounds @ $2.00)	$10.00
Direct labor (1/2 hour @ $14.00)	7.00
Variable overhead (1/2 hour @ $6.00)	3.00
Fixed overhead (1/2 hour @ $10.00)	5.00
	$25.00

The fixed-overhead rate was obtained by dividing budgeted fixed manufacturing overhead of $400,000 by expected volume of 40,000 direct-labor hours.

During June, the following actual results occurred: price of direct materials, $1.80 per pound; direct labor worked, 42,350 hours; and variable-overhead rate per hour, $6.20.

Required | Prepare a schedule of all manufacturing variances.

16-26 Direct-material spoilage variance. Moline Structural Metal Company uses a standard-costing system. One of its products requires 60 pounds of direct material at $3 per pound, a standard material cost of $180 per product unit. During a recent week, 90 units were produced, of which 12 were spoiled. Total direct materials purchased and used were 5,550 pounds at $3.20 per pound.

Required | 1. Compute all direct-material variances.
2. Prepare a journal entry to recognize these variances. Assume that the perpetual inventory of direct materials is carried in the accounts on an actual cost basis.

Nonmanufacturing Job Costing, Project Costing, Operation Costing, & JIT Costing

Job costing for control in nonmanufacturing • Control of projects • Hybrid costing • Operation costing • Constant-flow manufacturing and Just-in-Time (JIT) • JIT costing • Many available product-costing choices • Appendix: Accounting for payroll

This chapter extends our study of product costing. There are major sections devoted to professional service firms, long-run contracts, and the relationships of underlying production systems to the choice of product-costing systems. Special attention is given to hybrid systems that piece together features of job costing and process costing.

Each of the first two major sections (job costing in nonmanufacturing and control of projects) can be studied independently. However, the final sections (hybrid, operation, and JIT costing) are closely related.

The chapter appendix covers additional special features of a cost accounting system for payroll accounting.

JOB COSTING FOR CONTROL IN NONMANUFACTURING

Job-order costing is not confined to manufacturing companies. For example, this costing method is used by construction companies, service industries, and non-profit organizations. More specific examples are house builders, consulting firms, law firms, advertising agencies, and hospitals.

The emphasis in Chapter 4 was on product costing, not planning and control. We will now use a nonmanufacturing firm to emphasize how job costing helps planning and control.

Managers face challenging problems of how to apply costs to the specific services rendered. The degree of accuracy sought varies in accordance with many influences, including management styles, industry traditions, and competitive pressures.

Managers often use job costing for planning and control purposes. However, the managers in various industries may not use the job-costing terminology of Chapter 4. For example, law firms and hospitals have "cases"; consultants have "contracts" or engagements. Three different job-costing approaches used by non-manufacturing firms are

1. A single direct-cost item (usually direct labor) and a single overhead rate
2. Multiple direct-cost items (direct labor, photocopying, computer time, etc.), and a single overhead rate
3. Multiple direct-cost items and multiple overhead rates

This section illustrates the first two of these approaches. (Multiple overhead rates are rarely encountered in practice.)

Consider an auditing engagement of a public accounting firm. Like many professional service firms, this firm classifies the compensation of its professional personnel who work directly on the engagement as direct labor. All other costs are classified as overhead. (In the following discussion, we call this job-costing approach Alternative One.)

Suppose a public accounting firm has a condensed budget for 19_1 as follows:

Revenue	$15,000,000	100%
Direct professional labor (for professional hours charged to client engagements)	3,750,000	25
Contribution to overhead and operating income	$11,250,000	75%
Overhead (all other costs)	10,500,000	70
Operating income	$ 750,000	5%

In this illustration:

$$\text{Budgeted overhead rate} = \frac{\textbf{Budgeted overhead}}{\textbf{Budgeted direct labor}}$$

$$= \frac{\$10,500,000}{\$3,750,000} = 280\%$$

As each engagement is budgeted, the partner in charge of the audit predicts the expected number of direct professional hours needed. Direct professional hours are those worked on the audit by partners, managers, and subordinate accountants. The budgeted direct-labor cost is the pertinent hourly labor costs multiplied by the budgeted hours. Partners' time is charged to the engagement at much higher rates than those of subordinates. Overhead is applied accordingly. This practice implies that partners require proportionately more overhead support than their subordinates for each of their hours charged. Finally, the budgeted total cost of the engagement is the direct-labor cost plus the applied overhead (at 280% of direct labor in this illustration).

As in all decisions regarding pricing, the revenue for a particular engagement depends on competitive factors and the engagement partner's assessment of the client's willingness to pay. However, partners frequently use rules of thumb or formulas at least as a point of departure for setting a price. In our illustration, the formula might be:

$$\text{Markup rate for pricing individual engagements} = \frac{\text{Budgeted revenue}}{\text{Budgeted direct labor}}$$

$$= \frac{\$15,000,000}{\$3,750,000} = 400\%$$

Thus, if all the partners were able to obtain this 400% markup rate consistently, and the predicted direct-labor costs were accurate, budgeted revenue for the firm would be attained.

Specific control of work

The engagement partner usually has a budget for a specific audit that includes detailed scope and steps. For example, the budget for auditing cash or inventories would specify the exact work to be done, the number of hours, and the levels of skilled personnel needed.

The partner monitors progress by comparing the actual direct professional hours logged to date with the original budget *and* with the estimated hours remaining on the engagement. The degree of profitability of each engagement heavily depends on whether (a) the audit can be completed within the budgeted time limits and (b) the target revenue can be collected from the client.

Sometimes the scope of the work changes because of unanticipated early findings or special requests from the client. In these situations, the fees are renegotiated.

The costs of the previously described engagement might also include travel costs. These are often billed to the client at 100% of costs. Using assumed numbers, the engagement would have the following summarized costs:

Direct professional labor	$ 40,000
Applied overhead, 280% of $40,000	112,000
Total costs excluding travel costs	$152,000
Travel costs	11,000
Total costs of engagement	$163,000

Using the 400% markup rate, the expected revenue and operating income attributable to the engagement would be:

Revenue (400% of $40,000 + travel costs, or $160,000 + $11,000)	$171,000
Total costs	163,000
Operating income	$ 8,000

Note that the $8,000 here is 5% of the $160,000 revenue exclusive of travel costs; this is the same percentage of operating income shown earlier in the entire firm's budget ($750,000 ÷ $15,000,000 = 5%).

Our example described a relatively simple job-costing system for a professional service firm; only a single direct-cost item (labor) is used and only a single overhead rate is used. As competition increases, and as clients demand more thorough explanations of fees, professional service firms have increased their efforts to track more costs as direct costs rather than as overhead. We now consider an example of these efforts.

Many public accounting firms, law firms, and other professional service firms have refined their data-processing systems. Computers help gather information that is far more detailed than was feasible a few years ago. Thus costs have been shifted from being classified as overhead to being classified as a direct cost of the engagement. Using assumed numbers, an engagement might have the following summarized costs:

Direct professional labor	$ 40,000
Direct support labor, such as secretarial costs	10,000
Fringe benefits for all direct labor*	17,500
Photocopying	1,100
Telephone calls	1,000
Computer time (either used inside or acquired outside)	8,000
Total direct costs	$ 77,600
Applied overhead, assumed as 100% of total direct costs	77,600
Total costs excluding travel costs	$155,200
Travel costs	11,000
Total costs of engagement	$166,200

*35% assumed rate multiplied by ($40,000 + $10,000) = $17,500.

This more-detailed approach (termed Alternative Two) classifies the fringe benefits of all direct labor as a separate item. In contrast, many firms embed such fringe benefits as a basic part of their direct-labor rates. For instance, suppose fringe benefits are 35% of an auditor's hourly compensation of $20. Some firms will cost their labor at $20 plus 35% of $20, or $27. Other firms will do as implied in the tabulation, compiling direct professional labor at the $20 rate and separately compiling the related fringe benefits at the 35% rate.

How should we classify the compensation costs of the firm's computer-programmer employees directly tracked to the engagement? Some firms include such costs as direct professional labor; other firms classify them as direct support labor.

Alternative One used direct professional labor as a basis for a 400% markup. Alternative Two could use the total costs (excluding travel costs) as a basis for a percentage markup that would obviously be far lower than 400%.

What costs should be included in the total costs used as a basis for markup? Again, practices differ. For example, some firms will classify computer services purchased from outsiders as not being subject to markups. That is, such computer costs and travel costs will be billed to clients at 100% of the amounts incurred. Obviously, there are no single correct answers. These classifications are the result of the preferences of the managing partners of the firms.

Alternative Two has a lower overhead application rate, assumed as 100% of total direct costs instead of the 280% of direct labor used in Alternative One. Some firms prefer to continue to apply their overhead based on direct-labor costs rather than total direct costs. Why? Because the partners believe that overhead is principally affected by the amount of direct-labor costs rather than such items as photocopying, telephone calls, and outside computer services.

Note particularly that more than one overhead rate can be used to apply costs to engagements or jobs. For example, some overhead might be applied on the basis of direct labor, and other overhead might be applied on the basis of computer time. The latter base is becoming more widely used as expensive computers assume a more prominent role in rendering services to clients or customers.

No matter what overhead application base is chosen, Alternative Two will always have a lower overhead application rate than Alternative One. Why? Because many costs that firms previously regarded as part of overhead, an indirect cost, have been reclassified as direct costs.

Alternative Two results in different total costs. Depending on how prices are set, there may be a different total revenue for the engagement. Alternative Two illustrates a trend in the manufacturing and service industries. That is, as data processing becomes less expensive, more costs than just direct material and direct labor will be classified as direct costs wherever feasible. Alternative Two produces more accurate tracking of costs to specific jobs or engagements. In general, as competition intensifies, managers of all organizations seek more accurate costs of their products and services. In this way, managers have better guidance in setting prices and in allocating effort among particular jobs, products, services, and customers.

_____PROBLEM FOR SELF-STUDY_____

problem   The partner in charge of an audit engagement has prepared the following budget for making a proposal to a prospective client.

> Direct professional labor costs:
> | | | |
> |---|---|---|
> | Partner, 1 × 40 hrs. × $100 | $ 4,000 | |
> | Manager, 1 × 80 hrs. × $35 | 2,800 | |
> | Senior, 1 × 160 hrs. × $22 | 3,520 | |
> | Assistants, 2 × 150 hrs. × $15 | 4,500 | |
> | | $14,820 | |

The budgeted overhead rate is 250% of direct professional labor dollars. The normal markup for the pricing of engagements is 400% of direct-labor costs.

Required   1. Assume that a normal markup is used to quote a total fixed fee for the audit engagement. Compute the budgeted total revenue, total costs, and operating income.
2. What major factors may prevent obtaining the budgeted fee?

solution   1.

Fee revenue, 400% of $14,820		$59,280
Direct professional labor	$14,820	
Overhead, 250% of $14,820	37,050	
Total costs		51,870
Operating income		$ 7,410

2. Major factors that may cause the actual fee to differ from the budgeted fee include:
   a. Losing the engagement to a competing firm
   b. Reducing the proposed fee because of fear of being underbid by competing firms
   c. Increasing the proposed fee because of a strong relationship with the client
   d. Making changes in the scope of the work that require changes in the fee
   e. Failing to collect 100% of the agreed fee because of disputes or client's financial difficulties

---

CONTROL OF PROJECTS

Project features

What is a job? What is a project? What is an engagement? Distinctions are fuzzy. As we have seen, an accounting firm may use "engagements" to describe its audits for various clients. Still, an observer may regard the audit of the local country club as a "job," but the audit of a multinational company like Exxon as a "project." In general, then, a **project** is a complex job that often takes months or years to complete and requires the work of many different departments or divisions or subcontractors. For our purposes, we focus on long-term projects in such fields as construction (e.g., bridges, shopping centers, nuclear submarines); developing and introducing a new product model (e.g., automobile, computer); conducting complex lawsuits (e.g., antitrust cases); and launching a space vehicle. Note that the last is commonly described as a "mission" rather than a "project."

The planning and controlling of jobs and projects have common characteristics. However, projects are more challenging than jobs. Projects are unique, are nonrepetitive, have more uncertainties, involve more skills and specialties, and require more coordination over a longer time span.

As an example of prospective difficulties, consider the problem of coordination. There is usually a project manager who must obtain specialized personnel from various departments such as civil engineering, electrical engineering, and sanitary engineering. These engineers often give their primary loyalties to their respective department managers, not the project manager.

Managers' control of projects generally focuses on four key aspects: (a) scope, (b) quality, (c) schedule, and (d) costs. *Scope* is the technical description of the final product; for example, a nuclear aircraft carrier. Many projects are subjected to "change orders" as the work proceeds, whereby the final product has features different from those originally planned. Obviously, changes in scope usually also affect quality, schedule, and costs.

Managers use special control techniques for long-term projects. The projects are often subdivided into a series of work packages, each having its individual time schedules. Adherence to schedules is important. In addition, managers are concerned about quality and costs. Trade-offs are frequently necessary. For example, a manager may use more time and costs to obtain specified quality.

Project variances

The U.S. Department of Defense (DOD) spends billions of dollars each year on projects having varying schedules. The DOD requires that these expenditures be monitored by cost performance reporting (CPR). Exhibit 17-1 shows the essence of CPR:

BCWS—Budgeted cost of work *scheduled* to date. That is, as of August 31, the project should be 85% completed at a cost of $425,000.

EXHIBIT 17-1
Cost and Schedule Performance Report

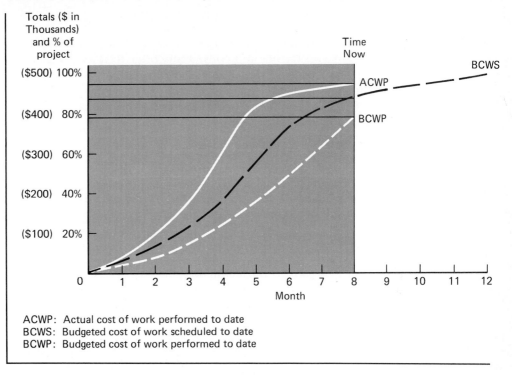

ACWP: Actual cost of work performed to date
BCWS: Budgeted cost of work scheduled to date
BCWP: Budgeted cost of work performed to date

BCWP—Budgeted cost of work *performed* to date. That is, as of August 31, the project is actually only 80% completed. The output achieved should cost $400,000.

ACWP—Actual cost of work performed to date, regardless of any budgets or schedules, $480,000.

Many more details are gathered and many variances are computed. Two variances are especially noteworthy in this CPR system:

Cost variance is ACWP—BCWP, or $480,000 − $400,000 = $80,000, unfavorable. This unfavorable variance is often called a cost overrun.

Schedule variance is BCWS − BCWP, or $425,000 − $400,000 = $25,000, unfavorable. This variance is unfavorable because it indicates that the project is behind schedule. When this variance is unfavorable, it is often called schedule slippage.

These two major variances underscore that the cost performance report system would be more accurately labeled as a *cost and schedule performance report system*. Moreover, the manager can use the unfolding information to predict final costs and completion dates.

Focus on future

The graph in Exhibit 17-1 also illustrates another key aspect of project control: a focus on what remains to be accomplished. That is, managers do not want surprises concerning future costs and future time for completion of a project. The "time now" label on the graph is the time for appraisal of where the project has been and where it is going. Such time may be at scheduled intervals, such as weeks or months, or at designated stages of completion called *milestones*. An example of a milestone is the completion of a building's foundation; a second milestone is the completion of a building's framing; and so forth.

Exhibit 17-1 shows a time scale of twelve months, but many projects have time scales that extend for several years.

This illustration is labeled as a cost and schedule performance report, but many contractors and consultants refer to it as simply *performance reporting* or as *earned value reporting* (also called *earned hour reporting*). The latter labels are often used when control of hours worked is the major determinant of success.

To illustrate earned hours reporting, suppose a management consultant has an engineering system project:

Original budget to complete, 1,500 hours.

BCWS—Budgeted cost (hours) of work scheduled to date, 1,000 hours.

BCWP—Budgeted cost (hours) of work performed to date, 700 hours. This amount is sometimes called earned value or earned hours.

ACWP—Actual cost (hours) of work performed to date, 600 hours.

The performance report could be expressed in hours, in dollars, or both. Suppose the budgeted and actual cost is $80 per hour. The variances would be:

Schedule variance is BCWS − BCWP, $80 × (1,000 − 700 hours), $24,000 unfavorable.

Cost variance is ACWP − BCWP, $80 × (600 − 700 hours), $8,000 favorable.

In this illustration, the schedule variance indicates that the project has fallen behind schedule, but the cost variance indicates that the work performed to date was done efficiently. Suppose, however, that the budgeted cost per hour of $80 was not met; it was affected by an unfavorable price variance of, say, $5 per hour. Then the cost variance would have two components, an efficiency variance and a price variance:

Efficiency variance, as calculated above	$8,000 F
Price variance, actual hours × difference in price per hour, or 600 hours × $5	3,000 U
Cost variance	$5,000 F*

*or ($85 × 600) − ($80 × 700) =
$51,000 − $56,000 = $5,000 F

In view of these variances, the project manager might predict a late completion date but a revised budgeted total final cost of $115,000 (or less), as follows:

Original budget, 1,500 hours × $80	$120,000
Less: Favorable cost variance to date	5,000
Subtotal	$115,000
Less: Additional favorable cost variance (prediction is needed)	?
Revised budget, final cost	?

Similarity of control of jobs and projects

The control of jobs is like the control of projects, although on a smaller, simpler scale. Moreover, jobs are usually more repetitive. For instance, consider the partner in charge of a routine audit engagement of a local country club. She must monitor progress and adjust her predictions of actual hours versus budgeted hours. Perhaps little can be done to alter performance or profitability of the current job. However, the information gathered on this year's job may be vital to the budgeting and negotiating of fees on next year's job.

Projects such as the development of weapons systems and computers are often undertaken despite high uncertainties and likely changes as work progresses. Should interim performance reports compare progress against the original budget or against a revised budget (much like a flexible budget)? Ideally, management should be provided with both budgets. In this way, the performance of managers as planners can be assessed by comparing the original budget against the revised budget. Similarly, the performance of managers regarding control of operations can be assessed by comparing the actual results against the revised budget.[1]

PROBLEM FOR SELF-STUDY

problem   Examine Exhibit 17-1, page 581. Suppose actual costs were $380,000 instead of $480,000. Compute the cost variance and the schedule variance.

solution   The cost variance would be $380,000 − $400,000, or $20,000, favorable. The schedule variance would be unchanged at $25,000, unfavorable.

HYBRID COSTING

Mixed-model manufacturing

Cost accounting systems for product costing may be placed along a continuum:

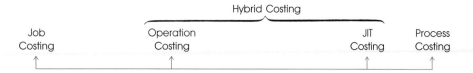

A particular organization may have features of one or more of the four product-costing systems identified here.

Obviously, a product-costing system should be tailored to the underlying production system. As we have seen, job costing usually accompanies the manufacture of relatively heterogeneous products or services (e.g., printing of posters, hand-tailoring of a suit, construction of a driveway). In contrast, process costing usually accompanies the mass production of homogeneous commodities (e.g., glass, paper, raw silicon wafers). An overview of these product-costing systems was presented in Exhibit 15-1, page 508.

As the continuum indicates, many product-costing systems are blends of ideas from both job costing and process costing. We call all these blends **hybrid costing.** The choice of a particular hybrid depends on the underlying production system.

The maker of a relatively wide variety of closely related standardized prod-

[1]For additional discussion, see D. Roman, *Managing Projects: A Systems Approach* (New York: Elsevier, 1986); C. Staffurth, ed., *Project Cost Control*, 2nd ed. (London: Heinemann, 1980); J. Stevenson, *Production/Operations Management*, 2nd ed. (Homewood, Ill.: Richard D. Irwin, 1986); and F. Biery, "The Accuracy of Military Cost and Schedule Forecasts," *Journal of Cost Analysis*, Spring 1986, pp. 13–23.

EXHIBIT 17-2
Different Approaches to Mixed-Model Manufacturing

TYPE OF PRODUCTION SYSTEM	RATE OF PRODUCTION OF FINISHED PRODUCTS	PRODUCT-COSTING SYSTEM	
		Hybrid Examples	Similar to
Batch manufacturing	Variable (uneven)	Operation Costing	Job Costing
Constant-flow manufacturing	Fixed (even)	JIT Costing	Process Costing

CHARACTERISTICS OF PRODUCTION SYSTEMS

Batch Manufacturing	Constant-flow Manufacturing
Operators and equipment grouped in work centers according to function (e.g., lathes, drill presses)	Operators and equipment placed by sequence of operations (e.g., extruding, forming, finishing)
Work orders or production orders initiate production activity (broad product variety)	Planned level of production rates for a family of standardized products
Nonlinear flow of material at varying rates	Linear flow of material at uniform rates
Volume or loads of individual work centers fluctuate over time	Volume and capacity of individual work centers balanced for the specified rates of output
Large work-in-process inventories to avoid idle time	Little or no storage of work in process or parts; hand-to-mouth flows of direct materials

ucts (e.g., Black and Decker tools, Jantzen swimwear, Hart, Schaffner, and Marx suits, Hewlett-Packard personal computers) is referred to here as a **mixed-model manufacturer.** The manufacturer has a choice between two basic modes of organizing production activity: batch manufacturing and constant-flow manufacturing. Exhibit 17-2 presents an overview of these two modes and their accompanying product-costing systems. First, consider batch manufacturing.

Batch production systems

Batch manufacturing is roughly similar to a job-shop environment, which approaches the procedures of a custom manufacturer. Production is initiated and governed by specific work orders or job orders or production orders. Operations and equipment are grouped in work stations (work centers) according to function (e.g., lathes, drill presses). Materials arrive at work stations at uneven rates and sometimes from a variety of previous work stations. The production volumes of individual work stations fluctuate over time.

The batch production system has buffers of inventories at each work station to keep workers busy. Larger stocks of materials, parts, and work-in-process inventories help avoid idle time. If units in process become defective, they can be tossed into a scrap or holding area for rework. To keep production moving, necessary parts can be drawn from nearby inventories.

OPERATION COSTING

Overview of operation costing

Operation costing (or **specification costing**) is a hybrid-costing system often used in the batch manufacturing of goods that have some common characteristics plus some individual characteristics. Examples include products of industries such as

584

textiles, shoes, clothing, and semiconductors. Such products are specifically identified by batches or production runs. They are often variations of a single design and require a varying sequence of standardized operations. For example, depending on quality or other specifications, a suit of clothes may contain different materials and require different hand operations.

Operation can be defined as a standardized method or technique that is repetitively performed regardless of the distinguishing features of the finished product. For example, a machining department may perform one or more of the following operations: milling, cleaning, grinding, and facing. As a term, *operation* is used loosely to describe assorted activities. An operation is most often one of several activities within a department. However, sometimes an operation may be another name for an entire department or process. For instance, some companies have a finishing department that may instead be called a finishing process or finishing operation.

An operation cost system collects cost of direct labor and factory overhead by operations. These conversion costs are then applied to all physical units passing through the operation by using a single average unit conversion cost for the operation. The direct-material costs are traced specifically to the product or product lines in the same manner as a job-cost system.

Exhibit 17-3 illustrates batch manufacturing and operation costing. Note how various batches move through some, but perhaps not all, operations. The T-accounts show how costs move through the ledger. Of course, the accounts for each operation could be grouped as a subsidiary ledger or as a single general-ledger account, Work in Process.

To illustrate, if a company produces lamp bases, the shape of the base may not vary, but the operations needed may differ, depending on the type of metal or finish used. Some metals must be annealed before being worked. Some lamp bases may be plated or painted while others may not. Cutting, stamping, or shaping operations may be identical regardless of the type of metal or finish. Thus the costs of a given lamp model will consist of direct material used plus only the conversion costs applied by the operations used. **Essentially, this system requires collecting conversion costs by operations and applying an average operation cost to those physical units that pass through the operations.**

Illustration of operation costing

An operation-costing system uses work orders that delineate the needed direct materials and step-by-step operations. Work orders differ mainly because each batch contains various combinations of finished units, direct materials, and operations undergone. For instance, consider women's jackets:

	BATCH ONE	BATCH TWO
Direct materials	Wool	Polyester
	Deluxe lining	Ordinary lining
	Deluxe buttons	Ordinary buttons
Conversion costs, each operation has a specific average rate per unit, per hour, or per minute	5 operations, such as cutting, sewing	3 operations

The product costs are compiled by batch. Direct materials would be specifically identified with the batch. Direct labor and factory overhead would not be specifically tracked to the batch. For example, workers would customarily punch in and out for their shifts, but not according to the timing as the batch moves through their operations. Instead an average unit conversion cost of each operation or each minute or hour of operation time would be applied to the products.

Suppose there are work orders for batches of 100 wool jackets and 200 polyester jackets:

	PRODUCTION ORDERS	
	For 100 Wool Jackets	For 200 Polyester Jackets
Direct materials (actual costs applied)	$6,000	$1,000
Conversion costs (costs applied on the basis of machine-hours, labor-hours, product units multiplied by a budgeted rate):		
Operation 1	580	1,160
Operation 2	400	800
Operation 3	500	—
Operation 4	1,900	3,800
Operation 5	300	—
Total manufacturing costs applied to products	$9,680	$6,760

The highlight of this operation cost system is the use of a budgeted or estimated costing rate for applying both the direct labor and the factory overhead of each operation. Direct labor vanishes as a separate classification for product costing. For example, the costs for Operation 1 might be budgeted as follows (amounts assumed):

$$\text{Budgeted application rate for conversion costs} = \frac{\text{Conversion cost (that is, Budgeted direct labor + Budgeted factory overhead)}}{\text{Budgeted machine-hours in Operation 1}}$$

$$= \frac{\$180,000 + \$400,000}{20,000} = \$29 \text{ per machine-hour}$$

Suppose it takes 20 machine-hours to process 100 jackets in Operation 1. Then the conversion cost of Operation 1 for 100 wool jackets is $20 \times \$29 = \$580$, and the conversion cost for 200 polyester jackets is $2 \times 20 \times \$29 = \$1,160$.

As goods undergo Operation 1, conversion costs are applied to them by multiplying the application rate times the machine-hours used in that operation. Any underapplication or overapplication of Operation 1 conversion costs is disposed of at the end of the year in the same manner as underapplied or overapplied factory overhead in job-costing systems.

EXHIBIT 17-3
Overview of Operation Costing

PHYSICAL FLOWS

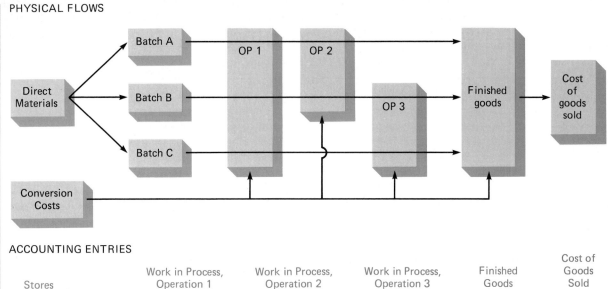

ACCOUNTING ENTRIES

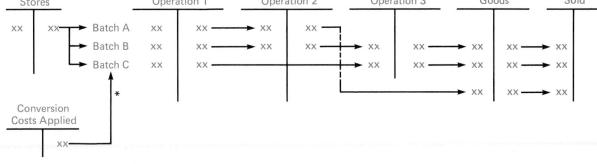

*Conversion costs would be applied to the batches in stages as the units moved through the designated operations. Many companies would use the term factory overhead applied instead of conversion costs applied. Moreover, if direct labor is a significant cost, it might be accounted for separately instead of being considered a subpart of factory overhead or conversion costs.

Note: Exhibit 17-5, page 596, provides an overview of JIT costing.

Summary journal entries for applying costs to the polyester jackets follow:

Work-in-process inventory	1,000	
Stores		1,000

To apply actual direct materials
used on 200 polyester jackets.

Work-in-process inventory	5,760	
Conversion costs applied		5,760

To apply conversion costs of Operations 1,
2, and 4 that were undergone on 200
polyester jackets ($1,160 + $800 +
$3,800 = $5,760).

For years, accountants have divided total manufacturing costs into three major elements: direct materials, direct labor, and factory overhead. Operation-costing systems often have two major elements: direct materials and conversion costs. Direct labor is no longer accounted for as a separate component of product costs.

CONSTANT-FLOW MANUFACTURING AND JUST-IN-TIME (JIT)

Major features
of JIT

Exhibit 17-2 (page 584) lists the characteristics of constant-flow manufacturing. The physical characteristics of constant-flow production systems include sequential operations, no work orders, linear flow of material at fixed or even rates, balancing of output throughout all work centers, and lower inventories of raw materials, parts, and work in process than in batch manufacturing. **Just-in-Time (JIT) Production** is a system whereby each component in a production line is produced immediately as needed by the next step in the production line. It is near-stockless production. Ideally, JIT operates with zero inventories. Many related terms describe the JIT approach, including MAN (Materials as Needed), MIPS (Minimum Inventory Production System), and ZIPS (Zero Inventory Production System).

In contrast to a batch production system, the JIT system has two major features. *First, inventory is regarded as an evil.* Therefore rigid limits are imposed on the inventories of direct materials, parts, and work in process at all points, from stores through various stages of production.

Second, production must be interrupted if parts are absent or defects are discovered. The latter approach differs from the common practice of building around a missing part, adding it later when the part becomes available. Chapter 21 contains further discussion of how the very sizable costs associated with defective units and inventories are significantly reduced by the adoption of JIT by some firms.

In a JIT production line, manufacturing activity at any particular work station is authorized or triggered by usage of that station's output at downstream stations. Ideally, the sale of a unit of finished goods triggers the completion of a unit in final assembly, and so forth, backward in the sequence of manufacturing. This is often referred to as the "demand-pull" feature of a JIT production line. For example, at Hewlett-Packard (HP), workers and managers frequently quote the following demand-pull slogan: "Never build nothing, nowhere for nobody, unless they *ask* you for it."

Employee
involvement
and total quality
control

When a factory switches from batch manufacturing to constant-flow manufacturing, personal observation (as distinguished from accounting reports or cost records) is a key to better control. Employees can see how the product is made by observing the flow of production; when something is wrong, it is apparent.

Factories that have switched to the JIT approach for constant-flow manufacturing have also used *employee involvement* as the major means of control. The managers and all other employees (the team approach) are expected to be sufficiently familiar with daily operations to take prompt action for keeping production on schedule and for controlling costs.

The pursuit of *total quality control* (TQC) also tends to get more attention in constant-flow manufacturing than in batch manufacturing. Each worker assumes responsibility for his or her own work. Vendors guarantee that parts and materials are free from defects. JIT is usually accompanied by an emphasis on employee involvement and on total quality control, but these ideas are conceptually distinct. For example, TQC programs can be used in any production system.

Good relationships with one or a few vendors are a critical component of JIT. These vendors provide high-quality items and make frequent deliveries to the factory; in turn, materials and parts are immediately placed into production. This procedure skips the storeroom and the corresponding Stores account completely.

Financial benefits of JIT

Switching from batch manufacturing to constant-flow manufacturing plus JIT, employee involvement, and TQC should lead to many financial benefits, including

1. Lower investments in inventories
2. Reductions in carrying and handling costs of inventories
3. Reductions in risks of obsolescence of inventories
4. Lower investments in factory space for inventories and production
5. Reductions in total manufacturing costs:
   a. Direct materials:
      (1) Quantity discounts, one vendor
      (2) Improved quality
   b. Other costs:
      (1) Lower labor costs from increased overall efficiency despite increases in downtime
      (2) Reductions of scrap and rework
      (3) Reductions in paperwork

Examples of reductions in paperwork include the issuance of blanket long-term orders to suppliers instead of purchase orders. Reductions can be dramatic. For example, a Taiwan factory was processing 10,000 purchase orders, receiving reports, and material requisitions per week. After switching to JIT, a simpler accounting system emerged. Ideally, there are no individual purchase orders, no receiving reports, no stores requisitions, no work orders, no tracking of direct labor as a separate cost element.

Cost accounting for batch manufacturing often focuses narrowly on the control of *direct labor*. In contrast, cost accounting for constant-flow manufacturing plus JIT tends to focus more broadly on the control of *total manufacturing costs*. For example, idle time may rise because production lines are starved for material more frequently than before. Still, many overhead costs will decline. For example, consider probable reductions in the costs of material handling and special inspectors for quality control.

Dramatic reductions in investments in inventories and in needs for factory space have been reported by some adopters of JIT. In addition, savings in total manufacturing costs have been substantial. Consider the Vancouver division of Hewlett-Packard. HP's manufacturing of printers had been based on work orders for small batches. These products are produced repetitively, so the work-order system had led to inefficiencies. The Vancouver division reported the following benefits two years after the adoption of JIT:

Work-in-process inventory dollars	Down 82%
Space used	Down 40%
Scrap/rework	Down 30%
Production time:	
Impact printers	Down 7 days to 2 days
Thermal printers	Down 7 days to 3 hours
Labor efficiency	Up 50%
Shipments	Up 20%

Chapter 21 expands the discussion of JIT. In particular, see Exhibit 21-7, page 730, for a summary of the beneficial effects of JIT production.

JIT COSTING

Cost accounting in a JIT environment

JIT costing is defined here as a *hybrid-costing* system that is used in conjunction with Just-in-Time production systems.[2] The cost accounting system used by HP for divisions adopting JIT is remarkably simple. Exhibit 17-4 compares the accounting system HP uses for JIT manufacturing with the accounting system for batch manufacturing. Under JIT, the distinction between raw materials and work in process (WIP) is replaced by "resources in process" (RIP), actually called "raw and in-process." The "dock-to-production" arrow indicates that the materials arrive at the receiving dock or area and are whisked immediately to the factory production area. Thus the Stores account vanishes.

The "post-deduct" arrow in Exhibit 17-4 denotes the HP method of crediting the RIP account *as goods are completed* and moved to Finished Goods.

EXHIBIT 17-4
Batch vs. Just-In-Time Manufacturing

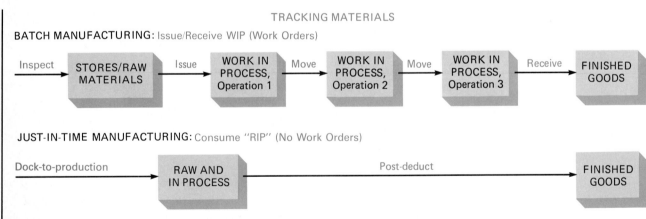

Chapter 17
590

[2]The discussion in this section illustrates one approach to cost accounting in a JIT environment. There is no single "best" approach to cost accounting in a JIT environment, just as there is no single best approach to cost accounting in a job-shop environment.

The most noteworthy aspects of HP's JIT accounting system are

1. The absence of a separate Stores account.
2. The absence of work orders or detailed tracking of actual raw materials and direct labor through a series of operations. (This aspect generated the comment: "Hello JIT; goodbye Stores and WIP; farewell Stores and WIP accounting.")

Journal entries for JIT costing

Exhibit 17-4 will become clearer if we compare the journal entries that accompany batch manufacturing and JIT costing. Consider HP purchases of raw materials. Numbers are assumed:

OPERATION COSTING		
Stores	20,000	
Accounts payable		20,000
To record purchases.		
Work in process, Operation 1	20,000	
Stores		20,000
Materials issued to the first operation.		
Work in process, Operation 2	19,800	
Work in process, Operation 1		19,800
Materials transferred.		
Work in process, Operation 3	19,400	
Work in process, Operation 2		19,400
Materials transferred.		
Finished goods	19,000	
Work in process, Operation 3		19,000
To record raw materials in completed units.		

JIT COSTING		
Raw and in-process inventory	20,000	
Accounts payable		20,000
To record purchases.		
Finished goods	19,000	
Raw and in-process inventory		19,000
To record raw materials in completed units. This is the post-deduct step.		

Direct-labor costs and factory-overhead costs are not tracked to specific work orders. There are no work orders. Direct labor is now regarded as just another subpart of factory overhead. In short, conversion costs are equal to factory overhead because there is no longer a separate category of direct labor. Moreover, factory overhead is accounted for as follows:

Virtually all of the manufacturing overhead incurred each month, now including direct labor, flowed through to cost of goods sold in the same month. Tracking overhead through work-in-process and finished goods inventory provided no useful information. Management decided, therefore, to treat manufacturing overhead as an expense charged directly to cost of goods sold. Overhead remaining in work-in-process and finished goods is maintained with end-of-month adjusting entries.[3]

Distinguish between the *incurrence* of factory overhead and its *application* to products. The incurrence of overhead is charged to responsibility centers under JIT costing in the same way as in other costing systems. However, overhead application is different. In our illustration, assume that the application of all factory costs (other than direct materials) is $16,000. The entry is made directly to cost of goods sold:

Cost of goods sold	16,000	
Factory overhead applied (or conversion costs applied)		16,000

At the end of each month, an adjusting entry is made for the standard-costing amounts (or similar estimates) of overhead associated with any raw and in-process or finished-goods inventories. Suppose the amount is $1,000 to RIP and $3,000 to finished goods:

Raw and in-process inventory	1,000	
Finished goods	3,000	
Cost of goods sold		4,000
To remove overhead costs from cost of goods sold that belong in the ending inventory accounts.		

Standard-cost variances

The cost accounting literature often erroneously distinguishes among job costing, process costing, and standard costing as though they were mutually exclusive categories of product costing. Standard costing can be used in conjunction with any product-costing system (job, process, operation, JIT, or some other hybrid). Indeed, regardless of the type of production system or product-costing system, standard costing is enormously popular.[4]

The accounting for variances in a JIT is insignificantly different whether operation costing or JIT costing is used. Reconsider our HP example. Suppose raw

---

[3]R. Hunt, L. Garrett, and C. M. Merz, "Direct Labor Cost Not Always Relevant at H-P," *Management Accounting,* February 1985, p. 61. Also see P. Chalos, "High-Tech Production: The Impact on Cost Reporting Systems," *Journal of Accountancy,* March 1986, pp. 106–12, and B. Neumann and P. Jaouen, "Kanban, Zips and Cost Accounting: a Case Study." *Journal of Accountancy,* August 1986, pp. 132–41.

[4]For example, a survey of 112 manufacturing firms indicated that 85% used standard costs. See H. Schwarzbach, "The Impact of Automation on Accounting for Indirect Costs," *Management Accounting,* December 1985.

materials were acquired for \$1,800 in excess of a standard cost of \$20,000:

JOB, PROCESS, AND OPERATION COSTING SYSTEMS

Stores	20,000	
Raw material purchase price variance	1,800	
Accounts payable		21,800

JIT COSTING SYSTEM

Raw and in-process inventory	20,000	
Raw material purchase price variance	1,800	
Accounts payable		21,800

JIT production systems force management to ask whether it is worthwhile to track detailed costs of products step by step to the point of completion. There is still physical tracking of units, but there is no "costs attach" tracking via work orders. Instead the production process is regarded as a pipeline. When the pipeline is filled, any costs entering at the start of the period will reappear as the costs of completed products before the end of the period.

Under JIT conditions, actual material and other factory costs are accumulated at the department level for each month. The good units produced are measured. Their standard costs allowed are also measured. Variances are computed at the department level monthly.

MANY AVAILABLE PRODUCT-COSTING CHOICES

Operation costing and JIT costing are only two examples of many hybrid approaches to product costing for mixed-model manufacturing. The many variations of these product-costing systems depend on the underlying production process and the desires of management for varying degrees of accuracy. For example, Hewlett-Packard uses JIT costing in some factories but operation costing in others. In general, as production processes change from job or batch methods to constant-flow or process methods, cost accounting systems become simpler and less expensive.

Additional choices under each system are also available. Examples: Should we use actual, normal, or standard costs? Should we use plantwide, departmental, or work station overhead rates? Should we use direct materials, direct labor, machine-hours, or units produced as an overhead allocation base? Should we use more than one overhead allocation base?

Every company seems to have its own peculiar production problems that result in systems choices that blend features of various product-costing systems or have imposing overhead application aspects. For example, a JIT system may have a constant production flow through many (but not all) operations, and each operation may have two individual overhead application rates based on, say, direct materials and machine-hours, respectively.

1. A factory has an operation-costing system. It has a storeroom and several buffer stocks of parts and in-process inventories at various work centers along the production lines. No special major cost category for direct labor exists; all labor is a subpart of factory overhead. For simplicity, assume there are no beginning inventories.

Prepare summary journal entries (without explanations) based on the following data for a given month:

Raw materials purchased	$30,000
Raw materials used	30,000
Factory overhead applied	22,500
Costs transferred to finished goods	49,700
Cost of goods sold	41,700

For simplicity, you are given sufficient data to prepare journal entries for each underlying movement from, say, Work in Process, Operation 1 to Work in Process, Operation 2 to Work in Process, Operation 3. Instead assume there is only a single account, Work in Process, that is supported by subsidiary work in process accounts for each operation.

2. The factory adopts a JIT system. Prepare summary journal entries (without explanations) based on the following data for a given month:

Raw materials purchased	$30,000
Raw materials used	30,000
Raw materials transferred to finished goods when units completed	28,500
Raw materials transferred from finished goods to cost of goods sold	23,500
Factory overhead applied	22,500
Amounts of factory overhead in ending inventories:	
Raw and in-process	1,300
Finished goods	3,000

3. Post the entries in requirements 1 and 2 to T-accounts for inventories and cost of goods sold.
4. Examine Exhibit 17-3, page 587. Prepare a similar exhibit for a JIT product-costing system. Include the same three operations in your diagram as those shown in Exhibit 17-3.

1. a. Stores   30,000
    Accounts payable   30,000

b. Work in process   30,000
    Stores   30,000

c. Work in process   22,500
    Factory overhead applied   22,500

d. Finished goods   49,700
    Work in process   49,700

e. Cost of goods sold   41,700
    Finished goods   41,700

2. a. Raw and in-process inventory   30,000

        Accounts payable   30,000

   b. Finished goods   28,500

          Raw and in-process inventory   28,500

      This is the "post-deduct" step.

   c. Cost of goods sold   23,500

          Finished goods   23,500

   d. Cost of goods sold   22,500

          Factory overhead applied   22,500

   e. Raw and in-process inventory   1,300

     Finished goods   3,000

          Cost of goods sold   4,300

3. The first row of T-accounts relates to requirement 1; the second, to requirement 2.

Stores		Work in Process		Finished Goods		Cost of Goods Sold	
(a) 30,000	(b) 30,000	(b) 30,000	(d) 49,700	(d) 49,700	(e) 41,700	(e) 41,700	
Bal. 0		(c) 22,500		Bal. 8,000			
		Bal. 2,800					

Raw and In-process Inventory				Finished Goods		Cost of Goods Sold	
(a) 30,000	(b) 28,500			(b) 28,500	(c) 23,500	(c) 23,500	(e) 4,300
(e) 1,300				(e) 3,000		(d) 22,500	
Bal. 2,800				Bal. 8,000		Bal. 41,700	

      To ease comparisons between the entries for operation cost accounting and JIT cost accounting, the numbers used for the various inventory balances are identical. However, advocates of JIT would insist that inventories would decline substantially, particularly inventories of raw materials and work in process.

     4. See Exhibit 17-5 on page 596.

SUMMARY

Job costing in nonmanufacturing settings differs little from that in manufacturing settings. The focus is on obtaining the total cost of a specific service or engagement. The major means of control is careful budgeting and use of direct-labor hours.

The major costs of professional service firms are the compensation and related costs of labor. Control of the number of employees and the use of their time is a major managerial challenge.

Project costing is more complex than ordinary job costing. Projects tend to have more uncertainties and require coordination over a longer time span.

The physical processes of production are the keys to the design of cost accounting systems. If the processes change, the cost accounting systems should also change. Hybrid-costing systems have various characteristics. Examples of hybrid systems are operation and JIT cost accounting systems.

EXHIBIT 17-5
Overview of JIT Costing

PHYSICAL FLOWS

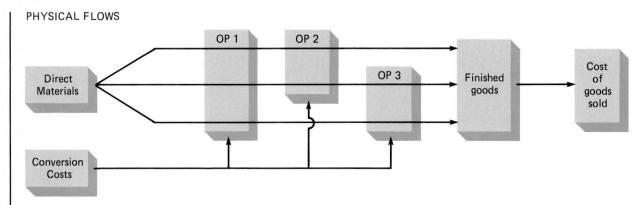

ACCOUNTING ENTRIES

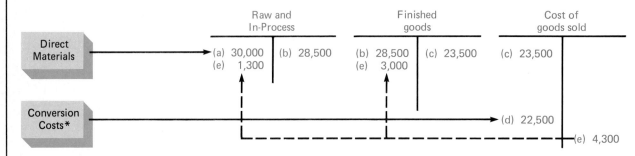

Many companies (e.g., Hewlett-Packard) use factory overhead instead of conversion costs to describe all costs other than direct materials.

Terms to Learn

This chapter and the Glossary at the end of this book contain definitions of the following important terms:

hybrid costing (p. 583)   JIT costing (590)   just-in-time (JIT) production (588)
mixed-model manufacturer (584)   operation (585)   operation costing (584)
project (580)   specification costing (584)

Special Points and Pitfalls

Ponder the changes from operation-costing to JIT-costing systems:

1. Inventory levels of raw materials and work in process plummet, so detailed accounting is reduced for acquisition, storage, and issuance of materials, and for parts in process.

2. JIT production systems tend to reduce material-handling costs, space costs, and the accounting costs of elaborate internal controls and tracking these overhead items. The accompanying cost accounting systems have been simplified in the sense that there are fewer transactions and no work orders.

APPENDIX 17: ACCOUNTING FOR PAYROLL

The tasks of accounting for payrolls are complicated by the necessity for withholding specified amounts from employee earnings, measuring costs of employment fringe benefits, and meeting the government requirements for taxation and regulation. There are three major problems: (a) allocating labor costs to functions, departments, and products; (b) accurately computing earnings and promptly paying individual employees; and (c) computing and remitting withholdings and fringe benefits. Many of the aspects of classifying and controlling labor costs—point (a) above—have been covered previously (Chapters 4 and 6). This appendix concentrates on other facets of payroll.

Individuals who are responsible for payroll accounting agree that, from the viewpoint of employees at least, promptness of payment and pinpoint accuracy are the foremost criteria for judging the merits of any payroll system. Whatever their educational level, be it twenty years of schooling or two, employees are excellent auditors of their own paychecks. Employees demand prompt and accurate payment, and they voice their dissatisfaction with vigor.

GOVERNMENT IMPACT

Complexity of payroll accounting

Fifty years ago, an employee who earned $60 per week received $60 in cash on payday. The bookkeeping problems for payroll were relatively simple. Only two parties (employer and employee) were involved.

Nowadays, the data-processing problems of accounting for payroll are staggering, and the clerical expenses for payroll accounting have soared accordingly. The rash of withholdings, fringe benefits, and incentive pay schemes requires an intricate network of accounts and supporting documents. Accounting for payroll has become so voluminous that new machine or computer installations invariably handle payroll as one of their first routine tasks. An extensive array of computer software packages for payroll accounting is now available for many organizations.

Government requirements regarding payroll records play a big role in systems and forms design. **The government has at least two major influences: (a) it requires the employer to be its collection agent for income taxes from employees, and (b) it levies special payroll taxes on the employer.**

Withholding taxes

The employer must withhold ordinary income taxes. As used here, "ordinary" refers to all federal, state, and municipal income taxes. Hereafter, these will simply be called *income taxes*. U.S. employers must also withhold a special income tax, commonly called the *Social Security tax*. Other terms for the Social Security tax are *federal insurance contributions act tax* (F.I.C.A. tax) and *federal old-age benefits tax* (F.O.A.B. tax). The amounts and timing of these tax payments to the government vary as specified by (changing) laws.

The basic journal-entry pattern is as follows:

Work-in-process control	120,000	
Factory-overhead control	30,000	
Selling-expense control	40,000	
Administrative-expense control	10,000	
Accrued payroll (gross)		200,000
Accrued payroll	35,000	
Withheld income taxes payable		29,000
Withheld Social Security taxes payable		6,000
Withheld income taxes payable	29,000	
Withheld Social Security taxes payable	6,000	
Cash (or some similar credit that has this ultimate effect on cash)		35,000

These entries show that the *gross* payroll cost is the measure of the various basic labor costs incurred by the employer. The taxes *on employees* are withheld and remitted (usually monthly) to the government.

Other withholdings   A flock of other withholdings from employees also exists. Withholdings as such are not employer costs. **They are merely portions of the employee's gross earnings that are being funneled via the employer to third parties, primarily for the employee's convenience.** Examples include employee contributions to group life insurance plans, hospitalization insurance, pension funds, employee savings plans, donations, and union dues.

FRINGE BENEFITS

Large size of fringe benefits   The gross earnings (gross payroll costs) of employees are only partial measures of the payroll costs really borne. U.S. employers not only must pay payroll taxes like Social Security (which match employee Social Security taxes) and unemployment levies but must also incur many more fringe costs. The following breakdown of payroll costs illustrates the general pattern:

Gross earnings of employee	100%
Employer payroll taxes (for Social Security, unemployment, workmen's compensation)	10
Vacations (and paid holidays)	12
Employer contributions to pension, medical, dental, and life insurance funds	16
Grand total payroll costs incurred by many employers	138%

The fringe costs of labor are no longer a dribble; their waterfall proportions have caused an increasing number of companies to recast their account classifications. Instead of treating all fringe costs as overhead, some companies add an average (that is, "equalized" or "leveled") fringe rate to the basic direct-labor rate to bring into focus a better measure of direct-labor costs (say 138%, as in the table above). **However, perhaps because of inertia, most companies continue to treat fringe costs as a part of overhead.**

Timing of cost recognition

As in many other phases of accounting, there is often a time lag between incurrence and payment of various payroll fringe costs. For example, the liability for vacation payments really accrues from week to week as each employee accumulates a claim to vacation pay. Thus many companies use an estimate to spread total vacation costs over a year instead of recognizing such costs as payments are made:

Work-in-process control (direct labor)	19,000	
Factory-overhead control (indirect labor plus $3,000 vacation pay)	9,000	
Estimated liability for vacation pay		3,000
Accrued payroll		25,000

To accrue vacation pay throughout the year because it is related to work done throughout the year. Leveled rate is 12% of Accrued Payroll. Entry here is, say, for January.

Accrued payroll	25,000	
Estimated liability for vacation pay	900	
Cash		22,600
Withholdings payable (various)		3,300

The liability account for vacation pay is debited as actual vacation payments are made.

Similar treatment can be given to contributions for other employee benefits such as pension funds. The decision to adopt such leveling arrangements in accounting for fringe costs largely depends on the significance of the amounts involved and on the distortion of month-to-month costs that may arise from failure to spread charges over the year.

EMPLOYER PAYROLL TAXES: THEORY AND PRACTICE

Employers must pay Social Security taxes and other payroll taxes on specified compensation paid to each employee every calendar year—up to maximum statutory taxable-wage limits that are changed by Congress from time to time. In most cases, this procedure means that heavier tax outlays will be made in the earlier months of the calendar year than in the later months, because the employer liability diminishes as wage payments to an increasing number of employees gradually reach and pass the yearly statutory taxable-wage limit.

The problem of timing charges for employer payroll taxes raises some special theoretical questions. The employer's legal liability is ordinarily a function of wages *paid* rather than of wages *accrued*. Yet in practice, employer payroll taxes are usually accrued as wages are *earned*. Furthermore, such payroll tax accrual diminishes as months pass because more and more employees' earnings gradually surpass the maximum taxable limit.

To illustrate, assume that a company has a gross payroll of $25,000 per month, $19,000 of which is direct labor, and $6,000 of which is indirect factory labor. For simplicity, assume that the total tax rate on employers is 10%.

Early months:	Work in process	19,000	
	Factory overhead		
	($6,000 + $2,500)	8,500	
	Accrued payroll		25,000
	Employer's payroll taxes payable		2,500
	Payroll tax is .10 × $25,000 = $2,500.		
Late months:	Work in process	19,000	
	Factory overhead	6,000	
	Accrued payroll		25,000
	Payroll is not subject to payroll tax because every employee's salary has passed the maximum taxable limits.		

In theory, employer payroll taxes (a) should be accrued as wages are earned (this practice is widely followed) and (b) should be spread over the year, using a leveled rate. Thus payroll taxes would be handled in a fashion similar to the immediately preceding illustration on vacation pay. The reasoning in support of spreading payroll taxes over the year is that, for a going concern, the commitment to hire employees is made for a year; the payroll tax is an annual tax that is related to the year as a whole. Because it benefits the entire year's operations, such a tax should not be loaded on the early months of the calendar year.

Illustration of payroll accounting

The Stengal Company has a gross factory payroll of $10,000 per day, based on a five-day, forty-hour, Monday-through-Friday workweek. Withholdings for income taxes amount to $1,000 per day. There are additional withholdings for Social Security; the employee Social Security tax rate is assumed to be 8%. Payrolls for each week are paid on the following Tuesday.

Gross daily payrolls consist of $7,000 direct labor and $3,000 indirect labor. The general-ledger entry to record the total of the payroll cost incurred (including accrued employer payroll fringe costs) is made on the last day of each month. Fringe costs borne by the employer are:

	PERCENTAGE OF GROSS PAYROLL
Vacation pay (and other fringe benefits such as pensions)	30%
Employer payroll taxes	10%
	40%

For our purposes, assume that the company starts business on March 3.

		MARCH				
S	M	T	W	T	F	S
						1
2	3	4	5	6	7	8
9	10	11	12	13	14	15
16	17	18	19	20	21	22
23	24	25	26	27	28	29
30	31					

		APRIL				
S	M	T	W	T	F	S
		1	2	3	4	5
6	7	8	9	10	11	12
13	14	15	16	17	18	19
20	21	22	23	24	25	26
27	28	29	30			

Assume that all taxes withheld on *paydays* are paid to the government on the final day of each month.

Try to solve the following requirements by yourself before examining the solution.

Required

1. All journal entries for payroll for March 11, 18, 25, and 31; April 1, 8, 15, 22, 29, and 30.

2. All postings to Accrued Payroll and Withheld Taxes Payable.

solution

1. Journal entries follow:

March 11	Accrued payroll (5 × $10,000)	50,000	
	Cash		41,000
	Withheld taxes payable		9,000
	(5 × $1,000) + (.08 × $50,000)		
	To pay payroll.		

The identical entry would be repeated every Tuesday, March 18 through April 29. Note that payroll settlements are made every *payday*, regardless of when payroll costs are recognized as being incurred.

The entry below is based on 21 days of work done in March.

March 31	Work in process		
	(21 days × $7,000)	147,000	
	Factory overhead		
	(21 days × $3,000) + .40(21 × $3,000)		
	+ .40($147,000)	147,000	
	Accrued payroll (21 days × $10,000)		210,000
	Estimated liability for vacation pay		
	(and other fringe benefits)		
	(.30 × $210,000)		63,000
	Employer's payroll taxes payable		
	(.10 × $210,000)		21,000
	To record incurrence of labor costs		
	and related payroll taxes and other		
	fringe costs for March.		

Such an entry is usually made and posted monthly. If desired, it could be made weekly, biweekly, or at any other interval. As contrasted with the preceding entry, this entry recognizes cost incurrence rather than payment. Its amounts depend on the number of work days in a calendar month.

Examine the postings to the Accrued Payroll account below. At the close of business on March 31, the balance represents the unpaid amount of *gross* earnings of employees applicable to the last six days worked in March. Note that the entries on *paydays* are the same for April as for March.

The entry below is based on 22 days of work done in April.

April 30	Work in process		
	(22 days × $7,000)	154,000	
	Factory overhead		
	(22 days × $3,000) + .40(22 × $3,000)		
	+ .40($154,000)	154,000	
	Accrued payroll (22 days × $10,000)		220,000
	Estimated liability for vacation pay		
	(.30 × $220,000)		66,000
	Employer's payroll taxes payable		
	(.10 × $220,000)		22,000
	To record incurrence of labor costs and related payroll taxes and fringe benefits for April.		

The journal entries for reductions of liabilities for withheld taxes paid in cash to the government on March 31 and April 30 follow:

March 31	Withheld taxes payable	27,000	
	Cash		27,000
	3 paydays × $9,000. The reduction of the liability is based on when the payroll is *paid*, not when it is *earned*.		
April 30	Withheld taxes payable	45,000	
	Cash		45,000
	5 paydays × $9,000.		

The timing of the company payments varies for employer payroll taxes, vacation pay, and liabilities for other fringe benefits. These details are beyond the scope of this book.

2. Postings for March and April follow:

Accrued Payroll

March 11	50,000	March 31	210,000
March 18	50,000		
March 25	50,000		
		March 31 balance, six days' gross earnings	60,000
April 1	50,000	April 30	220,000
April 8	50,000		
April 15	50,000		
April 22	50,000		
April 29	50,000		
		April 30 balance, three days' gross earnings	30,000

		Withheld Taxes Payable		
March 31	27,000	March 11, 18, 25		27,000
April 30	45,000	April 1, 8, 15, 22, 29		45,000

QUESTIONS, PROBLEMS, AND CASES

17-1 "Job-order costing is not confined to manufacturing companies." Give three examples of industries or types of companies that use job-order costing.

17-2 Give an example of a rule of thumb or a formula used for pricing by professional service firms.

17-3 Many professional service firms have refined their data-processing systems. How have such refinements affected classifications of costs?

17-4 If the total costs are unchanged, what effect will a reclassification of overhead costs as direct costs have on overhead rates?

17-5 "Projects are more challenging than jobs." Explain.

17-6 "Managers' control of projects generally focuses on four key aspects." Identify the four.

17-7 What is the relationship between cost and schedule performance reporting and earned value reporting?

17-8 Why is operation costing often called hybrid costing?

17-9 "Operation costing means that *conversion costs* and *factory overhead* are synonyms." Do you agree? Explain.

17-10 Give three examples of industries that are likely to use operation costing.

17-11 "In contrast to a batch production system, JIT production has two major elements." Identify the two elements.

17-12 "The focus of JIT broadens beyond saving labor costs." Explain.

17-13 Identify two noteworthy aspects of Hewlett-Packard's JIT accounting system.

17-14 "JIT accounting is essentially process costing." Do you agree? Explain.

17-15 "Employee involvement is the major means of control in JIT systems." Explain.

17-16 "Many product-costing choices are available." Explain.

17-17 Cost and price of services. Consider the following data:

Revenue	$21,000,000
Direct labor for professional services	?
Contribution to overhead and operating income	$16,000,000
Overhead	?
Operating income	?

The budgeted overhead rate is 300% of direct labor. Fill in the blanks. Also compute the average markup rate of direct labor for the pricing of engagements.

17-18 CPA fees. The partner in charge of an audit engagement has prepared the following budget data for a proposal to a prospective client. These data are for direct professional hours and include all fringe benefits (which total 40% of the basic labor rates):

Partner, 1 × 50 hours × $120	$ 6,000
Manager, 1 × 100 hours × $40	4,000
Senior, 1 × 200 hours × $30	6,000
Assistants, 3 × 180 hours × $20	10,800
	$26,800

The budgeted overhead rate is 200% of direct professional labor dollars. The normal markup for the pricing of engagements is 350% of direct-labor costs.

Required
1. Suppose a normal markup is used to quote a total fixed fee for the audit engagement. Compute the budgeted total revenue, total costs, and operating income.
2. Identify three factors that may cause the actual fee to differ from the budgeted fee.

17-19 Cost and price of services. Consider the following budgeted data for an audit engagement of Finn and Company, Certified Public Accountants. The client wants a fixed price quotation.

Direct professional labor	$30,000
Travel costs	7,000
Direct support labor	9,000
Other operating costs applied at 100% of total direct costs (excluding travel)	?
Fringe benefits for all direct labor	13,000
Photocopying	1,000
Telephone calls	1,000
Computer time	6,000

Required
1. Prepare a schedule of the budgeted total costs of the audit engagement. Show subtotals for total direct costs and total costs as a basis for markup. The firm's policy is to charge clients for the actual costs of travel.
2. Assume that the partner's policy is to quote a fixed fee at 20% above the total costs used as a basis for markup. What fee would she quote?
3. Suppose a competing public accounting firm has the same set of costs. However, the cost accounting system traces only direct professional labor as a direct cost of an engagement. The firm's policy is to quote a fixed fee at 500% of direct professional labor. What fee would the competitor quote?
4. Compare and comment on the approaches to fee setting described in requirements 2 and 3.

17-20 Program budgeting and job costing. Nonprofit institutions such as health centers and colleges continually face decisions concerning how to allocate their limited resources. A technique called program budgeting has been developed to help in the making of these decisions. The "program" is an activity or set of activities with a particular goal such as placing children for adoption, helping ex-convicts on parole, aiding disabled veterans, or educating students of management.

Program budgeting is a philosophy or state of mind rather than a rigid set of procedures. Questions such as the following are raised: (1) What are the organization's objectives or goals? Program categories sometimes cut across organizational lines so that two or more departments work together toward a common goal. (2) How much does each program cost? Costs typically include specifically traceable costs such as direct labor plus applied overhead. (3) How is each program funded? Are cash receipts from donations, tuition, or government grants earmarked specifically for one purpose? Sometimes raising money for a specific program can dislodge general funds for other purposes.

As 19_5 began, Muriel Clayton, director of the Uppervale Health Center, faced a decision. She had talked recently with Theodore Rosenberg, an administrator in the State Health Department. He told her that the state might be able to increase its support to the center by $100,000. Ms. Clayton had to determine which of two activities, drug-addict rehabilitation or alcoholic rehabilitation, was more effective so she could write a formal request for the additional funds.

For purposes of cost analysis, the center's activities were divided into four programs: (1) alcoholic rehabilitation, (2) drug-addict rehabilitation, (3) children's clinical services, and (4) after-care (counseling and support of patients after release from a mental hospital).

Ms. Clayton felt that costs per program would help her decide where to invest additional funds. Of course, such costs would give her some idea of the inputs devoted to each program. The measure of outputs is far more troublesome. Should it be patients treated, patients cured, patients not requiring further treatment for two years, or what measure? Ms. Clayton decided that cost per patient per year would be a helpful statistic for making her decision. She felt that it would be too expensive and too difficult to develop a more elegant measure of effectiveness. The center's board and staff agreed that if the cost per drug patient per year was not more than 20% higher than for the alcoholic patient, the drug program would receive the additional funds.

The center's simplified budget was typical for a nonprofit institution in the sense that it was a line-item budget, a mere listing of various costs classified by so-called natural descriptions:

Professional salaries:		
6 physicians @ $75,000	$450,000	
19 psychologists @ $50,000	950,000	
24 nurses @ $25,000	600,000	$2,000,000
Medical supplies		300,000
General overhead (administrative salaries, rent, utilities, etc.)		1,000,000
		$3,300,000

The budget and the accounting system did not show how the costs related to the four programs. Ms. Clayton decided to ask the professional staff to fill out a form indicating what percentage of time each devoted to the four programs. This was a critical form, and Clayton, who had earned uniformly high respect from the professional staff, stressed that it be filled out conscientiously.

Costs of medical supplies were to be allocated on the basis of physician-hours spent in each program. General overhead would be allocated on the basis of direct-labor cost (where direct labor is defined to include the time of doctors, psychologists, and nurses multiplied by the salary rate of each).

Clayton compiled the following data concerning allocations from individual time allocation forms:

	ALCOHOL	DRUG Counseling	DRUG Clinical	CHILDREN	AFTER-CARE	TOTAL
Physicians			2	4		6
Psychologists	6	4			9	19
Nurses	4	4	2	4	10	24

At any point in time, an average of 30 patients are in residence in the alcohol program, each staying about a half-year. Thus the clinic processed 60 patients but provided only 30 patient-years of service. Similarly, an average of 40 patients were involved in the drug program for about a half-year each; they received both counseling and clinical services.

<table><tr><td>Required</td><td>What is the cost of the alcohol and drug programs, using the Clayton approach to cost analysis? What action should be taken?</td></tr></table>

17-21 Job costing in an accounting firm.   A public accounting firm has a condensed budget for 19_2 as follows:

Revenue	$20,000,000
Direct labor (for professional hours charged to jobs)	5,000,000
Contribution to overhead and operating profit	15,000,000
Overhead (all other costs)	13,000,000
Operating income	$ 2,000,000

The firm uses a job-costing system for assorted purposes. For example, the partner in charge of an audit will plan the amount of professional time needed, including the time of the partners, managers, senior accountants, and assistants (often called junior accountants). The actual hours will be tabulated, comparisons made, and costs compiled, and the profitability of the job will be measured. The results will be used as a guide for managing future audits.

Required

1. The cost of each job is defined as actual direct labor plus overhead applied as a percentage of direct labor. Compute the budgeted overhead rate.
2. The markup rate for pricing jobs is intended to produce an operating income of 10% of revenue. Compute the markup rate as a percentage of direct labor.
3. The accounting firm's cost per hour of personnel assigned to Job 345, the audit of a local liquor distributor, is: partner, $60; manager, $35; senior, $25; assistant, $15. Last week's time sheets showed the following:

Partner	3
Manager	15
Senior	40
Assistants	160
Total	218

Compute the total costs added to Job 345 for the week. Suppose the accounting firm is able to realize normal billing rates for this work. Compute the addition to revenue because of this work.

17-22 Job costing in a service industry.   Howe and Halling, Certified Public Accountants, use a form of job-costing system. In this respect they are similar to many professional service firms, such as management consulting firms, law firms, and professional engineering firms.

An auditing client may be served by various staff who hold professional positions in the hierarchy from partners to managers to senior accountants to assistants. In addition, there are secretaries and other employees.

Suppose that Howe and Halling have the following budget for 19_2:

Compensation of professional staff	$4,000,000
Other costs	2,400,000
Total budgeted costs	$6,400,000

Each professional staff member must submit a weekly time report, which is used to assign costs to jobs. An example is the time report of a senior accountant:

WEEK OF JANUARY 8	S	M	T	W	T	F	S	TOTAL
CHARGEABLE HOURS								
Client A		8	8	5				21
Client B				3		4		7
Etc.								
NONCHARGEABLE HOURS								
Professional development								
(attending seminar on								
computer auditing)					8			8
Unassigned time						4		4
Total	0	8	8	8	8	8	0	40

In turn, these time reports are used for charging hours to a client job-order sheet, summarized as follows for Client A:

	WEEK OF		TOTAL	BILLING	TOTAL
EMPLOYEES CHARGED	Jan. 8	Jan. 15	HOURS	RATES	BILLED
Partners	4	4	8	$100	$ 800
Managers	4	4	8	60	480
Seniors	21	30	51	40	2,040
Assistants	48	70	118	20	2,360
Total hours	77	108	185		$5,680

In many cases, these job-cost sheets bear only a summary of the *hours* charged. Each class of labor is billed at an appropriate hourly rate, so that the job-cost sheet is the central basis for billing the client.

Required

1. Suppose this firm had a policy of charging overhead to jobs at a predetermined percentage of the salaries charged to the job. The experience of the firm has been that chargeable hours average 80% of available hours for all categories of professional personnel. The nonchargeable hours are regarded as additional overhead. What is the overhead rate as a percentage of the "direct labor," the chargeable professional compensation cost?

2. Compute the *total cost* of the Client A job for the two weeks that began January 8. Be as specific as possible. Assume that the average weekly compensation (based on a 40-hour week) of the personnel working on this job is: partners, $2,000; managers, $1,200; seniors, $800; assistants, $400.

3. As the tabulation for Client A implies, the job order often consists of only the time and no costs. Instead the revenue is computed via multiplying the time by the billing rates. Suppose the partners' income objective is 20% of the total costs budgeted. What percentage of the salaries charged to the jobs would be necessary to achieve a total billing that would ultimately provide the income objective? That is, what is the billing rate as a percentage of "direct labor"?

4. In addition to billing, what use might you make of the data compiled on the job orders?

17-23 Job costing in an accounting firm. Serra & Co., a public accounting firm, had the following costs in 19_2:

Direct professional labor	$10,000,000
Overhead	19,000,000
Total costs	$29,000,000

The following costs were included in overhead:

Fringe benefits to direct labor	$1,500,000
Secretarial costs	2,700,000
Telephone call time with clients (estimated but not tabulated)	600,000
Computer time	1,800,000
Photocopying	400,000
	$7,000,000

The firm's data-processing capabilities now make it feasible to document and trace these costs to individual jobs.

The managing partner is pondering whether more costs than just direct labor should be applied directly to jobs. In this way, the firm will be better able to justify billings to clients.

In late 19_2, arrangements were made to trace specified costs to seven audit engagements. Two job records showed the following:

	ENGAGEMENT	
	304	308
Direct professional labor	$20,000	$20,000
Fringe benefits to direct labor	3,000	3,000
Secretarial costs	2,000	6,000
Telephone call time with clients	1,000	2,000
Computer time	2,000	4,000
Photocopying	1,000	2,000
Total direct costs	$29,000	$37,000

Required

1. Compute the overhead application rate based on last year's direct-labor costs.
2. Assume that last year's costs were reclassified so that $7,000,000 would be regarded as direct costs instead of overhead. Compute the overhead application rate as a percentage of direct labor and as a percentage of total direct costs.
3. Using the three rates computed in requirements 1 and 2, compute the total costs of engagements 304 and 308.
4. Assume that the billing of clients was based on a 120% markup of total job costs. Compute the billings in requirement 3 for engagements 304 and 308.
5. Which method of job costing and overhead application do you favor? Explain.

17-24 Budgeting and control in accounting firms. The definitions of *direct labor* differ among and within industries. For example, some accounting, law, and consulting firms have secretaries and bookkeepers tabulate their time as worked for various clients. Other firms regard such work as general overhead. They confine their classification of direct labor to the time worked by their "professional staff." Similarly, some firms trace photocopying and phone calls to individual clients. If clients are billed by applying some multiple to direct-labor and other direct

EXHIBIT A
Summary Operating Revenue Budget

POSITION	NUMBER OF PEOPLE	TOTAL SALARIES	HOURS TO ACCOUNT FOR	BILLABLE PERCENTAGE	BILLABLE (CHARGEABLE) HOURS	DIRECT-LABOR COST	HOURLY COST	BILLING RATE	BUDGETED BILLINGS
Partner	1	$140,000	2,080	50%	1,040	$ 70,000	$67.31	$130	$135,200
Manager	1	60,000	2,080	75	?	?	?	75	?
Senior	2	80,000	?	85	3,536	?	19.23	50	176,800
Assistant	6	?	12,480	90	?	162,000	?	30	?
		?	?		?	?			?

costs, differences in cost classifications obviously might affect the total charges to individual clients.

Exhibit A displays the budgeting of 19_2 revenue for the Los Angeles office of Esposito and Company, a public accounting firm. The target billing rates are usually somewhere between two and three times the "direct-labor" costs. A partner's services are frequently quoted at the lower multiple or less because he or she will also get a partner's share of the income generated by the work of all members of the professional staff.

Required

Label your supporting computations.

1. Fill in the blanks indicated by the question marks in the accompanying exhibit.
2. Suppose overhead costs (all fixed), including the secretarial salaries but excluding any professional salaries, were $285,000. Fill in the blanks of the following budgeted income statement:

Fees earned for professional services	$?
Direct labor	?
Contribution to overhead and profit	?
Overhead, including professional salaries other than direct labor	?
Operating income (after deducting base salary of partner)	$?

3. Consider *each* of the following effects *independently*. That is, all the basic facts in requirements 1 and 2 would be unchanged with the exception of the new information given. Compute the new operating income if
   a. The assistants have a billable percentage of 85% instead of 90%.
   b. The partner has a billable percentage of 45% instead of 50%. Refer to the original data. Compare the results in 3a and 3b. What are their implications for management control?
   c. The budget should have provided for "write-downs" of 3% of gross revenue for billings not collectible. These usually take the form of "adjustments" when the client balks at paying too high a fee. They are typically accounted for as deductions from gross revenue to arrive at a net revenue amount. Refer to the original data. What is the implication of write-downs for management control?
4. As the partner in charge of the office, what detailed records and ratios would you want maintained to assist your planning and control? Be as specific as possible.

17-25 Project cost control. A defense subcontractor has a project entailing the design and production of a subsystem for guided missiles. The original budget to complete is 20,000 hours. The budgeted hours for the work scheduled to date are 12,000 hours. The budgeted hours for the work performed to date (earned hours) were 11,000. The actual hours of work performed to date were 11,400. The budgeted cost is $70 per hour. There was no price variance.

Required
1. Compute the cost variance and the schedule variance.
2. Prepare a revised budget that is designed to predict actual final cost. Assume that the cost variance will continue to be unfavorable at the same rate as shown to date.

17-26 Project cost control. Consider a research project on a new wing design for a fighter aircraft. The original budget to complete was 30,000 hours at an average cost of $120 per hour. The budgeted hours for the work scheduled to date are 21,000 hours. The budgeted hours for the work performed to date (earned hours) were 22,000 hours. The actual hours of work performed to date were 21,500. Actual costs were $2,795,000.

Required
1. Compute in dollars: the cost variance, efficiency variance, price variance, and schedule variance.
2. As the manager, how would you interpret these variances? If the cost variances persist at the same rate as shown to date, what is the expected actual final cost?

17-27 Project cost control. An engineering consulting firm has a large project, the design and testing of a production control system for an airline's maintenance base. The following data pertain to the project:

Original budget		$600,000
Add (deduct) cost variances to date:		
Unfavorable price variances	$42,000	
Favorable efficiency variances	(60,000)	(18,000)
Subtotal		$582,000
Add (deduct) additional expected variances		?
Revised budget of final cost		?

The budgeted cost per hour is $100. The budgeted hours for work performed to date were 3,000. The budgeted hours for work scheduled to date were 3,500.

Required
1. Compute the schedule variance and the cost variance for the work done to date.
2. Assume that there will be no further price variances. Assume also that the same relative efficiency will persist throughout the remainder of the project. Prepare an estimate of the revised budget of final cost. Will the manager of the consulting firm be pleased? Explain.

17-28 Basic operation costing. Werke Company manufactures a variety of tool boxes. The company's manufacturing operations and their cost for November were:

	CUTTING	ASSEMBLY	FINISHING
Direct labor	$2,600	$16,500	$4,800
Factory overhead	3,000	2,900	3,300

Three styles of boxes were produced in November. The quantities and direct-material costs were:

STYLE	QUANTITY	MATERIALS
Standard	1,200	$18,000
Home	600	6,660
Industrial	200	5,400

The industrial style requires no finishing operations.

Required | Compute the total cost and unit cost of each style produced.

17-29 Operation or hybrid costing. Penske Company manufactures a variety of plastic products. The company has an extrusion operation and subsequent operations to form, trim, and finish parts such as buckets, covers, and automotive interior components. Plastic sheets are produced by the extrusion operation. Many of these sheets are sold as finished goods directly to other manufacturers. Additional direct materials (chemicals and coloring) are added in the finishing operation.

The company's manufacturing costs applied to products for October were:

	EXTRUDE	FORM	TRIM	FINISH	TOTALS
Direct materials	$650,000	$ —	$ —	$ 80,000	$ 730,000
Direct labor	55,000	30,000	20,000	40,000	145,000
Factory overhead	270,000	90,000	40,000	60,000	460,000
	$975,000	$120,000	$60,000	$180,000	$1,335,000

In addition to plastic sheets, two types of automotive products (firewalls and dashboards) were produced:

	UNITS	PLASTIC SHEET DIRECT MATERIALS	ADDITIONAL DIRECT MATERIALS
Plastic sheets, sold after extrusion	10,000	$500,000	—
Firewalls, sold after trimming	1,000	50,000	
Dashboards, sold after finishing	2,000	100,000	$80,000
	13,000	$650,000	$80,000

For simplicity, assume that each of the items and units produced received the same steps within each operation.

Required | **1.** Tabulate the total conversion costs of each operation, the total units produced, and the conversion cost per unit.
2. Tabulate the total costs, the units produced, and the cost per unit. Be sure that the total costs are all accounted for.

17-30 Operation costing with ending work-in-process inventory. Gilhooley Products uses three operations in sequence to manufacture an assortment of picnic baskets. In each operation, the same procedures, time, and costs are used to perform that operation for a given quantity of baskets, regardless of the basket style being produced.

During April, a batch of materials for 1,100 baskets of Style X was put through the first operation. This was followed in turn by separate batches of materials for 400 baskets of Style Y and 1,300 of Style Z. All the materials for a batch are introduced at the beginning of the operation for that batch. The costs as shown below were incurred in April for the first operation:

Direct labor	$29,600
Factory overhead	13,135
Materials:	
Style X	18,700
Style Y	8,000
Style Z	13,000

All the units started in April were completed during the month and transferred out to the next operation except 350 units of Style Z, which were only partially completed at April 30. These were 40% completed as to conversion costs and 100% completed as to material costs. There were no work-in-process inventories at the beginning of the month.

1. For each basket style, compute the total cost of work completed and transferred out to the second operation.

2. Compute the total cost of the ending inventory in process.

17-31 Just-in-Time journal entries. A transistor radio factory has a JIT production system. Assume there are no beginning inventories. Prepare summary journal entries (without explanations) for the following for a given month:

a. Raw materials purchased and used	$400,000
b. Raw materials transferred to finished goods when units completed	390,000
c. Raw materials transferred from finished goods to cost of goods sold	365,000
d. Factory overhead applied	200,000
e. Amounts of factory overhead in ending inventories:	
Raw and in-process	5,000
Finished goods	12,500

17-32 Operation costing and JIT entries.

1. A computer terminal factory has an operation-costing system. It has a storeroom and several buffer stocks of parts and in-process inventories at various work centers along the production lines. All direct labor is a subclassification of factory overhead. For simplicity, assume there are no beginning inventories.

Prepare summary journal entries (without explanations) for the following for a given month:

a. Raw materials purchased	$200,000
b. Raw materials used	200,000
c. Factory overhead applied	80,000
d. Costs transferred to finished goods	266,000
e. Cost of goods sold	238,000

2. The factory adopts a JIT system. Prepare summary journal entries for the following transactions for a given month:

a. Raw materials purchased and used	$200,000
b. Raw materials transferred to finished goods when units completed	190,000
c. Raw materials transferred from finished goods to cost of goods sold	170,000
d. Factory overhead applied	80,000
e. Amounts of factory overhead in ending inventories:	
Raw and in-process	4,000
Finished goods	8,000

3. Post the entries in requirements 1 and 2 to T-accounts for inventories and cost of goods sold.

17-33 Payroll liability and payments. Study the appendix. The Raimundo Company had the following liabilities, March 31, 19_1:

Withheld income taxes payable	$400,000
Withheld Social Security taxes payable	220,000
Employer's payroll taxes payable	250,000

In April the gross payroll for employee earnings was $3,000,000, and employer costs for fringe benefits such as pensions and vacation pay (credit Estimated Liability for Vacation Pay) were $900,000. Employer's payroll tax payable on these earnings was $270,000.

The company paid the entire April payroll. However, $660,000 of income taxes were withheld. Social Security taxes withheld were $200,000.

<table>
<tr><td>Required</td><td>Prepare journal entries to record</td></tr>
</table>

1. The payment of all March 31 liabilities for taxes.
2. The recognition of the gross payroll liability and related liabilities for the month of April. (Debit Labor Costs and Overhead Costs.)
3. The payment, less withholdings, of the April payroll to employees.

17-34 Journal entries for payroll. Study the appendix. The Stable Company operates the year-round with a gross payroll of $5,000 a day. Withholdings for Social Security taxes and federal income taxes amount to $1,500 a day. The concern works five days a week, and the payroll period covers Monday to Friday, both inclusive. Payrolls for the week are paid on the following Tuesday.

Gross payrolls consist of $3,000 direct labor, $1,000 indirect labor, $700 selling expense, and $300 general and administrative expense each day. The general-ledger entry to record the total of the payroll cost incurred each month is made on the last day of the month. These totals are obtained by summarizing the Payroll Cost Recapitulation records. This firm uses a "leveled" percentage of 10% to estimate its own contribution to Social Security.

Required   Using the calendar as a guide, answer the following questions:

			APRIL			
S	M	T	W	T	F	S
		1	2	3	4	5
6	7	8	9	10	11	12
13	14	15	16	17	18	19
20	21	22	23	24	25	26
27	28	29	30			

1. What is the balance in Accrued Payroll as of the close of business on March 31?
2. What journal entries should be made on (a) April 1? (b) April 29? (c) April 30?
3. What is the ending balance in Accrued Payroll as of the close of business on April 30?

17-35 Journal entries for payroll. (J. March) Study the appendix. The balance of the Accrued Wages of Kem Industries, Inc., was $12,120 on October 31, 19_1. The company has a job-order cost system. The cost accounts are in the general ledger. Time tickets for pay periods falling wholly or partly in November are summarized as follows:

PAY PERIOD	DIRECT LABOR	FACTORY OVERHEAD	TOTAL
Nov. 1–7	$8,250	$4,510	$12,760
Nov. 8–14	8,450	4,490	12,940
Nov. 15–21	8,570	4,570	13,140
Nov. 22–28	7,920	4,060	11,980
Nov. 29–Dec. 5	8,430	4,470	12,900

Of the wages earned in the pay period ending December 5, one-third is applicable to November.

Payrolls for pay periods ending in November are summarized as follows:

PAY PERIOD ENDING	GROSS EARNINGS	WITHHOLDINGS, INCOME AND SOCIAL SECURITY TAXES
Oct. 31	$12,120	$2,750
Nov. 7	12,760	2,790
Nov. 14	12.940	2,840
Nov. 21	13,140	2,810
Nov. 28	11,980	2,675

The payroll for the period ending November 28 was paid December 2.

Required

Journal explanations in all cases should state clearly how you arrived at your amounts.

1. Journal entry for labor-cost incurrence for November earnings.
2. Journal entry for payrolls paid in November.
3. Postings in the Accrued Wages account.
4. Journal entry for accrual of employer's payroll taxes for the month of November at a leveled rate of 10% of gross earnings.
5. Answer the following questions:
   a. Theoretically, should the accrual of employer's payroll taxes be based on wages earned or on wages paid during the month?
   b. What does the balance of Accrued Wages represent?

17-36 **Accounting for idle time.** Study the appendix. The labor-cost allocation of the Dunne Desk Company is made from its payroll, all the wages of its twenty shop employees, except the foreman's, being treated as direct labor. The company pays for idle time of employees caused by material shortages, and this amounts to a substantial portion of the payroll.

For the year 19_1, the direct labor, according to the ledger, was $400,000 and the overhead $320,000. Accordingly, an overhead rate of 80% was used in 19_2 for the purpose of estimating costs of new products. The manager thinks that the estimates are wrong, for the income statement shows a gross margin of only $6 a desk, whereas selling prices are at least $30 a desk above the estimated costs. She suspects that the idle-time factor is not being included in the cost estimates, and she asks you to investigate the situation.

1. How would you proceed to determine whether the manager's suspicions are correct?
2. Recompute the overhead rate for 19_1 on the assumption that $40,000 was paid for idle time that should be treated as overhead instead of as direct labor.
3. Suggest a change in the method of labor-cost allocation that would result in a more accurate accounting for idle time.

17-37 **Just-in-time production, material control, changes in accounting system.** Solve Problem 21-25, page 741, which logically could have been placed here.

18

Decision Models, Uncertainty, and the Accountant

Characteristics of uncertainty • Coping with uncertainty • Buying perfect and imperfect information •
Applications in accounting • Recognizing complexity • Appendix: Value of imperfect information

The first part of Chapter 1 indicated that the results of an operating process, a decision, or a collection of decisions are affected by the environment. That is, the predictions and decisions of managers and accountants are made in a world of uncertainty. **Uncertainty** is defined as the possibility that an actual amount will deviate from an expected amount. This chapter explores the characteristics of uncertainty and describes how managers and accountants can cope with uncertainty.

CHARACTERISTICS OF UNCERTAINTY

Role of a decision model

The manager has a method, often called a *decision model*, for deciding among courses of action. A formal decision model measures the predicted effects of alternative actions. It usually has the following characteristics:

1. **Choice criterion**, which is an objective that can be quantified. This objective can take many forms. Most often it is expressed as a maximization (or minimization) of some form of profit (or cost). The choice criterion, also called an **objective function**, provides a basis for choosing the best alternative action.
2. A set of the alternative actions under explicit consideration.
3. A set of all the relevant **events** that can affect the outcomes (sometimes called **states** or **states of nature**), where an event is a possible occurrence. Because this set should be

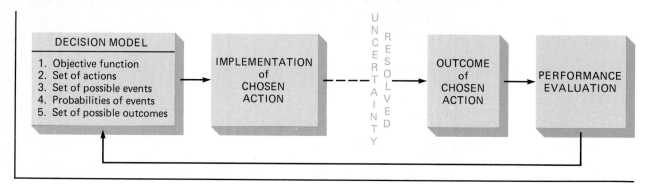

mutually exclusive and collectively exhaustive, only one of the events will actually occur. Two events are mutually exclusive if they have no element in common. Events are collectively exhaustive if, taken together, they make up the entire set of possible events. Examples of events include win contract or lose contract, rain or no rain, war or peace, and so on.

4. A set of **probabilities**, where a probability is the likelihood of occurrence of an event.

5. A set of possible **outcomes** (often called **payoffs**) that measure, in terms of the objective function, the predicted consequences of the various possible combinations of actions and events. Each outcome is conditionally dependent on a specific action and a specific event.

Exhibit 18-1 presents an overview of the link between a decision model, the implementation of the chosen action, its outcome, and subsequent performance evaluation. Chapter 1 explained how feedback can play an essential role in management control. A major form of feedback is a performance report, which often compares a budget with actual results. Using this historical information and other information (such as the general state of the economy or industry), the manager makes predictions. In turn, the predictions become inputs into a decision model, action occurs, and performance is evaluated and fed back to management.

Decisions under certainty

Decisions are frequently classified as those made under certainty and those made under uncertainty. **Certainty** exists when there is no doubt about what the outcome will be; there is a single outcome for each possible action. The probability of a certain event is 1.0. For example, the expected cash inflow on a federal treasury note might be, say, $4,000 for certain next year, graphed as shown in Exhibit 18-2.

Decisions under certainty are not always obvious. There are often numerous possible actions, each of which will offer a certain outcome. The problem then is finding the best action. For example, the problem of allocating twenty different job orders to twenty different machines, any one of which could do the job, can literally involve *millions* of different combinations. Each way of assigning these jobs is another possible action. In some cases, decision models have been developed to help choose among these many combinations. The linear-programming technique outlined in Chapter 22 is an example of such a decision model.

A **decision table** (sometimes called a **payoff table** or **payoff matrix**) is a convenient summary of the contemplated actions, events, probabilities, and outcomes. For

EXHIBIT 18-2
Single Outcome Under Certainty

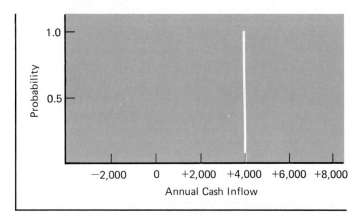

allocating the twenty jobs to the twenty machines, the decision table would appear as follows:

	EVENT: SUCCESSFUL IMPLEMENTATION
Probability of Event	1.0
ACTION:	
Combination 1	Measure of outcome (production costs)
Combination 2	Measure of outcome (production costs)
Combination 3	Measure of outcome (production costs)
(and so forth)	(and so forth)

As the table indicates, in a world of certainty, each action has only a single possible outcome. The decision obviously consists of choosing the action that will produce the most desirable outcome. The above decision table has many *rows* but only one event *column* because the costs of production using the various machines are assumed to be known with certainty.

Decisions under uncertainty

Of course, decision makers typically contend with uncertainty rather than certainty. A useful approach is to assign probabilities that represent the likelihood of various events occurring. A **probability distribution** describes the likelihood or probability of each of the collectively exhaustive and mutually exclusive set of events. In some cases, there will be much evidence to guide the assignment of probabilities. For example, the probability of obtaining a head in the toss of a fair coin is $\frac{1}{2}$; that of drawing a particular playing card from a complete and well-shuffled deck is $\frac{1}{52}$. In business, the probability of having a specified percentage of defective units may be assigned with great confidence, based on production experience with thousands of units. In other cases, there will be little evidence for estimating probabilities. For example, the probability of the success or failure of a new product may have to be assigned without the help of any related experience. No two individuals will necessarily assign the same probabilities.

EXHIBIT 18-3
Comparison of Probability Distributions

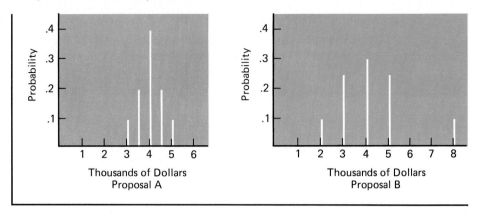

The concept of uncertainty can be illustrated by considering two investment proposals on new projects. The manager believes that the following *probability distribution* describes the relative likelihood of cash inflows for the next year (assume that the useful life of the project is one year):

PROJECT A		PROJECT B	
Probability	Cash Inflow	Probability	Cash Inflow
0.10	$3,000	0.10	$2,000
0.20	3,500	0.25	3,000
0.40	4,000	0.30	4,000
0.20	4,500	0.25	5,000
0.10	5,000	0.10	8,000

Exhibit 18-3 shows a graphical comparison of the probability distributions. Both Project A and Project B require identical certain investments of $2,000 at the start of the year. (For simplicity, we ignore the time value of money here. See Chapter 19 for discussion.)

Expected value

An **expected value** is a weighted average with the probabilities serving as the weights. The expected value of the cash inflows in Project A, denoted $E(A)$, is $4,000:

$$E(A) = 0.1(\$3{,}000) + 0.2(\$3{,}500) + 0.4(\$4{,}000) + 0.2(\$4{,}500) + 0.1(\$5{,}000)$$

$$= \$4{,}000$$

The expected value of the cash inflows in Project B is $4,200:

$$E(B) = 0.1(\$2{,}000) + 0.25(\$3{,}000) + 0.3(\$4{,}000) + 0.25(\$5{,}000) + 0.1(\$8{,}000)$$

$$= \$4{,}200$$

The expected value criterion is widely used as a decision criterion. For a decision maker wanting to maximize the expected monetary outcome of a chosen alternative, Project B is preferable to Project A. The next section contains a step-by-step outline of the use of the expected value approach in decision making.

Many statisticians and accountants favor presenting the entire probability distribution directly to the decision maker. Others first divide the information into three categories: optimistic, most likely, and pessimistic. Still others provide summary measures of dispersion, such as the standard deviation. Such presentations portray underlying phenomena more realistically than presentations that portray the data as if they came from a world of certainty.

COPING WITH UNCERTAINTY

Illustrative problem

The following problem will be used to demonstrate the general approach to uncertainty outlined in this chapter.[1] Suppose a decision maker, a manager named Mark Eastman, must choose between purchasing two molding machines, M1 and M2. Each machine will be used to produce a souvenir toy. M2 wastes less material and uses less direct labor but costs more to acquire and maintain. For simplicity, assume that each machine has a useful life of one year. Comparative operating incomes are:

$$\text{Buy M1: Operating income} = \$20x - \$15,000$$

$$\text{Buy M2: Operating income} = \$24x - \$21,000$$

where x = demand in units.

In words, the first equation says that the operating income from M1 will be a unit contribution margin of $20 times the number of units sold minus the fixed cost of acquiring and maintaining M1 ($15,000). If M2 is acquired, the unit contribution margin rises to $24 because less variable manufacturing costs will be used, but the fixed cost rises to $21,000 because M2 is a more-complex machine.

General approach to uncertainty

The construction of a model for decision making contains five steps that are keyed to the five characteristics described at the outset of this chapter:[2]

Step 1. Identify the objective of the decision maker. Assume that Eastman's choice criterion or objective function is to maximize expected operating income.

Step 2. Identify the set of actions under consideration. Eastman has two possible actions:

$$a_1 = \text{Buy M1}$$

$$a_2 = \text{Buy M2}$$

---

[1] This chapter outlines what is called the expected utility approach to decision making under uncertainty. For more-detailed expositions, see C. Holloway, *Decision Making under Uncertainty: Models and Choices* (Englewood Cliffs, N.J.: Prentice-Hall, 1979); and R. Magee, *Advanced Managerial Accounting* (New York: Harper & Row, 1986), Chaps. 2 and 3. For a thorough analysis of several alternative approaches to decision making under uncertainty, see R. Hilton, *Probabilistic Choice Models and Information* (Sarasota, Fla.: American Accounting Association, 1985).

[2] The presentations here and in Appendix 18 draw (in part) from teaching notes prepared by R. Williamson.

Step 3. Identify the set of relevant events that can occur. Eastman's only uncertainty is the level of future demand:

$$x_1 = \text{Demand is 1,200 units}$$

$$x_2 = \text{Demand is 2,000 units}$$

Step 4. Assign probabilities for the occurrence of each event. Eastman thinks that there is a 40% chance that future demand will equal 1,200 units and a 60% chance that it will equal 2,000 units. Therefore he has assessed the following probabilities:

$$P(x_1) = .4$$

$$P(x_2) = .6$$

Step 5. Identify the set of possible outcomes that are dependent on specific actions and events. The outcomes in this example take the form of four possible operating incomes, which are displayed in a decision table in Exhibit 18-4.

Eastman now has all the necessary information for making a decision. As shown in Exhibit 18-4, he can compute the expected value of each action. He would decide to buy M2 because its expected operating income is higher than that of M1 by $19,320 − $18,600, or $720.

Exhibit 18-5 illustrates how the five steps can be summarized using a decision tree. The following conventions are widely used in drawing a decision tree:

☐ represents a decision node
◯ represents an event node

Attached to each decision node will be all the individual actions being considered by the decision maker. Attached to each event node will be the total set of mutually exclusive and collectively exhaustive events.

EXHIBIT 18-4
Decision Table Presentation of Data

	EVENTS	
Probability of Events	$x_1 = 1,200$ $P(x_1) = .4$	$x_2 = 2,000$ $P(x_2) = .6$
ACTION:		
a_1: Buy M1	$OI = \$9,000^*$	$OI = \$25,000†$
a_2: Buy M2	$OI = \$7,800‡$	$OI = \$27,000§$

OI = Operating income
$E(OI)$ = Expected value of operating income
Expected values:
  Buy M1: $E(a_1) = .4(\$9,000) + .6(\$25,000) = \$18,600$
  Buy M2: $E(a_2) = .4(\$7,800) + .6(\$27,000) = \$19,320$

$^*\$20(1,200) - \$15,000 = \$\ 9,000$
$†\$20(2,000) - \$15,000 = \$25,000$
$‡\$24(1,200) - \$21,000 = \$\ 7,800$
$§\$24(2,000) - \$21,000 = \$27,000$

EXHIBIT 18-5
Decision Tree Presentation of Data

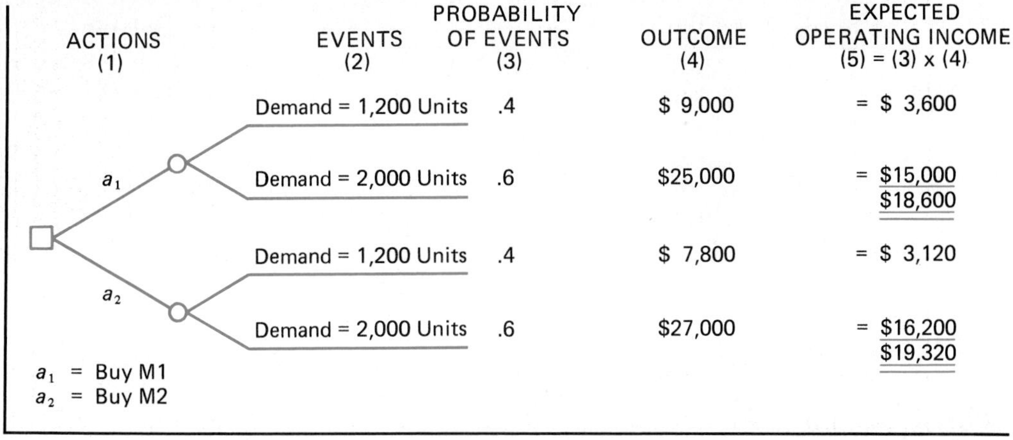

ACTIONS (1)	EVENTS (2)	PROBABILITY OF EVENTS (3)	OUTCOME (4)	EXPECTED OPERATING INCOME (5) = (3) x (4)
	Demand = 1,200 Units	.4	$ 9,000	= $ 3,600
a_1	Demand = 2,000 Units	.6	$25,000	= $15,000
				$18,600
	Demand = 1,200 Units	.4	$ 7,800	= $ 3,120
a_2	Demand = 2,000 Units	.6	$27,000	= $16,200
				$19,320

a_1 = Buy M1
a_2 = Buy M2

Good decisions and bad outcomes

Always distinguish between a good decision and a good outcome. One can exist without the other. By definition, uncertainty rules out guaranteeing after the fact that the best outcome always will be obtained. It is possible that "bad luck" will produce unfavorable consequences even when "good" decisions have been made.

Consider the following example. Suppose you are offered a gamble for a mere $1, a fair coin toss where heads you win and tails you lose. You will win $20 if the event is heads, but you will lose $1 if the event is tails. As a rational decision maker, you proceed through the logical phases: gathering information, assessing consequences, and making a choice. You accept the bet. The coin is tossed. You lose. From your viewpoint, this was a good decision but a bad outcome.

A decision can only be made on the basis of information available at the time of the decision. Hindsight is often flawless, but a bad outcome does not necessarily mean that it flowed from a bad decision; "the best protection we have against a bad outcome is a good decision."[3]

BUYING PERFECT AND IMPERFECT INFORMATION

In many cases, a decision maker can gather additional information about which event will occur when faced with uncertainty in a decision. This section discusses an approach that aids decisions about how much to invest to obtain more information.

Buying perfect information

Even though the expected value of the operating income is $720 higher under M2, Eastman might be concerned. The only uncertainty is what event (demand) will occur. *Eastman's assessments of probabilities are based on his existing information.* The worst possible operating income, $7,800, will occur if M2 is acquired and demand is 1,200 units. Suppose Eastman's present marketing staff is overloaded with other work, but he can hire a consultant, Mary O'Leary, to study the demand situation.

[3]D. North, "A Tutorial Introduction to Decision Theory," *IEEE Transactions on Systems Science and Cybernetics*, September 1968, p. 201.

Assume that she has the ability to make perfect or flawless predictions in these matters. What is the maximum amount Eastman should be willing to pay for the consultant's errorless wisdom? This amount is called the *expected value of perfect information* (EVPI).

The basic decision here is whether to purchase advance revelation (perfect information) *without knowing what the revelation will be.* There are five steps in computing EVPI:

Step 1. Identify the optimal action conditional on knowing what event will occur. If the consultant tells Eastman that demand will be 1,200, he will buy M1 and obtain an operating income of $9,000; similarly, if demand is predicted at 2,000, he will buy M2 and obtain an operating income of $27,000.

Step 2. Identify the probabilities of each event's being revealed after the purchase of advance event revelation. Eastman's best estimates of the two demands being revealed are his current assessments of probabilities, .4 and .6, respectively.

Step 3. Compute the expected value of a decision made with perfect information. The perfect information in advance of each occurrence of the events will contain only one of the two predictions. Therefore the expected value of the decision *with* perfect information is the sum of the optimum outcome for each event multiplied by its probability:

$$(.4 \times \$9,000) + (.6 \times \$27,000) = \$19,800$$

Step 4. Compute the expected value of the preferred action based on existing information. Using the earlier data in Exhibit 18-4, Eastman computed an expected value for M2 of $19,320, which is the higher of the expected values with existing information for the two actions in this example.

Step 5. Compute the expected value of perfect information. The top price Eastman should be willing to pay for perfect advance information would be the difference between the expected value with *perfect* information and the highest expected value with *existing* information. This *difference* is the **expected value of perfect information (EVPI):**

Expected value of a decision made *with* perfect information (from Step 3)	$19,800
Expected value of preferred action made *with* existing information (from Step 4)	19,320
Expected value of perfect information (EVPI)	$ 480

Time for reflection

Information gathering is costly, so the cost-benefit test must be met. In a general sense, the consultant may be considered as an *accounting system* or *information system.* The decision maker's action will depend on the message or *signal* (the specific prediction) supplied by the system. That is, the decision maker buys the system without knowing the forthcoming signal.

Eastman's action will depend on the particular signal. Indeed, if Eastman

EXHIBIT 18-6
Sequence of Analysis in Making Decisions to Purchase Perfect Information

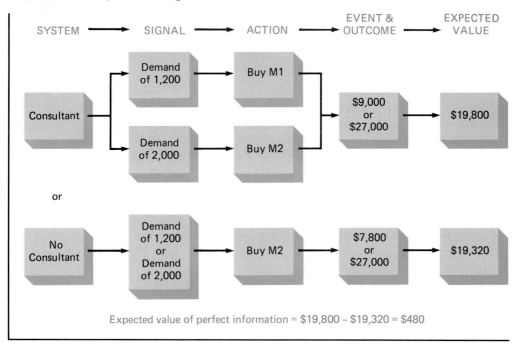

Expected value of perfect information = $19,800 – $19,320 = $480

chooses the same action regardless of the signal, he will be unwilling to pay anything for the information system. Moreover, Eastman will be unwilling to pay for a system unless it is expected to generate an increase in expected value of the action in excess of the cost of the system. In the example above, Eastman would be willing to pay up to $480 for the consultant's perfect predictions.

The sequence of analysis is straightforward but crucial. Its ultimate focus is on changes in expected value of the available actions. But the model moves from the *system* to the *signals* to the *actions* induced by the expected value of the decision maker's objective function. Exhibit 18-6 summarizes this sequence.

Finally, the choice of an optimal information system is "decision specific." That is, the choice depends on the existing information available to the decision maker, the decision table (as in Exhibit 18-4), the cost of the information system, and the objective function of the decision maker.

Buying imperfect information

Eastman's only uncertainty is whether x_1 or x_2 will occur. Obviously, *perfect* information is generally unobtainable (except in textbooks), but *imperfect* information may still be worth buying. Note that knowledge of EVPI permits outright rejection of any additional information gathering whose cost exceeds EVPI. Thus, if the consultant's fee exceeds $480, Eastman can cease pondering whether to buy more information.

Suppose the consultant's fee will be $300. Should Eastman acquire the imperfect information system offered by the consultant? Again, the answer depends on whether the expected value with the new information system exceeds the expected value with existing information. In turn, expected values depend on what type of outcome Eastman foresees. (See the appendix to this chapter for additional discussion.)

Cost-benefit is paramount

This chapter focuses on a single decision problem made by a single individual. In this context, the cost-benefit perspective can easily be illustrated. In many situations, however, data will be collected for a multitude of decisions. A cost-benefit perspective would then focus on the collective effect of these decisions. Even though given data may have little or no value in a particular decision situation, the system that provides such data may nevertheless be economically justifiable in a collective sense. For example, an expensive computer-based model for budgeting may be part of an accounting system that supports the planning of operations. For any particular decision, such as whether to acquire 100 or 150 units of material, a simpler model may be good enough because the data provided by the computer-based model would not change the action choice. *Therefore the models or systems may be valueless for a particular decision but may still be economically justifiable when their impact on the entire class of decisions is considered.*

APPLICATIONS IN ACCOUNTING

Sensitivity analysis

Throughout much of this book, we assume that items such as the level of variable costs, fixed costs, and volume can be represented by a single number. This assumption helps focus on a few key concepts.

A widely used approach to recognizing uncertainty about individual items is *sensitivity analysis*. This approach is a "what-if" technique that measures how the predictions of a decision model will be affected by changes in the critical data inputs. In the context of cost-volume-profit analysis, sensitivity analysis answers such questions as "What will my operating income be if the unit variable costs or the sales price changes by some amount from the original prediction?"

The major benefit of sensitivity analysis is its provision of an immediate financial estimate of the consequences of possible prediction errors. It helps focus on those aspects that are very sensitive indeed, and it eases the manager's mind regarding those predictions that have little impact on decisions.

The advantages of using certainty models coupled with sensitivity analysis are their relative simplicity and economy. The major disadvantage is the possible overlooking of "better" actions that might be forthcoming if more-formal models that include uncertainty are used.

Use of probabilities

A major objective of this chapter is to increase awareness that accountants and managers generally prepare single-number estimates without conducting formal analysis encompassing probabilities. Given our world of uncertainty, there are potential benefits of explicitly stating probabilities when analyzing alternatives. In this way, a manager is less likely to analyze alternatives too simplistically.

For example, the presentation of three possible outcomes, together with their respective probabilities, may seem warranted for major decisions. Suppose a company is contemplating rearranging some equipment, with the following costs and probabilities.

	EVENTS		
Probability of Event	Large Decrease in Manufacturing Costs .5	Minimal Decrease in Manufacturing Costs .2	Large Increase in Manufacturing Costs .3
ACTION:			
a_1: Do nothing	$200,000	$200,000	$200,000
a_2: Rearrange	$120,000	$180,000	$270,000

The expected costs of the two actions are:

Do nothing: $E(a_1) = .5(\$200{,}000) + .2(\$200{,}000) + .3(\$200{,}000) = \$200{,}000$

Rearrange: $E(a_2) = .5(\$120{,}000) + .2(\$180{,}000) + .3(\$270{,}000) = \underline{177{,}000}$

Difference in expected manufacturing costs $\underline{\underline{\$\ 23{,}000}}$

A probabilistic analysis provides the decision maker with a rich picture of what is faced in a world of uncertainty.

Expected monetary value and utility

The approach used so far in this chapter has had all the computations expressed in monetary terms. This monetary approach is appealing to many managers. It is the currency they buy and sell with and in which their reports are expressed. In some cases, however, a more general approach using utils rather than money is appropriate. The more general approach recognizes that individuals differ in how they value the loss of a given dollar amount and how they value the gain of the same dollar amount.

Utility value can be defined as the value of a specific outcome to a particular decision maker. A decision maker's utility function depends on attitudes toward risks. There are three basic attitudes: **risk neutral**, **risk averse**, and **risk seeking**. These attitudes are portrayed in Exhibit 18-7 where monetary amounts (dollars) are plotted on the horizontal axis and *utils* are plotted on the vertical axis. Utility is arbitrarily measured in **utils**, which are quantifications of the utility value of given monetary amounts.

EXHIBIT 18-7
Types of Risk Attitudes and Utility Functions

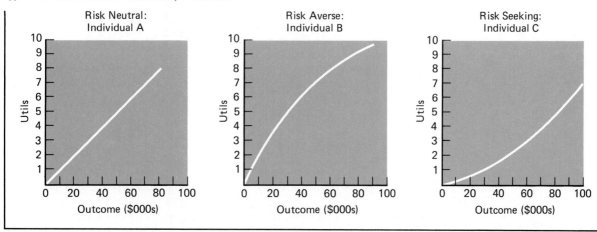

RISK NEUTRAL The left-hand box of Exhibit 18-7 represents the utility function of a risk-neutral decision maker, individual A. Utility is directly proportional to monetary amounts. In other words, the decision maker weighs each dollar as a full dollar (no more, no less). There is equal utility and disutility from a gain and a loss of the same dollar amount.

RISK AVERSE The middle box in Exhibit 18-7 represents the utility function of a risk-averse decision maker, individual B. There is more disutility from a loss of a given dollar amount than there is utility from a gain of the same dollar amount.

RISK SEEKING The right-hand box in Exhibit 18-7 represents the utility function of a risk-seeking decision maker, individual C. There is more utility from a gain of a given dollar amount than there is disutility from the loss of the same dollar amount.

Exhibit 18-7 reveals the nature of the trade-offs made between risks and returns. Individual A may be financially secure and will get as much pleasure from increasing her wealth by $20,000 as pain from decreasing her wealth by $20,000.

Individual B increases his utility from 6 to 8 utils when the payoff increases from $40,000 to $60,000. In contrast, B's utility decreases from 5 to 2 utils when the payoff decreases from $30,000 to $10,000. B puts a large penalty on decision outcomes where high losses may occur. Consequently, risk-averse managers may obtain a widely diversified set of projects so that the likelihood of a large overall loss is reduced.

Individual C increases her utility from 3 to 6 utils when the payoff increases from $60,000 to $90,000. In contrast, C's utility only decreases from 3 to 1 when the payoff decreases from $60,000 to $30,000. C puts high value on large gains and would be quite willing to invest much of her wealth in a single project that has a chance of major gains.

Risk and cost-volume-profit model

The cost-volume-profit model provides a simple illustration of why single numbers and expected monetary values often do not suffice for guiding decisions.[4] Suppose that owner and manager Amy Anton is going to choose between the production and sale of Product 1 and Product 2. Both products will require the same amounts of manufacturing facilities. The following data are available:

	PRODUCT 1	PRODUCT 2
Unit contribution margin	$4	$4
Increment in annual fixed costs	$400,000	$400,000
Breakeven volume	100,000 units	100,000 units

Anton's current wealth is $300,000.

Given these facts, Anton should be indifferent between the two products. Both products will apparently have the same total contribution margin for any level

---

[4]This section considers uncertainty in only the sales volume variable in cost-volume-profit analysis. Uncertainty can also be recognized in other variables such as selling price, variable costs, and fixed costs. See D. Driscoll, W. Lin, and P. Watkins, "Cost-Volume-Profit Analysis under Uncertainty: A Synthesis and Framework for Evaluation," *Journal of Accounting Literature,* Spring 1984, pp. 85–115.

of sales. However, consider some additional data:

| | PROBABILITY DISTRIBUTION | |
SALES VOLUME IN UNITS	Product 1	Product 2
50,000	.1	.2
75,000	.2	.3
100,000	.3	.2
125,000	.3	.1
150,000	.1	.1
225,000	.0	.1
	1.0	1.0

The expected values of sales volume in units are:

For Product 1:
$$.1(50,000) + .2(75,000) + .3(100,000) + .3(125,000) + .1(150,000) = 102,500$$

For Product 2:
$$.2(50,000) + .3(75,000) + .2(100,000) + .1(125,000) + .1(150,000)$$
$$+ .1(225,000) = 102,500$$

Both products have the same expected values for unit sales and hence the same expected values for contribution margins of $102,500 \times \$4 = \$410,000$. With Product 2 there is a .5 (.2 + .3) probability that sales will be below breakeven (i.e., less than or equal to 75,000 units). In contrast, the comparable probability for the unit sales of Product 1 being below breakeven is .3 (.1 + .2). Moreover, Product 2 has the probability of .7 of being just at breakeven sales or below; the comparable probability for Product 1 is .6. Product 2 has a higher dispersion around its expected sales and a higher probability of loss. Both products have the same expected profits of $\$410,000 - \$400,000 = \$10,000$.

Anton's choice will depend on her utility function. When using utils in the calculations, it is necessary to know the precise shape of functions such as those presented in Exhibit 18-7. Assume Amy Anton is risk averse and that her utility can be quantified by a logarithmic function:

$$\text{Utility (Ending Wealth)} = \text{Log}_{10}(\text{Ending Wealth})$$

Utility is defined by ending wealth and not profit or loss because it is assumed that it is wealth that determines the decision maker's attitude towards risk. This utility function can be illustrated by the possible outcomes with Product 1 or Product 2:

UNITS SOLD	PROFITS	ENDING WEALTH	LOG$_{10}$(ENDING WEALTH)*
(1)	(2)	(3) = $300,000 + (2)	(4)
50,000	−$200,000	$100,000	5.00
75,000	−100,000	200,000	5.30
100,000	0	300,000	5.48
125,000	100,000	400,000	5.60
150,000	200,000	500,000	5.70
225,000	500,000	800,000	5.90

*From a table of logarithms not included in this book.

627

The expected utilities from the choice of each product are:

Product 1

$$E(\text{Utility}) = .1(5.00) + .2(5.30) + .3(5.48) + .3(5.60) + .1(5.70)$$

$$= 5.454$$

Product 2

$$E(\text{Utility}) = .2(5.00) + .3(5.30) + .2(5.48) + .1(5.60) + .1(5.90)$$

$$= 5.406$$

Given Anton's logarithmic risk-averse preference function, she would choose Product 1 because its expected utility exceeds that from the choice of Product 2. Note that if Anton were risk neutral, she would be indifferent between a choice of Product 1 and Product 2.[5] This example illustrates how the risk preferences of managers can affect their decisions. These decisions include which information system to use within an organization as well as decisions such as what product to make and what price to charge customers.

RECOGNIZING COMPLEXITY

Although the analysis in this chapter may appear burdensome in terms of computations, the situations underlying the model are relatively simple. In our examples, we considered settings where there is only one decision maker and where decisions have consequences for only one period ahead. Consider a more-complex case where there are three parties—the owner of a firm (who makes decisions about what information system to use) and two operating managers. The illustration at the top of the next page depicts such a situation.

The information system chosen by the owner can perform several roles in this more-complex setting:

1. Improve the quality of decisions made by operating managers.
2. Motivate operating managers to make decisions that are in the best interest of the owner.
3. Assist the owner in evaluating the performance of *each* operating manager and of the activities that each manager directs.

The first role is illustrated in this chapter. The latter two roles are discussed in Chapters 11, 25, and 26.

The information available to the owner includes that conveyed by the operat-

---

[5]As a general rule, expected utility computations should consider the ending wealth level rather than just the incremental profits or cash flows associated with a specific decision. The intuition behind this general rule is that a loss of (say) $100,000 can have differing amounts of disutility depending on the wealth level of the decision maker. See R. Dillon and J. Nash, "The True Relevance of Relevant Costs," *Accounting Review* L111 (No. 1), pp. 11–17; and J. Demski, *Information Analysis*, 2nd ed. (Reading, Mass.: Addison-Wesley, 1980), pp. 34–35. Only under special conditions (such as risk neutrality) is it valid to make expected utility computations without explicitly considering the wealth level of the decision maker.

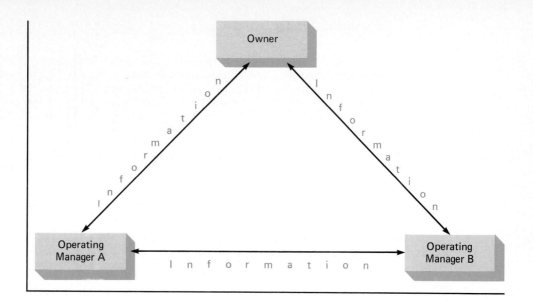

ing managers. These managers may not have incentives to communicate their information in an honest, timely way. Instead some operating managers individually (or in collusion) may withhold important information from higher management; they may even distort the information transmitted if such information could be used against them. Moreover, some operating managers may distort or delay the information transmitted to other operating managers; for example, information about capacity levels or cost structures may not be honestly communicated between operating managers. (Chapter 25 provides examples that illustrate this observation.)

These complexities do not diminish the importance of a cost-benefit perspective. Instead they serve to underscore the challenge of applying that perspective in the uncertain world in which owners and managers find themselves.

SUMMARY

Accountants must be acquainted with the entire decision process. They must focus on decision objectives, prediction methods, decision models, and alternative outcomes.

Formal decision models are increasingly being used because they are becoming cheaper to implement and because they replace or supplement hunches and implicit rules with explicit assumptions and criteria. The decision maker must choose the decision model to use. Both the choice criterion (objective function) and the complexities of the decision situation affect the choice of model. What information is to be compiled depends on the chosen prediction method and the decision model.

Managers and accountants are often prone to regard quantification as precise just because numbers are somehow supposed to be accurate. However, almost all data, whether they depict the past or the future, are subject to uncertainty. Accounting reports for decision making are increasingly being aimed toward the formal, explicit recognition of uncertainty. Cognizance of probability distributions is often essential to providing information for decisions, and the use of utility values provides a systematic way of measuring risk-return trade-offs.

problem Cheri Martel, a cost analyst for the air force, is currently reviewing the cost estimates made by Erland Corp. and Rex Inc., the final two bidders for a jet fighter contract. The decision on the contract will be made by a committee of four air force generals. Martel must make a presentation to this committee on the expected costs of the jet fighter project for each of the two contractors. The company awarded the contract will be reimbursed on an "actual cost plus a fixed fee" basis. The fixed fee is 8% of the cost bid at the time the contract is awarded.

Erland has made a cost bid of $600 million for the contract while Rex has made a bid of $650 million. Martel decides to use the past experience of both companies on government contracts to assess the probability distribution of actual costs on the jet fighter contract to the air force. She collects data on the cost bid at the time each contract was awarded and the eventual actual cost (before payment of the 8% fixed fee) for all past contracts awarded to Erland and for all past contracts awarded to Rex. The distribution is[6]:

	ERLAND	REX
10% cost underrun	.05	.15
No underrun or overrun	.10	.25
10% overrun	.10	.25
20% overrun	.15	.20
30% overrun	.20	.10
40% overrun	.25	.05
50% overrun	.10	—
60% overrun	.05	—
	1.00	1.00

Required 1. What is the probability distribution of the actual costs to the air force (including the 8% fixed fee) if the contract is awarded to (a) Erland and (b) Rex? Compute the expected value of the distribution of actual costs to the air force for each contractor.
2. Evaluate the approach used by Martel to compute the probability distribution of actual costs on the jet fighter contract.

solution 1. A three-step procedure is used to assess the probability distribution of actual costs to the air force:
   a. Determine the actual cost each contractor will report with a 10% underrun, . . . , 50% overrun, and 60% overrun,
   b. Add the fixed fee, which is 8% of the cost bid, and
   c. Use the past distribution for each underrun/overrun category to determine the probability distribution for the actual costs to the air force for the air fighter contract.

Exhibit 18-8 presents the computations, which can be summarized as follows:

CONTRACTOR	CURRENT BID (IN MILLIONS)	EXPECTED VALUE OF COST TO AIR FORCE (IN MILLIONS)	RANGE OF PROBABILITY DISTRIBUTION (IN MILLIONS)
Erland	$600 + $48 = $648	$813	$588 to $1,008
Rex	$650 + $52 = $702	$767	$637 to $962

---

[6]Evidence on the distribution of cost overruns on government contracts is summarized in N. Augustine, "A Viewpoint of Industry," *Journal of Cost Analysis*, Spring 1985, pp. 1–20, and F. Biery, "The Accuracy of Military Cost and Schedule Forecasts," *Journal of Cost Analysis*, Spring 1986, pp. 13–23.

EXHIBIT 18-8
Probability Distribution of Actual Costs to Air Force with Alternative Contractors

A. ERLAND CORP. AWARDED CONTRACT

COST UNDERRUN/ OVERRUN CATEGORY	CONTRACTOR'S ACTUAL COST	CONTRACTOR'S ACTUAL COST + 8% OF BID	PROBABILITY	
(1)	(2)	(3) = (2) + $48	(4)	(5) = (3) × (4)
10% cost underrun	$540	$ 588	.05	$ 29.4
No underrun/overrun	600	648	.10	64.8
10% overrun	660	708	.10	70.8
20% overrun	720	768	.15	115.2
30% overrun	780	828	.20	165.6
40% overrun	840	888	.25	222.0
50% overrun	900	948	.10	94.8
60% overrun	960	1,008	.05	50.4
			1.00	$813.0

B. REX INC. AWARDED CONTRACT

COST UNDERRUN/ OVERRUN CATEGORY	CONTRACTOR'S ACTUAL COST	CONTRACTOR'S ACTUAL COST + 8% OF BID	PROBABILITY	
(1)	(2)	(3) = (2) + $52	(4)	(5) = (3) × (4)
10% cost underrun	$585	$637	.15	$ 95.55
No underrun/overrun	650	702	.25	175.50
10% overrun	715	767	.25	191.75
20% overrun	780	832	.20	166.40
30% overrun	845	897	.10	89.70
40% overrun	910	962	.05	48.10
50% overrun	—	—	—	—
60% overrun	—	—	—	—
			1.00	$767.00

Rex has a lower expected value of the actual cost than Erland. The magnitude of the largest possible cost overrun with Rex ($962 million) is less than with Erland ($1,008 million).

2. The approach Martel used to assess probabilities assumes that the past track record of a contractor on all government contracts is a good predictor of likely performance on the jet fighter contract. Martel might consider two factors in evaluating the reasonableness of this assumption:

   a. Explanations for the past cost underruns or overruns for each contractor. These include
      (1) Unanticipated inflation,
      (2) Changes in specifications or quantity mandated by the government after the contract was awarded, and
      (3) Deliberate underbidding by contractor (this is frequently alleged, although it is difficult to document).

   If the appropriate explanations are unlikely to persist over the life of the jet fighter contract, a change in the probability distribution for underestimates or overestimates may be appropriate.

   b. The current management of each contractor. Has the management existing at the time of past contracts been replaced? Because of allegations of poor internal control for government contracts, excessive overruns, and so on? Then a reduction in the probability of large overruns may be appropriate.

Special Points and Pitfalls

Sensitivity analysis is a widely used way of dealing with uncertainty. However, the formal use of probability distributions is also receiving more attention.

Accountants increasingly recognize that expected *monetary* value ignores risk. If accountants work with expected *utility* value, the risk attitudes of the decision maker are contained in the utility function. Then maximizing expected utility does indeed explicitly make risk-return trade-offs.

The practical problems of developing utility functions are enormous. The accountant can avoid such problems by providing expected monetary values *plus* probability distributions. Then decision makers can explicitly or implicitly apply their own risk attitudes to the different probability distributions when choosing an action.

APPENDIX: VALUE OF IMPERFECT INFORMATION

This appendix explores the decision of whether to buy imperfect information. It explains how probabilities are revised, using Bayes's rule.

Effects of imperfect information

Review the Eastman illustration (pages 619–21). Recall that the expected value of perfect information (EVPI) was $480. However, no consultant or information system has flawless predictive powers. Thus the question is, How much should Eastman pay for the imperfect information system (the consultant)? Suppose the consultant has requested a fee of $300. Eastman should pay no more than the value of the imperfect information, which we will now compute.

In advance of each occurrence of the events in this illustration, the consultant is expected to produce only one of the two signals (reports). A pessimistic report will be a prediction of low demand, $x = 1,200$; an optimistic report will be a prediction of high demand, $x = 2,000$. The original decision table in Exhibit 18-4, page 620, would be changed by each of these reports, as shown in Exhibit 18-9.

Exhibit 18-9 summarizes the expected values with imperfect information. Note that the operating incomes are identical in the decision tables in Exhibits 18-4 and 18-9. The only substantial difference between the exhibits is the *change in probabilities* (and hence the change in expected values) caused by the imperfect

EXHIBIT 18-9

Expected Values with Imperfect Information

	EVENTS	
	$x_1 = 1{,}200$	$x_2 = 2{,}000$
If a pessimistic report, probability of events	.727*	.273*
If optimistic report, probability of events	.143*	.857*
ACTION:		
a_1: Buy M1	OI = \$9,000†	OI = \$25,000†
a_2: Buy M2	OI = \$7,800†	OI = \$27,000†

Assume pessimistic report:

$E(a_1) = .727(\$9{,}000) + .273(\$25{,}000) = \$13{,}368$

$E(a_2) = .727(\$7{,}800) + .273(\$27{,}000) = \$13{,}042$

Assume optimistic report:

$E(a_1) = .143(\$9{,}000) + .857(\$25{,}000) = \$22{,}712$

$E(a_2) = .143(\$7{,}800) + .857(\$27{,}000) = \$24{,}254$

*See the next section for an explanation of how these probabilities are computed.

†As in Exhibit 18-4.

information. The computation of these probabilities is explained in the next section, but let us obtain some perspective first. The **expected value of imperfect information** (sometimes called the *expected value of sample information*) is defined as the difference between the expected value of the optimal action with the additional information and the expected value of the optimal action with the existing information.

In our example, suppose Eastman assesses the probability of getting a pessimistic report as .44; an optimistic report, .56. (The computation of these probabilities is explained in the next section: if a pessimistic report is received, a_1 is chosen, while if an optimistic report is received, a_2 is chosen. Therefore:

Expected value with imperfect information	
$(.44 \times \$13{,}368) + (.56 \times \$24{,}254) =$	\$19,464
Expected value with existing information from Exhibit 18-4	19,320
Expected value of imperfect information	\$ 144

Thus the most that Eastman should pay for the consultant's report is \$144, which is considerably less than the \$300 fee requested.

Suppose the consultant lowers the fee from \$300 to \$100. Eastman hires her and the report is pessimistic. What should Eastman do now? Make the relevant computations, as before, using the revised probabilities. As Exhibit 18-9 shows, the expected value is \$13,368, considerably lower than the expected value of \$19,320 in Exhibit 18-4. Does this mean the decision to engage the consultant was wrong? No. The additional information has revised Eastman's probabilities and resulting expected values. The additional information has changed the optimal decision from M2 to M1.

Computing the value of imperfect information

The Eastman illustration included a revision of probabilities and resulting expected values, as summarized in Exhibit 18-9. There are five steps in computing the expected value of imperfect information.

Step 1. Determine the set of signals that the information system may provide. Assume that the consultant will provide only one of two possible reports, pessimistic or optimistic:

$$y_1 = \text{Pessimistic report: Prediction of } x_1 \text{ to be 1,200}$$

$$y_2 = \text{Optimistic report: Prediction of } x_2 \text{ to be 2,000}$$

Step 2. Determine the probability of receiving each signal. Eastman determines that the consultant's predictions are correct only 80% of the time. If the actual demand is 1,200, the consultant will give an optimistic report 20% of the time. If the actual demand is 2,000, the consultant will give a pessimistic report 20% of the time. These probabilities are summarized as follows:

$$P(y_1|x_1) = .8 \qquad P(y_2|x_2) = .8$$

$$P(y_2|x_1) = .2 \qquad P(y_1|x_2) = .2$$

where P = probability; y_1 = pessimistic report; y_2 = optimistic report; x_1 = demand of 1,200; and x_2 = demand of 2,000.

Given that $P(x_1) = .4$ and $P(x_2) = .6$, use the following formula (which is developed in many books on elementary decision theory and statistics) to derive the probabilities of obtaining a pessimistic or optimistic report:

$$P(y_k) = \sum_{i=1}^{n} P(y_k|x_i) \cdot P(x_i)$$

where P = probability; y_k = specific report (or signal); x_i = specific event (demand); and n = number of events.

Then

$$P(y_1) = (.8 \times .4) + (.2 \times .6) = .44$$

$$P(y_2) = (.8 \times .6) + (.2 \times .4) = .56$$

In words, if the consultant is correct 80% of the time, and if the probability of x = 1,200 is 40%, then the probability of a pessimistic report is 44%. The computation follows:

Probability of pessimistic report	=	$\left(\begin{array}{l}\text{Probability of pessimistic}\\ \text{report, given low demand } \textit{times}\\ \text{the Probability of low demand}\end{array}\right)$	+	$\left(\begin{array}{l}\text{Probability of pessimistic}\\ \text{report, given high demand } \textit{times}\\ \text{the Probability of high demand}\end{array}\right)$
	=	$(.8 \times .4)$		$+ (.2 \times .6)$
	=	$.32$		$+ .12$
	=	$.44$		

Probability of optimistic report	=	$\left(\begin{array}{l}\text{Probability of optimistic}\\ \text{report, given high demand } \textit{times}\\ \text{the Probability of high demand}\end{array}\right)$	+	$\left(\begin{array}{l}\text{Probability of optimistic}\\ \text{report, given low demand } \textit{times}\\ \text{the Probability of high demand}\end{array}\right)$
	=	$(.8 \times .6)$		$+ (.2 \times .4)$
	=	$.48$		$+ .08$
	=	$.56$		

Step 3. Determine the revised probabilities of each event occurring, conditional upon receiving a particular signal from the information system. Eastman is fundamentally interested in whether additional information will change his initial assessment of probabilities of x_1 and x_2. Bayes's rule, which is also developed in textbooks on basic decision theory, permits these *prior probabilities* to be revised to *posterior probabilities*. The revision depends on specification of the prior probabilities and the probabilities of obtaining a specific signal from the information system (that is, a pessimistic or optimistic report). The Bayes formula would be used as follows:

$$P(x_i|y_k) = \frac{P(x_i) \cdot P(y_k|x_i)}{P(y_k)}$$

$$P(x_1|y_1) = \frac{.4 \times .8}{.44} = .727$$

$$P(x_2|y_1) = \frac{.6 \times .2}{.44} = .273$$

$$P(x_1|y_2) = \frac{.4 \times .2}{.56} = .143$$

$$P(x_2|y_2) = \frac{.6 \times .8}{.56} = .857$$

These computations are often tabulated as follows:

	PRIOR PROBABILITY $P(x_i)$	LIKELIHOOD $P(y_k\|x_i)$	JOINT PROBABILITY $P(y_k, x_i)$	POSTERIOR PROBABILITY $P(x_i\|y_k)$
If pessimistic report (y_1):				
Demand of 1,200 (x_1)	.4	.8	.32	.727
Demand of 2,000 (x_2)	.6	.2	.12	.273
			.44	1.000
If optimistic report (y_2):				
Demand of 1,200 (x_1)	.4	.2	.08	.143
Demand of 2,000 (x_2)	.6	.8	.48	.857
			.56	1.000

In words, there is a 72.7% chance that $x = 1,200$ if a pessimistic report is provided and an 85.7% chance that $x = 2,000$ if an optimistic report is provided. Note especially that "being right 80% of the time" does not mean that $P(x_1|y_1) = .8$.

Step 4. Determine the optimal action conditional upon each signal from the information system. Each signal (optimistic report or pessimistic report) will generally cause Eastman's posterior probabilities to differ from his prior probabilities. The optimal action will depend on the signal. (If it did not, the sample information would be of no value to Eastman.) Therefore it is necessary to redo the five-step analysis that was originally performed with the prior information for each signal. Exhibit 18-9 shows these computations of expected values, one conditional upon receiving a pessimistic report and one conditional upon receiving an optimistic report.

Step 5. Determine the expected value with the (imperfect) information system. This step was performed earlier in conjunction with the explanation of Exhibit 18-9. The expected value with imperfect information depends on the probabilities of receiving a pessimistic or optimistic report:

$$(.44 \times \$13,368) + (.56 \times \$24,254) = \$19,464$$

As the previous section explained, Eastman should purchase the information system only if its price does not exceed $144, which is $19,464 minus the $19,320 expected value with existing information.

_____QUESTIONS, PROBLEMS, AND CASES_____

18-1 "Determining the problem is the key to successful decision making." Comment.

18-2 "Taking no action must always be listed among alternative actions." Discuss.

18-3 What steps should be taken in determining which action has the highest expected value of the objective function?

18-4 "A wisdom born after the event is the cheapest of all wisdom." Do you agree?

18-5 How would you respond to the following statement?

> Why learn about decision making under conditions of uncertainty? When all the computer runs have been digested (if that is possible), and when all the decision trees have shed their leaves, the decision maker has no guarantee that the final outcome will be more desirable than that which would have occurred by making a decision without a detailed analysis.

18-6. Distinguish between a decision maker who is (a) risk neutral, (b) risk averse, and (c) risk seeking.

18-7 What is the benefit of explicitly recognizing probabilities in decision making?

18-8 Size of inventory. Once a day, a retailer stocks bunches of fresh-cut flowers, each of which costs 40¢ and sells for $1. The retailer never cuts the selling price; leftovers are given to a nearby church. The retailer estimates demand characteristics as follows:

DEMAND	PROBABILITY
0	.05
1	.20
2	.40
3	.25
4	.10
5 or more	.00
	1.00

How many units should the retailer stock in order to maximize expected profits? Why?

18-9 Perfect information. Refer to the preceding problem. Compute the most the retailer should be willing to pay for a faultless prediction concerning the number of units to be sold on any given day.

18-10 Purchase of a new lathe, demand uncertainty. (A. Atkinson) The manager of operations at Purcell's Cove Machine Shop is considering the purchase of a new lathe to replace existing equipment.

The new lathe will increase annual fixed costs by $9,000 per year and will reduce variable costs by $8 per job.

The manager believes that the annual number of jobs processed by the company will be 900 or 1,200 or 1,500 with the possibilities of each of these events to be equally likely. Purcell uses an expected monetary value choice criterion in its decision making.

Required | Should the company buy the new lathe? Support your conclusion with appropriate calculations.

18-11 Setting prices and uncertainty. Assume that the unit cost of a product is known with certainty to be $1.60. The top executives are trying to decide whether to set a selling price of $2.00 or $2.20. The top price has been $2.00 for the past 30 months. Average monthly sales are forecast as follows:

AT A PRICE OF $2.00	
Units	Probability
1,050	.05
1,000	.90
950	.05

AT A PRICE OF $2.20	
Units	Probability
800	.10
750	.60
700	.30

Required | Which is the optimal price? Show computations.

18-12 Risk aversion and utilities. Reconsider the initial data of the purchase of M1 or M2 in the chapter. Suppose the decision maker was risk averse, so that the monetary values are reexpressed as utility values or utils that are not linear:

Monetary values	$7,800	$9,000	$25,000	$27,000
Utils	0.9	1.0	2.3	2.4

Required | 1. If the decision maker maximizes expected operating income expressed in utils instead of monetary values, will the decision change? Show calculations.
2. Suppose the utils for $9,000 were 1.1 instead of 1.0. Would the decision change? Show calculations.

18-13 Bidding for a contract, uncertainty over amount to bid. (A. Atkinson) Lunenburg Landscaping is considering submitting a bid to provide landscaping services at the site of a new Canadian hotel.

The job will require 400 labor-hours, $4,000 of material cost, and $2,000 of rental cost relating to the equipment that the company must rent to do this job.

The company's regular employees are paid $8 per hour. Normally, these employees work on lawns that the company contracts to maintain on an annual basis. The contribution margin per labor-hour devoted to lawn maintenance is $4. The company has learned that it can hire summer students at the rate of $5 per hour to mow lawns.

637

Kelly Burns, the owner-manager of Lunenburg Landscaping, figures that the probability is 100% that she can win the contract if she bids $8,500 on the job. Bids must be
submitted in multiples of $500. Burns figures that the probability of winning the contract
falls by 20% for every increment of $500 over $8,500 (for example, she assesses the probability of winning the contract with a $10,000 bid as 40%). Burns uses an expected monetary
value choice criterion in her decision making.

Required   What bid should Kelly Burns submit on this contract?

18-14 Alternative servicing policies for television sets.   As an appliance dealer, you are deciding how to
service your one-year warranty on the 1,000 color television sets you have just sold to a large
local hotel. You have three alternatives:

1. A reputable service firm has offered to service the sets, including all parts and labor, for
    a flat fee of $18,000.

2. For $15,000, another reputable service firm would furnish all necessary parts and pro-
    vide up to 1,000 service calls at no charge. Service calls in excess of that number would be
    $4 each. The number of calls is likely to be:

EVENT	CHANCE OF OCCURRENCE	PROBABILITY OF OCCURRENCE	TOTAL COST
1,000 calls or less	50%	0.5	$15,000
1,500 calls	20	0.2	17,000
2,000 calls	20	0.2	19,000
2,500 calls	10	0.1	21,000
	100%	1.0	

3. You can hire your own labor and buy your own parts. Your past experience with similar
    work has helped you to formulate the following probabilities and costs:

EVENT	CHANCE OF OCCURRENCE	PROBABILITY OF OCCURRENCE	TOTAL COST
Little trouble	10%	0.1	$ 8,000
Medium trouble	70	0.7	10,000
Much trouble	20	0.2	30,000
	100%	1.0	

Required   Using the expected monetary value approach, compare the three alternatives. Which
plan do you favor? Why?

18-15 Cost-volume-profit under uncertainty.   (J. Patell) In your recently obtained position as supervisor of
new product introduction, you have to decide on a pricing strategy for a specialty product
with the following cost structure.

$$\text{Variable cost per unit} = \$50$$

$$\text{Fixed cost of production} = \$200,000$$

The units are assembled upon receipt of orders, so the inventory levels are insignificant.
Your market research assistant is very enthusiastic about probability models and has presented the results of his price analysis in the following form.

a. If you set the price at $100/unit, the probability distribution of total sales dollars is
    uniform between $300,000 and $600,000.

b. If you lower the price to $70/unit, the distribution remains uniform, but it shifts up to
    the $600,000 to $900,000 range.

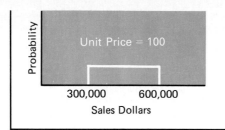 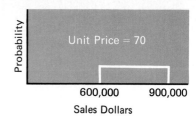

1. This is your first big contract and, above all, you want to show a profit. You decide to select the strategy that maximizes the probability of breaking even or earning a positive profit.
   a. What is the probability of at least breaking even with a price of $100/unit?
   b. What is the probability of at least breaking even with a price of $70/unit?
2. Your assistant suggests that maximum expected profit might be a better goal to pursue. Which pricing strategy yields the higher expected profit?

18-16 Choice of a production-run length. (CMA) Jackston Inc. manufactures and distributes a line of Christmas toys. The company had neglected to keep its dollhouse line current. As a result, sales have decreased to approximately 10,000 units per year from a previous high of 50,000 units. The dollhouse has been redesigned recently and is considered by company officials to be comparable to its competitors' models. The company plans to redesign the dollhouse each year in order to compete effectively. Joan Blocke, the sales manager, is not sure how many units can be sold next year, but she is willing to place probabilities on her estimates. Blocke's estimates of the number of units that can be sold during the next year and the related probabilities are as follows:

ESTIMATED SALES IN UNITS	PROBABILITY
20,000	.10
30,000	.40
40,000	.30
50,000	.20

The units would be sold for $20 each.

The inability to estimate the sales more precisely is a problem for Jackston. The number of units of this product is small enough to schedule the entire year's sales in one production run. If the demand is greater than the number of units manufactured, then sales will be lost. If demand is below supply, the extra units cannot be carried over to the next season and would be given away to various charitable organizations. The production and distribution cost estimates are as follows:

	UNITS MANUFACTURED			
	20,000	30,000	40,000	50,000
Variable costs	$180,000	$270,000	$360,000	$450,000
Fixed costs	140,000	140,000	160,000	160,000
Total costs	$320,000	$410,000	$520,000	$610,000

The company intends to analyze the data to facilitate making a decision as to the proper size of the production run.

1. Prepare a decision table for the different sizes of production runs required to meet the four sales estimates prepared by Joan Blocke for Jackston Inc. If Jackston Inc. relied solely on the expected monetary value approach to make decisions, what size of production run would be selected?

2. Identify the basic steps that are taken in any decision process. Explain each step by reference to the situation presented in the problem and your answer for requirement 1.

18-17 Uncertainty and cost-volume-profit analysis. (R. Jaedicke and A. Robichek, adapted) The Jaedicke and Robichek Company is considering two new products to introduce. Either can be produced by using present facilities. Each product requires an increase in annual fixed expenses of $400,000. The products have the same selling price and the same variable cost per unit: $10 and $8, respectively.

Management, after studying past experience with similar products, has assessed the following probability distribution:

EVENT (UNITS DEMANDED)	PROBABILITY— PRODUCT A	PROBABILITY— PRODUCT B
50,000	—	0.1
100,000	0.1	0.1
200,000	0.2	0.1
300,000	0.4	0.2
400,000	0.2	0.4
500,000	0.1	0.1
	1.0	1.0

Required

1. What is the breakeven point for each product?
2. Which product should be chosen? Why? Show computations.
3. Suppose management was absolutely certain that 300,000 units of Product B would be sold. Which product should be chosen? Why? What benefits are available to management from the provision of the complete probability distribution instead of just a lone expected value?

18-18 New product introduction, uncertainty. (CMA) Sofak Company is a manufacturer of precision sensing equipment. Jerry Adams, one of Sofak's project engineers, has developed a prototype of an automatic testing kit that could continually evaluate water quality and chemical content in hot tubs. Adams believes that this kit will permit domestic tub owners to control water quality better at substantially reduced costs and with less time invested. The management of Sofak is convinced that the kit will have strong market acceptance. Furthermore, this new equipment uses the same technology that Sofak employs in the manufacture of some of its other equipment. Therefore Sofak can use existing facilities to produce the product.

Adams is ready to proceed with developing cost and profit plans for the testing kit. He asked the marketing department to develop a suggested selling price and estimate the sales volume. The marketing department contracted with Statico, a marketing research company, to develop price and volume estimates.

Based on an analysis of the market, Statico considered unit prices between $80 and $120. Within this price range, it recommended a price of $100 per kit. The frequency distribution of the unit sales volume that Sofak could expect at this selling price is presented below.

ESTIMATED UNIT SALES VOLUME AT $100

Annual Unit Sales Volume	Probability
50,000	.25
60,000	.45
70,000	.20
80,000	.10
	1.00

Sofak's profit planning department accumulated cost data that Adams had requested. The new product will require direct materials costing $25.00 per unit and will require two hours of direct-labor time to manufacture. Sofak is currently in contract negotiations with its union, making any projections of labor costs difficult. The current direct-labor cost is $8.00 per direct-labor hour (DLH). Representatives of management who are negotiating with the union have estimated the possible settlements and related probabilities that are shown below.

PROBABILITY OF SETTLEMENT AMOUNTS

Direct-Labor Cost Per Hour	Probability
$8.50	.30
$8.80	.50
$9.00	.20
	1.00

Sofak applies manufacturing overhead to its products using a plantwide rate of $15.00 per DLH. This rate was based on a planned activity level of 900,000 DLH which represents 75% of practical capacity. The budgeted manufacturing overhead costs for the current fiscal year are presented below.

Sofak Company
Schedule of Budgeted Manufacturing Overhead Costs
For the Fiscal Year Ending November 30, 19_6

	BUDGETED ANNUAL COST	COST PER DLH
Variable:		
Supplies	$ 360,000	$ .40
Material handling	315,000	.35
Heat, light, power	1,125,000	1.25
Fixed:		
Supervisory salaries	1,440,000	1.60
Depreciation—building	4,410,000	4.90
Depreciation—equipment	3,420,000	3.80
Property taxes on factory	1,620,000	1.80
Insurance	810,000	.90
Total budgeted costs	$13,500,000	$15.00

The introduction of the new product will require some changes in the manufacturing plant. While the plant is below capacity and current facilities can be used, a new production line requiring a supervisor would be opened. The annual cost of the supervisor would be $28,000. In addition, one piece of equipment that Sofak does not own would have to be obtained under an operating lease at an annual cost of $150,000.

Sofak has already paid Statico $132,000 for the marketing study that was mentioned previously. Statico has agreed to conduct the promotion and distribution of the new product for a fee of $6.00 per unit once Sofak introduces it.

Required | Determine the annual pretax advantage (disadvantage) that Sofak Company could expect from the introduction of the new product by using

1. A deterministic approach based on the most likely outcome for each quantity that is not known with certainty
2. An expected monetary value approach

18-19 Cost estimation for navy, actual cost plus fixed fee reimbursement to contractor. Barry Windham, a cost analyst for the navy, is currently reviewing the cost estimates for a nuclear submarine contract. Windham must make a presentation to a selection committee of three admirals. His presentation will compare the costs that the navy will incur if each of the following three companies is individually awarded the contract:

- Olympus Inc.—has bid $220 million
- Pisces Ventures—has bid $230 million
- Scorpio Corporation—has bid $200 million

The company awarded the contract will be reimbursed on an "actual cost incurred plus fixed fee" basis. The fixed fee is 5% of the cost bid at the time the contract is awarded.

Windham collects data on the past cost underrun/overrun experience in government contracting of each of the three potential contractors. He will use these data to assess the probability distribution of underruns/overruns on the nuclear submarine project. Windham summarized these data by comparing the cost bid at the time the contract was awarded and the eventual actual cost (before inclusion of the 5% fixed fee). The distribution for each of the three contractors is:

	OLYMPUS	PISCES	SCORPIO
10% cost underrun	.10	—	—
No underrun or overrun	.15	.60	.10
10% overrun	.20	.40	.15
20% overrun	.30	—	.20
30% overrun	.10	—	.25
40% overrun	.10	—	.20
50% overrun	.05	—	.10
	1.00	1.00	1.00

Required

1. What is the probability distribution of the actual costs to the navy (including the 5% fixed fee) if the contract is awarded to (a) Olympus, (b) Pisces, or (c) Scorpio? Compute the expected value of the distribution of actual costs to the navy for each contractor.
2. Windham observes that Pisces has not previously built a nuclear submarine. He also notes that Pisces' past contracts with the government have been projects with a relatively low degree of uncertainty as to technical feasibility. How might Windham incorporate this information into his presentation to the contract selection committee?

18-20 Distribution of a new product, decision tree. (CMA, adapted) Sarah Eaton, a financial analyst with the Marketing Division of Ajax Industries, has been asked to evaluate the distribution alternatives for a new product. Eaton obtains the aid of a knowledgeable market analyst in the division to estimate the possible cash inflows from the alternatives and to assess the probabilities of each alternative.

The alternatives being considered are immediate national distribution or regional distribution with national distribution to follow if it is economically feasible. Ajax uses the expected monetary value choice criterion in its decisions. The possible cash flows and the probabilities associated with each alternative are presented below.

	CASH INFLOWS (In millions of dollars)	PROBABILITY OF CASH INFLOW
Immediate National Distribution Only:		
High national results	$+10.0	.30
Medium national results	+ 2.0	.40
Low national results	− 3.0	.30
		1.00

Regional Distribution Only:

Excellent regional results	+ 2.0	.40
Moderate regional results	+ .5	.40
Poor regional results	− 1.0	.20
		1.00

National Distribution Following Regional Distribution

National Distribution as a Consequence of Excellent Regional Results:

High national results	$+ 9.0	.70
Medium national results	+ 2.0	.20
Low national results	− 2.7	.10
		1.00

National Distribution as a Consequence of Moderate Regional Results:

High national results	$+ 8.0	.30
Medium national results	+ 1.8	.40
Low national results	− 3.0	.30
		1.00

National Distribution as a Consequence of Poor Regional Results:

High national results	$+ 7.0	.10
Medium national results	+ 1.5	.30
Low national results	− 4.0	.60
		1.00

Required

1. Formulate the decision tree framework for analyzing whether Ajax Industries should use (a) national distribution or (b) regional distribution with national distribution to follow if it is economically feasible. Identify the probabilities and expected cash flows for each branch in the tree.
2. Should Ajax select (a) national distribution or (b) regional distribution with national distribution to follow if it is economically feasible? Support your decision with appropriate calculations.
3. Eaton and her associates are aware that determination of cash flows involves subjectivity. Therefore, if any of these values are significantly in error, the reliability of the decision tree analysis could be in doubt. Describe a method by which the management can evaluate the possible consequences of errors in the estimates.

18-21 Bidding for a contract, expected value of perfect information. (A. Atkinson) Chester Steel Fabrication (CSF) is considering submitting a bid to construct a metal bridge for a new highway.

The company controller thinks that a bid of $1,000,000 will cover both the costs associated with this project and the opportunity costs of the equipment and labor that would be used on this project. Julie Dawson, the company president, figures that a CSF bid of $1,000,000 is sure to get the job. Dawson intends to bid that amount, but she wonders about some of the cost estimates that are included in the controller's report.

After some study, Dawson has determined that the total of all costs associated with this project could actually be $800,000, $900,000, $1,000,000, or $1,200,000 with respective probabilities of 0.10, 0.30, 0.40, and 0.20.

Chester Steel uses an expected profit maximization criterion in its decisions.

Required

1. Given the information provided, what is Dawson's optimal action (bid or not bid)?
2. What is the maximum that Dawson should be willing to pay for the controller to undertake a new study to determine precisely the costs associated with this project?

18-22 Buying perfect information. As a manager of a post office, you are trying to decide whether to rearrange a production line and facilities in order to save labor and related costs. Assume that the only alternatives are to "do nothing" or "rearrange." Assume also that the choice criterion is that the expected savings from rearrangement must equal or exceed $11,000.

Based on your experience and currently available information, you predict:

a. The "do nothing" alternative will have operating costs of $200,000.

b. The "rearrange" alternative will have operating costs of $100,000 if it is a success and $260,000 if it is a failure. You think there is a 60% chance of success and a 40% chance of failure.

Required

1. Compute the expected value of the costs for each alternative. Compute the difference in expected costs.
2. You can hire a consultant, Joan Zenoff, to study the situation. She would then render a flawless prediction of whether the rearrangement would succeed or fail. Compute the maximum amount you would be willing to pay for the errorless prediction. (The next problem explores imperfect information.)

18-23 Buying imperfect information. Study the appendix to this chapter. Refer to the preceding problem. Zenoff's eventual prediction of success or failure will be imperfect. The following analysis is provided:

	EVENTS	
PROBABILITY OF EVENTS	Success	Failure
If optimistic report	.818	.182
If pessimistic report	.333	.667

Required

1. Compute the expected costs, assuming an optimistic report.
2. Compute the expected costs, assuming a pessimistic report.
3. The probability of getting an optimistic report is .55; a pessimistic report, .45. (The computation of these probabilities is not necessary for solving this problem. The next problem covers that computation, which is explained in the appendix of this chapter.) Compute the expected value of imperfect information. Compare it with the expected value of existing information as computed in the preceding problem. The consultant's fee is $1,000. Should she be hired?
4. Suppose you hire the consultant. The report is pessimistic. Should you proceed with the rearrangement? Explain.

18-24 Revising probabilities. Study the appendix to this chapter. This problem explores how the probabilities in the preceding problem were computed. You determined that Zenoff's predictions were correct only 75% of the time. For example, if Zenoff supplies an optimistic prediction of success, a failure will occur 25% of the time.

Let P = probability; y_1 = optimistic report; y_2 = pessimistic report; x_1 = success; and x_2 = failure.

Then
$$P(y_1|x_1) = .75 \qquad P(y_2|x_2) = .75$$
$$P(y_2|x_1) = .25 \qquad P(y_1|x_2) = .25$$

Required

1. Given the existing information, the probability of success is .6 and of failure is .4. Compute the probabilities of obtaining a pessimistic or optimistic report.
2. Compute the revised probabilities of each event's occurring, conditional upon receiving a particular optimistic or pessimistic report. That is, revise your prior probabilities into posterior probabilities.

18-25 Nursery planting decision, expected value of perfect and imperfect information. (A. Atkinson) Study the Appendix for this chapter. It is midwinter and Arnie Lindberg, the owner-manager of Kentville Nurseries, is planning his planting activities for the upcoming season. In another few weeks Arnie will begin planting in his greenhouse. In mid to late spring these plants will be sold to garden centers for resale to customers.

Based on his sales over the last several years, Arnie figures that in the upcoming season, his sales could be $200,000, $250,000, or $300,000 with respective probabilities of 0.25, 0.50, and 0.25. The problem is that Arnie must plant his seeds and incur his costs before the actual sales level is known. Plants that remain unsold by mid-June are removed from Arnie's greenhouse and donated to a local nursing home. Arnie's total variable costs are 60% of the level of sales planted for, and fixed costs amount to $60,000. Arnie's three options are to plan for a sales level of $200,000 or $250,000 or $300,000.

Kentville Nurseries uses an expected profit maximization choice criterion in its decisions.

Required

1. Based on the information provided, for what level of sales should Arnie plant?
2. How much is it worth to Arnie to obtain perfect information about what level of sales will occur?
3. By investing $2,500 Arnie can travel and visit all his customers. On the basis of his discussions with his customers, Arnie can form an impression of whether the upcoming selling season will be good, fair, or poor. The characteristics of Arnie's likelihood function are as follows:

PROBABILITY OF ASSESSMENT GIVEN EVENT

Event	Good	Fair	Poor
Sales, $200,000	0.1	0.2	0.7
Sales, $250,000	0.3	0.5	0.2
Sales, $300,000	0.6	0.3	0.1

For example, the probability is 0.3 that Arnie's assessment of sales will be good given that the sales level will prove to be $250,000.

Should Arnie invest $2,500 to develop an assessment of whether sales will be good, fair, or poor?

18-26 Alternative contracts for a movie producer, uncertainty about production cost and demand. Jillian Armstrong, an independent movie producer, is negotiating with Roadshow Productions on the contract for the production and marketing of her next film, titled *Forward to the Past*. The budget for the film is $10 million. Roadshow offers Armstrong one of three contracts:

Contract A:

1. Roadshow pays all costs of production and marketing.
2. Armstrong receives a fixed fee of $1 million.
3. Armstrong receives 10% of gross revenues for the film in excess of $100 million. (No % payment is made for gross revenues up to $100 million.)

Contract B:

1. Roadshow pays 80% of costs of production and marketing up to $10 million and 50% of costs of production and marketing in excess of $10 million.
2. Armstrong receives 10% of *all* gross revenues for the film.

Contract C:

1. Roadshow pays 50% of costs of production and marketing up to $10 million and zero % thereafter.
2. Armstrong receives 30% of *all* gross revenues for the film.

Armstrong assesses the following probabilities for the gross revenues:

$$P \text{ (high demand of \$200 million)} = .1$$
$$P \text{ (medium demand of \$50 million)} = .3$$
$$P \text{ (low demand of \$10 million)} = .6$$

She assesses the following probabilities for the costs of production:

$$P \text{ (at budgeted cost of \$10 million)} = .6$$
$$P \text{ (at high cost of \$20 million)} = .4$$

Armstrong assesses the following probabilities for six possible events:

EVENT	PROBABILITY
High demand—budgeted cost	.06
High demand—high cost	.04
Medium demand—budgeted cost	.18
Medium demand—high cost	.12
Low demand—budgeted cost	.36
Low demand—high cost	.24
	1.00

Required

1. Compute the payoff to Armstrong under each contract for each of the six possible events.
2. Armstrong will choose the contract that maximizes her expected monetary value from the film. Which contract should she choose? Show calculations.
3. What information might Armstrong use in assessing the probability distribution for the costs of production and marketing of the *Forward to the Past* film?

Capital Budgeting and Cost Analysis

Should we add more factories, warehouses, hospitals, hotels, or student housing? Buy the new computer mainframe? Add the new product or service? Such special decisions frequently entail large dollar amounts, have long time spans, and uncertain outcomes. Accounting data often help managers make these long-range decisions, which are frequently called *capital-budgeting* decisions. This chapter examines the role of accounting data in the popular decision models for capital budgeting. We also study the relationship of the decision models to the performance evaluation models that are used to help judge the results of the capital-budgeting decisions.

At this stage we again focus on purpose. Income determination and the planning and controlling of routine operations primarily focus on the *current time period*. Special decisions and long-range planning primarily focus on the *project* or *program* with a far-reaching time span.

For simplicity, this chapter (along with Chapter 20) assumes that all cash outflows and cash inflows occur at the beginning or end (as specified) of each period.

CONTRAST IN PURPOSES OF COST ANALYSIS

Exhibit 19-1 illustrates how the project focus of capital budgeting differs from the current time-period focus of income determination. The vertical dimension signi-

EXHIBIT 19-1
The Project Orientation of Capital Budgeting

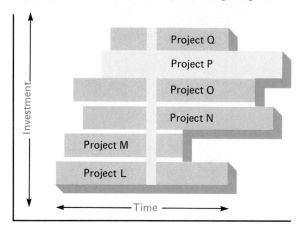

fies the total investment (assets) of the company. The horizontal dimension represents successive years in a company's life.

Each individual project is represented in Exhibit 19-1 as a distinct horizontal rectangle. Each can entail commitments over a prolonged span of time, not just one year. The focus is on an individual investment venture throughout its life. The interest or other income that can be earned over a period of time (that is, the time value of money) often looms large in these decisions.

The distinct vertical rectangle in Exhibit 19-1 illustrates the focus of income determination and current-period planning and control. This cross-sectional emphasis is on the company's overall performance and status for a year or less. Because the time period is relatively short, the time value of money usually is not directly involved. There is a great danger in basing capital-budgeting decisions on an indiscriminate use of the data routinely reported in the existing general-purpose accounting system.

DEFINITION AND STAGES OF CAPITAL BUDGETING

Capital budgeting is the making of long-term planning decisions for investments and their financing. The stages in capital budgeting, after a potential project has been identified, include

1. Definition of the project and prediction of its outcomes. The final section of this chapter notes the importance of including items that are not easily quantifiable in these predictions.
2. Choice of a project. A detailed analysis of financial and other aspects of each project should be made. The following project selection methods are discussed in this chapter:
   a. Net present value
   b. Internal rate of return
   c. Payback
   d. Accrual accounting rate of return
   e. Urgency
   Our discussion will emphasize methods a and b. Both of these methods explicitly recognize the time value of money as a critical factor in decisions having long time spans.

3. Financing of a project. Sources of finance include internally (within the organization) generated cash, the equity-security capital market, and the debt-security capital market.

4. Implementation of a project and monitoring of its performance. In some cases, monitoring may also include a postdecision audit in which the predictions made at the time a project was selected are compared with the subsequent outcomes.

The discussion in this chapter focuses on investment-decision aspects of capital budgeting. However, in understanding which projects within an organization are approved and which are rejected, the influence of individual personalities is often pivotal. Those managers who are best at selling their own projects to the decision maker will often get the lion's share of the available money, whereas the other managers either get nothing or wait, and then wait some more. Economic considerations can become secondary as individual managers war with words, often citing their impressive operating performance that may or may not be relevant to the capital-budgeting decision at hand.

DISCOUNTED CASH FLOW

The essence of discounted cash flow (DCF) is to represent the cash inflows and outflows of a project at a common point in time so that they can be compared (added, subtracted, etc.) in an appropriate way.

Time value of money

The *discounted cash-flow* model for capital-budgeting decisions recognizes that the use of money has a cost (interest), just as the use of a building or an automobile may have a cost (rent). A dollar in hand (or paid) today is worth more than a dollar to be received (or spent) five years from today. For instance, in the interim a dollar can be invested in a savings institution; the dollar would grow markedly during a five-year span because it would earn interest. **Because the discounted cash-flow model explicitly and routinely weighs the time value of money, it is usually the best model to use for long-range decisions.**

Another major aspect of DCF is its focus on *cash* inflows and outflows rather than on *net income* as computed in the conventional accrual accounting sense. Cash is invested now with the hope of receiving cash in a greater amount in the future. Try to avoid injecting accrual concepts of accounting into DCF analysis.

There are two main variations of DCF: (a) *net present value (NPV)* and (b) *internal rate of return (IRR)*. The compound interest tables and formulas used in DCF analysis are included in Appendix B, pages 942–50. **BEFORE READING ON, BE SURE YOU UNDERSTAND THIS APPENDIX.**

Both variations of DCF require as an input the **required rate of return (RRR)**, which is the minimum desired rate of return on an investment. This rate is also called the **hurdle rate, cutoff rate, cost of capital,** or **discount rate**. Chapter 20 discusses issues encountered in estimating this rate.

EXAMPLE

The following situation will be used to illustrate the various capital-budgeting decision models. A manager of a nonprofit entity, a hospital, is considering buying a new machine that will aid productivity in the X-ray department. The machine will cost $3,791 now, is expected to have a five-year useful life and a zero terminal disposal value, and will result in cash-operating savings of $1,000 annually. The hospital is not subject to income taxes.

In other words, Alternative A is to continue to operate the X-ray department without change (i.e., do nothing different). Alternative B is to buy the new machine, which will reduce hand processing. Because no change in revenue is indicated, the only element of difference is the savings in cash-operating costs.

Required

1. Compute the project's net present value. Assume that the required rate of return is 8%. (This relatively low interest rate is not unusual for a nonprofit institution.)
2. Compute the internal rate of return on the project.

Net present value model

Net present value (NPV) is a method of calculating the expected net monetary gain or loss from a project by discounting all expected future cash inflows and outflows to the present, using some predetermined minimum desired rate of return. Using the NPV method entails the following steps:

1. Draw a sketch of relevant cash inflows and outflows. The right-hand side of Exhibit 19-2 shows how these cash flows are portrayed. Outflows are placed in parentheses. Although such a sketch is not absolutely necessary, it clarifies relationships. It lets the decision maker organize the data in a systematic way. Note that Exhibit 19-2 includes the outflow at time zero, the date of the new machine acquisition.
2. Choose the correct compound interest table. Find the discount factor from the appropriate row and column. To obtain the present value, multiply the discount factors by the cash amounts in the sketch.
3. Sum the present values. If the total is zero or positive, the project should be accepted because its rate of return equals or exceeds the desired minimum. If the total is negative, the project is undesirable because its rate of return is below the desired minimum.

Exhibit 19-2 indicates a net present value of $202, assuming a hurdle rate of 8%; therefore the investment is desirable.

The higher the hurdle rate, the less willing the manager would be to invest in this project. At a rate of 12%, the net present value would be −$186 (that is, $1,000 × 3.605, the present value annuity factor from Table 4, = $3,605, which is $186 less than the required investment of $3,791). When the hurdle rate is 12%, rather than 8%, the machine is undesirable at its purchase price of $3,791.

Assumptions of model

Before reading on, ponder the meaning of the net present value model. First, the model assumes a world of certainty. That is, we are absolutely sure that the predicted cash flows will occur in the amounts and at the times indicated. Second, the model assumes that the original amount of investment can be viewed as either borrowed by us or loaned by us at the specified minimum desired interest rate.

Thus the net present value of $202 in Exhibit 19-2 means that if we borrowed $3,791 from a bank at 8% per annum, invested in the project, and repaid the loan and interest with the project cash inflows, we would accumulate the same net amount of money as if we deposited $202 in a bank at 8% interest. Exhibit 19-3 demonstrates these relationships. Suppose somebody approached us at time zero and offered $202 for the project that we had invested in ten seconds before. Also suppose that the buyer would assume the obligation to repay the bank loan. If we accept the buyer's offer, we would invest the $202 in the bank at an interest rate of 8%. In our assumed world of certainty, we would be completely indifferent between (a) keeping the original investment and (b) accepting the buyer's offer and investing the $202 in the bank.

EXHIBIT 19-2
Net Present Value Model

Original investment	$3,791	
Useful life	5 years	
Annual cash savings from operations	$1,000	
Hurdle rate of return, which is the discount rate	8%	

APPROACH 1: Discounting each year's cash inflow separately*

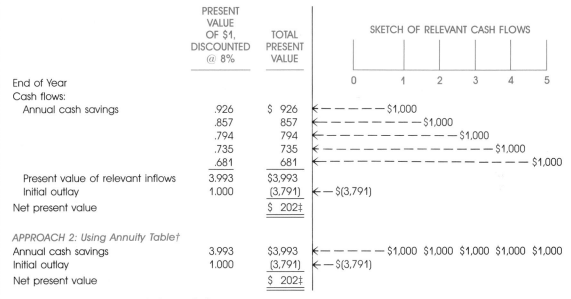

End of Year	PRESENT VALUE OF $1, DISCOUNTED @ 8%	TOTAL PRESENT VALUE	SKETCH OF RELEVANT CASH FLOWS
Cash flows:			0 1 2 3 4 5
Annual cash savings	.926	$ 926	←－－－－$1,000
	.857	857	←－－－－－－$1,000
	.794	794	←－－－－－－－－$1,000
	.735	735	←－－－－－－－－－－$1,000
	.681	681	←－－－－－－－－－－－－$1,000
Present value of relevant inflows	3.993	$3,993	
Initial outlay	1.000	(3,791)	←－ $(3,791)
Net present value		$ 202‡	

APPROACH 2: Using Annuity Table†

Annual cash savings	3.993	$3,993	←－－－－$1,000 $1,000 $1,000 $1,000 $1,000
Initial outlay	1.000	(3,791)	←－ $(3,791)
Net present value		$ 202‡	

*Present values from Table 2, Appendix B.
†Present annuity values from Table 4, Appendix B.
‡Rounded.
Note: *Throughout these exhibits regarding discounted cash-flow models, parentheses or negative signs will denote relevant cash outflows.*

Caution: Do not proceed until you thoroughly understand Exhibits 19-2 and 19-3. Furthermore, compare Approach 1 with Approach 2 in Exhibit 19-2 to see how the two compound interest tables in Appendix B relate to one another. Note how Table 4 is merely a compilation of the present value factors of Table 2. That is, the fundamental table is Table 2; Table 4 exists merely to reduce calculations when there is a series of equal cash flows at equal intervals.

Internal rate-of-return model

The internal rate of return (IRR) is the rate of interest at which the present value of expected cash inflows from a project equals the present value of expected cash outflows of the project. IRR is sometimes called the **time-adjusted rate of return.** Requirement 2 of our basic example calls for computation of the IRR. Exhibit 19-4 displays this computation.

Expressed in other ways, the internal rate of return can be described as

1. The interest rate that makes the net present value of a project equal to zero, as Exhibit 19-4 shows.

EXHIBIT 19-3
Rationale Underlying Net Present Value Model
(Same Data as in Exhibit 19-2)

ALTERNATIVE ONE: Invest and Hold the Project.

YEAR	(1) LOAN BALANCE AT BEGINNING OF YEAR	(2) INTEREST AT 8% PER YEAR	(3) (1) + (2) ACCUMULATED AMOUNT AT END OF YEAR	(4) CASH FOR REPAYMENT OF LOAN	(5) (3) − (4) LOAN BALANCE AT END OF YEAR
1	$3,791	$303	$4,094	$1,000	$3,094
2	3,094	248	3,342	1,000	2,342
3	2,342	187	2,529	1,000	1,529
4	1,529	122	1,651	1,000	651
5	651	52	703	1,000	(297)*

*After repayment of the final $703 loan installment, the investor would have $297 left over from the $1,000 cash provided by the project at the end of the fifth year; he would be $297 wealthier at the end of five years.

ALTERNATIVE TWO: Invest, Sell the Project for $202 an Instant Later, and Deposit the $202 in a Bank.

YEAR	(1) INVESTMENT BALANCE AT BEGINNING OF YEAR	(2) INTEREST AT 8% PER YEAR	(3) (1) + (2) ACCUMULATED AMOUNT AT END OF YEAR
1	$202	$16	$218
2	218	17	235
3	235	19	254
4	254	20	274
5	274	22	296†

†The investor would have the same amount of wealth at the end of five years as in Alternative One. (The $1 difference between the $296 and the $297 in Alternative One is because of rounding.) Note that stating the net present value at $202 at time zero is equivalent to stating the future amount at $296; the investor is indifferent as to having $202 today or $296 five years hence.

2. The maximum rate of interest that could be paid to a financial institution for borrowing the money invested over the life of the project to exactly break even. Here "break even" means arriving at the point where the net present value is zero or the internal rate of return equals the required rate of return.

The step-by-step computations of an internal rate of return are not too difficult when the cash inflows are equal. In Exhibit 19-4, the following equation is used:

$3,791 = Present value of annuity of $1,000 at X% for
5 years, or what factor F in Table 4 (p. 950)
will satisfy the following equation:

$$3,791 = \$1,000F$$

$$F = 3.791$$

On the period-5 line of Table 4, find the percentage column that is closest to 3.791. It happens to be exactly 10%. If the factor (F) fell between the columns,

EXHIBIT 19-4
Two Proofs of Internal Rate of Return

Original investment			$3,791
Useful life			5 years
Annual cash inflow from operations			$1,000
Internal rate of return			10%*

PROOF 1: Discounting each year's cash inflow separately†

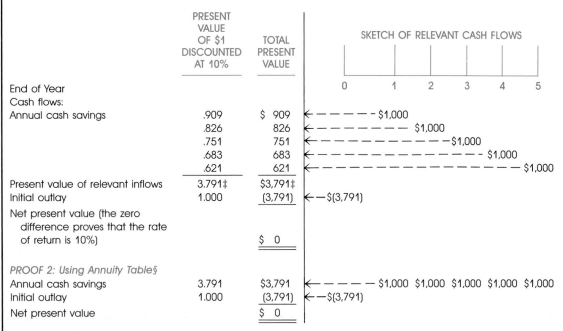

	PRESENT VALUE OF $1 DISCOUNTED AT 10%	TOTAL PRESENT VALUE	SKETCH OF RELEVANT CASH FLOWS
End of Year			0 1 2 3 4 5
Cash flows:			
Annual cash savings	.909	$ 909	◄ — — — — - $1,000
	.826	826	◄ — — — — — — — $1,000
	.751	751	◄ — — — — — — — — — $1,000
	.683	683	◄ — — — — — — — — — — — - $1,000
	.621	621	◄ — — — — — — — — — — — — — $1,000
Present value of relevant inflows	3.791‡	$3,791‡	
Initial outlay	1.000	(3,791)	◄ — $(3,791)
Net present value (the zero difference proves that the rate of return is 10%)		$ 0	

PROOF 2: Using Annuity Table§

Annual cash savings	3.791	$3,791	◄ — — — — $1,000 $1,000 $1,000 $1,000 $1,000
Initial outlay	1.000	(3,791)	◄ — $(3,791)
Net present value		$ 0	

*The rate of return would be computed by methods explained later in the chapter.
†Present values from Table 2, Appendix B.
‡Sum is really $3,790 but is rounded.
§Present values of annuity from Table 4, Appendix B.

---

straight-line interpolation would be used to approximate the internal rate of return. For an illustration, see Problem 1 of the Problems for Self-Study, page 666. In many cases, users will have access to a calculator or computer that is programmed to calculate the internal rate of return.[1]

Note in Exhibit 19-4 that $3,791 is the present value, at a rate of return of 10%, of a five-year stream of cash inflows of $1,000 per year. Ten percent is the rate that equates the amount invested ($3,791) with the present value of the cash inflows ($1,000 per year for five years). In other words, *if* money were borrowed at an interest rate of 10%, the cash inflow produced by the project would exactly

---

[1]A favorite expression of some instructors is "Dependence on programmed calculators is dangerous to your learning." Instructors often require students to use specific rounded discount factors on assignment problems or exams in the belief that this will better test student understanding of DCF (as distinguished from blind reliance on programmed calculators). A second rationale is that it aids grading, as student answers will not vary due to differences in the number of decimal digits in the calculator or computer used.

repay the hypothetical loan plus interest over the five years. If the minimum desired return is less than 10%, the project will be profitable. If the minimum desired return exceeds 10%, the cash inflow will be insufficient to pay interest and repay the principal of the hypothetical loan. Therefore 10% is the internal rate of return for this project.

Explanation of compound interest

The internal rate of return is computed on the basis of the investment tied up in the project from period to period instead of solely the original amount of the investment. See Exhibit 19-5. The internal rate of return in that exhibit is 10% *of the capital invested during each year.* The $1,000 inflow is composed of two parts, as analyzed in columns 3 and 4. Consider year 1. Column 3 shows the interest on the $3,791 invested capital as .10 × $3,791 = $379. Column 4 shows that $1,000 − $379, or $621, is the amount of investment recovered at the end of the year. In this example, the five-year cash inflow exactly recovers the original investment plus annual interest at a rate of 10% on the as-yet-unrecovered capital.

Exhibit 19-5 can be interpreted from both the borrower's and the lender's viewpoints. Assume the hospital borrowed $3,791 from a bank at an interest rate of 10% per annum, invested in the project, and repaid the loan with relevant cash savings of $1,000 per year. The lender would earn exactly 10% per year. The borrower would end up with an accumulated wealth of zero. Obviously, if the hospital could borrow at 10%, and the project could generate cash of greater than $1,000 annually, the hospital could keep some cash. Then the internal rate of return, *by definition,* would exceed 10%.

EXHIBIT 19-5
Rationale Underlying Internal Rate-of-Return Model
(Same Data as in Exhibit 19-4)

	Original investment	$3,791
	Annual cash savings from operations	1,000
	Useful life	5 years
	Internal rate of return	10%*

YEAR	(1) UNRECOVERED INVESTMENT AT BEGINNING OF YEAR	(2) ANNUAL CASH SAVINGS	(3) INTEREST AT 10% PER YEAR (1) × 10%	(4) AMOUNT OF INVESTMENT RECOVERED AT END OF YEAR (2) − (3)	(5) UNRECOVERED INVESTMENT AT END OF YEAR (1) − (4)
1	$3,791	$1,000	$ 379	$ 621	$3,170
2	3,170	1,000	317	683	2,487
3	2,487	1,000	249	751	1,736
4	1,736	1,000	173	827	909
5	909	1,000	91	909	0
		$5,000	$1,209	$3,791	

*Assumptions: Unrecovered investment at beginning of each year earns interest for whole year. Annual cash inflows are received at the end of each year. For simplicity in the use of tables, all operating cash inflows are assumed to take place at the end of the years in question. This is unrealistic because such cash flows ordinarily occur uniformly throughout the given year, rather than in lump sums at the end of the year. Compound interest tables especially tailored for these more stringent conditions are available, but we will not consider them here. See J. Bracken and C. Christenson, *Tables for Use in Analyzing Business Decisions* (Homewood, Ill.: Richard D. Irwin).

Comparison of
net present value
and internal rate-
of-return models

We can summarize the decision rules offered by the two discounted cash-flow models as follows:

INTERNAL RATE OF RETURN	NET PRESENT VALUE
1. Compute the internal rate of return.	1. Calculate the net present value, using the hurdle rate of return as the discount rate.
2. If this rate equals or exceeds the hurdle rate, accept the project; if not, reject the project.	2. If the net present value is positive or zero, accept the project; if negative, reject the project.

The net present value model is emphasized in this text. It has the important advantage that the end product of the computations is dollars, not a percentage. The result is that one can add up the net present values of individual independent projects and obtain a valid estimate of the effect of accepting a combination of projects.[2] In contrast, the internal rates of return of individual independent projects cannot be added to derive the internal rate of return of the combination of projects.

A second advantage is that the net present value method can handle situations where there is not a constant minimum desired return over each year of the project. For example, assume in the equipment replacement example that the hospital has a minimum desired rate of return of 8% in years 1, 2, and 3, and 12% in years 4 and 5. The total present value of the cash inflows is calculated as follows:

YEAR	CASH INFLOW	DISCOUNT RATE	PRESENT VALUE OF $1 DISCOUNTED AT DISCOUNT RATE	TOTAL PRESENT VALUE OF CASH INFLOWS
1	$1,000	8%	.926	$ 926
2	1,000	8	.857	857
3	1,000	8	.794	794
4	1,000	12	.636	636
5	1,000	12	.567	567
				$3,780

Given the initial outlay of $3,791, the project is unattractive. The internal rate-of-return model cannot be applied in the above context because there is not a single desired rate of return with which to compare its IRR.

---

[2]We view the net present value criterion as conceptually appealing because it recognizes the time value of money. This feature is important for both publicly traded companies and privately held companies, and for both profit and nonprofit organizations. The finance literature is currently examining the relationship between (a) use of the maximize net present value criterion and (b) maximizing the market value of a firm having publicly traded equity securities. Issues being considered include how the capital market prices the risk associated with future cash flows, and how information differences between internal managers and external investors can lead to lack of synchronization between (a) and (b). See R. Brealey and S. Myers, *Principles of Corporate Finance,* 2nd ed. (New York: McGraw-Hill, 1984); T. Copeland and J. Weston, *Financial Theory and Corporate Policy,* 2nd ed. (Reading, Mass.: Addison-Wesley, 1983); and J. Van Horne, *Financial Management and Policy,* 7th ed. (Englewood Cliffs, N.J.: Prentice-Hall, 1986).

To highlight the basic differences among various decision models, this chapter deals only with the expected values of cash flows as though they will occur for certain. Obviously, managers know that such predictions inevitably are imperfect. Chapter 18 describes how to contend with uncertainty in these and other situations. For now, we concentrate on *sensitivity analysis,* which was introduced in Chapter 3. **Sensitivity analysis** is a "what-if" technique that measures how the expected values in a decision model will be affected by changes in the critical data inputs. In the realm of capital budgeting, sensitivity analysis answers the question, How will the internal rate of return or net present value be affected if the predictions of cash flows vary as to their amounts or timing?

Of course, sensitivity analysis can take various forms. For instance, management may want to know how far annual cash savings will have to fall to break even on the investment. For the data in Exhibit 19-2, let X = annual cash inflows and let net present value = 0. The initial cash outlay is $3,791 and the present value factor at the 8% required rate for a five-year annuity of $1 is 3.993. Then:

$$NPV = 0$$

$$3.993X - \$3,791 = 0$$

$$3.993X = \$3,791$$

$$X = \$3,791 \div 3.993 = \$949$$

Thus the amount by which annual cash savings can drop before they reach the point of indifference regarding the investment is $1,000 − $949 = $51.

Another critical factor is useful life. If useful life were only four years, instead of five years, the gross present value would be $1,000 times 3.312 (from the period-4 line in the 8% column of Table 4), or $3,312, producing a negative net present value, $3,312 − $3,791, or −$479.

These calculations also apply to testing the sensitivity of rates of return. A fall in the annual cash savings from $1,000 to $900 reduces the internal rate of return from 10% (which was determined in Exhibit 19-5) to 6%:

$$NPV = 0$$

$$\text{Investment} - \text{PV of annuity of \$900 at } X\% \text{ for 5 years} = 0$$

We are seeking the factor (F) in Table 4 that will satisfy the following equation:

$$\$3,791 - \$900F = 0$$

$$900F = 3,791$$

$$F = 3,791 \div 900 = 4.212$$

Examine the five-year line in Table 4. Find the percentage column closest to 4.212. In this instance, we do not have to interpolate; the rate is exactly 6%.

Of course, sensitivity analysis works both ways. It can measure the potential increases in net present value or internal rate of return as well as the decreases. The major contribution of sensitivity analysis is that it provides an immediate financial measure of the possible errors in forecasting. Therefore it can be very useful. Why? Because it helps focus on those decisions that may be very sensitive indeed, and it eases the manager's mind about those decisions that are not so sensitive.

ANALYSIS OF TYPICAL ITEMS UNDER DISCOUNTED CASH FLOW

The following is a summary of how some common items are analyzed in DCF models:

1. CURRENT ASSETS Additional investments in plant and equipment, or in sales promotions of product lines, are invariably accompanied by additional investments in the cash, receivables, and inventories required to support these new activities. In the discounted cash-flow model, *all* investments at time zero are alike, regardless of how they may be accounted for by the accrual accounting model. That is, the initial outlays are entered in the sketch of relevant cash flows at time zero. At the end of the useful life of the project, the original outlays for machines may not be recovered at all, or they may be only partially recovered in the amount of the terminal disposal values. In contrast, the entire original investments in receivables and inventories are usually recouped when the project is terminated. **Therefore all investments at time zero are typically regarded as outflows at time zero, and their terminal disposal values, if any, are regarded as inflows at the end of the project's useful life.**

To illustrate, suppose a company buys some new equipment to make a new product. The required investment would also necessitate additional working capital in the form of cash, receivables, and inventories. Such investments would be shown in the format of Exhibit 19-2 as follows (numbers and lives assumed, investments in millions of dollars):

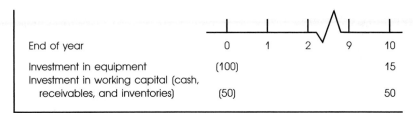

End of year	0	1	2	9	10
Investment in equipment	(100)				15
Investment in working capital (cash, receivables, and inventories)	(50)				50

As the sketch shows, the terminal disposal value of the equipment might be relatively small. However, the entire investment in working capital would ordinarily be recovered when the product is no longer being manufactured. The difference between the initial outlay for working capital and the present value of its recovery is the present value of the cost of using working capital in the project.

Where a capital-budgeting project will reduce working capital, the reverse of the above holds. Assume that a computer-integrated manufacturing project will reduce working capital by $20 million. This reduction will be represented as a decrease of $20 million in the total cash outflow for the project at time 0, and a decrease of $20 million in the cash inflow for the project at its date of termination.

2. BOOK VALUE AND DEPRECIATION Book value and depreciation are ignored in DCF approaches to cash flows from operations (before income taxes). Because the

DCF approach is fundamentally based on inflows and outflows of *cash* and not on the *accrual* concepts of revenues and expenses, no adjustments should be made to the cash flows for the periodic allocation of the asset cost called depreciation expense (which is not a cash flow). In the DCF approach, the initial cost of an asset is usually regarded as a *lump-sum* outflow of cash at time zero. **Therefore it is wrong to deduct depreciation from operating cash inflows.** To deduct periodic depreciation would be a double counting of a cost that has already been considered as a lump-sum outflow. (See the next chapter for a discussion of how book value and depreciation affect after-tax cash flows from operations, as distinguished from before-tax cash flows from operations.)

3. **CURRENT DISPOSAL VALUES AND REQUIRED INVESTMENT** In a replacement decision, how should the current disposal value affect the computations? For example, suppose that the current disposal value of old equipment is $5,000 and that new equipment is available for $40,000. There are a number of correct ways to analyze these items, all of which will have the same ultimate effect on the decision. Generally, the required investment is most easily measured, for example, by offsetting the current disposal value of the old assets ($5,000) against the gross cost of the new assets ($40,000) and by showing the net cash outflow at $35,000.

4. **FUTURE DISPOSAL VALUES** *The disposal value at the date of termination of a project is an increase in the cash inflow in the year of disposal.* Errors in forecasting disposal value are seldom crucial because their present value is usually small, especially for amounts to be received in the distant future.

5. **INCOME TAXES** In practice, comparison between alternatives is best made after considering income tax effects because the tax impact may alter the picture. (The effects of income taxes are considered in Chapter 20.)

6. **OVERHEAD ANALYSIS** In the relevant cost analysis of overhead, only the overhead that will differ between alternatives is pertinent. There is need for careful study of how much, if any, fixed overhead is relevant under the available alternatives. In practice, this is a difficult phase of capital budgeting because it is hard to relate the individual costs to any single project.

PAYBACK

Fundamental model

The payback model measures the time it will take to recoup, in the form of cash inflow from operations, the initial dollars invested in a project. A synonym is the **payout** model. Recall that in our example $3,791 was spent for a machine having a five-year expected useful life and a $1,000 annual cash inflow from operations. The payback calculations follow:

$$\text{Payback time} = \frac{\text{Initial incremental amount invested}}{\text{Uniform annual incremental cash inflow from operations}}$$

$$P = I \div O_c$$

$$P = \$3,791 \div \$1,000 = 3.8 \text{ years}$$

The payback measure highlights liquidity, which is often an important factor in business decisions. Payback has the benefit of being easily understood. Like the DCF methods described previously, it is not affected by accrual accounting conventions such as depreciation and depletion. Advocates of payback argue that it is a handy measure (a) where precision in estimates of profitability is not crucial and preliminary screening of many proposals is necessary, and (b) where the contemplated project is extremely risky.

The major weakness of the payback model is its neglect of profitability. The mere fact that a project has a satisfactory payback time does not mean that it should be selected in preference to an alternative project with a longer payback. To illustrate, consider an alternative to the $3,791 machine mentioned earlier. Assume that another machine requires only a $3,000 investment and will also result in cash savings of $1,000 per year. Compare the two payback periods:

$$P_1 = \$3,791 \div \$1,000 = 3.8 \text{ years}$$

$$P_2 = \$3,000 \div \$1,000 = 3.0 \text{ years}$$

The payback criterion would favor buying the $3,000 machine. However, one fact about this machine has purposely been withheld. Its useful life is only three years. Ignoring the complexities of compound interest for the moment, we find that the $3,000 machine results in zero profits, whereas the $3,791 machine (which has a useful life of five years) yields profits for 1.2 years beyond its payback period.[3]

Nonuniform cash inflows

The payback formula is designed for uniform cash inflows. When cash inflows are not uniform, the payback computation takes a cumulative form. That is, each year's net cash inflows are accumulated until the initial investment has been recovered. For example, assume that a $4,500 machine is expected to produce a total cash savings of $10,000 over ten years, but not at a rate of $1,000 annually. Instead the inflows are expected as follows:

YEAR	CASH SAVINGS	ACCUMULATED CASH SAVINGS	YEAR	CASH SAVINGS	ACCUMULATED CASH SAVINGS
1	$2,000	$2,000	6	$800	$ 8,300
2	1,800	3,800	7	600	8,900
3	1,500	5,300	8	400	9,300
4	1,200	6,500	9	400	9,700
5	1,000	7,500	10	300	10,000

---

[3]In the investment literature, the reciprocal of the payback time is (to no great surprise) called the payback reciprocal:

$$\text{Payback reciprocal} = \frac{1}{\text{Payback time}}$$

Gordon has demonstrated that the payback reciprocal approximates the internal rate of return reasonably well when two conditions hold: (1) the annual cash inflows are equal, and (2) the useful life of the project is at least twice the payback period. See M. Gordon, "Payoff Period and Rate of Profit," *Journal of Business*, XXVIII, No. 4, pp. 253–60.

Even when the conditions derived by Gordon hold, however, it is preferable to calculate directly the internal rate of return rather than to rely on an approximation of it.

The payback time is slightly beyond the second year:

YEAR	CASH SAVINGS	ACCUMULATED CASH SAVINGS	CASH INVESTMENT YET TO BE RECOVERED AT END OF YEAR
0	—	—	$4,500
1	$2,000	$2,000	$2,500
2	1,800	3,800	700
3	1,500	5,300	—

Straight-line interpolation within the third year reveals that the final $700 (that is, $4,500 − $3,800) needed to recover the investment would be forthcoming in about the middle of year 3:

$$2 \text{ years} + \left(\frac{\$700}{\$1,500} \times 1 \text{ year} \right) = 2.47 \text{ years}$$

The bailout factor: a better approach to payback

The typical payback computation as illustrated above tries to answer the question, How soon will it be before I can recoup my investment *if operations proceed as planned?* However, a more fundamental question is, Which of the competing projects has the best bailout protection if things go wrong? To answer such a question, we must consider the disposal value of the equipment throughout its life, an item that is ignored in the usual payback computations.

For instance, disposal values of general-purpose equipment far exceed those of special-purpose equipment. These disposal values can be incorporated into a bailout approach to payback. Assume that Equipment A (general-purpose) costs $100,000 and that Equipment B (special-purpose) costs $150,000. Each has a ten-year life. A is expected to produce uniform annual cash savings of $20,000; B, $40,000. A's disposal value is expected to be $70,000 at the end of year 1; it is expected to decline at a rate of $10,000 annually thereafter. B's disposal value is expected to be $80,000 at the end of year 1; it is expected to decline at a rate of $20,000 annually. Note the difference in results under the traditional payback and the bailout payback methods. The "bailout payback time" is reached when the cumulative cash operating savings plus the disposal value at the end of a particular year equal the original investment:

TRADITIONAL PAYBACK				BAILOUT PAYBACK			
If operations go as expected:				If the project fails to meet expectations:			

		AT END OF	CUMULATIVE CASH OPERATING SAVINGS	DISPOSAL VALUE	CUMULATIVE TOTAL
A: $P = \dfrac{I}{O_c} = \dfrac{\$100,000}{\$20,000} = 5 \text{ years}$		A: Year 1	$20,000	+ $70,000	= $ 90,000
		Year 2	40,000	+ 60,000	= 100,000
		Therefore bailout payback is 2 years.			
B: $P = \dfrac{I}{O_c} = \dfrac{\$150,000}{\$40,000} = 3.75 \text{ years}$		B: Year 1	$ 40,000	+ $80,000	= $120,000
		Year 2	80,000	+ 60,000	= 140,000
		Year 3	120,000	+ 40,000	= 160,000
		Therefore bailout payback is between 2 and 3 years. The exact time depends on assumptions regarding cash flows during the third year.			

The analysis above demonstrates how different interpretations of the payback method can produce different results. If the objective is to measure risk (in the sense of how to avoid loss), the bailout method is better than the traditional method.

ACCRUAL ACCOUNTING RATE-OF-RETURN MODEL

Fundamental model

The **accrual accounting rate of return** is an accounting measure of income divided by an accounting measure of investment. It is also called **accounting rate of return.** The denominator is frequently the initial increase in required investment:

$$\frac{\text{Accrual accounting}}{\text{rate of return}} = \frac{\text{Increase in expected average annual operating income}}{\text{Initial increase in required investment}}$$

Sometimes the denominator is expressed as the average increase in investment, rather than the initial increase.

The facts in our payback illustration would yield the following accounting rate of return (average depreciation is $3,791 \div 5 = \$758$) when the denominator is the initial increase in required investment:

$$R = \frac{\$1,000 - \$758}{\$3,791} = 6.4\%$$

If the denominator is the "average" investment, the rate would be doubled to 12.8% *assuming* the average increase in investment is the average book value over the useful life ($3,791 divided by 2, or $1,896) and the terminal disposal value is zero.[4]

The label for the *accrual accounting model* is not uniform. Synonyms are *financial statement method, book-value method, rate-of-return-on-assets method, approximate rate-of-return method, and unadjusted rate-of-return method.* Its computations supposedly dovetail most closely with conventional accounting models for calculating operating income and required investment. However, the dovetailing objective is not easily attained because the purposes of the computations differ. The most troublesome aspects are depreciation and decisions concerning capitalization versus expense.

---

[4]The cash inflow in the example is $1,000 a year. The amount of average annual depreciation is $3,791 \div 5 = \$758$. The average investment would be the beginning book value plus the ending book value ($3,791 + 0) divided by 2, or $1,896. Thus the rate of return on the average investment would be:

$$R = (\$1,000 - \$758) \div \$1,896 = 12.8\%$$

However, if the project has a nonzero terminal disposal value and straight-line depreciation is used, the *average* investment is computed by *adding* the terminal disposal value to the original cost and dividing by 2. For example, assume that the machine in Exhibit 19-2 has a terminal disposal value of $1,000 instead of zero. The annual depreciation would be ($3,791 - $1,000) \div 5 = \$558$. The average investment is ($3,791 + $1,000) \div 2 = \$2,396$. The accrual accounting rate of return with the denominator calculated as the "average" investment is:

661

$$R = (\$1,000 - \$558) \div \$2,396 = 18.45\%$$

For example, advertising and research are usually expensed under generally accepted accounting principles, even though they are really long-range investments.

Practice is not uniform as to whether initial investment or average investment in fixed assets should be used in the denominator. Companies defend the use of the initial-investment base because it does not change over the life of the investment; therefore follow-ups and comparisons are eased regarding actual rate of return against predicted rate of return. This follow-up is crucial for control and for improving future capital planning and comparison on a year-to-year, plant-to-plant, and division-to-division basis. The initial base is unaffected by depreciation methods.

In most cases, the rankings of competing projects will not differ regardless of whether the initial or average investment base is used. Of course, using the average base will show substantially higher rates of return; however, the desirable rate of return used as a basis for accepting projects should also be higher.

Current assets, such as cash, receivables, and inventories, often are expanded in order to sustain higher volume levels. In our example, if a $1,000 increase in current assets is required, the denominator will be $3,791 plus $1,000, or $4,791. This $1,000 increase in current assets will be fully committed for the life of the project; so, under the average-investment method, the average base would be $2,896 ($1,896 average investment in equipment plus $1,000 average investment in current assets, or alternatively [($4,791 starting + $1,000 terminal recovery of working capital) ÷ 2].

The gross or initial investment in the project should include the following: all additional required current assets, fixed assets, research costs, engineering costs, market-testing costs, startup costs, initial costs of sales promotion, and similar outlays. The omission of any of these items from the base can give misleading results.

Although the *accrual accounting model* for investment decisions tries to approximate the figures as they will eventually appear in financial statements, there is not always an exact agreement between figures on conventional statements and figures used for decision making. The tendency in accounting practice is to write costs off to expense quickly. Thus the assembly of figures for special decisions requires care to avoid understating investment. Often the investment base for decision making should include items, such as research and sales-promotion costs, that the accountant ordinarily writes off immediately as expenses.

Note that the *accounting rate of return* is based on the familiar financial statements prepared under accrual accounting. It is simple and easily understood. **Unlike the payback model, the accounting rate of return model at least has profitability as a consideration. However, its most serious drawback is that it ignores the time value of money.** Expected future dollars are unrealistically and erroneously regarded as being equal to present dollars. The discounted cash-flow model explicitly allows for interest and considers the exact timing of cash flows. In contrast, the accounting rate-of-return model is based on *annual averages*.

The use of the conventional accrual accounting model for evaluating performance is a stumbling block to the implementation of DCF models for capital-budgeting decisions. To illustrate, John Kent, the manager of a division of a multidivision company, took a course in management accounting in an executive program. He learned about discounted cash flow. He was convinced that such a model would lead to decisions that would better achieve the long-range profit goals of the company.

Upon returning to his company, he was more frustrated than ever. Top management used the accounting rate of return of his division to judge his performance. That is, each year divisional net income was divided by average divisional assets to obtain his rate of return on investment (ROI). Such a measure usually inhibits investments in plant and equipment that might clearly be attractive using the DCF models. Why? Because a huge investment often boosts depreciation inordinately in the early years under accelerated depreciation methods, thus reducing the numerator in the ROI computation. Also, the denominator is increased substantially by the initial cost of the new assets. As one manager said, "Top management is always giving me hell about my new flour mill, even though I know it is the most efficient we've got regardless of what the figures say."

Another illustration of the potential conflict between the decision model and the performance evaluation model is provided by the first example in this chapter. Recall that the internal rate of return is 10%, but the accounting rate of return on the initial investment of $3,791, as computed in the preceding section, is only 6.4%.

Obviously, there is an inconsistency between citing DCF models as being best for capital-budgeting decisions and then using quite different concepts for evaluating subsequent performance. As long as such practices continue, managers will frequently be tempted to make decisions that may be suboptimal under the DCF models but optimal, at least over short or intermediate spans of time, under the accrual accounting model of evaluating operating performance. Such temptations become more pronounced when managers are subject to frequent transfers and promotions.

URGENCY

Many phases of business operations are managed in the same manner in which many individuals care for their cars. How many of us keep cars going until that bald tire suddenly becomes useless or the old battery refuses to perform? Then what happens? Stop-gap action may be taken so that the car can be put back into service quickly. When a machine part fails, a belt breaks, or a generator wears out, routine replacements are made to avoid disruption in production. If the old machine on the assembly line suddenly falls apart, there may be a fast but uneconomic replacement so that downtime is minimized. Ideally, all repairs, maintenance, and replacements should be implementations of an overall equipment policy that considers future-cost comparisons and timing.

Often the urgent action taken is correct on logical grounds. But it is correct by coincidence rather than methodical analysis. The pressures of the moment lead to quick remedial action. When a contemplated outlay is large and far-reaching in its effects, urgency should not be a convincing influence in capital budgeting decisions.

Numerous surveys have been conducted regarding the capital-budgeting practices of firms.[5] Several patterns appear in the results of these surveys:

1. The trend is toward an increasing use of DCF models (either NPV or IRR). For example, a survey of large U.S. firms classified capital-budgeting projects into seven categories, which illustrate the diversity of areas in which capital-budgeting decisions are made. The following percentages indicate use of DCF as the "primary evaluation" method:[6]

CAPITAL-BUDGETING PROJECT CATEGORY	1970	1975	1980
Replacement Projects	28%	45%	56%
Expansion—Existing Operations	44	62	75
Expansion—New Operations	41	58	71
Foreign Operations	45	59	72
Abandonment	36	47	55
General and Administrative	21	29	36
Social Expenditures	10	14	14

The survey reported that the most frequent "primary evaluation" method used for both the general and administrative and the social expenditures categories was urgency.

2. Many firms use several methods when evaluating projects. For instance, many that report using DCF as the primary method also report using payback as a supplemental consideration.

COMPLEXITIES IN CAPITAL-BUDGETING APPLICATIONS

The most challenging stage in capital budgeting is definition of the project and the prediction of its outcome. Textbook examples typically assume away much of the complexity associated with this stage. This section illustrates some of the complexity often found in practice.

Consider a firm deciding whether to invest in computer-integrated manufac-

---

[5]For a summary of eleven individual surveys, see D. Scott and J. Petty, "Capital Budgeting Practices in Large American Firms: A Retrospective Analysis and Synthesis," *Financial Review*, March 1984, pp. 111–23. Other surveys include J. Moore and A. Reichert, "An Analysis of the Financial Management Techniques Currently Employed by Large U.S. Corporations," *Journal of Business Finance and Accounting*, Winter 1983, pp. 623–45; P. Lilleyman, "Capital Budgeting: Current Practices of Australian Organizations," *Australian Accountant*, March 1984, pp. 130–33; and M. Stanley and S. Block, "A Survey of Multinational Capital Budgeting," *Financial Review*, March 1984, pp. 36–54. See also the survey cited in footnote 6.

There is little systematic evidence of capital-budgeting practices in nonprofit organizations. See Chapter 20.

[6]T. Klammer and M. Walker, "The Continuing Increase in the Use of Sophisticated Capital Budgeting Techniques," *California Management Review*, Fall 1984, pp. 137–48.

turing (CIM) technology.[7] CIM in its most extreme form can result in a highly automated factory where the role of labor is largely restricted to computer programming, engineering support, and maintenance of the robotic machinery. The amounts at stake in CIM decisions can be large (in the billions of dollars for such companies as General Motors and Toyota). The time horizon of the decision can stretch well beyond ten years, or even twenty years. Many of the costs are incurred and are highly visible in the early years of adopting CIM. In contrast, important benefits may only be realized many years after the adoption of CIM. Capital-budgeting procedures that use too high a discount rate or too short a time horizon, or that ignore benefits not easily quantifiable, can result in CIM proposals appearing to have a negative net present value.

The costs of purchasing CIM technology and associated machinery from outside vendors are readily available. Some of the benefits (typically cost savings) associated with CIM are also reasonably quantified. Examples include the cost savings due to lower inventory levels, reduced floor space requirements, improved product quality, and lower accounts receivable.

There are also both costs and benefits that are more difficult to quantify. Such costs include:

1. Costs of retraining the operating and maintenance personnel. Examples of companies underestimating these costs by several orders of magnitude are not uncommon.
2. Costs of developing and maintaining the software and maintenance programs to operate the automated manufacturing activities.

Benefits difficult to quantify include:

1. Greater flexibility in manufacturing. For example, machine units can easily accommodate engineering changes and product redesigns. The benefits of this greater flexibility, however, will depend (in part) on subsequent investment decisions made by the firm. To quantify this benefit requires some notion of capital-budgeting decisions yet to be made.
2. Faster response to marketing changes. An automated factory can, for example, make major design modifications (such as switching from a two-door to a four-door car) in a relatively short time period. To quantify this benefit requires some notion of consumer demand changes that may occur many years in the future.
3. Willingness of workers to seek out additional areas where automation can be introduced and to wholeheartedly support and assist in the implementation of subsequent CIM projects. This change in the "mind-set" of workers (assuming a positive experience with the first CIM project) can be a major benefit to a firm.

Costs and benefits that are difficult to quantify may well be crucial in a firm's decision whether to invest in CIM. Failure to include them in the analysis means that they are estimated implicitly at zero.

The DCF models provide the opportunity to incorporate systematically into a decision the benefits and costs that occur many years hence. Where it is diffi-

---

[7]This section draws on R. Kaplan, "Must CIM be justified by faith alone?," *Harvard Business Review,* March-April 1986, pp. 87–93.

cult to quantify individual items, sensitivity analysis can be used; the very act of asking "what-if" questions for such items can provide much insight into the critical issues in a capital-budgeting decision.[8]

_____SUMMARY_____

Capital budgeting is long-term planning for proposed capital outlays and their financing. Because discounted cash-flow (DCF) models explicitly weigh the time value of money, they are the best models to use for such decisions.

DCF has two variations: net present value and internal rate of return. Both methods measure the timing of cash flows and are thus superior to other methods.

The payback model is a widely used approach to capital-spending decisions. It is simple and easily understood, but it neglects profitability.

The accrual accounting rate-of-return model is also widely used, although it is much cruder than the DCF models. It fails to recognize explicitly the time value of money. Instead the accrual accounting model depends on averaging techniques that may yield inaccurate answers, particularly when cash flows are not uniform throughout the life of a project.

A serious practical impediment to the adoption of DCF models is the widespread use of accrual accounting models for evaluating performance. Frequently, the optimal decision under DCF will not produce a good showing in the early years when performance is measured by accrual accounting methods. For example, heavy depreciation charges and the expensing rather than capitalizing of initial development costs will reduce reported income for the first year of a project's life.

The difficult forecasting problem makes capital budgeting one of the most imposing tasks of management. Although judgment and attitudes are important ingredients of capital budgeting, the correct application of the models described in this chapter should crystallize the relevant factors and help management toward intelligent decision making.

Special difficulties in relevant costs and capital budgeting, including income tax factors and inflation, are discussed in Chapter 20.

_____PROBLEMS FOR SELF-STUDY_____

problem 1   Refer to Exhibit 19-2, page 651. Suppose the expected annual cash savings were $1,300 instead of $1,000. All other facts are unchanged: a $3,791 original investment, a five-year useful life, a zero terminal disposal value, and an 8% required rate of return. Compute the following:
   1. Net present value
   2. Internal rate of return
   3. Payback period
   4. Accounting rate of return on initial investment

solution 1   1. NPV = ($1,300 × 3.993) − $3,791
                = $5,191 − $3,791 = $1,400
          2. $3,791 = $1,300F

$$F = \frac{\$3,791}{1,300} = 2.916$$

_____
[8] An alternative approach involves a two-step procedure: first, conduct DCF analysis on those items most amenable to quantification; second, judge those items not quantified in the first step to see if the decision implied by the DCF calculations should be accepted or changed. Ideally, the second step should be conducted by senior management.

On the period-5 line of Table 4, the column closest to 2.916 is 22%. This may be close enough for most purposes. To obtain a more accurate rate, interpolation is needed:

	PRESENT VALUE FACTORS	
20%	2.991	2.991
True rate		2.916
22%	2.864	
Difference	.127	.075

$$\text{Internal rate of return} = 20\% + \frac{.075}{.127}(2\%) = 21.2\%$$

3. $P = I/O_c = \$3{,}791/\$1{,}300 = 2.9$ years

4. $R = \dfrac{\text{Increase in expected average annual operating income}}{\text{Initial increase in required investment}}$

$= \dfrac{\$1{,}300 - \text{Average depreciation}}{\$3{,}791}$

$= \dfrac{\$1{,}300 - (\$3{,}791 \div 5)}{\$3{,}791} = 14.3\%$

problem 2 A company owns a packaging machine that was purchased three years ago for $56,000. The machine has a remaining useful life of five years but will require a major overhaul at the end of two more years of life, at a cost of $10,000. Its disposal value now is $20,000; in five years its terminal disposal value is expected to be $8,000, assuming that the $10,000 major overhaul will be done on schedule. The cash-operating costs of this machine are expected to be $40,000 annually.

A salesperson has offered a substitute machine for $51,000, or for $31,000 plus the old machine. The new machine will slash annual cash operating costs by $10,000, will not require any overhauls, will have a useful life of five years, and will have a terminal disposal value of $3,000.

Required Assume that the required rate of return is 14%. Using the net present value model, show whether the new machine should be purchased. Try to solve before examining the solution.

solution 2 A difficult part of long-range decision making is the structuring of the data. We want to see the effects of each alternative on future cash flows. The focus here is on *cash* transactions, not on opportunity costs. Using an opportunity-cost approach may yield the same answers, but repeated classroom experimentation with various analytical methods has convinced the authors that the following steps are likely to be the clearest:

Step 1. Arrange the relevant cash flows by project, so that a sharp distinction is made between total-project flows and incremental flows. The top part of Exhibit 19-6 is labeled as the *total-project* approach because the cash flows for *each* alternative are sketched. In contrast, the bottom part of the exhibit is called the *incremental* approach. The incremental flows are merely algebraic differences between two alternatives. (Note that there are always at least two alternatives. One is the status quo, the alternative of continuing with the present mode of operating.)

Step 2. Discount the expected cash flows and choose the project with the least cost or the greatest benefit. Whether you use the total-project approach or the incremental approach is a matter of preference. However, to develop confidence in this area, work with both at the start. In this example, the $8,425 net difference in favor of replacement is the ultimate result under either approach.

EXHIBIT 19-6 *Place a clip on this page for easy reference.)*
Total-Project versus Incremental Approach to Net Present Value
(Data from Self-study Problem)

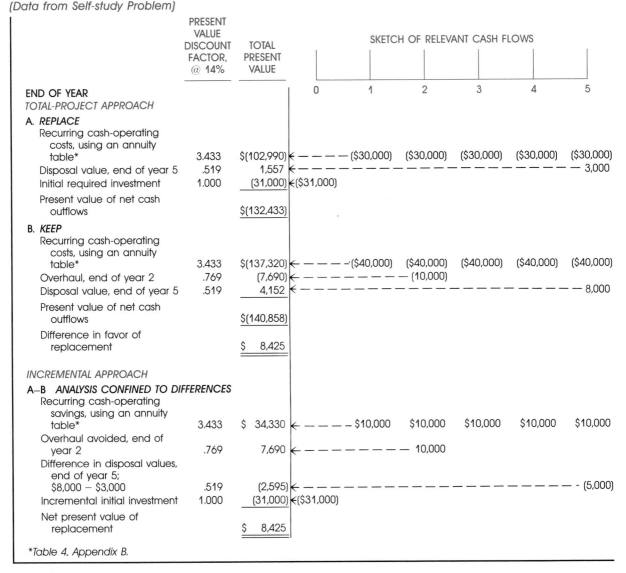

	PRESENT VALUE DISCOUNT FACTOR, @ 14%	TOTAL PRESENT VALUE	SKETCH OF RELEVANT CASH FLOWS				
			0	1	2	3	4	5
END OF YEAR								
TOTAL-PROJECT APPROACH								
A. *REPLACE*								
Recurring cash-operating costs, using an annuity table*	3.433	$(102,990)	($30,000)	($30,000)	($30,000)	($30,000)	($30,000)
Disposal value, end of year 5	.519	1,557						3,000
Initial required investment	1.000	(31,000) ($31,000)						
Present value of net cash outflows		$(132,433)						
B. *KEEP*								
Recurring cash-operating costs, using an annuity table*	3.433	$(137,320)	($40,000)	($40,000)	($40,000)	($40,000)	($40,000)
Overhaul, end of year 2	.769	(7,690)		(10,000)			
Disposal value, end of year 5	.519	4,152						8,000
Present value of net cash outflows		$(140,858)						
Difference in favor of replacement		$ 8,425						
INCREMENTAL APPROACH								
A–B *ANALYSIS CONFINED TO DIFFERENCES*								
Recurring cash-operating savings, using an annuity table*	3.433	$ 34,330	$10,000	$10,000	$10,000	$10,000	$10,000
Overhaul avoided, end of year 2	.769	7,690		10,000			
Difference in disposal values, end of year 5; $8,000 − $3,000	.519	(2,595)						- (5,000)
Incremental initial investment	1.000	(31,000) ($31,000)						
Net present value of replacement		$ 8,425						

*Table 4, Appendix B.

Special Points and Pitfalls

The essence of DCF is representing the cash inflows and outflows of a project at a common point in time so that they may be compared (added, subtracted, etc.) in an appropriate way. When doing DCF computations, sketch the relevant cash flows (see Exhibit 19-2, page 651).

Common errors in DCF computations include the deduction of depreciation from operating cash flows, and the use of the wrong present value table.

When solving assignment problems or taking exams, check to see whether a problem requires use of certain rounded discount factors (as distinguished from the number of decimal digits possible on a calculator or computer). Some instructors believe that the use of rounded discount factors provides a better test of student learning.

QUESTIONS, PROBLEMS, AND CASES

19-1 Define *capital budgeting*.

19-2 What are the four stages in capital budgeting after a potential project has been identified?

19-3 What is the essence of the discounted cash-flow method?

19-4 Define *internal rate of return*.

19-5 What is the payback method? What is its main weakness?

19-6 "The trouble with discounted cash-flow techniques is that their use ignores depreciation costs." Do you agree? Why?

19-7 "Let's be more practical. DCF is not the gospel. Managers should not become so enchanted with DCF that practical strategic considerations are overlooked." Do you agree? Why?

19-8 The president of a company accepts a capital-budgeting project advocated by Division X; this is the division in which the president spent his first ten years with the company. On the same day, the president rejects a project proposal from Division Y. The manager of Division Y is both despondent and incensed. He believes the Division Y project has an internal rate of return at least ten percentage points above the Division X project. He comments: "What is the point of all our detailed DCF analysis? If the president is visibly panting over a project, subordinates will supply the requisite DCF projections." What advice would you give the manager of Division Y?

19-9 Exercises in compound interest.   To be sure that you understand how to use the tables in Appendix B at the end of this book, solve the following exercises. Do the exercises on your own before checking your answers. The correct answers rounded to the nearest dollar are printed after the last problem in this chapter.

1. You have just won $5,000. How much money will you have at the end of ten years if you invest it at 6% compounded annually? At 14%? Ignore income taxes in this and other parts of this problem.
2. Ten years from now, the unpaid principal of the mortgage on your house will be $8,955. How much do you have to invest today at 6% interest compounded annually just to accumulate the $8,955 in ten years?
3. You plan to save $500 of your earnings each year for the next ten years. How much money will you have at the end of the tenth year if you invest your savings compounded at 12% per year?
4. If the unpaid mortgage on your house in ten years will be $8,955, how much money do you have to invest annually at 6% to have just this amount on hand at the end of the tenth year?
5. You hold an endowment insurance policy that will pay you a lump sum of $20,000 at age 65. If you invest the sum at 6%, how much money can you withdraw from your account in equal amounts each year so that at the end of ten years there will be nothing left?
6. You have estimated that for the first ten years after you retire, you will need an annual cash inflow of $50,000. How much money must you invest at 6% at your retirement age to obtain this annual cash inflow? At 20%?
7. The following table shows two schedules of prospective operating cash inflows, each of which requires the same initial investment:

	ANNUAL CASH INFLOWS	
YEAR	Plan A	Plan B
0	$ 1,000	$ 5,000
1	2,000	4,000
2	3,000	3,000
3	4,000	2,000
4	5,000	1,000
Total	$15,000	$15,000

The minimum desired rate of return is 6% compounded annually. In terms of present values, which plan is more desirable? Show computations.

19-10 Basic nature of present value. A company is considering investing in a project with a two-year life and no residual value. Cash inflow will be equal payments of $4,000 at the end of each of the two years. How much would the company be willing to invest to earn an internal rate of return of 8%? Use Table 2, Appendix B to get your answer. Then prepare a tabular analysis of each payment. The column headings should be year, investment at beginning of year, operating cash inflow, return @ 8% per year, amount of investment received at end of year, and unrecovered investment at end of year.

19-11 Comparison of decision models. The Block Company is thinking of buying, at a cost of $22,000, some new material-handling equipment that is expected to save $5,000 in cash-operating costs per year. Its estimated useful life is ten years, and it will have zero terminal disposal value.

Required | Compute:

1. Net present value if the required rate is 16%
2. Payback period
3. Internal rate of return
4. Accrual accounting rate of return based on (a) initial investment and (b) average investment. Assume straight-line depreciation.

19-12 Comparison of approaches to capital budgeting. Refer to Problem 9-12, page 327. Use the pertinent data there.

1. Compute the net present value of the proposed investment in new equipment, assuming that the required rate of return is 18%. Compute the solution in the two ways illustrated in the second Problem for Self-Study in the chapter, the "incremental" way and the "total-project" way.
2. Compute the internal rate of return and the payback period on the incremental investment.

19-13 Comparison of approaches to capital budgeting. City Hospital estimates that it can save $2,800 a year in cash-operating costs for the next ten years if it buys a special-purpose machine at a cost of $11,000. No terminal residual value is expected. The company's minimum desired rate of return is 14%.

(Round all computations to the nearest dollar. Ignore income taxes.)

1. Net present value
2. Payback period
3. Internal rate of return
4. Accrual accounting rate of return based on (a) initial investment and (b) average investment. Assume straight-line depreciation.

19-14 Capital budgeting with uneven cash flows. The Braddock Corporation is considering the purchase of a special-purpose machine for $28,000. It is expected to have a useful life of seven years with no terminal salvage value. The corporation's controller estimates the following savings in cash-operating costs:

YEAR	AMOUNT
1	$10,000
2	8,000
3	6,000
4	5,000
5	4,000
6	3,000
7	3,000
Total	$39,000

Compute:

1. Net present value if the required rate of return is 16%
2. Payback period
3. Internal rate of return
4. Accrual accounting rate of return based on (a) initial investment and (b) average investment. Assume straight-line depreciation.

19-15 Evaluating a government copper-mining project, delay in timing of cash inflows, sensitivity analysis. Tim Sung, the minister of Public Works, prides himself on having an awareness of modern capital-budgeting techniques. He is considering a proposed copper mine project that his army corps of engineers recommend be adopted. The mine and its related infrastructure (transportation for the copper to the nearest port, housing for workers, etc.) will be constructed by a foreign firm. The firm estimates construction time of three years for the mine and the related infrastructure. No copper will be mined or sold during the construction phase of the project. The foreign firm requires a $100 million payment (the full cost) at the start of construction.

The engineers estimate that after the mine is operational, the copper mine will provide an annual net cash inflow of $25 million (to be received at the *end* of each year). They also predict that this annual $25 million net inflow will occur for fifteen years from the start of copper mining. Zero terminal disposal value for the mine and the related infrastructure is expected. Legislation requires that a 6% hurdle rate of return be used in public works projects.

1. Present a sketch of the relevant cash inflows and cash outflows of the copper mine project.
2. What is the net present value of the copper mine project?
3. What is the payback period of the project?
4. Sung's past experience with the army corps of engineers leads him to seriously question their estimate of an annual net cash inflow of $25 million. Overestimates of 200% and more have occurred in the past. What annual net cash inflow will make the copper mine project a breakeven proposition (that is, net present value would be zero)?
5. Sung views a five-year rather than a three-year construction period as more realistic. How will use of a five-year period for construction affect your estimate of breakeven annual net cash inflow in requirement 4?
6. What other factors should Sung consider in analyzing the proposed copper-mining project?

19-16 Salvage value, current assets, and evaluation of performance. Hammerlink Company has been offered a special-purpose machine for $110,000. The machine is expected to have a useful life of eight years with a terminal salvage value of $30,000. Savings in cash-operating costs are expected to be $25,000 per year. However, additional current assets are needed to keep the machine running efficiently and without any stoppages. These assets include such items as filters, lubricants, bearings, abrasives, flexible exhaust pipes, and endless belts. These must be continually replaced, so that an investment of $8,000 must be maintained at all times in these items, but this investment is fully recoverable (will be "cashed in") at the end of the useful life.

1. Compute the net present value if the required rate of return is 14%.
2. Compute the internal rate of return.
3. Compute the accrual accounting rate of return (a) on the initial investment and (b) on the "average" investment. Assume straight-line depreciation.
4. You have the authority to make the purchase decision. Why might you be reluctant to base your decision on the DCF model?

19-17 Current assets, residual values, and choice of models. The manager of a local department store, one of a national company's two hundred stores, is considering whether to renovate some space in order to increase sales volume. New display fixtures and equipment will be needed. They will cost $70,000 and are expected to be useful for six years with a terminal salvage value of $4,000. Additional cash-operating inflows are expected to be $25,000 per year.

However, experience has shown that in order to sustain the higher sales volume, similar renovations have required additional investments in current assets, such as merchandise inventories and accounts receivable from customers. An initial investment of $40,000 is needed to finance or "carry" these current assets, and this level must be maintained continuously. If and when it may be decided to terminate this plan or to use the store space for other purposes, the inventories and receivables can soon be liquidated or "cashed in."

1. Compute (a) net present value, using a required rate of 12%; (b) internal rate of return; (c) accrual accounting rate of return on the initial investment; and (d) accrual accounting rate of return on the "average" investment. Assume straight-line depreciation.
2. As the store manager, which type of model would you prefer for the purposes of making this decision and for evaluating subsequent performance? Give reasons and compare the principal types of models.

19-18 Sensitivity analysis, payback reciprocal. Yale University is considering the replacement of some old research equipment with some new equipment that should save $5,000 per year in net cash-operating costs.

The old equipment has zero disposal value, but it could be used indefinitely. The estimated useful life of the new equipment is twelve years and it will cost $20,000.

1. Payback time.
2. Internal rate of return.
3. Management is unsure about the useful life. What would be the internal rate of return

if the useful life were (a) six years instead of twelve and (b) twenty years instead of twelve?

4. Suppose the life will be twelve years, but the savings will be $3,000 per year instead of $5,000. What would be the internal rate of return?

5. Suppose the annual savings will be $4,000 for six years. What would be the internal rate of return?

6. Professor Myron Gordon has pointed out that the payback reciprocal can be a crude approximation of the internal rate of return where (a) the project life is at least twice the payback period, and (b) the cash earnings or savings are uniformly received in equal amounts throughout the investment's life. The payback reciprocal, using the original data, will be $5,000 ÷ $20,000, or 25%.
   (i) How close is this to the internal rate of return?
   (ii) Compute the payback reciprocals for requirements 3a and 3b. How close are they to the internal rates of return?
   (iii) Compute the payback reciprocals for requirements 4 and 5. How close are they to the internal rates of return?

19-19 Capital budgeting for a sporting franchise. The Midwest Goalbusters are the leading team in a nationwide soccer league. Over the past five years, the team has consistently sold out all the 30,000 individual seats and the 100 corporate boxes at its home stadium. The stadium has a current book value of $19 million; annual depreciation using the straight-line method is $1.5 million. The estimated terminal value of the stadium at the end of ten years is $4 million. This $4 million is based on an agreement Midwest signed with the local city authorities. This agreement grants the city the option to repurchase the stadium for $4 million ten years hence from the current year. The owner of the stadium must pay the city $1 million each year that the stadium is not owned by the city.

Jeannette Ochoa, the owner of the Midwest Goalbusters' sporting franchise, predicts the following for each of the next ten years:

10,000 season "A" tickets sold at $300 per year
20,000 season "B" tickets sold at $200 per year
100 corporate boxes sold at $5,000 a box per year

Annual operating costs in addition to the $1 million payment to the city will be $5.5 million; these costs include salaries to coaches, players, and administrators, as well as the cost of operating the stadium. Television and radio royalties will be $5 million a year. For simplicity, assume that all the annual cash inflows and annual cash outflows occur at the end of each year.

Ochoa views the sporting franchise as having two assets:

(i) The player contracts and goodwill associated with the Midwest Goalbusters name
(ii) The stadium, which she believes the city will repurchase in ten years' time

She receives an offer from a local city real estate developer to buy both assets for $80 million. The real estate developer proposes to keep the team at its current stadium. Ochoa would invest the $80 million at 8% per annum. In considering this offer, Ochoa estimates the total value of the Midwest Goalbusters' sporting franchise at the end of ten years will be $100 million. (This $100 million *includes* the $4 million payment from the city for repurchase of the stadium.)

Ignore income tax considerations in your analysis.

Required

1. Using the discounted cash-flow method, would you recommend that Ochoa accept the $80 million offer? Her required rate of return on investments is 8% per annum.

2. What other factors would you recommend that Ochoa consider in deciding whether to accept the $80 million offer?

3. Assuming Ochoa decides to keep the sporting franchise, what will be her accrual accounting rate of return on the average investment over the next ten years. (Assume the stadium asset is the investment base.)

19-20 Capital budgeting for a new sports stadium. (Continuation of Problem 19-19) Jeannette Ochoa, the owner of the Midwest Goalbusters' sporting franchise, has long viewed the existing home sports stadium as an embarrassment. A national TV sports commentator stated that the stadium "redefined global minimum standards for fan comfort." The city mayor has recently offered Ochoa a new land area on which a modern domed stadium can be built. The land will be given free to the sporting team if it commits itself to construction of the stadium. The cost of constructing the new stadium is $60 million, to be payable in cash at the start of construction.

The new stadium will be ready by the start of the next season. In addition to its 60,000 individual seating capacity, there would be 300 super-deluxe corporate boxes. Ochoa predicts the following for the forthcoming and subsequent seasons over the next ten years if the new stadium is constructed:

> 20,000 season "A" tickets sold at $400 per year
> 20,000 season "B" tickets sold at $250 per year
> 10,000 season "C" tickets sold at $200 per year
> 250 corporate boxes sold at $20,000 a box per year

The annual operating costs of the franchise (including the costs of operating the new stadium) will be $9 million. Television and radio royalties of $5 million a year will be unaffected by the decision concerning the new stadium.

The city authorities require the Midwest Goalbusters to continue paying $1 million a year for the next ten years on the existing stadium even if it is not used. Ochoa expects the city to repurchase the existing stadium for $4 million ten years hence from the current year, irrespective of whether the Goalbusters remain in the existing stadium or move to the new stadium. The estimated resale value of the new stadium at the end of ten years is $30 million. Ignore income tax considerations in your analysis.

Required

1. What is the net present value of the proposed move to the $60 million stadium?
2. What is the payback period on the move to the new stadium? (Use the incremental cash inflow from the move as the denominator.)
3. What other factors might be important when deciding whether to construct the new stadium?

19-21 Equipment replacement, sensitivity analysis. A toy manufacturer that specializes in making fad items has just developed a $50,000 molding machine for automatically producing a special toy. The machine has been used to produce only one unit so far. It is planned to depreciate the $50,000 original cost evenly over four years, after which time production of the toy will be stopped.

Suddenly a machine salesman appears. He has a new machine that is ideally suited for producing this toy. His automatic machine is distinctly superior. It reduces the cost of materials by 10% and produces twice as many units per hour. It will cost $44,000 and will have zero disposal value at the end of four years.

Production and sales would continue to be at a rate of 25,000 per year for four years; annual sales will be $90,000. The current disposal value of the toy company's machine is now $5,000. Its terminal disposal value in four years time will be $2,600.

With its present equipment, the company's annual expenses will be: direct materials, $10,000; direct labor, $20,000; and variable factory overhead, $15,000. Variable factory overhead is applied on the basis of direct labor dollars. Fixed factory overhead, exclusive of depreciation, is $7,500 annually, and fixed selling and administrative expenses are $12,000 annually.

Required

1. Assume that the hurdle rate of return is 18%. Using the net present value method, show whether the new equipment should be purchased. Use a total-project approach and an incremental approach. What is the role of the book value of the old equipment in the analysis?
2. What is the payback period for the new equipment?
3. As the manager who developed the $50,000 molding machine, you are trying to justify

not buying the new $44,000 machine. You question the accuracy of the expected cash-operating savings. By how much must these cash savings fall before the point of indifference, the point where net present value of the project is zero, is reached?

19-22 Three alternatives, effects on inventory investments. The Dull Company has a very stable operation that is not marked by detectable variations in production or sales.

The Dull Company has an old machine with a net disposal value of $5,000 now and $1,000 five years from now. A new Rapido machine is offered for $25,000 cash or $20,000 with a trade-in. The new machine promises annual operating cash outflows of $2,000 as compared with the old machine's annual outflow of $10,000. A third machine, the Quicko, is offered for $45,000 cash or $40,000 with a trade-in; it promises annual operating cash outflows of $1,000. The disposal values of the new machines five years hence will be $1,000 each.

Because the new machines will produce output more swiftly, the average investment in inventories will be as follows:

Old machine	$100,000
Rapido	80,000
Quicko	50,000

The minimum desired rate of return is 20%. The company uses discounted cash-flow techniques to evaluate decisions.

Required

Which of the three alternatives is the most desirable? Show calculations. This company uses discounted cash-flow techniques for evaluating decisions. When more than two machines are being considered, the company favors computing the present value of the future costs of each alternative. The most desirable alternative is the one with the least cost.

PV of $1 at 20% for 5 years = .40
PV of annuity of $1 at 20% for 5 years = 3.00
Amount of $1 at 20% for 5 years = 2.20
Amount of annuity of $1 at 20% for 5 years = 8.00

19-23 Capital budgeting and relevant costs. The city of Los Angeles has been operating a *cafeteria* for its employees, but it is considering a conversion from this form of food service to a completely automated set of *coin vending machines,* in which case the old equipment would be sold now for whatever cash it might bring.

The vending machines would be purchased immediately for cash. A catering firm would take complete responsibility for servicing and replenishing the vending machines and would simply pay the city a predetermined percentage of the gross vending receipts.

The following data are available (in thousands of dollars):

Cafeteria cash revenues per year	$120
Cafeteria cash expenses per year	$124
Present cafeteria equipment (10-year remaining life):	
Net book value	$ 84
Annual depreciation expense	$ 6
Current cash value (zero value in 10 years)	$ 4
New vending machines:	
Purchase price	$ 64
Estimated useful life (yrs.)	10
Forecasted terminal scrap value	$ 5
Expected annual gross receipts	$ 80
City's percentage share of receipts	10%
Expected annual cash expenses (negligible)	
Present values at 14%:	
$1 due in 10 years	$0.27
Annuity of $1 a year for 10 years	$5.20

(Concerning the vending alternative compared with the cafeteria plan.)

1. Expected increase in net annual operating cash inflow
2. Payback period
3. Net present value
4. Point of indifference (zero NPV) in terms of annual gross vending machine receipts

19-24 Cost-volume-profit analysis and discounted cash flow. The Student Center of Great State University wants to make doughnuts to supply all of its food operations. Two machines are proposed for the production of the doughnuts: semiautomatic and automatic. The center now buys doughnuts from an outside supplier at $.25 each. Manufacturing costs would be:

	SEMIAUTOMATIC	AUTOMATIC
Variable costs per doughnut	$.21	$.20
Fixed costs:		
Annual cash-operating outlays	$ 4,500	$ 6,500
Initial cost of machines	$10,000	$28,000
Useful life of machines in years	4	4
Salvage value at the end of 4 years	—	$ 4,000

Required

1. The manager wants to know how many doughnuts must be sold in order to have total average annual costs equal to outside purchase costs for the (a) semiautomatic machine and (b) automatic machine. Assume straight-line depreciation.
2. At what annual volume of doughnuts would the total annual costs be the same for both machines? Which machine is preferable if the volume exceeds the volume you computed? Why?
3. Assume that the sales forecast over the next four years is 600,000 doughnuts per year. The minimum desired rate of return is 20%. Should the automatic machine be purchased? Why? Show calculations. Ignore income taxes.

PV of $1.00 at 20% for 4 periods is .5
PV of annuity of $1.00 at 20% for 4 periods is 2.6

Compare your answer with that in requirement 2. Do the answers differ? How? Why?

19-25 Capital investment in a baseball player. William Brenner, president of the Chicago Chartreuse Sox, is currently considering a player deal in which he will acquire Ian Winfield, a great gate attraction, from the New York Confederates in exchange for $3,800,000 cash plus George Bumble, a regular Sox outfielder who is currently receiving a salary of $60,000 a year. Winfield is to be Bumble's replacement in the regular outfield. Brenner and his fellow executives have assembled the following data:

Estimated useful life of Winfield	5 years
Estimated residual value of Winfield	$80,000
Estimated useful life of Bumble	5 years
Estimated residual value of Bumble	None
Current cash offer for Bumble received from the Atlanta Carpetbaggers Baseball Club	$160,000
Applicable minimum desired rate of return	20%

Other data:

YEAR	WINFIELD'S SALARY	ADDITIONAL CLUB GATE RECEIPTS BECAUSE OF WINFIELD	ADDITIONAL EXPENSES OF HANDLING HIGHER VOLUME
1	$600,000	$3,200,000	$320,000
2	700,000	3,000,000	300,000
3	800,000	2,000,000	200,000
4	800,000	1,000,000	100,000
5	700,000	400,000	40,000

(Ignore income taxes.)

1. Based on the data as given, should the Sox buy Winfield? Use the following present value factors for $1 at 20%:

	FOR END OF YEAR				
	1	2	3	4	5
Factor	.83	.69	.58	.48	.40

2. What other factors should be considered before making the decision? How much confidence do you have in the available data?

19-26 Capital-budgeting approaches, computer-integrated manufacturing. Craig Young, the production manager of Brittania Tools, is concerned about Brittania's ability to maintain its competitive position in the industrial machine tool market. A recent surge of imports is priced 30% below Brittania's absorption cost. A major domestic competitor recently switched to a computer-integrated manufacturing (CIM) operation for its machine tool plant.

Young attends a trade exhibition titled "Automate, Emigrate, or Evaporate" and starts negotiations with a vendor of CIM equipment. This vendor will provide the necessary machines and associated equipment for a cost of $80 million. Young estimates the following annual cost savings from implementing CIM:

1. Reduction in rental payments due to reduced floor space requirements	$ 4.0 million
2. Lower number of product defects and reduced reworking of products	$22.0 million

Another benefit of CIM is reduced levels of working capital. The average combined level of inventories and accounts receivable for Brittania Tools at present is $14 million. Young estimates that following implementation of CIM, the average combined level of inventories and accounts receivable would be $4 million. (For simplicity, assume that this reduction in working capital occurs instantaneously at the time the investment in CIM is made.)

The one-time internal cost of implementing CIM is estimated to be $40 million; this cost includes the retraining of operating and maintenance personnel plus any lost production during the changeover. For internal reporting purposes, the $40 million internal cost is capitalized along with the $80 million purchase price when determining the investment required for the CIM proposal. (For simplicity, assume that this $40 implementation cost is incurred at the same time the $80 million equipment purchase is made.) The cost of maintaining the software programs and of the CIM hardware equipment and machinery is estimated to be $8 million annually. The vendor of the CIM equipment maintains that, if properly maintained, a twenty-year useful life is to be expected.

The estimated disposal value of the CIM equipment is $30 million at the end of ten years and $10 million at the end of twenty years. Brittania currently requires investment proposals to return a minimum of 14%. The maximum time period Brittania currently considers for any investment proposal is ten years.

Ignore income tax considerations in your analysis.

1. Compute the payback period for the CIM proposal.
2. Compute the net present value of the CIM proposal. Should Brittania adopt CIM, given its existing investment criteria?
3. Compute the accrual accounting rate of return based on (a) initial investment and (b) average investment. Assume straight-line depreciation and a ten-year useful life for the investment.
4. Young reads an article that argues that many companies are rejecting CIM proposals due to the use of either (a) too high a discount rate in DCF analysis or (b) too short a time period over which the benefits are considered. He believes that Brittania should

use a 8% discount rate and that a twenty-year horizon period should be used in the CIM analysis. Prepare a report for Young on the effects of making these changes in the DCF calculations.

5. What other factors would you recommend that Brittania Tools consider in deciding whether to adopt the CIM proposal?

Answers
to exercises
in compound
interest
(problem 19-9)

The general approach to these problems centers on a key question: Which of the four basic tables am I dealing with? No computations should be made until after this basic question is answered with confidence.

1. From Table 1. The $5,000 is a present value. The value ten years hence is an *amount* or *future worth*.

$$S = P(1 + r)^n; \text{ the conversion factor, } (1 + r)^n, \text{ is on line 10 of Table 1.}$$

Substituting at 6%: $S = 5,000(1.791) = \$8,955$

Substituting at 14%: $S = 5,000(3.707) = \$18,535$

2. From Table 2. The $8,955 is an *amount* or *future worth*. You want the present value of that amount.

$$P = S/(1 + r)^n; \text{ the conversion factor, } 1/(1 + r)^n, \text{ is on line 10 of Table 2.}$$

Substituting: $P = \$8,955(.558) = \$4,997$

3. From Table 3. You are seeking the *amount* or *future worth* of an annuity of $500 per year.

$$S_n = \$500 \, F, \text{ where } F \text{ is the conversion factor}$$

$$S_n = \$500(17.549) = \$8,775$$

4. From Table 3. The $8,955 is a future worth. You are seeking the uniform amount (annuity) to set aside annually.

$$S_n = \text{Annual deposit } (F)$$

$$\$8,955 = \text{Annual deposit } (13.181)$$

$$\text{Annual deposit} = \frac{\$8,955}{13.181} = \$679$$

5. From Table 4. When you reach age 65, you will get $20,000. This is a present value at that time. You must find the annuity that will just exhaust the invested principal in ten years.

$$P_n = \text{Annual withdrawal } (F)$$

$$\$20,000 = \text{Annual withdrawal } (7.360)$$

$$\text{Annual withdrawal} = \frac{\$20,000}{7.360} = \$2,717$$

6. From Table 4. You need to find the present value of an annuity for ten years.

At 6% $\begin{cases} P_n = \text{Annual withdrawal } (F) \\ P_n = \$50,000(7.360) \\ P_n = \$368,000 \end{cases}$

At 20% $\begin{cases} P_n = \$50,000(4.192) \\ P_n = \$209,600, \text{ a much lower figure} \end{cases}$

7. Plan B is preferable. Its present value exceeds that of Plan A by $1,038:

YEAR	PV FACTORS AT 6% FROM TABLE 2	PV OF PLAN A	PV OF PLAN B
0	1.000	$ 1,000	$ 5,000
1	.943	1,886	3,772
2	.890	2,670	2,670
3	.840	3,360	1,680
4	.792	3,960	792
		$12,876	$13,914

Capital Budgeting: A Closer Look

Income tax factors • Capital budgeting and inflation • Required rate of return •
Applicability to nonprofit organizations • Administration of capital budgets •
Implementing the net present value rule • Implementing the internal rate-of-return rule •
Appendix: Accelerated Cost Recovery System

An old adage says two things in life are certain: death and taxes. A third might be added: changing prices. This chapter examines how income taxes and changing prices are analyzed in capital budgeting. (We also recognize death in this chapter, although only of projects, not of the individuals who select projects.) Also covered in this chapter are the estimation of the required rate of return, capital budgeting in nonprofit organizations, administration of capital budgets, and some issues in using the net present value rule and the internal rate-of-return rule.

Uncertainty about long-run events makes capital budgeting difficult and challenging. The uncertainty surrounding prediction should preclude any analyst's tendency to split hairs concerning controversial aspects. However, a few guideposts should help in making intelligent decisions. Some were discussed in Chapters 18 and 19. Others are discussed in this chapter.

For simplicity, this chapter (along with Chapter 19) assumes that all cash outflows and cash inflows occur at the beginning or end (as specified) of each period.

INCOME TAX FACTORS

Importance of income taxes

Income taxes often have a tremendous influence on decisions. Even where tax rates and timing are the same for all alternatives, the before-tax differences between alternatives are usually heavily reduced by application of current income tax rates, so that after-tax differences become narrower. This reduction of differences often results in the rejection of alternatives that are attractive on a pretax basis.

The role of taxes in capital budgeting does not differ from that of any other cash disbursement. *The two major impacts of income taxes are (1) on the amounts of cash inflow and outflow and (2) on the timing of cash flows.*

The intricacies of the income tax laws are often bewildering.[1] To highlight a general approach to the problem, this chapter will concentrate on a few pertinent provisions of the tax law, especially those relating to depreciation. We will confine the discussion to corporations rather than partnerships or individuals.

Managers have a responsibility to minimize tax payments through arrangements allowed by the law. Tax minimization is not evasion. Evasion is the use of illegal means to minimize tax payments.

<table>
<tr><td>

Treatment
of depreciation
for taxation

</td><td>

Taxation rules for depreciation vary considerably among countries. Even within a single country, marked changes can occur over short periods of time. Taxation rules typically cover three factors that influence depreciation.

</td></tr>
</table>

AMOUNT ALLOWABLE FOR DEPRECIATION. In many cases, the amount allowable for depreciation is the cost of the asset purchased. However, sometimes either less than the cost or more than the cost is allowable for depreciation. Where corporations have the option of claiming an investment tax credit,[2] the amount allowable for depreciation may be reduced below the cost of the asset acquired. In some countries, corporations may be permitted to write off more than the cost (as measured by nominal monetary units) for depreciation purposes. For example, when determining the amount allowable for periodic depreciation, Brazilian corporations may write up the cost of assets using inflation indexes.

TIME PERIOD OVER WHICH THE ASSET IS TO BE DEPRECIATED. Throughout the years and in various countries, tax authorities have used three main alternatives:

a. Estimate of useful life is made by the corporation.
b. Estimate of useful life is made by the tax authority, an industry trade association, or some other source external to the corporation.
c. Table of allowable lives is specified in tax legislation. This table need not be based on estimates of useful life made by the corporation or other parties. An example is the property-class life categories used in the Accelerated Cost Recovery System applicable in the United States (see the Appendix to this chapter).

---

[1] Many tax-service publications are available that describe and illustrate existing tax laws. For example, see C. McCarthy, D. Crumbley, and P. Davis, *The Federal Income Tax: Its Sources and Applications* (Englewood Cliffs, N.J.: Prentice-Hall, updated annually). See also W. Raby and V. Tidwell, *Introduction to Federal Taxation* (Englewood Cliffs, N.J.: Prentice-Hall, updated annually).

[2] An **investment tax credit (ITC)** is a direct reduction of income taxes arising from the acquisition of depreciable assets. The ITC aims to stimulate investments in specific assets or in specific industries. It also provides firms with an immediate reduction in income taxes. To illustrate, if a firm purchases an asset costing $1,000 and there is a 4% ITC, the firm obtains an immediate tax credit of $40; this credit increases the net present value of an asset purchase by $40. In the United States, the ITC option has been made available (and then subsequently withdrawn) several times since 1962.

Other things being equal, the shorter the allowable life, the higher the project's net present value.

PATTERN OF ALLOWABLE DEPRECIATION (FOR A GIVEN TIME PERIOD). Three main alternatives have been used by taxation authorities:

a. **Straight-line depreciation (SL)**, in which an equal amount of depreciation is allowed each year.

b. Accelerated depreciation methods, such as double-declining balance (DDB) or sum-of-the-years'-digits (SYD).[3] **Accelerated depreciation** is defined as any pattern of depreciation that writes off depreciable assets more quickly than does ordinary straight-line depreciation.

c. Table of allowable percentage write-offs each year as set out in tax legislation.

All other things being equal, the more accelerated the pattern of depreciation, the higher the project's net present value.

An example

Assume that Martina Enterprises is considering the purchase of equipment for a research and development project. Martina operates in a country in which the cost of the equipment (less any predicted terminal disposal value) is the amount allowable for depreciation. The time period used to depreciate assets is based on an estimate of useful life made by the taxpayer (Martina). Only the straight-line depreciation method is permitted by the tax authorities. The cost of the R & D equipment is $90,000, payable in cash immediately. Martina estimates that the equipment will have an expected useful life of five years with a zero terminal disposal value. The current corporate tax rate of 40% is expected to apply each year over this five-year period. The required rate of return the company uses in discounting after-tax cash flows associated with this class of investments is 10%.

Exhibit 20-1 shows the relationship between depreciation, income taxes, and net income. The purchase cost of $90,000 is tax-deductible in the form of yearly depreciation. The present value of the tax savings from depreciation to Martina Enterprises is calculated as follows:

YEAR	INCOME TAX DEDUCTION FOR DEPRECIATION	INCOME TAX SAVINGS AT 40%	10% DISCOUNT FACTOR	PRESENT VALUE AT 10%
1	$18,000	$ 7,200	.909	$ 6,545
2	18,000	7,200	.826	5,947
3	18,000	7,200	.751	5,407
4	18,000	7,200	.683	4,918
5	18,000	7,200	.621	4,471
				$27,288

---

[3]**Double-declining balance depreciation (DDB)** is a form of accelerated depreciation that results in first-year depreciation being twice the amount of straight-line depreciation when zero terminal value is assumed. DDB is illustrated in Exhibits 20-2 and 20-12.

Sum-of-the-years'-digits (SYD) depreciation is a form of accelerated depreciation based on the following formula:

$$S = n \left(\frac{n + 1}{2} \right)$$

where S = sum-of-the-years'-digits and n = number of years of estimated useful life. Assume that $n = 5$; thus $S = 15$. The depreciation pattern would be year 1 (5/15), year 2 (4/15), year 3 (3/15), year 4 (2/15), and year 5 (1/15). SYD is illustrated in Exhibit 20-12.

EXHIBIT 20-1
Basic Analysis of Income Statement, Income Taxes, and Cash Flow for Martina Enterprises
(Data Assumed)

TRADITIONAL INCOME STATEMENT

(S)	Sales	$100,000
(E)	Less: Expenses, excluding depreciation	$ 62,000
(D)	Depreciation (straight-line of $90,000 ÷ 5 years)	18,000
	Total expenses	$ 80,000
	Income before income taxes	$ 20,000
(T)	Income taxes at 40%	8,000
(I)	Net income	$ 12,000

Total after-tax effect on cash inflow from operations is either

$$S - E - T = \$100,000 - \$62,000 - \$8,000 = \$30,000$$

or

$$I + D = \$12,000 + \$18,000 \qquad = \$30,000$$

ANALYSIS FOR CAPITAL BUDGETING

	Cash Effects of Operations	
(S − E)	Cash inflow from operations: $100,000 − $62,000 =	$ 38,000
	Income tax outflow at 40%	15,200*
	After-tax effects of operations (excluding depreciation)	$ 22,800
	Effect of depreciation	
(D)	Straight-line depreciation: $90,000 ÷ 5 = $18,000	
	Income tax savings at 40%	7,200*
	Total after-tax effect on cash	$ 30,000†

*Net cash outflow from income taxes: $15,200 − $7,200 = $8,000.
†Letting t equal the income tax rate, this can also be expressed as

$$(S - E)(1 - t) + Dt = (\$100,000 - \$62,000)(1 - .4) + \$18,000(.4)$$
$$= \$22,800 + \$7,200 = \$30,000$$

The $27,288 amount represents the present value of the tax savings from having the $18,000 depreciation deduction each year for five years. The present value of the tax savings is influenced by the depreciation method used, the applicable tax rate, and the interest rate used for discounting future cash flows.

The existence of this often sizable present value of tax savings from depreciation illustrates that there is an upside associated with income tax laws. The tourist in Paris who stated that "the Eiffel Tower is the Empire State Building after taxes" may have been overly pessimistic in outlook.

Effects of income taxes on cash flow

The effect of income taxes on cash flow may best be visualized by a step-by-step analysis of an example.

EXAMPLE

The Lindo Company is considering the replacement of an old packaging machine with a new, more efficient machine. The old machine originally cost $22,000. Accumulated straight-line depreciation is $12,000, and the remaining useful life is five years. The old machine can be sold outright now for $4,000. The predicted residual value at the end of five years is $600. Annual cash-operating costs are $50,000 per year.

Company engineers are convinced that the new machine, which costs $15,000, will have annual cash-operating costs of only $46,000 per year. The new machine will have a useful life of five years (based on an industry standard), with an estimated terminal disposal value of $700.

The Lindo Company operates in a country in which the initial cost of the asset is the amount allowable for depreciation. The time period over which the asset is to be depreciated is based on industry standards. Straight-line is the pattern of depreciation required to be used for the old machine. The new machine, however, would qualify for a special tax provision that would permit use of the double-declining balance (DDB) depreciation method. The depreciation pattern under this method is $6,000 (year 1), $3,600 (year 2), $2,160 (year 3), $1,296 (year 4), and $1,944 (year 5).[4] For income tax purposes, no account is taken of predicted terminal disposal value when computing depreciation for either the old or the new machine. When an existing asset is sold, any difference between the sale proceeds and the book value (i.e., cost less any accumulated depreciation) at the time of the sale is treated as ordinary income (or loss) and taxed at the ordinary income rate of 40%.

Required

Using the net present value method, demonstrate whether Lindo should keep the old machine or replace it with the new machine. Assume that the required after-tax rate of return is 10%. Use two ways to get your answer, the total-project approach and the incremental approach, as described in Chapter 19 on page 668.

SOLUTION

See Exhibits 20-2 and 20-3 for the complete solution. The following steps are recommended. The pertinent income tax aspects are considered for each step. For simplicity, we assume that all cash outflows or inflows occur at the start or the end of a year.

Step 1. General Approach. The inclusion of tax considerations does not change the general approach to these decisions. Review Chapter 19, pages 649–51.

Step 2. Cash-Operating Costs and Depreciation. Cash-operating costs and their income tax effects are separated from the tax effects of depreciation. *These could be combined if preferred. However, the treatment illustrated helps comparisons of alternative depreciation effects and allows the use of annuity tables for the cash-operating costs if they are equal per year.*

In this illustration we assume that any cash receipts or disbursements and their related tax effects occur in the same period. For simplicity, we are neglecting the possibility that some tax payments related to the pretax operating cash inflows of year 1 actually may not occur until sometime in year 2. *The analysis could be refined to account for any possible lags. For simplicity, we are ignoring this possibility.*

Step 3. Disposal of Equipment. Rules on the tax rates and other impacts on taxes vary considerably, depending on the specific asset, time held, and other factors. For our purposes, assume that gains and losses on disposal of equipment by Lindo are taxed in the same way as ordinary gains and losses. Exhibit 20-2 analyzes the alternative dispositions of the old equipment. Disposal at the end of year 5 results in a taxable gain, the excess of the selling price over book value (zero in this case). The cash effect is the selling price less the 40% tax on the gain.

---

[4]The DDB depreciation pattern is calculated as follows:
a. Compute the rate (ignoring the terminal disposal value) by dividing 100% by the years of useful life. Then double the rate. In the Lindo example, $100\% \div 5$ years = 20%. The DDB rate would be $2 \times 20\%$, or 40%.
b. To compute the depreciation for any year, multiply the beginning book value (cost less any accumulated depreciation) by the DDB rate: $40\% \times \$15,000 = \$6,000$ for the first year; $40\% \times (\$15,000 - \$6,000) = \$3,600$ for the second year; etc. Unmodified, this method would never fully depreciate the existing book value. In the Lindo example, the depreciation in the fifth year is simply the book value at the start of the fifth year.

Immediate disposal of the old equipment results in a loss that is fully deductible from current income. The net loss must be computed to isolate its effect on current income tax, but the total cash inflow is the selling price plus the current income tax benefit.

Step 4. Total-Project or Incremental Approach? Exhibits 20-2 and 20-3 demonstrate these approaches. Both result in the same net present value in favor of replacement. Where there are only two alternatives, the incremental approach is faster. However, the incremental approach rapidly becomes unwieldy when there are more than two alternatives or when computations become intricate.

Clarification of role of depreciation

Consider the impact of depreciation on various decision models for capital budgeting, as illustrated by the old equipment in Exhibit 20-2. Study Exhibit 20-4. Note that *the inputs to the decision model are confined to the predicted income tax effects on cash.* Book values and depreciation amounts may be necessary for making *predictions.* By themselves, however, they are not inputs to DCF *decision models.*

The following points summarize the role of depreciation regarding the replacement of equipment:

1. *Accrual accounting rate-of-return model.* As we noted in Chapter 9, depreciation on old equipment is irrelevant for decisions to replace or not replace. The total book value is ultimately written off regardless of whether it takes the form of annual depreciation or a lump-sum charge against the proceeds from disposal. In contrast, depreciation on new equipment is relevant because it is an expected future cost that will differ between the alternatives of replace or do not replace.

2. *Discounted cash-flow model.* Depreciation on the old equipment is irrelevant because it is not a future cash outflow. Depreciation on the new equipment is irrelevant because otherwise the investment would be double-counted. The investment is usually a one-time outlay at time zero, so it should not be deducted again in the form of depreciation.

3. *Relation to income tax cash flows.* Given the definition of relevance in Chapter 9, book values and past depreciation are irrelevant in all capital-budgeting models. The relevant items are the *income tax cash effects,* not the book values. Using the approach in Exhibit 9-1 (page 299), the book values and any depreciation charges are essential data for the *prediction method,* but the impacts on expected future income tax cash disbursements are the relevant data for the *decision model.*

EXHIBIT 20-4
Relevant Costs in Capital Budgeting

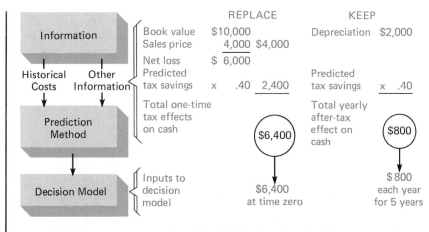

		REPLACE		KEEP	
Information	Book value	$10,000		Depreciation $2,000	
	Sales price	4,000	$4,000		
	Net loss	$ 6,000			
Historical Costs / Other Information	Predicted tax savings	× .40	2,400	Predicted tax savings	× .40
Prediction Method	Total one-time tax effects on cash		$6,400	Total yearly after-tax effect on cash	$800
Decision Model	Inputs to decision model		$6,400 at time zero		$800 each year for 5 years

EXHIBIT 20-2
Lindo Company, After-Tax Analysis of Equipment Replacement: Total-Project Approach

		PRESENT VALUE DISCOUNT FACTORS @ 10%	TOTAL PRESENT VALUE
End of Year			
(A) REPLACE			
Recurring cash-operating costs	$46,000		
Income tax savings, @ 40%	18,400		
After-tax effect on cash each year for 5 years	27,600	3.791	($104,632)

Depreciation deductions (DDB):

Year	Income Tax Deduction	Cash Effects Of Income Tax Savings @ 40%		
1	$6,000	$2,400	.909	2,182
2	3,600	1,440	.826	1,189
3	2,160	864	.751	649
4	1,296	518	.683	354
5	1,944	778	.621	483

Residual value at end of year 5, all subject to tax because book value will be zero and gain equals proceeds	$ 700		
Less: 40% tax on gain	280		
Total after-tax effect on cash	$ 420	.621	261
Cost of a new machine	$15,000	1.000	(15,000)

Disposal of old equipment:

Book value now ($22,000 − $12,000)	$10,000		
Selling price now	4,000		
Net loss	$ 6,000		
Tax savings	× .40		
Total after-tax effect on cash	$ 6,400	1.000	6,400
Total present value of all cash flows			($108,114)

(B) KEEP

Recurring cash-operating costs	$50,000		
Income tax savings, @ 40%	20,000		
After-tax effect on cash each year for 5 years	$30,000	3.791	($113,730)

Depreciation deductions ($10,000 ÷ 5)

	$ 2,000		
Income tax savings each year for 5 years at 40%	$ 800	3.790*	3,032

Residual value at end of year 5,

gain equals proceeds	$ 600		
Less 40% tax on gain	240		
Total after-tax effect on cash	$ 360	.621	224
Total present value of all cash flows			($110,474)

NET PRESENT VALUE DIFFERENCE IN FAVOR OF REPLACEMENT $2,360

Note: Rounded to avoid discrepancies between Exhibits 20-2 and 20-3 due to rounding differences: 3.790 = (.909 + .826 + .751 + .683 + .621)

SKETCH OF RELEVANT CASH FLOWS

	0	1	2	3	4	5
		($27,600)	($27,600)	($27,600)	($27,600)	($27,600)
		$2,400	$1,440	$864	$518	$778
						$420
	($15,000)					
	−$6,400					
		($30,000)	($30,000)	($30,000)	($30,000)	($30,000)
		$800	$800	$800	$800	$800
						$360

EXHIBIT 20-3
Lindo Company, After-Tax Analysis of Equipment Replacement: Incremental Approach

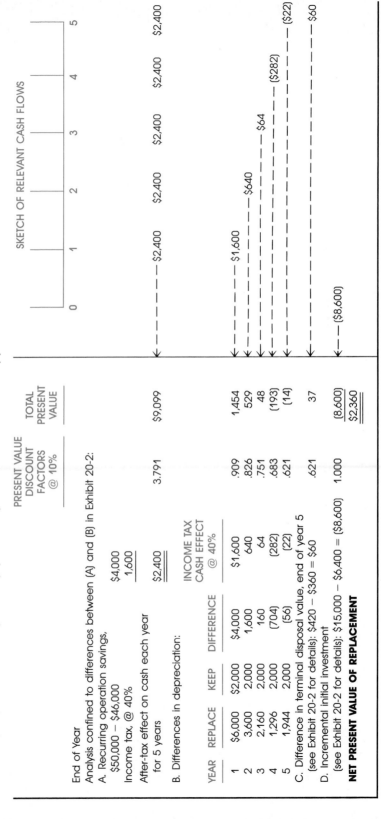

	PRESENT VALUE DISCOUNT FACTORS @ 10%	TOTAL PRESENT VALUE
End of Year		
Analysis confined to differences between (A) and (B) in Exhibit 20-2:		
A. Recurring operation savings,		
$50,000 − $46,000	$4,000	
Income tax, @ 40%	1,600	
After-tax effect on cash each year		
for 5 years	$2,400	
	3.791	$9,099
B. Differences in depreciation:		

YEAR	REPLACE	KEEP	DIFFERENCE	INCOME TAX CASH EFFECT @ 40%	PRESENT VALUE DISCOUNT FACTORS @ 10%	TOTAL PRESENT VALUE
1	$6,000	$2,000	$4,000	$1,600	.909	1,454
2	3,600	2,000	1,600	640	.826	529
3	2,160	2,000	160	64	.751	48
4	1,296	2,000	(704)	(282)	.683	(193)
5	1,944	2,000	(56)	(22)	.621	(14)

C. Difference in terminal disposal value, end of year 5		
(see Exhibit 20-2 for details): $420 − $360 = $60	.621	37
D. Incremental initial investment		
(see Exhibit 20-2 for details): $15,000 − $6,400 = ($8,600)	1.000	(8,600)
NET PRESENT VALUE OF REPLACEMENT		$2,360

Accelerated cost recovery system	The tax rules in the United States change almost every year. A major change occurred in 1981. The current rules are called the **Accelerated Cost Recovery System (ACRS)**. The ACRS is a federal tax regulation that classifies depreciable assets into one of several property class-life categories, each of which has a designated pattern of allowable depreciation. Two purposes of ACRS were to simplify prior depreciation laws and to encourage increased capital investments. The Appendix to this chapter summarizes some key provisions of ACRS and illustrates its use with the data from Exhibit 20-1. This Appendix can be read now without any interruption of the flow of the material in this chapter.				

_____PROBLEM FOR SELF-STUDY_____

problem Review the Lindo example, Exhibits 20-2 and 20-3, pages 686–87. Suppose the tax authorities specified the following depreciation schedule over the new asset's five-year life: 15%, 22%, 21%, 21%, and 21%. Compute the new net difference in present values in favor of replacement.

solution The only difference between the $2,360 answer in Exhibit 20-3 and the answer here is the present value of the tax savings from the depreciation deduction. The total present value of the difference in depreciation in Exhibit 20-3 is $1,824. The total present value of the difference in depreciation with the 15%, 22%, 21%, 21%, and 21% schedule is $1,466:

YEAR	REPLACE	KEEP	DIFFERENCE	INCOME TAX CASH EFFECT AT 40%	PV DISCOUNT FACTOR AT 10%	TOTAL PRESENT VALUE
1	$2,250	$2,000	$ 250	$100	.909	$ 91
2	3,300	2,000	1,300	520	.826	430
3	3,150	2,000	1,150	460	.751	345
4	3,150	2,000	1,150	460	.683	314
5	3,150	2,000	1,150	460	.621	286
						$1,466

Using the data in Exhibit 20-3 for A, C, and D and $1,466 for B:

A. Difference in present value of recurring operating savings	$9,099
B. Difference in present value of depreciation	1,466
C. Difference in present value of disposal value	37
D. Incremental initial investment	(8,600)
Net present value difference in favor of replacement	$2,002

CAPITAL BUDGETING AND INFLATION

Inflation can be defined as the decline in the general purchasing power of the monetary unit. In recent years, organizations have faced much volatility in inflation rates. Inflation rates of 15% or more in a single year have occurred in many countries. The International Monetary Fund made the following estimates of inflation in 1985:[5]

United States	3.2%	Middle East countries	16.4%
Canada	3.9	European countries	33.3
Asian countries	4.6	Latin American countries	185.4
African countries	13.9		

Such rates of inflation reinforce the importance of explicitly recognizing inflation in capital-budgeting decisions.

Real and nominal interest rates

When analyzing inflation, distinguish between the real rate of interest and the nominal rate of interest:

1. **Real rate of interest.** This rate is comprised of two elements: (a) a risk-free element—the "pure" rate of interest that is paid on long-term government bonds, and (b) a business-risk element—the "risk" premium above the pure rate that is demanded for undertaking risks.
2. **Nominal rate of interest.** This rate is comprised of two elements: (a) the real rate of interest, and (b) an inflation element—the premium demanded because of the anticipated decline in the general purchasing power of the monetary unit.

The relationship between the real rate of interest and the nominal rate of interest can be illustrated as follows. Assume that the real rate of interest for a project is assessed at 10% and an inflation rate of 20% is predicted. The nominal rate of interest is:[6]

Real rate of interest	.10
Inflation rate	.20
Combination (.20 × .10)	.02
Nominal rate of interest	.32

Discounted cash-flow models and inflation

The watchwords when incorporating inflation into DCF analysis are *internal consistency*. There are two internally consistent approaches:

APPROACH A: Predict cash inflows and outflows in nominal dollars *and* use a nominal discount rate.

APPROACH B: Predict cash inflows and outflows in real dollars *and* use a real discount rate.

---

[5]See "Inflation Continues to Plague Much of World," *Wall Street Journal*, December 26, 1985.

[6]The formula for deriving the nominal rate of return from the real rate of return is:

$$\text{Nominal rate} = (1 + \text{Real rate})(1 + \text{Inflation rate}) - 1$$

$$= (1 + .10)(1 + .20) - 1 = 1.32 - 1 = .32$$

The real rate of return can be derived from the nominal rate of return as follows:

$$\text{Real rate} = \frac{(1 + \text{Nominal rate})}{(1 + \text{Inflation rate})} - 1$$

$$= \frac{(1 + .32)}{(1 + .20)} - 1 = .10$$

Many managers find Approach A easier to understand because it uses numbers that will be recorded in their accounting systems. Moreover, it provides a planning basis that can be audited in terms of the future monetary units rather than in terms of "real" cash flows. In this way, managers may feel compelled to be more concerned with predicted inflation rates.[7]

An often overlooked adjustment under Approach B is necessary in countries (such as the United States) where tax rules restrict the amount allowed for depreciation to an asset's purchase price *in nominal dollars* at the time of the purchase. In these cases, the tax savings each year will be in nominal dollars and will need to be discounted for inflation before they are discounted in real terms.

The most frequently encountered error when accounting for inflation in capital budgeting is to keep cash inflows and outflows in real terms while using a nominal discount rate. This approach is internally inconsistent. It creates a bias against the adoption of many worthwhile capital investment projects.

An illustration

To illustrate the two internally consistent approaches, assume that an equipment rental company is considering expanding its holdings. The cost of the new equipment associated with the expansion is $150,000 payable immediately. The equipment is estimated to have a five-year useful life with zero terminal disposal value. An annual inflation rate of 20% is expected in this period. The predicted net cash inflows (before payment of the $150,000 and any tax payment) are:[8]

(1) YEAR	(2) REAL DOLLARS	(3) CUMULATIVE INFLATION RATE	(4) = (2) × (3) NOMINAL DOLLARS
1	$80,000	(1.20)	$ 96,000
2	80,000	$(1.20)^2$	115,200
3	80,000	$(1.20)^3$	138,240
4	60,000	$(1.20)^4$	124,416
5	40,000	$(1.20)^5$	99,533

The firm requires a real rate of return of 10% from this project. The corporate tax rate is 40%. Under a tax law designed to encourage increased capital investment, the firm can write off the cost of the asset over a three-year period; depreciation will be 25% of the cost in year 1, 38% in year 2, and 37% in year 3.[9]

Exhibit 20-5 presents the capital-budgeting approach for predicting cash flows in nominal dollars and using a nominal discount rate. Exhibit 20-6 presents the approach of predicting cash flows in real terms and using a real discount rate. (The present value factors in Exhibits 20-5 and 20-6 have six-decimal digits to

---

[7]Survey evidence indicates that Approach A is more widely used in practice than Approach B. See J. Hendricks, "Capital Budgeting Practices Including Inflation Adjustments: A Survey," *Managerial Planning*, January-February 1983, pp. 22–28.

[8]The cumulative inflation rate in the example is calculated using six-decimal digits to eliminate doubt about the equivalence of the two approaches. In practice, the cumulative inflation factor (to three-decimal digits) can be obtained using Table 1 (Compounded Amount of $1) on page 947. The Problem for Self-Study at the end of this chapter illustrates this approach.

[9]These depreciation percentages are those that would apply under the ACRS system described in the appendix for Chapter 20.

eliminate doubt about the equivalence of the two approaches.) Both approaches indicate that the project has a net present value of $42,960. Using a net present value criterion, acquisition of the rental equipment should be adopted.

REQUIRED RATE OF RETURN

The *required rate of return (RRR)* is a critical variable in discounted cash-flow analysis. It is the minimum acceptable rate of return on a project. Alternative names for RRR include the *discount rate,* the *hurdle rate,* and the *cost of capital.* Choosing the RRR for each project is complex and is discussed in finance texts.[10] A safe generalization is: The higher the risk, the higher the required rate of return.

When estimating the RRR, use a concept that is consistent with the approach used to estimate cash inflows and outflows. The options include various combinations of (a) the real rate or the nominal rate, and (b) pretax and after-tax rates. The numerical magnitude of differences among these rates can be sizable, given corporate tax rates of 40% or more and estimates of inflation that in some cases may exceed 15%. As noted previously in this chapter, the key words are *internal consistency* in the analysis.[11]

Required rate of return differs among projects

Companies usually possess an array or portfolio of projects having different risks. These differences should be recognized in capital budgeting. For instance, a petroleum company might well use after-tax RRRs of 6% for carrying accounts receivable and deciding whether to expand credit to customers, 10% for further development work on a currently operating oil field, and 16% for exploration activities in new areas.

Companies should not use the same RRR for all divisions. Managers may erroneously accept projects with excessive risk if a uniform rate is used. A risk-taking division may accept a project with an expected return higher than the uniform rate. But such higher rates may be lower than the division should earn, given the greater risk involved. In contrast, a division may reject a "safe" project with small risk because its rate is lower than the company's uniform stated rate. From a companywide viewpoint, some of these latter projects are desirable. Why? Because they will produce expected returns greater than the "true" divisional required rate.

Approaches used to recognize risk

Organizations typically use at least one of the following approaches to recognize the risks associated with projects:

1. *Varying the Payback Time.* Firms that use payback as a project selection criterion can vary the required payback time to reflect differences in project risk. A shorter payback time is required for higher-risk projects, and vice versa.

---

[10]See J. Van Horne, *Financial Management and Policy,* 7th ed. (Englewood Cliffs, N.J.: Prentice-Hall, 1986.)

[11]The approaches used to estimate the required rate of return include (a) reliance on the past returns on stocks and bonds, (b) surveys of security analysts, and (c) inferences derived from existing security prices and estimates of future earnings. These issues are summarized in a symposium on "Cost of Capital Estimation," *Financial Management,* Spring 1985, pp. 33–58. See also *Practice and Techniques: Cost of Capital* (Montvale, N.J.: National Association of Accountants, 1984).

EXHIBIT 20-5
Inflation Approach A: Predict Cash Inflows and Outflows in Nominal Dollars and Use a Nominal Discount Rate

CASH SAVINGS FROM OPERATIONS

YEAR	NET OPERATING CASH INFLOWS	TAX PAYMENTS (40%)	AFTER-TAX NET OPERATING CASH INFLOWS	PRESENT VALUE FACTOR (32%)	PRESENT VALUE
0	—	—	—	—	—
1	$96,000	$38,400	$57,600	.757576	$ 43,636
2	115,200	46,080	69,120	.573921	39,669
3	138,240	55,296	82,944	.434789	36,063
4	124,416	49,766	74,650	.329385	24,589
5	99,533	39,813	59,720	.249534	14,902
					$158,859

DEPRECIATION TAX SAVINGS

YEAR	DEPRECIATION*	TAX SAVINGS (40%)	PRESENT VALUE FACTOR (32%)	PRESENT VALUE
0	—	—	—	—
1	$37,500	$15,000	.757576	$ 11,364
2	57,000	22,800	.573921	13,085
3	55,500	22,200	.434789	9,652
4	—	—	—	—
5	—	—	—	—
				$ 34,101

Investment in equipment in year 0   ($150,000)

Net present value $ 42,960

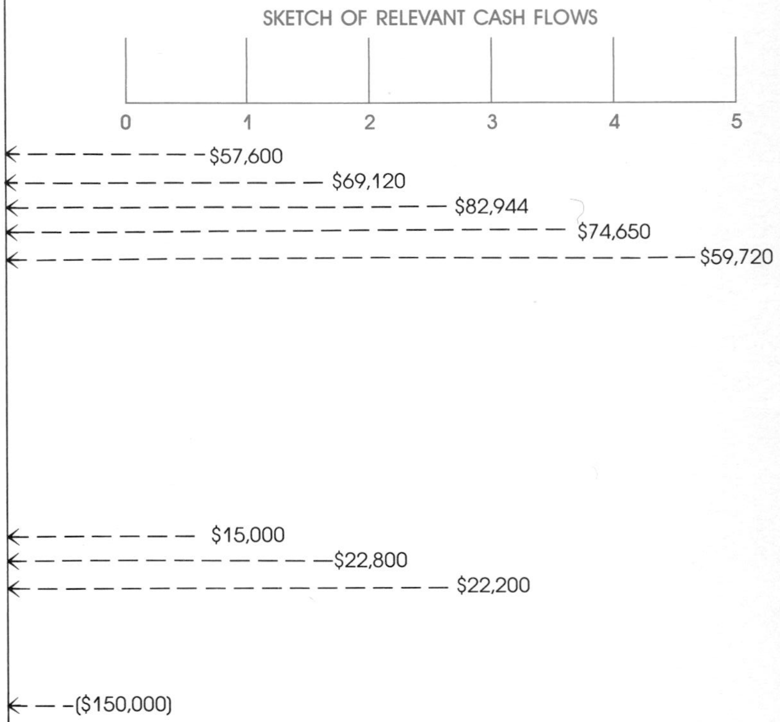

*Depreciation is $37,500 ($150,000 × .25) for year 1, $57,000 ($150,000 × .38) for year 2, and $55,500 ($150,000 × .37) for year 3.

SKETCH OF RELEVANT CASH FLOWS

0   1   2   3   4   5

-$57,600 $69,120 $82,944 $74,650 $59,720

$15,000 $22,800 $22,200

-($150,000)

EXHIBIT 20-6
Inflation Approach B: Predict Cash Inflows and Outflows in Real Dollars and Use a Real Discount Rate

CASH SAVINGS FROM OPERATIONS

YEAR	NET OPERATING CASH INFLOWS	TAX PAYMENTS (40%)	AFTER-TAX NET OPERATING CASH INFLOWS	PRESENT VALUE FACTOR (10%)	PRESENT VALUE
0	—				
1	$80,000	$32,000	$48,000	.909091	$ 43,636
2	80,000	32,000	48,000	.826446	39,669
3	80,000	32,000	48,000	.751315	36,063
4	60,000	24,000	36,000	.683031	24,589
5	40,000	16,000	24,000	.620921	14,902
					$158,859

DEPRECIATION TAX SAVINGS

YEAR	DEPRECIATION*	TAX SAVINGS (40%) IN NOMINAL DOLLARS	INFLATION FACTOR (20%)	TAX SAVINGS IN REAL DOLLARS	PRESENT VALUE FACTOR (10%)	PRESENT VALUE
0	—	—	—			
1	$37,500	$15,000	.833333	$12,500	.909091	$ 11,364
2	57,000	22,800	.694444	15,833	.826446	13,085
3	55,500	22,200	.578704	12,847	.751315	9,652
4	—	—	—	—	—	
5	—	—	—	—	—	
						$ 34,101

Investment in equipment in year 0   ($150,000)

Net present value $ 42,960

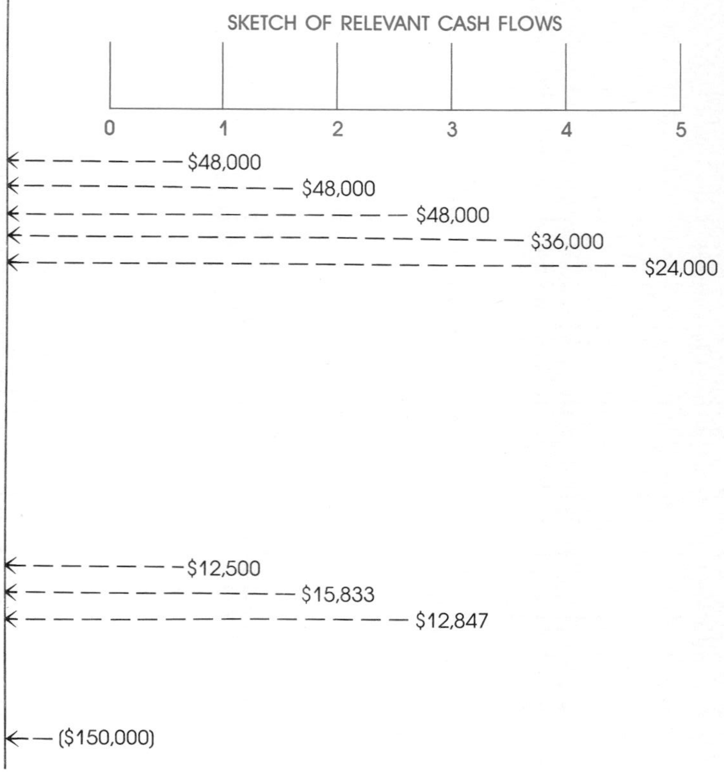

*Depreciation is $37,500 ($150,000 × .25) for year 1, $57,000 ($150,000 × .38) for year 2, and $55,500 ($150,000 × .37) for year 3.

SKETCH OF RELEVANT CASH FLOWS

	0	1	2	3	4	5
		$48,000				
			$48,000			
				$48,000		
					$36,000	
						$24,000
		-$12,500				
			$15,833			
				$12,847		
	($150,000)					

2. *Adjusting the Required Rate of Return.* The higher the risk, the higher the required rate of return. Estimating a precise risk factor for each project is difficult. Some organizations simplify the task by having three or four general-risk categories (for example, very high, high, average, and low). Each potential project is assigned to a specific category. Then a discount rate, which is preassigned by management to that category, is used as the required rate of return.

3. *Adjusting the Estimated Future Cash Flows.* The estimated future cash inflows of projects viewed as higher risk are systematically reduced.

4. *Sensitivity ("What-If?") Analysis.* This approach involves examining the consequences of changing key assumptions underlying a capital-budgeting project. For example, a copper-mining company might examine changes in the economic attractiveness of a mine if the world price of copper changes 10%, 20%, or 30%.

5. *Estimating the Probability Distribution of Future Cash Inflows and Outflows for Each Project.* This approach to uncertainty is discussed in Chapter 18. Although the task of determining these distributions is imposing, such an endeavor can help managers focus on important issues.

The first three of the above approaches are widely used in practice. One poll of U.S. and European managers asked what adjustments were made in capital budgeting for higher-risk projects. The most frequently mentioned adjustments were:[12]

	U.S. FIRMS	EUROPEAN FIRMS
1. Shorten payback period	34%	55%
2. Increase required rate of return	38	45
3. Decrease estimates of future cash inflows	19	36

Many respondents reported using more than one adjustment when considering higher-risk projects.

APPLICABILITY TO NONPROFIT ORGANIZATIONS

Discounted cash-flow applies to both profit-seeking and nonprofit-seeking organizations. For example, almost all organizations must decide which fixed assets will accomplish various tasks at the least cost. Moreover, all organizations, including governments, have to bear the costs of money. The required rate of return used in capital budgeting by U.S. federal agencies is 7% for water projects and 10% for all other projects.

---

[12]J. Baker, "Capital Budgeting in American and European Companies," *Mid-Atlantic Journal of Business,* Summer 1984, p. 21.

Studies of the capital-budgeting practices of government agencies at various levels (federal, state, and local) and in several countries report similar findings:[13]

1. Urgency is a common method of project selection. For example, capital budgeting for roads often starts with a list of the physical deficiencies in an existing highway rather than starting from a systematic analysis of whether it would be preferable to build an alternative highway.
2. Systematic biases are often found in project estimates. For example, studies of irrigation projects by the U.S. Bureau of Reclamation report overestimates of the benefits, underestimates of the costs, and underestimates of the time taken to construct dams and other irrigation infrastructure.
3. Tendency to cut capital items first when there is a strong push to balance a budget or reduce a deficit.

The General Accounting Office (GAO), in a study of capital-budgeting practices by U.S. federal agencies, gave "low points" to many agencies but "high points" to the U.S. Postal Service (USPS).

USPS uses return on investment, internal rate of return, and discounted cash flow. The Postal Service also performs a sensitivity analysis . . . Only the Postal Service conducts follow-up studies to find out if a completed project accomplished its objectives. . . . USPS uses its postaudits to determine the continuing applicability of previous conclusions, to highlight any continuing undesirable trends that warrant management action, to project cost changes through the life of the project, and to compare the results of the project's original economic evaluation.[14]

ADMINISTRATION OF CAPITAL BUDGETS

The first feature of effective capital-budgeting administration is the awareness on the part of all managers that long-run expenditures should be generators of long-run profits. This notion engenders a constant search for new methods, processes, and products.

Approval of overall capital budgets is usually the responsibility of the board of directors. Capital budget requests in many organizations are made semiannually or annually. They are reviewed as they move upward through managerial levels. They finally reach a committee that examines the requests and submits recommendations to the board of directors. Many organizations have formalized the administration of their capital budgets via the use of a standard set of forms and a specified

---

[13]See, for example, the following two studies: Report to the Congress of the United States by the Comptroller General, *Federal Capital Budgeting: A Collection of Haphazard Practices* (Washington, D.C.: General Accounting Office, 1981); and Report to the Committee on Environment and Public Works, United States Senate, *Effective Planning and Budgeting Practices Can Help Arrest the Nation's Deteriorating Public Infrastructure* (Washington, D.C.: General Accounting Office, 1982). See also R. Anthony and D. Young, *Management Control in Nonprofit Organizations*, 3rd ed. (Homewood, Ill.: Richard D. Irwin, 1984), Chaps. 8 and 9.

[14]*Federal Capital Budgeting: A Collection of Haphazard Practices*, p. 67.

routine for processing requests. Often there will be a full-time capital budget staff that analyzes proposals made within the organization.[15]

When projects are authorized, there is a threefold desirability of follow-up: (1) to see that spending and specifications conform to the plan as approved, (2) to increase the likelihood that capital-spending requests are sharply conceived and honestly estimated, and (3) to improve estimation on future capital-budgeting projects. The very existence of follow-up helps in this regard.

Systematic procedures are used for both implementing capital budgets and auditing the profitability performance of projects. This function is vital to a successful capital-budgeting program. The comparison of performance with original estimates not only helps ensure careful forecasts but also helps sharpen the tools for improving future forecasts.[16]

IMPLEMENTING THE NET PRESENT VALUE RULE

This section discusses problems in using the net present value rule when there is a restriction on the total funds available for capital spending. Such constraints may appear irrational in profit-seeking enterprises; after all, they can lead to the rejection of projects with positive net present values. Nevertheless, executives frequently must work within an overall capital-budgeting limit. In nonprofit enterprises, restrictions on the total funds available for capital spending are the norm. For example, an annual government budget typically will provide an upper limit on the funds available to each of the individual government departments.

Ranking schemes using excess present value index

The **excess present value index** (also sometimes called the *profitability index*) is the total present value of future net cash inflows divided by the initial cash outflow. This index has been proposed by some writers as a means of ranking projects in descending order of attractiveness. If capital rationing does not exist, and if there are no mutually exclusive or indivisible projects, the rankings by index and by net present value will produce the same answers. That is, there is no conflict because all projects will be accepted that have an index of 100% or above; these will also have a net present value of zero or above. However conflicts in decisions may be generated if projects are mutually exclusive, or if certain conditions of capital rationing exist.

Mutually exclusive alternatives and budget constraints

Suppose a company is considering two projects that are mutually exclusive—that is, where the acceptance of one alternative automatically results in the rejection of the other. The company can invest in either general-purpose (GP) equipment or spe-

---

[15] In a survey of budgeting practices for capital expenditure by U.S. manufacturing firms, W. Cress and J. Pettijohn report that 27.9% use a time horizon of one to two years, 23.3% use three to four years, 37.0% use five to nine years, and only 4.1% use ten or more years (7.7% gave no response): "A Survey of Budget-Related Planning and Control Policies and Procedures," *Journal of Accounting Education*, Fall 1985, pp. 61–78. For a collection of papers by practitioners, see M. Kaufman, ed., *The Capital Budgeting Handbook* (Homewood, Ill.: Dow-Jones Irwin, 1986).

[16] A report of the results of a questionnaire survey of large U.S. firms showed that "90% of the respondents indicate that their firms conducted post-audits in 1980 versus 51% in 1960." See T. Klammer and M. Walker, "The Continuing Increase in the Use of Sophisticated Capital Budgeting Techniques," *California Management Review*, Fall 1984.

cial-purpose (SP) equipment, as follows:

	(1) COST	(2) PRESENT VALUE AT 10% RRR	(2) ÷ (1) EXCESS PRESENT VALUE INDEX	(2) − (1) NET PRESENT VALUE
GP equipment	$1,000,000	$1,400,000	140%	$400,000
SP equipment	3,000,000	3,900,000	130%	900,000

The GP equipment promises a higher return per dollar invested; if all other things (such as risk and alternative uses of funds) were equal, the GP equipment would seem to be an obvious choice. But "all other things" are rarely equal.

Assume that $5,000,000 is the total capital budget for the coming year and that the allocation of resources, using GP equipment for Project A, is as shown under Alternative One in Exhibit 20-7. Note that the rationing used in Alternative Two is superior to Alternative One, despite the greater profitability per dollar invested in GP equipment compared with SP equipment. Why? Because the $2,000,000 incremental investment in SP equipment has an incremental net present value of $500,000, whereas the $2,000,000 would otherwise be invested in

EXHIBIT 20-7
Allocation of Capital Budget: Comparison of Two Alternatives

ALLOCATION OF $5,000,000 BUDGET

	Alternative One				Alternative Two		
PROJECT*	Investment Required	Excess Present Value Index	Total Present Value at 10%	PROJECT*	Investment Required	Excess Present Value Index	Total Present Value at 10%
C	$ 600,000	167%	$1,000,000	C	$ 600,000	167%	$1,000,000
A(GP)	1,000,000	140%	1,400,000				
D	400,000	132%	528,000	D	400,000	132%	528,000
				A(SP)	3,000,000	130%	3,900,000
F	1,000,000	115%	1,150,000	F	1,000,000	115%	1,150,000
					$5,000,000†		$6,578,000§
E	800,000	114%	912,000	E	$ 800,000	114%	Reject
B	1,200,000	112%	1,344,000	B	1,200,000	112%	Reject
	$5,000,000†		$6,334,000‡				
H	$ 550,000	105%	Reject	H	550,000	105%	Reject
G	450,000	101%	Reject	G	450,000	101%	Reject
I	1,000,000	90%	Reject	I	1,000,000	90%	Reject

*Each of the specific plans for the projects listed may have been selected from alternative mutually exclusive proposals. For example, Project D may be for new Ford trucks, selected after considering competing brands. Thus the capital budget is the crystallization of many "subcapital budgeting" decisions.

†Total budget constraint.

‡Net present value, $1,334,000.

§Net present value, $1,578,000.

Projects E and B, which have a lower combined incremental net present value of $256,000:

	COST	PRESENT VALUE	INCREASE IN NET PRESENT VALUE
SP equipment	$3,000,000	$3,900,000	
GP equipment	1,000,000	1,400,000	
Increment	$2,000,000	$2,500,000	$500,000
Project E	$ 800,000	$ 912,000	
Project B	1,200,000	1,344,000	
Total	$2,000,000	$2,256,000	$256,000

This example illustrates that decisions involving mutually exclusive investments of different sizes cannot be based on the excess present value index (or the internal rate of return, for that matter). The net present value method is the best general guide.

IMPLEMENTING THE INTERNAL RATE-OF-RETURN RULE

The net present value method will always indicate the project (or set of projects) that will maximize the net present value of future cash flows. However, surveys of practice report the widespread use of the internal rate-of-return model. Why? Probably because managers find it easier to understand and because, in most instances, their decisions would be unaffected by using one model or the other. In some cases, however, the two models will not indicate the same decision.

Conflict of ranking techniques Exhibit 20-8 illustrates how the two methods produce conflicting rankings of mutually exclusive investment proposals. (Use tables to check your understanding of the computations in Exhibit 20-8.)

What is the difference between these two variations of the discounted cash-flow approach? Essentially, differing assumptions are made with respect to the *rate of return on the reinvestment* of the cash proceeds at the end of the shorter investment's life. The two methods make different implicit assumptions as to the reinvestment rate of return.

EXHIBIT 20-8
Ranking of Projects Using Internal Rate of Return and Net Present Value

PROJECT	LIFE	INITIAL INVESTMENT OUTLAY	ANNUAL NET CASH EARNINGS	RANKING BY INTERNAL RATE OF RETURN		RANKING BY NET PRESENT VALUE		
				Internal Rate of Return	Ranking	Present Value of Earnings at 10% Hurdle Rate	Net Present Value Amount	Rank
A	5	$2,864	$1,000	22%	1	$3,791	$ 927	3
B	10	4,192	1,000	20%	2	6,145	1,953	2
C	15	5,092	1,000	18%	3	7,606	2,514	1

The internal rate-of-return model implicitly assumes that the reinvestment rate is equal to the indicated rate of return for the shorter-lived project. The net present value model assumes that the funds obtainable from competing projects can be reinvested only at the rate of the company's required rate of return.

Unequal lives and unequal investments

Where mutually exclusive projects have unequal lives or unequal investment outlays, the internal rate-of-return model can rank projects differently from the net present value model if there is exclusive focus on individual projects. Consider Exhibit 20-8.[17] The ranking by the internal rate-of-return model favors Project A, while the net present value model favors Project C.

The rankings of projects in Exhibit 20-8 are subject to the limitation that the projects differ in both life (5, 10, and 15 years) and initial investment outlay ($2,864, $4,192, and $5,092). Comparisons among the three projects should explicitly consider the same life and the same outlay. This requires assumptions about reinvestment for the shorter-life projects, and about investment for the difference in the initial investment outlays of the three projects.

Corporate finance textbooks cover (in great detail) problems of ranking projects with unequal lives or unequal investment outlays. Ideally, there should be a common terminal date for all projects with explicit assumptions as to the appropriate reinvestment rates of funds. The practical difficulties of predicting future profitability on reinvestment are greater than those of predicting profitability of immediate projects. But reinvestment opportunities should be considered where they can be foreseen and measured.

SUMMARY

Income tax factors almost always play an important role in decision making. Recognition of the tax savings from depreciation deductions can greatly improve the net present values of projects. Tax rules typically are both intricate and everchanging.

Inflation can be accounted for in several ways in capital budgeting. One correct approach is to predict cash inflows and outflows in nominal terms and and use a nominal discount rate. A second correct approach is to predict cash inflows and outflows in real terms and use a real discount rate. Both approaches are internally consistent.

The required rate of return should vary according to the riskiness of assets, projects, and divisions. The higher the risk, the higher the required return.

Restrictions on available capital funds are frequently encountered in many organizations (at least in the short run). Use caution when analyzing rankings based on percentages (such as the internal rate of return) to select the total set of investment projects. As a general rule, the net present value method is preferred when selecting investment projects.

PROBLEM FOR SELF-STUDY

(This is a comprehensive review problem. In particular, it illustrates both income tax factors and capital budgeting with inflation.)

problem Stone Aggregates operates ninety-two plants across the country. Each plant produces crushed stone aggregate used in many construction projects. Transportation is a major cost item. The existing system requires scale clerks—those who read all data pertaining to the

---

[17]Exhibit 20-8 concentrates on differences in project lives. Similar conflicting results can occur when the terminal dates are the same, but the sizes of the investment outlays differ.

weighing process—to prepare a delivery ticket (called a dray ticket) using a customer master plate and to enter data pertaining to each shipment manually. The clerk enters the weights of product shipped, derived from manual entries of scale and tare weights; the specific product shipped; freight charges, where appropriate; and the tax status of the product shipped, taxable or nontaxable.

Stone Aggregates is considering a proposal to use a computerized ticket-writing system for all of its ninety-two plants. It has already used one plant as a test pilot for the past twelve months, with cash-operating cost savings of $300,000. These savings arose mainly from a reduction in labor costs at the plant and from a reduction in overshipments (amounts shipped in excess of amounts ordered) to customers. The cost analyst estimates that had the computerized ticket system been operating at all its plants for the past year, cost savings would have been $25 million (in today's dollars). This cost savings estimate takes into account the estimated $5 million cash-operating cost of the computerized ticket-writing system for all of its plants in the past year.

The cost of the equipment for all ninety-two plants is $50 million, payable immediately. This equipment has an expected useful life of four years and a terminal disposal value of $10 million (in today's dollars). Under a tax law designed to encourage increased investment, Stone Aggregates can deduct as depreciation 25% of the $50 million cost in year 1, 38% in year 2, and 37% in year 3. The disposal value in nominal dollars will be taxed at the ordinary income tax rate in the year disposal is made. Stone Aggregates has a 30% income tax rate.

Required

1. Does the automated delivery ticket-writing proposal meet Stone Aggregates' 16% after-tax required rate-of-return criterion? An 8% inflation-rate prediction is already included in this 16% required rate of return. This 8% inflation rate is predicted to apply to both the cost savings and the terminal disposal value of the equipment. Conduct a net present value analysis using nominal dollars and a nominal required rate of return.

2. What factors would you recommend that Stone Aggregates consider in more detail when analyzing the proposal using net present value analysis?

solution

1. Exhibit 20-9 presents the net present value analysis. The format of Exhibit 20-9 differs from that of Exhibit 20-2 to illustrate an alternative presentation found in practice. The proposal for an automated delivery ticket-writing system should be implemented, as its net present value is $25.005 million. Note especially how the tax law enables Stone Aggregates to fully depreciate the equipment by the end of the third year. No depreciation expense occurs in year 4.

2. The analysis in Exhibit 20-9 assumes that the cost of operating the system is $5 million each year. However, costs in the year of changeover to the computerized system would probably be very high. Many companies find that actual implementation and operating costs in the changeover year exceed by a factor of 200% or more the operating costs in subsequent years.

The example in this problem was motivated by an article describing Vulcan Materials' adoption of a computerized ticket-writing system.[18] The benefits Vulcan reported included the following:

- "Hauler productivity increased because the new system improved the movement of product across the scales."

- "Scale clerks benefited through job enrichment and a much more predictable work load."

- "Communication between the scale-house microcomputers and the division office computers has afforded Vulcan several benefits. The first was the opportunity to eliminate costs associated with transporting the punch cards required under the old system. The second was the elimination of transferring transaction data from punch cards to computer tape. Vulcan also has benefited markedly from the

[18] J. Bush and R. Stewart, "Vulcan Materials Automates Delivery Ticket Writing," *Management Accounting*, August 1985, pp. 52–55.

EXHIBIT 20-9

Net Present Value Analysis of Computerized Ticket-Writing System for Stone Aggregates
(n.d. = nominal dollars)

	TOTAL PV	END OF YEAR 1	END OF YEAR 2	END OF YEAR 3	END OF YEAR 4
OPERATING SAVINGS					
1. Cash-operating savings (real dollars)	—	$25.000	$25.000	$25.000	$25.000
2. Cumulative inflation factor (from Table 1 on p. 947 for 8% p.a.)	—	1.080	1.166	1.260	1.360
3. Cash-operating savings (n.d.)	—	27.000	29.150	31.500	34.000
4. Tax payments (30%)	—	8.100	8.745	9.450	10.200
5. After-tax cash-operating savings (n.d.)	—	18.900	20.405	22.050	23.800
6. Present value factor (16%)	—	.862	.743	.641	.552
7. PV of after-tax cash-operating savings (n.d.): 5 × 6	$58.725	16.292	15.161	14.134	13.138
DEPRECIATION/DISPOSAL VALUE					
8. Depreciation*	—	12.500	19.000	18.500	—
9. Income tax savings (30%)	—	3.750	5.700	5.550	—
10. After-tax disposal value of equipment†	—	—	—	—	9.520
11. Total income tax savings + disposal value	—	3.750	5.700	5.550	9.520
12. Present value factor (16%)	—	.862	.743	.641	.552
13. PV of income tax savings + disposal value: 11 × 12	16.280	3.232	4.235	3.558	5.255
PV of total cash inflows: 7 + 13	$75.005	19.524	19.396	17.692	18.393
PV of cash outflows	(50.000)				
NET PRESENT VALUE =	$25.005				

*Depreciation of Year 1: 50.000 × .25 = $12.500
Year 2: 50.000 × .38 = $19.000
Year 3: 50.000 × .37 = $18.500

†Disposal value of $10 million in today's dollars will be $13.600 million ($10 million × 1.360) in year 4 nominal dollars. At a 30% tax rate, the after-tax disposal value in nominal dollars is $9.520 million.

SKETCH OF RELEVANT CASH FLOWS

0	1	2	3	4
	$27.000	$29.150	$31.500	$34.000
	−$3.750	$5.700	$5.550	
				$9.520
($50.000)				

reduction of errors contained in the transaction data and reduced costs associated with making corrections. In addition to improving accuracy, the system has accelerated the issuance of Vulcan's invoices."

- "Overshipments are eliminated because up-to-date status of a customer's sales order is available at the plant."

- "Cash on delivery customers are identified by the system to prevent unintentional credit sales."

- "Faster flow of data has narrowed the time lag in detecting and correcting problems."

Note that the dollar magnitude of many of these benefits would not be isolated individually in most accounting systems.

Terms to Learn

This chapter and the Glossary contain definitions of the following important terms:

Accelerated Cost Recovery System (ACRS) (p. 688)
accelerated depreciation (682)
double-declining balance depreciation (DDB) (682)
excess present value index (696)   *investment tax credit (ITC) (681)*
nominal rate of interest (689)   *real rate of interest (689)*
straight-line depreciation (SL) (682)
sum-of-the-years'-digits depreciation (SYD) (682)

Special Points and Pitfalls

The role of depreciation in capital-budgeting models is often misunderstood. Be sure to review the chapter subsection on "Clarification of Role of Depreciation" (page 685). Taxation deductions for depreciation result in valuable savings in cash outflows for taxes.

When including inflation in capital budgeting, maintain consistency between how cash inflows and outflows are expressed and the discount rate used. For example, if cash inflows and outflows are predicted using nominal dollars, a nominal discount rate should also be used. Where tax rules restrict depreciation to the cost of the asset expressed in nominal dollars at the time of purchase, depreciation deductions should not be adjusted for inflation.

Tax rules typically are both intricate and everchanging. This chapter has stressed general concepts associated with the role of taxes in capital budgeting. Always examine the most recent tax regulations (and consult experts on possible changes in them) before determining the after-tax consequences of decision alternatives.

APPENDIX: ACCELERATED COST RECOVERY SYSTEM

The current tax rules governing depreciation in the United States are called the Accelerated Cost Recovery System (ACRS). Two purposes of ACRS are to simplify the pre-1981 depreciation laws and to encourage increased capital investments. Some highlights of ACRS follow.

AMOUNT ALLOWABLE FOR DEPRECIATION.   Generally, the amount allowable for depreciation is the cost of the asset. The ACRS uses the phrase "capital recovery" to describe the amount allowable each year as a "depreciation" deduction. Estimates of future disposal or salvage values are not required under ACRS. If the asset is sold after the end of its "recovery period" (see below), any disposal value is taxed at the same rate as ordinary income.[19]

TIME PERIOD OVER WHICH THE ASSET IS TO BE DEPRECIATED.   The time period is specified in a "table of allowable lives" (termed *recovery periods*). Exhibit 20-10 illustrates several categories of ACRS property class lives.

PATTERN OF ALLOWABLE DEPRECIATION (FOR A GIVEN TIME PERIOD).   Exhibit 20-11 outlines the pattern of allowable depreciation associated with the 3-year, 5-year, 10-year, and 15-year property class-life categories.[20]

Comparison of present value of tax savings

Consider the R & D equipment being purchased by Martina Enterprises in Exhibit 20-1, page 683. Exhibit 20-10 reveals that R & D equipment has a 3-year class life for ACRS purposes. Exhibit 20-11 shows the ACRS pattern of depreciation allowed is 25% in year 1, 38% in year 2, and 37% in year 3. Thus, with a cost of $90,000, depreciation is:

Year 1: $90,000 × .25 = $22,500

Year 2: $90,000 × .38 = $34,200

Year 3: $90,000 × .37 = $33,300

EXHIBIT 20-10
Examples of Property Class Lives Allowed in
Accelerated Cost Recovery System (ACRS)

CLASS LIFE	EXAMPLES OF TYPES OF PROPERTY
3-Year	Property that is used in connection with research and development (R & D) or has a present class life* of four years or less. Examples include equipment used for R & D, automobiles, taxicabs, and light trucks.
5-Year	Most machinery, equipment, furniture and fixtures, and heavy-truck property. This category is a residual one and includes property not in the other categories.
10-Year	Public utility property with a present class life of more than 18 years but not more than 25 years. Category also includes railroad tank cars, large mobile homes, and amusement park structures.
15-Year	Longer-lived public utility property and general real estate property.

The "present class life" of an asset refers to the class life allowable under the legislation preceding ACRS.

---

[19]If the asset is sold before the end of its "recovery period" the tax treatment of the disposal value is more complex, especially when investment tax-credit considerations arise. See M. Holbrook and L. MacKirdy, *Depreciation and Investment Credit Manual, 1985 Edition* (Englewood Cliffs, N.J.: Prentice-Hall, 1985).

[20]The ACRS recovery schedule for "15-year General Real Estate" property in Exhibit 20-11 assumes the property is placed in service in the first month of the tax year. For more details, see Holbrook and MacKirdy, *Depreciation and Investment Credit Manual.*

EXHIBIT 20-11

ACRS Depreciation Schedules for Different Property Class-Life Categories

RECOVERY YEAR	PROPERTY CLASS-LIFE CATEGORY*				
	3-Year	5-Year	10-Year	15-Year Public Utility	15-Year General Real Estate
1	25%	15%	8%	5%	12%
2	38	22	14	10	10
3	37	21	12	9	9
4		21	10	8	8
5		21	10	7	7
6			10	7	6
7			9	6	6
8			9	6	6
9			9	6	6
10			9	6	5
11				6	5
12				6	5
13				6	5
14				6	5
15				6	5
	100%	100%	100%	100%	100%

*See Exhibit 20-10 for examples of types of property in each property class-life category.

Exhibit 20-12 shows the present value of the tax savings from the use of ACRS by Martina Enterprises. It also shows the present value of the tax savings if Martina could use the straight-line depreciation method, the double-declining balance depreciation method, or the sum-of-the-years'-digits method.

The present value of the tax savings associated with the use of each method in Exhibit 20-12 is:

A. ACRS	=	$29,484
B. Straight-line	=	$27,288
C. Double-declining balance	=	$29,142
D. Sum-of-the-years'-digits	=	$29,013

ACRS creates an additional incentive to invest in property. Why? Because ACRS increases the present value of the tax savings. How? ACRS specifies depreciable lives for income tax purposes that are shorter than the economic useful lives of the assets.

Straight-line depreciation option under ACRS

The ACRS system has reduced U.S. corporations' options when depreciating assets for tax purposes. However, corporations may still select a modified "straight-line" depreciation in lieu of the ACRS method outlined in Exhibits 20-10 and 20-11. This straight-line option is attractive for firms expected to suffer taxable losses in the early years of an asset's life. Many newly established companies fall into this category. To these companies, the benefit of the straight-line option over the ACRS system is that it defers more of the depreciation tax deductions to years in which the company expects to have taxable income.

EXHIBIT 20-12
Comparison of Tax Effects of Four Depreciation Methods for Martina Enterprises

A. ACRS METHOD

YEAR	INCOME TAX DEDUCTION	INCOME TAX SAVINGS AT 40%	10% DISCOUNT FACTOR	PRESENT VALUE AT 10%
1	$22,500	$ 9,000	.909	$ 8,181
2	34,200	13,680	.826	11,300
3	33,300	13,320	.751	10,003
Cash Effects: Saving in Income Taxes				$29,484

B. STRAIGHT-LINE METHOD

YEAR	INCOME TAX DEDUCTION	INCOME TAX SAVINGS AT 40%	10% DISCOUNT FACTOR	PRESENT VALUE AT 10%
1	$18,000	$ 7,200	.909	$ 6,545
2	18,000	7,200	.826	5,947
3	18,000	7,200	.751	5,407
4	18,000	7,200	.683	4,918
5	18,000	7,200	.621	4,471
Cash Effects: Saving in Income Taxes				$27,288

C. DOUBLE-DECLINING BALANCE METHOD

YEAR	INCOME TAX DEDUCTION	INCOME TAX SAVINGS AT 40%	10% DISCOUNT FACTOR	PRESENT VALUE AT 10%
1	$36,000	$14,400	.909	$13,090
2	21,600	8,640	.826	7,137
3	12,960	5,184	.751	3,893
4	7,776	3,110	.683	2,124
5	11,664	4,666	.621	2,898
Cash Effects: Saving in Income Taxes				$29,142

D. SUM-OF-THE-YEARS'-DIGITS METHOD

YEAR	INCOME TAX DEDUCTION	INCOME TAX SAVINGS AT 40%	10% DISCOUNT FACTOR	PRESENT VALUE AT 10%
1	$30,000	$12,000	.909	$10,908
2	24,000	9,600	.826	7,930
3	18,000	7,200	.751	5,407
4	12,000	4,800	.683	3,278
5	6,000	2,400	.621	1,490
Cash Effects: Saving in Income Taxes				$29,013

Other tax considerations

Income taxes are affected by many items not discussed in this chapter, including investment tax credits, loss carrybacks and carryforwards, state income taxes, short- and long-term capital gains, and distinctions between capital assets and other assets. Because income tax planning is exceedingly complex, professional tax counsel should be sought whenever the slightest doubt exists.

Questions that require analysis of the tax effects of depreciation include in their title the depreciation method to be used. Questions requiring use of the Accelerated Cost Recovery System (ACRS) are grouped at the end of the assignment material.

20-1 "Accelerated depreciation provides higher cash flows in early years." Do you agree? Why?

20-2 What are the two major aspects of the role of income taxes in decision making?

20-3 "It doesn't matter what depreciation method is used. The total dollar tax bills are the same." Do you agree? Why?

20-4 Distinguish between the real rate of interest and the nominal rate of interest.

20-5 What are the two internally consistent approaches to incorporating inflation into DCF analysis?

20-6 Name four approaches used to recognize risk in capital budgeting.

20-7 "In practice there is no single rate that is used as a guide for sifting among all projects." Why? Explain.

20-8 "In the case of mutually exclusive investments, smaller profitability indexes may enhance overall economic returns." How?

20-9 "The crux of the problem in replacement decisions is the lack of a realistic common terminal date for both proposals." Briefly describe two practical approaches to the problem.

20-10 Recapitulation of role of depreciation in Chapters 9, 19, and 20. A president of a large steel company remarked, "I've read three chapters that have included discussions of depreciation in relation to decisions regarding the replacement of equipment. I'm confused. Chapter 9 said that depreciation on old equipment is irrelevant, but that depreciation on the new equipment is relevant. Chapter 19 said that depreciation was irrelevant in relation to discounted cash-flow models, but Chapter 20 indicated that depreciation was indeed relevant."

Required | Prepare a clear explanation for the president that would minimize his or her confusion.

20-11 New equipment purchase, straight-line and DDB depreciation. The Mayo Corporation estimates that it can save $35,000 a year in cash-operating costs for the next five years if it buys a special-purpose machine at a cost of $75,000. No terminal disposal value is expected. Assume an overall income tax rate of 40% and a minimum desired rate of return of 12% after taxes.

Required | 1. Assume straight-line depreciation. Compute (a) net present value, (b) payback period, and (c) internal rate of return.
2. Assume double-declining balance depreciation, with depreciation for the fifth year being the book value at the start of the fifth year. Compute (a) net present value, (b) payback period, and (c) internal rate of return.

20-12 Discounted cash-flow analysis, including straight-line and SYD depreciation. The Dudley Company is trying to decide whether to launch a new household product. Through the years, the company has found that its products have a useful life of six years, after which the product is dropped and replaced by other new products. Available data follow:
A. The new product will require new special-purpose equipment costing $900,000. The useful life of the equipment is six years, with a $140,000 estimated disposal value at that time. However, the income tax authorities will not allow a write-off based on a life shorter than nine years. Therefore the new equipment would be written off over nine

years for tax purposes, using the sum-of-the-years'-digits depreciation and no salvage value.

B. The new product will be produced in an old plant already owned. The old plant has a book value of $30,000 and is being depreciated on a straight-line basis at $3,000 annually. The plant is currently being leased to another company. This lease has six years remaining at an annual rental of $9,000. The lease contains a cancellation clause whereby the landlord can obtain immediate possession of the premises upon payment of $6,000 cash (fully deductible for tax purposes). The estimated sales value of the building is $80,000; this price should remain stable over the next six years. The plant is likely to be kept for at least ten more years.

C. Certain nonrecurring market-research studies and sales-promotion activities will amount to a cost of $500,000 during year 1. The entire amount is deductible in full for income tax purposes in the year of expenditure.

D. Additions to working capital will require $200,000 at the outset and an additional $200,000 at the end of two years. This total is fully recoverable at the end of six years.

E. Net cash inflow from operations before depreciation and income taxes will be $400,000 in years 1 and 2, $600,000 in years 3 through 5, and $100,000 in year 6.

The company uses discounted cash-flow techniques for evaluating decisions. For example, in this case tabulations of differential cash flows would be made from year 0 through year 6. Yearly cash flows are estimated for all items, including capital outlays or recoveries. An applicable discount rate is used to bring all outlays from year 1 through year 6 back to year 0. If the summation in year 0 is positive, the project is desirable, and vice versa.

The minimum desired after-tax rate of return is 12%. Income tax rates are 60% for ordinary income.

Required

1. Using an answer sheet, show how you would handle the data listed above for purposes of the decision. Note that you are *not* being asked to apply discount rates. You are being asked for the detailed impact of each of items A through E on years 0 through 6.

Note, too, that each item is to be considered separately, including its tax ramifications. *Do not combine your answers to cover more than one item.*

Assume that all cash flows take place at the end of each period. Assume that income taxes are due or refundable at the end of the period to which they relate.

Sample Answer Sheet for Problem 20-12

		CASH FLOWS IN YEAR						
ITEM	EXPLANATION	0	1	2	3	4	5	6
A.	[Allow ample							
B.	space between							
C.	items]							
D.								
E.								

2. Total each column. Compute the net present value of the project.

20-13 Multiple choice, including straight-line depreciation. (CPA, adapted) Choose the best answer for each question. The Apex Company is evaluating a capital-budgeting proposal for the current year. The relevant data follow:

YEAR	PRESENT VALUE OF AN ANNUITY IN ARREARS OF $1 AT 15%
1	$ .870
2	1.626
3	2.284
4	2.856
5	3.353
6	3.785

The initial investment would be $30,000. It would be depreciated on a straight-line basis over six years with no terminal disposal value. The before-tax annual cash inflow due to this investment is $10,000, and the income tax rate is 40% paid the same year as incurred. The desired rate of return is 15%. All cash flows occur at year-end.

1. What is the after-tax accounting rate of return on Apex's capital-budgeting proposal? (a) 10%, (b) 16⅔%, (c) 26⅔%, (d) 33⅓%.
2. What is the after-tax payback time (in years) for Apex's capital-budgeting proposal? (a) 5, (b) 3.75, (c) 3, (d) 2.
3. What is the net present value of Apex's capital-budgeting proposal? (a) $(7,290), (b) $280, (c) $7,850, (d) $11,760.
4. How much would Apex have had to invest five years ago at 15% compounded annually to have $30,000 now? (a) $12,960, (b) $14,910, (c) $17,160, (d) cannot be determined from the information given.

20-14 Replacement of a machine, including straight-line and SYD depreciation. (CMA, adapted) The WRL Company makes cookies for its chain of snack food stores. On January 2, 19_1, WRL Company purchased a special cookie-cutting machine; this machine has been utilized for three years. WRL Company is considering the purchase of a newer, more efficient machine. If purchased, the new machine would be acquired on January 2, 19_4. WRL Company expects to sell 300,000 dozen cookies in each of the next four years. The selling price of the cookies is expected to average $.50 per dozen.

WRL Company has two options: (1) continue to operate the old machine, or (2) sell the old machine and purchase the new machine. No trade-in was offered by the seller of the new machine. The following information has been assembled to help decide which option is more desirable.

	OLD MACHINE	NEW MACHINE
Original cost of machine at acquisition	$80,000	$120,000
Salvage value at the end of useful life for depreciation purposes	$10,000	$ 20,000
Useful life from date of acquisition	7 years	4 years
Expected annual cash operating expenses:		
Variable cost per dozen	$.20	$.14
Total fixed costs	$15,000	$ 14,000
Depreciation method used for tax purposes	Straight-line	Sum-of-years'-digits
Estimated cash value of machines:		
January 2, 19_4	$40,000	$120,000
December 31, 19_7	$ 7,000	$ 20,000

WRL Company is subject to an overall income tax rate of 40%. Assume that all operating revenues and expenses occur at the end of the year. Assume that any gain or loss on the sale of machinery is treated as an ordinary tax item and will affect the taxes paid by WRL Company at the end of the year in which it occurred.

Required

1. Use the net present value method to determine whether WRL Company should retain the old machine or acquire the new machine. WRL requires an after-tax return of 16%. Round your discount factor to two decimal places before using them.
2. Without prejudice to your answer to requirement 1, assume that the quantitative differences are so slight between the two alternatives that WRL Company is indifferent to the two proposals. Identify and discuss the nonquantitative factors that are important to this decision that WRL Company should consider.

20-15 Inflation and nonprofit institution, no tax aspects. A university is considering the purchase of a photocopying machine for $3,791 on December 31, 19_0, useful life five years, and no terminal disposal value. The cash-operating savings are expected to be $1,000 annually, measured in 19_0 dollars. The hurdle rate is 20%, which includes an element attributable to anticipated inflation of 12%.

Required

Use the 20% hurdle rate for requirements 1 and 2:

1. Compute the net present value of the project without adjusting the cash-operating savings for inflation.
2. Repeat requirement 1, adjusting the cash-operating savings upward in accordance with the 12% inflation rate.
3. Compare your results in requirements 1 and 2. What generalizations seem applicable about the analysis of inflation in capital budgeting?

20-16 Capital budgeting with inflation, tax aspects with straight-line depreciation. W. Hoverling, the president of a Liverpool trucking company, is considering whether to invest £110,000 in new semiautomatic loading equipment that will last five years, have zero scrap value, and generate cash-operating savings in labor usage of £36,000 annually, using 19_0 prices and wage rates. It is December 31, 19_0.

The minimum desired rate of return is 18% per year after taxes.

Required

1. Compute the net present value of the project. Assume a 40% tax rate and straight-line depreciation.
2. Hoverling is wondering if the model in requirement 1 provides a correct analysis of the effects of inflation. She maintains that the 18% rate embodies an element attributable to anticipated inflation. For purposes of this analysis, she assumes that the existing rate of inflation, 10% annually, will persist over the next five years. Repeat requirement 1, adjusting the cash-operating savings upward in accordance with the 10% inflation rate.
3. What generalizations about the effects of inflation on capital-budgeting models and decisions seem warranted?

20-17 Capital budgeting with inflation. (Extension of Problem 20-16.) Footnote 6 gives the formula for deriving the real rate of return from the nominal rate of return and the inflation rate. Compute the real rate of return for the data in Problem 20-16. How would this real rate be used in capital budgeting? Footnote 6 is on p. 689.

20-18 Comparison of projects with unequal lives. The manager of the Robin Hood Company is considering two investment projects, which happen to be mutually exclusive.

The cost of capital to this company is 10%, and the anticipated cash flows are as follows:

PROJECT NO.	INVESTMENT REQUIRED NOW	CASH FLOWS (INCOME)			
		Year 1	Year 2	Year 3	Year 4
1	$10,000	$12,000	0	0	0
2	$10,000	0	0	0	$17,500

Required

1. Calculate the internal rate of return of both projects.
2. Calculate the net present value of both projects.
3. Comment briefly on the results in requirements 1 and 2. Be specific in your comparisons.

20-19 Ranking projects. (Adapted from *N.A.A. Research Report No. 35*, pp. 83–85) Assume that six projects in the table that follows have been submitted for inclusion in the coming year's budget for capital expenditures:

	YEAR	A	B	C	D	E	F
Investment	0	$(100,000)	$(100,000)	$(200,000)	$(200,000)	$(200,000)	$(50,000)
	1	0	20,000	70,000	0	5,000	23,000
	2	10,000	20,000	70,000	0	15,000	20,000
	3	20,000	20,000	70,000	0	30,000	10,000
	4	20,000	20,000	70,000	0	50,000	10,000
	5	20,000	20,000	70,000	0	50,000	
Per year	6–9	20,000	20,000		200,000	50,000	
	10	20,000	20,000			50,000	
Per year	11–15	20,000					
Internal rate of return		14%	?	?	?	12.6%	12.0%

Required

1. Internal rates of return (to the nearest half percent) for Projects B, C, and D and a ranking of all projects in descending order. Show computations. What approximations of rates of return for Projects B and C do you get by using payback reciprocals?
2. Based on your answer in requirement 1, state which projects you would select, assuming a 10% hurdle rate (a) if $500,000 is the limit to be spent, (b) if $550,000 is the limit, and (c) if $650,000 is the limit.
3. Assuming a 16% minimum desired rate of return, and using the net present value method, compute the net present values and rank all the projects. Which project is more desirable, C or D? Compare your answer with your ranking in requirement 2. If Projects C and D are mutually exclusive proposals, which would you choose? Why?
4. What factors other than those considered in requirements 1 through 3 would influence your project rankings? Be specific.

20-20 Comprehensive equipment replacement decision, tax aspects with straight-line depreciation. A manufacturer of automobile parts acquired a special-purpose shaping machine for automatically producing a special part. The machine has been utilized for one year; it is expected to be useless after three more years. The machine is being depreciated on a straight-line basis for income tax purposes. It cost $88,000, has a current disposal value of only $29,000, and has an expected terminal value of $6,000. However, no terminal value was provided for in computing straight-line depreciation for tax purposes.

A new machine has become available and is far more efficient than the present machine. It will cost $63,000, will cut annual cash-operating costs from $60,000 to $40,000, and will have no terminal value at the end of its useful life of three years. Sum-of-the-years'-digits depreciation would be used for tax purposes. The applicable income tax is 30%. The required rate of return is 14%.

Required Using the net present value model, show whether the new machine should be purchased (a) under a total-project approach or (b) under an incremental approach.

20-21 Capital budgeting with inflation, tax aspects with straight-line depreciation. (J. Fellingham, adapted) Abbie is considering buying a machine that costs $10,000. The machine will last five years. Abbie estimates that the incremental pretax cash savings from using the machine will be $3,000 annually. The $3,000 is measured at current prices and will be received at the end of each year. For tax purposes, she will depreciate the machine straight-line, assuming zero terminal disposal value. Abbie requires a 10% real rate of return (that is, the rate of return is 10% when all cash flows are denominated in 19_0 dollars).

Required Treat each of the following cases separately.

1. Abbie lives in a world without taxes and without inflation. What is the net present value of the machine in this world?
2. Abbie lives in a world without inflation, but there is a tax rate of 40%. What is the net present value of the machine in this world?
3. There are no taxes, but the annual inflation rate is 20%. What is the net present value

of the machine? The cash savings each year will be increased to reflect the inflation rate.

4. The annual inflation rate is 20%, and the tax rate is 40%. What is the net present value of the machine?

20-22 Automated materials-handling capital project, depreciation, Accelerated Cost Recovery System. Ontime Distributors operates a large distribution network for health-related products. It is considering an automated materials-handling (AMH) proposal for its major warehouse. The before-tax cash operating savings from the automation are estimated to be $2.5 million a year. These savings arise from reduced storage space requirements, increased labor productivity, less product damage, and higher inventory recordkeeping accuracy. This $2.5 million annual savings is calculated as $3.5 million gross cash operating savings minus the $1.0 million costs of operating and maintaining the AMH equipment. The AMH equipment will cost $6 million, payable immediately. The equipment has a useful life of four years and zero terminal disposal value. The lease on the warehouse expires in four years and is not expected to be renewed. The company has an income tax rate of 40% and a minimum desired rate of return of 12% after taxes. The $6 million equipment cost qualifies under ACRS as a three-year class-life asset.

Required

1. Compute (a) the net present value, (b) the payback period, and (c) the internal rate of return on the automated materials-handling project.
2. Assume the AMH equipment has a $1 million terminal disposal value at the end of the fourth year instead of a zero terminal disposal value. How will this $1 million terminal disposal value affect the net present value?
3. What other factors should Ontime Distributors consider in its decision?

20-23 Make or buy, depreciation, Accelerated Cost Recovery System. (CMA, adapted) Lamb Company manufactures several lines of machine products. One unique part, a valve stem, requires specialized tools that need to be replaced. Management has decided that the only alternative to replacing these tools is to acquire the valve stem from an outside source. A supplier is willing to provide the valve stem at a unit sales price of $20 if at least 70,000 units are ordered annually.

Lamb's average usage of valve stems over the past three years has been 80,000 units each year. Expectations are that this volume will remain constant over the next five years. Cost records indicate that unit manufacturing costs for the last several years have been as follows:

Direct material	$ 3.80
Direct labor	3.70
Variable overhead	1.70
Fixed overhead*	4.50
Total unit cost	$13.70

*Depreciation accounts for two-thirds of the fixed overhead. The balance is for "other fixed-overhead costs" of the factory that require cash expenditures. These "other fixed-overhead costs" will be incurred irrespective of whether the new specialized tools are purchased or the outside supplier provides the valve stem.

If the specialized tools are purchased, they will cost $2,500,000 and will have a disposal value of $100,000 after their expected economic life of five years. Straight-line depreciation is used for book purposes, but ACRS is used for tax purposes. The specialized tools are considered three-year property for ACRS purposes. The company has a 40% marginal tax rate, and management requires a 12% after-tax return on investment.

The sales representative for the manufacturer of the new tools stated, "The new tools will allow direct labor and variable overhead to be reduced by $1.60 per unit." Data from another manufacturer (provided by the sales representative) using identical tools and experiencing similar operating conditions, confirms the direct-labor and variable-overhead savings. However, the manufacturer told the sales representative that it experienced an increase in raw-material cost due to the higher quality of material that had to be used with the new tools. The other manufacturer indicated that its variable costs have been as follows:

Direct material per unit	$4.50
Direct labor per unit	$3.00
Variable overhead per unit	$ .80

Lamb believes that its variable costs will be the same as those of the other manufacturer.

Required

1. Present a net present value analysis covering the economic life of the new specialized tools to determine whether Lamb Company should replace the old tools or purchase the valve stem from an outside supplier.
2. Identify additional factors Lamb Company should consider before a decision is made to replace the tools or purchase the valve stem from an outside supplier.

20-24 Make or buy, investment tax credit.   (Extension of Problem 20-23) Assume the same information as that in Problem 20-23 with one additional item. Lamb Company can claim an investment tax credit of 8% of the cost of the asset purchase price. No reduction will be made to the $2,500,000 amount available for depreciation.

Required

How will this investment tax credit affect the net present value of the alternative of purchasing the new specialized tools?

20-25 Oil and gas project evaluation, depreciation, Accelerated Cost Recovery System.   Deborah Regent, project analyst for Richfield Oil, is considering a capital-budgeting project relating to enhanced recovery from one of Richfield's existing oil fields. The oil field is in Prudhoe Bay, Alaska. Enhanced recovery will involve the construction of a special drilling rig that will recover oil that is deeper in the ground than the current drilling rig can reach. The new drilling rig will be assembled in Anchorage and floated to the north slope of Alaska. The drilling rig project will cost $50 million, payable immediately. The new rig will enable an extra one million barrels of oil to be extracted each year for each of the next seven years. Regent estimates the following operating data:

Revenue per barrel	$21
Variable cost per barrel	$ 5
Fixed operating cost per year for the new drilling rig	
(excluding depreciation)	$ 1 million

The drilling rig has an expected useful life of seven years with zero terminal value. It will qualify under the Accelerated Cost Recovery System guidelines for a five-year class life. Richfield uses an after-tax required rate of return of 8% for low-risk enhanced recovery projects such as the Prudhoe Bay project. Its income tax rate is 30%.

Required

1. Calculate (a) the net present value, (b) the payback period, and (c) the internal rate of return on the enhanced recovery project.
2. Suppose the $21 figure for revenue per barrel is based on the current world price of oil. What is the revenue-per-barrel figure at which the enhanced recovery project is a breakeven proposition from a net present value perspective?

20-26 Replacement of newspaper printing equipment, depreciation, Accelerated Cost Recovery System. It is January 1, 19_5, and Anna Murdoch has gained control of the *Morning News*. Her first task is to consider possible replacement of the existing printing machines. The machines were bought secondhand four years ago at a total cost of $10 million. Their book value now (January 1, 19_5) is $2.1 million. If the old machines are not replaced, this $2.1 million will be fully written off as depreciation in the current year (which ends December 31, 19_5).

Disposal value as of January 1, 19_5, is $1 million. The old machines could be used for another seven years before they are ready to be scrapped, with zero terminal disposal value. Annual cash-operating costs (before depreciation and before taxes) with the old machines will be $40 million.

Murdoch has already obtained a bid from a manufacturer of printing machines. This manufacturer can immediately install state-of-the-art printing machines for $20 million, payable on January 1, 19_5. The Printers' Union at the *Morning News* has strongly opposed the acquisition by Murdoch. They will only partially cooperate with Murdoch, with the result that the annual cash-operating costs (before depreciation and before taxes) with the new machines will be $36 million. The new machines qualify for a five-year class life under the Accelerated Cost Recovery System. They have a useful life of seven years and a terminal disposal value of $3 million. Murdoch uses a 10% required after-tax rate of return in her analysis. The current income tax rate is 35%.

Required

1. Using a net present value approach, should Murdoch replace the existing printing machines with the new state-of-the-art printing machines?
2. The head of the Printers' Union has had second thoughts about the opposition to Murdoch. He agrees to further labor reductions at the *Morning News* that will reduce cash-operating costs (before depreciation and before taxes) with the new machines to $30 million a year. What is the net present value of the new machines to the *Morning News* with this revised union proposal?
3. What other factors should Murdoch consider in deciding whether to replace the existing printing machines?

20-27 Robotics capital project, inflation, tax aspects with Accelerated Cost Recovery System. Rustbelt America Inc. purchases secondhand pipeline equipment and "rehabilitates" it for resale. A major problem area in its plant is the spot-welding function. There have been many industrial accidents involving workers at this function. Rustbelt looks into the possibility of investing in robots. Robots are programmable machines capable of performing repetitive tasks such as spot welding. The investment in robots will cost $10 million payable immediately and will reduce labor costs, worker insurance costs, and materials usage costs by a total of $7 million (in 19_0 dollars) a year. The robots require an addition to annual cash-operating costs of $3 million (in 19_0 dollars) a year. Hence the net cash-operating savings from use of the robots will be $4 million annually (in 19_0 dollars). Rustbelt anticipates that use of robots will eliminate industrial accidents involving workers at the spot-welding function.

The robots have a four-year useful life with a terminal disposal value of $1 million (in 19_0 dollars). The robots qualify in the three-year property class category of the Accelerated Cost Recovery System (ACRS). Rustbelt anticipates inflation in its operating costs and in the terminal disposal value of the robots of 20% per annum. It uses a 10% required rate of return for investments expressed in real dollars. Rustbelt's income tax rate is 40%.

Required

1. What is the nominal required rate of return of Rustbelt America for investments expressed in nominal dollars?
2. What is the net present value of the $10 million investment in robots? Use the approach of predicting cash inflows and outflows in nominal dollars *and* using a nominal discount rate.
3. What are the advantages of the approach to capital budgeting for inflation in requirement 2 relative to the approach of predicting real cash inflows and outflows *and* using a real discount rate?
4. What factors other than the net present value figure in requirement 2 should Rustbelt America consider in deciding whether to invest in robots?

Operations Management and the Accountant (I): Materials and Inventory

Managing goods for sale in retail organizations • Accounting data and managing goods for sale •
Just-in-time purchasing • Managing materials in manufacturing organizations
Measuring the costs of product quality

The business press is extolling the "fresh allure of operations" and "the newfound interest in the shop floor." Global competition in many industries has put a premium on reducing operating costs, improving product quality, and increasing customer service. Managers now give high priority to operations management.

Operations management focuses on the management of resources to produce or deliver the products or services provided by an organization. Many specific decisions fall under the operations management umbrella. Examples include the mix of products or services to sell or manufacture; the layout of a retail outlet, distribution warehouse, or manufacturing plant; and the purchasing and handling of inventories by retailers and manufacturers.

Accounting information can play a key role in operations management. This chapter illustrates the importance of accounting information in two areas:

1. The management of goods for sale in retail organizations
2. The management of materials, work in process, and finished goods in manufacturing organizations

The next chapter examines the role of accounting information in decisions about the mix of products to sell or manufacture. Readers wishing to pursue operations management topics further can use one or more of the growing list of textbooks in this area.[1]

Cost of goods sold constitutes the largest single cost item for most retailers. For example, a survey of retail food chains reported the following breakdown of operating costs:[2]

Cost of goods sold	78.07%	Fringe benefits	3.01%
Payroll	11.11	Other costs	4.45
Store occupancy	3.36		

Net income of retail firms in the survey averaged 0.93% of sales. This paper-thin net income percentage means that better decisions relating to the purchasing and managing of goods for sale can cause dramatic increases in net income.

Two decisions central to the management of goods for sale in a retail organization are:

1. How much to order (the economic-order-quantity decision)
2. When to order (the reorder decision)

This section discusses models that assist managers in making these decisions. Both the basic features of these models and their assumptions and simplifications are covered in this chapter.

Costs associated
with goods
for sale

When managing goods for sale in a retail organization, five cost categories are important:

1. *Purchasing costs:* These are usually the largest single category. They can be affected by discounts available for different purchase-order sizes and by credit terms offered by the supplier.
2. **Ordering costs**: These consist of the clerical costs of preparing a purchase order, and the special processing and receiving costs related to the number of orders processed.
3. **Carrying costs**: These costs arise when stocks of goods for sale are held. They consist of the opportunity cost of the investment tied up in inventory (see Chapter 9, page 313) and the costs associated with storage, such as space rental and insurance.
4. *Stockout costs:* A **stockout** arises when a unit of stock is demanded but is not readily available to the customer. A firm may respond to the shortfall by expediting an order from an outside supplier. Expediting costs include the additional ordering costs plus any special associated transportation costs. Alternatively, the firm may lose a sale due to the stockout. In this case, stockout costs include the lost contribution margin on the sale plus any customer ill will generated by the stockout.

---

[1]Representative texts include R. Chase and N. Aquilano, *Production and Operations Management*, 4th ed. (Homewood, Ill.: Richard D. Irwin, 1985); J. McClain and L. Thomas, *Operations Management*, 2nd ed. (Englewood Cliffs, N.J.: Prentice-Hall, 1985); and R. Schmenner, *Production/Operations Management*, 2nd ed. (Chicago, Ill.: SRA, 1984).

[2]From *Food Marketing Outlook* (Washington, D.C.: Food Marketing Institute, 1984).

5. *Quality costs:* The **quality** of a product or service is its conformance with a prespecified (and often preannounced) standard. Quality costs are of two kinds: (i) costs incurred to increase the probability that a delivered product is in conformance with its specifications and (ii) costs incurred when a delivered product is not in conformance with its specifications. Inspection costs are an example of (i). The cost of a replacement product is an example of (ii).

Economic-order-quantity decision model

The **economic-order-quantity (EOQ)** decision model focuses on the trade-off between ordering costs and carrying costs. Assumptions made when using this model include the following:

1. The same fixed quantity (E) is ordered at each reorder point.
2. Demand for the good for sale is known with certainty. There is also certainty about the **purchase-order lead time**, the time between the placement of an order and its delivery.
3. Purchasing cost per unit is unaffected by the quantity ordered. This assumption makes purchasing costs irrelevant to determining the optimal EOQ size.
4. The cost of a stockout is so prohibitively high that inventory is always replenished before a stockout occurs.
5. Costs of quality are recognized in purchase-order size decisions only to the extent that they can be included as a component of ordering costs or carrying costs.

Given these assumptions, the total relevant costs for determining the optimal EOQ will be the sum of the total ordering costs and the total carrying costs:

Total relevant costs = Total ordering costs + Total carrying costs

EXAMPLE

A retailer, Computer Everything Inc., purchases computer diskettes from an outside supplier at $4 per diskette. Annual demand is 5,000 diskettes at a rate of 20 per working day. The lead time for diskette purchases is two weeks. The following cost data are available:

Desired annual return on investment, 10% × $4.00	$ 0.40
Relevant insurance, taxes, breakage per unit per year	0.10
Carrying costs per unit per year	$ 0.50

Costs per purchase order:
Clerical costs, stationery, postage, telephone, receiving, etc. $10.00

What is the economic order quantity for diskettes?

SOLUTION

Exhibit 21-1 deserves careful study. It tabulates the total annual relevant costs under various order sizes. The larger the order size, the higher the annual carrying cost and the lower the annual purchase-order cost. The smaller the order size, the lower the annual carrying cost and the higher the annual purchase-ordering cost. Exhibit 21-2 analyzes the behavior of these two cost functions graphically. The total annual relevant costs will be at a minimum where total purchase-ordering costs and total carrying costs are equal. The EOQ that minimizes the total annual relevant costs in Exhibits 21-1 and 21-2 is 448 units. This optimal EOQ is most easily found by using the formula in the next section.

EOQ formula

The formula underlying the EOQ model is:

$$E' = \sqrt{\frac{2AP}{S}}$$

EXHIBIT 21-1

Annualized Relevant Costs for EOQ Model at Various Order Levels
by Computer Everything Inc. for Diskettes (Assuming 250 Sale Days)

							MINIMUM COST ↓					
A	Demand	5,000	5,000	5,000	5,000	5,000	5,000	5,000	5,000	5,000	5,000	5,000
E	Order size	50	100	200	300	400	448	500	600	800	1,000	5,000
E/2	Average inventory in units*	25	50	100	150	200	224	250	300	400	500	2,500
A/E	Number of purchase orders	100	50	25	16.7	12.5	11.2	10	8.3	6.2	5	1
S(E/2)	Annual carrying costs @ $0.50	$ 12.5	$ 25	$ 50	$ 75	$100	$112	$125	$150	$200	$250	$1,250
P(A/E)	Annual ordering costs @ $10.00	1,000	500	250	167	125	112	100	83	62	50	10
C	Total annual relevant costs	$1,013	$525	$300	$242	$225	$224	$225	$233	$262	$300	$1,260

E = Order size
A = Annual demand in units: 5,000
S = Annual cost of carrying one unit in stock one year: $0.50
P = Cost per purchase order $10.00
C = Total annual relevant costs
*Assume that stock is zero when each order arrives. (Even if a certain minimum inventory were assumed, it has no bearing on the choice here as long as the minimum is the same for each alternative.) Therefore the average inventory relevant to the order decision will be one-half the order quantity. For example, if 600 units are purchased, the inventory on arrival will contain 600. It will gradually diminish at a constant rate until no units are on hand. Therefore the average inventory would be 300; the carrying cost, $0.50 × 300, or $150.

EXHIBIT 21-2

Graphic Analysis of Economic Order Quantity
for Computer Everything Inc.

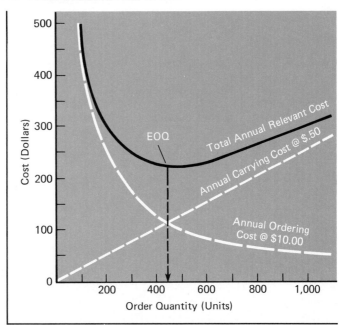

where E' = economic order quantity; A = demand in units; P = cost per purchase order; and S = cost of carrying one unit in stock for the time period used for A (one year in this example).

This formula can be illustrated with the data for Computer Everything Inc.:

$$E' = \sqrt{\frac{2(5,000)(\$10)}{\$0.50}} = \sqrt{\frac{\$100,000}{\$0.50}} = \sqrt{200,000}$$

$$E' = 447.21$$

$$E' = 448 \text{ units}$$

The total relevant costs can be calculated using the following formula:[3]

$$C = \frac{AP}{E} + \frac{ES}{2}$$

$$C = \frac{5,000 \times \$10}{448} + \frac{448 \times \$0.50}{2}$$

$$C = \$112 + \$112 = \$224 \text{ (rounded to nearest dollar)}$$

When to order assuming certainty

The **reorder point** is the quantity level of the inventory that triggers a new order being placed. The reorder is simplest to compute when there is certainty about both the demand and the lead time. Consider our Computer Everything Inc. example of diskette purchases:

Economic order quantity	448 diskettes
Sales per week	100 diskettes
Lead time for diskette purchases	2 weeks

$$\text{Reorder point} = \text{Sales per unit of time} \times \text{Lead time}$$

$$= 100 \times 2 = 200 \text{ diskettes}$$

---

[3]This formula for total relevant costs can be used to illustrate the derivation, via calculus, of the EOQ formula:

$$(1) \qquad C = \frac{AP}{E} + \frac{ES}{2}$$

$$(2) \qquad \frac{dC}{dE} = \frac{-AP}{E^2} + \frac{S}{2}$$

$$(3) \qquad \text{Set } \frac{dC}{dE} = 0; \quad \frac{S}{2} - \frac{AP}{E^2} = 0$$

$$(4) \qquad SE^2 = 2AP$$

$$(5) \qquad E^2 = \frac{2AP}{S}$$

$$(6) \qquad E = \sqrt{\frac{2AP}{S}}$$

EXHIBIT 21-3

Inventory Level of Diskettes at Computer Everything Inc. Assuming Certainty of Demand and Lead Time

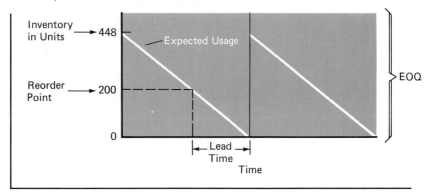

The graph in Exhibit 21-3 presents the behavior of the inventory level of diskettes assuming demand occurs uniformly throughout each week.[4] If the lead time is two weeks, a new order will be placed when the inventory level reaches 200 diskettes.

Safety stocks

Exhibit 21-3 assumes that there is certainty about both the demand for diskettes and the lead time. Where there is uncertainty about the demand or about the timing or amount that suppliers can provide, retailers often hold safety stocks. **Safety stock** is the minimum or buffer inventory that is held as a cushion against unexpected increases in demand. Assume that Computer Everything Inc. believes that while the expected weekly demand is 100 diskettes per week, a maximum demand of 140 diskettes may occur in some weeks. If Computer Everything decides that the cost of a stockout is prohibitive, it may decide to hold safety stock of 80 diskettes (maximum excess demand of 40 per week for 2 weeks of lead time).

Computation of safety stocks

In our example, we used 80 diskettes as a safety stock. The computation of safety stocks hinges on demand forecasts. The executive will have some notion—usually based on past experience—of the range of daily demand: the percentage chance (probability) that exists for usages of various quantities.

A frequency distribution based on prior daily or weekly levels of demand will offer data for constructing the associated costs of maintaining safety (minimum) stocks. The major relevant costs are the carrying costs and the stockout costs. For example, suppose a customer calls Computer Everything Inc. to buy ten diskettes. The store has none at the moment, but it can supply them within 24 hours at an extra payment to the supplier of $0.80 per diskette. The customer is willing to wait the 24 hours. The stockout cost in this case is a minimum of $0.80 per diskette. **The optimum safety-stock level exists where the costs of carrying an extra unit are exactly counterbalanced by the expected stockout costs.** This would be the level that minimizes the annual total stockout costs and carrying costs.

---

[4]This handy but special formula does not apply where the receipt of the standard order fails to increase stocks to the order-point quantity; for example, where the lead time is three weeks and the standard order is a one-week supply. In these cases, there will be overlapping of orders. The order point will be average usage during lead time plus safety stock *minus orders placed but not yet received*. This is really the general formula for computing the reorder point. For elaboration, see almost any book on inventory systems.

Suppose the total demand for diskettes at Computer Everything during the two-week lead time is expected to be:

								TOTAL PROBABILITY
Total demand	80	120	160	200	240	280	320	
Probability	.04	.06	.20	.40	.20	.06	.04	1.00

Thus, if we decide to use a reorder point equal to 200 units plus a safety stock, we could expect the following stockout results:

Probability of stockout	.20	.06	.04
Total actual demand during lead time	240	280	320
Less expected demand provided for	200	200	200
Stockouts if provision is also made for a safety stock of:			
zero units	40	80	120
40 units	0	40	80
80 units	0	0	40
120 units	0	0	0

Exhibit 21-4 presents the total sum of stockout and carrying costs assuming the stockout cost is $0.80 per diskette and the carrying cost is $0.50 per unit per year. Of the safety-stock levels presented in Exhibit 21-4, the total stockout and carrying costs are minimized at $54 when a safety stock of 80 diskettes is maintained.

EXHIBIT 21-4
Computation of Safety Stock

		STOCKOUT COSTS					
SAFETY-STOCK LEVELS IN UNITS	PROBABILITY OF STOCKOUT	Stockout In Units	Stockout Cost*	Orders Per Year†	Expected Stockout Cost‡	CARRYING COST§	TOTAL COSTS
0	.20	40	$32	11.2	$ 72		
	.06	80	64	11.2	43		
	.04	120	96	11.2	43		
					$158	$ 0	$158
40	.06	40	$32	11.2	$ 22		
	.04	80	64	11.2	29		
					$ 51	$20	$ 71
80	.04	40	$32	11.2	$ 14	$40	$ 54
120	.00	0	$ 0	11.2	$ 0	$60	$ 60

*Stockout units × stockout cost of $0.80.
†Annual demand 5,000 ÷ 448 EOQ = 11.2 orders per year.
‡Stockout cost × probability × number of orders per year.
§Safety stock × annual carrying cost of 50¢ per unit. Assumptions: Safety stock is on hand at all times and there is no overstocking caused by decreases in expected usage.

Extensions of the basic EOQ model

The EOQ model described in this section has been extended in several different directions. One extension incorporates a stockout cost into the model. The result is that carrying costs, ordering costs, and stockout costs are simultaneously considered in computing the economic order quantity. Another extension is to allow for price breaks because of (say) quantity discounts being available. The result is that acquisition costs, carrying costs, ordering costs, and stockout costs are simultaneously considered in computing the economic order quantity. A third extension is to allow for an announced price increase that comes into effect after a time period in which the existing price is available. Use of this model can result in an increase in the order size made while the existing purchase price is in effect.

Control classifications and the ABC method

Sometimes it is difficult to comprehend the enormous number of items that retailers must keep in stock—up to 50,000, and often more. An effective inventory-control system typically will not have all items in the inventory treated in the same manner under the same control techniques.

The ABC Method is an inventory control technique that divides items into subclassifications and uses different control systems for each classification. For example, one firm reported the following breakdown of its inventory:

	ITEMS		DOLLARS	
CLASS	Number of Items	Percent of Total	Total Cost	Percent of Total
A	2,500	5%	$14,400,000	72%
B	12,500	25	3,800,000	19
C	35,000	70	1,800,000	9
	50,000	100%	$20,000,000	100%

Note that only 5% of the items represent 72% of the total cost. In general, the greatest degree of continuous control would be exerted over these A items.

ACCOUNTING DATA AND MANAGING GOODS FOR SALE

Difficulties of estimating cost parameters

Obtaining accurate estimates of the cost parameters used in EOQ models is a challenging task. For example, the relevant carrying costs in the EOQ models consist of *outlay* costs for such items as insurance and property taxes, plus the *opportunity cost* of capital. How is the opportunity cost to be computed? Most internal reporting systems do not formally record opportunity costs. Suppose the required rate of return is 20% on invested capital. To what items is the 20% applicable?

Many simplifying assumptions underlie the EOQ model. In particular, the opportunity cost of capital pertains only to costs that vary with the number of units purchased and that are incurred at the time the units are received. In other words, an "interest" opportunity cost must be charged because of the decision to carry inventory. The theory is that such a cost would not exist if the units could be acquired at the instant of their use or sale.

721

The following table summarizes how some commonly encountered issues that arise in estimating the opportunity cost of capital should be handled:

ITEMS TO WHICH OPPORTUNITY COST OF CAPITAL PERTAINS	
Yes	*No*
1. Invoiced acquisition cost of goods.	1. Fixed overhead, whether expressed as a total or as a cost per unit.
2. Freight in, when variable and identified with units.	2. The costs of ordering, which are identified as P in the EOQ formula. These costs are unaffected by the number of units ordered. Examples include clerical costs, setup costs, and flat freight costs per truck or ship where the total costs are unaffected by the number of units ordered.
3. Unloading, inspection, cleaning, and placing in stock upon receipt.	3. Inspection or cleaning costs while in inventory or upon withdrawal for sale.
	4. Insurance costs that depend on the number of units in inventory. These are regarded as part of S, the costs of carrying, but not as part of the invested capital.

Opportunity costs not recorded in many internal accounting systems are also relevant to estimating stockout costs. When a sale is forgone because of an item being out of stock, the opportunity cost includes the lost contribution margin on that sale, as well as lost contribution margins on potential future sales that will not be made to the disgruntled customer.

Cost of a prediction error

Return to Exhibit 21-2. Note that the total annual relevant cost curve is relatively flat over the range from 300 to 600 order quantity sizes. The square root in the EOQ model formula reduces the sensitivity of the model to errors in predicting its inputs.

Suppose the actual carrying cost of Computer Everything Inc. is $1.00 instead of the $0.50 prediction used in Exhibits 21-1 and 21-2. The cost of this prediction error can be calculated using the three-step procedure outlined in Appendix 9A (pp. 322–24):

Step One: Compute the monetary outcome from the best action that could have been taken, given knowledge of the actual value of the cost input. The appropriate inputs are $A = 5,000$ units, $S = \$1.00$, and $P = \$10.00$. The optimal order quantity size is:

$$E' = \sqrt{\frac{2AP}{S}}$$

$$E' = \sqrt{\frac{2 \times 5,000 \times \$10}{\$1.00}} = \sqrt{\frac{\$100,000}{\$1.00}} = \sqrt{100,000}$$

$$E' = 316.23 \approx 316$$

The total relevant cost when $E' = 316$ is:

$$C = \frac{AP}{E} + \frac{ES}{2}$$

$$C = \frac{5,000 \times \$10}{316} + \frac{316 \times \$1.00}{2}$$

$$C = \$158 + \$158 \approx \$316 \text{ (rounded to nearest dollar)}$$

Step Two: Compute the monetary outcome from the planned course of action when the decision is based on the predicted value of the cost input. The planned cost of action when carrying costs are predicted to be $0.50 is to purchase in order quantities of 448 units. The total relevant cost using this order quantity size when $A = 5,000$ units, $S = \$1.00$, and $P = \$10.00$ is:

$$C = \frac{AP}{E} + \frac{ES}{2}$$

$$C = \frac{5,000 \times \$10}{448} + \frac{448 \times \$1.00}{2}$$

$$C = \$112 + \$224 \approx \$336 \text{ (rounded to nearest dollar)}$$

Step Three: Compute the difference between the monetary outcome from Step One and the monetary outcome from Step Two.

	MONETARY OUTCOME
Step One	$316
Step Two	336
Difference	$ (20)

The cost of the prediction error is only $20. A salient feature of the EOQ model is that the total relevant cost is rarely sensitive to minor variations in cost predictions.

Goal-congruence issues

The EOQ decision model highlights that opportunity costs are important components of the total relevant costs associated with goods for resale. However, the absence of recorded opportunity costs in conventional accounting systems raises the possibility of a conflict between the order size that the EOQ model indicates as optimal and the size that the stores manager regards as optimal.

Reconsider Exhibit 21-1 (p. 717). **If annual carrying costs are not included in the measures used to evaluate the performance of store managers, they may favor purchasing larger order sizes than is implied by the EOQ decision model. Of course, the answer to this conflict is to design the performance evaluation system so that the carrying costs are charged to the appropriate manager.** For example, we frequently see systems where an "imputed interest" charge is levied against managers for the inventories under their responsibility. This practice inhibits managers from overbuying stocks, a common temptation.

The inventory area provides another illustration of why accountants and managers must be alert to the motivational implications of failing to dovetail a performance-evaluation model with the decision model favored by top management.

JUST-IN-TIME PURCHASING

Organizations are giving increased attention to the potential gains from (i) making smaller and more frequent purchase orders and (ii) restructuring their relationship with suppliers. Both (i) and (ii) are related to the heightened interest in just-in-time purchasing systems. Just-in-time (JIT) purchasing involves the purchase of goods such that delivery immediately precedes demand or use; in the extreme, no inventories (goods for sale for a retailer; raw materials for a manufacturer) would be held with JIT purchasing.

Organizations that have moved toward JIT purchasing have made substantial changes in their purchasing practices:[5]

- A reduction in the number of suppliers for each item, with an associated reduction in negotiation time. For example, a division of Xerox reduced its suppliers from 5,000 to 300.
- The use of longer-term contracts with suppliers, with minimal paperwork involved in each individual transaction. Each purchase transaction may involve only a single telephone call or a single computer entry.
- Minimal checking by purchasers of the quantity and quality of goods shipped. In the initial negotiations, suppliers are made aware of the premium placed on the delivery of high-quality goods of the exact quantity ordered.
- Payment to suppliers is made for batches of deliveries rather than for each individual delivery. For example, the materials receiving group at one Hewlett-Packard plant sends receiving documents to Accounts Payable only on a weekly basis. Computer software programs then guide the "matching" of each receiving document with the purchase-order number. A computer program then sums all amounts due to each supplier, and a single check is written to each supplier.

These changes in purchasing practices can give rise to substantial reductions in the cost of placing each individual purchase order.[6]

Organizations using JIT purchasing will often stress the "hidden costs" associated with holding high inventory levels. Retailers have long recognized these costs in relation to perishable goods. For example, daily deliveries of bread and milk to supermarkets have occurred for many years. Retailers using JIT purchasing now are attempting to extend daily deliveries to as many areas as possible so that the goods spend less time in warehouses.

Some vendors are highly cooperative in attempts by firms to adopt JIT pur-

---

[5]C. Hahn, P. Pinto, and D. Bragg, "Just-in-Time Production and Purchasing," *Journal of Purchasing and Materials Management,* Fall 1983, pp. 2–10; and R. Schonberger, *World Class Manufacturing* (New York: Free Press, 1986), Chap. 9.

[6]Note that these changes in purchasing practices do not require adoption of a JIT purchasing policy. Indeed, for most retailers, some level of inventory holdings is inevitable unless customers are willing to inform retailers of their demands in advance.

chasing. For example, consider the Frito-Lay company, which has a dominant market share in potato chips and other snack foods. Frito-Lay operates with more frequent deliveries than many of its competitors. Its corporate strategy emphasizes service to retailers and consistency of product quality delivered to consumers. A subsequent section of this chapter illustrates how the costs of ensuring quality products and services can be quantified. **Companies moving toward JIT purchasing often argue that the costs of carrying inventories (especially those related to ensuring product quality) have been dramatically underestimated in the past.**

Successful adoption of just-in-time purchasing has been reported by both retail and manufacturing organizations. Firms with large-scale manufacturing facilities (such as Ford, General Motors, and General Electric) encourage suppliers to locate their plants in geographic proximity; the benefits to the purchasing firm include greater supply reliability and lower costs if vendors pass along some of the savings in transportation costs. JIT purchasing can also be applied by firms buying raw materials from several countries or even several continents. For example, Coleco used JIT purchasing at its two assembly plants—in Amsterdam (New York) and Tustin (California)—for Cabbage Patch Doll kits at the height of their popularity. The dolls were manufactured in Hong Kong and Taiwan; the diapers and clothes were obtained from Hong Kong, Taiwan, and North Carolina; and the adoption papers were prepared by various vendors in the United States. Coleco used daily deliveries by an international air courier service to help implement its JIT purchasing policy.

Exhibit 21-5 uses the EOQ model to illustrate the economics of smaller and

EXHIBIT 21-5

Effect of Changes in Cost Estimates for Parameters P and S on Total Cost Functions and on EOQ for Computer Everything Inc.

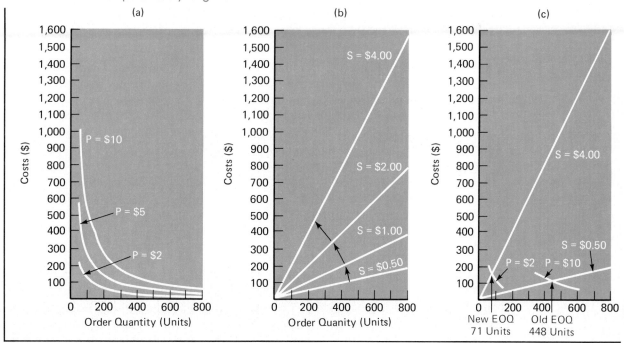

more frequent purchase orders. Reductions in the economic order quantity can be driven by:

(i) Reductions in the estimated cost of placing purchase orders, or
(ii) Increases in the estimated cost of carrying inventories.

The data in Exhibit 21-5 use the data in Exhibit 21-2. Panel A of Exhibit 21-5 shows how total annual purchase-order costs decrease when the purchase cost per order (P) is reduced from $10 to $5 to $2. Panel B of Exhibit 21-5 shows how total annual carrying costs increase when the annual carrying cost per unit (S) is increased from $0.50 to $1.00 to $2.00 to $4.00. Panel C of Exhibit 21-5 compares the EOQ at several combinations of P and S:

$P = \$10;\ S = \$0.50$	$P = \$2;\ S = \$4.00$
EOQ = 448 units	EOQ = 71 units

With an EOQ of 448 units and sales of 100 diskettes per week, deliveries are made every 31 days: $(448 \div 100) \times 7 \simeq 31$ days. With an EOQ of 71 units and sales of 100 diskettes per week, deliveries are made every 5 days: $(71 \div 100) \times 7 \simeq 5$ days.

The analysis in Exhibit 21-5 is a convenient way to present the economic intuition underlying JIT purchasing. Do not assume, however, that a JIT purchasing policy will always be guided by an EOQ model. The EOQ model assumes a constant order size for every order. If demand fluctuates, a JIT purchasing policy may well require differing order sizes for each order.

MANAGING MATERIALS IN MANUFACTURING ORGANIZATIONS

Managers in manufacturing organizations face the challenging task of producing high-quality products at competitive-cost levels. These managers can select from several basic approaches, including batch manufacturing and constant-flow manufacturing (see Exhibit 17-2 on page 584). Numerous techniques have been developed to assist managers in their planning or implementation activities. These techniques include computer-integrated manufacturing (CIM), flexible-manufacturing systems (FMS), just-in-time (JIT), materials requirements planning (MRP), and optimized production technology (OPT). The jargon used in describing techniques in this area can be overwhelming. One production manager commented: "Producing high-quality, low-cost products in competition with the Japanese is challenging but manageable. Understanding how CIM, FMS, JIT, MRP, and OPT relate to each other is both unmanageable and a time-sink."

This section outlines the key features of MRP and JIT and the role of accounting information in each of these techniques. Our descriptions of MRP and JIT are necessarily brief and simple. Be careful when examining the manufacturing systems of individual firms. They vary in the labels used to describe their system. Moreover, the vendors of manufacturing techniques use much license in labeling their individual products.

Materials requirements planning (MRP) is a planning system that focuses first on the amount and timing of finished goods demanded and then determines the derived demand for raw materials, components, and subassemblies at each of the prior stages of production.[7] A production structure diagram is a useful way to gain an overview of the production process and its materials requirements. Exhibit 21-6 presents such a diagram that has three end products (FG 1, FG 2, and FG 3). Working backward, each end product is sequentially exploded (that is, separated) into its necessary components and raw materials. Exhibit 21-6 illustrates that four direct materials (DM 1, DM 2, DM 3, and DM 4) are purchased for finished goods. For both FG 1 and FG 3, the raw materials are used to produce components before production of the end product. For FG 2, no intermediary components are produced.

Key components of an MRP system include the following:

1. Master Production Schedule, which specifies both the quantity and the timing of each item to be produced.
2. Bill of Materials File, which outlines the materials, components, and subassemblies for each end product. MRP distinguishes outside purchases from components derived from prior steps in the production process.
3. Inventory Report for Each Part, Component, or Subassembly, in which each such item is carried in a separate computer file with details on the number of items on hand and the arrival times and quantities of items scheduled to be received.
4. Lead times of all items to be purchased, and standard construction times for all components and subassemblies produced internally.

EXHIBIT 21-6
Production Structure Diagram Underlying an MRP System

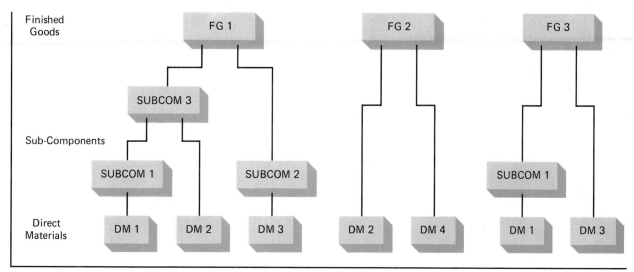

---

[7]MRP is sometimes used to describe materials resource planning, which is a planning system that considers such items as capacity planning and labor scheduling as well as materials planning. Common terminology is MRP I for materials requirements planning and MRP II for materials resource planning.

Given the information in the MRP system, computer algorithms can determine how changes in the demand for individual finished goods will affect the demand for raw materials, components, and subassemblies. For instance, when a customer requests that a large order be deferred for one month, an MRP system will help readjust the raw-materials purchases and the production schedules.

The accountant can play several important roles in the design and operation of an MRP system.[8] First, MRP requires much detailed information pertaining to inventories, work in process, and finished goods. A major cause of unsuccessful attempts to implement MRP has been the problem of collecting and updating inventory reports. The chances of its successful operation will be improved by combining the talents of manufacturing personnel and accountants in the early stages of implementing an MRP system. For complex multistage manufacturing systems, the required records can cover thousands of parts, raw materials, components, and finished goods. Unless this information is both accurate and timely, many of the benefits of using an MRP approach can be lost.

A second role of the accountant consists of providing estimates of the cost of setting up each unit of a plant, the cost of downtime, and the cost of holding inventory. Some operations managers attempt to combine MRP with decisions about optimal production lot sizes for substages of the production process. Where the costs of setting up machines or subunits of the production line are high (e.g., as with a blast furnace in an integrated steel mill), the benefits from using optimal production lot sizes can be considerable. Similarly, where the costs of downtime are high, there can be sizable benefits from maintaining a continuity of production. The challenge facing the accountant in this context is to recognize interdependencies in the product line. For example, downtime at one stage of a production line can also have ripple effects at subsequent stages in the production line.

Just-in-time
production

Just-in-time (JIT) production is a system whereby each component on a production line is produced immediately as needed by the next step in the production line. JIT production includes three key features:

1. The production line is run on a demand-pull basis, so that activity at each work station is authorized by the demand of downstream work stations.

2. Emphasis is placed on minimizing the production lead time of each unit. The **production lead time** is the interval between the first stage of production and the time that the finished good comes off the production line.

3. The production line is stopped if parts are absent or defective work is discovered. Stoppage creates an urgency about correcting problems that cause defective units. Each employee puts a premium on minimizing potential sources of stoppages (such as defective raw-material parts).

JIT production has as its underlying philosophy the simplification of the production process so that only essential activities are conducted. This simplification has been extended by several JIT adopters to the internal reporting sys-

---

[8]For a discussion of the role of accounting data in an MRP system, see P. Deis, "Using an MRP System for Financial Decision Support," *Journal of Accounting and EDP*, Winter 1986, pp. 38–48. See also R. Vollum, "Cost Accounting: The Key to Capturing Cost Information on the Factory Floor," *Journal of Accounting and EDP*, Summer 1985, pp. 44–51.

tem.[9] The bill of materials in several JIT plants has only two entries: first, when raw materials are put on the start of the production line; and second, when finished goods leave the production line. The rationales for using simplified bills of materials with JIT include the following:

1. Materials control in JIT plants can best be accomplished by a manager's personal observations. The absence of large amounts of raw materials and work-in-process inventory means that managers can quickly observe and monitor the existing material and work in process.
2. Work in process constitutes a lower percentage of the total cost of production because of the reductions in lead time and the demand-pull feature of production.
3. There is more homogeneity in the units processed with JIT because of the reduction in rework.

Firms adopting JIT production report a reduction in the role of cost accounting in the day-to-day control of operations at the plant level. Emphasis is likely to be placed on nonfinancial performance measures such as

- Production lead time

- $\dfrac{\text{Total setup time for machines}}{\text{Total production time}}$

- $\dfrac{\text{Number of defective units}}{\text{Total number of units started}}$

This heavy use of nonfinancial performance measures in the control of operations at the plant level also occurs at plants using process costing. For example, chemical-processing plants and oil-refining plants rely heavily on physical yield measures per gallon of material inputs when monitoring the day-to-day operating performance at plants.

Exhibit 21-7 summarizes the effects Hewlett-Packard reported from adopting JIT at several of its production plants. More details on JIT production and JIT accounting are in Chapter 17, pp. 588–93. Readers who have not read this section of Chapter 17 are encouraged to do so.

MEASURING THE COSTS OF PRODUCT QUALITY

The manufacturing and delivery of high-quality products is a pivotal objective for many organizations. More and more firms are publicly committing themselves to delivering high-quality products or services to their customers.[10] The following public release by the Commercial Tape Division of 3M is illustrative:

It is our basic operating philosophy to concentrate on prevention methods to make quality a way of life and perpetuate an attitude of "Do It Right the First Time."

---

[9] Chapter 10 of Schonberger, *World Class Manufacturing*, gives examples of simplifications in cost accounting being associated with simplifications in production methods. See also J. Patell, "Adapting a Cost Accounting System to Just-in-Time Manufacturing: The Hewlett-Packard Personal Office Computer Division," (Working paper, Stanford University, 1986).

[10] For an overview of quality programs at corporations, see P. Crosby, *Quality without Tears* (New York: McGraw-Hill, 1984).

EXHIBIT 21-7
Effects of JIT Production

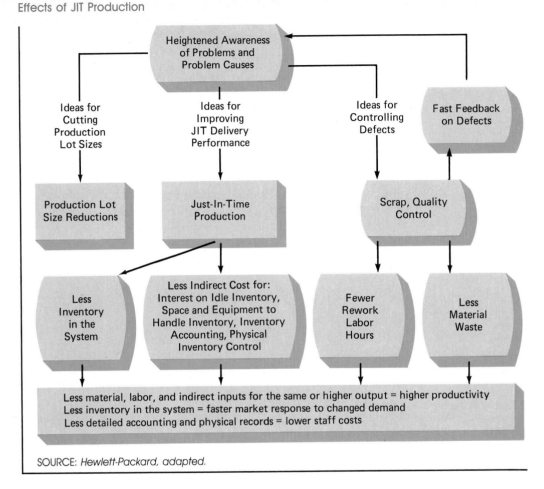

SOURCE: *Hewlett-Packard, adapted.*

Quality of a product or service means its conformance with a prespecified (and often preannounced) standard. Using this definition, a McDonald's hamburger can be a high-quality product, while filet mignon at a five-star restaurant can be a low-quality product.

Cost accounting can make a significant contribution to product quality programs. Accountants can collect and report the many diverse costs that fall under the product quality umbrella. Reports can highlight trends in these costs, as well as their often very high absolute level. Four categories of costs associated with product quality programs that several firms have found useful are:

1. **Prevention costs:** These focus on preventing the production of products that do not conform to specification. Individual cost components include supplier evaluations and supplier quality seminars, employee training, equipment design reviews, machine-tooling calibration, and preventive maintenance.

2. **Appraisal costs:** These focus on detecting which individual products of those produced do not conform to specification. Individual cost components include inspection and testing programs for materials, work in process and finished goods, and engineering programs (such as statistical quality control).

3. **Internal failure costs:** These focus on costs incurred when a nonconforming product is detected *before* its shipment to customers. Individual components include rework costs, scrap, space costs for rework and scrap, tooling changes, and downtime costs.

4. **External failure costs:** These focus on costs incurred when a nonconforming product is detected *after* its shipment to customers. Individual components include the cost of returned products, work done under warranty, product liability costs, and the customer ill will created by the sale of defective products. Consumer surveys are one approach used to estimate the loss of potential future sales because of defects in existing products.

The individual cost items included in these categories come from many different functional areas, such as purchasing, production, distribution, and marketing. The cost of initially developing, and then maintaining, a cost of quality internal-reporting system can be high. However, firms implementing these systems are enthusiastic advocates of their value. Two benefits frequently cited are (i) the ability to monitor trends in the aggregate costs of quality, as well as in individual items; and (ii) the increased importance that product quality assumes when the total costs of quality are communicated to all members of the organization.[11]

Exhibit 21-8 presents the cost of quality reporting format developed by the

EXHIBIT 21-8
Cost of Quality Reporting at Celanese Fibers Operations

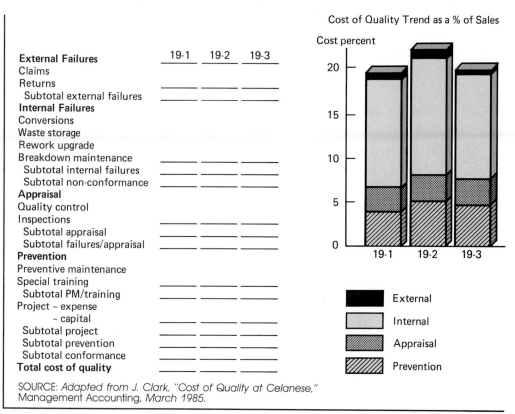

SOURCE: *Adapted from J. Clark, "Cost of Quality at Celanese,"* Management Accounting, *March 1985.*

[11] Articles discussing quality cost measures include W. Morse, "Measuring Quality Costs," *Cost and Management*, July-August 1983, pp. 16–20; and J. Clark, "Cost of Quality at Celanese," *Management Accounting*, March 1985, pp. 42–46.

Fibers Operations Division of Celanese Corporation. This division presents each report in dollar terms and as a percentage of sales. The cost of quality at Celanese's Fibers Operations Division has ranged between 18% and 22% of sales. (Celanese does not include estimates of future lost sales because of defects in existing products in its external failure cost computations.)

SUMMARY

The delivery to customers of competitively priced, high-quality products or services is fundamental to the success (even survival) of many organizations. There is now increased effort involved in reducing product costs while improving product quality.

Five cost categories important to managing goods for sale in a retail organization are purchasing costs, ordering costs, carrying costs, stockout costs, and quality costs. The economic-order-quantity (EOQ) model highlights the implications of ordering costs and carrying costs for the total relevant costs of different purchase-order quantity sizes. Accounting information that is used to estimate inputs for the EOQ model includes those routinely recorded in the accounting system, as well as opportunity costs not routinely recorded.

A major trend in organizations is a reduction in the level of inventories held. This trend in part reflects downward revisions in estimates of ordering costs, and upward revisions in estimates of carrying costs. The trend also reflects the growing body of evidence that the costs of delivering a high-quality product increase:

1. When goods are held in warehouses or sit for a long time on a retailer's shop floor
2. When raw materials or finished goods are held in storage areas, and when work in process is allowed to accumulate beyond that immediately demanded by subsequent stages in the production process

Where major changes occur in manufacturing practice or philosophy, accountants should consider whether a change in their existing reporting system can provide better information for planning and control. Some manufacturing changes can reduce the accountant's role in day-to-day operations. For example, bill of materials records are less detailed in many JIT production plants; control of materials relies heavily on personal observation by plant operating line workers. Other manufacturing changes can increase the accountant's role. For example, several firms have made sizable investments in accounting systems that measure the costs associated with their product quality programs.

Terms to Learn

The chapter and the Glossary contain definitions of the following important terms:

appraisal costs (p. 730)   *carrying costs (715)*
economic order quantity (EOQ) (716)   *external failure costs (731)*
internal failure costs (731)   *just-in-time (JIT) production (728)*
just-in-time (JIT) purchasing (724)
materials requirements planning (MRP) (727)   *operations management (714)*
ordering costs (715)   *prevention costs (730)*   *production lead time (728)*
purchase-order lead time (716)   *quality (716)*   *reorder point (718)*
safety stock (719)   *stockout (715)*

Special Points and Pitfalls

The management of materials and inventories is one of many specific topics in the operations management area. We chose to focus on this topic for two reasons:

1. Materials costs (goods for sale in retail; cost of products in manufacturing) are one of the largest single cost categories in most nonservice organizations.
2. Accounting information plays a key role in decisions relating to the management of materials and inventories.

The EOQ model illustrates how total carrying costs and total ordering costs behave differently as changes in the order quantity size are made. It also provides insight into how reductions in ordering costs and increases in carrying costs can make more frequent orders of smaller order quantities the optimal purchasing policy.

The potential conflict between decision models and performance evaluation models is exemplified by the EOQ model. The opportunity cost of the interest on the investment in inventory plays a key role in the EOQ decision model. Still, many organizations measure managerial performance on the basis of total costs or total profits without providing for any opportunity cost of interest.

PROBLEMS FOR SELF-STUDY

problem 1   Consumer Numero Uno (CNO) is deciding on the economic order quantity for the two brands of potato chips it carries: Frito Special and Captain Crisp. The following information is collected:

	FRITO SPECIAL	CAPTAIN CRISP
Annual demand	12,000 lots	6,000 lots
Ordering cost per lot	$5	$6
Annual carrying cost per lot	$11	$9

A *lot* is a carton containing 100 one-pound packages of potato chips. The wholesale price per lot to CNO is $100 for Frito Special, and $90 for Captain Crisp. The supermarket is open 300 days each year.

Required
1. Compute the EOQ for Frito Special and Captain Crisp.
2. How regularly will deliveries be made to CNO by the distributor for Frito Special and the distributor for Captain Crisp?

solution 1   1.

FRITO SPECIAL	CAPTAIN CRISP
$A = 12,000$	$A = 6,000$
$P = \$5$	$P = \$6$
$S = \$11$	$S = \$9$

$$E' = \sqrt{\frac{2(12,000)(\$5)}{(\$11)}} \qquad E' = \sqrt{\frac{2(6,000)(\$6)}{\$9}}$$

$$E' = 104.45 \qquad\qquad E' = 89.44$$

$$E' \simeq 104 \text{ lots per order} \qquad E' \simeq 89 \text{ lots per order}$$

2. Number of deliveries per year is $A \div E'$:

$$\text{Frito Special: } 12,000 \div 104 = 115.38$$

$$\approx 115 \text{ deliveries}$$

$$\text{Captain Crisp: } 6,000 \div 89 = 67.41$$

$$\approx 67 \text{ deliveries}$$

Average time between deliveries is the number of working days ÷ number of deliveries per year:

$$\text{Frito Special: } 300 \div 115 = 2.61 \text{ working days}$$

$$\text{Captain Crisp: } 300 \div 67 = 4.48 \text{ working days}$$

problem 2   CNO signs a long-term contract with the Frito Special distributor that changed its procedure for making purchase orders. The new procedure involves a single entry into a computer network operated by the Frito Special distributor. CNO's new ordering cost per lot will be $2. CNO reexamined its sales pattern and reestimated its annual carrying cost per lot to $14.

Required
1. Consider the new estimated ordering and carrying costs. Compute CNO's economic order quantity and the number of deliveries per year for Frito Special.
2. How might your answers to requirement 1 provide insight into a just-in-time purchasing policy?

solution 2   1.

$$\text{Frito Special: } A = 12,000$$

$$P = \$2$$

$$S = \$14$$

$$E' = \sqrt{\frac{2(12,000)(\$2)}{\$14}}$$

$$E' = 58.55 \text{ lots per order}$$

$$E' \approx 59 \text{ lots per order}$$

Number of deliveries per year:

$$\frac{A}{E} = \frac{12,000}{59} = 203.39 \approx 203 \text{ deliveries per year}$$

2. A just-in-time purchasing policy involves the purchase of goods such that delivery immediately precedes demand. The decrease in CNO's EOQ from 104 lots to 59 lots would increase the number of deliveries from 115 to 203 per year. By restructuring relationships with its supplier, CNO has dramatically reduced its ordering costs. This pattern is a familiar one with firms adopting JIT purchasing.

_____QUESTIONS, PROBLEMS, AND CASES_____

21-1   What is *operations management?*

21-2   Give two examples of decisions that fall under the operations management umbrella.

21-3   Name five cost categories important when managing goods for sale in a retail organization.

21-4 Give three examples of specific cost items associated with managing goods for sale that typically are not routinely recorded in the accounting system.

21-5 "Identical space costs for inventory can be zero during some months and sizable during other months." Explain.

21-6 "The practical approach to determining economic order quantity is concerned with locating a minimum cost range rather than a minimum cost point." Explain.

21-7 What is *just-in-time purchasing?*

21-8 Name two cost factors that can explain why an organization finds it cost effective to make smaller and more frequent purchase orders.

21-9 "We have placed inventories on the wrong side of the balance sheet. They are a liability, not an asset." Comment on this statement.

21-10 What is *materials requirements planning?*

21-11 Define *product quality.*

21-12 Name four categories of costs associated with product quality programs.

21-13 Economic order quantity for retailer. True-Value Hardware (TVH) is deciding the purchase-order size for its standard line of neon light fittings. Annual demand is 18,000 units. Cost per purchase order is $16. Carrying cost per light fitting unit is $1.50 per year. TVH uses an economic-order-quantity model in its purchasing decisions. The store is open 360 days a year.

Required
1. Calculate TVH's economic purchasing order quantity for neon light fittings.
2. Assume demand is known with certainty and the purchasing lead time is five days. Calculate TVH's reorder point for neon light fittings.

21-14 Economic order quantity for retailer. The Cloth Centre sells fabrics to a wide range of industrial and consumer users. One of its products is denim cloth, used in the manufacture of jeans and carrying bags. The purchasing officer of the Cloth Centre has collected the following information:

Annual demand for denim cloth	20,000 yards
Cost of placing each purchase order	$60
Cost of carrying each yard per year	20% of cost
Safety stock requirements	None
Cost of denim cloth	$3 per yard

The purchasing lead time is two weeks. The Cloth Centre is open 250 days a year (50 weeks for 5 days a week).

Required
1. Calculate the economic order quantity for denim cloth.
2. Calculate the number of orders that will be placed each year.
3. Calculate the reorder point for denim cloth.

21-15 Inventory control computations. Lt. Brighteyes, supply officer at a remote radar site, has been informed that the lead time for his supplies will be reduced from the present 180 days to 90 days.

The maximum daily usage of 12AU6 tubes has been 10 per day; average, 8 per day; minimum, 6 per day. Average inventory during the past two years has been 1,360 tubes.

1. Determine the safety stock, reorder point, normal maximum stock level, absolute maximum stock level, and the economic order quantity that Lt. Brighteyes has been submitting.
2. Do the same for the new 90-day level, *assuming that the economic order size is unchanged*.

21-16 Purchase-order size for retailer, EOQ, just-in-time purchasing. (Alternate is 21-17.) The *24 Hour Mart* operates a chain of supermarkets. Its best-selling soft drink is Fruitslice. Demand in April 19_2 for Fruitslice at its Memphis supermarket is estimated to be 6,000 cases (24 cans in each case). In March 19_2, the Memphis supermarket estimated the cost of placing each purchase order (P) for Fruitslice to be $30. The cost of carrying (S) each case of Fruitslice in inventory for a month was estimated to be $1.

At the end of March 19_2, the Memphis *24 Hour Mart* reestimated its cost of carrying to be $1.50 per case per month to take account of an increase in warehouse-related costs.

During March 19_2, *24 Hour Mart* restructured its relationship with suppliers. It reduced the number of suppliers from 600 to 180. Long-term contracts were signed only with those suppliers that agreed to make product quality checks before products were shipped to each supermarket. Each purchase order would be made by linking into the supplier's computer network. The Memphis *24 Hour Mart* estimated these changes would reduce the cost of placing each order to $5.

The *24 Hour Mart* is open 30 days in April 19_2.

1. Calculate the optimal order quantity in April 19_2 for Fruitslice. Use the EOQ model and assume in turn:
   (a) $A = 6,000$; $P = \$30$; $S = \$1$
   (b) $A = 6,000$; $P = \$30$; $S = \$1.50$
   (c) $A = 6,000$; $P = \$5$; $S = \$1.50$
2. How does your answer to requirement 1 give insight into the retailers' movement toward just-in-time purchasing policies?

21-17 Purchase-order size for retailer, EOQ, just-in-time purchasing. (Alternate is 21-16.) The Family Discount Store (FDS) operates a chain of retail discount stores. Its best-selling brand of baby diapers is Baby Care. Demand in October 19_4 for Baby Care at its Quebec City store is 800 cases (100 one-pound packages of Baby Care are in each case). In October 19_4, the Quebec City store estimated the cost of placing each purchase order (P) for Baby Care to be $40. The cost of carrying (S) each case of Baby Care diapers in inventory for a month was estimated to be $6.

At the end of September 19_4, the Quebec City store reestimated its cost of carrying to be $10 per case to take account of an increase in warehouse-related costs.

During September, FDS restructured its relationship with suppliers. It reduced the number of suppliers from 950 to 370. Only those suppliers that agreed to ship in the exact quantities ordered, and with quality control checks before shipment, were given long-term supply contracts by FDS. Each individual purchase order involved minimal paperwork, and no quality checks were to be made by FDS when each delivery arrived. The Quebec City store estimated its cost of placing each order to be $4.20 after these changes were made. FDS is open 31 days in October 19_4.

1. Calculate the optimal order quantity in October 19_4 for FDS for Baby Care. Use the EOQ model and assume in turn:
   (a) $A = 800$; $P = \$40$; $S = \$6$
   (b) $A = 800$; $P = \$40$; $S = \$10$
   (c) $A = 800$; $P = \$4.20$; $S = \$10$
2. How does your answer to requirement 1 give insight into the retailers' movement toward just-in-time purchasing policies?

21-18 EOQ, cost of prediction error. Ralph Menard is the owner of a truck repair shop. He uses an economic-order-quantity model for each of his truck parts. He initially predicts the annual demand for heavy-duty tires to be 2,000. Each tire has a purchase price of $50. The incremental cost of processing a purchase order is $40. The incremental cost of carrying is $4 per unit plus 10% of the supplier purchase price.

1. Calculate the EOQ for heavy-duty tires, along with the total sum of ordering and carrying costs.
2. Suppose Ralph is precisely correct in all his predictions but is wrong about the purchase price. He ignored a new law that abolished tariff duties on imported heavy-duty tires. If he had been a faultless predictor, he would have foreseen that the purchase price would have dropped to $30 at the beginning of the year and would have been unchanged throughout the year. What is the cost of the prediction error?

21-19 Economic order quantity, price discounts. Quality Inns uses 50 barrels of soap per year in one of its motels. It costs the company $1 per year to store a barrel, and a purchase order costs $10 to process.

The following discount schedule applies to the purchase price of the soap:

QUANTITY	DISCOUNT
1–9	None
10–49	$0.50 per barrel
50–99	$1.00 per barrel
100–up	$2.00 per barrel

Determine the economic order quantity, and briefly show why it is at that level.

21-20 EOQ, uncertainty, safety stock, reorder point. (CMA, adapted) The Starr Company distributes a wide range of electrical products. One of its best-selling items is a standard electric motor. The management of Starr Company uses the economic-order-quantity formula (EOQ) to determine the optimum number of motors to order. Management now wants to determine how much safety stock to order.

Starr Company estimates annual demand to be 30,000 electric motors (300 working days). Using the EOQ formula, the company orders 3,000 motors at a time. The lead time for an order is five days. The annual cost of carrying one motor in safety stock is $10. Management has also estimated that the cost of being out of stock is $20 for each motor they are short.

Starr Company has analyzed the demand during past reorder periods. The records indicate the following patterns:

DEMAND DURING LEAD TIME	NUMBER OF TIMES QUANTITY WAS DEMANDED
440	6
460	12
480	16
500	130
520	20
540	10
560	6
	200

1. Using an expected-value approach, determine the level of safety stock for electric motors that Starr Company should maintain in order to minimize costs. When computing carrying costs, assume that the safety stock is on hand at all times and that there is no overstocking caused by decreases in expected demand.
2. What would be Starr Company's new reorder point?
3. What factors should Starr Company have considered to estimate the out-of-stock costs?

21-21 EOQ, estimation of cost parameters, demand uncertainty. (CMA) SaPane Company is a regional distributor of automobile window glass. With the introduction of the new subcompact car models and the expected high level of consumer demand, management recognizes a need to determine the total inventory cost associated with maintaining an optimal supply of replacement windshields for the new subcompact cars introduced by each of the three major manufacturers. SaPane is expecting a daily demand for 36 windshields. The company's purchase price of each windshield is $50.

Other costs associated with ordering and maintaining an inventory of these windshields are as follows:

- The historical ordering costs incurred in the purchase order department for placing and processing orders for the past three years is shown below:

YEAR	ORDERS PLACED AND PROCESSED	TOTAL ORDERING COSTS
19_6	20	$12,300
19_7	55	12,475
19_8	100	12,700

Management expects the ordering costs to increase 16% over the amounts and rates experienced the past three years.
- The windshield manufacturer charges SaPane a $75 shipping fee per order.
- A clerk in the receiving department receives, inspects, and secures the windshields as they arrive from the manufacturer. This activity requires 8 hours per order received. This clerk has no other responsibilities and is paid at the rate of $9 per hour. Related variable overhead costs in this department are applied at the rate of $2.50 per hour.
- Additional warehouse space will have to be rented to store the new windshields. Space can be rented as needed in a public warehouse at an estimated cost of $2,500 per year plus $5.35 per windshield.
- Breakage cost is estimated to be 6% of the average inventory value.
- Taxes and fire insurance on the inventory are $1.15 per windshield.
- The desired rate of return on the investment in inventory is 21% of the purchase price.

Six working days are required from the time the order is placed with the manufacturer until it is received. SaPane uses an economic-order-quantity model in its purchase-order decisions. It uses a 300-day work year when making economic-order-quantity calculations.

1. Calculate the following values for SaPane Company:
   a. The value for purchase ordering cost that should be used in the EOQ formula
   b. The value for carrying cost that should be used in the EOQ formula
   c. The economic order quantity
   d. The minimum annual relevant cost at the economic-order-quantity point
   e. The reorder point in units
2. Without prejudice to your answer to requirement 1, assume the economic order quantity is 400 units, the carrying cost is $28 per unit, and the stockout cost is $12 per unit. SaPane wants to determine the proper level of safety stock in order to minimize its relevant costs of stockouts and carrying. Using the following probability schedule for excess demand during the reorder period, determine the proper amount of safety stock.

NUMBER OF UNITS SHORT DUE TO EXCESS DEMAND DURING REORDER PERIOD	PROBABILITY OF OCCURRENCE
60	.12
120	.05
180	.02

21-22 Purchase-order size decision by importer, EOQ, goal congruence. Outback Artifacts is a U.S. importer of distinctive cultural items from Australia. Its three best-selling items are hand-carved boomerangs, bark paintings, and digereedoos. The purchasing department is headed by Hobie Leland, Jr. Outback's purchasing policy calls for the use of an economic-order-quantity (EOQ) model to determine purchase-order sizes.

Outback's sole supplier of boomerangs is Bill King Enterprises, based in Alice Springs. Next period's contract with Bill King calls for an annual retainer of $20,000 and an additional payment of $2,500 per purchase order to cover packaging and handling costs. The purchase price includes air freight costs to San Francisco. The $20,000 annual retainer was up significantly from the $10,000 paid during the prior period. All payments to Bill King Enterprises are in U.S. dollars.

When each purchase order arrives from Australia, the boomerangs are placed into storage (accomplished at a work rate of 30 per hour). Similarly, when each sale is made, the boomerangs are taken out of storage (also at a work rate of 30 per hour). The average cost per hour of labor is $30. Outback Artifacts requires a before-tax rate of return of 10% per year on its investment. The internal processing cost of Outback Artifacts for each order is estimated to be $500.

Leland's compensation package comprises a fixed salary of $30,000 plus a bonus designed to encourage him to seek out cost-effective sources of supply. The bonus is calculated as:

20% × (Standard unit purchase price − Actual unit purchase price)
× Actual units purchased

The bonus system comes into effect when the actual price is less than the standard price. The standard unit purchase price was set by the president of Outback Artifacts after consultation with Hobie Leland. Leland spends two weeks in Australia each year to consult with Bill King and other suppliers.

The demand for the next period is estimated by the sales manager of Outback Artifacts to be 10,000 boomerangs. The standard price is $100 per boomerang. After the standard was set, Outback received a new price schedule from Bill King. It provides a $1 discount for purchases in order sizes of 10,000 boomerangs. Prior to this period, Bill King had steadfastly refused to give any price discount for large purchase-order sizes. Leland quickly decided to place an order for 10,000 boomerangs when he received the new price schedule.

Required

1. Using the EOQ model, calculate the optimal order size assuming the purchase price is the standard price of $100 per boomerang.
2. Calculate the sum of the total purchase cost, total ordering cost, and total carrying cost of the optimal order size policy from requirement 1.
3. Calculate the sum of the total purchase cost, total ordering cost, and total carrying cost when Hobie Leland purchases in a single-order size of 10,000 boomerangs. Comment on the difference between this answer and your answer to requirement 2.
4. What changes would you recommend in the compensation package of the purchasing officer of Outback Artifacts?

21-23 Accounting for cost of product quality, classification of cost items. Home Quality Products (HQP) assembles and distributes household electrical products. The president of the company, with the enthusiastic backing of the board of directors, publicly announces a commitment by HQP to "excellence in product quality." A cost of product quality program is implemented to assist senior management in their decisions in this area.

Marci Young, an accountant at HQP, is charged with developing the cost accounting system to report on product quality. Individual cost items will be grouped into one of four categories: (i) prevention costs, (ii) appraisal costs, (iii) internal failure costs, and (iv) external failure costs.

Young receives the following cost items pertaining to the steam iron product line of HQP:

1. Labor and materials costs of reworking a batch of steam iron handles at the Charlotte plant are $4,268.

2. Seminar costs for "Vendor Day," a program aiming to communicate to vendors the new quality requirements of HQP for all purchased components, are $20,492.

3. Costs of conformance tests at the Charlotte plant to test the heating unit in steam irons are $8,409.

4. Replacement cost of 1,000 steam irons sold in the Pittsburgh area but returned due to a faulty water-spray unit is $28,628.

5. Costs of inspection tests at the Raleigh packaging plant to ensure a complete set of warranty papers included in each steam iron box are $3,107.

Required

1. Classify the individual cost items marked 1 to 5 into one of the four categories of product quality cost (prevention, appraisal, internal failure, and external failure).
2. How might the cost of customer ill will created by the sale of defective products be estimated?
3. The production manager at the Charlotte plant is not enthusiastic about the extra work associated with HQP's cost of product quality program. He commented: "We are making detailed efforts to track quality costs at this plant. The time involved in adapting our reporting system to fit your format could be better spent on producing high-quality goods at a competitive cost." How should Young respond to this comment?

21-24 Measuring costs of product quality for manufacturer. Clean Shaven Inc. (CSI) produces electric shavers at its St. Louis, Missouri, plant. CSI, the sole North American manufacturer of electric shavers, has a 45% share of the North American market. Four manufacturers from Asia and Europe share the remainder of the market. Price and product quality are the two key factors along which companies compete in the electric shaver market.

CSI's manufacturing plant generally operates for one eight-hour shift, five days per week. Over 20,000 shavers can be produced on each eight-hour shift. The most important components in the shaver are the cutting system (made up of the cutter and the screen) and the motor. To manufacture the cutters, roles of steel are machine-stamped into rough blades that are then flattened and sharpened in lapping machines. In turn, these blades are fitted together to form the cutter unit that then passes through an ultrasonic cleaning system. The screens and the motors are purchased from outside suppliers. The cutters, screens, and motors pass through work stations where they are assembled along with electric cords and plastic molding into finished products. Finished products are packaged and sent to the finished goods warehouse for shipment.

Tory Kiam, the president of CSI, has a strong marketing focus. In recent years he has become concerned about the increasing quality level of the electric shavers sold by CSI's competitors. Two months ago, Consumer Magazine rated CSI's main brand of electric shaver as third in product quality of the five leading brands examined. A similar survey twelve months ago rated CSI's brand as first in product quality. Kiam decided to focus more resources on product quality.

Kiam set up a task force that he headed to implement a formal quality improvement program. Part of this program involved developing a cost accounting system to track product quality costs. Mary Peterson was given responsibility for this project. She started with a system that several other consumer-oriented companies had used. Four categories of product quality costs were distinguished: prevention, appraisal, internal failure, and external failure. Kiam's task force was set up in November 19_1. The following January (a low-production month), the product design staff held many seminars with all the employees of CSI. Starting in February, seminars were held with suppliers to CSI.

Mary Peterson's cost accounting project was implemented in January 19_2. She decided that for the first year (at least) she would restrict the cost of product quality system to items already recorded in the existing internal-reporting system. She viewed the task of collecting already recorded items in diverse parts of CSI, and then presenting them in a single cost of quality format, as challenging enough. At a later date she would consider recording opportunity costs that might be important when measuring the cost of product quality.

The exhibit at the top of page 741 presents the monthly cost of product quality reports for the January 19_2 to August 19_2 period.

Cost of Quality Reporting by Clean Shaven Inc. for Eight Months of 19_2 (in 000s)

	JANUARY	FEBRUARY	MARCH	APRIL	MAY	JUNE	JULY	AUGUST
PREVENTION								
Preventive machine maintenance	$ 166	$ 211	$ 196	$ 185	$ 209	$ 191	$ 211	$ 197
Seminars with suppliers	0	61	32	0	11	0	13	0
Product design reviews	202	166	167	159	179	185	192	189
	368	438	395	344	399	376	416	386
APPRAISAL								
Purchase inspection tests	67	72	69	31	24	25	23	21
Production line quality control	128	131	126	287	321	389	368	374
Final inspections and testing	157	161	154	191	327	317	347	326
	352	364	349	509	672	731	738	721
INTERNAL FAILURE								
Rework	647	623	631	651	550	496	421	396
Scrap	211	191	223	220	186	147	123	131
	858	814	854	871	736	643	544	527
EXTERNAL FAILURE								
Consumer repair claims	59	62	68	63	71	53	31	24
Product returns	235	247	221	262	251	122	116	87
	294	309	289	325	322	175	147	111
TOTAL COST OF QUALITY	$1,872	$ 1,925	$1,887	$ 2,049	$2,129	$1,925	$ 1,845	$ 1,745
TOTAL SALES	$8,508	$10,167	$8,986	$10,302	$8,406	$8,947	$11,206	$10,107

Required

1. What advantages might arise from developing a separate monthly cost of product quality report if the system is based only on items already recorded in the existing internal-reporting system?
2. What problems might Mary Peterson face in developing the cost of product quality system at CSI?
3. What trends are apparent in the monthly Cost of Product Quality reports for the January 19_2 to August 19_2 period? Comment on the uses management could make of the information in these reports.
4. What extensions might Mary Peterson consider if she is subsequently asked to develop a more comprehensive picture of the costs of product quality at CSI?

21-25 Just-in-time production, materials control, changes in cost accounting system. Silicon Valley Computer (SVC) was founded in 19_1 to manufacture the hard-disk drives used for data storage in a variety of computer products. Its customers are computer manufacturers who incorporate the disk drives into their computer systems. Competition in the hard-disk-drive market is intense. There is a large amount of idle capacity at many of the major manufacturing firms.

The exhibit on p. 742 outlines the manufacturing process at the Santa Clara plant of SVC. There is a raw-materials stockroom, five work stations on the production line, and a finished goods inventory stockroom. Raw materials (typically subassembled items) are used at each of the first three work stations.

THE PRE-JIT PRODUCTION ERA

From 19_1 to 19_4, SVC used a push approach to production. Production would start in response to a push launched from the front end of the system with the issuance of a work order at the Base & Motor Assembly work station. The work-order system was intended to track actual labor costs for each work-order batch. Shop floor laborers or managers would judge the distribution of labor time across work orders and would then record the information on work tickets. Later, clerks entered the work-ticket information into the computerized work-order system.

SVC used a batch manufacturing process. Work-in-process inventories developed at each of the five major work stations on the assembly line. Each work station

741

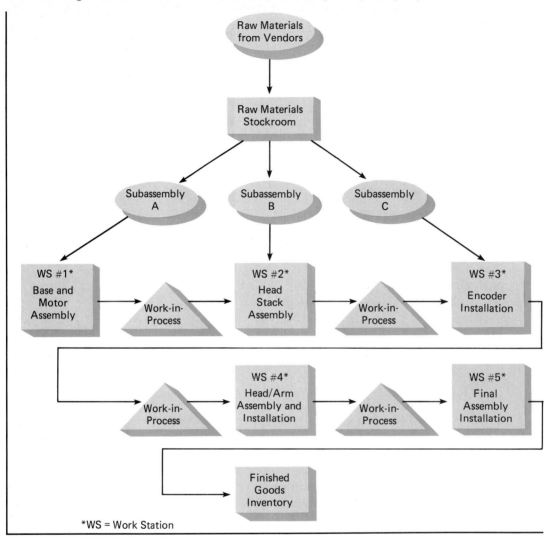

*WS = Work Station

had its own rework loop in which defective units were reworked. Rework activities did not appear as a separate cost center in each work station. Items relegated to rework were not separately recorded; they appeared in the tracking system as an item of work in process.

The cost accounting system had a job-costing orientation, based on standard costs. Three basic cost categories (raw materials, labor, and overhead) were separately tracked through the system.

PROBLEMS ARISING IN THE PRE-JIT PRODUCTION ERA

By 19_4, management had become aware of some major problems at the Santa Clara plant:

1. Large amounts of work-in-process inventory were accumulating at each work station. Work stations accumulated inventory to avoid not stopping production. In this way, each work station avoided depending on previous work stations for the flow of product. When a work station encountered a defective unit, it was put into a defective parts pool. At one point, over 3,000 defective disk drives had accumulated in rework.

2. Labor time was not accurately recorded. Workers and managers often recorded labor in a somewhat arbitrary fashion; blocks of labor time were rounded off and distributed haphazardly across work orders. In many months, the recorded labor time on the work orders was less than 80% of total labor-hours that should have been recorded.

3. The internal reporting system was exceedingly complex. The sheer cost and volume of paperwork associated with the system was overwhelming the production managers and staff.

THE JIT PRODUCTION ERA

In 19_5, SVC moved toward a JIT production system for its work in process. Demand pull became the driving force on the production line. Production is on a constant flow rather than a batch process. Approximately three days' inventory resides at each work station. (In 19_4, up to three months' inventory had resided at some work stations.) As customer demand pulls products out of finished goods, replacements move from work in process into finished goods, and each work station pulls partially assembled items from the prior work station. When a three-day buffer is filled at each work station, production at that work station stops. If a defective part is encountered at a work station, the product line at that work station is shut down until the problem is solved.

SVC's JIT system did not fully extend to either the raw materials or the finished goods. SVC held up to three months' supply of one of its key components in the raw-materials stockroom. The supplier of this component was the sole high-quality manufacturer and was unwilling to become a JIT supplier to SVC. The demand for SVC's hard-disk drives was unpredictable. SVC kept up to one month's supply of finished goods as a precaution against stockouts. The major customers of SVC were implementing JIT purchasing themselves and were not enthusiastic about holding large inventories of hard-disk drives. In the last two quarters of 19_5, a severe slump in demand by SVC's customers led to a quick buildup in finished-goods inventories.

COST ACCOUNTING IN THE JIT PRODUCTION ERA

SVC made major changes to its cost accounting system in 19_5. It moved away from the work-order concept and instituted a work center approach for tracking work in process. Each work station operates with an open-ended center record. That is, raw materials and overhead are charged to a work center, not a work order. As units are completed and transferred, standard costs are used to track the transfers. This procedure avoids the time-consuming and (sometimes) ambiguous activity of closing out work orders for each batch of production. SVC monitors total work-in-process flow at five points with five corresponding work center records. (In effect, each separate work station uses a version of process costing.) The new cost accounting system regards rework as a "separate cost" category within work in process. That is, rework costs are accumulated as a separate and distinct subpart of WIP. In this way, the costs of rework can be closely tracked.

SVC decided to include labor costs as a component of overhead costs. Eliminating the tracking of labor reduced management cost at the job level. The labor content for each disk drive in 19_5 ranged from 3% to 7% of total costs.

The quarterly financial data for selected items of Silicon Valley Computer for the 19_4 to 19_5 period (in millions) are as set out on page 744.

Required

1. Name four differences between the production process at SVC in 19_5 compared to the one in the 19_1 to 19_4 period.
2. Name three differences between the cost accounting system at SVC in 19_5 compared to the one in the 19_1 to 19_4 period. How do these differences relate to your answer in requirement 1?
3. What evidence is there that the changes documented in requirements 1 and 2 solved some of the problems at the Santa Clara plant that management became aware of in 19_4?
4. A commentator described SVC's manufacturing approach as "an abridged version of JIT." Explain this comment. What factors might prevent SVC from adopting a JIT approach in all phases of its manufacturing activities?

Silicon Valley Computer: Quarterly Data for 19_4 and 19_5 (millions)

	SALES	COST OF GOODS SOLD	TOTAL ASSETS	RAW MATERIALS	WORK IN PROCESS	FINISHED GOODS	TOTAL INVENTORIES
19_4, Quarter 1	$25.4	$16.4	$ 79.3	$11.8	$8.4	$5.7	$25.9
19_4, Quarter 2	30.1	18.8	79.8	9.7	6.8	6.2	22.7
19_4, Quarter 3	31.8	18.8	89.3	7.8	6.7	5.6	20.1
19_4, Quarter 4	33.1	19.7	99.5	11.8	5.9	5.2	22.9
19_5, Quarter 1	34.0	20.7	103.8	9.8	5.0	4.8	19.6
19_5, Quarter 2	29.1	18.3	106.1	8.3	3.1	3.4	14.8
19_5, Quarter 3	30.5	17.3	116.8	7.1	1.6	8.2	16.9
19_5, Quarter 4	27.6	16.6	126.2	6.9	1.5	9.1	17.5

22

Operations Management and the Accountant (II): Linear Programming

The linear-programming model • LP example: deriving an optimal product mix •
Substitution of scarce resources • Implications for managers and accountants •
Other illustrative uses of linear programming • Assumptions and limitations

Accountants can play an important role in providing inputs to decision models used by operating managers. This chapter illustrates the role of accounting data in linear-programming decision models. **Linear programming** (hereafter often referred to as **LP**) is concerned with how to best allocate scarce resources to attain a chosen objective such as maximization of operating income or minimization of operating costs; the distinctive feature of LP is that all the relationships in the model are linear.

The accountant who is able to interpret the inputs, outputs, assumptions, and limitations of LP can play a vital role in managing the operations of the organization. We begin by examining the LP model. Then we explore LP's implications for accounting systems and measurements. Our cost-benefit theme persists; the worth of formal models and more elaborate systems ultimately depends on whether decisions will be collectively improved.

THE LINEAR-PROGRAMMING MODEL

Although the linear-programming model can be used for a variety of decisions, its most widespread application is as a short-run allocation model. All such short-run models assume that a given set of resources is available that generates a specified level of fixed costs. The objective is to choose what types and amounts of products or services to produce or sell, given a set of revenue and cost behaviors and a set of resources. A detailed example concerning the choice of an optimal product mix is presented below. Other examples of LP are briefly discussed in a subsequent section of this chapter.

Linkage
to previous
chapters

The relationships of costs to volume and to profits were introduced in Chapter 3. That chapter dealt mostly with a single product or a combination of products being sold without restriction. The focus was on maximizing contribution margin, given a level of fixed costs. In Chapter 9, the importance of considering the scarcity of resources in product-mix decisions was illustrated. The most profitable product is not necessarily the product with the highest contribution margin per unit. Instead the preferable product is the one that produces the highest contribution per unit of the scarce resource or constraining factor, such as total available machine-hours (see pp. 310–11).

The basic idea presented in Chapter 9 still holds, but in practice there is usually more than one constraint. **Therefore the problem becomes one of maximizing total contribution margin, given many constraints. The LP model is designed to provide a solution to problems where the linear assumptions underlying the model are reasonable approximations.**

Building
the model

The most challenging aspects of using an LP model are (a) expressing a business problem in a format suitable to be solved by a linear-programming model, and (b) obtaining reliable estimates of the information inputs used in the model. As a minimum, accountants and managers should be able to recognize the types of problems in their organizations that are most susceptible to analysis by linear programming. They should also be able to help in the construction of the model—that is, in specifying the objective function, the constraints, and the variables. Ideally, they should understand the mathematics and be able to communicate effectively with those who are attempting to express the problem mathematically. However, the position taken here is that the accountant and the manager should concentrate on the formulation of the model and not worry too much about the technical intricacies of the solution. The latter responsibility can be delegated to the mathematicians; the feasibility of delegating the former is highly doubtful.

LP EXAMPLE: DERIVING AN OPTIMAL PRODUCT MIX

Consider Advanced Engineering, a company that makes two products, A and B. Each product requires processing in two departments, machining and finishing. Some data follow:

	AVAILABLE CAPACITY IN HOURS	USE OF CAPACITY IN HOURS PER UNIT OF PRODUCT		DAILY MAXIMUM PRODUCTION IN UNITS	
		A	B	A	B
Department 1, Machining	200	1	2	200	100
Department 2, Finishing	125	1	0.5	125	250

Suppose a department works exclusively on a single product. The table indicates that Department 1 can machine a maximum of 200 A (200 hours ÷ 1 hour per unit = 200 units) or 100 B (200 hours ÷ 2 hours per unit = 100 units). Similarly, Department 2 can finish 125 A (125 hours ÷ 1 hour per unit = 125 units) or 250 B (125 hours ÷ 0.5 hours per unit = 250 units).

Exhibit 22-1 summarizes these and other relevant data. Note that each unit of Product A has a contribution margin of $2.00; Product B, a contribution margin of $2.50. Moreover, material shortages for Product B will limit its production to a maximum of 90 units per day. How many units of each product should be produced daily to maximize operating income?

EXHIBIT 22-1
Advanced Engineering: Operating Data

	CAPACITIES (PER DAY) IN PRODUCT UNITS		
PRODUCT	Department 1: Machining	Department 2: Finishing	CONTRIBUTION MARGIN PER UNIT
If produce A only	200 units	125 units	$2.00
If produce B only	100 units	250 units	$2.50

Steps in solving an LP problem

Solving an LP problem involves the following three steps:

Step One: Determine the objective. For example, maximize operating income or minimize operating costs. The *objective function* of a linear program expresses the objective or goal to be maximized or minimized.

Step Two: Determine the basic relationships. These relationships include constraints expressed by using linear functions. A **constraint** is a mathematical inequality or equality that must be satisfied by the variables in the LP model.

Step Three: Compute the optimal solution. Where there are only two variables in the objective function and a minimal number of constraints, the graphical solution method or the trial-and-error solution method can be used. An understanding of both methods, which are outlined in this chapter, provides intuition about LP modeling. In most LP applications, standard computer software packages are used to compute the optimal solution.

Illustration of steps

The data in Exhibit 22-1 help illustrate these steps in solving an LP problem:

Step One: Determine the objective. The objective is to find the combination of products that maximizes the total contribution margin. The linear function expressing this objective is:

$$\text{Total contribution margin (TCM)} = \$2.00A + \$2.50B$$

where A equals the number of units of A produced, and B the number of units of B produced.

747

Step Two: Determine the basic relationships. The relationships can be depicted by the following inequalities:

Department 1 constraint (machining):	$A + 2B \leq 200$
Department 2 constraint (finishing):	$A + .5B \leq 125$
Material shortage constraint for Product B:	$B \leq 90$
Because negative production is impossible:	$A \geq 0$ and $B \geq 0$

The three solid lines on the graph in Exhibit 22-2 show the existing constraints for Departments 1 and 2 and of the material shortage constraint.[1] The feasible alternatives are those that are technically possible. The "area of feasible solutions" in Exhibit 22-2 shows the boundaries of those product combinations that are feasible— that is, combinations of quantities of A and B that satisfy all the constraining factors. The coefficients of the constraints are often called technical coefficients. For example, in Department 1 the technical coefficient of A is one hour, and the technical coefficient of B is two hours.

EXHIBIT 22-2
Linear Programming—Graphic Solution for Advanced Engineering

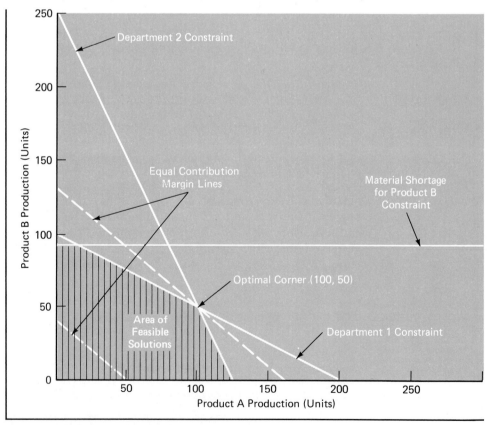

[1]As an example of how the lines are plotted in Exhibit 22-2, use equal signs instead of inequality signs and assume for Department 1 that $B = 0$; then $A = 200$. Assume that $A = 0$; then $B = 100$. Connect those two points with a straight line.

Step Three: Compute the optimal solution. In Step 2 we concentrated on physical relationships. We now return to the economic relationships expressed as the objective function in Step 1. The graphic solution approach and the trial-and-error solution approach will be presented.

Graphic solution approach

In the graphic approach, the optimal solution must lie on one of the corners of the "area of feasible solutions." Why? Consider all possible combinations that will produce an equal total contribution margin of, say, $100. That is, $2.00A + $2.50B = $100. This set of $100 contribution margins is a straight dashed line through (50,0) and (0,40). Other equal total contribution margins can be represented by lines parallel to this one. The equal total contribution margins increase as the lines get farther from the origin. The optimal dashed line is the one farthest from the origin that has a feasible solution on it; this happens at a corner (100,50). This solution will become apparent if you put a ruler on the graph and move it outward from the origin and parallel with the $100 line. In general, the optimal solution in a maximization problem lies at the corner where the dashed line intersects an extreme point of the area of feasible solutions.[2]

The slope of the objective function (the dashed line representing the equal total contribution margin, *TCM*) can be computed from the equation

$$TCM = \$2.00A + \$2.50B$$

To find the slope (the rate of change of *B* for one additional unit of *A*), divide by the coefficient of *B* and transfer *B* to the left-hand side of the equation:

$$\frac{TCM}{\$2.50} = \frac{\$2.00}{\$2.50} \cdot A + B$$

$$B = \frac{TCM}{\$2.50} - \frac{\$2.00}{\$2.50} \cdot A$$

Therefore the slope of the objective function is a negative $2.00/$2.50, or −⅘. The graphic solution approach provides intuitive insight into the computation of the optimal solution. However, its use is restricted to LP problems with two products in the objective function (so that the solution can be represented on a two-dimensional graph).

Trial-and-error solution approach

The optimal solution can also be found by trial and error, usually by working with coordinates of the corners of the area of feasible solutions. The approach is simple:

A. Start with any set of corner points and compute the total contribution margin. The corner points can be derived from Exhibit 22-2. It is useful to use simultaneous equations as a check on the coordinates read from a graph. To illustrate, the

---

[2]An exception occurs if the dashed line has the same slope as a constraint line. Then any combination along where the dashed line and constraint line are identical would provide the same maximum total contribution margin.

point (100,50) can be derived by solving the two pertinent constraint inequalities as simultaneous equations:

$$(1) \qquad A + 2B = 200$$

$$(2) \qquad A + .5B = 125$$

Subtract (2) from (1): $\qquad 2B - .5B = 200 - 125$

$$1.5B = 75$$

$$B = 75 \div 1.5 = 50$$

Substitute for B in (1): $\qquad A + (2 \times 50) = 200$

$$A = 200 - 100 = 100$$

Given $A = 100$ and $B = 50$:

$$TCM = (\$2.00 \times 100) + (\$2.50 \times 50) = \$325$$

B. Move from corner to corner to see if it will improve the result in A. These computations, corner by corner, are summarized as follows:[3]

TRIAL	CORNER	PRODUCT A	PRODUCT B	TOTAL CONTRIBUTION MARGIN		
1	0,0	0	0	$2.00(0)	+ $2.50(0)	= $ 0
2	0,90	0	90	2.00(0)	+ 2.50(90)	= 225.00
3	20,90	20	90	2.00(20)	+ 2.50(90)	= 265.00
4	100,50	100	50	2.00(100)	+ 2.50(50)	= 325.00*
5	125,0	125	0	2.00(125)	+ 2.50(0)	= 250.00

*The optimal product mix is 100 of A and 50 of B

SUBSTITUTION OF SCARCE RESOURCES

A common fallacy is to assume that the optimal solution is always to produce as much as possible of the product with the highest contribution margin per unit. In the above example, this would entail maximizing production of B and then devoting any remaining capacity to A. This approach ignores the fact that productive capacity is the scarce resource. **The key to the optimal solution rests in the relative rates of substitution and profitability per unit (per hour or per day) of productive capacity.** This point becomes clearer if we examine Exhibit 22-2. Moving from corner (20,90) to corner (100,50) implies that the company is transferring the scarce resource (productive capacity) between the products. In Department 1, each

---

[3]Although graphic or trial-and-error approaches can be useful for two or possibly three variables, they are impractical where many variables exist. Standard computer software packages rely on the simplex method. The **simplex method** is an iterative step-by-step procedure for determining the optimal solution to an LP problem; it starts with a specific feasible solution and then tests it by substitution to see if the solution can be improved. These substitutions continue until no further improvement is possible, and thus the optimum solution is obtained.

productive hour devoted to one unit of Product B may be given up (sacrificed or traded) for two units of Product A. Will this exchange add to profitability? Yes, as shown below:

Total contribution margin at (20,90):		
20 @ $2.00 + 90 @ $2.50		$265.00
Added contribution margin from Product A of moving to corner (100,50):		
100 − 20 or 80 more units @ $2.00	$160.00	
Loss of contribution margin from Product B of moving to corner (100,50):		
90 − 50 or 40 less units @ $2.50	100.00	
Net additional contribution margin		60.00
Total contribution margin at (100,50):		
100 @ $2.00 + 50 @ $2.50		$325.00

As we move from corner (20,90) to corner (100,50), we are contending with the Department 1 constraint. There is a net advantage of trading two units of A for one unit of B; each such substitution will add $1.50 to the total contribution margin (receive 2 @ $2.00 = $4.00, instead of 1 @ $2.50 = $2.50). The increase in total contribution margin, as shown above, is $60.00.

But the advantage of substituting A for B reverses when the Department 2 constraint takes effect. As we move from corner (100,50) to corner (125,0), the rate of substitution can be stated as follows: Each productive hour devoted to one unit of Product B may instead be devoted to .5 of a unit of Product A. This substitution would entail giving up a $2.50 contribution margin for each unit of Product B in exchange for a $1.00 contribution margin for each .5 units of Product A. Therefore corner (100,50) is the optimal solution.

Note again that the heart of the substitutions discussed above is a matter of swapping a given contribution margin per unit of scarce resource for some other contribution margin per unit of *scarce resource;* it is not simply a matter of comparing margins per unit of *product.*

IMPLICATIONS FOR MANAGERS AND ACCOUNTANTS

Many LP models include both accounting coefficients and technical coefficients. The contribution margins of Products A and B in Exhibit 22-1 are examples of accounting coefficients. Examples of technical coefficients in Exhibit 22-1 are the coefficients of the capacity constraints.

Sensitivity analysis   What are the implications of a faulty estimate of the accounting or technical coefficients used in the LP model? **Both sets of coefficients inevitably affect the slope of the objective function (the equal-contribution margin line in our example) or the area of feasible solutions.** Questions about measurement errors are frequently explored via sensitivity analysis (i.e., asking "What if?" questions).

In some cases, the optimal decision about product mix may be unchanged, even though there is a revision in the estimated contribution margin. Errors in approximations of costs and revenues per unit may reduce or increase unit contribution margins but may not tilt the slope of the equal-contribution margin line enough to alter the optimal solution.

751

An important question is, **How much measurement error can be tolerated before the optimal solution would change?** That is, what is the value where the (100,50) combination is no longer optimal? Concentrate on the constraint for Department 1. If the slope of the objective function is the same as that constraint, optimal solutions will be identical all along that constraint as long as it is binding. For example, if the contribution margin of Product A falls to $1.25, the objective function will be $1.25A + $2.50B, which is the same slope as the constraint for Department 1. Then the total contribution margin would be the same for corners (20,90) and (100,50):

CORNER	TOTAL CONTRIBUTION MARGIN
20,90	$1.25(20) + $2.50(90) = $250
100,50	$1.25(100) + $2.50(50) = $250

Suppose the material cost for A were $.90 higher than originally expected. Then the contribution margin for A would become $1.10 instead of $2.00. The slope of the objective function would change from $-\frac{4}{5}$ ($-$2.00/$2.50) to $-\frac{11}{25}$ ($-$1.10/$2.50). The new optimal solution would be different. If you put a ruler on the graph and move it outward from the origin using a $-\frac{11}{25}$ slope, the optimal corner will now be (20,90), providing a contribution of $1.10(20) + $2.50(90) = $247.

Cost of a prediction error

The cost of incorrectly predicting a $2.00 contribution margin for A, instead of the correct $1.10 value, can be computed using the cost of a prediction error approach outlined in Appendix 9A (pp. 322–24):

Step One: Compute the monetary outcome of the best action, given the actual value of the predicted variables. Given a $1.10 contribution margin for A, the optimal combination is (20,90). The total contribution margin is

$$TCM = \$1.10(20) + \$2.50(90) = \$247.$$

Step Two: Compute the monetary outcome of the action based on the incorrect value of the predicted variable. The predicted $2.00 contribution margin for A leads to the selection of a (100,50) combination. The total contribution margin from this action, given the $1.10 actual contribution margin for A, is

$$TCM = \$1.10(100) + \$2.50(50) = \$235$$

Step Three: Compute the difference between the monetary outcomes in Steps One and Two:

	MONETARY OUTCOME
Step One	$247
Step Two	235
Difference	$ 12

The cost of the prediction error for the contribution margin of A is $12.

The above illustration shows the original solution as being relatively insensitive to a $0.90 error in predicting the unit material costs for A. Other complexities could be introduced to the decision. For example, the material costs of both A and B might change simultaneously. Moreover, a change in labor productivity would affect both the unit contribution margins and the technical coefficients. You can easily imagine more-complicated situations where heavy interdependencies (many constraints and many products) might make the decision very sensitive.

If prediction errors are costly, more resources should be spent initially to enhance the accuracy of the predictions before a decision is made. Once the choice is made, extra efforts may also be made to implement the decision so that the predicted outcomes (for example, costs or production volumes) are achieved. Such endeavors can be economically justifiable when the costs of prediction errors are high.

The accounting coefficients in the objective function typically are the contribution margin of each product or the variable cost of each resource input. If a firm reports absorption costs in its internal reporting system, the inputs to the LP model should exclude the allocated fixed costs included in the absorption cost numbers.

The output of computer programs frequently provides shadow prices. **Shadow prices** indicate how much the objective function will increase if one more unit of the limiting resource is available. Thus a shadow price of $1 for machining means that the total operating income of the firm would increase by $1 if machining capacity were increased by one unit. Shadow prices facilitate the computation of the possible changes in total operating income from expansion of capacity by Advanced Engineering.

Shadow prices should be interpreted cautiously. They are valid quantifications of opportunity costs only if the basic solution (the chosen types of products and idle facilities) does not change. For example, the shadow prices would not change as long as some A, some B, and some idle facilities were present. But the shadow prices would change if another constraint takes effect and alters the optimal solution.

OTHER ILLUSTRATIVE USES OF LINEAR PROGRAMMING

Linear-programming models have proved useful in a wide variety of decisions. Other applications include:[4]

Production Scheduling. LP models have helped production planning so that demand requirements are met at minimum cost, subject to constraints concerning production capacity, subcontracting, and inventory holdings. Key cost inputs in this application include the cost per unit of production and the cost of holding each unit of inventory.

Blending of Raw Materials. A typical objective is cost minimization subject to constraints concerning raw-material availability and final end-product quality. Success-

---

[4]Industries with widespread use of LP include petroleum refining, chemicals, and food processing. See J. Moore and A. Reichert, "An Analysis of the Financial Management Techniques Currently Employed by Large U.S. Corporations," *Journal of Business Finance and Accounting*, Winter 1983, pp. 623–45.

ful applications have been reported in such diverse settings as the mixing of paint, the mixing of meats to make sausages, the blending of chocolate products, and the blending of petroleum products. Key cost inputs include the costs of the individual raw materials and the processing costs for individual materials and combinations of materials.

Transportation/Distribution. The typical aim of this application is to meet demand from geographically dispersed product areas using several geographically dispersed plants while minimizing transportation and distribution costs. A critical input is the cost of transporting products from each plant to each market area.

People Planning. An example of an LP application of this type is the assignment of nurses to departments of a hospital when there are peaks and troughs in demand. Key inputs in these applications include the cost of each grade of nurse for normal hours and the cost of overtime and supplemental staff.[5]

With a cost minimization problem, the feasible solution area lies beyond the constraints rather than within the constraints for the total contribution maximization problem in Exhibit 22-2.

ASSUMPTIONS AND LIMITATIONS

When you encounter applications of LP, be aware that there are several assumptions underlying the output of an LP model:

1. All relationships are linear.
2. All constraints and coefficients are known with certainty. (However, probabilities can be used to forecast the specific amounts involved in the construction of the LP model.)
3. Solutions in fractional units are permissible, even though fractional units may not make economic sense in the decision setting.

Few actual situations completely satisfy these assumptions. **The optimal solution to an LP problem should not automatically be the chosen decision. Managers should always assure themselves that the assumptions underlying the LP model are reasonable for the decision being made.**

SUMMARY

Linear programming is a popular formal decision model for determining how to optimize the use of a given set of scarce resources. Accountants and managers should be especially alert to the sensitivity of the solution to possible measurement errors in the accounting coefficients and the technical coefficients of the LP model.

---

[5]For more-detailed analysis of linear programming and its applications, see G. Eppen and F. Gould, *Introductory Management Science* (Englewood Cliffs, N.J.: Prentice-Hall, 1984).

Special Points and Pitfalls

The linear-programming model is often regarded as a multiple-product extension of the cost-volume-profit model that was introduced in Chapter 3. In addition, it extends the resource-allocation model that was introduced in Chapter 9, where only one constraint was discussed.

Accountants and managers should periodically remind themselves that LP solutions may be highly sensitive to the measurements of the costs used in the model.

_____PROBLEM FOR SELF-STUDY_____

problem

1. Suppose the budgeted contribution margins for Products A and B of Advanced Engineering in Exhibit 22-1 were calculated as follows:

	A	B
Selling price per unit	$18.00	$38.00
Variable cost per unit	16.00	35.50
Contribution margin per unit	$ 2.00	$ 2.50

The actual contribution margin for A was $2.00 per unit as budgeted, but B had an actual contribution margin of $5.00 per unit. What is the cost of predicting a $2.50 contribution margin for B instead of the actual $5.00 contribution margin?

2. The production manager is contacted by a new supplier of the materials used in the production of B. This supplier can provide, at the same purchase price as the old supplier, virtually unlimited amounts of the material. How much can Advanced Engineering increase its operating income by having no material shortage constraint for B? (Assume the contribution margin for B is $5.)

solution

1. Exhibit 22-3 presents the revised graphic solution using the $5 contribution margin for B. The new optimal solution is (20,90). This result can also be found using the trial-and-error solution approach:

TRIAL	CORNER	PRODUCT A	PRODUCT B	TOTAL CONTRIBUTION MARGIN
1	(0,0)	0	0	$2(0) + $5(0) = $ 0
2	(0,90)	0	90	$2(0) + $5(90) = $450
3	(20,90)	20	90	$2(20) + $5(90) = $490*
4	(100,50)	100	50	$2(100) + $5(50) = $450
5	(125,0)	125	0	$2(125) + $5(0) = $250

*The new optimal combination of (20,90) has a total contribution margin of $490.

EXHIBIT 22-3
Linear Programming—Revised Graphic Solution for Advanced Engineering

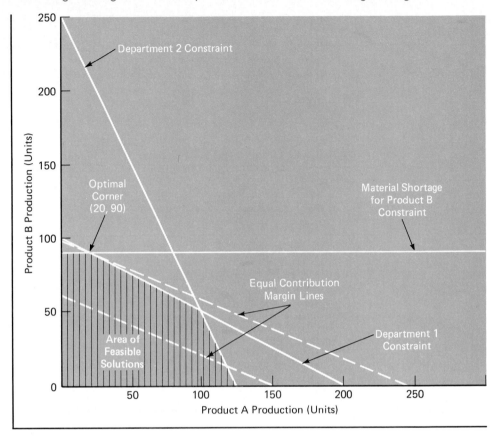

The cost of a prediction error can be computed as follows:

Step One: Compute the monetary outcome of the best action, given the actual value of the predicted variables:

$$TCM = \$2(20) + \$5(90) = \$490$$

Step Two: Compute the monetary outcome of the action based on the incorrect value of the predicted variable. The predicted $2.50 unit contribution margin for B leads to the selection of a (100,50) combination (see Exhibit 22-2). The total contribution margin from this action, given that the actual contribution margin for B is $5.00, is

$$TCM = \$2(100) + \$5(50) = \$450$$

Step Three: Compute the difference between the monetary outcomes in Steps One and Two:

	MONETARY OUTCOME
Step One	$490
Step Two	450
Difference	$ 40

The cost of the prediction error for the contribution margin of B is $40.

2. The exclusion of the material shortage constraint (B ≤ 90) changes the area of feasible solutions. The new corner points are:

TRIAL	CORNER	PRODUCT A	PRODUCT B	TOTAL CONTRIBUTION MARGIN
1	(0,0)	0	0	$2(0) + $5(0) = $ 0
2	(0,100)	0	100	$2(0) + $5(100) = $500
3	(100,50)	100	50	$2(100) + $5(50) = $450
4	(125,0)	125	0	$2(125) + $5(0) = $250

Advanced Engineering can achieve a total contribution margin of $500 when there is no material-shortage constraint for B. This outcome is an increase of $10 over the $490 total contribution margin computed in requirement 1.

_____QUESTIONS, PROBLEMS, AND CASES_____

22-1. What are the three steps in solving a linear-programming problem?

22-2 How might the optimal solution of an LP problem be determined?

22-3 What is the main limitation of the graphic solution method?

22-4 "The LP model is an extension of the cost-volume-profit model." Do you agree? Explain.

22-5 "The optimal product mix will maximize the production of the product with the highest contribution margin." Do you agree? Explain.

22-6 "Measurement error in an LP model can be tolerated as long as the cost of the prediction error is zero." Do you agree? Explain.

22-7 Name five areas where LP models have proved useful in decision making.

22-8 List three assumptions underlying the output of an LP model.

22-9 Optimal production plan, computer manufacturer. Information Technology, Inc. assembles and sells two products, printers (X) and desk-top computers (Y). Customers can purchase either (i) a computer or (ii) a computer plus a printer; the printers are *not* sold without the accompanying purchase of a computer. The result is that the quantity of printers sold is equal to or less than the quantity of desk-top computers sold.

Each printer requires 6 hours assembly time on production line 1, and 10 hours assembly time on production line 2. Each computer requires 4 hours assembly time on production line 1 only. (Many of the components of each computer are subassembled by external vendors.)

Production line 1 has 24 hours of available time per day, while production line 2 has 20 hours of available time per day.

The contribution margins are $200 per printer and $100 per computer.

Required

757

1. Express the relationships in a linear-programming format.
2. Which combination of printers and computers will maximize the operating income of Information Technology?

22-10 Minimum cost combination, fertilizer mix. The local agricultural center has advised Sam Bowers to spread at least 4,800 pounds of a special nitrogen fertilizer ingredient and at least 5,000 pounds of a special phosphate fertilizer ingredient in order to increase his crop yield. Neither ingredient is available in pure form.

A dealer has offered 100-pound bags of VIM at $1 each. VIM contains the equivalent of 20 pounds of nitrogen and 80 pounds of phosphate. VOOM is also available in 100-pound bags, at $3 each; it contains the equivalent of 75 pounds of nitrogen and 25 pounds of phosphate.

How many bags of VIM and VOOM should Bowers buy in order to obtain the required fertilizer at minimum cost? Solve graphically.

22-11 Optimal sales mix for a retailer, sensitivity analysis. Always Open, Inc. operates a chain of food stores open twenty-four hours a day. Each store has a standard 40,000 square feet of floor space available for merchandise. Merchandise is grouped in two categories: grocery products and dairy products. Always Open requires each store to devote a minimum of 10,000 square feet to grocery products, and a minimum of 8,000 square feet to dairy products. Within these restrictions, each store manager can choose the mix of products to carry.

The manager of the Winnipeg store estimates the following weekly contribution margins per square foot:

Grocery products	$10
Dairy products	3

Required

1. Formulate the decision facing the store manager as a linear-programming model.
2. Why might Always Open set lower bounds on the floor space devoted to each line of product?
3. Compute the optimal mix of grocery products (X) and dairy products (Y) to carry at the Winnipeg store. Use both the graphic solution approach and the trial-and-error solution approach.
4. Suppose the contribution margin for dairy products is believed accurate. How much measurement error in the contribution margin of grocery products can be tolerated before the optimal solution from requirement 3 would change?

22-12 Formulation of an LP model. (CMA) SmyCo manufactures two types of display boards that are sold to office supply stores. One board is a hard-finished marking board that can be written on with a water-soluble felt-tip marking pen and then wiped clean with a cloth. The other is a conventional cork-type tack board.

Both boards pass through two manufacturing departments. All of the raw materials—board base, board covering, and aluminum frames—are cut to size in the cutting department. Both types of boards are the same size and use the same aluminum frame. The boards are assembled in one of SmyCo's two assembly operations—the automated assembly department or the labor assembly department.

The automated assembly department is a capital intensive assembly operation. This department has been in operation for 18 months and was intended to replace the labor assembly department. However, SmyCo's business expanded so rapidly that both assembly operations are needed and used. The final results of the two assembly operations are identical. The only difference between the two is the proportion of machine time versus direct labor time in each department and, thus, different costs. However, workers have been trained for both operations so that they can be switched between the two operations.

Data regarding the two products and their manufacture are presented in the following schedules.

Sales Data

	MARKING BOARD	TACK BOARD
Selling price per unit	$ 60.00	$ 45.00
Variable selling expenses per unit	$ 3.00	$ 3.00
Annual fixed selling and administrative expenses (allocated equally between the two products)	$900,000	$900,000

758

Unit Variable Manufacturing Costs

	CUTTING DEPARTMENT		LABOR ASSEMBLY DEPARTMENT*	AUTOMATED ASSEMBLY DEPARTMENT*
	Marking Board	Tack Board		
Raw materials				
Base	$ 6.00	$6.00	$ —	$ —
Covering	14.50	7.75	—	—
Frame	8.25	8.25	—	—
Direct labor				
(@$10/DLH)	2.00	2.00	—	—
(@$12/DLH)	—	—	3.00	.60
Manufacturing overhead				
Supplies	1.25	1.25	1.50	1.50
Power	1.20	1.20	.75	1.80

*The unit costs for the marking board and the tack board are the same within each of the two assembly departments.

Machine-Hour Data

	CUTTING DEPARTMENT	LABOR ASSEMBLY DEPARTMENT	AUTOMATED ASSEMBLY DEPARTMENT
Machine-hours required per board	.15	.02	.05
Monthly machine-hours available	25,000	1,500	5,000
Annual machine-hours available	300,000	18,000	60,000

SmyCo produced and sold 600,000 marking boards and 900,000 tack boards last year. Management estimates that the total unit sales volume for the coming year could increase 20% if the units can be produced. SmyCo has contracts to produce and sell 30,000 units of each board each month.

Sales, production, and cost incurrence are uniform throughout the year. SmyCo has a monthly maximum labor capacity of 30,000 direct-labor hours in the cutting department and 40,000 direct-labor hours for the assembly operations (automated assembly and labor assembly departments combined).

Required

1. SmyCo's management believes that linear programming could be used to determine the optimum mix of marking and tack boards to produce and sell. Explain why linear programming can be used by SmyCo.
2. SmyCo plans to employ linear programming to determine its optimum production mix of marking and tack boards. Formulate and label the (a) objective function, (b) constraint functions.

   Be sure to define your variables.

22-13 Formulation of LP problem, assumptions of LP model. (CMA, adapted)   The Tripro Company produces and sells three products, hereafter referred to as Products A, B, and C. The company is currently changing its short-range planning approach in an attempt to incorporate some of the newer planning techniques. The controller and some of his staff have been conferring with a consultant on the feasibility of using a linear-programming model for determining the optimum product mix.

Information for short-range planning has been developed in the same format as in prior years. This information includes expected sales prices and expected direct-labor and material costs for each product. In addition, variable-overhead and fixed-overhead costs were assumed to be the same for each product, because approximately equal quantities of the products were produced and sold.

759

	A	B	C
Selling price	$25.00	$30.00	$40.00
Direct labor	7.50	10.00	12.50
Direct materials	9.00	6.00	10.50
Variable overhead	6.00	6.00	6.00
Fixed overhead	6.00	6.00	6.00

All three products use the same type of direct material, which costs $1.50 per pound. Direct labor is paid at the rate of $5.00 per hour. There are 2,000 direct-labor hours and 20,000 pounds of direct materials available in a month.

Required

1. Formulate and label the linear-programming objective function and constraint functions necessary to maximize Tripro's contribution margin. Use Q_A, Q_B, Q_C to represent units of the three products.
2. What underlying assumptions must be satisfied to justify the use of linear programming?

22-14 Effect of change in contribution margins, cost of a prediction error. United Foods processes and packages three frozen vegetable products for a chain of restaurants: carrots (C), peas (P), and zucchini (Z). Linear programming is used by United Foods to determine the optimal product mix. The objective function of this linear program in July was

$$\text{maximize } \$1C + \$2P + \$4Z$$

The optimal product mix for July was C = 100,000 packages, P = 200,000 packages, and Z = 300,000 packages.

Later, additional investigation of cost behavior revealed that the unit contribution margins should have been $1.10, $2.80, and $4.30 for C, P, and Z, respectively. Although these better-cost approximations provided a more accurate estimate of the individual product contribution margins, the optimal decision of 100,000, 200,000, and 300,000 packages for C, P, and Z respectively, was unchanged.

Required

1. Compute the predicted total contribution margin at the time the July optimal product mix was originally determined.
2. Compute the total contribution margin using the revised estimates of the unit contribution margins per package of C, P, and Z.
3. What is the cost of the error in predicting the July contribution margins of C, P, and Z?

22-15 Multiple choice. (CPA) A company markets two products, Alpha and Gamma. The unit contribution margins per gallon are $5 for Alpha and $4 for Gamma. Both products consist of two ingredients, D and K. Alpha contains 80% D and 20% K, while the proportions of the same ingredients in Gamma are 40% and 60%, respectively. The current inventory is 16,000 gallons of D and 6,000 gallons of K. The only company producing D and K is on strike and will neither deliver nor produce them in the foreseeable future. The company wishes to know the numbers of gallons of Alpha and Gamma that it should produce with its present stock of raw materials in order to maximize its total revenue. Let X_1 = 1 unit of Alpha, X_2 = 1 unit of Gamma, X_3 = 1 unit of D, and X_4 = 1 unit of K.

1. The objective function for this problem could be expressed as
   a. $f_{max} = 0X_1 + 0X_2 + 5X_3 + 5X_4$
   b. $f_{min} = 5X_1 + 4X_2 + 0X_3 + 0X_4$
   c. $f_{max} = 5X_1 + 4X_2 + 0X_3 + 0X_4$
   d. $f_{max} = X_1 + X_2 + 5X_3 + 4X_4$
   e. $f_{max} = 4X_1 + 5X_2 + X_3 + X_4$

2. The constraint imposed by the quantity of D on hand could be expressed as
   a. $X_1 + X_2 \geq 16,000$
   b. $X_1 + X_2 \leq 16,000$
   c. $.4X_1 + .6X_2 \leq 16,000$
   d. $.8X_1 + .4X_2 \geq 16,000$

e. $.8X_1 + .4X_2 \leq 16,000$

3. The constraint imposed by the quantity of K on hand could be expressed as
   a. $X_1 + X_2 \geq 6,000$
   b. $X_1 + X_2 \leq 6,000$
   c. $.8X_1 + .2X_2 \leq 6,000$
   d. $.8X_1 + .2X_2 \geq 6,000$
   e. $.2X_1 + .6X_2 \leq 6,000$

4. To maximize total contribution margin, the company should produce and market
   a. 106,000 gallons of Alpha only
   b. 90,000 gallons of Alpha and 16,000 gallons of Gamma
   c. 16,000 gallons of Alpha and 90,000 gallons of Gamma
   d. 18,000 gallons of Alpha and 4,000 gallons of Gamma
   e. 4,000 gallons of Alpha and 18,000 gallons of Gamma

5. Assuming that the contribution margins per gallon are $7 for Alpha and $9 for Gamma, the company should produce and market
   a. 106,000 gallons of Alpha only
   b. 90,000 gallons of Alpha and 16,000 gallons of Gamma
   c. 16,000 gallons of Alpha and 90,000 gallons of Gamma
   d. 18,000 gallons of Alpha and 4,000 gallons of Gamma
   e. 4,000 gallons of Alpha and 18,000 gallons of Gamma

22-16 Optimal production plan for manufacturing plant, contribution margin per scarce resource. (CMA)
Calen Co. manufactures and sells three products. The three products are manufactured in a factory consisting of four departments. Both labor and machine time are applied to the products as they pass through each applicable department. The nature of the machine processing and labor skills required in each department is such that neither machines nor labor can be switched from one department to another.

Calen's management is attempting to plan its production schedule for the next several months. The planning is complicated by the fact that there are labor shortages in the community and some machines will be down several months for repairs.

The following information regarding available machine and labor time by department and the machine-hours and direct-labor hours required per unit of product has been accumulated to aid in the decision. These data should be valid for at least the next six months.

		DEPARTMENT			
		1	2	3	4
MONTHLY CAPACITY AVAILABILITY					
Normal machine capacity in machine-hours		3,500	3,500	3,000	3,500
Capacity of machine being repaired in machine-hours		(500)	(400)	(300)	(200)
Available machine capacity in machine-hours		3,000	3,100	2,700	3,300
Labor capacity in direct-labor hours		4,000	4,500	3,500	3,000
Available labor in direct-labor hours		3,700	4,500	2,750	2,600

LABOR AND MACHINE SPECIFICATIONS PER UNIT OF PRODUCT					
Product	Labor and Machine Time				
401	Direct-labor hours	2	3	3	1
	Machine-hours	1	1	2	2
403	Direct-labor hours	1	2	—	2
	Machine-hours	1	1	—	2
405	Direct-labor hours	2	2	2	1
	Machine-hours	2	2	1	1

The sales department believes that the monthly demand for the next six months will be as follows:

PRODUCT	MONTHLY SALES VOLUME IN UNITS
401	500
403	400
405	1,000

Inventory levels are at satisfactory levels and need not be increased or decreased during the next six months. The unit price and cost data that will be valid for the next six months are presented below.

	PRODUCT		
	401	403	405
Unit Costs:			
Direct material	$ 7	$ 13	$ 17
Direct labor			
Department 1	12	6	12
Department 2	21	14	14
Department 3	24	—	16
Department 4	9	18	9
Variable overhead	27	20	25
Fixed overhead	15	10	32
Variable selling	3	2	4
Unit selling price	$196	$123	$167

Required

1. Calculate the monthly requirement for machine-hours and direct-labor hours for the production of products 401, 403, and 405 to determine whether the monthly sales demand for the three products can be met by the factory.
2. What monthly production schedule should Calen Co. select in order to maximize its dollar profits? Explain how you selected this production schedule, and present a schedule of the contribution to profit that would be generated by your production schedule.
3. Identify the alternatives Calen Co. might consider so it can supply its customers with all the product they demand.

22-17 Optimal production plan, certainty v. uncertainty analysis. (SMA, adapted)   Z LTD. produces two products, A and B. Product A sells for $50 per unit and requires 3 hours of direct-labor time to produce. Product B sells for $30 per unit and requires 2 hours of direct-labor time. Assume, for simplicity, that direct labor is the only variable production cost. The cost of direct labor is $7 per hour.

Fixed costs of Z LTD. are $500 per period.

Owing to the specialized nature of Z LTD.'s direct-labor requirements, the amount of direct labor available for production cannot be varied in the short run. For next period the maximum number of direct-labor hours available is 120 hours.

Z LTD.'s marketing expert advises that the maximum number of units that could be sold next period is 30 units of A and 45 units of B.

Required

1. Z LTD. must decide how many units of A and B to produce next period in order to maximize its operating income. To assist in this decision problem, you are asked to formulate it as a linear-programming problem—i.e., set up the objective function and the constraints.
2. What is the optimal combination of A and B to produce? Use both the graphic solution approach and the trial-and-error solution approach.

3. A linear-programming problem is an example of a *deterministic* model; i.e., the various numbers and relationships within the model are assumed to be known with certainty. Given, however, that most firms operate in an uncertain environment, do you think it is wise to ignore uncertainty in decisions such as this? Why?

22-18 Effect of a change in contribution margins, cost of a prediction error. (J. Demski and C. Horngren) Mary Demhorn is the manager of the Tollman Company. Tollman produces two products in two departments. Mary has great confidence in her cost accounting data regarding direct materials and direct labor, but she is less sure about the manufacturing overhead. She has been using a plantwide total factory overhead prediction equation in which the variable factory overhead rate is $4 per direct-labor hour. The plantwide total factory overhead equation is:

$$\$9,000 \text{ per month} + \$4 \text{ per direct-labor hour}$$

Mary collects the following price, cost, and technical data:

	PRODUCT	
	X	Y
Selling price per unit	$114	$149
Incremental selling cost per unit sold	$ 4	$ 8
Direct materials per unit	$ 20	$ 30
Direct-labor hours per unit:		
Machining	1 hr.	2 hrs.
Finishing	4 hrs.	3 hrs.

The wage rate is $7 per hour in machining and $9 per hour in finishing.

A linear-programming model was used to determine the optimal production combination of X and Y. The coordinates of the corners of the area of feasible solutions are:

CORNER	X	Y
1	0	0
2	200	400
3	0	500
4	250	0

Required

1. Compute the individual contribution margins of Products X and Y.
2. Determine the product combination of X and Y that will maximize the total contribution margin of Tollman Company.
3. The day after Mary has made an irrevocable decision about the combination of X and Y to produce (see requirement 2), she is presented with an impeccable regression analysis of manufacturing overhead costs in each department:

Machining overhead = $6,000 per month
+ $3.00 per machining direct-labor hour
Finishing overhead = $3,000 per month
+ $5.00 per finishing direct-labor hour

Mary is convinced that these prediction models give a "truer" or "more accurate" picture than the plantwide total factory overhead model she used. What is the cost of the prediction error associated with using the plantwide model for predicting variable factory overhead costs of each product?

22-19 Optimal production plan, food processor, fixed v. variable overhead costs. (A. Atkinson, adapted) Coldbrook Manufacturing produces two special concentrates that are derived from processing apples. These two products, which are known as Delicious (D) and Tasty (T), are used for flavoring in the food-manufacturing industry. Because of the quality of these products, Coldbrook Manufacturing can sell all the output it can produce at the existing prices. The characteristics of the two products are summarized as follows:

	PRODUCT D	PRODUCT T
Selling price	$20	$35
Direct materials used	$12.40	$17
Direct-labor hours used	0.2 hr.	0.5 hr.
Machine-hours used	1 hr.	2 hrs.

The company applies manufacturing overhead to production at the rate of $18 per direct-labor hour worked. The fixed component of the overhead charge per direct-labor hour was estimated by dividing the estimated fixed manufacturing overhead of $450,000 by the total direct-labor hours (45,000) available for production during the year.

Factory workers are paid $10 per hour worked, and the machine-hours available for production amount to 200,000 during the year. All selling and administrative expenses are fixed and are expected to be $300,000 during the upcoming year.

Required

1. Determine the optimal production mix for the upcoming year.
2. Suppose the company controller decides that by using dual rates, better estimates of variable overhead costs can be obtained. The new function used to estimate variable overhead costs (V.OVH) will be

V.OVH per unit = $1.00 (direct-labor hours) + $2.50 (machine-hours)

How might the use of this approach to variable-overhead cost estimation affect the optimal production mix determined in requirement 1?

22-20 Optimal assembly mix, cost of a prediction error, change in a technical constraint. Video Unlimited assembles and distributes video-recording machines (VCRs). At its Brisbane plant, a standard model and a deluxe model are assembled. The standard model requires two hours of assembly time in Department 1 and one hour of assembly time in Department 2. The deluxe model requires two hours of assembly time in Department 1 and three hours of assembly time in Department 2. There are multiple-production lines in each department. The total assembly time available in Department 1 is 1,200 hours per month. The total assembly time available in Department 2 is 900 hours per month. A shortage of the microchips used in the deluxe model limits its production to 250 units per month.

The unit contribution margins are $100 for the standard model and $160 for the deluxe model.

Required

1. Formulate the Brisbane product-mix decision as a linear-programming model.
2. Compute the mix of standard VCRs (S) and deluxe VCRs (D) that will maximize the total contribution margin. Use both the graphic solution approach and the trial-and-error solution approach.
3. After the production schedule is set, Video Unlimited finds that it must reduce the wholesale price of its standard model by $50 per unit to match unexpected competition from an overseas supplier. (All other data are unchanged.) Compute the cost of the prediction error for the contribution margin of the standard model.
4. The microchip supplier informs Video Unlimited that it can supply additional microchip units. Now production is feasible up to 500 deluxe VCRs per month. How will the increased supply of microchip units affect the optimal assembly mix of Video Unlimited? (Assume the contribution margin for the standard VCR unit is $50, as explained in requirement 3.)

Cost Behavior and Regression Analysis

23

Guidelines for regression analysis • Presentation of regression analysis • Choosing among regressions • Criterion 1: economic plausibility • Criterion 2: goodness of fit • Criterion 3: significance of independent variables • Criterion 4: specification analysis • Multiple regression • Appendix: Regression analysis

Chapter 10 provided an overview of how to determine cost behavior patterns (cost functions) so that predictions will be as accurate as possible. This chapter extends Chapter 10 by concentrating on the role of regression analysis in the estimation of how costs behave. **Before reading this chapter, be sure you are comfortable with the contents of Chapter 10.**

"Regression analysis" uses a formal model to measure the *average* amount of change in the dependent variable that is associated with unit changes in the amounts of one or more independent variables. When only one independent variable is used, the analysis is called **simple regression**; when more than one independent variable is used, it is called **multiple regression**.

Regression analysis has several attractive features. First, it produces measures of probable error. Second, procedures can be performed to examine how well its assumptions describe the data being analyzed. Third, regression can be applied where there are several independent variables instead of only one.

The remainder of this chapter assumes that you are already familiar with the fundamentals of both simple and multiple regression. Therefore, before reading on, if you need a review, consult the Appendix to this chapter (or an introductory book on statistics). Suppose you begin the body of the chapter and are puzzled by some of the language and concepts. Stop immediately. Study the Appendix thoroughly. Then return to the body of the chapter.

GUIDELINES FOR REGRESSION ANALYSIS

When using regression analysis, it is critical to consider the data collection issues discussed in Chapter 10. In particular, knowledge of both operations *and* cost accounting is required for intelligent regression analysis. For example, consider repair costs. Repairs may be scheduled when output is low because machines may be taken out of service at these times. In this case, regression analysis would indicate that the higher the output, the lower the repair costs. And if these costs were pooled with other overhead costs, the estimated variability of cost with output would be understated. Thus the true extent of the variation of overhead cost would be masked.

The engineering link of repairs to output can usually be clearly established. There is a cause-and-effect relationship; the higher the volume, the higher the repairs. However, a mechanical application of regression analysis would produce just the opposite picture. This example illustrates the following guidelines:

1. To the extent that physical relationships or engineering data are available for establishing cause-and-effect links, use them.
2. To the extent that relationships can be implicitly established via logic and knowledge of operations, use them (preferably in conjunction with guideline 3).
3. To the extent that the relationships in guideline 1 or 2 can be buttressed by an appropriate statistical analysis of data, use it. Regression analysis is often the best available check on guidelines 1 and 2.

Plotting the data on a graph is always recommended when using these guidelines.

PRESENTATION OF REGRESSION ANALYSIS

Regression analysis uses a *sample* of past costs to estimate how the *population* of costs behaves. The least-squares line is often presented as follows, where y' is the estimated total cost:

$$y' = a + bx$$

Consider the data in columns (2) and (3) of Exhibit 23-1 for the direct-labor costs (y') and the units produced (x) at Southern Rugs. This company produces large woven rugs. Direct-labor costs have typically been the largest single cost item in the income statement of Southern Rugs. The cost function estimated with a simple regression model is:

$$y' = 77.08 + 6.10x$$

Exhibit 23-2 presents a convenient format for summarizing the regression results. This regression model, and the results in Exhibit 23-2, will be used in several subsequent sections of this chapter.

CHOOSING AMONG REGRESSIONS

Often the accountant or the manager must choose among various possible regressions that use different independent variables or combinations thereof. For exam-

EXHIBIT 23-1

Explaining Direct-Labor Cost Behavior at Southern Rugs

WEEK NUMBER	DIRECT-LABOR COSTS	UNITS PRODUCED	MACHINE-HOURS	KILOWATTS OF ELECTRICITY USED
(1)	(2)	(3)	(4)	(5)
1	$340	34	45	130
2	346	44	41	117
3	287	31	38	119
4	262	36	35	102
5	220	30	34	99
6	416	49	42	131
7	337	39	46	145
8	180	21	29	96
9	376	41	37	105
10	295	47	33	101
11	215	34	29	95
12	275	24	41	128

ple, one regression may use units produced as the independent variable, another may use machine-hours, and another may use both as independent variables. How does the decision maker pick from among these alternative regressions? There are four important selection criteria:

1. *Economic Plausibility.* The regression equation should make economic sense and be intuitive to both the operating manager and the accountant.
2. *Goodness of Fit.* The independent variable(s) should explain a considerable percentage of the variation in the dependent variable. The *coefficient of determination* (r^2) is a frequently used measure of goodness of fit. The **coefficient of determination** or r^2 is a measure of the extent to which the independent variable accounts for the variability in the dependent variable.
3. *Significance of Independent Variable(s).* The absolute value of the *t*-statistic (the regression coefficient of each independent variable divided by its standard error) should be "respectable"—say, at least 2.00.
4. *Specification Analysis.* Testing of the basic assumptions underlying regression analysis is termed **specification analysis**. If the statistical model satisfies these assumptions, greater confidence can be placed in the estimates of cost behavior derived from using the model.

CRITERION 1: ECONOMIC PLAUSIBILITY

The first criterion, economic plausibility, places regression analysis in perspective. Does a high correlation between two variables mean that either is a cause of the

EXHIBIT 23-2

Regression Results for Simple Regression

VARIABLE	COEFFICIENT	STANDARD ERROR	*t*-VALUE
Constant	77.08	62.21	1.24
Independent variable 1:			
Units produced	6.10	1.69	3.61

$r^2 = .57$; Standard error of residuals = 48.62; Durbin-Watson = 2.09

other? Correlation, by itself, cannot answer that question: x may cause y, y may cause x, x and y may interact on one another, both may be affected by z, or the correlation may be due to chance. High correlation merely indicates that the two variables move together. No conclusions about cause and effect are warranted. For example, church attendance and beer consumption correlate over the years, but this correlation does not mean that attending church makes one thirsty or that drinking beer incites piety; they both simply increased with population growth. In summary, correlation does not imply causation.

But high correlation coupled with economic plausibility is desirable. Thus if a factory-overhead cost had a high r^2 in relation to advertising space committed, you might doubt the plausibility of the relationship. But if a factory-overhead cost had a high r^2 in relation to direct-machine hours worked, you might have greater confidence in the plausibility of the relationship. Our knowledge of cost behavior and the production function confirms the latter relationship; in contrast, there is no theoretical basis to support the former. **Without any economic plausibility to a relationship, it is less likely that the level of correlation observed in one set of data will be similarly found in other sets of data.**

For the regression reported in Exhibit 23-2, the relationship is an economically plausible one. Given the nature of the product (woven rugs), a positive relationship between direct-labor costs and units produced would be predicted by those knowledgeable about the manufacturing operations.

CRITERION 2: GOODNESS OF FIT

Other things being equal, the preferable regression model has higher rather than lower goodness of fit or explanatory power. The r^2 test for goodness of fit is an intuitive measure of the extent to which the independent variable(s) explains or accounts for the variability in the dependent variable. The range of the r^2 is from zero (implying no explanatory ability) to one (implying perfect explanatory ability).[1]

Relying exclusively on the goodness-of-fit criterion can be dangerous. It can lead to the indiscriminate inclusion of variables that increase r^2 but have no economic plausibility. The term **data mining** is sometimes used to describe a search for independent variables that is aimed at solely the maximization of r^2. Determining the dividing line between (i) reasonable data analysis and experimentation and (ii) data mining is a difficult judgment call.[2]

The r^2 for the regression reported in Exhibit 23-2 is .57, implying that varia-

---

[1]Computer programs frequently report an adjusted r^2, which is calculated thus:

$$\text{Adjusted } r^2 = r^2 - \frac{(k-1)}{(n-k)}(1 - r^2)$$

where k is the number of independent variables and n is the number of observations. The adjusted r^2 penalizes the unadjusted r^2 as extra independent variables are added to the regression. The adjusted r^2 measure can in some cases be negative (where there is a low r^2 and many independent variables in the regression). See P. Newbold, *Statistics for Business and Economics* (Englewood Cliffs, N.J.: Prentice-Hall, 1984), pp. 510–11.

[2]See J. Johnston, *Econometric Methods*, 3rd ed. (New York: McGraw-Hill, 1984), pp. 501–4. See also M. Lovell, "Data Mining," *Review of Economics and Statistics*, February 1983, pp. 1–12.

tion in the independent variable (units produced) explains 57% of the variability in direct-labor costs of Southern Rugs. A useful benchmark is that an r^2 of .30 or higher passes a goodness-of-fit test.

CRITERION 3: SIGNIFICANCE OF INDEPENDENT VARIABLES

The coefficient of the chosen independent variable should be significantly different from zero. Such a result implies that there is a significant relationship between changes in the dependent variable and changes in the independent variable(s). The t-value of the slope coefficient (that is, b) is used to assess significance. A t with an absolute value greater than 2.00 is consistent with the b coefficient being significantly different from zero.[3]

The t-value for a is seldom important because regression is rarely concerned with predicting the value of y when x is equal to zero. Instead the major objective is to predict how costs behave as activity changes over a relevant range, which seldom encompasses zero activity. As noted in Chapter 10, it is best to think of the intercept as that amount of total cost that does not vary with output *over the relevant range*.

An example may clarify why the t-value of a may be unimportant. Suppose a company had a nonlinear cost function but used a linear approximation over the relevant range of activity, as in Exhibit 23-3.

Note that a has a high t-value, but a is negative! How can a cost be negative at zero activity? It is virtually impossible, but who cares? The cost analyst should be unconcerned because what is wanted is a reliable basis for prediction within the relevant range; the t-value for b is critical for this purpose. Its extremely high value

EXHIBIT 23-3
Interpretation of Intercept

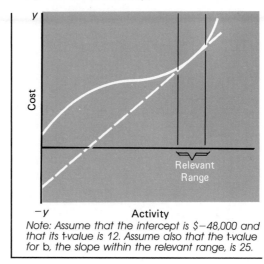

Note: Assume that the intercept is $-48,000$ and that its t-value is 12. Assume also that the t-value for b, the slope within the relevant range, is 25.

---

[3]This benchmark of $t > 2.00$ (or < -2.00) is for sample sizes of 60 or more, using a 95% confidence interval. With samples smaller than 60, a higher t value is necessary to conclude that b is significantly different from zero at the 95% confidence level. (Benchmarks for smaller samples are $t > 2.23$ for $n = 10$ for a two-tailed test and $t > 2.09$ for $n = 20$ for a two-tailed test.)

of 25 indicates that great confidence can be placed in *b* as a predictor *only within the relevant range*. Thus, in this case of a nonlinear cost function, the cost analyst would find the linear approximation offered by regression analysis very comforting.

Fixed-cost component

The foregoing example illustrates why the often-called "fixed-cost" component of a total-cost function should be carefully interpreted and labeled.

As seen in Exhibits 23-3 and 23-4, which should be examined now, a cost function that is estimated for a mixed (semivariable) cost may yield a good approximation to the actual cost function over the relevant range. However, that relevant range rarely includes zero activity. *Therefore, rather than thinking of the intercept (the fixed component) as a fixed cost, think of it as merely the intercept at* $x = 0$. For example, see Exhibit 23-4. Note that *a* would be a valid estimate of fixed cost if the actual observations included the point where activity was zero and the relationship between activity and output was linear. If more observations were available, perhaps the dashed curve would be a better approximation and *a* would be zero. Therefore the value of the constant term, *a*, is not the expected cost at zero activity; it is only the value that is computed as a result of the regression line calculated from the available data. Too often, cost analysts unjustifiably extrapolate beyond the range of the data upon which the regression equation was estimated.

In cases where a cost function is hypothesized to be wholly variable, a coefficient for *a* insignificantly different from zero (say, $t = 0.67$) would be expected. To illustrate, direct-material costs would be expected to have a coefficient for *a* insignificantly different from zero in many production settings.

EXHIBIT 23-4
Demonstration of Relevant Range

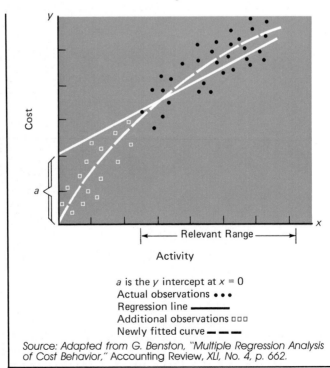

a is the *y* intercept at $x = 0$
Actual observations ● ● ●
Regression line ▬▬▬
Additional observations ▫▫▫
Newly fitted curve ▬ ▬ ▬

Source: Adapted from G. Benston, "Multiple Regression Analysis of Cost Behavior," Accounting Review, XLI, No. 4, p. 662.

Chapter 23

770

For the regression reported for Southern Rugs in Exhibit 23-2, the t-value for the slope coefficient (b) is 3.61, which exceeds the benchmark of 2.00 offered earlier. The coefficient on the units-produced independent variable is therefore significantly different from zero. The relevant range for the units-produced variable in Exhibit 23-1 is from 21 to 49 units. Thus the intercept of 77.08 should only be interpreted as the amount of direct-labor costs that does not vary with units produced in the 21-to-49-unit production range.

CRITERION 4: SPECIFICATION ANALYSIS

Although regression analysis can be a helpful tool for predictions and decisions, it can easily be misused. **There is no shortcut or substitute for the scrutiny of a particular situation to ensure that the assumptions of regression analysis are applicable to the data.**

Probably the major limitation of regression analysis is the assumption that the relationships will persist—that there is an ongoing, stable relationship between cost and the independent variable(s) used to estimate the cost. For example, if Southern Rugs changed its operations from a labor-intensive plant to a highly automated plant, the cost function in Exhibit 23-2 would probably no longer be descriptive. The Problem for Self-Study at the end of this chapter illustrates how in an automated plant, machine-hours rather than labor-hours can better explain variations in plant-overhead costs.

When four key assumptions are met, the sample values of a and b from a least-squares regression model are the best available efficient, unbiased estimates of the population values A and B. These assumptions are (1) linearity, (2) constant variance of residuals, (3) independence of residuals, and (4) normality of residuals. Most computer regression programs include tests that may be systematically applied to see whether these and other assumptions hold. These tests are often referred to as *specification analysis*.

Linearity and relevant range

First, linearity must exist between x and y in the relevant range for the population. The hypothesized relationship is

$$y = A + Bx + u$$

and we assume $E(u) = 0$. This leads to

$$E(y) = A + Bx$$

where A and B are the true (but unknown) parameters of the regression line. The deviation of the *actual* value of y from the regression line is called the **residual term** u (also called the **disturbance term** or **error term**):

$$u = y - E(y)$$

The average or expected value of u is zero. The residual term includes the effect of all variables excluded from the regression model plus the effect of measurement error in the variables included in the model.

Where there is one independent variable, the presence of linearity can be checked most easily by studying the data on a scatter diagram, a step that often is unwisely skipped. Exhibit 10-3 on page 347 presents a scatter diagram for the direct-labor cost and units-produced variables for Southern Rugs in Exhibit 23-1. Linearity appears to be a reasonable assumption for these data.

An example of a nonlinear model occurs when costs are "sticky" downwards. That is, costs may rise in response to increases in volume over time but may not decline in the same way as volume declines. A second example is the learning curve phenomenon discussed in Chapter 10; costs increase with volume increases, but less than would occur with a linear model.

Constant variance of residuals

The second assumption is that the standard deviation and variance of the u's is constant for all values of x. This assumption implies that there is a uniform scatter or dispersion of points about the regression line.[4] Again, the scatter diagram is the easiest way to check for **constant variance**. This assumption is valid for the left-hand chart in Exhibit 23-5, but not for the right-hand chart.

The constant variance assumption implies that the distribution of the u's is unaffected by the size of the independent variables. If the assumption does not hold, the reliability of the estimates of the standard errors is reduced; the a and b regression coefficients are still unbiased. **Bias** in statistics does not mean prejudice because of race or religion. Instead it means failure of a random sample to represent a population because of some systematic error. Violation of the constant variance assumption is likely in many cost-volume-profit relationships. As the right-hand chart in Exhibit 23-5 indicates, the higher the volume, the higher the probability of more scatter of the residuals.

With a small number of observations (as with the Exhibit 23-1 data for Southern Rugs), tests for constant variance are not very powerful. Data sets of at least twenty observations are necessary before even moderately reliable tests of the nonconstant variance assumption can be made.

EXHIBIT 23-5
Analysis of Constant Variance of Residuals Assumptions

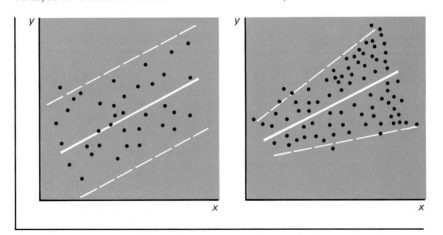

[4]Constant variance also is known as homoscedasticity. Violation of this assumption is called heteroscedasticity.

The third assumption is that the u's are independent of each other. That is, the deviation of one point about the line (its u value, where $u = y - E(y)$) is unrelated to the deviation of any other point. If the u's are not independent, the problem of **serial correlation** in the residuals (also called **autocorrelation**) is present. Serial correlation means that there is a systematic pattern in the residuals such that knowledge of the residual in time t conveys information about the residual in time $t + 1$, $t + 2$, etc.

Serial correlation affects the efficiency (but not the unbiasness) of the regression estimates of a and b. Efficiency is important because with positive (negative) correlation, the estimates of the standard errors will be understated (overstated) relative to the underlying population standard errors. Thus one may infer that the parameter estimates are more (less) precise than they actually are.

The Durbin-Watson statistic is one measure of serial correlation in the estimated residuals. For samples of ten to twenty observations, a Durbin-Watson statistic in the 1.30 to 2.70 range is consistent with the residuals being independent. For the regression model for Southern Rugs in Exhibit 23-2, the Durbin-Watson statistic is 2.09. An assumption of independence in the estimated residuals seems reasonable for this regression model.

Normality

The fourth assumption is that the points around the regression line are normally distributed. That is, the u values are normally distributed. This assumption is necessary concerning inferences about y', a, and b. For example, the normality assumption is necessary to make probability statements using the standard error of the residuals.

Tests for normality can be conducted by inspecting plots of the residuals or by examining statistics such as the skewness coefficient and the kurtosis coefficient.[5] As with tests for constant variance, data sets of at least twenty observations are necessary before even moderately reliable tests of the normality of the residuals assumption can be made.

Overview

Exhibit 23-6 presents a convenient overview of the four assumptions examined in specification analysis.[6] Three topics are covered for each assumption:

1. A description of the assumption and the consequences of its violation
2. Ways to detect if a violation occurs in the sample of data being examined
3. Examples of causes of a violation and their possible solution

Many of the items presented in Exhibit 23-6 reinforce two points stressed in Chapter 10: the gains from plotting data, and that the most difficult step in cost analysis is collecting reliable data on the dependent and independent variables.

---

[5]The skewness coefficient examines whether the distribution of the data departs from the bell-shaped curve of the normal distribution in either the upper or lower parts of the distribution. The kurtosis coefficient examines whether the distribution of the data is more or less fat-tailed than would be expected from the normal distribution. For an illustration of the use of these statistics when examining accounting data, see G. Foster, *Financial Statement Analysis*, 2nd ed. (Englewood Cliffs, N.J.: Prentice-Hall, 1986), Chap. 4.

[6]An overview of regression analysis assumptions in exhibit form is also in R. Magee, *Advanced Managerial Accounting* (New York: Harper & Row, 1986), p. 128.

EXHIBIT 23-6
Specification Analysis for Regressions Using Accounting Data

WHAT IS THE ASSUMPTION AND WHAT ARE THE CONSEQUENCES OF ITS VIOLATION?	HOW TO DETECT IF A VIOLATION OCCURS IN THE SAMPLE OF DATA BEING EXAMINED	EXAMPLES OF CAUSES OF THE VIOLATION AND THEIR POSSIBLE "SOLUTION"
A. LINEARITY Relationship between the dependent variable and the independent variable can be approximated by a linear function. One consequence of violation of this assumption is that the fitted cost function may not describe cost behavior very well; there can be high prediction errors. Different forms of nonlinearity can lead to violations of the constant variance, independence, or normality assumptions described below.	1. Plotting of the data and inspecting for nonlinearities. 2. Include nonlinear variable in the regression model, such as x^2 or $\sqrt{x}$, and examine their statistical significance. 3. Estimate nonlinear cost functions, such as a learning-curve function, and conduct specification analysis on its residuals. (Alternatively, the data may be transformed to examine if the linearity assumption is appropriate.)	1. Data-recording problems, e.g. (a) time period for the dependent variable is weekly, whereas the time period for the independent variable is monthly, (b) materials costs reported when materials are purchased and not when materials are used, and (c) pension expenses are recorded only in the final quarter rather than being accrued for each pay period. *Possible solution:* (a) Use the same unit of time to measure all variables, and (b) use an accrual-accounting basis for recording costs. 2. Learning by workers causes increases in labor productivity. *Possible solution:* Estimate a cost function that explicitly incorporates learning effects. 3. Inflation in input prices. *Possible solution:* Deflate the variables affected by inflation by a price index. 4. "Cost stickiness" (costs decline less than predicted when activity declines). *Possible solution:* Estimate a cost function including a dummy variable that assumes a value of 1 if activity declines, and 0 otherwise.
B. CONSTANT VARIANCE OF RESIDUALS The variance of the residuals around the "true" regression line should be the same over the entire range of the independent variable. A consequence of violating this assumption is that the standard error used to test the significance of the independent variable(s) is less reliable; it will depend on the range of the independent variable. Estimates of the regression coefficients are still unbiased.	1. Plotting the data and inspecting for non-constant variance. 2. Examining the equality of the variance of the estimated residuals in different ranges of the independent variable. 3. Testing for specific violations of nonconstant variance (e.g., residuals are proportional to the expected value of the dependent variable).	1. Stoppages, defective raw materials, etc., have larger dollar effects at higher activity levels. *Possible solution:* Transform the dependent variable (y_i) to, say, (log y_i). 2. Increasing levels of inflation occur as the firm is expanding activity. *Possible solution:* Deflate variables affected by inflation by a price index. 3. Repairs and maintenance conducted during periods of low activity. *Possible solution:* Estimate a separate cost function for repairs and maintenance.

C. INDEPENDENCE OF RESIDUALS

Knowledge of the sign or magnitude of a residual should not help predict the sign or magnitude of the residual in the next (or subsequent) periods. Autocorrelation affects the efficiency (but not the unbiasness) of the regression estimates of the a and b coefficients. Positive (negative) autocorrelation results in the estimated standard errors of the regression coefficients being understated (overstated).

1. Plotting the pattern of the residuals around the fitted line and examining for systematic patterns.

2. Computing the Durbin-Watson statistic, which tests for (first-order) serial correlation.

3. Computing the autocorrelation function of the residuals, which facilitates testing for serial correlation at any specific lag structure.

1. Underlying cost function is nonlinear. *Possible solution:* See the above section for the linearity assumption.

2. Underlying cost function is linear, but it includes more variables than are currently being analyzed. *Possible solution:* Include additional independent variables in the regression analysis.

3. High autocorrelation is induced by successive activity levels having a high percentage of commonality. *Possible solution:* Estimate the cost function using successive changes in the dependent and independent variables rather than successive values of the variables.

D. NORMALITY OF RESIDUALS

The distribution of the "true" residuals should be well approximated by a normal distribution. One consequence of violating this assumption is that the standard error may not be a good measure of dispersion, causing the significance tests to be less reliable.

1. Plotting the residuals and inspecting whether the distribution approximates the bell-shaped normal curve.

2. Computing distribution statistics for the residuals, such as the skewness coefficient and the kurtosis coefficient.

1. Extreme (nonnormal) observations can arise from errors in recording the data. (This is a very common situation. All extreme values should be checked against their source records.) *Possible solution:* Correct the recording error.

2. Extreme observation arises from an "unusual" event such as a fire or a strike. *Possible solution:* Delete the extreme observation or make an adjustment to exclude the effect of the "unusual" event.

3. Technological change, such as a marked change in the level of automation, can cause the distribution of residuals to be bimodal (that is, to have two separate groupings of observations). *Possible solution:* Restrict the data being analyzed to a period with a low level of technological change.

In some cases, satisfactory predictions of a cost may be based on only one independent variable, such as direct-labor hours. In many cases, however, accuracy can be improved by basing the prediction on more than one independent variable. The most widely used equations to express relationships between a dependent variable and two or more independent variables are linear equations of the form

$$y = a + b_1x_1 + b_2x_2 + b_3x_3 + \cdots + u$$

where y is the variable to be predicted; x_1, x_2, and x_3 are the independent variables on which the prediction is to be based; b_1, b_2, and b_3 are unknown coefficients; and u is the "residual term" that includes the net effect of other factors. For cost predictions, there may be two, three, or more independent variables such as direct-labor hours, direct-labor cost, machine-hours, weight of materials, temperature, types of machines, and types of labor skill.

Consider again the data in Exhibit 23-1. The earlier sections of this chapter discussed a simple regression model. Exhibit 23-7 presents results for the following multiple regression model (using data in columns (2), (3) and (4) of Exhibit 23-1):

$$y' = a + b_1(\text{Units produced}) + b_2(\text{Machine-hours})$$
$$= -137.53 + 4.68 \text{ Units produced} + 7.08 \text{ Machine-hours}$$

It is economically plausible that both machine-hours and units produced would help explain variations in direct-labor costs at Southern Rugs; workers use machine-operated tools in the production of each woven rug, and there is no standard number of hours spent on each unit produced. The t statistics on both of the independent variables are significantly different from zero ($t = 4.46$ for the coefficient on units produced and $t = 4.44$ for the coefficient on machine-hours). The r^2 of .57 with the simple regression in Exhibit 23-2 increases to .86 with the multiple regression in Exhibit 23-7. This multiple regression model satisfies both economic and statistical criteria, and it explains sizably more variation in direct-labor costs than does the simple regression model in Exhibit 23-2.

In Exhibit 23-7 the slope coefficients, 4.68 and 7.08, measure the change in the dependent variable (direct-labor costs) associated with a unit change in each independent variable (assuming that the other independent variable is held constant). For example, the effect of producing one more unit is to increase direct-labor costs by $4.68, assuming that the number of machine-hours is held constant.

EXHIBIT 23-7
Regression Results for Multiple Regression with Two Independent Variables

VARIABLE	COEFFICIENT	STANDARD ERROR	t-VALUE
Constant	−137.53	60.59	−2.27
Independent variable 1:			
Units produced	4.68	1.05	4.46
Independent variable 2:			
Machine-hours	7.08	1.59	4.44

$r^2 = .86$; Standard error of residuals = 28.68; Durbin-Watson = 2.58

A major concern that arises with multiple regression is multicollinearity. **Multicollinearity** exists when two or more independent variables are highly correlated with each other; a correlation greater than .7 is a frequently used benchmark for designating a correlation as high. In many cost accounting contexts, high correlation is to be expected.

Exhibit 23-1 (column 5) lists the units of electricity used each week at the Southern Rugs plant. The correlation between machine-hours (column 4) and units (kilowatts) of electricity used (column 5) is .94; given that machines are the largest users of electricity at Southern Rugs, this .94 correlation is economically plausible. Multicollinearity has the effect of increasing the standard errors of the coefficients of the individual variables. Exhibit 23-8 presents results for the following multiple regression model:

$$y' = a + b_1(\text{Units produced}) + b_2(\text{Machine-hours}) + b_3(\text{Kilowatts of electricity})$$

$$= -129.75 + 4.58 \text{ Units produced} + 8.64 \text{ machine-hours}$$
$$-0.55 \text{ Kilowatts of electricity}$$

The standard error of the slope coefficient on the machine-hours variable (b_2) in Exhibit 23-7 is 1.59. When the highly collinear units of electricity variable is added in Exhibit 23-8, the standard error of b_2 increases to 5.11. The result is that there is greater uncertainty about the underlying value of the coefficient on machine-hours in the Exhibit 23-8 regression, relative to the value of the coefficient on machine-hours in Exhibit 23-7. The 95% confidence interval for b_2 in Exhibit 23-7 is 3.90 to 10.26 (7.08 ± (2)1.59). In contrast, the 95% confidence interval for b_2 when the highly collinear kilowatts of electricity variable is added to the regression increases to −1.58 to 18.86 (8.64 ± (2)5.11). Another limitation of using the regression model in Exhibit 23-8 is that the negative b_3 coefficient on kilowatts of electricity is economically implausible.

SUMMARY

Regression analysis is a systematic approach to cost estimation. Unlike several other cost estimation approaches, it has measures of probable error and can be applied when there are several independent variables instead of only one. Ideally, the relationships underlying a regression model should be established via logic and knowledge of operations.

EXHIBIT 23-8
Regression Results for Multiple Regression with Three Independent Variables

VARIABLE	COEFFICIENT	STANDARD ERROR	t-VALUE
Constant	−129.75	68.31	−1.90
Independent variable 1:			
Units produced	4.58	1.15	3.98
Independent variable 2:			
Machine-hours	8.64	5.11	1.69
Independent variable 3:			
Kilowatts of electricity	−0.55	1.70	−0.32

$r^2 = .87$; Standard error of residuals = 30.22; Durbin-Watson = 2.58

Four important criteria when choosing among regression models are (1) economic plausibility, (2) goodness of fit, (3) significance of independent variable(s), and (4) conformance of data with assumptions as to linearity, constant variance of residuals, independence of residuals, and the residuals being normally distributed. The Problem for Self-Study illustrates a systematic approach to using these criteria when comparing alternative regression models.

_____PROBLEM FOR SELF-STUDY_____

problem Krystal Carrington was given the task of developing a cost function for predicting indirect overhead costs for the Denver personal computer manufacturing plant of Electronic Horizons. The production plant is highly automated. The following information has been collected:

MONTH	INDIRECT OVERHEAD COSTS ($)	MACHINE-HOURS	DIRECT-LABOR HOURS
January	2,530	2,730	324
February	1,900	1,810	210
March	4,710	3,403	347
April	1,270	2,200	331
May	4,380	3,411	272
June	4,020	2,586	202
July	3,730	3,364	342
August	3,070	2,411	247
September	4,980	3,964	347
October	3,310	2,897	328
November	1,270	2,207	293
December	3,510	2,864	307

She examines two cost functions using regression analysis:

REGRESSION MODEL A:
Indirect Overhead Costs = f(Machine-Hours)

VARIABLE	COEFFICIENT	STANDARD ERROR	t-STATISTIC
Constant	−1,707.70	912.94	−1.87
Independent variable 1:			
Machine-hours	1.75	0.32	5.52

$r^2 = .75$; Standard error of residuals = 657.44; Durbin-Watson = 2.59

REGRESSION MODEL B:
Indirect Overhead Costs = f(Direct-Labor Hours)

VARIABLE	COEFFICIENT	STANDARD ERROR	t-STATISTIC
Constant	1,914.10	2,264.60	0.84
Independent variable 1:			
Direct-Labor hours	4.43	7.55	0.59

$r^2 = .03$; Standard error of residuals = 1,300.77; Durbin-Watson = 2.45

EXHIBIT 23-9
Cost Behavior Patterns at Electronic Horizons

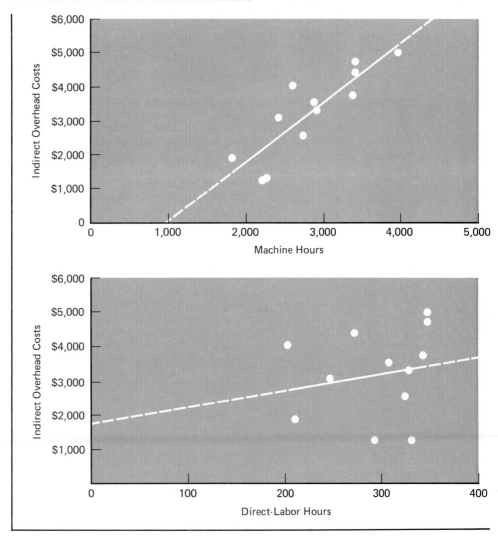

Required Which cost function should Carrington adopt for predicting indirect overhead costs? Why?

solution Plots of the data underlying each regression model are presented in Exhibit 23-9. Exhibit 23-10 presents a systematic approach to comparing these two regression models. The regression using machine-hours is preferable to the regression using direct-labor hours.

Terms to Learn

This chapter, the chapter appendix, and the Glossary contain definitions of the following important terms:

autocorrelation (p. 773)   *bias (772)*   *coefficient of determination (767)*
confidence interval (786)   *constant variance (772)*   *data mining (768)*

EXHIBIT 23-10
Comparison of Alternative Regression Models

CRITERION	REGRESSION A (MACHINE-HOURS)	REGRESSION B (DIRECT-LABOR HOURS)
1. Economic Plausibility	Positive relationship between overhead costs and machine-hours is economically plausible in a highly automated plant.	Positive relationship between overhead costs and direct-labor hours is economically plausible, but less so than machine-hours on a month-by-month basis.
2. Goodness of Fit	$r^2 = .75$ Excellent goodness of fit.	$r^2 = .03$ Minimal goodness of fit.
3. Significance of Independent Variables	t-statistic on machine-hours of 5.52 is significant.	t-statistic on direct-labor hours of 0.59 is insignificant.
4. Specification Analysis A. Linearity	Appears reasonable from a plot of the data.	Appears questionable from a plot of the data.
B. Constant Variance of Residuals	Appears reasonable, although 12 observations do not facilitate the drawing of reliable inferences.	Appears questionable, although 12 observations do not facilitate the drawing of reliable inferences.
C. Independence of Residuals	Durbin-Watson = 2.59 Assumption of independence is not rejected.	Durbin-Watson = 2.45 Assumption of independence is not rejected.
D. Normality of Residuals	Data base too small to make reliable inferences.	Data base too small to make reliable inferences.

Special Points and Pitfalls

Evaluation of a regression model should be conducted in a systematic way. The format in Exhibit in 23-10 is a useful way to summarize comparisons across alternative regression models. One regression model will seldom be preferred to competing models for every one of the categories in Exhibit 23-10. A cost analyst will typically be making a choice among "imperfect" cost functions, in the sense that one or more of the assumptions underlying ordinary least squares will not be perfectly met by the data of any single cost function.

Simple regression analysis exists when only one independent variable is used. Multiple regression analysis exists when two or more independent variables are used. A common problem with multiple regression is multicollinearity. High multicollinearity can lead to an increase in the standard errors of the coefficients of the independent variables.

The most difficult step in cost analysis is collecting reliable data on the dependent and independent variables. Mechanical use of regression analysis without detailed attempts to collect "high-quality" data can result in major problems. Such problems include nonlinearity, nonconstant variance of the residuals, autocorrelation of the residuals, and nonnormality of the residuals.

APPENDIX: REGRESSION ANALYSIS

The data in columns (2) and (3) of Exhibit 23-1 will be used to illustrate regression analysis. The dependent variable is direct-labor costs. The independent variable is units produced. Note that the data are paired. For example, week 11 consists of a units-produced observation (independent variable) of 34 with an *associated* direct-labor cost (dependent variable) of $215.

The scatter diagram of these twelve points in Exhibit 23-11 indicates that a straight line should provide a reasonable approximation of the relationship that prevailed during the sample history between direct-labor costs and units produced. Using the least-squares technique, the sum of the squares of the vertical deviations (distances) from the points to the straight line is smaller than it would be from any other straight line. *Note especially that, as the graph in Exhibit 23-11 shows, the deviations are measured vertically to the regression line.*

The object is to find the values of the a and b coefficients in the predicting equation $y' = a + bx$, where y' is the calculated value as distinguished from the observed value of y. We wish to find the numerical values of the coefficients a and b that minimize $\Sigma(y - y')^2$, the difference between the observed y and the y' value predicted by the equation relating y to changes in x. This calculation is accomplished by using two equations, usually called *normal equations:*

$$\Sigma y = na + b(\Sigma x)$$

$$\Sigma xy = a(\Sigma x) + b(\Sigma x^2)$$

EXHIBIT 23-11
Least-Squares Criterion

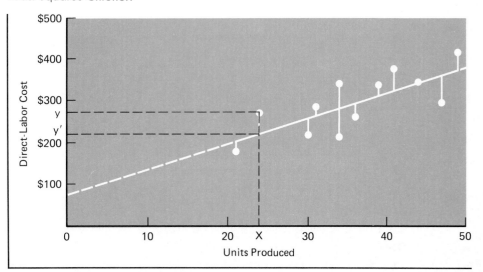

781

EXHIBIT 23-12
Computation for Least Squares

WEEK	UNITS PRODUCED	DIRECT LABOR COSTS				TOTAL VARIANCE OF y	UNEXPLAINED VARIANCE	TOTAL VARIANCE OF x
	x	y	x^2	xy	y'	$(y - \bar{y})^2$	$(y - y')^2$	$(x - \bar{x})^2$
1	34	340	1,156	11,560	284.48	1,958	3,082	3
2	44	346	1,936	15,224	345.48	2,525	0	67
3	31	287	961	8,897	266.18	77	433	23
4	36	262	1,296	9,432	296.68	1,139	1,203	0
5	30	220	900	6,600	260.08	5,738	1,606	34
6	49	416	2,401	20,384	375.98	14,460	1,602	173
7	39	337	1,521	13,143	314.98	1,702	485	10
8	21	180	441	3,780	205.18	13,398	634	220
9	41	376	1,681	15,416	327.18	6,440	2,383	27
10	47	295	2,209	13,865	363.78	1	4,731	125
11	34	215	1,156	7,310	284.48	6,520	4,827	3
12	24	275	576	6,600	223.48	431	2,654	140
	430	3,549	16,234	132,211	$\approx$3,549	54,389	23,640	825

where n is the number of pairs of observations; Σx and Σy are, respectively, the sums of the given x's and y's; Σx^2 is the sum of the squares of the x's; and Σxy is the sum of the products obtained by multiplying each of the given x's by the associated observed value of y.

Using our numerical illustration, we obtain the ingredients of our normal equations from the table in Exhibit 23-12. Substituting into the two simultaneous linear equations, we obtain:

$$3,549 = 12a + 430b$$

$$132,211 = 430a + 16,234b$$

The solution is $a = 77.08$ and $b = 6.10$, which can be obtained by direct substitution if the normal equations are reexpressed symbolically as follows:

$$a = \frac{(\Sigma y)(\Sigma x^2) - (\Sigma x)(\Sigma xy)}{n(\Sigma x^2) - (\Sigma x)(\Sigma x)}$$

$$b = \frac{n(\Sigma xy) - (\Sigma x)(\Sigma y)}{n(\Sigma x^2) - (\Sigma x)(\Sigma x)}$$

And for our illustration we now have:

$$a = \frac{(3,549)(16,234) - (430)(132,211)}{12(16,234) - (430)(430)} = 77.08$$

$$b = \frac{(12)(132,211) - (430)(3,549)}{(12)(16,234) - (430)(430)} = 6.10$$

Placing the amounts for a and b in the equation of the least-squares line, we have:

$$y' = \$77.08 + \$6.10x$$

where y' is the predicted direct-labor cost for any number of units produced. A prime is placed on the y to distinguish between the value of y that is predicted using the equation of the line and that which is actually observed for a specified value of x. If we apply the equation, we would predict, for example, that production of 30 units would have direct-labor costs on average of $\$77.08 + \$6.10(30) = \$260.08$.

CORRELATION AND GOODNESS OF FIT

How much of the total variation of the y's can be attributed to chance? How much can be attributed to the relationship between the two variables x and y? The coefficient of determination (r^2) is a measure of the extent to which the independent variable accounts for the variability in the dependent variable. Note in Exhibit 23-13 that the total deviation of the dependent variable y from its mean $\bar{y}$ (that is, $y - \bar{y}$) can be divided into two parts: first, the deviation of the value on the line (y') from the mean $\bar{y}$, or ($y' - \bar{y}$), which is explained by the given value of x; and second, the deviation of y from the regression line ($y - y'$), which is not explained by x.

The measure of the goodness of fit of a regression line is made by comparing $\Sigma(y - y')^2$ with the sum of the squares of the deviations of y's from their mean $\Sigma(y - \bar{y})^2$. Using our illustration from Exhibit 23-12, $\Sigma y = 3,549$ and $\bar{y} = 3,549 \div 12 = 295.75$. Therefore:

$$\Sigma(y - \bar{y})^2 = (340 - 295.75)^2 + (346 - 295.75)^2 + \cdots + (275 - 295.75)^2 = 54,389$$

EXHIBIT 23-13
Fundamental Measure of Variation

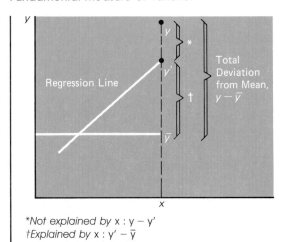

*Not explained by x : y − y'
†Explained by x : y' − ȳ

Chance variation is measured by the deviations of the points from the regression line, by the quantity $\Sigma(y - y')^2$. If all the points actually fell on a straight line, $\Sigma(y - y')^2$ would equal zero. To compute this quantity for our illustration, the predicted values y' must be calculated by substituting the given values of x into the least-squares equation:

$$y' = 77.08 + 6.10x$$

Therefore we obtain $y' = 77.08 + 6.10(34) = 284.48$ for the first week's production, $y' = 77.08 + 6.10(44) = 345.48$ for the second week's production, and so on. Substituting these values and the observed y's into $\Sigma(y - y')^2$, we get

$$\Sigma(y - y')^2 = (340 - 284.48)^2 + (346 - 345.48)^2 + \cdots$$
$$+ (275 - 223.48)^2 = 23,640$$

Therefore,

$$\frac{\Sigma(y - y')^2}{\Sigma(y - \bar{y})^2} = \frac{23,640}{54,389} = .43 = 43\%$$

of the variation in the direct-labor cost of the units produced can be attributed to random variation (chance) and the effect of other variables not explicitly incorporated into the model. The remaining 57% (100% − 43%) of the variation in the direct-labor costs is accounted for by differences in the number of units produced.

The coefficient of determination is often called **r-square** (**r^2**). It indicates the proportion of the variance, $(y - \bar{y})^2$, that is explained by the independent variable x. The coefficient of determination is also expressed more informatively as 1 minus the proportion of total variance that is not explained:

$$r^2 = 1 - \frac{\Sigma(y - y')^2}{\Sigma(y - \bar{y})^2} = 1 - \frac{\text{Unexplained variance}}{\text{Total variance}}$$

$$= 1 - \frac{23,640}{54,389} = 1 - .43 = .57$$

The square root of the proportion .57 (that is, the proportion of the total variation in direct-labor costs that is accounted for by differences in the number of units produced) is called the coefficient of correlation, r:

$$r = \pm \sqrt{1 - \frac{\Sigma(y - y')^2}{\Sigma(y - \bar{y})^2}}$$

The sign attached to r is the sign of b in the predicting equation:

$$r^2 = .57$$
$$r = +\sqrt{.57} = .755$$

The coefficient of correlation is a relative measure of the relationship between two variables. The range is from −1 (perfect negative correlation) to +1 (perfect positive correlation); a correlation of zero implies no correlation between the two variables.

How accurate is the regression line as a basis for prediction? We are using a sample of historical events. If we duplicated that sample using different data, we would not expect to obtain the same line. The values for a and b would differ for each sample taken. What we really want to know is the true regression line of the entire population,

$$y = A + Bx$$

where A and B are the true coefficients. The values of a and b are estimates based on a sample. Therefore they are subject to chance variation, as are all sample statistics.

To judge the accuracy of the regression line, we examine the dispersion of the observed values of y around the regression line. A measure of this dispersion assists in judging the probable accuracy of a prediction of the average direct-labor cost of, say, 41 units produced. The measure of the scatter of the actual observations about the regression line is called the **standard error of the residuals**. (It is also called the **standard error of the estimate**.) The standard error of the residuals for the population may be calculated from a sample in a simple linear regression as follows:

$$S_e = \sqrt{\frac{\Sigma(y - y')^2}{n - 2}}$$

where n is the size of the sample.

Using the data in Exhibit 23-12:

$$S_e = \sqrt{\frac{23,640}{10}} = 48.62$$

If the assumptions of regression analysis are met (e.g., constant variance of residuals and normality of residuals), we can use the standard error to help gauge our confidence in the predictions. Consider the prediction of direct-labor costs when 41 units are produced: $y' = 77.08 + 6.10(41) = 327.18$. Approximately two-thirds of the points in a normal distribution should be within the band $y' \pm$ one standard error:

$$\$327.18 \pm (1.0)(\$48.62)$$

Thus the band is $279 to $376 (rounding to the nearest dollar). Management can predict that a production level of 41 units will result in costs between $279 and $376, with approximately two chances out of three that the confidence interval constructed in this manner will contain the true value of y. (For predicting costs beyond the data set used to estimate the regression model, an extra adjustment is necessary that will increase the standard error of prediction.[7])

---

[7]See P. Newbold, *Statistics for Business and Economics* (Englewood Cliffs, N.J.: Prentice-Hall, 1984), p. 480.

Does a significant explanatory relationship exist between x and y? For example, the regression coefficient of x of \$6.10 implies a change in cost of \$6.10 for each additional unit produced. The regression coefficient \$6.10 is an estimate of a population parameter. A particular sample may indicate a relationship, even when none exists, by pure chance. If there is no relationship, then the slope B of the true regression line would be zero. A null hypothesis can be set up that $B = 0$. If the sample value b is significantly different from zero, we would reject the hypothesis and assert that there is a definite relationship between the variables.

To test this null hypothesis, we need to calculate the **standard error** of the b coefficient:

$$S_b = \frac{S_e}{\sqrt{\Sigma(x - \bar{x})^2}}$$

For the data in Exhibit 23-12:

$$S_b = \frac{48.62}{\sqrt{825}} = \frac{48.62}{28.72} = 1.69$$

The procedure for deciding whether a positive relationship exists between units produced and direct-labor costs is this:

Null hypothesis: $B = 0$ (no relationship)
Alternative hypothesis: $B \neq 0$ (relationship exists between direct-labor costs and units produced)

The value of b is \$6.10. If the null hypothesis is true, $B = 0$, and b is \$6.10 units from B. In terms of its standard error, this is \$6.10 ÷ \$1.69 = 3.61. Therefore b is 3.61 standard errors from $B = 0$. A deviation of more than two standard errors is usually regarded as significant. Therefore the probability is low that a deviation as large as 3.61 standard errors could occur by chance. Consequently, we reject the null hypothesis and accept the alternative hypothesis that there is a significant relationship between the variables.

The amount of 3.61 standard errors just computed is called the t-value of the regression coefficient:

$$\textbf{\textit{t}-value} = \frac{\text{Coefficient}}{\text{Standard error of the coefficient}} = \frac{6.10}{1.69} = 3.61$$

High t-values enhance confidence in the value of the coefficient as a predictor. Low t-values (as a rule of thumb, under 2.00) are indications of low reliability of the predictive power of that coefficient.

Confidence intervals and t-values

The standard error of the regression coefficient and the table of values of t permit us to assess a probability that the "true" B is between specified limits. These limits are usually called **confidence intervals.** The 95% confidence interval is computed with the use of the appropriate t-value from the table in Exhibit 23-14.

EXHIBIT 23-14

Selected Values of t

d.f.	$t_{.100}$	$t_{.050}$	$t_{.025}$	$t_{.010}$	$t_{.005}$	d.f.
1	3.078	6.314	12.706	31.821	63.657	1
5	1.476	2.015	2.571	3.365	4.032	5
8	1.397	1.860	2.306	2.896	3.355	8
10	1.372	1.812	2.228	2.764	3.169	10
12	1.356	1.782	2.179	2.681	3.055	12
15	1.341	1.753	2.131	2.602	2.947	15
20	1.325	1.725	2.086	2.528	2.845	20
inf.	1.282	1.645	1.960	2.326	2.576	inf.

Note: The t-value describes the sampling distribution of a deviation from a population value divided by the standard error.

Degrees of freedom (d.f.) are in the first column. The probabilities indicated as subvalues of t in the heading refer to the sum of a one-tailed area under the curve that lies outside the point t.

For example, in the distribution of the means of samples of size $n = 10$, d.f. $= n - 2 = 8$; then .025 of the area under the curve falls in one tail outside the interval $t \pm 2.306$.

For instance, with a sample size of 12, we use the row in Exhibit 23-14 with $n - 2 = 10$ degrees of freedom, and the column $t_{.025}$ (for a two tail test) to find the confidence interval:

$$b \pm t_{.025}(S_b)$$

$$6.10 \pm 2.228(1.69)$$

$$= 6.10 \pm 3.77$$

There is a .95 probability that the population (true) value of B lies in the $2.33 to $9.87 range. (Alternatively speaking, there is a .025 probability that the true value of B lies below $2.33 and a .025 probability that the true value of B lies above $9.87.)

_____QUESTIONS, PROBLEMS, AND CASES_____

23-1 What is the role of the relevant range in interpreting a scatter diagram?

23-2 Give two synonyms for *residual term*.

23-3 "Multicollinearity exists when the dependent and the independent variable are highly correlated." Do you agree? Explain.

23-4 "High correlation between two variables means that one is the cause and the other is the effect." Do you agree? Why?

23-5 Name two advantages of using regression analysis for cost estimation relative to the use of the high-low approach.

23-6 Identify two possible causes of the linearity assumption in regression analysis being violated. Give one possible solution for each cause.

23-7 Identify two possible causes of the constant variance of the residuals assumption in regression analysis being violated. Give one possible solution for each cause.

23-8 Identify two possible causes of the independence of the residuals assumption in regression analysis being violated. Give one possible solution for each cause.

23-9 Identify two possible causes of the normality of the residuals assumption in regression analysis being violated. Give one possible solution for each cause.

23-10 Interpretation of regression coefficient. A manager learned about linear regression techniques at an evening college course. He decided to apply regression in his study of repair costs in his plant. He plotted 24 points for the past 24 months and fitted a least-squares line:

$$\text{Total repair cost per month} = \$80,000 - \$.50x$$

where x = number of machine-hours worked.

He was baffled because the result was nonsense. Apparently, the more the machines were run, the less the repair costs. He decided that regression was a useless technique.

Required | Why was the puzzling regression coefficient negative? Do you agree with the manager's conclusion regarding regression? Explain.

23-11 Account analysis and cause and effect. The costs of maintenance of way and structures (M of W & S) are incurred by a railroad to continue in usable condition the fixed facilities employed in the carrier's railway operations. These costs are usually very material in relation to revenue and net income. A substantial portion of M of W & S costs is incurred on a cyclical program. For example, the costs are influenced by the tonnage that moves over the road for periods of up to or more than ten years. The costs are also influenced by management policy decisions and other nontraffic factors.

Required | 1. What are likely to be heavy influences (the influential independent variables) on the M of W & S costs for any given year? Be as specific as possible.
2. If M of W & S costs were estimated by simple regression using a measure of traffic (such as train-miles or gross ton-miles) as the independent variable, would the variable-cost portion (the b-coefficient) tend to be too high or too low? Why?

23-12 Fundamentals of least squares. (Adapted from *Separating and Using Costs as Fixed and Variable*, N.A.A. *Bulletin*, Accounting Practice Report No. 10) Assume that nine monthly observations of power costs are to be used as a basis for developing a budget formula. A scatter diagram indicates a mixed cost behavior in the form $y = a + bx$. The observations are:

MONTH	TOTAL MIXED COST (y)	MACHINE-HOURS (x)
1	$ 23	22
2	25	23
3	20	19
4	20	12
5	20	12
6	15	9
7	14	7
8	14	11
9	16	14
	$167	129

23-13 Rudiments of least-squares regression analysis. (H. Nurnberg) ABC Corporation wishes to set flexible budgets for each of its operating departments. A separate maintenance department performs all routine and major repair work on the corporation's equipment and facilities. It has been determined that maintenance cost is primarily a function of machine-hours worked in the various production departments. The maintenance cost incurred and the actual machine-hours worked during the first four months of 19_1 are as follows:

	MAINTENANCE COST (y)	MACHINE-HOURS (x)
January	$350	800
February	350	1,200
March	150	400
April	550	1,600

(This example simply illustrates the methods that can be used for determining similar information. If, as in this instance, the number of observations is small, additional analysis should be performed to determine whether the results are reliable.)

Required

1. Draw a scatter diagram.
2. Compute variable maintenance cost per machine-hour and fixed maintenance cost per month, using the high-low method.
3. Compute variable maintenance cost per machine-hour and fixed maintenance cost per month, using least-squares regression analysis.
4. Compute the coefficient of determination, the r^2.

23-14 Multiple choice. (CMA) The Alpha Company, which produces several different products, is making plans for the introduction of a new product that it will sell for $6 a unit. The following estimates have been made for manufacturing costs on 100,000 units to be produced the first year:

Direct materials	$50,000
Direct labor	$40,000 (the labor rate is $4 an hour)

Overhead costs have not yet been estimated for the new product, but monthly data on total production and overhead costs for the past 24 months have been analyzed using simple linear regression. The following results were derived from the simple regression and will provide the basis for overhead cost estimates for the new product.

SIMPLE REGRESSION ANALYSIS RESULTS ($y = a + bx$)

Dependent variable (y)—factory-overhead costs	
Independent variable (x)—direct-labor hours	
Computed values:	
y-intercept	$40,000
Coefficient of independent variable	$2.10
Coefficient of correlation (r)	.953
Standard error of residuals	$2,840
Standard error of regression coefficient	.42
Mean value of independent variable	$18,000
Coefficient of determination (r^2)	.908

1. What percentage of the variation in overhead costs is explained by the independent variable? (a) 90.8%, (b) 42%, (c) 48.8%, (d) 95.3%, (e) some amount other than those mentioned.
2. To determine a confidence interval for the parameter estimated by b in the regression computation, an appropriate t-value would be selected from a table of values from a t distribution corresponding to the desired level of confidence and having (a) 0 degrees of freedom, (b) 2 degrees of freedom, (c) 10 degrees of freedom, (d) 22 degrees of freedom, (e) 24 degrees of freedom.
3. Assuming that the appropriate t-value is 2.07, a 95% confidence interval for the b values would be (a) (1.23, 2.97), (b) (.10, 4.10), (c) (2.1, 2.97), (d) (.22, 3.97), (e) some amount other than those mentioned.
4. The total overhead cost for an estimated activity level of 20,000 direct-labor hours would be (a) $42,000, (b) $82,000, (c) $122,000, (d) $222,000, (e) some amount other than those mentioned.
5. The expected contribution margin per unit to be earned during the first year on 100,000 units of the new product would be (a) $4.49, (b) $4.89, (c) $0.30, (d) $5.10, (e) some amount other than those mentioned.

23-15 Choosing a prediction method. (CMA, adapted) The Ramon Co. manufactures a wide range of products at several different plant locations. The Franklin Plant, which manufactures electrical components, has been experiencing some difficulties with fluctuating monthly overhead costs. The fluctuations have made it difficult to estimate the level of overhead that will be incurred for any one month.

Management wants to be able to estimate overhead costs accurately in order to plan its operation and financial needs better. A trade association publication to which Ramon Co. subscribes indicates that, for companies manufacturing electrical components, overhead tends to vary with direct-labor hours.

One member of the accounting staff has proposed that the cost behavior pattern of the overhead costs be determined. Then overhead costs could be predicted from the budgeted direct-labor hours.

Another member of the accounting staff suggested that a good starting place for determining the cost behavior pattern of overhead costs would be an analysis of historical data. The historical cost behavior pattern would provide a basis for estimating future overhead costs. The methods proposed for determining the cost behavior pattern included the high-low method, the scatter-graph (visual fit) method, simple linear regression, and multiple regression. Of these methods Ramon Co. decided to employ the high-low method, the scatter-graph method, and simple linear regression. Data on direct-labor hours and the respective overhead costs incurred were collected for the previous two years. The raw data follow:

	19_3		19_4	
	DIRECT-LABOR HOURS	OVERHEAD COSTS	DIRECT-LABOR HOURS	OVERHEAD COSTS
January	20,000	$84,000	21,000	$86,000
February	25,000	99,000	24,000	93,000
March	22,000	89,500	23,000	93,000
April	23,000	90,000	22,000	87,000
May	20,000	81,500	20,000	80,000
June	19,000	75,500	18,000	76,500
July	14,000	70,500	12,000	67,500
August	10,000	64,500	13,000	71,000
September	12,000	69,000	15,000	73,500
October	17,000	75,000	17,000	72,500
November	16,000	71,500	15,000	71,000
December	19,000	78,000	18,000	75,000

Using linear regression, the following data were obtained:

VARIABLE	COEFFICIENT	STANDARD ERROR	*t*-VALUE
Constant	39,859	2,668.3	14.94
Independent variable:			
Direct-labor hours	2.1549	0.1437	15.00

$r^2 = .911$; Standard error of residuals = 2,840.2; Durbin-Watson = 1.2

The true *t*-statistic for a 95% confidence interval (22 degrees of freedom) is 2.074.

Required

1. Using the high-low method, determine the cost behavior pattern of the overhead costs for the Franklin Plant.
2. Using the scatter-graph (visual fit) method, determine the cost behavior pattern of the overhead costs for the Franklin Plant.
3. Using the results of the regression analysis, calculate the estimate of overhead costs for 22,500 direct-labor hours.
4. Of the three proposed methods (high-low, scatter-graph, linear regression), which one should Ramon Co. employ to determine the historical cost behavior pattern of Franklin Plant's overhead costs? Explain your answer completely, indicating the reasons why the other methods should not be used.

23-16 Regression assumptions. (CMA) The controller of the Connecticut Electronics Company believes that the identification of the variable and fixed components of the firm's costs will enable the firm to make better planning and control decisions. Among the costs the controller is concerned about is the behavior of indirect supplies expense. He believes there is some correlation between the machine-hours worked and the amount of indirect supplies used.

A member of the controller's staff has suggested that a simple linear-regression model be used to determine the cost behavior of the indirect supplies. The regression equation shown below was developed from 40 pairs of observations using the least-squares method of regression. The regression equation and related measures are as follows:

$$S = \$200 + \$4H$$

where S = total monthly costs of indirect supplies, and H = machine-hours per month.

Standard error of residuals: $S_e = 100$

Coefficient of correlation: $r = .87$

Required

1. When a simple linear-regression model is used to make inferences about a population relationship from sample data, what assumptions must be made before the inferences can be accepted as valid?
2. Assume the assumptions identified in requirement 1 are satisfied for the indirect supplies expense of Connecticut Electronics Company.
   a. Explain the meaning of "200" and "4" in the regression equation $S = \$200 + \$4H$.
   b. Calculate the estimated cost of indirect supplies if 900 machine-hours are to be used during a month.
3. Explain briefly what the
   a. Coefficient of correlation measures
   b. Value of the coefficient of correlation ($r = .87$) indicates in this case if Connecticut Electronics Company wishes to predict the total cost of indirect supplies on the basis of estimated machine-hours

23-17 Evaluating alternative regression functions, accrual accounting adjustments. Trevor Kennedy, the cost analyst at a can-manufacturing plant of United Packaging, used a regression model to examine the relationship between total engineering support costs reported in the plant records and machine-hours. After further discussion with the operating manager, Kennedy discovers that the materials and parts numbers reported in the monthly records are on an "as purchased" basis and not on an "as used" basis. By examining materials and parts usage records, Kennedy is able to restate the materials and parts costs to an "as used" or accrual accounting basis. (No restatement of the labor costs was necessary.) The reported and restated costs are:

MONTH	LABOR: REPORTED COSTS	MATERIALS AND PARTS: REPORTED COSTS	MATERIALS AND PARTS: RESTATED COSTS	TOTAL ENGINEERING SUPPORT: REPORTED COSTS	TOTAL ENGINEERING SUPPORT: RESTATED COSTS	MACHINE-HOURS
(1)	(2)	(3)	(4)	(5) = (2) + (3)	(6) = (2) + (4)	(7)
March	$347	$847	$182	$1,194	$529	30
April	521	0	411	521	932	63
May	398	0	268	398	666	49
June	355	961	228	1,316	583	38
July	473	0	348	473	821	57
August	617	0	349	617	966	73
September	245	821	125	1,066	370	19
October	487	0	364	487	851	53
November	431	0	290	431	721	42

The regression results, when total engineering support reported costs (column 5) are used as the dependent variable, are:

REGRESSION 1:
Engineering Support Reported Costs = f(Machine-Hours)

VARIABLE	COEFFICIENT	STANDARD ERROR	t-STATISTIC
Constant	1,393.20	305.68	4.56
Independent variable 1:			
Machine-hours	−14.23	6.15	−2.31

$r^2 = .43$; Standard error of residuals = 291.83; Durbin-Watson = 2.26

The regression results, when total engineering support restated costs (column 6) are used as the dependent variable, are:

REGRESSION 2:
Engineering Support Restated Costs = f(Machine-Hours)

VARIABLE	COEFFICIENT	STANDARD ERROR	t-STATISTIC
Constant	176.38	53.99	3.27
Independent variable 1:			
Machine-hours	11.44	1.08	10.59

$r^2 = .94$; Standard error of residuals = 51.54; Durbin-Watson = 1.31

Required

1. Present a plot of the data for the cost function relating the total engineering support reported costs to machine-hours. Present a plot of the data for the cost function relating the total engineering support restated costs to machine-hours. Comment on the plots.
2. Contrast and evaluate the cost function estimated with regression using restated data for materials and parts with the cost function estimated with regression using the data reported in the plant records. Use the comparison format employed in Exhibit 23-10 (p. 780) for the Problem for Self-Study.
3. What problems might Kennedy encounter when restating the materials and parts costs recorded to an "as used" or accrual basis?

23-18 Choosing one of two regression analyses. (CMA) The Alma Plant manufactures the industrial product line of CJS Industries. Plant management wants to be able to get a good, yet quick, estimate of the manufacturing-overhead costs that can be expected to be incurred each month. The easiest and simplest method to accomplish this task appears to be to develop a flexible-budget formula for the manufacturing-overhead costs.

The plant's accounting staff suggested that simple linear regression be used to determine the cost behavior pattern of the overhead costs. The regression data can provide the basis for the flexible-budget formula. Sufficient evidence is available to conclude that manufacturing-overhead costs vary with direct-labor hours. The actual direct-labor hours and the corresponding manufacturing-overhead costs for each month of the last three years were used in the linear-regression analysis.

The three-year period contained various occurrences not uncommon to many businesses. During the first year, production was severely curtailed during two months due to wildcat strikes. In the second year, production was reduced in one month because of material shortages and increased overtime during two months to meet the units required for a one-time sales order. At the end of the second year, employee benefits were raised significantly as the result of a labor agreement. Production during the third year was not affected by any special circumstances.

Various members of Alma's accounting staff raised some issues regarding the historical data collected for the regression analysis. These issues were as follows.

1. Some members of the accounting staff believed that the use of data from all 36 months would provide a more accurate portrayal of the cost behavior. While they recognized that any of the monthly data could include efficiencies and inefficiencies, they believed these efficiencies/inefficiencies would tend to balance out over a longer period of time.

2. Other members of the accounting staff suggested that only those months that were considered normal should be used so that the regression would not be distorted.

3. Still other members felt that only the most recent 12 months should be used because they were the most current.

4. Some members questioned whether historical data should be used at all to form the basis for a flexible-budget formula.

The accounting department ran two regression analyses of the data—one using the data from all 36 months and the other using only the data from the last 12 months. The information derived from the two linear regressions is:

Least-Squares Regression Analyses

	DATA FROM ALL 36 MONTHS	DATA FROM MOST RECENT 12 MONTHS
Coefficients of the regression equation:		
Constant	$123,810	$109,020
Independent variable (DLH)	$1.6003	$4.1977
Coefficient of correlation	.4710	.6891
Standard error of the residuals	13,003	7,473
Standard error of the regression coefficient for the independent variable	.9744	1.3959
Calculated t-statistic for the regression coefficient	1.6423	3.0072
t-statistic required for a 95% confidence interval		
34 degrees of freedom (36 − 2)	1.960	
10 degrees of freedom (12 − 2)		2.228

Required

1. From the results of Alma Plant's regression analysis that used the data from all 36 months:
   a. Formulate the flexible-budget equation that can be employed to estimate monthly manufacturing-overhead costs.

b. Calculate the estimate of overhead costs for a month when 25,000 direct-labor hours are worked.

2. Using only the results of the two regression analyses, explain which of the two results (12 months versus 36 months) you would use as a basis for the flexible-budget formula.
3. How would the four specific issues raised by the members of Alma's accounting staff influence your willingness to use the results of the statistical analyses as the basis for the flexible-budget formula? Explain your answer.

23-19 Choosing independent variables. A post office department has used a flexible-overhead budget for years:

$$\text{Budgeted overhead} = a + bx_1$$

where a = the intercept; b = rate per direct-labor hour; and x_1 = number of direct-labor hours.

In recent years, much automated machinery has been introduced. The actual (but not measured) cost behavior pattern is

$$\text{Budgeted overhead} = a + bx_1 + cx_2$$

where c = rate per machine-hour and x_2 = number of machine-hours.

The department, which is managed by Richard, has two foremen. George is in charge of the machinery area. Harold is in charge of an area where direct laborers work intensively.

For the month of June, actual direct-labor hours of input exceeded the standard hours allowed for the output achieved by 20%. Moreover, the actual overhead incurred for the 6,000 actual direct-labor hours of input actually worked was $36,000.

Required

1. Prepare a graph of the flexible budget being used by the department. Let a = $14,000 and b = $3 per direct-labor hour. Compute and graph the budget, spending, and efficiency variances.
2. Which of the three managers is traditionally held responsible for each variance? What are the likely effects on the attitudes of the three managers under the existing budgeting formula?

23-20 Evaluating alternative simple regression models, university business school. Teri Bush, executive assistant to the president of Western University, has been hearing many complaints from university administrators that the nonacademic overhead costs of the business school are out of control. The business school has grown from fourteen full-time faculty to sixty-one full-time faculty in the last twelve years. The nonacademic overhead costs include the salaries of administrators and other nonacademic staff, the costs of handling student applications, and numerous individual supply items such as photocopying paper.

Bush decides that some data analysis is warranted. She collects the following information pertaining to the business school:

YEAR	NONACADEMIC OVERHEAD COSTS (000's)	NUMBER OF NONACADEMIC STAFF	NUMBER OF STUDENT APPLICATIONS	NUMBER OF ENROLLED STUDENTS
1	$ 2,200	29	1,010	342
2	4,120	36	1,217	496
3	3,310	49	927	256
4	4,410	53	1,050	467
5	4,210	54	1,563	387
6	5,440	58	1,127	492
7	5,600	88	1,892	513
8	4,380	72	1,362	387
9	5,270	83	1,623	346
10	7,610	73	1,646	487
11	8,070	101	1,870	564
12	10,388	103	1,253	764

She finds the following results for three separate simple regression models.

REGRESSION 1:
Overhead Costs = f(Number of Nonacademic Staff)

VARIABLE	COEFFICIENT	STANDARD ERROR	t-STATISTIC
Constant	112.04	1,119.40	0.10
Independent variable 1:			
Number of staff	79.68	15.89	5.02

$r^2 = .72$; Standard error of residuals = 1,269.20; Durbin-Watson = 1.82

REGRESSION 2:
Overhead Costs = f(Number of Student Applications)

VARIABLE	COEFFICIENT	STANDARD ERROR	t-STATISTIC
Constant	1,147.40	2,710.00	0.42
Independent variable 1:			
Number of applicants	3.10	1.91	1.62

$r^2 = .21$; Standard error of residuals = 2,118.70; Durbin-Watson = 0.89

REGRESSION 3:
Overhead Costs = f(Number of Enrolled Students)

VARIABLE	COEFFICIENT	STANDARD ERROR	t-STATISTIC
Constant	−1,382.20	1,350.30	−1.02
Independent variable 1:			
Number of students	14.83	2.84	5.22

$r^2 = .73$; Standard error of residuals = 1,233.00; Durbin-Watson = 1.09

Required

1. What problems might arise in measuring the nonacademic costs of the business school?
2. Plot the relationship between nonacademic overhead costs and each of the following three variables: (a) number of nonacademic staff, (b) number of student applications, and (c) number of enrolled students.
3. Compare and evaluate the three simple regression models estimated by Bush. Use the comparison format employed in Exhibit 23-10 (p. 780).
4. What other variables might Bush collect to explain the behavior of non-academic overhead costs of the business school?

23-21 **Evaluating alternative multiple regression models, university business school.** (Extension of Problem 23-20). Teri Bush decides that the simple regression analysis reported in Problem 23-20 could be extended to a multiple regression analysis. She finds the following results for several multiple regressions:

REGRESSION 4:
Overhead Costs = f(Number of Staff; Number of Applications)

VARIABLE	COEFFICIENT	STANDARD ERROR	t-STATISTIC
Constant	1,243.00	1,630.20	0.76
Independent variable 1:			
Number of staff	93.81	21.73	4.32
Independent variable 2:			
Number of applications	−1.50	1.57	−0.96

$r^2 = .74$; Standard error of residuals = 1,274.40; Durbin-Watson = 1.92

REGRESSION 5:
Overhead Costs = f(Number of Staff; Number of Students)

VARIABLE	COEFFICIENT	STANDARD ERROR	t-STATISTIC
Constant	−2,114.70	894.79	−2.36
Independent variable 1:			
Number of staff	48.62	12.62	3.85
Independent variable 2:			
Number of students	9.37	2.32	4.03

r^2 = .90; Standard error of residuals = 798.40; Durbin-Watson = 1.82

REGRESSION 6:
Overhead Costs = f(Number of Applications; Number of Students)

VARIABLE	COEFFICIENT	STANDARD ERROR	t-STATISTIC
Constant	−3,178.60	1,714.20	−1.85
Independent variable 1:			
Number of applications	1.68	1.08	1.55
Independent variable 2:			
Number of students	13.70	2.76	4.97

r^2 = .79; Standard error of residuals = 1,154.40; Durbin-Watson = 1.65

The correlation coefficient between pairwise combinations of the variables is:

	OVERHEAD COSTS	NUMBER OF STAFF	NUMBER OF APPLICATIONS
Number of staff	.846		
Number of applications	.455	.679	
Number of students	.855	.610	.264

Required

1. Compare and evaluate the three multiple regression models estimated by Bush. Use the comparison format employed in Exhibit 23-10 (p. 780).
2. What problems may arise in multiple regressions that do not arise in simple regressions? Is there evidence of such problems in any of the multiple regressions presented in this question?
3. Of what use might the regression results be to the president of Western University in attempting to control the nonacademic overhead costs of the business school?

23-22 Regression analysis. (J. Patell, adapted) Mike Mean, controller of Acro-Cel, has hired you as a consultant with data analysis skills to help him construct a flexible budget for overhead costs in 19_7. He has supplied you with the following monthly data from 19_6:

MONTH	OVERHEAD COSTS	DIRECT-LABOR HOURS	MATERIAL COSTS
Jan.	$8,900	1,295	$19,810
Feb.	8,444	1,108	17,001
Mar.	8,056	1,330	19,208
Apr.	8,209	1,302	22,137
May	9,621	1,264	22,793
June	8,747	1,340	19,596
July	6,701	830	11,032
Aug.	6,924	766	4,930
Sept.	8,474	1,298	20,304
Oct.	8,453	1,200	20,393
Nov.	8,262	1,135	21,867
Dec.	7,596	1,090	19,237

You have run a number of regression analyses and are now in the process of explaining the output. In all the regressions shown below, the *dependent* variable is overhead costs.

PART A

Mike initially felt that both labor-hours and material costs might be related to overhead expenditures, but he had no idea of their relative merits. Therefore you ran regression 1.

REGRESSION 1:
Overhead Costs = f(Direct-Labor Hours, Material Costs)

VARIABLE	COEFFICIENT	STANDARD ERROR	t-VALUE
Constant	4,663.20	1,095.60	4.26
Independent variables:			
1. Direct-labor hours	2.24	1.65	1.36
2. Material costs	0.05	0.06	0.83

r^2 = .684; Standard error of residuals = 505.20; Durbin-Watson = 2.19

Included with this regression output was the following table of correlation coefficients:

	OVERHEAD COSTS	DIRECT-LABOR HOURS	MATERIAL COSTS
Overhead costs	1.00		
Direct-labor hours	.81	1.00	
Material costs	.79	.88	1.00

Required

1. State in equation form the overhead flexible budget indicated by regression 1.
2. "What do you mean, 'the *t*-statistics indicate that both labor-hours and material costs are insignificant'?" State in no more than two sentences the meaning of the *t*-statistics shown above.
3. "Look, I may not understand 'regression analysis' but I understand this company and I know that when we work more hours and use more material I get higher bills for indirect costs." If Mike is correct, how do you explain (in no more than three data analytic sentences) the *t*-statistics in regression 1?

PART B

Knowing that Mike was really interested in an inexpensive, easy-to-understand budget system, you also ran regressions 2 and 3.

REGRESSION 2:
Overhead Costs = f(Direct-Labor Hours)

VARIABLE	COEFFICIENT	STANDARD ERROR	t-VALUE
Constant	4,188.10	922.42	4.54
Independent variable:			
Direct-labor hours	3.45	0.78	4.40

r^2 = .660; Standard error of residuals = 497.53; Durbin-Watson = 2.3

REGRESSION 3:
Overhead Costs = f(Material Costs)

VARIABLE	COEFFICIENT	STANDARD ERROR	t-VALUE
Constant	5,951.30	578.12	10.29
Independent variable:			
Material costs	0.12	0.03	4.00

r^2 = .619; Standard error of residuals = 526.45; Durbin-Watson = 1.73

"I'm not sure I follow exactly what's going on, but I'm glad you got both labor-hours and material costs to be 'significant' by doing things separately. Now let's just take the individual labor and material coefficients and plug them into the joint model you went after in the first regression. I think both effects really are important."

4. If Mike is correct about the form of the "true relation" he seeks, will his suggestion give you a good approximation of the coefficients? Explain thoroughly why or why not in no more than four sentences.

5. What is the meaning of the Durbin-Watson Statistic obtained for regression 3, and what does its numerical value of 1.73 indicate?

6. Using a *t*-probability table, construct a "95% confidence interval" for the direct-labor hour coefficient in *regression 2*. In no more than two sentences, what do you mean by a confidence interval?

7. Mike is intrigued by the idea of using labor-hours as a predictor of all costs, including material costs. Estimate the percentage of explained variance you would expect to achieve in a regression in which labor-hours were used to predict material costs.

Variances: Mix, Yield, and Investigation

A principal function of comparing results with plans is to help explain what has happened. In this way, managers can see the impact of key variables on the actual results and focus on areas that deserve more investigation. Chapters 6 and 7 illustrated various uses of variance information relating to direct materials, direct labor, and overhead.

This chapter surveys some major areas of the analysis of accounting variances that have been covered only briefly in earlier chapters. Three subjects are discussed: (1) the analysis of sales variances (sales-volume, sales-quantity, sales-mix, market-size, and market-share variances), (2) the analysis of production variances (direct material-yield, direct material-mix, direct labor-yield, and direct labor-mix variances), and (3) the problem of when to investigate variances. Since each subject can be studied independently, the chapter is divided into three major parts.

PART ONE: SALES VARIANCES

Most organizations produce more than one product or service. Therefore overall plans for revenue usually specify the quantity of each product to be sold. **Sales mix is the relative proportion or combination of the quantities of products that comprise total sales.** Managers want help in tracing deviations from original plans.

Chapter 6 showed how price, efficiency, and sales-volume variances assist managers in single-product situations. We now explore the complications that may arise in multiple-product situations when the sales quantity or the sales mix differ from the original plan.[1]

The literature on variance analysis in multiple-product situations is sizable and bewildering. It almost seems that every organization has a pet way of attacking the problem. Therefore be on guard whenever you see the terms *quantity variance, volume variance, activity variance, mix variance,* or *yield variance.* In any discussion, be sure that all parties agree on the definitions involved.

SALES-VOLUME VARIANCES

Consider an illustration. Suppose Ajax Company sells two products, A and B. Ajax has a budgeting system, basing its budget on a combination of last year's performance, a forecast of general economic conditions, and its expected share of predicted industry sales.

Ajax prepared a static (master) budget for a given period, expecting to sell 160,000 units of output:

Sales	$1,000,000
Variable costs	600,000
Contribution margin	400,000
Fixed costs	300,000
Operating income	$ 100,000

Flexible budgets and standards were introduced in Chapter 6, which emphasized that managers can evaluate performance by seeking various levels of detail. Exhibit 6-6, page 187, provided an overview of variances. Pause and review that exhibit before reading further.

Distinctions among variances may be made at various levels of detail. Even in companies having multiple products, the simplest, most informative analysis usually concentrates on a product-by-product analysis that has three components: *price, efficiency,* and *sales-volume* variances. Chapter 6 dwelled on the price and efficiency variances; we now focus on the sales-volume variance.

The *sales-volume variance* is the difference between the amount of the contribution margin in the budget based on actual sales volume (the flexible budget) and that amount in the static (master) budget. Budgeted selling prices and budgeted unit variable costs are held constant. This variance is measured in terms of contribution margin because fixed costs are the same in a flexible budget and the static budget.[2]

---

[1]The illustration in this chapter deals with two products. The analysis is unchanged if A and B are thought of as two services.

[2]There are many differences across authors in the labels used to describe individual variances. For example, Kaplan uses the phrase "sales-activity variance" to describe what we call the "sales-volume variance." He then uses the terms "sales-volume variance" and "sales-mix variance" to describe the two components of his "sales-activity variance." We use the terms "sales-quantity variance" and "sales-mix variance" to describe these two components. R. Kaplan, *Advanced Management Accounting* (Englewood Cliffs, N.J.: Prentice-Hall, 1982), p. 307.

EXHIBIT 24-1

Variance Analysis Using Flexible Budget

	ACTUAL RESULTS	FLEXIBLE-BUDGET VARIANCES	FLEXIBLE BUDGET	SALES-VOLUME VARIANCES	STATIC (MASTER) BUDGET
Physical units of output	160,000		160,000		160,000
Revenue	$1,125,000	$75,000 F	$1,050,000	$50,000 F	$1,000,000
Variable costs	620,000	30,000 U	590,000	10,000 F	600,000
Contribution margin	$ 505,000	$45,000 F	$ 460,000	$60,000 F	$ 400,000
Fixed costs	305,000	5,000 U	300,000	—	300,000
Operating income	$ 200,000	$40,000 F	$ 160,000	$60,000 F	$ 100,000

Static budget variance, $100,000 F

F = Favorable; U = Unfavorable.

Assume that Ajax actually sold 160,000 units during the period. Exhibit 24-1 analyzes the results. (Exhibit 24-1 is a Level 2 analysis in the terminology used in Chapter 6). The favorable static-budget variance of $100,000 is made up of a favorable flexible-budget variance of $40,000, and a favorable sales-volume variance of $60,000.

Effects of more than one product

Exhibit 24-1 provides a useful overview of the variances, but most managers want more detail. For example, the final three columns have a puzzling aspect. How can the flexible-budget amounts differ from those of the static (master) budget amounts if the number of units actually sold equals the 160,000 units originally budgeted? The reason, as explained in this section, is that this is a multiple-product company. If this were a single-product company, no such puzzle would arise.

In a multiple-product company, each product will have its own standards and flexible budgets. If the *mix* of products sold changes, the flexible budget is affected because it is merely a *summation* of the flexible budgets for the individual products sold.

Exhibit 24-2 shows how the original budgeted contribution margin of $400,000 was the sum of the budgeted contribution margins for 120,000 units of A and 40,000 units of B. But 110,000 units of A and 50,000 units of B were actually sold! The flexible budget based on actual sales of 160,000 units differs from the static budget because the mix changed.

Exhibit 24-2 provides individual product details of the sales-volume variance. It shows how the flexible budget based on actual units sold is really a sum of individual flexible budgets; it also shows how the total flexible-budget amounts can easily differ from the static-budget amounts. The details of the sales-volume variance tell the manager a straightforward story. Consider the sales-volume variance for the contribution margin:

$$\text{Sales-volume variance} = \left(\begin{array}{c}\text{Actual sales} \\ \text{volume in units}\end{array} - \begin{array}{c}\text{Budgeted sales} \\ \text{volume in units}\end{array}\right) \times \left(\begin{array}{c}\text{Budgeted individual product} \\ \text{contribution margin per unit}\end{array}\right)$$

For A: = (110,000 − 120,000) × $1 = $10,000 U
For B: = (50,000 − 40,000) × $7 = 70,000 F
Total $60,000 F

801

EXHIBIT 24-2
Sales-Volume Variances by Product

	PRODUCT A			PRODUCT B			TOTAL		
	Flexible Budget*	Static (Master) Budget	Sales-Volume Variance	Flexible Budget*	Static (Master) Budget	Sales-Volume Variance	Flexible Budget*	Static (Master) Budget	Sales-Volume Variance
Sales in units	110,000	120,000	10,000 U	50,000	40,000	10,000 F	160,000	160,000	—
Sales @ $5 and @ $10	$550,000	$600,000	$50,000 U	$500,000	$400,000	$100,000 F	$1,050,000	$1,000,000	$50,000 F
Variable costs @ $4 and @ $3	440,000	480,000	40,000 F	150,000	120,000	30,000 U	590,000	600,000	10,000 F
Contribution margin @ $1 and @ $7	$110,000	$120,000	$10,000 U	$350,000	$280,000	$ 70,000 F	$ 460,000	$ 400,000	$60,000 F
Fixed costs							300,000	300,000	—
Operating Income							$ 160,000	$ 100,000	$60,000 F

*Based on actual units sold during the period.
F = Favorable; U = Unfavorable.

Before reading on, study Exhibit 24-2 carefully. Some readers prefer to label the sales-volume variance as a "marketing variance." Other things being equal, the failure to sell the originally expected 120,000 units of Product A would cause a decline in operating income of 10,000 units × $1 = $10,000. However, the selling of 10,000 more units of Product B than originally expected would cause an increase in operating income of 10,000 units × $7 = $70,000.

Use by managers   Consider the appropriate variance at three levels of management: (1) the individual product manager, (2) the manager of the two-product line consisting of A and B, and (3) management at corporate headquarters in a company that markets numerous product lines.

The individual managers of Products A and B using Exhibit 24-2 will be primarily concerned with why their volume levels differed from their individual budgets. We have already discussed this type of variance analysis (Chapter 6, p. 183).

The manager of the two-product line consisting of A and B may concentrate on the "total" columns in Exhibit 24-2. However, these total columns offer the manager only an analytical beginning. *First,* note that the budgeted and actual *aggregated* units were equal. But is this informative? Adding units together may produce a meaningless result. For example, Product A may be shaving lotion and Product B may be shampoo. The point is that as we move beyond a one-product situation, aggregated units fail to provide a common denominator for measuring overall sales volume. Instead units are converted into monetary equivalents such as sales dollars or contribution margins. But we should not forget that the fundamental inputs and outputs of organizations are products or services.

Second, the aggregated dollars give an overall picture of the product line, but decisions typically must focus on individual products. The variances in the total columns are merely the sums of the individual product sales-volume variances.

Third, there can be enormous confusion regarding the sales-volume variances of $50,000, $10,000, and $60,000 in the right-hand column of Exhibit 24-2. Taken together, *the total sales volume in units* was unchanged, but the original proportions or mix changed. The fundamental explanation is that the actual volumes of *individual* products deviated from what was expected. If the original budget in total units is attained, but a larger proportion of higher-than-average budgeted contribution margin products are sold than was specified in the original mix, higher operating income will ensue.

Fourth, if the product-line manager wants a full explanation, he or she must get the individual product analyses contained in the other columns. This point is not trivial. Many accounting systems do not routinely prepare current reports by individual products, so the manager may have to work with only the totals in dollars (not even including the total units).

Managers at corporate headquarters usually receive summary monetary figures rather than a flood of detail. For example, corporate management would probably receive only the dollar amounts (not the number of units) in the total column in Exhibit 24-1. However, advances in the amount of data stored on computer networks are reducing the limitations of highly summarized data presentations. Corporate management, in some organizations, can link into a computer network to seek further explanations for individual items in their summary variance reports. Indeed, they may be able to access on-line the same detailed product-by-product variance information typically examined only by individual product managers or division managers.

SALES-QUANTITY AND SALES-MIX VARIANCES

Many accountants favor probing the sales-volume variances further. The analysis in Exhibit 24-2 reveals how the overall sales-volume variances can be affected by two major factors: (i) the actual quantity of units sold and (ii) the relative proportions of products bearing different contribution margins. The sales-quantity variance captures factor (i), while the sales-mix variance captures factor (ii). To simplify the computations, focus solely on contribution margins, even though these variances could be computed separately for revenues and variable costs.

The **sales-quantity variance** is the difference between the amount of contribution margin in the flexible budget based on actual sales volume at budgeted mix and that amount in the static (master) budget. Budgeted selling prices and budgeted unit variable costs are held constant. This variance is measured in terms of contribution margin because total fixed costs are the same in a flexible budget and the static budget.

The **sales-mix variance** is the difference between the amount of contribution margin in the flexible budget based on actual sales volume at actual mix and that amount in the flexible budget based on actual sales volume at budgeted mix. Budgeted selling prices and budgeted unit variable costs are held constant. This variance is measured in terms of contribution margin because total fixed costs are unchanged in the flexible budgets.[3]

Exhibit 24-3 presents the formulas and computations for Products A and B

---

[3]The discussion on sales-mix variance draws extensively on J. Harris and J. Persons, "Toward Identification and Resolution of the Issues Regarding Sales-Mix Variances" (Working paper, University of Tulsa, 1986). Harris and Persons provide an excellent discussion of the many diverse approaches to computing sales-mix variances found in the literature.

for both the sales-quantity variance and the sales-mix variance:

	SALES-QUANTITY VARIANCE	SALES-MIX VARIANCE
For A:	$25,000 U	$15,000 F
For B:	25,000 F	45,000 F
Total	$ 0	$60,000 F

Observe that the sales-quantity variance weights all units at a single overall budgeted-average contribution margin per unit. For a given change in actual volume, the total contribution margin would be expected to change at the $2.50 rate of the average unit margin. With a positive contribution margin, a favorable sales-quantity variance arises when the total number of physical units sold exceeds the budgeted amount.

Ponder the role of the *average* unit contribution margin. It helps focus on *overall* results, not *individual product* results. By itself, an individual sales-quantity variance for A does not help understanding if it is based on an average margin. However, the total sales-quantity variance can enhance understanding. The manager can see how income should fluctuate if the budgeted product mix is maintained as total actual volume departs from the total budgeted volume.

The sales-mix variance measures the impact of deviations from the budgeted percentage mix for each product, taking into account how that product's contribution margin differs from the budgeted average contribution margin. In the static budget, the budgeted sales mix is 75% for A and 25% for B. The actual sales mix was 68.75% for A and 31.25% for B. The $1.00 budgeted contribution

EXHIBIT 24-3
Sales-Quantity and Sales-Mix Variance Analysis

$$\text{Sales-quantity variance} = \left(\begin{array}{c} \text{Actual sales volume in units} - \text{Static budgeted sales volume of individual product in units} \end{array} \right) \times \left(\begin{array}{c} \text{Budgeted average contribution margin per unit} \end{array} \right)$$

For A: = (110,000 − 120,000) × $2.50* = $25,000 U
For B: = (50,000 − 40,000) × $2.50* = 25,000 F
Total $ 0

*From the total static budget: $400,000 ÷ 160,000 units = $2.50 per unit.

$$\text{Sales-mix variance} = \left(\left(\begin{array}{c} \text{Actual sales-mix percentage} - \text{Budgeted sales-mix percentage} \end{array} \right) \times \begin{array}{c} \text{Actual total sales volume of all products in units} \end{array} \right) \times \left(\begin{array}{c} \text{Budgeted individual contribution margin per unit} - \text{Budgeted average contribution margin per unit} \end{array} \right)$$

For A: = ((.6875 − .75) × 160,000)×($1.00 − $2.50)
     = (−.0625 × 160,000) × (−$1.50) = $15,000 F
For B: = ((.3125 − .25) × 160,000)×($7.00 − $2.50)
     = (.0625 × 160,000) × ($4.50) = $45,000 F
Total $60,000 F

margin for A is $1.50 below the overall average contribution margin of $2.50. The $7.00 budgeted contribution margin for B is $4.50 above the overall average contribution margin of $2.50.

Favorable sales-mix variances arise if there is (i) a decrease in the percentage sold of units with below-average contribution margins, or (ii) an increase in the percentage sold of units with above-average contribution margins. Product A in Exhibit 24-3 illustrates (i), while Product B in Exhibit 24-3 illustrates (ii).

Unfavorable sales-mix variances arise if there is (i) an increase in the percentage sold of units with below-average contribution margins, or (ii) a decrease in the percentage sold of units with above-average contribution margins.

If the original sales mix of 75% of A and 25% of B were maintained, but actual volume increased by 5%, there would be no sales-mix variance, only a sales-quantity variance. The actual sales would be 126,000 units of A (160,000 × 1.05 × .75) and 42,000 of B (160,000 × 1.05 × .25). The sales-quantity variance would be:

$$
\begin{aligned}
\text{For A:} &= (126,000 - 120,000) \times \$2.50 = \$15,000 \text{ F} \\
\text{For B:} &= (\ 42,000 - \ 40,000) \times \$2.50 = \ \underline{\ 5,000} \text{ F} \\
\text{Total} &= (168,000 - 160,000) \times \$2.50 = \underline{\underline{\$20,000}} \text{ F}
\end{aligned}
$$

This result is consistent with the idea that, given an unchanging sales mix, a 5% increase in actual unit volume should produce a 5% increase in sales dollars and a 5% increase in contribution margin. The budgeted contribution margin would increase from $400,000 to $420,000, or the $20,000 increase calculated above.

MARKET-SIZE AND MARKET-SHARE VARIANCES

Many companies regard their fate as being heavily affected by (a) overall demand for the products of an industry and (b) a company's ability to maintain its share of the market. Sometimes industry statistics are readily available, so the company's market share can easily be monitored. Examples are automobiles, television sets, and toothpaste. For other products, industry statistics are not easy to obtain in a timely fashion.

Suppose our illustrative company had reliable statistics and expected to maintain a 5% share of an industry market of 3,200,000 units during the budget period: .05 × 3,200,000 = 160,000 units. Suppose further that the industry market was actually 4,000,000 units, but the company got only a 4% share: 160,000 ÷ 4,000,000 = .04. The sales-quantity variance can be subdivided into the *market-size variance* and the *market-share variance*.[4] Exhibit 24-4 presents the formulas and computations for these two variances:

$$
\begin{aligned}
\text{Market-size variance} &= \$100,000 \text{ F} \\
\text{Market-share variance} &= \underline{\ 100,000} \text{ U} \\
&\quad \underline{\underline{\$\qquad 0}}
\end{aligned}
$$

[4]See J. Shank and N. Churchill, "Variance Analysis: A Management-Oriented Approach," *Accounting Review*, October 1977, p. 955.

EXHIBIT 24-4
Market-Size and Market-Share Variance Analysis

$$\begin{array}{c} \text{Market-size} \\ \text{variance} \end{array} = \left(\begin{array}{c} \text{Budgeted} \\ \text{market} \\ \text{share} \\ \text{percentage} \end{array} \right) \times \left(\begin{array}{c} \text{Actual} \\ \text{industry} \\ \text{sales} \\ \text{volume} \\ \text{in units} \end{array} - \begin{array}{c} \text{Budgeted} \\ \text{industry} \\ \text{sales} \\ \text{volume} \\ \text{in units} \end{array} \right) \times \left(\begin{array}{c} \text{Budgeted} \\ \text{average} \\ \text{contribution} \\ \text{margin} \\ \text{per unit} \end{array} \right)$$

$$= .05 \times (4{,}000{,}000 - 3{,}200{,}000) \times \$2.50$$

$$= \$100{,}000 \text{ F}$$

$$\begin{array}{c} \text{Market-share} \\ \text{variance} \end{array} = \left(\begin{array}{c} \text{Actual} \\ \text{market} \\ \text{share} \\ \text{percentage} \end{array} - \begin{array}{c} \text{Budgeted} \\ \text{market} \\ \text{share} \\ \text{percentage} \end{array} \right) \times \left(\begin{array}{c} \text{Actual} \\ \text{industry} \\ \text{sales} \\ \text{volume} \\ \text{in units} \end{array} \right) \times \left(\begin{array}{c} \text{Budgeted} \\ \text{average} \\ \text{contribution} \\ \text{margin} \\ \text{per unit} \end{array} \right)$$

$$= (.04 - .05) \times 4{,}000{,}000 \times \$2.50$$

$$= \$100{,}000 \text{ U}$$

Managers are likely to gain some insights from these variances. They measure the additional contribution margin, $100,000, that would be expected because the market size expanded. Unfortunately, the company attained only 4% of the industry market. This failure to maintain market share was accompanied by an equal offsetting variance. (Obviously, the dollar amounts will seldom be exactly offsetting.)

_____ PROBLEM FOR SELF-STUDY _____

problem Review Exhibit 24-2 (p. 802). Suppose 144,000 units of Product A and 36,000 units of Product B were sold. Focus on the contribution-margin line. Compute the sales-volume variances for each product and in total. Subdivide the sales-volume variance into sales-quantity and sales-mix variances. Using your numerical results, comment on the meaning of the three types of variances.

solution

$$\begin{array}{c} \text{Sales-volume} \\ \text{variance} \end{array} = \left(\begin{array}{c} \text{Actual sales} \\ \text{volume in units} \end{array} - \begin{array}{c} \text{Budgeted sales} \\ \text{volume in units} \end{array} \right) \times \left(\begin{array}{c} \text{Budgeted individual product} \\ \text{contribution margin per unit} \end{array} \right)$$

For A: = (144,000 − 120,000) × $1.00 = $24,000 F
For B: = (36,000 − 40,000) × $7.00 = <u>28,000 U</u>
Total   <u>$ 4,000 U</u>

This variance is straightforward. The manager can see that selling 24,000 more units of A increased the total contribution margin by $24,000. However, selling 4,000 fewer units of B, which is more profitable per unit, more than offset the favorable effects of A.

$$\begin{array}{c} \text{Sales-quantity} \\ \text{variance} \end{array} = \left(\begin{array}{c} \text{Actual sales} \\ \text{volume} \\ \text{in units} \end{array} - \begin{array}{c} \text{Static budgeted sales} \\ \text{volume of individual} \\ \text{product in units} \end{array} \right) \times \left(\begin{array}{c} \text{Budgeted average} \\ \text{contribution} \\ \text{margin per unit} \end{array} \right)$$

For A: = (144,000 − 120,000) × $2.50 = $60,000 F
For B: = (36,000 − 40,000) × $2.50 = <u>10,000 U</u>
Total = (180,000 − 160,000) × $2.50 = <u>$50,000 F</u>

Given an unchanging mix, exceeding the budgeted unit quantity of 160,000 units would produce a favorable sales-quantity variance of 180,000 − 160,000, or 20,000 units multiplied by the budgeted average unit contribution of $2.50, for a total of $50,000.

$$\begin{matrix} \text{Sales-mix} \\ \text{variance} \end{matrix} = \left(\left(\begin{matrix} \text{Actual} \\ \text{sales-mix} \\ \text{percentage} \end{matrix} - \begin{matrix} \text{Budgeted} \\ \text{sales-mix} \\ \text{percentage} \end{matrix} \right) \times \begin{matrix} \text{Actual total} \\ \text{sales volume} \\ \text{of all} \\ \text{products} \\ \text{in units} \end{matrix} \right) \times \left(\begin{matrix} \text{Budgeted} \\ \text{individual} \\ \text{contribution} \\ \text{margin} \\ \text{per unit} \end{matrix} - \begin{matrix} \text{Budgeted} \\ \text{average} \\ \text{contribution} \\ \text{margin} \\ \text{per unit} \end{matrix} \right)$$

For A: $= ((.80 - .75) \times 180,000) \times (\$1.00 - \$2.50)$
$\quad = (.05 \times 180,000) \times (-\$1.50) = \qquad\qquad$ \$13,500 U

For B: $= ((.20 - .25) \times 180,000) \times (\$7.00 - \$2.50)$
$\quad = (-.05 \times 180,000) \times (\$4.50) = \qquad\qquad$ 40,500 U

Total $\qquad\qquad\qquad\qquad\qquad\qquad\qquad\qquad\qquad$ \$54,000 U

The actual sales mix is 80% of A (compared with 75% in the static budget) and 20% of B (25% in the static budget). Thus there was (i) an increase in the percentage sold of Product A, which has a lower-than-average contribution margin, and (ii) a decrease in the percentage sold of Product B, which has a higher-than-average contribution margin. Both changes are unfavorable.

A summary of these three variances follows:

Sales-quantity variance	$50,000 F
Sales-mix variance	54,000 U
Sales-volume variance	$ 4,000 U

PART TWO: PRODUCTION VARIANCES

Manufacturing processes often entail the combination of a number of different direct-materials and a number of different direct-labor skills to obtain a unit of finished product, or the use of a single direct-material or direct-labor skill to produce several joint products. For example, chemicals, lumber, fruit, vegetables, and fabrics can sometimes be combined in various ways without affecting the specified quality characteristics of a finished product. Similarly, the composition of teams of labor may differ from hour to hour or day to day.

What is usually meant by the terms *yield* and *mix* in a production setting? *Yield* refers to the quantity of finished output produced from a budgeted or standard mix of inputs. *Mix* refers to the relative proportion or combination of the various inputs required to produce the quantity of finished output.

DIRECT MATERIAL-YIELD AND DIRECT MATERIAL-MIX VARIANCES

When we initially examined material and labor variances in Chapter 6, we saw that managers sometimes make trade-offs between price and efficiency variances. For example, a shoe manufacturer may try some variations in grades of leather if the potential savings exceed the potential costs of waste or rejects.

In addition to considering whether to make deliberate changes, managers must contend with technical characteristics that are frequently uncontrollable, at least in the short run. For example, humidity, temperature, molecular structure, or other physical characteristics can dramatically affect the relationships between inputs and outputs.

Consider a specific example of multiple inputs and a single output. Suppose a chemical company, Polymer Products, has the following input standards to produce 9 gallons of a single output (Product K):

5 gallons of material F at $0.70 per gallon	$3.50
3 gallons of material G at $1.00 per gallon	3.00
2 gallons of material H at $0.80 per gallon	1.60
	$8.10

The standard cost of the single output (Product K) is $0.90 per gallon ($8.10 ÷ 9 gallons of output).

Suppose, for simplicity, that no inventories of direct materials are kept. Purchases are made as needed, so that all price variances relate to materials used. Actual results show that 100,000 gallons of the three inputs in total were used during a certain period:

45,000 gallons of material F at actual cost of $0.80	$36,000
33,000 gallons of material G at actual cost of $1.05	34,650
22,000 gallons of material H at actual cost of $0.85	18,700
100,000	$89,350
Finished product output was 92,070 gallons of K	
at a standard cost of $0.90 per gallon	82,863
Total variance to be explained	$ 6,487 U

Given the standard that 10 gallons of input are required to produce 9 gallons of the Product K output, 102,300 gallons is the standard input required to produce 92,070 gallons of K: 92,070 ÷ .9 = 102,300. The budgeted share of material inputs F, G, and H of this 102,300 standard gallons of total material inputs is:

Material F: .5 × 102,300 = 51,150 gallons
Material G: .3 × 102,300 = 30,690 gallons
Material H: .2 × 102,300 = 20,460 gallons

Exhibit 24-5 presents the usual approach to analyzing the budget variance that was discussed in Chapter 6. Further explanation of the $6,487 unfavorable budget variance in Exhibit 24-5 can be obtained by computing individual price variances and individual efficiency variances. The material price variances are:

MATERIAL	(1) DIFFERENCE IN UNIT PRICE OF MATERIAL INPUTS	(2) ACTUAL MATERIAL INPUTS USED	(3) = (1) × (2) MATERIAL PRICE VARIANCE
F	($0.70 − $0.80) = −$0.10	45,000	$4,500 U
G	($1.00 − $1.05) = −$0.05	33,000	1,650 U
H	($0.80 − $0.85) = −$0.05	22,000	1,100 U
Total			$7,250 U

EXHIBIT 24-5
Material-Price and Material-Efficiency Variance Analysis

MATERIAL	ACTUAL COSTS INCURRED: ACTUAL INPUTS × ACTUAL PRICES		FLEXIBLE BUDGET: BASED ON ACTUAL INPUTS × STANDARD PRICES		FLEXIBLE BUDGET: BASED ON STANDARD INPUTS ALLOWED FOR ACTUAL OUTPUTS × STANDARD PRICES	
F	45,000 × $0.80 =	$36,000	45,000 × $0.70 =	$31,500	51,150 × $0.70 =	$35,805
G	33,000 × $1.05 =	34,650	33,000 × $1.00 =	33,000	30,690 × $1.00 =	30,690
H	22,000 × $0.85 =	18,700	22,000 × $0.80 =	17,600	20,460 × $0.80 =	16,368
Total	100,000	$89,350	100,000	$82,100	102,300	$82,863

Price variance, $7,250 U   Efficiency variance, $763 F

Flexible-budget variance, $6,487 U

The material efficiency variances can also be computed in the usual manner (see Chapter 6, p. 191):

MATERIAL	DETAILED COMPUTATIONS FOR COLUMN (1)	(1) STANDARD UNITS OF MATERIAL INPUTS ALLOWED FOR ACTUAL OUTPUTS	(2) ACTUAL UNITS OF MATERIAL INPUTS USED	(3) = (1) − (2) DIFFERENCE	(4) BUDGETED PRICE PER UNIT OF MATERIAL INPUT	(5) = (3) × (4) MATERIAL EFFICIENCY VARIANCE
F	(.5 × 102,300)	51,150	45,000	6,150	$0.70	$4,305 F
G	(.3 × 102,300)	30,690	33,000	−2,310	1.00	2,310 U
H	(.2 × 102,300)	20,460	22,000	−1,540	0.80	1,232 U
Total		102,300	100,000	2,300		$ 763 F

The budgeted *average* price per unit of material input is $0.81:

$$(.5 \times \$0.70) + (.3 \times \$1.00) + (.2 \times \$0.80) = \$0.81$$

where .5, .3, and .2 are the budgeted (standard) proportions of material inputs required to produce one unit of output.

The analysis above may suffice where managers control each input on an individual basis and where no discretion is permitted regarding the physical mix of material inputs. For example, there is often a predetermined mix of materials needed for the assembly of microcomputers, radios, and washing machines (or at least a predetermined mix for major subcomponents of these products). In these cases, all deviations from the engineered input-output relationships are deemed to be attributable to efficiency; the price and efficiency variances individually computed for each material typically provide all the necessary information for decisions. Why? Because no deliberate substitutions of inputs are tolerated.

Role of material-yield and material-mix variances

Where managers have the opportunity for substitutions among materials, the yield and mix variances can provide additional insights. Exhibit 24-6 presents a subdivision of the $763 favorable material efficiency variance into its yield and mix components:

	MATERIAL-YIELD VARIANCE	MATERIAL-MIX VARIANCE
For F:	$4,981.50 F	$550 U
For G:	1,871.10 U	570 U
For H:	1,247.40 U	20 F
	$1,863.00 F	$1,100 U

The material-yield variance in Exhibit 24-6 shows that if the combination of ingredients were held constant, and 2,300 units less of input were used, the savings would have been $1,863, solely because of improved yield of a given mix of inputs. In effect, the yield variance holds budgeted average unit price constant and views all units of input as if they were alike.

As the word *mix* implies, the material-mix variance in Exhibit 24-6 concentrates on the changes in the percentages (proportions) of the individual inputs used. Favorable materials-mix variances arise if there is (i) an increase in the percentage use of the material input with the below-average price per unit or (ii) a decrease in the percentage use of the material input with the above-average price per unit. Material H in Exhibit 24-6 illustrates (i). Unfavorable material-mix variances arise if there is (i) an increase in the percentage use of the material input with the above-average price per unit or (ii) a decrease in the percentage use of the material input with the below-average price per unit. Material G in Exhibit 24-6 illustrates (i), while material F illustrates (ii).

The material-yield variance in Exhibit 24-6 is $1,863 F, while the material-mix variance is $1,100 U. There was a trade-off among ingredients that boosted yield but caused the average budgeted unit cost of the overall material inputs to be

EXHIBIT 24-6
Material-Yield and Material-Mix Variance Analysis

$$
\text{Material-yield variance} = \left(\begin{array}{c} \text{Standard units} \\ \text{of material} \\ \text{inputs allowed for} \\ \text{actual outputs} \end{array} - \begin{array}{c} \text{Actual units} \\ \text{of material} \\ \text{inputs} \\ \text{used} \end{array} \right) \times \left(\begin{array}{c} \text{Budgeted} \\ \text{average price} \\ \text{per unit of} \\ \text{material input} \end{array} \right)
$$

For F: = (51,150 − 45,000) × $0.81 = 6,150 × $0.81 = $4,981.50 F
For G: = (30,690 − 33,000) × $0.81 = −2,310 × $0.81 = $1,871.10 U
For H: = (20,460 − 22,000) × $0.81 = −1,540 × $0.81 = $1,247.40 U
Total: = (102,300 − 100,000) × $0.81 = 2,300 × $0.81 = $1,863.00 F

$$
\text{Material-mix variance} = \left(\left(\begin{array}{c} \text{Actual} \\ \text{material-} \\ \text{mix} \\ \text{percentage} \end{array} - \begin{array}{c} \text{Budgeted} \\ \text{material-} \\ \text{mix} \\ \text{percentage} \end{array} \right) \times \begin{array}{c} \text{Actual total} \\ \text{units of} \\ \text{material} \\ \text{inputs} \\ \text{used} \end{array} \right) \times \left(\begin{array}{c} \text{Budgeted} \\ \text{individual} \\ \text{price per unit} \\ \text{of material} \\ \text{input} \end{array} - \begin{array}{c} \text{Budgeted} \\ \text{average} \\ \text{price per unit} \\ \text{of material} \\ \text{input} \end{array} \right)
$$

For F: = ((.45 − .50) × 100,000) × ($0.70 − $0.81) = −5,000 × −$0.11 = $ 550 U
For G: = ((.33 − .30) × 100,000) × ($1.00 − $0.81) = 3,000 × $0.19 = $ 570 U
For H: = ((.22 − .20) × 100,000) × ($0.80 − $0.81) = 2,000 × −$0.01 = $ 20 F
Total $1,100 U

higher than expected. The trade-off resulted in a net favorable variance of $763. Thus the material-yield and material-mix variances provide additional insights for the manager.[5]

DIRECT LABOR-YIELD AND DIRECT LABOR-MIX VARIANCES

As we have just seen, the standard costs of products are frequently developed by using specified combinations of materials bearing different individual prices. The same approach is often used for direct labor. Pursuing our example, suppose the production process required considerable labor input. The direct-labor rate per gallon of output is computed as follows:

(1) Budgeted (standard) labor price per hour:	
1 skilled worker @ $20	$20
2 unskilled workers @ $11	22
Total cost of standard combination of labor	$42
Budgeted average price per labor-hour, $42 ÷ 3 =	$14
(2) Standard labor price per gallon of output at 10 gallons per hour, $14 ÷ 10 =	$1.40
(3) Standard labor cost of 92,070 gallons of output, $1.40 × 92,070, or $14 × 9,207 hours =	$128,898
(4) Actual inputs, 9,000 hours consisting of:	
3,400 hours of skilled labor @ $21 an hour	$ 71,400
5,600 hours of unskilled labor @ $10 an hour	56,000
9,000 hours @ $14.1555 an hour	$127,400

The standard mix and actual mix of skilled and unskilled workers are:

	STANDARD MIX	ACTUAL MIX
Skilled labor	.3333 (1/3)	.3778 ($3,400/9,000$)
Unskilled labor	.6667 (2/3)	.6222 ($5,600/9,000$)
	1.0000	1.0000

The standard output is 10 gallons per hour. Thus the standard hours of labor allowed for the actual output of 92,070 gallons is:

Skilled labor:	1/3 × (92,070/10) =	3,069
Unskilled labor:	2/3 × (92,070/10) =	6,138
Total standard hours allowed		9,207

---

[5]For further discussion of production-mix variances, see A. Adelberg, "An Improved Analysis of Production-Mix Variances," *Production and Inventory Management,* Fourth Quarter 1984, pp. 35–41.

EXHIBIT 24-7
Direct-Labor Price and Direct-Labor Efficiency Variance Analysis

DIRECT-LABOR CATEGORY	ACTUAL COSTS INCURRED: ACTUAL INPUTS × ACTUAL PRICES		FLEXIBLE BUDGET: BASED ON ACTUAL INPUTS × STANDARD PRICES		FLEXIBLE BUDGET: BASED ON STANDARD INPUTS ALLOWED FOR ACTUAL OUTPUTS × STANDARD PRICES	
Skilled	3,400 × $21 =	$ 71,400	3,400 × $20 =	$ 68,000	3,069* × $20 =	$ 61,380
Unskilled	5,600 × $10 =	56,000	5,600 × $11 =	61,600	6,138† × $11 =	67,518
Total	9,000	$127,400	9,000	$129,600	9,207	$128,898

Price variance, $2,200 F ← → Efficiency variance, $702 U

Flexible-budget variance, $1,498 F

*1/3 × 9,207 = 3,069.
†2/3 × 9,207 = 6,138.

Exhibit 24-7 presents the direct-labor price and the direct-labor efficiency variances; the favorable price variance of $2,200 is partially offset by the unfavorable efficiency variance of $702. The labor-efficiency variance may be subdivided into yield and mix variances in the same way that we subdivided the material-efficiency variance in the previous section. Exhibit 24-8 presents formulas and computations for the labor-yield and labor-mix variances:

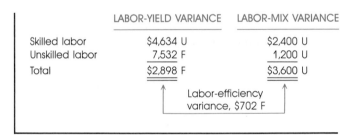

	LABOR-YIELD VARIANCE	LABOR-MIX VARIANCE
Skilled labor	$4,634 U	$2,400 U
Unskilled labor	7,532 F	1,200 U
Total	$2,898 F	$3,600 U

Labor-efficiency variance, $702 F

The financial effect of substitution on labor efficiency is measured by the yield and mix variances. In particular, since we are subdividing the labor-efficiency variance, all price variances are excluded from these calculations. The labor-yield variance shows that if the standard combination of skilled and unskilled labor were held constant, and 207 fewer labor-hours were used, the savings would be $2,898 F.

Favorable labor-mix variances arise if there is (i) an increase in the percentage use of the labor category with below-average price per hour or (ii) a decrease in the percentage use of the labor category with above-average price per hour. Neither (i) or (ii) occurred with the data in Exhibit 24-8. Unfavorable labor-mix variances arise if there is (i) an increase in the percentage use of the labor category with above-average price per hour or (ii) a decrease in the percentage use of the labor category with below-average price per hour. The skilled category of labor in Exhibit 24-8 illustrates (i), while the unskilled category in Exhibit 24-8 illustrates (ii).

This section highlighted the financial impact of the interaction of *all* variances. The flexible-budget variance in Exhibit 24-7 is $1,498 favorable. The manager may have deliberately decided to change the mix of skilled and unskilled

EXHIBIT 24-8
Labor-Yield and Labor-Mix Variance Analysis

$$\begin{array}{c}\text{Labor-yield}\\\text{variance}\end{array} = \left(\begin{array}{c}\text{Standard units}\\\text{of labor}\\\text{inputs allowed for}\\\text{actual outputs}\end{array} - \begin{array}{c}\text{Actual}\\\text{units}\\\text{of labor}\\\text{inputs used}\end{array}\right) \times \left(\begin{array}{c}\text{Budgeted}\\\text{average price}\\\text{per unit of}\\\text{labor input}\end{array}\right)$$

For skilled: $(3{,}069 - 3{,}400) \times \$14 = -331 \times \$14 = \$4{,}634$ U
For unskilled: $(6{,}138 - 5{,}600) \times \$14 =\ \ \ 538 \times \$14 = \underline{\$7{,}532}$ F
Total: $(9{,}207 - 9{,}000) \times \$14 =\ \ \ 207 \times \$14 = \underline{\$2{,}898}$ F

$$\begin{array}{c}\text{Labor-mix}\\\text{variance}\end{array} = \left(\left(\begin{array}{c}\text{Actual}\\\text{labor-mix}\\\text{percentage}\end{array} - \begin{array}{c}\text{Budgeted}\\\text{labor-mix}\\\text{percentage}\end{array}\right) \times \begin{array}{c}\text{Actual total}\\\text{units of}\\\text{labor}\\\text{inputs}\\\text{used}\end{array}\right) \times \left(\begin{array}{c}\text{Budgeted}\\\text{individual}\\\text{price per unit}\\\text{of labor}\\\text{input}\end{array} - \begin{array}{c}\text{Budgeted}\\\text{average}\\\text{price per unit}\\\text{of labor}\\\text{input}\end{array}\right)$$

For skilled: $= ((.3778 - .3333) \times 9{,}000) \times (\$20 - \$14)$
                        $= (.0445 \times 9{,}000) \times (\$6) = 400 \times \$6\ \ \ \ \ \ \ = \$2{,}400$ U
For unskilled: $= ((.6222 - .6667) \times 9{,}000) \times (\$11 - \$14)$
                        $= (-.0445 \times 9{,}000) \times (-\$3) = -400 \times -\$3 = \underline{\$1{,}200}$ U
Total $\underline{\$3{,}600}$ U

labor. The budgeted proportion of skilled labor was .3333, whereas the actual proportion was .3778. Moreover, the skilled labor was paid $21 per hour instead of the budgeted rate of $20. Even though a small unfavorable efficiency variance of $702 occurred, a favorable price variance of $2,200 was achieved because the unskilled workers were paid a rate of $10 rather than the budgeted rate of $11. Perhaps the manager made the trade-off because many of the unskilled workers were new, earning lower-than-budgeted rates, and were expected to be less efficient than the usual unskilled workers. By introducing a mix with a higher proportion of skilled workers, the overall budgeted efficiency was almost attained.

Computation burden in variance calculations

The examples presented in this chapter involve no more than three sales products or three direct-material or two direct-labor inputs. Even with such few products or inputs, the calculations underlying the variances discussed in this chapter are time-consuming (and tedious). Computer software packages can greatly reduce the computation burden in calculating variances. Where there are thousands of products sold, or thousands of direct-material inputs or direct-labor categories, the use of computer software packages is essential in variance analysis.

_____PROBLEM FOR SELF-STUDY_____

problem   Review the example on material variances summarized in Exhibits 24-5 (p. 809) and 24-6 (p. 810). Suppose 46,000 gallons of material F, 40,000 gallons of material G, and 14,000 gallons of material H were actually used to produce the 92,070 gallons of output. Compute the total price and total efficiency variances. Explain why the efficiency variance is no longer $763 favorable. Also compute the material-yield and material-mix variances.

MATERIAL	ACTUAL COSTS INCURRED: ACTUAL INPUTS × ACTUAL PRICES		FLEXIBLE BUDGET: BASED ON ACTUAL INPUTS × STANDARD PRICES		FLEXIBLE BUDGET: BASED ON STANDARD INPUTS ALLOWED FOR ACTUAL OUTPUTS × STANDARD PRICES	
F	46,000 × $0.80 =	$36,800	46,000 × $0.70 =	$32,200	51,150 × $0.70 =	$35,805
G	40,000 × $1.05 =	42,000	40,000 × $1.00 =	40,000	30,690 × $1.00 =	30,690
H	14,000 × $0.85 =	11,900	14,000 × $0.80 =	11,200	20,460 × $0.80 =	16,368
Total	100,000	$90,700	100,000	$83,400	102,300	$82,863

↑————— Price variance, $7,300 U —————↑————— Efficiency variance, $537 U —————↑

↑——————————————— Flexible-budget variance, $7,837 U ———————————————↑

The unfavorable price variance of $7,300 reflects the increase in the price of each of the three materials relative to their individual budgeted price per material unit. The favorable efficiency variance of $763 in the original situation has become $537 unfavorable. The new actual input combination is less economical than the old actual input combination:

MATERIAL	MATERIAL INPUTS USED				Difference
	Old Combination		New Combination		
F	45,000 × $0.70 =	$31,500	46,000 × $0.70 =	$32,200	$ 700 U
G	33,000 × $1.00 =	33,000	40,000 × $1.00 =	40,000	7,000 U
H	22,000 × $0.80 =	17,600	14,000 × $0.80 =	11,200	6,400 F
	100,000	$82,100	100,000	$83,400	$1,300 U

The material-yield and material-mix variances are:

$$\text{Material-yield variance} = \left(\begin{array}{c} \text{Standard units} \\ \text{of material} \\ \text{inputs allowed for} \\ \text{actual outputs} \end{array} - \begin{array}{c} \text{Actual units} \\ \text{of material} \\ \text{inputs} \\ \text{used} \end{array} \right) \times \left(\begin{array}{c} \text{Budgeted} \\ \text{average price} \\ \text{per unit of} \\ \text{material input} \end{array} \right)$$

For F: = (51,150 − 46,000) × $0.81 = 5,150 × $0.81 = $4,171.5 F
For G: = (30,690 − 40,000) × $0.81 = −9,310 × $0.81 = 7,541.1 U
For H: = (20,460 − 14,000) × $0.81 = 6,460 × $0.81 = 5,232.6 F
Total: = (102,300 − 100,000) × $0.81 = 2,300 × $0.81 = $1,863.0 F

$$\text{Material-mix variance} = \left(\left(\begin{array}{c} \text{Actual} \\ \text{material-} \\ \text{mix} \\ \text{percentage} \end{array} - \begin{array}{c} \text{Budgeted} \\ \text{material-} \\ \text{mix} \\ \text{percentage} \end{array} \right) \times \begin{array}{c} \text{Actual total} \\ \text{units of} \\ \text{material} \\ \text{inputs} \\ \text{used} \end{array} \right) \times \left(\begin{array}{c} \text{Budgeted} \\ \text{individual} \\ \text{price per unit} \\ \text{of material} \\ \text{input} \end{array} - \begin{array}{c} \text{Budgeted} \\ \text{average} \\ \text{price per unit} \\ \text{of material} \\ \text{input} \end{array} \right)$$

For F: = ((.46 − .50) × 100,000) × ($0.70 − $0.81) = −4,000 × −$0.11 = $ 440 U
For G: = ((.40 − .30) × 100,000) × ($1.00 − $0.81) = 10,000 × $0.19 = 1,900 U
For H: = ((.14 − .20) × 100,000) × ($0.80 − $0.81) = −6,000 × −$0.01 = 60 U
Total $2,400 U

The change in the efficiency variance is solely attributable to the change in the mix of materials because there is no change in the material-yield variance.

This computation of mix and yield variances tells the manager that the trade-off was unwise. That is, yield was better than standard, but the use of higher-cost materials more than offset the advantage of yield.

PART THREE: VARIANCE INVESTIGATION DECISIONS

Given feedback in the form of routine reports of cost variances, when should managers investigate a situation where variances occurred? These variances may lead to investigation or no investigation. In turn, investigation may prompt corrective action or no corrective action.

The accounting system often plays a key part in these decisions, but it is not an exclusive source of information. For example, a plant manager on a daily inspection of the production line may observe a sequence of defective units. An investigation into the cause of the defective units can be started immediately.

Managers typically do not investigate every variance that is reported, line by line. As usual, the decisions are based on layers of simplifications, assumptions, and incomplete knowledge about the relative costs and benefits. This section explores the dimensions of this investigation decision.[6]

SOURCES OF VARIANCES

There are at least six sources of a variance: (1) inappropriate standard, (2) mismeasurement of actual results, (3) implementation breakdown, (4) parameter prediction error, (5) inappropriate decision model, and (6) random variation. These six sources are discussed in sequence. Note that each source may call for different corrective actions.[7] All of these corrective actions are costly. Whether they are worth taking depends on comparing the costs of corrections against any predicted benefits (such as increased cost savings).

Inappropriate standard

Developing materials, labor, or overhead standards for numerous individual products or services is costly and time-consuming. Accurate standards are difficult to obtain for operations subject to a high level of technological change; an inappropriate standard in this context would be a standard based on the prior, rather than the current, technology of the operation. Inappropriate standards can also arise when individuals undermine the standard-setting process by deliberately working slowly or using more raw materials than necessary during the test period for setting standards. Correcting this source of a variance requires the setting of more accurate standards.

Mismeasurement of actual results

The recorded amounts for such items as actual cost, actual revenue, and actual materials used can differ from the actual amounts. For example, a worker may incorrectly count the ending inventory, resulting in an erroneous measure of total costs. Other sources of mismeasurement include improper classification of items

---

[6]For more-detailed analysis of the issues raised in this section, see R. Magee, *Advanced Managerial Accounting* (New York: Harper & Row, 1986), Chaps. 9 and 10.

[7]See J. Demski, "Optimizing the Search for Cost Deviation Sources," *Management Science,* 16 (No. 8), 486–94.

(e.g., including an indirect-labor-cost item with the direct-labor costs) and improper recording of items (e.g., recording an advertising payment as a prepayment rather than an expense of the current period).

Correcting this source of a variance largely depends on getting individual employees to obtain accurate documentation as part of their everyday work habits. Obtaining data with a high level of integrity is an especially troublesome problem of systems design and motivation that permeates all types of organizations. For example, employees sometimes falsify time records so that the true variances from standards on particular operations are masked.

Implementation breakdown

Employee actions do not always agree with plans. For example, consider the economic-order-quantity inventory model discussed in Chapter 21. Perhaps, because of improper motivation or instruction, the wrong quantity is ordered. For example, an employee may order too many units. Why? Because of the attractions of a lower-than-standard price for a larger order.

Correcting this source often entails restricting the employees' discretion. For example, purchasing officers may not be permitted to order quantity levels above a preset level unless the unit price is less than 85% of the standard price.

Parameter prediction error

Planning decisions are based on predictions, such as future costs, future selling prices, and future demand. In many cases, there will be a difference between the realized value and the predicted value of the cost, selling price, demand, and so forth; this difference is termed a *prediction error*. For example, one parameter predicted in the economic-order-quantity model is the cost of placing an order. The parameter may be incorrectly predicted because of a failure to recognize a recently negotiated increase in hourly labor costs.

Reducing this source of a variance requires the development of a better prediction model. Sensitivity analysis will help the manager decide the potential net benefits from maintaining a routine monitoring of possible prediction errors and of devoting resources to reduce these errors.

Inappropriate decision model

Decision models differ in their ability to capture reality. Variances can arise when the chosen decision model fails to capture important aspects affecting the decision. Consider the linear-programming (LP) model discussed in Chapter 22. The solution to an LP model can be used when setting standards for raw-material purchase prices. However, these standards may be inappropriate if the LP solution is not feasible due to the failure of the LP model to recognize a constraint on labor availability or storage capacity. Similar problems can arise if the objective function or the variables in the LP model are incorrectly specified.

Note that a decision model source of a variance is not the same as a parameter prediction error source. The decision model source pertains to an incorrect functional relationship, while the prediction error pertains to an incorrect parameter prediction.

Deciding to correct a decision model source of a variance usually necessitates a comparison of the cost of correction with the benefits over many future time periods. In contrast, the decision to correct a parameter prediction involves a similar analysis but typically relates to a shorter time period because these predictions are updated more frequently.

Random variation Standard cost systems typically represent a standard as a *single* acceptable measure. However, a more appropriate representation is that the standard is a *band* or *range* of possible acceptable measures. For example, the raw-material input per unit of output in a chemical process may fluctuate because of random variations that are inherent in the process. By definition, a random deviation in itself calls for no corrective action. Distinguishing random deviations from other sources of a variance is a helpful first step in deciding whether and when to investigate individual variances. **Recognizing the random variation source of a variance highlights that the concern should be whether the underlying process is behaving well rather than whether a single cost realization is deemed abnormal.**

The distinctions among the six sources of variances illustrate the complexities that decision makers face. The manager should be alert to these six sources because they focus on assumptions about standard setting, measurement, implementation, prediction methods, and decision models.

The nature of the search prompted by each of the six sources of variance can differ considerably. For example, an implementation breakdown source may require interviewing a specific worker; it may even require redesigning an incentive scheme. In contrast, a decision model source may require discussions with an engineer or a mathematician. As always, the expected costs of these investigators should be compared with their expected savings to determine if an investigation should be launched.

DIFFICULTIES IN ANALYSIS OF VARIANCES

Ideally, managers would like to have a variance information system that:

a. Is timely
b. Is itemized in sufficient detail, such that important individual variances are not hidden because they cancel each other out
c. Pinpoints the source(s) of each variance into one (or more) of the six categories listed above (or the categories appropriate in a particular setting)
d. Indicates the sequence of an investigation that will maximize overall net benefits

In practice, managers face interdependencies between the individual sources of variances. The problems of estimating costs and benefits can also be imposing.

The difficulties facing managers are well illustrated by one study of the use of variance investigation models in several cost centers of a grain process firm. The most useful variances to operating managers were those reported on a daily basis; weekly or monthly variances were less useful because of the difficulty involved in locating the cause of process problems that had occurred many days earlier. However, the daily physical quantities necessary to compute some variances were not available in the reporting system, so only a subset of variances could be computed. Moreover, difficult measurement problems arose with data that were available on a daily basis:

It was difficult to precisely measure inputs (e.g., direct material units) and outputs (finished output units) due to the difficulty of estimating large bin and tank inventory levels. Although a perennial cost accounting problem, it was more acute because of the daily reporting period. The second measurement problem was the difficulty of matching inputs and outputs. This was due to the often lengthy processing times in the grain firm. For example, a variable supply item was paired with output for the same day even though its purpose may have been to process output for the following day.[8]

COST-BENEFIT ANALYSIS OF VARIANCE INVESTIGATION DECISIONS

Decision analysis approach

The approach to decision making under uncertainty outlined in Chapter 18 can be used in variance investigation decisions.[9] Exhibit 24-9 presents a simple example involving two events and two actions:

Events: X_1 = In-control process (i.e., the activity in question is functioning properly)

X_2 = Out-of-control process (i.e., the activity in question is not functioning properly)

Actions: a_1 = Investigate process
a_2 = Do not investigate process

Examine Exhibit 24-9 carefully so that the facts of the example are clear.

The probability of the process being in control is .80 and the probability of its

EXHIBIT 24-9
Decision Table Presentation of Data

	EVENTS	
	X_1 = In-control Process $p(X_1)$ = .80	X_2 = Out-of-control Process $p(X_2)$ = .20
ACTIONS		
a_1 = Investigate process	C = $3,000	C + M = $10,000
a_2 = Do not investigate process	$0*	L = $37,000

C = Cost of investigation = $3,000
M = Cost of correction, if out-of-control process discovered = $7,000
L = Extra costs over the planning horizon of the process being out of control, which may be either the time until the process is expected to go out of control again or the time until a routine intervention is scheduled = $37,000
*All other amounts in this table are incremental in relation to this action and event combination. Note that the model underlying this decision table assumes (1) that a process that goes out-of-control stays out-of-control, and (2) that when an out-of-control process is corrected, it stays in-control until the end of the planning period.

---

[8]F. Jacobs, "When and How to Use Statistical Cost Variance Investigation Techniques," *Cost and Management*, January-February 1983, pp. 26–32.

[9]We present the simplest example of the decision approach to variance investigation decisions; only one period ahead is explicitly considered and only two events (in-control and out-of-control) are recognized. We assume risk-neutral decision makers. More-complex models are discussed in F. Jacobs and R. Marshall, "A Note on the Choice Structure of Cost Variance Investigation Models," *Journal of Accounting Literature*, Spring 1984, pp. 73–83. Critical comments on the relevance of these models to operating managers are presented in G. Boer, "Solutions in Search of a Problem: The Case of Budget Variance Investigation Models," *Journal of Accounting Literature*, Spring 1984, pp. 47–69.

being out of control is .20:

$$p(X_1) = .80 \qquad p(X_2) = .20$$

The expected costs from the investigate (a_1) and do not investigate (a_2) actions are:

Investigate:
$$E(a_1) = (p(X_1) \times C) + (p(X_2) \times (C + M))$$
$$= (.80 \times \$3,000) + (.20 \times \$10,000) = \$4,400$$

Do not investigate:
$$E(a_2) = (p(X_1) \times \$0) + (p(X_2) \times L)$$
$$= (.80 \times \$0) + (.20 \times \$37,000) = \$7,400$$

The optimal action is to investigate the process, because the expected cost is $3,000 less ($4,400 − $7,400) than the do-not-investigate alternative.

Role of
probabilities

The foregoing example illustrates the critical role of probabilities in deciding whether to investigate. A low probability, say .05, of the process being out of control will change the desirability of conducting an investigation:

Investigate:
$$E(a_1) = (.95 \times \$3,000) + (.05 \times \$10,000) = \$3,350$$

Do not investigate:
$$E(a_2) = (.95 \times \$0) \qquad + (.05 \times \$37,000) = \$1,850$$

With $p(X_2) = .05$, the optimal action is do not investigate.

The probability level at which a manager would be indifferent between investigating and not investigating whether a process is out of control is:[10]

$$p(X_2) = \frac{C}{L - M}$$

Given $C = \$3,000$, $L = \$37,000$, and $M = \$7,000$ (see Exhibit 24-9 for definitions of C, L, and M), then

$$p(X_2) = \frac{\$3,000}{\$37,000 - \$7,000} = .10$$

The expected cost when $p(X_2) = .10$ for both a_1 and a_2 is $3,700:

Investigate:
$$E(a_1) = (.90 \times \$3,000) + (.10 \times \$10,000) = \$3,700$$

Do not investigate:
$$E(a_2) = (.90 \times \$0) \qquad + (.10 \times \$37,000) = \$3,700$$

---

[10]This formula is derived as follows:

Given $\qquad\qquad\qquad p(X_1) + p(X_2) = 1$

then $\qquad\qquad\qquad p(X_1) = 1 - p(X_2)$

Equating the expected costs of a_1 and a_2 and substituting $(1 - p(X_2))$ for $p(X_1)$ yields:

$$[(1 - p(X_2)) \times C] + [p(X_2) \times (C + M)] = p(X_2) \times L$$

$$C - (C \times p(X_2)) + (C \times p(X_2)) + (M \times p(X_2)) = (L \times p(X_2))$$

$$C = p(X_2)(L - M)$$

$$p(X_2) = \frac{C}{L - M}$$

Investigation is only desirable in the Exhibit 24-9 example if the probability of the process being out of control exceeds .10.

Estimation of costs and benefits

The usefulness of the above cost-benefit calculation is critically dependent on having accurate estimates of $p(X_1)$ and $p(X_2)$ and of the C, M, and L parameters defined in Exhibit 24-9. Much care needs to be taken with such estimation.

Consider the estimation of C, the cost of investigation. In some operations, signals to a line manager that a process is potentially out of control can occur well before the cost-variance report is prepared. For example, line operators on a soft-drink bottling production line may complain about the quality of the glass bottles if they encounter a greater than expected number of breakages. The line manager may immediately direct that a different batch of bottles be used on the production line, pending investigation of the batch currently being used. By the time the line manager receives a materials-yield variance report, a preliminary investigation may already be completed. In this case, estimation of C should include only the incremental investigation costs beyond those already incurred. Similarly, estimation of M and L in Exhibit 24-9 should recognize those steps already taken to correct the glass-bottle breakage problem. This example illustrates how the timeliness of cost accounting data can affect the values of parameters used in cost-variance investigation models.

Rules of thumb

Again and again we have seen that managers use simple decision models or rules of thumb in complex situations.[11] In the area of variance analysis, rules of thumb observed in practice include the following:

1. Investigate all variances. This approach can involve numerous investigations but may be justified if the cost of the process being out of control is extremely high.
2. Investigate all variances greater than a preset percentage deviation from the standard (e.g., 5%, 10%, or 25%).
3. Investigate all variances greater than a preset absolute size (e.g., $100 or $500).
4. Investigate all variances greater than a preset point on the frequency distribution of variances (e.g., two standard deviations (2σ) or three standard deviations (3σ) from the budgeted amount).

STATISTICAL QUALITY CONTROL

Statistical quality control (SQC) is a formal means of distinguishing between random variation and other sources of variation in an operating process. SQC is one approach that can be used in decisions on whether to investigate a variance.[12] A key tool in SQC is a control chart. A **control chart** is a graph of successive observations of a series (or of successive arithmetic means of independent samples) in which each observation is plotted relative to preset points on the expected distribution (such as the .10 and .90 percentiles or the 2σ confidence intervals). Only those observations beyond these limits are ordinarily regarded as nonrandom and worth investigating.

---

[11]A survey found that only 4.6% of the respondents used statistical analysis to determine whether a particular cost variance should be investigated. W. Cress and J. Pettijohn, "A Survey of Budget-Related Planning and Control Policies and Procedures," *Journal of Accounting Education*, Fall 1985, p. 75.

[12]For a useful introduction to the SQC literature, see A. Feigenbaum, *Total Quality Control*, 3rd ed. (New York: McGraw-Hill, 1983), especially Chaps. 13–17.

EXHIBIT 24-10

Statistical Quality Control Charts: Daily Energy Use at Three Production Lines

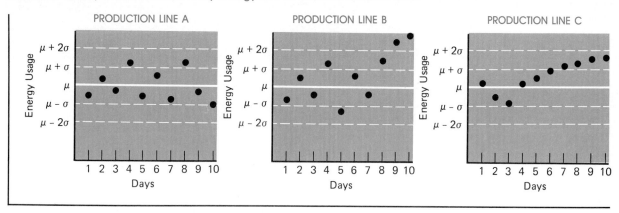

Exhibit 24-10 presents control charts for the daily energy usage (in kilowatt hours) of three production lines of an assembly plant. Energy usage in the prior sixty days for each plant was assumed to provide a good basis from which to calculate the distribution of daily energy usage. The arithmetic mean (μ) and standard deviation (σ) are the two parameters of the distribution that are used in the control charts in Exhibit 24-10. Based on past experience, the firm decides that any observation outside the 2σ range should be investigated.

For production line A in Exhibit 24-10, the process is deemed to require no investigation; all observations are within the 2σ from the mean range. For production line B in Exhibit 24-10, the last two observations signal a possible out-of-control state. Given the 2σ rule, both observations would lead to an investigation. Production line C in Exhibit 24-10 illustrates a process that would not prompt an investigation under the 2σ rule but may well be out of control. The last eight observations show an ever-increasing deviation from the mean daily energy use. Statistical procedures (called cumulative-sum or cusum procedures) have been developed that consider the trend in recent usage as well as the level of each day's energy use.

A major benefit of the SQC chart format is that managers find it easy to understand and, over time, can become relatively adept at recognizing patterns in sequences of observations. Most work on statistical quality control has focused on observations measured in engineering terms (such as labor time, material usage, and number of product rejects) rather than in the monetary terms traditionally found in accounting variance reports.

There are few reported instances where SQC charts have been applied to the analysis of cost variance reports. Several factors could explain this situation. First, adding dollar amounts to engineering items, such as material usage or the number of product rejects, may not provide any greater insight into how such items can be better controlled at the plant manager level. Second, it is often easier to estimate the distribution of items in quantity terms than it is to estimate the distribution of items in price times quantity terms. For example, when major decreases in oil prices occurred in the 1980s, airline companies found that the distribution of dollar fuel cost per mile traveled was changing; this made it difficult to estimate reliably the 1σ

and 2σ parameters used in SQC charts. In contrast, the distribution of gallons of fuel consumed per mile traveled by airline companies was more stable in this period.

PROBLEM FOR SELF-STUDY

problem   Refer to the example in Exhibit 24-9 (p. 818). Suppose $C = \$5,000$, $M = \$10,000$, and $L = \$30,000$. The probabilities as set out in Exhibit 24-9 are unchanged: $p(X_1) = .80$ and $p(X_2) = .20$. What would be the expected costs of investigate (a_1) and do not investigate (a_2)? What level of probability of the process's being out of control would make the expected costs of each action be the same?

solution

Investigate: $E(a_1) = (p(X_1) \times C) + (p(X_2) \times (C + M))$

$$= (.80 \times \$5,000) + (.20 \times \$15,000) = \$7,000$$

Do not investigate: $E(a_2) = (p(X_1) \times \$0) + (p(X_2) \times L)$

$$= (.80 \times \$0) + (.20 \times \$30,000) = \$6,000$$

The optimal action is do not investigate the process.
        The probability level for X_2 at which a manager would be indifferent between a_1 and a_2 is

$$p(X_2) = \frac{C}{L - M} = \frac{\$5,000}{\$30,000 - \$10,000} = .25$$

If the probability of the process being out of control exceeds .25, an investigation should be made.

SUMMARY

Accounting variances are a means of communicating what has happened. By this and other means, the manager enhances understanding and decides whether specified areas deserve more investigation.

The variances discussed in this chapter are supplemental to the price and efficiency variances introduced in Chapter 6. Quantity, mix, and yield variances are especially useful where sales or production managers have considerable discretion about the mix of products to sell or the way inputs are combined in the manufacture of a given product.

Decisions about whether to investigate a variance should consider the costs of investigation and correction, and the costs of a process being out of control (such as the costs associated with defective units and poor quality). Because these factors are difficult to quantify, rules of thumb are often used in practice for deciding when to investigate.

Terms to Learn

This chapter and the Glossary contain definitions of the following important terms:

control chart (p. 820)   labor-mix variance (813)
labor-yield variance (813)   material-mix variance (810)
market-share variance (806)   market-size variance (806)
material-yield variance (810)   sales mix (799)   sales-mix variance (803)
sales-quantity variance (803)   statistical quality control (820)   SQC (820)

This chapter illustrates the cost-benefit theme of this book. If the perceived benefits exceed the costs, managers will pay for more-detailed variance analysis and for formal models of when to investigate variances. Otherwise managers settle for less detail and rely on their individual experience and personal observations for judging when variances deserve a closer look.

Always consider possible interdependencies among individual variances. Standing alone, an individual variance is rarely sufficient for decision making. For example, decisions on material mix may depend on the relative prices of material and the relationships of mix to yield.

The examples presented in this chapter involve at most three products or three material or three labor inputs. Even with such few products or inputs, the computation is tedious. (We have no illusions about this.) The gains in speed and accuracy from using standardized computer packages are very large in the mix and yield variance area.

QUESTIONS, PROBLEMS, AND CASES

24-1 Distinguish between a *sales-quantity variance* and *sales-mix variance*.

24-2 "The sales-volume variance might be better labeled as a marketing variance." Explain why such a comment might be made.

24-3 Why might market-size and market-share sales variances not be computed?

24-4 "A company can sell exactly the same number of units as specified in the static budget and still have a flexible budget with numbers that differ from those in the static budget." Do you agree? Explain.

24-5 Distinguish between a *material-yield variance* and a *material-mix variance*.

24-6 "Production-mix and production-yield variances should be calculated as a routine part of a management accounting system." Do you agree? Explain.

24-7 "Price variances are excluded from all calculations of mix and yield variances." Do you agree? Explain.

24-8 Name five sources of a variance.

24-9 Contrast the accountant's and the statistician's concept of the word *standard*.

24-10 Name three rules of thumb used in practice to decide whether to investigate a variance.

24-11 Describe the basic approach of statistical quality control (SQC).

24-12 Sales-volume, sales-quantity, and sales-mix variances. Debbie's Delight Inc. operates a chain of cookie stores. Budgeted and actual operating data of the downtown store for August 19_2 follow.

BUDGET FOR AUGUST

	Selling Price per lb.	Variable Cost per lb.	Contribution Margin per lb.	Sales in lbs.
Chocolate chip	$4.50	$2.50	$2.00	45,000
Oatmeal raisin	5.00	2.70	2.30	25,000
Coconut	5.50	2.90	2.60	10,000
White chocolate	6.00	3.00	3.00	5,000
Macadamia nut	6.50	3.40	3.10	15,000
				100,000

ACTUAL FOR AUGUST

	Selling Price per lb.	Variable Cost per lb.	Contribution Margin per lb.	Sales in lbs.
Chocolate chip	$4.50	$2.60	$1.90	57,600
Oatmeal raisin	5.20	2.90	2.30	18,000
Coconut	5.50	2.80	2.70	9,600
White chocolate	6.00	3.40	2.60	13,200
Macadamia nut	7.00	4.00	3.00	21,600
				120,000

Required

1. Compute the individual product and total sales-volume variances for August 19_2.
2. Compute the individual product and total sales-quantity variances for August 19_2.
3. Compute the individual product and total sales-mix variances for August 19_2.
4. Comment on your results in requirements 1, 2, and 3.

24-13 Sales-volume, sales-quantity, and sales-mix variances.   Computer Horizons manufactures and sells three related microcomputer products:

1. Plum—sold mostly to college students and for use in small offices and in homes
2. Portable Plum—smaller version of the Plum that can be carried in a briefcase
3. Super Plum—has a larger memory and more capabilities than the Plum and is targeted at the business market

Budgeted and actual operating data for 19_4 follow.

BUDGET FOR 19_4

	Selling Price per Unit	Variable Cost per Unit	Contribution Margin per Unit	Sales Volume in Units
Plum	$1,200	$ 700	$ 500	700,000
Portable Plum	800	500	300	100,000
Super Plum	5,000	3,000	2,000	200,000
				1,000,000

ACTUAL FOR 19_4

	Selling Price per Unit	Variable Cost per Unit	Contribution Margin per Unit	Sales Volume in Units
Plum	$1,100	$ 500	$ 600	825,000
Portable Plum	650	400	250	165,000
Super Plum	3,500	2,500	1,000	110,000
				1,100,000

During 19_4, Computer Horizons bought key components at bargain prices because of a price war for computer chips sparked by overseas suppliers. Computer Horizons had budgeted for a major expansion into the lucrative business market in 19_4. Unfortunately, it underestimated the marketing power of the Big Blue Company.

Required

1. Compute the individual product and total sales-volume variances for Computer Horizons in 19_4.
2. Compute the individual product and total sales-quantity variances for 19_4.
3. Compute the individual product and total sales-mix variances for 19_4.
4. Comment on your results in requirements 1, 2, and 3.

24-14 Market-size and market-share sales variances. (continuation of Problem 24-13) Computer Horizons derived its total unit sales budget for 19_4 from an internal management estimate of a 20% market share and an industry sales forecast by Micro-Information Services of 5,000,000 units. At the end of 19_4, Micro Information reported actual industry sales of 6,875,000 units.

Required

Compute the market-size and market-share sales variances for Computer Horizons.

24-15 Sales-price and volume variances, sales-quantity and mix variances, market-size and market-share variances. (CMA, adapted) The Arsco Co. makes three grades of indoor-outdoor carpets. The sales volume for the annual budget is determined by estimating the total market volume for indoor-outdoor carpet, and then applying the company's prior-year market share, adjusted for planned changes due to company programs for the coming year. The volume is apportioned between the three grades based on the prior year's product mix, again adjusted for planned changes due to company programs for the coming year.

Given below are the company budget for 19_3 and the results of operations for 19_3.

BUDGET

	Grade 1	Grade 2	Grade 3	Total
Sales—units	1,000 rolls	1,000 rolls	2,000 rolls	4,000 rolls
Sales—dollars				
(000 omitted)	$1,000	$2,000	$3,000	$6,000
Variable expense	700	1,600	2,300	4,600
Contribution margin	$ 300	$ 400	$ 700	$1,400
Traceable fixed expense	200	200	300	700
Traceable margin	$ 100	$ 200	$ 400	$ 700
Selling and administrative expense				250
Net income				$ 450

ACTUAL

	Grade 1	Grade 2	Grade 3	Total
Sales—units	800 rolls	1,000 rolls	2,100 rolls	3,900 rolls
Sales—dollars				
(000 omitted)	$810	$2,000	$3,000	$5,810
Variable expense	560	1,610	2,320	4,490
Contribution margin	$250	$ 390	$ 680	$1,320
Traceable fixed expense	210	220	315	745
Traceable margin	$ 40	$ 170	$ 365	$ 575
Selling and administrative expense				275
Net income				$ 300

Industry volume was estimated at 40,000 rolls for budgeting purposes. Actual industry volume for 19_3 was 32,500 rolls.

Required

1. Prepare a comparison for each product, and for all products in total, of the original budgeted total contribution margin and the actual total contribution margin. Show price/variable cost variances and sales-volume variances.
2. What is the dollar impact on profits (using budgeted variable margins) of the shift in product mix from the budgeted mix? That is, split the sales-volume variance in requirement 1 into its quantity and mix components.
3. What portion of the variance, if any, can be attributed to the state of the carpet market?

24-16 Material-price and efficiency variances, material-yield and mix variances, food processing. Tropical Fruits Inc. processes tropical fruit into fruit salad mix, which it sells to a food service company. Tropical Fruits has in its budget the following standards for the raw-material inputs to produce 80 pounds of tropical fruit salad:

50 pounds of pineapple at $1.00 per pound	$50
30 pounds of watermelon at $0.50 per pound	15
20 pounds of strawberries at $0.75 per pound	15
100	$80

No inventories of raw materials are kept. Purchases are made as needed, so that all price variances relate to materials used. The actual raw-material inputs used to produce 54,000 pounds of tropical fruit salad for the month of October were:

36,400 pounds of pineapple at $0.90 per pound	$32,760
18,200 pounds of watermelon at $0.60 per pound	10,920
15,400 pounds of strawberries at $0.70 per pound	10,780
70,000	$54,460

Required

1. Compute the material-price and material-efficiency variances for each product and for the total output of tropical fruit salad in October.
2. Compute the individual product and total material-yield variances for October.
3. Compute the individual product and total material-mix variances for October.
4. Comment on your results in requirements 1, 2, and 3.
5. Why might material-yield and material-mix variances be especially informative to the management of Tropical Fruits Inc?

24-17 Material-yield and mix variances, perfume manufacturing. (SMA) The Scent Makers Company Ltd. produces a perfume for men. To make this perfume, three different types of fluids are used. Dycone, Cycone, and Bycone are applied in proportions of 2/5, 3/10, and 3/10, respectively, at standard, and their standard costs are $6.00, $3.50, and $2.50 per gallon, respectively. The chief engineer reported that in the past few months, the standard yield has been at 80% on 100 gallons of mix. The company maintains a policy of not carrying any direct materials, as storage space is costly. Current production has been set at 4,160,000 gallons of perfume for the year.

Last week the company produced 75,000 gallons of perfume at a total raw-materials cost of $449,500. Actual number of gallons used and costs per gallon for the three fluids are as follows:

	GALLONS	COST PER GALLON
Dycone	45,000	$5.50
Cycone	35,000	4.20
Bycone	20,000	2.75

1. Compute the price, yield, and mix variances for each of the three fluids. Reconcile these variances with the total material variance.
2. Explain the managerial significance of the price, yield, and mix variances in the above situation.

24-18 Material-price and efficiency variances, material-yield and mix variances, chemical processing. (CMA, adapted) Energy Products Company produces a gasoline additive, Gas Gain, at its chemical-processing plant. This product increases engine efficiency and improves gasoline mileage by creating a more complete burn in the combustion process.

Careful controls are required during the production process to ensure that the proper mix of input chemicals is achieved and that evaporation is controlled. If the controls are not effective, there can be loss of output and efficiency.

The standard cost of producing a 500-liter batch of Gas Gain is $138. The standard materials mix and related standard cost of each chemical material input used in the production of a 500-liter batch of Gas Gain are:

CHEMICAL MATERIAL INPUT	STANDARD INPUT QUANTITY IN LITERS	STANDARD COST PER LITER	TOTAL COST
Echol	180	$.20	$ 36.00
Protex	120	.40	48.00
Benz	240	.15	36.00
CT–40	60	.30	18.00
	600		$138.00

The quantities of chemicals purchased and used in production during February 19_3 are shown below. There were no inventories of any of the chemical inputs on February 1. A total of 140 batches of Gas Gain were manufactured in February; each batch contains 500 liters of Gas Gain. Energy Products determines its price and efficiency variances at the end of each month:

CHEMICAL MATERIAL INPUT	LITERS PURCHASED IN FEBRUARY	TOTAL PURCHASE PRICE	LITERS USED IN FEBRUARY
Echol	30,000	$ 6,600	26,600
Protex	14,000	7,000	12,880
Benz	40,000	4,800	37,800
CT–40	8,000	2,000	7,140
Total	92,000	$20,400	84,420

1. Compute the price and efficiency variances for the quantity used of each chemical material input in February.
2. Compute the individual product and total material-yield variances for February.
3. Compute the individual product and total material-mix variances for February.
4. Comment on your results in requirements 1, 2, and 3.

24-19 Labor price and efficiency variances, labor-yield and mix variances. A supervisor in a sheet metal operation of Mid-West Industries has the following direct-labor standard:

(a) Labor price per hour:

2 journeymen @ $22		$44
3 helpers @ $12		36
Total cost of standard combination of labor		$80
Average price per hour, $80 ÷ 5 =		$16

(b) Standard labor price per unit of output
at 8 units per hour, $16 ÷ 8 = $ 2

(c) Standard labor cost of 20,000 units of output,
20,000 × $2, or 2,500 × $16 = $40,000

(d) Actual inputs, 2,900 hours consisting of:

900 hours of journeymen @ $23	$20,700
2,000 hours of helpers @ $11	22,000
	$42,700

The supervisor had to pay a higher average wage rate to his journeymen because of the inclusion of some skilled workers who had bargained for a superior rate of pay. As a result, he tried to save some costs by using more helpers per journeyman than usual.

Required

1. Compute the price and efficiency variances.
2. Divide the efficiency variance into yield and mix components.
3. What would the actual costs probably have been if the standard labor mix had been maintained even though the actual labor prices were incurred?

24-20 Labor price and efficiency variances, labor-yield and mix variances, textile industry, performance evaluation. Home Textile Products manufactures and sells a diverse set of textile products. Lyn Randell, the chief operating officer, is evaluating the performance of the manager of the Savannah, U.S.A., plant and the manager of the Seoul, South Korea, plant. Both plants produce high-quality bed sheets. A key area of concern to Randell is direct-labor costs. The standards underlying the March budget for each batch of 1,000 sheets is (all amounts are expressed in U.S. dollars):

DIRECT-LABOR CATEGORY	SAVANNAH PLANT	SEOUL PLANT
Semiskilled	36 hours at $20 an hour	42 hours at $9 an hour
Skilled	60 hours at $25 an hour	44 hours at $12 an hour
Supervisory	24 hours at $36 an hour	14 hours at $16 an hour

In the first week of April, Randell received the actual results for March. The output of the Savannah plant was 800 batches of 1,000 sheets. The output of the Seoul plant was 600 batches of 1,000 sheets. The actual direct-labor costs (in $U.S.) were:

Direct-Labor Category	Savannah Plant (Hours)	Seoul Plant (Hours)
Semiskilled	29,600 at $20 an hour = $ 592,000	24,000 at $9.50 an hour = $228,000
Skilled	38,400 at $24 an hour = 921,600	27,600 at $13 an hour = 358,800
Supervisory	12,000 at $35 an hour = 420,000	10,200 at $18 an hour = 183,600
	$1,933,600	$770,400

The average direct-labor cost per batch was $2,417 for Savannah and $1,284 for Seoul.

Required

1. Compute the direct-labor price and direct-labor efficiency variances for the Savannah and Seoul plants.

2. Compute the direct labor-yield and direct labor-mix variances for the Savannah and Seoul plants.

3. Compare the performance of the managers of the Savannah and Seoul plants with regard to direct-labor costs.

24-21 Sources of variances. The chapter described six possible sources of variances: (1) inappropriate standard, (2) mismeasurement of actual results, (3) implementation breakdown, (4) parameter prediction error, (5) inappropriate decision model, and (6) random variation.

Required

Listed below are some examples of factors associated with a reported variance. Use one of the numbers (1) through (6) to identify the most likely source of the variance being described.

(a) A supervisor gets a year-end bonus that is really attributable to overtime that was worked seven months previously. The bonus is charged to overhead at year-end.

(b) Costs of supplies are charged to overhead as acquired rather than as used.

(c) Costs of setting up printing jobs are consistently pegged too low when bids are made.

(d) The salvage value of scrap from production is forecast incorrectly.

(e) Normal spoilage in a food-processing plant amounts to 5% of good output.

(f) The salvage value of scrap from production is ignored completely.

(g) A worker is inefficient because of daydreaming.

(h) A worker is inefficient because he is new at his job and is just learning how to do the work.

(i) A worker deliberately used more raw materials than necessary when the initial materials standards were set.

24-22 Cost-benefit analysis of variance investigation decision. When a process is investigated in an automated department, the costs of investigation are $1,000. If an out-of-control process is discovered, the cost of correction is $1,500. The manager is always indifferent about conducting an investigation when there is a probability of .60 that the process is in control.

Required

How large must the cost savings (L) be to warrant an investigation?

24-23 Cost-benefit analysis of variance investigation decision. You are the manager of a manufacturing process. A material efficiency variance of $10,000 has been reported for the past week's operations. You are trying to decide whether to investigate. You feel that if you do not investigate and the process is out of control, the cost savings (L) over the planning horizon is $3,800. The cost to investigate is $500. The cost to correct the process if you discover that it is out of control is $1,000. You assess the probability that the process is out of control at .30.

Required

1. Should the process be investigated? What are the expected costs of investigation and of no investigation?

2. What level of probability that the process is out of control would exist where the expected costs of each action would be the same?

3. If the cost variance is $10,000, why is L only $3,800?

24-24 Cost-benefit analysis of variance investigation decision. (by J. Harris for CMA) Cilla Company manufactures a line of handbags. An operations summary of Cilla's cutting department for May 19_4 included the analysis below.

Standard materials cost of production	$314,000
Materials price variance	0
Unfavorable materials efficiency variance	16,000
Actual materials cost of production	$330,000

Donna Cook, cutting department supervisor, gathered the following information for use in deciding whether or not the variance should be investigated.

Estimated cost of investigating the variance	$4,000
Estimated cost of making the necessary changes if the cutting department is operating improperly	8,000
Estimated costs that would be saved by making the necessary changes if the cutting department is operating improperly	40,000
Estimated probability of the cutting department operating properly during the current fiscal year	90%

Required

1. Recommend whether or not Donna Cook should investigate the unfavorable materials efficiency variance. Support your recommendation by (a) preparing a payoff table for use in making the decision, (b) computing the expected value of the cost of each possible action.
2. Donna Cook is uncertain about the probability estimate for proper operation of the cutting department (i.e., 90%). Determine the probability estimate of the cutting department operating properly that would cause Donna Cook to be indifferent between the two possible actions.

24-25 Cost-benefit analysis of variance investigation decision, production plant setting. San Diego Surf Products (SDSP) produces suntan lotion at its La Jolla plant. This plant operates six days a week. At the end of every third working day, a detailed investigation is made of the materials used, the mixing machinery, and the bottling operations. This investigation is part of SDSP's quality control program. On Tuesday, December 12, SDSP completed one of its regular three-day investigations.

On Wednesday, December 13, Hobie Leland, Jr., received the daily material usage report after the production line had stopped for the day. Leland was dismayed to find an unfavorable materials efficiency variance of $5,500. He believed that one of two underlying events existed:

1. Production line in control. Under this possibility, Leland expects no unfavorable material efficiency variance on either the fourteenth or fifteenth of December. The $5,500 unfavorable variance on the thirteenth is judged to be a random variance.
2. Production line out of control. Under this possibility, the $5,500 unfavorable material efficiency variance would continue each day on both December 14 and December 15.

Leland has a decision to make. Should an investigation be made overnight on December 13 of the materials used, the mixing machinery, and the bottling operations? The cost of the investigation would be $2,000. If the process is found to be out of control, it will cost an additional $1,000 to put it back in control.

Required

1. Specify the cash flows associated with the investigate and do-not-investigate actions for each of the two underlying events (in-control process and out-of-control process).
2. What is the probability of the process being out of control at which Leland would be indifferent between investigating and not investigating the process?
3. In requirements 1 and 2, it is assumed that the daily cost to the firm of the process being out of control is the $5,500 unfavorable materials efficiency variance. Give two reasons why this assumption need not be valid.

24-26 Statistical quality control, airline operations. People's Skyway operates daily roundtrip flights on the London–New York route using a fleet of three 747s. These three 747s are the Spirit of Birmingham, the Spirit of Glasgow, and the Spirit of Manchester. The standard quantity of fuel used on each flight is based on the mean fuel usage over the last twelve months. The distribution of fuel usage per roundtrip over this twelve-month period has a mean of 100 gallon units and a standard deviation of 10 gallon units. A gallon unit is 1,000 British gallons.

Cilla Black, the operations manager of People's Skyway, uses a statistical quality control (SQC) approach to decide whether to investigate variances from the standard fuel usage per roundtrip flight. Those flights with fuel usage greater than two standard deviations from the mean are investigated. In addition, Black monitors trends in the SQC charts to determine if additional investigation decisions should be made.

Black receives the following report for roundtrip fuel usage in October by the three planes operating on the London–New York route:

FLIGHT	SPIRIT OF BIRMINGHAM (Gallon Units)	SPIRIT OF GLASGOW (Gallon Units)	SPIRIT OF MANCHESTER (Gallon Units)
1	104	103	97
2	94	94	104
3	97	96	111
4	101	107	104
5	105	92	122
6	107	113	118
7	111	99	126
8	112	106	114
9	115	101	117
10	119	93	123

Required

1. Using the two standard deviations rule, what variance investigation decisions would be made?
2. Present SQC charts for roundtrip fuel usage by each of the three 747s in October.
3. What inferences can be drawn from the three SQC charts developed for requirement 2?
4. A proposal is made that the SQC charts developed by People's Skyway be expressed in dollar terms rather than in physical quantity terms (gallon units). What are the advantages and disadvantages of using dollar fuel costs rather than gallon units as the unit of analysis in an SQC chart?

831

25

Systems Choice: Decentralization and Transfer Pricing

Organization structure and decentralization • Transfer pricing • Illustration of transfer pricing •
Market-based transfer prices • Cost-based transfer prices • General rule for transfer pricing? •
Multinational transfer pricing • Surveys of company practice •
Appendix: Management control system design

Is General Motors' management control system better than Ford's? What role can accounting information play in management control systems? Should products exchanged between individual profit centers of an organization be transferred at market price or at absorption cost? Such questions are often asked of senior management or their advisers. Chapters 25, 26, and 27 cover important topics in this area. This chapter discusses the benefits and costs of centralized versus decentralized organizations, and the choice of a price to transfer products or services between subunits of the same organization;[1] the Appendix presents a framework for the design of management control systems. The topics of performance evaluation, executive compensation, and internal control are examined in the following two chapters.

Chapters 25, 26, and 27 contain a blend of cost accounting (narrowly conceived), general management, economics, and organization behavior. This material, along with Chapter 11, is "softer" than that in other chapters of this text.

---

[1]The literature on decentralization and transfer pricing is voluminous. For a good overview, see S. Grabski, "Transfer Pricing in Complex Organizations: A Review and Integration of Recent Empirical and Analytical Research," *Journal of Accounting Literature*, Spring 1985, pp. 33–75. For two classic studies, see D. Solomons, *Divisional Performance: Measurement and Control* (Homewood, Ill.: Richard D. Irwin, 1968); and R. Vancil, *Decentralization: Managerial Ambiguity by Design* (New York: Financial Executives Research Foundation, 1979).

"Softer" means that many issues raised here cannot be resolved merely by crunching some numbers. The responsibilities of a management accountant extend beyond the preparing of numerical reports.

ORGANIZATION STRUCTURE AND DECENTRALIZATION

As organizations grow, top managers face two continuing problems: (a) how to divide activities and responsibilities and (b) how to coordinate subunits. Inevitably, the power to make decisions is distributed among various managers. The essence of **decentralization** is the freedom to make decisions. **Decentralization is a matter of degree. Total decentralization means minimum constraints and maximum freedom for managers to make decisions at the lowest levels. Conversely, total centralization means maximum constraints and minimum freedom to make decisions.**

Benefits of decentralization

How should top managers decide on how much decentralization is optimal? Conceptually, they try to choose the degree of decentralization that maximizes the excess of benefits over costs. From a practical standpoint, top managers are seldom able to quantify either the benefits or the costs. Nevertheless, this cost-benefit approach helps focus on the central issues.

The claimed benefits of decentralizing decisions to the managers of subunits include the following:

1. Subunit managers can incorporate into decision making *more information* about local demand and supply conditions. This benefit can be sizable. The costs of transmitting information about local conditions to a central decision maker are often high. Moreover, the information transmitted may be incomplete or even intentionally distorted.

2. Subunit managers can make *more timely* decisions. With no need to seek approval from higher-level managers, subunit managers can more quickly respond to situations as they arise. This shortened response time can be very attractive to potential customers.

3. Subunit managers are usually *more highly motivated,* given that they can exercise greater individual initiative. The pride of "making one's own decisions" is heightened.

4. *The development of an experienced pool of managerial talent* is promoted by giving managers more responsibility. Not only is training provided to develop effective managers, but early warning signals are obtained about ineffective managers. A company (Tektronix) expressed this benefit as follows: "Decentralized units provide a training ground for general managers, and a visible field of combat where product champions may fight for their ideas."

5. By keeping management subunits small, the benefits from having *highly focused groups of people* can be obtained; for example, the subunit can custom-tailor itself to fit the market or to exploit its unique talents. This benefit is associated with the "small is beautiful" theme in several recent management books.

6. *Senior management,* relieved of the burden of day-to-day decision making, *can focus more of their time and energy on strategic planning* for the total organization.

833

The claimed costs of decentralizing decisions to the managers of subunits include the following:

1. **Dysfunctional decision making**—that is, decision making where the benefit to one subunit is more than offset by the costs or loss of benefits to the organization as a whole. This situation may be caused by (a) a lack of harmony or congruence among the overall organization goals, the subunit goals, and the individual goals of decision makers, or (b) a lack of information for guiding subunit managers concerning the effects of their decisions on other parts of the organization.

Dysfunctional decision making is most likely to occur where the subunits in the organization are highly interdependent—that is, where decisions affecting one segment of the organization influence the decisions and performance of another segment. Examples of interdependencies are:
- Subunits competing with each other for the same input factors such as raw materials, or for the same customers, and
- Subunits that are vertically related such that the end product of one subunit is the raw material of another subunit.

2. *Duplication of activities*—that is, the same activity is separately undertaken many times in individual subunits of the organization. For example, there may be a duplication of staff functions (such as accounting, employee relations, and legal) if there is a high degree of decentralization across all levels of an organization.

3. *Decreased loyalty toward the organization as a whole.* Individual subunit managers may regard the managers of other subunits in the same organization as being no different from external parties. Consequently, managers may be less willing to share significant information or to assist when another subunit faces an emergency situation.

Some organizations impose restrictions on the ability of subunits to purchase (source) from outside parties, products or services that are available from other internal subunits. Such restrictions mean that some degree of centralization exists in the organization. Various rationales are given for sourcing restrictions:

1. The attempt to build long-term commitments so that subunits can make capital budgeting and operating decisions with greater predictability
2. The attempt to improve long-term supply reliability or to reduce the average level of inventory held
3. The protection of an "infant" segment. A subunit may be in its infancy and the parent wants to protect it from "market forces" in its development stages by providing a guaranteed market for some of its products
4. The belief that products or services produced internally are of higher quality

The benefits and costs of decentralization must be compared by top managers, often on a function-by-function basis. For example, the controller's function may be highly decentralized for many attention-directing and problem-solving purposes (such as operating budgets and performance reports), but highly centralized for other purposes (such as accounts-receivables processing and income tax planning). Organizations are rarely totally centralized or totally decentralized.

Responsibility center choices and decentralization

Chapter 5 outlined four basic options for measuring the performance of subunits:

- Cost Center—reporting of costs only
- Revenue Center—reporting of revenues only
- Profit Center—reporting of both costs and revenues
- Investment Center—reporting of costs, revenues, and investments

These definitions do not mention centralization or decentralization. Each of these responsibility units can be found in the extremes of centralized and decentralized organizations.

A common misconception in both the accounting literature and the management literature is that the term *profit center* (and in some cases *investment center*) is a synonym for a decentralized subunit. Although it may seem strange at first, **profit centers could be coupled with a highly centralized organization, and cost centers could be coupled with a highly decentralized organization.** For example, a company may have many divisions called profit centers, but their managers may have little leeway in making decisions. Managers may be unable to buy or sell outside their company, may have to obtain approval from corporate headquarters for every capital expenditure over, say, $10,000, and may be forced to accept central-staff "advice." In another company that has only cost centers, managers may have great latitude on capital outlays and on where to purchase materials and services. **In short, the labels of profit center and cost center are sometimes deceptive as clues to the degree of decentralization.**

TRANSFER PRICING

Terminology

A **transfer price** is the price charged by one segment (subunit, department, division, etc.) of an organization for a product or service supplied to another segment of the same organization. Consider Product A, which is transferred from Division X to Division Y of the same company. Division Y then further processes Product A into Product B, which is sold in finished form to outside customers:

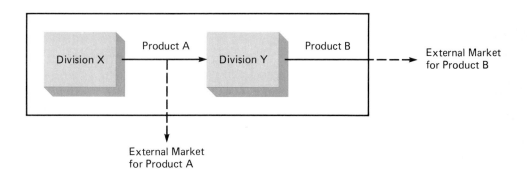

The product transferred from Division X to Division Y often is termed an **intermediate product**. Assume that Division X has the option of selling Product A to outside customers in its partly finished (intermediate) form. A market in which an interme-

835

diate product is bought or sold is termed an **intermediate market**; this market is a **perfectly competitive market** if there is a homogeneous product with equivalent buying and selling prices and for which no individual buyers or sellers can affect those prices by their own actions.

In a fundamental sense, all cost allocation is a form of transfer pricing. For example, although it is rarely thought of in this way, the allocation of service department costs to production departments (see pages 418–27) is essentially an imposed form of transfer pricing. In practice, however, the term *transfer price* is usually associated with exchanges involving at least one profit or investment center.

Alternative transfer-pricing methods

There are three general methods for determining transfer prices:

1. *Market-based transfer prices.* Examples include the use of publicly listed prices of similar products or services, and the prices a subunit charges to third parties where that subunit has both internal and external customers.
2. *Cost-based transfer prices.* Examples include either actual or standard variable costs or absorption costs. In many cases, full costs are used; that is, all manufacturing, selling, and administrative costs are allocated to the units of product transferred. In some cases, transfers are priced on a cost-plus basis—e.g., 120% of absorption costs.
3. *Negotiated prices.* In some cases, the subunits of a firm are free to negotiate the transfer price between themselves. Information about costs and market prices may be used in these negotiations, but there is no requirement that the chosen transfer price have any specific relationship to either cost or market price data.

Choice criteria

Ideally, transfer prices should communicate information that leads each subunit manager to make optimal decisions for the organization as a whole. Two specific criteria can help in choosing a transfer-pricing method:

1. Promotion of goal congruence. Goal congruence exists when individuals and groups aim at the organization goals desired by top management.
2. Promotion of a sustained high level of managerial effort. *Effort* is defined as exertion toward a goal.

If top management favors a high level of decentralization, a third criterion is also appropriate:

3. Promotion of a high level of subunit autonomy in decision making. *Autonomy* is the degree of freedom to make decisions.

These criteria are also explored in Chapter 11 (pp. 374–75) and in the Appendix to this chapter, which discusses criteria for judging management control systems.

The next section illustrates the use of market- and cost-based transfer-pricing methods in a petroleum company with production, transportation, and refining divisions. This example shows how the choice of a transfer-pricing method can dramatically affect division profits. The following sections of the chapter then discuss how the criteria of goal congruence, managerial effort, and subunit autonomy affect the choice of transfer-pricing methods within organizations.

Horizon Petroleum has three divisions. Each operates as a profit center:

1. Production Division—manages the production of crude oil from an oil field near Tulsa, Oklahoma.
2. Transportation Division—manages the operation of a pipeline that transports crude oil from the Tulsa area to Houston, Texas.
3. Refining Division—manages a refinery at Houston that processes crude oil into gasoline. (For simplicity, assume that gasoline is the only salable product made by the refinery, and that it takes two barrels of crude oil to yield one barrel of gasoline.)

The data in Exhibit 25-1 summarize the variable and fixed costs of each division. The fixed costs per unit are based on estimates of total budgeted volume of crude oil to be produced and transported, and total gasoline to be produced in the current year.

The Production Division can sell crude oil to other parties in the Tulsa area at $12 per barrel. The Transportation Division "buys" crude oil from the Production Division, transports it to Houston, and then "sells" it to the Refining Division. The pipeline from Tulsa to Houston can carry 40,000 barrels of crude oil per day. The

EXHIBIT 25-1
Horizon Petroleum: Operating Data

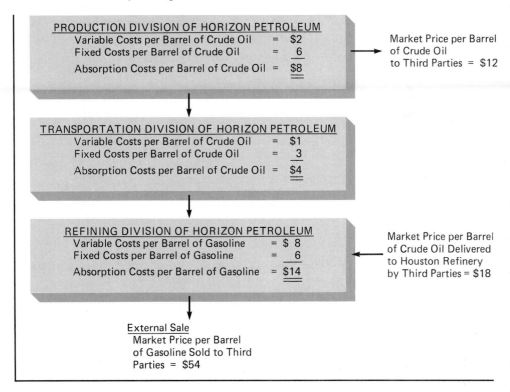

PRODUCTION DIVISION OF HORIZON PETROLEUM
Variable Costs per Barrel of Crude Oil	=	$2
Fixed Costs per Barrel of Crude Oil	=	6
Absorption Costs per Barrel of Crude Oil	=	$8

Market Price per Barrel of Crude Oil to Third Parties = $12

TRANSPORTATION DIVISION OF HORIZON PETROLEUM
Variable Costs per Barrel of Crude Oil	=	$1
Fixed Costs per Barrel of Crude Oil	=	3
Absorption Costs per Barrel of Crude Oil	=	$4

REFINING DIVISION OF HORIZON PETROLEUM
Variable Costs per Barrel of Gasoline	=	$ 8
Fixed Costs per Barrel of Gasoline	=	6
Absorption Costs per Barrel of Gasoline	=	$14

Market Price per Barrel of Crude Oil Delivered to Houston Refinery by Third Parties = $18

External Sale
Market Price per Barrel of Gasoline Sold to Third Parties = $54

Refining Division has been operating at capacity using oil from Horizon's Production Division (on average 10,000 barrels per day) and oil bought from other producers (on average 20,000 barrels per day) at $18 per barrel.

Exhibit 25-2 illustrates the effect on division operating income of using the following three transfer pricing methods for a series of transactions involving 100 barrels of crude oil produced by Horizon's Production Division:

Method A: 150% of variable costs, where variable costs are the cost of the transferred-in product plus the division's own variable costs

Method B: 125% of absorption costs, where absorption costs are the cost of the transferred-in product plus the division's own variable and fixed costs

Method C: Market price

EXHIBIT 25-2

Division Operating Income of Horizon Petroleum for 100 Barrels of Crude Oil under Alternative Transfer-Pricing Methods

	METHOD A Internal transfers at 150% of variable costs	METHOD B Internal transfers at 125% of absorption costs	METHOD C Internal transfers at market price
1. PRODUCTION DIVISION			
Revenues:			
$3, $10, $12, × 100 barrels crude oil	$ 300	$1,000	$1,200
Division variable costs:			
$2 × 100 barrels crude oil	200	200	200
Division fixed costs:			
$6 × 100 barrels crude oil	600	600	600
Division operating income	$ (500)	$ 200	$ 400
2. TRANSPORTATION DIVISION			
Revenues:			
$6, $17.50, $18, × 100 barrels crude oil	$ 600	$1,750	$1,800
Transferred-in costs:			
$3, $10, $12, × 100 barrels crude oil	300	1,000	1,200
Division variable costs:			
$1 × 100 barrels crude oil	100	100	100
Division fixed costs:			
$3 × 100 barrels crude oil	300	300	300
Division operating income	$ (100)	$ 350	$ 200
3. REFINING DIVISION			
Revenues: $54 × 50 barrels gasoline	$2,700	$2,700	$2,700
Transferred-in costs:			
$6, $17.50, $18, × 100 barrels crude oil	600	1,750	1,800
Division variable costs:			
$8 × 50 barrels gasoline	400	400	400
Division fixed costs:			
$6 × 50 barrels gasoline	300	300	300
Division operating income	$1,400	$ 250	$ 200

The transfer prices per barrel of crude oil under each method are:

> 150% of Variable Costs
> - Production Division to Transportation Division = 1.5($2) = $3
> - Transportation Division to Refining Division = 1.5($3 + $1) = $6
>
> 125% of Absorption Costs
> - Production Division to Transportation Division = 1.25($2 + $6) = $10
> - Transportation Division to Refining Division = 1.25($10 + $1 + $3) = $17.50
>
> Market Price
> - Production Division to Transportation Division = $12
> - Transportation Division to Refining Division = $18

The division operating income per 100 barrels of crude oil reported under each transfer-pricing method is (see Exhibit 25-2):

DIVISION	150% OF VARIABLE COSTS	125% OF ABSORPTION COSTS	MARKET PRICE
Production	$ (500)	$200	$400
Transportation	(100)	350	200
Refining	1,400	250	200
Total company	$ 800	$800	$800

The total operating income to Horizon Petroleum from producing, transporting, and refining the 100 barrels of crude oil is $800, regardless of the set of internal transfer prices used. However, the division operating incomes differ dramatically under the three methods in Exhibit 25-2. Little wonder that division managers take considerable interest in the setting of transfer prices, especially those managers whose compensation is directly affected by division operating income.

Exhibit 25-2 illustrates that the choice of a transfer-pricing method can affect how a pie is divided among individual divisions. Subsequent sections of this chapter illustrate that the size of the pie also can be affected by the choice of a transfer-pricing method.

MARKET-BASED TRANSFER PRICES

Where the intermediate market is perfectly competitive and where interdependencies of subunits are minimal, transferring products or services at market prices generally leads to optimal decisions.[2] There are no inherent conflicts in abiding by

---

[2]A landmark article is J. Hirshleifer, "On the Economics of Transfer Pricing," *Journal of Business*, July 1956, pp. 172–84. Hirshleifer shows that the transfer price that maximizes corporate profitability is the marginal cost of the selling division; if a perfectly competitive market exists, this marginal cost will be the same as the market price. The Hirshleifer analysis assumes there is cooperative behavior between the managers of the individual divisions.

all three criteria—goal congruence, managerial effort, and subunit autonomy. The guidelines are these:

    a. A market price or negotiated market price should be used
    b. The seller should have the option of selling internally or selling externally
    c. An arbitration procedure should be available for settling disputes

These guidelines assume that managers of the divisions have access to perfectly competitive outside markets and are fully informed about existing market prices. **Where market prices are relevant for making economic decisions, and if the costs of maintaining such a system are justifiable, they are also relevant to the preservation of subunit autonomy and the maintenance of managerial effort.**

    Reconsider the Horizon Petroleum example in Exhibits 25-1 and 25-2. Assume that there is a perfectly competitive market for crude oil in the Tulsa area; crude oil can be sold or purchased at $12 per barrel. Consider the decisions that would be made by Horizon's division managers if each had the option of selling or buying crude oil externally. If the transfer price between Horizon's Production Division and Transportation Division is set below $12, the manager of the Production Division will be motivated to sell all production to outside buyers at $12 per barrel. If the transfer price is set above $12, the manager of the Transportation Division will be motivated to purchase all its crude oil requirements from outside suppliers. A transfer price of $12 per barrel will approximate an arm's-length, bargained, open-market price. It reflects independent evidence of the company's sacrifice by using the transferred product internally.

    In most cases, internal procurement is expected where the selling division's products and services are equal to or more attractive than those of outsiders in terms of quality and price. The buying division often obtains benefits such as better quality, assurance of supply, and dependable delivery.

    In sum, if a company's participation in a market has no effect on price, market prices typically establish the ceiling for transfer pricing. In many instances a lower price may be justified, particularly when selling costs are less, when no bad debts are likely, or when an advantage is obtained through an exclusive supplier contract or through a cost-plus arrangement ensuring profits in all cases. (Each of these justifications implies that the intermediate market is not perfectly competitive.) These situations lead to the notion of negotiated market prices, whereby the cost savings to the company as a whole, from an internal exchange, are split between the selling and buying divisions through bargaining.

    Arbitration or umpiring is sometimes necessary. However, if arbitration is used frequently, it indicates a step toward centralization. Why? Because it usually elevates the decision to a higher-level manager in the organization. Consequently, too much reliance on arbitration indicates the division managers' inability to operate smoothly on a decentralized basis.

Limitation of market prices

The use of market prices has innate appeal for purposes of inducing both goal congruence and managerial effort. *Without routine checks on market prices, managers often obtain critical information only in a haphazard or tardy fashion.* Profit centers compel an approximation of what revenue might be if a division were operated as a completely independent entity; in this way, the managers become more sensitive to market conditions.

    Market prices are not always readily available. Few markets are perfectly competitive. In some cases, no intermediate market may exist for the exact product or service in question. A quoted price for a product or service is strictly comparable only if the credit terms, grade, quality, delivery terms, and auxiliary considerations are precisely the same. For example, the crude oil from Horizon Petroleum's Production Division may have a heavier tar content than other crude oil available in Tulsa, it may require extra processing, or it may have a lower gasoline yield at the Houston refinery.

Many product parts are unique, creating a situation that adds considerably to the costs of preparing bids. Suppose an outside supplier prepares a few bids and discovers that the internal supplier division always wins. The so-called market prices either will not be forthcoming or will be unreliable. After all, the frequently rejected bidder can reduce the costs of submitting a bid by simply and deliberately submitting an artificially high price. Some companies allocate part of their purchases to outside suppliers on a regular basis to maintain alternative sources of supply and to provide for continuous monitoring of market prices.

Distress prices When an industry has idle capacity, unusually low prices may occur. These prices are sometimes called "distress prices" because they are regarded as being caused by temporary conditions. What transfer-pricing scheme should be used for judging performance if distress prices are believed to prevail? Some companies use these distress transfer prices, but others use long-run average or "normal" market prices. The decision as to which transfer-pricing basis is preferable depends on subjective judgments regarding the costs and benefits of each alternative.

If distress pricing is used, in the short run the manager of the supplier division will meet the price as long as it exceeds the incremental costs of supplying the product or service. In the long run, the manager must decide whether disposal of some manufacturing facilities would be desirable. If long-run average price is used, managers may be forced to buy internal products at above-current market prices; consequently, the short-run performance of the buying division will be hurt.

The use of current market prices (even distress prices) is generally preferable to some long-run average price, especially if a long-run perspective is taken when deciding whether to dispose of production facilities. In this way, two evaluations can be made. The first is a comparison of long-run predictions and current prices; this gives insights into past and current capital-budgeting decisions. The second evaluation entails assessing the current performance of both the buying and supplying divisions in relation to existing opportunities in the form of current market prices.

Deciding whether a current market price is a "distress price" is often difficult. Just because market prices precipitously drop from prior levels does not mean the current market price will subsequently increase. The market prices of several agricultural commodities and minerals have stayed at what observers initially believed were temporary "distress levels" for many years.

COST-BASED TRANSFER PRICES

Sometimes market prices are unavailable, inappropriate or too costly to be used for transfer pricing. Many organizations use cost-based measures as transfer prices. This section explores examples of these measures and the problems that may arise with their use.

Full-cost bases

The use of actual full or actual absorption costs as a transfer price provides the supplying division with few incentives to control costs. Any inefficiencies at the supplying division are passed on to the buying division. Indeed, if the transfer price is actual cost *plus* a percentage of actual cost, the supplying division can make an additional margin on each dollar of cost inefficiency! Many companies use standard or budgeted absorption costs to promote cost efficiency at each of their divisions.

A major limitation of using full or absorption costs as the basis for transfer prices (be they actual or standard costs) is that they can lead to suboptimal decisions for the company as a whole. Assume that Horizon Petroleum in Exhibits 25-1 and 25-2 makes internal transfers at 125% of absorption costs. The purchasing officer at the Houston Refining Division is attempting to reduce the cost of crude oil provided by outside suppliers. At present it is purchased from a Houston supplier at $18 per barrel. Assume now that the market for crude oil in Tulsa is not perfectly competitive. The purchasing officer of the Refining Division locates an independent Tulsa producer that will sell to Horizon Petroleum 20,000 barrels of crude oil per day, at $13 per barrel, delivered to Horizon's pipeline in Tulsa. Given Horizon's organization structure, the Transportation Division will purchase the 20,000 barrels of crude oil in Tulsa, ship it to Houston, and then sell it to Horizon's Refining Division. The pipeline has excess capacity and can ship the 20,000 barrels at its variable costs of $1 per barrel without affecting the shipping of the crude oil from its own Production Division. Should Horizon Petroleum purchase crude oil from the independent producer in Tulsa? Will the Refining Division show lower costs of purchasing crude oil by using oil from the Tulsa producer or from using its current Houston supplier?

Horizon Petroleum will prefer to purchase oil from the Tulsa independent producer:

Alternative 1: Buy 20,000 barrels from Houston supplier at $18 per barrel

Total cost to Horizon Petroleum = 20,000 × $18 = $360,000

Alternative 2: Buy 20,000 barrels in Tulsa at $13 per barrel and transport it to Houston at $1 per barrel variable cost

Total cost to Horizon Petroleum = 20,000 × ($13 + $1) = $280,000

There is a reduction in total costs to Horizon Petroleum of $80,000 by using the Tulsa independent producer.

The Refining Division of Horizon Petroleum will see its reported division costs increase if the crude oil is purchased from the independent producer in Tulsa when the transfer price from the Transportation Division to the Refining Division is 125% of absorption costs:

$$\begin{array}{l} \text{Transfer} \\ \text{price} \end{array} = 1.25 \left(\begin{array}{l} \text{Purchase} \\ \text{price from} \\ \text{Tulsa} \\ \text{producer} \end{array} + \begin{array}{l} \text{Variable} \\ \text{costs of} \\ \text{Transportation} \\ \text{Division} \end{array} + \begin{array}{l} \text{Fixed} \\ \text{costs of} \\ \text{Transportation} \\ \text{Division} \end{array} \right)$$

$$= 1.25(\$13 + \$1 + \$3) = \$21.25 \text{ per barrel}$$

Alternative 1: Buy 20,000 barrels from Houston supplier at $18 per barrel

$$\text{Total cost to Refining Division} = 20,000 \times \$18 = \$360,000$$

Alternative 2: Buy 20,000 barrels from the Transportation Division of Horizon Petroleum that are purchased from the independent producer in Tulsa

$$\text{Total cost to Refining Division} = 20,000 \times \$21.25 = \$425,000$$

Given that the Refining Division is run as a profit center, it can maximize its short-run division profitability by purchasing from the Houston supplier. By choosing the alternative that maximizes the profitability of the company as a whole, the Refining Division will increase its own division operating costs by $425,000 − $360,000 = $65,000.

This situation is a clear example of goal incongruence that is induced by a transfer price based on full or absorption costs. **The transfer-pricing scheme has led the Refining Division to regard the fixed costs (and the 25% markup) of the Transportation Division as variable costs.** From the viewpoint of the company as a whole, the absorption cost-based transfer price can lead to dysfunctional decisions in the short run.

Cost-plus as a synthetic market price

Despite the obvious limitations of the approach, transfer prices based on full cost, or on full cost plus some markup, are in common use. A major reason for the wide use of cost-based transfer pricing is its clarity and administrative convenience. Moreover, the transferred product or service in question is often slightly different in quality or other characteristics from that available from outside sources. As a result, cost-plus pricing is often viewed as yielding a "satisfactory" approximation of an outside market price. Therefore the resulting synthetic market price is regarded as a good practical substitute for market price. The alternative of obtaining "actual" market prices is perceived as being too costly to be incorporated into a management control system.

When market prices are unavailable, full cost plus some markup can be a defensible way to administer transfer prices that are "reasonable" in the eyes of some of the affected parties. For example, the Internal Revenue Service proposed using the gross profit percentage (profits as a percentage of sales) on the domestic sales of a multinational company as the suitable gross profit percentage for its international sales: "This process was accepted by the court, even though it was somewhat arbitrary, because it was not considered to have reached unreasonable results."[3]

Variable costs plus lump sum

Top management often wants the buyer–division manager to make month-to-month purchasing decisions based on the variable costs of the supplier division. Otherwise, as the example in the preceding section showed, the buyer division may be led toward a dysfunctional decision. One way to satisfy the needs of the two divisions, and the company as a whole, is to transfer at the standard variable costs per unit. A separate budgeted lump-sum charge is made for fixed costs, to which is

---

[3]R. Benke and J. Edwards, *Transfer Pricing: Techniques and Uses* (New York: National Association of Accountants, 1980), p. 128, describing the case of Eli Lilly and Co. v. U.S., 372 F.2d 520 (9th Cir.).

added a lump sum for profit. This charge can be made annually or monthly and is based on an *annual expectation,* not on actual purchases. In any event, the buyer's month-to-month decisions are not influenced by the supplier's fixed costs or the supplier's profit.

Recall the example of Horizon Petroleum purchasing crude oil from the independent producer in Tulsa at $13 per barrel. The variable costs to transport each barrel from Tulsa to Houston are $1 per barrel. What transfer price will encourage goal congruence and managerial effort for both the Transportation Division and the Refining Division?

The minimum transfer price is $14 per barrel; a transfer price below this amount will not provide incentives for the Transportation Division to purchase crude oil from the independent producer in Tulsa. The maximum transfer price is $18 per barrel; a transfer price above this amount will not provide incentives for the Refining Division to purchase crude oil from the Transportation Division.

A popular solution is to impose a variable-cost transfer price, but credit each division for a prorated share of the $4 per barrel overall contribution to corporate operating income. The proration of the contribution can be negotiated in any number of ways. Suppose that it were in proportion to the standard variable costs incurred by each division. Using the data in Exhibit 25-2 (p. 838):

Variable costs of Transportation Division	$100
Variable costs of Refining Division	400
	$500

The $4-per-barrel overall contribution would be allocated thus:

$$\text{To Transportation Division: } \frac{\$100}{\$500} \times \$4.00 = \$0.80$$

$$\text{To Refining Division: } \frac{\$400}{\$500} \times \$4.00 = \$3.20$$

The transfer price between the Transportation Division and the Refining Division would be $14.80 per barrel of crude oil ($13 purchase cost + $1 variable cost + $0.80 allocated contribution). With this transfer price, both divisions will increase their own reported division operating income by purchasing crude oil from the independent producer in Tulsa. Essentially, this approach is a standard-variable-cost plus transfer-pricing system; the "plus" is a function of the overall contribution to corporate operating income.

To decide on the $0.80 and $3.20 allocation of the $4.00 contribution to total corporate operating income per barrel, it is necessary that both divisions share information about their variable costs. In effect, each division does not operate (at least for this transaction) in a totally decentralized manner. Because most organizations are hybrids of centralization and decentralization anyway, this approach deserves serious consideration where such transfers are significant.

Dual pricing	There is seldom a *single* transfer price that will simultaneously meet the criteria of goal congruence, managerial effort, and subunit autonomy. One approach is **dual pricing**, which uses two separate transfer-pricing methods to price each interdivision transaction. An example is a 125% of absorption costs transfer price to the selling division, and a market-based transfer price to the buying division. Assume Horizon Petroleum purchases crude oil from the independent producer in Tulsa at $13 per barrel. One way of recording the transfer between the Transportation Division and the Refining Division is:

1. Credit the Transportation Division with the 125% of absorption costs transfer price of $21.25 per barrel of crude oil.
2. Debit the Refining Division with the market-based transfer price of $18 per barrel of crude oil.
3. Debit a corporate account for the $3.25 ($21.25 minus $18.00) difference between the two transfer price methods.

This dual-pricing system essentially gives the Transportation Division a corporate subsidy. The profit for Horizon Petroleum as a whole will be less than the sum of the division profits.

This dual-pricing method is not widely used in practice, despite its ability to reduce the goal incongruence problems associated with a pure cost-plus-based transfer-pricing method. One concern of managers is that the supplying division will not have sufficient incentives to control costs with a dual-price system. A second concern is that use of a dual-price system does not provide clear signals to division managers about the level of decentralization sought by top management.

GENERAL RULE FOR TRANSFER PRICING?

The preceding section demonstrated that market price was not a cure-all answer to the problem of setting transfer prices. The most obvious example is the nonexistence of an intermediate market for a highly specialized product component.

Outlay costs and opportunity costs	Is there an all-pervasive rule for transfer pricing that will lead toward optimal economic decisions? The answer is negative because the three criteria of goal congruence, managerial effort, and subunit autonomy must all be considered simultaneously.

The following general rule has proved to be a helpful *first step* in setting a transfer price:

The minimum transfer price should be

a. **The additional outlay costs per unit incurred to the point of transfer (sometimes approximated by variable costs), plus**
b. **The opportunity costs per unit to the firm as a whole.**

The term *outlay costs* in this context represents the cash outflows that are directly associated with the production and transfer of the products and services. These cash outflows do not necessarily have to be made at a particular instant, but the action of production and transfer will result sooner or later in some cash outflows that will be termed outlay costs.

Opportunity costs are defined here as the maximum contribution forgone by the firm as a whole if the products or services are transferred internally.

The distinction between outlay costs and opportunity costs is made because the accounting system originally records the outlay costs of the alternative selected but fails to record the outlay costs of the alternative rejected.[4] Opportunity costs may be forgone contribution margins in some instances, or even forgone net proceeds from the sale of facilities in other instances.

If a perfectly competitive intermediate market exists, the opportunity cost is market price less outlay cost (i.e., the cost of the opportunity forgone by the internal supplier). For example, if the outlay cost is $1 per unit and the market price is $4 per unit, the transfer price is $1 + ($4 − $1) = $4, which happens to be the market price. However, if no market exists for the intermediate product or alternative products that might utilize the same supplying division's facilities, the opportunity cost may be zero. In the latter case, outlay costs (perhaps approximated by variable costs) may be the correct transfer price.

To recapitulate:

Minimum transfer price	= Outlay costs per unit	+ Opportunity costs per unit to company as a whole	
If idle capacity exists:	= $1	+ Probably $0	= $1
If no idle capacity exists:	= $1	+ (Market price − Outlay cost)	
	= $1	+ ($4 − $1)	= $4

Imperfect markets

The problems in transfer pricing would be trivial if the intermediate market were perfect. But in many cases the intermediate markets are nonexistent, ill structured, or imperfect. Imperfect competition exists when one seller or buyer, acting alone, can affect the market price. If the intermediate market is imperfectly competitive, additional volume can be obtained only if selling prices are lowered. This schedule of demand means that the existing market price at a particular volume level is no longer applicable to the decision regarding how much to produce and sell. The additions to revenue will be less than the sales of the additional units at the new selling price because the new lower price will apply to the entire sales volume. For example, suppose the current selling price is $1 per unit and 80,000 units are being sold. Revenue is $80,000. A cut in price from $1.00 to $0.90 may increase unit sales to 90,000. The increase in revenue is $1,000 (90,000 × $.90, minus $80,000).

In these situations, the analysis can become exceedingly complex. The optimal transfer price from the viewpoint of the corporation as a whole is different for each situation, depending on the existence of cost interdependencies and demand interdependencies. An example of a cost interdependency occurs where the price of a certain raw material may be dependent on the total purchases by two or more divisions. An example of a demand interdependency is any vertically integrated operation where there is no intermediate market for a unique component part of a

---

[4]The jungle of terminology in this area is too dense to dwell on at length in this book. The "general rule" has been expressed in the hope that it will ease the understanding of those who are more comfortable with the terminology of accountants than with that of economists. For example, some economists would examine this general rule and say that both part (a) and part (b) together are opportunity costs.

finished product. Then the total number of finished products sold depends on the total number of components available, and vice versa.

As we saw earlier, market price is a special case rather than a universal guide. The key computation is the opportunity cost component part of the general rule above. It is easy to say, "Measure the forgone contribution from transferring products or services internally." However, it actually is not easy to make such a measurement. For example, consider a supplier division with idle capacity and an imperfect demand in the intermediate market. Is its opportunity cost zero? Probably not. One alternative may be to cut price so as to increase demand and hope to increase overall operating income. But measuring the probable effect is difficult, so measuring the opportunity costs is also difficult. Clearly, the transfer price must be determined in relation to constantly changing levels of supply and demand. There is not just one transfer price; rather, there is a schedule of transfer prices (a transfer-price function) for various quantities supplied and demanded.

How do you design a performance-evaluation (motivation) scheme that induces goal congruence when high interdependencies exist? Obviously, if management control systems were costless, the ideal solution would be to have a flexible (though necessarily complex) transfer-pricing policy that would ensure goal-congruent decisions. But management control systems are not costless, so simple rules tend to be used for various classes of transactions. For example, market prices may be used for some transfers and cost-based prices for others. Unusual cases tend to be negotiated or settled by central management. The greater the opportunities and interdependencies, the greater the desire for centralized control.

MULTINATIONAL TRANSFER PRICING

Many organizations have divisions located in different countries. Deciding on a set of transfer prices to use for exchanges between these divisions requires consideration of additional factors. These factors include:

1. *Taxation.* Countries have different tax rates, allowable deductions, and enforcement of their tax codes. For example, consider a transfer of motor vehicle parts by Division A of World Motors in country X to Division B of World Motors in country Y. Country X has a 20% income tax rate and country Y has a 50% income tax rate. World Motors has an incentive to use a high transfer price for transfers from Division A to Division B to maximize the income reported in the lower-tax-rate country. (The tax authorities in country Y are fully aware of these incentives and will make efforts to maximize the taxes paid by Division B of World Motors.)

2. *Income or Dividend Repatriation Restrictions.* Some countries restrict the repatriation of income or dividends. By increasing the prices of goods or services transferred into divisions in these countries, firms can increase the funds repatriated out of these countries without violating any income or dividend restrictions.

Other factors that arise in multinational transfer pricing include tariffs, custom duties, and risks associated with movements in foreign currency exchange rates.

There is considerable evidence on the transfer-pricing practices of companies. Exhibit 25-3 summarizes the factors that executives consider important when determining transfer prices for both domestic and multinational operations. Exhibit 25-4 summarizes the results of studies of domestic transfer-pricing methods and multinational transfer-pricing methods. Observe the widespread use of both market-based and absorption or full-cost-based transfer prices.

For companies using cost-based methods, standard costs are more widely used than actual costs. One survey of U.S. companies reported that standard costs were used by 54% of respondents, actual costs by 16%, and some of each by 30%.[5]

Case studies and interviews with managers stress the key role that both corporate strategy and performance evaluation play in decisions about transfer pricing. For example, companies that use market-based (cost-based) transfer prices have been found to put more (less) emphasis on division profit-oriented performance criteria in the evaluation of division managers.[6]

SUMMARY

A transfer-pricing system must be judged in relation to its impact on (a) goal congruence, (b) managerial effort, and (c) subunit autonomy. Some version of market price as a transfer price will often best motivate managers toward optimal economic decisions; moreover, the

EXHIBIT 25-3
Factors Stated by Executives to Be Important in Decisions on Transfer Pricing (in Order of Importance)

A. *DOMESTIC TRANSFER PRICING**
   1. Performance evaluation—to measure the results of each operating entity
   2. Managerial motivation—to provide the company with a "profit-making" orientation throughout each organizational entity
   3. Pricing driven—to better reflect "costs" and "margins" that must be received from customers
   4. Market driven—to maintain an internal competitiveness so that the company stays in balance with outside market forces

B. *MULTINATIONAL TRANSFER PRICING†*
   1. Overall income to the company
   2. The competitive position of subsidiaries in foreign countries
   3. Performance evaluation of foreign subsidiaries
   4.‡Restrictions imposed by foreign countries on repatriation of profits or dividends
   5.‡The need to maintain adequate cash flows in foreign subsidiaries
   6. Maintaining good relationships with host governments

*Source: Price Waterhouse, *Transfer Pricing Practices of American Industry* (1984), p. 2.
†Source: R. Tang, "Environmental Variables of Multinational Transfer Pricing: A U.K. Perspective," Journal of Business Finance & Accounting, Summer 1982, p. 182.
‡Ranked equal in importance.

---

[5]Price Waterhouse, *Transfer Pricing Practices of American Industry* (1984).

[6]See P. Yunker, "A Survey Study of Subsidiary Autonomy, Performance Evaluation and Transfer Pricing in Multinational Corporations," *Columbia Journal of World Business,* Fall 1983, pp. 51–64; and R. Eccles, *The Transfer Pricing Problem: A Theory for Practice* (Lexington, Mass.: Lexington Books, 1985).

EXHIBIT 25-4
Surveys of Transfer Pricing Methods

A. DOMESTIC TRANSFER-PRICING METHODS

METHODS	UNITED STATES*	AUSTRALIA†	CANADA‡	JAPAN*	INDIA§	UNITED KINGDOM‖
1. Market-price based	30%	46%	34%	34%	47%	41%
2. Cost-based:						
Variable costs	4	8	6	2	6	6
Absorption or full costs	45	37	37	44	47	19
Other	1	—	3	—	—	4
Total	50%	45%	46%	46%	53%	29%
3. Negotiated	18%	9%	18%	19%	—	24%
4. Other	2%	—	2%	1%	—	6%
	100%	100%	100%	100%	100%	100%

B. MULTINATIONAL TRANSFER-PRICING METHODS

METHODS	UNITED STATES*	AUSTRALIA†	CANADA‡	JAPAN*	INDIA§	UNITED KINGDOM‖
1. Market-price based	35%	—	37%	37%	—	31%
2. Cost-based:						
Variable costs	2	—	5	3	—	5
Absorption or full costs	42	—	26	38	—	28
Other	2	—	2	—	—	5
Total	46%	—	33%	41%	—	38%
3. Negotiated	14%	—	26%	22%	—	20%
4. Other	5%	—	4%	—	—	11%
	100%	—	100%	100%	—	100%

SOURCES:
*R. Tang, C. Walter, and R. Raymond, "Transfer Pricing—Japanese vs. American Style," Management Accounting, January 1979, pp. 12–16.

†R. Chenhall, "Some Elements of Organisational Control in Australian Divisionalised Firms," Australian Journal of Management, April 1979 Supplement, pp. 1–36.

‡R. Tang, "Canadian Transfer-Pricing Practices," CA Magazine, March 1980, pp. 32–38.

§V. Govindarajan and B. Ramamurthy, "Transfer Pricing Policies in Indian Companies: A Survey," Chartered Accountant, November 1983, pp. 296–301.

‖A. Mostafa, J. Sharp, and K. Howard, "Transfer Pricing—A Survey Using Discriminant Analysis," Omega, 12, No. 5 (1984), 465–74.

evaluation of performance will then be consistent with the concept of decentralization. However, where there are interdependencies between subunits, and where the markets for intermediate goods are not perfectly competitive, market prices will not always lead to optimal decisions. In such instances, some centralization of control may be desired to prevent dysfunctional decisions. If so, serious thought should be given to whether profit centers and decentralization provide the best organizational design. Above all, the perceived costs and benefits of alternative levels of decentralization should be explicitly considered when choosing a transfer-pricing scheme.

There is rarely a single transfer price that will serve all needs. Instead there may be one transfer price for making a particular production decision, another for evaluating performance, and yet another for minimizing tariffs or income taxes.

Profit (or investment) centers usually accompany decentralization, but one can exist without the other. The desirability of a profit (or investment) center versus a cost center should be judged by their predicted relative impacts on collective decisions.

problem A transportation equipment manufacturer, the Pillercat Corporation, is heavily decentralized. Each division head has full authority on all decisions regarding sales to internal or
external customers. Division P has always acquired a certain equipment component from
Division S. However, when informed that Division S was increasing its unit price to $220,
Division P's management decided to purchase the component from outside suppliers at a
price of $200.

Division S had recently acquired some specialized equipment that was used primarily
to make this component. Juan Gomez, the manager, cited the resulting high depreciation
charges as the justification for the price increase. He asked the president of the company to
instruct Division P to buy from S at the $220 price. He supplied the following information:

P's annual purchases of component, in units	2,000
S's variable costs per unit	$ 190
S's fixed costs per unit	$ 20

1. Suppose there are no alternative uses for the S facilities. Will the company as a whole
benefit if P buys from the outside suppliers for $200 per unit? Show computations.
2. Suppose internal facilities of S would not otherwise be idle. The equipment and other
facilities would be assigned to other production operations and would result in annual
cash-operating savings of $29,000. Should P purchase from outsiders?
3. Suppose there are no alternative uses for S's internal facilities and that the selling price
of outsiders drops $15. Should P purchase from outsiders?
4. What rule would you favor for setting transfer prices in the Pillercat Corporation?
5. As the president, how would you respond to the request of the manager of S? Would
your response differ according to the specific situations described in parts 1–3 above?
Why?

solution 1–3. The analyses of the first three parts are summarized below (in thousands of dollars):

	(1)	(2)	(3)
Total purchase costs from outsider	$400	$400	$370
Total outlay costs if bought inside	380	380	380
Total opportunity costs if bought inside	—	29	—
Total relevant inside costs	380	409	380
Net advantage (disadvantage) to company as a whole from buying inside	$ 20	$ (9)	$ (10)

4. Of course, in part 1, if the manager of S understood cost-volume-profit relationships,
and if he wanted to maximize his short-run operating income, he would probably
accept a price of $200. This would bring a contribution to the divisional operating
income of 2,000 × ($200 − $190), or $20,000. The information given indicates that the
best rule might be a market price with the seller having the option to refuse to sell
internally. This rule would have led to the correct decision from the viewpoint of both
the divisions and the company as a whole.

In situation 1, S would obtain a contribution of $200 − $190, or $10 per unit. In 2,
S would lose a contribution of $10 per unit, or $20,000; but its $29,000 cost saving on
other work would lead to a net saving of $9,000, or $4.50 per unit. In 3, S would lose $5
per unit, or $10,000, if the units were bought inside.
5. As president, you probably would not want to become immersed in these disputes. If
arbitration is necessary, it should probably be conducted by some other officer on the

corporate staff. One possibility is to have the immediate line boss of the two managers make a decision.

If decentralization is to be strictly adhered to, the arbitrator should probably do nothing under any of the conditions described. If no forced transfer were made, P would go outside, resulting in an optimal decision for the overall company in parts 2 and 3 but not in part 1.

Suppose in part 1 that S refuses to meet the price of $200. This decision means that the company will be $20,000 worse off in the short run. Should top management interfere and force a transfer at $200? This interference would undercut the philosophy of decentralization. Many managers would not interfere because they would view the $20,000 as the price that has to be paid for mistakes made under decentralization. But how high must this price go before the temptation to interfere would be irresistible? $30,000? $40,000?

In sum, the point of this question is that any superstructure that interferes with lower-level decision making weakens decentralization. Of course, such interference may occasionally be necessary to prevent very costly blunders. But recurring interference and constraints simply transform a decentralized organization into a centralized organization. Indeed, the trade-offs among goal congruence, managerial effort, and autonomy may justify more centralization in many instances.

Despite the intuitive attractions of market price, the chapter contains illustrations where market price will not lead to optimal decisions. For example, sometimes the adherence by a supplying division to a high market price despite having low variable costs may force the consuming division not to buy even though the company as a whole would benefit.

Note that the "general rule" described in the chapter also might be applied, although it frequently might be subject to suspicion because it seems more awkward than the "market-price" rule. Also, as Case 1 below shows, the goal-congruent decision may be obvious at a transfer price of $190, but the S manager has no particular motivation to favor transfer:

TRANSFER PRICE	=	OUTLAY COSTS	+	OPPORTUNITY COSTS	
1.	=	$190	+	0	= $190
2.	=	$190	+	($29,000 ÷ 2,000)	= $204.50
3.	=	$190	+	0	= $190

P would buy inside in Case 1 and outside in 2 and 3; these decisions would provide goal congruence for the company as a whole.

Terms to Learn

This chapter (including the appendix) and the Glossary at the end of this book contain definitions of the following important terms:

decentralization (p. 833)   *dual pricing (845)*
dysfunctional decision making (834)   *industry economics (856)*
intermediate market (836)   *intermediate product (835)*
managerial style (857)   *organization culture (857)*   *organization goals (855)*
organization structure (856)   *perfectly competitive market (836)*
strategic planning (856)   *transfer price (835)*

Transfer prices convey information that often affects many critical decisions concerning the acquisition and allocation of an organization's resources, just as prices in the entire economy affect decisions concerning the allocation of a nation's resources. Ideally, transfer prices should guide managers to choose inputs and outputs in coordination with other subunits so as to maximize the operating income of the organization as a whole. The three motivational criteria (goal congruence, managerial effort, and subunit autonomy) provide insights when designing and judging a transfer-pricing system.

Do not confuse *profit center* and *decentralized subunit*. They are not synonyms. For example, a factory may have heavily decentralized management even though it is a cost center rather than a profit center. Similarly, the managers of some profit centers, such as a unit in a chain of grocery stores, may have little latitude in making decisions.

Distinguish sourcing restrictions by firms from transfer-pricing restrictions by firms. Sourcing restrictions occur where subunits are restricted in their ability to purchase, from outside parties, products or services available from internal sources. Pricing restrictions occur where there are limitations on the price at which internal transfers are made. Firms can have sourcing restrictions but no pricing restrictions, or pricing restrictions but no sourcing restrictions. Firms that have sourcing restrictions can encounter problems in obtaining reliable estimates of market prices for their internal transfers.

APPENDIX: MANAGEMENT CONTROL SYSTEM DESIGN

The primary criterion for judging a management control system is cost benefit. To make the cost-benefit criterion more specific, Chapter 11 (pages 374–75) introduced the secondary criteria of goal congruence and managerial effort. This Appendix outlines four areas in which management control system design choices are made: responsibility centers, performance measurement, performance motivation, and information transmission. A framework is then outlined that provides more structure when examining control system issues in organizations such as corporations, government departments, hospitals, and consulting partnerships.[7] Exhibit 25-5 presents an overview of the key concepts in this Appendix.

Accounting reports provide only one source of information for decision making. There are many other sources. Consequently, accountants should never become preoccupied with their own importance. Although their role in measuring revenues, costs, assets, liabilities, and so forth, is valuable and important, accountants have no monopoly on supplying information. Other sources often produce much data more efficiently. For example, a manager's personal observation of an assembly line may provide knowledge about efficiency more quickly than an accountant's performance report.

CONTROL SYSTEM DESIGN CHOICES

Responsibility centers

The following options are available for measuring the financial performance of responsibility units:

[7]More-detailed discussion of management control system design can be found in K. Merchant, *Control in Business Organizations* (Boston: Pitman, 1985).

1. Cost center: accountable for costs only,
2. Revenue center: accountable for revenues only,
3. Profit center: accountable for both costs and revenues, and
4. Investment center: accountable for costs, revenues, and investments.

Performance measurement

Performance measurement can relate to activities or to the individuals managing those activities. It is essential to distinguish between performance of activities and performance of individuals. A manager assigned to a troublesome division may be doing a stellar job even if that division is reporting a loss of $10 million. (It could have been $50 million with a less able manager!) While there may be overlap in the measures used for the performance of activities and individuals, this overlap should be by design rather than default. Questions that arise in this area include the following:

1. What general measures should be used to represent organization goals? Operating income? Rate of return on investment? Sales? There may be several other measures capturing subgoals. For example, there may be measures of defective work or market share.
2. How should the measures be defined? What is operating income? What is investment? What is defective work? What is market share?
3. How should assets and liabilities be measured? Historical cost? Replacement cost?
4. What dollar amounts (if any) should be put on transfers of products and services between subunits of the organization?

Performance motivation

Individuals are motivated to perform in a way that leads to rewards and personal fulfillment. Rewards take both pecuniary and nonpecuniary forms: bonuses, promotion, pay, fancy offices, and other perquisites. Personal fulfillment can encom-

EXHIBIT 25-5
Criteria and Choices for Management Control Systems

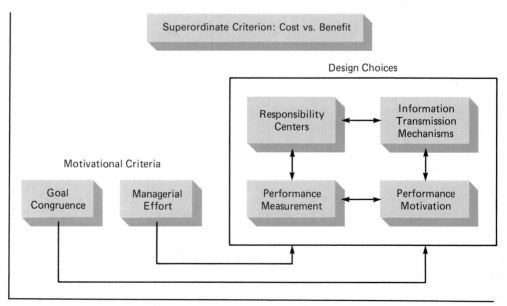

pass being pleased with one's own accomplishments as well as having fun and feeling challenged. Questions that arise in this area include the following:

1. What mix between salary and piece rate compensation to use for employees doing highly repetitive tasks? What mix between salary and bonus to use for employees eligible to participate in the bonus pool?
2. What mix between the current year's results and changes in subsequent years' results should be reflected in bonuses, promotion decisions, etc?
3. Should the rewards of divisional managers be based on divisional results or corporate results, or both?
4. Should academic faculty at a university be rewarded on research publications, textbook writing, teaching, or service to the university? If some combination is desired, what weights should be assigned to each of these areas?

Information transmission

Accounting information is only a part of a very rich and diverse information network that exists in an organization. Information can flow from central management to subunits, from subunits to central management, and from subunit to subunit:

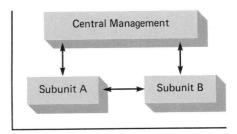

Three possible scenarios describe how information could be transmitted among different parts of an organization:

1. Complete sharing of information and cooperative (and honest) behavior by all individuals
2. Incomplete sharing of information, but cooperative (and honest) behavior by all individuals
3. Incomplete sharing of information and noncooperative (possibly dishonest) behavior by one or more individuals

Some executives argue that scenario 3 (incomplete information and noncooperative behavior) best describes most organizations. **Within a cost-benefit framework, the management control system should promote the integrity of information flows within an organization and help reduce the amount of noncooperative behavior.**

Questions raised in this area include the following:

1. What mix between accounting and nonaccounting forms of quantitative information should be transmitted? How should qualitative information be sent?
2. What mix between written and nonwritten forms of information should be transmitted? What use should be made of meetings?
3. Should information be sent at daily, weekly, or monthly intervals? Who should be the recipient of information sent: Central management? Other subunit managers?

4. What penalties should be imposed on individuals who distort information (e.g., overstate the costs of supplying a product or service to another unit) or deliberately delay sending important information to, or even withhold it from, others?

FRAMEWORK FOR EXAMINING MANAGEMENT CONTROL SYSTEM ISSUES

Exhibit 25-6 presents a framework for examining management control system issues. This section discusses each of the factors included in Exhibit 25-6. The key role of organization goals is apparent in this exhibit. The five boxes underneath organizational goals represent influential variables, so named because they also influence the individual choices made in designing a management control system.

Organization goals

The largest influence on systems design should be **organization goals,** which are the objectives the organization is aiming to accomplish. In commercial organizations, top management typically specifies these goals. Examples of stated organization goals include the following:

- Maximize shareholder wealth via maximization of current share price
- Attain a preset accounting rate of return, say 16%
- Exceed a preset growth rate in earnings, say 10%
- Maintain maximum responsiveness to customer wants

For many nonprofit organizations, government legislation specifies the goals. An example for an air-traffic controller's unit is to attain maximum aircraft safety, both in the air and on the ground.

Some organizations also have subgoals that provide specific indications of the tasks viewed as essential to achieving their main goals. For example, McDonald's Corporation emphasizes quality, service, cleanliness, and value. McDonald's regards these factors as critical not only to the success of each individual restaurant but also to the willingness of customers to return to other locations of McDonald's.

EXHIBIT 25-6
Framework for Evaluating Management Control Systems

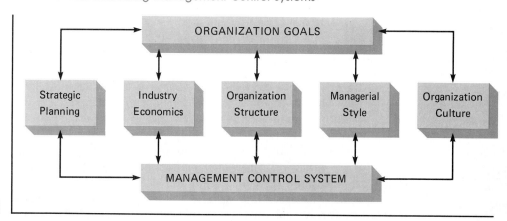

Subgoals are usually more concrete. Employees can relate better to attributes such as cleanliness and service than to a more abstract notion such as return on investment.

Strategic planning is planning in regard to the general direction of the organization; it considers the resources of the organization, the likely behavior of competitors, the direction of technological change, and the projected demands of the marketplace. Managers desire information systems that help the strategic planning process. For example, consider a steel company that has a strategy of specializing in those steel products in which it has a sustainable, relatively low cost position. The control system that provides useful information for this company will include product-by-product cost information about the firm and each of its major competitors.

Industry economics are factors such as supply, demand, and competition that affect the goals and subgoals of the organization. An analysis of industry economics helps managers focus on the dimensions on which organizations compete. Consider building construction companies. They compete in terms of cost, technical competence, quality, and adherence to time schedules. Control systems that monitor such attributes help construction companies maintain their reputation regarding the key factors of their distinctive competence. Chapter 17 (pp. 580–83) illustrates how both financial and nonfinancial measures can be incorporated into a control system for construction companies.

A second illustration of industry economics is the "Product Review and Evaluation" reports used by Holiday Inns to evaluate individual motels in its chain of motels (see Chapter 26, pp. 884–86, for discussion). These reports cover financial and nonfinancial factors—e.g., the attire and grooming of personnel. They signal to all employees the critical attributes that top management of Holiday Inns wants every employee to demonstrate.

Organization structure is defined as the arrangement of lines of responsibility within an organization. It embraces such factors as:

a. The lines of reporting (e.g., does a divisional controller have primary reporting responsibility to a central corporate controller or to the division manager?)
b. The grouping of decision-making responsibilities in an organization (e.g., by functions such as manufacturing and marketing, or by divisions each with authority concerning both manufacturing and marketing)
c. The degree of decentralization that top management aims for in the organization

Such factors affect the costs of collecting information in a management control system and the willingness of division managers to share information among themselves. Consider goal-incongruence problems in a firm that uses 125% of absorption costs for setting transfer prices. One approach to reducing these problems is for individual division managers to share information about their own fixed and variable costs and about their own opportunity costs. Such an approach, however, may conflict with a top-management edict that individual division managers operate in a highly decentralized manner. Managers of independent competitive firms certainly do not share such information in their day-to-day negotiations about the price to be paid for external purchases. One survey of U.S. transfer-pricing practices reported that 33% of the respondents viewed information about the "true cost" to the selling division as confidential to that division and not to be disclosed to the buying division.[8]

Managerial style

Managerial style is the set of behaviors exhibited by key managers in an organization. Some managers are authoritarian; others depend on extensive participation and consensus in reaching decisions. Some managers emphasize written communication; others emphasize oral communication and personal observation. Some managers emphasize financial numbers; others place more emphasis on nonfinancial aspects such as product innovation, service, quality, and employee morale. The control system should fit the style of key managers.

Top-management support is essential for the success of any management control system. For example, a chief executive officer who fervently believes in continuous financial monitoring of each division would be unenthusiastic about a system that focused primarily on a division's product innovations. Without clear top-management backing, the goals specified by the system are less likely to gain acceptance by subordinates as group goals or as personal goals.

Organization culture

Organization culture is the set of beliefs and values shared by members of the organization.[9] Examples of these beliefs and values include acceptable forms of interpersonal behavior, personal mannerisms such as dress, and work style. Consider an organization that promotes only those individuals who meet budget targets, without any questions asked about the means used to reach those targets. Such a culture encourages managers to delay necessary maintenance on equipment until after the fiscal year-end, and even to circumvent an internal control system by fraudulently recording current-period expenses as prepayments. Chapter 27 provides an illustration of such a corporate culture.

_____QUESTIONS, PROBLEMS, AND CASES_____

25-1 Name three benefits of decentralization.

25-2 Name two costs of decentralization.

25-3 Distinguish between _sourcing restrictions_ and _transfer-pricing restrictions._

25-4 "Transfer pricing is confined to profit centers." Do you agree? Why?

25-5 What three motivational criteria are applicable to transfer pricing?

25-6 What conditions must exist for an intermediate market to be perfectly competitive?

25-7 What are three major bases for pricing intracompany transfers?

---

[8]Price Waterhouse, _Transfer Pricing Practices,_ p. 15.

[9]Many variants of this definition are given in the numerous individual papers in P. Frost, L. Moore, M. Louis, C. Lundberg, and J. Martin, _Organizational Culture_ (Beverly Hills, Calif.: Sage Publications, 1985).

25-8 What is the major limitation to transfer prices based on cost?

25-9 What is the most common example in transfer pricing of a clash between divisional action and overall company profitability?

25-10 If an optimal economic decision is wanted in a particular situation, what is a general rule for transfer pricing?

25-11 What is outlay cost in the context of transfer pricing?

25-12 Compare the significance of the following three statements by executives on the major problems with their current transfer-pricing system:
   a. "Because of our transfer-pricing system, we may be forgoing economic benefits to the corporation in total."
   b. "The biggest weakness in our transfer-pricing system is that tempers sometimes flare up during negotiations."
   c. "The time involved in the negotiation of transfer prices could be more productively utilized in other ways."

25-13 Transfer-pricing methods, goal congruence. British Columbia Lumber has a Raw Lumber Division and Finished Lumber Division. The variable costs are:

Raw Lumber Division: $100 per 100 board feet of raw lumber

Finished Lumber Division: $125 per 100 board feet of finished lumber

Assume there is no weight loss in processing raw lumber into finished lumber. Raw lumber can be sold at $200 per 100 board feet. Finished lumber can be sold at $275 per 100 board feet.

Required

1. Should British Columbia Lumber process raw lumber into its finished form?
2. Assume that internal transfers are made at 110% of variable costs. Will each division maximize its division operating income contribution by adopting the action that is in the best interests of British Columbia Lumber?
3. Assume that internal transfers are made at market prices. Will each division maximize its division operating income contribution by adopting the action that is in the best interests of British Columbia Lumber?

25-14 Transfer pricing. The Plastics Company has a separate division that produces a special molding powder (MP). For the past three years, about two-thirds of the output (measured in pounds) has been sold to another division within the company. The remainder has been sold to outsiders. Last year's operating data follow:

	TO OTHER DIVISION		TO OUTSIDERS	
Sales	10,000 MP. @ $70*	$700,000	5,000 MP. @ $100	$500,000
Variable costs @ $50		$500,000		$250,000
Fixed costs		150,000		75,000
Total costs		$650,000		$325,000
Gross margin		$ 50,000		$175,000

*The $70 price is ordinarily determined by the outside sales price less selling and administrative expenses wholly applicable to outside business.

The buying-division manager has a chance to get a firm contract with an outside supplier at $65 per pound for the ensuing year.

Assume that the molding-powder division manager asserts that no margin can be earned if sales are made at $65 per pound. As the buying-division manager, write a short reply. Assume that the 10,000 pounds cannot be sold by the molding-powder division to other customers.

25-15 Transfer-pricing dispute. Allison-Chambers Corp., manufacturer of tractors and other heavy farm equipment, is organized along decentralized lines, with each manufacturing division operating as a separate profit center. Each division head has been delegated full authority on all decisions involving the sale of that division's output both to outsiders and to other divisions of Allison-Chambers. Division C has in the past always purchased its requirement of a particular tractor-engine component from Division A. However, when informed that Division A was increasing its price to $150, Division C's management decided to purchase the engine component from outside suppliers.

The component can be purchased by C for $135 on the open market. Division A insists that owing to the recent installation of some highly specialized equipment and the resulting high depreciation charges, A would not be able to make an adequate profit on its investment unless it raised its price. A's management appealed to top management of Allison-Chambers for support in its dispute with C and supplied the following operating data:

C's annual purchases of tractor-engine component	1,000
A's variable costs per unit of tractor-engine component	$120
A's fixed costs per unit of tractor-engine component	$ 20

Required
1. Assume that there are no alternative uses for internal facilities. Determine whether the company as a whole will benefit if Division C purchases the component from outside suppliers for $135 per unit.
2. Assume that internal facilities of A would not otherwise be idle. By not producing the 1,000 units for C, A's equipment and other facilities would be assigned to other production operations and would result in annual cash-operating savings of $18,000. Should C purchase from outsiders?
3. Assume that there are no alternative uses for A's internal facilities and that the price from outsiders drops $20. Should C purchase from outsiders?

25-16 Transfer-pricing problem. Refer to Problem 25-15. Assume that Division A could sell the 1,000 units to other customers at $155 per unit with variable selling costs of $5 per unit. If this were the case, determine whether Allison-Chambers would benefit if C purchased the 1,000 components from outsiders at $135 per unit.

25-17 Market prices and transfers. (SMA) The Caplow Company is a multidivisional company, and its managers have been delegated full profit responsibility and complete autonomy to accept or reject transfers from other divisions. Division A produces a subassembly with a ready competitive market. This subassembly is currently used by Division B for a final product that is sold outside at $1,200. Division A charges Division B market price for the subassembly, which is $700 per unit. Variable costs are $520 and $600 for Divisions A and B, respectively.

The manager of Division B feels that Division A should transfer the subassembly at a lower price than market because at this price, Division B is unable to make a profit.

Required
1. Compute Division B's profit contribution if transfers are made at the market price, and also the total contribution to profit for the company.
2. Assume that Division A can sell all its production in the open market. Should Division A transfer goods to Division B? If so, at what price?
3. Assume that Division A can sell in the open market only 500 units at $700 per unit, out of the 1,000 units that it can produce every month, and that a 20% reduction in price is necessary to sell full capacity. Should transfers be made? If so, how many units should it transfer and at what price? Submit a schedule showing comparisons of contribution margins under three different alternatives to support your decision.

25-18 The pertinent transfer price. The XYZ Company has two divisions, A and B. For one of the company's products, Division A produces a major subassembly and Division B incorporates this subassembly into the final product. There is a market for both the subassembly and the final product, and the divisions have been delegated profit responsibility. The transfer price for the subassembly has been set at long-run average market price.

The following data are available to each division:

Estimated selling price for final product	$300
Long-run average selling price for intermediate product	200
Outlay cost for completion in Division B	150
Outlay cost in Division A	120

The manager of Division B has made the following calculation:

Selling price—final product		$300
Transferred-in cost (market)	$200	
Outlay cost for completion	150	350
Contribution (loss) on product		$ (50)

Required

1. Should transfers be made to Division B if there is no excess capacity in Division A? Is market price the correct transfer price?
2. Assume that Division A's maximum capacity for this product is 1,000 units per month and sales to the intermediate market are now 800 units. Should 200 units be transferred to Division B? At what relevant transfer price? Assume for a variety of reasons that A will maintain the $200 selling price indefinitely; that is, A is not considering cutting the price to outsiders regardless of the presence of idle capacity.
3. Suppose A quoted a transfer price of $150 for up to 200 units. What would be the contribution to the firm as a whole if the transfer were made? As manager of B, would you be inclined to buy at $150?

25-19 Pricing in imperfect markets. Refer to Problem 25-18.

1. Suppose the manager of Division A has the option of (a) cutting the external price to $195 with the certainty that sales will rise to 1,000 units or (b) maintaining the outside price of $200 for the 800 units and transferring the 200 units to Division B at some price that would produce the same income for Division A. What transfer price would produce the same income for Division A? Does that price coincide with that produced by the "general rule" in the chapter, so that the desirable decision for the company as a whole would ensue?
2. Suppose that if the selling price for the intermediate product is dropped to $195, outside sales can be increased to 900 units. Division B wants to acquire as many as 200 units if the transfer price is acceptable. For simplicity assume that there is absolutely no outside market for the final 100 units of Division A capacity.
   a. Using the "general rule," what is (are) the relevant transfer price(s) that should lead to the correct economic decision? Ignore performance evaluation (incentive) considerations.
   b. Compare the total contributions under the alternatives to show why the transfer price(s) recommended lead(s) to the optimal economic decision.

25-20 Conflict of interests of profit centers and company as a whole. (D. Solomons, adapted) Division A of a company is the only source of supply for an intermediate product that is converted by Division B into a salable final product. Most of A's costs are fixed. For any output up to 1,000 units per day, its total costs are $500 per day. Total costs increase by $100 per day for every additional thousand units made. Division A judges that its own results will be optimized if it sets its internal transfer price at 40¢ per unit, and it acts accordingly.

Division B incurs additional costs in converting the intermediate product supplied by A into a finished product. These costs are $1,250 for any output up to 1,000 units, and $250 per thousand for outputs in excess of 1,000. On the revenue side, B can increase its revenue only by spending more on sales promotion and by reducing selling prices. Its sales forecast is:

SALES IN UNITS	AVERAGE NET REVENUE PER THOUSAND UNITS
1,000	$1,750.00
2,000	1,325.00
3,000	1,100.00
4,000	925.00
5,000	800.00
6,000	666.67

Required

1. Prepare a schedule comparing B's costs, including its purchases from A, revenues, and net income at various levels of output.
2. What is B's maximum net income? At that level, what is A's net income? At that level, what is the corporation's aggregate net income?
3. Suppose the company abandons its divisionalized structure. Instead of being two profit centers, A and B are combined into a single profit center with responsibility for the complete production and marketing of the product. Prepare a schedule similar to that in requirement 1. What volume level will provide the most net income?
4. Evaluate the results in requirement 3. Why did the circumstances in requirement 1 lead to less net income than in requirement 3? How would you adjust the transfer-pricing policy to ensure that overall company net income will be maximized where separate profit centers A and B are maintained?

25-21 Effect of alternative transfer-pricing methods on division profits. Oceanic Products is an integrated tuna-fishing company based in San Diego. It has three divisions:
1. Tuna Harvesting: operates a fleet of 20 trawling vessels
2. Tuna Processing: processes the raw tuna into tuna fillets
3. Tuna Marketing: packages tuna fillets in 2-pound packets that are sold to wholesale distributors at $12 each

The Tuna Processing division has a yield of 500 pounds of tuna fish fillets from 1,000 pounds of raw tuna provided by the Tuna Harvesting division. The Tuna Marketing division has a yield of three hundred 2-pound packets from every 500 pounds of tuna fish fillets provided by the Tuna Processing division. (The weight of the packaging material is included in the 2-pound weight.) Cost data for each division are:

Tuna Harvesting Division
Variable costs per pound of raw tuna   = $0.20
Fixed costs per pound of raw tuna   = $0.40
Tuna Processing Division
Variable costs per pound of processed tuna = $0.80
Fixed costs per pound of processed tuna   = $0.60
Tuna Marketing Division
Variable costs per 2-pound packet   = $0.30
Fixed costs per 2-pound packet   = $0.70

Fixed costs per unit are based on the estimated volume of raw tuna, processed tuna, and 2-pound packets to be produced during the current fishing season.

Oceanic Products has chosen to process internally all raw tuna brought in by the Tuna Harvesting division. Other tuna processors in San Diego purchase raw tuna from boat oper-

861

ators at $1 per pound. Oceanic Products also has chosen to process internally all tuna fillets into the 2-pound packets sold by the Tuna Marketing division. Several fish marketing companies in San Diego purchase tuna fillets at $5 per pound.

Required

1. Compute the overall operating income to Oceanic Products of harvesting 1,000 pounds of raw tuna, processing it to tuna fillets, and then selling it in 2-pound packets.
2. Compute the transfer prices that will be used for internal transfers (i) from the Tuna Harvesting Division to the Tuna Processing division, and (ii) from the Tuna Processing division to the Tuna Marketing division under each of the following transfer pricing methods:
   a. 200% of variable cost: Variable cost is the cost of the transferred-in product (if any), plus the division's own variable cost.
   b. 150% of absorption cost: Absorption cost is the cost of the transferred-in product (if any), plus the division's own variable and fixed costs.
   c. Market price.
3. Oceanic rewards each division manager with a bonus, calculated as 10% of division operating income (if positive). What is the amount of the bonus that will be paid to each division manager under each of the three transfer-pricing methods in requirement 2? Which transfer-pricing method will each division manager prefer to use?

25-22 Goal-congruence problems with cost-plus transfer-pricing methods, dual-pricing methods. (Extension of Problem 25-21) Assume that Oceanic Products uses a transfer price of 150% of absorption cost. Pat Forgione, the managing director, attends a seminar on the virtues of decentralization. Forgione decides to implement decentralization at Oceanic Products. A memorandum is sent to all division managers: Starting immediately, each division of Oceanic Products is free to make its own decisions regarding the purchase of its raw materials or the sale of its finished product.

Required

1. Give two examples of goal-congruence problems that may arise if Oceanic continues use of the 150% of absorption costs transfer-pricing method and a policy of decentralization is adopted.
2. Forgione is investigating whether a dual transfer-pricing policy will reduce goal-congruence problems at Oceanic Products. Transfers out of each selling division will be made at 150% of absorption cost; transfers into each buying division will be made at market price. Using this dual transfer-pricing policy, compute the operating income of each division for a harvest of 1,000 pounds of raw tuna that is further processed and marketed by Oceanic Products.
3. Compute the sum of the division operating incomes in requirement 2. Why might this sum not equal the overall corporate operating income from the harvesting of 1,000 pounds of raw tuna and its further processing and marketing?
4. What problems may arise if Oceanic Products uses the dual transfer-pricing system described in requirement 2?

25-23 Multinational transfer pricing, global tax minimization. Industrial Diamonds Inc., based in Los Angeles, has two divisions:
1. Philippine Mining Division—operates a mine containing a rich body of raw diamonds
2. U.S. Processing Division—processes the raw diamonds into polished diamonds used in industrial applications

The costs of the Philippine Mining Division are:

Variable costs = 2,000 pesos per lb. of raw industrial diamonds
Fixed costs   = 4,000 pesos per lb. of raw industrial diamonds

Industrial Diamonds Inc. has a corporate policy of further processing in Los Angeles all raw diamonds mined in the Philippines. Several diamond-polishing companies in the Philippines buy raw diamonds from other local mining companies at 8,000 pesos per pound. The current foreign exchange rate is 20 pesos = $1 U.S.

The costs of the U.S. Processing Division are:

Variable costs = $200 per lb. of polished industrial diamonds
Fixed costs   = $600 per lb. of polished industrial diamonds

Assume that it takes two pounds of raw industrial diamonds to yield one pound of polished industrial diamonds. Polished diamonds sell for $4,000 per pound.

Required

1. Compute the transfer price (in $U.S.) for one pound of raw industrial diamonds transferred from the Philippine Mining Division to the U.S. Processing Division under two methods: (a) 300% of absorption costs, (b) market price.
2. Assume a world of no income taxes. One thousand pounds of raw industrial diamonds are mined by the Philippine Division and then processed and sold by the U.S. Processing Division. Compute the operating income (in $U.S.) for each division of Industrial Diamonds Inc. under each transfer-pricing method in requirement 1.
3. Assume the corporate income tax rate is 20% in the Philippines and 35% in the United States. Compute the after-tax operating income (in $U.S.) for each division under each transfer-pricing method in requirement 1. (Income taxes are *not* included in the computation of the cost-based transfer price. Industrial Diamonds does not pay U.S. taxes on income already taxed in the Philippines.)
4. Which transfer-pricing method in requirement 1 will maximize the total after-tax operating income of Industrial Diamonds?
5. What factors, in addition to global tax minimization, might Industrial Diamonds consider in choosing a transfer-pricing method for internal transfers between its two divisions?

25-24 Multinational transfer pricing, effect of alternative transfer-pricing methods on division operating income and global income tax minimization. User Friendly Computer Inc., with headquarters in San Francisco, manufactures and sells desk-top computers for business users. User Friendly has three divisions, each of which is located in a different country:

1. China Division—manufactures memory devices and keyboards
2. South Korea Division—assembles desk-top computers, using internally manufactured parts and memory devices and keyboards from the China Division
3. United States Division—packages and distributes desk-top computers

Each division is run as a profit center. The costs for the work done in each division that is associated with a single desk-top computer unit are:

China Plant:	Variable costs = 1,000 Yuan
	Fixed costs = 2,000 Yuan
South Korea Plant:	Variable costs = 30,000 Won
	Fixed costs = 40,000 Won
U.S. Plant:	Variable costs = $100
	Fixed costs = $200

Each desk-top computer is sold to retail outlets in the U.S. for $3,200. Assume that the current foreign exchange rates are:

10 Yuan = $1 U.S.
100 Won = $1 U.S.

Both the China and the South Korea plants sell part of their production under private label. The China plant sells the comparable memory/keyboard package used in each User Friendly desk-top computer to a Chinese manufacturer for 7,000 Yuan. The South Korea plant sells the comparable desk-top computer to a South Korean distributor for 150,000 Won.

863

1. Assume a world with no income taxes. Compute the operating income (in $U.S.) to User Friendly Computer Inc. of manufacturing and distributing each desk-top computer.
2. Assume a world with no income taxes. Compute the operating income (in $U.S.) of each division under each of the following transfer-pricing methods: (a) 300% of variable costs, (b) 200% of absorption costs, (c) market price.
3. Assume the following corporate income tax rates: China, 40%; South Korea, 20%; and United States, 30%. Compute the after-tax operating income (in $U.S.) of each division under each of the transfer-pricing methods in requirement 2. (Income taxes are *not* included in the computation of the cost-based transfer prices.)
4. Which transfer pricing method(s) will maximize the total after-tax operating income of User Friendly Computer Inc? (Assume User Friendly does not pay U.S. taxes on income already taxed in other countries.)
5. What factors, in addition to global tax minimization, might User Friendly consider in choosing a transfer-pricing method for internal transfers among its divisions?

25-25 Transfer pricing in banks. The Jackson Stone National Bank is a two-branch bank servicing retail and wholesale customers in the greater Big City metropolitan area. The head-office staff consists of the president and the controller. With minor exceptions, the branch managers are permitted to conduct their affairs like the heads of two independent banks. The planning and control system centers on branch income statements prepared by the controller.

The Big City branch, located in the growing downtown area, serves primarily commercial customers. The manager, Mr. Jones, has found in recent years that while he faces a number of vigorous competitors, the principal constraint on his ability to generate new loan business is a lack of supporting deposits. The *only* alternative source of lendable funds is the purchase of Eurodollars, which are dollar deposits held in a bank outside the United States. This option is considered less than acceptable by Jones, as the 22% interest he would have to pay for such funds is higher than the rate he is able to charge loan customers, currently 20%.

The new Sun City branch, on the other hand, is located outside of town in a large and growing retirement community and is primarily a retail branch. Mr. Smith, the manager, is in his first year with the Stone Bank. In his attempts to sell the bank's services to the Sun City residents, he has found that his only success is in the area of savings deposits. Loan business, on the other hand, is both competitive and scarce. The interest rate he can charge is constrained by the fact that the manager of the local branch of the Behemoth Bank, while not actively soliciting loan business, is apparently charging rates below the prevailing Big City prime rate. Additionally, there seems to be a fundamental resistance on the part of the Sun City residents to the idea of borrowing, even at the 12% rates Smith has been offering. In spite of his frequent lectures on the merits of leverage, the best Smith has been able to do is to generate a few golf-cart installment and Social Security check receivable loans. As a result, he finds himself with substantial excess savings deposits on which he is paying 10% interest but earning nothing. Aside from the deposits, which he has to keep in the vault to satisfy the government's 20% (of deposits) reserve requirement, the vault additionally contains excess lendable funds equal to almost 70% of total savings deposits. The controller has suggested that he lend these funds to Jones at the Big City branch. This was acceptable to both managers, although some disagreement arose as to the interest rate appropriate for such a loan. The argument was finally settled by the controller, who indicated that the theoretically correct rate was the rate Smith was paying on savings deposits, 10%. It has been further agreed that if Smith could find additional loans, any or all of the funds lent to Jones would be returned.

1. Evaluate the 10% interbranch loan rate, and suggest appropriate changes in relation to the following criteria:
   a. Motivating managers to act in a manner consistent with the best interests of the bank as a whole
   b. Evaluating the performance of individual *branches*
2. Would your answer change if the Sun City loan rate were to rise to 14% while all other rates, as well as the level of loan demand at Sun City, remained the same?
3. Would your answer change if all rates were the same as in requirement 1 except that the cost of Eurodollars dropped to 18%?

4. Based on your answers to the questions above, what general statements can you make about the interbranch loan rate appropriate for evaluating individual *managers?*

25-26 Paper company. (Copyright 1986 by the President and Fellows of Harvard College. Reproduced by permission.) "If I were to price these boxes any lower than $480 a thousand," said Mr. Brunner, manager of Birch Paper Company's Thompson division, "I'd be countermanding my order of last month for our sales representatives to stop shaving their bids and to bid full-cost quotations. I've been trying for weeks to improve the quality of our business, and if I turn around now and accept this job at $430 or $450 or something less than $480 I'll be tearing down this program I've been working so hard to build up. The division can't very well show a profit by putting in bids which don't even cover a fair share of overhead costs, let alone give us a profit."

Birch Paper Company was a medium-sized, partly integrated paper company, producing white and kraft papers and paperboard. A portion of its paperboard output was converted into corrugated boxes by the Thompson division, which also printed and colored the outside surface of the boxes. Including Thompson, the company had four producing divisions and a timberland division which supplied part of the company's pulp requirements.

For several years each division had been judged independently on the basis of its profit and return on investment. Top management had been working to gain effective results from a policy of decentralizing responsibility and authority for all decisions but those relating to overall company policy. The company's top officials felt that in the past few years the concept of decentralization had been successfully applied and that the company's profits and competitive position had definitely improved.

In early 19_7 the Northern division designed a special display box for one of its papers in conjunction with the Thompson division, which was equipped to make the box. Thompson's package design and development staff spent several months perfecting the design, production methods, and materials that were to be used. Because of the unusual color and shape these were far from standard. According to an agreement between the two divisions, the Thompson division was reimbursed by the Northern division for the cost of its design and development work.

When the specifications were all prepared, the Northern division asked for bids on the box from the Thompson division and from two outside companies. Each division manager was normally free to buy from whichever supplier he wished, and, even on sales within the company, divisions were expected to meet the going market price if they wanted the business.

In early 19_7 the profit margins of converters such as the Thompson division were being squeezed. Thompson, as did many other similar converters, bought its board, liner, or paper and its function was to print, cut, and shape it into boxes. Though it bought most of its materials from other Birch divisions, most of Thompson's sales were to outside customers. If Thompson got the business, it would probably buy the linerboard and corrugating medium from the Southern division of Birch. The walls of a corrugated box consist of outside and inside sheets of linerboard sandwiching the fluted corrugating medium. About 70% of Thompson's out-of-pocket cost of $400 represented the cost of linerboard and corrugating medium. Though Southern had been running below capacity and had excess inventory, it quoted the market price, which had not noticeably weakened as a result of the oversupply. Its out-of-pocket costs on both liner and corrugating medium were about 60% of the selling price.

The Northern division received bids on the boxes of $480 a thousand from the Thompson division, $430 a thousand from West Paper Company, and $432 a thousand from Erie Papers, Ltd. Erie Papers offered to buy from Birch the outside linerboard with the special printing already on it, but would supply its own inside liner and corrugating medium. The outside liner would be supplied by the Southern division at a price equivalent of $90 per thousand boxes, and would be printed for $30 a thousand by the Thompson division. Of the $30, about $25 would be out-of-pocket costs.

Since this situation appeared a little unusual, William Kenton, manager of the Northern division, discussed the wide discrepancy of bids with Birch's commercial vice-president. He told the vice-president: "We sell in a very competitive market, where higher costs cannot be passed on. How can we be expected to show a decent profit and return on investment if we have to buy our supplies at more than 10% over the going market?"

Knowing that Mr. Brunner had on occasion in the past few months been unable to operate the Thompson division at capacity, the vice-president found it odd that Mr. Brunner would add the full 20% overhead and profit charge to his out-of-pocket costs. When asked about this, Mr. Brunner's answer was the statement that appears at the beginning of the case. He went on to say that having done the developmental work on the box, and having received no profit on that, he felt entitled to a good markup on the production of the box itself.

The vice-president explored further the cost structures of the various divisions. He remembered a comment that the controller had made at a meeting the week before to the effect that costs that were variable for one division could be largely fixed for the company as a whole. He knew that in the absence of specific orders from top management, Mr. Kenton would accept the lowest bid, which was that of the West Paper Company for $430. However, it would be possible for top management to order the acceptance of another bid if the situation warranted such action. And though the volume represented by the transactions in question was less than 5% of the volume of any of the divisions involved, other transactions could conceivably raise similar problems later.

Required

1. In the controversy described, which alternative seems best for the company as a whole? Prepare an analysis of the cash flows under each alternative.
2. As the commercial vice-president, what action would you take?

25-27 Utilization of capacity. (J. Patell) The California Instrument Company (CIC) consists of the semiconductor division and the minicomputer division, each of which operates as an independent profit center. The semiconductor division employs skilled workers who produce two different electronic components, the new high-performance Super-chip and an older product called Okay-chip. These two products have the following cost characteristics:

	SUPER-CHIP		OKAY-CHIP	
Material	Parts	$ 2	Parts	$1
Labor	2 hours @ $14	28	½ hour @ $14	7

Annual overhead in the semiconductor division totals $400,000, all fixed. Owing to the high skill level necessary for the workers, the semiconductor division's capacity is set at 50,000 hours per year.

To date, only one customer has developed a product utilizing Super-chip, and this customer orders a maximum of 15,000 Super-chips per year, at a price of $60 per chip. If CIC cannot meet his entire demand, the customer curtails his own production. The rest of the semiconductor division's capacity is devoted to Okay-chip, for which there is unlimited demand at $12 per chip.

The minicomputer division produces only one product, a process-control unit, which requires a complex circuit board imported from Sweden at a price of $60. The control unit's costs are:

	CONTROL UNIT	
Material	Circuit board	$60
	Other parts	8
Labor	5 hours @ $10	50

The minicomputer division is composed of only a small assembly plant, and all overhead is fixed at a total of $80,000 per year. The current market price for the control unit is $140 per unit.

A joint research project has just revealed that with minor modifications, a single Super-chip could be substituted for the circuit board currently used by the minicomputer division. The modification would require an extra 1 hour of labor by minicomputer's staff, for a new total of 6 hours per control unit. Minicomputer has therefore asked semiconductor to declare a transfer price at which the semiconductor division would sell Super-chip internally.

Required

1. Minicomputer expects to sell 5,000 control units this year. From the overall viewpoint of California Instrument, how many Super-chips should be transferred to minicomputer to replace circuit boards?
2. If demand for the control unit is sure to be 5,000 units, but its *price is uncertain* what should the transfer price of Super-chip be to ensure proper decisions? (All other data unchanged.)
3. If demand for the control unit rises to 12,000 units at a price of $140 per unit, how many of the 12,000 units should be built using Super-chip? (All other data unchanged.)

25-28 Transfer pricing for a motorcar dealership, goal congruence. European Motors is the largest Mercedes-Benz dealership in the Midwest. The company was started by Stephanie Mortimer, Les Johns, and Kevin Ryan. Mortimer is president. For the first ten years, the company operated with only two divisions:

1. Car Sales Division, with Les Johns as manager. Mercedez-Benz cars were purchased from a German distributor who delivered the cars to the dealership. An independent finance company provided car loans to new car customers. Cars traded in by new car purchasers were sold by an independent auction company for a 10% commission.
2. Car Service Division, with Kevin Ryan as manager. Approximately 40% of the work done in this division was on Mercedes-Benz cars previously sold by the Car Sales Division of European Motors.

This organization structure operated smoothly. Mortimer stipulated that any work done by the Car Service Division for warranties on cars sold by the Car Sales Division be charged out to the Car Sales Division at 200% of actual cost, the normal charge for work done for external customers. Her rationale was to provide the Service Division with the incentive to maintain a high quality of service for the car-purchasing customers of European Motors.

European Motors recently expanded its activities to include the sales of used cars and the provision of financing. The new organization structure was:

1. New Car Sales Division—Les Johns, manager
2. Used Car Sales Division—Terry Lamb, manager
3. Service Division—Kevin Ryan, manager
4. Car Financing Division—Georgianna Peponis, manager

Lamb and Peponis were recently hired by European Motors. Mortimer mandated that all trade-ins be first worked on by the Service Division and then sold by the Used Car Sales Division.

Mortimer labeled each of the four divisions as profit centers. Each division manager was paid a salary plus a bonus equal to 20% of the division operating income. Used cars traded in to the New Car Sales Division were transferred to the Used Car Sales Division at the trade-in price negotiated by the New Car Sales Division; Johns had the final approval on each trade-in price. Work done by the Service Division on traded-in used cars before their sale by the Used Car Division was at 200% of actual costs, the normal charge for external work; Ryan had the final approval on the amount of service work done on each trade-in. The Car Financing Division borrowed money from a bank at 14% per annum. The Car Financing Division was credited with the difference between the actual rate charged to a customer and the 14% cost of money. The target spread between the rate charged to a customer and the cost of money is 4%.

Problems arose quickly with the current transfer-pricing methods in the new organization structure chosen by Mortimer. Lamb and Peponis used a set of related transactions to illustrate the source of their frustration. The New Car Division recently sold a Mercedes-Benz 190; the list price was $30,000 and the cost from the German distributor was $18,000. A five-year-old Ford Supreme was traded in by the purchaser of the Mercedes 190. The "blue-book" price (an approximation of the market price) for dealers buying a five-year-old Ford Supreme was $12,000.

Sale of Mercedes 190 by New Car Division
1. Sale price of Mercedes 190, $29,500
2. Trade-in price on Ford Supreme, $15,000
3. Cash down payment, $4,500; and a $10,000 one-year loan at 12% per annum

Work Done By Service Division on Ford Supreme
1. General maintenance, $800 (200% of actual costs of $400)
2. Repair of transmission, $700 (200% of actual costs of $350)

Sale of Ford Supreme by Used Car Division
1. Sale price of Ford Supreme, $16,000
2. Cash down payment, $8,000; and a $8,000 one-year loan at 18% per annum

No car was traded in by the buyer of the Ford Supreme.

Lamb argued that the Service Division spent more hours than was standard on the Ford Supreme due to their having limited experience with work on non-Mercedes-Benz cars. He also questioned whether the high-quality maintenance and service work approved by Ryan was necessary for the sale of a used car, especially a non-Mercedes-Benz used car. Peponis was livid at Johns' approving financing at 12% per annum on the Mercedes 190 $10,000 loan.

Required

1. Compute the operating income of European Motors on the combined sales of the Mercedes-Benz and the Ford Supreme.
2. Compute the individual operating income for *each* of the four divisions on the combined sales of the Mercedes-Benz and the Ford Supreme.
3. What problems may arise with the current transfer pricing methods in the new organization structure chosen by Mortimer?
4. Assume that Mortimer wishes to implement a policy of decentralization at the division level. Recommend an alternative transfer-pricing system for European Motors.

26

Systems Choice: Performance Measurement and Executive Compensation

Steps for choosing an accounting-based performance measure • Alternative performance measures •
Definitions of income and investments • Measurement alternatives for evaluating activities •
Measurement alternatives for evaluating managers • Nonfinancial measures of performance •
Executive compensation plans •
Appendix: Compound interest depreciation and models for measuring performance

This chapter examines the general problem of designing a management control system for measuring performance. Performance measurement of both activity units and managers is discussed; emphasis is placed on the importance of distinguishing between the two. The difficulties of relating income to invested capital are given special consideration. Performance measurement using non-accounting-based variables, and executive compensation, are covered in the final sections of the chapter. Those sections emphasize that the accounting system, although important, is not the only source of information used in performance measurement.

Performance measurement of activities should be a prerequisite for allocating resources in an organization. When new activities are undertaken, projections of revenues, expenses, and investments are made. An ongoing comparison of the actual revenues, expenses, and investments with the budgeted amounts can help guide decisions about possible expansion or contracting of activities.

Performance measurement of managers is used in decisions about the assignment of managers to activities, their salaries and bonuses, and their future assignments and status. Moreover, the very act of measuring managers' performance can motivate them to strive for the targets used to evaluate performance.

There are five general steps for choosing among accounting-based performance measures, particularly as they bear on subunits and their managers:

1. Choose a measure of accomplishment that represents *top-management goals*. Should it be operating income, net income, rate of return on investment, sales, or some other measure? Should the measure be maximized?

2. Whatever measure is chosen, the designer must then select *definitions of such items as income and investment*. Should income be based on variable or absorption costing? Should central corporate costs be allocated? Should investment consist of assets, or assets minus liabilities, or some other grouping?

3. How should items such as income and investment be *measured*? Historical cost? Replacement cost? Realizable value? Historical cost adjusted for changes in the general price level?

4. What *standards* should be applied? Should all divisions be required to earn the same rate of return on all their investments?

5. What *timing of feedback* is needed? Quarterly? Annually? Should feedback on the performance of managers be timed differently from feedback on the performance of activities such as divisions?

The first three steps will be discussed in subsequent sections of this chapter. The fourth step was discussed in Chapter 19, where it was pointed out that different required rates of return should be used for different divisions. The fifth step, the timing of feedback, has been discussed in many places in this book; timing depends largely on the specific level of management that is receiving the feedback.

These five steps need not be taken sequentially. The issues considered in each step are interdependent. A decision maker will often proceed through these steps several times before deciding on a preferred set of accounting-based performance measures. The answers to the questions raised in each step will depend on predictions of how the information alternatives fulfill, in a cost-effective manner, the behavioral criteria of goal congruence, managerial effort, and subunit autonomy discussed in Chapter 25 (p. 836). As with other chapters of this text, the overlay of cost-benefit analysis is ever present.

ALTERNATIVE PERFORMANCE MEASURES

Alternative performance measures will be illustrated with an example from the lodging industry. Hospitality Inns owns and operates three motels, one each in San Francisco, Chicago, and New Orleans. Exhibit 26-1 summarizes data for each of the three motels and corporate headquarters (in San Francisco) for the most recent year (19_8). At present, Hospitality Inns does not allocate, to the three separate motels, the operating costs and assets of corporate headquarters or the total long-term debt of the company. Exhibit 26-1 indicates that the New Orleans motel generates the highest operating income of $480,000 as compared with $300,000 for Chicago and $240,000 for San Francisco. However, this comparison ignores potential differences in the investment base used to generate the operating income.

EXHIBIT 26-1
Hospitality Inns: Annual Financial Data for 19_8 ($000s)

	SAN FRANCISCO MOTEL	CHICAGO MOTEL	NEW ORLEANS MOTEL	CORPORATE HEAD-QUARTERS	TOTAL
	(1)	(2)	(3)	(4)	(1) + (2) + (3) + (4)
Motel revenues	$1,200	$2,000	$3,000	—	$6,200
Motel variable costs	540	750	840	—	2,130
Motel fixed costs	420	950	1,680	—	3,050
Motel operating income	240	300	480	—	1,020
Central corporate variable costs	—	—	—	$ 80	80
Central corporate fixed costs	—	—	—	120	120
Interest on long-term debt	—	—	—	400	400
Interest before income taxes	—	—	—	—	420
Income taxes	—	—	—	—	150
Net income	—	—	—	—	$ 270
Average Book Values for 19_8:					
Current assets	400	500	600	200	1,700
Fixed assets	600	1,500	2,400	300	4,800
Total assets	$1,000	$2,000	$3,000	$ 500	$6,500
Current liabilities	230	320	350	100	1,000
Long-term liabilities	—	—	—	4,000	4,000
Shareholders' equity	—	—	—	—	1,500
Total					$6,500

Two approaches used to incorporate the amount of invested capital into a performance measure are the return on investment (ROI) ratio and residual income:

$$\text{Return on investment} = \frac{\text{Income}}{\text{Invested capital}}$$

Residual income = Income − Imputed interest charge for invested capital

Both approaches are described in this section. ROI is often called the accounting rate of return or the accrual accounting rate of return.

ROI as an investment tool

Return on investment (ROI) is income divided by invested capital. It is the most popular approach to incorporating invested capital into a performance measure. Conceptually, ROI has appeal because it blends into one number all the major ingredients of profitability; the ROI statistic by itself can be compared with opportunities elsewhere, inside or outside the company. From a practical standpoint, however, ROI is an imperfect measure that should be used with caution and in conjunction with other performance measures.

The ROI measure can often provide more insight into performance when it is divided into the following components:

$$\text{Capital turnover} \times \text{Income percentage of revenues} = \text{Return on investment}$$

$$\frac{\text{Revenues}}{\text{Invested capital}} \times \frac{\text{Income}}{\text{Revenues}} = \frac{\text{Income}}{\text{Invested capital}}$$

This approach is widely known as the Du Pont method of profitability analysis. The components of the Du Pont method lead to the following generalizations: ROI is increased by any action that (A) decreases costs, (B) increases revenues, or (C) decreases invested capital—while holding the other two factors constant. Put another way, there are two basic ingredients in profit making: capital turnover and profit margins. An improvement in either without changing the other will enhance return on invested capital.

Consider the ROI of each of the three Hospitality Inns motels in Exhibit 26-1. Our definitions here are motel operating income for the numerator of the ROI ratio and total assets of each motel for the denominator:

MOTEL	MOTEL OPERATING INCOME	÷	TOTAL ASSETS	= ROI
	(In Thousands)		(In Thousands)	
San Francisco	$240	÷	$1,000	= 24%
Chicago	$300	÷	$2,000	= 15%
New Orleans	$480	÷	$3,000	= 16%

Using these ROI figures, the San Francisco motel appears to make the best use of its total assets.

Assume that the top management of Hospitality Inns adopts a 30% target ROI for the San Francisco motel. How can this return be attained? The Du Pont method can be used to illustrate the present situation and three alternatives (in $000s):

	$\dfrac{\text{REVENUES}}{\text{TOTAL ASSETS}}$ $\times$	$\dfrac{\text{OPERATING INCOME}}{\text{REVENUES}}$ $=$	$\dfrac{\text{OPERATING INCOME}}{\text{TOTAL ASSETS}}$
Present situation	$\dfrac{1,200}{1,000}$ $\times$	$\dfrac{240}{1,200}$ $=$	$\dfrac{240}{1,000}$, or 24%
Alternatives			
A. Increase operating income by decreasing costs	$\dfrac{1,200}{1,000}$ $\times$	$\dfrac{300}{1,200}$ $=$	$\dfrac{300}{1,000}$, or 30%
B. Increase operating income by increasing revenues	$\dfrac{1,500}{1,000}$ $\times$	$\dfrac{300}{1,500}$ $=$	$\dfrac{300}{1,000}$, or 30%
C. Decrease total assets	$\dfrac{1,200}{800}$ $\times$	$\dfrac{240}{1,200}$ $=$	$\dfrac{240}{800}$, or 30%

Alternative A demonstrates a popular way of improving performance; margins can be increased by reducing costs. Alternative B can be achieved by increasing the price per unit charged (the room rate) or by increasing the number of units sold (rooms rented). Alternative C shows that a reduction in the level of total assets (such as inventories or accounts receivable) will also improve the ROI performance measure.

The ROI measure highlights the benefits that managers can obtain by reducing their investments in current or fixed assets. Some managers are conscious of the need to control costs and boost revenues but give much less attention to controlling the level of investment. Investments in cash, inventory, accounts receivables, and fixed assets should be minimized for any level of effective performance. This approach means investing idle cash, determining proper inventory levels, managing credit judiciously, and spending carefully on fixed assets.

Residual income

Residual income is income minus an imputed interest charge for invested capital. Assume that Hospitality Inns defines residual income for each motel as motel operating income minus an imputed interest charge of 10% of the total assets of the motel:

MOTEL	MOTEL OPERATING INCOME	−	IMPUTED INTEREST CHARGE	=	RESIDUAL INCOME
San Francisco	$240		− $100 (10% of $1,000) =		$140
Chicago	$300		− $200 (10% of $2,000) =		$100
New Orleans	$480		− $300 (10% of $3,000) =		$180

Given the 10% imputed interest charge, the New Orleans motel is performing best in terms of residual income.

The objective of maximizing residual income assumes that as long as the division earns a rate in excess of the imputed charge for invested capital, the division should expand. Some firms have favored the residual-income approach because managers will concentrate on maximizing an absolute amount (dollars of residual income) rather than a percentage (rate of return on investment).

The objective of maximizing ROI may induce managers of highly profitable divisions to reject projects that, from the viewpoint of the organization as a whole, should be accepted. To illustrate, assume that the top management of Hospitality Inns regards 10% as the minimum required rate of return on investments. Assume also that an expansion of the San Francisco motel will increase motel operating income by $160,000 and increase motel total assets by $800,000. The ROI for the expansion is 20% ($160,000 ÷ $800,000), which makes it attractive to Hospitality Inns. However, by making this expansion, the San Francisco manager will see that motel's ROI decrease (in $000s):

$$\text{Preexpansion ROI} = \frac{\$240}{\$1,000} = 24\%$$

$$\text{Postexpansion ROI} = \frac{\$240 + \$160}{\$1,000 + \$800} = \frac{\$400}{\$1,800} = 22.2\%$$

The annual bonus paid to the San Francisco manager may well decrease if ROI is a key factor in the bonus calculation and the expansion option is selected.

If the annual bonus is a function of residual income, the San Francisco manager will view the expansion favorably:

873

$$\text{Preexpansion residual income} = \$240 - (10\% \times \$1,000) = \$140$$

$$\text{Postexpansion residual income} = \$400 - (10\% \times \$1,800) = \$220$$

Goal congruence is more likely to be promoted by using residual income rather than ROI as a division manager performance measure.

Both ROI and residual income represent the results for a single time period (such as twelve months). Managers can take actions that cause short-run increases in ROI or residual income, but that are in conflict with the long-run interests of the organization. For example, research and development and plant maintenance can be curtailed in the last three months of a fiscal year to achieve a target level of annual operating income.

Distinction between managers and investments

As noted in several chapters, **performance evaluation of a manager should be distinguished from performance evaluation of an activity unit such as a division of the company.** The most skillful division manager is often put in charge of the sickest division in an attempt to change its fortunes. Such an attempt may take years, not months. Furthermore, it may result in merely bringing the division up to a minimum acceptable ROI. The division may continue to be a poor profit performer in comparison with other divisions. If top management relied solely on the absolute ROI to judge management, the skillful manager would be foolhardy to accept such trouble-shooting assignments.

Comparisons of income or rates of return among investment centers should be made cautiously. Why? Because there tend to be too many peculiarities that destroy their validity. Even for similar factories making similar products, local conditions often cause a variety of environments and costs. *Therefore a manager would usually be more appropriately judged by performance against some budget target rather than against other investment centers.*

Surveys of company practice

The financial criteria used by organizations to evaluate managers or activities rely heavily on accounting measures. To illustrate, one survey polled U.S. and U.K. managers on the financial criteria used to evaluate the performance of division managers. Most respondents reported using multiple measures:[1]

	U.S. FIRMS	U.K. FIRMS
1. Achievement of target ROI imposed by company	51.7%	44.7%
2. Ability to stay within budget	49.3	43.7
3. Achievement of target profit before interest and taxes	45.4	50.5
4. Achievement of target profit after charging interest on total capital employed by the divisions	28.8	37.4
5. Achievement of target cash flow	21.5	41.7

---

[1] R. Scapens, J. Sale, and P. Tikkas, *Financial Control of Divisional Capital Investment* (London: Institute of Cost and Management Accountants, 1982), p. 128. Other survey evidence is reported in W. Abdallah and D. Keller, "Measuring the Multinational's Performance," *Management Accounting*, October 1985, pp. 26–30.

Many firms do not use the same financial criteria for each division or responsibility center. For example, the ability to stay within a budget criterion is more commonly found in activities set up as cost centers than as investment centers.

DEFINITIONS OF INCOME AND INVESTMENTS

Alternative income definitions

There is considerable diversity among companies in the definition of division or segment income used in the ROI formula. Exhibit 26-2 outlines six alternatives definitions, marked (A) through (F), that have been used by companies. As one moves from (A) through (F), the number of allocated items increases. The main argument favoring the use of definitions such as (A) or (B) is that only those items controllable by the manager are included in the income measure. The main arguments favoring the use of definitions such as (C), (D), (E), and (F) are that these costs are part of doing overall business; division managers should be made aware of both their existence and their magnitude. Chapters 12 and 13 discuss the issues that arise in choosing which of the above (or other) definitions of income might be used. Few topics cause more heartburn within organizations than do corporate cost allocation issues. Almost any approach is subject to criticism.

Possible investment bases

The base that is used for defining invested capital may appropriately differ among companies and within segments of the same company. The possible alternative bases include:

1. *Total assets available.* This base includes all business assets, regardless of their individual purpose.
2. *Total assets employed.* This base excludes excess or idle assets, such as vacant land or construction in progress. For example, if the New Orleans motel in Exhibit 26-1 has unused land set aside for potential expansion, the total assets employed by the motel in the performance measure would exclude the book value of that unused land.
3. *Working capital (current assets minus current liabilities) plus other assets.* This base is really the same as base 1 except that current liabilities are deducted from current assets. In a sense, this base represents an exclusion of the portion of current assets that is supplied by short-term creditors.

EXHIBIT 26-2
Alternative Income Definitions for Segment Performance Evaluation

```
        Net Revenues of Segment
        − Variable Costs of Segment
(A) =   Contribution Margin of Segment
        − Fixed Costs of Segment Controllable by Segment Managers
(B) =   Contribution Controllable by Segment Managers
        − Fixed Costs of Segment Controllable by Others
(C) =   Operating Income of Segment
        − Allocated Central Corporate Costs
(D) =   Income Before Interest and Income Taxes
        − Allocated Interest Costs on Long-Term Debt
(E) =   Income Before Income Taxes
        − Allocated Income Taxes
(F) =   Net Income
```

4. *Stockholders' equity.* This base centers attention on the rate of return that will be earned by the business owners. Use of this measure for the three motels in Figure 26-1 would require allocation of the long-term liabilities of Hospitality Inns to the three motels.

Most firms that use ROI for performance measurement choose among total assets available, total assets employed, and working capital plus other assets. Total assets available is very informative when the division manager's acknowledged mission is to utilize all assets without regard to their financing. However, where a top-management directive forces the division manager to carry extra assets, use of total assets employed can be more informative than total assets available. The most common rationale given for using working capital plus other assets is that the manager often does have direct influence over the amount of short-term credit that a division utilizes. An able manager should maximize the use of such credit, within some overall constraints, to prevent endangering the company's credit standing. By deducting current liabilities from the total assets, the denominator of the ROI measure will show the actions of the manager who maximizes the use of such credit.

The main criticism of stockholders' equity as the investment base at the division or segment level is that it combines the effects of decisions made mainly at two different levels: operating decisions made at the individual motel level and financing decisions made at the corporate level. In addition, arbitrary decisions are often necessary when allocating long-term corporate debt to individual divisions or segments.

Companies are not constrained to use the same income and investment definitions for both evaluating the performance of divisions and evaluating the performance of division managers. For evaluating the performance of divisions, the aim is to identify all those assets of the organization (be they division assets or corporate assets) that are attributable to the operation of individual divisions. For evaluating the performance of division managers, many firms are concerned that divisional managers view the chosen definitions as reasonable.

MEASUREMENT ALTERNATIVES FOR EVALUATING ACTIVITIES

How should we measure the assets that are included in the investment base? Should assets be measured at present value, current cost, disposal value, or historical cost? Should gross book value or net book value be used for depreciable assets? The relevant measure depends on the decisions being affected and evaluated.

This section discusses measurement issues relating to the performance evaluation of segment activities. The next section discusses additional issues that arise when the performance of segment managers is evaluated.

Total present value

Chapters 19 and 20 discuss the relevance of discounted cash-flow (DCF) analysis for both asset acquisition and disposal decisions. **Present value** is the asset measure that is based on DCF estimates. To illustrate, consider an existing motel that has an expected useful life of ten years, expected net cash inflows of $1,200,000 each year, and an expected terminal disposal value of $2,000,000. The required rate of return is 12%. The present value of the asset would be $7.424 million:

Present value of annuity of $1,200,000 for ten years discounted at 12%:	
$1,200,000 × 5.650	$6,780,000
Present value of $2,000,000 ten years hence discounted at 12%:	
$2,000,000 × .322	644,000
Present value of motel	$7,424,000

For new asset acquisition decisions, the present value of the cash inflows should be compared with the present value of the cash outflows associated with the investment. Those asset purchases with a zero or positive net present value should be purchased. For decisions concerning the disposal of currently held assets, the present value of cash inflows from continuing to retain the asset should be compared with the current disposal value (often called the current selling price) of the asset. The very act of continuing to hold an asset implies that, at a minimum, the continuance or disposal decision has been made (either explicitly or implicitly).

The relevance of discounted cash-flow analysis to asset acquisition and disposal decisions has led to proposals to use total present value as the ideal investment measure for evaluating the performance of activities. The use of such a measure in an ROI calculation requires a concept of income (an income model) that differs from the conventional accrual accounting model. *Annual income* under this income model is defined as the difference between total present values at the beginning and at the end of a year (assuming no cash dividends or additional investments). This approach requires an annual computation of a new total present value of the expected cash inflows. The resulting income would be affected by more than just current operating activities. Income depends on a measurement of total present value at the end of the year, so it would also be affected by other events influencing future cash flows (such as new inventions, the entry of new competitors, and changes in government regulations) and by changes in the required rate of return on investments.

Several firms (e.g., Cadbury-Schweppes in the United Kingdom and Westinghouse Electric Corporation in the United States) are experimenting with the use of present value asset valuations in evaluating individual division performance. These firms recognize the subjectivity of the cash-flow estimates underlying the individual asset values. However, they argue that the sizable problems in implementing the approach should not detract senior management attention from the relevance of information about changes in total present values.

Where firms do not systematically incorporate total present value (and disposal value) information into their routine accounting reports, periodic attempts should be made to approximate present values (and disposal values) in judging the desirability of investment in assets. Otherwise managers will overlook obsolescence and investment opportunities.[2]

---

[2]Where a company's equity securities are publicly traded, the market capitalization should be compared with the internal management estimates of present value. Explanations for differences between the two numbers include: (1) the capital market does not have access to the same information as internal management, (2) the capital market uses a different discount rate or a different time horizon than does internal management, and (3) either the capital market or internal management misestimates the underlying future cash flows.

Current-cost measures for assets are frequently proposed as one means of reducing the comparability problems that arise with historical-cost measures. **Current cost** is the cost today of purchasing an asset currently held if identical assets can currently be purchased; it is the cost of purchasing the services provided by that asset if identical assets cannot currently be purchased. Consider the following comment by American Standard, an enthusiastic advocate of current-cost measures when evaluating the performance of both its activities and its managers:

> [For some years] American Standard has been modifying its financial measurements to eliminate the distortions and inequities of historic cost accounting. [Under historical cost accounting] a company will find that some of its divisions have higher return on book investment than others. This performance criterion is one factor considered in allocating capital resources. A considerable amount of the difference in returns on book assets between units, however, can just be a reflection of when a unit acquired its fixed assets. The unit that acquired its assets some time ago at deflated dollars in today's terms can look very good compared with a unit that acquired its fixed assets recently. It may be that the converse relation is actually true in terms of economic returns on new investments. Then too, the units with high returns may be inhibited from making necessary fresh investments because the investments will depress the historic return on book assets. The internal accounting system should have correct incentives for management to make economic capital investment decisions.
>
> By trying to maintain unrealistically high book returns, management can be inhibited from investing in the business. Book returns [under historical cost accounting] can lead management into a trap of "milking the business" and shying away from necessary replacements with new and better equipment and facilities.[3]

The American Standard argument can be illustrated using the Hospitality Inns example discussed earlier in this chapter (see Exhibit 26-1). Assume the following information about the fixed assets of each motel (amounts are in $000s):

	SAN FRANCISCO	CHICAGO	NEW ORLEANS
Age of facility (at end of 19_8)	8 years	4 years	2 years
Gross book value	$1,400	$2,100	$2,800
Accumulated depreciation	$ 800	$ 600	$ 400
Net book value (at end of 19_8)	$ 600	$1,500	$2,400
Depreciation for 19_8	$ 100	$ 150	$ 200

Hospitality Inns uses a fourteen-year estimate of useful life, assumes no terminal disposal value for the physical facilities, and calculates depreciation on a straight-line basis.

An index of construction costs for the eight-year period that Hospitality Inns has been operating (19_0 year-end = 100) is as follows:

---

[3]This extract is from an internal document ("Managerial Uses of Inflation-Adjusted Accounting Data: The American Standard Approach") by K. Todd. For a detailed discussion of current cost and alternative measures, see R. Bloom and A. Debessay, *Inflation Accounting: Reporting of General and Specific Price Changes* (New York: Praeger, 1984).

Year	19_1	19_2	19_3	19_4	19_5	19_6	19_7	19_8
Construction Cost Index	110	122	136	144	152	160	174	180

Earlier in this chapter we computed the ROI of 24% for San Francisco, 15% for Chicago, and 16% for New Orleans (see page 872). One possible explanation of the high ROI for San Francisco is that the fixed assets are expressed in terms of 19_0 construction price levels, whereas the fixed assets for Chicago and New Orleans are expressed in terms of more recent construction price levels.

Exhibit 26-3 illustrates a step-by-step approach for incorporating current-cost estimates for fixed assets and depreciation into the ROI calculation. The current-cost adjustment dramatically reduces the ROI of the San Francisco motel:

	ROI: HISTORICAL COST	ROI: CURRENT COST
San Francisco	24%	10.81%
Chicago	15%	11.05%
New Orleans	16%	13.79%

Thus the 24% ROI of the San Francisco motel can give a highly misleading picture of the returns that Hospitality Inns should expect from subsequent investments in motel facilities.

Obtaining current-cost estimates for some assets can be difficult. The exact assets currently held by an organization may no longer be traded or manufactured. The focus when making current-cost estimates should be on the expected cash flows from the assets held, not their precise physical or technological features. The aim is to approximate how much it would cost to obtain similar assets that would produce the same expected operating cash inflows as the assets currently held. Managers rarely replace assets with new assets having identical operating and economic characteristics.

Current cost or historical cost?

Some form of current-cost accounting, akin to that in Exhibit 26-3, has been required in the annual reports of companies in several countries. For example, U.S. firms were required under FASB 33 to include current-cost information in their annual reports sent to shareholders. The main rationale for regulatory bodies requiring this information was its presumed relevance to decisions made by external parties such as investors.

Despite the availability of current-cost information for external reporting, there was no evident rush toward including current costs in the routine reports developed for internal reporting. One survey asked U.S. managers to rank "the extent of use and reporting of FASB 33 information for internal company purposes such as management decision making." Respondents used a 7-point scale, with 1 being "never use" and 7 "always use". The mean response of U.S. managers polled was 1.6.[4] Similar surveys of Canadian and United Kingdom managers like-

---

[4]K. Rosenzweig, "Companies Are Not Using FAS 33 Data," *Management Accounting*, April 1985, p. 52.

EXHIBIT 26-3

Hospitality Inns: ROI Computed Using Current-Cost Estimates as of 19_8
for Depreciation and Fixed Assets

STEP ONE: Restate fixed assets from gross book value at historical cost to current cost as of 19_8.

$$\frac{\text{GROSS BOOK VALUE}}{\text{AT HISTORICAL COST}} \times \frac{\text{CONSTRUCTION COST INDEX IN 19\_8}}{\text{CONSTRUCTION COST INDEX IN YEAR OF CONSTRUCTION}}$$

San Francisco: $1,400 × (180/100) = $2,520
Chicago: $2,100 × (180/144) = $2,625
New Orleans: $2,800 × (180/160) = $3,150

STEP TWO: Derive net book value of fixed assets at current cost as of 19_8. (The estimated total useful life of each motel is 14 years.)

$$\frac{\text{GROSS BOOK VALUE}}{\text{AT CURRENT COST IN 19\_8}} \times \frac{\text{ESTIMATED USEFUL LIFE REMAINING}}{\text{ESTIMATED TOTAL USEFUL LIFE}}$$

San Francisco: $2,520 × 6/14 = $1,080
Chicago: $2,625 × 10/14 = $1,875
New Orleans: $3,150 × 12/14 = $2,700

STEP THREE: Compute current cost of total assets in 19_8. (Assume current assets of each motel expressed in 19_8 dollars.)

$$\frac{\text{CURRENT ASSETS}}{\text{(FROM EXHIBIT 26-1)}} + \frac{\text{FIXED ASSETS}}{\text{(FROM STEP TWO ABOVE)}}$$

San Francisco: $400 + $1,080 = $1,480
Chicago: $500 + $1,875 = $2,375
New Orleans: $600 + $2,700 = $3,300

STEP FOUR: Compute current-cost depreciation expense in 19_8 dollars.

GROSS BOOK VALUE AT CURRENT COST IN 19_8 × 1/14

San Francisco: $2,520 × 1/14 = $180
Chicago: $2,625 × 1/14 = $187.50
New Orleans: $3,150 × 1/14 = $225

STEP FIVE: Compute 19_8 operating income using 19_8 current-cost depreciation.

$$\frac{\text{HISTORICAL-COST}}{\text{OPERATING INCOME}} - \left(\frac{\text{CURRENT-COST}}{\text{DEPRECIATION}} - \frac{\text{HISTORICAL-COST}}{\text{DEPRECIATION}} \right)$$

San Francisco: $240 − ($180 − $100)   = $160
Chicago: $300 − ($187.50 − $150) = $262.50
New Orleans: $480 − ($225 − $200)   = $455

STEP SIX: Compute ROI using current-cost estimates for fixed assets and depreciation.

$$\frac{\text{OPERATING INCOME (FROM STEP FIVE)}}{\text{TOTAL ASSETS (FROM STEP THREE)}}$$

San Francisco: $160/$1,480   = 10.81%
Chicago: $262.50/$2,375 = 11.05%
New Orleans: $455/$3,300   = 13.79%

wise report minimal use of current-cost or price-level adjusted data in routine internal accounting reports.[5]

What factors could explain the widespread inclusion of historical costs and the limited inclusion of current-cost data in routine internal reporting?

1. *Managers are unaware of the defects of historical costs and of the benefits of alternative systems.* This explanation is not a persuasive one. Managers live in a highly competitive environment. They are always seeking an edge. Managers will invest in a more elaborate accounting system if they think a better set of collective operating decisions will ensue (i.e., if benefits exceed costs).

2. *Benefits of including current costs in routine internal reporting systems are overstated.* One reason for firms continuing to use historical-cost information could be that many of the so-called defects of historical cost are already being minimized via use of a budgeting system. Although critics of historical cost portray the choice as historical cost versus current cost, this is misleading. The choices are better expressed as:

System A: Budgeted data and historical-cost data

or

System B: Budgeted data and current-cost data

Managers seeking to improve their control system may well decide that it is better to upgrade their budgeting system than to install a current-cost reporting system.

Many advocates of current-cost accounting assert that "bad" decisions are being made because accounting systems are not based on current costs. But the evidence is very limited. Consider some decision models in wide use today: cost-volume-profit, inventory planning, production scheduling, pricing, and capital budgeting. What types of data are common among those models? Budgeted data! For example, in capital budgeting, expected inflation is built in to forecasts. Current costs (or historical costs) are not direct inputs into these decisions.

3. *Costs of including current costs in routine internal reporting systems are understated.* A key aspect of the definition of systems is regularity. For example, historical data are recorded in an orderly fashion as a part of everyday operations. Continuous compilation tends to be more expensive than occasional compilation. Other data may be gathered as desired; for example, current costs may be sought via special cost studies when specific equipment or an individual plant is being evaluated.

4. *Managerial self-interest is not maximized by the inclusion of current-cost data in routine internal reports.* Managers who are being evaluated on an ROI basis may prefer the use of historical-cost-based numbers as compared with the typically shriveled numbers reported with a current-cost system.

---

[5]J. Waterhouse, "Reporting Non-Historical Accounting Data to Canadian Managers" (Canadian Certified General Accountants' Research Foundation, 1984); and A. McCosh and S. Howell, "Planning and Control Systems and Their Evolution during Inflation," in *Management Accounting Research and Practice*, ed. D. Cooper, R. Scapens, and J. Arnold (London: Institute of Cost and Management Accountants, 1983).

The above explanations should be interpreted as being neither for nor against historical-cost or current-cost accounting. Indeed, unless a budget is also used, a strong case can be made for rejecting historical costs as a basis for performance measurement. **For management accounting purposes, the main issue for a given organization is whether the costs of a new current-cost system, including all indirect costs of educating users, will yield a greater benefit than an existing or improved budgeting system. As always, that benefit should be calibrated by predicting how collective decisions will be affected by one system versus another.**

General price-level adjustments

Some companies are exploring the use of historical cost data adjusted for general price-level changes. This approach entails restating *historical* data in terms of current general purchasing power by use of a general index such as a consumer price index or a gross national product-implicit price deflator index. Companies in Argentina, Brazil, and other high-inflation countries use this approach. As explained more thoroughly in the literature on external reporting, the use of *general* price-level adjustments represents a restatement of historical costs. Conceptually, restated historical costs are *not* the same as current costs, which are sometimes approximated via the use of *specific* price indexes. (However, a separate line of reasoning claims that general price-level accounting is a practical, cost-effective way of getting crude approximations of results that would be obtained under current-cost accounting.)

Plant and equipment: gross or net book value?

Because historical-cost investment measures are used most often in practice, there has been much discussion about the relative merits of using gross book value (original cost) or net book value (original cost minus accumulated depreciation). Those who favor using gross book value claim that it helps comparisons among plants and divisions. If income decreases as a plant ages, the decline in earning power will be made evident. In contrast, if net book value is used, the constantly decreasing base can show a higher rate of return on investment in later years; this higher rate may mislead decision makers. The Appendix to this chapter presents the example of an asset with equal cash inflows of $2,000 each year for three years, but for which the use of net book value (and straight-line depreciation) gives a rate of return on investment of 14% in year 1, 21% in year 2, and 42% in year 3 (see Exhibit 26-4 on page 890).

Defenders of gross book value frequently claim that it partially compensates for the impact of the changing price level on historical cost. However, if a company desires to use current cost as a base, it should face the problem squarely by using appraisal values or specific price indexes. Reliance on gross book value is an unreliable means of approximating current cost.

The proponents of using net book value as a base maintain that it is less confusing because (a) it is consistent with the total assets shown on the conventional balance sheet, and (b) it is consistent with net income computations that include deductions for depreciation. If net book value is used in a manner that is consistent with the planning model, it can be useful for auditing past decisions (see the chapter Appendix on compound interest depreciation for further discussion of this point).[6]

---

[6]One survey of eighty-eight multinationals reported that 80% used net book value when computing ROI for assessing foreign subsidiary performance: *Assessing Foreign Subsidiary Performance* (New York: Business International Corporation, 1982), p. 163.

Individual components of a management control system should be consistent and mutually reinforcing. Goal congruence problems can arise where the measures used to evaluate a manager's performance conflict with the decision models advocated by top management.

Limitations of accrual accounting performance measures

As discussed in Chapter 19, capital investment decisions in many firms are supposed to be based on discounted cash-flow (DCF) models. However, these same firms often use accrual accounting models for evaluating the performance of managers. Such managers may not make capital outlays that are justified by DCF methods but produce poor performance records in the first year or two after the initial investment. Such behavior is especially likely if the total initial investment is immediately expensed (as is the case with research and development expenditures for external reporting purposes by publicly held U.S. corporations).

Several approaches can be used to promote consistency between the DCF model used to select projects and the model used for performance evaluation:

1. Directly compare the cash-flow predictions made in the DCF project analysis with the actual cash flows.
2. Select projects using DCF, but make predictions of both the cash flows and the implied accrual accounting rate of return for each year of the life of the project; performance evaluation is based on a comparison of the predicted accounting rate of return made when the project was chosen with the actual accrual accounting rate of return.
3. Integrate the discounted cash-flow analysis explicitly into the computation of the accrual accounting rate of return. The Appendix to this chapter illustrates this approach.

Comparability problems with historical-cost measures

The preceding section of this chapter illustrated how historical-cost measures make comparisons difficult. Reconsider the Hospitality Inns example:

	ROI: HISTORICAL COST	AGE OF PHYSICAL FACILITY
San Francisco	24%	8 years old
Chicago	15%	4 years old
New Orleans	16%	2 years old

The managers of the Chicago and New Orleans motels could legitimately claim that the 24% ROI makes the manager of the San Francisco motel appear relatively more effective than would be the case if all three motels had been constructed in the same year.

Hospitality Inns could use one of several approaches to increase the reliability of its performance evaluation of individual motel managers:

1. Restate the fixed assets and depreciation of each motel to a current-cost basis. This approach calculates the ROI figures that would be reported if all three motels had been constructed in the same year. As illustrated earlier in this chapter (p. 879), this approach shows the New Orleans manager to be achieving the highest return on investment.

2. Retain the historical-cost system to compute ROI, but set a budget target for each motel that recognizes the effect of historical-cost rules for motels built at different time periods. For example, the target ROIs could be 26% for San Francisco, 18% for Chicago, and 16% for New Orleans.

The second alternative is frequently overlooked in the literature. Critics of historical cost have indicated how high rates of return on old assets may erroneously induce a manager not to replace assets. However, the manager's mandate is often, "Go forth and attain the budgeted results." The budget should be carefully negotiated with full knowledge of historical-cost accounting pitfalls. The desirability of tailoring a budget to a particular manager and a particular accounting system cannot be overemphasized. For example, many problems of asset valuation and profit measurement (whether based on historical cost or current cost) can be satisfactorily solved if top management gets everybody to focus on what is attainable in the forthcoming budget period.

NONFINANCIAL MEASURES OF PERFORMANCE

While accounting measures such as ROI and residual income capture important aspects of performance, each has its limitations (as does any single measure of performance). For example, these measures fail to capture explicitly nonfinancial aspects such as customer service, product quality, and the safety record of manufacturing plants.

Some organizations have developed very explicit and detailed systems to monitor these nonfinancial aspects. As an illustration in the lodging industry, consider the "Product Review and Evaluation Summary" system used by Holiday Inns Inc., an operator of a worldwide chain of over eighteen hundred motels.[7] This system is administered by the Quality Assurance Division of Holiday Inns to ensure that a traveler staying at any motel has a consistently good experience. Seventeen individual areas of each motel facility (e.g., the entrance and lobby, public rest rooms, guest room, guest bathroom, and outdoor pool) are examined for any deviation from the standards set by headquarters. Each area has a detailed set of items to be checked for conformance with company standards. For instance, the items checked in each guest room include cleanliness, lighting, the sleep package, and television set. The score on a "Product Review and Evaluation Summary" from a motel visit by the Quality Assurance Division is used in determining the compensation of the manager of that motel. The Holiday Inns system provides clear signals to all employees about the specific areas top management views as critical to the success of the company.

Many management control systems include a combination of both financial and nonfinancial performance measures. For example, the variables monitored by the Fabrication Division of one semiconductor firm include the following:[8]

---

[7]Reprinted with permission of Holiday Inns, Inc.

[8]R. Kaplan, "Accounting Lag: The Obsolescence of Cost Accounting Systems," *California Management Review,* Winter 1986, pp. 174–99.

Yield: ratio of wafer chips in to wafer chips out; rework %

Production: % of delivery commitments met

Productivity: wafer chips produced/payroll dollars

Equipment: % of hours with no unscheduled downtime

Financial: cost per chip; revenue per chip

The design of an effective management control system for many companies now requires the joint effort of accountants, engineers, information technologists, marketing personnel, and production or operations managers.

EXECUTIVE COMPENSATION PLANS

A reward system is an integral part of a management control system. The chosen reward system should strengthen the link between goal congruence and managerial effort. Rewards include monetary items such as base salary, bonus payments, and stock options, as well as nonmonetary items such as an office with a view, a personal secretary, authority, and status.[9]

Executive compensation plans are one component of the reward system. They include a diverse set of short-run and long-run plans that detail the conditions under which, and the forms in which, compensation is to be made to executives of the organization. A major issue in designing an executive compensation plan is the appropriate mix between (1) base salary, (2) annual incentives (e.g., cash bonuses based on annual reported income), (3) long-term incentives (e.g., stock options based on achieving a set level of ROI by the end of a five year period), and (4) benefits (e.g., life insurance).[10]

Objectives of executive compensation

Objectives cited as important by designers of executive compensation plans include the following:

1. To provide incentives for better current and future performance
2. To reward past performance
3. To attract new managers
4. To retain existing superior performing managers
5. To better align the risk attitudes of individual managers with those of corporate shareholders
6. To reduce the taxation paid by the manager as an individual or by the corporation
7. To promote an "entrepreneurial spirit" within an organization

Simultaneous attainment of all the above objectives is unlikely. The challenge facing the designer of an executive compensation package is to choose that mix of rewards (e.g., salary, cash bonus, stock options, and perquisites), and the timing of

---

[9]Further discussion of the issues raised in this section can be found in R. Kaplan, *Advanced Management Accounting* (Englewood Cliffs, N.J.: Prentice-Hall, 1982), Chaps. 15–17; and R. Magee, *Advanced Managerial Accounting* (New York: Harper & Row, 1986), Chaps. 11–12.

[10]A survey of the one hundred largest U.S. industrial corporations reported the following total (median) compensation mix for senior executives: base salary, 42%; annual incentive, 20%; long-term incentive, 31%; and benefits, 7%. *Top 100 Industrial Executive Compensation Study* (Philadelphia: Towers, Perrin, Forster, and Crosby, 1985).

payment, that best achieves the chosen set of objectives viewed by top management as being of overriding importance.[11]

The framework for evaluating management control systems outlined in the Appendix to Chapter 25 (pp. 855–57) should be explicitly considered in designing an executive compensation plan. For example, the chosen compensation plan should reinforce the organization's strategy and should capture the key economic success factors that determine the organization's ability to achieve its goals. Two factors given considerable weight by many designers of compensation plans are administrative ease and the likelihood that managers affected by the plan will view it as fair.

Role of accounting measures

In many executive compensation plans, accounting performance measures are a key component. Short-run plans can make the payment of a bonus contingent on attaining a budgeted net income or ROI figure. Some long-run plans, termed **performance plans,** make payment of a definite number of performance units (each assigned a fixed dollar value) contingent on the ROI (net income, etc.) at the end of an extended time period (say five years) being at a set level; for example, being in the top 25% of the largest one thousand industrial corporations in the United States. By explicitly including a five-year period in the plan, management is encouraged to adopt a long-term focus in decision making.[12]

ROI or residual income need not induce a short-run focus by managers. The focus on the short run in many compensation plans comes not from the ROI or residual income measure itself, but from a plan that does not take account of time periods longer than the current year. For example, note the long-run focus of the performance plans just described.

Accounting measures can be combined with nonaccounting measures in an executive compensation plan. For example, there are four components of the compensation paid to the senior executives of Holiday Inns Inc.: (1) base salary, (2) team profit sharing, (3) individual bonuses, and (4) discretionary incentives. The team profit-sharing component requires attainment of two goals at the company level:

1. Financial Target: "The Hotel Group reaches at least 95% of its planned operating income for that year," and
2. Customer Satisfaction Target: "The Holiday Inns hotel system achieves an established level of customer satisfaction as measured by:
   - Guest inspection scores: The annual number of overall C, D, and F responses on guest inspection cards per 1,000 room-nights sold must be less than 1.670.
   - Guest complaint letters: The annual number of guest complaint letters per 1,000 room-nights sold must be less than 0.457."

---

[11]*Compensation and Benefit Review*, a journal published by the American Management Association, is a good source of information on existing practice. Research studies with a strong economics foundation can be found in J. Pratt and R. Zeckhauser, eds., *Principals and Agents: The Structure of Business* (Boston: Harvard Business School Press, 1985). For a good summary of the empirical research literature, see R. Lambert and D. Larcker, "Executive Compensation, Corporate Decision-Making and Shareholder Wealth: A Review of the Evidence," *Midland Corporate Financial Journal*, Winter 1985, pp. 6–22.

[12]Sixty-six of the one hundred largest U.S. industrial corporations include performance plans as part of their compensation package for senior executives. See *Top 100 Industrial Executive Compensation Study* (1985), p. 6.

The fast-food industry is similar to the lodging industry in its use of both financial targets and customer service/satisfaction targets in executive compensation plans.[13]

SUMMARY

Performance reports should distinguish between the performance of the manager of an activity and the performance of the activity as an economic investment.

Choices about the measure of accomplishment (such as ROI or residual income), about the definitions of components of that measure (such as income and investment), and about the accounting measurements (such as current cost or historical cost) should not be made independently. Top management may compensate for known deficiencies of, say, accounting measures by choosing a definition of a component that minimizes the effect of those deficiencies.

Accounting measures such as ROI or residual income can capture important aspects of both manager performance and activity performance. In many cases, however, they need to be supplemented with nonfinancial measures of performance, such as those relating to customer service, product quality, and productivity.

A common criticism of accounting performance measures is that they bias managers toward short-run actions and away from actions that benefit the long-run health of the organization. This criticism is misplaced. Accounting measures can be an integral part of a long-term executive compensation plan that rewards managers for achieving net income, ROI, or residual income targets over a three- or five-year period. As with nearly all accounting techniques, accounting performance measures are inanimate devices. Some criticisms should properly focus on the way these measures are used by organizations rather than on the measures themselves.

PROBLEMS FOR SELF-STUDY

problem 1   Suppose a division's budgeted data are as follows:

Average available assets:	
Receivables	$ 300,000
Inventories	200,000
Fixed assets, net	500,000
	$1,000,000
Fixed costs	$ 225,000
Variable costs	$5 per unit
Target rate of return on average available assets	27.5%
Expected volume	200,000 units

a. What average unit sales price is needed to obtain the target rate of return on average available assets?

b. What would be the expected turnover of assets?

c. What would be the net-income percentage of dollar sales?

d. What rate of return would be earned on assets available if sales volume is 300,000 units, assuming no changes in prices or variable costs per unit?

[13]Detailed surveys of compensation practices in individual industries are often available from accounting or other consulting firms. An example is *Executive Compensation and Benefits in the Foodservice Industry* (National Restaurant Association and Laventhol and Horwath, 1985).

a. 27.5% of $1,000,000 = $275,000 target net income

$$\text{Let } X = \text{Unit sales price}$$

$$\text{Dollar sales} = \text{Variable costs} + \text{Fixed costs} + \text{Net income}$$

$$200,000\, X = 200,000\ (\$5) + \$225,000 + \$275,000$$

$$X = \$1,500,000 \div 200,000$$

$$X = \$7.50$$

b. Expected asset turnover $= \dfrac{200,000 \times \$7.50}{\$1,000,000} = \dfrac{\$1,500,000}{\$1,000,000} = 1.5$

c. Net income as a percentage of dollar sales $= \dfrac{\$275,000}{\$1,500,000} = 18.33\%$

d. At a volume of 300,000 units:

Sales @ $7.50	$2,250,000
Variable costs @ $5.00	1,500,000
Contribution margin	$ 750,000
Fixed costs	225,000
Net income	$ 525,000
Rate of return on $1,000,000 assets	52.5%

Note that an increase of 50% in unit volume almost doubles net income. This result occurs because fixed costs do not increase as volume increases.

problem 2   A division managed by Wendy Bonini has total assets of $200,000 and net income of $60,000.

a. What is the division's ROI?

b. If interest is imputed at 14% of total assets, what is the residual income?

c. What effects on Bonini's management behavior can be expected if ROI is used to gauge performance?

d. What effects on Bonini's management behavior can be expected if residual income is used to gauge performance?

a. $60,000 \div $200,000 = 30\%$

b. $60,000 - .14($200,000) = $32,000$

c. If ROI is used, the manager is prone to reject projects that do not earn an ROI of at least 30%. From the viewpoint of the organization as a whole, this action may be undesirable because its best investment opportunities may lie in that division at a rate of, say, 22%. If a division is enjoying a high ROI, it is less likely to expand if it is judged via ROI than if it is judged via residual income.

d. If residual income is used, the manager is inclined to accept all projects whose expected ROI exceeds the minimum desired rate. The division is more likely to expand, because the goal is to maximize a dollar amount rather than a rate.

This chapter (and the Appendix) and the Glossary contain definitions of the following important terms:

Annuity method of depreciation (p. 889)
compound interest depreciation method (889)   *current cost (878)*
executive compensation plan (885)   *performance plan (886)*
present value (876)   *residual income (873)*   *return on investment (871)*
ROI (871)

Special Points and Pitfalls

Chapters 11 and 25 cover topics that are central to decisions on performance measures. For example, performance measures emphasizing the ability to stay within a cost budget are more appropriate in engineered-cost centers than in discretionary-cost centers. As a second example, performance measures emphasizing division profitability are more appropriate for organizations with a high level of decentralization than for those with a high level of centralization.

Do not become preoccupied with the defects of any one component of a management control system. Managers are often aware of these defects and attempt to minimize their dysfunctional consequences by putting more emphasis on other components of the control system. For example, top management of a motel chain may be aware that book values based on historical cost understate market values. However, they may not routinely record market values in the control system because of the high cost of updating these values. Thus, for evaluating subordinates, top management may put more emphasis on meeting an operating income target than on meeting an ROI target.

Increasing emphasis is explicitly being given to incorporating nonfinancial measures of performance into executive compensation plans. Examples include measures of product defects in automobile plants and measures of quality, service, and cleanliness in fast-food restaurant chains.

APPENDIX: COMPOUND INTEREST DEPRECIATION AND MODELS FOR MEASURING PERFORMANCE

Compound interest depreciation was developed to promote consistency between the use of DCF for project choice and the use of accrual accounting rate of return for performance evaluation. The **compound interest depreciation method** calculates depreciation in such a manner that the year-by-year accounting rate of return on beginning period investment is equal to the DCF internal rate of return on the investment. When the cash inflows are the same each period, this depreciation method is frequently called the **annuity method of depreciation.**

Assume that (in a world of certainty) a manager is considering a $4,212 investment in an energy-savings equipment unit. This unit is expected to generate an annual after-tax operating cash inflow of $2,000 for three years. The predicted terminal disposal value is zero. The internal rate of return on this investment is 20%. (Using Table 4 in Appendix B, the present value of an annuity of $1 for 3 years at 20% is $4,212 ÷ $2,000 = 2.106.)

Study Exhibit 26-4. Suppose subsequent performance adhered to predictions. The income statement that dovetails with the assumptions of the DCF model would be shown in the first three columns of Exhibit 26-4. **If cash inflows are equal each year, the compound interest method results in an increasing charge for depreciation over the useful life of the asset. In contrast, as Exhibit 26-4 shows, straight-line depreciation generates equal charges; sum-of-years'-digits depreciation generates decreasing charges.**

As explained in Chapter 19, DCF methods assume a capital-recovery factor that is related to funds in use. Each period's income under the compound interest depreciation method is *defined* as the internal rate of return times the beginning investment. Each cash payment consists of income (rate of return on investment) plus recovery of principal (depreciation):

YEAR	(1) INVESTMENT AT BEGINNING OF YEAR	(2) OPERATING CASH INFLOW	(3) OPERATING INCOME @ 20% PER YEAR	(4): (2) − (3) "DEPRECIATION" ("INVESTMENT"), RECOVERED DURING YEAR	(5): (1) − (4) NET BOOK VALUE, UNRECOVERED INVESTMENT AT END OF YEAR	(6): (3) ÷ (1) OPERATING INCOME TO INVESTMENT AT BEGINNING OF YEAR
1	$4,212.00	$2,000	$842.40	$1,157.60	$3,054.40	20%
2	3,054.40	2,000	610.88	1,389.12	1,665.28	20%
3	1,665.28	2,000	≈334.72	1,665.28	—	20%

By construction, the ratio of income to beginning investment is equal each year (and is the same as the internal rate of return).

Effects on performance

Exhibit 26-4 assumes steady cash flows. Under these conditions, the commonly used depreciation models show increasing profitability as the asset ages. Such varying rates of return have no relation to the DCF planning models. Many critics of straight-line and sum-of-the-years'-digits depreciation worry that managers are motivated to hold on to existing assets too long. Why? Because, as Exhibit 26-4 shows, in the late years the rates of return on old assets appear very high.

EXHIBIT 26-4
Alternative Depreciation Methods and Accounting Rates of Return

YEAR	COMPOUND INTEREST			STRAIGHT LINE			SUM-OF-YEARS'-DIGITS		
	1	2	3	1	2	3	1	2	3
Cash operating income	$2,000	$2,000	$2,000	$2,000	$2,000	$2,000	$2,000	$2,000	$2,000
Depreciation	1,158*	1,389*	1,665*	1,404†	1,404†	1,404†	2,106‡	1,404‡	702‡
Operating income	842	611	335	596	596	596	(106)	596	1,298
Investment base— beginning balance	4,212	3,054	1,665	4,212	2,808	1,404	4,212	2,106	702
Rate of return on beginning balance	20%	20%	20%	14%	21%	42%	−3%	28%	185%

*See the text on this page.
†$4,212 ÷ 3 = $1,404 per year.
‡Sum of digits = 1 + 2 + 3 = 6. Therefore year 1, $2,106 (3/6 × $4,212); year 2, $1,404 (2/6 × $4,212); year 3, $702 (1/6 × $4,212).

Using the data in Exhibit 26-4, the compound interest method of depreciation would show the following effects on residual income:[14]

YEAR	YEAR 1	YEAR 2	YEAR 3
Cash operating income	$2,000	$2,000	$2,000
Depreciation: Based on predicted cash flows at start of investment	1,158	1,389	1,665
Imputed interest: Charged against subunit at 20% required rate of return	842	611	335
Residual income	$ 0	$ 0	$ 0

Any actual cash flow that deviated from the predicted cash flow would affect residual income. Suppose actual cash flows were as follows:

YEAR	YEAR 1	YEAR 2	YEAR 3
Cash operating income	$2,247	$1,964	$1,683
Depreciation: Based on predicted cash flows at start of investment	1,158	1,389	1,665
Imputed interest: Charged against subunit at 20% required rate of return	842	611	335
Residual income	$ 247	$ (36)	$ (317)

The depreciation pattern under the compound interest method is based on *predicted* cash flows, not *actual* cash flows. The deviations between budgeted performance and actual performance can be explained by various operating and economic conditions, not by the depreciation pattern.

Firms' adoption of the compound interest depreciation method has been limited. Why? Explanations include the following:

1.   The conventional depreciation methods have become firmly entrenched in external reporting, and some companies cling to using the same depreciation method for internal reporting and shareholder reporting.

---

[14]The example in this Appendix assumes that the required rate of return on investment is the same as the internal rate of return of 20%. Alternative approaches of handling those cases where the two rates differ include:

a. Use the internal rate of return for the imputed interest charge in the residual income calculation, and

b. Increase the "cost" of the investment to the present value of the cash inflows. Then use the revised "cost" figure as the beginning investment base for year one, and the required rate of return in computing the depreciation on the investment. In the year that a new project is adopted, income would include an additional item representing the net present value of that project.

   One feature of (b) is that a new manager of a division will not receive a benefit from past investment decisions that had a positive net present value. (One chairman commented: "In some of our businesses, managers enjoy tail winds not of their own making; in others, they fight unavoidable head winds.")

2. If cash flows are equal per year, compound interest methods produce an increasing charge over the useful life of an asset. For instance, in the example used previously in this Appendix, there is a uniform cash inflow of $2,000 each year, but the depreciation charge (rounded) is $1,158 in year 1, $1,389 in year 2, and $1,665 in year 3. Intuitively, managers do not see the justification for an increasing charge for depreciation if cash flows remain constant. Moreover, many executives believe that most investments in depreciable assets tend to generate higher cash inflows in earlier years. If so, straight-line depreciation may give approximately the same results as compound interest depreciation.

3. The compound interest method works clearly if projected annual operating flows are reasonably equal, but the implicit principal-recovery pattern is more difficult to compute and explain if projected cash flows differ markedly through the years. Indeed, for some cash-flow configurations there can be negative depreciation in some years. For example, consider a $4,212 investment that will generate annual operating after-tax cash inflows of $500 in year 1, $2,400 in year 2, and $3,679 in year 3. The predicted terminal disposal value at the end of year 3 is zero. The compound interest depreciation (rounded) is −$342 in year 1, $1,489 in year 2, and $3,065 in year 3:

YEAR	(1) INVESTMENT AT BEGINNING OF YEAR	(2) OPERATING CASH INFLOW	(3) OPERATING INCOME @ 20% PER YEAR	(4) "DEPRECIATION" ("INVESTMENT") RECOVERED DURING YEAR	(5) NET BOOK VALUE, UNRECOVERED INVESTMENT AT END OF YEAR	(6) OPERATING INCOME TO INVESTMENT AT BEGINNING OF YEAR
1	$4,212.00	$ 500	$842.40	$ (342.40)	$4,554.40	20%
2	4,554.40	2,400	910.88	1,489.12	3,065.28	20%
3	3,065.28	3,679	613.72	3,065.28	—	20%

Many managers would find it counterintuitive to see an asset purchased for $4,212 at the start of year 1 have a book value of $4,554 at the end of year 1. Yet this is what can result with a compound interest depreciation method for projects that have low cash inflows in the early years but high internal rates of return.

_____QUESTIONS, PROBLEMS, AND CASES_____

26-1 What are the steps in choosing an accounting-based performance measure?

26-2 "Income divided by revenues is the most important single measure of business success." Do you agree? Why?

26-3 "The accounting rate-of-return tool is so hampered by limitations that we might as well forget it." Do you agree? Why?

26-4 "Too much stress on the current years accounting rate of return can hurt the corporation." How?

26-5 What measures besides the accounting rate of return are commonly used to judge managerial performance?

26-6 Proponents of net book value as an investment base usually cite two major reasons for their position. What are these reasons?

26-7 How should interest expense and nonrecurring expenses be considered in computing incomes that are related to investment bases?

26-8 List four possible bases for computing the cost of invested capital.

26-9 What factors could explain the widespread inclusion of historical-cost data and the limited inclusion of current-cost data in routine internal reporting systems?

26-10 What approaches can be used to promote consistency between the DCF model used to select capital budgeting projects and the model used for performance evaluation?

26-11 Name four objectives of an executive compensation plan.

26-12 Peta Milano made the following comment when her friend Jake Ali was made manager of the Nuclear Construction Division of General Projects: "It was like putting a new captain on the bridge of the Titanic after it had hit the iceberg. That division has no prospect of ever being profitable. It is a dinosaur that should have died a long time ago." How can Jake Ali be motivated to make a sustained effort to achieve General Projects' goal of maximizing companywide accounting rate of return?

26-13 Analysis of return on capital; comparisons of three companies. (Adapted from *N.A.A. Research Report No. 35*, pp. 34–35.)

1. Rate of return on capital is often expressed as follows:

$$\frac{\text{Income}}{\text{Invested capital}} = \frac{\text{Sales}}{\text{Invested capital}} \times \frac{\text{Income}}{\text{Sales}}$$

What advantages can you see in the breakdown of the computation into two separate components?

2. Fill in the blanks:

	COMPANIES IN SAME INDUSTRY		
	A	B	C
Sales	$1,000,000	$500,000	$ —
Income	100,000	50,000	—
Invested capital	500,000	—	5,000,000
Income as a percent of sales	—	—	0.5%
Turnover of invested capital	—	—	2
Return on invested capital	—	1%	—

After filling in the blanks, comment on the relative performance of these companies as thoroughly as the data permit.

26-14 Pricing, rate of return, and measuring efficiency. A large motorized bicycle company follows a pricing policy whereby "normal" or "standard" activity is used as a base for pricing. That is, prices are set on the basis of long-run annual-volume predictions. They are then rarely changed except for notable changes in wage rates or material prices.

You are given the following data:

Materials, wages, and other variable costs	$1,320 per unit
Fixed overhead	$300,000,000 per year
Desired rate of return on invested capital	20%
Normal volume	1,000,000 units
Invested capital	$900,000,000

Required

1. What net-income percentage based on dollar sales is needed to attain the desired rate of return?
2. What rate of return on invested capital will be earned at sales volumes of 1,500,000 and 500,000 units, respectively?
3. The company has a sizable management bonus plan based on yearly divisional performance. Assume that the volume was 1,000,000, 1,500,000, and 500,000 units, respectively, in three successive years. Each of three managers served as division manager for one year before being killed in an automobile accident. As the major heir of the third manager, comment on the bonus plan.

26-15 Analysis of return on invested assets, comparison of three divisions. Quality Products, Inc., is a major soft drink and food product company. It has three divisions: soft drinks, snack foods, and family restaurants. Results for the past three years are:

	SOFT DRINK DIVISION	SNACK FOODS DIVISION	RESTAURANT DIVISION	QUALITY PRODUCTS, INC.
Operating Revenues:				
19_1	$2,800	$2,000	$1,050	$5,850
19_2	3,000	2,400	1,250	6,650
19_3	3,600	2,600	1,530	7,730
Operating Income:				
19_1	$120	$360	$105	$585
19_2	160	400	114	674
19_3	240	420	100	760
Invested Assets:				
19_1	$1,200	$1,240	$ 800	$3,240
19_2	1,250	1,400	1,000	3,650
19_3	1,400	1,430	1,300	4,130

Required

Use the Du Pont method (p. 872) to explain changes in the operating income to invested assets ratio over the 19_1 to 19_3 period for the (a) Soft Drink Division, (b) Snack Foods Division, (c) Restaurant Division, and (d) Quality Products, Inc. Comment on the results.

26-16 ROI and residual income. (D. Solomons, adapted) Consider the following for General Electric Company (in $000s):

	DIVISION A	DIVISION B
Invested capital	$1,000	$5,000
Income	$200	$750
Return on investment	20%	15%

Required

1. Which is the more successful division? Why?
2. General Electric has used residual income as a measure of management success, the variable it wants a manager to maximize. *Residual income* is defined as income minus an imputed interest charge for invested capital. Using this criterion, what is the residual income for each division if the imputed interest rate is (a) 12%, (b) 14%, (c) 18%? Which division is more successful under each of these imputed interest rates?

26-17 ROI and residual income. (D. Kleespie) The Gaul Company produces and distributes a wide variety of recreational products. One of its divisions, the Goscinny Division, manufactures and sells "menhirs," which are very popular with cross-country skiers; the demand for these menhirs is relatively insensitive to price changes. The Goscinny Division is considered to be an investment center and in recent years has averaged a return on investment of 20%. The following data are available for the Goscinny Division and its product:

Total annual fixed costs	$1,000,000
Variable costs per menhir	$300
Average number of menhirs sold each year	10,000
Average operating assets invested in the division	$1,600,000

Required

1. What is the minimum per-unit selling price that the Goscinny Division should charge in order to avoid a negative performance rating for Mary Obelix, the division manager? (You may assume that the judgment of Obelix's performance is based on the division's ROI record.)
2. Assume that the Gaul Company's judgment of the performance of its investment center managers is based on the residual income rather than ROI as was assumed in requirement 1 above. The company's minimum acceptable earning rate is considered to be 15%. What is the minimum per-unit selling price that the Goscinny Division should charge in order to avoid a negative performance rating for Obelix?

26-18 Various measures of profitability. When the Coronet Company formed three divisions a year ago, the president told the division managers that an annual bonus would be paid to the most profitable division. However, absolute profit as conventionally computed would not be used. Instead the ranking would be affected by the relative investments in the three divisions. Options available include ROI and residual income; invested capital can be measured using gross book value or net book value. Each manager has now written a memorandum claiming entitlement to the bonus. The following data are available:

DIVISION	GROSS BOOK VALUE AT START OF YEAR	NET INCOME AS COMPUTED FOR CONVENTIONAL EXTERNAL ANNUAL REPORT COMPILATION
X	$400,000	$47,500
Y	380,000	46,000
Z	250,000	30,800

All the assets are fixed assets that were purchased ten years ago and have ten years of usefulness remaining. A zero terminal disposal value is predicted. The Coronet required rate of return on invested assets is 10%. All computations of annual return should be based on invested capital at the start of the year.

Required

Which method for computing profitability did each manager choose? Make your description specific and brief. Show supporting computations. Where applicable, assume straight-line depreciation.

26-19 ROI, Residual income, expansion decisions. (CMA) Lawton Industries has manufactured prefabricated houses for over 20 years. The houses are constructed in sections to be assembled on customers' lots.

Lawton expanded into the pre-cut housing market when it acquired Presser Company, one of its suppliers. In this market, various types of lumber are pre-cut into the appropriate lengths, banded into packages, and shipped to customers' lots for assembly. Lawton decided to maintain Presser's separate identity and thus established the Presser Division as an investment center of Lawton.

Lawton uses return on average investment (ROI) as a performance measure with investment defined as operating assets employed. Management bonuses are based in part on ROI. All investments in operating assets are expected to earn a minimum return of 15% before income taxes.

Presser's ROI has ranged from 19.3% to 22.1% since it was acquired in 19_1. Presser had an investment opportunity in 19_6 that had an estimated ROI of 18%. Presser's management decided against the investment because it believed the investment would decrease the division's overall ROI.

The 19_6 operating statement for Presser Division is presented below. The division's operating assets employed were $12,600,000 at the end of 19_6, a 5% increase over the 19_5 year-end balance.

Presser Division
Operating Statement
For The Year Ended December 31, 19_6
($000 omitted)

Sales revenue		$24,000
Cost of goods sold		15,800
Gross profit		$ 8,200
Operating expenses		
Administrative	$2,140	
Selling	3,600	5,740
Income from operations before income taxes		$ 2,460

Required

1. Calculate the following performance measures for 19_6 for the Presser Division of Lawton Enterprises:
   a. Return on average investment in operating assets employed (ROI).
   b. Residual income calculated on the basis of average operating assets employed.
2. Would the management of Presser Division have been more likely to accept the investment opportunity it had in 19_6 if residual income were used as a performance measure instead of ROI? Explain your answer.
3. The Presser Division is a separate investment center within Lawton Industries. Identify the items Presser must control if it is to be evaluated fairly by either the ROI or residual income performance measures.

26-20 ROI and residual income as performance measures, adoption of investment proposals. The budget of World Wide Brands for the coming year (19_9) includes the following items for its five divisions (in millions):

	OPERATING INCOME	IDENTIFIABLE ASSETS
Tobacco products	$528	$1,650
Hardware and security	40	400
Distilled beverages	66	300
Food products	32	200
Office products	20	400
	$686	$2,950

The manager of each division is paid a base salary plus a bonus that is positively related to the magnitude of the division's return on investment (defined as operating income divided by identifiable assets). World Wide Brands uses a uniform 12% required rate of return for new investments in all divisions.

The chief financial officer of World Wide Brands is very concerned about the current bonus scheme. Each division recently submitted its best investment proposal, based on a discounted cash-flow criterion; each had a positive net present value using the 12% required rate of return. The 19_9 increase in operating income and the increase in identifiable assets of each investment proposal is:

INVESTMENT PROPOSAL FROM DIVISION	19_9 INCREASE IN OPERATING INCOME	19_9 INCREASE IN IDENTIFIABLE ASSETS
Tobacco products	$120	$ 500
Hardware and security	26	200
Distilled beverages	38	200
Food products	9	50
Office products	14	100
	$207	$1,050

Required

1. How will adoption of the proposed investment by each division affect the 19_9 ROI (operating income divided by identifiable assets) of that division? Calculate the ROI of each division before the proposed investment, the ROI of the proposed investment, and ROI of the division including the proposed investment. Comment on the results.
2. How will adoption of the proposed investment by each division affect the 19_9 residual income of that division? In calculating residual income, a 12% imputed interest charge for identifiable assets is used. Calculate the residual income of each division before the proposed investment, the residual income of the proposed investment, and the residual income of the division including the proposed investment. Comment on the results.
3. The chief financial officer questions the reasonableness of the uniform required rate of return for all divisions. How might differences across divisions in their required rate of return be incorporated into accounting-based performance measures?

26-21 Alternative measures for the investment base of gasoline stations. Atlantic Richfield is having trouble in deciding whether to continue to use its old gasoline stations and in evaluating the performance of these stations and their managers in terms of return on investment. Top management has explored various ways of measuring invested capital for such stations:

a. *Historical cost:* original cost of land and buildings less accumulated depreciation (sometimes called net book value)
b. *Current cost:* cost to currently replace the services provided by the existing gasoline station
c. *Disposal value:* the current selling price

Information on three currently owned gasoline stations was collected to help clarify the issues:

	FRESNO STATION	LAS VEGAS STATION	MODESTO STATION
Operating income	$100,000	$120,000	$ 60,000
Historical cost of invested capital	$400,000	$200,000	$260,000
Current cost of invested capital	$640,000	$480,000	$290,000
Disposal value of invested capital	$600,000	$2,500,000	$300,000
Age	6 years old	15 years old	2 years old

The Las Vegas station is located next to the largest casino on the Las Vegas Strip and was purchased before the current boom in casinos. The current-cost estimate of the Las Vegas station is for a site one mile away from the existing site with equivalent ability in regard to the generation of operating income. The current-cost estimates for the Fresno and Modesto stations are for the same site as the existing station in each city.

1. Which of the three invested capital measures is relevant for deciding whether to dispose of any one or more of the currently owned gasoline stations? Why?
2. Compute the ratio of operating income to invested capital for the Fresno, Las Vegas, and Modesto stations under each of the three measures of investment.
3. Which of the three measures is applicable for judging the performance of a gasoline station as an investment activity?
4. Which of the three measures is applicable for judging the performance of the manager of a gasoline station? Is your answer the same as, or different from, your answers in requirements 1 and 3?
5. What measures of performance, in addition to ROI, might be used to evaluate the performance of a manager of a gasoline station?

26-22 ROI performance measures based on historical cost and current cost.   Mineral Waters Ltd. operates three divisions that process and bottle sparkling mineral water. The historical-cost accounting system reports the following for 1987 ($000s):

	CALISTOGA DIVISION	ALPINE SPRINGS DIVISION	ROCKY MOUNTAINS DIVISION
Revenues	$500	$ 700	$1,100
Operating expenses (excluding depreciation)	300	380	600
Depreciation	70	100	120
Operating income	$130	$ 220	$ 380
Current assets	$200	$ 250	$ 300
Fixed assets—plant	140	900	1,320
Total assets	$340	$1,150	$1,620

Mineral Waters estimates the useful life of each plant to be 12 years with zero terminal disposal value. The straight-line depreciation method is used. The respective age of each plant at the end of 1987 is Calistoga (10 years old), Alpine Springs (3 years old), and Rocky Mountains (1 year old).

An index of construction costs of plants for mineral water production for the ten-year period that Mineral Waters has been operating (1977 year-end = 100) is:

1977	1984	1986	1987
100	136	160	170

Given the high turnover of current assets, management believes that the historical-cost and current-cost measures of current assets are approximately the same.

1. Compute the ROI (operating income to total assets) ratio of each division using historical-cost measures. Comment on the results.
2. Use the approach in Exhibit 26-3 (p. 880) to compute the ROI of each division incorporating current-cost estimates as of 1987 for depreciation and fixed assets. Comment on the results.
3. What advantages might arise from using current-cost asset measures as compared with historical-cost measures for evaluating the performance of the managers of the three divisions?
4. What factors could explain the widespread inclusion of historical-cost data, and the limited inclusion of current-cost data, in routine internal reporting systems used for evaluating managerial performance?

26-23 Compound interest depreciation.   Study the Appendix to this chapter. A hospital X-ray department is considering investing in a machine costing $7,132 having an expected useful life of two years and no terminal disposal value. As compared with an existing machine, the new machine will save $4,000 in cash operating costs.

Required

1. Compute the internal rate of return.
2. Prepare a tabular comparison of the effect of the investment on operating income, using compound interest, straight-line, and sum-of-years'-digits depreciation for each of the two years. Also show the yearly rate of return on the beginning balance of the investment.
3. How closely do the answers in requirement 2 approximate the internal rate of return? Why do they differ?
4. Assume that compound interest depreciation is used. Compute the residual income in each of two years. Assume that the cash operating savings were (a) $4,000 in each year and (b) $4,500 in the first year and $3,800 in the second year.

26-24 ROI based on gross and net book value, compound interest depreciation. Study the Appendix to this chapter. The Ezra Company is considering investing $21,084 in plant and equipment having a four-year useful life and a terminal disposal value of zero. The operating cash savings with the plant and equipment are $2,000 in year 1, and $10,000 each year in years 2, 3 and 4. The internal rate of return, based on a discounted cash-flow analysis, is 16%. Ezra Company uses the straight-line depreciation method on plant and equipment. Ignore income taxes.

Required

1. Compute the predicted accrual accounting return on investment each year over the four-year useful life of the investment. Use (a) the gross book value of the plant and equipment as the investment base, and (b) the beginning net book value each year of the plant and equipment as the investment base. Comment on the results.
2. If the accrual accounting rate of return is used to evaluate management performance, why might a manager be reluctant to make the $21,084 investment in plant and equipment?
3. Compute the depreciation each year under the compound interest method of depreciation. Will the use of this depreciation method reduce the problem(s) noted in requirement 2?

26-25 ROI, compound interest depreciation. (CMA, adapted) Study the Appendix to this chapter. Peterdonn Corporation made a capital investment of $100,000 in new equipment two years ago. The analysis made at that time indicated the equipment would save $36,430 in operating expenses per year over a five-year period. The equipment has a zero terminal disposal value. Using a discounted cash-flow analysis, the internal rate of return on the equipment is 24%.

The department manager believed that the equipment had "lived up" to its expectations. However, the departmental report showing the overall return on investment (ROI) rate for the first year in which this equipment was used did not reflect as much improvement as had been expected. The department manager asked the accounting department to "break out" the figures related to this investment to find out why it did not contribute more to the department's ROI.

The accounting department was able to identify the equipment and its contribution to operations. The report presented to the department manager at the end of the first year is shown below.

Reduced operating expenses due to new equipment	$ 36,430
Less: Depreciation—20% of cost	20,000
Contribution before taxes	$ 16,430
Investment—beginning of year	$100,000
Investment—end of year	$ 80,000
Average investment for the year	$ 90,000

$$ROI = \frac{16,430}{90,000} = 18.26\%$$

The department manager was surprised that the ROI was less than 24% because the new equipment performed as expected. The staff analyst in the accounting department replied that the company ROI for performance evaluation differed from that used for capital investment analysis. The analyst commented that the discrepancy could be solved if the company used the compound interest method of depreciation for its performance evaluation reports.

Required

1. Discuss the reasons why the return on investment of 18.26% for the new equipment as calculated in the department's report by the accounting department differs from the 24% internal rate of return calculated at the time the machine was approved for purchase.

2. Compute the depreciation each year under the compound interest method of depreciation. Will this method solve the discrepancy as the analyst claims? Explain your answer.

3. Compute the predicted operating income to average investment ratio for each year of the investment. Explain how this predicted set of ROIs can be used to reduce the discrepancy between the DCF model used to choose projects and the accrual accounting ROI used to evaluate subsequent performance.

26-26 Alternative bonus schemes for a multiactivity firm, companywide bonus pool or separate division bonus pools, residual income. Consumer Products Inc. is one of the largest manufacturers and marketers of tobacco products in the world. Three years ago, as part of a diversification drive, two acquisitions were made:

1. High-Life Beverage, a major beer company
2. Maxwell Products, a major food products company

The table below provides information on the operating revenues, operating income, and invested assets of each of the three lines of business of Consumer Products Inc. for the 19_7 and 19_9 period.

Consumer Products: Operating Data (Millions)

	TOBACCO DIVISION	BEER DIVISION	FOOD PRODUCTS DIVISION	CONSUMER PRODUCTS INC.
Operating Revenues:				
19_7	$ 9,000	$3,200	$8,000	$20,200
19_8	10,000	3,000	8,300	21,300
19_9	10,500	2,900	8,600	22,000
Operating Income:				
19_7	$ 1,620	$ 224	$ 608	$ 2,452
19_8	2,100	120	731	2,951
19_9	2,625	87	675	3,387
Invested Assets:				
19_7	$ 5,300	$2,000	$3,800	$11,100
19_8	5,700	1,800	4,300	11,800
19_9	6,000	1,700	4,500	12,200

The current compensation scheme for senior executives covers all high-ranking managers (except the president, chief executive officer, and chief operating officer of Consumer Products Inc.). The following table shows the number of senior executives covered by the current scheme:

YEAR	TOBACCO DIVISION	BEER DIVISION	FOOD PRODUCTS DIVISION	TOTAL
19_7	280	80	140	500
19_8	320	80	150	550
19_9	350	75	175	600

A key component of the current compensation scheme is the annual bonus award. All senior executives share equally in a bonus pool that is calculated as 10% of the annual residual income (if positive) of Consumer Products Inc. Residual income is defined as operating income of Consumer Products Inc. minus an imputed interest charge of 14% of invested assets of Consumer Products Inc.

Required

1. Using the Du Pont approach (see page 872), explain differences over the 19_7 to 19_9 period in the profitability of Consumer Products Inc. and in each of its three individual divisions.
2. Compute the size of the annual bonus pool to be shared by the senior executives of Consumer Products Inc. each year of the 19_7 to 19_9 period under the current compensation scheme. Compute the annual bonus to be paid to each senior executive in the 19_7 to 19_9 period.
3. The president of the Tobacco Division proposes that the annual bonus pool be calculated for each division separately. Compute the annual bonus to be paid to each senior executive of each division in the 19_7 to 19_9 period if the bonus pool is defined as 10% of division residual income (if positive); division residual income is defined as division operating income minus an imputed interest charge of 14% of invested assets of the division. Comment on the results.
4. Discuss the pros and cons to Consumer Products Inc. of basing the bonus pool on the residual income of the company as a whole as compared with the residual income of each division.

26-27 Performance evaluation using historical-cost, current-cost, and present value measures. Embassy Hotels Inc. is a privately held company operating in the lodging and gambling (gaming) industry. The accompanying exhibit details the number of wholly owned, partially owned, managed, franchised, and gambling hotels of Embassy Hotels over the 19_1 to 19_7 period.

The existing bonus scheme for senior executives is based on net income computed using historical-cost accounting rules; 10% of historical-cost net income is set up as a bonus pool that is allocated among the top 20 executives of Embassy Hotels.

Embassy Hotels Inc.: Operating Data

	19_1	19_2	19_3	19_4	19_5	19_6	19_7
Number of Properties at Year-end							
Wholly owned or leased	15	15	14	14	13	11	11
Partially owned	14	14	15	14	13	13	14
Managed	17	15	16	19	23	22	23
Franchised	145	163	171	188	194	204	218
Gambling	2	2	3	3	3	3	4
Percentage of Occupancy							
Hotels owned or managed	71	69	65	61	60	64	64
Gambling	86	81	81	72	80	84	86
Total Revenues ($millions)	$1,026	$1,114	$1,196	$1,238	$1,345	$1,479	$1,562
Long-Term Debt ($millions)	125	121	120	180	242	276	284
Shareholders' Equity ($millions)							
Historical cost	389	459	533	569	634	593	651
Current cost	712	848	1,083	1,182	1,295	1,362	1,405
Present value	1,582	1,942	2,134	2,048	2,251	2,304	2,362
Net Income ($millions)							
Historical cost	99	106	113	83	113	114	100
Current cost	75	93	94	62	53	69	84

For internal reporting purposes, Embassy Hotels collects information using the historical-cost, current-cost, and present value measures:

Historical cost: Depreciation is based on original cost and is computed using the straight-line method with the following estimated useful lives: buildings and improvements—average of approximately 44 years; leasehold improvements—the remaining lives of existing leases; furniture and equipment—average of eight years.

Current cost: Current costs of property and equipment are based on replacement cost and are based primarily on appraisals made by professional appraisers. No adjustment is made for inventories due to their high turnover rate, which results in current costs being reflected in the historical-cost financial statements.

Present value: Arrived at by "calculating the present worth of estimated future income streams accruing to the owner utilizing rates of return ranging from 9% to 12%, and various terms of financing and conditions of sale and profitability factors with respect to individual properties." As an example, the value of one property was based on a ten-year horizon period. The future annual revenues and future annual expenses for the property were predicted and then used to calculate the "most probable net operating income and pretax cash flow to be generated by the property." An estimate of the residual value of the property at the end of the tenth year was also made. The discount rate was that "yield which would attract a prudent investor to a property with comparable degrees of risk, non-liquidity, and management burdens." Embassy Hotels employed outside appraisal companies to derive the present value measures.

Embassy Hotels calculated shareholders' equity under each of the historical-cost, current-cost, and present value measures. Net income was computed using the historical-cost and current-cost measures. The exhibit on p. 901 reports this information for each of the most recent seven years.

The difference between shareholders' equity using present value and shareholders' equity using historical cost was termed *revaluation equity*. Details of changes in revaluation equity over the 19_1 to 19_7 period are:

	19_1	19_2	19_3	19_4	19_5	19_6	19_7
Balance, January 1	$ 895	$1,193	$1,483	$1,601	$1,479	$1,617	$1,711
Increase:							
Operating properties and others	211	188	62	(113)	123	6	(77)
Management and franchise agreements	28	31	35	47	22	74	76
Other	59	71	21	(56)	(7)	14	1
Total	298	290	118	(122)	138	94	0
Balance, December 31	$1,193	$1,483	$1,601	$1,479	$1,617	$1,711	$1,711

The decline in present value in 19_4 was associated with a "protracted recession that brought about a decline in business, leisure, and international travel as well as reduction in the Nevada gambling market."

1. Use the Du Pont approach (see page 872) to explain changes in the net income to shareholders' equity ratio of Embassy Hotels over the 19_1 to 19_7 period based on (a) the historical-cost and (b) the current-cost measures. Use the year-end measure of shareholders' equity as the denominator. Comment on the results.
2. Assume that the annual change in the present value of shareholders' equity is defined as income under the present value measure. Compute the net income to shareholders' equity (measured at year-end present value) ratio of Embassy Hotels over the 19_2 to 19_7 period. Compare the results with the numbers derived in requirement 1.
3. Why might differences arise between the (a) historical-cost, (b) current-cost, and (c) present value measures of shareholders' equity? Compare and contrast the costs of developing the (a), (b), and (c) measures.
4. What asset measures would be appropriate for evaluating existing individual hotels as activities?
5. What asset measures would be appropriate for evaluating the managers of individual hotels? What nonfinancial measures might also be appropriate for evaluating the manager of each hotel?
6. Critique the existing bonus scheme for senior executives.

26-28 Consulting engagements for university professors, alternative incentive fee arrangements. Strategic Horizons Group (SHG) is a management consulting firm with offices in ten different cities. SHG provides a broad range of consulting services in the profit and nonprofit sectors. It was originally set up by four university professors to coordinate their consulting activities. In the next twenty years SHG retained a close connection with professors at many universities. Over this same twenty years, SHG also built up the professional status of its own staff. The average revenues to SHG per consulting assignment are currently over $100,000, independent of the payments made to university professors.

Each university professor can receive compensation from SHG in either one or both of two forms:

1. Hourly rate. This rate is set by each professor and is charged out to clients as a direct cost of each project. These costs are not included in the staff billings SHG reports for each project.
2. Attribution fee. This fee is designed by SHG to provide professors with a monetary incentive to include SHG in their consulting activities. An attribution fee is paid on those projects for which a professor is the initial source of the contact (or for which the client hires SHG, conditional on that professor's being the academic member of the project team). The attribution fee is paid irrespective of whether the professor is a member of the project team.

The existing attribution scheme bases the fee on the following formula:

$$\frac{\text{Income of SHG in 19\_X}}{\text{Revenues of SHG in 19\_X}} \times \text{SHG staff billings on projects initiated by professor}$$

SHG staff billings are calculated as total billings to the client minus the billings of the professor included in the total billings.

Bob Davis, a professor at Academic University, has worked on many SHG project teams in the last ten years. Davis's expertise includes the design of executive compensation plans for senior executives; all of his projects are managed by an SHG vice-president at its San Francisco office.

The income to revenue ratio of SHG (companywide) and of the San Francisco office for each of the past five years is:

	19_4	19_5	19_6	19_7	19_8
SHG	.14	.16	.18	.12	.07
San Francisco	.19	.21	.22	.18	.16

The San Francisco office specializes in consulting for litigation work and in executive compensation plan design; both specialties are highly profitable consulting areas for SHG.

Columns (1) to (7) in the exhibit at the bottom of this page presents Davis's compensation report for the 19_4 to 19_8 period. Column (8) of the exhibit reports the operating income ratio for each project in the compensation report:

Project operating income ratio =

$$\frac{\text{SHG staff billings on project} - \text{Identifiable project cost}}{\text{SHG staff billings on project}}$$

SHG has had a policy of not disclosing the operating income ratio of each project to its university associates. The identifiable project costs do not include the hourly fees paid to a professor or the attribution fees paid if a professor is the source of the project.

Davis was upset when he received the 19_8 $11,200 attribution fee ($3,500 for Project L and $7,700 for Project M). He was expecting at least $20,000. The 19_8 income to revenue ratio of 7% for SHG was an unpleasant surprise.

SHG's chief financial officer informed Davis that the large drop in the income to revenue ratio in 19_8 was because of three main factors: (1) high development costs in opening SHG offices in London and Paris, (2) several large-cost overruns on fixed fee contracts (of which Davis was *not* a member), and (3) the bankruptcies of two clients of the New York office of SHG, leaving large write-offs for unpaid billings.

Davis called Carolyn Harper, the president of SHG, to complain about the formula currently used to compute the attribution fee. Harper's response to Davis was, "What took you so long to complain, Bob? In the last two weeks, twenty-seven other professors have chewed my ear off about the current formula." She asked for Davis's advice on redesigning the existing attribution scheme.

Davis collected data that indicated that the percentage of SHG's projects sourced by university professors was 100% in its first two years of existence. Over the last five years, this percentage has declined from 55% to 42%.

Five-Year Compensation Report from SHG to Bob Davis

(1) PROJECT	(2) DAVIS AS SOURCE OF PROJECT INITIATION	(3) TOTAL BILLINGS TO CLIENT	(4) BILLINGS OF DAVIS TO CLIENT	(5) SHG STAFF BILLINGS	(6) SHG INCOME TO REVENUE RATIO	(7) = (5) × (6) ATTRIBUTION PAYMENT TO DAVIS	(8) OPERATING INCOME RATIO OF PROJECT
19_4:A	YES	$130,000	$15,000	$115,000	.14	$16,100	.48
19_4:B	NO	70,000	30,000	40,000	.14	—	.40
19_5:C	NO	80,000	20,000	60,000	.16	—	.34
19_5:D	YES	50,000	20,000	30,000	.16	4,800	.39
19_5:E	YES	100,000	—	80,000	.16	12,800	.42
19_6:F	NO	40,000	10,000	30,000	.18	—	.24
19_6:G	YES	160,000	30,000	130,000	.18	23,400	.38
19_7:H	YES	300,000	10,000	290,000	.12	34,800	.46
19_7:I	NO	200,000	20,000	180,000	.12	—	.35
19_7:J	YES	210,000	—	160,000	.12	19,200	.43
19_8:K	NO	150,000	20,000	130,000	.07	—	.29
19_8:L	YES	80,000	30,000	50,000	.07	3,500	.36
19_8:M	YES	120,000	10,000	110,000	.07	7,700	.42

1. What is the purpose of the attribution fee? Would you recommend that SHG continue to include an "attribution fee" in the compensation paid to university professors?
2. What information would you collect for evaluating whether the current attribution scheme needed changing?
3. Assume that SHG decides to continue the attribution fee concept. What criteria should it use in deciding on the specific scheme to be adopted?
4. Using the criteria in requirement 3, evaluate the following alternative schemes put forward for consideration by Davis:
    a. The existing attribution fee scheme based on SHG's companywide income to revenue ratio.
    b. Attribution fee is a fixed percentage (say 14%) of SHG's staff billings on professor-initiated projects.
    c. Attribution fee is a percentage of SHG's staff billings on professor-initiated projects, where the percentage is the maximum of (i) 10% or (ii) SHG's companywide income to revenue ratio.
    d. Same as (c) except that (ii) is the income to revenue ratio of the SHG office at which the professor-initiated project is managed.
    e. Attribution fee is a fixed percentage (say 50%) of the operating income to SHG on each professor-initiated project; operating income on a project is SHG's staff billings on the project minus the identifiable project costs.

26-29 Designing a compensation scheme for unit restaurant managers of McDonald's Corporation. (Comprehensive review of Chapter 26 and Appendix to Chapter 25). The chief operating officer of McDonald's Corporation is considering changes in the compensation package of the manager of each of its company-owned restaurants. The history of McDonald's dates back to 1955 whey Ray Kroc opened the first restaurant in the chain. It is now the largest chain of restaurants in the world serving fast food. A recent annual report included the following comments in a section headed "The McDonald's restaurants: Where technology meets Q.S.C. and V." (*Q.S.C. and V.* stands for quality, service, cleanliness, and value):

> In the tradition of entrepreneurial giants, Ray Kroc built a new type of production system. McDonald's took the guesswork out of the foodservice business by applying procedures that geometrically increased productivity while ensuring quality and an enjoyable eating-out experience. The secret of McDonald's success, one expert claimed, was "the rapid delivery of a uniform high-quality mix of prepared foods in an environment of obvious courtesy." The secret, claimed another expert, was McDonald's ability to initiate and maintain its quality control systems through a network of hardworking, dedicated franchisees, and company employees.

McDonald's maintains a year-round training program for all levels of operations. The central training center is Hamburger University at Elk Grove, Illinois. Managers of company-owned restaurants must take an intensive course at Hamburger University at which the Q.S.C. and V. system of values is emphasized (and emphasized, and emphasized . . .).

The options regarding the unit manager compensation scheme that the chief operating officer was considering included the following.

OPTION A: The existing plan in which the unit manager's annual compensation consisted of (1) a base salary and (2) a quarterly bonus that rewarded the ability to meet preset objectives in the areas of (i) labor costs, (ii) food and paper costs, (iii) Q.S.C. and V., and (iv) volume projections.

1. The fixed salary: After surveying each market in which it owned restaurants, McDonald's established three salary ranges according to prevailing labor rates and other

economic factors. Range I, the highest, usually applied to very large metropolitan areas; Range II applied to somewhat smaller areas where industrial and rural influences on the labor market were about equal; and Range III applied to small-town markets with little industrial influence. In addition, annual merit increases were awarded within each range according to whether an employee was judged superior, satisfactory, or still in the new employee bracket.

2. The bonus: Meeting the optimal labor crew expenses—figured according to projected sales volume and labor crew needs for each month of the quarter—entitled the manager to a bonus of 5% of the base salary.

Together the area supervisor and the unit manager determined the food and paper cost objective based on current wholesale prices, product mix, and other operating factors peculiar to the unit. By meeting the previously agreed objective, the manager earned another 5% bonus.

The accompanying exhibit on p. 907 is an excerpt from the monthly management visitation report by which each store's Q.S.C. and V. is rated. Based on the average score for the quarter, units were designated "A," "B," or "C." Managers of "A" stores received a bonus of 10% of base salary; "B" store managers, 5%; and "C" store managers, no bonus.

In addition, the manager received a bonus of 2.5% of the increase over the previous year's sales, up to 10% of the base salary. If unit volume was significantly affected by operating circumstances beyond the manager's control, the regional manager could grant a semiannual payout of 5% of base salary.

Therefore the maximum annual incentive bonus to an "A" store manager who met all the objectives was 20% of the base salary plus an additional 10% of the salary because of the volume gain at the restaurant.

Bonuses for meeting cost objectives were paid quarterly, while those for meeting the Q.S.C. and V. standards and volume increases were paid semiannually.

A group of the unit managers protested that the existing plan was much too complicated. Some managers also complained about its undue subjectivity and the overemphasis on volume increases.

OPTION B: The unit manager's base salary would initially be determined according to the range system described in Option A. Thereafter the manager would be rated monthly by the regional operations staff on six factors: quality, service, cleanliness, training ability, volume, and profit. Each factor would be rated 0 for unsatisfactory, 1 for satisfactory, and 2 for outstanding. A manager whose semiannual total is 12 would warrant a bonus of 40% of the base salary for half a year, a score of 11 would warrant a 35% bonus, and so on. At the end of the year, the two semiannual scores would be averaged and the manager would receive a salary increase of 12% for a score of 12, 11% for a score of 11, and so on, down to a point where the manager would presumably be encouraged to seek a future with a competitor.

OPTION C: The unit manager's base salary would be determined by the range system in Option A. The bonus would be 10% of any sales gain plus 20% of the income (provided that gross profit amounted to at least 10% of the gross sales). The maximum bonus paid would be 50% of the base salary.

A survey of the compensation schemes used by competitors of McDonald's Corporation led to several other options being included in the analysis:

OPTION D: The unit manager's compensation scheme has a relatively low base salary with a six-month bonus of 10% of any sales gain above the previous highest six-month sales level. There is no restriction on the size of the bonus paid.

OPTION E: The unit manager's compensation scheme has a relatively low base salary with a six-month bonus of 20% of the operating income of the restaurant. There is no restriction on the size of the bonus pool.

OPTION F: The unit manager is paid a high base salary, which is based on the prior year's sales of the restaurant. No bonus scheme is included in the compensation package. Above-average performers can seek promotions to manage restaurants with higher sales levels.

Required	**1.** What criteria should the chief operating officer of McDonald's Corporation consider when designing a compensation plan for the managers of its individual restaurants?
	2. Using the criteria that you listed in requirement 1, evaluate the six (A–F) compensation scheme options outlined in this problem.
	3. Which plan would you recommend that the chief operating officer of McDonald's adopt? (You are not restricted to the six options outlined in this problem.)

EXTRACT FROM VISITATION REPORT

Question No.	SECTION I (Outside)	Item Score
1.	Is area within one block of the store free of all litter?	
2.	Are flags being displayed properly and are they in good condition? Are entrance and exit and road signs in excellent condition?	
3.	Are waste receptacles in an excellent state of repair and clean? Is trash being emptied as necessary?	
4.	Is the parking lot and landscaping as clean, litter-free, and well picked up as you could reasonably expect for this business period? Do these areas reflect an excellent maintenance program? Is traffic pattern well controlled?	
5.	Do the sidewalks surrounding the building and the exterior of the building reflect an excellent maintenance program? Were these areas being maintained properly during this visit?	
6.	Were all inside and outside lights which should have been on, on, and were windows clean?	
	SECTION TOTAL	

Question No.	SECTION II (Inside Store Pre-Purchase of Food)	Item Score
7.	Was the restroom properly maintained? Was the inside lobby and dining area properly maintained?	
8.	Does point of promotion in the store present a unified theme?	
9.	Is menu board in excellent repair and clean? Are napkins and straws available near all registers?	
10.	Is the general appearance of all stations good? Is all stainless steel properly maintained?	
11.	Is there an adequate number of crew and management people working for this business period and are they positioned properly?	
12.	Are all crew members wearing proper McDonald's uniforms, properly groomed, and does their general conduct present a good image?	
13.	Are all counter persons using the Six Step Method and does their serving time per customer meet McDonald's standards?	
	SECTION TOTAL	

907

Question No.	SECTION IV (After Food Order)	Item Score
14.	Was the sub total, tax, and total charged to you exactly correct and did you receive the correct change?	
15.	Was your order placed properly in the proper size bag, on the correct tray, and did the total packaging appear neat? Was the bag double folded?	
16.	Was the Production Caller controlling production properly?	
17.	Did sandwiches appear neat and do they reflect that the prescribed operational procedures were used when preparing the food?	
18.	Were all sandwiches hot and tasty?	
19.	Were your fries a full portion, hot, and did they meet finished fry standards?	
20.	Did all soft drinks, shakes, or coffee meet McDonald's standards?	
	SECTION TOTAL	

27

Accounting Systems and Internal Control

Overview of internal control • Examples of internal control breakdowns •
Forces operating to promote internal control • Legislation relating to internal control •
Reporting relationships within organizations • Checklist of internal control •
Control of inventories in retailing

A corporation overcharged the government on a contract. An executive overstated
a division's sales. White-collar crime is higher than ever. These types of news stories
appear frequently. Their common denominator is the alleged breakdown or failure of an internal control system. Questions are invariably raised as to whether top
management knew, or should have known, about the alleged overcharging, manipulation, or fraud. **Internal control is a central responsibility of top management.**

The systems and techniques for implementing internal control are aimed
mainly at improving the accountability for actions, the accuracy and reliability of
records, the safeguarding of assets, and the overall efficiency of operations. This
chapter explains internal control, with emphasis on its role in a management control system.[1]

---

[1]Internal control is covered in other accounting books, such as C. Horngren and G. Sundem,
Introduction to Financial Accounting, 3rd ed. (Englewood Cliffs, N.J.: Prentice-Hall, 1987),
Chap. 8; and A. Arens and J. Loebbecke, *Auditing*, 3rd ed. (Englewood Cliffs, N.J.: Prentice-
Hall, 1984).

Definition of internal control

Internal control is the set of accounting and administrative controls and practices that helps ensure that approved and appropriate decisions are made in an organization. This definition is broader than some advanced in the literature.[2] Note especially that it includes both accounting control and administrative control:

1. **Accounting control** comprises the methods and procedures that are mainly concerned with the authorization of transactions, the safeguarding of assets, and the accuracy of the accounting records. Good accounting controls help *increase* efficiency; they help *decrease* waste, unintentional errors, and fraud.
2. **Administrative control** comprises the plan of organization (for example, the formal organization chart concerning who reports to whom) and all methods and procedures that help management planning and control of operations. Examples are departmental budgeting procedures and performance reports.

This chapter focuses on internal accounting controls; internal administrative controls have been covered in previous chapters of this book (see especially Chapters 1, 5, 11, 25, and 26).

Importance of internal control

Regardless of an organization's size or type, and whether it is held privately or publicly, managers and accountants should know the rudiments of its accounting systems and controls. **Accounting serves a variety of purposes. A major purpose is to help managers operate their organizations more efficiently and effectively.** Any person who forms a business soon discovers that recordkeeping is absolutely essential. For instance, records of receivables and payables must be maintained for transactions with customers and creditors, and cash receipts and disbursements must be traced to the individual accounts. Even the simplest organizations must have some records. The cost-benefit test is easily met. Unless orderly compilation occurs, intolerable chaos results. In short, an accounting system is a wise business investment.

An **accounting system** is a set of records, procedures, and equipment that *routinely* deals with the events affecting the financial performance and position of the organization. The focus of the accounting system is on repetitive, voluminous transactions, which generally fall into four categories:

1. Cash disbursements
2. Cash receipts
3. Purchases of products and services, including employee payroll
4. Sales of products and services

This chapter emphasizes the *general* features of accounting systems. The purpose here is not to develop skills as a systems designer, but to develop an acquaintance with the scope and nature of accounting systems and controls. **No manager or would-be manager can afford the risks of not knowing the primary attributes of a suitable internal control system.**

---

[2]For a discussion of the broadening responsibilities of internal auditors, see R. Mautz, P. Tiessen, and R. Colson, *Internal Auditing: Directions and Opportunities* (Altamonte Springs, Fla.: Institute of Internal Auditors, 1985).

This section illustrates two categories of breakdowns in an internal control system: (1) undetected fraud and (2) managers misrepresenting the timing, amount, or intent of transactions in the accounting records, which are not discovered by the internal control system.

Types of fraud

Fraud involves taking something of value from someone else through deceit. A survey of internal auditors in the electric and gas utility industry reported the following types of fraud in order of frequency of occurrence:[3]

1. Theft of cash
2. Theft of material and supplies
3. Theft of gas or electricity services
4. Expense reports overstated or falsified
5. Payroll-related falsification or theft
6. Collusion between an employee and a vendor
7. Kickbacks to contractors or vendors
8. Erroneous or improper contractor billings

Numerous examples of fraud can be found in law cases. A subsequent section of this chapter outlines a checklist that can be used to reduce the likelihood of fraud occurring.

Cooking the books

An important aspect of internal control is ensuring the integrity of the reported accounting numbers. Documented instances where management has misrepresented the timing, amount, or intent of transactions have been given much publicity in the financial press. Phrases such as "cooking the books" and "paper entrepreneurialism" have been used to describe these instances.

One publicized instance involved McCormick & Company, a diversified specialty U.S. food company with products (such as spices) sold in over eighty countries. This case focused on the padding of the sales and net income. Exhibit 27-1 lists the reported and restated results for a four-year period investigated by the audit committee of McCormick's board of directors.[4] The investigation focused on the Grocery Products Division of McCormick. Among the practices disclosed by the audit committee were the following:

Sales Related
- Recognizing as sales of the current year items "picked and staged" but not shipped.
- Recognizing as sales of the current year items "picked and staged" after midnight on the last day of the fiscal year.
- Altering shipping documents to attribute sales to an earlier period.

---

[3]T. Agee, "Fraud Challenges in the Utility Industry," *Internal Auditor,* December 1984, pp. 34–38. Numerous examples of fraud are cited in W. Albrecht, K. Howe, and M. Romney, *Deterring Fraud: The Internal Auditor's Perspective* (Altamonte Springs, Fla.: Institute of Internal Auditors Research Foundation, 1984); and J. Bologna, *Corporate Fraud: The Basics of Prevention and Fraud* (Boston: Butterworth Publishers, 1984).

[4]This information is from the Form 8-K that *McCormick & Company, Incorporated,* filed with the Securities and Exchange Commission on May 27, 1982.

EXHIBIT 27-1

McCormick & Company: Reported and Restated Results (000,000s)

	19_1	19_2	19_3	19_4
Net sales as previously reported	$355.151	$400.357	$457.165	$547.966
Net reduction resulting from restatement	5.469	8.270	13.668	20.365
Net sales as restated	$349.682	$392.087	$443.497	$527.601
Net income as previously reported	$ 14.816	$ 16.735	$ 19.430	$ 14.840
Correction of accounting for certain customer allowances and sales	(0.919)	(2.366)	(1.117)	(2.184)
Correction of accounting for advertising and other expenses	(0.458)	0.218	(0.284)	(1.067)
Income tax effect	0.676	1.099	0.680	1.607
Net income as restated	$ 14.115	$ 15.686	$ 18.709	$ 13.196

Expense Related

- Understating allowances to customers to reduce the reported expenses of the current period.
- Delaying the internal processing of sales allowances until next period.
- Deferring the recognition of advertising expenses (via the advertising agency delaying its billing or via the altering of invoices to conceal earlier billing dates).

Other documented instances of division managers "cooking the books" were reported at PepsiCo (see Problem 27-24) and H. J. Heinz (see Problem 27-25).

A survey of reported cases of division managers "cooking the books" found several common factors:[5]

1. The companies operated with a high level of decentralization; there was little oversight by corporate headquarters of the auditing, accounting, and internal controls at each division.
2. Top management set financial goals for each division without advance communication with division managers about the realism of the goals.
3. Division managers perceived that the accounting and auditing aspects of running a business were of minor importance.
4. There was a team spirit among the division employees that led them to ignore any personal misgivings about the acceptability of the practices.

FORCES OPERATING TO PROMOTE INTERNAL CONTROL

Forces that promote internal control within an organization include (a) the board of directors, audit committee, and top management, (b) performance and reward criteria, (c) codes of conduct and ethics, (d) internal and external audit procedures, and (e) legal requirements.

[5]J. Treadway, "Unsound Financial Reporting—Pressures That Cause Companies To Stray" (Address to Georgia Bar Association, Atlanta, February 7, 1985).

Board of directors, audit committee, and top management

The board of directors must monitor the actions taken by top management of the organization. **The board should urge top management to send clearcut signals that any attempts to undermine the internal control system will not be tolerated.**

Many companies have an audit committee that assists the board of directors. The objective of the audit committee is to oversee the accounting controls, financial statements, and financial affairs of the corporation. The committee represents the full board and provides personal contact and communication among the board, the external auditors, the internal auditors, the financial executives, and the operating executives.[6]

Audit committees typically are composed of three or more "outside" board members. Not being everyday employees of the company, outside board members are usually considered to be more independent than the "inside" directors, who, as employees, also serve as part of the corporation's management. The New York Stock Exchange now requires, as a condition for initial and continued listing, the establishment of an audit committee; the membership of this committee is restricted to directors independent of management.

Performance and reward criteria

What performance evaluation criteria and reward criteria are used for employees? Are performance evaluations and rewards closely linked? Employers' choice of these criteria give important signals about internal control. For example, suppose promotion is based on results alone. The ends, not the means, are senior management's primary concern. Rewards are given accordingly. Such a company "culture" may induce year-end accounting manipulations and perhaps even bribes and kickbacks. In contrast, suppose senior management demotes or terminates the employment of individuals found violating internal control guidelines. Such actions establish a culture in which both accounting and administrative control gain high status within the organization.

Codes of conduct and ethics

Codes of "Business Conduct" are circulated in some organizations to signal appropriate or inappropriate individual behaviors. An illustration is Caterpillar Tractor's "Code of Worldwide Business Conduct and Operating Principles":

> The law is a floor. Ethical business conduct should normally exist at a level well above the minimum required by law. . . . Caterpillar employees shall not accept costly entertainment or gifts (excepting mementos and novelties of nominal value) from dealers, suppliers and others with whom we do business. And we won't tolerate circumstances that produce, or reasonably appear to produce, conflict between personal interests of an employee and interests of the company.

An example of a potential conflict of interest occurs when Caterpillar employees are also the owners of a supplier firm. Such employees would tend to favor purchasing services from their own firms and not make concerted efforts to locate the lowest-cost suppliers that can meet Caterpillar's quality requirements.

---

[6]For background on the development of audit committees, see J. Samet and J. Sherman, "The Audit Committee: In Search of a Purpose," *Corporation Law Review*, Winter 1984, pp. 42–55. The activities of the audit committee of one company (South Central Bell) are discussed in M. Jenkins and L. Robinson, "The Corporate Audit Committee," *Management Accounting*, December 1985, pp. 31–35.

The National Association of Accountants (NAA) has published a set of *Standards of Ethical Conduct for Management Accountants:*

> Management accountants have an obligation to the organizations they serve, their profession, the public, and themselves to maintain the highest standards of ethical conduct.

The NAA standards cover five areas: competence, confidentiality, integrity, objectivity, and resolution of ethical conflict. Exhibit 27-2 presents an extract from the standard covering resolution of ethical conflict.

Internal and external audit procedures

Internal auditors are full-time employees of the organization being audited. External auditors are also called independent auditors or outside auditors because they are public accountants hired for a fee to issue their independent opinion regarding financial statements. A survey of corporate audit costs reported that the ratio of internal audit costs to external audit costs for a broad set of U.S. corporations was 1.73.[7]

Internal auditors have several roles: first, monitor the existing system of accounting and administrative controls; second, identify areas where improvements in existing controls might be made; third, investigate alleged breakdowns in the existing system.

EXHIBIT 27-2
Extract from NAA Standard Covering "Resolution of Ethical Conflict"

When faced with significant ethical issues, management accountants should follow the established policies of the organization bearing on the resolution of such conflict. If these policies do not resolve the ethical conflict, management accountants should consider the following courses of action:

- Discuss such problems with the immediate superior except when it appears that the superior is involved, in which case the problem should be presented initially to the next higher managerial level. If satisfactory resolution cannot be achieved when the problem is initially presented, submit the issues to the next higher managerial level.

  If the immediate superior is the chief executive officer, or equivalent, the acceptable reviewing authority may be a group such as the audit committee, executive committee, board of directors, board of trustees, or owners. Contact with levels above the immediate superior should be initiated only with the superior's knowledge, assuming the superior is not involved.
- Clarify relevant concepts by confidential discussion with an objective advisor to obtain an understanding of possible courses of action.
- If the ethical conflict still exists after exhausting all levels of internal review, the management accountant may have no other resource on significant matters than to resign from the organization and to submit an informative memorandum to an appropriate representative of the organization.

Except where legally prescribed, communication of such problems to authorities or individuals not employed or engaged by the organization is not considered appropriate.

SOURCE: *Statement on Management Accounting,* Standards of Ethical Conduct for Management Accountants *(Montvale, N.J.: National Association of Accountants, 1983).*

---

[7] D. Garner, "Internal Auditing—A Growth Profession," *Internal Auditor,* April 1985, pp. 39–41.

External auditors are mainly concerned with the financial statements of a company as a whole; however, these auditors also make an important contribution by detecting weak points in the existing system of accounting controls.

Legal requirements

Specific provisions of enacted legislation impose responsibilities on management and restrictions on their behavior. Two examples described in the next section are the *Foreign Corrupt Practices Act* and the *Federal Managers' Financial Integrity Act*. The provisions of the civil and criminal legal codes can also guide management behavior; for example, theft of property can be punished by fines or imprisonment. Management will not seek prosecution of alleged legal violations in all cases. Sometimes the employee may be confronted with the allegations and merely discharged. Some organizations require that employees sign a statement annually indicating that they are aware of specific laws (e.g., those outlawing restrictive pricing agreements) and that they have complied with those laws when conducting the business of the organization.

LEGISLATION RELATING TO INTERNAL CONTROL

Foreign Corrupt Practices Act

In the mid-1970s, many U.S. multinational corporations disclosed illegal political contributions, bribes, kickbacks, and other improprieties. In part because of these disclosures, the U.S. Congress passed the *Foreign Corrupt Practices Act* (FCPA). The title is misleading because the act's provisions pertain to the internal control systems of all publicly held companies, *even if they do no business outside the United States*. (A former chairman of the Securities and Exchange Commission commented: "If this act were a prospectus, the issuer would be jailed for using a misleading title.")

The **Foreign Corrupt Practices Act** contains not only specific prohibitions against bribery and other corrupt practices but also requirements (a) for maintaining accounting records in reasonable detail and accuracy and (b) for maintaining an appropriate system of internal accounting controls. These responsibilities are now explicitly codified as part of a federal U.S. law!

Under the FCPA, public reporting on the adequacy of internal control has become an explicit responsibility of management. Consequently, management in general, not just accountants, has focused on systems of internal control as never before. Boards of directors can assure themselves of compliance with the FCPA and with SEC requirements by (a) obtaining far more documentation of a system than previously existed and (b) compiling written evidence of management's evaluation and ongoing review of a system. The biggest impact of the FCPA has been the mandatory documentation of the evaluation of internal control by management.

The documentation should systematically refer to (a) management's cost-benefit choices regarding the system and (b) management's evaluation of how well the system is working. Documentation includes memos, minutes of meetings discussing the FCPA and internal control concepts with all affected individuals, written statements of intention to comply, flow charts, procedure manuals, and the like. Moreover, there should be a written program for ongoing review and evaluation of the system. Finally, there should be letters from external auditors stating that they found no material weaknesses in internal control during their audit, or that necessary improvements have been made.

The act specifies that internal accounting controls should provide reasonable assurance concerning:

1. *Authorization.* Transactions are executed in accordance with management's general or specific intentions.
2. *Recording.* All authorized transactions are recorded in the correct amounts, periods, and accounts. No fictitious transactions are recorded.
3. *Safeguarding.* Precautions and procedures appropriately restrict access to assets.
4. *Reconciliation.* Records are compared with other independently kept records and physical counts. Such comparisons help ensure that other control objectives are attained.
5. *Valuation.* Recorded amounts are periodically reviewed for impairment of values and necessary write-downs.

The first three objectives—authorization, recording, and safeguarding—relate to establishing the system of accountability and are aimed at *prevention* of errors and irregularities. The other two objectives—reconciliation and valuation—are aimed at *detection* of errors and irregularities.

In our opinion, *a sixth objective of an internal control system should be added: promoting operating efficiency. Although the FCPA is not particularly concerned with efficiency, management should recognize that an internal control system's purpose is as much a positive one (promoting efficiency) as a negative one (preventing and detecting errors and fraud).*

Federal Managers' Financial Integrity Act

The **Federal Managers' Financial Integrity Act** requires the heads of federal U.S. government agencies to report annually on the status of their internal control and accounting systems, and it provides for the disclosure and correction of material weaknesses. A key section of this act includes the following provision:

> The internal accounting and administrative controls of each executive agency are to be established in accordance with the standards prescribed by the Comptroller General, in order to provide assurance that:
> 1. obligations and costs are in compliance with applicable law;
> 2. funds, property, and other assets are safeguarded against waste, loss, unauthorized use, or misappropriation; and
> 3. revenues and expenditures applicable to agency operations are properly recorded and accounted for to permit the preparation of accounts and reliable financial and statistical reports and to maintain accountability over the assets.[8]

A review by the General Accounting Office (GAO) of compliance with the act found that most agencies had material weaknesses in their internal control or accounting systems. Areas where widespread evidence of weaknesses was found were accounting/financial management systems, procurement, property management, and cash management.[9]

---

[8]For further discussion, see F. Heim and H. Steinberg, "Implementing the Internal Control Evaluation, Improvement and Reporting Process in the Federal Government," *Government Accountants Journal,* Winter 1983–84, pp. 1–15.

[9]*Financial Integrity Act: The Government Faces Serious Internal Control and Accounting Systems Problems* (Washington, D.C.: United States General Accounting Office, December 1985).

Internal audit reporting responsibilities

Organizations differ in the designated corporate position to which the manager of internal audit has a direct reporting responsibility. But there is an unmistakable trend that reinforces our earlier observation that internal control is a central responsibility of top management. Exhibit 27-3 shows how internal auditors increasingly have reporting responsibilities to the very top levels of the organization, such as the audit committee of the board of directors or the chief executive officer. Exhibit 27-4 presents the organization chart of Hewlett-Packard. The internal audit function reports directly (solid line) to the chief executive officer. The head of internal audit also independently meets with the audit committee of the board of directors three times a year.

Division controller reporting responsibilities

Division controllers can perform two main roles, with varying degrees of emphasis, in any one organization:

1. Financial advisory role to the division manager
2. Oversight role regarding financial reporting to corporate headquarters

Exhibit 27-5 on page 919 presents two alternative reporting relationships, each of which can be observed in individual organizations.[10]

The most common reporting responsibility is the one in which the division controller has direct (solid line) reporting responsibility to the division manager, and indirect (dashed line) to the corporate controller. Under this approach, the division controller is likely to be viewed as part of the "division team" and to participate fully in decision making about operating aspects of the division.

Organizations in which the division controller reports directly (solid line) to the corporate controller, and indirectly (dashed line) to the division manager, are found less frequently. However, an increasing number of firms are adopting this approach. This trend is consistent with the increase in top management interest in,

EXHIBIT 27-3
Reporting Responsibilities of Internal Audit Manager

DESIGNATED POSITION FOR RECEIVING REPORTS	% AS OF 1977	% AS OF 1982
• Audit Committee of Board of Directors	20%	31%
• Chief Financial Officer (often entitled Vice-President, Finance)	30%	31%
• Controller	28%	14%
• Chief Executive Officer or President	8%	12%
• Other	14%	12%

SOURCE: B. Baird and A. Michenzi, "Impact of the Foreign Corrupt Practices Act," Internal Auditor, June 1983, pp. 20–22.

---

[10]Extensive discussion of these two reporting relationships can be found in V. Sathe, *Controller Involvement in Management* (Englewood Cliffs, N.J.: Prentice-Hall, 1982).

EXHIBIT 27-4
Hewlett-Packard Corporate Organization Chart

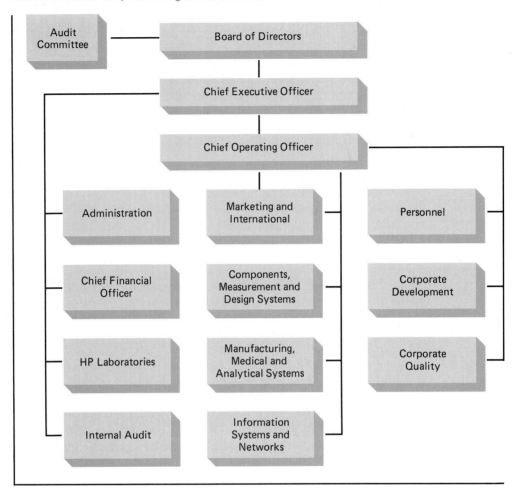

and responsibility for, internal control. International Telephone and Telegraph (ITT) is a strong advocate of the division controller's having direct reporting responsibility to the corporate controller: "We believe that because of the special nature of a controller's responsibilities, the importance of neutrality, objectivity, and integrity—as well as the watchdog function—it is necessary that the prime duty and loyalty be directly to the total corporation and its shareholders, and not to the individual section of the company or division."[11]

---

[11]R. Alleman, "Comptrollership at ITT," *Management Accounting,* May 1985, pp. 24–30. For an alternative view of the role of the division controller, see K. Williams, "The Magic of 3M Management Accounting Excellence," *Management Accounting,* February 1986, pp. 20–27. Although division controllers at 3M report directly to the corporate controller, they play a more active role in operating decisions at the division level than do the division controllers at ITT.

EXHIBIT 27-5
Alternative Reporting Relationships for a Division Controller

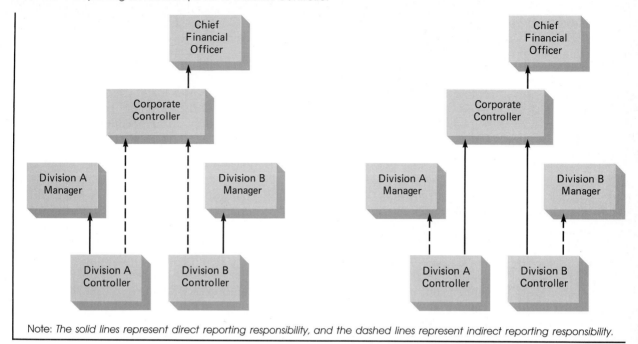

Note: *The solid lines represent direct reporting responsibility, and the dashed lines represent indirect reporting responsibility.*

CHECKLIST OF INTERNAL CONTROL

All good systems of internal control have certain features in common. These features can be termed a *checklist of internal control,* which may be used to appraise any specific procedures for cash, purchases, sales, payroll, and the like. Several of these checklist items are a substitute for top management personally observing whether their strategies are being appropriately implemented at all levels of the organization.

The following checklist summarizes the guidance that is found in much of the systems and auditing literature:[12]

1. **Reliable personnel with clear responsibilities.** *The most important element of successful control is personnel. Incompetent or dishonest individuals can undermine a system, no matter how well it meets the other items on the checklist.* Individuals obviously must be given authority, responsibility, and duties commensurate with their abilities, interests, experience, and reliability. Yet many employers use low-cost talent that may prove exceedingly expensive in the long run, not only because of fraud but also because of poor productivity.

---

[12]For an expanded discussion, see Arens and Loebbecke, *Auditing,* Chap. 7. Accounting firm publications cover internal control in much detail.

Reliability begins at the top of the organization. The entire system deserves surveillance by operating management to see if it is working as prescribed and if changes are warranted. In addition, appropriate oversight and appraisal of employees are essential. The most streamlined accounting system is deficient if its prescribed procedures are not being followed conscientiously.

Responsibility means tracking actions as far down in the organization as is feasible so that results may be related to individuals. It means having salesclerks sign sales slips, inspectors initial packing slips, and workers sign time cards and requisitions. The psychological impact of fixing responsibility tends to promote care and efficiency. Employees often perform better when they must explain deviations from required procedures.

2. Separation of duties. This element not only helps ensure accurate compilation of data but also limits the chances for fraud that would require the collusion of two or more persons. This extremely important and often neglected element can be subdivided into four parts:

a. *Separation of operational responsibility from recordkeeping responsibility.* The entire accounting function should be divorced from operating departments so that objective, independent records may be kept either by other operating people or by clerks. For example, product inspectors, not machine operators, should count good units produced; stores record clerks or computers, not storekeepers, should keep perpetual inventory counts.

b. *Separation of the custody of assets from accounting.* This practice reduces temptation and fraud. For example, the bookkeeper should not handle cash, and the cashier should not have access to ledger accounts such as the individual records of customers. In a computer system, a person with custody of assets should not have access to programming or any input records. Similarly, an individual who handles programming or input records should not have access to tempting assets.

c. *Separation of the authorization of transactions from the custody of related assets.* To the extent feasible, persons who authorize transactions should not have control over the related asset. For instance, the same individual should not authorize the payment of a supplier's invoice and also sign the check in payment of the bill. Nor should an individual who handles cash receipts have the authority to indicate which accounts receivable should be written off as uncollectible.

d. *Separation of duties within the accounting function.* An employee should not be able to record a transaction from its origin to its ultimate posting in a ledger. Independent performance of various phases will help ensure control over errors and fraud.

3. Proper authorization. This element is stressed in the Foreign Corrupt Practices Act. Authorization can be either *general* or *specific*. General authorization is usually found in writing. It often sets definite limits on what costs to charge (whether to fly economy or first class), on what price to charge (whether to offer a sales discount), on what credit limits to grant to customers, and so forth. There may also be complete prohibitions (against paying extra fees, bribes, or overtime premiums).

Specific authorization usually means that a superior manager must sanction (typically in writing) any particular deviations from the limits set by general authorization. For example, the plant manager, rather than the lathe supervisor, may have to approve overtime. Another example is the need for approval from the board of directors regarding expenditures for capital assets in excess of a specific limit.

4. **Adequate documents.** Documents and records vary considerably—from source documents, such as sales invoices and purchase orders, to bookkeeping records, such as journals and ledgers. Immediate, complete, and tamperproof recording is the aim. It is encouraged by having all source documents prenumbered and accounted for, by using devices such as cash registers and locked compartments in invoice-writing machines, and by designing forms for ease of recording.

Immediate recording is especially important for handling cash sales. Devices used to ensure immediate recording include cash registers with loud bells and compiling tapes, private detectives, guaranteeing "rewards" to customers if they are not offered a receipt at the time of sale, and forcing clerks to make change by pricing items at $1.99, $2.99, and $3.99 rather than at $2.00, $3.00, and $4.00.

5. **Proper procedures.** Most organizations have *procedures manuals,* which specify the flow of documents and provide information and instructions to facilitate adequate recordkeeping.

Routine and automatic checks are major ways of attaining proper procedures. In a phrase, this means doing things "by the numbers." Just as manufacturing activities tend to be made more efficient by the division and specialization of repetitive activities, so can recordkeeping activities be made less costly and more accurate. Repetitive procedures may be prescribed for nonmanufacturing activities such as order taking, order filling, collating, and inspecting. The use of general routines permits specialization of effort, division of duties, and automatic checks on previous steps in the routine.

6. **Physical safeguards.** Obviously, losses of cash, inventories, and records are minimized by safes, locks, guards, and limited access. This item also includes safeguards for documents that provide access to assets (such as blank checks).

7. **Bonding, vacations, and rotation of duties.** Key people may be subject to excessive temptation; top executives, branch managers, and individuals who handle cash or inventories should have understudies, be forced to take vacations (so that they are away from the workplace for extended periods), and be bonded.

A facet of this idea is also illustrated by the common practice of having receivables and payables clerks periodically rotated in duties. Thus a receivables clerk may handle customer accounts from A to C for three months and then be rotated to accounts M to P for three months, and so forth.

Incidentally, the act of bonding, that is, buying insurance against embezzlement, is not a substitute for vacations, rotation of duties, and similar precautions. Insurance companies will pay only when a loss is proven; establishing proof is often difficult and costly in itself.

8. **Independent check.** All phases of the system should be subjected to periodic review by outsiders (for example, by external auditors) and by internal auditors who do not ordinarily have contact with the operation under review.

The idea of an independent check extends beyond the work performed by professional auditors. For example, bank statements should be reconciled with book balances. The bank provides an independent record of cash. Furthermore, the monthly bank reconciliations should be conducted by some clerks other than those working with cash, receivables, or payables. Other examples of independent checks include monthly statements sent to credit customers and periodic unannounced physical counts of inventory to check against perpetual records.

One of the main jobs of internal auditors and external auditors is to appraise the effectiveness of internal control; such appraisal affects the extent of the sampling of transactions needed to test the validity of account balances.

9. **Cost-benefit analysis.** Highly complex systems tend to strangle people in red tape, so that the system impedes rather than promotes efficiency. Besides, there is "a cost of keeping the costs" that sometimes gets out of hand. Investments in more costly systems must be judged in the light of expected benefits. Unfortunately, such benefits are difficult to measure. It is much easier to relate new lathes or production methods to cost savings in manufacturing than a new computer to cost savings in the form of more accurate, more rapid, and more tamperproof processing of accounts payable or accounts receivable.

The relationship of costs to benefits sometimes leads to using sampling procedures. Although many companies implement more-complex procedures to improve internal control, a few have taken a reverse course. They have decided that the increased costs of additional scrutiny are not worth the expected savings from finding some mistakes or a theft. For example, an aerospace manufacturer routinely pays suppliers' invoice amounts without checking supporting documentation except on a random-sampling basis. An aluminum company sends out a blank check with its purchase orders, and then the supplier fills out the check and deposits it.

No framework for internal control is perfect in the sense that it can prevent some shrewd individual from "beating the system" either by outright embezzlement or by producing inaccurate records. The task is not total prevention of fraud, nor is it implementation of operating perfection; rather, the task is designing a cost-effective tool that will help achieve efficient operations and reduce temptation.

CONTROL OF INVENTORIES IN RETAILING

Inventory shrinkage

Retail merchants must contend with a major operating problem that is often called inventory shrinkage, a polite term for shoplifting by customers and embezzling by employees. Some department stores have suffered shrinkage losses of 4% to 5% of their sales volume; compare this expense with the typical net-income margin of 5% to 6%.

Experts on controlling inventory shrinkage generally agree that the best deterrent is an alert employee at the point of sale. But other means are also used. Some retail stores use tiny sensitized tags on merchandise (termed electronic article surveillance devices); if not detached or neutralized by a sales clerk, these miniature transmitters trip an alarm as the culprit begins to leave the store. Macy's has continuous surveillance with numerous television cameras at its main New York department store. *Retailers must also scrutinize their own personnel, because they account for 30% to 40% of inventory shortages.*

Some stores have hired actors to pose as shoplifters, who are then subjected to fake, calm arrests. If potential thieves see the arrests, they may be deterred. Such ploys have helped reduce thefts by employees of major retail chains.

The problem of stealing is not confined to profit-seeking organizations. According to the student newspaper at Northwestern University, $14,000 worth of silverware, glasses, and china is stolen from the university dining halls annually. That amounts to $4.71 for every regular customer. Signs are posted at the end of each school term requesting the return of "borrowed" items, but they have not been very successful. The food service director commented, "Two years ago, we put up really nice signs and set out boxes for returns. Kids saw the boxes and stole them for packing."

The imposing magnitude of retail inventory shrinkage demonstrates how management objectives may differ among industries. For example, consider the grocery business, where the net income percentage on sales hovers around 1%. **You can readily see why a prime responsibility of the store manager is to control inventory shrinkage rather than boost gross sales volume. The trade-off is clear: If the operating income on sales is 1%, to offset a $1,000 increase in shrinkage requires a $100,000 boost in gross sales.**

Retail method of inventory control

A widely used inventory method, known as the retail method, is utilized as a control device as well as for obtaining an inventory valuation for financial statement purposes. The wide variety, low unit value, and high volume of most retail merchandise operations prevent any economical use of a perpetual inventory system as commonly conceived. The **retail inventory method** deducts the recorded sales for one period from the goods available for sale during that period to obtain the estimated closing inventory level at retail prices. The following is a general version of how food stores use the retail method to control grocery inventories at the store level. All merchandise is accounted for at retail prices as follows:

	RETAIL PRICES
Inventory, January 5 (by count of branch auditors) at retail prices	$ 15,000
Add purchases stated in initial retail prices	101,000
Add markups from initial retail prices	2,000
Deduct markdowns from initial retail prices	5,000
(1): Total merchandise to account for	$113,000
Deduct sales per cash-register records	100,000
Add allowable shrinkage (for shoplifting, breakage, etc; usually a budgeted % of sales)	1,000
(2): Total recorded sales and allowable shrinkage	$101,000
(1) − (2): Inventory, February 11, should be	$ 12,000
Deduct inventory, February 11, by physical count	11,100
Inventory shrinkage in excess of allowable limit	$ 900

If there is an inventory shrinkage in excess of the allowable limit, the manager usually bears prime responsibility. There are worrisome behavioral implications here. For utmost accuracy, the retail method requires the prompt application of the directed changes in retail prices that are ordered by the branch managers. For example, to help ensure a good performance regarding their control of shrinkage, store managers may be inclined to delay the entering of markdowns on price tags and may be inclined to overstate the retail prices of merchandise if possible. The branch manager typically relies on other means, such as surprise spot checks, to ensure that markup and markdown directives are being followed.[13]

[13]Inventory measured at retail prices can be restated in terms of an average cost of goods for financial statement purposes by applying an average cost-of-goods ratio. For example, if the average gross profit is 20% of sales price, $11,100 inventory (at retail) would be shown at a cost of .80 × $11,100, or $8,880.

Internal control is a central responsibility of top management. Top management should signal to all levels of the organization their unwavering commitment to ensuring that approved and appropriate decisions are made and that attempts to undermine the control system will not be tolerated.

Documented instances of division managers "cooking the books" illustrate how internal control can break down in an organization. Division managers in these instances were under high pressure to meet unrealistic short-run financial targets and operated with little oversight by central management. Moreover, the promotion and reward system created an environment where misrepresenting the timing, amount, or intent of financial transactions was viewed as acceptable behavior.

An effective system of internal control is built on an elaborate set of checks and balances. A breakdown in any one component should not lead to a breakdown in the whole system. The individual components include

1. Reliable personnel with clear responsibilities
2. Separation of duties
3. Proper authorization
4. Adequate documents
5. Proper procedures
6. Physical safeguards
7. Bonding, vacations, and rotation of duties
8. Independent check
9. Cost-benefit analysis

PROBLEM FOR SELF-STUDY

problem The following figures pertain to the Zenith Gift Store for the two-month period November and December, 19_8:

Sales (per cash-register records)	$170,000
Markups (from initial retail prices)	10,000
Markdowns (from initial retail prices)	25,000
Purchases (at cost price)	52,000
Purchases (at initial retail prices)	80,000
Inventory, November 1, 19_8:	
At cost price	105,000
At retail selling price	160,000

Required
1. Compute the inventory amount on December 31, 19_8, using the retail inventory method before any adjustment for shrinkage.
2. Suppose the allowable shrinkage is 2% of sales. The physical inventory at retail prices on December 31, 19_8, amounts to $50,000. What is the inventory shortage?

solution 1.

	RETAIL PRICES
Inventory, November 1, 19_8, at retail prices	$160,000
Add purchases stated in initial retail prices	80,000
Add markups from initial retail prices	10,000
Deduct markdowns from initial retail prices	25,000
Total merchandise to account for	$225,000
Deduct sales per cash-register records	170,000
Inventory, December 31, 19_8, should be	$ 55,000

2.

Inventory, December 31, 19_8, at retail prices should be (see solution to requirement 1)	$55,000
Deduct allowable shrinkage (2% × $170,000)	3,400
Inventory, December 31, 19_8, should be	$51,600
Deduct inventory, December 31, 19_8, by physical count	50,000
Inventory shrinkage in excess of allowable limit	$ 1,600

Explanations for this $1,600 excess inventory shrinkage include abnormal theft, clerical error, and random variation.

Terms to Learn

This chapter and the Glossary contain definitions of the following important terms:

Accounting control (p. 910)   *accounting system (910)*
administrative control (910)   *Federal Managers' Financial Integrity Act (916)*
Foreign Corrupt Practices Act (915)   *fraud (911)*   *internal control (910)*
retail inventory method (923)

Special Points and Pitfalls

This chapter introduces a subject that is covered in great detail in auditing and internal control texts. Our focus is on both the forces promoting internal control and the essential components of an effective internal control system. Top management should first gain an overview of internal control and then gain skill in asking appropriate questions to pinpoint weaknesses in the current system.

Internal control issues arise in both the profit and nonprofit sectors of the economy. For example, the U.S. General Accounting Office estimated that twenty-nine thousand staff days were spent on reviewing compliance by twenty-two federal departments and agencies in the first year after enactment of the Federal Managers' Financial Integrity Act.[14]

The Institute of Internal Auditors (Altamonte Springs, Florida) operates an active program aimed at keeping the members of its profession abreast of developments in this field. Individual trade associations are also an excellent source of information on internal control problems that are of importance in specific industries. For example, the National Retail Merchandise Association (New York) monitors ways to reduce inventory shrinkage.

_____QUESTIONS, PROBLEMS, AND CASES_____

27-1 Distinguish *accounting control* from *administrative control*.

27-2 Into what four categories can the most repetitive, voluminous transactions in most organizations be divided?

_____
[14]G. Frank and J. Steinhoff, "Implementing the Federal Managers' Financial Integrity Act," *GAO Review*, Spring 1985, p. 15.

27-3 Give two examples of a breakdown in an internal control system.

27-4 Name five forces promoting internal control within an organization.

27-5 What is the primary objective of the audit committee?

27-6 Name five objectives of the Foreign Corrupt Practices Act with respect to internal accounting controls.

27-7 Give three examples of documentation of an internal accounting control system.

27-8 Name the designated person to whom the internal audit manager most frequently reports in organizations.

27-9 What is the essential idea of separation of duties?

27-10 "Business operations would be a hopeless tangle without the paperwork that is often regarded with disdain." Explain.

27-11 "There are nine check points that I always use as a framework for judging the effectiveness of an internal control system." Name them.

27-12 "The words *internal control* are commonly misunderstood. They are thought to refer to those facets of the accounting system that are supposed to help prevent embezzling." Do you agree? Why?

27-13 "Internal control systems have both negative and positive objectives." Do you agree? Explain.

27-14 The branch manager of a national retail grocery chain has stated, "My managers are judged more heavily on the basis of their merchandise-shrinkage control than on their overall sales volume." Why? Explain.

27-15 Use of credit cards. A business-school student used a VISA card for a variety of purchases. When checking his monthly bill, he compared his original copy with a duplicate copy for a gasoline purchase made at a local discount-store shopping center. The original copy showed a purchase of $14.25; the duplicate was raised to $16.25.

Required | Who obtained the extra $2? How can the system be improved to prevent such thievery?

27-16 Retail method of inventories, fraud. Contemporary Clothes, Inc., operates a chain of clothing stores. The following data pertain to merchandising operations for the first quarter of 19_1 for one of the stores:

Beginning inventory:	
At cost prices	$ 80,000
At retail prices	130,000
Sales (per cash-register records)	200,000
Markups (from initial retail prices)	10,000
Markdowns (from initial retail prices)	30,000
Purchases:	
At cost prices	90,000
At initial retail prices	140,000

During this period, an investigation revealed the theft of a number of suits costing $2,900 and bearing retail price tags totaling $5,000. A salesperson had attempted to cover the theft by making false markdown entries in the supplementary records maintained as part of assigned duties.

1. Compute the ending inventory at retail price:
   a. Assuming you were unaware of the theft and its cover-up
   b. Assuming the theft had not taken place
2. Assume that the actual physical inventory at retail was $48,300. Compute the inventory shrinkage due to causes other than this particular theft.
3. Explain briefly how the false markdown entries would mask the theft.
4. See the checklist of internal control (pp. 919–22). Identify the items that would be relevant to such a theft, and describe briefly any different procedure that should have been followed by Contemporary Clothes.

27-17 Retail inventory method, comparison of effectiveness of internal control at three stores. Best-Value Family Stores operates a chain of supermarket food stores. The regional manager of the Eastern Division is evaluating the effectiveness of the inventory internal control policies at three of the large stores in the chain. The following information pertains to July 19_1 (000s):

	STORE X	STORE Y	STORE Z
Sales (per cash-register records)	$1,000	$1,500	$2,000
Inventory, July 1 (at retail prices)	300	480	550
Purchases (at initial retail prices)	1,200	1,600	1,900
Markups (from initial retail prices)	30	40	50
Markdowns (from initial retail prices)	80	60	70
Allowable shrinkage (% of sales)	2%	1%	1.5%
Inventory, July 31, by physical count (at retail prices)	414	530	405

1. Why might the allowable shrinkage percentage differ across the three stores?
2. Compute the inventory as of July 31, 19_1, at retail prices using the retail inventory method for each of the three stores. Include the allowance for inventory shrinkage in your computation.
3. Which store has been the most effective in its inventory internal control policies in July 19_1?

27-18 Audit committee, reporting responsibility of internal audit. The accompanying partial organization chart depicts the place of the audit committee in American Building Maintenance Industries, a large company (revenues of $500 million) whose major business is janitorial service in large office buildings.

Comment on these relationships. Explain any changes you favor.

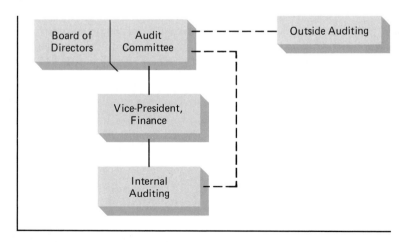

27-19 Reporting relationships between line and staff, controller. (CMA) The Arjohn Corporation is a multidivisional firm. Each division has a manager who is responsible for division operations.

The controller for each division is assigned to the division by the corporate controller's office. The division controller manages the division's accounting system and provides analysis of financial information for the division management. The division manager evaluates the performance of the division controller and makes recommendations for salary increases and promotions. However, the final responsibility for promotion evaluation and salary increases rests with the corporate controller.

Each division of Arjohn is responsible for product design, sales, pricing, operating costs and expenses, and profits. However, corporate management exercises very tight control over the financial operations of the divisions. For example, all capital expenditures above a very modest amount must be approved by corporate management. The method of financial reporting from the division to corporate headquarters provides further evidence of the degree of financial control. The division manager and the division controller submit to corporate headquarters separate and independent commentary of the financial results of the division. The corporate management states that the division controller is there to provide an independent view of the division's operations and not as a spy.

Required

1. Discuss the concept of line, staff, and functional reporting using the facts presented in the question as examples of each.
2. Arjohn Corporation's dual reporting system for divisions may create problems for the division controller.
   a. Identify and discuss the factors that make the division controller's role difficult in this type of situation.
   b. Discuss the effect of the dual reporting relationship on the motivation of the division controller.

27-20 Internal control breakdowns, recommended changes. (CMA) The management of Bertly Company has always recognized that a well-designed accounting system provides many benefits including reliable financial records for decision making and a control system that increases the probability of preventing or detecting errors or irregularities. Thus Bertly has developed an adequate system of internal accounting control.

Bertly's internal audit department periodically reviews the company's accounting records to determine if the internal accounting control system is functioning effectively. The internal audit director believes such reviews are important because inconsistencies or discrepancies can serve as a warning that something is amiss.

The seven conditions listed below were detected by Bertly's internal audit staff during a routine examination of the accounting records:

1. Daily bank deposits do not always correspond with cash receipts.
2. Bad checks from customers are consistently approved by the same employee.
3. Physical inventory counts sometimes differ from perpetual inventory records, and there have been alterations to physical counts and perpetual records.
4. There is a high percentage of customer refunds and credits.
5. There is an excessive use of substitute documents because originals are lost or missing.
6. An unexplained and unexpected decrease in gross profit percentage has occurred.
7. Many documents are not countersigned.

Required

For each of the seven conditions detected by Bertly Company's internal audit staff:

1. Describe a possible cause of the condition.
2. Recommend actions to be taken and/or controls to be implemented that would correct the condition.

Use the following format to present your answer.

CONDITION NUMBER	POSSIBLE CAUSE	RECOMMENDED ACTIONS AND/OR CONTROLS TO CORRECT CONDITION

27-21 Internal control, plant and machinery. (CMA) Superior Co. manufactures automobile parts for sale to the major U.S. automakers. Superior's internal audit staff is to review the internal controls over machinery and equipment and make recommendations for improvements where appropriate.

The internal auditors obtained the following information on five items during the assignment:

Item 1: Requests for purchase of machinery and equipment are normally initiated by the supervisor in need of the asset. The supervisor discusses the proposed acquisition with the plant manager. A purchase requisition is submitted to the purchasing department when the plant manager is satisfied that the request is reasonable and if there is a remaining balance in the plant's share of the total corporate budget for capital acquisitions.

Item 2: Upon receiving a purchase requisition for machinery or equipment, the purchasing department manager looks through the records for an appropriate supplier. A formal purchase order is then completed and mailed. When the machine or equipment is received, it is immediately sent to the user department for installation. This procedure allows the economic benefits from the acquisition to be realized at the earliest possible date.

Item 3: The property, plant, and equipment ledger control accounts are supported by lapsing schedules organized by year of acquisition. These lapsing schedules are used to compute depreciation as a unit for all assets of a given type that are acquired in the same year. Standard rates, depreciation methods, and terminal salvage values are used for each major type of fixed asset. These rates, methods, and terminal salvage values were set ten years ago during the company's initial year of operation.

Item 4: When machinery or equipment is retired, the plant manager notifies the accounting department so that the appropriate entries can be made in the accounting records.

Item 5: There has been no reconciliation since the company began operations between the accounting records and the machinery and equipment on hand.

Required | Identify the internal control weaknesses and recommend improvements that the internal audit staff of Superior Co. should include in its report regarding the internal controls employed for fixed assets. Use the following format in preparing your answer.

WEAKNESS   RECOMMENDATION

Item 1:
Item 2:

27-22 Internal control, pharmacy department of a hospital. You are hired by the president of the Hospital Corporation Group (HCG). Two financial objectives of HCG are (1) to have total revenue exceed total expenses by 6% and (2) to minimize hospital cost to the patient in the face of tremendous past price increases.

Your first project is in the pharmacy. Upon discussing the issue of drug usage and control, various pharmacists have indicated a suspicion that a significant quantity of drugs is not accounted for. There were three possible sources of loss: (a) breakage, spillage, and wastage; (b) failure to charge patients for drugs actually delivered; and (c) theft.

The chief pharmacist estimates that the revenue value of these losses is about $120,000 per year. The three causes listed earlier probably each account for one-third of this amount. The actual invoice cost of drugs is about one-quarter of the billing price that patients pay. Drugs are ordered in bulk, and large quantities are held in inventory to minimize stockouts. Ordering and handling costs account for another 10% of the drug invoice cost. The remaining drug markup covers miscellaneous pharmacy overhead and contribution to hospital overhead.

Under the present system, the source document for billing purposes is the medical record sheet filled out by the nurse each time she administers medication. When the doctor prescribes a specific drug, the request is sent to the pharmacy, where the order is filled and sent up to the floor along with the rest of the drugs for that ward. The medication containers have the patients' names on them and are placed in open bins in the storeroom according to room number. The storeroom is located in the central nursing area, adjacent to the head nurse's office. The storeroom is never locked, since many different nurses and doctors use the room around the clock to prepare medication.

When the pharmacist fills the order, he includes the number of doses that will probably be required during the next three or four days. Unused portions of the order that can be reused (i.e., pills, sealed immunization ampules) are returned to the pharmacy when the patient no longer requires them. The actual number of units in the container is not tallied because it is irrelevant, as billing comes from the medical record sheet. So, if any medication is lost either through accident, neglect, or mischief, no one would really be able to trace the actual amount lost.

Two new systems have been proposed to improve the situation. One involves charging patients for all medication when the orders are filled by the pharmacist and crediting each patient for any usable returns. This "front-end-billing" is commonly used in some other hospitals. With this system, there is no lost revenue; the patient pays for all drugs that theoretically have been allocated to him or her. It is estimated that revenue would increase by $120,000 annually if this system were implemented. A new clerk would be needed to handle credits at a total annual cost of $16,000.

The other system involves installation of three satellite pharmacies in strategic locations in the wards. These would replace the present medication storerooms. Full-time pharmacists would be in charge of these satellites. They would be responsible for all inventory and would place the exact medication needed for each shift in a tray for the nurse. If the pharmacist felt that a particular nurse might be neglectful in recording drug administration, he could compare her medical record sheet with his records. Since the pharmacist would be the only person to have access to the satellite inventory, and since this inventory would be accurately quantified as it left the central pharmacy and had to be completely accounted for, it was felt that losses would be almost entirely eliminated. Rescheduling of personnel and shifting of inventory from the central pharmacy would enable satellite operation at an increased annual cost of $24,000.

Required | 1. What is the actual current loss of net income due to the drug-control problem?
| 2. Of the systems being considered, which would you recommend? Explain fully.

27-23 Payment of supplier invoices, internal control, cost-plus reimbursement contracts. Failure Proof Systems (FPS) specializes in operating and maintaining meltdown safeguard security units at nuclear power plants. It operates these units at thirty nuclear power plants in North America.

Pacific Nuclear Energy (PNE) commenced operations at its Shasta nuclear power plant in 1976. Included at the Shasta plant was an FPS meltdown safeguard security unit. The contract between PNE and FPS stipulated that PNE would reimburse FPS on the basis of "120% of the actual costs identified with operating and maintaining the meltdown safeguard security unit." One of the identifiable cost items was electricity. The electricity used by the FPS unit in the nuclear power plant is provided by Mountain Electric (ME). The relationship between these three firms is:

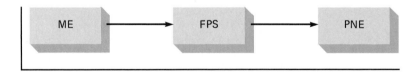

When the Shasta plant commenced operations, ME incorrectly set the meter used to record FPS's electricity usage. The meter incorrectly reported five kilowatt hours used by FPS for each kilowatt hour actually used by FPS. This error was undetected for twelve years. In May 1987, ME discovered the error when it replaced the old meter. ME promptly notified FPS of its overbilling. In turn, FPS promptly notified PNE of its overbilling on the 120% of actual costs reimbursement contract.

The actual payments made by FPS to ME during the period in which the meter was incorrectly set were (in 000s):

1976	$ 40	1982	$ 90
1977	40	1983	100
1978	50	1984	120
1979	60	1985	120
1980	80	1986	140
1981	100	1987	50

Based on these reported payments, PNE reimbursed FPS at 120% of reported cost.

PNE requested that FPS return the amount (with interest) it was overcharged during this twelve-year period. FPS then requested that ME return the amount (with interest) it was overcharged during this twelve-year period. ME offered to repay FPS for only the overcharges in the 1983 to 1987 period. ME argued that FPS shared the responsibility for the overcharging because FPS's internal control system failed to detect the overcharging for a prolonged time. FPS used a similar argument to claim that PNE share the responsibility for its overcharging.

ME, FPS, and PNE could not reach agreement. Lawyers and expert witnesses were hired and a court battle ensued.

Required

1. How much did ME overcharge FPS during this twelve-year period?
2. How much did FPS overcharge PNE during this twelve-year period?
3. Assume you are hired as an expert witness by ME to evaluate the FPS internal control system regarding payments to suppliers. Using the checklist of internal control (pp. 919–22), identify the specific issues you would investigate when examining FPS's internal control system.
4. Comment on the failure of two independent internal control systems (FPS's and PNE's) to detect an overbilling of this magnitude over such an extended time.

27-24 Cooking the books, division managers, internal control. PepsiCo's three main divisions are beverages (main product is the Pepsi soft drink), food products (main products are Frito-Lay chips and other snack foods), and food service (mainly Pizza Hut and Taco Bell).

Over the 19_1 to 19_5 period, the beverage division was organized into Pepsi-Cola Company (U.S. operations) and PepsiCo International. PepsiCo International bottled soft drinks in more than six hundred foreign plants.

In November 19_5, PepsiCo included the following in a press release:

Internal auditors at PepsiCo, Inc. recently discovered significant accounting irregularities in certain company-owned foreign bottling operations of its International division. The foreign subsidiaries involved accounted for less than five percent of PepsiCo's operating profit in 19_4.

It appears that these irregularities involve the overstatement of assets and understatement of expenses over several years, going back at least to 19_1.

The company's investigation, being conducted by a task force which includes special legal counsel and public accountants retained for this purpose, has shown that accounts were falsified by managers of these foreign subsidiaries, principally in Mexico and the Philippines, to improve the apparent performance of their operations. Extensive collusion, creation of false documentation, and the evasion of company internal controls combined to make these misstatements possible. It does not presently appear that these misrepresentations were designed to divert company funds to personal, improper or illegal use.

PepsiCo is terminating and replacing the appropriate individuals, including the U.S.-based manager of the bottling unit of the International division.

In a December 19_5 press release, PepsiCo reported the following details on a restatement of earnings for the 19_1 to 19_5 period based on the investigation (in $ millions):

	19_1	19_2	19_3	19_4	19_5
Net Income as reported	225.8	264.9	291.8	333.5	273.0
Net Reduction resulting from restatement		2.6	14.5	31.1	36.0	8.1
Net Income as restated	223.2	250.4	260.7	297.5	264.9

A former SEC commissioner stated that "numerous techniques were used (by the foreign subsidiaries of PepsiCo) to report false profits, including falsifying expenses, failing to write off broken or unusable bottles and uncollectible accounts receivable, and writing up bottle inventories above cost. To further these schemes, certain individuals made false statements to PepsiCo and its independent auditors concerning the financial condition of certain subsidiaries and, at various times, participated in, or were aware of the falsifications of the books and records of the foreign beverage operations."

The operating income of PepsiCo's three main divisions over the 19_1 to 19_5 period, before any adjustments for the practices disclosed in the investigation, were (in $ millions):

DIVISION	19_1	19_2	19_3	19_4	19_5
Beverage	227.0	254.0	274.7	281.9	217.7
Food Products	158.2	195.4	245.8	298.5	326.4
Food Service	64.1	49.9	59.5	81.9	119.3

Required

1. For each year, compute the percentage that the "restatement of net income" is of (a) net income of PepsiCo as reported and (b) operating income of the beverage division. Comment on the results.
2. What factors may have motivated the Mexico and Philippine senior managers who engaged in the documented practices?
3. One press commentator described the practices reported by the investigation as "business as usual in a company with a high pressure to perform. It is the proverbial storm in a teacup. I don't think the issue is a serious one for PepsiCo's top management." Do you agree? Explain your answer.

27-25 **Cooking the books, decentralization, internal control.** In 19_9 the general counsel of H. J. Heinz became aware of allegations about the internal control and financial reporting in one of its divisions. The audit committee of the board of directors engaged an outside law firm and an accounting firm to fully investigate these and related allegations. Heinz subsequently filed with the SEC a "Report of Audit Committee to the Board of Directors: Income Transferral and Other Practices."

The report concluded that during the years 19_1 to 19_9 certain Heinz divisions (termed "affiliates") "engaged in the practices of improperly accounting for income and expense items and sales, which had the effect of transferring income between fiscal years." The table at the top of page 933 summarizes the restatements to reported sales and net income made by the company.

One set of restatements was due to prior "improper recognition of advertising and market research expenses. These practices generally resulted in an overstatement of expenses in the year in which the item was expensed and a comparable understatement of expenses in a succeeding year when the previously expensed amount was recovered." The percentage of total advertising and market research expenses improperly recognized ranged from 10.8% in 19_3 to 0.2% in 19_5. For example, in 19_3, Heinz USA (HUSA) solicited $2 million of invoices from an advertising agency for services that would be rendered in 19_4. Such invoices were recorded as expenses in 19_3.

Another set of restatements was attributable to "improper recognition of sales. Certain divisions recorded sales in a fiscal period other than the period in which such sales should have been recorded." The percentage of total sales improperly recognized ranged from

H. J. Heinz Income Transferral Practices ($000s)

YEAR	TOTAL NET INCOME BEFORE TAX: BEFORE RESTATEMENT	IMPROPER RECOGNITION OF EXPENSES	IMPROPER RECOGNITION OF SALES	OTHER PRACTICES	INCREASE (DECREASE) NET INCOME BEFORE TAX	TOTAL NET INCOME BEFORE TAX: AFTER RESTATEMENT	% EFFECTS OF RESTATEMENT
(1)	(2)	(3)	(4)	(5)	(6)	(7)	(8)
19_1	$ 75,381	$ 513	—	—	$ 513	$ 75,894	.7%
19_2	80,995	1,814	$ 1,968	—	3,782	84,777	4.5
19_3	92,250	4,250	309	$1,364	5,923	98,173	6.0
19_4	116,525	(2,476)	(1,527)	615	(3,388)	113,137	(3.0)
19_5	127,633	111	1,815	(877)	1,049	128,682	.8
19_6	154,936	4,139	1,294	(268)	5,165	160,101	3.2
19_7	168,731	(734)	2,872	(671)	1,467	170,198	.9
19_8	199,547	(8,888)	(7,085)	(396)	(16,369)	183,178	(8.9)
19_9	203,823	(76)	354	233	511	204,334	.3

0.0% in 19_1 to 1.3% in 19_2 (and 1.1% in 19_9). For example, in 19_4 and 19_5, the report stated that HUSA's books "may have been kept open for a period of time after year end, or documents may have been misdated to include additional sales in those years." In 19_6 and 19_7, HUSA deferred processing vendor credits through its accounting system in the year in which they were received and recorded them in the succeeding fiscal year.

H. J. Heinz's organizational structure consists of its World Headquarters located in Pittsburgh and divisions located in many different countries. These divisions in the 19_1– 19_9 period were "largely self-sufficient enterprises conducting business with their own operating officers and managements." Heinz operated as a highly decentralized organization.

During the 19_1 to 19_9 period, Heinz publicly stated that its objective was to seek an increase in company earnings at a steady and consistent rate. World Headquarters placed great emphasis on each division's ability to meet budgeted targets; these targets were set by World Headquarters without heavy participation with the division managers. The audit committee noted that the "overall aim was to meet the projected consolidated earnings goals. Predictability was the watchword, and surprises were to be avoided." At the end of the third fiscal quarter, reviews were conducted by World Headquarters with division managers. If there was to be any shortfall in the expected results, the division managers "might be encouraged to show extra profit, which could be accomplished by various means, including the reduction of discretionary expenses."

H. J. Heinz maintained a management incentive program (MIP) that covered management at World Headquarters and the senior managers of most of the divisions. The audit committee noted that "goals were stated in terms of a 'fair' goal of a certain earnings figure and a higher 'outstanding goal' . . . The emphasis of the MIP program was on the achievement of short-term (one year) earnings results." The amount paid to each MIP participant represented a significant portion (in some cases as much as 40%) of total compensation. Several of the income transferral practices were designed to ensure that the divisions met, but did not substantially exceed, their income targets, since each year's goals were based on the previous year's results.

The financial and accounting officers of each division reported, and were solely responsible to, the manager of that division. They were not responsible to any executives at the corporate level.

Required

1. What similarities and differences are there between the practices uncovered in the Heinz investigation and those uncovered in the McCormick investigation described in the chapter (see pp. 911–12)?
2. What factors may have motivated the "income transferral and other practices" documented in the audit committee report? Distinguish between the motivations of

933

(a) management at the division level and (b) senior management at World Headquarters.

3. The audit committee report stated that "there is no evidence that any employee of [Heinz] sought or obtained any direct personal gain in connection with any of the transactions or practices described in this Report." Do you agree with this statement?

4. What changes would you recommend in the reporting relationship of the financial and accounting officers of each division?

FOR ADDITIONAL ASSIGNMENT MATERIAL ON THE ROLE OF FINANCIAL EXECUTIVES IN THE ORGANIZATION, SEE PROBLEMS 1-30 THROUGH 1-33, WHICH COULD HAVE BEEN LOGICALLY PLACED HERE.

28

Cost Accounting in Professional Examinations

Types of Professional Examinations • Review for Examinations

This chapter describes the role of cost accounting in United States professional examinations. The suggestions offered are also applicable to professional examinations in other nations.

Cost/managerial accounting receives abundant attention in professional examinations. The assignment materials in the previous chapters of this book have included numerous illustrations of the variety and degrees of difficulty that may be encountered. A conscientious reader who has solved a representative sample of the problems at the end of the chapters will be well prepared for the professional examination questions dealing with cost accounting. The major purposes of this chapter are to provide perspective, instill confidence, and encourage readers to take the examinations.

TYPES OF PROFESSIONAL EXAMINATIONS

CPA and CMA designations

Many American readers may eventually take the Certified Public Accountant (CPA) examination or the Certified Management Accountant (CMA) examination. Similar examinations are conducted in other countries. Certification is important to professional accountants for many reasons, such as:

1. Recognition of achievement and technical competence by fellow accountants and by users of accounting services
2. Increased confidence in professional abilities
3. Membership in professional bodies having programs of career-long education
4. Enhancement of career opportunities
5. Personal satisfaction

The CPA certificate is issued by individual states; it is necessary for obtaining a state's license to practice as a Certified Public Accountant. A prominent feature of financial accounting is the use of independent (external) auditors to give assurance about the reliability of the financial statements supplied by managers. These auditors are called Certified Public Accountants in the United States and Chartered Accountants in many other English-speaking nations. The major U.S. professional association in the private sector that regulates the quality of external auditors is the American Institute of Certified Public Accountants (AICPA).[1]

The CMA designation is offered by the Institute of Certified Management Accountants. The ICMA was created by the National Association of Accountants (NAA), the largest association of management accountants in the world.[2] The major objective of the CMA certification is to enhance the development of the management accounting profession. In particular, focus is placed on the modern role of the management accountant as an active contributor to and a participant in management.

The CMA examination has five parts: (1) economics and business finance, (2) organization and behavior, including ethical considerations, (3) public reporting, standards, auditing, and taxes, (4) internal reporting analysis, and (5) decision analysis, including modeling and information systems. The CMA designation is gaining increased stature in the business community as a credential parallel to the CPA designation.[3]

The CMA certificate is not "in competition" with the CPA certificate. The two fields of management accounting and public accounting are compatible, not com-

---

[1] The AICPA also prepares the Uniform CPA Examination. Information regarding this examination may be obtained from the Director of Examinations, AICPA, 1211 Avenue of the Americas, New York, N.Y., 10036. Information regarding *specific requirements* for taking the CPA Examination in a particular state is available from that state's Board of Public Accountancy. The *Journal of Accountancy* contains numerous advertisements for CPA review materials and courses.

[2] The NAA has a wide range of activities, including many committees. For example, consider the Management Accounting Practices Committee. It issues statements on both financial accounting and management accounting. The NAA also has an extensive continuing education program.

[3] Information regarding the CMA program can be obtained from the Institute, 10 Paragon Drive, P.O. Box 405, Montvale, N.J. 07645–0405. CMAs are expected to comply with the provisions of the Standards of Ethical Conduct for Management Accountants. The periodical *Management Accounting* contains numerous advertisements of CMA review materials and courses. A Certified Cost Analyst program is administered by the Institute of Cost Analysis, 7111 Marlan Drive, Alexandria, VA 22307. The Institute's primary purpose is to further the effectiveness of cost and price analysis in government and industry.

petitive. The CMA designation identifies the holder as having a required level of professional achievement in management accounting.

Taking both examinations

Students should plan to take both the CMA and CPA examinations. **There are almost three times as many management accountants as there are public accountants. Many students work in public accounting immediately after graduation but spend most of their careers elsewhere.** The material covered in both examinations is comparable in rigor and overlaps considerably. Therefore, candidates should try to prepare for both examinations at about the same time.

Students should take the CMA and CPA examinations as soon as possible after attaining their university degrees in accounting. At that point, if they conduct an appropriate review of their courses, students are likely to be as adequately prepared as they ever will be. The examinations are essentially academic in nature. They are really aimed at determining whether a candidate is a qualified *entrant* into a profession rather than a full-fledged, highly qualified practitioner.

REVIEW FOR EXAMINATIONS

Prominence of cost accounting

Cost/managerial accounting questions are prominent in the CMA examination; the CPA examination also includes such questions, although they are less extensively covered when compared with financial reporting, auditing, and business law. As Exhibit 28-1 shows, on the average, cost/managerial accounting represents 33% of the CMA examination and 5% of the content of the CPA examination. This book includes numerous questions and problems used in past CMA and CPA examina-

EXHIBIT 28-1
Content Comparison of CMA and CPA Examinations

SUBJECT AREAS	CMA†	CPA‡
Cost/managerial accounting including quantitative methods*	33%	5%
Financial reporting	13	35
Auditing	9	25
Taxation		
Individual	—	3
Corporate	4	2
Governmental accounting	—	5
Business law	—	25
Business finance	10	—
Economics	9	—
Management and organization behavior	17	—
Information systems	5	—
	100%	100%

*Essentially material covered in this textbook.
†Source: R. DePasquale, "Does the Typical Curriculum Prepare You for the CMA Exam?" Management Accounting, *November 1985, pp. 44–46.*
‡Source: AICPA Content Specification Outlines for the Uniform Certified Public Accountant Examination. Effective for May 1986 examination and beyond.

tions.[4] In addition, a supplement to this book, *Review Manual for Classroom Exams* (John K. Harris [Englewood Cliffs, N.J.: Prentice Hall, 1987]), contains over 300 CMA and CPA questions and explanatory answers. The organization of the Harris supplement is keyed to the chapters in this textbook.

Exhibit 28-2 classifies the cost accounting in CMA and CPA examinations by topical area, indicating the relative depth of knowledge required. The most popular topics are standard costs, flexible budgets, analyses of variances, cost-volume-profit analysis, variable (direct) costing, relevant costs for special decisions, and discounted cash-flow analysis. Problems on product costing are also covered regularly. They emphasize process costing and joint costs.

EXHIBIT 28-2

Competency Levels for Topics Currently Covered
in CMA and CPA Examinations,
Cost/Management Accounting, Including Quantitative Methods

TOPIC	CMA EXAM	CPA EXAM	CHAPTER REFERENCE IN THIS BOOK
Planning: short-run budgets	3	2	5
Planning: long-run forecasts	3	2	5, 19, 20
Cost accumulation systems—job order and process, absorption and variable	3	3	4–8, 15, 16
Cost control—flexible budgets and standard costs	3	3	6–8, 24
Divisional performance and transfer pricing	3	2	25, 26
Cost-volume-profit relationships	3	3	3, 8, 18
Tax implications of alternative decisions	2	2	20
Capital budgeting	3	2	19, 20
Behavioral science applications in accounting	2	1	5, 11, 25, 26
Probability	2	2	18
Regression analysis	3	2	23
Decision models and operations research	3	2	18, 21, 22

Levels of competency:

Level 1: Introductory level knowledge, implying an awareness and general understanding of principal topics.

Level 2: Application of knowledge and demonstration of analytical capability in the solution of specific problem situations.

Level 3: An extension of Level 2 capabilities to include interpretation, evaluation, and synthesis of complex situations. Level 3 implies an in-depth understanding of the topic and the ability to communicate conclusions.

Source: *Adapted from the Report of the Committee on Professional Examinations,* Accounting Review, *Supplement to Vol. XLXI, pp. 6–7.*

---

[4]These are designated in this book as "(CMA)" and "(CPA)." In addition, the problems designated "(SMA)" in this book are from the set of regular examinations (which are graduated by levels of difficulty) of the Society of Management Accountants of Canada, and the ones designated "(CGAA)" are from the examinations of the Certified General Accountants Association of Canada. Some of the professional examination questions and problems in this book have been adapted to bring out particular points in the chapter for which they were chosen. Note that examinations are also given by the U.S. Institute of Internal Auditors; however, cost accounting is covered lightly in these examinations.

Cost accounting is an important part of professional examinations. Candidates should be aware of which cost accounting topics are likely to appear in a professional examination. Exhibit 28-1 provides guidance. An analysis of the five or six most recent examinations also gives helpful clues.

Careful study of appropriate topics in this book will fortify candidates with sufficient background for success in the cost accounting portions of the professional examinations. Chapters 2–10, 14–16, and 19–20 should be particularly helpful for the CPA examination. Chapters 11–13, 18, and 21–26 should be of additional help for the CMA examination.

QUESTIONS, PROBLEMS, AND CASES

28-1 Why is certification important to professional accountants?

28-2 "It is a good idea for the entry-level accountant to take both the CMA and CPA examinations." Do you agree? Explain.

28-3 What are the significant differences between the content of the CMA and CPA examinations? Be specific.

> **Note:** *Additional problems for professional examinations can be found in nearly every chapter in this book, designated as (CMA), (CPA), or (SMA). Also see the supplement to this book by John K. Harris,* **Review Manual for Classroom Exams: CPA and CMA Questions with Explanatory Answers** *(Englewood Cliffs, N.J.: Prentice-Hall, 1987).*

Recommended Readings

The literature on cost accounting and related areas is vast and varied. The footnotes in this book contain citations to over two hundred articles and books.

Advanced textbooks and casebooks related to topics covered in this book include:

ANTHONY, R., J. DEARDEN, and N. BEDFORD, *Management Control Systems,* 5th ed. Homewood, Ill.: Richard D. Irwin, 1984.

ANTHONY, R., and D. YOUNG, *Management Control in Nonprofit Organizations,* 3rd ed. Homewood, Ill.: Richard D. Irwin, 1984.

BARRETT, M., and W. BRUNS, *Case Problems in Management Accounting,* 2nd ed. Homewood, Ill.: Richard D. Irwin, 1985.

KAPLAN, R., *Advanced Management Accounting.* Englewood Cliffs, N.J.: Prentice-Hall, 1982.

MACIARIELLO, J., *Management Control Systems.* Englewood Cliffs, N.J.: Prentice-Hall, 1984.

MAGEE, R., *Advanced Managerial Accounting.* New York: Harper & Row, 1986.

RAMANATHAN, K., *Management Control in Nonprofit Organizations: Text and Cases.* New York: John Wiley, 1982.

ROTCH, W., and B. ALLEN, *Cases in Management Accounting and Control Systems.* Richmond, Va.: Robert F. Dame, 1982.

SHANK, J., *Contemporary Managerial Accounting: A Casebook.* Englewood Cliffs, N.J.: Prentice-Hall, 1981.

Books that explore specific topics in more detail include:

ALSTON, F., F. JOHNSON, M. WORTHINGTON, L. GOLDSMAN, and F. DEVITO, *Contracting with the Federal Government.* New York: John Wiley, 1984.

ATKINSON, A., *Intra-firm Cost and Resource Allocations: Theory and Practice.* Society of Management Accountants of Canada and Canadian Academic Accounting Association Research Monograph, 1987.

BEDINGFIELD, J., and L. ROSEN, *Government Contract Accounting.* Washington, D.C.: Federal Publications Inc., 1985.

COOPER, D., R. SCAPENS, and J. ARNOLD, *Management Accounting Research and Practice.* London: Institute of Cost and Management Accountants, 1983.

EUSKE, K., *Management Control: Planning, Control, Measurement and Evaluation.* Reading, Mass.: Addison-Wesley, 1984.

MERCHANT, K., *Control in Business Organizations.* Boston: Pitman, 1984.

VANCIL, R., *Decentralization: Managerial Ambiguity by Design.* New York: Financial Executives Research Foundation, 1979.

Books of readings and handbooks related to cost or management accounting include:

ASHTON, R., ed., *The Evolution of Behavioral Accounting Research.* New York: Garland Publishing, 1984.

Bell, J., ed., *Accounting Control Systems: A Behavioral and Technical Integration*. New York: Markus Wiener, 1983.

Berry, E., and G. Harwood, eds., *Governmental and Nonprofit Accounting: A Book of Readings*. Homewood, Ill.: Richard D. Irwin, 1984.

Bulloch, J., D. Keller, and L. Vlasho, eds., *Accountants' Cost Handbook*, 3rd ed. New York: John Wiley, 1983.

Chenhall, R., G. Harrison, and D. Watson, eds., *The Organizational Context of Management Accounting*. Boston: Pitman, 1981.

Ramanathan, K., and L. Hegstad, eds., *Readings in Management Control in Nonprofit Organizations*. New York: John Wiley, 1982.

Rappaport, A., ed., *Information for Decision Making*, 3rd ed. Englewood Cliffs, N.J.: Prentice-Hall, 1982.

Rosen, L., ed., *Topics in Management Accounting*. Toronto: McGraw-Hill, 1984.

Shim, J., and L. Geller, eds., *Readings in Cost and Managerial Accounting*. Dubuque, Iowa: Kendall/Hunt, 1980.

Thomas, W., ed., *Readings in Cost Accounting, Budgeting, and Control*, 6th ed. Cincinnati: South-Western Publishing, 1983.

Vargo, R., and P. Dierks, eds., *Readings and Cases in Governmental and Nonprofit Accounting*. Houston: Dame Publications, 1982.

Zimmerman, V., ed., *Managerial Accounting: An Analysis of Current International Applications*. Urbana-Champaign: University of Illinois, 1984.

Two detailed annotated bibliographies of the cost and management accounting research literatures are:

Clancy, D., *Annotated Management Accounting Readings*. Management Accounting Section of the American Accounting Association, 1986.

Klemstine, C., and M. Maher, *Management Accounting Research: 1926–1983*. New York: Garland Publishing, 1984.

Both of these publications classify numerous individual studies into one or more of the following categories: (1) general literature, (2) product cost, (3) cost allocation, (4) cost estimation, (5) decision making, (6) planning and control, and (7) literature reviews.

Professional associations that specialize in serving members with cost and management accounting interests include:

National Association of Accountants, 10 Paragon Drive, P.O. Box 433, Montvale, N.J., 07645. Publishes the *Management Accountant* journal. Also publishes monographs on many topics covered in cost accounting and management accounting courses.

Financial Executives Institute, 10 Madison Avenue, P.O. Box 1938, Morristown, N.J., 07960. Publishes *FE: The Magazine for Financial Executives.* The Financial Executives Research Foundation publishes monographs on many topics covered in cost accounting and management accounting courses.

The Institute of Cost Analysis, 7111 Marlan Drive, Alexandria, Va., 22307. Publishes the *Journal of Cost Analysis* and monographs related to cost and price analysis in government and industry.

The Institute of Internal Auditors, 249 Maitland Avenue, Altamonte Springs, Fla., 32701. Publishes *The Internal Auditor* journal. Also publishes monographs on topics related to internal control.

Society of Management Accountants of Canada, 154 Main Street East, MPO Box 176, Hamilton, Ontario, L8N 3C3. Publishes the *CMA* magazine six times a year. Also publishes monographs on many topics covered in cost accounting and management accounting courses.

The Institute of Cost and Management Accountants, 63 Portland Place, London, WIN 4AB. Publishes the *Management Accounting* journal. Also publishes monographs covering cost and managerial accounting topics.

In many countries, individuals with cost and management accounting interests belong to professional bodies that serve members with financial reporting and taxation, as well as cost and management accounting, interests. An example is the Australian Society of Accountants.

Notes on Compound Interest and Interest Tables

Interest is the cost of using money. It is the rental charge for funds, just as rental charges are made for the use of buildings and equipment. Whenever a time span is involved, it is necessary to recognize interest as a cost of using invested funds. This requirement applies even if the funds in use represent ownership capital and if the interest does not entail an outlay of cash. The reason why interest must be considered is that the selection of one alternative automatically commits a given amount of invested funds that could otherwise be invested in some other opportunity. The measure of the interest in such cases is the return forgone by rejecting the next-best alternative use.

Interest is rarely unimportant, even when short-term projects are under consideration, and it looms large when long-run plans are being considered. For this reason, the rate of interest is of telling import. The rate used will often influence the ultimate decision. For example, $100,000 invested now and compounded annually for ten years at 8% will accumulate to $215,900; at 20%, to $619,200.

INTEREST TABLES

Four basic tables are used for computations involving interest. Tables 2 and 4 are the most pertinent for our purposes.

Table 1—future amount of $1

Table 1 shows how much $1 invested now will accumulate in a given number of periods at a given compounded interest rate per period. The future proceeds (often simply called *amount*) of an investment of $1,000 for three years at 8% compound interest could be sketched as follows:

Accumulate
$1,000 × (1.08)³ or $1,000 × 1.2597* (from Table 1) = $1,259.70

END OF YEAR 0   3
Present Value ⟵─────────────────────────────────── Future Amount
                            Discount

*To minimize discrepancies from rounding, the four-place factor (1.2597) is used here instead of the three-place factor (1.260) shown in Table 1.

TABULAR CALCULATION

YEAR	INTEREST PER YEAR	CUMULATIVE INTEREST, CALLED COMPOUND INTEREST	TOTAL AT END OF PERIOD
0	$ —	$ —	$1,000.00
1	80.00	80.00	1,080.00
2	86.40	166.40	1,166.40
3	93.30	259.70	1,259.70

Note that what is really being done in the tabular presentation is a series of computations that could appear as follows:

$$S_1 = \$1,000(1.08)$$

$$S_2 = \$1,000(1.08)^2$$

$$S_3 = \$1,000(1.08)^3$$

The formula for the "amount of 1," often called the "future value of $1" or "future amount of $1," can be written:

$$S = P(1 + r)^n$$
$$S = 1,000(1 + .08)^3 = \$1,259.70$$

S is the *amount*, the future value; P is the present value, $1,000 in this case; r is the rate of interest, n is the number of periods.

Fortunately, tables make key computations readily available, so that a facility in selecting the *proper* table will minimize computations. Check the accuracy of the answer above against Table 1, page 947.

Table 2—present value of $1

In the previous example, if $1,000 compounded at 8% per annum will accumulate to $1,259.70 in three years, then $1,000 must be the present value of $1,259.70 due at the end of three years. The formula for the present value can be derived by reversing the process of *accumulation* (finding the future amount) that we just finished. Look at the earlier sketch to see the relationship between accumulating and discounting.

943

If

$$S = P(1 + r)^n$$

then

$$P = \frac{S}{(1 + r)^n}$$

$$P = \frac{\$1,259.70}{(1.08)^3} = \$1,000$$

Use Table 2, page 948, to check this calculation.

When accumulating, we advance or roll forward in time. The difference between our original amount and our accumulated amount is called *compound interest*. When discounting, we retreat or roll back in time. The difference between the future amount and the present value is called *compound discount*. Note the following formulas (where $P = \$1,000$):

$$\text{Compound interest} = P[(1 + r)^n - 1] = \$259.70$$

$$\text{Compound discount} = S\left[1 - \frac{1}{(1 + r)^n}\right] = \$259.70$$

Table 3—amount of annuity of $1

An (ordinary) *annuity* is a series of equal payments (receipts) to be paid (or received) at the *end* of successive periods of equal length. Assume that $1,000 is invested at the end of each of three years at 8%:

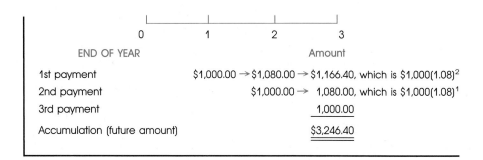

The arithmetic shown above may be expressed algebraically as the amount of an ordinary annuity of $1,000 for three years = $1,000(1 + r)^2 + $1,000(1 + r)^1 + $1,000.

We can develop the general formula for S_n, the amount of an ordinary annuity of $1, by using the example above as a basis:

1. $S_n = 1 + (1 + r)^1 + (1 + r)^2$

2. Substitute: $S_n = 1 + (1.08) + (1.08)^2$

3. Multiply (2) by $(1 + r)$: $(1.08)S_n = 1.08 + (1.08)^2 + (1.08)^3$

4. Subtract (2) from (3): $1.08S_n - S_n = (1.08)^3 - 1$
   Note that all terms on right-hand side are removed except $(1.08)^3$ in equation (3) and 1 in equation (2).

5. Factor (4):

$$S_n(1.08 - 1) = (1.08)^3 - 1$$

6. Divide (5) by $(1.08 - 1)$:

$$S_n = \frac{(1.08)^3 - 1}{1.08 - 1} = \frac{(1.08)^3 - 1}{.08}$$

7. The general formula for the amount of an ordinary annuity of $1 becomes:

$$S_n = \frac{(1 + r)^n - 1}{r} \quad \text{or} \quad \frac{\text{Compound interest}}{\text{Rate}}$$

This formula is the basis for Table 3, page 949. Look at Table 3 or use the formula itself to check the calculations.

Table 4—present value of an ordinary annuity of $1

Using the same example as for Table 3, we can show how the formula of P_n, the *present value of an ordinary annuity*, is developed.

END OF YEAR		0	1	2	3
1st payment	$\frac{1,000}{1.08} = \$\ 926.14 \leftarrow \$1,000$				
2nd payment	$\frac{1,000}{(1.08)^2} = \$\ 857.52 \leftarrow\!- \$1,000$				
3rd payment	$\frac{1,000}{(1.08)^3} = \$\ 794.00 \leftarrow\!- \$1,000$				
Total present value	$\$2,577.66$				

For the general case, the present value of an ordinary annuity of $1 may be expressed:

1.

$$P_n = \frac{1}{1 + r} + \frac{1}{(1 + r)^2} + \frac{1}{(1 + r)^3}$$

2. Substituting,

$$P_n = \frac{1}{1.08} + \frac{1}{(1.08)^2} + \frac{1}{(1.08)^3}$$

3. Multiply by $\frac{1}{1.08}$:

$$P_n\frac{1}{1.08} = \frac{1}{(1.08)^2} + \frac{1}{(1.08)^3} + \frac{1}{(1.08)^4}$$

4. Subtract (3) from (2):

$$P_n - P_n\frac{1}{1.08} = \frac{1}{1.08} - \frac{1}{(1.08)^4}$$

5. Factor:

$$P_n\left(1 - \frac{1}{1.08}\right) = \frac{1}{1.08}\left[1 - \frac{1}{(1.08)^3}\right]$$

6. or

$$P_n\left(\frac{.08}{1.08}\right) = \frac{1}{1.08}\left[1 - \frac{1}{(1.08)^3}\right]$$

7. Multiply by $\frac{1.08}{.08}$:

$$P_n = \frac{1}{.08}\left[1 - \frac{1}{(1.08)^3}\right]$$

The general formula for the present worth of an annuity of $1.00 is:

$$P_n = \frac{1}{r}\left[1 - \frac{1}{(1+r)^n}\right] = \frac{\text{Compound discount}}{\text{Rate}}$$

Solving,

$$P_n = \frac{.2062}{.08} = 2.577$$

The formula is the basis for Table 4, page 950. Check the answer in the table. **The present value tables, Tables 2 and 4, are used most frequently in capital budgeting.**

Note that the tables for annuities are not really essential. That is, with Tables 1 and 2, compound interest and compound discount can be readily computed. Then it is simply a matter of dividing either of these by the rate to get values equivalent to those shown in Tables 3 and 4.

TABLE 1

Compound Amount of $1.00 (The Future Value of $1.00)

$S = P(1 + r)^n$. In this table $P = \$1.00$.

PERIODS	2%	4%	6%	8%	10%	12%	14%	16%	18%	20%	22%	24%	26%	28%	30%	32%	40%	PERIODS
1	1.020	1.040	1.060	1.080	1.100	1.120	1.140	1.160	1.180	1.200	1.220	1.240	1.260	1.280	1.300	1.320	1.400	1
2	1.040	1.082	1.124	1.166	1.210	1.254	1.300	1.346	1.392	1.440	1.488	1.538	1.588	1.638	1.690	1.742	1.960	2
3	1.061	1.125	1.191	1.260	1.331	1.405	1.482	1.561	1.643	1.728	1.816	1.907	2.000	2.097	2.197	2.300	2.744	3
4	1.082	1.170	1.262	1.360	1.464	1.574	1.689	1.811	1.939	2.074	2.215	2.364	2.520	2.684	2.856	3.036	3.842	4
5	1.104	1.217	1.338	1.469	1.611	1.762	1.925	2.100	2.288	2.488	2.703	2.932	3.176	3.436	3.713	4.007	5.378	5
6	1.126	1.265	1.419	1.587	1.772	1.974	2.195	2.436	2.700	2.986	3.297	3.635	4.002	4.398	4.827	5.290	7.530	6
7	1.149	1.316	1.504	1.714	1.949	2.211	2.502	2.826	3.185	3.583	4.023	4.508	5.042	5.629	6.275	6.983	10.541	7
8	1.172	1.369	1.594	1.851	2.144	2.476	2.853	3.278	3.759	4.300	4.908	5.590	6.353	7.206	8.157	9.217	14.758	8
9	1.195	1.423	1.689	1.999	2.358	2.773	3.252	3.803	4.435	5.160	5.987	6.931	8.005	9.223	10.604	12.166	20.661	9
10	1.219	1.480	1.791	2.159	2.594	3.106	3.707	4.411	5.234	6.192	7.305	8.594	10.086	11.806	13.786	16.060	28.925	10
11	1.243	1.539	1.898	2.332	2.853	3.479	4.226	5.117	6.176	7.430	8.912	10.657	12.708	15.112	17.922	21.199	40.496	11
12	1.268	1.601	2.012	2.518	3.138	3.896	4.818	5.936	7.288	8.916	10.872	13.215	16.012	19.343	23.298	27.983	56.694	12
13	1.294	1.665	2.133	2.720	3.452	4.363	5.492	6.886	8.599	10.699	13.264	16.386	20.175	24.759	30.288	36.937	79.371	13
14	1.319	1.732	2.261	2.937	3.797	4.887	6.261	7.988	10.147	12.839	16.182	20.319	25.421	31.691	39.374	48.757	111.120	14
15	1.346	1.801	2.397	3.172	4.177	5.474	7.138	9.266	11.974	15.407	19.742	25.196	32.030	40.565	51.186	64.359	155.568	15
16	1.373	1.873	2.540	3.426	4.595	6.130	8.137	10.748	14.129	18.488	24.086	31.243	40.358	51.923	66.542	84.954	217.795	16
17	1.400	1.948	2.693	3.700	5.054	6.866	9.276	12.468	16.672	22.186	29.384	38.741	50.851	66.461	86.504	112.139	304.913	17
18	1.428	2.026	2.854	3.996	5.560	7.690	10.575	14.463	19.673	26.623	35.849	48.039	64.072	85.071	112.455	148.024	426.879	18
19	1.457	2.107	3.026	4.316	6.116	8.613	12.056	16.777	23.214	31.948	43.736	59.568	80.731	108.890	146.192	195.391	597.630	19
20	1.486	2.191	3.207	4.661	6.727	9.646	13.743	19.461	27.393	38.338	53.358	73.864	101.721	139.380	190.050	257.916	836.683	20
21	1.516	2.279	3.400	5.034	7.400	10.804	15.668	22.574	32.324	46.005	65.096	91.592	128.169	178.406	247.065	340.449	1171.356	21
22	1.546	2.370	3.604	5.437	8.140	12.100	17.861	26.186	38.142	55.206	79.418	113.574	161.492	228.360	321.184	449.393	1639.898	22
23	1.577	2.465	3.820	5.871	8.954	13.552	20.362	30.376	45.008	66.247	96.889	140.831	203.480	292.300	417.539	593.199	2295.857	23
24	1.608	2.563	4.049	6.341	9.850	15.179	23.212	35.236	53.109	79.497	118.205	174.631	256.385	374.144	542.801	783.023	3214.200	24
25	1.641	2.666	4.292	6.848	10.835	17.000	26.462	40.874	62.669	95.396	144.210	216.542	323.045	478.905	705.641	1033.590	4499.880	25
26	1.673	2.772	4.549	7.396	11.918	19.040	30.167	47.414	73.949	114.475	175.936	268.512	407.037	612.998	917.333	1364.339	6299.831	26
27	1.707	2.883	4.822	7.988	13.110	21.325	34.390	55.000	87.260	137.371	214.642	332.955	512.867	784.638	1192.533	1800.927	8819.764	27
28	1.741	2.999	5.112	8.627	14.421	23.884	39.204	63.800	102.967	164.845	261.864	412.864	646.212	1004.336	1550.293	2377.224	12347.670	28
29	1.776	3.119	5.418	9.317	15.863	26.750	44.693	74.009	121.501	197.814	319.474	511.952	814.228	1285.550	2015.381	3137.935	17286.737	29
30	1.811	3.243	5.743	10.063	17.449	29.960	50.950	85.850	143.371	237.376	389.758	634.820	1025.927	1645.505	2619.996	4142.075	24201.432	30
35	2.000	3.946	7.686	14.785	28.102	52.800	98.100	180.314	327.997	590.668	1053.402	1861.054	3258.135	5653.911	9727.860	16599.217	130161.112	35
40	2.208	4.801	10.286	21.725	45.259	93.051	188.884	378.721	750.378	1469.772	2847.038	5455.913	10347.175	19426.689	36118.865	66520.767	700037.697	40

TABLE 2 *(Place a clip on this page for easy reference.)*
Present Value of $1.00.

$$P = \frac{S}{(1 + r)^n}. \text{ In this table } S = \$1.00.$$

PERIODS	2%	4%	6%	8%	10%	12%	14%	16%	18%	20%	22%	24%	26%	28%	30%	32%	40%	PERIODS
1	0.980	0.962	0.943	0.926	0.909	0.893	0.877	0.862	0.847	0.833	0.820	0.806	0.794	0.781	0.769	0.758	0.714	1
2	0.961	0.925	0.890	0.857	0.826	0.797	0.769	0.743	0.718	0.694	0.672	0.650	0.630	0.610	0.592	0.574	0.510	2
3	0.942	0.889	0.840	0.794	0.751	0.712	0.675	0.641	0.609	0.579	0.551	0.524	0.500	0.477	0.455	0.435	0.364	3
4	0.924	0.855	0.792	0.735	0.683	0.636	0.592	0.552	0.516	0.482	0.451	0.423	0.397	0.373	0.350	0.329	0.260	4
5	0.906	0.822	0.747	0.681	0.621	0.567	0.519	0.476	0.437	0.402	0.370	0.341	0.315	0.291	0.269	0.250	0.186	5
6	0.888	0.790	0.705	0.630	0.564	0.507	0.456	0.410	0.370	0.335	0.303	0.275	0.250	0.227	0.207	0.189	0.133	6
7	0.871	0.760	0.665	0.583	0.513	0.452	0.400	0.354	0.314	0.279	0.249	0.222	0.198	0.178	0.159	0.143	0.095	7
8	0.853	0.731	0.627	0.540	0.467	0.404	0.351	0.305	0.266	0.233	0.204	0.179	0.157	0.139	0.123	0.108	0.068	8
9	0.837	0.703	0.592	0.500	0.424	0.361	0.308	0.263	0.225	0.194	0.167	0.144	0.125	0.108	0.094	0.082	0.048	9
10	0.820	0.676	0.558	0.463	0.386	0.322	0.270	0.227	0.191	0.162	0.137	0.116	0.099	0.085	0.073	0.062	0.035	10
11	0.804	0.650	0.527	0.429	0.350	0.287	0.237	0.195	0.162	0.135	0.112	0.094	0.079	0.066	0.056	0.047	0.025	11
12	0.788	0.625	0.497	0.397	0.319	0.257	0.208	0.168	0.137	0.112	0.092	0.076	0.062	0.052	0.043	0.036	0.018	12
13	0.773	0.601	0.469	0.368	0.290	0.229	0.182	0.145	0.116	0.093	0.075	0.061	0.050	0.040	0.033	0.027	0.013	13
14	0.758	0.577	0.442	0.340	0.263	0.205	0.160	0.125	0.099	0.078	0.062	0.049	0.039	0.032	0.025	0.021	0.009	14
15	0.743	0.555	0.417	0.315	0.239	0.183	0.140	0.108	0.084	0.065	0.051	0.040	0.031	0.025	0.020	0.016	0.006	15
16	0.728	0.534	0.394	0.292	0.218	0.163	0.123	0.093	0.071	0.054	0.042	0.032	0.025	0.019	0.015	0.012	0.005	16
17	0.714	0.513	0.371	0.270	0.198	0.146	0.108	0.080	0.060	0.045	0.034	0.026	0.020	0.015	0.012	0.009	0.003	17
18	0.700	0.494	0.350	0.250	0.180	0.130	0.095	0.069	0.051	0.038	0.028	0.021	0.016	0.012	0.009	0.007	0.002	18
19	0.686	0.475	0.331	0.232	0.164	0.116	0.083	0.060	0.043	0.031	0.023	0.017	0.012	0.009	0.007	0.005	0.002	19
20	0.673	0.456	0.312	0.215	0.149	0.104	0.073	0.051	0.037	0.026	0.019	0.014	0.010	0.007	0.005	0.004	0.001	20
21	0.660	0.439	0.294	0.199	0.135	0.093	0.064	0.044	0.031	0.022	0.015	0.011	0.008	0.006	0.004	0.003	0.001	21
22	0.647	0.422	0.278	0.184	0.123	0.083	0.056	0.038	0.026	0.018	0.013	0.009	0.006	0.004	0.003	0.002	0.001	22
23	0.634	0.406	0.262	0.170	0.112	0.074	0.049	0.033	0.022	0.015	0.010	0.007	0.005	0.003	0.002	0.002	0.000	23
24	0.622	0.390	0.247	0.158	0.102	0.066	0.043	0.028	0.019	0.013	0.008	0.006	0.004	0.003	0.002	0.001	0.000	24
25	0.610	0.375	0.233	0.146	0.092	0.059	0.038	0.024	0.016	0.010	0.007	0.005	0.003	0.002	0.001	0.001	0.000	25
26	0.598	0.361	0.220	0.135	0.084	0.053	0.033	0.021	0.014	0.009	0.006	0.004	0.002	0.002	0.001	0.001	0.000	26
27	0.586	0.347	0.207	0.125	0.076	0.047	0.029	0.018	0.011	0.007	0.005	0.003	0.002	0.001	0.001	0.001	0.000	27
28	0.574	0.333	0.196	0.116	0.069	0.042	0.026	0.016	0.010	0.006	0.004	0.002	0.002	0.001	0.001	0.000	0.000	28
29	0.563	0.321	0.185	0.107	0.063	0.037	0.022	0.014	0.008	0.005	0.003	0.002	0.001	0.001	0.000	0.000	0.000	29
30	0.552	0.308	0.174	0.099	0.057	0.033	0.020	0.012	0.007	0.004	0.003	0.002	0.001	0.001	0.000	0.000	0.000	30
35	0.500	0.253	0.130	0.068	0.036	0.019	0.010	0.006	0.003	0.002	0.001	0.001	0.000	0.000	0.000	0.000	0.000	35
40	0.453	0.208	0.097	0.046	0.022	0.011	0.005	0.003	0.001	0.001	0.000	0.000	0.000	0.000	0.000	0.000	0.000	40

TABLE 3
Compound Amount of Annuity of $1.00 in Arrears* (Future Value of Annuity)

$$s_n = \frac{(1+r)^n - 1}{r}$$

PERIODS	2%	4%	6%	8%	10%	12%	14%	16%	18%	20%	22%	24%	26%	28%	30%	32%	40%	PERIODS
1	1.000	1.000	1.000	1.000	1.000	1.000	1.000	1.000	1.000	1.000	1.000	1.000	1.000	1.000	1.000	1.000	1.000	1
2	2.020	2.040	2.060	2.080	2.100	2.120	2.140	2.160	2.180	2.200	2.220	2.240	2.260	2.280	2.300	2.320	2.400	2
3	3.060	3.122	3.184	3.246	3.310	3.374	3.440	3.506	3.572	3.640	3.708	3.778	3.848	3.918	3.990	4.062	4.360	3
4	4.122	4.246	4.375	4.506	4.641	4.779	4.921	5.066	5.215	5.368	5.524	5.684	5.848	6.016	6.187	6.362	7.104	4
5	5.204	5.416	5.637	5.867	6.105	6.353	6.610	6.877	7.154	7.442	7.740	8.048	8.368	8.700	9.043	9.398	10.946	5
6	6.308	6.633	6.975	7.336	7.716	8.115	8.536	8.977	9.442	9.930	10.442	10.980	11.544	12.136	12.756	13.406	16.324	6
7	7.434	7.898	8.394	8.923	9.487	10.089	10.730	11.414	12.142	12.916	13.740	14.615	15.546	16.534	17.583	18.696	23.853	7
8	8.583	9.214	9.897	10.637	11.436	12.300	13.233	14.240	15.327	16.499	17.762	19.123	20.588	22.163	23.858	25.678	34.395	8
9	9.755	10.583	11.491	12.488	13.579	14.776	16.085	17.519	19.086	20.799	22.670	24.712	26.940	29.369	32.015	34.895	49.153	9
10	10.950	12.006	13.181	14.487	15.937	17.549	19.337	21.321	23.521	25.959	28.657	31.643	34.945	38.593	42.619	47.062	69.814	10
11	12.169	13.486	14.972	16.645	18.531	20.655	23.045	25.733	28.755	32.150	35.962	40.238	45.031	50.398	56.405	63.122	98.739	11
12	13.412	15.026	16.870	18.977	21.384	24.133	27.271	30.850	34.931	39.581	44.874	50.895	57.739	65.510	74.327	84.320	139.235	12
13	14.680	16.627	18.882	21.495	24.523	28.029	32.089	36.786	42.219	48.497	55.746	64.110	73.751	84.853	97.625	112.303	195.929	13
14	15.974	18.292	21.015	24.215	27.975	32.393	37.581	43.672	50.818	59.196	69.010	80.496	93.926	109.612	127.913	149.240	275.300	14
15	17.293	20.024	23.276	27.152	31.772	37.280	43.842	51.660	60.965	72.035	85.192	100.815	119.347	141.303	167.286	197.997	386.420	15
16	18.639	21.825	25.673	30.324	35.950	42.753	50.980	60.925	72.939	87.442	104.935	126.011	151.377	181.868	218.472	262.356	541.988	16
17	20.012	23.698	28.213	33.750	40.545	48.884	59.118	71.673	87.068	105.931	129.020	157.253	191.735	233.791	285.014	347.309	759.784	17
18	21.412	25.645	30.906	37.450	45.599	55.750	68.394	84.141	103.740	128.117	158.405	195.994	242.585	300.252	371.518	459.449	1064.697	18
19	22.841	27.671	33.760	41.446	51.159	63.440	78.969	98.603	123.414	154.740	194.254	244.033	306.658	385.323	483.973	607.472	1491.576	19
20	24.297	29.778	36.786	45.762	57.275	72.052	91.025	115.380	146.628	186.688	237.989	303.601	387.389	494.213	630.165	802.863	2089.206	20
21	25.783	31.969	39.993	50.423	64.002	81.699	104.768	134.841	174.021	225.026	291.347	377.465	489.110	633.593	820.215	1060.779	2925.889	21
22	27.299	34.248	43.392	55.457	71.403	92.503	120.436	157.415	206.345	271.031	356.443	469.056	617.278	811.999	1067.280	1401.229	4097.245	22
23	28.845	36.618	46.996	60.893	79.543	104.603	138.297	183.601	244.487	326.237	435.861	582.630	778.771	1040.358	1388.464	1850.622	5737.142	23
24	30.422	39.083	50.816	66.765	88.497	118.155	158.659	213.978	289.494	392.484	532.750	723.461	982.251	1332.659	1806.003	2443.821	8032.999	24
25	32.030	41.646	54.865	73.106	98.347	133.334	181.871	249.214	342.603	471.981	650.955	898.092	1238.636	1706.803	2348.803	3226.844	11247.199	25
26	33.671	44.312	59.156	79.954	109.182	150.334	208.333	290.088	405.272	567.377	795.165	1114.634	1561.682	2185.708	3054.444	4260.434	15747.079	26
27	35.344	47.084	63.706	87.351	121.100	169.374	238.499	337.502	479.221	681.853	971.102	1383.146	1968.719	2798.706	3971.778	5624.772	22046.910	27
28	37.051	49.968	68.528	95.339	134.210	190.699	272.889	392.503	566.481	819.223	1185.744	1716.101	2481.586	3583.344	5164.311	7425.699	30866.674	28
29	38.792	52.966	73.640	103.966	148.631	214.583	312.094	456.303	669.447	984.068	1447.608	2128.965	3127.798	4587.680	6714.604	9802.923	43214.343	29
30	40.568	56.085	79.058	113.283	164.494	241.333	356.787	530.312	790.948	1181.882	1767.081	2640.916	3942.026	5873.231	8729.985	12940.859	60501.081	30
35	49.994	73.652	111.435	172.317	271.024	431.663	693.573	1120.713	1816.652	2948.341	4783.645	7750.225	12527.442	20188.966	32422.868	51869.427	325400.279	35
40	60.402	95.026	154.762	259.057	442.593	767.091	1342.025	2360.757	4163.213	7343.858	12936.535	22728.803	39792.982	69377.460	120392.883	207874.272	1750091.741	40

*Payments (or receipts) at the end of each period.

TABLE 4
(Place a clip on this page for easy reference.)

Present Value of Annuity of $1.00 in Arrears*

$$P_n = \frac{1}{r}\left[1 - \frac{1}{(1+r)^n}\right]$$

PERIODS	2%	4%	6%	8%	10%	12%	14%	16%	18%	20%	22%	24%	26%	28%	30%	32%	40%	PERIODS
1	0.980	0.962	0.943	0.926	0.909	0.893	0.877	0.862	0.847	0.833	0.820	0.806	0.794	0.781	0.769	0.758	0.714	1
2	1.942	1.886	1.833	1.783	1.736	1.690	1.647	1.605	1.566	1.528	1.492	1.457	1.424	1.392	1.361	1.331	1.224	2
3	2.884	2.775	2.673	2.577	2.487	2.402	2.322	2.246	2.174	2.106	2.042	1.981	1.923	1.868	1.816	1.766	1.589	3
4	3.808	3.630	3.465	3.312	3.170	3.037	2.914	2.798	2.690	2.589	2.494	2.404	2.320	2.241	2.166	2.096	1.849	4
5	4.713	4.452	4.212	3.993	3.791	3.605	3.433	3.274	3.127	2.991	2.864	2.745	2.635	2.532	2.436	2.345	2.035	5
6	5.601	5.242	4.917	4.623	4.355	4.111	3.889	3.685	3.498	3.326	3.167	3.020	2.885	2.759	2.643	2.534	2.168	6
7	6.472	6.002	5.582	5.206	4.868	4.564	4.288	4.039	3.812	3.605	3.416	3.242	3.083	2.937	2.802	2.677	2.263	7
8	7.325	6.733	6.210	5.747	5.335	4.968	4.639	4.344	4.078	3.837	3.619	3.421	3.241	3.076	2.925	2.786	2.331	8
9	8.162	7.435	6.802	6.247	5.759	5.328	4.946	4.607	4.303	4.031	3.786	3.566	3.366	3.184	3.019	2.868	2.379	9
10	8.983	8.111	7.360	6.710	6.145	5.650	5.216	4.833	4.494	4.192	3.923	3.682	3.465	3.269	3.092	2.930	2.414	10
11	9.787	8.760	7.887	7.139	6.495	5.938	5.453	5.029	4.656	4.327	4.035	3.776	3.543	3.335	3.147	2.978	2.438	11
12	10.575	9.385	8.384	7.536	6.814	6.194	5.660	5.197	4.793	4.439	4.127	3.851	3.606	3.387	3.190	3.013	2.456	12
13	11.348	9.986	8.853	7.904	7.103	6.424	5.842	5.342	4.910	4.533	4.203	3.912	3.656	3.427	3.223	3.040	2.469	13
14	12.106	10.563	9.295	8.244	7.367	6.628	6.002	5.468	5.008	4.611	4.265	3.962	3.695	3.459	3.249	3.061	2.478	14
15	12.849	11.118	9.712	8.559	7.606	6.811	6.142	5.575	5.092	4.675	4.315	4.001	3.726	3.483	3.268	3.076	2.484	15
16	13.578	11.652	10.106	8.851	7.824	6.974	6.265	5.668	5.162	4.730	4.357	4.033	3.751	3.503	3.283	3.088	2.489	16
17	14.292	12.166	10.477	9.122	8.022	7.120	6.373	5.749	5.222	4.775	4.391	4.059	3.771	3.518	3.295	3.097	2.492	17
18	14.992	12.659	10.828	9.372	8.201	7.250	6.467	5.818	5.273	4.812	4.419	4.080	3.786	3.529	3.304	3.104	2.494	18
19	15.678	13.134	11.158	9.604	8.365	7.366	6.550	5.877	5.316	4.843	4.442	4.097	3.799	3.539	3.311	3.109	2.496	19
20	16.351	13.590	11.470	9.818	8.514	7.469	6.623	5.929	5.353	4.870	4.460	4.110	3.808	3.546	3.316	3.113	2.497	20
21	17.011	14.029	11.764	10.017	8.649	7.562	6.687	5.973	5.384	4.891	4.476	4.121	3.816	3.551	3.320	3.116	2.498	21
22	17.658	14.451	12.042	10.201	8.772	7.645	6.743	6.011	5.410	4.909	4.488	4.130	3.822	3.556	3.323	3.118	2.498	22
23	18.292	14.857	12.303	10.371	8.883	7.718	6.792	6.044	5.432	4.925	4.499	4.137	3.827	3.559	3.325	3.120	2.499	23
24	18.914	15.247	12.550	10.529	8.985	7.784	6.835	6.073	5.451	4.937	4.507	4.143	3.831	3.562	3.327	3.121	2.499	24
25	19.523	15.622	12.783	10.675	9.077	7.843	6.873	6.097	5.467	4.948	4.514	4.147	3.834	3.564	3.329	3.122	2.499	25
26	20.121	15.983	13.003	10.810	9.161	7.896	6.906	6.118	5.480	4.956	4.520	4.151	3.837	3.566	3.330	3.123	2.500	26
27	20.707	16.330	13.211	10.935	9.237	7.943	6.935	6.136	5.492	4.964	4.524	4.154	3.839	3.567	3.331	3.123	2.500	27
28	21.281	16.663	13.406	11.051	9.307	7.984	6.961	6.152	5.502	4.970	4.528	4.157	3.840	3.568	3.331	3.124	2.500	28
29	21.844	16.984	13.591	11.158	9.370	8.022	6.983	6.166	5.510	4.975	4.531	4.159	3.841	3.569	3.332	3.124	2.500	29
30	22.396	17.292	13.765	11.258	9.427	8.055	7.003	6.177	5.517	4.979	4.534	4.160	3.842	3.569	3.332	3.124	2.500	30
35	24.999	18.665	14.498	11.655	9.644	8.176	7.070	6.215	5.539	4.992	4.541	4.164	3.845	3.571	3.333	3.125	2.500	35
40	27.355	19.793	15.046	11.925	9.779	8.244	7.105	6.233	5.548	4.997	4.544	4.166	3.846	3.571	3.333	3.125	2.500	40

*Payments (or receipts) at the end of each period.

Glossary

Abnormal spoilage. Spoilage that is not expected to arise under efficient operating conditions; it is not an inherent part of the selected production process. *(p. 546)*

Absorption costing. Method of product costing where fixed manufacturing overhead is included in the inventoriable costs. *(p. 55)*

Accelerated cost recovery system. Federal U.S. tax regulation that classifies depreciable assets into one of several property class-life categories, each of which has a designated pattern of allowable depreciation. Abbreviated as *ACRS*. *(p. 688)*

Accelerated depreciation. Any pattern of depreciation that writes off depreciable assets more quickly than does ordinary straight-line depreciation. *(p. 682)*

Accounting control. Comprises the methods and procedures that are mainly concerned with the authorization of transactions, the safeguarding of assets, and the accuracy of the accounting records. *(p. 910)*

Accounting rate of return. See *accrual accounting rate of return.*

Accounting system. Set of records, procedures, and equipment that routinely deals with the events affecting the financial performance and position of the organization. *(p. 910)*

Accrual accounting rate of return. Accounting measure of income divided by an accounting measure of investment. Also called *accounting rate of return.* *(p. 661)*

ACRS. Abbreviation for *accelerated cost recovery system.* *(p. 688)*

Activity variance. See *production volume variance.*

Actual costs. Amounts determined on the basis of costs incurred (historical costs), as distinguished from predicted or forecasted costs. *(p. 21)*

Administrative control. Comprises the plan of organization (for example, the formal organization chart concerning who reports to whom) and all methods and procedures that help management planning and control of operations. *(p. 910)*

Annuity method of depreciation. See *compound interest depreciation method.*

Applied overhead. *Factory overhead* allocated to products (or services), usually by means of some budgeted (predetermined) rate. *(p. 95)*

Appraisal costs. Costs of detecting which individual products of those produced do not conform to specification. Component of quality costs. *(p. 730)*

Artificial cost. See *complete reciprocated cost.*

Authoritative budgeting. Budgeting approach where top management imposes the budget on all managers without consulting them. *(p. 394)*

Autocorrelation. See *serial correlation.*

Average cost. Cost computed by dividing some total cost (the numerator) by some denominator. *(p. 26)*

Bias. Failure of a random sample to represent a population because of some systematic error. *(p. 772)*

Book value. Original cost less any accumulated depreciation. *(p. 315)*

Breakeven point. Point of activity (sales volume) where total revenues and total expenses are equal. *(p. 48)*

Budget. Quantitative expression of a plan of action and an aid to coordination and implementation. *(pp. 3, 139)*

Budgeted factory-overhead rate. Budgeted total overhead divided by the budgeted rate base. *(p. 98)*

Budgeted volume. See *master-budget volume*.

Byproducts. Products that (1) have minor sales value as compared with the sales value of the major product(s) and (2) are not separately identifiable as individual products until their split-off point. *(p. 478)*

Capacity variance. See *production volume variance*.

Capital budgeting. The making of long-term planning decisions for investments and their financing. *(p. 648)*

Carrying costs. Arise when stocks of goods for sale (or production) are held. They consist of the opportunity cost of the investment tied up in inventory and the costs associated with storage, such as space rental and insurance. *(p. 715)*

CASB. See *Cost Accounting Standards Board*.

Cash budget. Schedule of expected cash receipts and disbursements. *(p. 162)*

Cash cycle. See *self-liquidating cycle*.

Certainty. Exists when there is no doubt about what the outcome will be. *(p. 616)*

Certified Management Accountant. Internal accountant's counterpart of the CPA (Certified Public Accountant). Designation given by the Institute of Certified Management Accountants to those who pass an examination and meet specified experience and education requirements. Abbreviated as *CMA*. *(p. 2)*

Choice criterion. An objective that can be quantified. *(p. 615)*

Clock card. Document used as a basis for determining individual earnings; contrast with *work ticket*. *(p. 89)*

CMA. Abbreviation for *Certified Management Accountant*. *(p. 2)*

Coefficient of determination. Measure of the extent to which the independent variable(s) in a regression model accounts for the variability in the dependent variable. Also called r^2, *r-square*. *(pp. 767, 784)*

Committed costs. Costs that arise from having property, plant, equipment, and a functioning organization. *(p. 378)*

Common cost. Cost of operating a facility that is shared by two or more users. *(p. 428)*

Complete reciprocated cost. The actual incurred cost of the service department plus a part of the costs of the other service departments that provide services to it. Also called *artificial cost*. *(p. 425)*

Compound interest depreciation method. Calculates depreciation in such a manner that the year-by-year accounting rate of return on beginning period investment is equal to the DCF internal rate of return on the investment. Also called *annuity method of depreciation*. *(p. 889)*

Confidence intervals. Limits within which the true value of a coefficient of a regression model lies (in a probabilistic sense). *(p. 786)*

Constant gross-margin percentage NRV method. Allocates joint costs so that the overall gross-margin percentage is identical for each individual product. *(p. 484)*

Constant variance. Uniform scatter or dispersion of points about the regression line. Assumption made in *regression analysis*. *(p. 772)*

Constraint. Mathematical inequality or equality that must be satisfied by the variables in a linear-programming model. *(p. 747)*

Contribution margin. Equal to revenue (sales) minus all variable expenses. *(p. 48)*

Contribution-margin ratio. Total *contribution margin* divided by the total sales. *(p. 58)*

Control. (a) Action that implements the planning decision, and (b) performance evaluation that provides feedback of the results. *(p. 3)*

Control chart. Graph of successive observations of a series (or of successive arithmetic means of independent samples) in which each observation is plotted relative to preset points on the expected distribution (such as the .10 and .90 percentiles or the 2σ confidence intervals). *(p. 820)*

Control-factor unit. Measure of workload. *(p. 384)*

Controllability. The degree of influence that a specific manager has over the costs or revenues or other items in question. *(pp. 157, 452)*

Controllable cost. Any cost that is primarily subject to the influence of a given manager of a given responsibility center for a given time span. *(p. 157)*

Controllable variable. See *independent variable*.

Controller. Financial executive who is primarily responsible for both management accounting and financial accounting. *(p. 9)*

Conversion costs. Consist of *direct-labor costs* and *factory-overhead*. *(p. 29)*

Correlation. Degree of relationship between two variables, such as cost and volume. *(p. 346)*

Cost. Resources sacrificed or forgone to achieve a specific objective. *(p. 20)*

Cost accounting. *Management accounting*, plus a small part of financial accounting—to the extent that its product-costing function satisfies the requisites of external reporting. *(p. 2)*

952

Cost Accounting Standards Board. Created by Congress in 1970 and ceased operations in 1980. Formed to promulgate cost accounting standards designed to achieve uniformity and consistency in the cost accounting principles followed by defense contractors and subcontractors under federal contracts. Abbreviated as *CASB*. (*p. 456*)

Cost accumulation. Collection of cost data in an organized way via an accounting system. (*p. 21*)

Cost allocation. The assignment and reassignment of a cost or group of costs to one or more cost objectives. Terms with assorted shades of meaning are *cost reallocation, cost assignment, cost reassignment, cost apportionment, cost reapportionment, cost distribution, cost redistribution, cost tracing,* and *cost retracing.* (*p. 411*)

Cost allocation base. A systematic means of relating a given cost or cost pool with a cost objective. (*p. 415*)

Cost apportionment. See *cost allocation.*

Cost assignment. See *cost allocation.*

Cost-benefit approach. Primary criterion for choosing among alternative accounting systems or methods—how well they help achieve management goals in relation to their costs. (*p. 6*)

Cost center. Responsibility center that is accountable for costs only. (*pp. 87, 153*)

Cost distribution. See *cost allocation.*

Cost estimation. Attempt to measure historical-cost relationships by specifying some underlying relationship between a dependent variable (costs) and one or more independent variables. Contrast with *cost prediction.* (*p. 341*)

Cost object. See *cost objective.*

Cost objective. Any activity for which a separate measurement of costs is desired. Also called *cost object.* (*p. 21*)

Cost of capital. See *required rate of return.*

Cost pool. A grouping of individual costs. (*p. 415*)

Cost prediction. Forecasting of future costs. Contrast with *cost estimation.* (*p. 341*)

Cost reallocation. See *cost allocation.*

Cost reapportionment. See *cost allocation.*

Cost reassignment. See *cost allocation.*

Cost redistribution. See *cost allocation.*

Cost-reimbursement contract. Price to be received by the contractor is based on the actual costs incurred by the contractor. (*p. 455*)

Cost retracing. See *cost allocation.*

Cost tracing. See *cost allocation.*

Cross-allocation method. See *reciprocal allocation method.*

Cumulative average-time learning model. Model in which the cumulative average time per unit is reduced by a constant percentage each time the cumulative quantity of units produced is doubled. (*p. 354*)

Current cost. The cost today of purchasing an asset currently held if identical assets can currently be purchased; it is the cost of purchasing the services provided by that asset if identical assets cannot currently be purchased. (*p. 878*)

Currently attainable standards. Standards that should be reached under very efficient operating conditions. They are difficult but possible to achieve. (*p. 196*)

Cutoff rate. See *required rate of return.*

Data mining. Search for independent variables in *regression analysis* that is aimed solely at the maximization of r^2. (*p. 768*)

DCF. Abbreviation for *discounted cash flow.* (*p. 649*)

DDB. Abbreviation for *double-declining-balance depreciation.* (*p. 682*)

Decentralization. Freedom to make decisions. Total decentralization means minimum constraints and maximum freedom to make decisions at the lowest levels. (*p. 833*)

Decision model. Formal method for making a choice that often involves quantitative analysis. (*p. 298*)

Decision table. Summary of the contemplated actions, events, probabilities, and outcomes. Also called *payoff table, payoff matrix.* (*p. 616*)

Denominator activity. See *denominator volume.*

Denominator level. See *denominator volume.*

Denominator variance. See *production volume variance.*

Denominator volume. The preselected production volume level used to set a budgeted fixed-factory-overhead rate for applying costs to products. Also called *denominator activity, denominator level.* (*p. 223*)

Dependent variable. The cost to be predicted in a cost function. (*p. 344*)

Differential costs. See *incremental cost.*

Direct allocation method. Method for allocating service department costs that ignores any service rendered by one service department to another; it allocates each service department's total costs directly to the production departments. Also called *direct method.* (*p. 423*)

Direct cost. Cost item that can be identified specifically with a single cost objective in an economically feasible manner. (*p. 411*)

Direct costing. See *variable costing.*

Direct-labor costs. Wages of all labor that is identified with the production of finished goods in an economically feasible manner. (*p. 29*)

Direct-materials costs. Acquisition costs of all materials that are identified as part of the finished goods and may be traced to the finished goods in an economically feasible manner. *(p. 29)*

Direct-materials inventory. Materials on hand and awaiting use in the production process. *(p. 30)*

Direct method. See *direct allocation method.*

Discounted cash flow. Method that represents the cash inflows and outflows of a project at a common point in time so that they can be compared (added, subtracted, etc.) in an appropriate way. Abbreviated as *DCF. (p. 649)*

Discount rate. See *required rate of return.*

Discretionary costs. Costs (1) that arise from periodic (usually yearly) appropriation decisions regarding the maximum amounts to be incurred, and (2) have no well-specified function relating inputs and outputs. Also called *managed costs, programmed costs. (p. 378)*

Disturbance term. See *residual term.*

Double-declining-balance depreciation. Form of accelerated depreciation that results in first-year depreciation being twice the amount of straight-line depreciation when zero terminal disposal value is assumed. Abbreviated as *DDB. (p. 682)*

Double-distribution allocation method. See *reciprocal allocation method.*

Dual pricing. Use of two separate transfer-pricing methods to price each interdivision transaction. *(p. 845)*

Dual-rate method. Cost allocation method in which two cost pools are used (typically one cost pool for fixed costs and another cost pool for variable costs). *(p. 418)*

Dysfunctional decision making. Decision making where the benefit to one subunit is more than offset by the costs or loss of benefits to the organization as a whole. *(p. 834)*

Economic order quantity. Purchase order size determined by a decision model that focuses on the trade-off between carrying costs and ordering costs. Abbreviated as *EOQ. (p. 716)*

Effectiveness. The degree to which a predetermined objective or target is met. *(p. 184)*

Efficiency. The degree to which inputs are used in relation to a given level of outputs. *(p. 184)*

Efficiency variance. The difference between the quantity of actual inputs (such as pounds of materials) and the quantity of inputs that should have been used (the flexible budget for any quantity of units of good output achieved), multiplied by the budgeted price. *(p. 190)*

Effort. Exertion toward a goal. Embraces all conscious actions that accompany the behavior of individuals. *(p. 374)*

Engineered costs. Costs that result specifically from a clear-cut measured relationship between inputs and outputs. *(p. 378)*

Environment. Set of uncontrollable factors that affect the success of a process. *(p. 4)*

EOQ. Abbreviation for *economic order quantity. (p. 716)*

Equivalent units. Measures of the output in terms of the quantities of each of the factors of production applied thereto. An equivalent unit is a collection of inputs (work applications) necessary to produce one complete physical unit of output. *(pp. 108, 511)*

Error term. See *residual term.*

Estimated net realizable value method. Allocates joint costs on the basis of their relative estimated net realizable value (predicted sales value in the ordinary course of business less the predicted separable costs of production and selling). *(p. 483)*

Event. An occurrence that may happen. Also called *states, states of nature. (p. 615)*

EVPI. Abbreviation for *expected value of perfect information. (p. 622)*

Excess materials requisition. Form filled out by production employees to obtain any materials needed in excess of the standard amount allowed for the scheduled output. *(p. 199)*

Excess present value index. Total present value of future net cash inflows divided by the initial cash outflow. Also called *profitability index. (p. 696)*

Executive compensation plan. One component of the reward system. It includes a diverse set of short-run and long-run plans that detail the conditions under which, and the forms in which, compensation is to be made to executives of the organization. *(p. 885)*

Expected annual activity. See *master-budget volume.*

Expected annual capacity. See *master-budget volume.*

Expected annual volume. See *master-budget volume.*

Expected value. A weighted average with the *probabilities* serving as the weights. *(p. 618)*

Expected value of imperfect information. The difference between the expected value of the optimal action with additional information and the highest expected value with existing information. *(p. 633)*

Expected value of perfect information. The difference between the expected value with perfect information and the highest expected value with existing information. Abbreviated as *EVPI. (p. 622)*

Expected variance. Anticipated variances stipulated in the budget for cash planning. *(p. 196)*

Experience curve. Function that shows how total costs (e.g., manufacturing, marketing, and distribution) per unit decline as units of output are increased. Broader concept than *learning curve. (p. 353)*

Explanatory variable. See *independent variable.*

External failure costs. Costs incurred when a nonconforming product is detected *after* its shipment to customers. Component of quality costs. *(p. 731)*

Factory burden. See *factory overhead.*

Factory overhead. All costs other than *direct materials costs* and *direct labor costs* that are associated with the manufacturing process. Also called *factory burden, indirect manufacturing costs, manufacturing expenses,* and *manufacturing overhead. (p. 29)*

Federal Manager's Financial Integrity Act. Requires the heads of U.S. government agencies to report annually on the status of their internal control and accounting systems, and provides for the disclosure and correction of material weaknesses. *(p. 916)*

Feedback. In control systems, consists of a comparison of the budget with actual results. *(p. 5)*

Financial accounting. External reporting, emphasizes the historical, custodial, and stewardship aspects of accounting. Heavily constrained by generally accepted accounting principles. Contrast with *management accounting. (p. 2)*

Financial budget. Part of the master budget that comprises the capital budget, cash budget, budgeted balance sheet, and budgeted statement of changes in financial position. *(p. 144)*

Financial-planning models. Mathematical statements of the relationships among all operating and financial activities, as well as other major internal and external factors that may affect decisions. *(p. 152)*

Finished-goods inventory. Goods fully completed but not yet sold. *(p. 30)*

Fixed cost. Cost that remains unchanged in total for a given time period despite wide changes in the related total activity or volume. *(p. 22)*

Fixed-price contract. Price to be received by the contractor is established at the outset. It is not subject to any adjustment due to the actual cost experience of the contractor. *(p. 455)*

Flexible budget. Budget that is adjusted for changes in volume. Based on a knowledge of how revenues and costs should behave over a range of activity. Also called a *variable budget.* Contrast with *static budget. (p. 181)*

Flexible-budget variance. The difference between actual amounts and the flexible-budget amounts for the actual output achieved. *(p. 183)*

Foreign Corrupt Practices Act. U.S. law that contains prohibitions against bribery and other corrupt practices, and also requirements (a) for maintaining accounting records in reasonable detail and accuracy and (b) for maintaining an appropriate system of internal accounting controls. *(p. 915)*

Fraud. Involves taking something of value from someone else through deceit. *(p. 911)*

Full cost. Absorption cost plus an allocation of selling and administrative cost. Also called *fully distributed cost, fully allocated cost. (p. 304)*

Fully allocated cost. See *full cost.*

Fully distributed cost. See *full cost.*

Functional authority. Right to command action laterally and downward with regard to a specific function or specialty. *(p. 8)*

Goal congruence. Individuals and groups aim at the organization goals desired by top management. *(p. 374)*

Goods in process. See *work-in-process inventory.*

Gross margin. Excess of sales over the inventory cost of the goods sold. Also called *gross profit. (p. 58)*

Gross profit. See *gross margin.*

High-low approach. Approach to cost estimation that entails using only the highest and lowest values of the independent variable within the relevant range. *(p. 347)*

Homogeneous cost pool. Cost pool in which each activity whose costs are included therein has the same or a similar cause-and-effect relationship to a cost objective. *(p. 446)*

Hurdle rate. See *required rate of return.*

Hybrid costing. Product-costing systems that are blends of ideas from both *job (order) costing* and *process costing. (p. 583)*

Idle capacity variance. See *production volume variance.*

Idle time. Typically represents wages paid for unproductive time caused by machine breakdowns, material shortages, sloppy production scheduling, and the like. *(p. 34)*

Incremental cost. The difference in total cost between two alternatives in a decision. Also called *differential cost. (p. 301)*

Incremental-unit time learning model. Model in which the incremental unit time (the time needed to produce the last unit) is reduced by a constant percentage each time the cumulative quantity of units produced is doubled. *(p. 354)*

Independent variable. The variable(s) used to predict the dependent variable in a cost function. Usually a measure of volume subject to the influence of a decision maker. Also called *controllable variable, explanatory variable. (p. 344)*

Indirect cost. Cost item that cannot be identified specifically with a single cost objective in an economically feasible manner. *(p. 411)*

Indirect cost pool. Any grouping of individual costs that cannot be identified directly with a single cost objective in an economically feasible manner. *(p. 415)*

Indirect labor costs. All factory labor wages other than for direct labor. *(p. 29)*

Indirect manufacturing costs. All costs other than *direct materials* and *direct labor* that are associated with the manufacturing process. Also called *factory burden, factory overhead, manufacturing expenses,* and *manufacturing overhead.* *(p. 29)*

Industrial engineering approach. Approach to cost estimation in which the relationships between inputs and outputs are analyzed and quantified in physical terms. The physical measures are then transformed into standard or budgeted costs. *(p. 345)*

Industry economics. Factors such as supply, demand, and competition that affect the goals and subgoals of the organization. *(p. 856)*

Intercept. The estimated component of total costs that, in the relevant range, does not vary with the activity level of the explanatory variable. *(p. 342)*

Intermediate market. Market in which an *intermediate product* is bought or sold. *(p. 836)*

Intermediate product. The product transferred from one segment of an organization to another segment of the same organization. *(p. 835)*

Internal accounting. See *management accounting.*

Internal control. The set of accounting and administrative controls and practices that helps ensure that approved and appropriate decisions are made in an organization. *(p. 910)*

Internal failure costs. Costs incurred when a nonconforming product is detected *before* its shipment to customers. Component of quality costs. *(p. 731)*

Internal rate of return. The rate of interest at which the present value of expected cash inflows from a project equals the present value of expected cash outflows of the project. Abbreviated as *IRR.* Also called *time-adjusted rate of return.* *(p. 651)*

Inventoriable cost. See *product costs.*

Investment center. Responsibility center that is accountable for costs, revenues, and investments. *(p. 153)*

Investment tax credit. Direct reduction of income taxes arising from the acquisition of depreciable assets. Abbreviated as *ITC.* *(p. 681)*

IRR. Abbreviation for *internal rate of return.* *(p. 651)*

ITC. Abbreviation for *investment tax credit.* *(p. 681)*

JIT costing. Hybrid costing used in conjunction with just-in-time production systems. *(p. 590)*

JIT production. Abbreviation for *just-in-time production.* *(pp. 588, 728)*

JIT purchasing. Abbreviation for *just-in-time purchasing.* *(p. 724)*

Job-cost sheet. See *job order.*

Job-cost record. See *job order.*

Job order. Basic document used by job-order costing to apply *product costs.* Also called *job-cost record* and *job-cost sheet.* *(p. 88)*

Job-order costing. System used by organizations whose products or services are readily identified by individual units or batches, each of which receives varying inputs of direct materials, direct labor, and factory overhead. *(p. 87)*

Joint cost. Cost of a single process that yields two or more products (or services) simultaneously. *(p. 478)*

Joint products. Two or more products that (1) have relatively significant sales values and (2) are not separately identifiable as individual products until their split-off point. *(p. 478)*

Just-in-time production. System whereby each component on a production line is produced immediately as needed by the next step in the production line. Abbreviated as *JIT production.* *(pp. 588, 728)*

Just-in-time purchasing. Involves the purchase of goods such that delivery immediately precedes demand or use. In the extreme, no inventories (goods for sale for a retailer; raw materials for a manufacturer) would be held with JIT purchasing. Abbreviated as *JIT purchasing.* *(p. 724)*

Labor-mix variance. [(Actual labor-mix percentage − Budgeted labor-mix percentage) × (Actual total units of labor inputs used)] × (Budgeted individual price per unit of labor input − Budgeted average price per unit of labor input). *(p. 813)*

Labor-paced manufacturing environment. Worker dexterity and productivity determine the speed of production. Machines function as tools that aid production workers. *(p. 450)*

Labor-yield variance. (Standard units of labor inputs allowed for actual outputs − Actual units of labor inputs used) × (Budgeted average price per unit of labor input). *(p. 813)*

Learning curve. Function that shows how labor hours per unit decline as units of output are increased. *(p. 353)*

Linear programming. Decision model concerned with how best to allocate scarce resources to attain a chosen objective such as maximization of operating income or minimization of operating costs. Abbreviated as *LP.* *(p. 745)*

Line authority. Authority that is exerted downward over subordinates. *(p. 8)*

LP. Abbreviation for *linear programming. (p. 745)*

Machine-paced manufacturing environment. Machines conduct most (or all) phases of production, such as shipment of materials to the production line, assembly and other activities on the production line, and shipment of finished goods to the delivery dock areas. *(p. 451)*

Managed costs. See *discretionary costs.*

Management accounting. Identification, measurement, accumulation, analysis, preparation, interpretation, and communication of information that assists executives in fulfilling organizational objectives. Also called *internal accounting. (p. 2)*

Management by exception. Practice of concentrating on areas that deserve attention and ignoring areas that are presumed to be running smoothly. *(p. 3)*

Management by objectives. Budgeting procedure under which a subordinate and his or her superior jointly formulate the subordinate's set of goals and plans for attaining those goals for a subsequent period. Abbreviated as *MBO. (p. 158)*

Management control system. Means of gathering data to aid and coordinate the process of making decisions throughout the organization. *(p. 4)*

Managerial style. The set of behaviors exhibited by key managers in an organization. *(p. 857)*

Manufacturing. Transformation of materials into other goods through the use of labor and factory facilities. *(p. 27)*

Manufacturing expenses. See *factory overhead.*

Manufacturing overhead. See *factory overhead.*

Margin of safety. Excess of budgeted sales over the breakeven sales volume. *(p. 54)*

Market-share variance. (Actual market-share percentage − Budgeted market-share percentage) × (Actual industry sales volume in units) × (Budgeted average contribution margin per unit). *(p. 806)*

Market-size variance. (Budgeted market-share percentage) × (Actual industry sales volume in units − Budgeted industry sales volume in units) × (Budgeted average contribution margin per unit). *(p. 806)*

Master budget. Summarizes the objectives of all subunits of an organization—sales, production, distribution, and finance. *(p. 139)*

Master-budget activity. See *master-budget volume.*

Master-budget volume. The anticipated level of capacity utilization for the coming year. Also called *budgeted volume, expected annual volume, expected annual capacity,* *expected annual activity,* or *master-budget activity. (p. 264)*

Master operations lists. Lists compiled for routing and scheduling a variety of products through a series of operations or processes. *(p. 201)*

Material requisition. See *stores requisition.*

Material-mix variance. ([Actual material-mix percentage − Budgeted material mix percentage] × [Actual total units of material inputs used]) × (Budgeted individual price per unit of material input − Budgeted average price per unit of material input). *(p. 810)*

Materials requirements planning. Planning system that focuses first on the amount and timing of finished goods demanded and then determines the derived demand for raw materials, components, and subassemblies at each of the prior stages of production. Abbreviated as *MRP. (p. 727)*

Material-yield variance. (Standard units of material inputs allowed for actual outputs − Actual units of material inputs used) × (Budgeted average price per unit of material input). *(p. 810)*

Matrix allocation method. See *reciprocal allocation method.*

MBO. Abbreviation for *management by objectives. (p. 158)*

Merchandising. Selling of goods without changing their basic form. *(p. 27)*

Mixed cost. Cost function that has both fixed and variable elements. Also called *semivariable cost. (p. 342)*

Mixed-model manufacturer. The maker of a relatively wide variety of closely related standardized products. *(p. 584)*

Motivation. Desire for a selected goal (the goal congruence aspect) together with the resulting drive or pursuit (the effort aspect) toward that goal. *(p. 374)*

MRP. Abbreviation for *materials requirements planning. (p. 727)*

Multicollinearity. Exists when two or more independent variables in a multiple regression model are highly correlated with each other; a correlation greater than .7 is a frequently used benchmark for designating a correlation as high. *(p. 777)*

Multiple regression. *Regression analysis* in which more than one independent variable is used. *(p. 765)*

NAA. Abbreviation for *National Association of Accountants. (p. 2)*

National Association of Accountants. Largest association of internal accountants in the United States. Abbreviated as *NAA. (p. 2)*

Negotiated static budget. Budget in which a fixed amount of costs is appropriated based on negotiations at the start of the budget period. *(p. 381)*

Net present value. Method of calculating the expected net monetary gain or loss from a project by discounting all expected future cash inflows and outflows to the present, using some predetermined minimum desired rate of return. Abbreviated as *NPV*. *(p. 650)*

Nominal rate of interest. Rate comprised of two elements: (a) the real rate of interest and (b) an inflation element—the premium demanded because of the anticipated decline of the general purchasing power of the monetary unit. *(p. 689)*

Normal costing. Method of charging costs to products using actual *direct-materials costs,* actual *direct-labor costs,* and *applied overhead* (using budgeted overhead rates times actual inputs). Termed normal costing because the overhead is applied to products on an average or "normalized" basis. *(p. 106)*

Normal spoilage. Spoilage that arises under efficient operating conditions; it is an inherent result of the particular process and is thus uncontrollable in the short run. *(p. 546)*

Normal volume. The level of capacity utilization (which is less than 100% of practical capacity) that will satisfy average consumer demand over a span of time (often five years) that includes seasonal, cyclical, and trend factors. *(p. 264)*

NPV. Abbreviation for *net present value*. *(p. 650)*

Objective function. Choice criterion that provides a basis for choosing the best alternative action. *(p. 615)*

Operating budget. Budget of the income statement and its supporting schedules. *(p. 143)*

Operating cycle. See *self-liquidating cycle*.

Operation. Standardized method or technique that is repetitively performed regardless of the distinguishing features of the finished product. *(p. 585)*

Operation costing. System often used in the manufacture of goods that have some common characteristics plus some individual characteristics. Distinctions are made between batches of products. It is a hybrid system. Also called *specification costing*. *(pp. 109, 584)*

Operations management. Focuses on the management of resources to produce or deliver the products or services provided by an organization. *(p. 714)*

Opportunity cost. The maximum contribution that is forgone by using limited resources for a particular purpose. *(p. 314)*

Ordering costs. Consist of the clerical costs of preparing a purchase order, and the special processing and receiving costs related to the number of orders processed. *(p. 715)*

Ordinary incremental budget. Budget that considers the previous period's budget and actual results. The budget amount is then changed in accordance with experience during the previous period and expectations for the next period. *(p. 382)*

Organization culture. The set of beliefs and values shared by members of the organization. *(p. 857)*

Organization goals. Objectives the organization is aiming to accomplish. *(p. 855)*

Organization structure. The arrangement of lines of responsibility within an organization. *(p. 856)*

Outcomes. Measure (in terms of the objective function) of the predicted consequences of the various possible combinations of actions and events. Also called *payoffs*. *(p. 616)*

Outlay cost. Cost that requires a cash disbursement sooner or later. *(p. 315)*

Overapplied overhead. Applied overhead that exceeds the actual overhead incurred. *(p. 102)*

Overtime premium. Cost of the wages paid to all factory workers (for both direct labor and indirect labor) in excess of their straight-time wage rates. Overtime premium is usually considered a part of overhead. *(p. 34)*

Parameter. A constant or coefficient in a model or system of equations. *(p. 342)*

Participative budgeting. Budgeting approach where the individuals influenced by the budget are fully involved in the setting of the budget. *(p. 394)*

Payback. Measures the time it will take to recoup, in the form of cash inflow from operations, the initial dollars invested in a project. Also called *payout*. *(p. 658)*

Payoff matrix. See *decision table*.

Payoffs. See *outcomes*.

Payoff matrix. See *decision table*.

Payoff table. See *decision table*.

Payout. See *payback*.

Perfectly competitive market. Market in which there is a homogeneous product with equivalent buying and selling prices and for which no individual buyers or sellers can affect those prices by their own actions. *(p. 836)*

Performance plan. Long-run executive compensation plan that makes payment of a definite number of performance units (each assigned a fixed dollar value) contingent on the ROI (net income, etc.) being at a set level at the end of an extended time period (say five years). *(p. 886)*

Performance reports. Measurements of activities. These reports often consist of comparisons of budgets with actual results. *(p. 3)*

Period costs. Costs always expensed in the same period in which they are incurred; they do not go through an inventory stage. *(p. 30)*

Periodic inventory method. Does not require a day-to-day record of inventory changes. Costs of materials used or costs of goods sold cannot be computed accurately until ending inventories, determined by physical count, are subtracted from the sum of the opening inventory, purchases, and other purchasing costs. *(p. 32)*

Perpetual inventory method. Requires a continuous record of additions to and reductions in materials, work in process, and finished goods, thus measuring on a day-to-day basis not only these three inventories but also the cumulative cost of goods sold. *(p. 32)*

Physical measure method. Allocates joint costs on the basis of their relative proportions at the split-off point using a common physical measure such as weight or volume. *(p. 481)*

Planning. Delineation of goals, predictions of potential results under various ways of achieving goals, and a decision of how to attain the desired results. *(p. 3)*

Practical capacity. Maximum level of capacity at which the plant or department can operate efficiently. *(p. 264)*

Predatory pricing. Involves temporary price cuts intended to eventually restrict supply and then raise prices rather than to enlarge demand or meet competition. *(p. 308)*

Present value. The asset measure that is based on discounted cash flow (DCF) estimates. *(p. 876)*

Prevention costs. Costs of preventing the production of products that do not conform to specification. Component of quality costs. *(p. 730)*

Previous department costs. See *transferred-in costs*.

Price variance. Difference between actual unit prices and budgeted unit prices multiplied by the actual quantity of goods or services in question (for example, purchased or used). *(pp. 185, 190)*

Prime costs. Consist of *direct-materials costs* plus *direct-labor costs*. *(p. 29)*

Priority incremental budget. Budget similar to incremental budgets, with the addition of a description of what incremental activities or changes would occur, first, if the budget were increased by, say, 10%, and second, if the budget were decreased by a similar percentage. *(p. 382)*

Probabilities. Likelihoods of occurrence of an event. *(p. 616)*

Probability distribution. Describes the likelihood or probability of each of the collectively exhaustive and mutually exclusive set of events. *(p. 617)*

Process. Collection of decisions or activities that should be aimed at some ends. *(p. 4)*

Process costing. System for applying costs to like products that are mass produced in continuous fashion through a series of production steps called *processes*. *(pp. 107, 507–8)*

Product costing. Accumulation of the costs of an organization's products and services. *(p. 2)*

Production cost report. Report of the units manufactured during a specified period together with their related costs. *(p. 514)*

Product costs. Costs allocated to inventory when incurred. Become expenses (as cost of goods sold) only when the units in inventory are sold. Also called *inventoriable costs*. *(p. 30)*

Production lead time. Time from the first stage of production to when the finished good comes off the production line. *(p. 728)*

Production volume variance. Measure of the cost of departing from the denominator level of volume used to set the fixed-overhead rate: (Budgeted fixed factory overhead − Applied fixed factory overhead). Arises only in an absorption-costing system. Also called *capacity variance, activity variance, denominator variance, idle capacity variance, volume variance*. *(p. 227)*

Profitability index. See *excess present value index*.

Profit center. Responsibility center that is accountable for costs and revenues. *(p. 153)*

Pro-forma statements. Budgeted financial statements. *(p. 143)*

Programmed costs. See *discretionary costs*.

Project. Complex job that often takes months or years to complete and requires the work of many different departments or divisions or subcontractors. *(p. 580)*

Proration. Spreading of underapplied or overapplied overhead among various inventories and cost of goods sold. *(p. 103)*

Purchase-order lead time. The time between the placement of an order and its delivery. *(p. 716)*

P/V chart. Profit-volume graph showing the impact of changes in volume on net income. *(p. 59)*

Quality. Conformance of a product or service with a prespecified (and often preannounced) standard. *(p. 716)*

Quantity variance. *Efficiency variance* pertaining to direct materials and direct labor. Also see *sales-quantity variance*. *(p. 193)*

r^2. See *coefficient of determination*.

Rate variance. *Price variance* for direct labor. *(p. 193)*

Real rate of interest. Rate comprised of two elements: (a) a risk-free element—the "pure" rate of interest that is paid on long-term government bonds, and (b) a business-risk element—the "risk" premium above the pure rate that is demanded for undertaking risk. *(p. 689)*

Reciprocal allocation method. Method for allocating service department costs by explicitly including the mutual services rendered among all departments. Also called *cross-allocation method, matrix allocation method, double-distribution allocation method.* (p. 425)

Regression analysis. Statistical model to measure the average amount of change in the dependent variable that is associated with a unit change in the amounts of one or more independent variables. (p. 346)

Relevant costs. Expected future costs that will differ under alternatives in a decision. (p. 301)

Relevant range. Band of activity (volume) in which a specific form of budgeted sales and cost (expense) relationships will be valid. (p. 23)

Relevant revenues. Expected future revenues that will differ under alternatives in a decision. (p. 301)

Reorder point. Quantity level of inventory that triggers a new order being placed. (p. 718)

Required rate of return. The minimum desired rate of return on an investment. Abbreviated as *RRR.* Also called *hurdle rate, cutoff rate, cost of capital,* and *discount rate.* (p. 649)

Residual income. Income minus an imputed interest charge for invested capital. (p. 873)

Residual term. The deviation of the actual value of *y* (the dependent variable) from the regression line. Also called *disturbance term, error term.* (p. 771)

Responsibility accounting. System that measures the plans and actions of each responsibility center. (p. 153)

Responsibility center. Subunit (part or segment) of an organization whose manager is accountable for a specified set of activities. (pp. 87, 153)

Retail inventory method. Deducts the recorded sales for one period from the goods available for sale during that period to obtain the estimated closing inventory level at retail prices. (p. 923)

Return on investment. Income divided by invested capital. Abbreviated as *ROI.* (p. 871)

Revenue center. Responsibility center that is accountable for revenues only. (p. 153)

Reworked units. Unacceptable units of production that are subsequently reworked and sold as acceptable finished goods. (p. 545)

Risk averse. More disutility from a loss of a given dollar amount than there is utility from a gain of the same dollar amount. Opposite of *risk seeking.* (pp. 625–26)

Risk neutral. Equal utility and disutility from a gain and a loss of the same dollar amount. Utility is directly proportional to monetary amounts. (pp. 625–26)

Risk seeking. More utility from a gain of a given dollar

amount than there is disutility from the loss of the same dollar amount. Opposite of *risk averse.* (pp. 625–26)

ROI. Abbreviation for *return on investment.* (p. 871)

RRR. Abbreviation for *required rate of return.* (p. 649)

***r*-square.** See *coefficient of determination.*

Safety stock. The minimum or buffer inventory that is held as a cushion against unexpected increases in demand. (p. 719)

Sales mix. Relative proportions or combination of the quantities of products that comprise total sales. (pp. 60, 799)

Sales-mix variance. The difference between the amount of contribution margin in the flexible budget based on actual sales volume at actual mix, and that amount in the flexible budget based on actual sales volume at budgeted mix. Budgeted selling prices and budgeted unit variable costs are held constant. (p. 803)

Sales-quantity variance. The difference between the amount of the contribution margin in the flexible budget based on actual sales volume at budgeted mix and that amount in the static (master) budget. Budgeted selling prices and budgeted unit variable costs are held constant. (p. 803)

Sales value at split-off method. Allocates joint costs on the basis of the products' relative sales value at the split-off point. (p. 481)

Sales-volume variance. The difference between the amount of the contribution margin in the budget based on actual sales volume (the flexible-budget) and that amount in the static (master) budget. Budgeted selling prices and budgeted unit variable costs are held constant. (pp. 183, 800)

Scrap. Inputs that do not become part of the outputs but have relatively minor economic values. (p. 545)

Segment. Any line of activity or part of an organization for which separate determinations of costs or revenues or both are desired. Also called *subunit.* (p. 452)

Self-liquidating cycle. The movement from cash to inventories to receivables and back to cash. Also called *cash cycle, operating cycle,* and *working-capital cycle.* (p. 164)

Semivariable cost. See *mixed cost.*

Sensitivity analysis. "What-if" technique that essentially asks how a result will be changed if the original predicted data are not achieved or if an underlying assumption changes. (pp. 54, 656)

Separable costs. Costs incurred beyond the split-off point. Called separable costs because they are not part of the joint production process; they are identifiable with individual products. *(p. 478)*

Sequential allocation method. See *step-down allocation method.*

Serial correlation. Arises when residuals (in a regression model) are not independent. Also called *autocorrelation.* *(p. 773)*

Service department. Department in which the main (and in some cases exclusive) rationale of the department is the provision of services to other departments in the organization. *(p. 417)*

Setup time. Time needed to prepare equipment and related resources for producing a specified number of finished units or operations. *(p. 201)*

Shadow prices. Indicate how much the objective function will increase if one more unit of the limiting resource is available. Used in linear programming. *(p. 753)* .

Simple regression. *Regression analysis* in which only one independent variable is used. *(p. 765)*

Simplex method. Iterative step-by-step procedure for determining the optimal solution to a linear-programming problem; it starts with a specific feasible solution and then tests it by substitution to see if the solution can be improved. *(p. 750)*

SL. Abbreviation for *straight-line depreciation.* *(p. 682)*

Slope coefficient. The amount of change in *y* (the dependent variable) for each unit change in *x* (the independent variable). *(p. 342)*

Specification analysis. Testing of the basic assumptions underlying *regression analysis.* These assumptions include linearity, constant variance of the residuals, and independence of the residuals. *(p. 767)*

Specification costing. See *operation costing.*

Spending variance. Actual amount of overhead incurred minus the expected amount based on the flexible budget for actual inputs. *(p. 220)*

Split-off point. The juncture of production where the joint products and byproducts become individually identifiable. *(p. 478)*

Spoilage. Unacceptable units of production that are discarded and sold for disposal value. *(p. 544)*

SQC. Abbreviation for *statistical quality control.* *(p. 820)*

Staff authority. Authority to advise but not command others. *(p. 8)*

Standard bill of materials. Specifies the physical quantities allowed for manufacturing a specified number of acceptable finished units. *(p. 198)*

Standard costs. Carefully predetermined costs that are usually expressed on a per-unit basis; they are target costs—costs that should be attained. *(p. 188)*

Standard error. Obtained by dividing the standard error of the residuals by a measure of the dispersion of the *x* values around their mean. Used in regression analysis. *(p. 786)*

Standard error of the estimate. See *standard error of the residuals.*

Standard error of the residuals. Measure of the scatter of the actual observations about the regression line. Also called *standard error of the estimate.* *(p. 785)*

Standard hours allowed. Number of standard hours that should have been used to obtain any given quantity of output (that is, actual goods produced or actual outputs achieved). Also called *standard hours earned, standard hours worked,* or *standard hours of input allowed for good output produced.* *(p. 191)*

Standard hours earned. See *standard hours allowed.*

Standard hours of input allowed for good output produced. See *standard hours allowed.*

Standard hours worked. See *standard hours allowed.*

States. See *event.*

States of nature. See *event.*

Static budget. Has a single planned volume level. The budget is not adjusted or altered regardless of changes in volume or other conditions during the budget period. Contrast with *flexible budget.* *(p. 181)*

Statistical quality control. Formal means of distinguishing between random variation and other sources of variation in an operating process. Abbreviated as *SQC.* *(p. 820)*

Step allocation method. See *step-down allocation method.*

Step-down allocation method. Method for allocating service department costs that makes a limited recognition of services rendered by service departments to other service departments. See *step allocation method, sequential allocation method.* *(p. 424)*

Step-function cost. Cost function whereby the cost of the input is constant over various small ranges of output, but the cost increases by discrete amounts (that is, in steps) as activity moves from one range to the next. *(p. 352)*

Stockout. Arises when a unit of stock is demanded but is not readily available to the customer. *(p. 715)*

Stores requisition. Form used to charge job-cost records for direct materials used. Also called *material requisition.* *(p. 88)*

Straight-line depreciation. Equal amount of depreciation is allowed each year. Abbreviated as *SL.* *(p. 682)*

Strategic planning. Planning in regard to the general direction of organization; it considers the resources of the organization, the likely behavior of competitors, the direction of technological change, and the projected demands of the marketplace. *(p. 856)*

Subunit. See *segment.*

Sum-of-the-years'-digits. Form of accelerated depreciation based on the following formula: $S = n [(n + 1)/2]$, where $S =$ sum-of-the-years'-digits and $n =$ number of years of estimated useful life. *(p. 682)*

SYD. Abbreviation for *sum-of-the-years'-digits* depreciation. *(p. 682)*

Theoretical capacity. Measurement of capacity that assumes the production of output 100% of the time. *(p. 264)*

Time-adjusted rate of return. See *internal rate of return.*

Transfer price. Price charged by one segment (subunit, department, division, etc.) of an organization for a product or service supplied to another segment of the same organization. *(p. 835)*

Transferred-in costs. Costs incurred in a previous department that have been received by a subsequent department. Also called *previous department costs.* *(p. 526)*

Treasurer. Financial executive who is primarily responsible for obtaining investment capital and managing cash. *(p. 9)*

t-value. Computed as the coefficient of a parameter in a regression model divided by the standard error of the coefficient. *(p. 786)*

Uncertainty. Possibility that an actual amount can deviate from an expected amount. *(p. 54, 615)*

Underapplied overhead. *Applied overhead* is less than the actual overhead incurred. *(p. 102)*

Usage variance. *Efficiency variance* pertaining to direct materials or direct labor. *(p. 193)*

Utility. The value of a specific outcome to a particular decision maker. *(p. 625)*

Utils. Quantifications of the utility value of given monetary amounts. *(p. 625)*

Variable budget. See *flexible budget.*

Variable cost. Cost that changes in total in direct proportion to changes in the related total activity or volume. *(p. 22)*

Variable costing. Method of product costing where fixed manufacturing overhead is *excluded* from the inventoriable costs. Also called *direct costing.* *(p. 55)*

Variable-cost ratio. Total *variable cost* divided by the total sales. *(p. 58)*

Variances. Deviations of actual results from budget. *(p. 3)*

Volume variance. See *production volume variance.*

Waste. Inputs that do not become part of the outputs. *(p. 545)*

Working-capital cycle. See *self-liquidating cycle.*

Work-in-process inventory. Goods undergoing the production process but not yet fully completed. Costs include the three major manufacturing costs (direct materials, direct labor, and factory overhead). Also called *goods in process* and *work in progress.* *(p. 30)*

Work in progress. See *work-in-process inventory.*

Work measurement. Careful analysis of a task, its size, the method used in its performance, and its efficiency. The objective of work measurement is to determine the workload in an operation and the number of workers needed to perform that work efficiently. *(p. 383)*

Work ticket. Form used to charge jobs for direct labor used. Indicates the time spent on a specific job. *(p. 88)*

ZBB. Abbreviation for *zero-base budgeting.* *(p. 382)*

Zero-base budgeting. Budgeting from the ground up as though the budget were being initiated for the first time. Abbreviated as *ZBB.* *(p. 382)*

Author Index

Subject Index

Internal control breakdowns, 911–12
Internal failure costs, 731
Internal (time-adjusted) rate of return (IRR)
model, 649, 651–57, 664, 698–99
on compound-interest depreciation-method
for investment, 889–92
rule for, 698–99
Inventory(-ies):
in batch production, 584
change of, 57
control, retailing, 922–23
cost allocation of, 30–31, 480, 485, 490–93
of goods for sale, retailing, 715–26, 733
MRP system and, 728
opportunity-cost for, 313–15
recorder point of, 718–20
standard-cost impact of, 193
Inventory, merchandise, costs, 30–33, 56
Inventory, work-in-process (progress), 30
Inventory, work-in-process costing, 507–34,
549–54, 563–65 (see also FIFO;
Weighted-average methods; Process-
costing)
Inventory control, retail method, 923
Inventory costing, 30–31, 253–70, 313–15, 507–
34, 549–54, 563–65
Inventory model, economic-order-quantity,
716–18, 721–26, 733, 816
Inventory quantity level, recorder point, 718–20
Inventory shrinkage, 922–23
Investment, capital:
cash-flow models for, 648–66
definitions of, 875–76
in performance measuring models, 871–79,
883, 889–92
profitability index and, 696–99
See also Return on investment
Investment base, 662, 876
Investment center, 153, 835, 836, 849, 853, 874,
875
Investment tax credit, 681
IRR (see Internal rate of return)

JIT (see Just-in-time)
Job-cost accounting for spoilage, 554–55
Job-cost record (sheet), 88–89, 94–96
Job-costing, 34, 87–107, 508, 575–80, 583–84
for nonmanufacturing control, 575–79
See also Hybrid costing
Job-order (-cost record/-sheet), 88–89, 91–96
Job-order costing, 87–107, 112–16, 575–80
general ledgers for, 90–92, 112–16, 555
process-costing compared, 508–9
Job-order sheet (record), 88–96 passim
Jobs and labor costs, 34–35, 575–80
Joint products, 478
Journal entries:
for JIT costing, 591–92, 594–96

Journal entries (cont.)
for job-cost records, 90–96
for operation costing, 587, 591, 594–95
for overhead, 225–26
for payroll costs, 91–95, 598, 603
for process-costing, 509, 510, 515–16, 528,
532–33
spoilage loss in, 552–54
Junk, production unit, 555 (see also Scrap)
Just-in-time costing, 588–93, 595
inventory systems with, 544, 575, 590
journal entries, 591, 594–96
production with, 728–29
constant-flow and, 588–90
purchasing with, 724–26

Kurtosis coefficient, specification analysis, 773

Labor costs (see Direct labor)
Labor costs, direct or indirect, 29, 34
Labor costs, direct professional, in job-costing,
576–79
Labor-mix variance, direct, 811–13
Labor-paced manufacturing environments, 450–
51
Labor price variances, 198
Labor-yield variance, direct, 811–13
Language of accounting, 31–36
Learning and cost function estimation, 353–57
Learning curve, 353, 354, 355
Least square criterion, regression analysis, 781–
83
Ledger procedure for product-costing (see Gen-
eral ledger entries)
Ledger relationships (see General ledger entries)
Ledger treatment (see General ledger entries;
Journal entries; Subsidiary ledgers)
Legislation, internal control, 915–16
Linear programming (LP), 745
Linear programming model, 745–55
assumptions/limitations of, 754
other uses of, 753–54
variables in, 816
Linear programming problem-solving, 747–50
Linearity assumption, 24, 25
Linearity, relevant range, specification analysis,
771–72
Line authority, 7, 8
Line relationship and staff, 7–9
Loss from Abnormal Spoilage account, 546, 547,
552
Low-cost producer, 341
LP (see Linear programming)
Lump sum plus variable costs, 843–44

Machine hours:
in cost-function estimation, 360–61